BUSINESS

The American Challenge for Global Competitiveness

BUSINESS

The American Challenge for Global Competitiveness

William G. Zikmund
Oklahoma State University

R. Dennis Middlemist
Colorado State University

Melanie R. Middlemist
Colorado State University

IRWIN

Burr Ridge, Illinois
Boston, Massachusetts
Sydney, Australia

Publisher: William Schoof
Acquisitions Editor: Mary Fischer
Production Manager: Bob Lange
Marketing Manager: Kurt Messersmith

Design and project management provided by
Elm Street Publishing Services, Inc.

Compositor: Elm Street Publishing Services, Inc.
Typeface: 10/12 Helvetica Condensed
Printer: Von Hoffmann Press, Inc.

Library of Congress Cataloging-in-Publication Data

Zikmund, William G.
Business: the American challenge for global competitiveness / William G. Zikmund, R. Dennis Middlemist, Melanie R. Middlemist.
p. cm.
Includes index.
ISBN 0-256-11412-9
1. Business. 2. Management. I. Middlemist, R. Dennis. II. Middlemist, Melanie R. III. Title.
HF5351.Z54 1994
650—dc20 94-10914

Printed in the United States of America
1 2 3 4 5 6 7 8 9 0 VH 9 8 7 6 5 4

Address editorial correspondence:
Austen Press
18141 Dixie Highway
Suite 111
Homewood, IL 60430

Address orders:
Richard D. Irwin, Inc.
1333 Burr Ridge Parkway
Burr Ridge, IL 60521

Austen Press
Richard D. Irwin, Inc.

Cover sources: Sky image—Superstock; doorway image—Al Francekevich.

To Bill, Mary, and John—three entrepreneurs in an industry enamored with conglomerate thinking.

—William G. Zikmund and R. Dennis Middlemist

To the ones who provide my inspiration—my children and my mother.

—Melanie Middlemist

PREFACE

This book originated with an idea—the conceptualization of the four Cs of business. The four Cs stemmed from our concern that business is sometimes taught as sets of independent activities, such as marketing, management, and finance. It is difficult to impress upon students that these are not independent activities but that they work together to affect business outcomes. For instance, customers are affected not only by marketing activities but by management decisions, production activities, and financial arrangements. Thus, the notion of the four Cs evolved. The four Cs are

Company

Customers

Competitors

Collaborators

Each of these is critical to business success, and each is affected by nearly all business activities. Structuring a book around the four Cs enables students to organize their thoughts and integrate the various topics of business. Students are reminded that marketing decisions also affect collaborators such as suppliers and distributors. Finance decisions affect (and are affected by) customers and competition.

Many professors who have experience teaching the introduction to business course will recognize that our book is quite different from its competitors, especially those textbooks conceptualized in a different era of business. We will use the four Cs concept to elaborate on some of these differences. Most of our venerable **competitors**, published by large conglomerate organizations, were in tune with the business environment of the 1980s. Today, however, many are not close to their customers. Our situation could not be more different. Everything about this project is new, forward looking, and customer oriented. Our publisher, Austen Press, is the right kind of **company** for this project. Its three principals live and work in different states. Telecommunications and working with **collaborators**, two of the foremost trends in today's global business environment, are essential to its entrepreneurial style and flexible way of doing business. Austen consulted with business professors around the country to learn their needs. The design and production of the book were performed in collaboration with Elm Street Publishing Services, a successful new service business that was created as the result of a major publishing corporation's downsizing. Freelance professionals, including several working mothers operating out of their homes, were involved in creating contemporary graphics and a look that will strongly appeal to Generation X students. All our efforts are to satisfy our **customers**—professors and students. To ensure you receive the service so necessary in today's world, Austen works in collaboration with Richard D. Irwin's marketing and sales organizations to provide support for this and other Austen products. This is the key to any company's success. A later section of this preface discusses distinctive features the professor will like about *Business.* At this point, we would like to discuss how our student customers will be satisfied with their purchase of this book.

We feel that students must be particularly aware of the collaborators of business. The business world is rapidly changing. Business is moving away from an era when organizations performed all operations internally without any help from other collaborating organizations. In the present business era where companies operate in a global economy, strategic alliances, networks, partnerships, and other organizational collaborations are vitally important. Collaborative relationships have dramatically changed the way business is conducted around the world. Our book is the first introductory business textbook to stress the role of collaborators and new forms of business organization. Simply put, *Business: The American Challenge for Global Competitiveness* was written to respond to a changing business world.

Our book looks at business from a global perspective. Examples such as AMP, a Pennsylvania company that gets 60 percent of its revenues from wholly owned foreign subsidiaries, and The Body Shop, a British retailer doing business in the United States and several European countries, fill the pages of this book.

This book was also written to provide students with some delightful surprises. Business is a fascinating subject, one that is important in our society. Students will be able to relate to examples about Sega, Nike, The Limited, and other familiar companies. Students will find engaging stories about both successes and failures associated with unique goods and services. Learning what went wrong can be as instructive as knowing how business principles are supposed to work.

Our book explains the nature of business today in both large and small companies. Its purpose is to discuss how students can make a success of themselves as an employee or owner of a customer-oriented business.

This book also springs from the belief that students need to be **street smart** as well as book smart. Academic business concepts are vitally important in business. However, many an "A" student who only understands academic theories has been surpassed by street smart "C" students. Our Street Smart feature relates practical lessons that business people have learned in the school of hard knocks. Each chapter of this book includes at least one Street Smart selection. We want every student who reads the book to be both book smart and street smart.

The graphic design of the book symbolically represents its contemporary nature. Students will be pleased with many aspects of *Business's* modern design. The design uses computer art and virtual reality effects, an art form that has become more and more popular with the current generation of young Americans.

THE ORGANIZATION OF THIS BOOK

Although the content of this book is quite different from the standard introduction to business textbook, *Business: The American Challenge for Global Competitiveness* is organized around traditional topics.

Part One, "Business Foundations," introduces students to business fundamentals. Chapter 1, "The Nature of Business," jumps right into a discussion of business by introducing the four Cs concept. It sets the stage for the entire book. Chapter 2, "Capitalism and Contemporary Economics," illustrates why communism has faltered and why capitalism is the hope for developing economies around the world. Chapter 3, "Economic and Global Issues in Our Service Economy," addresses the economic goals our society hopes to achieve. It also points out that the services sector of our economy is becoming the major economic force in America. The chapter highlights several global economic issues such as NAFTA. Chapter 4, "Forms of Business Ownership," discusses the nature of sole ownerships, partnerships, and corporations and how these businesses are organized. Chapter 5, "The Business Mission and Social Responsibility," explains that every company must decide the nature of its business, what it hopes to accomplish, and what products it will sell. The chapter also addresses ethical issues in business. Chapter 6, "Small Business, Entrepreneurship, and Franchises," explains the importance of small business and how to start a business.

Part Two, "Organizational Management," introduces students to the basic activities of management. Chapter 7, "The Function of Management," explains the traditional activities of planning, organizing, directing, and controlling, but with a flair for how they are seen in current approaches such as total quality management (TQM). Chapter 8, "Organizational Structure," examines the process of departmentalization and organizing in a global environment. Students see how Johnson and Johnson and other firms use structure to maintain control over their large, complex companies. Chapter 9, "Production, Logistics, and Quality Improvement Processes," covers production functions, and how successful modern companies like Rubbermaid and Electrolux are thriving by incorporating new approaches to production issues.

Part Three, "Human Resources," describes how organizations are applying traditional and modern solutions to problems of motivating and maintaining effective work forces. Chapter 10, "Human Resources, Motivation, and Performance," looks at common motivation models, as well as novel approaches used by such companies as the Kalinin Cotton Mill in Russia which is now entering the global business arena. Chapter 11, "Human Resource Management," emphasizes the need for manpower planning, an especially relevant topic in view of the emerging "contingency work force." Examples such as McDonald's flagship restaurant in Beijing, China, make interesting and informative reading. Chapter 12, "Employee Relations," looks at labor unions and contemporary issues such as downsizing in the workplace.

Part Four, "Marketing Management," includes four chapters dealing with marketing. Chapter 13, "Marketing Principles," introduces the marketing concept and market segmentation. It discusses the importance of studying consumer behavior with marketing research. Chapter 14, "Products, Brands, and Prices," discusses the various types of goods and services and the marketing strategies associated with them. The importance of branding and proper pricing strategies is emphasized. Chapter 15, "Distribution," stresses the importance of placing the product in the right outlets at the right time. Chapter 16, "Promotion," deals with the fascinating topics of advertising, public relations, personal selling, and sales promotion. The promotional strategies of the Beverly Hills Sports Council, Guess Jeans, the Girl Scouts, and many other companies are discussed.

Part Five, "Tools for Business Decision Making," explains two vital tools of business—information systems and accounting. Chapter 17, "Information for Managers," describes the most recent aspects of information including such developments as the internet, voice mail, e-mail, and interactive television. Chapter 18, "Accounting," portrays the experiences of a small jewelry store to explain why companies must track financial information and how they do it.

Part Six, "Finance," examines the nature of money, and how it is managed in the world of business. Chapter 19, "Money and Financial Institutions," explains the role of money in our business economy and how it is managed by the Federal Reserve and the nation's banking system. Chapter 20, "The Securities Markets," focuses on stocks, bonds and related financial instruments, and the collaborator role played by Wall Street and other financial markets such as the Hong Kong stock market. Chapter 21, "Financial Management," describes the sources of funds and how they are used in business activities. Gotham Apparel and Rizzo Associates are two of the growing companies that show how different means can be used to raise capital. Chapter 22, "Managing Risk and Insurance," is a review of how managers control risk in business activities. Insurance is viewed as only one way of managing risk.

Part Seven, "Business Opportunities and Constraints," examines business laws and government regulations, and the types of opportunities students may find in a business career. Chapter 23, "Business Law and Government Regulation," covers many of the basic laws that affect business, such as sales law, contract law, and intellectual property law. Differences in laws between nations highlight a discussion of trademark laws and problems faced by Levi Strauss and other U.S. companies in the international business arena. The Epilog, "Your Future in Business," looks at many career opportunities in the fields of business. Information is provided for students regarding how they can prepare themselves to enter these fields.

SOME DISTINCTIVE FEATURES THE PROFESSOR WILL LIKE

STREET SMART

The Street Smart boxes feature practical lessons from business people who have learned about business in the school of hard knocks. For example, Chapter 8, "Organizational Structure," has a Street Smart box in a section about decentralization (p. 176). It makes the point that "You don't reduce costs by dividing a problem up and shipping it out of town." The Street Smart box in Chapter 13, "Marketing Principles," provides students with practical advice explaining "Ways to Market Yourself" (p. 305). Every chapter of this book includes at least one Street Smart section. We want every student who reads the book to be both book smart and street smart.

FOCUS SECTIONS

This book revolves around the four Cs of business. Special sections of the book have been written as *Focus on Company, Focus on Customers, Focus on Competitors,* and *Focus on Collaborators.* For example, one *Focus on Company* tells how one of the top real estate salesmen in New York state uses his other career as an art teacher to help him sell (p. 377). A *Focus on Collaborators* discusses how Apple Computer, American Telephone and Telegraph, and Time-Warner are forming complex alliances in the emerging digital media business (p. 79).

In Question: Take a Stand

The definition of success has changed among most young people. They would like to have a job that helps make the world better. They want to do the right thing. The *In Question: Take a Stand* feature focuses student attention on ethical dilemmas, debatable international policies, and controversial behavior by small businesses. Students are confronted with a controversial issue and asked to take a stand. The purpose of the *In Question: Take a Stand* feature is to induce spirited classroom debate.

DISCUSSION QUESTIONS

The end-of-chapter questions are organized around the four Cs to reinforce the major theme of this book. These questions were carefully designed to promote student involvement in the classroom.

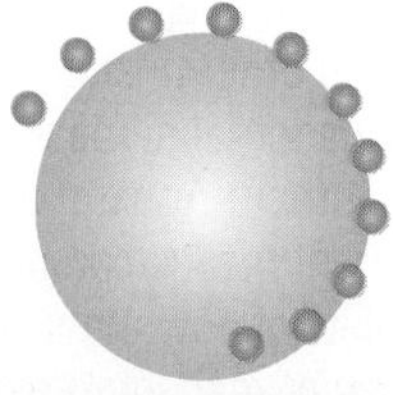

END-OF-CHAPTER CASES

The cases present real-world companies and actual situations that require students to make thoughtful decisions. The cases are designed to stimulate students' thinking by applying topics in the textbook to real-life business situations.

INTEGRATIVE VIDEO CASE

A comprehensive video case at the end of the book features the Specialized Bicycle Components Company. End-of-case questions and the accompanying video materials allow the instructor to impress upon the student that the various business activities work together rather than independently.

SMART SUPPLEMENTS

The Smart Supplements created to accompany *Business* are as innovative as the text itself. Printed supplements are available on disk and visual supplements are supplied on the Video Disc. Elements from these media can be combined to create a customized package that meets the professor's teaching needs at all levels. A description of each of the Smart Supplements and how it can enrich students' learning experiences follows.

THE BUSINESS VIDEO SERIES

A series of videos has been developed especially for *Business* to assist students and instructors in understanding the use of the four Cs from the text: company, customers, competitors, and collaborators. The video included for each chapter focuses on the chapter's content by presenting real-life experiences of both small businesses and large corporations. In addition, students will discover how all the bits and pieces of business fit together into a unified whole by watching "Specialized Bicycle Components"—an integrative video that correlates with the major sections of the book.

Custom-made multimedia presentations can be created to fit every instructor's needs with *Business's Video Disc.* Included are topical and integrative videos, critical thinking exercises, selected transparencies, learning objectives, key terms, chapter reviews, graphics, photos, and illustrations.

ANNOTATED INSTRUCTOR'S EDITION

Clear, concise sidebars on every page of the text make it easy for instructors to supplement their lectures and get students involved in *Business.* Extra examples, teaching tips, and valuable hints for integrating the visuals in the supplemental packages are included. Ann Bresingham of Robert Morris College is the author of the *Annotated Instructor's Edition.*

INSTRUCTOR'S MANUAL

The *Instructor's Manual,* which is also available on disk, features helpful information on how to use the manual and how to coordinate it with the *Annotated Instructor's Edition* and other Smart Supplements components.

Pedagogical elements in each chapter of the text are covered in the *Instructor's Manual:*

1. "Chapter at a Glance" provides an overview of each chapter plus a brief note about the opening vignettes.
2. Key terms with corresponding text page numbers.
3. Suggested Learning Objectives. These are pulled from the text and expanded.
4. Chapter Outlines.
5. Answers to Discussion Questions.
6. Notes on boxed material—"Street Smart," and the four Cs: "Focus on Company," "Focus on Competitors," "Focus on Collaborators," and "Focus on Customers."
7. Synopsis of chapter cases along with suggested solutions and answers to questions.
8. Supplemental hand-outs, self-quizzes, and exercises are provided for students.

Throughout the *Instructor's Manual,* selected transparency masters of text exhibits include detailed teaching notes that describe and highlight key points in each exhibit. In addition, a lecture outline keyed to the transparencies includes fresh examples not found in the text. Gene Hastings of Portland Community College and Dennis Middlemist are the authors of the *Instructor's Manual.*

TEST BANK AND COMPUTERIZED TEST BANK

The importance of a high-quality test bank is a well-known fact in teaching. With that in mind, the development of the *Business Test Bank* succeeds—not only by supplying instructors with a useful teaching tool, but also by providing detailed direction on how to construct tests to suit individual needs.

The *Test Bank* contains more than 3,400 questions and is available in both printed and computerized formats. Each chapter includes multiple-choice questions with mini cases to allow application of the principles, true/false questions, fill-in-the-blanks, short essays, matching, and crossword puzzles. Answers are given for each question, along with corresponding text page numbers and the answers' rationale. All questions are organized according to the text's learning objectives and are classified by level of difficulty and by type: recall, comprehension, calculation, or application.

The *Test Bank* is also available in a computerized version. Professors can quickly tailor their own quizzes and exams by using either IBM-PC compatible or Macintosh formatted computer disks. The *Test Bank* was prepared by Sylvia Ong of Scottsdale Community College.

TELETEST

If using the keyboard to select questions and develop your own testing protocols is not for you, make use of Irwin's free customized exam preparation service. Select your desired questions from the *Test Bank,* then phone Irwin's Educational Software Services (ESS) at 1-800-331-5094. ESS will send you a master test with answer key within 24 hours of receiving your order.

TRANSPARENCY ACETATES

It's no secret that there is a great need for supplemental overheads of exhibits not found in the text that are clear, legible, and effective even in large classrooms. *Business's* transparency package includes 10 acetates with 6–7 *new* overheads per chapter. Each acetate was designed with visual clarity in mind—excessive wording has been eliminated to accentuate readability.

All transparencies include teaching notes that summarize and outline key points for students. Joyce Stockinger of Portland Community College developed and organized the transparency package for use with the *Instructor's Manual.*

STUDY GUIDE

How does a student succeed in *Business?* Using the *Study Guide* provides that extra edge—it was designed especially for students who wish to improve their comprehension of text concepts. The *Study Guide* allows students to test their knowledge of text material and helps them identify areas requiring further study. The following items are included:

1. Chapter Outline.
2. "What This Chapter Is About"
3. "Important Terms and Concepts." Definitions, text key terms, and marginal glossary terms are reviewed.
4. 1–2 "Application Exercises" per chapter. These are integrated with sample "Business Papers."
5. Test questions: multiple choice, true/false, matching, and fill-in-the-blanks. Answers are given at the end of the chapter.

Mary Lou Lockerby of the College of DuPage is the author of the *Study Guide.* The Sample Business Plan in the *Business* appendix is also available on disk.

Using Smart Supplements and the capability for customized supplement packages enables the professor to create a stimulating environment for students at all levels. It's the smart thing to do!

ACKNOWLEDGMENTS

Business: The American Challenge for Global Competitiveness is the result of a team effort. The authors have great esteem for the confidence that Bill Schoof, Mary Fischer, and John Weimeister showed in us. Their willingness to commit to a project of this magnitude based strictly on a handshake is truly appreciated. We see them as three entrepreneurs in a industry enamored with conglomerate thinking.

Jane Perkins and everyone at Elm Street Publishing Services, even the White Sox fans, are the most cheerful bunch of people who must cope daily with tight deadlines and perfectionist authors. Martha Beyerlein is especially appreciated for her sense of humor and willingness to put up with our obsession for ever revising manuscript, galleys, and pages again and again just to make the book better in our eyes. Nancy Maybloom's skill as a wordsmith will be noticed by everyone who reads this book. We thank her very much. Stephanie Riley's help in photo research is also appreciated. Jessica Philip cannot be thanked enough. She truly created a work of art of which we are very proud. Sue Langguth's electronic paging skills transformed a great design into the finished book. Kelly Spiller's scheduling talents ensured a timely publication date.

Over a longer period of time, each of the authors' lives has been touched by the University of Colorado-Boulder. We all have a warm feeling for this university that nurtured our intellects.

ACKNOWLEDGMENT OF REVIEWERS

Several professors assisted us by reviewing the manuscript at varying stages of development. We sincerely appreciate the helpful comments and recommendations of the following individuals:

Rex Bishop, *Charles County Community College*
Ann Bresingham, *Robert Morris College*
Bob Cox, *Salt Lake Community College*
Gene Hastings, *Portland Community College*
Ron Herrick, *Mesa Community College*
George Katz, *San Antonio College*
Dave Kelson, *Ferris State College*
Mary Lou Lockerby, *College of DuPage*
Sylvia Ong, *Scottsdale Community College*
Gus Petrides, *Borough of Manhattan Community College*
Leon Singleton, *Santa Monica College*
Carl Sonntag, *Pikes Peak Community College*
Joyce Stockinger, *Portland Community College*
Ron Young, *Kalamazoo Valley Community College*

ABOUT THE AUTHORS

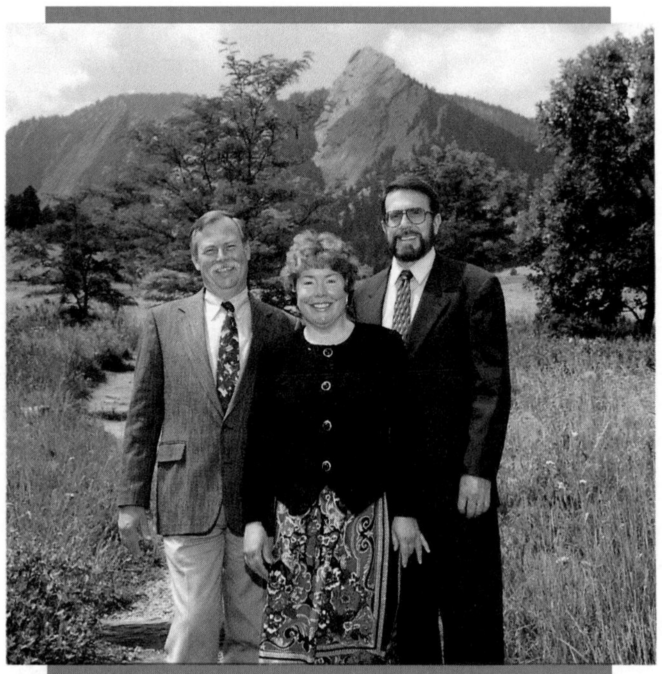

William G. Zikmund is a professor of marketing at Oklahoma State University. He received his bachelor of science in marketing from the University of Colorado, a master of science from Southern Illinois University, and a PhD in business administration from the University of Colorado. Professor Zikmund worked in marketing research for Conway/Millikin Company and Remington Arms Company before beginning his academic career. In addition, he has extensive consulting experience with many business and not-for-profit organizations.

Professor Zikmund has published many articles and successful textbooks. His books include *Marketing, Effective Marketing, Exploring Marketing Research,* and *Business Research Methods.* He is an active teacher who strives to be creative and innovative in the classroom.

R. Dennis Middlemist is a professor of management at Colorado State University. His bachelor of science in small business management and MBA were received from the University of Colorado. Following several years of banking and other industrial experience, he earned a PhD in business from the University of Washington. He previously taught at the University of Wisconsin-Green Bay and Oklahoma State University. Professor Middlemist consults regularly with private and public organizations, including Phillips Petroleum, Anheuser Busch, and the Washington State Department of Transportation.

Professor Middlemist has published many articles and textbooks including *Management: Concepts and Effective Practices, Organizational Behavior: Managerial Strategies for Performance,* and *Personnel Management: Jobs, People, and Logic.* His graduate course—Human Relations Concepts—was televised nationally for several years by Mind Extension University.

Melanie R. Middlemist is an assistant professor of accounting at Colorado State University. She received a bachelor of arts in mathematics and English from the University of Colorado. She taught math and English at the secondary level for several years before earning a master of science and PhD in accounting from Oklahoma State University. She is student oriented and is a faculty advisor to many student organizations. She has received several teaching and service awards from student groups at Colorado State University and has published articles in *The Small Business Controller* and *Internal Auditing.*

CONTENTS IN BRIEF

CONTENTS

PART 6 FINANCE 449

A NOTE TO THE INSTRUCTOR

Austen Press texts are marketed and distributed by Richard D. Irwin, Inc. For assistance in obtaining supplementary material for this and other Austen Press titles, please contact your Irwin sales representative or the customer service division of Richard D. Irwin at (800) 323-4560.

PART 1

Business Foundations

CHAPTER 1

THE NATURE OF BUSINESS

When you have studied this chapter, you will be able to:

1. Discuss how business affects our daily lives.
2. Define *business.*
3. Identify the four Cs of business.
4. Describe the activities and relationships in the business value chain.
5. Trace the historical development of business in the United States.
6. Explain why it is important to study business.

A wave of exotic aromas is the first thing that greets shoppers as they enter The Body Shop. The shop itself is very orderly. Products with names like Rhassoul Mud Shampoo, White Grape Skin Tonic, and Peppermint Foot Lotion line the shelves. The colorful shampoos, lotions, soaps, and cosmetics all bear the claim: "Not tested on animals." Stacks of pamphlets with titles like "What is Natural" abound because The Body Shop develops its products from ingredients that are natural or have been used by humans for centuries. The plastic bottles with black caps and green labels are returnable for a discount. They leave the shop in biodegradable plastic bags. Part of the profits from the sale of these products goes to fund environmental campaigns such as saving the Amazon rain forests.

Based in the United Kingdom, The Body Shop is now rapidly expanding in the United States, Germany, France, and Spain. It offers consumers clean hair and a clean conscience at the same time. One New York customer who is willing to pay a bit more for shampoo at The Body Shop than at the local drugstore says, "I liked what they had to say, and I like what they have to use."

Pineapple facial wash and orchid oil cleansing milk appeal to the growing environmental consciousness of young people—the ones who shun fur and scorn disposable diapers. Although they wouldn't buy these products if they didn't smell good, regardless of The Body Shop's ethic, these consumers don't see themselves as buying a soap, a perfume, or a shampoo. They believe they are shopping with social responsibility. They are buying ethics.[1]

What do consumers really want from a shampoo and the store that sells it? How important is the price of a product? What does The Body Shop do that motivates shoppers to buy? Is being socially responsible an important concern for the ownership and management of The Body Shop? What impact will an economic recession have on a company like The Body Shop? The answers to questions like these lie in the field of business—the subject of this book.

This chapter describes the basic activities of business and how American business evolved. It also explains why the study of business is important whether or not you plan to pursue a business career.

BUSINESS AFFECTS OUR DAILY LIVES

Perhaps you thought of some possible answers to the above questions. After all, you have visited shopping centers, examined retail displays, compared prices, dealt with salespeople, and evaluated and purchased products shipped from other states or countries. You may have worked in a retail store or a fast-food restaurant. If you think about it, you have had some experience with the business system throughout most of your life. Thus, you already know something about business. Like most people, however, you may be familiar with some aspects of business but may not fully understand its place in society or how to manage a business.

Business is a fascinating subject and is vital to our society. This book explains the nature of business today. Its purpose is to help you be a success as an employee or an owner of a business.

WHAT IS BUSINESS?

Business
All activities involved in the production and distribution of goods and services for profit to satisfy consumer needs and wants.

Business consists of all activities involved in the production and distribution of goods and services for profit to satisfy consumer needs and wants. There are many different businesses. Farms, factories, retailers, banks, transportation companies, and many other enterprises are all businesses. They all encounter problems that are unique to their situations. For example, a neighborhood movie theater faces a different set of problems than those faced by a large manufacturer like General Motors.[2] A manufacturer of compact disks faces problems different from those of a retailer of high-fashion clothing. As a result, these businesses operate in very different ways.

Is there a way to look at all businesses? Can we generalize about what all businesses have in common? The answer is yes. However, before we explain the fundamental ideas common to all businesses, let's look at the many activities involved in a particular business.

Suppose you decide to open a restaurant. You want your restaurant to stand out from others in the area. Your idea is to offer a healthy meal at a good price. To start your business you may have to borrow money, perhaps from a bank. You have to find a good location that is available for rent. You have to buy cooking equipment. You have to hire people to work as cooks and servers. You may need an accountant to do the book work. You have to provide friendly service to your customers. You must make sure you have enough cash to pay your bills. In short, you have to do many things in business.

THE FOUR Cs OF BUSINESS

Is there any way to organize all these different activities? The answer is yes. It is useful to group these activities into four basic categories:

When many students think of business, they often think of large manufacturing corporations or local retail stores. However, the principles of business this book will explain are used by such diverse businesses as filmmakers, welding services, and professional basketball teams. Even government agencies and not-for-profit organizations, such as the San Diego Zoo shown here, use many of the same business principles to run their organizations.

- **C**ompany
- **C**ustomers
- **C**ompetitors
- **C**ollaborators

We will call these categories the *four Cs*. Each C represents a participant that performs essential business activities.[3]

COMPANY

Company
An arrangement for running the business. The term *company* refers to the business itself: the organization of people, the buildings and equipment, and other resources needed to operate the business.

A **company** is an arrangement for running the business. The term *company* refers to the business itself. More specifically, it refers to the organization of people, the buildings and equipment, and other resources needed to operate the business. A company or business is the process or system of core activities necessary to run the business.

Every business must have people who perform certain tasks. At The Body Shop, there are people who make the soaps and shampoos. Employees serve as sales clerks inside the store. Accountants keep the store's records for income tax purposes. Janitors keep the store clean.

Many companies begin when an individual starts the business as the company's sole "employee." Most owners of small businesses, however, plan to expand beyond their own labor to "bigger and better things." Many companies have more than one owner. A large corporation such as IBM or General Mills can have thousands of owners.

You should realize that when we use the word *company,* companies can take many forms, ranging from an individual who works on his or her own to a large corporation that operates in dozens of countries. Our focus, however, is on "making it" and "making it big." So, although we will discuss starting a business as a one-person operation, we will spend considerable time discussing organizations that have many employees. After all, you may go to work for Disney, United Air Lines, Procter & Gamble, or another large company. Understanding the nature of such a company is an important part of "making it big."

Exhibit 1.1 **TYPICAL COMPANY ACTIVITIES**

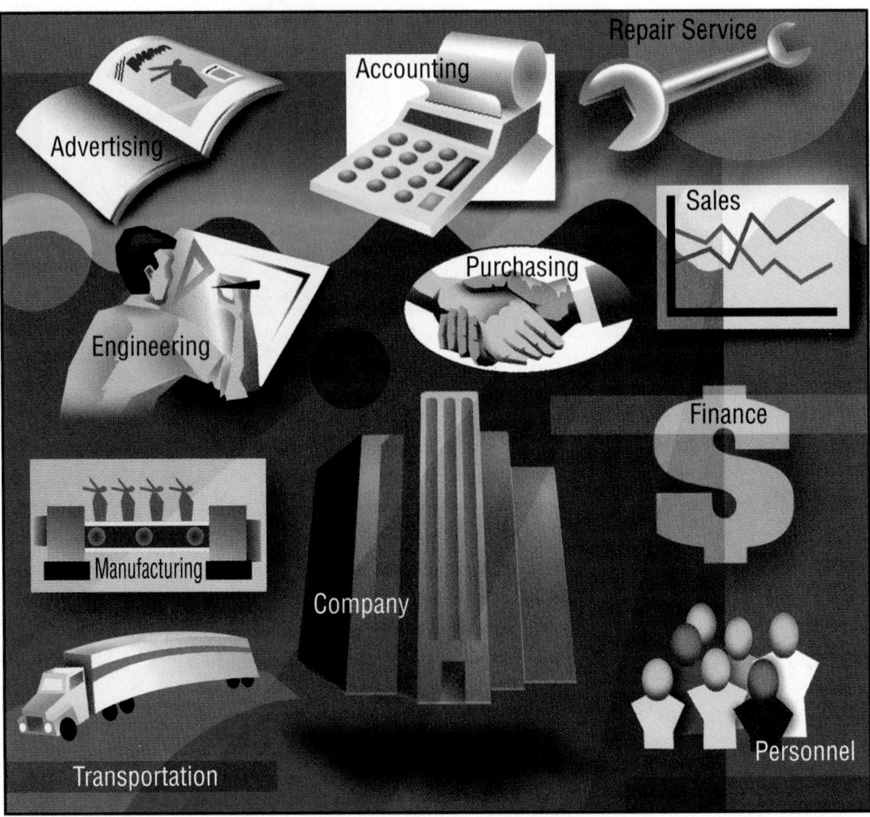

Exhibit 1.1 shows some of the major activities people perform in a large manufacturing company, including manufacturing, engineering, purchasing, sales, accounting, finance, advertising, and personnel. These activities and the people who perform them have to be managed. *Management* is the art of getting things done through the efforts of other people and by using necessary resources. Managers are responsible for the company's operations. Effective managers achieve desired results by planning, organizing, and efficiently coordinating human and material resources.

We will not define every company activity here; rather, we will briefly identify a few activities to help you understand the basic nature of a company.

Engineering and *manufacturing,* as you probably already know, involve design and production of the company's products. These are essential business activities for many companies, discussed later in Chapter 9, "Production, Logistics, and Quality Improvement Processes."

Running a company also requires money. *Finance* and *accounting* are business activities that deal with acquiring and managing the money needed to start and maintain the company.

Personnel management involves hiring, training, and other aspects of the business concerned with the administration of human resources.

Sales and *advertising* activities involve informing and persuading customers—our second C.

CUSTOMERS

Customers
Those who buy the company's products or services.

Customers buy the company's products or services. The purpose of business is to sell products or services to customers. Customers are so important that Ray Kroc, founder of

Exhibit 1.2 **THE COMPANY-CUSTOMER RELATIONSHIP**

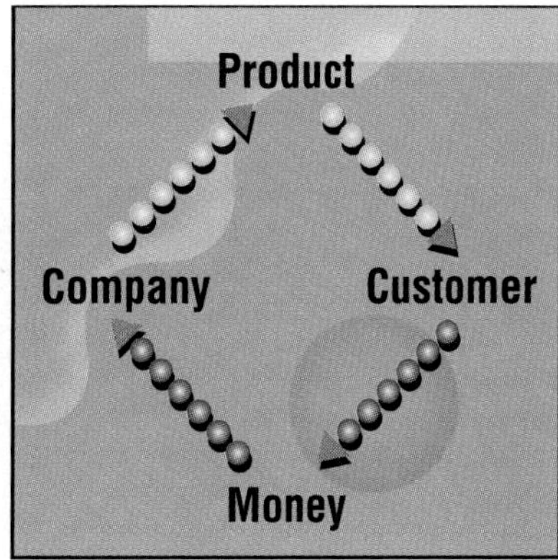

McDonald's, said, "The customer is number one. After all, that is the name of the game." Every company needs to satisfy its customers.

Exhibit 1.2 shows the relationship between the company and the customer. The company exchanges goods and services for a price. Goods and services flow from the company to the customer. Money flows from customers to the company. A price determines how much money a customer gives the company. The money a company receives is called *revenue*.

Market
A group of customers.

A group of customers is known as a **market**. Marketing activities within a company, such as personal selling, are focused to bring about an exchange between the company and its customers (the market). The most typical marketing exchange occurs when an item is bought and sold. The customer gives money to the company in exchange for the product or service.

Marketing
Planning and distributing products to satisfy customer needs at a profit.

Marketing is the major business activity for satisfying customers. Marketing involves planning and distributing products. Advertising, personal selling, pricing, wholesaling, retailing, and many other activities are marketing activities.

STREET SMART

What Is a Customer?

Many companies display signs on office walls to remind employees of important ideas. The following definition gives some shrewd advice.

A *customer* is the most important person ever in this office—in person or by mail.

A customer is not dependent on us; we are dependent on him.

A customer is not an interruption of our work...he is the purpose of it. We are not doing a favor by serving him...he is doing us a favor by giving us the opportunity to do so.

A customer is not someone to argue or match wits with. Nobody ever won an argument with a customer.

A customer is a person who brings us his wants. It is our job to handle them profitably to him and to ourselves.

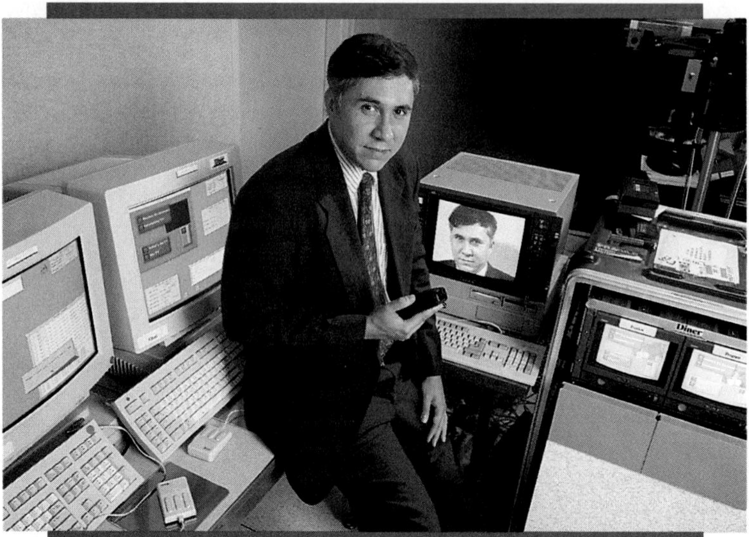

Conducting business to obtain a competitive advantage often requires working with collaborators. AT&T recognizes the ongoing merging of telecommunications and computers. Thus, AT&T is collaborating with Viacom, a cable television programmer, to market a two-way video service that will allow people to view movies at home whenever they want. AT&T is also collaborating with Sega Enterprises to enable Sega game players to take on opponents over AT&T's phone lines. These businesses mutually recognize that the success of each company depends in part on the other company.

A fundamental purpose of marketing—indeed, one of the major goals of a company—is to satisfy customer needs at a profit. Marketing is covered in Chapters 13 through 16. For now, remember that most successful companies believe customers *are* the business—and the key to business success is to satisfy customer needs better than competitors do.

COMPETITORS

Competitors
Rival companies engaged in the same business.

Industry
All competitive producers of a good or service.

Competitive advantage
Having an edge or being superior to or different from competitors in some beneficial way.

Economics
Concerned with the production, distribution, and consumption of goods and services.

Pepsico and Coca-Cola are competitors. So are two plumbing companies in your neighborhood. **Competitors** are rival companies engaged in the same business. Your competitors are interested in selling their products and services to your company's existing and potential customers.

Businesspeople refer to all the competitive producers of a good or service as an **industry**. A company strives to obtain an edge or a *competitive advantage* over industry competitors. To establish and maintain a **competitive advantage** means to be superior to or different from competitors in some way. This may be accomplished by operating a more efficient factory, offering better-quality products, selling at a lower price, or satisfying customers in other ways. We will spend a great deal of time in this book discussing how to outfox and outperform competitors. Successful companies are "street smart" companies. This idea is a major theme of this book.

In the United States, we are familiar with competition because American business operates in a *capitalistic* or *free enterprise economic system.* **Economics** is concerned with the production, distribution, and consumption of goods and services. Students of business need to know about economics because economic theory helps explain the nature of competition.

The nature of competition is influenced by the economic system and by many environmental factors. These are the subject of Chapter 2.

Exhibit 1.3 **COLLABORATORS HELP WITH MANY BUSINESS ACTIVITIES**

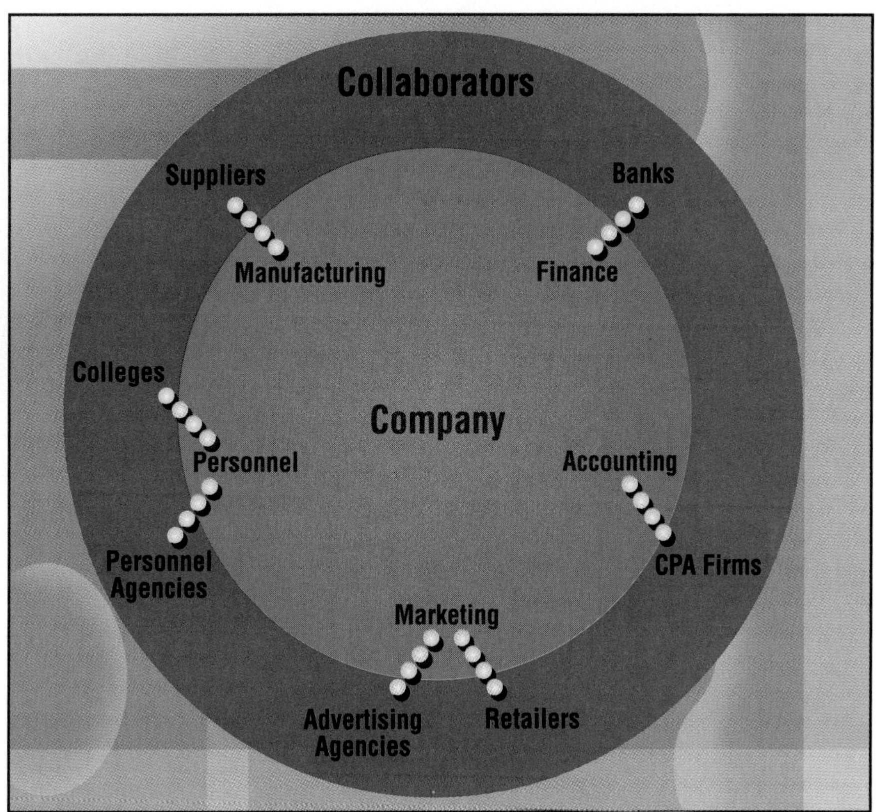

Collaborator
A person or an organization that works with the company but is not part of it.

COLLABORATORS

Hiring an accountant, buying materials and supplies, or getting a loan from a bank requires that the company engage one or more collaborators. A **collaborator** is a person or an organization that works with the company. Collaborators help the company run its business without actually being part of it. Often they are specialists who provide special services or supply raw materials, component parts, or production equipment for use in the production of other goods and services.

For example, a large company like Whirlpool works with many collaborators that provide special services or contribute unique talents that strengthen and support Whirlpool as a business. Whirlpool may borrow money from Chase Manhattan Bank. It buys the steel for its appliances from North American companies like Inland Steel in Chicago and Dofasco Inc. in Hamilton, Ontario, Canada. Whirlpool works with its advertising agency to create exciting television commercials. It uses Roadway Express and FedEx to transport its products to Sears stores, where customers receive personalized service. In Taiwan, it works with Teco Electric & Machinery Company Ltd. to distribute Whirlpool's home appliances in Asia.

Collaborators have been called *alliances, networks, informal partnerships,* and other names. However, the term *collaborators* works well because it implies a company and another party engaged in an ongoing relationship. In today's business climate, companies must be flexible and able to change quickly. Working with collaborators helps companies achieve this.

Exhibit 1.3 shows many business activities for which a company can use collaborators. For example, banks, suppliers, accounting firms, advertising agencies, and retailers are all collaborators.

Exhibit 1.4 **THE BUSINESS VALUE CHAIN**

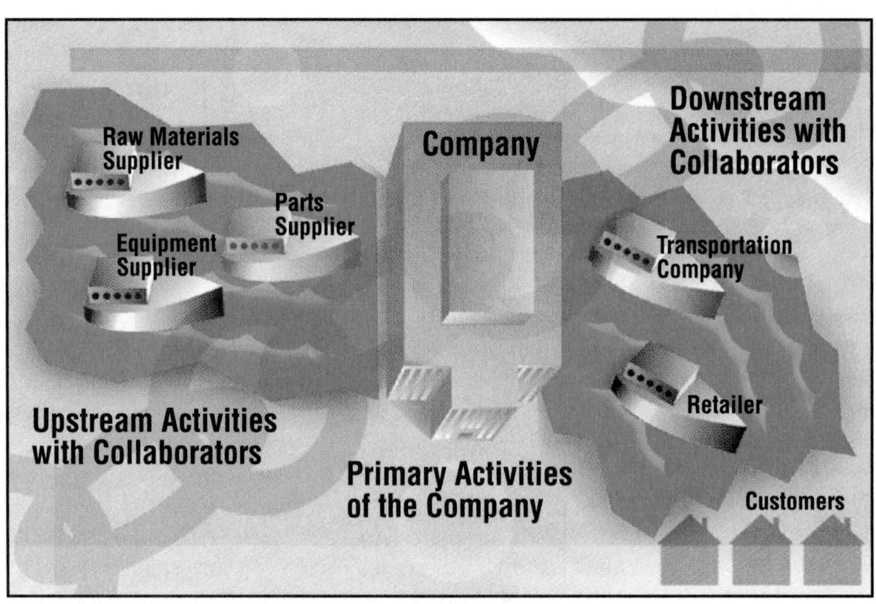

Supplier
A person or a company that provides goods or services needed to make a final product.

Let's take the relationship between a manufacturing company and a supplier. **Suppliers** provide the organization with raw materials, equipment, software, and services that help it operate its business. For example, G. D. Searle and Company supplies Pepsico with NutraSweet for Pepsico's diet soft drinks. Collaboration with a supplier like G. D. Searle eliminates the need for Pepsico to make all of its ingredients. In other situations, companies purchase equipment or other items used to run the business, such as Macintosh computers and NCR cash registers, from suppliers.[4] The typical supplier exchanges goods or services for a price.

Personnel agencies specialize in placing the right people in the right jobs. A company that collaborates with a personnel agency need not interview a large number of job candidates before finding the most qualified people.

Business value chain
A system of activities and relationships, both inside and outside the firm, that a company needs to run its business.

Exhibit 1.4 shows what we will call the **business value chain**—a system of activities and relationships in which each link in the chain adds value to the product customers ultimately buy. The exhibit illustrates the relationships between a company and its customers and some of its collaborators by dividing activities into primary, upstream, and downstream activities. Notice that before the company engages in its *primary operations,* such as production, accounting, or sales, it performs *upstream activities* such as purchasing equipment and materials from suppliers. *Downstream activities*—those performed after the product is produced—require dealing with other collaborators, such as transportation companies and retailers.

Different companies use collaborators in different ways. Although the need for and number of collaborators vary from one situation to another, almost all businesses work with collaborators to some degree. This is because when a company works with a collaborator, it expands its own resources and capacities. We will soon see that major changes in the way modern business is carried out have increased the importance of collaborators.

Much of this book deals with how **C**ompanies effectively and efficiently deal with **C**ollaborators, **C**ustomers, and **C**ompetitors. The four Cs help us understand what business requires and how a company operates. Throughout this book, we will refer back to the four Cs to help explain why one business has succeeded while another has failed.

Before we continue with our discussion of the principles of contemporary business, we will take a look backward in time. Knowledge about the development of business in America and around the globe will help future businesspeople avoid repeating the mistakes of the past.

THE EVOLUTION OF AMERICAN BUSINESS PHILOSOPHY

Business has played an important role in the history of the United States. Business and the American economy have changed along with changes in the nation itself.

THE COLONIAL ERA: BARTER IN AN AGRARIAN SOCIETY

In colonial America, most people were self-sufficient. They lived off the land. Although land was abundant, few goods were manufactured. Farmers and most other people produced their own soap, candles, and clothing. If they produced a surplus of some items, they would barter the surplus for items they could not make themselves. **Barter**, the exchange of one good for another, was common. Colonial America was basically a subsistence economy: If you needed something, you made it or traded for it.

Barter
The exchange of one good for another.

As the nation grew, silversmiths, blacksmiths, and other craftspeople began to appear. Businesses such as these made all the parts for their products and assembled them by hand. Businesses were small. Poor transportation facilities caused products to be produced and sold locally. The business orientation was to make profits by charging high prices to cover the high costs of skilled craftsmanship and limited production.[5]

These small businesses prospered because colonial society clearly valued the rights to own private property and to freely engage in whatever enterprise an individual desired. The individual's right to make a profit has a long historical tradition in America.

After the Revolutionary War, the nature of business and the American economy remained much the same. Grain, tobacco, cotton, and other crops were the mainstay of the economy. Trade with England provided goods not manufactured in the colonies. Gradually, however, the industrialization that had begun in England during the 18th century began to change our nation. Improvements in agricultural production created enough food to allow surpluses, which enabled some Americans to move from the farm and produce goods in the city that they could sell to farmers in exchange for the farmers' surplus food.

THE INDUSTRIAL ERA: THE TRANSITION FROM FARM TO FACTORY

The first half of the 19th century saw many changes. The development of the factory system, the innovation of agricultural machines, and improvements in transportation had the biggest impact on the economy and on business thinking. By 1820, three out of every four persons gainfully employed worked in agriculture. By 1910, only three in ten worked on farms.[6] The transition from farm to factory was the result of the Industrial Revolution (and a transportation revolution) and the development of machines that allowed each farmer to do work that previously required many workers.

Industrialization changed both rural and urban America. The canal boat, the steamboat, the railroads, and the telegraph improved transportation and communication. Improved transportation, especially the construction of a nationwide railroad network in the 1840s, changed the nature of agricultural markets. Many farmers began to specialize in growing one crop. Others started concentrating on raising only cows, pigs, or sheep.[7] Transportation, along with inventions such as the cotton gin, also helped bring about changes in the production of goods.

Factory system
A simple concept for mass production in the industrial age in which unskilled workers use machines to manufacture interchangeable parts and other workers assemble the parts into a standardized product.

The foundation of the Industrial Revolution was the factory system. The **factory system** of manufacturing is a simple concept for the mass production of goods. Under a factory system, unskilled workers use machines to manufacture interchangeable parts, while other unskilled workers assemble the parts to construct a standardized product. This specialization and a division of labor in the factory system greatly improved productivity. The fundamental business philosophy of the time focused on developing systems that embodied **specialization** and **division of labor**.

Specialization
Assigning different activities to different individuals to attain greater efficiency.

Division of labor
Subdividing a company's work into different components.

Factory workers received wages. Consumers purchased soap, clothing, and other basic products in the marketplace. Specialty stores began to compete with the general stores that were prominent in the previous era. Barter became less important, and the market economy was born.

THE AGE OF TITANS: THE BIRTH OF THE CORPORATION

Age of Titans
Also called the Second Industrial Revolution, the second half of the 19th century and the first decades of the 20th century, when big-business tycoons owned large industrial corporations in urban areas.

The second half of the 19th century and the first decades of the 20th century were called the **Age of Titans**. (Some historians call it the Second Industrial Revolution.) It was an age when business leaders like Isaac Merritt Singer, Cyrus McCormick, John D. Rockefeller, and Henry Ford built business empires. Large industrial corporations in urban areas became a dominant form of business enterprise. Big business needed large amounts of money, and the banking industry grew in response to this need. Individuals who invested money in stocks became the "owners" of the corporations. For the first time, managers and owners were not one and the same individuals.

Production orientation
A business philosophy during the era of the factory systems that stressed production and engineering to mass produce products.

As industrialization became firmly established in the United States, the prevailing business philosophy of the time was a **production orientation**. Managers tried to improve factory systems by eliminating workers' wasted motions. Henry Ford's creation of the assembly line in 1913 was a classic implementation of a production-oriented philosophy. The Ford philosophy stressed the use of production and engineering to produce a low-cost automobile:

> I will build a motor car for the great multitude...constructed of the best materials, by the best men to be hired, after the simplest designs that modern engineering can devise...so low in price that no man making a good salary will be unable to own one....[8]

Ultimately businesses with a production orientation began to give more attention to the efforts of their sales forces and to advertising.

SALES ORIENTATION: CHANGE THEIR MINDS

After the Great Depression (1929–1933) ended, many organizations perfected their production processes. Manufacturers now could produce as much as they wanted. The number of competitors grew. Customers now had many alternatives for spending their money. This led to the development of a *sales-oriented* philosophy. Businesses that wanted to sell more set out to change consumers' minds to fit the product. The slogan "Push! Push! Sell! Sell!" epitomized this sales orientation.

Organizations stressed aggressive personal selling efforts and advertising campaigns to "push" their existing products. These organizations concentrated on selling what they made rather than on learning what would best satisfy consumers and then producing and marketing those products. Sales-oriented organizations emphasized the goal of short-term sales maximization over customer satisfaction. This philosophy prevailed until the end of World War II.

THE BEGINNING OF THE CONSUMER ERA

Consumer orientation
A business philosophy that believes customer needs and wants are the focus of a business enterprise.

After World War II, business began to view the consumer as the hub of every business—the central point about which the business operates for the balanced interests of all concerned. Organizations began to create products and services aimed at satisfying the customer's needs. This business philosophy of **consumer orientation** holds that a business's first priority is to determine what the customer wants. It suggests that it is better to find out what the customer wants and offer that product than to first make a product and then try to sell it to somebody.

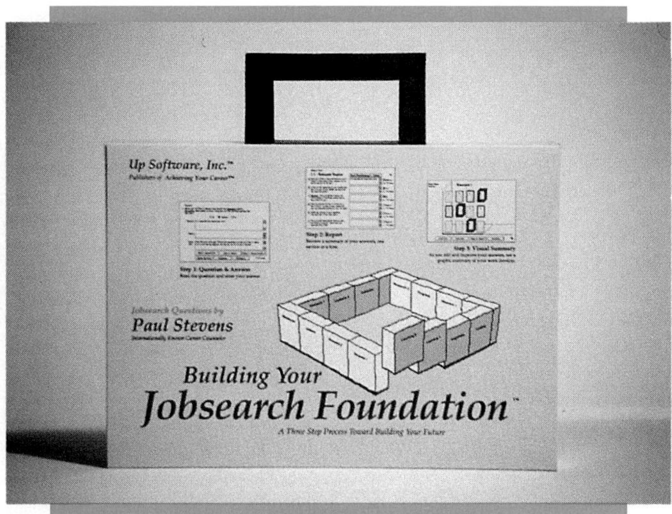

To succeed in the 1990s, companies must offer products that fulfill customer needs. Up Software is a San Francisco company that offers its customers software products such as Building Your Jobsearch Foundation. *This program helps Macintosh users maximize their efforts in preparing résumés, writing letters, and interacting in interviewing and negotiating sessions. The software uses a 3D graphical interface and visual reinforcement to help users improve their job search effectiveness.*

In a way, even the great inventor Thomas Edison, usually thought of as a production genius, was consumer oriented. Though he did no formal consumer research, he identified people's needs and sought to develop products that would fulfill those needs. Edison literally made a list of potential products such as a device for lighting houses without a gas flame, a machine that could talk, and pictures that could move to tell a story.

This consumer orientation remains an essential focus for running a business. According to most contemporary business thinkers, consumer orientation—the satisfaction of customer wants—is the reason for an organization's existence. We will elaborate on this topic in Chapter 13, "Marketing Principles."

THE INFORMATION AGE: GAINING COMPETITIVE ADVANTAGE IN A GLOBAL ECONOMY

Today most businesspeople have personal computers. They routinely use fax (facsimile) machines, electronic mail, electronic libraries, and satellite technology for video conferencing. Computer and electronic technology have moved business into the **information age**.

Information age
The current era of global business where electronic information is communicated worldwide. A business enterprise must try to gain competitive advantage, yet put a greater emphasis on its social responsibilities.

The information age has been called the *computer age,* the *electronic age,* the *service era,* the *global era,* and various other names describing the impact of electronic technology on business worldwide. In years to come, historians may reach some agreement about the appropriate label for our present era of business. Whatever name historians select, however, the point is that business operates in an environment where electronic technology *instantaneously* communicates information from around the world. This has dramatically changed the nature of business.

It is difficult to identify the exact start of the information age. No doubt, the development of the first practical computers, the widespread availability of television sets, and the invention of other electronic technologies set the stage. The first electronic digital computer was built at Bell Telephone Laboratories in 1939, but computers were not used widely until the late

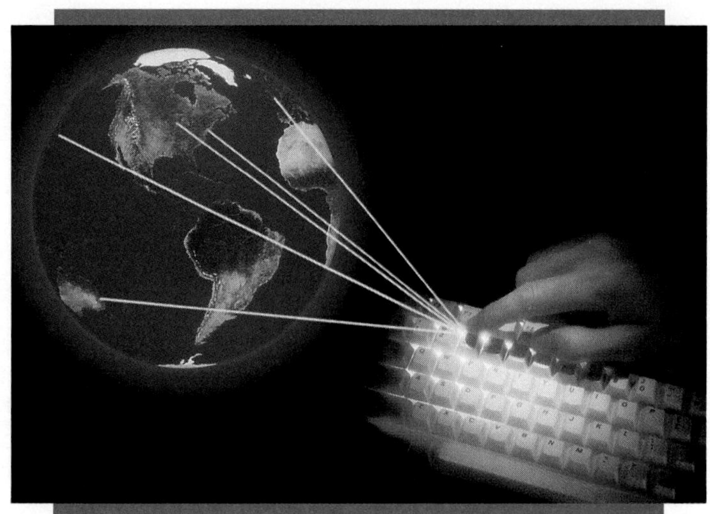

We live in the information age. Information from around the world is instantaneously communicated via electronic technology. This development has dramatically changed the nature of business. It allows companies from around the world to keep in touch with business markets tens of thousands of miles away. Today's business is global.

1950s. Television was born before World War II, but most homes did not have a TV set until the 1950s. The development of transistors and microchips rapidly accelerated the growth of the information age. Today we have instantaneous communication around the globe. Much business is conducted by computers "talking" to other computers. In the 1990s it is very difficult to imagine life without cable television, computers, and microprocessors. We are clearly in a new era.

The information age has radically changed the complexion of our work force. Factories and offices have become automated. Industrial robots have revolutionized the manufacturing process. These changes have made factory workers more productive and reduced the number of factory workers needed. Today most Americans do not work in factories. They are engaged in the delivery of services rather than the production of manufactured goods.

Many call the information age the electronic age because electronic technology gives businesspeople access to so much information. We need only think back to the Persian Gulf war of 1990 to see how electronic technology affects our daily lives. Modern computer, satellite, and fax technology have crumbled communication borders. And, as we will see in Chapters 7 and 8, changes in electronic technology have dramatically changed the nature of jobs in large, bureaucratic organizations. For example, it has increased companies' ability to work with collaborators. Many modern companies link their computers with those of collaborating suppliers.

Electronic technologies have fostered international trade and hence global competition. Global business has become so important in today's business environment that we mention aspects of it throughout the book. We also devote much of Chapter 3, "Economic and Global Issues in Our Service Economy," to this topic.

Modern communications media, which provide instantaneous reports from around the globe, have made citizens and businesspeople more aware of the impact of business actions on environmental and social issues. Today business must deal with issues such as pollution, discrimination, and illiteracy. We discuss these topics in Chapter 5, "The Business Mission and Social Responsibility."

The prevailing business philosophy of the information age is complex. Consumer orientation and other ideas from previous eras have not been abandoned. Yet the characteristics of the information age have led to new ways of thinking about business. Today's business understands that the production of *high-quality goods and services* has become paramount to consumers and our economy. Business clearly recognizes the influence of *global competition* and *advanced technology* on business activity. Business focuses on gaining a *competitive edge* and on the need to have ongoing relationships with *collaborators.* Finally, business has adopted a *societal orientation,* a recognition that the needs of society at large are a vital aspect of business.

Thus, the prevailing business philosophy recognizes the world as the marketplace. It stresses the importance of the creation of a *competitive advantage* through a consumer orientation and efficient production of quality products and services to satisfy *society's* needs.

Of course, we do not expect you to understand every aspect of this philosophy after reading this first chapter. After all, the purpose of this book is to explain what business is like today and what it will be like in the 21st century. The remaining chapters have much to say about the business philosophies that will prevail during your business career.

WHY STUDY BUSINESS?

One practical reason for studying business is the many career opportunities business offers. Career possibilities include banking, sales, product management, retail store management, computer work, and many other options. The Epilog at the end of this book provides additional information to help you learn what career options are available and the preparation required for employment in these fields.

The study of business is valuable even for students who are not planning a career in business. Many students will work for not-for-profit organizations in some capacity. It may surprise you to learn that most not-for-profit organizations actively engage in business activity. Therefore, the study of business principles can help students who work for these organizations become more efficient workers. If you plan to work for yourself, business is the name of the game, and you must understand it to succeed. After you finish this course, you will know why this is so.

We already noted that business is used by organizations and people outside the business world. Indeed, when you look for a job, you will be actively involved in marketing yourself. The business principles and skills you will learn in this course will help you achieve the goals you have set for your career. You will learn how business skills can help you in many of your daily activities.

Studying business will help you become a more knowledgeable consumer. You will better understand the business practices that influence your purchases.

Finally, learning how business is viewed by society and how it functions in an increasingly global environment is part of being an educated person. Business is a pervasive aspect of our culture that has a dramatic impact on world affairs. It is also a fascinating subject, and we hope you will enjoy studying it.

SUMMARY

1. ***Discuss how business affects our daily lives.***
   Every person deals with some aspect of the business world in one way or another. For instance, when working at a fast-food restaurant, visiting a shopping center, comparing prices, or evaluating and purchasing products, a person in fact plays a part in a much broader business world.

2. ***Define* business.**
   Business consists of all activities involved in the production and distribution of goods and services for profit to satisfy consumer needs and wants.

3. ***Identify the four Cs of business.***
   All business activities can be organized under one of the four Cs: **C**ompany, **C**ustomers, **C**ompetitors, and **C**ollaborators. A company or business is the system of core activities necessary to run the business. Customers are individuals or organizations that buy the company's products and services. Competitors are rival companies engaged in the same business. A collaborator is a person or a company that works with the company and helps it run its business without actually being part of it.

4. ***Describe the activities and relationships in the business value chain.***
   The business value chain involves a system of activities and relationships, both inside and outside the firm, necessary for the company to run its business. These activities include primary operations such as production and accounting; upstream activities like purchasing equipment and materials from suppliers; and downstream activities such as dealing with other collaborators like transportation companies, advertising agencies, and retailers to make the final product available to the ultimate consumers.

5. ***Trace the historical development of business in the United States.***
   Business and the American economy have changed along with changes in the nation itself. During the colonial era, the United States was a self-sufficient, agrarian economy in which people engaged in barter to obtain goods they could not produce themselves. By the beginning of the 19th century, the United States had become an industrial economy as a result of the industrial and transportation revolutions. The new industrial economy was based on a factory system, which focused on manufacturing goods in mass quantities. The fundamental business philosophy of the time emphasized developing systems that embodied specialization and division of labor. In the second half of the 19th century and the early 20th century, called the Age of Titans, large industrial corporations in urban areas became a dominant form of business enterprise. The business philosophy of that time was a production orientation, with a greater emphasis on improving the efficiency of the production process. This gradually evolved into the current philosophy of consumer orientation, which puts customer needs and wants at the hub of a business enterprise. Today we live in an information age where every business enterprise tries to gain a competitive advantage but also recognizes its social responsibilities (societal orientation).

6. ***Explain why it is important to study business.***
   One practical reason for studying business is the many career opportunities business provides. Even not-for-profit organizations and self-employed individuals actively engage in business activities. Knowledge of business helps you to become a more knowledgeable consumer and to market yourself effectively while looking for a job. Moreover, learning how business is viewed by society and how it functions in an increasingly global environment is part of becoming an educated person.

KEY TERMS AND CONCEPTS

Business (p. 4)
Company (p. 5)
Customers (p. 6)
Market (p. 7)
Marketing (p. 7)
Competitors (p. 8)
Industry (p. 8)
Competitive advantage (p. 8)
Economics (p. 8)
Collaborator (p. 9)
Supplier (p. 10)
Business value chain (p. 10)
Barter (p. 11)
Factory system (p. 11)
Specialization (p. 12)
Division of labor (p. 12)
Age of Titans (p. 12)
Production orientation (p. 12)
Consumer orientation (p. 12)
Information age (p. 13)

DISCUSSION QUESTIONS

Company

1. What are some companies in your local community? Describe the general nature of their business.
2. What activities do you think every company performs? Select two companies (e.g., Coca-Cola and Delta Air Lines) to illustrate your answer.
3. What is the history of business philosophy in America? How have companies' ways of doing business changed over the years?

Customers

4. Why are customers so important to a company?
5. What is a market?
6. What does the term *consumer orientation* mean?

Competitors

7. Identify two competitors in your local community. How are their businesses the same? How do they differ?
8. What does the term *competitive advantage* mean?

Collaborators

9. What is a collaborator?
10. What are some examples of a collaborator? Pick a company (e.g., a local restaurant or Nike, Inc.) to illustrate your answer.
11. What is the business value chain? Use frozen pizza sold in supermarkets to explain your answer.
12. In your opinion, how has the role of collaborators in business changed over the last 100 years?
13. We are said to be in an information age. How does this influence the nature of business today?

In Question: Take a Stand

A number of very successful businesspeople did not study business in college. In fact, some billionaires who believed hard work prevails never even went to college. Is studying business in college really worth the effort?

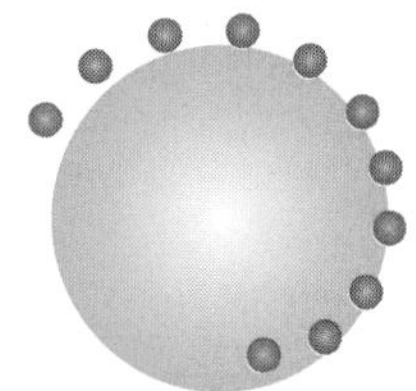

CASE 1.1
TOUR EDGE[9]

When David Glod attended Florida Southern University a decade ago, he was nearly as good a player on the golf team as Rocco Mediate, who today is a star on the pro tour. But while teammates were spending long hours honing their swings, Glod was in his dormitory room happily regripping and repairing clubs. Glod never did make the jump to a lucrative professional playing career, but his love affair with the equipment side of the game has never waned.

Today he's president of fast-growing Tour Edge Golf Manufacturing Inc., one of the dozens of small clubmakers around Chicago that has found a retail niche within the crowded cadre of national brand names. Along with Southern California, Chicago has long been one of the golf manufacturing capitals of the nation. Brands such as Wilson, Ram, Northwestern, and Tommy Armour are all headquartered in Chicago.

A second tier of equipment producers has cropped up, sporting such unfamiliar names as Vulcan, Allied, Pro Select, and Apollo Shafts. Officials of each company dream of repeating the success of Calloway Golf Company in California, which zoomed past $100 million in sales from virtually a standing start over the past decade.

Tour Edge is still a long way from the level of Calloway, which took the market by storm with an oversized driver called Big Bertha. However, Tour Edge's sales jumped 50 percent to top $1 million during the 1993 season, and Glod is laying plans for his first national efforts.

Tour Edge clubs are already carried by 110 of the 300 or so golf shops around Chicago. Glod figures that the potential for further growth in Illinois, where the firm enjoys 90 percent of its revenues, is limited. "Going national is a real challenge, but it's time to move beyond our backyard. I want to double the company's size over the next two years," says Glod, who recently hired his first national sales manager.

The 31-year-old Glod has been interested in golf clubs since he was a youngster. At age 16, he had his own business, David Glod Golf Classics, that included a typewritten catalog and classified ads in *Golf Digest* magazine. "I'd buy an old Tommy Armour driver for $50, fix it up and resell it for $400," he remembers. Glod tried the life of a teaching professional at a public course in a Chicago suburb. Soon he was doing a thriving business in club repair on the side.

In the 1980s, computer entrepreneurs like Michael Dell found they could buy component parts from Far Eastern suppliers and assemble their own finished products in the United States. Golf club makers like Glod were discovering foundries in Taiwan and China willing to produce high-quality cast clubheads for independent assemblers, who then got shafts and grips from U.S. sources.

In 1987, Glod moved into his own plant—with the help of $50,000 in loans from friends and family and $50,000 from a local bank—and began assembling and customizing clubs. It was a modest start. Tour Edge sales amounted to only $100,000 its first year, with three employees, and didn't make a profit until 1989. There are now fifteen employees and Glod has gone beyond stock products from component suppliers to his own exclusive designs. The clubheads are cast from original molds in the Far East.

Tour Edge has a thoughtful design and high quality-control standards. Its best set of irons retails for about $300. This puts Tour Edge at a price level between the low-quality $150 sets available from mass merchants and the pro-line $600 sets sold in golf shops.

Most nationally known club brands sponsor tournaments and pay top players to use their products. Such expenses would force Tour Edge to boost its prices substantially. "Tour Edge makes a very good product but if it goes national, the company is going to have to do some things differently," says Robert Held, owner of AGC Custom Golf, who consults with many large manufacturers.

Questions

1. *In your own words explain the basic nature of this company.*
2. *Who are Tour Edge's customers?*
3. *Who are Tour Edge's competitors?*
4. *Who are Tour Edge's collaborators?*

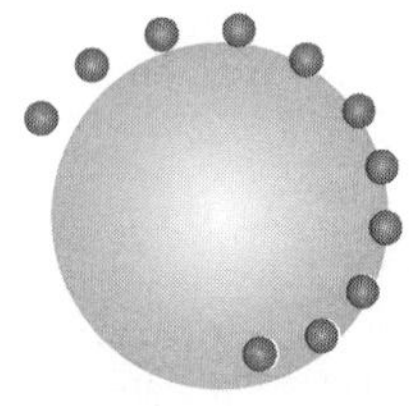

CASE 1.2
TREADCO[10]

Retreads are only a small part of the tire market for cars, but they make up more than 60% of all sales of replacement tires for trucks. Treadco, in Fort Smith, Arkansas, is the United State's second-largest retreader (behind Goodyear). It has 45 sales warehouses throughout the South, but it sells mostly through a team of 130 salesmen. They travel with truckloads of tires, making regular visits to customers to help check and consult about old tires and to sell new ones. That one-on-one service has helped the company grow strongly despite a sluggish tire market.

Treadco uses a "cold bonding" process of retreading, which it franchises from Bandag, Inc. of Iowa. Cold bonding requires much lower temperatures than traditional methods to attach new tread to a worn tire, resulting in less damage to the core tire. Retreads sell for about one-third the price of new truck tires.

Questions

1. *In your own words, explain the basic nature of this company.*
2. *Who are Treadco's customers?*
3. *Who are Treadco's competitors?*
4. *Who are Treadco's collaborators?*

CHAPTER 2

CAPITALISM AND CONTEMPORARY ECONOMICS

When you have studied this chapter, you will be able to:

1. Define *capitalism*.
2. Identify the basic building blocks of capitalism.
3. Define *economics* and identify its branches.
4. Understand that the degree of competition within markets varies.
5. Describe the purpose of an economic system and identify the two basic economic systems that exist around the world.
6. Explain how a market economy operates.
7. Define Adam Smith's market economy (laissez-faire capitalism).
8. Identify the characteristics of pure communism.
9. Describe the nature of mixed economic systems.

The Shanghai Orient Shopping Centre opened in 1993. It is in China but it could just as well be in Los Angeles or Seattle. A piano tinkles in the lobby. On the first floor, fashionably dressed Chinese women shop for Christian Dior cosmetics, Rado watches, and gold jewelry. Downstairs shoppers stock up on Unilever Lux shampoo, Heinz infant cereal, Nestlé powdered milk, and other Western brands. In the electric appliance section, newlyweds look over Toshiba refrigerators, Panasonic color TV sets, and Pioneer stereo systems.[1]

Fifty miles away is Suzhou, a quiet city of graceful ancient pagodas and gardens. Suzhou still has a socialist aura. At the state-owned Beita store, clerks nap on the counters or munch on watermelon seeds and spit out the husks on the garbage-strewn floor of the dimly lit shop. But even Beita brims with Western brand goods.

China's economy is still in part a planned, socialist economy, but that part is shrinking. In China's vast and rapidly growing underground economy, many urban residents report to their official jobs and, knowing they can't be fired, quickly depart for second or even third jobs either in the underground or in the new private sector. Socialist taxation is widely ignored. Almost no one reports his or her true income, and incentive payments at primary jobs often go unreported. In fact, few workers pay income taxes.

Fueled with money from second jobs, disregarding of taxes, and underground economic activity, the Chinese economy is growing 9 percent a year, even though it's prone to boom-bust cycles. At this rate, each year China creates a new market as big as Argentina's.

In recent years, the world has seen the collapse of communist rule and the end of the Union of Soviet Socialist Republics. China is changing dramatically. Vietnam is becoming a hotbed of business activity. Politics and economics, especially in communist countries, are closely intertwined. They determine the nature of business.

This chapter clarifies the relationship between economics and business. It begins by comparing the various types of economic systems. Then it explains the differences between capitalism and other economic systems that exist worldwide. Finally, the chapter describes how our economic system works to provide a high quality of life for American citizens who strive for success.

CAPITALISM: THE BASIC BUILDING BLOCKS

Our opening vignette points out the failure of communism. Now let's expand on the success story that opens Chapter 1 to highlight the fundamental aspects of capitalism.

Anita Roddick, the founder of The Body Shop, was not an experienced businessperson when she decided to start her own business. She was a 33-year-old homemaker with two young daughters and a husband who had a longing for adventure. She started the business with the idea that people wanted a store that sold natural products for the body. Shortly after she took out a bank loan to start the shop, her husband left for South America. When he returned ten months later, she had opened a second store.

Entrepreneur
Someone who takes a financial risk in the hope of making a profit.

Capital
Material resources intended for use in the production of other goods and services.

Profit
A company's reward for taking risks and doing a good job of management.

Anita Roddick is a classic example of an entrepreneur who owns and operates her own business in the free enterprise system. An **entrepreneur** is someone who takes a financial risk in the hope of making a profit.

Roddick took out a loan because she needed *capital* for her business. In this situation, **capital** refers to the money necessary to purchase what one needs to operate the company.

In addition to the satisfaction she receives from her work, Roddick makes a profit. **Profit** is a company's reward for taking risks and doing a good job of management. A profit is the amount of money remaining from sales revenues after costs have been deducted.

Finally, Anita Roddick's business exists in an economic system that allows her the freedom to choose the nature of her business.

Entrepreneurship, capital, profit, and freedom of choice, then, are the building blocks of capitalism. These ideas are familiar to you because you live in a capitalistic country. You already know something about economics. However, now that we have looked at a simple explanation of capitalism, we can examine the fundamentals of economic theory in greater detail. We begin with the concept of scarcity.

THE CONCEPT OF SCARCITY

Scarcity
The concept that there are only finite resources to meet infinite human needs and wants.

When we speak of **scarcity**, we mean that people have an infinite number of needs and wants but only a limited amount of resources to satisfy those needs and wants. For example, John Kim is an American community college student who works part time at McDonald's. He uses his paycheck to pay for clothing, tuition, books, and recreational activities. He would like to purchase a car, but he doesn't have enough money. He would like to spend more on recreational activities, but he can't. There are many spending alternatives for Kim.

John Kim recognizes that money is a scarce resource. When he determines his weekly budget, he considers alternative spending choices. Should he set money aside for savings? Should he earmark some money for a day at the ballpark? He must determine how to budget and allocate—distribute—the money he has.

Businesses also face problems of resource allocation. The economic system in which a business operates largely determines how scarce resources will be allocated within a society.

ECONOMICS: THE STUDY OF THE ALLOCATION OF SCARCE RESOURCES

Economics
The study of the way society uses its limited resources, which have alternative uses, to produce goods and services for present and future consumption.

Macroeconomics
The study of how scarce resources are allocated within the economy as a whole or within an entire industry.

Microeconomics
The study of the economic behavior of individual firms.

Factors of production
The resources used in the production process include material resources (land and capital) and human resources (labor and entrepreneurship).

Economics is concerned with the production, distribution, and consumption of goods and services. More specifically, **economics** deals "chiefly with the way society employs its limited resources, which have alternative uses, to produce goods and services for present and future consumption."[2]

There are two branches of economics. **Macroeconomics** investigates how scarce resources are allocated within the economy as a whole or within an entire industry such as the steel industry. This can be distinguished from **microeconomics**, which is the study of the economic behavior of individual firms.

In this chapter we will focus on macroeconomics, or the ways a society employs its limited resources. From an economist's standpoint, *resources* refer to anything that can be used to produce products, that is, either goods or services. Because economic resources are used to produce goods and services, they are called the **factors of production**.

THE FACTORS OF PRODUCTION

Our economic system uses four factors of production, or resources: land, capital, labor, and entrepreneurship. Land and capital are referred to as *material resources.* Labor and entrepreneurship are referred to as *human resources.* These are resources for the economy as a whole.

Land Economists use the term *land* in a broad sense to include not only agricultural land and land for building sites but also other natural resources like minerals, water, and timber.

Capital In economic terms, *capital* refers to material resources intended for use in the production of other goods and services. Equipment, buildings, and tools are capital goods.

Economics—more specifically macroeconomics—investigates the economy as a whole. Business, as we will discuss it in this book, concerns the operation of a single company. Sometimes economists and businesspeople use different terminology. We will point out differences in terms when clarification is needed. For example, to a businessperson capital includes *financial capital* (money) and *capital goods* (material resources). Economists do not include financial capital when discussing capital as a factor of production. To the economist, real capital refers to a resource that is directly linked to the production of a good or service.

Labor The efforts of a factory worker, a lawyer, a sales representative, or anyone who works for a business are defined as labor. *Labor* therefore means the physical activities and mental efforts of people engaged in operating the business.

Entrepreneurship As mentioned earlier, an *entrepreneur* is someone who takes a financial risk in the hopes of making a profit. A person who creates and owns a business is an entrepreneur. Entrepreneurship involves making business decisions about the other factors of production.

ECONOMIC SYSTEMS

Every society has an economic system that determines who will control the factors of production and how the society will allocate its scarce resources. More specifically, every economic system must answer the following questions:

1. *What* goods and services should be produced? (What quantity should be produced?)
2. *How* can resources be efficiently used in production?
3. Who will consume the goods and services? (*For whom* will the goods and services be produced?)[3]

Throughout history these *what, how,* and *for whom* questions have been answered in many and very different ways. Different societies have stressed different values and created many different economic systems.[4]

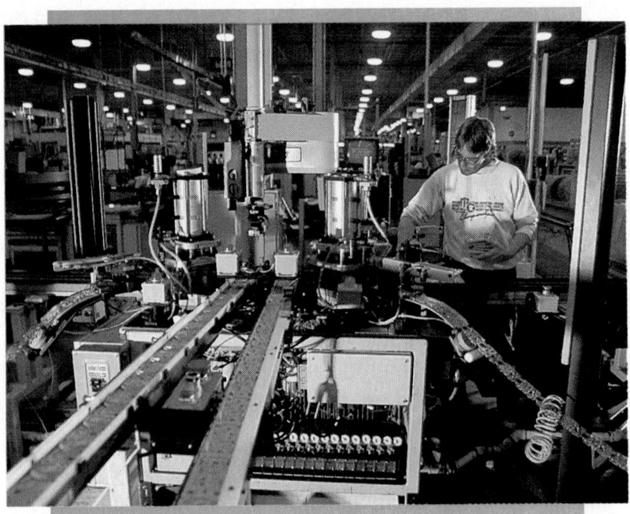

What, how, *and* for whom *are the basic macroeconomic questions. The factory shown here would not exist if there were not a consumer demand for its product. Goods must be produced efficiently if they are to be competitive. Thus, how or the way goods are produced is determined by the economic system. To whom goods are allocated is also determined by price and the laws of supply and demand.*

TWO BASIC TYPES OF ECONOMIC SYSTEMS

To begin our discussion of economic systems, we will look at two basic theories: *capitalism* and *communism.* (These should not be confused with political systems known as democracy and communism.) First, we will examine these systems in their pure form, or as they ought to be. Then we will look at modified economic systems as they exist in our modern world.

We do this because economists describe the world in two ways: *as it is* and *as it ought to be.* In other words, although neither pure capitalism nor pure communism exists in any economy today, we believe you need to understand these theories before you can understand the modified economic systems of the world today.

PURE CAPITALISM

Pure capitalism
An economic system characterized by private property, free enterprise and freedom of choice, profit incentives, and a free market economy with competition.

Pure capitalism is an economic system that has the following characteristics:

1. Private property
2. Free enterprise and freedom of choice
3. Profit as an incentive
4. A free market economy with competition

Private Property Capitalism is also called the *private enterprise system* because private individuals control the factors of production. Governments do not control labor or entrepreneurship, and governments do not own the land and capital. Individuals have the right to own land or other personal property and to protect that property.

The right of private property allows individuals to undertake enterprises that will benefit the individual businesses rather than public institutions. Businesses may be run by private individuals and are not restricted to operations run by the government or other public institutions. This feature distinguishes capitalism from communism.

Some Asian governments consider satellite television a threat to their cultural identity. Singapore and Malaysia restrict the private ownership of satellite television dishes. China and Vietnam prohibit private ownership of satellite television dishes.

Free Enterprise and Freedom of Choice Capitalism has also been called the *free enterprise system* because businesses and consumers have freedom of choice. Individuals are free to choose the nature of their work, free to choose how they will make a living, and free to enter whatever enterprise they desire. Consumers are free to buy what they wish. Of course, while individuals may make their own decisions, a person's education or income may restrict the choices that are available.

Profit Capitalism gets its name because ownership of capital is rewarded with profits. Profits provide the owners of a business with an incentive, or motive, for taking entrepreneurial risks.

Profits are the driving force within a capitalistic system. Profits determine the allocation of capital, labor, and entrepreneurs within an economy. Scarce resources flow to the enterprises and opportunities that offer the greatest profits.

Profits serve as the primary source of capital funds for expanding the business. Growth-oriented businesses "plow profits back" into the enterprise.

Market economy
An economy in which competition exists and supply and demand determine the prices of goods and services.

A Market Economy: Self-Interest and Competition A capitalistic system operates under a *market economy.* The term **market economy** refers to the fact that competition exists and the market forces of supply and demand determine the prices of goods and services. Through the price system, the forces of supply and demand determine what will be produced, what quantities of goods and services will be produced, and who will consume the goods and services. For example, diamonds are distributed to those who demand them and have the means to pay for them. When products are scarce or in short supply, prices are high and wealthier people are better able than poorer people to afford them. When a produce item such as beets is not in great demand, the price for this item is low. Thus, in a market economy price allocates available goods and services by determining who will get them.

The topic of supply and demand is important, and we will discuss it in greater detail later in this chapter. At this point, you need only understand the basic principle. When the price of a good or service is low, buyers are willing to buy more of it (demand is high). Suppliers' reaction to prices is opposite to that of buyers: The lower the market price, the less suppliers are willing to sell (supply is low). In a market economy, if the quantity brought to the market is sufficient to supply consumers' needs, the economy will create a natural market price.

Adam Smith's Market Economy The title "father of modern economics" usually goes to Adam Smith (1723–1790), who wrote *An Inquiry into the Nature and Causes of the Wealth of Nations* in 1776. In the same year Americans declared political freedom, Smith wrote about economic freedom and the market economy. He believed each individual in society should be allowed to pursue his or her own self-interest without the interference of government. Smith wrote that if no governmental obstacles exist, people (businesses) trying to enhance their own economic well-being will be led as though by an "*invisible hand*" to attain the greatest economic good for society. In other words, if each person (or business) is free to work at maximizing his or her economic rewards, the economy will prosper.

Adam Smith's theory that the government should not interfere with business is known as *laissez-faire capitalism.* This French term came about when a French businessman responded *laissez nous faire* ("leave us alone") after being asked how government could help business. This principle of pure capitalism as Smith saw it has been modified within most modern economies. Nevertheless, within our modified capitalistic system, competitive markets exist and the market economy determines price.

PURE COMMUNISM

In the 19th century Karl Marx, a German economist (1818–1883), wrote *The Communist Manifesto* and *Das Kapital* to criticize capitalism. Marx claimed the free market system exploited the laboring classes because owners of capital earned excessive profits. He believed a more equal and just society would come about if workers owned all the capital. According to Marx, workers needed to be free of the "tyranny of the marketplace" and capitalism's servant, private property. Marx argued for a "class struggle" between workers and capitalists (the bourgeoisie) to achieve a truly classless society without managers. His theory suggested that government would "temporarily" own the factors of production until such a society could evolve.

Pure communism
An economic system characterized by public ownership of property, central planning, an absence of economic incentives for workers, and an absence of entrepreneurship.

Pure communism is an economic system that has the following characteristics:

1. Public ownership of property
2. Central planning
3. An absence of economic incentives for workers
4. An absence of entrepreneurship

Public Ownership In direct contrast to capitalism, pure communistic economic systems involve public ownership of the factors of production. In theory, the public shares all the wealth of a society. In practice, the government controls all business resources.

Central Planning Hand in hand with government ownership of business is the idea of central planning as an allocator of resources. No market economy determines how much of a good or service it will produce. The central planning authority determines what will be produced and in what quantity. The central planners also decide where individuals will work and live. Workers, consumers, and citizens have little economic freedom. Freedom of choice for employment and housing does not exist. Because planners make all the economic decisions, the economy is called a *command economy.*

Absence of Economic Incentives In theory, in a communist economy each worker receives what he or she needs or, according to Karl Marx's famous phrase, "From each according to his ability; to each according to his need." In other words, a worker with low productivity would receive the same pay as the most productive worker. In a pure communistic economy, there

STREET SMART

Creating Capitalists

It is said that when Franklin D. Roosevelt was asked what American book he would place in the hands of every Russian communist should such an opportunity arise, his response was not a biography of one of our great political leaders—Washington, Jefferson, Lincoln. Neither was it a poetic or novelistic treatment of American themes by such as Hawthorne, Twain, or Whitman. Nor was it a scholarly examination of the themes defining the American experience. Possible choices here might have included works by Turner, Parrington, Beard, Henry Adams, or even by his own fifth cousin once removed, Theodore.

Roosevelt's selection was not really a book at all. It was the Sears catalog.

Although the original Sears catalog featuring a wide array of products no longer exists, in Roosevelt's time it embodied a prosperous society's wide selection of goods. If Roosevelt were alive today, he would probably pick a catalog from The Sharper Image, Williams-Sonoma, or Neiman Marcus to reflect the differences between capitalism and communism.

are no wage incentives to attract the best workers. Workers who do not perform at high levels of output still get to keep their jobs.

Likewise, profits do not exist in a pure communistic economy. In government-owned businesses, there are no profits to serve as a motivator. The lack of wage and profit incentives suppresses ambition and inhibits innovation. This is one of the main reasons for the failure of communism in the Soviet bloc countries.

Absence of Entrepreneurship In pure communism, labor creates all value. There is no need for managers or government. According to Marx, workers would carry out the managerial functions. However, even Marx said this could not be achieved immediately after a "communistic revolution." He saw the need for a transitional economic system known as *socialism,* discussed in the next section.

MIXED ECONOMIC SYSTEMS

We have described capitalism and communism as Adam Smith and Karl Marx thought they ought to be. Most countries, however, have neither a pure capitalistic nor a pure communistic economic system. These countries are said to have **mixed economies** because they combine free enterprise and government regulation of economic resources. Some economic resources are government owned, and some are privately owned.

Mixed economy
An economy in which there is a mixture of free enterprise and government regulation of economic resources.

Before we discuss how the United States and other countries deviate from the pure economic systems prescribed by theories, which suggest the way the world ought to be, let's take a look at socialism.

Socialism Karl Marx addressed socialism as an economic system because it falls in the middle between pure capitalism and pure communism. He saw it as an economic system that would facilitate the transition from capitalism to communism. Today socialistic economic systems exist in countries such as Sweden, Finland, and Norway.

Exhibit 2.1 **THREE ECONOMIC SYSTEMS COMPARED**

Issue	Pure Capitalism	Pure Communism	Mixed Economy
Private enterprise: Who owns the factors of production?	Companies or private individuals	The public	Both private companies and government
Free enterprise: Are enterprises free to do as they choose?	Yes, companies make the decisions	No, central planners decide	Choices are distributed between government and companies
Incentives and motivators: What is the role of profits?	Ownership of capital is rewarded with profits	There are no profits	Profits are highly taxed
Freedom of consumer choice: Do consumers have freedom of choice?	Yes, the marketplace encourages competition	No, planners decide what will be produced/consumed	Consumer choice is restricted
Allocation of supply: Is there a market economy?	Yes, a laissez-faire economy	No, it is a planned economy	There is a limited market economy

Socialism
An economic system in which private property is allowed but the government owns primary industries.

In **socialism**, private property is allowed, but the government owns primary industries such as health care, transportation, and banking. Individuals typically own businesses in industries that do not touch on all citizens' welfare. It is common for small businesses, such as retail stores and restaurants, to be privately owned.

Profits are allowed in private enterprises. In most socialist countries, however, governments impose high tax rates on these profits. In 1989, income tax rates in Sweden were as high as 72 percent. After radical tax reforms in 1991, the highest rate became only 51 percent.[5]

In general, both workers and consumers have considerable freedom of choice. Yet government programs often offer incentives for some occupations, and certain goods may be banned or highly regulated.

In state-owned industries, government bureaucrats engage in central planning to coordinate the activities of critical industries within the economy and to monitor political occurrences. Governments typically allot state subsidies to critical businesses to make them competitive. Exhibit 2.1 summarizes the characteristics of pure capitalism, pure communism, and mixed economies.

AMERICAN CAPITALISM

You probably know our economy was founded on capitalistic principles. Like most world capitalistic systems, however, American capitalism is actually a *modified* capitalistic system.

In Adam Smith's world, every industry consisted of many small producers and consumers who had complete information about all products. Buyers did not know other buyers, buyers did not know sellers, and sellers did not know other sellers. No individual producer could raise or lower price unless market demand or market supply changed. Adam Smith's economic theory of capitalism explained a world of commodities. All products were the same. Competition occurred through price. Prices were established via the mechanism of an impersonal market—the "invisible hand" that ensured consumer well-being. Under Smith's description of capitalism, business managers did not lose sleep over the question of whether or not to compete on price. Competition was defined as price competition, which could occur only in the short run. Producers in markets where no product differences existed had no options. They had to accept the market price.[6]

It is easy to see that not all products in our modern world are the same. Also, big business dominates many industries. But perhaps the most important reason America's capitalistic system fits into the category of a mixed economy is that the government regulates economic activity. For example,

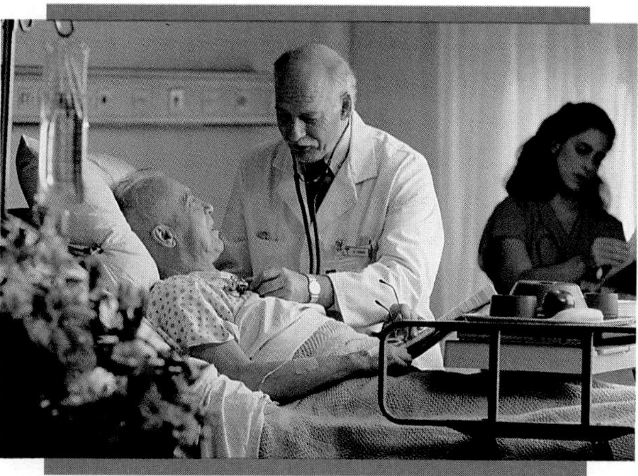

In England and Canada, the government makes many decisions about the allocation of health care resources. In the United States, where health care is a major part of the economy, President Clinton believes the federal government should become increasingly involved in deciding how our health care system operates.

- Government ownership of the space program, which is run by NASA, is an example of why the American free enterprise system does not fit with the "pure" theory of capitalism.
- The United States has a number of laws, such as the minimum wage laws, that regulate business's freedom to do as it pleases.
- The government pays subsidies to farmers to decrease the supply of some agricultural products.
- The government imposes taxes on business income that reduce the amount of profits a company can make.

We will take another look at the role of government in the American capitalistic system at the close of this chapter. However, because government plays such a large role in communist economic systems (as they exist in today's world rather than according to Marx's theory), we will now examine the reality of communistic economies.

POLITICAL AND ECONOMIC REFORM IN EASTERN EUROPE: FALTERING ECONOMIES

August 1991 marked an historic event: the collapse of communist rule in the Soviet Union. Indeed, it marked the beginning of the end of the Union of Soviet Socialist Republics. The desire to change from a centrally planned economy toward capitalism and a market economy was a major underlying reason for the political change. Politics and economics, especially in communist countries, are intertwined. The political change from a communist government toward democracy in the individual republics also led to changes in Eastern European economic systems.

Before August 1991, the Soviet Union had made minor strides toward changing its economic system. Things had gotten so bad that many communists realized that the economic system had to change. The seeds of economic change had been planted because communism, as practiced, did not deliver what it promised.

Communism had created a shortage of goods and shabby living conditions for most citizens. Productivity of factories was low by Western standards. Goods were often of poor quality, and

Now that communism has fallen, many Eastern European countries are adapting to a market economy. In Hungary, the government has sold thousands of shops and restaurants to businesses in the private sector.

even for shoddy goods the distribution system did not work. Farm produce often rotted because the trucks needed to deliver them to state-owned stores in the cities were broken down and repair parts were impossible to find.

Goods often went to Communist party bosses and labor leaders rather than to the stores. Bureaucratic corruption by communist officials was widespread. Many goods were sold on the "black market" at 10 times the official price. In state-owned stores, shelves were often bare. When food and other goods were available in stores, customers often faced long waiting lines for everyday items.

Health care items also were in short supply. Disposable items such as syringes, needles, catheters, and intravenous tubing could rarely be found in hospitals and clinics. Patients faced a higher rate of infection when these items were reused. Furthermore, when intravenous needles and scalpels became dull, patients suffered increased pain and discomfort.[7]

Stories about how the Soviet economic system worked before August 1991 are difficult for Americans to believe. More than one-half of all industrial production was for weapons, military transportation vehicles, and other military goods. Soviet consumers who wanted to buy a car might have had to wait 10 years for a new Soviet-built Ladas if they were lucky enough or had enough clout to get their names on the list. Because of the long wait, car owners could sell used Ladas for more than twice the price of a new Ladas.

Taxi drivers insisted that passengers pay with cartons of cigarettes rather than with Soviet rubles (currency). Why? Cigarettes were worth more than the ruble.[8]

Bureaucrats and hard-line communists made it very difficult for Western companies to conduct business within the Soviet Union. No consistent laws governed business activity. Western companies often had to deal with red tape and complex bureaucratic procedures that took years before any action was taken. Complicating matters was the lack of a hard currency. Because rubles could not be converted to dollars or other foreign currencies, transactions took place using a barter system, such as trading Pepsi for Stolichnaya vodka.

Mikhail Gorbachev, the former president of the Soviet Union, had foreseen the need for economic reform and restructuring (called *perestroika*) but had underestimated citizens' dissatisfaction with the economic realities in the Soviet Union. Citizens not only clamored for democracy but desired the high living standards capitalism and a market economy provide.

Exhibit 2.2 **CHANGES IN NUMBER OF CAR WASHES DEMANDED AS PRICES INCREASE**

Price	Car Washes per Month
$ 1	4
2	2
20	0

Thus, the goal of supplying a minimal standard of living to all citizens was barely met by most Soviet bloc economies. Citizens faced perennial food shortages and long waiting lines to make other purchases.

The output of the communist economies as a whole lagged far behind that of Western countries. Communist countries were inefficient. Productivity and technological innovation were far behind what Western countries had accomplished.

For the most part, business decision making was characterized by large bureaucracies where decisions were based more on political than on economic factors. Air and water pollution in certain sectors of Eastern Europe were unbearable by Western standards. By all accounts, the communist economic system in Europe was a failure.

Nevertheless, communist economic systems still exist in other parts of the world. Communism remains the economic system operating in the People's Republic of China. However, change is going on in China, too. While the government still controls most factors of production, China now allows limited use of capitalism. Perhaps in the 21st century, major economic change will occur in China, Cuba, Vietnam, and other communist economies.

Americans often take the freedom to choose for granted. The failure of the Soviet bloc economy should remind us that when governments are assigned the task of allocating goods, consumers may be unable to consume what they desire when they desire.

HOW THE MARKET ECONOMY WORKS

Now that we have discussed the foundations for economic systems, we will look at how markets in free enterprise economies work.

Industry market
A market consisting of all buyers and all sellers who engage in the exchange of a good or service.

Every economy has many industries and many markets. In macroeconomics, a *market* (or, more formally, an **industry market**) consists of all buyers and all sellers who engage in the exchange of a good or service. This fits with our earlier definition of a market as a group of customers, but the macroeconomist's perspective includes all sellers as well as buyers.

Most items of value are distributed to those who demand them and have the means to pay for them. As mentioned earlier, when products are scarce or in short supply, prices are high and wealthier citizens are better able than poorer ones to afford them. Thus, from an economic perspective price allocates available goods and services within our economy by determining who will get them. Economists focus on price as the exchange mechanism. It is the interaction of demand and supply that determines how much an economy will produce and consume.

Demand
The quantity of a good or service consumers are willing and able to buy at a given price.

Demand curve
A graphic representation of the relationship between the various prices sellers charge for a good or service and the amount of that product or service buyers will desire at each price.

THE DEMAND CURVE

Demand is the quantity of a good or service consumers are willing and able to buy at a given price. Usually the quantity demanded changes as price changes, and we can use a demand curve to represent this change. Thus, you might be willing to pay someone $1 to wash your car each week. But you might have the car washed only every two weeks if the price rose to $2, and not at all at a price of $20. At $20, you would either wash the car yourself or leave it dirty! (See Exhibit 2.2.)

If potential buyers of a particular product are grouped together, we have a demand schedule. The **demand curve**, or *schedule of demand,* is a graphic representation of the rela-

Exhibit 2.3 **A DEMAND CURVE**

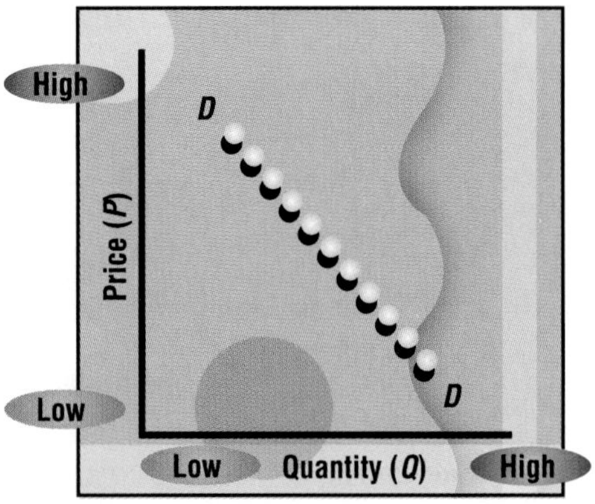

tionship between the various prices sellers charge for a good or service and the amount of that good or service buyers will desire at each price.

A demand curve for a local car wash industry is represented as the line labeled *D* in Exhibit 2.3. Note that as price *(P)* declines, more and more quantity *(Q)* of the product is demanded.

THE SUPPLY CURVE

Supply
The quantity of a good or service marketers are willing and able to sell at a given price in a given time period.

Supply curve
A graphical representation of the amount of goods or services marketers will supply at various prices.

Supply is the quantity of a good or service marketers are willing and able to sell at a given price in a given time period. The **supply curve**, or *schedule of supply* (labeled *S* in Exhibit 2.4), graphically represents the amount of goods or services marketers will supply at various prices.

A supply curve shows that as prices become more attractive to suppliers (marketers), those suppliers will try to provide more of the good or service. For example, if the price of car washes rises from $2 to $4 per wash, a car wash operation may hire more workers so that more cars can be washed in a day. Thus, in most cases, as prices rise suppliers are encouraged to supply more of the product, and as prices fall suppliers will prefer to supply less.

The intersection of the industry demand and supply curves establishes the market price (P_1) and the quantity produced (Q_1), or the *size* of the market (see Exhibit 2.5). The market is

Exhibit 2.4 **A SUPPLY CURVE**

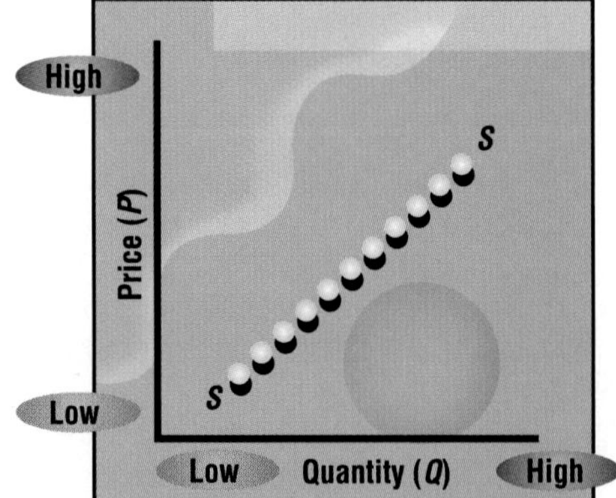

Exhibit 2.5 **THE INTERSECTION OF SUPPLY AND DEMAND**

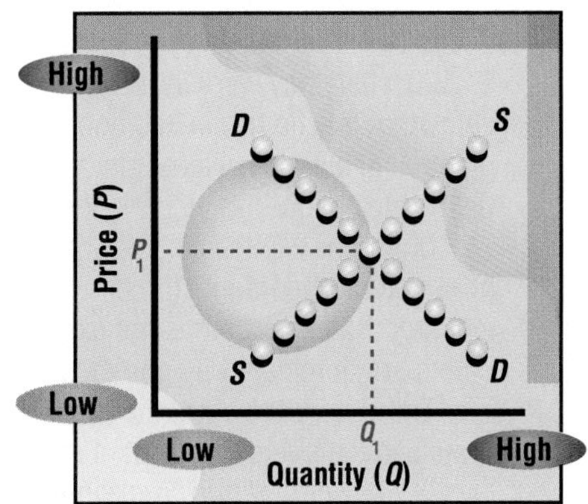

Equilibrium
The market situation where the quantity supplied equals the quantity demanded.

said to be at **equilibrium** because the quantity supplied is equal to the quantity demanded. Thus, economic theory shows how price determines how much will be produced and distributed to members of society. (Note that this discussion deals with price for an industry, not for an individual company marketing a product.)

Let's go back to the car wash industry and look at a numerical example illustrating what happens when all customers and all suppliers are combined. In Exhibit 2.6, the interaction of supply and demand occurs at $4. At this equilibrium price, car wash companies are willing to provide 500 units of the car wash service. If the price temporarily rose to $5, car wash suppliers would be willing to provide 700 car washes. However, there would be an *excess supply,* or a surplus of car wash capacity, because buyers would demand only 300 car washes. If the market price were lowered to $3, car owners would demand more car washes. Suppliers, being less interested in this low price, would offer only 300 units of the car wash service. After all, why work overtime supplying extra car washes when there is little money in it? This condition would be called *excess demand* because a supply shortage would exist.

Exhibit 2.6 **THE INTERSECTION OF SUPPLY AND DEMAND IN THE CAR WASH INDUSTRY**

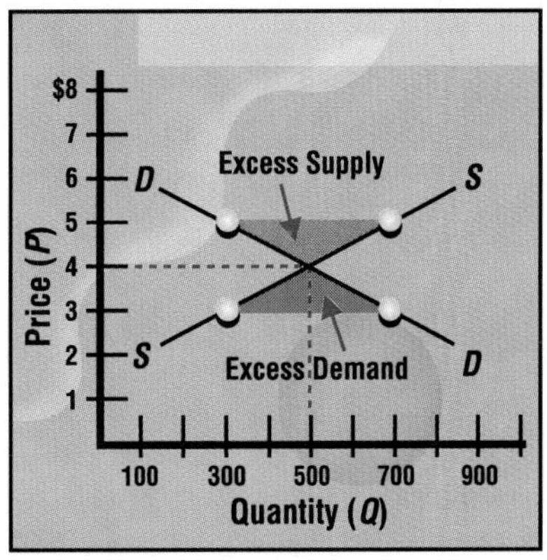

THE DEGREE OF COMPETITION WITHIN MARKETS

Economic competition, or rivalry among competitors, often leads to lower prices and the introduction of differentiated products. For example, videocassette recorders sold for more than $1,500 when they were introduced. After a few short years, the price dropped to less than 20 percent of that figure. In addition, the first videocassettes could record only two hours of programming, but today eight-hour videocassettes are available from numerous new competitors. Cellular telephones have gone the same route.

Under the capitalistic system, foreign and domestic competition influence the interaction of supply and demand forces. The degree of competition varies widely from industry to industry. Some industries are extremely competitive, with numerous competing firms, while others are dominated by one or two companies with large shares of the market.

The *competitive market structure of an industry*—that is, the number of competing firms and the size of the market each competitor holds—strongly influences business strategies. *Pure competition, monopolistic competition, oligopoly,* and *monopoly* are the four basic types of competitive market structure.

Pure competition
An industry in which no barriers to competition exist.

Pure competition exists when there are no barriers to competition. Many small competing firms offer almost identical products, and there are many buyers. This means there is a steady supply of and demand for the product, and therefore the price is controlled by neither the buyers nor the sellers; rather, the forces of supply and demand determine prices. An individual producer can make more money by producing and selling more. The markets for basic food commodities such as rice or mushrooms approximate this pure competition market structure.

Monopolistic competition
An industry in which a large number of sellers sell similar products differentiated only by minor changes in product design, style, or technology.

On the other hand, the principal characteristic of **monopolistic competition** is product differentiation—a large number of sellers, for example, selling similar products differentiated (distinguished) by only minor changes in product design, style, or technology. Firms engaged in monopolistic competition have enough influence on the marketplace to exert some control over their own prices. The fast-food industry is a good example of monopolistic competition. A Big Mac is similar to a Big Classic at Wendy's, but it has its own special sauce and comes on a sesame seed bun.

Oligopoly
An industry controlled by a few large firms.

Oligopoly, the third type of market structure, is an industry controlled by a few large firms. The commercial aircraft industry, for example, is dominated by Boeing, McDonnell Douglas, and Airbus Industrie. Getting established in an oligopoly like the commercial aircraft industry often requires a huge capital investment, which presents a barrier to new firms wishing to enter the industry. The distinguishing characteristic of an oligopoly, however, is not the size of the company as measured by assets or sales volume but its control over the marketplace as measured by its share of the market. Each company in an oligopoly has a strong influence on product offering, price, and market structure within the industry.

Monopoly
An industry that has only one producer firm and in which no substitute products are available.

Industries with only one producer firm, such as local cable TV companies and electric utilities, are called *monopolies.* In a **monopoly**, no substitute products are available and the monopolist may charge any price. The monopolist will set the price to maximize its profits.

Of course, local electric utilities are regulated by law. Thus, they are restricted in setting prices. Federal laws strictly control monopolies in the United States.

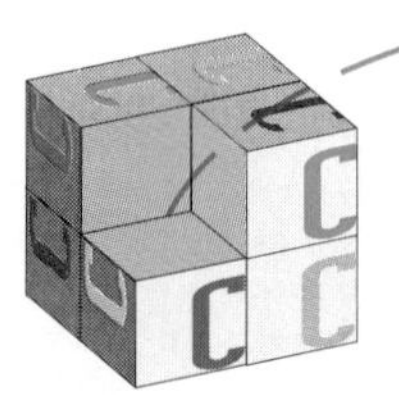

FOCUS ON COMPETITORS

Bobby Bonilla

The salary of a professional baseball player is a price—the price a team is willing to pay for the player's services. The player's position, whether he is a pitcher, infielder, or outfielder, in part determines how much the player is in demand. However, a pitcher with a low E.R.A. or a position player with a high batting average is in greater demand. Outstanding hitters like Bobby Bonilla are in great demand and the supply is limited.

When Bobby Bonilla, at age 27, made $2.4 million with the Pittsburgh Pirates, he was disappointed because he had lost his appeal in salary arbitration for higher pay. At the end of the 1991 season, when he had hit .302 with 18 home runs, Bonilla became a free agent. His services at the plate and in the outfield became highly demanded.

The Pittsburgh Pirates were the first to bid for Bonilla's services. Bonilla rejected several offers from the Pirates. The last offer of $22.5 million for a five-year contract just wasn't enough. After the Angels, Cubs, Phillies, and White Sox made higher offers, Bonilla decided to supply his services to the New York Mets for a $29 million, five-year contract. The Mets, who really wanted his services, established Bonilla's value at a price of $5.8 million per year. After some negotiation, supply for his services was brought into equilibrium with market demand.

POLITICAL ECONOMY: GOVERNMENT'S ROLE IN OUR ECONOMIC WELL-BEING

In Adam Smith's world of capitalism, many small businesses competed strictly on price. All products were the same. An "invisible hand" controlled the market. The American capitalistic system is a free enterprise system, but it is not the world of Adam Smith. Government plays a large role in today's global economy.

In the United States, the government plays a role in determining our economic well-being. It accomplishes this with a number of laws that regulate business. This is a major reason the United States is a modified capitalistic system rather than a pure free enterprise system. So many laws regulate business that we will discuss government's role in business throughout this book.

The most important laws pertaining to an economy's market structure are designed to promote free enterprise principles and safeguard our free enterprise system. Many laws have been passed to restrict monopolies. The Sherman Antitrust Act (1890), Clayton Antitrust Act (1914), Federal Trade Commission Act (1914), and Wheeler-Lea Act (1938) all deal with this issue. We will discuss these laws in Chapter 23.

Another role of government in the American economic system is to develop programs to assist the needy and otherwise help specific groups in society. The government influences economic activity by providing money, training, and other assistance to homeless, poor, and unemployed individuals and to other groups in need. Government programs for minorities, women, and other special-interest groups are discussed throughout this book.

The government also engages in economic policies that influence the level of the economy as a whole. Government actions influence economic growth, low unemployment, and low inflation. Monetary and fiscal policy are discussed in Chapter 3.

Another reason for government action is to provide roads, airports, weather services, disaster relief, and other *public goods and services.* Private companies are unable or unwilling to provide these goods and services, so government provides them in exchange for taxes.

FOCUS ON COLLABORATORS

Keiretsu

The Japanese practice of *keiretsu* provides a good example of a fundamental difference in the way American and Japanese companies conduct business. *Keiretsu* are groups of companies that form a "corporate family." Bound by mutual shareholdings or other financial ties, mem-

Exhibit 2.7 **THE RANGE OF ECONOMIC UTILITY**

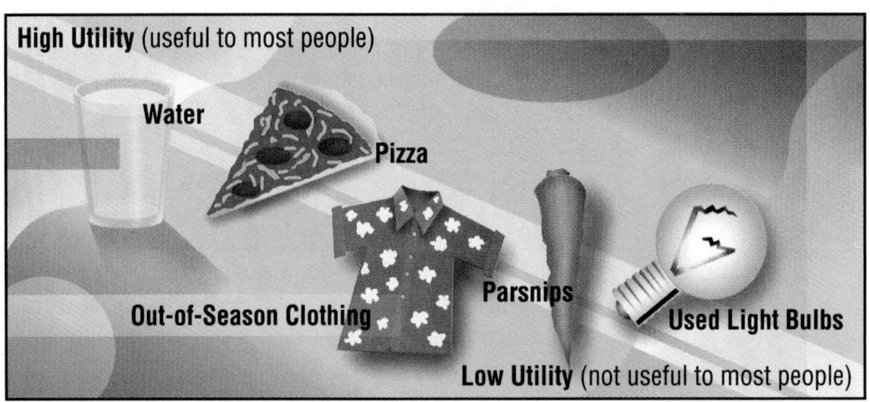

bers of the *keiretsu* engage in cooperative business strategies. Because Toyota's *keiretsu* includes Koito Manufacturing, an automobile parts company, Koito has special privileges when supplying parts to Toyota. The laws in Japan regulating the economy are very different from those in the United States. The Japanese government strongly supports the economic activity associated with *keiretsu.* Other outside companies find it difficult to market products in the same way.

ECONOMIC UTILITY

Economic utility
A product's ability to satisfy potential customers' wants.

Demand is influenced by the amount of economic utility a product offers. **Economic utility** is a product's ability to satisfy potential customers' wants. Exhibit 2.7 shows a hypothetical range of economic utility for several products to illustrate how most consumers evaluate the utility of various products.

Form utility
Economic utility created by conversion of raw materials into finished goods with a more useful form.

Place utility
Economic utility created by making products available at the right place, or where buyers want them to be.

Time utility
Economic utility created by storing products so they are available when consumers need them.

Possession utility
Economic utility created by ownership, which satisfies the consumer's need to have control over a product's use or consumption.

Four specific types of economic utility satisfy consumers' needs: form, place, time, and possession utility. In converting raw materials into finished goods, an organization's production department alters the materials' form. In doing so, it creates **form utility**. However, transforming a sheet of leather and some thread into a purse does not create form utility unless the new shape is designed to satisfy a consumer need. Marketing helps production people create form utility by communicating consumer needs for products of various configurations and formulations to production planners.

Products available at the right place—that is, where buyers want them—have **place utility**. A bottle of Pepsi-Cola at a bottling plant far from a consumer's hometown has considerably less place utility than does a Pepsi in the refrigerator.

Storing products so they are available when consumers need them creates **time utility**. A bank may close at 5:00 P.M., but by maintaining a 24-hour automatic teller machine, it produces additional time utility for its customers.

Homeowners enjoy greater freedom to alter their homes, such as the right to paint walls a bright orange, than do house renters because they have possession utility. **Possession utility** satisfies the consumer's need to own the product and have control over its use or consumption. It is created at the conclusion of a sale when the transfer of ownership occurs.

Notice that of the four types of utility identified, only one—form utility—is not developed and enhanced mostly by marketing activities. In fact, place, time, and possession utilities are created almost entirely by marketing. Provision of these economic utilities is marketing's reason for being in society.

SUMMARY

1. ***Define* capitalism.**
   Capitalism is an economic system characterized by private property, free enterprise and freedom of choice, profit incentives, and a free market economy with competition.

2. ***Identify the basic building blocks of capitalism.***
   The basic building blocks of capitalism include entrepreneurship, capital, profit, and freedom of choice. An entrepreneur is someone who takes a financial risk in the hope of making a profit. Profit is a company's reward for taking risk and doing a good job of management. Capital refers to material resources intended for use in the production of other goods and services. Freedom of choice means individuals are free to choose how they will make a living, free to enter whatever enterprise they desire, and free to buy what they wish.

3. ***Define* economics *and identify its branches.***
   Economics is concerned chiefly with the way society uses its limited resources, which have alternative uses, to produce goods and services for present and future consumption. There are two branches of economics. Macroeconomics investigates how scarce resources are allocated within the economy as a whole or within an entire industry. Microeconomics is the study of the economic behavior of individual firms.

4. ***Understand that the degree of competition within markets varies.***
   The competitive market structure of an industry is defined by the number of competing firms and the size of market share each competitor holds, which in turn strongly influences business strategies. Pure competition, monopolistic competition, oligopoly, and monopoly are the four basic competitive market structures. Pure competition exists when there are no barriers to competition and many small competing firms sell nearly identical products to many buyers. Monopolistic competition is characterized by product differentiation, where a large number of sellers sell similar products differentiated by only minor changes. In an oligopoly, a few large firms control the market. In a monopoly, there are no substitute products available and the monopolist will set the price to maximize its profits.

5. ***Describe the purpose of an economic system and identify the two basic economic systems that exist around the world.***
   An economic system determines who will control the factors of production and how society will allocate its scarce resources. There are two basic economic systems: capitalism and communism.

6. ***Explain how a market economy operates.***
   A capitalistic system operates under a market economy. The term *market economy* refers to the fact that competition exists and the market forces of supply and demand determine the prices of goods and services, what will be produced, and who will consume the goods and services.

7. ***Define Adam Smith's market economy (laissez-faire capitalism).***
   According to Adam Smith, the father of modern economics, if each person (or business) is free to work at maximizing his or her economic rewards under the guidance of the "invisible hand" (the market mechanism), the economy will prosper.

8. ***Identify the characteristics of pure communism.***
   Pure communism is an economic system characterized by public ownership of property, central planning, an absence of economic incentives for workers, and an absence of entrepreneurship. In theory, public ownership means the public shares all of society's wealth. In practice, the government controls all business resources. Because central planners make all economic decisions, the economy is also called a *command economy*.

9. ***Describe the nature of mixed economic systems.***
   Most countries are said to have mixed economies because they combine free enterprise and government regulation of economic resources. Examples are socialism and the American capitalistic system. In socialism, private property is allowed, but the government owns primary industries such as health care, transportation, and banking. American capitalism fits into this category because the government regulates economic activity to some extent and prices of all goods and services are not determined through the market mechanism.

KEY TERMS AND CONCEPTS

Entrepreneur (p. 22)
Capital (p. 22)
Profit (p. 22)
Scarcity (p. 22)
Economics (p. 23)
Macroeconomics (p. 23)
Microeconomics (p. 23)
Factors of production (p. 23)
Pure capitalism (p. 24)
Market economy (p. 25)
Pure communism (p. 26)
Mixed economy (p. 27)
Socialism (p. 28)
Industry market (p. 31)
Demand (p. 31)
Demand curve (p. 31)
Supply (p. 32)
Supply curve (p. 32)
Equilibrium (p. 33)
Pure competition (p. 34)
Monopolistic competition (p. 34)
Oligopoly (p. 34)
Monopoly (p. 34)
Economic utility (p. 36)
Form utility (p. 36)
Place utility (p. 36)
Time utility (p. 36)
Possession utility (p. 36)

DISCUSSION QUESTIONS

Company

1. What advantages does the free enterprise system offer a small company?
2. What is an entrepreneur? Provide an example.
3. What is capital?
4. In your opinion, how do companies define profits?

Customers

5. What is economic utility?
6. Think about a product you would like to own. What type of economic utility does the company offer its customers?

Competitors

7. What is economics? What role does scarcity play in economics?
8. Distinguish between macroeconomics and microeconomics.
9. What are the factors of production?
10. What are the two basic types of economic systems in the world?
11. How does a market economy work? Does America's market economy differ from Adam Smith's theory of a market economy?
12. What role does competition play in pure communism?
13. What is a demand curve?
14. What is a supply curve?
15. What is the importance of the intersection of the industry demand curve and supply curve?
16. What are the different types of competitive market structures?

Collaborators

17. What is government's role in a modified capitalistic system?

In Question: Take a Stand

There are a lot of poor people in the world. In fact, millions of people go to bed hungry every night. While capitalism works in rich countries like the United States, wouldn't communism be a better system for helping the starving people of the world?

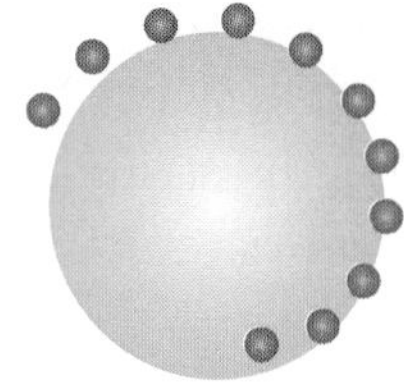

CASE 2.1
THE WESTERNIZATION OF CHINA[9]

In evaluating China's economy, most Western companies find that not all figures are what they appear to be because the Chinese government has muddled economic reality. Officially, per capita income in China is under $400 a year. But nearly every independent study by academics and multilateral agencies puts incomes, adjusted for black market activity and purchasing power parity, at three or four times that level—in other words, at $1,000 to $2,000. Multiply that by 1.2 billion people and you get a huge economy, the world's third largest after the United States and Japan. Many of these studies project that China will have the world's largest economy in a generation.

Because the remnants of the socialist state still shower urban workers with huge subsidies, most of workers' income gains go right down to disposable income. For instance, according to a 1993 study by McKinsey & Company, Chinese families spend less than 5 percent of household income on housing, health care, education, and transportation combined, compared with 30 to 40 percent in other Asian countries. A typical Chinese urban worker spends $1 or $2 a month on housing and eight times as much on cigarettes and liquor. Penetration of refrigerators in urban households has mushroomed from under 5 percent in 1984 to over 50 percent today—great for chilling that Coke and Pabst. Washing machine penetration in the cities is over 80 percent, creating a market for detergents like P&G's Ariel and Unilever's Omo. Now many urban residents are moving on to telephones, microwave ovens, CD players, VCRs, and laser disc players (great for Hollywood).

Business analysts say that once an economy breaks through an annual per capita income barrier of roughly $1,000, consumers move beyond buying staples and begin shopping for durables like TV sets; nonessential processed foods like ice cream; and packaged goods, including branded vanities such as P&G's Oil of Olay skin cream. How many Chinese consumers have crossed that $1,000 threshold? Ron Cromie, general manager of J. Walter Thompson China, which serves clients like Nestlé, Unilever, and S. C. Johnson in China, gives this advice: "Forget about the 1.2 billion [overall population]; focus on the 350 million urban residents—100 million households. The vast majority have values and lifestyles that we would characterize as middle class. They're already buying shampoo, cigarettes, beer, and biscuits."

Questions

1. *China is a communist country. How does that fact influence business in this country?*
2. *Why are businesses in the United States concerned with China?*
3. *How important is China as an economic power?*

CHAPTER

3

ECONOMIC AND GLOBAL ISSUES IN OUR SERVICE ECONOMY

When you have studied this chapter, you will be able to:

1. Explain the basic nature of today's economy.
2. Describe the importance of the service sector in the American economy.
3. Define the goals of the American economy.
4. Discuss the nature of the business cycle.
5. Describe measures of economic well-being.
6. Define monetary and fiscal policies.
7. Explain how the world economy strongly influences the American economy.
8. Describe changing U.S. economic trends.

Wu Wen-Shuo, a Taiwanese student only a year away from finishing medical school at UCLA, has decided he would like to remain in the United States. So would many non-U.S. residents. But Wu has an edge: cash—and lots of it. Under one provision of the sweeping new immigration law that took effect in October 1991, investors who put at least $1 million—or half that amount in rural or depressed areas—into an American business that employs 10 or more workers can get permanent residency. So Wu, 22, is injecting $1.1 million, which he got mostly from his family, into a new gas station and car wash in Chula Vista, California. David Liang, a San Diego real estate broker who led Wu to the investment, claims plenty of other prospective Americans are ready to plunk down their money for a fast track to permanent residency, the major step toward citizenship. "This is only my first project," he says. "If it turns out well, I have 11 other people who would like me to help them get a business started here."

It may be time to expand the plaque at the base of the Statue of Liberty that bears the famous lines by Emma Lazarus: "Give me your tired, your poor, your huddled masses...." These days the call is also out for "your skilled, your rich, and your lucky." That change is the result of the Immigration Act of 1990, the most fundamental revision of immigration policy since the 1965 law, which opened the door to large numbers of non-Europeans. At a time when America is losing ground in the global economic competition, the new law represents a major shift in philosophy about who should get permanent residency, the "green card" status that makes immigrants eligible for full citizenship in five years. The old system stressed family reunification: Ninety percent of slots went to the relatives of earlier arrivals. Now brainpower and purchasing power will also count.[1]

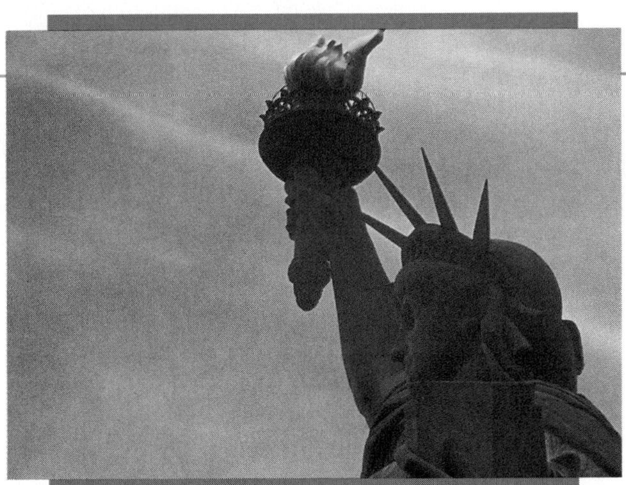

Throughout America's history, the labor market has been influenced by immigration patterns as well as by the condition of the economy. Today business and governments collaborate to enhance economic well-being. This chapter describes the nature of the American economy, the world economy, and the role global competition plays in creating a high quality of life in America.

THE NATURE OF TODAY'S AMERICAN ECONOMY

In the century following the Industrial Revolution, the image of American business was one of smokestacks and factories. The American economy changed from an agricultural economy to a manufacturing economy. Today our economy continues to change.

In the last few decades, the United States has shifted from a manufacturing economy to a service economy. This does not mean all the factories and industrial businesses have shut down. Rather, it means there has been an explosive growth of jobs for service workers and a profound change in the nature of the work force.

Before we discuss our service economy, we should explain the difference between goods and services. A business may sell *durable goods, nondurable goods,* or *services.* Goods have a tangible form—that is, you can see, hear, feel, taste, or smell them. **Durable goods**, such as automobiles and refrigerators, last over an extended period of time. **Nondurable goods** are quickly used, worn out, or outdated and are consumed in a single usage or a few uses.[2] Chewing gum, paper towels, and hand soap are examples of nondurables.

Durable good
A good that lasts over an extended period of time.

Nondurable good
A good that is quickly used, worn out, or outdated and is consumed in a single usage or a few uses.

Service
Any task (work) performed by another person or business.

A **service** is any task (work) performed by another person or business. A service may provide a product or facility for someone's temporary use, but ownership is not transferred to the customer.[3] Services differ from goods because they are intangible. You can take a Corvette for a test drive, smell a rose, and see and hear the quality of the picture and sound of a Sony television set. However, you cannot touch, smell, see, or hear a service before it is purchased.

The production of a service may be linked to a tangible good. For example, the transportation service an airline provides is tied to its fleet of airplanes. Renting a videotaped movie is tied to the temporary usage of the videocassette. Still, a service is intangible because buyers cannot see, feel, smell, hear, or taste it before they buy it. A company that produces intangible services operates its business differently than one that manufactures durable or nondurable goods.

Most services are delivered by people. Because not all workers are the same, variability among services can be great. Dealing with a friendly clerk or having other positive experiences with the people who provide the service may be a major reason why people keep using the service. Think about your regular hairstylist. Why do you go there rather than to another hairstylist? If you think about hairstyling, dental care, insurance, subway and bus transportation, and all the other services you buy, you will appreciate the importance of services in our economy.

HOW LARGE IS THE SERVICE ECONOMY?

Who belongs to the swelling ranks of the U.S. service economy? Service workers are often depicted as a legion of hamburger flippers and computer programmers, but in fact they make up a huge, diverse group whose members range from cashiers to airline pilots. The vast majority of the U.S. labor force (128,633,000 workers in 1993)—more than 75 percent—belong to the service sector. The Department of Labor defines the goods-producing sector as manufacturing, mining, and construction, but the rapidly growing service-producing sector is much broader, encompassing many new types of jobs that do not seem to fit into any other category.

The government is a major part of the service economy. Private services include such important sectors as health care; finance, insurance, and real estate; and retailing, wholesale trade, transportation, utilities, and communications.

Service jobs fit every imaginable description, from powerful (U.S. senators) to humble (janitors), from noisy (auctioneers) to quiet (librarians), and from outdoorsy (ski instructors) to indoorsy (accountants). Among the largest job classifications are professionals (15 million), executives and managers (14.2 million), sales workers (13.7 million), and secretaries (4 million). In more specific categories, the Department of Labor counts 152,000 dentists, 116,000 economists, 73,000 professional athletes, 141,000 messengers, 324,000 bartenders, and 108,000 news vendors. The country employs eight times as many hairdressers and cosmetologists (769,000) as it does barbers (94,000).

While the service economy offers a far brighter employment picture than manufacturing does, many of its jobs are relatively low paying. It was estimated that about 304,000 new cashier jobs would become available between 1988 and 2000, but average weekly earnings for such workers at the beginning of that period was only $192. Some 613,000 registered nurses will be hired by the year 2000; their average weekly earnings are projected to be $516. The service sector also includes such highly paid groups as lawyers and psychiatrists.[4]

We can subdivide the service sector of the economy into many different service businesses:

- *Business services*—companies that perform work for other companies (accounting, maintenance, advertising, and consulting services)
- *Repair services*—companies that repair machines or goods (automobile, air conditioning, and television repair services)
- *Personal services*—companies that perform tasks for consumers (maid services, hairstyling, taxis, and ski instruction)
- *Travel and lodging services*—companies that specialize in vacation and business travel (travel agencies, hotels, and resorts)
- *Entertainment and recreational services*—companies that concentrate on providing leisure time, amusement, and fun (theme amusement parks, sports teams, golf courses, ski areas, and video rental stores)

WHAT ARE THE GOALS OF THE AMERICAN ECONOMY?

The well-being of the American economy—indeed, the health of the world economy—influences most businesses. For this reason, businesspeople and economists continuously evaluate whether our economy is meeting its goals. But what *are* the goals of the American economy?

Economists, like all people, do not agree completely on the goals for the American economy. Nevertheless, most economists would agree on the following economic goals:

- *Full employment:* Full employment exists when every person who is able and willing to work has a job.
- *Economic efficiency:* Economic efficiency exists when the economy is getting the most out of its limited resources. Economic efforts are productive and well spent.
- *Economic growth:* Economic growth is an increase in the production (and usually consumption) of goods and services.
- *Price stability:* Price stability exists when prices remain relatively constant. Prices do not rapidly change upward or downward.[6]

When healthy, the economy comes close to achieving each of these goals.

We will now investigate the economic issues related to these goals. Then we will show how to measure whether the economy is meeting them.

IBM, Xerox, Southwestern Bell, and many other major companies initiated "downsizing" programs to become more globally competitive. Downsizing in the 1990s has created much unemployment among middle managers in major corporations. It has also created a demand for collaborating organizations that offer temporary workers—even temporary executives. A contingency work force, consisting of part-timers, freelancers, subcontractors, consultants, and independent service providers, now exists because companies want to be lean and flexible. The growth in the contingency work force reflects the changing nature of the global economy: Companies are increasingly using collaborators.

Business cycle
Reflects recurring fluctuations in general economic activity.

Prosperity
The phase of the business cycle in which the economy operates at or near full employment and both consumer spending and business output (GDP) are high.

THE BUSINESS CYCLE

Recession
The downward phase of the business cycle, in which consumer spending, business output, and employment are decreasing.

Depression
The low phase of the business cycle, in which unemployment is highest and consumer spending and business output are low.

Recovery
The upward phase of the business cycle, in which employment, consumer spending, and business output are rising.

The **business cycle** reflects recurring fluctuations in general economic activity. The various booms and busts in the health of an economy influence unemployment, inflation, and consumer spending and savings patterns, which in turn influence business activity. The four phases of the business cycle are

1. **Prosperity**: The phase in which the economy operates at or near full employment and both consumer spending and business output (GDP) are high. It is a period of economic growth.
2. **Recession**: The downward phase, in which consumer spending, business output (growth), and employment are decreasing.
3. **Depression**: The low phase, in which unemployment is highest. Consumer spending is low, and business output has declined drastically.
4. **Recovery**: The upward phase, in which employment, consumer spending, and business output are rising.

The business cycle affects most economic activity and our economic well-being.

MEASURES OF ECONOMIC WELL-BEING

A number of measures of economic well-being have been developed to determine whether our economy is meeting its goals. These measures include unemployment, productivity, economic growth, consumer spending, and price stability.

Exhibit 3.1 **THE UNEMPLOYMENT RATE IN THE UNITED STATES AND SEVERAL OTHER COUNTRIES**

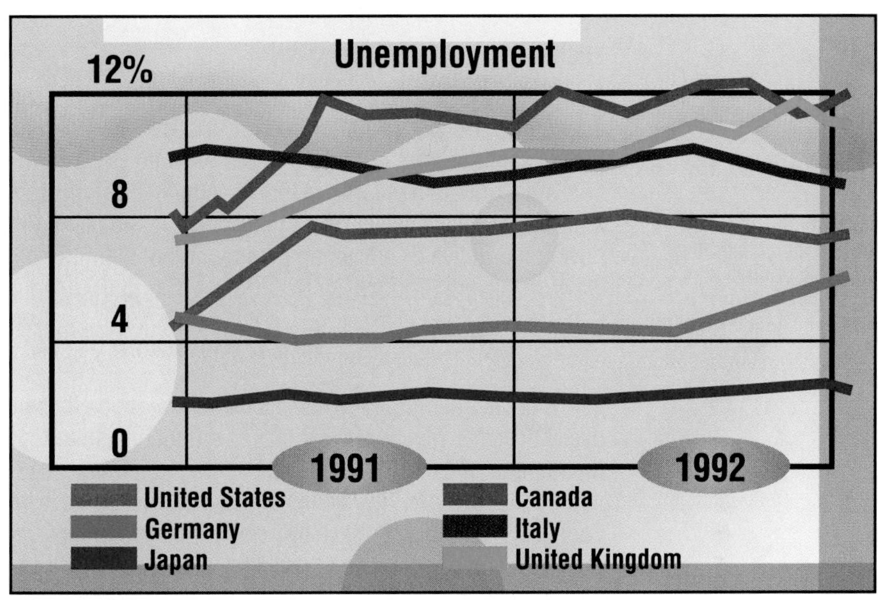

UNEMPLOYMENT

Unemployment rate
A measure of the percentage of individuals in the work force who are willing and able to work but cannot find full-time jobs.

To the person who cannot find work, the unemployment rate is the most significant measurer of economic well-being. The **unemployment rate** measures the percentage of individuals in the work force who are willing and able to work but cannot find full-time jobs.

At the end of 1993, the U. S. unemployment rate was 6.4 percent. Exhibit 3.1 compares the unemployment rate in the United States with those of several other countries using the latest comparable figures.

People may be unemployed for a variety of reasons. The economy slows down and oil pipeline workers are laid off. Ski season ends and the ski slopes close down until the next season. A restaurant worker, when asked to clean the floor with his good pants on, says, "Take this job and shove it." A typesetter at an urban newspaper loses her job to a modern, computerized typesetting machine. Typesetting jobs no longer exist; her work skills are obsolete. If she does not learn new skills, she will become one of the *hard-core unemployed.* These four types of unemployment are referred to as *cyclical, seasonal, transitional,* and *structural (hard core) unemployment.* Exhibit 3.2 defines these forms of unemployment.

Exhibit 3.2 **THE DIFFERENT TYPES OF UNEMPLOYMENT**

Structural unemployment: The loss of jobs due to a basic change in the economy. *Example:* After the collapse of the Soviet Union, the need for weapons, combat airplanes, and other military goods declined. This resulted in the loss of many defense industry jobs. Workers who cannot learn new skills become hard-core unemployed.

Cyclical unemployment: The loss of jobs because the economy or an industry is in a recession or a depression. *Example:* Oil exploration workers and automobile factory workers lose their jobs as the economy slows down.

Seasonal unemployment: The loss of jobs because the business declines at certain times of the year. *Example:* Restaurants in beach towns such as South Padre Island, Texas, lay off workers in the off season. Construction workers are laid off in the winter.

Transitional unemployment: Unemployment that occurs because people are between jobs or in the process of changing jobs. *Example:* A student about to receive an associate's degree from a community college quits her food server job because she has a job offer to work for a travel agency after graduation.

Unemployment rates vary by region of the country, age group, ethnic group, and level of education. For example, the unemployment rate among African-American teenagers is much higher than the unemployment rate for the country at large.

PRODUCTIVITY AND EFFICIENCY

Our discussion of the economic changes in Eastern Europe in Chapter 1 implied that these economies are not productive—that the quality of economic well-being is poor because these economies are not efficient. But what do *productivity* and *efficiency* really mean?

A person or an enterprise that is economically productive creates economic value. Such a person or enterprise is constructive, that is, efficient. **Productivity** is a measure indicating how constructive or efficient a person, an operation, or an enterprise is. The most common way to measure productivity is as a ratio of output to input:

Productivity
A measure indicating how constructive or efficient a person, operation, or enterprise is; a ratio of output to input.

$$\textit{Productivity} = \frac{\textit{Output}}{\textit{Input}}.$$

A measure of productivity in a factory might be the amount of output for a single worker over a specified period of time, that is, output per labor hour. For an entire automobile factory, the number of cars produced in a day might be the measure of productivity.

Productivity for the economy can be measured with average output per labor hour. Changes in productivity, seen by comparing the current year with past years, influence the cost of production of goods and services for the economy as a whole.

ECONOMIC GROWTH

Economic growth results in increased output of goods and services. If the economy grows, the society enjoys a higher standard of living.

The health of an economy is measured by a country's *gross domestic product* and its *gross national product.* The U.S. **gross domestic product (GDP)** measures the value of *all* the goods and services produced by workers and capital *in the United States.* The U.S. **gross national product (GNP)** measures the value of all the goods and services produced by U.S. residents or corporations *regardless of location.* Thus, profits on overseas operations of American companies are included in GNP but not in GDP. Profits foreign companies make in the United States are included in GDP but not in GNP. Both GDP and GNP provide economic yardsticks of business output. The difference between these two measures concerns whether we wish to know what is produced inside our borders or what is produced by Americans around the world.

Gross domestic product (GDP)
Measures the value of all the goods and services produced by the workers and capital in a country.

Gross national product (GNP)
Measures the value of all the goods and services produced by a country's residents or corporations regardless of location.

Economic growth is measured by recording changes in GDP or GNP. In 1993, GDP exceeded $6 trillion. (A trillion is a thousand billion, and a billion is a thousand million.) In 1995, GDP is estimated to be $6.5 trillion. In April 1993, per capita GDP in the United States amounted to $24,733.

CONSUMER SPENDING

A number of economic measures are related to GNP. Consumer spending is one of the most important. A country's GNP refers to the amount of goods and services *produced.* **Consumer spending,** which measures how much people are buying, is an early indicator of an economy's well-being. In general, if workers believe bad economic times are ahead, they will cut back on spending and put aside a "nest egg" in the event they are laid off from work.

Consumer spending
An early indicator of an economy's well-being that measures how much people are buying.

You will often hear reports of Sears's, Wal-Mart's, and Kmart's retail sales on the news. These reports of retail sales reflect consumer spending on general merchandise. Many economists use the early information about the sales of top retailers to forecast economic activity. Consumer spending represents approximately two-thirds of GNP.

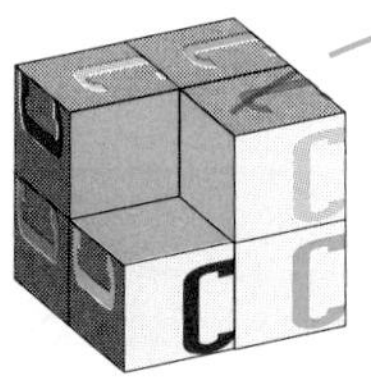

FOCUS ON CUSTOMERS

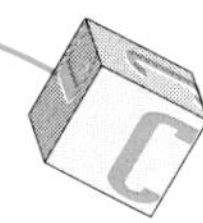

The Conference Board

Many economists use measures of consumer confidence to evaluate the health of the economy. The Conference Board, a New York–based economic research organization, produces a monthly index based on surveys of consumers in 5,000 households. The survey asks many questions. For example, consumers are asked if they think "business conditions are good" and if they think "jobs are plentiful." Then the answers are combined to form an index. The index is based on a standard of 100, which was set in 1985. In February 1992, the index stood at 46.3. At the beginning of 1994, it was at 70.

In February 1992, the index slumped to its lowest level since 1974, when the economy was in the middle of a severe recession. By the end of 1993, however, consumer confidence had increased. Consumers believed business conditions had improved and expected better times in the immediate months ahead.

The consumer confidence index usually indicates whether consumers will spend or borrow money in the near future. It is a widely watched and crucial indicator, as consumer spending accounts for approximately two-thirds of total economic activity in the United States.

PRICE STABILITY AND INFLATION

Inflation
A rise in price levels over an extended period of time.

Consumer Price Index (CPI)
A measure that reflects the average prices for many goods and services purchased by the typical household.

Inflation is defined as a rise in price levels over an extended period of time. Inflation reduces purchasing power if income levels remain the same as general price levels rise. The federal government compiles the **consumer price index (CPI)** to reflect the average prices for many goods and services purchased by the typical household. Changes in the consumer price index from one year to the next reflect the annual *inflation rate.* In 1993, the U.S. inflation rate was less than 3 percent.

Economists identify two basic causes of inflation. *Cost-push inflation* arises when the costs of production increase and are passed on to buyers. You may read in the newspaper that Chrysler does not want to give large pay increases to automobile workers because this would increase the costs of its cars. If prices rise due to labor or materials cost increases, cost-push inflation results. *Demand-pull inflation* occurs when buyers' demand for goods and services increases, causing prices to rise. When referring to all goods and services in an economy, demand-pull inflation is related to the amount of money in the economy. Demand-pull inflation decreases the value of money because "too much money is chasing too few products."

MONETARY AND FISCAL POLICY

Monetary policy
Policy that promotes or restricts economic activity by controlling the size of the country's money supply.

Fiscal policy
A policy that involves the government's power to tax and spend.

Governments influence economic activity with monetary policies and fiscal policies.

Monetary policies deal with money. A **monetary policy** promotes or restricts economic activity by controlling the size of the country's money supply. An increase in the money supply makes borrowing less expensive. With more money available, both consumer and business spending may increase. Governments normally increase the supply of money when they wish to stimulate the economy or bring about economic recovery. Reducing the supply of money generally has the opposite effect. Government economists reduce the money supply when the economic goal is to reduce inflation by "cooling down" the economy.

A **fiscal policy** involves the government's power to tax and spend. A candidate for office who recommends tax decreases suggests a change in fiscal policy. A government economist

Exhibit 3.3 **HOW THE NATIONAL DEBT AND DEFICIT HAVE GROWN OVER RECENT YEARS**

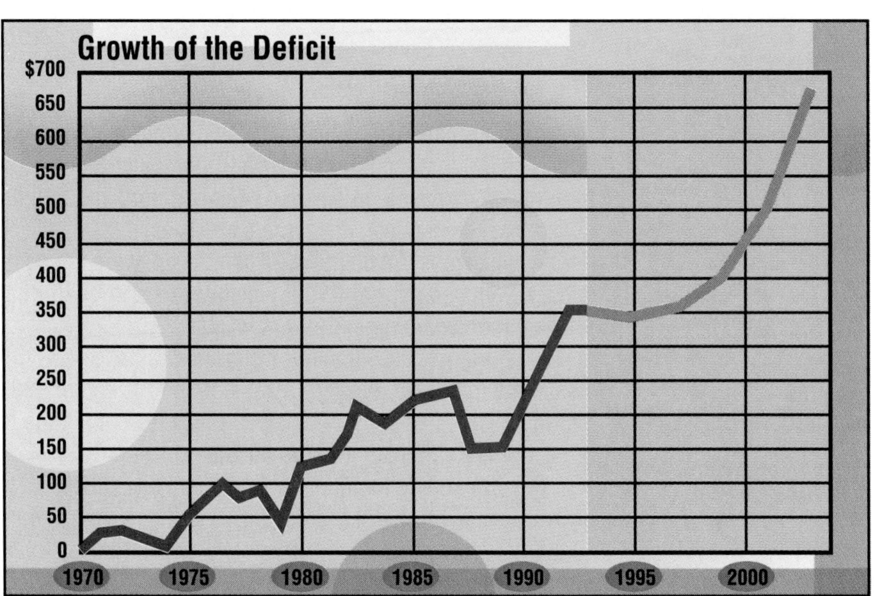

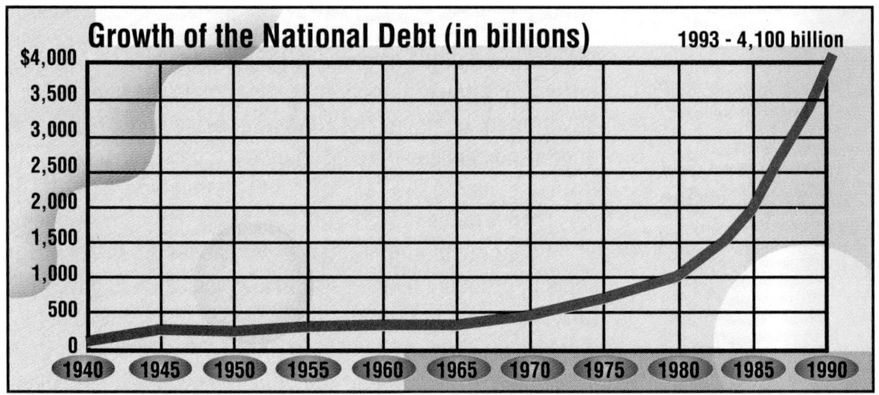

who suggests a reduction in defense spending so the money can be used for the homeless in America is recommending a new fiscal policy.

All businesses pay a portion of their income to the government. Many businesses are directly influenced by government spending. For example, manufacturers of weapon systems are influenced by the defense budget. Landlords of low-income apartment complexes are influenced by the welfare budget and taxes on low-income households. How the government taxes and spends shapes the economic conditions under which most businesses operate.

Budget deficit
Exists when the federal government's spending exceeds its tax revenues for a given year.

National debt
Money borrowed by the federal government to finance budget deficits over several years.

When the federal government's spending exceeds its tax revenues for a given year, a **budget deficit** exists. After years of borrowing to cover federal deficits (also called *deficit spending*), our federal government has amassed a large **national debt**. You may have heard the claim that "the next generation will have to pay for today's generation's reckless spending." This statement implies deficit spending cannot go on forever: Our government, like the average worker, cannot keep on borrowing without causing economic problems.

The 1994 earthquake in southern California had a major impact on the Los Angeles infrastructure. Highways, urban transportation systems, telephone and communications systems, and other economic foundations basic to a healthy economy are "invisible" to most of us until a tragedy makes us realize how important they are to a local economy.

Today the *gross national debt*—or the sum the government owes its creditors—exceeds $4.1 trillion. In the time it took you to read the last sentence, the national debt increased by $40,000. Also, just like the average working person, the federal government must pay interest on the money it borrows. Annual interest payments on the gross national debt exceed $300 billion each year (the estimate for 1995 is $400 billion). This amounts to about 6 percent of GNP. With recent cuts in defense spending, interest on the national debt is now the most expensive item in the federal budget.

Exhibit 3.3 shows how the national debt and the federal deficit have changed over recent years. The deficit is growing at $1 billion a day, or $11,574 per second.[7]

A relationship exists between government borrowing and the inflation rate. When the government borrows, the deficit increases and interest payments rise. What impact does this have on the economy? Usually interest rates go up when government borrowing increases.

A large portion of the money we borrow comes from foreigners who buy U.S. government bonds and Treasury bills. Some believe this is a cause for concern. Others conclude this is just another sign that our economy is becoming more global.

Gramm-Rudman-Hollings Act
A law passed in 1985 to achieve automatic spending cuts to help reduce the deficit.

Many critics of U.S. fiscal policy suggest that the government should reduce its deficit spending. In 1985, the **Gramm-Rudman-Hollings Act** was passed to achieve automatic spending cuts. However, in 1987 and again in 1990, political actions were taken to adjust the law to account for "emergencies" such as aid to refugees in Iraq.

INFRASTRUCTURE

Infrastructure
The basic, underlying framework of an economic system that is necessary for a healthy economy.

Another important issue in economics is the infrastructure of an economy. According to one dictionary, an *infrastructure* is the basic, underlying framework or features of something.[8] In economics, **infrastructure** refers to roads, urban transportation systems, telephone and communications systems, and other economic foundations necessary for a healthy economy. For example, when economists discuss problems in urban America, they often point to infrastructure problems. That is, many urban areas lack an underlying framework of factories,

Many U. S. citizens who travel to Banff National Forest in Alberta stay in hotels, purchase recreational services, and buy souvenirs. As this example illustrates, international business between Canada and the United States, the world's largest trading partners, involves both goods and services.

supermarkets, and other economic institutions needed to support thriving economic activity. Governments often strengthen infrastructures to improve economic productivity.

Companies considering doing business in other countries look closely at infrastructure before investing heavily abroad. For example, modern airports are essential to most international business.

GLOBAL COMPETITION AND INTERNATIONAL BUSINESS

You may drive a Toyota, a Mazda, or a Volvo. You may fill your tank at a Shell service station with gasoline refined from crude oil from Nigeria or Venezuela. The attendant may ask you to sign the credit slip with a Bic pen. Each of these products comes from a foreign company and is made available in the United States as a result of *international business.* Today the American economy is strongly influenced by the world economy. It is difficult to think of matters that do not affect or are not themselves affected by other areas of the world. Jet age transportation, satellite television, computers, facsimile (fax) transmissions, and other electronic technologies are reshaping and restructuring the patterns of business.

IMPORTS AND EXPORTS

Imports
Products that are produced in other countries and sold in the home country.

Exports
Products that are produced in the home country and sold in other countries.

Products that are produced in other countries and sold in the home country are **imports**. Products that are produced in the home country and sold in other countries are **exports**. For example, official Swiss army knives, which bear the familiar white cross, are manufactured by Wenger S.A. in Switzerland. Wenger S.A. operates its international business in Swiss army knives by exporting to the U.S. market with the help of Precision International in Orangeburg, New York. Precision International is thus an *importer,* while Wenger S.A. is an *exporter.*

Countries import foreign products to fill needs that domestic producers are not satisfying. Because the United States cannot supply all of its oil-related needs, it must import oil from other nations. In this sense, imported products are a necessary way of life. World trade helps countries meet certain needs that their domestic economies are not meeting. With con-

Exhibit 3.4 **THE UNITED STATES' TOP TEN TRADING PARTNERS**

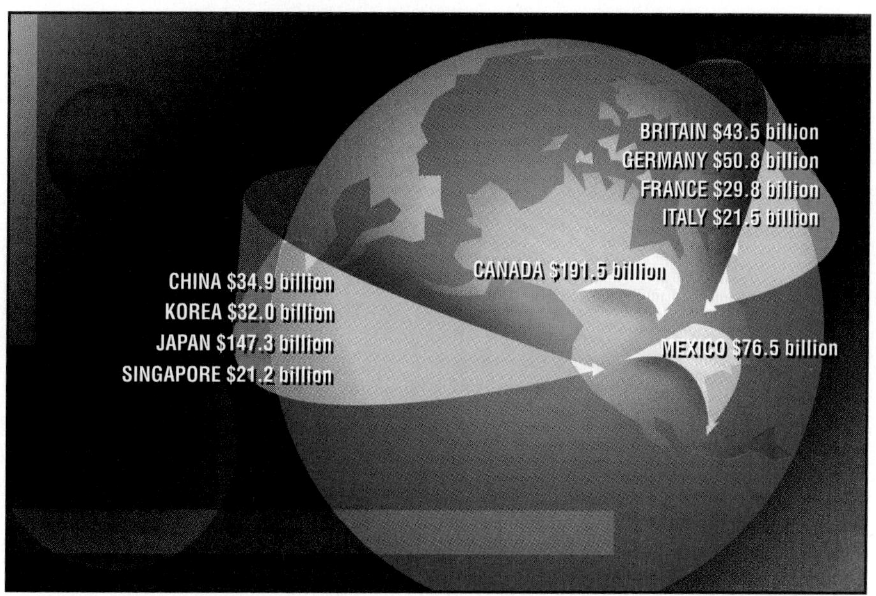

tinued growth of multinational business activity, world trade can be expected to raise the standard of living in many parts of the world.

Exhibit 3.4 shows America's top export customers. Canada is America's biggest trading partner in total volume of imports and exports. Japan is second, and Mexico is third.

Exhibit 3.5 lists America's leading imports and exports in 1993. Crude oil was the largest import and agricultural products the biggest U.S. export.

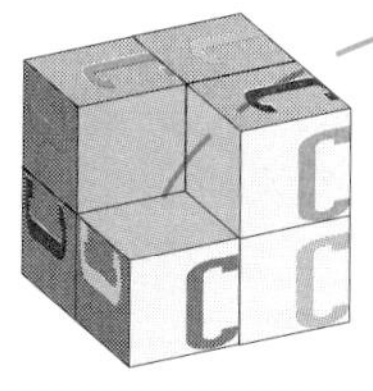

FOCUS ON COMPETITORS

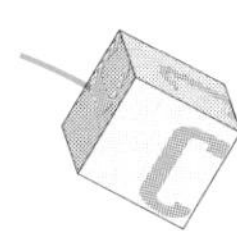

Sushi Boy

A trial shipment of 960 pieces of sushi was held in storage at Osaka airport until it was released after passing its sanitary inspection. This may not seem an important event. However, it was a victory for free trade and the American rice industry when Japan's government decided to approve the plan for a restaurant chain to import frozen sushi from the United States. Fujio Matsumoto, president of the Sushi Boy chain, said the company had been told by the branch of Japan's food agency in Osaka,where the company is based, that imports of sushi would not violate the nation's prohibition on imported rice.

Sushi Boy wanted to manufacture sushi, slices of raw fish on top of chunks of rice, at its factory in Escondido, California, and import the products to serve in its 44 restaurants. Matsumoto said the company could cut the price of its sushi nearly in half by using California rice, which costs one-fifth or less of the cost of Japanese rice, and making the sushi in an automated factory rather than by hand at each restaurant.

But the Japanese food agency said no. Japan bans rice imports to protect its rice farmers and remain self-sufficient in its staple food. But it permits imports of processed food containing rice if other ingredients make up at least 20 percent of the total weight.

Exhibit 3.5 **TOP U.S. IMPORTS AND EXPORTS, 1993 (BILLIONS OF DOLLARS)**

Imports		*Exports*	
Motor cars and other vehicles	$52.5	Aircraft and associated equipment	$31.9
Crude oil	38.4	Thermionic, cold cathode, photocathode valves	20.1
Data processing machines	26.5	Parts and accessories for motor vehicles	19.7
Thermionic, cold cathode, photocathode valves	20.6	Data processing machines	18.0
Parts and accessories for motor vehicles	14.0	Motor cars and other vehicles	15.0
Telecommunications equipment	13.7	Parts for data processing and office machines	12.4
Parts for data processing and office machines	11.6	Telecommunications equipment	10.9
Baby carriages, toys, games, and sporting equipment	11.2	Measuring and analysis instruments	9.7

Sushi Boy claimed its sushi met this requirement. The food agency, however, was worried that the rice could be separated from the fish too easily. But top officials at the Ministry of Finance, which has jurisdiction over customs, and of the Ministry of Agriculture, which oversees the food agency, said that sushi is, in the words of finance vice minister Mamoru Ozaki, "one entity" rather than separate pieces of rice and fish.

Both the American embassy in Tokyo and the U.S. Rice Millers Association issued statements in support of the sushi imports. Matsumoto of Sushi Boy said international pressure clearly played a role in guiding the government to make this culinary distinction.

Now Sushi Boy faces another challenge: getting Japanese consumers, who generally like their sushi fresh and home grown, to eat the prefabricated American product.

TRADE DEFICITS AND SURPLUSES

In our modern economy, businesses engage in international business or trade with other nations. A *trade deficit* or a *trade surplus* indicates whether a country is buying more than it sells to other countries or selling more than it buys from other countries. The United States

STREET SMART

There's Nothing Simple about a Business Trip to Osaka, Japan

The complexities of doing business in Osaka, Japan, can be overwhelming. Not only is the language foreign but the rituals and business practices are quite different from our own. For this reason, the power of having just a little knowledge beforehand should never be underestimated.

Try to type up all your ideas and the points you want to make at your meetings so you can hand them out before you start. The Japanese understand written English much better than they do the spoken word.

Although friendly, Osaka's taxi drivers speak almost no English, so get all your directions written in Japanese before you leave the hotel. Osaka is an enormous and congested city, so make sure to allow time for traffic delays.

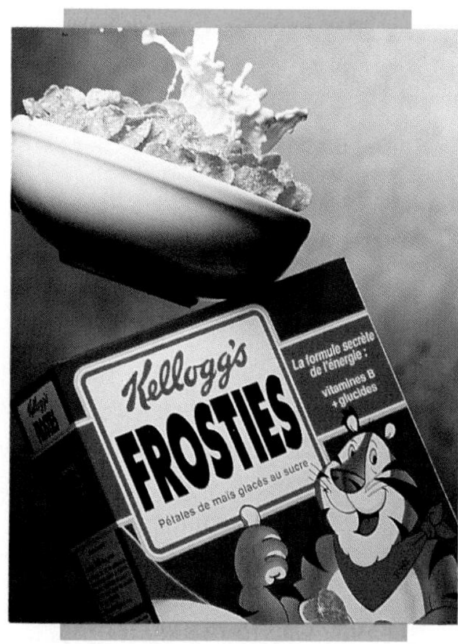

Kellogg Company, the maker of Kellogg's Corn Flakes®, Kellogg's Rice Krispies®, and Kellogg's Frosted Flakes®, distributes its ready-to-eat cereals in over 150 countries. The global marketplace is exceedingly important to Kellogg. It earns more than 35 percent of its profits outside of the United States.

has a trade deficit with Japan, because it imports more goods from Japan than it exports to Japan. With Canada it has a trade surplus, because it exports more products to Canada than it imports from there. Since 1976, the United States has had a trade deficit with the rest of the world. In 1994, the trade deficit was approximately $11 billion.

Balance of payments
A record of the flow of money between a nation and the rest of the world.

The **balance of payments** is a record of the flow of money between a nation and the rest of the world. The relationship between a country's imports and its exports plays a major part in the country's balance of payments. However, money flows are not restricted to import and export activity. The government's aid to undeveloped countries, military spending abroad, tourists vacationing in foreign lands, foreign investments in the home country, and other financial transactions influence the flow of money into and out of the country.

Governments that wish to reduce a trade deficit or a balance of payments deficit often adopt monetary policies to influence the currency exchange rate.

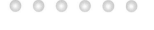

EXCHANGE RATES

Exchange rate
Indicates the value of one country's currency relative to another country's currency.

If you go to Japan, you will spend yen. If you do business in Venezuela, you will do so in bolivars. Just how many dollars equal a yen or a bolivar? The answer to this question lies in the exchange rate. Almost every country has its own currency or form of money. The **exchange rate** indicates the value of one country's currency relative to another country's currency. In 1985 a Swiss franc could be exchanged for $2.25, but in 1994 a Swiss franc bought only $1.40. In the last few years, the Swiss franc has lost value relative to many countries' currencies. This loss of value of the dollar is known as *devaluation.* In contrast, the U.S. dollar has grown in value compared to the Swiss franc. American companies like this *revaluation* of the dollar because it makes a business trip to Switzerland more affordable.

After devaluation of the Swiss franc, economists say the franc is weaker. The weaker the franc is to the dollar, the more expensive American exports are to Swiss consumers. On the other hand, in the United States a devaluation of the franc may have the same impact as cutting prices of Swiss imports 10 to 20 percent.

The stronger the dollar is in relation to the franc, the less attractive Swiss imports become to Americans. A strong dollar also makes travel to America more costly for Swiss tourists and businesspeople. When exchange rates change quickly, the risk of doing international business increases.

COUNTERTRADE

Pepsi-Cola has been sold in Russia for years, but Pepsico doesn't get paid in dollars or rubles. Rather, it trades the ingredients for its products for Stolichnaya vodka. This occurs because Russia, like many Eastern European countries with emerging market economies, does not have a convertible currency. A *convertible currency,* also know as hard currency, is one that can be easily exchanged for another country's currency. In the many Eastern European countries, currency exchanges—that is, cash transactions—do not occur because other countries and banks do not buy and sell the currency as they do U.S. dollars or Japanese yen.

What does this mean for international business? Using Russia as an example, it has meant that rubles obtained in business transactions could not be taken out of Russia. Thus, the only way to market a product or a service in Russia or another country without a convertible currency was to engage in countertrade. *Countertrade* is a form of international barter on a large scale. Countertrading can be extremely complex because prices, the exchange rate, and what will be received in return (sometimes from a third party in another country) must be negotiated.

WORLD MARKETS AND POLITICAL ACTIONS

Tariff
A tax imposed by a nation on an imported good.

Import quotas
Limits on the number or types of imported goods.

In some cases, businesses that sell their products around the world find that political or legal actions in another country discourage business by multinational firms. **Tariffs** are taxes imposed by a nation on an imported good. Tariffs attempt to make imported goods more expensive. **Import quotas** are limits on the number or types of imported goods. Foreign governments impose both tariffs and import quotas to stimulate domestic production by discouraging domestic consumption of foreign goods. For example, in 1993 the Hungarian government imposed import quotas on cars because General Motors and Suzuki both manufacture cars in Hungary and there is "domestic" competition for imported cars.

However, the realization that the world is turning to a global economy has led to many changes in world markets. Perhaps the most important change has been the growth of economic communities. An *economic community* is a group of nations that work together to eliminate tariffs and import quotas and to reduce other differences in trade laws and currencies among nations.

FOCUS ON COLLABORATORS

The European Union

European Union (EU)
Also called the **European Community (EC)**, an economic and potential political union of western Europe.

Perhaps the best-known economic community is the **European Union (EU)**, also known as the **European Community (EC)**. It consists of Portugal, France, Ireland, the United Kingdom, Spain, Denmark, Germany, Netherlands, Belgium, Luxembourg, Italy, and Greece. The EU illustrates how businesses must collaborate with governments to achieve economic goals.

Although Europeans have been working on a "borderless" economy for its 12 member nations for more than 30 years, 1992 marked the deadline for eliminating national trade barriers, differing tax laws, conflicting product standards, and other restrictions that kept the member nations from being a single market. In 1992, trade within Europe began to parallel trade among the states of the United States—trade without border and customs controls.

A single market with more than 325 million consumers means enormous opportunities. Since 1992, the European Union has become the largest single market in the world, with market spending of more than $44 trillion. Each year American companies sell more than $500 billion of goods and services in the EC.

Even more impressive is the fact that the European Union will grow. By the year 2000, this group of economic partners may include most of the continent. The European Free Trade Association (EFTA), which consists of Austria, Finland, Iceland, Norway, Sweden, and Switzerland, recently approved a pact that, beginning in 1993, will integrate the six EFTA members with the European Union. Three former communist countries—the Czech Republic, Hungary, and Poland—are seeking associate status with the EU, and they may become full members by the turn of the century. Some economists estimate that in the year 2000, the trading area will consist of 450 million people

THE NORTH AMERICAN FREE TRADE AGREEMENT (NAFTA)

North American Free Trade Agreement (NAFTA)
This agreement, approved in 1993, allows for increased trade among Mexico, Canada, and the United States.

In 1988, the United States–Canada Trade Act was passed to establish an economic community in North America. This paved the way for the **North American Free Trade Agreement (NAFTA)**, which was approved in 1993. This agreement, which allows for increased trade among Mexico, Canada, and the United States, will have a major impact on production location, imports, exports, and unemployment in selected industries. As a result of NAFTA, in 1994 the United States canceled tariffs on 60 percent of Mexican goods that had been subject to taxes. Other tariffs are being phased out over a 15-year period. NAFTA will lead to the development of a single American trading market of more than 350 million people in the 21st century.

THE GENERAL AGREEMENT ON TARIFFS AND TRADE (GATT)

General Agreement on Tariffs and Trade (GATT)
A series of agreements reached by member nations that are located in different parts of the world but want to encourage global trade by reducing international trade restrictions and tariffs.

Not all efforts at encouraging trade are undertaken by countries in the same geographic area. The **General Agreement on Tariffs and Trade (GATT)** is a series of agreements reached by member nations that are located in different parts of the world but want to encourage global business by reducing international trade restrictions and tariffs. In the Western world, several separate agreements have been signed by many industrialized and developing nations. Almost two-thirds of all developed nations are member nations.

GLOBAL PRODUCTION

Coca-Cola owns several bottling plants in China and hopes to build one in Vietnam. Several Japanese and German automobile manufacturers have built auto plants in the United States to minimize shipping expenses and political pressures associated with selling foreign-made cars to the U.S. market. Moreover, an organization that directly invests in plant operations in developing countries may take advantage of low-cost labor. Whatever the reason, direct investment in manufacturing facilities and marketing operations reflects a long-term commitment to international marketing.

Many risks are associated with a long-term direct investment strategy. For example, Iraq's invasion of Kuwait had a major impact on Exxon, Aramco, and other oil companies whose oil exploration facilities were destroyed or damaged during the Gulf War. In some countries, a change in government may lead a foreign power to transfer the company's assets to the new government. If nationalization of a multinational's operations poses a potential risk, a direct investment becomes less attractive.

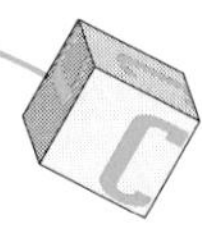

FOCUS ON CUSTOMERS

John Deere

Town council members in Greece, New York, were considering the purchase of a dirt-moving excavator to use for creek clearing. The choice was between John Deere and its only competitor, Komatsu. When a member of Japan's legislature called American workers lazy, the council got a lot of phone calls demanding "Buy American." The council voted to buy the John Deere excavator even though the Komatsu machine was $15,000 cheaper.

Shortly after the decision was made, however, the residents and the council learned the Komatsu brand is made by Komatsu Dresser, an American-Japanese joint venture with headquarters in Lincolnshire, Illinois, and 95 percent of the company's dirt movers are made in the United States. Furthermore, the John Deere excavators are produced under a joint venture between Deere and Hitachi. The engines for the John Deere brand are made in the United States, but the machines themselves are made in Japan.

This very complicated buying situation reflects how business is conducted in our new global environment. "Who is us?" is how a Harvard professor illustrated the point that, in today's world of U.S.–owned corporations with foreign manufacturing facilities and foreign-owned corporations with assembly plants in the United States, the multinational corporation is truly a world enterprise.

THE CHANGING ECONOMY

Predictions about what business will have to face in the year 2000 and beyond hold many challenges. Business must be able to adapt to a changing society and new economic realities. The nature of the American work force is changing. Placing factories outside the United States is increasingly becoming a major consideration for American corporations. Rapid technological changes will require different ways of running businesses. The changing nature of the American population will call for new and different products. World markets are becoming more important. The demands of a global marketplace will become increasingly important to survival.

Many U.S. companies are thoroughly involved in multinational business. Gillette, Coca-Cola, and Johnson & Johnson earn well over 50 percent of their profits overseas. The U.S. government encourages American companies to enlarge their international efforts. The United States is, in fact, a major exporting country in terms of absolute dollar volume. Yet other measures indicate that our degree of commitment to international marketing is relatively low.

American exports typically amount to approximately 7.5 percent of our gross national product (GNP). Compared to trading nations such as Germany and Canada, which regularly exceed 20 percent of their GNPs, this is a low percentage.[9] The explanation for this low figure is partly the result of the large, highly developed domestic market in the United States relative to those of most other countries. Other nations, such as the Netherlands, have had to emphasize international business activities to maintain economic growth.

Global competition has a major impact on the domestic economy of every nation. We will discuss issues in international business throughout the book.

FOCUS ON COMPANY

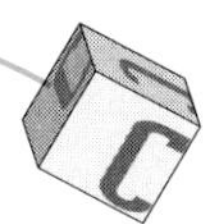

Mitsubishi Electric Corporation

Many Japanese companies, like Mitsubishi Electric Corporation, achieve an enormous advantage in product innovation and development of quality products through a process of steady, step-by-step improvements that keep them at least a step ahead of their competitors. Every year between 1979 and 1988, Mitsubishi added a new feature or made a major design change in its three-horsepower heat pump. In 1980, Mitsubishi introduced integrated circuits to control the heat pump cycle.

Not until the mid-1980s did any American company even consider the use of integrated circuits in its residential heat pump. One company concluded it would have taken four to five years to bring the product to market, and by 1990 it would have had a product comparable only to the 1980 Melco heat pump made by Mitsubishi. The American company threw in the towel, purchasing its advanced air conditioners, heat pumps, and components from the Japanese competition. Mitsubishi had gotten so far ahead of the U.S. company's new-product development cycle that its American rival had to surrender.

SUMMARY

1. ***Explain the basic nature of today's economy.***
   Following the Industrial Revolution, American business was dominated by a manufacturing economy. In today's information age, our economy is called a *service economy.* At present, a vast majority of the U.S. labor force works in the service sector. Service workers make up a huge, diverse group whose members range from cashiers to airline pilots.

2. ***Describe the importance of the service sector in the American economy.***
   Of the nearly $3.9 trillion in private services generated in 1988, 22 percent came from finance, insurance, and real estate. Retail business accounted for 14 percent, wholesale trade for 11 percent, transportation and utilities for 12 percent, and communications for 5 percent.

3. ***Define the goals of the American economy.***
   Most economists support economic goals like full employment, efficiency, economic growth, and price stability. Full employment exists when every person who is able and willing to work has a job. An efficient economy or business gets the most out of its limited resources, and its economic efforts are productive and well spent. Economic growth is an increase in the production (and usually consumption) of goods and services. Price stability exists when prices remain relatively constant.

4. ***Discuss the nature of the business cycle.***
   The business cycle reflects recurring variations in general economic activity. The four phases of the business cycle are prosperity, recession, depression, and recovery. Prosperity is a period of economic growth in which the economy operates at or near full employment and both consumer spending and business output (GNP) are high. Recession is the downward phase, in which consumer spending, business output, and employment are decreasing. Depression is the low phase, in which unemployment is highest and consumer spending and output are low. Recovery is the upward phase, when employment, consumer spending, and business output are rising.

5. ***Describe measures of economic well-being.***
   Measures of economic well-being determine whether our economy is meeting its goals. Some of these measures are the unemployment rate, productivity, gross domestic product, gross national product, consumer spending, inflation, and the consumer price index. The unemployment rate measures the percentage of individuals in the work force who are willing and able to work but cannot find full-time jobs. Productivity measures how constructive or efficient a person, operation, or enterprise is; it is a ratio of output to input. Gross domestic product (GDP) measures the value of all the goods and services produced by the workers and capital in a country. Gross national product (GNP) measures the value of all the goods and services produced by a country's residents or corporations regardless of location. Consumer spending is an early indicator of an economy's well-being and measures how much people are buying. Inflation is defined as a rise in price levels over an extended period of time. The consumer price index (CPI) reflects the average prices for many goods and services purchased by the typical household.

6. ***Define monetary and fiscal policies.***
   Governments influence economic activity via monetary and fiscal policies. A monetary policy promotes or restricts economic activity by controlling the size of a country's money supply. Governments normally increase the supply of money when they wish to stimulate the economy or bring about economic recovery, but this action usually increases the inflation level. Reducing the money supply generally has the opposite effect. Fiscal policy involves the government's power to tax and spend. For instance, a government economist who recommends a reduction in taxes is suggesting a new fiscal policy.

7. ***Explain how the world economy strongly influences the American economy.***
   Today other areas of the world influence almost all economic activity. The United States heavily engages in international trade. Imports are products produced in other countries and sold in the home country. Exports are products produced in the home country and sold in other countries. A trade deficit indicates that a country is buying more than it sells. A trade surplus indicates that a country is selling more than it buys. Both trade deficits and trade surpluses affect the balance of payments. The balance of payments is a record of the flow of money between a nation and the rest of the world.

8. ***Describe changing U.S. economic trends.***
   Business must be able to adapt to a changing society and new economic realities. The nature of the American work force is changing. Placing factories outside America is increasingly becoming a major consideration for U.S. corporations. Rapid technological changes will require different ways of running businesses. The changing nature of the American population will require new and different products. World markets are becoming increasingly important.

KEY TERMS AND CONCEPTS

Durable good (p. 42)
Nondurable good (p. 42)
Service (p. 42)
Business cycle (p. 44)
Prosperity (p. 44)
Recession (p. 44)
Depression (p. 44)
Recovery (p. 44)
Unemployment rate (p. 45)
Productivity (p. 46)
Gross domestic product (GDP) (p. 46)
Gross national product (GNP) (p. 46)
Consumer spending (p. 46)
Inflation (p. 47)
Consumer price index (CPI) (p. 47)
Monetary policy (p. 47)
Fiscal policy (p. 47)
Budget deficit (p. 48)
National debt (p. 48)
Gramm-Rudman-Hollings Act (p. 49)
Infrastructure (p. 49)
Imports (p. 50)
Exports (p. 50)
Balance of payments (p. 53)
Exchange rate (p. 53)
Tariff (p. 54)
Import quotas (p. 54)

European Union (EU) (p. 54)

North American Free Trade Agreement (NAFTA) (p. 55)

General Agreement on Tariffs and Trade (GATT) (p. 55)

DISCUSSION QUESTIONS

Company

1. What is the difference among a durable good, a nondurable good, and a service? Give some examples.
2. What are some examples of service businesses in your hometown?

Competitors

3. How large is the service economy? What types of businesses operate in a service economy?
4. What are the goals of the American economy?
5. How does the business cycle influence competition and other economic activity?

Customers

6. In your opinion, what are the best measures of economic well-being?
7. What are the different types of unemployment?
8. Is customer spending an indicator of an economy's well-being? Explain.
9. What is inflation?
10. What is an import?
11. What is an export?

Collaborators

12. What role does the government play in economic activity?
13. What is a monetary policy?
14. What is a fiscal policy?
15. What is a budget deficit?
16. How large is the U.S. gross national debt?
17. How important is infrastructure in an economy?
18. What is the balance of payments?
19. How does an exchange rate influence business for a company?
20. What is countertrade?
21. What is the General Agreement on Tariffs and Trade?

In Question: Take a Stand

1. Comment on the following statement: "Americans should not buy foreign products. Good citizens avoid buying Japanese cars. The more American products there are, the better off American workers will be."

2. MNC Financial Inc. sold the American Security Bank building, which is pictured on every $10 bill. A French investment firm purchased the American landmark, located kitty-cornered from the White House and across the street from the U.S. Treasury, for about $26 million.[10] The 1905 building is the latest prominent site bought by a non-U.S. company. Others include Rockefeller Center in New York and the Watergate Hotel in Washington. Should overseas buyers be able to buy slices of Americana?

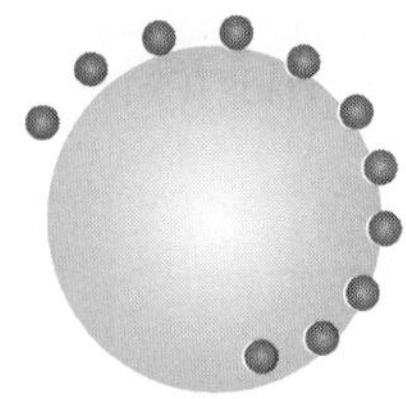

CASE 3.1
PEARL JAM[11]

Pearl Jam is the intense Seattle-based band that has become the top rock act in the country.

Ticketmaster is the colossus of American ticket brokers, a tough, aggressive computerized service that sells more that $1 billion in sports and entertainment tickets annually.

A bitter fight between the band and ticket service has now landed in the U.S. Department of Justice and the outcome could change the way tickets to major events are priced and sold.

Pearl Jam believes rock concert tickets are often too expensive, priced so high that many of the youngsters who most ardently support the music can't afford to buy them. Top prices for rock concerts have broken the $100 barrier in some venues, and it is common for concertgoers across the country to shell out $25 to $50 per ticket. The price includes the face value of the ticket and a service charge for the ticketing agency that issues it.

Pearl Jam, which has a strong teen-age following, has wanted to keep the total cost of its tickets below $20. The band members, fabulously rich now, remember what is was like just a few years ago when they were broke. They empathize with the 50 percent or so of their fans who earn less than $12,000 a year. They don't think those fans should be frozen out of Pearl Jam concerts. So the band proposed that its concert tickets sell for $18 plus a 10 percent service charge.

That was a problem. A $1.80 service charge is well below the average for concert tickets. Such charges often run $6 to $10 each, and sometimes higher. The service charge for a $350 Barbra Streisand ticket was $18.

Ticketmaster, to put it delicately, did not find Pearl Jam's proposal congenial.

Pearl Jam tried to find other ways to distribute its tickets but that is not so easy. In 1991 the Justice Department scrutinized and then gave the green light to a deal in which Ticketmaster purchased the contracts of its only viable competitor, Ticketron. Since then, according to Steven Holley, a lawyer for Pearl Jam, Ticketmaster has dominated the field, becoming the only national distribution service that handles rock concerts.

The fight between Pearl Jam and Ticketmaster escalated. Pearl Jam argued that greed is what keeps service charges high. The group noted that promoters and concert halls get a portion of the service-charge revenues, and thus there is no incentive to lower the charges. Ticketmaster has said it wants to compromise, but Pearl Jam won't negotiate its demands.

Then Pearl Jam dropped a bomb. It charged in a memorandum filed with the Antitrust Division of the Justice Department that it had to cancel its summer tour because of a group boycott organized by Ticketmaster. According to Pearl Jam's complaint, members of a national association of top concert promoters, prompted by Ticketmaster, refused to deal with Pearl Jam as long as the band stuck to its demand for a $1.80 service charge.

The memorandum also charged that Ticketmaster, because of its lack of competition and its exclusive contracts with nearly all of the major promoters, has a virtual monopoly on the national distribution of tickets to rock concerts. According to Pearl Jam, there is no reasonable alternative to doing business with Ticketmaster.

In March 1994, Ben Liss, executive director of the North American Concert Promoters Association, told his members in a memo that Fredric D. Rosen, president and chief executive officer of Ticketmaster, "intends to take a very strong stand on this issue." Mr. Liss urged his members "to be very careful about entering into a conflicting agreement which could expose you to a lawsuit."

A spokeswoman for the Justice Department said on Thursday, "We are investigating possible anti-competitive practices in the ticket distribution industry." She did not specifically name Ticketmaster and would give no details of the investigation.

Ticketmaster has vigorously denied all of Pearl Jam's allegations. "Our perspective is that we are being victimized by the band," said Ned Goldstein, the company's general counsel. He especially denied that Ticketmaster had engaged in any monopolistic practices.

When asked if there were any other nationwide ticket distribution services that handled rock concerts, Mr. Goldstein replied, "I don't know that that's the point."

Questions

1. *How important is price in a person's decision to attend a Pearl Jam concert?*
2. *How do the forces of supply and demand operate when the product is a rock concert?*
3. *In your opinion, is Ticketmaster violating antitrust laws?*

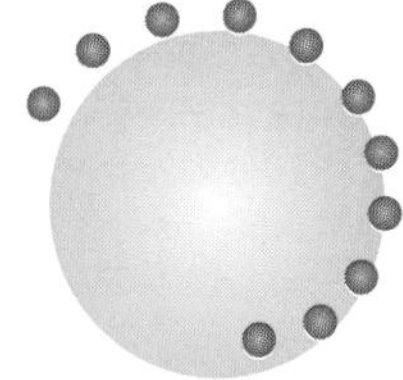

CASE 3.2
MARS INC. IN RUSSIA

Mars Inc. is reshaping the appetites of Russians, from street toughs to executives, most of whom have never seen a Milky Way.

The disintegration of the Soviet Union threw open a vast Russian market hungry for consumer goods—especially imported goods that had been banned under communism. Yet foreign companies face a volatile political landscape in Russia, where laws governing business change almost weekly. But Mars stormed in and within eighteen months established its products. It now virtually owns the chocolate market.

When the Soviet Union expired, so did state subsidies to confectioners, who lacked the hard currency to pay for the imported cocoa and sugar essential to chocolate production. Factories sat idle. Russians grumbled about the hard candies and grainy Turkish chocolate growing stale in stores. By 1992, there was no locally made chocolate in Russia.

Mars barreled over Russia's roadblocks with a gutsy business strategy. While many Western enterprises offer goods only for hard currency, Mars sells its products for rubles. Its candy bars cost about 300 rubles (25 cents) in Moscow and are among the most affordable Western status symbols. Its advertising blitz has made "Sneekerz" a Russian word. And in a sprawling country with a threadbare infrastructure, Mars keeps shelves across Russia stocked with its goods.

Mars embarked on a glitzy advertising campaign even before its chocolate appeared in stores. Full-color billboards on Moscow's main street made Russians curious about the "chocolate that melts in your mouth, not in your hands." (Actually, M&Ms don't sell as well as other Mars confections because locals don't find them as filling.) Snickers has been a runaway success. Distinctly Western television commercials show a hip young man enthusiastically biting into a Snickers bar to the Rolling Stones' song "Satisfaction."

Questions

1. *Use economic terms to classify Mars candies. Are they durable or nondurable goods? Imports or exports?*
2. *How important is business outside the United States to a company like Mars? What impact will it have on the American economy?*
3. *What impact did hard currency have on candy companies in Russia? Why is Mars Inc. willing to accept rubles when many other American companies will not?*
4. *Does the Russian infrastructure change the way American companies do business there?*

CHAPTER

4

FORMS OF BUSINESS OWNERSHIP

When you have studied this chapter, you will be able to:

1. Describe the sole proprietorship form of business ownership.
2. Explain the advantages and disadvantages of sole proprietorships.
3. Identify the areas covered in a standard partnership agreement.
4. Discuss the nature of general and limited partnerships.
5. Explain the rights and obligations of partners under the Uniform Partnership Act.
6. Identify the advantages and disadvantages of partnerships.
7. Describe the nature of corporations.
8. Identify the advantages and disadvantages of corporations.
9. Discuss the nature of corporate mergers and acquisitions.
10. Describe three collaborative forms of business ownership.

In 1978 Leslie Hindman, the daughter of Donald Hindman, who owns the thriving Clark Foodservice Company, decided to start her own business in Chicago, specializing in the auctioning of fine art and rare antiques. Unlike many people who aspire to own their own businesses, Hindman was in a unique position. She had many assets that would be valuable in the auction business, including her social status, her knowledge of the art market, and her family's business connections. But she had no money.

Like most entrepreneurs, Hindman's first problem was to find a way to raise capital to start her company. First, Hindman approached her father, but he thought her proposed business was a poor idea and refused to lend her any money. So Hindman turned to her mother's wealthy cousin, who loaned her $30,000. This sum gave credibility to her project, and Hindman was able to raise additional debt and equity capital.

Hindman rented space in Chicago's trendy River North section, hired three employees, and began rounding up merchandise and customers. But Leslie Hindman Auctioneers' first auction, in the fall of 1982, was not very successful, and a few months later she was again out of money. She obtained some additional capital from her investors, which allowed her to send out more catalogs, place advertisements in art magazines, and buy advertising time on local classical music stations. Eventually her auctions became fashionable social events in Chicago. By 1985, her auction business began to earn a profit.

Hindman has had some major successes in the auction world. In 1989 her firm convinced creditors of William Stoecker, a bankrupt Chicago swindler, to let her company handle the sale of his art and antique collection. In 1990, Hindman's agents located a formerly unknown Van Gogh in the hallway of a Milwaukee ranch house, and her firm auctioned it for $1.4 million to a Japanese buyer. In 1991, Hindman auctioned a large collection of furniture and paintings owned by heirs to Kohler Company.

Today Hindman is opening new auction houses in several midwestern cities. Now she would like to buy out her investors and assume sole ownership. But with profits coming in, none of the investors are willing to sell their shares of the business.[1]

Leslie Hindman had easier access to start-up capital than many new entrepreneurs, but her story is otherwise a familiar one. Sometimes people must find partners to be able to start a new business. But if they later want to assume sole ownership of the business, they may find the partnership hard to dissolve. As we will see in this chapter, people have several options other than partnership in choosing the form of ownership their businesses will take.

THE BASIC FORMS OF BUSINESS OWNERSHIP

Few countries provide as many opportunities for individuals to be involved in business as the United States does. In some societies, the only way a person can enter the business world is as an employee of a state-run organization. But in the United States, one can be a single owner of a business, an active partner, or an inactive part owner. One can own the whole business or share ownership with thousands of other investors. Each form of business ownership has many advantages as well as disadvantages. Each form also presents many exciting opportunities for individuals in our society.

As Leslie Hindman's story illustrates, a great many problems must be overcome when first establishing a business. Many of these problems are financial in nature: getting the money necessary to start the business, buying equipment, advertising the service or product, and paying employees' initial salaries. Tax considerations may be the single most important reason for choosing the legal form of a business, since different forms of business face different tax rates. Also, most owners are concerned about what will happen to the business after their death and whether it will continue to provide income for their survivors.

The first decision to make regarding the form of business is whether the business will be owned by only one or more than one person. While people like Leslie Hindman who start a new business often prefer to be the only owner, the need to raise start-up capital often forces them to take on other "partners." Even established businesses that wish to expand their operations may find it necessary to take on additional owners to obtain the capital they need.

But, as Leslie Hindman discovered, once a business is successful, shedding unwanted partners is not easy. While the skills of the major owner may be critical to the success of the business, the money the other owners provide is equally important. Also, the expansions Hindman is planning may require additional capital, and she would face this dilemma in the future even if she were able to buy out her partners' interests at that time.

Sharing ownership of a business with co-owners, then, poses both advantages and disadvantages. Co-owners can provide assets that one person acting alone cannot. Also, co-owners share the risks associated with failure, minimizing potential losses to any one person. But co-owners will share in the profits of the business, even if they do not "work" nine to five in the daily operations. Also, their co-ownership entitles them to take part in making major decisions for the business.

The three major forms of business ownership are the sole proprietorship, the partnership, and the corporation. As Exhibit 4.1 shows, although most businesses in the United States are sole proprietorships, corporations account for the vast majority of sales revenues. Thus, we can conclude that most proprietorships are small and only a few large corporations can significantly affect our country's economic well-being.

We will now look at each form of business ownership in turn.

THE SOLE PROPRIETORSHIP

Sole proprietorship
A business that is owned by only one person.

By far the most common form of business ownership is the *sole proprietorship.* A **sole proprietorship** is a business that is owned by only one individual. Sole proprietorships typically are managed by the owner, and they usually are small in terms of sales and number of employees. For example, restaurants, landscape nurseries, child care centers, construction companies, and air conditioning, electrical, and plumbing repair services are often sole pro-

Exhibit 4.1 **OWNERSHIP AND REVENUES**

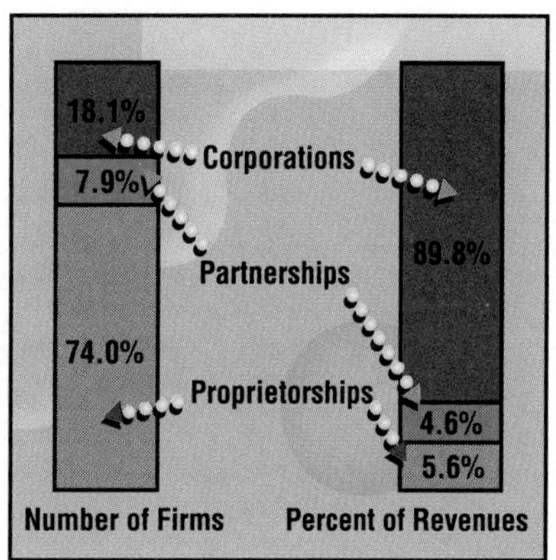

prietorships. As Exhibit 4.1 shows, although 74 percent of all businesses in the United States are sole proprietorships, they sell less than 7 percent of goods and services in this country.

A sole proprietorship is the simplest form of business to start. It involves very few legal steps. Anybody can establish his or her own business simply by getting the necessary local licenses.

The sole proprietorship also is flexible. The owner makes all the decisions; no votes need to be taken. The owner can hire whomever he or she pleases, keep all the profits, and be responsible to no one else.

ADVANTAGES OF THE SOLE PROPRIETORSHIP

Being the sole proprietor of one's own business offers many advantages. For some people, the major advantage is the ability to "be your own boss." Owners can set their own hours, take a vacation when they please, and never be chewed out by a supervisor for making a mistake. There are several other advantages as well.

Simplicity of Creating and Dissolving. All you need to start a sole proprietorship is an idea, money, and desire. You may already have owned your own business without realizing it. For example, if you ever had a newspaper route, mowed neighbors' lawns, or ran a lemonade stand, you operated a sole proprietorship. More complicated businesses operated by sole proprietors are florist shops, clothing boutiques, and providers of industrial services. The list is endless. In addition, a sole proprietorship is as easy to stop as it is to start. You don't have to reach an agreement with unwilling partners. You don't have to consult anyone. All you have to do is simply put a sign on the door saying, "Out of Business."

Low Cost of Creating the Business. The sole proprietorship is usually one of the least costly forms of business to create. Because legal papers are not necessary, start-up legal expenses will be minimal. Since the owner is usually the boss—and sometimes the only employee—the new business will have few labor costs.

Total Command over Decisions and Profits. Since the owner has complete control over the business, he or she can make decisions without consulting others and can withdraw money from the business whenever the need arises. Motivation to increase the company's revenues and profits is high, since all benefits will go only to the owner. Sole proprietors (often called *self-employed persons*) usually come to work early and stay late because they know that doing so is to their benefit.

Uncomplicated Tax Basis. All profits of a sole proprietorship are taxed as normal, personal income of the owner. There are no special business taxes. However, the owner must file esti-

Exhibit 4.2 **BUSINESS FAILURES AND BANKRUPTCIES**

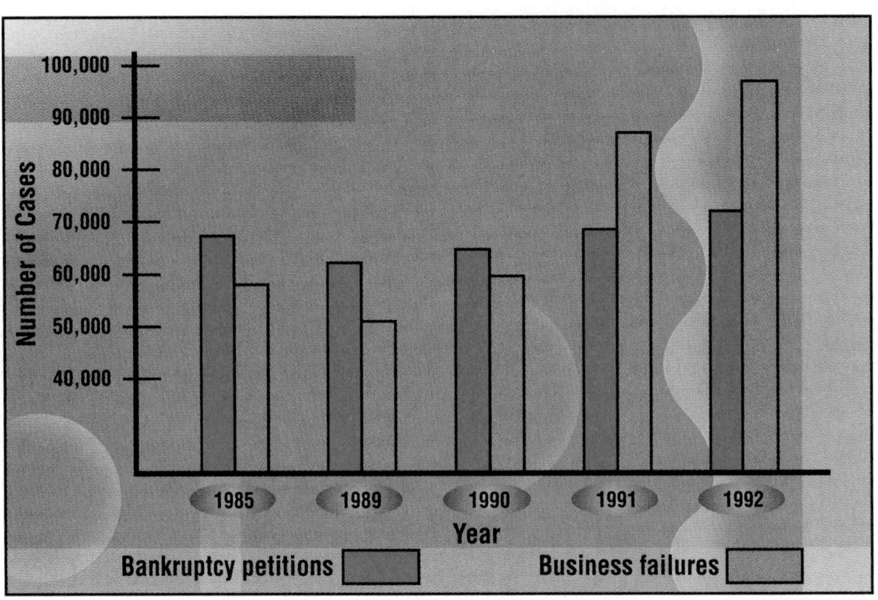

mated taxes on a quarterly basis and submit payroll taxes if he or she employs other people. However, these taxes are common to all businesses; they are not a problem unique to the sole proprietorship.

DISADVANTAGES OF THE SOLE PROPRIETORSHIP

While the sole proprietorship offers many benefits, it also has several disadvantages. As the opening case illustrated, it often is difficult to raise enough money to start one's own business. Although the sole proprietorship is usually the least costly form of business to start, the costs may still be substantial. For instance, the owner can expect costs associated with inventory, office supplies, insurance, advertising, rent, and perhaps a small staff. There are other disadvantages as well.

Risk of Financial Loss. When you work for another person, the only financial risk you face is that the owner may be unable to pay you this week's wages. If you are the owner of a business, however, you risk the loss of all the money you put into the business to start it, plus all the outstanding debts from doing business. As the sole proprietor, you have no partners with whom to share these losses. You have unlimited liability and may lose all of your personal assets as well as business assets if the business turns sour.

As Exhibit 4.2 shows, the risk of business failure and bankruptcy is not insignificant. In 1991 and 1992, the number of business failures and bankruptcies jumped by nearly 50 percent. Of those failures, more than half were small businesses owned by single proprietors or families.[2]

Lengthy Time Commitment. Perhaps the most unique disadvantage of the sole proprietorship is long hours and few vacations. Since sole proprietorships often have limited funds with which to attract high-quality employees, the owners tend to take on work that might otherwise be performed by others. Also, sole proprietors tend to perform all managerial duties and are reluctant to delegate these time-consuming tasks to others. Thus, people who own their own businesses often work 12 or more hours a day and 6 days a week. Vacations are rare, since there are no employees or skilled assistants to trust with the business operations.

STREET SMART

Some Partners Are Not What They Appear to Be

The street-smart businessperson recognizes that many types of partnerships are not disclosed. First, there are *real partners*—the actual co-owners of the business. A real partner may be silent, secret, or dormant. A *silent partner* may be known to the public but has no voice and takes no part in the partnership's business. A *secret partner* is a real partner who can take an active part in managing the firm but who is not disclosed to the public. A *dormant partner* is both a silent and a secret partner. In other words, he or she takes no active part in conducting business and remains unknown to the public. In contrast to the real partner is the *ostensible partner.* This person is not an actual partner but presents himself or herself to others as a partner or permits others to consider him or her as such. To prevent injustice to third parties, this person may be held liable much like a real partner, operating in a relationship called *partnership by estoppel.*

Growth Problems. The fact that the sole proprietorship depends heavily on the time and skills of the owner is a significant disadvantage when the firm is in a position to grow. In addition, the owner's financial resources may be inadequate to allow for expansion. It is often very difficult to obtain financing for a sole proprietorship. However, the Small Business Administration (SBA) often makes low-interest loans to sole proprietorships. In 1990 the SBA loaned over $4.3 billion to small businesses, and by 1992 it had loaned over $6.3 billion.[3]

Lack of Continuity. The sole proprietorship is established by the initial owner, operated by the owner, and tends to die with the owner. There is no means for continuing the business after the owner dies or if he or she becomes disabled or ill. Unless the owner's children have been trained to take over the business, the company will likely dissolve when the owner is no longer there to run it. Even if the children are trained to assume the business, there may be too many of them to allow them to make a decent living by sharing the business. In that case, they may simply sell off the assets and divide the spoils.

While owning one's own business is very exciting and invigorating for many persons, it presents many risks (especially financial ones) that others prefer to avoid. For some people, the dream is more realistic when they share the rigors and risks of ownership with other people.

THE PARTNERSHIP

Partnership
An arrangement in which two or more people co-own the business.

A **partnership** is an arrangement in which two or more people co-own the business. This arrangement permits the owners to enjoy many of the benefits of owning one's own business while reducing the costs and risks.

In a partnership, the co-owners share the assets, liabilities, and profits of the business. They may share profits on an equal basis, such as one-half for each of two partners or one-third for each of three partners. Or they may agree to some unequal arrangement, especially if one of the partners has invested more in terms of money, effort, or creativity than the others.

Some of today's most prominent businesses were once partnerships. Names like Procter & Gamble, Johnson & Johnson, and Lever Bros. suggest their business beginnings. However, the most common partnerships in business today occur among doctors, lawyers, accountants,

Exhibit 4.3 **PARTNERSHIP AGREEMENT ITEMS**

Item	Specifies
Name of the partnership	What the business will be called.
Location of the business	Where the business will be located.
Purpose of the business	The mission statement for the business (e.g., perform accounting services).
Duration of the partnership	How long the partners will operate the business as a partnership (may be for a specified or unspecified time period).
Names and addresses of the partners	Who the partners are and where they reside.
Agreement on salaries for the partners	Which partners will be paid a salary, in addition to their share of profits.
Profit and loss distributions	How profits and losses will be shared among the partners, as well as how much of earnings will remain in the business (if any).
Contributions by each partner	What each partner has given to the partnership, including cash, equipment, patents, ideas, and other assets.
Addition of new partners at some future time	Conditions for adding new partners to the business.
Selling of partners' interest	How one partner can sell his or her interest without formally dissolving the business. Often a veto privilege is provided for the other partners to protect them from getting stuck with a new partner they don't want. Also, remaining partners may get first opportunity at buying the exiting partner's interest in the business.
Dissolution of the partnership	How assets will be divided when the partnership is ended and who retains the right to use business names and patents.
Death of a partner	How the business will continue in the event of the death of one partner. Surviving partners may not wish to include the heirs of the deceased partner in the business, but all may wish to protect the interests of heirs in the deceased partner's assets.

and other professionals. One reason professionals often form partnerships is that they need partners to share otherwise unmanageable workloads.

PARTNERSHIP AGREEMENTS

Partnership agreement
A written document stating the terms of the partnership for the protection of each partner.

A **partnership agreement** is a document stating the terms of the partnership for the protection of each partner. Partnership agreements (also called *articles of partnership*) are not legally required among business partners. However, it is wise to work out a partnership agreement with legal counsel. Because this agreement identifies the status and responsibilities of each partner, it helps prevent arguments from arising at a later time.

When no agreement exists, the partnership will be governed by a law called the Uniform Partnership Act. However, the provisions of this law may not be as favorable to the partners as a specific agreement mutually arrived at when forming the business. Standard partnership agreements may include all of the items listed in Exhibit 4.3.

LIMITED PARTNERSHIPS

Limited partnership
A partnership in which some partners invest money or other assets but have no managerial responsibilities or liability for losses.

General partner
A partner who participates in managing the business and has unlimited liability for its debts.

Limited partner
A partner who does not participate in managing the company and is liable for its indebtedness only to the extent of his or her investment in the firm.

In a **limited partnership**, some partners invest money or other assets but have no managerial responsibilities or liability for losses. Two basic types of partners exist in a limited partnership. A **general partner** participates in managing the business and has unlimited liability for its debts. General partners also have the authority to bind the partnership to contracts and the right to share in profits and losses. A **limited partner** does not participate in managing the business and is liable for its indebtedness only to the extent of his or her investment in the firm.

In the event of some business catastrophe, such as bankruptcy, limited partners have much less risk regarding their personal assets. The personal assets of general partners may be used to settle business debts.

The Tax Reform Act of 1986 made the tax advantages of limited partnerships attractive to potential investors. This act reduced personal income taxes while closing many of the loopholes in the corporate profits tax structure. However, the Internal Revenue Service (IRS) has recently considered changing this law because of its impact on tax revenues.

UNIFORM PARTNERSHIP ACT

The *Uniform Partnership Act (UPA)* was first passed in 1914 by the state of Pennsylvania. Since then, nearly all states (except Georgia, Louisiana, and Mississippi) have adopted the act. The UPA offered a legal definition of *partnership* and established the rights and obligations of partners.

Rights of the Partners. Under the UPA, each partner has the right to

1. Share in the management and operations of the business
2. Receive interest on additional investments made by a partner
3. Be compensated for expenses incurred in the name of the partnership
4. Share in any profits the company earns
5. Have access to the company's books and records
6. Receive a formal accounting of the business affairs of the partnership

Obligations of the Partners. Under the UPA, each partner also has several obligations, including the obligations to

1. Share in any losses incurred by the business, except as noted in the limited partnership agreement
2. Work for the partnership without salary as necessary
3. Submit to majority vote or arbitration of differences that may arise among the partners
4. Give other partners complete information about all affairs of the partnership
5. Give a formal accounting of the business affairs of the partnership

While the UPA provides for a certain degree of consistency in partnership arrangements, good business relationships among partners must go beyond legal requirements. Partners must demonstrate trust, loyalty, and earnest efforts. If the partners do only what is legally required, the relationship may become strained. This, of course, weakens one of the primary benefits of partnerships: the ability to share efforts.

ADVANTAGES OF PARTNERSHIPS

While the partnership is the least common form of business ownership, it may offer more advantages than either the sole proprietorship or the corporation in certain situations.

Pooled Resources. Unlike sole proprietorships, partnerships permit the pooling of capital and labor resources. While a single owner may have difficulty raising start-up money for the business, two co-owners together may have the necessary resources. In addition, the co-owners may possess different levels of managerial skills and other resources important to the business, such as business contacts or patents.

Ease of Creation. Like the sole proprietorship, a partnership can be established easily and inexpensively. The co-owners must obtain the necessary licenses and permits, but they avoid the complex arrangements of corporations.

No Double Taxation. Profits of partnerships are not subject to separate federal income taxes beyond personal income taxes. All net income from the partnership is either distributed directly to the partners or charged to them as personal income. Partners pay personal income tax on their shares, but the partnership has no taxes to pay. Thus, double taxation, to which owners of a corporation are subject, is avoided.

Division of Work and Sharing of Skills. Managing even a small business may demand more effort and time than one person can provide. By sharing the work, partners can ease the demands on their time and effort. This is especially true for doctors and lawyers who, despite jokes to the contrary, are often unable to schedule vacations or holidays or even rely on a day of rest each week. By acquiring partners, doctors and lawyers can cover for one another when they need time away from work.

In addition, partners may bolster one another's skills. In some law offices, for instance, the partners specialize in different types of legal cases. Thus, a law partnership may have a divorce specialist, a tax lawyer, and a personal injury specialist. With such specialists, the partnership can retain business that might otherwise go to another firm.

Finally, if the partners are good friends, working with one another may be a lot of fun. However, good friendships may be ruined if business pressures build up, so the decision to form a partnership must be made with care.

Attraction of Additional Investment. While a sole proprietor either has to provide his or her own capital or borrow the money, partnerships may attract additional capital by adding more partners. Even if the original partners do not want to give up management control, they can offer any number of limited partnerships. In this way, new partners can realize substantial returns on their investments while enjoying limited risks to their personal assets.

DISADVANTAGES OF PARTNERSHIPS

The partnership form of business also has some important disadvantages that may account for its relative lack of popularity among business owners.

Unlimited Liability of General Partners. At least one member of every partnership must be a general partner. All general partners have unlimited personal liability for the lawsuits, contracts, and debts of the partnership. In this respect, their personal assets face the same risk that those of sole proprietors do. This is true even in cases where one of the other partners has created the business liability.

Transferring Ownership Without Dissolving the Business. Partnerships legally end when one of the general partners ends his or her partnership. But if the other partners do not want to end the business, problems may arise. Thus, it is common for partners to have an agreement stating that a partner who leaves the business must sell his or her interest to the remaining partners. But this means the other partners must have capital available to buy those interests when the one partner wants to leave. Otherwise they may be forced to either accept a new partner or dissolve the partnership.

Disputes among Partners. Some disagreement among partners can't be avoided and may be difficult to resolve. Even among relatives disputes may disrupt the business. For example, a dispute between the founder of Boyer Coffee Company and his sons led to the creation of separate businesses and a legal suit over the name of the sons' competing business.

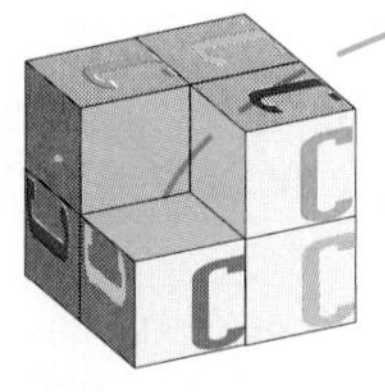

FOCUS ON COMPETITORS

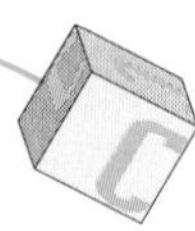

Boyer Coffee Company versus Boyer Gourmet Products Manufacturing

For more than a year, Boyer Gourmet Products Manufacturing, Inc., was involved in a legal squabble over trade-name rights with Boyer Coffee Company. While companies often argue in the courts over the rights to trade names, it is unusual when the parties involved are father and sons.

Bill Boyer started Boyer Coffee Company in 1965. The firm, which supplies coffee for institutional customers, Burger King restaurants, and Conoco convenience stores, has a roasting and wholesale coffee sales facility in the Denver area. The company's sales have grown rapidly during the past few years.

Dennis and Sam Boyer were working with their father, Bill, in the family business in 1985 and helped start Boyer Gourmet under the umbrella of Boyer Coffee. But in 1988, a dispute between father and sons led the two companies to separate. Since both companies were in the coffee business, lawyers hashed out an agreement regarding the use of the Boyer trademarks.

Boyer Gourmet sells coffee at more than 3,000 grocery stores, operates an office coffee service, and supplies institutional customers such as hotels and hospitals. The company roasts more than 8 million pounds of coffee a year at its plant located near Stapleton Airport. Sales grew from just over $600,000 in 1985 to more than $30 million in 1992.

In 1991, the sons filed a federal court suit asking for protection for their right to use the Boyer Bros. trade name and logo on their coffee products. Later that year Bill Boyer filed his own suit, charging that his sons had forfeited the right to use trademarks with the Boyer name under the terms of the initial agreement. Finally, the sons agreed to take the Boyer name off their product labels and renamed their company Brothers Gourmet Coffees.

Limited Access to Capital. Although some capital can be added to the original capital base of the business, it must come either from the partners themselves or by adding new partners. The amount of additional capital that can be raised this way is limited, however, since new partners are hard to find and existing partners may have few additional assets available. Also, partners are naturally reluctant to further share their business with other co-owners and may prefer to finance growth from the profits of the business. This means growth of the business is likely to be slow, even when the market for the products and services is large.

DISSOLUTION OF PARTNERSHIPS

A partnership is *dissolved* when one of the general partners ceases to be associated with the business. Dissolving a partnership requires canceling the partnership agreement, which in turn requires agreement among all of the partners. A partnership can be dissolved by any of the following events:

- The death of a partner
- Completion of the project or time period identified in the partnership agreement that created the business relationship
- The expressed desire of any general partner to cease operation (of course, one of the partners may choose to "recreate" the business as a sole proprietorship, if the others agree to this)
- Expulsion of a partner according to the terms of the partnership agreement
- Bankruptcy of the partnership business or personal bankruptcy of any general partner

In addition, legal actions against the partnership for either criminal or other wrongful acts may cause the partnership to dissolve. In general, dissolving a partnership is more difficult than discontinuing a sole proprietorship but less difficult than dissolving a corporation.

Corporation
An entity owned by stockholders and granted by government charter certain powers, privileges, and liabilities separate from those of the individual stockholders.

THE CORPORATION

A **corporation** is similar to a partnership in that the business has multiple co-owners. However, large corporations such as Du Pont or General Foods may have thousands of owners, many of whom have never even visited one of the business's facilities. Most have never reprimanded an employee, and few have participated in the actual management of the firm. In contrast to these giant corporations are many small, privately owned businesses with relatively few employees that have incorporated to take advantage of tax laws. The owners of these small corporations rarely intend to sell stock to the general public and usually know all of their employees by name.

The corporation is the most complex form of business ownership. The U.S. Supreme Court has defined the corporation as "an artificial being, invisible, intangible, and existing only in the contemplation of the law." This means the corporation is a distinct, legal entity in itself; that is, it has a legal life separate from its owners. As a legal entity, a corporation often has been likened to a real person. This is because a corporation can write contracts, borrow money, sue and be sued, and pay taxes just like a person.

One other unique feature of a corporation is that it can have an indefinite life span. Since the corporation exists independently of the owners, the owners can sell or trade their interests in the business, and their deaths will not affect its continuation.

Ownership in a corporation is represented by shares of stock in the corporation. A corporation owns its own stock until the stock is issued or sold to investors. By selling its stock, a corporation raises the capital needed to establish the business and to finance growth. However, when one stockholder sells his or her stock to another investor, the money from that secondary transaction goes from one person to the other. The corporation receives money only from stock that *it* sells.

Perhaps the major advantage of the corporation is that it limits the liability of its owners. All stockholders can lose is the amount they have invested to buy the stock. Since the corporation is a legal entity, it alone is responsible for the liabilities of the company. If the business goes bankrupt, the stockholders will lose whatever they paid for their shares, but not their personal property. This feature makes the corporate form of business ownership unique from either a sole proprietorship or a partnership.

We should note at this point that the number of people who own shares in a corporation can range from one or two to as many as there are shares of stock. Some large U.S. corporations have thousands of investors, while many small corporations are owned by only one or two shareholders and operate much like any other small business.

Board of directors
Group of individuals selected by the corporation's stockholders to hire the chief executive officer (CEO), make decisions about the corporation's stocks and dividends, and oversee major policy decisions.

Large corporations have *boards of directors.* A **board of directors** is a group of individuals selected by the stockholders to hire the corporation's chief executive officer (CEO), make decisions about the corporation's stocks and dividends, and oversee major policy decisions. For example, the board of directors might approve or disapprove top executives' decision to construct a manufacturing plant in South Africa.

ADVANTAGES OF CORPORATIONS

The corporate form of business ownership offers several distinct advantages over other forms of ownership.

Access to Capital. To raise money for business purposes, a corporation sells stock to interested investors. This means millions of small investors can become owners in American business. Since corporations often sell their stock for less than $100 per share, no investor is too small. And since corporations may sell 10 million or more shares, they can easily raise more than $1 billion from issuing shares in their business. This gives the corporation a major advantage over the sole proprietorship and the partnership. This advantage helped the United States become one of the most prosperous nations in the world.

Limited Liability. In addition to the relative ease of raising capital, the corporation offers all its shareholders limited liability. *Limited liability* means all the shareholders or owners of the corporation are responsible for losses only in the amount they invested in buying the shares. Their personal assets cannot be seized to pay debts owed by the corporation. This advantage also helps the corporation raise capital, since it reduces investors' fear that they will lose their personal assets if the business fails.

Perpetual Life. Corporations have permanence beyond the lives of their owners. Since the corporation is an entity in itself, it does not cease upon the death of a shareholder. This allows corporate managers to plan far into the future, whereas partners and sole proprietors must limit their planning to events that will occur in the near future.

Ease of Transferring Ownership. Owners of corporate stock can transfer their ownership by merely selling their stock certificates to another person. Ownership of large corporations changes daily as investors buy and sell their shares according to shifts in market prices of the stocks. Wall Street traders make changing ownership easy for investors whose desire to increase their wealth comes before any loyalty they may feel toward any particular corporation.

Global Acceptance. While we tend to think of the corporation as a uniquely capitalistic form of business ownership, it is becoming an important tool in the development of Eastern Europe and China. For example, the People's Republic of China is becoming an important global competitor, and many of its businesses are incorporating. Stock in these corporations is being sold in the international business community. These investments are proving attractive to many "capitalists" around the globe.[4]

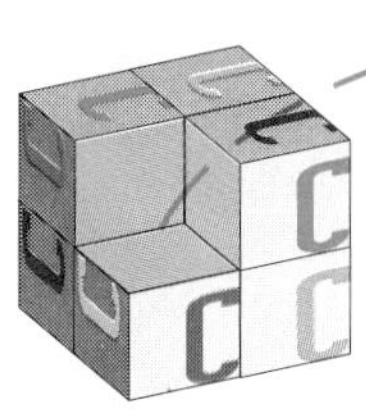

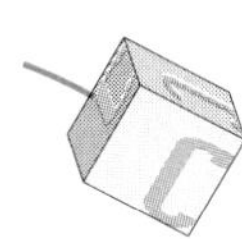

FOCUS ON COMPETITORS

Hong Kong Telecommunications Corporation

Southern China is becoming a hot economy, spurred by a GNP that is racing ahead at a 15 percent annual rate. The economy is being paced by Hong Kong manufacturers that have capitalized on cheap labor and free-market reforms. All this new business keeps Hong Kong Telecommunications Corporation phone lines busy. The company's profits have grown 18 percent annually over the past five years. In 1991, the company earned profits of $556 million on $2.1 billion in revenues.

With only three phones per 100 people, China's telecommunications market represents vast growth potential. Experts expect that China's phone traffic will expand at about 35 percent each year through 1995. If current rate regulation disputes between the Hong Kong government and Hong Kong Telecommunications are resolved, the company's stock price may explode. While some people expect that after the final settlement phone rates may be permitted to increase only at the same rate as inflation, most think even this restriction will not deter the company's profit march. One expert explains that increasing volume will keep the company's earnings growing 15 percent annually for several years regardless of the outcome of the rate discussions.

DISADVANTAGES OF CORPORATIONS

It might seem that corporations have no disadvantages, but this is not true. Corporations have some very important drawbacks.

Double Taxation. Since the corporation is an entity, like a person it must pay income taxes on the net income it earns *before* that income is distributed to the owners. Owners must again pay personal taxes on any of the remaining corporate income that is paid to the investors in the form of dividends. Thus, a corporation's earnings are actually taxed twice, a practice called *double taxation.*

Exhibit 4.4 **ADVANTAGES AND DISADVANTAGES OF THE THREE FORMS OF BUSINESS OWNERSHIP**

Form of Ownership	Advantages	Disadvantages
Sole proprietorship	1. Easy to establish 2. Simple structure, owner maintains high degree of control over operations and decisions 3. Earnings taxed only once, as personal income of owner	1. Unlimited liability of owner, whose personal assets may be seized to settle business debts 2. Limited ability to raise capital for growth or expansion 3. Problems associated with death of owner and lack of continuity of ownership
Partnership	1. Permits owners to share work and management responsibilities 2. Easier to raise money than with sole proprietorships 3. Earnings taxed only once, as personal incomes of owners.	1. Unlimited liability of owners, whose personal assets may be seized to settle business debts 2. Potential for major conflicts among partners 3. Harder to raise money than with corporations 4. Problems arising from the death of a partner or when a partner wishes to sell his or her interest in the business
Corporation	1. Limited liability for owners, who cannot lose personal assets to settle business debts 2. Company continues despite the death of any shareholders 3. Ease of raising capital	1. Owners are taxed twice, once as profits of the corporation and again when dividends are paid to individual owners 2. Loss of control by shareholders (owners) 3. May become unmanagement in size, resulting in inflexibility and slow response to changing business conditions

Lack of Distinct Decision-Making Authority. Since a corporation has so many owners, they cannot exert much individual influence over corporate decisions. Only wealthy owners or ownership groups have much influence over the affairs of the corporation. In addition, the board of directors, chosen by owners to represent them, creates extra steps in important decisions.

Legal Issues. Corporations must file a large number of reports to various government agencies such as the Securities and Exchange Commission (SEC). These reports are required because of the limited liability and widespread ownership. Sole proprietorships and partnerships do not require such reports.

Possible Loss of Control by Founder(s) of the Corporation. When a corporation issues a large amount of stock to raise capital, the founder may lose control over the business. Steve Jobs, one of the main creators of Apple Computer, discovered this when John Sculley, then chairperson of Apple, persuaded the board of directors to remove Jobs's authority because he believed Apple's management was ineffective under Jobs's leadership. Even though the Apple computer was largely his idea, Jobs could no longer control the company's destiny.

Large Size. Since it is relatively easy for corporations to raise the capital they need to finance growth, they can grow quite large. In fact, all of the largest businesses in the United States are corporations. While large companies have more money, have more employees, and are able to make large investments in new products, they also suffer from inflexibility and red tape. Control of large corporations depends on established rules and procedures that all employees are expected to follow. In a small company, in contrast, the influence of the owner is the primary means of control. Thus, the corporation's size can make the company slow to respond to changing business conditions.

We can conclude from our discussion of sole proprietorships, partnerships, and corporations that no single form of business ownership is ideal for all owners. For instance, to gain the advantage of obtaining additional capital, a sole proprietor gives up total control of the busi-

The increased focus on global business has created a need for multinational corporations. The merger of Mattel and Fisher-Price gives Hasbro Inc., the world's No. 1 toy company, a much stronger competitor in global markets. The biggest benefit of the merger is Mattel's ability to extend Fisher-Price's foreign distribution to Germany, Spain, Italy, Australia, New Zealand, and the Far East. Mattel's chairman says, "We hope to put (Fisher-Price) teethers or rattles in every newborn's hand."[5]

ness as it becomes a partnership or a corporation. Owners of corporations are taxed on both profits and owner dividends. As Exhibit 4.4 shows, every advantage to be gained from one form of ownership seems to have one or more accompanying disadvantages.

GROWTH OF CORPORATIONS THROUGH MERGERS AND ACQUISITIONS

Corporations can grow quite large over the years because of their ability to generate additional investment by selling shares of stock. But corporations can grow even larger, faster, by merging with other companies, or simply acquiring them.

MERGERS

Merger
The result of two firms formally joining their assets, liabilities, and ownership.

Vertical merger
The combining of firms engaged in related businesses.

Horizontal merger
The joining of firms in the same industry.

Conglomerate merger
The combining of firms that do business in completely unrelated industries.

A **merger** occurs when two firms formally join their assets, liabilities, and ownership. Both companies gain strength by combining their resources. Three types of mergers are the vertical merger, the horizontal merger, and the conglomerate merger.

In a **vertical merger** the combined firms are engaged in related businesses, such as a large supermarket chain and a milk-processing facility. This type of merger ensures a constant and cheaper supply of milk for the supermarket chain, and a constant and dependable customer for the dairy producer.

A **horizontal merger** is the joining of firms that may be competitors in the same industry, such as two large banks. For both banks, this type of merger enlarges their total market relative to other banks and strengthens their financial position. This is especially useful if one bank has resources that the other needs, such as branches in a different state or region.

When two firms in completely unrelated industries merge, it is called a **conglomerate merger**. This type of merger helps the firms diversify their operations. This makes the companies less vulnerable to shifts in product sales. Avco Corporation is a large conglomerate corporation that began as a finance company and now has holdings that include movie studios and other unrelated businesses.

Exhibit 4.5 **MERGER AND ACQUISITION ACTIVITY IN THE UNITED STATES**

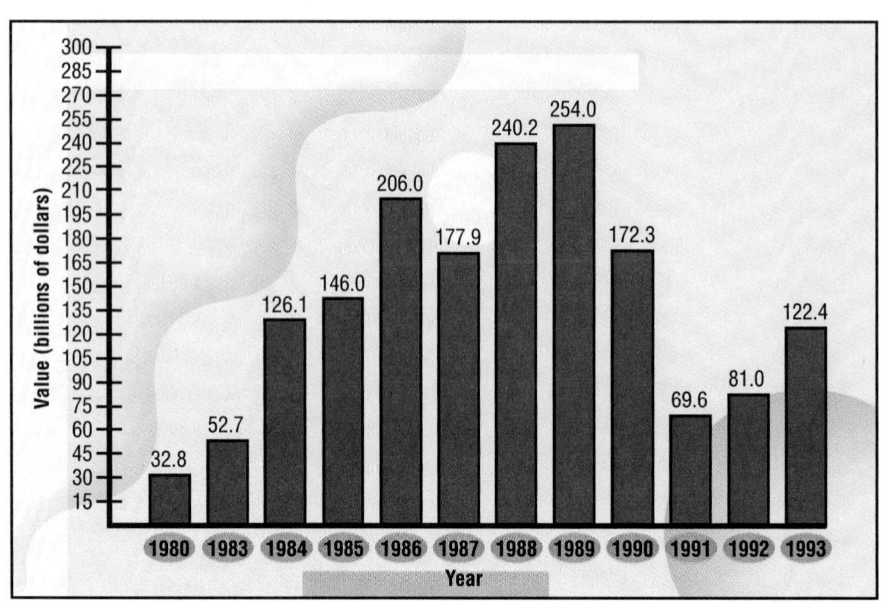

Acquisition
The result of one firm simply buying the assets and obligations of another company.

Tender offer
An offer to the shareholders of a company to purchase all of their stock at a price above current market value.

Hostile takeover
Occurs when a firm acquires another company whose managers do not want the company to be sold.

ACQUISITIONS

Most mergers occur as a result of friendly negotiations between companies that both have something to gain from the merger. However, one company may simply buy another company by purchasing its assets and liabilities. This type of transaction is called an **acquisition**. Acquisitions can occur in several ways. Company A can acquire Company B by purchasing its stock in the stock market. Company A can also make a **tender offer**: an offer to buy the stock held by shareholders of Company B at a price above market value. An acquisition becomes a **hostile takeover** when the managers of Company B do not want it to be sold.

Hostile takeovers were common during the 1980s, when corporation managers were more concerned about making financial profits from Wall Street transactions than about achieving real growth in products and profits. Their concern was not to improve the acquired corporations, but rather to take advantage of a financial situation, such as a large cash flow in the company. Some individuals, such as T. Boone Pickens and Carl Icahn made substantial profits from these mergers and acquisitions, but other investors as well as the acquired companies suffered. As seen in Exhibit 4.5, merger and acquisition activities peaked by the end of the 1980s.[6] However, these activities still run in the billions of dollars.

In the 1990s, the main concerns in a merger are to improve a corporation's competitive position and to combine technologies. For example, in 1991 AT&T bought NCR (a computer company) for $7.5 billion. AT&T hoped to strengthen its own computer operations and prepare for the emerging blend of telephone, cable television, and computer technologies into large information networks. These "information superhighways" are being developed by MCI, Sprint, AT&T, IBM, and numerous other companies. The acquisition of NCR may give AT&T an edge in this highly competitive field.[7] Corporate growth through merger and acquisition will probably continue to be an important business activity for the rest of this decade.

SPECIAL FORMS OF COMMON BUSINESS OWNERSHIP

In the search for a better form of business ownership, two special types have evolved: the master limited partnership and the S corporation.

MASTER LIMITED PARTNERSHIPS

Master limited partnership Similar to a limited partnership, except that shares of ownership can be traded on stock exchanges.

The **master limited partnership** is a relatively new form of business ownership. Master limited partnerships, such as the Boston Celtics, are like regular limited partnerships except that the owners' shares are traded on stock exchanges in much the same way shares of corporations are traded. Thus, the master limited partnership provides many of the same advantages of the corporation—limited liability of the owners and ease of raising capital—but it avoids the burden of being taxed twice. A master limited partnership looks and acts like a corporation, but it is taxed like a partnership.[8]

A master limited partnership also offers the limited partners an easier way to sell their interests in the business and to keep the business going if any partner dies. However, the accounting process for master limited partnerships is very complex. Whereas sole proprietorships and corporations need only report their total net income, master limited partnerships must divide all income and expenses among perhaps thousands of partners. Congress is considering taxing master limited partnerships as corporations, which would eliminate the major advantage of these partnerships.

S CORPORATIONS

S corporation (subchapter S) A form of business that is distinct from other corporations only in the way it is taxed; taxed similarly to sole proprietorships and partnerships.

The **S corporation** (sometimes called **subchapter S**) is a form of business that, according to the Internal Revenue Service, is distinct from other corporations only in the way it is taxed. It also has the following legal restrictions:

1. It must be a domestic corporation.
2. It cannot have a nonresident alien (citizen of a foreign country who is not living in the United States) as a shareholder.
3. It can issue only one class of common stock (although it can issue voting and nonvoting common stock).
4. It must limit its shareholders to individuals, estates, and certain trusts.
5. It cannot have more than 35 shareholders.
6. No more than 20 percent of its income can come from passive activities (such as owning stock in another corporation).

These restrictions prevent most large corporations from qualifying as S corporations. But if a corporation meets these requirements and its shareholders vote to be treated as an S corporation, its income will be taxed in the same way as a sole proprietorship and a partnership.

These restrictions are designed to make small corporations competitive with sole proprietorships and partnerships in terms of the tax laws. While there is no upper limit on the earnings of an S corporation, most of these businesses are small.

COLLABORATIVE FORMS OF BUSINESS OWNERSHIP

While the three common forms of business ownership generally are sufficient for business purposes, there are times when a different form may be appropriate. This is especially true when the purpose of the business is not to maximize profit, but to provide a service to the owners at lower cost. It is also true when the company's financial and other resources are insufficient for the firm to achieve some broad or expensive goal. For these reasons, collaborative forms of organization may be needed.

A *collaborative form of organization* is one that combines the resources of individuals and companies without depending on a common business ownership arrangement. Collaborative forms of organization include cooperatives, joint ventures, and nonprofit organizations.

Cooperatives are a common form of "agribusiness." They offer better prices because they are owned by the people who do business with them and because they deal with large volumes.

COOPERATIVES

Cooperative
A business that is owned and managed by its customers or members, who pay annual dues or membership fees and share in any profits made.

A **cooperative** is a business that is owned and managed by its customers or members, who pay annual dues or membership fees and share in any profits made. Although cooperatives usually are not created for the purpose of making profits, they may accumulate profits from the sale of goods and services to nonmembers at prices above those offered to members. The basic reason for forming cooperatives is to allow members to get better prices for the goods they buy (or sell) by buying in larger volumes than individuals acting alone could buy. Members can get lower prices because the cooperative does not try to earn profits from sales to its own members.

Cooperatives are often associated with farming and buyers' clubs. While buyers' clubs typically do not permit sales to nonmembers, farming cooperatives often do.

FOCUS ON COLLABORATORS

Farmland Industries

Some farming cooperatives have grown quite large. Farmland Industries is a $5 million business. It owns manufacturing facilities, oil wells and refineries, fertilizer plants, feed mills, and other manufacturing operations. In addition to selling products at low cost to members, it provides insurance, financial, and technical services for over 750,000 members.

Today the United States has over 7,500 farming cooperatives. Although most are considerably smaller than Farmland Industries, together they do over $1 billion worth of business a year.

Joint venture
An alliance in which two or more people or companies join together to undertake a specific, limited, or short-term project.

JOINT VENTURES

A **joint venture** is an alliance in which two or more persons or companies join together to undertake a specific, limited, or short-term project. Joint ventures are common in the global,

Mazda Motor Corporation has aggressively attacked the U.S. car market, but not always successfully. In the 1992 model year, its sales were down 4 percent in a market that was up 4 percent. But Jan Thompson, Mazda's marketing boss, sees strong sales and profit from a pickup truck that Ford is building for Mazda. Based on the restyled Ford Ranger compact pickup pictured above, it will be the second Ford truck sold as a Mazda. Ford ranks high among truck buyers, and Thompson thinks this benefits Mazda.[9]

market. For example, General Motors and Toyota formed a joint venture to manufacture the GEO Prizm, and Ford and Mazda formed one to produce the Ford Escort. In the technological fields, Apple Computer and IBM formed a joint venture to develop and share new system software that will permit their customers to work with both computer systems. These companies did not completely merge their businesses; rather, they formed cooperative agreements on specific products or projects.

Joint ventures are taxed as partnerships, and each person or company has unlimited liability while it exists. This, of course, subjects the companies to the same risk any sole proprietor would face on the project, but does not subject individual stockholders to increased liability.

Management of joint ventures is often the most difficult part of the venture. Typically, management is assigned to one individual, but this limits the authority of the other partners in the joint venture. Often the partners divide the authority among several managers chosen from the different companies. The result is a division of authority, which can weaken the management structure of the joint venture.

New motivation for forming joint ventures is the emerging markets in high-tech consumerism. This is especially true in the digital media business, which presents possibilities for combining computer, television, cable, telephone, and other information technologies.

FOCUS ON COLLABORATORS

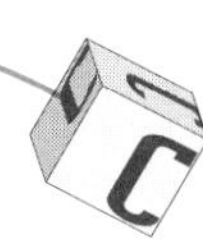

Partnerships across Industries

Apple Computer, Inc., American Telephone & Telegraph Company (AT&T), and Time Warner Inc. are among the many corporations forming complex alliances in the emerging digital media business. Apple, AT&T, and Time Warner are jockeying for position in what they expect to be three distinct new businesses:

- The *content* of digital transmissions, such as databanks, consumer services, music, books, and movies
- The *delivery* of information over telephone lines, cable TV, satellites, or other wireless networks
- The *manipulation* of information with operating software, personal computers, hand-held communicators, TV controllers, and the like

Which combinations might work are uncertain, since so many new and different technologies are involved. No single player possesses all of the skills to be competitive, but by forming collaborative alliances, each company hopes to be part of the business. The deal-makers admit they don't know which products and services could turn into big markets. But many executives say they are compelled to go ahead with alliances precisely because future markets look so foggy. The international nature of this market finds shaky alliances between competitors such as Motorola and AT&T; Sony, Matsushita, and Phillips; and Microsoft, Intel, and Compaq Computer.

Nonprofit organizations like the Advertising Council, the Red Cross, the Salvation Army, and the March of Dimes complement the services provided by thousands of for-profit businesses. Without organizations such as these, many people would be unable to acquire needed goods and services.

NONPROFIT ORGANIZATIONS: MEETING SOCIETY'S DIVERSE NEEDS

Although many people think of business as limited to profit-making organizations, one of the most rapidly growing segments of our economy is the nonprofit organization. Over 850,000 nonprofit organizations exist today, and they provide a wide variety of services that meet needs not fulfilled by the common forms of business. They are perhaps the ultimate form of collaborative organization. Among the many types of nonprofit organizations are churches, hospitals (although some hospitals now are for-profit organizations), research foundations (the March of Dimes, the American Cancer Society), and volunteer organizations (Boy Scouts, Girl Scouts).

These organizations do not pay taxes on their fund-raising operations and do not make profits that enable them to provide services. But they do provide important services and allow profit-making businesses to make tax-deductible charitable contributions. Corporations give some $5 billion a year to nonprofit organizations, which in turn distribute these funds to needy people and organizations. Without nonprofit organizations, many needy children probably wouldn't have presents at Christmas and medicine wouldn't have advanced as far as it has today. Although nonprofit organizations may not be the typical "business" form, they certainly are a necessary form.

You should note that nonprofit organizations provide a valuable training ground for college students who want business careers or simply want to learn organizational, managerial, and "people" skills. Nonprofit organizations often rely on volunteers and give these people large responsibilities that not only provide a valuable community service but also provide meaningful work experience. Experience in these organizations can help you market yourself to prospective employers.

SUMMARY

1. ***Describe the sole proprietorship form of business organization.***
   The sole proprietorship, the most common form of business ownership in the United States, is a business that is owned by only one individual, who is often the manager and sometimes the only employee. It is easy to establish and is the preferred means of employment for many Americans.

2. ***Explain the advantages and disadvantages of sole proprietorships.***
   The advantages of sole proprietorships are that (1) they are simple to create and dissolve, (2) they require relatively little money to start, (3) the owner has complete control over business decisions and profits, and (4) they have an uncomplicated tax basis.

   The disadvantages of sole proprietorships are that (1) the owner has unlimited liability for all business losses and may lose personal assets if the business fails, (2) operating the business may take long hours each day and limit vacations and holidays, (3) resources with which to finance business growth are limited, and (4) the business may cease to exist if the owner dies or becomes disabled.

3. ***Identify the areas covered in a standard partnership agreement.***
   Standard partnership agreements include the name of the partner, the location of the business, the purpose of the business, the duration of the partnership, the names and addresses of the partners, salaries for the partners, distribution of profits and losses, contributions by each partner, possible addition of new partners in the future, selling of partners' interests, dissolution of the partnership, and continuity of the business if one of the partners dies.

4. ***Discuss the nature of general and limited partnerships.***
   In a general partnership, all partners share all assets, liabilities, and profits of the business according to some agreed-on percentage. Each partner tends to be active in managing the business and is personally responsible for its debts. In a limited partnership, some partners invest money or other assets in the business but have no managerial responsibilities or personal liability for losses.

5. ***Explain the rights and obligations of partners under the Uniform Partnership Act.***
The Uniform Partnership Act established six rights of partners: (1) to share in the management and operations of the business, (2) to receive interest on additional investments made by a partner, (3) to be compensated for expenses incurred in the name of the partnership, (4) to share in any profits the company earns, (5) to have access to the company's books and records, and (6) to receive a formal accounting of the business affairs of the partnership. Each partner also has several obligations: (1) to share in any losses incurred by the business, except as noted in the limited partnership agreement, (2) to work for the partnership without salary as necessary, (3) to submit to majority vote or arbitration of differences that may arise among the partners, (4) to give other partners complete information about all affairs of the partnership, and (5) to give a formal accounting of the business affairs of the partnership.

6. ***Identify the advantages and disadvantages of partnerships.***
The advantages of partnerships are (1) the ability to pool resources, (2) ease of creation, (3) avoidance of double taxation, (4) the ability to divide work and share skills, and (5) the ability to attract additional investment. The disadvantages are (1) unlimited personal liability of the general partners, (2) the difficulty of transferring ownership without dissolving the partnership, (3) the possibility of disputes among the partners, and (4) limitations on how additional capital can be raised.

7. ***Describe the nature of corporations.***
The corporation is a unique business form. A corporation may have thousands of owners, some of whom have never visited the business, or only one or two owners who operate it much like a sole proprietorship or a partnership. The corporation is a legal entity in itself and must pay taxes on the profits before distributing them to the owners. Also, a corporation can be sued, write contracts, borrow money, and do other things people do in conducting business. The owners have very limited liability, and the corporation can easily raise additional money by attracting new stockholders.

8. ***Identify the advantages and disadvantages of corporations.***
The advantages of corporations are (1) the ability to raise additional capital by selling stock, (2) limited liability of the shareholders or owners, (3) perpetual life even when shareholders die, and (4) the ease of transferring ownership. The disadvantages are (1) double taxation, (2) lack of distinct decision-making authority, (3) the need to file a large number of reports to various government agencies, and (4) large size, which can cause the founders to lose control over the business.

9. ***Discuss the nature of corporate mergers and acquisitions.***
A merger occurs when two firms formally join their assets, liabilities, and ownership. Most mergers result from friendly negotiations between two companies that each has something to gain from the merger. In an acquisition, one company simply buys the assets and obligations of another company.

10. ***Describe three collaborative forms of business ownership.***
Three collaborative forms of business are the cooperative, the joint venture, and the nonprofit organization. Cooperatives are businesses that are owned and managed by customers or members, who pay membership fees and share in any profits the business makes. Their primary purpose is to buy goods and services at lower prices for members by buying in volume and minimizing profit markups.

Joint ventures occur when two or more people or companies join together to undertake a specific, limited, or short-term project. As in partnerships, resources and profits are shared, and the projects typically are large and costly.

Nonprofit organizations provide services and goods not offered by for-profit businesses. Examples are the Boy Scouts, the Girl Scouts, the Salvation Army, and the March of Dimes.

KEY TERMS AND CONCEPTS

Sole proprietorship (p. 64)
Partnership (p. 67)
Partnership agreement (p. 68)
Limited partnership (p. 68)
General partner (p. 68)
Limited partner (p. 68)
Corporation (p. 71)
Board of directors (p. 72)
Merger (p. 75)
Vertical merger (p. 75)
Horizontal merger (p. 75)
Conglomerate merger (p. 75)
Acquisition (p. 76)
Tender offer (p. 76)
Hostile takeover (p. 76)
Master limited partnership (p. 77)
S corporation (p. 77)
Cooperative (p. 78)
Joint venture (p. 78)

DISCUSSION QUESTIONS

Company

1. Why might a person wish to establish a new company as a sole proprietorship rather than as a corporation?
2. Which form of business might be best for a company that expected fairly rapid growth in the future? Why?

Customers

3. Which form of business caters most to the needs of its customers? How might other forms of business become more customer oriented?
4. Why might customers prefer to do business with small proprietorships rather than with large corporations?

Competitors

5. How might a sole proprietorship compete successfully with larger partnerships and corporations?
6. Do nonprofit organizations compete unfairly with for-profit businesses? Why or why not?

Collaborators

7. What benefits do companies that participate in joint ventures receive?
8. In what ways are corporate shareholders like collaborators rather than business owners?

In Question: Take a Stand

Korn/Ferry, an executive recruiting firm, reported that in its 20th Annual Board of Directors Study, which surveyed 327 Fortune 1000 companies, 60 percent of corporate boards include at least one woman compared with 11 percent in 1973.[10] In addition, minorities have increased 37 percent, up from just 9 percent two decades ago. In the companies surveyed by another company, board representation by women has increased 35 percent since 1987. However, the actual number of board seats held by women and minorities shows women accounted for 9 percent of the 9,707 directors at public Fortune 1000 companies. Only 135 of these companies have two or more female directors.

Should stockholders be concerned with how many of its directors are women or minorities? Is it more important to choose competent directors than to be concerned with having diversity on the board?

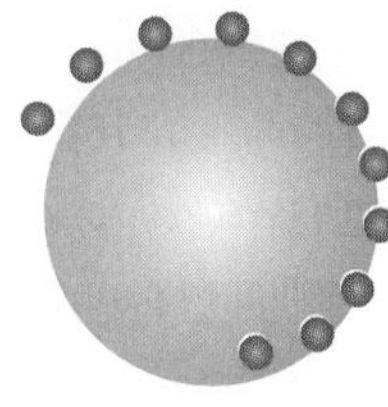

CASE 4.1
NATURAL RESOURCES

Mary Kessler had a degree in Child and Family Relations and several years experience in preschool education when she, her husband, and their five-year-old daughter moved to Wausaw, Wisconsin.

Although she loved small-town life, Kessler wasn't happy with Wausaw's preschools. Then Kessler met Becky Mohs who had a B.S. in early childhood education. They struck up a friendship and within six months decided to go into business together.

They found an old building that had once been a school in the central business district of Wausaw. It seemed like a perfect place for their preschool, kindergarten, and day care business. The partners took out a personal bank loan and started Natural Resources, an "S" corporation. The school's name was inspired by a quote by Walt Disney: "Our greatest natural resource is the minds of our children."

Mary was now her own boss and she and Mohs were free to make all the decisions for their business. She knew this freedom came with a price—hard work and risks to her personal wealth. However, she didn't realize how many long, hard hours of work would be required to run the business.

The school started with twelve students. Kessler and Mohs employed one teacher, one teacher's aide, one cook, and one aerobics instructor. The school stressed quality care and provided students with both group activities and individual attention.

The first few years were very lean. Profit was not in Natural Resources' vocabulary. However, over time their high-quality service became well known in the Wausaw area. After three years Kessler and Mohs were employing five teachers, one teacher's aide, one cook, three part-time people, a music teacher, and an aerobics instructor. The school had individual learning centers dedicated to art, science, computers, music, and reading. Aerobic exercises were available for both children and parents. The hard work was paying off.

In the spring of 1994, Mary was approached by the Wausaw area Catholic schools who wanted to buy out Natural Resources to handle the overflow at Catholic schools. Their plan was to take over Natural Resources' building lease, buy all the equipment and toys, and hire Kessler and Mohs as co-principals.

It was a sweet deal—the Wausaw area Catholic schools would pay off Kessler and Mohs' loans and they would reap an additional $30,000. And there were the attractive salaries, health care, and other employee benefits that went along with the co-principal jobs.

Questions

1. *In your opinion, why did Mary and Becky choose an "S" Corporation? What are the advantages of this type of business organization?*
2. *What alternative forms of business organization might Mary and Becky have chosen?*
3. *Should Mary and Becky sell the business? What alternatives might they have to selling the business?*

CHAPTER

5

THE BUSINESS MISSION AND SOCIAL RESPONSIBILITY

When you have studied this chapter, you will be able to:

1

Define and explain the nature of a business mission.

2

Identify socially responsible behavior and define *business ethics*.

3

Explain how ethical dilemmas arise.

4

Identify some ethical issues that can develop within a company.

5

Describe a firm's responsibility to its customers and the environment.

6

Explain a firm's responsibility to its competitors.

7

Explain a firm's responsibility to its collaborators.

8

Describe some approaches companies use to foster ethical behavior within the organization.

Nobody who worked at the Imperial Food Products plant in Hamlet, North Carolina, had much love for the place. The job—cooking, weighing, and packing fried chicken parts for fast-food restaurants—was hot, greasy, and poorly paid. The conveyor belts moved briskly, and the few rest breaks were so strictly timed that going to the bathroom at the wrong moment could lead to dismissal. But in the sleepy town of 6,200, there was not much else in the way of work. So most of the plant's 200 employees, predominantly black and female, were thankful just to have the minimum-wage job. Until last week, that is.

The morning shift had just started when an overhead hydraulic line ruptured, spilling its volatile fluid onto the floor. Gas burners under the frying vats ignited the vapors and turned the 30,000-square-foot plant into an inferno of flame and thick, yellow smoke. Panicked employees rushed for emergency exits, only to find several of them locked. "I thought I was gone, until a man broke the lock off," said Letha Terry, one of the survivors. Twenty-five of Terry's fellow employees were not so lucky. Their bodies were found clustered around the blocked doorways or trapped in the freezer, where the workers had fled in vain from the fire's heat and smoke.

The disaster brought to light the mostly invisible body count of the American workplace. By some estimates, more than 10,000 workers die each year from on-the-job injuries—about 30 every day. Perhaps 70,000 more are permanently disabled. The fire also exposed the weakness of measures for ensuring job safety. The 11-year-old Imperial Food Products plant had never been inspected. Like a lot of American workplaces, it fell through the gaping cracks of a system in which there are too few inspectors, penalties are mostly trifling and the procedures for reporting dangerous conditions can leave workers to choose between risking their jobs and risking their lives.[1]

Business has an important responsibility to society. This chapter focuses on how businesses view their mission in society and highlights the various issues of social responsibility they face.

THE BUSINESS MISSION

Business mission
A statement defining what the company business is and how the company will operate the business.

Every company must decide on the nature of its business. Owners and managers define the essence of the business—what it hopes to accomplish and what products the company will sell. The **business mission** defines what the company business is and how the company will operate the business. It is a broad statement about the reasons for the company's existence. For example, when Ford Motor Company was founded in 1903, Henry Ford clearly understood that the average American family, not just the rich, had a need for economical transportation in the form of a low-priced car. Ford also knew that product standardization and assembly line technology could be used to accomplish this mission.

Modern companies should strive to have an equally clear sense of the nature of their business. Consider these excerpts from The Limited, Inc.'s mission statement:

1. To offer the absolutely best customer shopping experience anywhere—the best store—the best merchandise—the best merchandising presentation—the best customer service—the best "everything" that a customer sees and experiences and to treat all the women, men, and children who enter our stores with the same respect and dignity we accord to our family and friends.
2. To become the world's foremost retailer of life-style fashions.
3. To be known as a high-quality business with an unquestioned reputation for integrity and respect for all people.
4. To maintain a revolutionary and restless, bold and daring business spirit noted for innovation and cutting-edge style.[2]

These statements make it clear what type of store The Limited wishes to be. It provides direction for the organization.

Let's look at another example of how mission statements usually go far beyond the description of existing products. JCPenney's business mission, shown in Exhibit 5.1, is a broad statement of the company's purpose. It discusses the way the company will deal with customers, employees, and society at large. It outlines the organization's *purpose* and *responsibilities.* It describes how the company will treat competitors and collaborators.

TOTAL QUALITY MANAGEMENT

Total quality management (TQM)
A business philosophy that a company must operate with an emphasis on customer-driven quality throughout the organization.

Total quality management is a business philosophy that frequently appears in business mission statements. **Total quality management (TQM)** expresses the belief that the company must operate with an emphasis on customer-driven quality throughout the organization. Such a mission makes TQM a top priority. Production quality control is a necessary aspect of TQM programs.

Exhibit 5.1 **JCPENNEY'S BUSINESS MISSION**

1. To serve the public, as nearly as we can, to its complete satisfaction.
2. To expect for the service we render a fair remuneration and not all the profit the traffic will bear.
3. To do all in our power to pack the customer's dollar full of value, quality, and satisfaction.
4. To continue to train ourselves and our associates so that the service we give will be more and more intelligently performed.
5. To improve constantly the human factor in our business.
6. To reward men and women in our organization through participation in what the business produces.
7. To test our every policy, method, and act in this way: "Does it square with what is right and just?"

For many years, American corporations' product quality failed to keep pace with the product quality of a number of overseas competitors. For example, Xerox Corporation lost a substantial portion of its business to Ricoh, Canon, and other Japanese copier producers because the Japanese companies offered copying machines not only at lower prices but with higher quality as well. Xerox closely examined its product and production strategies and discovered that sloppiness and inefficiency were destroying the company. Managers concluded that Xerox—and many other American companies—had lost sight of "an axiom as old as business itself...focusing on quality that meets the customer's requirements."[3]

The following statement by a Burger King executive illustrates the philosophy behind the implementation of a quality management strategy: "The customer is the vital key to our success. We are now looking at our business through the customers' eyes and measuring our performance against their expectations, not ours."[4] A company that employs a quality strategy must evaluate its quality through the eyes of its customers.

We will discuss additional aspects of companies' business missions in Chapters 7 and 13. However, because a company's role in society is an important part of its mission, we now turn to issues involving ethics and social responsibility.

BUSINESS ETHICS AND SOCIALLY RESPONSIBLE BEHAVIOR

In recent years, many highly publicized stories about corporate wrongdoing or about individuals who failed to act with high ethical standards have appeared on television and in newspapers and magazines. For example, a storm of criticism erupted over the Exxon *Valdez* and *Braer* oil spills and the weakness of each company's efforts to reduce the resulting damage to the environment. McDonald's received so much flak about the fat content of some of its menu items that it stopped cooking french fries in beef tallow and introduced McLean Deluxe, a burger with only 9 percent fat.

Social responsibility
Refers to the ethical consequences of a person's or organization's acts as they might affect the interests of others.

Ethics
Involves values about right and wrong conduct.

Business ethics
Concerns the principles that guide an organization's conduct and the values the company expects to express in certain situations.

Moral behavior
Reflects how well an individual's or organization's business activities demonstrate ethical values.

Norms
Suggest what ought to be done under given circumstances.

Ethical dilemma
A predicament in which the businessperson must resolve whether an action, although benefiting the organization, the individual, or both, may be considered unethical.

Society clearly expects companies to obey the law, but a socially responsible organization has an obligation broader than *legal* responsibility. **Social responsibility** refers to the ethical consequences of a person's or organizations's acts as they might affect the interests of others.[5] Every manager makes decisions with ethical implications.

Ethics involves values about right and wrong conduct. **Business ethics** concerns the principles that guide an organization's conduct and the values the company expects to express in certain situations.[6] A businessperson's **moral behavior** reflects how well an individual's or organization's business activities demonstrate these ethical values.

Ethical principles reflect the social values and cultural norms of a society. **Norms** suggest what ought to be done under given circumstances. They indicate approval or disapproval—what is good or bad. Many norms in Western society are based in the Judeo-Christian ethical philosophy. Being truthful is good. Being fair—doing unto others as you would have them do unto you—meets with approval.

Some norms dictated by broad-ranging ethical principles for personal conduct have a direct counterpart in business actions. Being truthful—a societal norm—and avoiding deceptive or untruthful advertising are closely linked. In these situations, the expected moral behavior is relatively clear. Some actions, such as killing a competitor, are so obviously linked to norms that they seem to be morally inexcusable in all circumstances. Although morally accepted behavior may be clear-cut in many circumstances, in other situations determining what is ethical is a complicated and debatable matter.

An **ethical dilemma** is a predicament in which a businessperson must resolve whether an action, although benefiting the organization, the individual, or both, may be considered unethical.[7] An ethical dilemma may arise when two norms or values are in conflict. Suppose a corporation president values both high profits and a pollution-free environment. When one of these two goals interferes with achieving the other goal, the businessperson faces an ethical dilemma.

He ran a 4.4 40, a 9.5 100 and a 50 sec. 440.
Unfortunately, he made a 1.0 in high school.
Russell Corporation salutes those athletes who choose to have a good mind, as well as a good time. For they are the true winners.
42
A quality education wears well on everybody.

Socially responsible organizations believe they have a responsibility broader than legal responsibility. Russell Corporation, an athletic wear maker, made posters of this ad available to teachers and coaches to help remind student athletes of the importance of an education.

Problems also arise if others do not share the principles or values that guide a businessperson's actions. For instance, is it wrong to pay a bribe in a country where bribery is a standard business practice? Should MTV avoid airing a Snoop Doggy Dogg video if its overtones of violence and racism offend some viewers but not others? How a business answers these questions involves resolving ethical dilemmas.

In many situations, individuals agree on the principles or values, but no fixed measure or standard exists by which to judge actions. An engineer can calculate exactly how strong a steel girder is, and a chemist can offer the right formulation of chemicals necessary to perform a task. But the business executive cannot be so precise. Even in instances where specific laws would seem to guide actions, the laws and their applications are almost always subject to debate. Although businesspeople often pride themselves on their rational, problem-solving abilities, the lack of permanent, objective ethical standards for all situations continues to trouble the person seeking the ethical course of action in business.

Thus, an absolute consensus rarely exists on what should be done when ethical behavior is involved. Different people, and even any one person, can evaluate a question using several different perspectives. For example, the belief that smoking is harmful to health has led to regulations restricting smoking in airplanes and other public places and barring cigarette commercials from radio and television. Yet to some people this is a controversial matter. Of course, good health is important, but what about individuals' freedom of choice? What about the effects of secondhand smoke?

In general, when business decision makers encounter ethical dilemmas, they consider the impact of the organization's actions and operate in a way that balances the organization's short-term profit needs and society's long-term needs. More specifically, businesspeople must ask what is ethical in a particular situation. Is it wrong to market a product that contains chlorofluorocarbons, which, according to many but not all scientists, may damage the earth's ozone layer? Businesspeople must establish the facts and determine whether their plans are compatible with the organization's ethical values. They must determine at what point certain business practices become ethically questionable. Is it ethical for a sales representative to pay for a purchasing agent's lunch? To give the agent a gift on his or her birthday? To arrange for an expenses-paid vacation if the sales representative's company gets a big contract?

WHAT VALUES DO WE USE TO MAKE ETHICAL JUDGMENTS?

Social value
A value that reflects the goals a society views as important and expresses a culture's shared ideas about preferred ways of acting.

A **social value** reflects the goals a society views as important and expresses a culture's shared ideas about preferred ways of acting. Social values express abstract ideas about what is good, right, and desirable. For example, we learn from those around us that it is wrong to lie or steal.

Some social values that reflect the beliefs of the majority of Americans are

- *Freedom.* The freedom of the individual to act as he or she pleases is a fundamental value in American culture.
- *Achievement and success.* The achievement of wealth and prestige through honest efforts is highly valued because it leads to a higher standard of living and improves the quality of life.
- *Work ethic.* Americans believe it is important to work on a regular basis. Idle people are considered lazy.
- *Equality/equity.* Most Americans have a high regard for human equality, especially equal opportunity, and generally relate to one another as equals. Americans respect fair and impartial behavior.
- *Patriotism/nationalism.* Americans take pride in living in the "best country in the world." They are proud of our country's democratic heritage and its achievements.
- *Individual responsibility and self-fulfillment.* Americans are oriented toward developing themselves as individuals. They value being responsible for their achievements. The U.S. army slogan "Be all that you can be" succinctly expresses the desirability of personal growth.[8]

You probably share all or most of these values. In the next section, we will see how these and other values are applied in business situations.

ETHICAL QUESTIONS AND THE FOUR Cs

Throughout this book, we will see that laws and ethical considerations can affect every aspect of a business. Business ethics involves the behavior of a company's owners, managers, and workers and the company's relationships with its customers, competitors, and collaborators. Exhibit 5.2 presents some possible ethical questions that apply to all four Cs of business. In considering these questions, remember that ethical issues are in fact philosophical in nature and there may not be general agreement among all parties about answers to ethical dilemmas.[9] However, a definite trend has emerged toward broadening the social responsibility of business organizations beyond the limitations of their traditional role as economic forces.

We will now examine key issues regarding business's social responsibility for each of the four Cs.

Exhibit 5.2 **SELECTED ETHICAL QUESTIONS RELATED TO THE FOUR Cs**

Company

- How much employee training for "fire drills" is necessary?
- What should an employee consider to be a conflict of interest?
- Should a company hire a certain quota of Asian employees?

Customers

- Is protective packing a source of unnecessary environmental pollution?
- Can advertising persuade us to purchase products we don't really want?
- What effect does advertising have on children?

Competitors

- Should we discuss our prices with our competitors?
- Is it good business practice to spread a rumor that our competitor's company symbol is a "devil's symbol"?

Collaborators

- Does the bank really need to know everything about our debts?
- Should we exaggerate how many units we expect to buy to get a good price on raw materials?

RESPONSIBILITY WITHIN THE COMPANY

Individuals who work for business organizations have certain rights as well as obligations to the company. Many of these rights have been clearly spelled out. Other rights are hotly debated. We will discuss the most important ethical issues dealing with individuals and activities within the company.

WORKING CONDITIONS

The example that opens this chapter illustrates the potential horrible consequences if a company fails to concern itself with its workers' most basic right: the right to a safe workplace. Few owners or managers would say they are not concerned with employee safety. However, this is not a black-and-white issue. The ethical question that is debated usually boils down to two words: "How safe?" Different jobs involve various degrees of danger. Ethical dilemmas tend to arise if productivity can be increased or cost can be decreased by making the workplace a "little" more dangerous. Managers use their own judgment to determine what is safe—and different managers can have big differences of opinion.

Workplace conditions have been an issue throughout America's history. Upton Sinclair's novel *The Jungle* dealt with unhealthy and unsafe working conditions in Chicago's meat-packing houses in the early 1900s. The revelations in the book resulted in laws that regulated this business.

More recently, the Occupational Safety and Health Act of 1970 (OSHA) was passed to provide regulation standards such as the wearing of protective clothing and equipment and controlling toxic chemicals in the workplace. It also provides for government inspection of workplaces, which may occur on a surprise basis.

EQUAL EMPLOYMENT OPPORTUNITY IN A DIVERSE WORKPLACE

A socially responsible organization's hiring policies provide an equal opportunity for all people, regardless of race, sex, religion, age, and ethnic affiliation. This does not mean a company cannot hire individuals who are best qualified for the job. It does mean competent and experienced individuals should be allowed the opportunity for employment and promotion without discrimination.

Of course, we do not live in a perfect world. Discrimination against minorities has existed in the past, and it exists today. As we discussed earlier, not everyone shares the same

Exhibit 5.3 **PAY LEVELS OF MEN AND WOMEN HAVE NOT BEEN EQUAL**

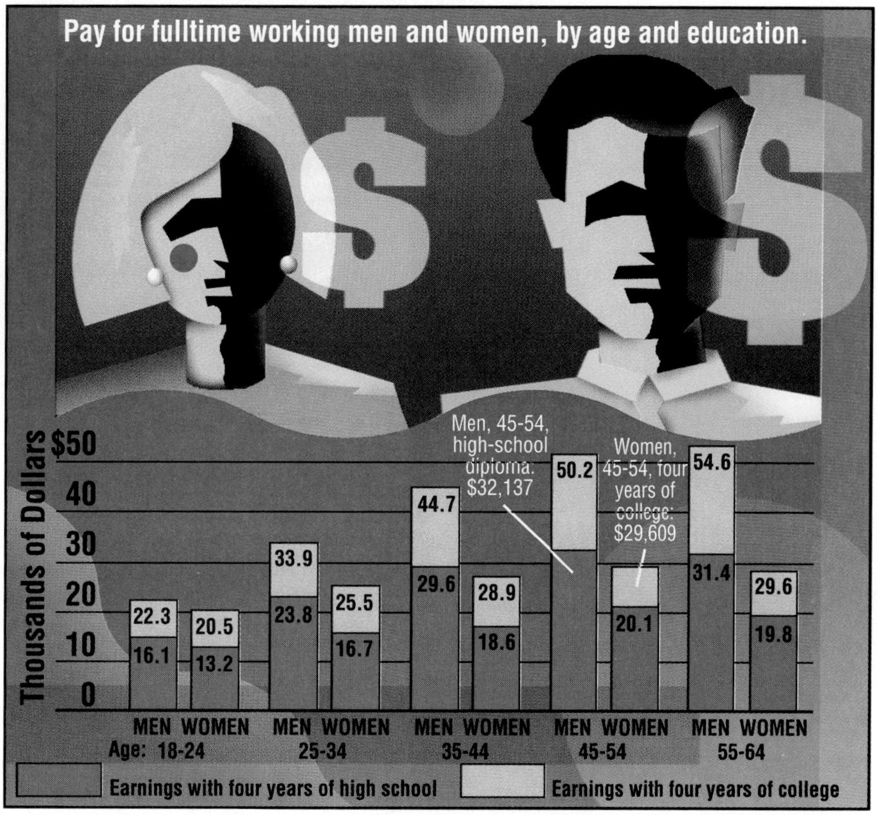

Pay for fulltime working men and women, by age and education.

Thousands of Dollars
$50
40
30
20
10
0

Men, 45-54, high-school diploma: $32,137
Women, 45-54, four years of college: $29,609

Age	18-24		25-34		35-44		45-54		55-64	
	MEN	WOMEN	MEN	WOMEN	MEN	WOMEN	MEN	WOMEN	MEN	WOMEN
Earnings with four years of high school	16.1	13.2	23.8	16.7	29.6	18.6		20.1	31.4	19.8
Earnings with four years of college	22.3	20.5	33.9	25.5	44.7	28.9	50.2		54.6	29.6

values. The average woman earns only 70 cents for every dollar earned by the average man. The Census Bureau estimates that this is up from 60 cents thirty years ago—which means women's earnings have gained on men's by approximately one-third of one percent a year.

Exhibit 5.3 shows that women between ages 18 to 24 with college degrees earn an average 92 cents for every dollar earned by men of the same age and education level. At every education level, women make less money than men with the same education.[10]

Exhibit 5.4 shows that race makes a difference in unemployment rates. Historically, African-American teenagers have had the highest unemployment rates. Discrimination plays a part here, but the fact that teenagers are the least skilled segment of the labor force also contributes to this situation.[11]

Congress has passed several laws aimed at discrimination in employment. The most important impact of these laws was the creation of the Equal Employment Opportunity Commission (EEOC). Congress granted this agency the power to investigate complaints of

Exhibit 5.4 **RACE MAKES A DIFFERENCE IN UNEMPLOYMENT RATES**

Unemployment by Race

Race	Average Annual Unemployment, May 1993
Black	12.9%
Hispanic	9.7
White	6.0
Total	6.7

The work force is becoming increasingly diverse. Growth in participation rates of major ethnic minority groups in the U.S. labor force between 1988 and 2000 is expected to be dramatic. The Bureau of Labor Statistics projects growth from 13.3 million to 16.5 million for African-Americans, from 9.0 million to 14.3 million for Hispanic-Americans, and from 3.6 million to 5.6 million for Asian-Americans and others.[12]

employment discrimination. The EEOC also has the power to take legal action against companies that use discriminatory practices.

AFFIRMATIVE ACTION

Affirmative action programs Programs that attempt to remedy historical problems of discrimination by increasing the number of minority employees in organizations.

Affirmative action programs attempt to remedy historical problems of discrimination by increasing the number of minority employees in organizations. They also try to correct imbalances at the top management and middle management levels. For example, the number of Asian-Americans, African-Americans, Hispanic-Americans, and women executives differs dramatically from their proportions in the work force. However, the work force is changing and is expected to be even more diverse by the year 2000.

Not all companies support affirmative action programs. Many employers hold that affirmative action programs force a quota system on the company. They argue that a quota system interferes with the company's right to operate its own business as a free enterprise. They also claim that these programs encourage **reverse discrimination** by making it more difficult for nonminority groups to be hired or promoted.

Reverse discrimination Discrimination that makes it more difficult for non-minority groups to be hired or promoted.

DIVERSITY TRAINING

Companies like Sun Microsystems Inc. have launched diversity training programs to accommodate the changing work force.[13] Diversity training picks up where affirmative action programs leave off. While affirmative action programs have brought minorities into the work force, they have done little to accommodate the multicultural nature of today's workers.

Diversity training programs Programs that attempt to get workers to understand and value individual cultural differences within the organization's work force.

Diversity training programs attempt to get workers to understand and value individual cultural differences within the organization's work force. Sun Microsystems began its Strategic Cultural Initiatives in 1990, when it recognized its work force as one that couldn't be treated as a homogeneous group. "We recognized that the workforce will continue to become increasingly multicultural. The idea of being assimilated into a corporate culture has gone the way of the dinosaurs," said the manager of Sun's Strategic Cultural Initiatives group.[14]

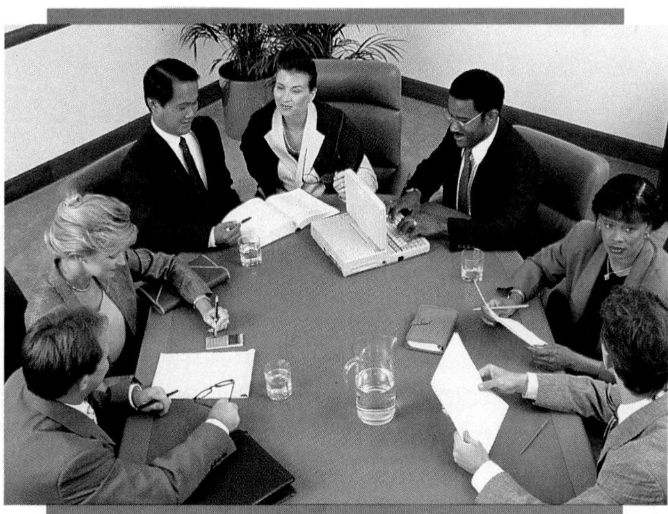

Workplace conflicts stemming from a work force's ethnic and religious diversity can seriously hurt productivity. Diversity training attempts to ease tensions springing from multiculturalism in the workplace. Diversity training programs attempt to get employees to understand and value individual cultural differences in the context of corporate culture.

However, diversity training consultants caution that training workshops, which typically last only one day, have limited impact without any follow-up. "The biggest myth is that we give the training, we hold hands and sing 'We Are the World,' and things are all better—but that's not true," says one consultant. "If the boss uses diversity training as a Band-Aid, the problems often recur."[15]

ECONOMIC SECURITY

Economic security takes two forms. First, it means the employee has steady, uninterrupted employment that provides a living wage. Most companies find it undesirable to have their employees constantly being laid off. Nevertheless, layoffs do occur. Socially responsible companies try to ensure that their workers are provided for in the event of bad times.

In this chapter, we can only mention that companies often face ethical dilemmas when demand for their products or services decreases, when rapid changes in technology eliminate jobs, or when it becomes more economical to move the factory to another country. These are complex issues that pit economic security against productivity or other business goals. We will address these issues more fully elsewhere in the book.

The second aspect of economic security deals with providing for those who are no longer able to provide for themselves. It means providing economic assistance if accidental injury occurs or giving an employee the opportunity to retire in old age.

Most companies recognize their responsibility to provide economic security. American business has always believed that loyalty over the years should be rewarded. For more than 100 years, American companies have been granting pensions to their long-time employees. A **pension** is a fixed amount of money paid to a retired employee on a regular basis.

Pension
A fixed amount of money paid to a retired employee on a regular basis.

Recent years have seen several scandals about pension funds that were used for purposes other than paying for former employees' golden years. For example, Harcourt Brace Jovanovich used its pension fund, which was tied to the value of its stock, as a source of capital to ward off a hostile takeover attempt. The company also borrowed extensively. The stock price declined in value, and employees' retirement funds became almost worthless.

FOCUS ON COLLABORATORS

The American Guild of Musical Artists

A ballet may appear like poetry in motion, but all that delicate movement comes at a price. Like many athletes, ballet dancers often use up their bodies by age 40. Some of them are questioning why they should have to wait around another quarter-century—until age 65—to get their pensions. They want economic security.

Recently a group of ballet dancers from the American Ballet Theater, the New York City Ballet, the Joffrey Ballet, and the Dance Theater of Harlem filed a suit against their union, the American Guild of Musical Artists, in federal district court in Manhattan, charging it with discrimination and seeking $20 million as well as changes in how the plan is run. The usual retirement age "bears no rational relationship to the age at which dancers are compelled to retire and need income—almost always prior to age 40," the lawsuit contends.

"Dancers are always worried about their welfare," said Cynthia Gregory, age 45, who retired from the American Ballet Theater in June but is a guest artist with several companies. "They've been in one career, focused on that since they were small children. Nobody makes it to age 65."

Also joining the suit are such well-known dancers as Fernando Bujones, Cynthia Harvey, Judith Fugate, and Donald Williams.

Sanford I. Wolff, a lawyer and the executive director of the union, said programs were available to help dancers change careers. In addition, he said, they are entitled to disability benefits, which vary depending on how long a dancer has been working and how much he or she was paid. "The regular retirement age is 65, and that's what it is in this plan, and it covers a lot of people, some dancers, some singers," Wolff said. "There's nothing discriminatory about it."

But Miss Gregory said the suit makes sense. "This is such an unusual career," she said. "Our lives are run a little backward from most people's."

CHILD CARE AND PARENTAL LEAVE

A number of companies believe it is their responsibility to provide child care facilities. Some companies choose to grant parental leave (also called *family leaves of absence*). While some companies provide both child care and parental leave, others support neither.

As we will see, our work force has changed greatly in recent years. More than 60 percent of all married women work. The number of households run by women with no husband present doubled between 1980 and 1990. There are 10 million single-parent households, and the number of those households headed by men is growing twice as fast as the number headed by women. This trend has changed the way many companies think about their responsibility to their employees.

EMPLOYEE DIGNITY AND SEXUAL HARASSMENT

When a person accepts a job, he or she does not give up all rights as a private citizen. Most companies respect the individual worker's self-esteem. For example, in The Limited's business mission statement, the company states it wishes "to be known as a high-quality business with an unquestioned reputation for integrity and respect for all people." Humiliation of employees is unacceptable by most business standards. Employees do not leave their dignity at the doorstep when they go to work.

STREET SMART

A Sexual Harassment Policy

When it comes to issues like sexual harassment, the smart thing to do is to be specific. Experts consider AT&T's sexual harassment policy to be well written and to the point. Here are some excerpts:

> A.T. & T.'s sexual harassment policy prohibits sexual harassment in the workplace, whether committed by supervisory or non-supervisory personnel. Specifically, no supervisor shall threaten or insinuate, either explicitly or implicitly, that an employee's submission to or rejection of sexual advances will in any way influence any personnel decision regarding that employee's employment, wages, advancement, assigned duties, shifts, or any other condition of employment or career development....
>
> Other sexually harassing conduct in the workplace that may create an offensive work environment, whether it be in the form of physical or verbal harassment, and regardless of whether committed by supervisory or non-supervisory personnel, is also prohibited. This includes, but is not limited to, repeated offensive or unwelcome sexual flirtations, advances, propositions, continual or repeated verbal abuse of a sexual nature, graphic verbal commentaries about an individual's body; sexually degrading words used to describe an individual; and the display in the workplace of sexually suggestive objects or pictures....
>
> Sexual harassment in the workplace by any employee will result in disciplinary action up to and including dismissal and may lead to personal legal and financial liability. Employees are encouraged to avail themselves of A.T. & T.'s internal Equal Opportunity complaint procedure if they are confronted with sexual harassment or any prohibited form of harassment. Such internal complaints will be investigated promptly, and corrective action will be taken where allegations are verified. No employee will suffer retaliation or intimidation as a result of using the internal complaint procedure.

Sexual harassment is the most visible issue concerning employee dignity. A person's employment should not hinge on providing sexual favors in exchange for keeping his or her job, getting a raise, or receiving a promotion. Furthermore, a "hostile" or "offensive" environment can be a form of sexual harassment. People should be free to work in an environment in which they do not have to endure degrading comments, listen to lewd remarks, or be exposed to vulgar jokes.

As with several other issues of social responsibility, these practices do exist in some companies. One survey showed that one in four women reported having been sexually harassed.[16] Laws have been passed to deter sexual harassment and punish offenders.

Most everyone agrees that touching an employee or forcing a worker to submit to sex to keep her or his job is a clear violation of employee rights. However, there is less agreement on what a "hostile environment" is. The term is vague. Problems may arise if men and women do not view flirtatious behavior or certain remarks in the same way. If one person thinks he or she is just being a friendly manager while another thinks the person's actions are inappropriate, problems arise. What kinds of verbal remarks are insulting? Many companies that wish to avoid problems related to differences of opinion specifically identify what types of conduct are considered to be sexual harassment.

During the nomination hearing for appointment to the Supreme Court, Judge Clarence Thomas was accused of sexual harassment. Anita Hill alleged that when Thomas was her supervisor in a federal government agency 10 years earlier, he sexually harassed her. Thomas denied the charges. This situation dramatically highlighted the issue of sexual harassment in the workplace. In particular, a number of people asked why Anita Hill did not complain at the time the alleged harassment occurred. One reason given was that victims of sexual harass-

Exhibit 5.5 **THE HIGHEST-PAID EXECUTIVES IN AMERICA 1989–1993**

Company/Chief Executive	Total Compensation, 1993 ($ Thousands)	5-Year Total ($ Thousands)
Walt Disney/Michael D. Eisner	$203,020	$236,771
Travelers/Sanford I. Weill	53,111	141,605
HJ Heinz/Anthony J.F. O'Reilly	2,797	120,844
U.S. Surgical/Leon C. Hirsch	2,758	114,346
Fund American/John J. Byrne	16,172	80,809
Loral/Bernard L. Schwartz	33,690	64,753
Forest Labs/Howard Solomon	32,582	62,819
McCaw Cellular/Craig O. McCaw	102	52,833
Coca-Cola/Roberto C. Goizueta	14,652	51,896
Conseco/Stephen C. Hilbert	38,675	51,156

ment rarely report the incident because they are so emotionally devastated. Subordinates often fear they will lose their jobs or suffer other negative consequences. Researchers estimate that only 5 percent of individuals experiencing sexual harassment take any kind of formal action.[17]

EXCESSIVE EXECUTIVE COMPENSATION

In 1993 Michael Eisner, chief executive of The Walt Disney Company, made $203.1 million. This compensation made him the highest paid chief executive of a public corporation in history. He received this compensation despite the fact that the company's profit fell by 63 percent from the previous year. The second-highest paid executive of 1993 was Sanford Weill, head of Travellor Corp. He earned $52.8 million. In 1990, the top two executives at Time Warner received $99.6 million between them, and the company lost money.[18] Were these executives wildly overpaid? Some think so. Most corporations provide large incentives for executives who exceed sales and profit goals. Exhibit 5.5 lists the 10 highest-paid executives in America. Determining what is fair compensation for executives may be a controversial issue in many organizations. Answers to the question "How much is too much?" undoubtedly will vary among people, depending on their values.

Golden parachute
Compensation given to an executive whose company is purchased by another company in a hostile takeover.

A **golden parachute** is an agreement between an executive and his or her employer that the executive will be given extra compensation if the company is purchased by another company in a hostile takeover. These compensation packages are called golden parachutes because they "ease the landing" and allow executives to "land on their feet" when they get fired because of a takeover.

CONFLICT OF INTEREST

Executives and managers often make decisions that influence the company's interests. If an executive's judgment about what is best for the company is clouded by the chance for personal gain, a conflict of interest exists. The following excerpt from ITT's code of corporate conduct clearly explains what behavior the company expects:

> As long as you remain an ITT employee, your duty is to act in business matters solely for the benefit of the Corporation. Your salary and other corporate benefits are full compensation for your services to ITT. You must particularly avoid any act on behalf of ITT which might produce an unauthorized private financial benefit for yourself, your family, friends, or business associates. You and those under your supervision must not become involved for personal gain with competitors, customers, or suppliers to the ITT system.[19]

RESPONSIBILITY TO CUSTOMERS AND THE ENVIRONMENT

To help business act in a socially responsible manner, President John F. Kennedy outlined the consumer's basic rights: the *right to be informed,* the *right to safety,* the *right to choose,* and the *right to be heard.* Since Kennedy's pronouncement, others have argued that consumers have additional rights, such as the *right to privacy* and the *right to a clean and healthy environment.* Some argue that children have special rights because they lack mature reasoning powers.

THE RIGHT TO SAFETY

Right to safety
Right of customers to use products that do not unnecessarily put them in danger.

Consumers expect many things when they buy a product. They want it to work properly, last as long as expected, and so on. But the most basic expectation is probably that of safety. Although most of us are willing to take certain reasonable risks, we assume we have a **right to safety:** We do not want our use of a product to unnecessarily place us in danger.

Pepsico had to address questions of product safety when a woman called its consumer hotline to report she had found a hypodermic syringe in a can of Diet Pepsi. This was the first such report outside the Seattle area, where Pepsico was investigating a similar claim. After much investigation, Pepsico decided not to recall Diet Pepsi. First, the company knew its production processes did not include syringes. Second, although the company knew the public associated syringes with AIDS and hepatitis, a consultation with the Food and Drug Administration assured Pepsico's product safety experts that no health risk existed. The company's statements to the media showed it was impossible for its bottling plants to place syringes in cans or bottles. They assured the public their cans were 99.9 percent safe. Within days, they were able to announce that the entire affair was a hoax.

Most people would agree that consumers should be protected against products that are hazardous to life or health. In this sense, the right to safety is a move away from *caveat emptor* (let the buyer beware) to a philosophy that holds sellers responsible for their actions. Socially responsible companies make a great effort to ensure they are not negligent in the production and sale of products.

Although we have many laws designed to protect consumers, faulty products are sometimes produced and consumers are sometimes injured. Even when products are properly constructed, manufacturers are now expected to further protect consumers by means of warnings, instructions on safe product use, and directions about what to do in certain problem situations ("If swallowed, call physician immediately"). Although occasionally such requirements seem to go too far ("Remove plastic wrapper from pizza before eating pizza"), the fact remains that unsafe products do not benefit the business in the long run. Failure to protect customers is inconsistent with the goal of total quality management.

THE RIGHT TO BE INFORMED

Right to be informed
Right to be protected against fraudulent, deceitful, or grossly misleading information, advertising, labeling, or other practices, and to be given the facts one needs to make an informed choice.

Several years ago, a Chicago man discovered that his Oldsmobile had been equipped at the factory with an engine marked "Chevrolet." General Motors (GM) refused his demand for a "pure Oldsmobile," declaring that switching engines (which were all about the same anyway) to meet production schedules had been its practice for years. The motorist sued. Ultimately GM settled out of court with 66,000 owners of Buicks, Oldsmobiles, and Pontiacs who had been "deceived" in this manner. These buyers had insisted on their right to be informed about any modifications made to the products they purchased.

Most people would agree that the consumer has a right "to be protected against fraudulent, deceitful, or grossly misleading information, advertising, labeling, or other practices, and to be given the facts one needs to make an informed choice." The **right to be informed** is reflected in laws and practices involving nutritional labeling, product content and quality, and other information on labels, as well as requirements relating to truth in lending and package design.

Wrangler Earth Wash jeans are made with low-sulfide dyes, biodegradable enzymes, and less water to help protect our rivers and streams. Wrangler believes consumers have the right to a clean and healthy environment.

QUALITY OF LIFE

Quality of life
A value that reflects a lessening concern with being economically well off and an increasing concern with people's general well-being.

As the United States, Canada, and other nations became more affluent, their citizens' values changed. Concern with **quality of life** has been increasing. That term is difficult to define precisely, but it reflects a lessening of concern with being economically well off and an increasing concern with people's general well-being.

When applied to the business community, this value translates into a belief that companies should be expected to be more than economically efficient. Business organizations are called on to serve customers by safeguarding the environment in addition to being economically efficient. In other words, business has a responsibility for the long-run welfare of consumers (society) as well as for supplying products that provide consumers with immediate satisfaction.

Issues of quality of life spring from the idea that citizens have certain rights that no organization can be permitted to violate. Meeting quality of life expectations while fulfilling other missions has caused companies many problems. Yet if the demands of consumers, most of whom are interested in both quality of life issues and the demands of the law, are to be met, companies must address these problems.

ECOLOGY

Within the past 25 years, there has been a mounting realization that society must be concerned with ecology and protection of the environment. Do companies, as important members of society, have a responsibility not to tamper with or damage the environment? Satisfaction of the general public, which wants a clean environment, is a major quality of life issue that marketers must address. This is a complex issue because people want more than a clean environment. This fact means environmental issues often involve trade-offs such as the following examples:

- Producers of electric power are told that nuclear plants disturb the ecosystem and are very dangerous. Yet people want low-priced electricity and do not want to burn "dirty coal," which both causes air pollution and disfigures the earth through mining.
- Nonreturnable cans and bottles may create litter problems and damage the environment in other ways. But people do not like the bother and expense associated with returnable bottles and often throw them away for the sake of "convenience."
- People want to pay low prices for gasoline. But they also claim that oil spills from tankers could be prevented if oil companies took extra precautions—precautions that would raise the companies' costs and, ultimately, prices at the gas pump.

The packaging industry has developed biodegradable packages that, unlike bottles and cans, decompose over time. However, companies like Burger King and Taco Bell must spend considerable effort in keeping neighborhood litter under control even though many of their packages are biodegradable.

The fact that business has a social responsibility to our environment is obvious. What is not obvious is how it will meet that responsibility. The issue comes down to who will pay—in terms of dollars and inconvenience—for a cleaner environment. Is society willing to pay a higher price for products that reduce pollution? Does society place a higher value on lower-priced automobiles or on clean air?

The issue of a cleaner environment can be partially solved by recycling waste products to make "new" products. Recycling can be understood as requiring a role change. The consumer who drinks a can of beer becomes the seller of a raw material by recycling the empty can. The recycling process can reduce trash and litter and conserve natural resources. But again the trade-off problem arises. Both consumers and organizations must bear the costs and effort of the recycling effort. Also, in some cases recycling has proven more expensive than continuing to operate in the old way. Nevertheless, many companies now operate recycling centers to reduce solid-waste problems.

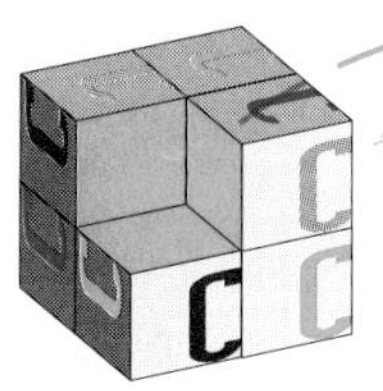

FOCUS ON CUSTOMERS

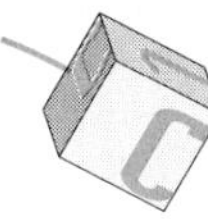

The Rainforest

Nuts to you, bud—Brazil nuts and cashews, specifically. That's what Jason Clay, director of the save the rainforest group Cultural Survival, answered when Ben Cohen of Ben & Jerry's asked how his ice cream company could help the cause. Clay's organization was just beginning to export the nuts—and hundreds of other rainforest resources—to help enable native dwellers to keep their land. After Cultural Survival and Ben & Jerry's made a deal, Rainforest Crunch ice cream was launched in 1990. It's become a top-five seller.

What's proven good for Ben & Jerry's is also proving good for the world's tropical wetlands. Not only do profits keep the land undeveloped, but the product concept has helped generate publicity for the rainforests.

They can use all the help they can get. Though the rainforests help keep the greenhouse effect at bay, they are being destroyed with lightning speed. Fully half have already been degraded or destroyed, and 100 acres continue to disappear every minute.

With celebrities, rock singers, and, increasingly, "ordinary folks" getting hot under the collar about the consequences of deforestation, it's not surprising that many companies are jumping into the cause. Rainforest products such as copaiba-oil soap are in the Rainforest

Essentials cosmetics line. Two major outdoor clothing companies feature jacket buttons from Equador's tagua palm. New York even boasts its own store, From the Rain Forest. And rainforest products won't be fading into the woodwork anytime soon. Many food, drug, and cosmetics companies are exploring products, and a major breakfast company is testing a cereal. Even moviemakers are even getting into the act; Twentieth Century-Fox plans an animated film on the dangers of rainforest destruction.

RESPONSIBILITY TO COMPETITORS

It has been said that business needs a level playing field. This means competitive conditions must allow *all* businesses an equal opportunity to survive and grow.[20] What would competition be like if lying, cheating, bribery, kickbacks, and monopolistic practices were common behavior rather than exceptions to the rule? Competition would be more like inner-city gang warfare than business.

Society expects companies to engage in behaviors that do not interfere with free enterprise. Competition in our American economy is expected to be fair and honest. Unfortunately, ethical business dealings with competitors have not always occurred during our business history.

The ethical standards for competition that have developed over the years are closely intertwined with laws. Government has passed much legislation to deal with problems involving companies' responsibilities toward competitors.

Federal antitrust legislation
Laws prohibiting acts such as restraint of trade, monopoly, price fixing, price discrimination, and other behavior that tends to lessen competition.

Federal antitrust legislation prohibits acts such as restraint of trade, monopoly, price fixing, price discrimination, and other behavior that tends to lessen competition. The federal government has passed many laws to restrict monopolies. The Sherman Antitrust Act (1890), the Clayton Antitrust Act (1914), the Federal Trade Commission Act (1914), and the Wheeler-Lea Act (1938) all deal with this issue.

Federal Trade Commission (FTC)
A major federal agency with broad powers of investigation and jurisdiction over unfair methods of competition.

One major federal agency, the **Federal Trade Commission (FTC)**, which was established in 1914, affects competitive activity on a regular basis. The FTC was given broad powers of investigation and jurisdiction over "unfair" methods of competition. For example, false advertising and other deceptive practices such as misrepresentations in the labeling of products are illegal under the FTC act. Initially the FTC was supposed to draft a fixed list of "unfair practices." However, it soon became clear that no list could cover all situations.

RESPONSIBILITY TO COLLABORATORS

A company has a responsibility to those who help it exist and prosper. It may face ethical issues concerning suppliers, creditors, investors, and the community at large.

SUPPLIERS AND CREDITORS

Most companies purchase materials, components, equipment, and supplies from their suppliers. As a commercial customer, a company has the responsibility to deal with its suppliers in a fair and honest manner. It is obliged to pay its bills on time. It is also obliged to avoid deception in negotiations.

Creditors should be shown authentic financial statements. The company's records should be accurate. Documents should not be falsified to allow the company to obtain credit. In short, the company should be truthful.

INVESTORS AND SHAREHOLDERS

In a capitalistic economic system, the purpose of a business is to make money for its owners, the investors or the stockholders. Classical economists argue that the only responsibility of business is to *maximize* the amount of money stockholders receive. They argue that issues such as environmental pollution are of no concern to business. In today's business environment, however, most organizations seek to earn enough money to *satisfy* their investors. Most businesses find that operating to maximize profits without considering issues of social responsibility is not the best long-run perspective for the organization or society. This is a complex issue, and at this point in the text, we cannot discuss the full debate. We simply point out that in our modified capitalistic system, the arguments for socially responsible actions outweigh the arguments by classical economists.

Insider trading
Occurs when a person buys or sells stocks of a company because he or she has inside information about the company's plans.

Another ethical issue involves whether executives of a company or their associates in the financial community should obtain personal gain because of their knowledge of the company's plans. **Insider trading** occurs when a person buys or sells (trades) stocks of a company because he or she has "inside information." For example, suppose the president of an aircraft company knows that its major customer, an airline, has just canceled an order for 20 planes. As soon as the company announces that this action will lower profits, the price of the company's stock is likely to fall. If the president and other individuals with inside information sell their stock at its higher price before this information becomes public, they will be engaging in insider trading.

Greenmail
The practice of threatening to take over a company and buying a significant portion of the company's stock in the hope of making a quick profit.

Another ethical issue is known as **greenmail**. *Greenmail* sounds like *blackmail* for a reason. A criminal blackmailer threatens to reveal something embarrassing about a person that the victim doesn't want known, perhaps something he or she did in the past. Similarly, a greenmailer buys a significant portion of a corporation's stock in the hope of making a quick profit on the sale of the stock. What's wrong with making a large profit? Nothing, except for the means the greenmailer uses. The greenmailer threatens to take over the company, often implying that once the hostile takeover has occurred, top managers will be removed, many employees will lose their jobs, and parts of the company may be sold off. To avoid the takeover, the company's board of directors votes to buy the greenmailer's stock at a price above the stock's market price.

Obviously companies do not like to be greenmailed, so they have devised a number of strategies to avoid this possibility. However, these solutions tend to weaken the company financially.

THE COMMUNITY

Many organizations feel a strong commitment to the communities in which they operate. Community support ranges from buying uniforms for a local Little League team to donating executives' time and company funds to running a United Way campaign.

Philanthropy
Company donations to charities and other social causes.

Philanthropy refers to company donations to charities and other social causes. The next time your local ballet, opera, or symphony orchestra plans a performance, count the number of corporate sponsors of the event. You may be surprised!

FOCUS ON COMPANY

Taylor Energy

Self-made Patrick Taylor, 54, is one of Louisiana's toughest and richest oil moguls. His tie, suspenders, and oversized diamond cufflinks all sport his company's motif: a knobby, T-shaped fitting for an oil well known to drillers as a "Christmas tree." His company, Taylor Energy, is one of the fastest-growing independent oil producers in the country, with 14 offshore rigs in the Gulf of Mexico.

But Taylor is also a committed philanthropist, specializing in the education of underprivileged kids. Like many successful Americans, Taylor credits his achievements to education. He had to work hard for his success. In 1955 he hitchhiked to Baton Rouge with $55 in his pocket to get into then tuition-free Louisiana State University, where he earned a degree in petroleum engineering. "I *wanted* that college education," he says. "I was qualified, and they didn't turn me away."

Like a lot of bootstrap millionaires, Taylor once thought that if he could make it himself, anyone could. He changed his mind three years ago after speaking to a class of 183 "problem" eighth-graders at a middle school in a New Orleans neighborhood plagued by drugs and crime.

Taylor was struck by their predicament. Their teachers seemed capable and committed, and the kids seemed bright enough. But even if they did graduate from high school, what then? Louisiana's state universities were no longer free. These kids probably wouldn't be able to afford college—and they knew it. Taylor figured they didn't need new curricula, new teachers, or a new building. What they needed was an incentive.

Taylor decided the best incentive was an open door to college. So he offered to provide college tuition, books, living expenses, and $1,000 a year in "pocket" money to any of those 183 students who graduated from high school with a B or better grade average and wanted to go on to college. His adopted class called themselves Taylor's Kids. Twenty-six members of that original class are high school seniors and on track to go to college.

A year later, Taylor launched his New Orleans project. Together with 17 other businesspeople, he pledged a $1,000 annual stipend to any New Orleans high school student entering college whose family lived below the poverty level (in this case, $13,000 a year). The cost was $1 million, but only part of it came from Taylor. "I probably had the million dollars," he says. "But I wanted the students to know that the money was coming from the community's corporate leaders. I wanted it to say, 'We believe in you. We're willing to invest in you. Because we want to hire you.'" So he raised the money for Project New Orleans from chief executives around the city. He gives a list of their names and their college degrees and majors to every student who receives a grant.

To date, over 400 New Orleans students have received support from Taylor's various projects. "We've laid out a pathway to success for people," Taylor says.

GOVERNMENT

Companies also have relationships with the government at the local, state, and federal levels. For example, the Immigration Reform and Control Act of 1986 makes it illegal for an employer to knowingly employ a non–U.S. resident who is not authorized to work in the United States. Compliance with the law is a primary social responsibility of business. We discuss various laws influencing business in Chapter 23 and elsewhere in the book.

FOSTERING ETHICAL BEHAVIOR

As you can see, ethical values influence many aspects of business strategy. What can a company do to encourage ethical behavior by its executives, managers, and workers? Two approaches are the code of conduct and the social audit.

CODES OF CONDUCT

Code of conduct
Establishes a company's or professional organization's guidelines indicating its ethical principles and specifying what behavior the organization considers proper.

A **code of conduct** establishes a company's or professional organization's guidelines indicating its ethical principles and specifying what behavior the organization considers proper. For example, Caterpillar Tractor's code of conduct begins, "The law is the floor. Ethical business conduct should exist at a level well above the minimum required by law."

Most company codes of conduct are extensive statements. They identify what behavior is considered dishonest. They explain what type of relationship employees and collaborators are expected to have. They point out potential conflicts of interest.

Following a code of conduct helps resolve some ethical dilemmas but not others. Many ethical issues are not clear-cut or without controversy. Individuals often have to resolve ethical dilemmas using judgments based on their own ethical values. The following checklist offers some good general advice when considering ethical dilemmas.

1. Recognize and clarify the dilemma.
2. Get all possible facts.
3. List the options—all of them.
4. Test each option by asking, "Is it legal? Is it right? Is it beneficial?"
5. Make your decision.
6. Double check your decision by asking, "How would I feel if my family found out about this? How would I feel if my decision were printed in the local newspaper?" Do you still feel you made the correct decision?
7. Take the action warranted by the decision.[23]

SOCIAL AUDITS

Social audit
A form of self-regulation in which the company attempts to monitor managers' and employees' ethical behavior

Many companies, especially large corporations, attempt to regulate themselves. They conduct **social audits** to monitor managers' and employees' ethical behavior. The social audit investigates how well the company's ethical policies are being carried out. Companies typically form ethics committees to systematically appraise the company's policies and practices from an ethical perspective. The basic question the social audit attempts to answer is: Are we doing the right things?

WHISTLE BLOWING

Whistle blower
An employee who informs management, a union, the press, or a government agency that some behavior within the organization is not as it should be.

A whistle blower is an informant—someone who "blows the whistle" to sound an alert. The term has a negative ring to it, but it should not. A **whistle blower** informs management, a union, the press, or a government agency that some behavior within the organization is not as it should be. Many organizations encourage employees to report unethical policies or actions.

Unfortunately, in some organizations the parties involved in the questionable behavior accuse whistle blowers of not being team players. Whistle blowers are often "punished." In some instances, whistle blowers have been demoted, passed up for promotion, transferred to undesirable locations, or treated as misfits by other employees.

In one of the most sensational cases of whistle blowing, Karen Silkwood alleged that her employer was causing plutonium contamination among workers. Silkwood later died in an automobile accident. Her death was said to be the result of her whistle blowing, but this was never proven in court.

SUMMARY

1. ***Define and explain the nature of a business mission.***
The business mission defines what the company business is and how the company will operate the business. It is a broad statement about the reasons for the company's existence and outlines the organization's purpose and responsibilities. Some business mission statements contain the business philosophy of total quality management. Total quality management (TQM) expresses the belief that the company must operate with an emphasis on customer-driven quality throughout the organization.

2. ***Identify socially responsible behavior and define* business ethics.**
Society expects business not only to obey the law but also to act in a socially responsible manner. *Social responsibility* refers to the ethical consequences of a person's or organization's acts as they might affect the interests of others. *Business ethics* concerns the principles that

guide an organization's conduct and the values it expects to express in certain situations. These ethical principles reflect the social values and cultural norms of the society.

3. ***Explain how ethical dilemmas arise.***
   In many instances, determining what is ethical is a complicated matter. This sometimes leads to a situation called an *ethical dilemma,* in which a businessperson must resolve whether an action, although benefiting the organization, the individual, or both, may be considered unethical. Problems also arise if others do not share the principles or values that guide a businessperson's actions. In many situations, individuals agree on the principles or values, but no fixed measure or standard exists by which to judge actions. In general, when business decision makers encounter ethical dilemmas, they consider the impact of the organization's actions and attempt to balance the company's short-term profit needs and society's long-term needs.

4. ***Identify some ethical issues that can develop within a company.***
   An organization's employees have certain rights as well as obligations to the company. Some of the most important ethical issues dealing with individuals and activities within the company are working conditions, equal employment opportunity, affirmative action, diversity training, economic security, child care and parental leave, employee dignity and sexual harassment, excessive executive compensation, and conflict of interest.

5. ***Describe a firm's responsibility to its customers and the environment.***
   A socially responsible company must satisfy certain basic rights of the consumer, including the right to be informed, the right to safety, the right to choose, the right to be heard, the right to privacy, and the right to a clean and healthy environment. The right to safety means the use of certain products or services offered by a firm should not unnecessarily put their users in danger. The right to be informed means the consumer has a right "to be protected against fraudulent, deceitful, or grossly misleading information, advertising, labeling, or other practices, and to be given the facts one needs to make an informed choice." Moreover, business organizations are called on to serve customers by being economically efficient and to safeguard the environment.

6. ***Explain a firm's responsibility to its competitors.***
   Society expects companies to engage in behaviors that do not interfere with free enterprise. Government has passed a great deal of legislation to address problems involving companies' responsibilities toward competitors. The Federal Trade Commission (FTC) has broad powers of investigation and jurisdiction to ensure fair competitive practices.

7. ***Describe a firm's responsibility to its collaborators.***
   A company has a responsibility to those who help it exist and prosper. These collaborators include suppliers, creditors, investors, shareholders, and governments. For instance, a business has a responsibility to satisfy its investors while fulfilling its responsibility to society.

8. ***Describe some approaches companies use to foster ethical behavior within the organization.***
   A company can use several approaches to encourage ethical behavior by its executives, managers, and workers. For instance, it can introduce a code of conduct, which sets forth guidelines indicating the organization's ethical principles and specifying what behavior it considers proper. It can conduct social audits to monitor ethical behavior by management and employees. Finally, the company can encourage whistle blowing to uncover unethical behavior.

KEY TERMS AND CONCEPTS

Business mission (p. 88)
Total quality management (TQM) (p. 88)
Social responsibility (p. 89)
Ethics (p. 89)
Business ethics (p. 89)
Moral behavior (p. 89)
Norms (p. 89)
Ethical dilemma (p. 89)

Social value (p. 91)
Affirmative action programs (p. 94)
Reverse discrimination (p. 94)
Diversity training programs (p. 94)
Pension (p. 95)
Golden parachute (p. 98)
Right to safety (p. 99)
Right to be informed (p. 99)
Quality of life (p. 100)
Federal antitrust legislation (p. 102)
Federal Trade Commission (FTC) (p. 102)
Insider trading (p. 103)
Greenmail (p. 103)
Philanthropy (p. 103)
Code of conduct (p. 104)
Social audit (p. 105)
Whistle blower (p. 105)

DISCUSSION QUESTIONS

Company

1. What is a business mission? Give some examples of possible mission statements.
2. Ray Kroc, the founder of McDonald's, did not invent the hamburger. He began his company by defining his business in terms of "mass-produced fast foods." In your opinion, what was McDonald's business mission in its early days, and what is it today?
3. What is total quality management?
4. How should a company define social responsibility?
5. What is an ethical dilemma? Provide some examples.
6. Can you think of any examples of sexual harassment at a company where you have worked or at your college?
7. What is a conflict of interest?
8. What is reverse discrimination?
9. What is affirmative action?
10. How can a company foster ethical behavior?
11. Should whistle blowing be encouraged in a company? Why or why not?

Customers

12. What ethical principles do customers expect companies to follow?
13. Think of your shopping experiences. Do you think any company's actions have been unethical?
14. What ethical obligations does a company have to the public?

Competitors

15. What role does competition play in a company's determination of its business mission?
16. What role does competition play in a company's determination of its business ethics?
17. What ethical obligations does a company have to its competitors?
18. What federal legislation deals with competition?

Collaborators

19. What role do labor unions play in determining a company's policies on economic security?
20. What ethical obligations does a company have to its collaborators?
21. What role does a company have to play when it deals with investors, suppliers, and the community at large?

In Question: Take a Stand

A New York businesswoman said,

> *A friend of mine, an elegant man of middle years who works in the same financial circuit where I earn my living, recently told me with some amusement about an evening reception he had attended.*
>
> *A major New York bank was playing host to an equally formidable Japanese institution. The wine flowed, the canapes circulated, the flowers nodded in the waft of conversation among several hundred polite and expensively clad people—almost all of them men.*
>
> *My pal is a man's man who likes to spend time with the boys. But this was no locker room; this was a party, for heaven's sake! Where were the women? His polite probing produced one inescapable conclusion: It was deemed important that the Japanese visitors be put at ease, that they feel at home. And at home is where the women in their lives traditionally stay. So their ever so tactful New York hosts apparently decided that their women—wives and executives—should stay home too.*
>
> *This is wrong. America is different from Japan. Businesswomen should be at parties for Japanese businessmen even if business suffers.*

Do you agree?

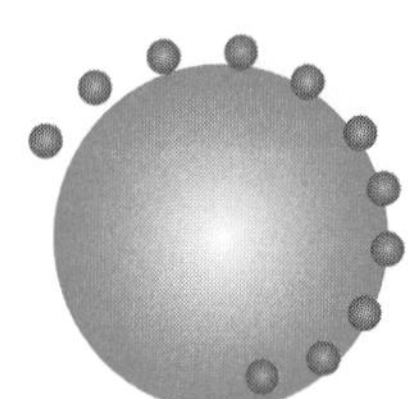

CASE 5.1
WORKPLACE DIVERSITY AND CONFLICT

For more than a year, two of Emma Colquitt's employees had argued about religion. Then one of them, a Hispanic Roman Catholic woman, approached her operations manager with a complaint: The other worker, an African-American follower of Jehovah's Witnesses, had listened sympathetically as a customer "bashed" Catholicism. A petty office squabble? Not to Colquitt, president and co-owner of Cardiac Concepts Inc., a Texas outpatient laboratory that specializes in cardiovascular tests. She worried that conflicts growing out of the ethnic and religious diversity of her tiny work force could seriously hurt production. Most of her eleven employees were women and minority members, representing half a dozen faiths.

Questions

1. *How should an employee treat a customer who makes a racial, ethnic, or religious slur?*
2. *What should Emma Colquitt do about the workplace conflicts that have arisen?*
3. *Can a small business act in the same way a large corporation would in this matter? Why or why not?*

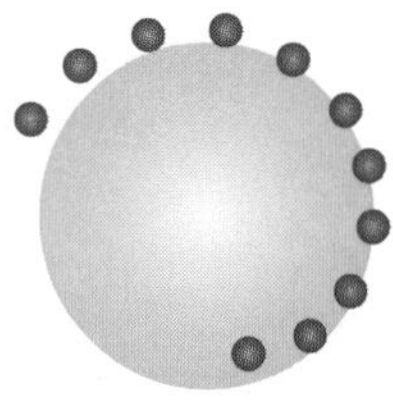

CASE 5.2
RED ROSE EXCAVATION[22]

Frankie Snead, whose company, Red Rose Excavation, in Houston does "anything dirt related," says the prospect of a health care tax terrifies her. She offers her 12 employees no health benefits. "We'd like nothing better than to give our personnel the best health care available," she says, "but it's just not in the numbers." An 8 percent health care tax, which she fears will wipe out some small businesses, will almost eliminate the profits on her annual revenues of just under $1 million. She can raise prices only if her competitors respond to the new tax by raising theirs. But she fears higher prices will squelch the slow recovery Houston's battered construction industry has managed over the past three years. "People just won't build as much," she says.

Questions

1. *Is it ethical for a company not to offer a health care plan?*
2. *Why would someone work for a company without a health care plan?*
3. *If heath care becomes government mandated, what can this company do to stay in business?*

CHAPTER

6

SMALL BUSINESS, ENTREPRENEURSHIP, AND FRANCHISES

When you have studied this chapter, you will be able to:

1
Discuss the nature and importance of small business.

2
Categorize the different types of small-business operations.

3
Explain what functions all businesses have in common.

4
Outline the basic questions to be answered in developing a new business venture.

5
Describe how to prepare a business plan.

6
Explain the major advantages of operating a small business.

7
Discuss the reasons many new small businesses fail.

8
Describe the characteristics of entrepreneurs.

9
Explain how collaborators help small businesses.

10
Define a *franchise* and discuss the nature of franchising.

11
Describe the advantages and disadvantages of franchising.

In the late 1970s, Tuan Huynh concentrated on surviving until the next day. Today he focuses on building his apparel-manufacturing company's sales to $100 million. Along the way, Huynh overcame huge obstacles. A captain in the South Vietnamese army when the United States pulled out of Vietnam in 1975, Huynh was captured by the victorious North Vietnamese and put into a "reindoctrination" camp. Following his release in 1978, Huynh rejoined his wife, Anh, and their seven children. But the family's life was not a happy one.

Huynh planned his family's escape from Vietnam for a year. One dark night, the Huynhs crammed into a boat with 254 other refugees. After they spent six months in an Indonesian refugee camp, a sponsor in Dallas brought them to the United States in 1980.

Huynh found work as an auto mechanic, and Ahn sewed at home for several Dallas apparel manufacturers. After Huynh's workday ended, he delivered Anh's clothing—and made business contacts. Five years later, the family had saved over $50,000. Huynh launched his own company, H&A Fashions. He hired five employees and set up shop in a 3,000-square-foot warehouse. Huynh and his general manager, Joe Allen, worked 12 hours a day 7 days a week.

Today H&A employs 120 people and recently completed its third move, into a 129,000-square-foot building. The company sells six different lines of women's apparel to some 3,000 customers, including Sears and Wal-Mart. It is the largest single supplier of women's dresses to JCPenney Company.

Joe Allen says Huynh's strong points are his willingness to work exceptionally hard, a broad practical streak, and patience. "We in this country have short-term business plans," Allen explains. "He plans ahead."

Management flexibility also separates H&A from some of its competitors, according to Penney buyer Nancy Hillis. Its production lines are set up for quicker turnaround than many companies can manage. Also, H&A maintains an unusually large inventory, so it can fill unexpected store needs almost overnight.

Huynh's plans call for building H&A to $100 million in sales within the next five years, through both internal growth and acquisitions, but he sounds like he will be content even if his company does not achieve his lofty goal. "I am happy here because I have freedom," Huynh says. "I work hard so I have money. I can sleep all night here. Why should I worry about anything?"[1]

Tuan Huynh is a successful entrepreneur who took on hard work and many risks to start his own small business. This chapter discusses what a small business is and what it takes to start your own business.

WHAT IS A SMALL BUSINESS?[2]

Small business
A business that is independently owned and operated, is not dominant in its field, and has fewer than 500 employees.

Small Business Administration (SBA)
A federal agency charged with protecting and assisting small businesses.

A **small business** is a business that is independently owned and operated, is not dominant in its field, and has fewer than 500 employees.[3] The word *small* is a bit deceiving. According to the **Small Business Administration (SBA)**, the federal agency charged with protecting and assisting small businesses, 99 percent of all American businesses are small.

A small restaurant, a small computer components manufacturer, and a small private hospital are very different small businesses. For this reason, the SBA does not have one single size definition of small business that fits all industries. However, the SBA has established two widely used size standards—500 employees for most manufacturing and mining industries and $3.5 million in annual receipts (sales) for most nonmanufacturing industries. To be a small business, the company must not exceed these limits. However, many exceptions exist. Exhibit 6.1 summarizes the general size standards for selected industries.

So what exactly is a small business? The answer is that it depends on the type of business, as Exhibit 6.1 shows. For example, in agriculture sales volume (annual receipts) for a small farm cannot exceed $3.5 million. A small construction company has sales volume below $17 million. A small retailer has sales volume below $13.5 million. In other industries, however, such as manufacturing and wholesaling, the business is defined in terms of the number of employees. A wholesaler, for example, must have no more than 100 employees to be classified as a small business.

SMALL BUSINESS: THE CORNERSTONE OF OUR ECONOMY

Historically small-business owners have always demonstrated an extraordinary ability to get the most out of their resources and generate new jobs.[4] Small-business owners generate the

Exhibit 6.1 **SUMMARY OF SBA SIZE STANDARDS BY INDUSTRY**

Manufacturing: There are 459 separate manufacturing industries. For 350 of these, the size standard is no more than 500 employees. Three industries have a 1,500-employee size standard and the remaining 106 industries have a standard of either 750 or 1,000 employees.

Mining: All mining industries, except mining services, have a size standard of 500 employees.

Construction: General building and heavy construction contractors have a size standard of $17 million in average annual receipts. Special trade construction contractors have a size standard of $7 million.

Services: For the 147 service industries, the most common size standard is $3.5 million in average annual receipts. Computer programming, data processing, and systems design have a size standard of $7 million. The highest annual receipts size standard in any service industry is $14.5 million, for motion picture production, distribution, and services.

Retail trade: Most retail trade industries have a size standard of $3.5 million in average annual receipts. A few, such as grocery stores, department stores, motor vehicle dealers, and electrical appliance dealers, have higher size standards. None are above $13.5 million.

Agriculture: In agriculture the basic size standard is sales volume (annual receipts). A small farm cannot exceed $3.5 million in sales volume. However, there is great variation depending on the crop.

Wholesale trade: For the 69 wholesale trade industries, a size standard of not more than 100 employees is applicable for loans and other financial programs.

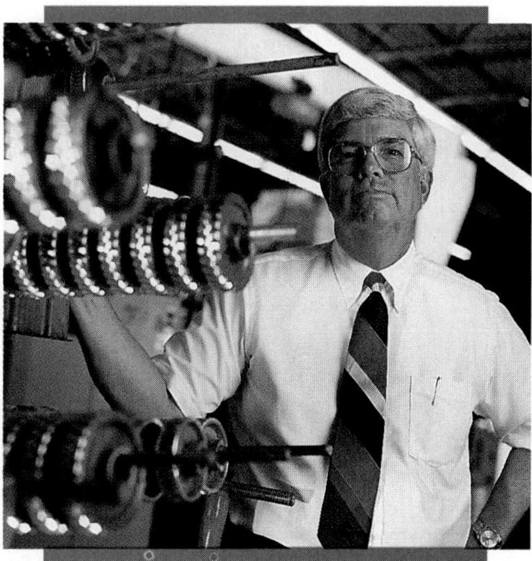

Over the past six years, Ron Bullock, CEO of Bison Gear & Engineering, which makes the gear motors used in power wheelchairs, X-ray tables, and commercial restaurant equipment, has expanded his company from $7 million to $24 million in annual sales and from 75 to 150 employees by investing heavily in research and development and in new equipment. Bullock says, "We basically have put every penny we've earned after taxes back into the business here."[5]

majority of jobs and produce a major share of the nation's goods and services. Firms with fewer than 500 employees accounted for 10 million of the 18.4 million new jobs created in the booming 1980s. In contrast, the Fortune 500 companies lost nearly 2 million jobs.

The importance of small business to America's economic well-being cannot be overstated. The entrepreneur—the small-business owner—is the seed for change and innovation. Small businesses are the cornerstone of our economy.

Year after year, statistics confirm the importance of new, small ventures:

- Small businesses account for over 99 percent of all U.S. firms.
- Small firms employ nearly half of the work force.
- Over 37 percent of the gross national product is generated by small business.
- Most new ideas and product innovations come from new, small ventures.
- Nearly two out of every three new jobs are created by small business.

Establishment
Any single physical location where a company conducts its business.

Enterprise
A company or business organization consisting of one or more establishments under the same ownership or control.

ENTERPRISES AND ESTABLISHMENTS

The SBA makes a distinction between enterprises (what we call the *company*) and establishments (branches, places of business.) An **establishment** is any single physical location where a company conducts its business. An **enterprise** is a company or business organization consisting of one or more establishments under the same ownership or control. Most small-business enterprises consist of a single establishment. When Pizzeria Uno began in 1943, it had a single establishment in downtown Chicago. Today Uno's business enterprise contains many restaurant establishments located in major cities throughout the United States.

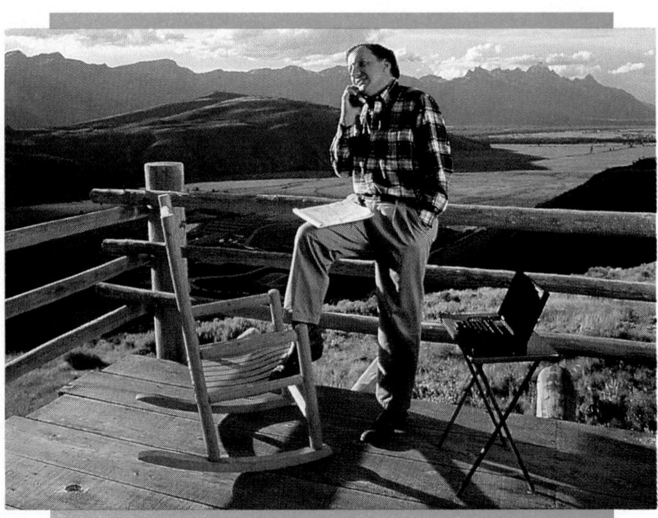

Almost 13 million people are self-employed in home-based businesses. Powerful personal computers, fax machines, cellular phones, and other advances in information technology have made running a small business from one's home a new way of doing business.

TYPES OF SMALL-BUSINESS OPPORTUNITIES

Small businesses range from small flower shops to high-technology computer disk manufacturers. In this section, we will discuss some typical small businesses.

RETAILERS

When asked to describe the typical small business, most people say retailing. A *retailer* is a "middleman" who sells to consumers. A typical retailer buys goods from manufacturers or wholesalers and sells merchandise in a store or shop.

The retail world is dominated by many gigantic corporations like Wal-Mart, Safeway, and Dayton-Hudson that have many chain stores throughout the country. Fortunately for the person who desires a small business, the retailing world also abounds with hundreds of thousands of small retail businesses. If you go to your local shopping mall, you will most likely find that the number of small retailers far exceeds the number of larger businesses. Retailing, which is discussed in depth in Chapter 14, provides big opportunities for small businesses.

SERVICE BUSINESSES

The United States has become a service economy, and many small businesses are service businesses. The Small Business Administration's definition of a small service business depends on the type of service provided. Sales volume may not exceed \$3.5 million to \$13.5 million, depending on the service industry.

Many small service businesses are started by individuals with a particular skill or specialized knowledge, such as an accountant or a golf professional. Service businesses often start off on a "shoestring" budget. For example, catering, auto detailing, and child care services often begin as *home-based businesses.* The SBA estimates that nearly 20 percent of all new small businesses begin operations in the owner's home.[6] Working out of one's home helps cut many of the costs of running the business.

CONSTRUCTION AND BUILDING TRADES

General building construction and the many associated building trades account for slightly less than ten percent of all small businesses. While companies that build skyscrapers tend to be large, most residential contractors are small businesses operating in a limited geographical area. Plumbers, electricians, and other building trades are dominated by small business. More than 6 million jobs exist because of this segment of the economy.

MANUFACTURERS

A small manufacturing business is defined by the maximum number of employees. According to the SBA, the maximum number of employees may range from 500 to 1,500, depending on the product manufactured.

Many small manufacturers are *high-technology businesses.* These organizations manufacture products using the highest levels of innovative technology. For example, Biocad Corporation's Catalyst System is a desktop computer-aided system for chemists working on drug discovery. California's Silicon Valley (the area surrounding San Jose) is known for the large number of creative engineers, inventors, and computer geniuses who founded these types of high-tech start-up businesses.

Many of these companies need large amounts of capital to engage in business. Firms known as *venture capitalists,* such as Southern California Ventures, and banks like Silicon Valley Bank specialize in lending large sums to high-tech small businesses that show promise of rapid growth. Venture capitalists often get a piece of the business (partial ownership) in exchange for their willingness to risk more on a new enterprise.

FARMS

The small family farm has always been an American tradition. As we mentioned in Chapter 1, our nation moved from a rural country during the post–Revolutionary War years to the urban economy it is today. The farm as a small business has undergone many transitions during this time.

Willy Nelson's Farm Aid concerts illustrate that not all farmers have experienced good times in recent years. Yet many farmers who looked at their farms as small businesses rather than a lifestyle are big successes. Today successful small farmers use computers and other modern equipment to run their farm businesses. They have adapted to the modern way of farming by becoming business oriented. The principles presented in this text apply as closely to agriculture as they do to manufacturing or retailing.

WHAT ALL BUSINESSES HAVE IN COMMON

Before we discuss how to start and operate a small business, we need to discuss what *all* businesses have in common.

All business activity can be categorized into four functional areas: production, marketing, finance, and management.

- *Production:* They must produce a good or offer a service.
- *Marketing:* They must market their offerings.
- *Finance:* They must acquire capital to finance their operations and control the flow of money within the company.
- *Management:* They must plan, organize, direct, and control the functional activities of production, marketing, and finance.

Exhibit 6.2 **THE FUNCTIONS OF BUSINESS**

Production Functions

Growing
Extracting/harvesting
Processing
Assembling and buying
Construction
Standardizing and grading
Servicing

Marketing Functions

Product conception and development
- Idea generation
- Pricing

Communication and exchange functions
- Selling
- Advertising

Physical distribution functions
- Transportation
- Storage

Finance Functions

Capitalization
Risk taking
Accounting

Management and Facilitating Functions

Planning
Organizing
Leading
Controlling
Information gathering

Exhibit 6.2 summarizes the essential elements of all businesses, large or small. Every business performs (or collaborates with others to perform) production, marketing, and finance functions. However, the nature of these general functions can vary dramatically in different business. For example, to a copper mining company, extracting is the primary production function. To a building contractor, construction is the primary production function. Since production, marketing, and finance activities must be managed, all businesses perform managerial functions as well.

A MODEL FOR STARTING AND OPERATING A SMALL BUSINESS

Many small businesses begin when an individual buys an existing business. Agreeing on a price for an existing company and then working long and hard to build it have been the road to success for many businesspeople. This is an important path for many individuals who want to own their own businesses. In this section, however, we will focus on starting a business from scratch. We will identify the path an enterprising individual takes when starting a new venture rather than the path an individual takes when acquiring an existing business.

Before getting started in a business, future small-business owners should ask themselves, "Is there an opportunity to start a business? Is my idea good enough?"

Getting a creative idea often leads to the creation of a new business. For example, Jean Giles-Ordonez of Boca Raton, Florida, started 2nd Moms without much money but with a great idea. Giles-Ordonez knew Florida is full of young couples who live far away from their

Exhibit 6.3 **SEVEN BASIC QUESTIONS TO ANSWER IN DEVELOPING A NEW BUSINESS VENTURE**

1. Is there a *customer* opportunity to start a business?
2. Is my idea good enough? Is it better than *competitors'* ideas?
3. What *company* resources are needed?
   a. What human resources are needed? How should they be managed?
   b. What capital is needed? How do I raise capital funds?
   c. What production operation or procedure is required to create my product or generate my service?
   d. How do I market my offering?
4. Whom must I *collaborate* with to run the business?
5. How should I organize the business?
6. After I start the business, how will I evaluate the company's performance?
7. What are the legal requirements for starting my business?

extended families. Many of these families have no one to help them care for a sick child or a newborn infant. So her idea was to start a service company that would train "second moms" to provide baby care and lactation coaching for new mothers. 2nd Moms also markets its service to corporations. This service was based on the idea that 2nd Moms could save companies money if they gave new mothers the option of a week of professional infant care instead of an extra day in the hospital.[7]

Once the entrepreneur has determined that the idea is good enough to start a business, he or she should ask, "What exactly is the nature of the business? Is there a need for this type of business?" Often an idea will require modification or further development before it becomes a realistic idea for a business. The prospective business owner may need to go to the library or to discuss the idea with potential customers to get information that will help him or her decide whether to start the business.

After determining that an opportunity for a business exists, there are still other questions to answer. Exhibit 6.3 summarizes the seven basic questions that must be answered in the process of developing a new business venture.

After answering these questions, the potential entrepreneur should incorporate the responses into a business plan.

THE BUSINESS PLAN

Having a sound new-business idea is a good starting point, but it is not enough. Those who are really serious about starting a business need a business plan.

Business plan
Lays out a direction for the company; describes the business operations and outlines the goals of the business.

The business plan is a key step in starting a business. The **business plan** serves the same purpose that a blueprint does for a building contractor. It lays out a direction for the company. It describes the business operations and outlines the goals of the business. A good business plan projects the expected results and indicates how the company plans to achieve them. The business plan provides a tool for evaluating each aspect of the business.

Often the business plan is shown to a bank or another collaborator. In these situations, the business plan normally includes an introduction and some appendixes in addition to the major sections. The introduction section includes the name and address of the business and other basic information about the company's purpose and its reasons for preparing the business plan. The major sections describe the company's goals and intentions with respect to the four Cs. The appendixes often show financial statements, the results of surveys, and other information too detailed for most readers of the business plan. Exhibit 6.4 outlines a typical business plan. Appendix A at the end of this book presents a complete sample business plan.

Exhibit 6.4 **AN OUTLINE FOR A BUSINESS PLAN**

Customers

This section identifies the markets for the business. It also defines the product or service the business will provide from the customers' perspective.

Who is the customer? What will they be buying? That is, what is the nature of your product or service? Why is it unique? Why will they buy it from your company?

Competitors

This section identifies the competition.

Are there any important industry trends that may influence the business? Who are your current competitors? What are their strengths and weaknesses? (For example, competitor A is a large, impersonal organization, while competitor B is a discount operation with low-quality products.) What companies may become future competitors?

Company

This section describes the business and its operating requirements and explains basic strategies.

Production and operations plans: What production processes or service delivery processes will be used?

Marketing plans: How will the product be distributed? Who will sell the product? Is advertising important?

Finance needs and plans: What are the company's capital needs? How much credit is needed? When will the money be needed? How will money needs change during the company's course of growth?

Management: What is the background of the managers/owners? How will the company be organized? What are the responsibilities of company personnel?

If the company already exists, this section may refer to an appendix that includes financial statements, for example, income statements and monthly cash flow statements for the first three years of operation.

Collaborators

This section identifies collaborators needed to fulfill the company's goals.

What bank will be used? Who will be the suppliers? Who will be the distributors? What shipping companies will be used? Who will be the company attorney? Who will be the public accountant? Who will help the company with hiring and training?

Appendix

Many business plans have one or more appendixes that include financial statements, research reports, and other information too technical or too detailed for most readers of the plan.

CUSTOMERS

As Exhibit 6.4 shows, this section of the business plan discusses customers' need for the product or service. Stated somewhat differently, it answers the questions "Is there an opportunity to start a business? Is my idea good enough?"

This section explains the creative idea and the nature of the business in terms of customers. It explains why customers will buy the product or service. It says how many customers will buy the product. In other words, it indicates the demand for the business. By identifying the demand, the business plan helps explain the need for the business.

COMPETITORS

Having a good idea that customers like may not be enough. The business plan must show that the company is able to operate in a competitive environment. It should show how the company will be different, better, or cheaper than the competition. It should identify existing and future competitors and indicate why the idea is good enough to survive competition.

COMPANY

The business plan should clearly identify the nature of the company and the resources needed to operate it. It should identify the production, marketing, finance, and management plans. This

STREET SMART

It's a Smart Idea to Communicate Effectively

Many great ideas for businesses didn't get off the ground because the business plan was not well written.

A business plan gives financiers their first impressions of a company and its principals. Investors are looking for evidence that the principals treat their own property with care—and will likewise treat the investment carefully. In other words, form as well as content is important. Good business plans incorporate the following tips.

- *Appearance.* The business plan should be neat and durable—not too amateurish or too lavish. A plan presented in plastic spiral binding with a one-color cover sheet looks serious and not inappropriately expensive.
- *Length.* The business plan should be no longer than 40 pages. Investors can be given additional background information in a separate volume after they express initial interest.
- *The cover and title page.* The cover contains the company name, address, phone number, and the month and year the plan is issued. The title page which follows the cover repeats this information with the addition of "Copy number ___" in the lower right corner. The copy number is useful for keeping track of the plans in circulation. No more than 20 plans should be in circulation at the same time.
- *The executive summary.* This concise two-page summary must sell potential investors on reading the rest of the business plan. It explains the company's current status, its products or services, the benefits to customers, the financial forecasts, the company's objectives in three to seven years, the amount of financing needed, and how investors will benefit.
- *The table of contents.* A well designed list of the plan's sections with page numbers.

section of the business plan answers many of the basic questions about starting a new business venture listed in Exhibit 6.3.

- *What human resources are needed? How should they be managed?* Am I prepared to operate or manage this business? What is the management plan?
- *How should I organize the company?* Most new small businesses are sole proprietorships, where the business is owned by one individual. However, the person considering a small business venture must decide which form of business ownership—sole proprietorship, partnership, or corporation—will be best. The advantages of these various types of ownership as well as the legal requirements for starting a small business are discussed in Chapter 4.
- *What capital is needed? How do I raise capital funds?* A lack of adequate capital funds may be the biggest barrier to starting a business. It is essential that a prospective start-up company owner estimate his or her capital needs and expected cash flow (when money will come into the business via sales). Chapters 14 and 18 explain breakeven analysis, balance sheets, and other financial tools that the small-business owner needs to understand.

  The source of capital funds should be determined. Will it be the local bank? Relatives? Friends? Can the Small Business Administration help?
- *How will I evaluate the company's performance?* After starting the business, the owner should establish procedures to evaluate the company's

performance. Accounting records should be maintained and sales forecasts made to set standards for the business. The owner must have enough information to determine whether the business is performing well enough to continue.

- *What are the legal requirements for starting my business?* In many instances, the company will need to obtain licenses or permits to operate. Some business plans mention contracts, leases, government regulations, or other legal issues essential for starting or operating the business.

COLLABORATORS

The business plan indicates with whom the company will collaborate to run the business. Indeed, the business plan is often intended for collaborators, such as banks, that will provide loans to the company. Many business plans identify major investors, certified public accountants, insurance companies, suppliers, and others who are or will be collaborators. For example, a Ford automobile dealership's business plan is highly dependent on Ford Motor Company, so its business plan will be developed in conjunction with that company.

ADVANTAGES OF A SMALL BUSINESS

Workweeks of 60, 70, and 80 hours are not uncommon for owners of small businesses. Why would someone work this long and hard? Small businesses provide a number of advantages that large companies find difficult to offer.

PERSONALIZED SERVICE AND PERSONAL CONTACT

Each and every customer is important to the small business. Small-business owners often know every customer by name. Customers who have personal contact with the owner value the personalized service they receive. The close relationship between the company and its customers is a major competitive advantage for most successful small businesses.

FLEXIBILITY

Small businesses are more flexible than large companies. Many businesses, especially service companies, are more efficient when run as small businesses. Small businesses can "turn on a dime." They can adapt quickly to change. The formal procedures and other red tape found in large corporations are absent in small businesses.

Large corporations achieve profits through volume production. Many multinational companies operate under the principle of standardization and thus fail to adapt to individual customers' needs. All products are the same for everyone. Unlike a small business, they cannot customize their operations or change quickly. This is an advantage for small businesses.

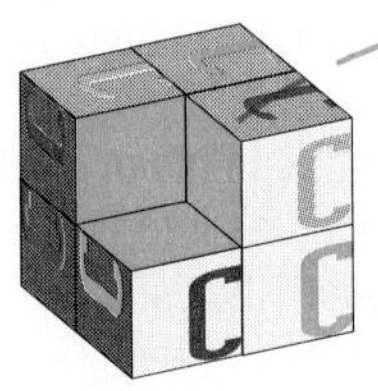

FOCUS ON CUSTOMERS

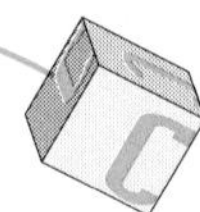

A. Schulman Company

Specialty plastics from A. Schulman Company go into everything from pens and candy wrappers to lawn furniture and automobiles. This relatively small company successfully competes with such giant organizations as Monsanto and Dow because it is able to fill special orders. While other industrial plastics manufacturers strive to market the lowest-cost commodity plastics, Schulman sticks to high-priced specialty items with features the competition can't easily match. For example, Polypur, a polyurethane-based compound used in auto trim, can be finished with only one coat of paint and molded without metal inserts, which add to costs.

Schulman's organizational customers benefit from the company's small size. Company strategists figured it was not economical for its larger competitors to fill special orders, but Schulman could make money and build long-term relationships with organizational buyers by operating this way. Schulman laboratories do not first develop plastic compounds and then go looking for a market. Its sales representatives regularly work with customers on ideas and then get engineers to develop them.

If Schulman's customers want a rush order, they get it. For example, suppose General Motors is running out of a particular color concentrate that would take an average supplier four weeks to deliver. Schulman's marketing managers will tell their production people to stop what they are doing and work over the weekend to do a special run. The price may be higher, but GM will keep its assembly line running.

LOWER COSTS

While survival is a goal of all businesses, many small-business owners regularly face money problems. You will often hear small business owners moan, "I just want to be able to make the payroll this month." What they mean is that they wish to generate enough business to keep the company going.

Often the need to keep the business going results in putting in long hours, reducing costs, and charging less for products and services. The owner who does not draw a salary or earn an hourly wage puts in long hours because he or she does not have a large permanent staff to help. Small firms rarely are overstaffed, and this helps to lower costs.

Small businesses extensively use collaborators to reduce the amount of money tied up in capital investments. They hire trucking services, attorneys, and accounting services only when needed. They reduce overhead costs by shipping their goods using common carriers such as UPS or Roadway Express rather than maintaining their own fleets of trucks. These practices also help them keep their prices lower.

Another reason small firms' prices are often lower is that the small business can operate with a lower profit margin than a large corporation can.

INNOVATION OPPORTUNITIES

Entrepreneurs who had new ideas for a business have started many successful small businesses. Most people know that Steve Jobs and Steve Wozniak started Apple Computer in a garage and subsequently launched the personal computer industry. There are thousands of similar stories about inventors and entrepreneurs who were first on the market with a new product or a new concept for running a business. Most true innovations come from entrepreneurial small business. We will discuss the nature of entrepreneurship later in this chapter.

WHY DO SMALL BUSINESSES FAIL?

The path to a successful small-business enterprise can be a rocky one, at least in terms of the time, care, and effort required. Unfortunately, most new businesses fail. Estimates vary, but most small-business experts say at least one out of three fail in their first year. After two years, only one-half are still operating the same business. After five years, more than two out of three have failed to survive.

Despite precautions, failures and near-failures occur somewhat regularly. For example, Cajun Cola tried to compete regionally against Pepsico and Coca-Cola but found the task impossible. Coca-Cola and Pepsico were engaged in an intensive "cola war" with reduced prices and increased advertising. Cajun Cola didn't have the same resources.

Exhibit 6.5 **SOURCES OF MONEY USED TO START SMALL BUSINESSES**

Commercial bank loan
A loan from a bank that provides a line of credit or money that will be repaid according to a contractual agreement
Government loan
A loan from a government agency such as the Small Business Administration
Commercial mortgage
A loan from a bank or other financial institution that is secured with the owner's personal property, such as house or land
Credit from collaborator
Sale of inventory or other equipment on credit to allow the owner to finance the business
Offering of stock
Sale of stock to investors via the stock market
NA 12½ TCS 25⅛ ZAA 2¼
Owner's personal resources
Savings, personal loans, credit card loans, help from friends and/or family
Small Business
Funds from venture capitalist
An ownership interest in the business given in exchange for money

Following are the most common reasons for new-business failures.

Limited Experience and Poor Management. The small-business owner must manage all aspects of the business. He or she often lacks experience or expertise in many of the activities involved in running the business. Learning by trial and error is possible, but often the necessary experience comes too late and the business fails. Even when a business succeeds, the small-business owner must make up for lack of experience with long hours.

Underestimating the strength of existing competition is a mistake often made by overly optimistic small-business managers. Such managers fail to anticipate future competitive reactions. All too often, the enthusiastic small-business manager finds that it takes more time and effort than expected to successfully launch a business.

Lack of Company Superiority or Uniqueness. If a "me too" business merely imitates competitors and fails to offer customers a unique advantage, the business may be doomed from the start. Consider Jerry, who collected guns as a hobby. He decided to open a small gun shop to combine his hobby with a business. The store failed within two years. Jerry didn't realize the tremendous price advantage large sporting goods stores offered on their guns. Failing to understand customers' needs and to develop realistic estimates of the acceptance of a store, product, or service is the cause of many failures. Gift Mates offered brightly colored batteries designed to coordinate with Christmas gift wrappings, but the idea generated little interest. This new venture lasted only two holiday seasons. People simply did not have a need for the product.

Some businesses fail because of technical problems with their products. The product does not do what it is supposed to do due to flaws in production or design, or the product breaks down often and is in constant need of repair.

Insufficient Capital or Funds. Owners of small businesses often finance their companies with their own funds. They may borrow from banks, from friends or family, or even from personal credit cards to start the business. Exhibit 6.5 shows how small businesses finance their operations.

Many businesses go into bankruptcy because they were launched with inadequate financing. No matter how good the idea for the business, adequate financial capital must exist if the company is to survive. Many small businesses fail because their managers think their product or service is so good it will sell itself and they fail to provide adequate funds to operate the business. Often no matter how well plans are implemented or how much energy managers put forth, there is not enough money to run the business.

Poor Timing. Some businesses fail because of poor timing. The company entered the market too early or too late. For example, the first video store in a town may be successful. However, by the time the third and fourth stores enter the market, the first store may have already developed loyal customers, and the newcomers can't compete. Some businesses are started just before a recession or just before inflation rises.

All businesspeople planning a new company have one thing in common: They must attempt to predict the future. The company planned in 1994 that opens its doors in 1996 may face a somewhat different environment than that of two years earlier. Hence, the business plan may not work as well as expected. New start-up companies must forecast the future, but, as the old adage goes, "Forecasts are dangerous, particularly those about the future." However, some of these businesses resurface when business strategies are adjusted and the timing is right.

ENTREPRENEURSHIP

ENTREPRENEURIAL ENTERPRISES

Entrepreneurs create new business ideas and then assume the risks associated with developing those ideas. Many small businesses are born to develop and manage an entrepreneurial idea. Entrepreneurs throughout the world have always been at the cutting edge of new-product development and changes in retailing. One should not underestimate the potential of a creative individual who risks his or her own money and works in the garage on weekends to make something happen.[8]

Many successful new products with novel technologies, such as in-line skates, are the result of the entrepreneurial activity of a single risk-taking individual. Succeeding with a novel idea with a low chance for success may require some bending of the concepts and "rules" that conservative managers in big businesses will not do.

FOCUS ON COMPANY

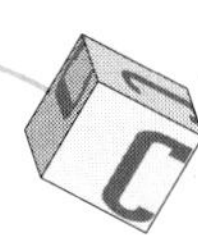

Spectrum Software, Inc.

Judy Sims is one of three children of a Fort Worth steelworker. From that rather humble start in life, Sims, now 40, has become a multimillionaire and chair of the board of one of America's 200 fastest-growing public companies, Spectrum Software, Inc. Judy Sims is, in short, a highly successful entrepreneur.

How do you get to be a successful entrepreneur in our success-oriented society? You need a reasonable amount of intelligence, a good deal of energy, and some luck. But beyond that, you need a desire to succeed that is so powerful that repeated failures only increase your determination. Entrepreneurship is a matter of try, try, and try again.

In her college days at Texas Tech University, Judy Sims had that desire. She worked one summer in a tiny tuxedo rental shop in Fort Worth. Instead of waiting around for business to walk in the door, she studied the social pages of newspapers, noting the names of couples announcing their engagements. Then she cold-called the prospects about renting them formal-

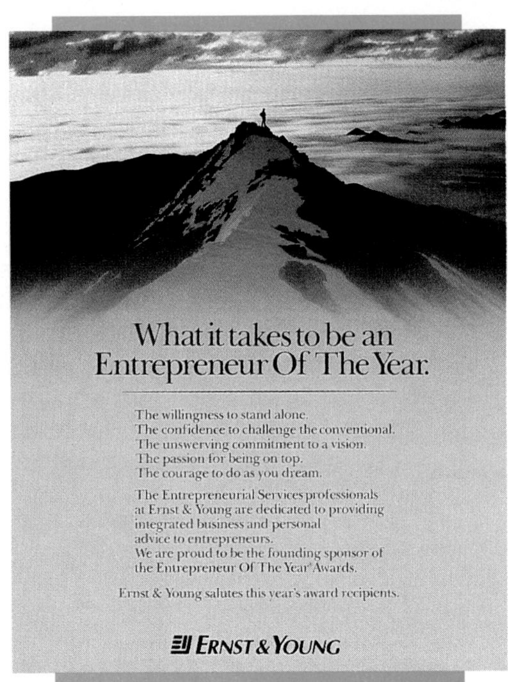

Ernst & Young, sponsor of the Entrepreneur Of The Year Award, asks what it takes to be an entrepreneur. The advertisement shown here identifies some characteristics that Ernst & Young believes are important: The willingness to stand alone. The confidence to challenge the conventional. The passion for being on top. The courage to do as you dream.

wear for their weddings. Her idea worked so well that she knew she had a flair for business and vowed that some day she would have her own.

In 1977 Judy, then a certified public accountant, married Richard Sims, also a CPA. He too wanted to be his own boss. They had no great business idea, but successful entrepreneurs frequently begin with nothing more than the desire to run a business.

In 1983, the Simses had a vague idea that the personal computer business offered lots of entrepreneurial opportunities. An industry study they had bought for $500 told them that games and educational software were the way to go. They put up $40,000 of their own money and started a store stocked with such products in a Dallas strip mall. The store was an immediate flop. After six weeks they decided they needed a new plan—and fast.

Remembering how she had sold tuxedo rentals by telephone, Sims started cold-calling local businesses about her business software. One early account she landed was Ross Perot's Electronic Data Systems. Others followed, and the Simses moved out of retailing to become a direct marketer of software to businesses. Today Spectrum Software's sales reps and telemarketers sell business software in 48 states. Big corporate customers like Mobil Oil and GTE have helped to raise the company's annual sales to more than $160 million.

The Simses credit their success not to their original idea but to their persistence and entrepreneurial drive. "You've got to set clear goals and stay focused," says Judy Sims.

CHARACTERISTICS OF ENTREPRENEURS

It has been said that it takes a certain personality to be an entrepreneur. Do all entrepreneurs share certain characteristics and backgrounds? Are all entrepreneurs extroverts? Nonconformists? Inventors? Highly educated? Are all entrepreneurs like Judy Sims?

Research on this issue shows that no true "entrepreneurial profile" exists.[9] Individuals start their own businesses for many reasons. Entrepreneurs have diverse educational backgrounds and work experiences. Both women and men can be entrepreneurs. People with previous career successes and career failures have become entrepreneurs.

Research also shows that entrepreneurs are motivated by different things. But probably all entrepreneurs seek *achievement, personal independence,* and *control.*

Achievement. Ben Cohen is one of the partners of Ben and Jerry's Homemade Inc. His advice to entrepreneurs like himself is, "When somebody tells you that something can't be done, all it really means is that it hasn't been done before."[10] Cohen's advice reflects a belief that businesspeople should strive to make things happen, that accomplishing goals is possible if you work hard. Cohen—and most entrepreneurs—have a high need to achieve, to succeed when facing a challenging task.

The number of successful entrepreneurs who were not discouraged by failure is astonishing. Their willingness to go the extra mile to get the job done is often the reason they achieve success.

Personal Independence. Mo Siegel, founder of Celestial Seasonings, Inc., says he knew early in life that he would not make a good employee. He did not want to conform to the rules imposed by a large corporation. He did not want to work for somebody else. He wanted independence. He wanted to be his own boss. Personal independence, the need to do it on one's own, is common to many entrepreneurs. In fact, it is the number one reason entrepreneurs give for creating a start-up company.

Entrepreneurs usually trade off the security of working for a large corporation for their independence. Although making money is not unimportant to entrepreneurs, it generally takes a back seat to their desire for independence. For the entrepreneur, the company's profit is his or her "salary," and the opportunity to make it big can be a major motive.

Control. The belief that you control your fate because you have the energy and drive to take charge of things is common among entrepreneurs. Most entrepreneurs believe they can realize their dreams. They believe that with persistence, they can control their businesses' success or failure. As you can see, the satisfaction gained from being in control is related to the needs for achievement and personal independence.

FOCUS ON COMPANY

Paschal Petroleum Inc.

David Paschal, president of the highly successful Paschal Petroleum Inc., is an entrepreneur. He describes how he believed he could control his own fate by being the owner of his own business:

> People looked at me quizzically when I started an oil company in Texas in 1983.... Despite the oil industry's downturn, I believed big profits could still be made from Texas's black gold. Since I had only a rudimentary [very basic] education in the oil business, I decided to learn the industry from the bottom, with a job as a landsman—a title researcher—and all-purpose gofer. [*Gofer* is business slang for a person who is told to "go for this and go for that."]
>
> It was 1980, and there I was—26, no job, a mortgage, a wife, and a child. I called every oil company in the Dallas Yellow Pages. I even called Bunker Hunt, the Texas oil millionaire, at home; I had found his number in the White Pages. I

told him I wanted to get into the oil business and asked him for five minutes of his time; he had me come to his office, and he gave me maybe 10 or 15 minutes. Meeting Bunker Hunt at this point in my life really gave me fire. He sent me to a company geologist, which led to my next job, as a landsman at Spindletop Oil & Gas Co. For three years I got my hands dirty learning every aspect of the oil business. In 1983, I was ready to go out on my own, ready to generate profits for myself as owner of Paschal Petroleum Inc.

I cajoled [coaxed] my banker into giving me a $10,000 signature loan to buy an oil lease in an unproven area in Knox County, Texas. I personally raised $70,000, enough to drill the well. It blew in 1984, spewing sizable profits for me and my investors. We have drilled many more wells, whose in-ground reserves total about $35 million.

I attribute my success to two things. I'm not afraid of taking risks—big risks. In fact, I prefer to take big risks because that's the only way to score big returns. And I'm not afraid of failure. I know that if I make the wrong decision and lose everything in some venture, I still could find another opportunity and become just as successful as I have been in the oil business.

One reason I enjoy risk is that I believe in my instincts. They are based on detailed observation of the market-place, which is my second secret of success.... I read many periodicals and get an overview of developments and directions in business. I can spot brewing trends and devise plans to take advantage of the opportunities they present.

Season that with a lot of hard work, and you have the formula for my success.

INTRAPRENEURS

Entrepreneurs, as we have defined them, create small start-up businesses. Entrepreneurial start-up companies grow into large corporations, as Apple Computers did, but the common bond is that a new company is started from scratch.

Intrapreneur
A person who works for a large corporation and experiments with new ideas, takes the initiative to do different things, and takes risks just as an entrepreneur does.

Intrapreneurs share many of the skills and characteristics of entrepreneurs. The difference is that they work for large corporations. Of course, there are major differences between large, bureaucratic corporations and small, start-up businesses. However, many big businesses realize they must have people who are allowed to create personal "pet" projects. Companies like Xerox and 3M encourage their intrapreneurs to experiment with new ideas, take the initiative to do different things, and take risks just as entrepreneurs who start their own businesses do. We discuss the role of intrapreneurial/entrepreneurial activity in large corporations further in Chapter 13.

COLLABORATORS WHO HELP SMALL BUSINESSES

Like all businesses, small businesses find collaboration with other companies to be an important part of running the business. One of the most important collaborators for small business is the U.S. government.

THE SMALL BUSINESS ADMINISTRATION (SBA)

Congress created the *Small Business Administration (SBA)* in 1953.[11] As we mentioned earlier, the SBA's mission is to stimulate and foster economic development through small business and help entrepreneurs form successful small-business enterprises. Simply put, the agency helps new businesses get started and helps established businesses grow. Congress established the SBA because small-business enterprises are the backbone of our economy and the driving force behind U.S. economic growth and prosperity.

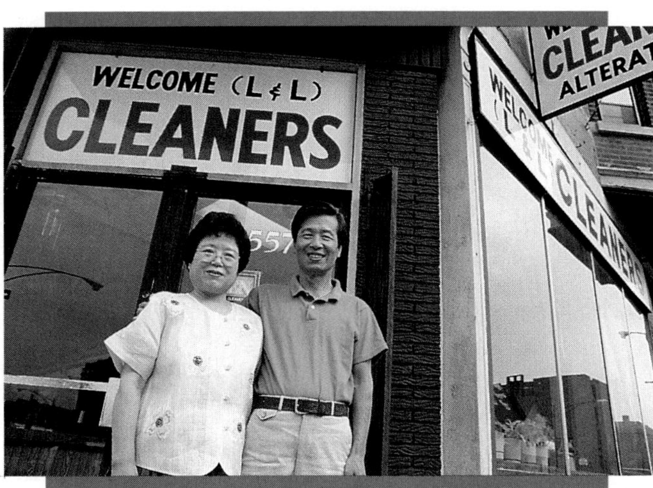

Small business and America's cultural diversity have always gone hand in hand. Often immigrants open shops to serve the particular needs of the residents of ethnic neighborhoods. Because Americans take pride in our mosaic society, our government strives to help minority-owned businesses succeed. The Minority Business Development Agency offers special assistance to help minority-owned businesses grow and prosper.

THE SERVICE CORPS OF RETIRED EXECUTIVES (SCORE)

The Service Corps of Retired Executives (SCORE) is composed of more than 13,000 volunteers—mostly retired business executives—who provide free consulting services in more than 750 counseling locations nationwide. SCORE's only reason for existence is to help small businesses with free information and advice on practically any business problem.

When a small business requests SCORE counseling, there's a good chance that the person chosen to help out has had years of experience in a business. A counselor (or team of counselors) meets with the business owner personally and as frequently as necessary. SCORE counselors analyze and define business problems and then help find solutions. They keep checking for as long as necessary, since they want to know how the solutions are working. SCORE counseling continues for as long as needed to get the job done, from one session to a year or more.[12]

SMALL BUSINESS DEVELOPMENT CENTERS (SBDCs)

Small Business Development Centers (SBDCs)
Agencies that sustain and encourage the small-business community through low-cost training and free one-on-one counseling programs.

The purpose of **Small Business Development Centers (SBDCs)** is to sustain and encourage the small-business community through low-cost training and free one-on-one counseling programs. SBDCs are run by universities in cooperation with the federal and state governments. Unlike SCORE counselors, SBDC staff are paid professionals. Resource people in the private sector, such as lawyers, are available to SBDCs. SBDC counselors can draw on the expertise of SCORE volunteers, and vice versa. They have access to the resources of state universities, the SBA, and private businesses to provide management assistance, research information, and technical assistance.

REACHING OUT TO MINORITY-OWNED BUSINESSES

Minority businesses grew quickly in the last decade. African-American–owned firms account for 3.1 percent of all firms,[13] and more than 90 percent of them are small businesses. Government statistics show that from 1982 to 1987, the number of African-American–owned

STREET SMART

Minority Entrepreneurs

What can minority entrepreneurs do to help one another? *Nation's Business* offers several recommendations:

1. *Buy from one another.* This is not always possible, but when it is, it strengthens minority business.
2. *Introduce good minority businesses to companies that might become customers.* Recommendations can help companies get a "foot in the door."
3. *Make and market quality products and services.* Companies that have a quality focus and give top performance get invited back.
4. *Be realistic and creative about capital.* Banks are very cautious about making loans to entrepreneurs, no matter what color or sex. Companies need to do their homework to find sources of capital. They need to communicate their strengths.
5. *Network and join forces with one another.* Work with other minority and nonminority businesspeople to get things done. Jointly exploit opportunities with groups like the local chamber of commerce.

firms grew by 424,000, or 38 percent, compared to 26 percent for all U. S. companies. The number of African-American–owned firms with paid employees grew three times as fast as those without paid employees. The number of businesses owned by Hispanic-Americans and Asian-Americans grew even faster.

The *Minority Business Development Agency* was established in 1969 to offer special assistance to help minority-owned businesses grow and prosper. The agency provides loans (venture capital), management assistance, and technical help to small businesses owned by minorities that historically have been socially and economically disadvantaged and to small businesses in areas of high unemployment.

According to the U.S. Commission on Minority Business Development, 80 percent of minority-business owners believe their biggest problem was getting adequate capital.[14] Minority-owned banks, federally chartered Minority Enterprise Small Business Investment Companies, and community development groups help minority-owned businesses acquire sufficient capital. For example, the Chicago Association of Neighborhood Associations (CANDO) is a coordinating group that helps dozens of neighborhood associations grant loans to minority-owned businesses.

Finally, the Minority Business Enterprise Legal Defense and Education Fund provides legal assistance to small minority-owned businesses. The National Center for American Indian Enterprise Development, the U.S. Hispanic Chamber of Commerce, the National Association of Black and Minority Chambers of Commerce, and the National Business League all engage in helping minority business development.

REACHING OUT TO WOMEN-OWNED BUSINESSES

At many large corporations, women who are qualified to become top managers remain stuck in the ranks of middle management. These women say they cannot be promoted

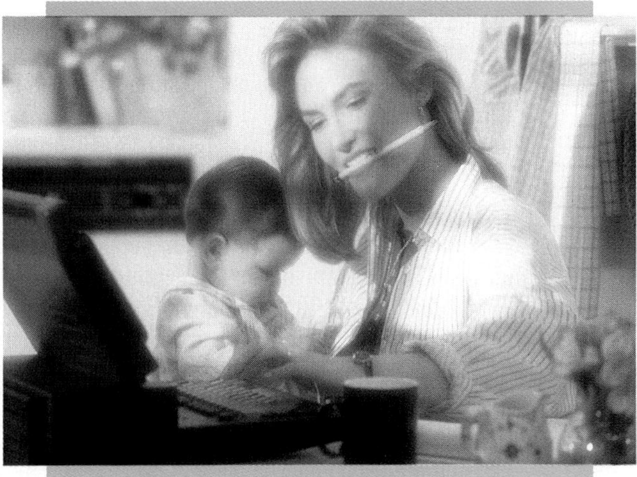

With a new baby girl and a new, fast-track management job at Allstate Insurance, Judith Wunderlich thought she had it all. But she soon realized that having it all can mean having less. She rarely saw the baby when she was awake, and she was constantly exhausted. Finally, her doctor told her to either slow down or risk physical breakdown.

Wunderlich quit her job and joined the growing ranks of "mom-preneurs." Baby in arm, she started a freelance typesetting business at home. Today Wunderlich has two kids and runs a $300,000-a-year temporary employment service from a spare bedroom in her home.[15]

because of the "glass ceiling." The *glass ceiling* refers to the invisible barrier that keeps women from moving higher up the corporate ladder. Many experienced women who start their own small businesses are ex-executives who became frustrated with the discrimination they faced in large organizations.

Today there are 5 million women-owned businesses in the United States that earn about $83 billion in revenues. The Small Business Administration forecasts that by the year 2000, a woman will be the chief executive in almost 40 percent of all small businesses.[16]

The *SBA's Office of Women's Business Ownership* helps women-owned businesses by providing resources and performing a wide range of services. For example, the Women's Entrepreneurial Training Network attempts to provide mentors for women who are new to business ownership.

Community organizations also help. In Denver, the Mi Casa Resource Center has a loan program especially targeted to low-income minority women.

FRANCHISING: A VERY FORMAL COLLABORATION

Franchise
An individually owned business that is operated as a part of a network of businesses; a contractual agreement between a franchisor and a number of franchisees.

Many aspiring small-business owners discover that buying a franchise is the ideal way to go into business for themselves. A **franchise** is an individually owned business that is operated as part of a network of businesses. More specifically, it is a contractual agreement between a *franchisor* (typically a manufacturer or a wholesaler) and a number of *franchisees* (usually independent retailers).

Franchise services or products are standardized so that a Big Mac bought in Miami is exactly the same as one purchased in San Juan. McDonald's Corporation (the franchisor) gives the individual businessperson (the franchisee) the right to market McDonald's products by using its brand names, trademarks, reputation, and way of doing business. The franchise agreement, or contract, may give the franchisee the exclusive right to sell the franchisor's product or service or otherwise represent the franchisor in a specified area.

In return, the franchisee agrees to pay a sum of money—a franchise fee, a percentage of the profits, or both—and frequently to buy equipment or supplies from the franchisor. The franchisee is usually responsible for paying for insurance, property taxes, labor, and supplies.

The franchise agreement often gives the franchisor considerable control over the planning of the small retailer's operations. The franchisor offers information from its own experts, technical assistance, and often supplies.

The franchise has been quite popular in the fast-food industry. Subway, Wendy's, Godfather's Pizza, and many other successful fast-food restaurants are franchises. Subway is one of the most rapidly growing fast-food franchise operations. Of the 4,760 outlets, only 10 are company owned. In 1993, Subway was second only to McDonald's in the number of restaurants in North America.

Franchising is also prominent in the service industry. Consider such familiar names in the automotive field as Brakeman, Midas, and AAMCO.

ADVANTAGES OF FRANCHISING[17]

There are some solid reasons for starting a business with a franchise. First, franchisees can begin business even if they have had limited experience, because they are using the franchisor's knowledge and experience. (Most franchisors provide training.) They can start with a relatively small amount of capital (sometimes a franchisor will loan a franchisee part of the start-up costs) and with a strengthened financial and credit standing (since a well-known franchise offers the recognition and prestige of a national name and product).

Second, a franchise offers a brand identity and a nationally recognizable storefront. It provides a well-developed consumer image and goodwill, since it offers proven products and services. It might take years for "Max's Hot Dogs" to achieve even a local reputation, but "Big Mac" is known everywhere. Likewise, Ethan Allen Carriage Houses, Holiday Inns, and other franchise operations have strong identities. A person driving past these establishments has a very clear idea of the products or services he or she will find there.

Third, a franchisee receives professionally designed facilities, layout, displays, and fixtures. He or she enjoys the quantity buying power of a chain of franchises. Also, the franchisee generally can rely on business training and continued management assistance from experienced franchisor personnel.

Finally, and perhaps most important, the franchisee benefits from national or regional promotion and publicity. In our mobile society, every television ad for Burger King, no matter where it's shown, will help sell Burger King hamburgers.

DISADVANTAGES OF FRANCHISING[18]

Franchising also has its drawbacks. First, the franchise owner must run a standardized operation. There is no such thing as "have it your way;" instead, it must be done the company way—by the book. Thus, a franchise may not be for people who want to be their own boss in *all* respects.

Second, nearly all franchisors charge a royalty or a percentage of gross sales, which ultimately comes out of the franchisee's profits. Sometimes this fee must be paid whether or not a profit has been made. Thus, the franchisor shares the profits but not the losses.

Third, many franchise arrangements lack flexibility. The contract may restrict the franchisee from meeting competitors' prices, dropping unprofitable items, or adding potentially profitable ones. The franchisee may be unable to make some very basic management decisions, since they are all made at headquarters.

Sometimes (but fortunately not often) the contract is heavily slanted in favor of the franchisor. It may contain unrealistic sales quotas, clauses that cancel the contract for minor reasons, or restrictions on how the franchise owner can sell or transfer the business. Therefore, potential franchise owners should have their attorneys review the franchise contract and point out possible trouble spots.

SUMMARY

1. ***Discuss the nature and importance of small business.***
   A small business is independently owned and operated, is not dominant in its field, and has fewer than 500 employees. Almost 99 percent of all American businesses are small. Small businesses are the cornerstone of our economy. Such firms employ nearly half of the work force and generate over 37 percent of the gross national product. Most new ideas and product innovations come from new, small ventures.

2. ***Categorize the different types of small-business operations.***
   Small businesses range from small flower shops to high-technology computer disk manufacturers. Some typical small businesses are retailers, service businesses, manufacturers, and farms. The Small Business Administration (SBA) has different standards to determine the size of businesses in different industries. The SBA's definition of a small business depends on the type of business. Sales volume may not exceed \$3.5 million to \$13.5 million, depending on the industry. A small manufacturing business is defined by the maximum number of employees. According to the SBA, this number may range from 500 to 1,500 depending on the product manufactured. The small family farm has always been an American business tradition.

3. ***Explain what functions all businesses have in common.***
   All business activity can be categorized into four functional areas: production, marketing, finance, and management. All businesses therefore must (1) produce a good or offer a service (production), (2) market their offerings (marketing), (3) acquire capital to finance their operations and control the flow of money within the company (finance), and (4) plan, organize, direct, and control the functional activities of production, marketing, and finance (management).

4. ***Outline the basic questions to be answered in developing a new business venture.***
   These questions are:
   1. Is there a *customer* opportunity to start a business?
   2. Is my idea good enough? Is it better than competitors' ideas?
   3. What *company* resources are needed?
      a. What human resources are needed? How should they be managed?
      b. What capital is needed? How do I raise capital funds?
      c. What production operation or procedure is required to create my product or generate my service?
      d. How do I market my offering?
   4. With whom must I *collaborate* to run the business?
   5. How should I organize the business?
   6. After I start the business, how will I evaluate the company's performance?
   7. What are the legal requirements for starting my business?

5. ***Describe how to prepare a business plan.***
   The business plan is a key step in starting a business. The business plan lays out a direction for the company. It describes the business operations and outlines the goals of the business. A good business plan projects the expected results and indicates how the company plans to achieve them. The business plan provides a tool for evaluating each aspect of the business. A well-written business plan is essential for getting needed financial resources from banks or other collaborators. A comprehensive business plan includes sections on the company and its potential customers, competitors, and collaborators.

6. *Explain the major advantages of operating a small business.*
Small businesses offer a number of advantages that large companies find difficult to offer, including personalized service and personal contact, flexibility, lower costs, and innovation opportunities. The close relationship between the small business and its customers is a major competitive advantage for most successful small businesses. Small businesses are more flexible than large businesses and can adapt quickly to change. The formal procedures and red tape found in large corporations are absent in small businesses.

7. *Discuss the reasons many new small businesses fail.*
Most new businesses fail in a few years or less. Some of the reasons are limited experience and poor management, lack of company superiority or uniqueness, inadequate capital or insufficient funds, and poor timing. Small-business owners must manage all aspects of the business. They often lack experience or expertise in many activities involved in running the business. If a new business merely imitates existing competitors and fails to offer customers a unique advantage, the business may be doomed from the start. Many small businesses fail because managers do not provide adequate funds to operate the business. Finally, some businesses fail because they entered the market too early or too late.

8. *Describe the characteristics of entrepreneurs.*
Entrepreneurs create new business ideas and then assume the risks associated with developing those ideas. Many small businesses are born to develop and manage an entrepreneurial idea. Research shows that no true "entrepreneurial profile" exists. Individuals start their own businesses for many reasons. Entrepreneurs have diverse educational backgrounds and work experiences and appear to be motivated by different things. But probably all entrepreneurs seek achievement, personal independence, and control.

9. *Explain how collaborators help small businesses.*
Like all businesses, small businesses find collaboration with other companies to be an important part of running the business. One of the most important collaborators for small business is the U. S. government. Congress created the Small Business Administration (SBA) in 1953. This agency helps new businesses get started and helps established businesses grow. The Service Corps of Retired Executives (SCORE) is composed of more than 13,000 volunteers—mostly retired business executives—who provide free consulting services to small businesses. Small Business Development Centers (SBDCs) sustain and encourage the small-business community through low-cost training and free one-on-one counseling programs. The Minority Business Development Agency offers special assistance to help minority-owned businesses grow and prosper. The SBA's Office of Women's Business Ownership (Assistant Administrator for Women's Business Enterprises) helps women-owned businesses.

10. *Define a* franchise *and discuss the nature of franchising.*
A franchise is an individually owned business that is operated as part of a network of businesses. A franchise is a contractual agreement between a franchisor (typically a manufacturer or a wholesaler) and a number of franchisees (usually independent retailers). The franchise agreement may give the franchisee the exclusive right to sell the franchisor's product or service or otherwise represent the franchisor in a specified area. In return, the franchisee agrees to pay a franchise fee, a percentage of the profits, or both and frequently to buy equipment or supplies from the franchisor.

11. *Describe the advantages and disadvantages of franchising.*
The advantages of franchising are that franchisees can begin business even if they have had limited experience, can start with a relatively small amount of capital, have the recognition and prestige of a national name, have the benefit of a well-developed consumer image, have the quantity buying power of a chain of franchises, and can rely on business training and continued management assistance from experienced franchisor personnel. Some of the disadvantages are that franchisees must run a standardized operation, the franchisor nearly always charges a roy-

alty or a percentage of gross sales, many franchise arrangements lack flexibility, and the contract may be heavily slanted in favor of the franchisor.

KEY TERMS AND CONCEPTS

Small business (p. 112)
Small Business Administration (SBA) (p. 112)
Establishment (p. 113)
Enterprise (p. 113)
Business plan (p. 117)
Intrapreneur (p. 126)
Small Business Development Centers (SBDCs) (p. 127)
Franchise (p. 129)

DISCUSSION QUESTIONS

Company

1. What is a small business? Give some examples.
2. What is the difference between an establishment and an enterprise?
3. What are some types of small businesses?
4. What are the advantages of running a small business?
5. What are the major reasons small businesses fail?
6. What do all small businesses have in common?
7. What are the seven basic questions to be answered in developing a new enterprise?
8. What is the business plan? What are the important sections of a business plan?
9. What does it take to be an entrepreneur? An intrapreneur?
10. What is thc glass ceiling?

Customers

11. In the business plan, what should be included in the section on customers?
12. In your opinion, does a company's focus on customers differ depending on whether the company is a small business or a large organization? Explain.

Competitors

13. Why do you think small business is important to our competitive economy?
14. In the business plan, what should be included in the section on competitors?
15. In your opinion, does the nature of a company's competition differ depending on whether the company is a small business or a large organization? Explain.

Collaborators

16. What sources of money do entrepreneurs use to start a small business?
17. In a business plan, what should the section on collaborators include?
18. What collaborators help small business?
19. What role does the Small Business Administration (SBA) play for small business?
20. What is SCORE?
21. Where can minority-owned businesses turn for help in developing their businesses?
22. What is franchising? Give some examples of franchises in your neighborhood.
23. What are the advantages of franchising? What are the disadvantages?

In Question: Take a Stand

The purpose of business is business: to make money. Spending extra time to hire women, minorities, and individuals with disabilities takes time away from conducting business. Everyone takes care of his or her own. A small business manager should be able to do what he or she wants so the company can make a profit. It's tough enough in business without all these government regulations telling you whom to hire. These laws should apply only to major corporations. Take a stand.

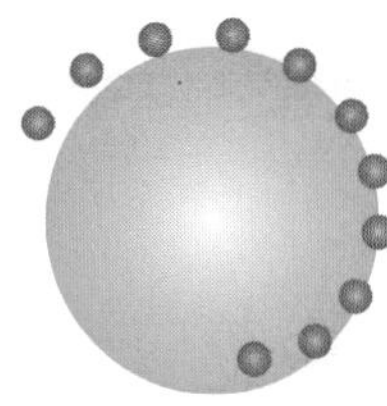

CASE 6.1
CRAZY SHIRTS INC.[19]

Thirty years ago, Frederick Carleton "Rick" Ralston spray-painted a design on a T-shirt, transforming it from underwear into fashion and launching a mass passion for T-shirts that remains today. Ralston is now called the "T-shirt king of America" and the "father" of the modern T-shirt. Ralston's company, Crazy Shirts Inc., located in suburban Honolulu, has two factories and 42 retail stores in Hawaii and on the mainland and takes in $65 million a year.

Ralston's entrepreneurial odyssey began in the summer of 1960, when he was just out of high school in Montebello, California. He and a buddy known as "Crazy Arab" headed for Santa Catalina Island to spray-paint designs on beach towels and sell them. "I practiced on an old T-shirt, doing an ugly monster shape," recalls Ralston. "I wore it down the street, and a tourist stopped me and bought it off my back for his daughter."

"Forget beach towels," he told Crazy Arab. "We're going into the T-shirt business."

They set up shop on the sidewalk. Tourists bought plain T-shirts from a local sporting goods shop, and Ralston and Crazy Arab embellished them with monsters, surfers, or hot rods at $2.85 apiece. Sometimes they made as much as $100 a day.

After another summer on Catalina and two years of studying automotive design at the Los Angeles Art Center School of Design, Ralston thought he'd try his luck selling T-shirts on the sidewalks of Waikiki. He fell under Hawaii's spell and decided to stay. The summer's tourism season had put enough money in his pockets, he says, "to pay rent, buy a bag of rice, do a little surfing, chase girls, and do the things that young men 20 years old do."

In 1964, Ralston opened a tiny shop in the bustling Waikiki bazaar known as the International Market Place. It was called Ricky's Crazy Shirts and, to Ralston's knowledge, was the first store anywhere devoted exclusively to T-shirts and sweatshirts. For greater speed, he turned from spray-painting to screen-printing his designs.

In 1970 Crazy Shirts, as it was called by then, opened a second shop in Honolulu's Ala Moana shopping center, and Ralston began to get his first competitors. "All of a sudden there were T-shirt shops opening every place," he says.

But most of them applied their designs with heat transfers. "We never did that," says Ralston, explaining that heat transfers tend to crack and peel. Even before the competition came along, he wanted to "upgrade the image of underwear" and make T-shirts the best they could be, with the best artwork and "the finest T-shirt that I could get."

When he had started out, Ralston bought plain T-shirts at retail from JCPenney. As his business grew, he was able to buy directly from the manufacturer. When his volume grew large enough to enable him to specify what he wanted, he ordered shirts of heavier weight than most T-shirts, with more stitches per inch, more tailoring, and Lycra fibers in collars and cuffs so they would hold their shape after repeated washings.

Ralston's shirts still sport an occasional hot rod or surfer, but they are more likely to portray fishing boats and porpoises. Among the most popular designs are those featuring the late B. Kliban's famous cat as lifeguard, surfer, or fitness nut.

Ralston says his business decisions are guided by three factors. About 60 percent of the weight goes to what he calls image, or "offering the best possible product so that our customer is going to think well of our product and our service." The next 30 percent is personnel, under which he considers such questions as: How will the decision affect the company's 750 employees? Will they feel positive about it? Will it create an undue workload? Profit gets the remaining 10 percent weight. Ralston acknowledges that "You can't carry on if you don't make a profit," but he adds that Crazy Shirts' experience shows that "if you have the image and you've got happy people," the profit will follow.

Crazy Shirts now comes under the umbrella of a parent company called Ralston Enterprises. Ralston has expanded to a number of other ventures, including one that acquires and restores historic properties.

Ralston admits to being a "Type A" personality—an aggressive, determined, outspoken, goal-oriented person. But he has chosen to live in a "Type B" environment, where the spirit of *aloha,* with its complex mix of welcome, love, caring, and respect, holds sway.

Does that spirit affect the way Ralston manages? "It sure does," he says, explaining that he sees Hawaii's management style as more laid-back, more patient with people, and more caring about them.

Although he is still a "let's-get-it-done" kind of person, Ralston says he has learned to temper himself. "We should enjoy our work," he says. "We should enjoy life. That's the first thing. Business should support that."

Questions

1. *What type of small business is Crazy Shirts?*
2. *In your opinion, what was the business opportunity presented to Rick Ralston when he first got his idea for a business?*
3. *Suppose that during Crazy Shirts' early days, the company asked you to prepare a business plan. What would be the main components of this business plan?*
4. *Does Rick Ralston fit the profile of the typical entrepreneur? Why or why not?*

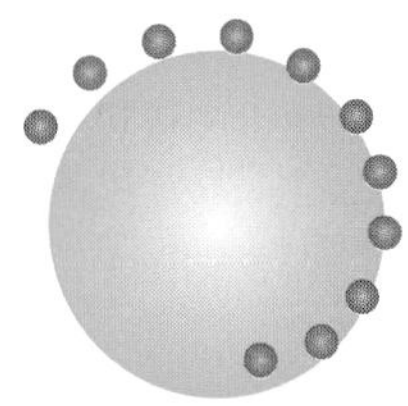

CASE 6.2
MJI BROADCASTING[20]

It's just past 5 a.m. in the control room of WMXV-FM, a New York City radio station with an adult contemporary format. Time for the daily trivia quiz. "Ancient superstition held that a rare little plant had powers to cure coughs, clean the blood and heal sores," intones the announcer, Dan Taylor. "Today this plant is mainly considered a symbol of good luck—especially on St. Patrick's Day. Can you name this botanical oddity?"

The phone panel lights up and the station awards a lucky caller with tickets to an off-Broadway show. Of such simple ideas are fortunes made: The brains behind this quiz and some half dozen others is a rumpled 44-year-old named Joshua Feigenbaum. Over the last dozen years he has turned his quizzes into an $11 million (1993 revenues) success named MJI Broadcasting.

Feigenbaum launched MJI in 1980, after a half-dozen years working in sales and marketing at *Rolling Stone* and Arista Records. He went into business for himself with $20,000 in savings and then suffered a string of failures. He launched a weekly radio musical variety show, which he traded to radio stations in exchange for advertising time, which he resold. But the show's star, comedian Robert Klein, pulled out after one year.

Entrepreneurs don't give up. Feigenbaum then developed Sports Line, hosted by Reggie Jackson, the loudmouthed New York Yankees outfielder. No go. Listeners flipped their dials. By mid-1981 Feigenbaum's savings were gone, and he owed $100,000 to suppliers.

Then he had a brainstorm. In the fall of 1981 he noticed that whenever a quiz came on the radio, one of his young employees would hit the phone. At that time most of these quizzes were slapdash affairs, dreamed up by a disc jockey. Recalls Feigenbaum: "I thought, 'Wouldn't it be great if we could produce a contest that stations could use on an ongoing basis?'"

This focus group of one evolved into Feigenbaum's version of interactive radio. Using trivia guides, encyclopedias and the trade press, his three-person staff put together a series of quizzes tailored for rock 'n' roll stations and using rock 'n' roll themes. By November 1981, 70 stations had signed up. MJI provided them with ten quizzes a week in return for ten minutes of commercial time, which it sold to Nestlé. MJI cut deals with electronics companies, book publishers and record companies, among others, to provide the prizes in return for getting their names mentioned on the air.

Rock Quiz was an instant hit; 40 more stations signed on within the first year. There followed a quiz for country stations, a trivia quiz, and a sports quiz.

By tailoring the quizzes to particular audiences, Feigenbaum enables advertisers to target their messages. For example, one of the sponsors of his trivia quiz on WMXV is Clorets, the breath freshener. Susan Rowe, now with Backer, Spielvogel & Bates, used MJI programs to advertise for such clients as the U.S. Army and JCPenney. She says of the programs: "They are the cable TV of radio."

These days MJI provides 13 programs to over 2,000 stations nationwide, and for 1993 will probably earn pretax profits of over $1.6 million. Feigenbaum, who owns 100% of the company, has diversified. Two of MJI's top moneymakers are the Grammy Awards, which MJI has produced for radio since 1986, and the Country Music Awards, since 1992.

These aren't one-night-a-year deals. The Grammys, which cover a broad range of musical styles, are packaged into seven two-hour shows, including the nominations press conference, interviews with the nominees, backstage interviews before the broadcast and talks with the winners after the show.

The Country Music Awards get similar treatment. This year Chevrolet Trucks picks up the tab for the country music shows.

At 7:15 on a brisk autumn morning, Josh Feigenbaum is standing outside the Opryland museum nursing his umpteenth cup of coffee. He's been there since 4 a.m., shepherding a parade of country singers—Vince Gill and Wyonna Judd among them. "It doesn't take a rocket scientist to succeed in this business," he explains with weary satisfaction. "You just have to work harder at it than anyone else." And be damned persistent.

Questions

1. *What type of small business is MJI Broadcasting?*
2. *In your opinion, what were the basic business functions of Joshua Feigenbaum's company when he first got the idea for the trivia quizzes?*
3. *Suppose during Feigenbaum's early days when he got the idea for the trivia quizzes, he was asked for a business plan. What would be the main components of the business plan?*
4. *Who are MJI Broadcasting's main collaborators?*
5. *Does Joshua Feigenbaum fit the profile of a typical entrepreneur? Why or why not?*

PART 2

Organizational Management

Chapter 7
The Function of Management

Chapter 8
Organizational Structure

Chapter 9
Production, Logistics, and Quality Improvement Processes

CHAPTER

THE FUNCTION OF MANAGEMENT

When you have studied this chapter, you will be able to:

1. Define *management* and describe the basic responsibility of a manager.
2. Discuss the three primary components of effective management.
3. Describe the four major functions of management.
4. Identify several activities in which all managers must engage.
5. Describe the management pyramid and the types of skills that are important at each level.
6. List Fayol's 14 traditional principles of management and contrast them with the principles described by Peters and Waterman.
7. Explain the importance of productivity in today's competitive, global market.
8. Describe total quality management (TQM) and its role in modern business.

Herb Kelleher, the chief executive officer (CEO) of Southwest Airlines, has set some difficult goals for the company. In an industry where poor performance and bankruptcy prevail, Kelleher insists on achieving productivity and profitability. Cost containment and employee productivity are the focus of his efforts and the key to Southwest Airlines' success.

Kelleher has established clear-cut objectives for controlling costs. Southwest does not assign seats to passengers, transfer their baggage, arrange connections, or serve food other than snacks. It does not sell tickets through the airline industry's computerized reservations system and it avoids flying to many of the newest large-city airports. This no-frills approach allows Southwest to offer its customers rock-bottom fares, yet remain profitable. But this cost control strategy would not work without employee commitment which in turn is due to Kelleher's remarkable management approach.

Southwest Airlines' employees do what is unthinkable at other airlines. Pilots and flight attendants often volunteer to help clean up planes, ramp workers sell tickets, and counter agents unload bags. Flight crews are paid by the trip rather than by the hour. As a result of energized and motivated employees, Southwest Airlines has managed to control costs and achieve profitability in a very competitive industry.

Kelleher's management style is, to say the least, unusual. He manages with a sense of humor. Kelleher once wore an evening gown to an employee's social affair. A photograph of him launching a paper airplane dominated the cover of a Southwest annual report. But his famed wackiness has a calculated purpose—to foster a gung-ho spirit that will boost employee productivity. And it works.

Kelleher is proud of the way his company operates. He says the reason for Southwest's success is that management values its employees. "At Southwest, we hire attitudes," he says. "We can teach someone anything they need to know, but they must start with the right attitude." And the right attitude spills over to Southwest's managers, who treat each employee as an individual who matters. Kelleher believes that treating employees right is something that the employees carry over to customers. "The kind of workplace that you provide creates the kind of people who will take care of customers. Your internal customers are your employees, and they directly affect your external customers," Kelleher says.[1]

It is an exciting time to be a manager! Today, managers of most businesses face an environment of great complexity. Rapidly advancing technology, dynamic and turbulent economic conditions, and growing international competition make a manager's job challenging and interesting. How managers deal with these conditions is central to a company's success or failure.

Southwest Airlines' operations are an extension of the personality and skills of CEO Herb Kelleher. His understanding of management, personal excitement, and managerial style of dealing with Southwest's complex environment are key elements in Southwest's success. This chapter examines the basic functions, principles, and activities of management and the knowledge and skills required to be an effective manager.

WHAT IS MANAGEMENT?

Management
The effective and efficient integration and coordination of resources to achieve desired objectives.

Efficiency
The ratio of benefits to costs as resources are used and depleted to produce goods and services.

Effectiveness
The degree to which the company's goals are being attained.

Management is the effective and efficient integration and coordination of resources to achieve desired objectives. **Efficiency** refers to the ratio of benefits to costs as resources are used and depleted to produce goods and services. **Effectiveness** refers to the degree to which the company's goals are being attained. Managers are those people responsible for ensuring that this happens. A **manager** integrates and combines human, capital, and technological resources in the best way possible to ensure that the organization's objectives are achieved.

Managers may not be directly involved in all the activities employees perform, such as operating a forklift or sending a collection letter to a past-due customer. But they must direct employees' efforts and provide employees with the technical and financial resources they need to do their jobs. For example, Herb Kelleher relies on the efforts of Southwest Airlines employees to carry out the activities necessary for operating the airline. If they do not perform those activities effectively, both operations and customer satisfaction will suffer.

COMPONENTS OF EFFECTIVE MANAGEMENT

Manager
A person responsible for integrating and combining human, capital, and technological resources in the best way possible to ensure that the organization's objectives are achieved.

Objectives
Targets, or desired levels of achievement.

The main ingredients of effective management are (1) achieving business objectives, (2) using resources in the best way possible, and (3) integrating and coordinating those objectives and resources. Let's look at each of these components in turn.

OBJECTIVES

All companies have some purpose to serve. Generally these purposes include the kind of business the company is in, the products or services it hopes to provide, and the financial goals it wishes to achieve. To accomplish these purposes, the business establishes targets, or desired levels of achievement, called **objectives.** Most companies set profit objectives, sales objectives, market share objectives, productivity objectives, and other objectives related to efficient performance. These objectives direct the efforts of all employees toward the same purposes, and also serve as milestones against which the organization's success or failure can be measured. The first decisions managers must make, then, involve setting objectives for the business.

For example, in recent years two of General Motors' passenger sedans, a Cadillac and a Buick, were ranked among the auto industry's top 10 in terms of customer satisfaction. But at the same time, GM faced major problems. It lagged behind its major competitors in almost every measure of efficiency. In some key areas—the number of worker-hours required to assemble a car, for example—GM was 40 percent less productive than Ford Motor Company. The introduction of the 1992 Cadillac Seville STS, a highly rated new model, was delayed for a year because of design problems, and the plant where it was manufactured ran at 50 percent of capacity. Neither the plant nor the vehicle met GM's profit objectives.[2]

GM once commanded a 46 percent share of the new-car market. Today its share has declined to 35 percent. In 1992 GM, the world's fourth largest company in terms of assets in

The watchmaking industry is a global business with historical roots in Switzerland. When Japanese quartz watches were introduced in the 1980s they took a huge share of worldwide business. Swatch, a Swiss business, almost single-handedly reversed the trend by introducing inexpensive, fashionable watches. It has sold almost 150 million timepieces to consumers around the globe. Unlike many global businesses, its managers have not moved its factories to cheap labor markets abroad. Swatch keeps its labor costs low by extensive use of automation in the production process.

1972, had dropped from the list of the top 20 most profitable firms.[3] GM's concerned managers saw a company that had met one of its primary objectives—building better cars and trucks—but that failed to meet its profit, productivity, or market share objectives.

RESOURCES

Resources
The people, financial capital, technology, and time used in achieving the organization's objectives.

Resources are all the people, financial capital, technology, and time used in achieving the organization's objectives. People include not only employees but also suppliers and customers. Financial capital includes the money invested by stockholders and other owners, money borrowed from banks and other financial institutions, and the revenues and profits earned from selling the company's goods and services.

Technology includes the production processes, computers used to track sales and receipts, equipment used to transport merchandise, and other equipment and processes that apply scientific knowledge. For example, technological developments in genetics have led to many new pharmaceutical products. Satellite communications technology, fax machines, scanning equipment, and cellular phones are relatively new technologies that have helped create the global business environment of the 1990s.

Finally, time is perhaps one of the most important—abused—of all business resources. This may be especially true for managers with considerable demands on their time. Techniques for time management can improve managers' effectiveness. Such techniques include prioritizing tasks and responsibilities and dealing with high-priority items first. Another technique is delegation—assigning work to others, especially subordinates. This fundamental skill is one of many that all managers must acquire.

INTEGRATING AND COORDINATING

Objectives and resources are essential to the success of any business. However, unless resources are used effectively, objectives will not be achieved. After accumulating the necessary resources, managers must integrate and coordinate them in ways that will maximize productivity. For example, if workers (a people resource) are not trained to operate the equipment used in the production line (a technology resource), products will be of inferior quality and produced in insufficient quantity. This is the type of problem Boeing managers address when they increase the level of automation in a 747 plant. New technologies may require investing in employee training (such as reading and math skills).

Integration and coordination of resources require management skills such as planning, leading, scheduling, and motivating. These skills enter into management activities like designing a secretary's job so that he or she canshare a laser printer with coworkers to perform the necessary tasks in less time. Integrating and coordinating also enter into creating a production schedule that will eliminate delays caused by waiting for parts to arrive or to be assembled.

People are not born with a knowledge of management principles. These principles must be learned. Management principles in today's business actually have evolved over a long period of time in industrialized societies. This chapter introduces some of the fundamental principles that all managers must master.

FOCUS ON COLLABORATORS

Saturn

Three important resources of the Saturn division of General Motors are its technology, its people, and its collaborators. Outdated production processes and unmotivated, untrained people decrease a company's ability to compete in our global business environment. When GM created the Saturn division, it recognized the importance of these resources and created a modern production facility with highly trained and motivated employees. But even more essential to GM's plan, Saturn was expected to build collaborative relationships between management and labor and between company and supplier—relationships in which everyone shared risks and rewards. Integrating and coordinating resources was the factor that would determine the new division's success.

Managers decided all Saturn stores would be called "Saturn of [Location]," thus stressing the Saturn name instead of the retailer. The collaborators decided they were in the retail business—not in the "deal" business, where haggling over price lowered a car's image among customers.

Saturn created several internal video communication pieces about the company. To prepare the story, the Spring Hill, Tennessee, factory workers were interviewed, and an "incredible emotional involvement" at Saturn was discovered. "These people believe so strongly, it's almost like a cult," said one observer. In April 1989, a 26-minute film, *Spring, in Spring Hill,* documented the start-up of a project that was dedicated to building cars "in a brand new way."

That film has played an extraordinary role in the Saturn story. The company has used it for training and to help explain itself to new employees, suppliers, and the media. Dealers have used it in presentations for bank loans and zoning variances. *Spring* was built around the simple idea of letting Saturn team members explain—often emotionally—just what the project was all about and what it meant to them.

MANAGEMENT FUNCTIONS

Management principles revolve around several essential functions: planning, organizing, directing, and controlling the business process. Each of these functions requires managers to have the skills needed to perform certain other activities. For example, effective managers

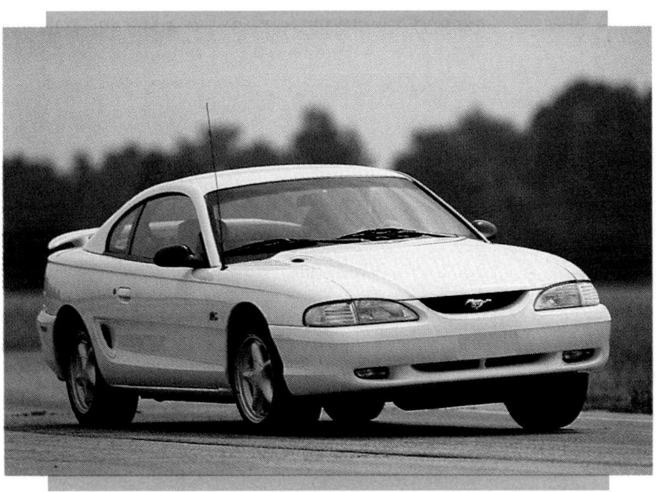

With a projected development cost of $1 billion, redesigning the Ford Mustang seemed too expensive when Ford executives first considered it in late 1989. But a group known as Team Mustang scrambled to save the Mustang from fading away. Good planning, commitment, and follow-through brought the new Mustang in at a cost of under $700 million in less than three years of development time.[4]

must be skilled decision makers. We will discuss these required management activities and skills later. First, we will look at the basic functions of all decision makers.

PLANNING

Planning
The process of assessing future business conditions and anticipating actions the business should take to reach its objectives.

Planning involves assessing future business conditions and anticipating actions the business should take to reach its objectives. Planning includes decisions about what kind of product or service the company should provide, how to finance the operation, where to market the goods or service, and what resources the company should use in its business. Since the environment in which the business operates is likely to be constantly changing, planning is a continuous process. Managers must continually assess their operations and make appropriate adjustments.

The importance of planning is illustrated by WellPoint Healthcare, a health maintenance organization (HMO). Like other HMOs, WellPoint faces a dilemma if the proposed Clinton health care reform plan takes effect. Unless managers can anticipate the kinds of actions to take in the next few years, WellPoint is unlikely to have any advantage over competitors like United Healthcare. WellPoint's managers must anticipate rapidly changing conditions in the health care industry, assess the company's own strengths and weaknesses, and determine appropriate actions to maintain market share and improve profitability.

Planning often is categorized as being strategic, tactical, or operational, depending on the scope and depth of the planning process.

Strategic planning
The process of setting organizational objectives, determining overall strategy for the business, and deciding on the appropriate allocation of resources for the business to reach its objectives.

Strategic Planning. Strategic planning is the process of setting organizational objectives, determining overall strategy for the business, and deciding on the appropriate allocation of resources for the business to reach its objectives. Strategic plans tend to be broad and long range in nature, often focusing on objectives that will have a major impact on the business over a long period of time, usually 3 to 15 years.

Consider E-Systems, a maker of top-secret surveillance and electronic warfare systems. The company currently is feeling the pinch of defense cutbacks. For E-Systems, strategic plans would entail decisions regarding research and development expenditures and where to expand operations in nonaerospace and defense businesses. The company already has been able to use its extraordinary data retrieval systems (formerly used to comb through classified intelligence data) to store all of Mobil Oil's seismic survey data.[5] For another business, such as a local restaurant, strategic plans may involve decisions regarding location, seating capacity, and when or where to expand the business.

Tactical planning
Focuses on specific actions to take to implement the organization's long-range strategies.

Tactical Planning. **Tactical planning** focuses on specific actions to take to implement the organization's long-range strategies. Tactical planning tends to be shorter term and involves decisions about near-term implementation activities. Campbell Soup Company, for example, tracks all major storms moving across the United States during the winter months. The information gathered allows managers to plan to advertise "hot soup for cold weather" on the radio on the days before, of, and after a storm.

Tactical plans often are implemented by middle managers and affect specific business divisions rather than the entire organization. Thus, one set of tactical plans at Marriott Corporation would be created for Marriott Resorts and another for its Fairfield Inns division.

Operational plans
Plans that are set for very short periods of time and outline activities and goals at department, work group, or individual employee levels.

Operational Planning. The lowest level of plans in terms of scope and depth are operational plans. **Operational planning** focuses on very short periods of time, such as a day or a week. Operational plans tend to outline activities and goals at department, work group, or individual employee levels and often are stated in terms of quotas, standards, and schedules for employees to meet.

Production schedules detailing how and when parts are to be assembled into the final product, shipping schedules specifying when and where the company's products are to be sent, and vacation schedules indicating which employees will be on vacation and which will be on duty are common examples of operational plans. Departmental and project budgets are other examples.

Planning Levels. Planning can be accomplished in several ways. While many people believe planning must begin at the very top of the organization and then filter its way down to the bottom, it can work the other way as well. When planning begins at the CEO level, the process is called a *top-down planning.* When employees at the bottom generate ideas and plans that are passed along to the top, *bottom-up planning* occurs. Additionally, managers and their employees often sit down together to generate plans in an interactive approach. This process is called *management by objectives.* In today's turbulent business environment, managers should be open to all the alternatives for generating useful plans.

ORGANIZING

Wal-Mart has become one of the most successful retailers in the United States because it organizes for profits. Its 1993 profit was $2.3 billion[6], while Sears suffered losses. Some of the differences, according to observers, lie in how the two firms are organized. Once plans have been established, the business must be organized. **Organizing** involves establishing the basic framework of formal relationships among tasks, activities, and people in the company. Essentially, all tasks and activities must be classified and divided into manageable units. Three steps are required to organize effectively:

Organizing
Establishing the basic framework of formal relationships among tasks, activities, and people in the company.

1. Determine specific work activities required to accomplish the organization's objectives and plans.
2. Group work activities into a rational structure of departments or units.
3. Assign work activities to specific positions and employees.

Wal-Mart is organized to work with many collaborators on a regular, almost daily, basis. Important questions that managers must ask themselves as they organize for profitability and productivity are:

- Are some employees working in the wrong positions?
- Is the manufacturing or service operation organized for maximum quality and efficiency?
- Is the distribution system organized to minimize delays and maximize customer satisfaction?

Managers must determine how much coordination can be achieved among the operating divisions. One way a company can achieve effective and efficient coordination is by expanding the "team concept." This will move power down the hierarchy and may minimize the tension so common between labor and management.

Differences in organization among businesses can be seen when comparing the structure of a giant organization such as at IBM and that of a growing high-tech firm like Autodesk, Inc. As the following "Focus on Company" feature shows, Autodesk appears to have very little formal structure compared to more traditional firms. This company has relied on a small group of technical employees—the core—and one introverted founder for all coordination and integration of activities.

FOCUS ON COMPANY

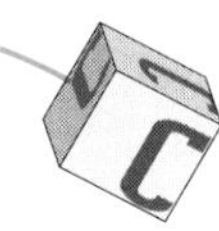

Autodesk, Inc.

Although largely unknown to the general public, Autodesk, Inc., is one of America's most profitable companies. Autodesk manufactures software that allows inexpensive personal computers to produce powerful architectural and engineering models. The company controls 71.8 percent of its market, and profits climbed from just over $10 million in 1987 to more than $57 million today. Just as Microsoft Corporation, the world's largest software supplier, is an extension of its founder, William Gates, Autodesk reflects the personality of its creator, John Walker. Walker is very skilled at identifying computer trends and spreading his vision to the troops.

However, as the company rapidly became the leading supplier of this software, Walker found he could not be all things to all people. He turned his CEO responsibilities over to the firm's chief financial officer. But the real power still rested with Walker and an elite group of programmers called "Core." These eccentric free-thinkers preferred to communicate by sending "flame mail"—biting electronic letters. The outbursts sometimes led to sudden changes in the software programs and even brought work to a complete stop. Disputes often broke out among programmers and managers, usually about the technical direction of the company. Over time, Autodesk became almost unmanageable due, some believed, to the freewheeling atmosphere within the company. Employees met and discussed things, but there was no organized structure in place to ensure that decisions were finalized and activities completed.

Ultimately, the CEO was replaced by Carol Bartz, who formerly ran worldwide field operations for Sun Microsystems Inc. Bartz plans to organize the firm to bring order to the chaos. She has said that she is no dictator, but she is also not a consensus manager. In fact, she told one interviewer, "I do not believe the best decision is a group grope." Her strategy is to create formal responsibility and authority relationships which will minimize the disruptive freewheeling communications.

DIRECTING

Once the organizational structure for accomplishing the firm's plans is in place, it might seem that little else needs to be done. However, organizational structures are not living things. Tasks

Directing
The process of guiding and motivating employees to accomplish the organization's objectives.

and activities are unlikely to be completed effectively unless someone directs them. **Directing** means guiding and motivating employees to accomplish the company's objectives.

Directing requires considerable people skills on the part of a firm's managers, in particular leading, guiding, and motivating. Although important at all levels, the directing function is especially critical at the supervisory level, where tasks and activities are completed. People skills take many shapes. For example, John Walker, former CEO of Autodesk, Inc., was a charismatic manager. He was able to draw key employees into his vision of the company. He led by example. In contrast, current CEO Carol Bartz is a rational persuader of employees who leads by planning and making decisions.

CONTROLLING

Controlling
The process of monitoring and evaluating the organization's performance and determining how to correct problems that detract from that performance.

Controlling is the process of monitoring and evaluating the organization's performance and determining how to correct problems that detract from that performance. Controlling is closely associated with planning, since performance can be evaluated only in terms of what managers think *should* have been accomplished—the company's planned activities.

Evaluation and control of the company's performance require four basic steps:

1. Establish rational performance standards that correspond to the company's plans.
2. Monitor the levels of performance achieved by employees and employee groups.
3. Compare actual performance to the company's plans to determine whether it deviated from the plans.
4. If deviations are found, determine why and what to do about them.

Businesses have made great progress during the past 10 to 15 years in exercising control over operations. In part this is due to changes in standard procedures such as inventory planning and control. It also is due to advances in computerized information systems that permit managers to anticipate changes in customer demand and react more quickly to those changes. For example, Tenneco's $1.7-billion-a-year auto parts division used to make its Monroe shock absorbers in batches of 2,000. Now it can profitably turn out 300 in one production run, meaning it can react more quickly to changes in customer demand.

Goodyear, a large tire manufacturer, also waits for information on customer demand before gearing up to supply automobile manufacturers. Modern manufacturing processes ensure that Goodyear will not have to stock large numbers of tires and will be able to respond quickly to changes in demand. Control processes such as these contribute to a business's productivity and profitability.

MANAGEMENT ACTIVITIES

Managers engage in a variety of activities as they perform their management functions of planning, organizing, directing, and controlling. To perform these functions effectively, managers must lead others (especially subordinate employees), motivate both employees and collaborators such as suppliers, make many decisions, and manage information and time. The variety and complexity of these activities are great.

LEADING

Leader
A person who guides others, often by example, to ensure that their work is done correctly and on time.

One of the most important activities for managers is to act as leaders. A **leader** guides others, often by example, to ensure that their work is done correctly and on time. Leading is closely related to the function of directing, since managers must provide the direction that others will follow.

Today effective companies reflect their leaders. Some of America's most admired companies are led by managers whose names are very familiar to us. Microsoft Corporation is inevitably associated with Bill Gates and when one mentions Walt Disney the leadership of

Michael Eisner comes to mind.[7] Employees follow these leaders because these managers passionately believe in the company's mission. Often this leadership spreads throughout the organization's culture and becomes the force that guides employees to willingly perform their jobs.

However, not all leaders are as forceful as Michael Eisner or Bill Gates. There are many different and effective leadership styles. Many high-tech firms successfully use democratic styles of leadership that permit maximum input from employees, customers, and collaborators. A democratic leadership style requires traits such as flexibility, good listening skills, the ability to coach and counsel subordinates, and empathy. Not all leaders are born with these skills, but most of these skills can be learned. More important, other leaders may choose a less democratic approach.

Research on leadership is extensive and sometimes contradictory, but the following conclusions can be drawn:

- Effective managers provide leadership by example. Employees follow leaders who are good models.
- Effective leaders communicate clearly and honestly with employees.
- Effective leaders provide frequent guidance and assistance to employees. The role of coaching uses many leadership activities.
- Effective leadership requires considerable people skills. Leaders get along with others, understand others, and believe in the importance of others.

MOTIVATING

Motivation
Energizing employees to exert high levels of effort and achieve superior performance.

Motivation is another important management activity. **Motivation** means energizing employees to exert high levels of effort and achieve superior performance. While high performance is often encouraged by leadership, it is usually enhanced by systematic motivation activities. Motivation is another people skill that separates effective from ineffective managers. Good motivational skills can be found in many companies, large and small. Motivated employees, as team members, can help the organization succeed in many different ways. As the opening story about Southwest Airlines shows, a motivated employee will work harder, will work smarter, and will likely provide better service to customers.

STREET SMART

The Value of Good Advice

"No one is competent in every area of expertise needed to succeed in business. The most successful entrepreneurs recognize their limitations and bring in people with complementary strengths to counter their weaknesses." This statement by Charles McCabe, president and CEO of Peoples Income Tax, typifies his approach to decision making. His business is a small tax preparation firm with 20 offices in the Richmond, Virginia, area. "If you want to build a company that will still have market value when you are no longer part of it, you'll need the advice and help of seasoned business experts with skills and knowledge that you lack," McCabe says. His philosophy of sharing decisions is good advice for managers who must make many decisions that require technical skills beyond their own personal abilities.

Exhibit 7.1 **THE DECISION-MAKING PROCESS**

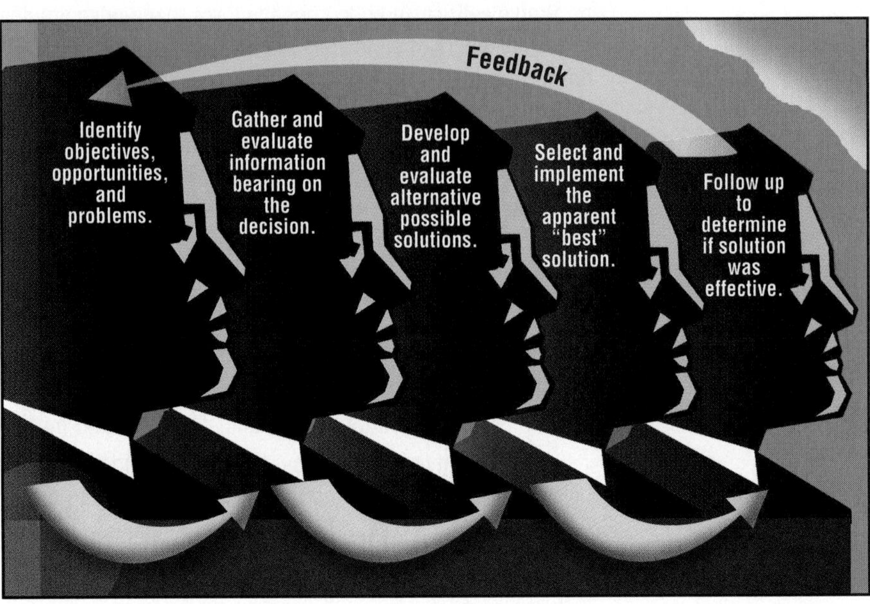

DECISION MAKING

Decision making
Choosing one action from among several possible alternatives.

One of the manager's most important activities is **decision making**—choosing one action from among several possible alternatives. Often managers are known as "good" or "bad" managers simply because of the decisions they make. This implies that managers are evaluated by the consequences of their decisions. If decisions prove successful, the company looks good to its customers and collaborators and unbeatable to its competitors. The importance of decision making is seen in a company that is attempting to bring out a new product or to deal with difficult labor problems. How its managers decide to deal with an important opportunity or a major problem will have an important bearing on the company's future.

Decision making is often described as a five-step process. Exhibit 7.1 outlines the steps effective decision makers use to arrive at good decisions.

Although decision making is an important management activity, effective companies often involve employees in this process. In fact, one of the basic decisions managers must make is to what extent they will share this activity with subordinates. Many managers have found that sharing decisions with employees can help make their companies more productive. When Monte Peterson became CEO of Thermos Company, he replaced a top-down bureaucratic management structure with a flexible team structure. The benefits of letting employee teams have a larger role in decision making were quickly realized. The new hot selling Thermos Thermal Electric Grill was created by one of the decision-making teams.[8] Gordon Forward, CEO of Chaparral Steel, is another manager who involves employees in almost every decision that affects them. In the process, Chaparral Steel has become one of the world's lowest cost producers of steel.[9]

MANAGING INFORMATION AND TIME

Managing Information. Managers receive a great deal of information regarding products, customers, suppliers, financial resources, and other data that affect business operations. Consider Citibank, where managers must cope with inflation, interest rates, international currency fluctuations, government regulation, changes in customer demands, and so on. To deal with these major issues, managers must obtain volumes of information regarding economic forecasts, technological developments, customer preferences, international developments, and employee information. Information-gathering and processing activities are critical to the decisions managers must make.

Communication and exchange of information help all employees perform their jobs better. If employees know the direction in which the manager plans to go, they can do their jobs more effectively. Distributing information also reduces misunderstandings among departments and divisions.

While gathering information has always been crucial to a company's success, it is especially important in today's rapidly changing business environment. Fortunately for managers, technological developments in information processing have made it possible for them to stay abreast of the information they need to make business decisions. The personal computer and business software have helped even small-business managers gather information more effectively.

Managing Time. Managers are busy people. They must perform many important activities and achieve organizational objectives in a limited amount of time. Thus, good managers know how to manage their limited time effectively.

Time management is a skill rarely taught in academic programs. However, many guidelines for managing one's time effectively have proven to work:

- Establish a list of objectives and prioritize them. Look at the list often, and begin at the top of the list. This helps you concentrate your efforts on the most important items.
- Delegate duties to others when appropriate. Managers do not have to do everything themselves; that's what subordinates are for. Delegating activities and responsibilities to others who have the skills to perform them will free time for you to concentrate on the most important items and on items that are best left to you alone.
- Arrange to work when you are feeling energetic rather than when you are tired. Taking a lot of work home will probably be less productive, since you are likely to be tired at the end of the workday. In fact, everyone needs a rest break to rebuild their energy. Trying to work too many hours is counterproductive.
- Spend more time on activities that have the greatest return and less time on those that have the least return.

MANAGEMENT LEVELS AND ASSOCIATED SKILLS

As companies grow, managerial functions and activities must be shared by several managers. Different levels of management are then created to establish authority relationships among managers. This allows managers to determine who has final responsibility for each decision. Each level of management requires different activities and skills.

THE MANAGEMENT PYRAMID

A small, independent grocery store has a very simple management structure. Typically it has one manager—the owner—and everyone else is an employee (checker, bagger, stocker, janitor). A larger organization, however, needs more than one manager. The management structure at a Safeway supermarket is more complex than that of the small grocery store. It may consist of store manager, assistant store manager, head checker, head bagger, and head stocker. Each of these people performs specific management duties. For example, the store manager is responsible for making decisions on pricing, advertising, and purchasing. The assistant store manager may make staffing decisions, set employee work schedules, and

Exhibit 7.2 **THE MANAGEMENT PYRAMID**

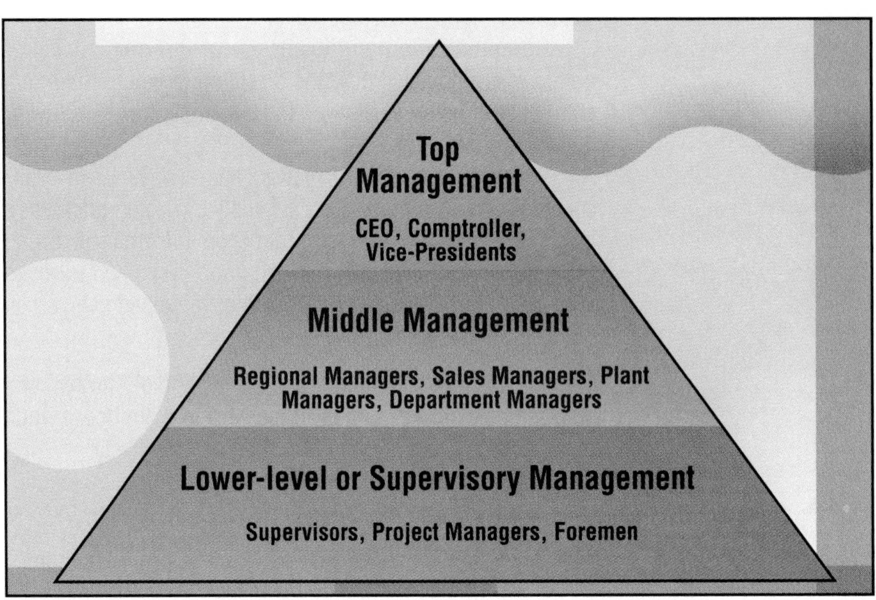

assign employees special tasks such as clearing snow from the entrance to the store following a storm. The head checker may decide which checker works at which cash register and usually trains new checkers. Thus, the various managers share the management activities.

However, there needs to be an order among the managers regarding who has final authority over the various decisions and some means for reaching decisions when managers can't agree. This order is accomplished through the organizational hierarchy, or the **management pyramid**—a structure of authority relationships among the managers. This pyramid may consist of a great many layers, but three basic levels of management are most common. These levels are top management, middle management, and supervisory or lower-level management (see Exhibit 7.2).

Management pyramid
A hierarchy of authority relationships among managers at different levels in the organization.

Top Management. **Top management** consists of managers who are responsible for setting the overall direction of the business and determining the organization's business strategy. In large organizations, the very top position is referred to as the *chief executive officer (CEO).* This person is responsible for setting the major objectives and plans of the company. The CEO also may serve as chairperson on the organization's board of directors.

Top management
Managers who are responsible for setting the overall direction of the business and determining the organization's business strategy.

In addition to the CEO, top management includes the chief financial officer (the comptroller or treasurer) and a variety of vice-presidents. At Procter & Gamble, top managers are in charge of the major divisions, such as bleach and laundry products (e.g., Oxydol, Cheer), cleansers (Comet, Mr. Clean), bar soaps (Camay, Ivory), diapers (Pampers), and mouthwash/toothpaste (Scope, Crest). Together these top managers set the direction for the firm and make decisions that lower-level managers must carry out.

Middle Management. **Middle management**, the second management level, is responsible for implementing the strategies and plans developed by top management. These managers are somewhat more difficult to identify, because they have no commonly accepted titles (such as CEO at the top level). The middle management level often includes regional managers, sales managers, plant and department managers (e.g., manager of customer service), and manager of production.

Middle management
Managers responsible for implementing the strategies and plans developed by top management.

Cindy Ransom is a middle manager (also called sponsor*) at Clorox Company. Four years ago, she asked her subordinates to redesign the plant's operations. Then she sat back and watched, intervening only to answer an occasional question. Ransom's employees changed traditional structures, set work rules, and reorganized into five customer-focused business units. Her plant was later recognized as the most improved plant in the company. But instead of a promotion to the ranks of top management, Ransom will get to attack problems at an overseas unit—something she looks forward to. Such project focus seems to be the new middle management role.[10]*

Middle managers must design specific procedures, detailed plans of action, and budgets to carry out top management's plans. Middle managers often hire employees, design jobs, purchase materials, and choose equipment. They leave the actual job assignments, daily monitoring of work, and disciplinary procedures to lower-level managers.

Supervisory management
Managers responsible for directing and coordinating the work of nonmanagement employees.

Supervisory Management. Supervisory management, the bottom management level, consists of those managers who directly supervise and coordinate the work of nonmanagement employees. Supervisors typically work on the line, side by side with their employees, and may fill in for an employee in an emergency. They are often chosen to be supervisors because they previously were outstanding employees in the nonmanagement ranks. New college graduates usually begin their management careers at this level.

This level is very important in establishing relationships with customers, suppliers, and the general public. It is the first point of contact for these groups, and how pleasant, efficient, and productive supervisors are will greatly affect how they perceive it. It is also an ideal training ground for new managers. By learning how things are done "in the trenches," these trainees can avoid making the mistakes often made by inexperienced managers.

MANAGEMENT SKILLS

It is widely recognized that all managers need three basic skills to perform their activities effectively. These skills are technical job skills, human relations skills, and conceptual skills. Although managers at each level need all three skills, the importance of each skill varies among the levels. Exhibit 7.3 illustrates the difference in the skill mix for the three management levels.

Exhibit 7.3 **MANAGEMENT SKILL MIX AT DIFFERENT LEVELS**

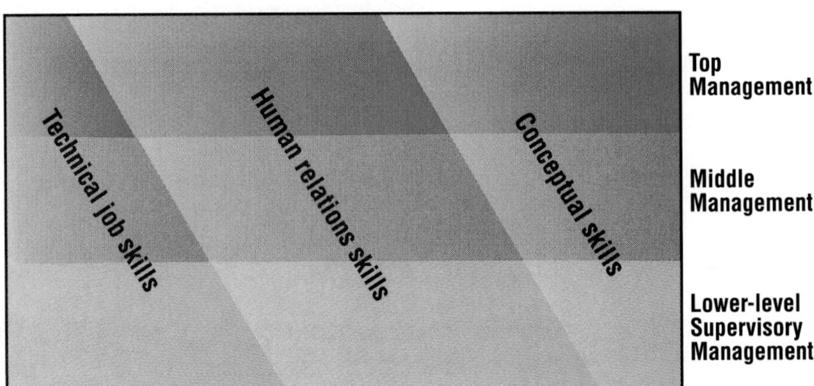

Technical job skills
Skills that require the ability to understand and use the specific tools, knowledge, and techniques of a discipline or function.

Technical Job Skills. **Technical job skills** are the manager's ability to understand and use the specific tools, knowledge, and techniques of a discipline or function. These skills are acquired through training and experience in the discipline and are especially important at the supervisory level. For example, when John Walker founded Autodesk, his considerable skills in computer programming were a major reason for the company's success. He personally wrote much of the software that was central to the company's product. Employees followed him because of his programming and computer skills. But as the company grew, so did his responsibilities. Now his management position (top level) required different skills, those in the areas of finance and marketing.[11] This is generally the case with top managers: The skills they needed as lower-level managers are no longer sufficient for effective performance at the higher levels.

Human relations skills
Skills that require the ability to get along with others and to lead and motivate them to accomplish what the organization needs.

Human Relations Skills. **Human relations skills** reflect the manager's ability to get along with others and to lead and motivate them to accomplish what the organization needs. Managers sometimes call these skills "people" skills. While it might seem that people skills come naturally to some individuals, this is incorrect. People skills must be learned and practiced and are present only among managers who consistently attend to the needs of others. People skills consist of the ability to motivate others, lead others, empathize, and create a positive work environment and team culture in the organization.

As Exhibit 7.3 shows, human relations skills may be the single most important management skill. This is one reason for the success achieved by companies like Chaparral Steel where employees are treated like responsible adults, are encouraged to make positive contributions, and are rewarded when they do. Even the most technically skilled managers are unlikely to run productive departments unless the people who work for them are positive contributors. In a sense, managers' accomplishments depend on the accomplishments of others.

Conceptual skills
Skills that require the ability to understand the whole organization, analyze and evaluate information, and make appropriate plans and decisions.

Conceptual Skills. The importance of conceptual skills increases as managers move up in the organization. **Conceptual skills** involve the ability to understand the whole organization, analyze and evaluate information, and make appropriate plans and decisions. Conceptual skills are especially important at the top level, since managers at this level must develop plans that integrate the entire business. Decision making is another management activity that conceptual skills enhance, since the evaluation of facts and alternatives relies on these skills.

One reason for Japan's success in the computer field has been well-developed conceptual skills among Japanese companies' managers. For example, several years ago Japan's Ministry of International Trade and Industry announced support for a large artificial intelligence project. Western companies responded with their own, lesser financed projects, believing artificial intelligence was an unachievable goal. Japan failed to produce a computer that could

Exhibit 7.4 **FAYOL'S PRINCIPLES OF MANAGEMENT**

Principle	Description
1. Division of work	This principle leads to the creation of work units, departments, and jobs that specialize in few rather than many skills.
2. Authority and responsibility	Authority is the right to give orders and obtain obedience. Responsibility follows from authority. This principle states that managers are responsible for achieving the goals of the business and are authorized to delegate duties to others (subordinates) that will accomplish those goals.
3. Discipline	Fayol viewed obedience to "rules of work" authorized by managers as fundamental to accomplishment of goals. He believed the best way to have productive employees was to set limits and impose penalties with good judgment.
4. Unity of command	This principle states that there should be one—and only one—boss for each employee. Fayol believed employees would be confused when issued conflicting demands from different managers.
5. Unity of direction	All units in the organization should be moving toward the same objective through coordinated and focused effort. Unity of direction is achieved by creating a structure, by communicating the objectives and plans, and through leadership.
6. Subordination of individual interest to general interest	Fayol believed, as do most managers, that the interest of the company must come before any needs or interests of individual managers or employees. Individual needs can be achieved only if the company first meets its goals and objectives.
7. Remuneration of employees	The overall pay and compensation for employees should be fair to both employees and the organization.
8. Centralization	Authority should be decentralized to include employees, with the final authority retained by managers and owners.
9. Scalar chain	Organizations should have a chain of authority and communication that runs from top to bottom in the hierarchy. Managers and subordinates should follow this chain when communicating and seeking advice and guidance.
10. Order	People and materials must be in the right places at the right times for maximum efficiency. This makes planning, scheduling, and similar management activities particularly important.
11. Equity	Good sense and experience are needed to ensure fairness to all employees. Employees should be treated as equally as possible and always based on their contributions to the company.
12. Stability of personnel	Employee turnover should be minimized to maintain organizational efficiency.
13. Initiative	Workers should be encouraged to develop and carry out their plans for improvements.
14. Esprit de corps	Management should promote a team spirit of unity and harmony among employees.

"think." But Japanese planners weren't really expecting this success. Rather, the project produced important side effects including a new computer research infrastructure that brought together scientists in business, government, and education. A new generation of well-trained computer scientists is now ready to tackle major new projects in Japan.[11]

MANAGEMENT PRINCIPLES: THEN AND NOW

The management of business organizations is not a new phenomenon. Business firms have existed for thousands of years, and managers have been practicing their skills for at least as long. Management skills were evident in the building of the pyramids, and modern business practices existed in the Venetian shipyards in the Middle Ages. Venice, then known for its military power and large production of ships, used assembly line techniques to outfit galley ships to go to war. In addition, double-entry accounting was created during this time, and employee wine breaks (as opposed to coffee breaks) were common.

FAYOL'S PRINCIPLES OF MANAGEMENT

As the field of management evolved, various principles of management were created. These principles provided the foundation on which modern management is practiced. While we will not review all of them, one set of principles in particular stands out as still applicable in our modern business world. This set, consisting of 14 principles, was described by Henri Fayol in the 19th century. Fayol divided management into five functions: *planning, organizing,*

Exhibit 7.5 **PETERS AND WATERMAN'S MANAGEMENT PRINCIPLES**

Principle	Description
1. Bias for action	A preference for doing something—anything—rather than sending an idea through endless cycles of analysis and committee reports.
2. Staying close to the customer	Learning the customer's preferences and catering to them.
3. Autonomy and entrepreneurship	Breaking the corporation into small companies and encouraging them to act independently and competitively.
4. Productivity through people	Creating in all employees the awareness that their best efforts are essential and that they will share in the rewards of the company's success.
5. Hands-on, value-driven	Insisting that executives keep in touch with the company's essential business and promote a strong culture.
6. "Stick to the knitting"	Remaining with the businesses the company knows best.
7. Simple form, lean staff	Few administrative layers, few people at the upper levels.
8. Simultaneous loose-tight properties	Fostering a climate of dedication to the central values of the company, combined with tolerance for all employees who accept those values.

commanding, coordinating, and *controlling.* These functions are very similar to the four functions of planning, organizing, directing, and controlling described earlier in this chapter. Within his group of five functions, Fayol developed a list of basic management principles for achieving an effective organization. Exhibit 7.4 lists these principles.

Fayol's principles contain many elements, but the basic idea is an emphasis on rationality and consistency. These principles remain with us, but often have been adapted to modern technologies and methods. For example, Fayol believed the best way to ensure productive employees was to set limits and administer penalties using good judgment (the principle of discipline). Today's managers are much less likely to expect strict obedience, but most business operations still have a set of work rules pertaining to attendance, absenteeism, work hours, and so on that employees are expected to follow.

Further, most modern managers know it is better not to overcentralize authority. Many companies such as Thermos Company have achieved good results by passing considerable authority to the lowest levels of employees.

Finally, esprit de corps—a shared devotion to a cause—is a positive force at work. Feeling like part of a team and enjoying one's coworkers are now considered to be strong motivators of employee effort.

MANAGING FOR EXCELLENCE: PETERS AND WATERMAN

Thomas Peters and Robert Waterman published *In Search of Excellence,* a book that was hailed as the new gospel of management.[13] This book contained many innovative ideas that would lead to higher levels of excellence among business firms. It was based on a review of 100 of the most successful U.S. companies according to criteria established by the authors. However, many believed that Peters and Waterman's ideas (see Exhibit 7.5) were simply refinements of long-standing principles established by early writers such as Fayol. In the extreme, they argued, the "new" principles demonstrated that little had changed in management.

While we do not share this view, many of Peters and Waterman's findings do have a familiar ring. For example, their principles of autonomy and entrepreneurship, productivity through people, stick to the knitting, and simple form, lean staff are very similar to Fayol's principles of stability of personnel, initiative, unity of direction, and order. However, new emphasis was placed on relationships with customers and collaborators. Concern for quality in products, customer relations, and other aspects of the business was brought to the company discussion table.

STREET SMART

Only the Most Productive Companies Are Going to Win

Jack Welch, CEO at General Electric since 1981, is known for breakthrough management ideas. The following is an excerpt taken from his new book that appeared in *Fortune*:

> Everywhere you go, people are saying, "Don't tell me about your technology, tell me your price." To get a lower price, customers are willing to sacrifice the extras they used to demand. The fact is, many governments are broke, and people are hurting, so there's an enormous drive to get value, value, value. ...[A] worldwide capacity overhang, coming at a time when everybody feels poor, is forcing ferocious price competition. As it intensifies, the margin pressure on all corporations is going to be enormous. Only the most productive companies are going to win. If you can't sell a top-quality product at the world's lowest price, you're going to be out of the game.

MANAGING FOR PRODUCTIVITY, QUALITY, AND EFFECTIVENESS

Successful companies depend on the skills and knowledge of their managers. Since the business world today is more competitive and challenging than it was just a few years ago, managers must be alert to the need to be productive and to strive for quality and effectiveness in their operations.

PRODUCTIVITY

Productivity
The total output of goods and services in a given period of time divided by the inputs needed to produce that output.

Productivity is the total output of goods and services in a given period of time divided by the inputs needed to produce that output. Productivity is increased by producing more goods and services using the same number of or fewer inputs.

New technologies are creating some productivity gains in the service sector of the U.S. economy. Computers, word processors, price scanners, electronic mail, and other advances have decreased the labor necessary to achieve good results in the service sector. Robots, lasers, computerized production lines, and other developments hold considerable promise for improving productivity in the manufacturing sector as well.

However, major gains in productivity lie in improved management practices. Developing improved work teams, creating better work climates, and increasing concern for quality and effectiveness throughout the company will achieve the desired improvement.

TOTAL QUALITY MANAGEMENT (TQM)

Most businesses now define *quality* as meeting or exceeding customer expectations. The dimensions of quality differ somewhat between goods and services. For example, the quality of a pair of women's jeans may be based on durability—how long the jeans will last—and aesthetics—the look and feel of the jeans. The quality of a computer may be judged based on performance features such as speed of operation and "bell and whistles" like a Sound Blaster card. Of course, since you can't pick up a service and examine tangible features, service quality is based on factors like how long a customer must wait to obtain the service like a car wash or how courteous the employee at the dry cleaning store is.

At Harley-Davidson, top executives and managers are expected to own and ride Harleys. The management philosophy is that managers must use the company's products if they are to understand consumer problems and manufacturing quality issues. They must know what makes the product good and what needs to be improved. Total quality management (TQM) is a companywide effort that involves all employees, suppliers, and customers in continuously improving the quality of the company's goods or services.

Total quality management (TQM)
A companywide effort that includes all employees, suppliers, and customers and seeks to continuously improve the quality of products and services to meet customer expectations.

Total quality management (TQM) is a companywide effort that includes all employees, suppliers, and customers, and seeks to continuously improve the quality of products and services to meet customer expectations. Thus, TQM affects all aspects of management.

The focus on quality by American businesses has been widely publicized during the past decade. While for many years American products and services were considered the best in the world, Japanese companies' improvements in the quality of their products took this competitive advantage away from the United States.

Total quality management is rooted in statistical quality control in the 1940s. These ideas were transplanted to Japan by W. Edwards Deming after World War II. Japanese companies, whose products were noted for their inferior quality at the time, embraced Deming's philosophies regarding quality. Deming emphasized the importance of employees in achieving high quality and in learning how quality can be improved. He described the fundamental forces driving TQM as empowering, energizing, and enabling employees to work with one another. By the 1970s, superior Japanese products were flooding markets around the world.

To understand the nature of TQM, we need only examine the success of companies that have applied the principles. Perhaps one of the best examples is Xerox Corporation, a leading manufacturer of copy machines. Throughout the 1960s Xerox dominated this market, introducing the first 914 copier. It had little competition, and profits soared. Xerox reached $1 billion in revenues more quickly than any other company in history. But by the 1970s, Japanese copiers of superior quality and at lower prices were taking sales away from Xerox. In response, Xerox established a total quality management program.

Benchmarking
Comparing a company's products and manufacturing processes to those of competitors to help gauge how much the company needs to improve.

As it began this program, Xerox established a process called **benchmarking**: comparing its products and manufacturing processes to those of competitors to help gauge how much it needed to improve. Xerox found it had 10 times as many assembly line rejects, twice the new-product development time, 7 times as many defects, and 9 times as many suppliers as its competitors had. Its manufacturing cost per unit equaled Japanese competitors' selling prices. By applying principles of TQM, Xerox emerged from this threatening competitive situation and is stronger today than ever.

TQM improves quality and productivity by seeking improvements along the entire manufacturing and service process. Under TQM, employees are encouraged to participate in the improvement of quality and to find and solve problems that affect productivity. Although TQM advocates admit their philosophy contains nothing new, the vocabulary of TQM, the dedication to total-quality products and services, and the emphasis on customer satisfaction are novel.[14] The basic principles of TQM include a customer focus, strategic planning and management, continuous improvement, and empowerment and teamwork.

Customer Focus. TQM is an element of management strategy directed toward customer satisfaction. Thus, customers are the judge of product and service quality. The quality system must provide value to the customer by enhancing the product or service. These enhanced features distinguish the product or service and lead to market share gain and customer retention. Knowing how customers use the product or service and what characteristics they value and perceive help managers respond rapidly and flexibly to needed changes. Customer focus is discussed in greater detail in Chapters 13 through 15.

Strategic Planning and Management. Managers must make long-term commitments to improving the quality of their products and services. Top managers must create clear quality values and high expectations and develop strategies and methods for reaching those goals. Commitment to quality becomes a priority, and leadership by managers becomes a key to getting all employees involved in reaching the quality goals.

Continuous Improvement. Managers should not expect their companies to reach lofty quality goals overnight. A step-by-step approach is much more realistic and more likely to succeed. Improvements through new and improved products and services, reduction of errors and waste, quicker responsiveness to customer needs, and improved effectiveness in the use of the company's resources may take a lot of time to achieve. But daily improvements in these activities are possible—and essential.

Empowerment and Teamwork. Since quality improvements are attained through all employees and not just managers, a great deal of teamwork among all workers and across all levels of the company must occur. Such teamwork is required vertically, that is, among top, middle, and lower-level managers and nonsupervisory employees. It is also required horizontally—within and across departments. Cross-functional teams—teams consisting of members from various departments or business functions—have become a successful team strategy. Finally, interorganizational teamwork between the company and its suppliers is needed to fully integrate suppliers' capabilities with those of the company.

Teamwork gives more power to employees and motivates them to work toward quality improvement goals. It gives employees a sense of "ownership" in the process and pride in their accomplishments. Suppliers become partners in product improvements and contribute valuable ideas for cost control.

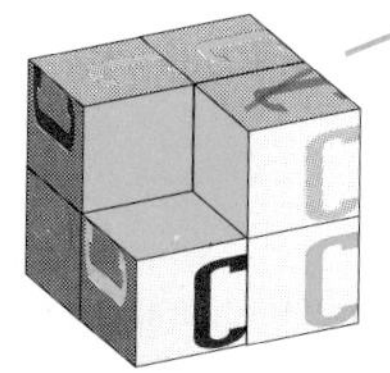

FOCUS ON CUSTOMERS

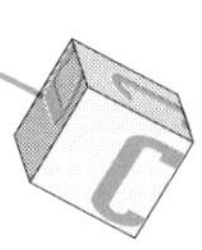

MasterCard International Inc.

A few years ago, a new management team took over the MasterCard Automated Point of Sale Program (MAPP), an unprofitable division of MasterCard International Inc. The team's mission was to determine whether MAPP could generate profits while providing consistently top-quality electronic transaction-processing services for the financial services sector. MAPP receives electronic credit card and sale information from banks and merchants, which speeds up credit approval and reduces fraud. This results in lower cost for the merchants and banks and is a valuable service to them. But the division was plagued with unhappy people, poor product quality, and autocratic management. It had no plan, no mission, and no future. All it had was a lot of people working very hard but achieving very little. It also had many unhappy customers.

During its first year, the new management team concentrated on empowering employees to help fix problems instead of blaming them for the problems. A central feature of this effort was the creation of PRIDE teams (*P*lanning & *R*esource *I*dentification for *D*eveloping *E*xcellence). PRIDE teams tackled project planning, internal communications, internal training, technical planning, high-quality customer service, product innovation, marketing planning, and problem solving.

In the second year, MAPP scaled the major projects back to five and designed new wholesale electronic payment systems and services. In the third year, the improvement program was officially called Total Service Quality (TSQ). This program focused employee efforts on the types of problems they should be solving and spurred even greater initiative.

The results at MAPP have been astounding. MAPP became one of the most profitable MasterCard divisions. Revenue per employee increased 65 percent in a one-year period. In addition, a survey of employees found that MAPP employees rate the division as an above-average place to work, claim they are proud to work for MAPP, and rate the senior management team as good or very good. And, perhaps most important, customers have returned to the division and are pleased with its services.

TQM improves quality and productivity by seeking improvements along the entire manufacturing and service process. Under TQM, employees are encouraged to participate in the improvement of quality, and to find and solve problems that affect the company's productivity. Although TQM advocates admit that their philosophy contains nothing new, the dedication to total quality products and services and the emphasis on customer satisfaction are necessary for surviving in our modern, global business environment.[15]

SUMMARY

1. ***Define* management *and describe the basic responsibility of a manager.***
   Management refers to the effective and efficient integration and coordination of resources to achieve desired objectives. Managers are the people who ensure that this happens. Managers integrate and combine the business's human, capital, and technological resources, in the best way possible to achieve the organization's objectives.

2. ***Discuss the three primary components of effective management.***
   Objectives are targets managers establish in terms of sales, revenues, profits, and performance. These targets serve to direct the efforts of all employees toward the same objectives. Resources are the people, capital, technology, and time managers use to achieve the business's objectives. By integrating and coordinating these resources, managers are able to effectively reach the objectives.

3. ***Describe the four major functions of management.***
   The four major management functions are planning, organizing, directing, and controlling. Planning involves assessing future conditions and anticipating actions to take to reach the organization's objectives. Three types of planning are strategic planning, tactical planning, and operational planning. Organizing involves establishing the basic framework of formal relationships among the organization's tasks, activities, and people. Directing refers to guiding and motivating

employees to accomplish the organization's objectives. Controlling is the process of monitoring and evaluating the business's performance and determining how to correct problems that detract from that performance.

4. ***Identify several activities in which all managers must engage.***
   Managers engage in several activities to accomplish their management functions. The most important activities are leading, motivating, decision making, and managing information and time.

5. ***Describe the management pyramid and the types of skills that are important at each level.***
   The management pyramid consists of three levels of management: top management, middle management, and supervisory management. Top management consists of the CEO and other vice-presidents who make major strategic decisions in the organization. Conceptual skills are very important at this level. Middle management consists of regional managers, sales managers, plant managers, and department managers who must implement the strategies and plans developed by top management. Although human relations skills are important at all levels, they are particularly important at this level. Supervisory management includes those managers who directly supervise and coordinate the work of nonmanagement employees. Technical skills are more important at this level than at the other levels.

6. ***List Fayol's 14 principles of management and contrast them with the principles described by Peters and Waterman.***
   Fayol's 14 principles of management were division of work, authority and responsibility, discipline, unity of command, unity of direction, subordination of individual interest to general interest, remuneration of employees, centralization, scalar chain, order, equity, stability of personnel, initiative, and esprit de corps. Fayol emphasized rationality and consistency. Peters and Waterman established eight more modern principles based on their analysis of effective organizations. These principles stress the customer, productivity, and flexibility. The principles are bias for action; staying close to the customer; autonomy and entrepreneurship; productivity through people; hands-on, value-driven; stick to the knitting; simple form, lean staff; and simultaneous loose-tight properties.

7. ***Explain the importance of productivity in today's competitive, global market.***
   Productivity is the total output of goods and services in a given period of time divided by the inputs needed to produce that output. Japanese firms were highly productive during the 1970s and 1980s and put great pressure on world competitors. Productivity can be affected by improving both production processes and human relations skills.

8. ***Describe total quality management (TQM) and its role in modern business.***
   Total quality management (TQM) improves quality and productivity by seeking improvements along the entire manufacturing and service processes. Employees are encouraged to contribute ideas for improving quality and increasing productivity. The basic principles of TQM are a customer focus, strategic planning and management, continuous improvement, and employee empowerment and teamwork.

KEY TERMS AND CONCEPTS

Management (p. 140)
Efficiency (p. 140)
Effectiveness (p. 140)
Manager (p. 140)
Objectives (p. 140)
Resources (p. 141)
Planning (p. 143)
Strategic planning (p. 143)
Tactical planning (p. 144)
Operational planning (p. 144)
Organizing (p. 144)
Directing (p. 146)
Controlling (p. 146)
Leader (p. 146)
Motivation (p. 147)
Decision making (p. 148)
Management pyramid (p. 150)
Top management (p. 150)
Middle management (p. 150)
Supervisory management (p. 151)

Technical job skills (p. 152)
Human relations skills (p. 152)
Conceptual skills (p. 152)
Productivity (p. 155)
Total quality management (TQM) (p. 156)
Benchmarking (p. 156)

DISCUSSION QUESTIONS

Company

1. Why must organizations have objectives?
2. What would be important resources for a local convenience store?

Customers

3. Should the needs of customers play a larger role in the planning process than it does today? Why or why not?
4. Which management skills are most important in maintaining good customer relations?
5. How have changes in the principles promoted by management writers such as Peters and Waterman affected relationships between companies and their customers?

Competitors

6. Do strategic plans truly improve a company's competitive strength, or does this strength come from shorter-term plans such as tactical or operational plans? Explain.
7. What new approaches seem to be helping U.S. firms regain their competitive position relative to international competitors?

Collaborators

8. How might a manager use suppliers and other collaborators to correct problems that detract from the company's desired performance?
9. Which level of management might play the largest role in coordinating the efforts of various collaborators such as suppliers, employment agencies, and distributors? Why?

In Question: Take a Stand

Many organizations today are hiring temporary managers and other employees to cope with declining profits. Does this practice take unfair advantage of people who desperately need jobs? What would it be like to have little job security and few job benefits such as a retirement plan and health insurance? How would these disadvantages affect the motivation and commitment of managers?

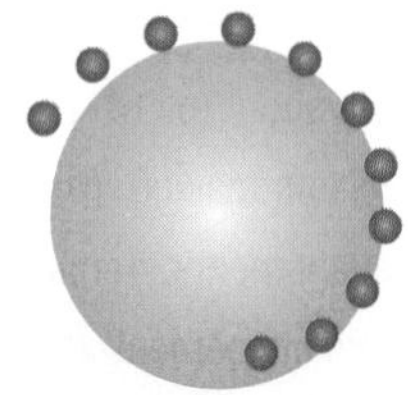

CASE 7.1
CHAPARRAL STEEL[16]

Executives from U.S. Steel are wondering how a small steel company in Midlothian, Texas, has become one of the world's lowest-cost steel producers. The company, Chaparral Steel, is a well-coordinated business with all the ingredients of good management—customer service, empowerment, emphasis on quality, training, and a team focus. To become a low-cost producer, the firm concentrates on three ideas: the classless corporation, universal education, and freedom to act.

In Chaparral's classless organization, top management treats employees like adults. Workers receive a salary and bonus based on their performance, company profits, and new skills learned. They don't have to punch a time clock and can set their own lunch hours and breaks. They can park where they wish and walk through executives' offices to get to their spotless locker room.

This high degree of freedom and trust placed in the workers motivates them to take the initiative, use their heads, and get the job done. Management further supports this motivational program by helping employees enroll in classes, receive cross-training, and participate in important decisions.

The payoff for all this effort by management is that employees contribute in countless ways to the success of the business. Two maintenance workers invented a machine for strapping together bundles of steel rods that cost only $60,000 compared to $250,000 for the old machines and did the job faster. Other employees developed technology that manufactures a product with just 8 to 12 passes versus traditional methods that required up to 50 passes. The effect has spilled over to the customer service area, where the employee motto is "to be the easiest steel company in the world to deal with."

CEO Gordon Forward says, "Real motivation comes from within. People have to be given the freedom to succeed or fail." The results at Chaparral certainly support this statement.

Questions

1. *What management functions are most important at an organization like Chaparral Steel?*
2. *How does motivation affect productivity at Chaparral Steel?*
3. *In your opinion, what is the main motivating force at Chaparral Steel? Why?*

CHAPTER

ORGANIZATIONAL STRUCTURE

When you have studied this chapter, you will be able to:

1. Identify eight types of strategic objectives.
2. Explain the difference between horizontal coordination and vertical coordination.
3. Describe specialization, job scope, and job depth.
4. Discuss authority and its components.
5. Describe the five ways of creating departments.
6. Describe three special forms of organizational structure, the profit center, committee organization, and matrix organization.
7. Discuss the importance of organizational culture.

Marvin L. Woodall, the independent-minded president of Johnson & Johnson Interventional Systems Company, doesn't check very often with his bosses, who are located at J&J's worldwide headquarters only an hour's drive away. When speaking about his international business trips, he says, "I just go. I don't ask permission. I'm almost never distracted by J&J management."

The presidents of J&J's 166 separately chartered companies are expected to act independently. They decide who will work for them and what products they will produce. They determine how much research and development their companies will conduct. They also prepare budgets and marketing plans. While they are ultimately accountable to headquarter executives, they rarely see them.

Johnson & Johnson's organizational structure has turned out many success stories. For example, Vistakon, a J&J company that makes Acuvue disposable contact lenses, beat major competitors like Bausch & Lomb to the market by six months or more. Vistakon was so small that its president could make rapid-fire marketing and other business decisions with little interference from headquarters.

Johnson & Johnson believes smaller, self-managing units are more manageable. Its decentralized structure makes it quicker to react to specialized markets and more accountable to its customers. In fact, J&J's extremely diverse mix of products almost demands a decentralized organizational structure.

Many other companies striving to be more competitive are trying to copy J&J's organizational structure. Du Pont is drastically trimming its middle management ranks and giving those who remain a lot more responsibility. Pepsico is pushing decisions to the lower levels, and Procter & Gamble is increasing individual managers' responsibilities. These companies believe decentralization will help them speed products to customers at lower cost.

However, Johnson & Johnson has found that its highly decentralized structure also has a downside. It frequently needs to fine-tune its approach to achieve a balance of entrepreneurial spirit and corporate structure. As it prepares for intense global competition in the 21st century, the company is trying to share more services among units, cut duplication among its sales force, and smooth relationships with its largest customers. For example, by establishing "customer support centers," Johnson & Johnson hopes to keep big retailers happy and reduce its own sales force.[1]

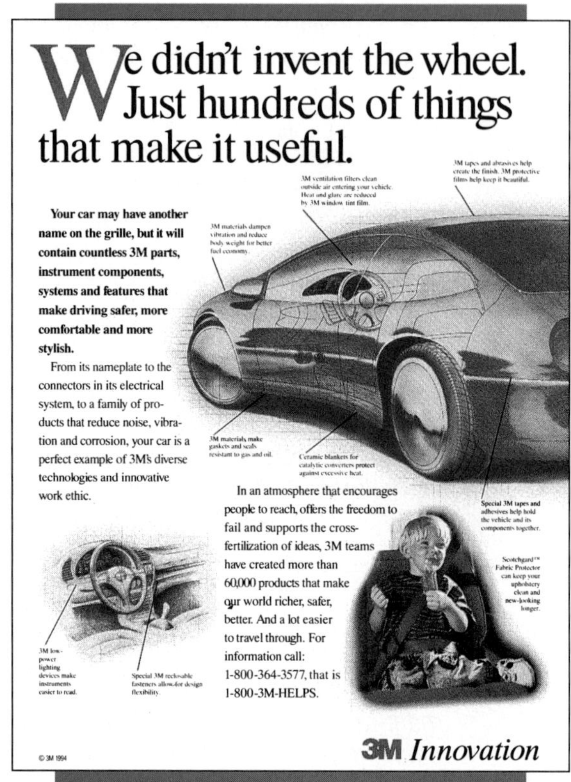

3M has a strong focus on technology. It developed Post-it note pads and many other unique products. Being a leader in innovation is one of 3M's primary objectives. To achieve its goal to innovate, 3M directs its organizational structure toward research and development.

A fundamental task of every manager is to organize the work, actions, and efforts of all people involved in the business—employees, subordinate managers, and collaborators. This chapter focuses on the organizing process used to group tasks and activities into the most effective organizational structure possible.

ORGANIZATION OBJECTIVES: THE FOUNDATION OF STRUCTURE

As you learned in Chapter 7, *objectives* are desired levels of achievement. One of the primary objectives of 3M Company, for example, is to be a leader in innovation. To achieve this goal, 3M has geared its organizational structure toward research and development. The result has been Post-it note pads, Ultrathon insect repellent, and a host of other unique products.

Thus, organization objectives serve as the foundation for planning organizational structure. **Organizational structure** is a formal grouping of employees and their tasks into logical working arrangements that will maximize the achievement of the organization's objectives.

Organizational structure
A formal grouping of employees and their tasks into logical working arrangements that will maximize the achievement of the organization's objectives.

In Chapter 5, we explained that the *business mission* defines what the company's business is and how the company will operate the business. The business mission is the company's primary strategic objective. *Strategic objectives* like the business mission are broad statements about what the organization wants to accomplish in its long-term future.

Strategic objectives set by top-level managers influence organizational structure at all levels of the company. When setting strategic objectives, managers generally consider the following issues which apply equally to large and small organizations:

1. *Innovation:* objectives that state intentions to develop new products or production techniques
2. *Managerial performance and development:* objectives that indicate desired levels of management productivity and growth
3. *Market standing:* objectives that set targets for market share and the organization's niche, or position, relative to competitors
4. *Physical and financial resources:* objectives that specify the acquisition, use, and maintenance of physical and capital resources
5. *Productivity:* objectives that set desired levels of production efficiency
6. *Profitability:* objectives that specify desired profit levels and other financial targets
7. *Public responsibility:* objectives that indicate the company's responsibility to its customers and to society at large
8. *Worker performance and attitudes:* objectives that pertain to desired employee achievements and work attitudes.[2]

Hierarchy of objectives
An arrangement of objectives beginning with the company's broad, long-term strategic objectives and ending with increasingly specific, shorter-range employee objectives.

A company identifies its major strategic objectives after it has considered each of these eight issues. Then it breaks down these objectives into smaller, more specific objectives toward which employees can work comfortably. Management theorists suggest creating a **hierarchy of objectives**, beginning with the company's broad, long-term strategic objectives and ending with increasingly specific, shorter-range employee objectives. The strategic objectives may be broken down into major objectives for various divisions, plants, departments, work groups, projects, and, finally, employees. Thus, if each employee meets his or her objective, the group will meet its objective. If each group meets its objective, the department objective will be satisfied. The process continues until the achievement of division objectives ensures that the overall company objectives will be met. Organizational structure thus typically corresponds to the hierarchy of objectives.

ORGANIZING: A STARTING POINT

As we saw in Chapter 7, organizing is the process of creating formal relationships among tasks, activities, and people in the organization. Exhibit 8.1 illustrates the steps in the organizing process. As the exhibit shows, two basic factors guide managers in this effort. These are *horizontal coordination* between tasks and activities and *vertical coordination* among people.

HORIZONTAL COORDINATION

The first step in designing an effective organizational structure is to focus on the various activities required to reach the company's objectives. Henri Fayol (see Chapter 7) described the essential principles for achieving coordination as division of work, unity of direction, and subordination of individual interests to general interests.

At a huge company like Johnson & Johnson, thousands of tasks and activities must be completed. Some of them pertain to developing new products, some to selling, some to tracking financial information, and some to manufacturing.

Managers are concerned with the division of work, that is, grouping some of these activities into a particular job that a single person can perform. Managers must be careful when grouping these activities, because a job can be either too broad or too narrow. If a job has too many different types of activities, it will be hard for the employee to master the job. Alternatively, if the job is too narrow (specialized), the employee will find it boring and monotonous. In any event, organizational structure begins when jobs are created with specific sets of activities assigned to them.

Exhibit 8.1 **HORIZONTAL AND VERTICAL COORDINATION**

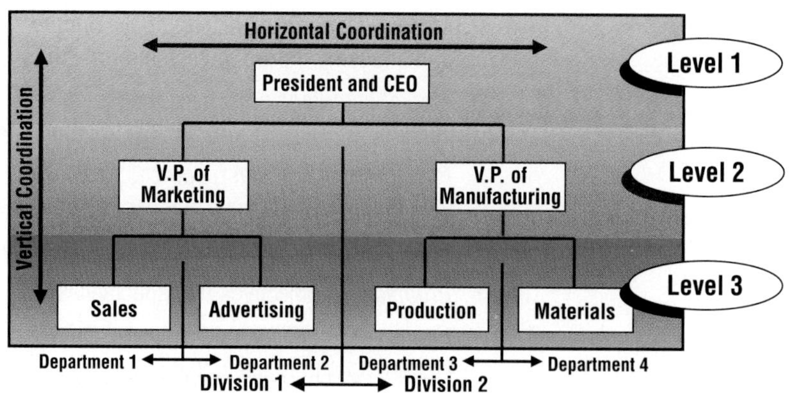

Once jobs have been created, managers must establish unity of direction by coordinating the jobs with one another. *Unity of direction* means providing for necessary communication, eliminating duplication of activities, and ensuring that all employees will work toward the same objectives. As Exhibit 8.1 shows, the most basic way to achieve unity of direction is to group jobs that share similar activities into departments. Thus, jobs that involve contacting customers who have already purchased the product might be grouped into a department called "customer relations." One set of jobs might involve conducting a satisfaction survey following the sale. Another set of jobs might be following up on customer complaints. Unity of direction among these jobs will be enhanced by the fact that they are performed in the same department.

VERTICAL COORDINATION

While a good deal of coordination is achieved by grouping activities and jobs into departments, conflicts, disagreements, and confusion will often occur. This is especially true when department objectives differ or when employees and managers disagree about objectives and how to achieve them. It is also true when there are a great many different jobs, departments, and divisions.

Consider the huge difficulty of coordinating the vast array of activities at Johnson & Johnson. In many cases, one J&J company may not know what another is doing. Imagine the confusion and loss of effectiveness that result when two J&J companies develop competing products, such as Carefree and Stayfree sanitary products. Such confusion is routine when retailers are visited by dozens of Johnson & Johnson sales representatives.

As Exhibit 8.1 illustrates, vertical coordination is achieved by assigning increasing levels of authority going from the bottom to the top of the organization. Fayol called this system the *chain of command* and referred to the principles of authority, responsibility, discipline, and unity of command. More authority allows a division manager to dictate answers to problems between two departments. More authority lets a manager demand a solution to a disagreement between employees. Increasing levels of authority also ensure that the general interests of the company are not put below an individual's specific interests. We discuss authority in more detail later in this chapter.

We can see, then, that a key objective in organizational structure is coordination. Coordination must be achieved both horizontally and vertically within the company. Although horizontal and vertical coordination may seem like entirely separate issues, managers most often consider them together as they design effective structures.

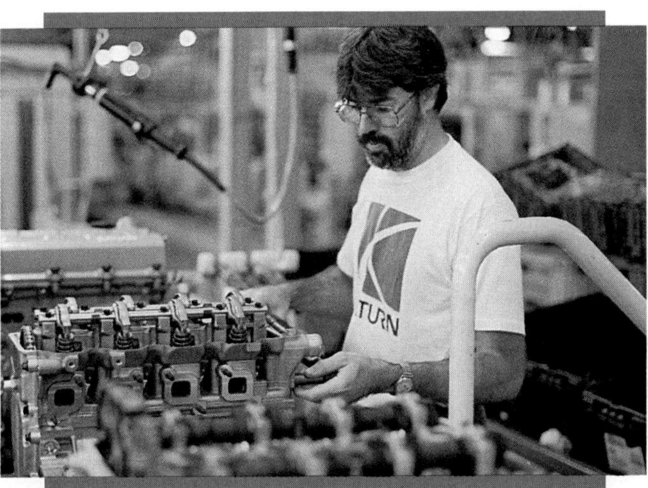

Saturn Corporation says it's a new kind of company—and according to most of its employees, it is. One employee in the Saturn plant in Tennessee said this about his role in Saturn's power train operations:

> *I like sports. And right now I feel like I imagine pro basketball players feel—they're doing exactly what they like to do and getting paid for it. That's the way it is at Saturn. People depending on each other. People pulling in the same direction. It feels good.*
>
> *After a while, at most places, work is just work, and it can get boring. But here it's like I'm waiting for the alarm clock to go off in the morning. Because every day I'm doing something different. And my input is just as important as anyone else's.*[3]

From his point of view, the job has a good deal of both job scope and depth. The importance of these job components is not lost on this employee. He seems motivated to work and to be productive on the job.

DESIGNING JOBS

Job design
A conscious effort to group activities and tasks into logical units of work.

Job design is a conscious effort to group activities and tasks into logical units of work. One of the first steps in designing jobs is to decide how many activities to allocate to any single job.

SPECIALIZATION

The smaller the variety of activities and tasks in a job, the more specialized the job is. Highly specialized jobs may consist of only one or two activities that are performed during the entire workday. This was commonly the case during the early 20th century, with the onset of assembly line production. Employees who worked in automobile assembly plants spent hours doing simple, repetitive jobs. One job might have been to put a windshield in each car that passed the work station. After doing this a few hundred or a few thousand times, employees became highly skilled at this job. However, many employees also became very bored and lost interest in their performance.

Still, job specialization to some extent is necessary in most organizations. There are three fundamental reasons for specializing jobs. First, rarely does any one person have the wide range of highly developed skills necessary for performing the entire array of tasks in a company. At Johnson & Johnson tasks include research, chemistry, package design, advertising, tracking revenues and expenses, shipping, inventorying, and countless other jobs. Although no one person possesses every skill, most individuals have certain skills that allow them to master a smaller, specialized set of activities.

Exhibit 8.2 **RELATIONSHIP BETWEEN JOB SCOPE AND DEPTH**

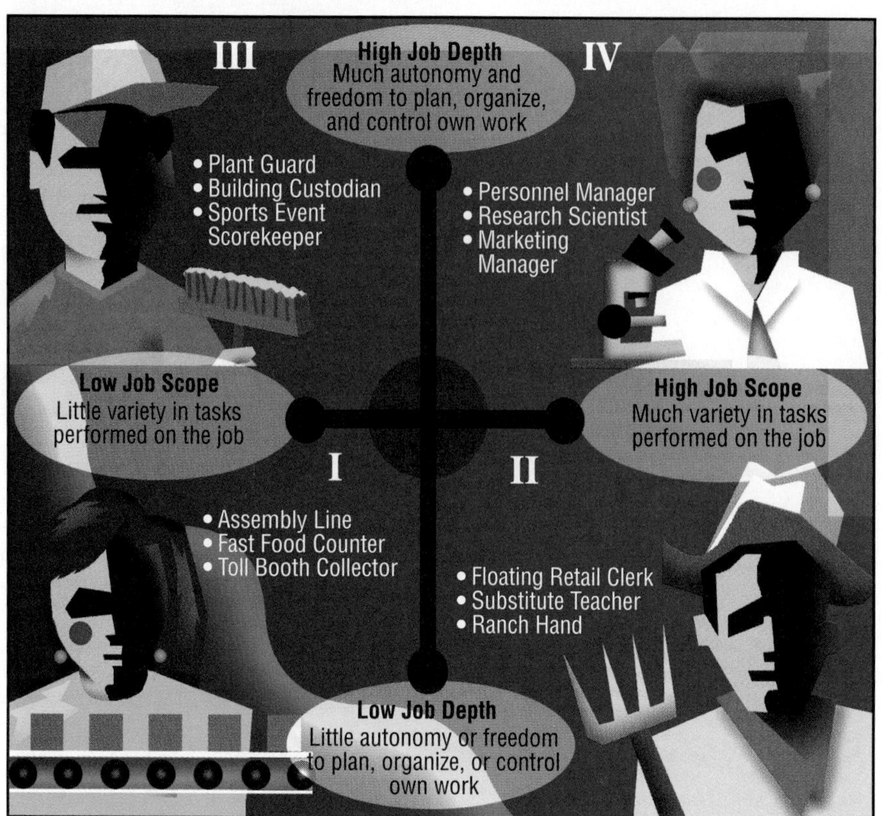

Second, the production of complex products and services requires the use of knowledge from several fields. Knowledge of medicine, chemical engineering, production, finance, and dozens of other fields are required at Johnson & Johnson. Even in less diversified companies like United Parcel Service (UPS), many fields of knowledge are required, such as human resources management, computer programming, communications technology, advertising, and others.

Third, specialization increases productivity. As employees become skilled in the limited variety of activities they perform, they can reach high levels of productivity. Since they perform the same physical and mental activities again and again, they acquire efficiency. In grocery stores, for example, checkers and baggers, who perform repetitive jobs, can quickly and efficiently process customers' orders.

Of course, one disadvantage of specialization is the loss of motivation due to boredom. Stockers, baggers, and checkers are often seen slacking off, perhaps playing games to break the monotony. Excessive specialization also leads to increased absenteeism, tardiness, and, in extreme cases, employee sabotage (e.g., theft).

BALANCING JOBS AND PEOPLE

Job scope
The variety of tasks that are included within a job.

The solution to the conflict between achieving the efficiency associated with highly specialized jobs and losing motivation is to make jobs have enough variety to be interesting and challenging, yet be specialized enough that individuals can become skilled at them. Two methods for accomplishing this are to increase job scope and to enhance job depth. **Job scope** refers

Job depth
The degree of responsibility, autonomy, and freedom an individual has in planning, organizing, and controlling his or her own work.

to the variety of tasks that are included within a job. **Job depth** refers to the degree of responsibility, autonomy, and freedom an individual has in planning, organizing, and controlling his or her own work.

Exhibit 8.2 illustrates the relationship between job scope and job depth. The jobs in quadrant I are low in both job scope and job depth. Individuals performing these jobs have little to say about how their jobs are performed, and their tasks are short and repetitive. Jobs in fast-food restaurants, in tollbooths, and on many assembly lines tend to be low in scope and depth. The jobs in quadrant II involve a wide variety of tasks that require few responsibilities. Although most decisions are made by the employees' bosses, the workers at least get to switch from one task to another during the course of the day. In quadrant III, jobs have little task variety, but employees are responsible for deciding when and how to do their tasks. Plant guards and building custodians have these kinds of jobs. Finally, quadrant IV jobs are high in both job scope and job depth. Managers, research scientists, and many service employees who belong to self-managed work teams have jobs like these.

The proper mix of job scope and job depth can add to a company's productivity and profitability because it balances the needs of people with the demands of their jobs. Wal-Mart Stores, Inc., one of the nation's largest and most profitable retailers, began as a small department store owned by the late Sam Walton. Wal-Mart eventually grew into a chain of more than 2,000 stores with $67.3 billion in annual sales.[4] Jobs at the store manager level are high in job scope and job depth, while jobs at the lowest clerical level have less scope and depth. Obviously, good job design at Wal-Mart has helped create an organizational structure that promotes productivity and growth.

FOCUS ON COMPANY

Wal-Mart Stores, Inc.

One of the marvels of Wal-Mart is that its huge size—over 2,000 stores and $67.3 billion in annual sales—hasn't led to the kind of bureaucracy that slows down other giant companies. Part of Wal-Mart's success is rooted in its folksy culture created by founder Sam Walton. Part of its success is also found in management's "bias for action" philosophy that filters down from the top executives to the lowest-level cashiers.

Still another important part of Wal-Mart's success is the way the company has designed its jobs. Department managers in the stores are expected to act as entrepreneurs, each running his or her own business. They receive the support and the information they need to perform their demanding jobs. This includes profit-and-loss statements, information on inventory turnover, and sufficient budgets.

Department managers are encouraged to experiment with their operations. The famous greeters who welcome shoppers to Wal-Mart and offer them shopping carts was the result of such an experiment. If the experiments don't work, no one is punished, unless the same mistake is made twice.

Sam Walton preferred to give his store managers considerable job depth. When Wal-Mart was still a small operation, Claude Harris, who was managing one of two Fayetteville stores, made a deal with McKesson-Robbins to buy health and beauty aids at unusually low prices. He wanted to create the first discount department in Wal-Mart. When he approached Sam Walton about his idea, Walton said to go ahead and try it. Many innovative ideas at Wal-Mart were the result of such job depth designed into managers' jobs.

The effectiveness of Wal-Mart's well-designed jobs is evident in employees' attitudes and motivation. Employees truly believe they are collaborators rather than employees.

Exhibit 8.3 **CHAIN OF COMMAND**

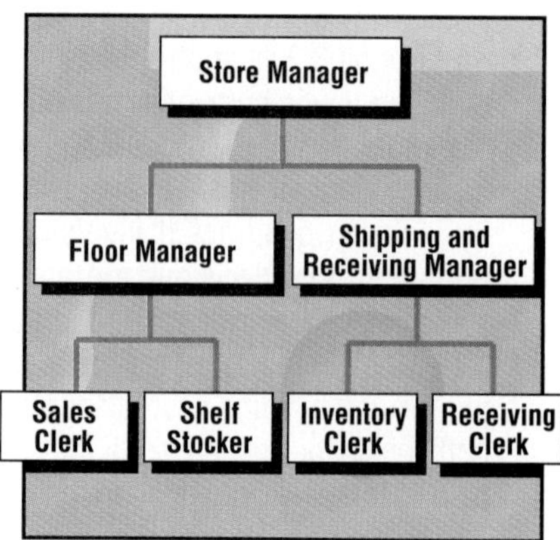

DELEGATING AUTHORITY

Delegating is the process of assigning authority to someone else. *Authority* is one of the basic means of achieving coordination between jobs and departments. It is a major factor in organizational structure. Authority often is confused with power, but in fact they differ.

Power
The ability to influence another person's behavior.

Authority
The right to make decisions due to the organization's delegation of that right.

Power is the ability to influence another person's behavior. This ability exists because one person is stronger than another or controls resources another person wants. Power often is viewed as coercive—stemming from force—or illegitimate influence. **Authority** refers to the right to make decisions due to the organization's delegation of that right. Thus, authority more often is viewed as legitimate, and the manager's power arises more because of the delegation of authority than because the manager is stronger than subordinates.

Some authority is assigned to nearly all jobs, but some jobs carry very little authority. Often this is because the manager is afraid to trust employees who perform the job, or simply because the manager thinks he or she must make all decisions as part of a manager's duties. But in some companies, such as Johnson & Johnson and Wal-Mart, employees are often quite capable of making job-related decisions. Decision-making authority, then, can be delegated by managers to lower levels in the company. As this happens, employees become more motivated and develop better attitudes toward their jobs.

Delegation of authority also affects four other aspects of the organizational structure: the chain of command, unity of command, span of control, and line/staff relationships.

CHAIN OF COMMAND

Chain of command
An unbroken hierarchy of authority that links managers and subordinates.

The **chain of command** is an unbroken hierarchy of authority that links managers and subordinates. Exhibit 8.3 is a partial organization chart that shows one chain of command (organization charts are discussed later in this chapter). In this chart, the sales clerk to floor manager to store manager (the dashed line) is one link in the chain of command. But other links exist as well. The entire chain of command also coordinates jobs at the same level. For example, the sales clerk is linked to the shelf stocker through their common superior, the floor manager. Similarly, the floor manager and the shipping and receiving manager are linked through their common manager, the store manager. Delegation of authority flows along the chain, communication and coordination follow the chain, and disagreements are resolved according to the authority points in the chain.

UNITY OF COMMAND

Unity of command
A principle of organizing stating that each employee should be responsible to only one manager.

The principle of **unity of command** states that each employee should be responsible to only one manager. If an employee has, say, two managers, one manager might instruct the employee to perform activity A, while the other manager commands the employee to complete activity B. Such conflict in instruction would lead to confusion and probably to poor morale on the part of the employee. Exhibit 8.3 indicates that each employee does in fact have one—and only one—supervisor. Thus, the chain of command and unity of command go together and lead to high levels of coordination among employees, departments, and divisions.

SPAN OF CONTROL

Span of control
The number of subordinates who report directly to a manager.

Span of control refers to the number of subordinates who report directly to a manager. Since authority and effective communication along the chain of command are key ingredients of effective coordination, managers should not have too many employees reporting directly to them. If the number of subordinates is too large, authority is weakened. As managers' time becomes too greatly divided, they will not have time to spend with each subordinate.

Early management writers suggested that appropriate spans of control range between 8 to 12 subordinates for lower-level managers and 4 for top-level managers. This structure led to fairly centralized organizations and many layers of management. Today, however, we realize there are many ways to coordinate employee efforts that increase the effectiveness of the span of control. Johnson & Johnson is but one example where managers control much larger numbers of employees. Whenever authority is delegated downward to employees, and when employees work in teams, the span of control can be successfully increased.

Decentralized organizations, then, tend to rely on the exercise of more authority by employees and employee work teams. Coordination among employees and teams occurs more informally from the employees and teams themselves rather than from the chain of command and management control. This increased span of control seems to satisfy both managers and employees and lead to higher productivity.

LINE/STAFF RELATIONSHIPS

Line-and-staff organization
A structure that combines the direct flow of vertical (line) authority with staff who specialize in a limited set of activities that support the line activities.

Line departments
Departments that perform activities directly associated with company objectives, such as production, marketing, finance, and customer service departments.

Staff departments
Departments that perform specialized activities that support line departments in activities such as human resources management, engineering, and accounting.

The fourth consideration when dividing authority among employees and managers is special cases involving exceptional skills or unusual knowledge. Examples of activities that require special skills are testing, hiring, and training employees. Although managers could perform these activities to some extent, a person with specialized knowledge would do so more effectively. The organizational solution to this problem is to create a set of "advisory" managers called *staff managers.*

The **line-and-staff organization**, found in most companies, is a structure that combines the direct flow of vertical (line) authority with staff who specialize in a limited set of activities that support the line activities. Line managers, departments, and employees are involved in activities directly associated with company objectives. **Line departments** typically include production, marketing, finance, and customer service departments. **Staff departments** support line departments in activities such as human resources management (testing, training, benefits), engineering, and accounting.

The major difference between line and staff departments is the nature of their authority. Line managers have full authority to make decisions about all activities affecting their operations. Staff managers can only consult with line managers and advise them regarding the specialized activities in which they have been trained. In the typical line-and-staff organization, line managers may use or ignore this advice.

Exhibit 8.4 **LINE-AND-STAFF ORGANIZATION**

Plant Manager
Assistant to Plant Manager for Human Resources
Production Department
Customer Service
Marketing Department
Tool Maintenance
Assembly
Materials Inventory
Sales
Advertising and Promotion
Staff relationship **Line relationship**

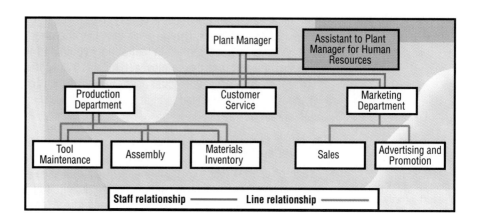

Exhibit 8.4 shows the authority relationship between line and staff departments. In this partial organizational chart, human resources management is a staff department. The dotted line running from the human resources department to the production, customer service, and marketing departments indicates that human resources management has no authority over the line departments. However, staff managers tend to follow the chain of command when working with lower-level departments. In this example, the human resources manager will go through the production department manager before consulting with the materials inventory manager.

DEPARTMENTALIZATION

Departmentalization
The logical grouping of jobs into distinct units located within the organizational structure.

Now that we have looked at horizontal coordination among tasks and activities and vertical coordination among people, let's see how departments are created. **Departmentalization** is the logical grouping of jobs into distinct work units located within the organizational structure. Grouping jobs into departments promotes efficiency. For instance, jobs might be grouped according to the kinds of skills used, such as a paint department, a tool design department, and a maintenance department, among others. Employees within these departments will use similar skills and can assist and learn from one another.

Five major methods for creating departments have been identified: grouping jobs by function, product, location, customer, and process. As Exhibit 8.5 shows, a company may use all five methods when creating departments, depending on its need.

DEPARTMENTALIZING BY FUNCTION

The most common method of grouping tasks into major departmental units is by the function performed. Functional departments in a typical company include finance, marketing, production, human resources, and research and development. This method groups jobs according to similar activities. For instance, all employees in the finance department will perform activities related to investments and business opportunities. Employees in the marketing department will engage in activities related to customers, such as selling, advertising, and public relations.

The principal advantages of functional departmentalization are simplification of training, coordination among employees, and common objectives. But there are some disadvantages as well, including possible overspecialization among employees and a lack of innovative ideas. Managers need to balance these factors when considering functional departmentalization.

Exhibit 8.5 **FORMS OF DEPARTMENTALIZATION IN ONE COMPANY**

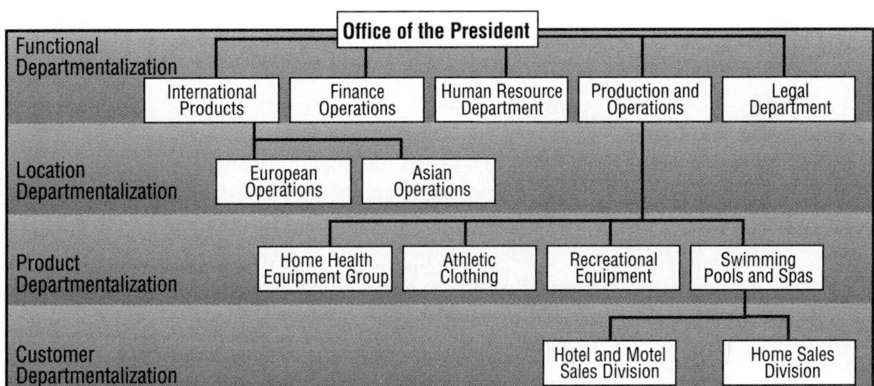

DEPARTMENTALIZING BY PRODUCT

Often jobs are grouped according to the types of products made. This method is especially appropriate for companies that manufacture a wide range of products, such as Johnson & Johnson. With such diverse products as disposable contact lenses, birth control pills, baby oil, toothbrushes, and Band-aids, structuring the company by product can avoid considerable confusion. Nearly all large corporations have at least some product divisions, such as Marriott Hotels and Resorts, Residence Inns, Fairfield Inns, and Roy Rogers Restaurants at Marriott Corporation.

A major advantage of creating product departments is that each product line has more independent authority. What works for making and selling Band-aids may be totally inappropriate for making and selling disposable contact lenses. Both the materials used and the distribution outlets differ for each product.

The product structure also permits faster response to customer and competitor changes. The presidents of Johnson & Johnson's independent companies emphasize this strategic advantage.

However, it is difficult for upper-level management to control independent product divisions. There is much duplication of effort, especially in sales. When dozens of sales representatives call on the same retailer, the retailer may wonder if the company knows what it is doing. Coordination of efforts among product divisions, then, is a major problem with this form of departmentalization.

DEPARTMENTALIZING BY LOCATION

Many organizations form departments based on the geographic locations where work activities are performed. The most obvious advantage to departmentalizing by location is that decision making can focus on local customers and competitors. Also, communication with local customers and collaborators is improved, since the operation will probably be staffed with local employees who are familiar with the geographic area. Departmentalization by location is common in companies with international operations that must deal with differing local customs, languages, and cultures.

However, it is difficult to maintain control of operations that may be continents away from headquarters. It is also difficult to take advantage of centralized functions like purchasing and human resources management.

FOCUS ON COMPETITORS

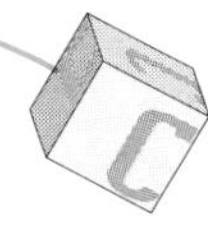

AMP Inc.

AMP Inc. is a rather unusual company. Although it ranks 150th on the Fortune 500 industrial list, few people have heard of it. But its competitors have. AMP is four times the size of its nearest competitor and outsells its Japanese and German rivals—even in Japan and Germany.

AMP is headquartered in Harrisburg, Pennsylvania, but gets 60 percent of its revenues from 30 wholly owned foreign subsidiaries. It controls about 18 percent of the $17-billion-a-year world market in electronic connectors. These connectors include insulated copper leads that link wires to circuit boards in IBM and Apple computers and entire connector systems that couple a car's on-board computers to the engine and transmission.

AMP established its commanding lead in the industry by creating a global organizational structure before its competitors did. Its market-leading Japanese operation began in 1957. Now every single automobile that Japan manufactures contains AMP connectors.

All of AMP's foreign operations, from Malaysia to Ireland, are locally managed. Most operations have their own engineering and production departments, so AMP can quickly detect customer needs and design, manufacture, and deliver new products while competitors are still scratching their heads. Local ties are so close that many overseas customers don't even know AMP has U.S operations. AMP sales engineers and product designers sit down with customers to help design the customers' products. This helps them determine which AMP subsystems can be designed into the customers' products. Sometimes it is hard to tell whether the customer is really a customer or a collaborator. General Electric, one of AMP's customers, was so impressed with AMP's customer service techniques that it studied the company to improve its own management practices.

DEPARTMENTALIZING BY CUSTOMER

Sometimes companies create organizational structures that serve the needs of especially important customers. A common example is a manufacturer that produces both its own brand of a product and another brand for a large retailer like Sears. For instance, Whirlpool makes its own brand of washers and dryers and also makes Sears's Kenmore brand. Because Sears is such a large customer, some manufacturers may create divisions called the "Sears Division."

Sometimes a group of customers create the need for a special division. For instance, selling products to large sporting goods stores such as SportsTown may pose unique problems or opportunities that differ from those of a company's other customers. In this case, the company may have a marketing division called "Sporting Goods Store Sales."

By creating customer-based departments, a company helps its salespeople better understand the unique needs of important groups of customers. However, coordination among customer-based divisions is sometimes difficult. Each customer division will make its own customers a priority, which may reduce cooperation among the divisions.

DEPARTMENTALIZING BY PROCESS

A less common method for creating departments is to group activities by process. For example, manufacturing large machinery often involves processes such as heat rolling, stamping, and casting. Each of these processes is quite complex and probably requires expensive equipment. Also, the equipment may take up a lot of plant space. Thus, the manufacturer may choose

STREET SMART

National Cultures Dictate Company's Actions

In today's global economy, corporations manufacture and market their products in many areas outside their home countries. U.S. companies marketing world brands like Coca-Cola have thrived in the international marketplace. To remain competitive, many companies have given their organizational structures an international focus.

Managing in the global organization has some unique problems that require managers to be street smart. For example, the chief executive officer (CEO) of a major Japanese manufacturer recently canceled several important meetings to attend the funeral of one of his company's local dealers. When Kenichi Ohmae, an international consultant, asked if he would have done the same for a dealer in Belgium who did a larger volume of business each year than his late counterpart in Japan, the CEO firmly replied no. At most he would have sent a letter of condolence. In Japan, however, tradition dictated that the CEO attend the funeral.

But Japanese tradition isn't everything, Ohmae reminded the CEO. After all, the CEO was the head of a global organization, not just a Japanese one. By violating the principle of equidistance—viewing all key customer accounts as equally distant from the corporate center—his attendance at the funeral made it seem like some customers were more important than others. He was sending the wrong signals and reinforcing the wrong values. The primary rule of equidistance is to see—and to think—global first.

to create a heat-rolling department, a stamping department, and a casting department. In this structure, all the equipment and employees involved in each process will be housed together.

The primary advantage of this method is that it groups employees with similar skills and minimizes space requirements. However, if the product is large, getting it from one process location to another may be a problem.

THE ORGANIZATION CHART

Organization chart
Diagram illustrating the chain of command, division of work activities, and departmentalization within the organization.

Organizational structures often are quite complex and hard to visualize. For this reason, most companies use an **organization chart**, a diagram illustrating the chain of command, division of work activities, and departmentalization within the organization. The "view" of the organization's structure that an organization chart provides helps managers coordinate activities and allows areas of responsibility and authority to be easily identified. The partial organization charts shown in Exhibits 8.1, 8.3, 8.4, and 8.5 show how they create an overview of the entire company.

Centralization
Keeping most authority at the top levels of management and maintaining control through several layers of intermediate management.

However, organization charts may also be misleading. Much of a company's structure is informal, existing in the culture and values of its employees, which cannot be illustrated in a chart. The interpersonal nature of working relationships cannot be shown in an organization chart. Thus, managers must understand that the company's organization chart is only a visual impression of the company's true organization structure.

CENTRALIZATION AND DECENTRALIZATION

The terms *centralization* and *decentralization* refer to the extent to which authority is delegated throughout the company. **Centralized** companies tend to delegate little authority downward

STREET SMART

Problems with Decentralization

Kentucky Fried Chicken had tastier food and happier customers in mind when it kicked off a quality improvement drive for its 2,000 company-owned restaurants two years ago. But the chain's independent regional divisions failed to coordinate their efforts. There was so much duplication of effort that decentralization was not practical.

While there are many good reasons to decentralize, there are also many good reasons not to. Many companies expected decentralizing to save money, but the notion just didn't work out. Says John Humphrey, chair and chief executive of Forum Corporation, a Boston-based training firm, "You don't reduce costs by dividing the problem up and shipping it out of town."

to lower levels. They usually have many layers of intermediate management and a narrow span of control. Control over decisions and activities is confined to top management.

Decentralization
Delegation of considerable authority to lower, operational levels and minimizing the number of intermediate levels of management.

Decentralized companies delegate considerable authority to lower, operational levels. These companies tend to have few layers of intermediate management. The span of control is wide, since there are fewer managers to go around. Middle and supervisory managers have more authority and more leeway in decision making than in centralized companies. Supporters of decentralization believe upper-level control is not lost. Rather, by delegating many decision-making activities, top managers can concentrate on strategic objectives and plans. Finally, decisions about day-to-day operations are made by the supervisors and employees who are closest to those operations.

FOCUS ON COLLABORATORS

Asea Brown Boveri

Asea Brown Boveri (ABB), a manufacturer of electrical equipment headquartered in Zurich, Switzerland, is the leanest, meanest company in the industry—bigger than Westinghouse and ready to take on GE. In four years, CEO Percy Barnevik has added 70 European and U.S. operations. ABB is now a world leader in high-speed trains, robotics, and environmental controls.

Success in this mammoth company has been achieved with just 250 global managers who lead 210,000 employees. One of Barnevik's secrets lies in his advice to cut headquarters staff and decentralize. He says, "Ideally you should have a minimum of staff to disturb the operation people and prevent them from doing their more important jobs." When Barnevik acquires a company, 30 percent of the headquarters staff go into new service companies, 30 percent are absorbed by operating units, and 30 percent are separated from the company. The other 10 percent still hang around headquarters, but some leave later to join other companies.

Lean staffs in decentralized companies like ABB can't handle traditional headquarters' tasks. So things like maintaining detailed personnel records are delegated to line managers, who prefer to keep their own records anyway. Some responsibilities are delegated to suppliers, who now act more like true collaborators. Building fewer but stronger collaborative relationships with suppliers keeps control at the local level rather than at headquarters.

So far, decentralization and a few twists are working at ABB. The company is profitable, effective, and growing.

OTHER ORGANIZATIONAL STRUCTURES

The simplest methods of organizing are the line and line-and-staff organizations. These are traditional organizational structures that follow established principles such as span of control, specialization, and chain of command. However, the business world today is more complex than it was when these principles were created. Many successful companies have developed special structures that adapt or even ignore traditional principles. Three organizational structures that serve special purposes are the profit center, the committee organization, and the matrix organization.

THE PROFIT CENTER

Profit center
A highly independent unit or division that is given broad decision-making authority as long as it makes acceptable profits.

The **profit center** concept of organizational structure creates highly independent units or divisions and gives them broad decision-making authority as long as they make acceptable profits. This approach decentralizes authority but holds operating managers responsible for generating profits. Johnson & Johnson uses this structure to some extent. Its 166 companies are all expected to produce profits, and as long as they do, headquarters staff stay away. J&J presidents run their own companies as though they were their own and make decisions without interference. Of course, the organization chart looks similar to those we have already seen, but the reason a division or department exists is to make a profit. This gives managers the freedom to pursue any product or any customer without antagonizing other divisions.

Profit centers encourage creativity and high motivation, but they can lead to some conflict among divisions. Also, managers must take care not to focus on profits at the expense of product development and customer service. If managers emphasize only profits, they may ignore long-term investments in R&D or market promotion and actually lower profits.

COMMITTEE ORGANIZATION

Committee organization
A structure in which authority is given to a group of individuals rather than to one person.

Committee organization is a structure in which authority is given to a group of individuals rather than to one person. It is often used at the highest level in the company and is a part of a more traditional line-and-staff structure.

Top-level managers in most organizations are called on to make many difficult decisions and have many demands on their time. Sometimes it is nearly impossible for one CEO to handle all of his or her duties effectively and make all the decisions required of a CEO. Therefore, some companies have created an office of the president position. The *office of the president* includes several executives, usually a president and at least two executive vice-presidents. They work together as a committee to combine their knowledge and experience to arrive at mutually acceptable decisions. Generally the office of the president makes only the most important strategic decisions. Other decisions are made by the individual members as part of their regular duties.

R. H. Macy & Company, the large department store retailer, is using the office of the president concept to help pull itself out of bankruptcy reorganization. When CEO Edward S. Finkelstein resigned under pressure, the board of directors appointed a two-person team to take over. Myron Ullman III and Mark Handler sit at one end of a long wooden table in

Macy's boardroom to reach decisions that affect the company. Their lines of responsibility are relatively clear-cut, but they make decisions together.[5]

Lower-level committees also exist in many companies. These committees work on specific projects and they usually include managers from different areas such as product design, production, and marketing. IBM and Toshiba formed a business alliance to develop liquid crystal displays in color. These two companies are competitors in several product lines, so it was necessary to create positive working relationships in their new joint company, Display Technologies Inc. Work teams were created for specific projects. The members of these teams, drawn from both parent companies, have a common-sense rule for preventing conflicts. They must put a ten-yen coin in a big jar if they mention the names of either parent company during meetings and work sessions.[6]

Committees have considerable authority, but they tend to be somewhat short-lived and often do not appear in the organization chart. They are effective in achieving coordination among functional departments, since their members are from these departments. However, committees tend to be slow, and sometimes their decisions are not very creative. Committees may also arrive at decisions through compromise rather than by pursuing the best alternative.

THE MATRIX ORGANIZATION

Companies that deal with large, complex production and service often choose the *matrix form of organizational structure.* This organizational structure is very common in companies that have many special projects and in high-tech companies that emphasize research and development.

Matrix organization
A structure that is built around a specific project or problem and usually has a line-based manager and a project manager in one work group.

The **matrix organization** is built around specific projects or problems. Employees with different specialized skills and knowledge are assembled from functional departments such as marketing, engineering, production, and finance. These employees combine their skills to work on the project or arrive at solutions to the problem. Each project has a project manager, but each employee is still responsible to the functional area from which she or he came. Thus, an engineer is responsible to the project manager for progress on the project, but the functional engineering manager will likely evaluate the engineer's performance.

Obviously the matrix organization violates the unity of command principle, since the employees on the project have two managers. However, companies that use the matrix structure try to establish distinct areas of responsibility when they create project teams. Thus, achieving coordination between functional managers and project managers is easier than it might appear. Still, since both managers can issue job orders and evaluate the employee's performance, job orders and evaluations may conflict. Therefore, both managers and employees must have good people skills to make the structure work. The dual-authority relationship created by the matrix organization can be effective only if conflicts are handled skillfully.

Asea Brown Boveri uses a matrix form of organizational structure. All employees have a country manager and a business sector manager. Country managers run traditional national companies with local boards of directors. Business sector managers track industry statistics and ensure coordination among countries. The matrix structure exists only at the top level, and employees are not bothered by it. Managers who are affected prefer it, since it maintains the local culture but keeps them tied to the global market.

Among the many companies that have successfully used the matrix structure are Sun Information Services, Boeing, Shell Oil, Dow Chemical, Chase Manhattan Bank, Procter & Gamble, and Lockheed Aircraft. The most famous example is one of the earliest organizations to perfect the approach, the National Aeronautics and Space Administration (NASA). While thousands of mechanical engineers, electrical engineers, aeronautical engineers, and other technicians worked for NASA in functional departments, NASA also recognized the importance of combining these skills for specific projects like the Mercury, Gemini, and Apollo mis-

Exhibit 8.6 **NASA'S MATRIX ORGANIZATION**

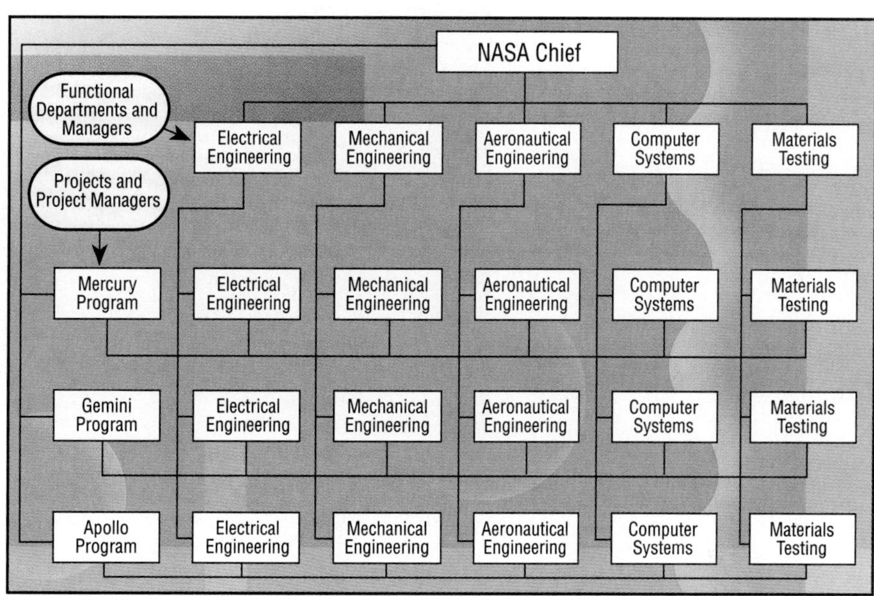

sions. NASA's organization chart would be far too large and complex to include here; Exhibit 8.6 shows an abbreviated version. The functional authority of line managers is crossed by the project lines of authority.

The major advantages of the matrix structure are its flexibility and the ability to concentrate employee skills and knowledge to solve specific, complex problems. But, as already mentioned, it requires excellent human relations skills, especially on the parts of the dual managers, who must avoid confusing and threatening subordinates.

GLOBAL ORGANIZATION

A company must adapt its structure to its environment, especially to the national and regional customs, traditions, and laws that surround it. This is difficult even for companies that do business primarily in one country. However, when companies do business globally, which has become increasingly common, their structures must be unique and creative. For example, the extensive use of work teams and the virtual guarantee of lifetime employment in Japanese firms would be less appropriate in nations like India, where social class distinctions are much larger.

Unique structural arrangements are common in global businesses. For example, Woodward Governor Corporation has widespread operations in England, Germany, Japan, the United States, and other countries. The company regularly rotates managers among these operations, so it is as likely that a Colombian manager will head up an operation in England as it is that an English manager will head up a Colombian plant. This is one of many structural features that help the company maintain a global focus.

As firms have expanded in global operations, they often lack all of the required skills. They need more partnerships and joint ventures to acquire needed skills. These firms may create business unit boundaries that cross national borders. Thus, employees who make decisions in Norway must respond to that marketplace but remain accountable to the basic business unit and to shareholders who may be spread across several European nations.

At Compaq Computers' headquarters, the building's architecture and interior design reflect the company's casual and relaxed organizational culture. Compaq's friendly, relaxed atmosphere is a major reason why many employees choose to work for the company.

ORGANIZATION CULTURE

Organization Culture
A pattern of shared expectations and norms that affects relationships among employees and their individual and group behaviors.

The term *organization culture* refers to a system of shared meaning. Often the unspoken but clearly understood customs within the organization dictate how all employees are expected to behave. The culture of an organization is interwoven with its structure and must be considered part of it. **Organization culture** is a pattern of shared expectations and norms that affects relationships among employees and their individual and group behaviors. All organizations have commonly accepted values, rituals, and behavior patterns that have emerged over time. These shared values and patterns affect how employees think about the organization and how they are likely to respond to it. When faced with problems, employees are likely to do what the organization culture suggests is the "correct" thing.

Since it is a shared system and contains statements about what employees are expected to do, the organization culture promotes coordination and cooperation among employees. If the shared values are strongly held and are positive for the company, the organization culture will promote motivation and positive job attitudes. However, if the culture is negative, employees will be less productive. The best organization cultures are consistent with total quality management goals and emphasize productivity, service to customers, less reliance on restrictive work rules, and fewer procedures and controls. These cultures are perceived as friendly and encourage employee loyalty and commitment to the job.

An organization's culture often reflects the vision or mission of the owners and top managers. These people have great influence on the organization's goals, and their behaviors and attitudes flow throughout the company. They project an image of what the company should be, and employees soon perceive it in this manner. Strong cultures, in which most employees strongly hold key values, have greater influence than do weak cultures.

The organization culture often is described as the informal organization that operates behind the formal structure. This culture is not planned but develops out of the interactions of people, both managers and employees.

Most effective companies have distinctive and strong cultures. For example, the culture at Apple Computer emphasizes entrepreneurial spirit and the use of nontraditional authority. Authority rests in employees with expertise and ideas, regardless of their positions. This culture helps ensure coordination among employees, departments, and work groups. A strong organization culture allows shared goals to develop among departments and leads to more cooperation and reduced conflict within the company.[7]

Sometimes, however, a company's culture can have negative effects. Nissan Motor Company's culture, at least among its U.S. dealers, consisted of pessimism and skepticism toward the company. Only 20 percent of the dealers rated a Nissan franchise as an excellent investment. An earlier company motto, "Mr. Dealer, you are my most important customer," was no longer part of Nissan's culture.

Changing a company's culture requires breaking with tradition and overcoming old beliefs and expectations. But this is difficult to do.

Changing a company's culture also is easier if there is some major crisis to be overcome. In this case, employees may work together to save their company and their jobs. At Nissan, change will be helped by the fact that the company is barely profitable and has been consistently losing market share. Finally, changing the culture is easier if some key person pushes for it. At Nissan, Thomas Mignanelli's efforts to change the culture are a key ingredient. Mignanelli, Nissan's U.S. sales and marketing boss, is a popular figure, and his strong personal influence will help dealers acquire the beliefs and expectations he hopes to create in the new culture.

The importance of organization culture is perhaps best illustrated by an excerpt from Sam Walton's memoir, *Made in America: My Story:*

> We don't pretend to have invented the idea of a strong corporate culture. We're constantly doing crazy things to capture the attention of our folks and lead them to think up surprises of their own. We like to see them do wild things in the stores, things that are fun for the customers and fun for the associates. If you're committed to the Wal-Mart partnership and its core values, the culture encourages you to think up all sorts of things to break the mold and fight monotony. I have a cheer I lead whenever I visit a store. For those of you who don't know, it goes like this:
>
> –Give me a W!
> –Give me an A!
> –Give me an L!
> –Give me a Squiggly!
> –(Here, everybody sort of does the twist.)
> –Give me an M!
> –Give me an A!
> –Give me an R!
> –Give me a T!
> –What's that spell?
> –Wal-Mart!
> –Who's No. 1?
> –THE CUSTOMER![8]

SUMMARY

1. ***Identify eight types of strategic objectives.***
   The eight types of strategic objectives relate to innovation, managerial performance and development, market standing, the use of physical and financial resources, desired levels of productivity, profitability, public responsibility, and desired levels of worker performance and attitudes.

These objectives influence organizational structure at the top levels and provide guidelines that influence behavior throughout the organization.

2. ***Explain the difference between horizontal coordination and vertical coordination.***
   Horizontal coordination is grouping activities together into particular jobs that people perform. In this process, the required activities, behaviors, and responsibilities are grouped into meaningful job sets. Vertical coordination involves allocating appropriate amounts of authority and often requires the creation of departments and assigning supervisory or management authority to the leaders. This permits employees and managers to resolve disputes and avoid confusion as they go about performing their individual jobs.

3. ***Describe specialization, job scope, and job depth.***
   Job specialization refers to a reduction in the variety and number of tasks included in any one job. A job that is highly specialized consists of very few tasks that are repeated time after time, while a nonspecialized job contains more tasks that are repeated less often. Job scope refers to the variety of tasks and activities performed in the job. Job depth is the degree of independence an employee has in planning, organizing, and performing the job.

4. ***Discuss authority and its components.***
   Authority is one of the basic means of coordinating among jobs, departments, and managers. It adds depth to jobs and is a primary component of organizational structure. Delegation is the process of assigning authority to someone else. Authority is affected by the chain of command, unity of command, span of control, and line/staff positions. The chain of command is an unbroken hierarchy of authority that links managers and their subordinates. Unity of command is the principle that each employee should be responsible to only one manager. Span of control refers to the number of subordinates a manager supervises. Finally, line employees have a direct flow of vertical authority associated with organizational objectives, while staff employees provide support to line employees and typically have limited authority.

5. ***Describe the five ways of creating departments.***
   The process of creating departments is called departmentalization. The five most common methods of departmentalization are by function, product, location, customer, and process. Grouping jobs according to similar activities is the function method. The product method groups jobs according to the type of product made. Creating departments by location is based on the geographic location where work activities are performed. Grouping by customer may be appropriate when there is either a large single customer or a large group of customers, such as discount stores. The least common method of departmentalizing is by the process used in creating the product or service.

6. ***Describe three special forms of organizational structure, the profit center, committee organization, and matrix organization.***
   A profit center is a highly independent unit or division that is given broad decision-making authority as it makes acceptable profits. This arrangement allows managers to make decisions without interference from top management. Committee organization is a structure in which authority is given to a group of individuals rather than to one person. At the top level, an office of the president structure consists of two or three executives who work together as a committee to reach top level decisions. Lower-level committees also can be created, especially to work on important projects. The matrix organization is built around specific projects or problems that are too large for committees. Project teams are created by grouping employees from functional departments such as engineering, design, production, and finance. These employees are still responsible to their functional departments but concentrate their efforts on the specific project. The matrix structure is commonly used by companies that have many special projects and in high-tech companies that emphasize research and development.

7. Discuss the importance of organizational culture.
The culture of an organization consists of the expectations, behaviors, values, and norms shared among employees and departments. Most companies have strong cultures that establish what is permitted and expected from employees as they perform their jobs. A well-managed culture helps promote coordination among employees, departments, and work groups.

KEY TERMS AND CONCEPTS

Organizational structure (p. 164)
Hierarchy of objectives (p. 165)
Job design (p. 167)
Job scope (p. 168)
Job depth (p. 169)
Power (p. 170)
Authority (p. 170)
Chain of command (p. 170)
Unity of command (p. 171)
Span of control (p. 171)
Line-and-staff organization (p. 171)
Line departments (p. 171)
Staff departments (p. 171)
Departmentalization (p. 172)
Organization chart (p. 175)
Centralization (p. 175)
Decentralization (p. 176)
Profit center (p. 177)
Committee organization (p. 177)
Matrix organization (p. 178)
Organization culture (p. 180)

DISCUSSION QUESTIONS

Company

1. How does a company's strategic objectives affect its organizational structure?
2. When is it appropriate to delegate authority to subordinate employees? Are there times when authority should not be delegated? If so, when are those times?

Customers

3. How might a company take customer needs into account as it decides on an appropriate organizational structure?
4. Chains of command reflect only the relationships between supervisors and subordinates. Where does the customer fit into a company's chain of command?
5. Would a decentralized or a centralized structure be more responsive to customer needs? Why?

Competitors

6. Describe the structure of two competing firms, such as Kmart and Wal-Mart. Why do their structures differ?
7. How can a company's choice of departmentalization method affect its ability to respond to competition?

Collaborators

8. Why do overspecialized jobs tend to decrease employee motivation? Why do companies specialize jobs if such jobs tend to affect employees negatively?
9. How do staff specialists resemble collaborators of the company?
10. How does a company's culture affect its relationships with collaborators?

In Question: Take a Stand

Today's joint ventures and strategic alliances may be just a glimpse into the future of business. The virtual corporation (the popular name for this new phenomenon) is a temporary network of companies that come together quickly to exploit fast-changing opportunities. Companies in a virtual corporation can share costs, skills, and access to global markets, with each partner contributing what it does best. Will arrangements like this have an effect on competition and result in higher prices to consumers? What are some of the advantages and disadvantages to our global business environment?

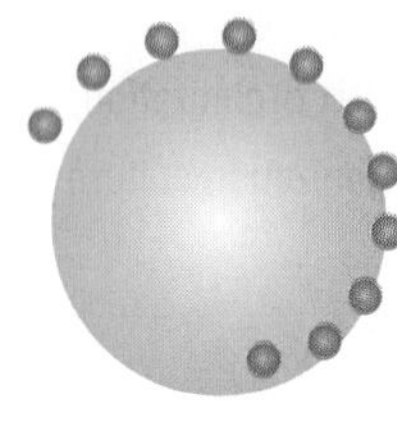

CASE 8.1 HILTON HOTELS CORPORATION[9]

In 1994, Hilton Hotels Corp. announced plans for a reorganization of its internal operations, including the relocation of some functions to Las Vegas.

The new corporate organization includes five key lines of responsibility—Gaming Operations, Hotel Operations, Finance and Administration, Gaming and Hotel Development and Marketing and Strategic Planning.

Gaming Operations and Gaming and Hotel Development will be based in Las Vegas, with Hotel Operations remaining in Beverly Hills. Hilton said it expects to make additional decisions on location of personnel and departments during the second quarter of this year. The direct day-to-day reporting responsibilities for this new organization are to Raymond C. Avansino, Jr., president and chief operating officer.

"This organization highlights the importance of the functions necessary to ensure continued and efficient growth as well as enhancing our leadership position in gaming and hotels," said Barron Hilton, chairman and chief executive officer. "It also allows us to consolidate departments and positions and invest the future of this company in a first-rate senior management team."

Each of the five functions will have responsibility for several operational areas:

- Gaming Operations. In addition to his responsibilities as president and chief operating officer of the company, Avansino will continue to oversee Hilton's domestic and international gaming operations—including Nevada hotel-casinos, riverboats and land-based facilities in Australia, Canada, Uruguay and Turkey.
- Hotel Operations. Hilton is conducting an executive search for the new position of executive vice president–hotel operations. Carl T. Mottek will retire as planned in April 1994 after 42 years with the company.
- Finance and Administration. The company is also conducting a search for an executive vice president–finance and administration. This new position will have increased management duties and will oversee not only finance but legal, information services, purchasing, corporate affairs and other extensive administrative responsibilities.
- Gaming and Hotel Development. All domestic and international gaming and hotel development activities will be directed by F. Michael O'Brien, senior vice president.
- Marketing and Strategic Planning. This new function will be led by Michael A. Ribero, who becomes its senior vice president, after serving as the company's senior vice president–marketing. Included are such responsibilities as corporate marketing, strategic planning and implementation of new business ventures and initiatives.

"One of the exciting prospects of this new organization is that it enables us to employ our best resources to move between our gaming and hotel businesses for the ultimate benefit of both, while putting the groundwork in place to explore new and potentially profitable areas of new business," Hilton said.

The company said the new organization was the result of several months of study and planning and was approved by Hilton's board of directors.

Questions

1. *On what basis is Hilton organized?*
2. *What are the advantages and disadvantages of Hilton's organizational structure?*
3. *Should Hilton's board of directors approve of the "new" organization? Why or why not?*

CHAPTER

9

PRODUCTION, LOGISTICS, AND QUALITY IMPROVEMENT PROCESSES

When you have studied this chapter, you will be able to:

1
Define and describe the nature of production.

2
Describe three factors that are important to increasing productivity.

3
Explain the production planning process.

4
Identify four factors to consider in designing products and services.

5
Explain two common production facility layouts.

6
Describe computer-aided design (CAD), computer-aided manufacturing (CAM), and flexible manufacturing systems (FMSs).

7
Discuss activities associated with logistics and physical distribution.

8
Describe four inventory management techniques.

9
Discuss eight keys to a successful quality improvement program.

According to Fortune *magazine, the most admired company in America is not a fashionable high-tech company or one of the decades-old automobile makers. Rather, it is Rubbermaid Incorporated, the maker of dustpans and drainers.*

The secrets to Rubbermaid's success in business as well as with consumers are innovation and quality production. Rubbermaid doesn't depend on only one product. Instead, it focuses on making small improvements to some 5,000 everyday products—such as mailboxes, storage containers, toys, mops, spatulas, and desk organizers—and then producing high-quality products at low cost. The company's attention to detail is impressive. For example, Rubbermaid learned that some consumers prefer to change their cars' oil themselves but hate getting dirty when the oil misses the pan during draining. So product designers created the Draintainer®, which featured an extra-wide 12-quart oil pan, a screw-on lid, a spigot for easy pouring, and a holder for draining the oil filter. And, like most Rubbermaid products, the Draintainer® container was produced with polymer to be extremely durable.

In fact, Rubbermaid's products are so durable that they almost never need replacing. So the company focus is on new-product development and quality production. CEO Wolfgang Schmitt has set a goal of entering a new-product category every 12 to 18 months. During 1993, Rubbermaid turned out new products at the rate of one a day. Nine out of ten were commercial successes.

Most new-product ideas come from 20 teams, each with 5 to 7 people from marketing, manufacturing, R&D, finance, and other departments. These teams focus on specific product lines, such as bathroom accessories.

Even Rubbermaid's top management sees new-product ideas everywhere. From an exhibit of Egyptian antiquities, CEO Schmitt and Dick Gates, head of Rubbermaid business development, came away with 11 new-product ideas. In their "War Room," they keep samples of competing products so that they can study their good and bad points. At Rubbermaid, attention to product design and quality is the key to successful business.[1]

Exhibit 9.1 **THE PRODUCTION PROCESS**

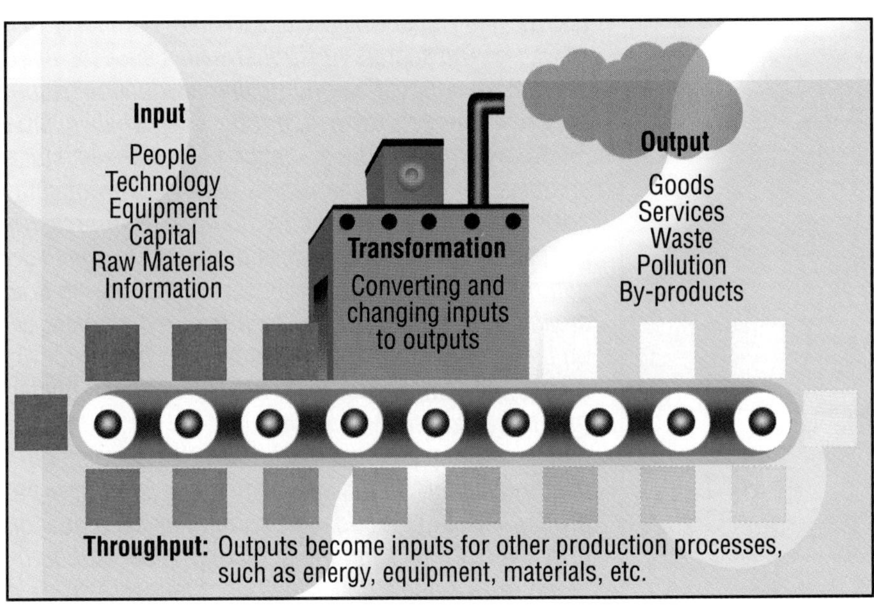

The purpose of this chapter is to describe the production process and various management activities performed in the effective production of goods and services. Rubbermaid is an example of how companies can achieve effective production.

THE IMPORTANCE OF PRODUCTION

Economists argue that a strong production sector is fundamental to a strong America. Political leaders, business executives, and consultants have voiced concern about whether U.S. industry can compete effectively against Japanese and German firms that seem to have the edge in both productivity and quality of consumer goods. Until very recently, U.S. manufacturers in industries like steel, automobiles, computer chips, and electronic goods seemed to be losing the battle. Many believed the United States was becoming too heavy in the service sector and losing jobs and products in the manufacturing sector. Today over 20 percent of total sales of manufactured products sold in the United States are imports—twice as much as in 1970.[2]

But companies like Rubbermaid counter the argument that America has lost its competitive edge. In fact, at many U.S. companies, production of quality goods and services is stronger than ever.

Production
The use of people, capital, and other resources (inputs) to convert raw materials into finished goods and services (outputs).

Production is the use of people, capital, and other resources (inputs) to convert raw materials into finished goods and services (outputs). Production management concerns the activities directly involved in producing the organization's goods or services. Both tangible goods (such as an elevator) and intangible services (such as legal services) require the conversion of inputs into outputs.

Typically the production process is thought of as an input-transformation-output system. Exhibit 9.1 illustrates this system. Inputs in the production system include the people who work for the company and collaborators such as consulting and engineering firms that provide useful services. Various materials, technology, and equipment used during the transformation stage are also important inputs. For example, inputs for a manufacturer of garden hoses include rubber, metal couplings, extruding equipment, inventory holding bins, and, of course, employees.

The transformation of inputs into outputs requires that some inputs perform operations that affect other inputs. In our garden hose example, extruding machines draw rubber, shape and mold it, and perhaps bond it with metal wire for strength. Thus, the extruding machines affect and change the raw material, rubber. The end result is output (transformed input), the finished hose and whatever by-products (waste, pollution) are created in the process. Effective production requires that waste and pollution be minimized, that the goods or services be of high quality, and that a minimum of inputs be consumed (used up) in the process.

MODERN PRODUCTION PROCESSES

The intended result of all production management activities is a high level of productivity. As we explained in Chapter 7, *productivity* means that the outputs (goods and services) are more valuable than the total of inputs consumed in producing them. Productivity is increased by producing more goods and services while using the same number of or fewer inputs. Increases in productivity typically depend on three factors: standardization of parts and processes, specialization of labor, and mechanization of work.[3]

STANDARDIZATION OF PARTS AND PROCESSES

Standardization involves adopting uniform, consistent parts and processes in producing a good or service. If an employee always uses the same type of screw or rivet, time will be saved and skills increased. If, however, the employee uses a different type of screw or rivet for each separate operation, time will be wasted looking for the right tools and parts. Thus, standardization saves both time and costs in the manufacture of many goods today.

The advantages of standardization are highlighted by problems faced by Electrolux, a Swedish appliance maker. Although there are 325 million European consumers, local and regional customs prevent standardization. Northern Europeans want large refrigerators because they shop once a week. But southern Europeans want small ones because they shop for fresh produce each day. Northerners want freezers on the bottom, southerners on the top. Britons insist 60 percent of the refrigerator be devoted to freezer space. In Europe Electrolux is only one of over 100 appliance makers, yet it must produce over 120 basic refrigerator designs with 1,500 variants. Manufacturing expenses necessitated by the great variety of designs have depressed Electrolux's profits for years.[4]

SPECIALIZATION OF LABOR

Specialization was described in Chapter 8 as an element of job design. As noted there, specialization can enhance productivity. As employees become increasingly skilled at the limited variety of activities they perform, they can reach high levels of productivity.

In addition to having employees simply repeat a few rather than many activities, managers of production processes can take other steps. For example, they can conduct time-and-motion studies, in which they carefully observe workers on the job to see exactly what movements they use while performing a task, such as bending over or "grasping" a tool. By doing this, they discover any repetitive movements or unnecessary "small" movements, called *therbligs*.[5] Then they can work to minimize these movements and thus help employees speed up the performance of their tasks. Another form of specialization is collaboration with another organization to perform the work. We address this important issue later in the chapter.

We should note here that standardization of parts and processes and specialization of labor go hand in hand. Without standardized parts and processes, specialization of labor would be much less effective. Together they allow great gains in productivity.

MECHANIZATION OF WORK

A human being is not a natural production tool. Flesh and bones are weak compared to steel, and muscles and brains are slow and undependable compared to robots and computers. Some

Exhibit 9.2 **THE PRODUCTION PLANNING PROCESS**

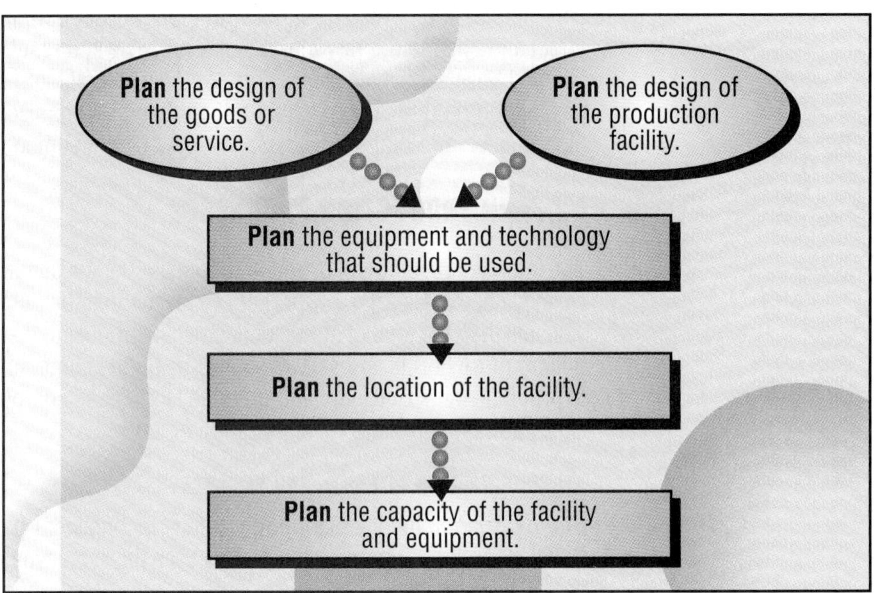

people argue that creativity and flexibility are important production inputs that cannot be replaced by machines, and this is probably true. But when jobs have been greatly specialized and parts and processes highly standardized, the activities to be performed no longer require great amounts of creativity and flexibility. Thus, certain production activities can be mechanized to great advantage. In fact, machines are much better at endless repetitions of identical motions. They can place rivets, drill holes, and so on precisely—and they never find the work boring or tedious.

ASSEMBLY LINE PRODUCTION

Standardization, specialization of labor, and mechanization of work made assembly line production possible. The assembly line process is a technique in which the product passes along a number of work stations, often by means of a conveyor belt. At each work station, only a few specialized actions are performed, using standardized parts. Thus, employees stay put, using endless repetitive motions, and much gets done in short periods of time. As soon as a worker completes his or her tasks, the product moves ahead, making room for the next one, on which the identical tasks are performed. Since most modern goods—and some services—require a great deal of assembly, the assembly line has become a fixture in today's production processes. In fact, when people hear the words *production* and *manufacturing,* they most often think of an assembly line.

However, many advances have been made in production processes during the past 30 years, and the repetitive assembly line is fast disappearing. In its place are a variety of computerized and robotized processes. In addition, both tangible goods and intangible services now receive a great deal more attention in the design stage to simplify both the product and the process by which it is made or serviced.

PRODUCTION PLANNING

The first step in improving production of goods and services is planning that production. Whatever inefficiencies were found in traditional assembly lines were usually caused by poor

Spalding president George Dickerman shows off the company's latest product in the ongoing golf ball wars. "Each new ball has to feel like satin. The stamp has to pop at you. Golfers are turned off by imperfections," he says. This statement underlies the attention Spalding gives to the design and production of its high-quality balls. A new $20 million investment in its production facilities ensures that its quality goals will be met.[6]

planning at some stage. As Exhibit 9.2 illustrates, high-quality, high-volume production requires planning the design of the product or service, the layout of the production facility, the equipment and technology to be used, the location of the facility, and the capacity of the facility and equipment.

DESIGN OF GOODS AND SERVICES FOR PRODUCTIVITY

One of the most important developments in production management is called *design for manufacturability and assembly (DFMA).* Engineers who design goods and services have tended to ignore the difficulties that might arise during the manufacture of the product. While they preferred to use standardized parts, they almost always used too many parts. Thus, an automobile manufactured in the United States had nearly 50 percent more parts than an equivalent car manufactured in Japan. Simply eliminating screws, rivets, and other fasteners can save up to 75 percent of assembly costs and improve the reliability of the product at the same time.[7] Improved, simplified product and service designs are now improving the competitiveness of American manufacturers.

FOCUS ON COMPANY

Chrysler Corporation

The guys on the assembly line knew a good idea when they saw one.

A gang of Chrysler veterans, preparing the plant in Belvidere, Illinois, to build the Neon small car, were nosing around a Subaru factory in Lafayette, Indiana, when they noticed an amazing thing. Subaru workers use just one wrench to install door glass.

Chrysler workers needed several, to accommodate nine different-size fasteners, tightened to five different settings. Subaru's window-glass fasteners, though different sizes, had the same-size heads and were tightened to the same specification. One wrench; one setting. Mistake-proof. No door rattles from loose windows.

"We went back and told our engineers. They said, 'You're crazy.' We said, 'Oh, yeah? How come those guys can do it?'" recalls Larry Bird, a manager on the Neon production team. Thus challenged, Chrysler engineers gave Belvidere workers the one-size-fits-all solution they wanted. That was part of a cost purge that eliminated 350 types of fasteners. Neon has about 300 kinds of screws, bolts and other threaded fasteners vs. 650 on an average Chrysler.

That kind of thinking could make Neon Detroit's first profitable small car. Already it has ignited an almost unimaginable turnaround in Detroit's once-dismal performance.

Producibility
The extent to which a product or service can be easily produced using existing facilities and processes.

Cost
The value of all inputs used to produce the product or service, including raw materials, labor, plant and equipment overhead and similar factors.

Quality
The serviceability and value of the product or service.

Reliability
The degree to which the product or service will perform its intended function for a reasonable length of time.

Factors in Product Design. Engineers must consider four factors when designing new products and services: producibility, cost, quality, and reliability.[8] **Producibility** is the extent to which a product or service can be easily produced using existing facilities and processes.

Cost refers to the value of all inputs used to produce the product or service, including raw materials, labor, plant and equipment overhead, and similar factors. Products that are less producible tend to cost more.

Quality is the serviceability and value found in the product or service. Japanese manufacturers have shown that high-quality goods and services are actually less costly to produce in the long run. This is because less scrap and rework are involved, and fewer purchases are returned by customers.

Finally, **reliability** is the degree to which the product or service will perform its intended function for a reasonable length of time. Products and services that are designed with too many parts are less reliable because more things can go wrong.

Proper design can affect intangible services as well as tangible goods. For example, ServiceMaster uses tools designed to minimize the number of steps needed to perform its cleaning services. This increases the quality and reliability of its services and improves productivity. Similarly, designing a simple restaurant menu results in low-cost food items that have great customer value. Hot food is hot and cold food is cold when a menu and the facility are designed to be easily serviceable by employees.

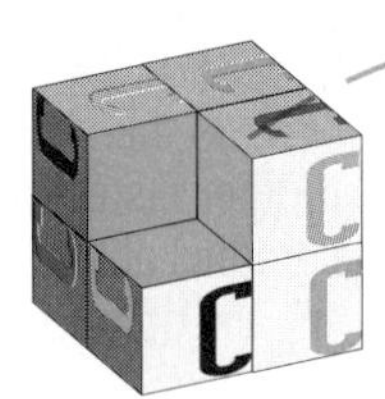

FOCUS ON CUSTOMERS

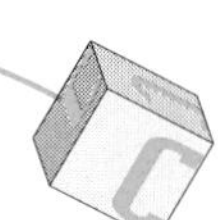

The Olive Garden Italian Restaurant

On Sunday nights in the Chicago suburb of Northbrook, the average wait for a table at The Olive Garden Italian restaurant is 45 minutes. Dinner portions of pasta are so enormous that customers leave with a doggie bag or two, and the price is just $10 per person. The food is not memorable, but that's not what customers really come for. Rather, they come for value and consistency—hot food that's hot, cold food that's cold, and clean restrooms. The secret for this General Mills–owned franchise is a food factory where economies of scale and automation bring down costs. These productivity gains are almost unheard of in the service sector.

Each Olive Garden restaurant makes its own pasta daily from raw ingredients. It costs less than 40 cents a pound, including labor, compared to 55 cents if the pasta were purchased already prepared. Computers track sales and predict what will be needed for each day's operation. Quality control is important. Managers carry thermometers in their shirt pockets to spot check food temperatures. The result is consistency, controlled costs, and satisfied customers.

Exhibit 9.3 **A PROCESS LAYOUT IN A RESTAURANT KITCHEN**

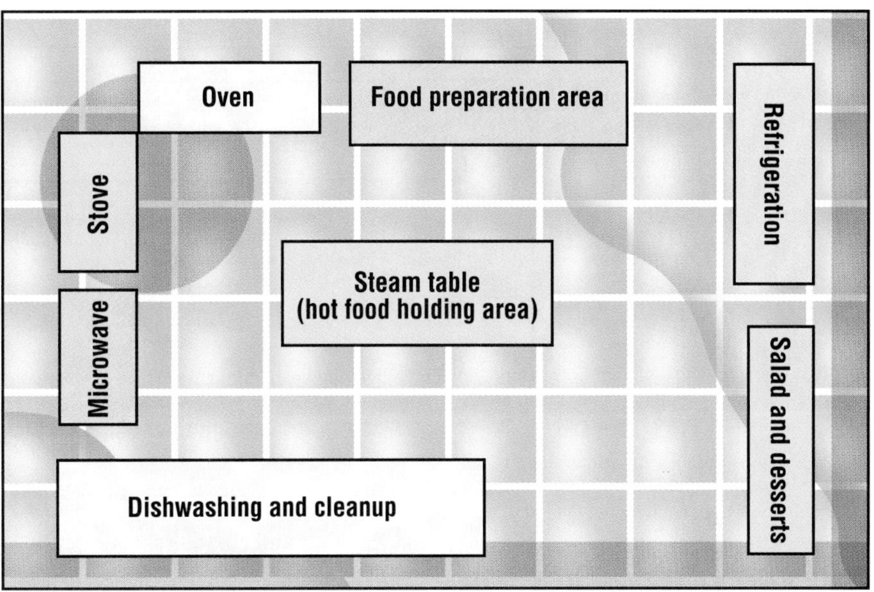

FACILITIES LAYOUT

While the product or service is being designed, other engineers consider the facility in which it will be made. Often these engineers are part of a project team that designs the product or service and the facility at the same time. This allows them to make changes in the product or service that ensure consistent production. Alternatively, if the design of the product or service is known, the facility can be modified before production begins. The layout of the facility design, then, depends on the nature of the product or service itself. Two common layouts in production are process and product.[9]

Process layout
A facilities design in which all production equipment that performs similar tasks is grouped together.

Process Layout. In a **process layout**, all production equipment that performs similar tasks is grouped together. This type of layout is very common in restaurants (see Exhibit 9.3), where ovens are grouped together in one area of the kitchen, refrigerators in a second section, dishwashing equipment in a third, and salad and cold dessert equipment in a fourth. It is also common in small machine shops; lathes are in one area, drill presses in a second, stamping machines in a third, and so on. Similar arrangements are found in banks and hospitals.

Process layouts offer several advantages. First, employees with similar skills are grouped together and can assist one another if a problem arises. Second, fewer machines and equipment may be necessary. However, grouping equipment this way means that the product or service must be transported between stations when more than one task is to be performed. Thus, in a hospital, a patient is moved from the surgery preparation area to the operating room, then to the recovery room, and finally to a regular room. Transportation can require additional employees and, in some industries, it can contribute to breakage and other losses.

Product layout
A facilities design in which equipment and activities are arranged for a single product or service in the sequence of steps that will be used to produce it.

Product Layout. An alternative to the process layout is the product layout. In the **product layout**, equipment and activities are arranged for a single product or service in the sequence of steps that will be used to produce it. Often this layout is combined with another layout design such as the process layout. Exhibit 9.4 shows a common layout in a pizza restaurant. The oven (process) area is arranged to facilitate the making of pizzas. In the sublayout (product), the pizza progresses from the automatic dough roller to pizza assembly, then to baking, and finally to cutting and serving.

Exhibit 9.4 **A PRODUCT LAYOUT WITHIN A PROCESS LAYOUT IN A RESTAURANT KITCHEN**

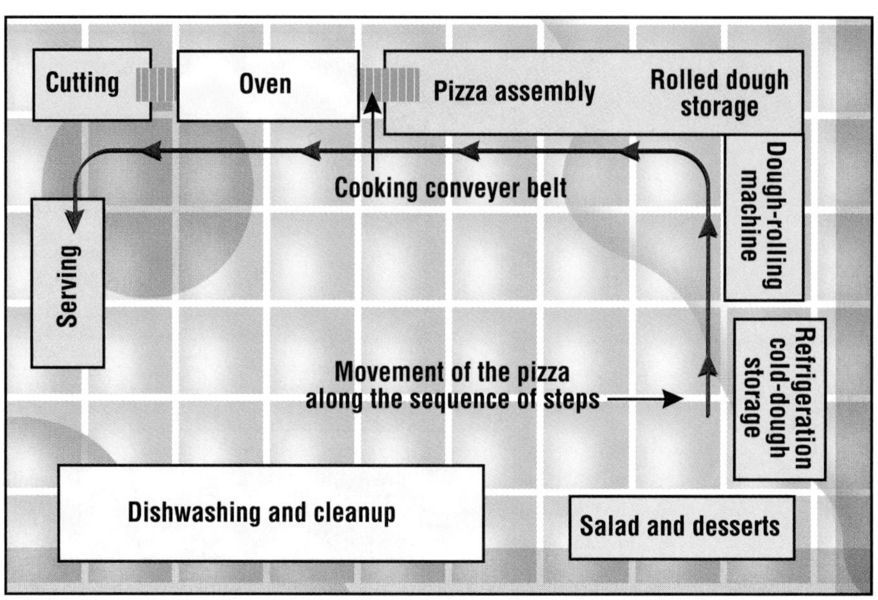

This layout is also common in the traditional automobile assembly line in which the car moves from the first point of assembly to the final point. At each progressive work station, a new step is performed. These assembly lines are specialized according to the unique features and parts of the car. Thus, only Buicks can be made at the Buick plant, and only Pontiacs can be made at the Pontiac plant.

The advantage of being able to handle large volumes of a single product or service, however, is somewhat offset by the inability to handle a second product on the same line. Thus, the company will need many duplicate machines, employees with identical skills, and more plants to make more than one product. If the pizza restaurant expanded its menu to include hamburgers and grilled chicken, it would need a second product layout. This would mean the addition of more ovens, stoves, and preparation areas, but dishwashing, salad and dessert, and refrigeration areas would remain unchanged.

Fixed-Position Layout. One other common facility design is the fixed-position layout. In the *fixed-position layout,* the product or service remains in one position while required activities, tools, and personnel are brought to it. This is how homes are constructed. The carpenters, roofers, electricians, plumbers, and finish workers are each brought to the home when their activities are required. When the home is finished, a new one is begun in a new location, and the process starts over again. This arrangement is not really a layout, however; it is simply one way of producing a product or service.

PRODUCTION EQUIPMENT AND TECHNOLOGIES

Once product design and facilities layout have been planned, managers must give attention to the various types of innovative technology that are available to assist in the design and production of goods and services. Mechanization is a key issue here. However, production technology today has progressed far beyond simple machines. Computers and robots are increasingly replacing people, especially on repetitive tasks. Further, some complex tasks that still require human intelligence and creativity can be improved by computerized processes.

General Motors

"They might get robots to do some jobs. But we'll be running the robots."

Robots are useful. Human beings, however, are indispensable. That's why, after years of training, Dave Klenk moved from a job on the assembly line to a job programming and repairing robots. And now, Dave is teaching the skills he's learned to Tim Pruyt. General Motors is changing the way it builds cars, and it's helping the people who work there change with it. After all, machines just do what they're made to do and no more. Machines can't have a flash of inspiration, or find a better way. Machines can't take pride in their work. General Motors workers can and do.

General Motors Corporation knows that, although robots are useful, human beings are indispensable in the production process. Dave Klenk moved from a job on the assembly line to a job programming and repairing robots. Production in our rapidly changing technological environment requires that workers (and management) be willing to change. Preparing workers to accept change and retraining will be increasingly more important.

Robot
A machine that can be programmed to perform a variety of tasks without direct employee involvement.

Robotics. Great use is being made of **robots**—machines that can be programmed to perform a variety of tasks without direct employee involvement. It is difficult to estimate the number of robotic machines used in industry today, but it is probably several hundred thousand. Robots are heavily used in the automobile industry, where they do work that previously was difficult, monotonous, or hazardous or required great precision. Robots now paint car bodies, reducing employee exposure to hazardous paint fumes and ensuring smooth, even coatings of paint. Robots deliver meals and reading materials in prisons, relieving guards of these less demanding tasks. Giant robots place wings for assembly in aircraft plants, and precision robots place intricate wiring assemblies in computer manufacturing facilities.

Robotic skills are greatly advanced from just a few years ago. Now robots have vision, touch sensing, odor sensing, physical strength, and dexterity. Robots can be programmed to perform many of the therblig movements observed in time-and-motion studies. A robot can pick up a part, transport it to another position, and hold it in place until another robot welds it to the mated piece. The robot can sense if the weld is too hot or too cold and can "see" via X-ray whether the weld contains voids that could weaken it. Not only is the process faster, but the weld is probably of higher quality. A human welder would be more likely to make a weld

STREET SMART

A Can-Do Ethic at Boeing

A can-do ethic prevails at The Boeing Company and military-style humor is appreciated. One example: "An airplane is several million parts flying in fairly close formation." Now Boeing is leading the way in designing new airplanes with a minimal use of paper. Called the "paperless airplane," it is designed and tested on computers. "We are good, and intend to remain good, at integrating everything that makes an airplane," said one executive. Boeing executives are driving technology ahead so that the company is not a sitting target to its competitors. If a manufacturing problem arises, Boeing employees "can do" whatever is necessary to overcome the problem.

that was weak and slightly misplaced. The widespread use of robots in Japanese automobile plants was a major reason for the many quality advantages they once enjoyed over American automobile producers.

Computer-aided design (CAD)
The use of computers that are specially programmed to aid in the design of parts, products, and buildings.

Computer-Aided Design (CAD). Advances in computer technology have led to the use of computers in the design of products and production processes. **Computer-aided design (CAD)** is the use of computers that are specially programmed to aid in the design of parts, products, and buildings. CAD provides engineers with the basic functions of drafting, documentation, analysis, testing, and modeling right at their desks. Designs can be modeled in three dimensions and tested for quality of fit before the first part is ever produced.

From the computer, an architect can lay out the design of a home, install cabinets, place sinks, locate plumbing and electrical fixtures, and print the plans. Then the computer can display the three-dimensional image, and a prospective customer can "walk through the home" and see the entire effect of color choices, interior design, and space. A CAD program can test parts of a fuel injection system for quality and producibility, permitting changes in both product and facility. It can even design the machines needed to manufacture the system. Landscape designers also like CAD, since it allows them to show the initial layout of the customer's yard and how it will look later on as the plants mature.

CAD provides many advantages to a business, including the obvious increase in quality of the product or service. CAD is an enormous drafting board that greatly reduces paperwork. It is also much faster, since an engineer can make and save changes on the computer in seconds and then relay them electronically to another engineer working in a different location. Without CAD such changes would require that several copies be made by hand and sent by mail to other locations. CAD also permits engineers to design the part or product; determine the manufacturing changes needed to produce it; estimate the amount of labor that will be required; estimate costs, weights, and size; and test the product for fit, appearance, and acceptability to the customer.

Computer-aided manufacturing (CAM)
A production technology in which computers guide and control the manufacturing process.

Computer-Aided Manufacturing (CAM). Computer-aided manufacturing (CAM), a natural extension of CAD, is a production technology in which computers guide and control the manufacturing process. CAM information is translated into instructions for the production equipment to guide robots' movements, schedule movement of the product from step to step, and

Workers at Kao Corporation, Japan's biggest soap and cosmetics company, deliver goods within 24 hours to some 280,000 shops, whose average order is for only 7 items. Signs on the production floor tell which product(s) a single production line will turn out each day. Maximizing the company's flexible response to customers' demands means effectively tracking over 10 gigabytes of information at any one time.[10]

detect any bottlenecks on the production line. CAM can schedule fabrication and assembly and coordinate those processes with both purchasing and inventory schedules. CAM can then schedule employee work hours, assign workers to specific tasks, and calculate labor costs. It can also estimate customer shipping dates very accurately and relay them to the sales staff. In this manner, all machines and personnel are fully coordinated. They are never too busy or too idle, waiting for someone else to complete their jobs.

Flexible Manufacturing Systems (FMS). To stay competitive in today's global environment, companies must be flexible enough to be able to change from one product or service to another in a very short time. Competitors can flood the market, the current product may prove less marketable, or customers may require changes in the product that need to be made quickly and inexpensively. Hence, many companies have created small and medium-size automated production lines that can be adapted quickly to produce different products. These are called **flexible manufacturing systems (FMS)**.

Flexible manufacturing system (FMS)
A small or medium-size automated production line that can be adapted or modified quickly to produce different products.

Both small and large companies can use an FMS, but the FMS itself tends to be somewhat small. CAD and CAM make an FMS possible, since computers can be reprogrammed easily and quickly. The typical system consists of CAD- and CAM-controlled equipment to produce parts and assemblies, robots to handle and transport the parts, and electronic linkages to ensure smooth, coordinated production. The computers instruct machines to change parts, specifications, and tools and tell them when a new product will come on line. Obviously an FMS requires many technicians who are highly skilled in product design, equipment design, and computer programming.

FACILITY LOCATION

The fourth step in the production planning process is to determine where to locate the production facilities. This is true for both a service company such as the First National Bank of Chicago and a producer of goods like Sony. First National Bank may need to open a new branch within the city. Sony may need to decide whether to locate a new plant in Japan or in Malaysia.

Location decisions are often based on cost-benefit analyses. In this approach, managers try to estimate the costs of land acquisition, building costs, local labor costs, shipping costs, and other relevant costs. They also estimate the volume of business that might be done at various possible locations, which in turn may be affected by the volume of customer traffic or ease of access by customers. By comparing the benefits to the costs of each possible location, managers can reach the best decision.

Other factors sometimes lead to location decisions. For instance, the owner of a company may wish to locate in the United States regardless of lower labor costs in Mexico or South Korea. Events such as the recent Los Angeles earthquake may discourage some businesses from locating there, regardless of the benefits LA may offer. When GM decided to locate its new Saturn plant in Tennessee, local labor, land, and shipping costs were only part of that decision. Executives also liked the physical beauty of the location and preferred to locate somewhere in the United States rather than in some other country. Also, they wanted to try a new approach to union-management relationships in a relatively nonunion location. Other factors that may play a role in location decisions include closeness to raw materials and customer markets, availability of transportation, and closeness to major research institutions and universities.

CAPACITY PLANNING

The final step in production planning is to coordinate the actual level of production with customer demand for the product or service. This essentially means matching the demand to the supply by anticipating what will be sold and adjusting output to this level.

Besides building a new facility, managers can do several things to increase (or decrease) capacity. Managers may decide to run additional shifts beyond the normal eight-hour daytime shift. Employees may work overtime or on holidays. Work may be subcontracted to other businesses, or the company may buy additional, faster equipment. If customer demand consistently exceeds existing capacity, the company may build additional plants.

By planning how to adjust capacity, managers can avoid making unnecessary expenditures on new plants or hiring too many employees who must be laid off later. AT&T, Southwest Bell, Apple Computer, Hewlett-Packard, Texas Instruments, and many other companies received national attention when they opened new plants and then closed those or other plants, laying off thousands of employees. Thus, managers prefer smaller plant facilities and adjusting to periodic increases in demand by having employees work overtime or by subcontracting work to other firms.

Gantt chart
A chart that lists necessary activities, their order of accomplishment, who is to perform each activity, and the time needed to complete it.

PERT (Program Evaluation and Review Technique) Chart
A chart that analyzes the tasks involved in completing a project, estimates the time needed to complete each task, identifies the minimum time needed to complete the total project, and identifies the path along which delays will hold up the project.

Production managers also use various planning techniques for scheduling and controlling production activities. One popular technique is the use of Gantt charts. A **Gantt chart** lists necessary activities, their order of accomplishment, who is to perform each activity, and the time needed to complete it. Bars on the chart show both the planned times for completion and the progress being made on each activity. A second technique is the **PERT (Program Evaluation and Review Technique) chart**. This chart analyzes the tasks involved in completing a given project, estimates the time needed to complete each task, and identifying the minimum time needed to complete the total project. It also identifies the path along which delays will hold up the project, as opposed to more minor delays.

As we have seen, the production planning process is a major management activity. Planning the design of the goods or services, the design of the production facility, the equipment or technology, the location of the facility, and the capacity of the facility and equipment contributes to the company's productivity and profitability.

ORGANIZATIONAL COLLABORATION: AN IMPORTANT TREND

In Chapter 1, we mentioned that modern business operates in the information age. Advances in computers, communications technology, and information systems have dramatically changed business activity. The most visible change is modern companies' focus on global

Exhibit 9.5 **LOGISTICS MANAGEMENT**

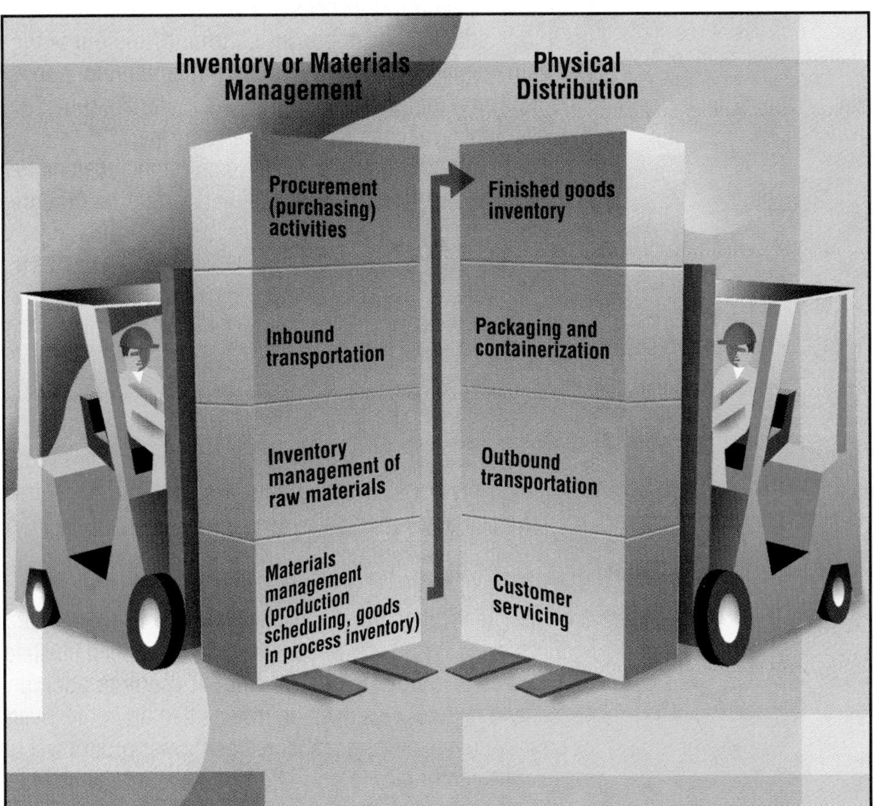

business. Equally important but less visible is the movement away from self-sufficient businesses to businesses that use collaborators that are essential to the company's operations.

For example, Nike, Inc., has many managers, shoe designers, and sales personnel, but few manufacturing personnel. It does not produce shoes in the United States. Rather, it contracts almost all of its manufacturing operations to factories in Indonesia, Thailand, and other Asian countries with low labor costs. Nike operates what it calls a "futures" program that requires U.S. retailers to place their shoe orders six months in advance.[11] This enables Nike to give clear production orders to its contract manufacturers in Asia. With 80 percent of its shoes presold, Nike avoids the risk of holding big inventories. This collaboration with its retailers and the Asian companies that manufacture its shoes is essential to Nike's operations.

In the service sector, Hyatt Corporation president Darryl Hartley-Leonard believes establishing long-term relationships with suppliers benefits all the involved companies.[12] Whether sheets and linen, emergency fire exit signs, or cheesecake, Hyatt buyers comb the globe looking for the highest-quality products. Once Hyatt settles on a supplier, the company works hard at maintaining that relationship.

In the case of cheesecake, Hyatt's team of talented chefs gave up their own efforts after tasting the product produced by Eli's Cheesecake, a small bakery in Chicago. The quality of Eli's cheesecake, which Hyatt now offers in its award-winning restaurants, is proof that collaboration between large and small companies can be a very sweet deal indeed.

Many suppliers are deeply involved in their customers' production and logisitics processes. We discuss the importance of logistical collaboration in the next section.

LOGISTICS

Logistics
The entire process of moving raw materials and component parts, in-process inventory, and finished goods into, through, and out of the firm.

Logistics is the entire process of moving raw materials and component parts, in-process inventory, and finished goods into, through, and out of the firm.[13] As Exhibit 9.5 shows, logistics management involves planning, implementing, and controlling the efficient flow of both inbound (raw) materials and outbound materials (finished products) through the production process until it reaches the ultimate customer.

The term *logistics* is broad in scope. It includes managing the movement and storage of raw materials and supply parts needed during the procurement (acquisition) and production processes. It also includes planning and coordinating the physical distribution of finished goods. Inventory or materials management consists of those activities performed up to the production point, whereas physical distribution includes activities that occur after production, namely getting the product or service to the customers. Collaborators such as transportation companies are vital to these processes.

INVENTORY MANAGEMENT

Inventory
The goods (raw materials, work in process, and finished products) that the company keeps on hand to produce the product or service.

Inventory management involves bringing raw materials and supplies to the point of production. **Inventory** consists of the goods (raw materials, work in process, and finished products) that the company keeps on hand to produce the product or service.

Inventory management begins with the purchase of merchandise, raw materials, and supplies that will be used in the production of the product or service. The intermediate stage involves the level of work in process, which requires materials and supplies. The final stage is the storing of products or services that have been finished but not yet shipped to customers.

Excess inventory is costly, since it requires additional personnel, equipment, storage space, and interest expenses on money tied up in the inventory. But having no inventory may be equally costly, since unexpected customer orders will go unfilled or be delivered late. This may cause customers to go to competitors for the product or service.

The goals of inventory management are to plan the overall inventory (raw materials, work in process, and finished goods) to maximize the probability of filling customer orders and minimize the costs associated with holding inventory. Effective inventory management systems usually have the following characteristics:

- They are computer based.
- They maintain accurate and timely records.
- They use a scientific approach.
- There is a high degree of manager understanding and involvement.
- High-cost items are tightly controlled.
- Inventory is minimized within short time frames.

Four specific inventory control techniques are economic order quantity, materials requirement planning, manufacturing resource planning, and just-in-time.

Economic order quantity (EOQ)
The amount of material that should be ordered at one time to minimize the cost of storing it in inventory.

Reorder point (ROP)
The inventory level at which an order for new material should be placed.

Economic Order Quantity (EOQ). A traditional method of controlling inventory costs is called the **economic order quantity (EOQ)**—the amount of material that should be ordered at one time to minimize the cost of storing it in inventory. If less can be ordered, fewer storage costs will be incurred. However, ordering less means materials will have to be ordered more often. Also, it costs money to place an order (clerical salaries, shipping and receiving costs, etc.), so those costs must be considered as well.

Once managers know *how much* to order at one time, they must determine *when* to order it. They can determine this by using a formula called the **reorder point (ROP)**—the inventory level at which an order for new material should be placed. For instance, if it takes three days for a restaurant to receive flour after placing the order, a three-day supply must

Exhibit 9.6 **IMPACT OF EOQ AND ROP ON FLOUR INVENTORY FOR A RESTAURANT**

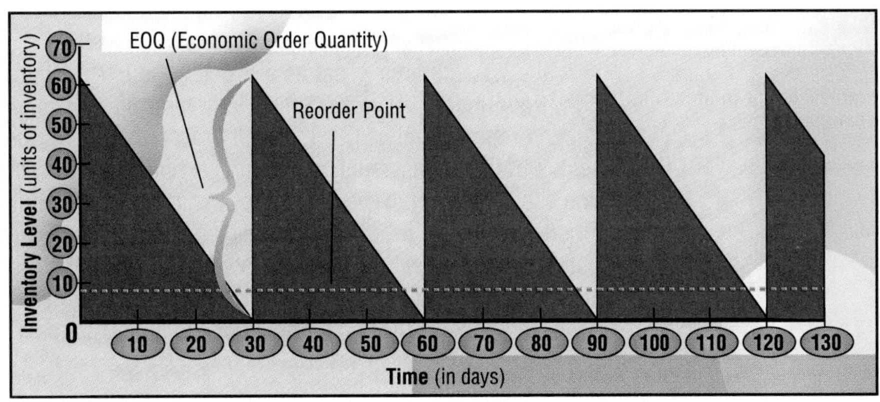

be on hand when the order is placed. Exhibit 9.6 shows the effect of EOQ and ROP on the level of inventory.

Materials Requirement Planning (MRP). EOQ results in an order quantity and a reorder point for each item in inventory. This works well for items that are not related to one another. For instance, the number of pizzas prepared is independent of the demand for beer and soft drinks. When materials used to make the product or service are related, however, the amount of inventory to carry is a more complicated matter. For example, when BMW managers make 50,000 cars, the process will require 200,000 tires, 1,000,000 lug nuts, 200,000 wheel rims, 50,000 steering wheels, and 100,000 windshield wipers. The demand for each of these items depends on the demand for cars.

Materials requirement planning (MRP)
An inventory management technique used when the demand for some materials depends on the demand for others.

Materials requirement planning (MRP) is an inventory management technique used when the demand for some materials depends on the demand for others. MRP has the widest use in the machine tool, electronics, and transportation manufacturing industries. MRP uses precise estimates of future demand rather than records of past sales. It is also computer assisted, since the dependent-demand characteristics will affect the need for perhaps thousands of items. In the BMW example, it would be enormously expensive to carry large supplies of the tires, lug nuts, and other parts in stock, as in EOQ. But given a precise number of cars to produce in the next week, MRP will determine the number needed for each of the many parts and subassemblies and coordinate the ordering and delivery of all these materials. This way, parts will be scheduled to arrive just shortly before they are needed, eliminating the need to store all these items in inventory.

Manufacturing resource planning (MRP II)
An inventory management method that coordinates inventory management with other company systems, such as capacity planning, accounting, and financial planning.

Manufacturing Resource Planning (MRP II). Developments in computerization and networking capabilities have permitted a more advanced control system. **Manufacturing resource planning (MRP II)** coordinates the inventory management system with other systems in the organization. MRP II integrates accounting, financial planning, cash flow, capacity planning, and inventory management. It also supports marketing and engineering, thus uniting all the functions of the business and providing control over most of the company's resources.

Managers use MRP II as a strategic planning technique to analyze the entire company's efforts. The computerized system generates plans for managers and permits them to anticipate and solve a variety of problems associated with their resources. Starting with the company's objectives, sales demand is forecast. The sales forecasts are used to generate production forecasts and determine the flows of materials and other resources (such as cash) needed to support all this activity. MRP II is complicated and expensive and is therefore used mostly in large companies.

Just-in-time (JIT)
An inventory management technique designed to create a zero inventory level by having materials arrive just in time for immediate use in the production process.

Just-in-Time. One reason manufacturing costs for Japanese products are so low is the ability to operate with very small inventory levels. The **just-in-time (JIT)** technique is designed to create a *zero* inventory level by having materials arrive just in time for immediate use in the production process.

The JIT technique requires a simple production layout, one that is well coordinated and tightly controlled. JIT moves parts into the production line only when the next stage of production requires them. This is called a *demand-pull system,* since *demand* at the next stage *pulls* parts or subassemblies into the next position. In contrast, the more traditional production line uses a *batch-push system,* in which parts and subassemblies are produced in large *batches* and then *pushed* to the next line position to wait until they are needed. The demand-pull system used with JIT results in very few idle parts that could get damaged while sitting around and thus often improves the quality of the product. JIT inventory systems have been used with great success by both large and small companies.

FOCUS ON COMPANY

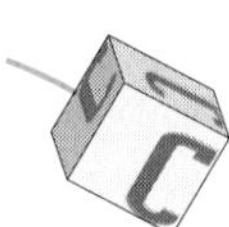

American Standard Inc.

American Standard's plant in Trenton, New Jersey, was built in 1925. Until recently the company's production processes were as dated as its plant. In the last few years, however, American Standard has converted all of its manufacturing operations—sinks, bathtubs, toilets, air-conditioning units, and automotive braking systems—to JIT or demand-pull manufacturing. As an American Standard fact sheet puts it, this move was customer driven rather than forecast driven. It was part of a total quality management program adopted to help bail the company out of $3.1 billion in outstanding debt.

Installing the demand-pull system requires starting with the last production stage before a product leaves the factory and working backward. The Trenton plant first applied demand-pull principles to work on a one-piece toilet, starting with its emergence from a 1,230-degree kiln through its placement in a carton for shipment. That process used to take American Standard about 180 hours. Now it's done in four. Of the company's 32,000 employees, more than half have been trained in demand-pull, including most top managers.

PHYSICAL DISTRIBUTION

Physical distribution
The broad range of activities concerned with efficient movement of finished products from the end of the production line to the customer.

Physical distribution is the broad range of activities concerned with efficient movement of finished products from the end of the production line to the customer. In short, physical distribution refers to the flow of products from producers to consumers. Its major focus is the physical aspects of that flow rather than the wholesaler's and retailer's activities dealing with buying, changing title of ownership, and facilitating exchanges.

Physical distribution consists of several tasks that must be performed to move products from place to place. The major activities in physical distribution are

1. *Finished goods inventory management*—activities that control inventory size. Managers must determine how many finished goods to hold in stock to meet customer orders.
2. *Order processing*—activities involved in recording and processing orders. The manufacturer receives an order for the product or service. Employees handle the paperwork and arrange for shipping and billing.

3. *Warehousing and storage*—holding and housing finished goods in inventory for a certain period of time. Finished goods are held by the manufacturer or distributors so that customers' orders are filled on a timely basis.
4. *Materials handling*—the use of employees and machines to identify, load, and unload products.
5. *Protective packaging and containerization*—packaging products to protect them against breakage, moisture, and temperature extremes. Packaging is also designed to make handling easier and to protect against theft.
6. *Transportation*—the physical movement or shipment of goods. Products are physically moved to customers using trucks, railroads, airplanes, or other available means.

Physical distribution can have significant effects on a business. Low-cost distribution must be combined with timely delivery to customers or the company may fail to be competitive with other producers.

FOCUS ON COMPETITORS

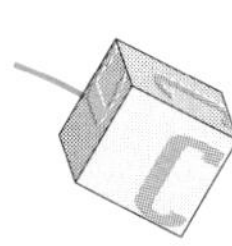

Formica

Formica is almost a generic name for laminated plastic countertops. At one point it dominated the construction market and few competitors could keep up with Formica's new products. According to CEO Ralph Wilson, when Formica was the market leader and every other company was an "also-ran," the Formica name was associated with arrogance. But Wilson recognized that service was important.

Wilson devised a warehousing strategy that allowed Formica to compete with other companies on delivery time. Formica has a network of 15 regional warehouses that provide one-day delivery of its products to distributors. In addition, the company designed its products to use a simplified (though more expensive) group of resins that allowed it to quickly manufacture any items distributors did not have in stock. This meant Formica could deliver almost any product within 10 days compared to 25 days for most competitors.

PRODUCT AND SERVICE QUALITY MANAGEMENT

Business managers sometimes resist investing money in processes designed to improve the quality of products and services. Traditionally, companies believed that putting money into quality improvements would reduce their productivity. However, Japanese firms demonstrated that improving quality actually *improved* productivity. Whenever a part or a product is made correctly the first time, less effort and money have to be spent on rework, scrappage, and servicing products after they have been sold. Poor quality also decreases customer loyalty, as many American firms have discovered. In the early 1980s, American business managers who lacked a true understanding of total quality management followed nearly every quality improvement fad. Many were disappointed with the results of their efforts. Today, we know that increasing the quality of products and services requires more than simply following popular fads. Successful quality programs require commitment from all managers and employees, especially top-level managers.

KEYS TO QUALITY IMPROVEMENT PROGRAMS

One survey of U.S. and international managers found that American managers are much less likely to involve employees in idea suggestion programs to improve quality.[16] It also found that American firms are less likely to use customer complaints as a way of identifying new product and service opportunities.

At a conference in Tokyo in 1991, J. M. Juran, an American quality consultant, predicted that in the 1990s America will again become a symbol of world-class quality. Already business schools in the United States are changing their programs to reflect a concern for quality. U.S. companies are establishing an office called "vice-president for quality." The top levels of U.S. corporations are committing to quality. Whether America succeeds in the push for quality depends on the lessons learned during the past two decades. Several experts have recommended the following keys to successful quality improvement programs.

Key 1: Product Planning. One key to success applies to the product or service planning period. If the product and manufacturing process design are excellent, it is very likely that quality will be as planned. Inspecting a product before it's made—in the design stage—and then making the manufacturing process stable and reliable is an important key to producing quality products.[17]

Product planning includes considering how the product will affect the environment. For example, Texaco Inc. has tested a process that uses tires as a fuel source for making electricity cleanly. The process recasts tires as an intermediate stage between crude oil and useful energy. The process is built around gasification (the idea that cooking hydrocarbon fuels into a gas before burning them results in far cleaner combustions and far more energy than is possible in traditional combustion). And it helps our environment at the same time.[18]

Key 2: Statistical Quality Control. W. Edwards Deming's primary contribution to Japanese quality was teaching Japanese companies statistical quality control. This method enables engineers to tell the difference between avoidable and unavoidable errors and track down the causes of controllable problems. One rule regarding quality is that any loss of quality, no matter how small, increases a product's ultimate costs. These costs include warranty liability and customer dissatisfaction, losses that U.S. firms once overlooked.

Key 3: Establish Good Benchmarks. Many companies have little idea of the benchmarks that would indicate improvements in productivity and quality. Other companies have benchmarks, but they are the wrong ones. One national brand manager recently told his accountant that top managers rarely see numbers that tell them what's happening to brand quality.[19]

Examples of good and bad benchmarks are seen throughout the product and service industries. Benchmarks that indicate decreasing quality in child care centers include teacher pay, turnover, and children's social, intellectual, and language development in these centers.[20] Benchmarks in other companies include product development speed (3M), frequency of mistakes (First Chicago Bank), and the number of parts that go into a product, since fewer parts means higher quality (Ford Motor Company).

Key 4: The Executive Suite. As stated earlier, quality improvement programs must have the support of top management. Companies now are looking for experts in quality concepts.

One typical quality manager is Harry Artinian, vice-president of corporate quality at Colgate-Palmolive Company. He has a staff of five with backgrounds in engineering, systems control, technology, manufacturing, and chemistry. He works with unit executives to find ways to improve quality in manufacturing and distribution and to focus on consumer needs. As an example of improved quality, he points to the achievement of a cross-functional team that improved "the timeliness and accuracy of orders delivered to supermarkets by 50 percent in only six months."[21]

Key 5: Worker Involvement. When Japanese companies applied Deming's quality concepts, they remembered the importance of workers in achieving quality. American managers, however, tended to overlook their workers, blaming them for being lazy and uncaring about the company's success. In fact, Japanese leaders believed American workers *were* lazy. But when one of Japan's top politicians sneered early in 1992 that U.S. workers are "too lazy" to compete and "cannot even read," U.S. journalists looked at the real story. They found that American workers are as motivated as any in the world. They take pride in their efforts and wish to contribute. However, many companies do not let them participate.

When given the chance, workers can add greatly to quality improvement programs. Some successful approaches are the use of self-managed teams (Digital Equipment Corporation and Corning Incorporated), computer-based teaching systems to train workers in statistical quality control, and simply having workers and managers eat in the same cafeteria (Honda of America).[22]

Key 6: Quality Service from Collaborators. It is important to remember that quality improvement must be gained throughout the company and must involve collaborators in the process. This involvement must include such issues as reliable materials and supplies that meet or exceed standards and on-time delivery. We have already discussed the vital role collaborators play in the production and logistical process.

Key 7: Read Everything You Can Get Your Hands On. Quality improvement depends on educating managers and workers in the methods of quality control. Japanese firms recognized this and provided education for their managers and workers in quality control methods. However, this key implies an even more extensive approach, reading and searching for materials that give ideas on how to improve quality. Reading what a competitor has done and what a researcher has discovered will provide valuable lessons.

Key 8: Serve the Customer. Quality is driven by the customer. Customers' demands that products meet high quality standards cause companies to seek quality improvements. Surveys of customer perceptions regarding the quality of a product or service will indicate whether the company's goods and services are of satisfactory quality. If customers are unhappy with the quality, increasing advertising won't help. Perceptions of poor quality are improved only when the quality of the product or service is improved.

U.S. firms that have learned the lessons of the past two or three decades are in a good position to improve both productivity and quality. Productivity and quality problems are not due to lazy or incompetent workers. Rather, their solutions are to be found in enlightened and informed management.

ISO 9000: QUALITY IN EUROPE

Quality management and assurance standards are now published by the International Organization for Standardization (ISO). The most recent of these standards is called *ISO 9000,* which provides international standards for quality that can be applied to any company in the world. The standards cover product design and development, manufacturing, testing, final inspection, installation, and service. For example, the standards for product design and development require a company to understand customer needs, control the design process to meet requirements, provide employees with correct documentation, assume responsibility for quality both within the company and from suppliers, and maintain appropriate records and documentation. These international standards are recognized by about 100 countries, including Japan, and are having a major impact on global competition. The European Community (EC) is demanding that companies that do business with the EC meet the standards set in ISO 9000. Over 15,000 European companies have been certified, but few U.S.

Precision Tube Technology, Inc., of Houston, Texas, was aware of the new ISO 9000 standards and their potential impact on this young business. After opening in 1990, the company quickly built an international customer base by gaining certification through the ISO 9000 series of quality assurance standards. Certification set Precision Tube apart from its competitors, many of which were not registered, and resulted in a sharp increase in sales.[14]

companies have.[15] To compete globally, U.S. companies must commit fully to total quality management and meet international standards.

SUMMARY

1. ***Define and describe the nature of production.***
   Production is the use of people, capital, and other resources (inputs) to convert raw materials into finished goods and services (outputs). The production process is an input-transformation-output system and requires the management of raw materials, production procedures, and finished inventory. Also, it involves assessment and control of the quality of the goods or services produced.

2. ***Describe three factors that are important to increasing productivity.***
   Increases in productivity result from standardization of parts and processes, specialization of labor, and mechanization of work. Standardized parts and processes save time and costs in the production process and ensure higher-quality products. Specialization of labor permits employees to become highly skilled in the activities they perform due to constant repetition of those activities. Mechanization of work permits machines to reliably perform certain activities that require few human skills and are excessively repetitive.

3. ***Explain the production planning process.***
   Production planning requires planning for the design of the product or service, the layout of the production facility, the equipment and technology to be used, the location of the production facility, and the capacity of the facility and equipment. One of the most important developments in production management today is called design for manufacturability and assembly (DFMA). This has resulted in improved, simplified product and service designs.

4. ***Identify four factors to consider in designing products and services.***
Four factors important in product and service design are producibility, cost, quality, and reliability. Producibility is the extent to which a product or service can be easily produced using existing facilities and processes. Cost is the value of all inputs used to produce the product or service. Generally, cost increases as producibility decreases. Quality is the serviceability and value of the product or service. Product quality has been a major concern for U.S. manufacturers. Reliability refers to the degree to which the product or service will perform its intended function for a reasonable length of time.

5. ***Describe two common production facility layouts.***
Two common production facility layouts are the process layout and the product layout. In a process layout all production equipment that performs similar tasks is grouped together. Process layouts are used in restaurants, machine shops, banks, and hospitals. In a product layout, equipment and activities are arranged for a single product or service in the sequence of steps that will be used to produce it. This layout is found in automobile assembly lines.

6. ***Describe computer-aided design (CAD), computer-aided manufacturing (CAM), and flexible manufacturing systems (FMS).***
Computer-aided design (CAD) and computer-aided manufacturing (CAM) involve the application of computer techniques to help solve product design and production problems. By using CAD, engineers can design products and see those designs in three dimensions before any product is actually made. Parts that are intended to fit together can be tested for fit and serviceability. CAM uses computers to guide and control the manufacturing process. Data and information in the computer are used to instruct production equipment, guide robots' movements, schedule movement of the product from step to step, and detect any bottlenecks on the production line. Finally, a flexible manufacturing system enables the company to change from making one product or service to another in a very short time. CAD and CAM make an FMS possible. An FMS requires many technicians who are highly skilled in product design, equipment design, and computer programming.

7. ***Discuss activities associated with logistics and physical distribution.***
Logistics is the entire process of moving raw materials and components parts, in-process inventory, and finished goods into, through, and out of the company. It consists of managing inventory as well as physical distribution of finished goods. Physical distribution, one part of logistics, involves activities that occur after production, namely getting the product or service to the customer. It includes finished goods inventory management, order processing, warehousing and storage, materials handling, protective packaging and containerization, and transportation.

8. ***Describe four inventory management techniques.***
Economic order quantity (EOQ) is a traditional method of controlling inventory costs by identifying the amount of material that should be ordered and when it should be ordered. The reorder point (ROP) is the level of inventory at which an order for new material should be placed. Materials requirement planning (MRP) is a newer inventory control technique that is appropriate when the demand for some materials depends on the demand for others. For example, the demand for cars will determine how many tires, steering wheels, and other parts will be needed. Manufacturing resource planning (MRP II) coordinates the inventory management system with other systems in the organization, thus providing control over most of the company's resources. MRP II used as a strategic planning technique that helps managers of various functions anticipate and solve problems associated with their resources. Just-in-time (JIT) is a technique designed to create a zero inventory level by having materials arrive just in time for immediate use in the production process. JIT uses a demand-pull system in which demand at the next production stage pulls parts and subassemblies into the next position.

9. ***Discuss product and service quality and the keys to a successful quality improvement program.*** Traditionally, product and service quality was not a major issue for U.S. manufacturers. Companies believed that investing money in quality improvements would reduce their productivity. However, international competitors found that improving the quality of their products actually increased their productivity, since it lowered the costs of rework, scrappage, and servicing. Today companies in more than 100 countries have committed to ISO 9000, a set of quality standards established by the International Organization for Standardization. More U.S. companies will have to commit to these standards to be able to compete globally.

   Eight keys to a successful quality improvement program are product planning, statistical quality control, establishing good benchmarks for improvement, support from top management, employee involvement, quality service from collaborators, reading materials on quality, and serving the customer.

KEY TERMS AND CONCEPTS

Production (p. 188)
Producibility (p. 192)
Cost (p. 192)
Quality (p. 192)
Reliability (p. 192)
Process layout (p. 193)
Product layout (p. 193)
Robot (p. 195)
Computer-aided design (CAD) (p. 196)
Computer-aided manufacturing (CAM) (p. 196)
Flexible manufacturing system (FMS) (p. 197)
Gantt chart (p. 198)
PERT (Program Evaluation and Review Technique) chart (p. 198)
Logistics (p. 200)
Inventory (p. 200)
Economic order quantity (EOQ) (p. 200)
Reorder point (ROP) (p. 200)
Materials requirement planning (MRP)(p. 201)
Manufacturing resource planning (MRP II) (p. 201)
Just-in-time (JIT) (p. 202)
Physical distribution (p. 202)

DISCUSSION QUESTIONS

Company

1. Does the mechanization of the production process lead to employee job losses? If so, what should companies do to provide some relief for displaced workers?
2. What types of jobs are best suited for the use of robotics and computer technology in a manufacturing firm? Why?

Customers

3. How has the standardization of parts and processes benefitted the consumers of goods and services?
4. What kind of production (service) layout do grocery stores use to maximize customer satisfaction?

Competitors

5. How has the shift from a production economy to a service economy affected the ability of the United States to compete in the global market?
6. How does an effective production planning process enable a company to remain competitive?

Collaborators

7. What effects have just-in-time and other inventory management techniques had on a company's suppliers?

8. How might the location of a company's suppliers affect decisions regarding the location of its facilities?
9. How might collaborators help a company in its quest to improve the quality of its products and services?

In Question: Take a Stand

Deep in the rain forest on Papua, New Guinea, Chevron Corporation and its partners have spent more than $1 billion developing a new kind of eco-friendly oil project. The company has gone to unusual lengths to blunt the impact of its operations on the environment. Burying the pipeline and minimizing road construction cost tens of millions of dollars. Road construction will clear only 1,500 of the 88 million rain forest acres in the country. Chevron officials are convinced that modern production and quality control methods will eliminate the possibility of oil spills.[23] With the increase in public awareness of environmental issues during the past three decades, companies need to include protection of the environment as one of their quality improvement goals. Do you feel that the steps taken by Chevron Corporation to protect the environment are necessary? Are they sufficient?

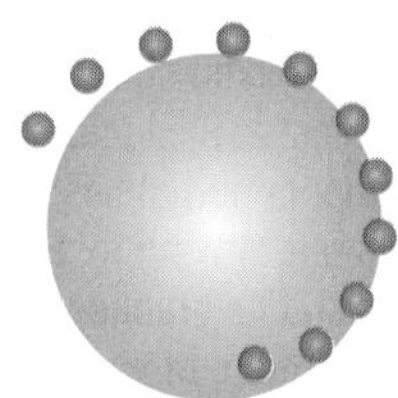

CASE 9.1
GENERAL MOTORS

When managers use the term *production,* many people immediately think of the American automobile industry. This industry created many of the modern processes used in the mass production of consumer goods. Assembly lines, inventory management techniques, unionization, and many other industrial processes have their roots in these giant manufacturers.

However, the automobile industry also calls up some negative images. In his book *Rivethead: Tales from the Assembly Line,* Ben Hamper, a worker on an auto assembly line for many years, portrays the decline of the auto industry and its effect on the city of Flint, Michigan. Hamper refers to this experience as an "inferno." For several years, Hamper was "ball-and-chained" to a job on the Rivet Line "that kept me forever in motion." Also, it was a job with "no champions for the masses" (his coworkers on the assembly line).

Hamper was a third-generation autoworker who found no dignity in labor in the auto plants. Working on the Rivet Line, "the starting point for all that went on during the three-day snake trail needed to assemble a truck," was, he wrote, "like being paid to flunk high school the rest of your life." He finally lost his job when he placed himself in therapy, the victim of anxiety caused by one of the most humdrum jobs on earth.

One question raised by *Rivethead* is: How was it possible for an earlier generation of workers to find self-respect on the assembly line and for a later generation to find only self-contempt? Hamper thinks that by the late 1970s and early 1980s, whatever General Motors had done right had been lost. GM was now, according to the book, a completely "lunatic" corporation. It was the kind of place where, to inspire its workers to produce higher-quality output, management created a mascot, a "quality cat" called Howie Makem. "Howie Makem stood five feet nine. He had light brown fur, long synthetic whiskers and a head the size of a Datsun. He wore a long red cape emblazoned with the letter Q for Quality," Hamper wrote. From the Cab Shop or the Rivet Line, the management style at GM was a mixture of paternalism, contempt, and brutality to Hamper and his coworkers.

Despite Hamper's portrayal of GM as a personal hell, evidence suggests that the American automobile industry is not such a bad place to have a career. Much has changed in manufacturing and production during the past 15 years, and the Rivet Line is probably little more than a symbol of the past. Still, the memory lingers on and the lessons learned must be applied on the factory floor if U.S. companies are to regain their international leadership role in business.

Questions

1. *How has the production process changed at General Motors over the years?*
2. *In your opinion, what have been the most important changes in the auto industry? Which changes have been the most positive from the workers' viewpoint?*
3. *In your opinion, would a career with a company like General Motors be desirable? Why or why not?*
4. *Are American automobile manufacturers better off or worse off from the competition from Japanese manufacturers during the past 25 years? Why?*

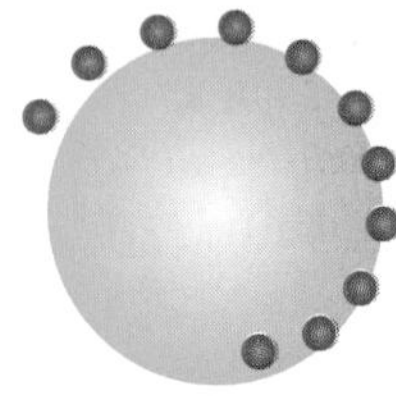

CASE 9.2
WESTERN ATLAS[24]

Richard Mixon is one of the new breed who is actively managing his career. A senior electronics engineering technician in the seismic testing division of the Western Atlas oil exploration company in Houston, Mixon early on made it his mission to seek out jobs that would allow him to grow. "I wanted to have a broad enough spectrum of skills to be able to fit into any technical environment," he says.

The son of a construction worker, Mixon studied electronics for two years at the University of Houston with the aim of working in the computer industry. Lacking the funds to continue his studies, however, he took a job with IBM repairing office equipment. The five years he spent as a service representative taught him valuable lessons in how to deal with customers, but it wasn't getting him any closer to his goal of working with engineers who design computer circuit boards. He left IBM in 1978 to join Texas Instruments which hired him to repair integrated-circuit test systems.

Inside a year, Mixon realized that without a four-year engineering degree his chances for advancement with TI were limited. But he could see that printed-circuit technology was beginning to spread to many other industries besides computers—and with it, his opportunities to take on more challenging projects. So when he learned about an opening for an electronics lab technician at Halliburton, an oil-field services company that was booming in the energy-short years of the early 1980s, he jumped.

The move exposed Mixon to the kind of work he had been longing to do. Over the next nine years at Halliburton and later at Schlumberger, which offered him both more money and more interesting assignments, Mixon assisted electronics design engineers in developing circuit boards that would go into the latest geologic data-acquisition equipment. Despite the challenge, Mixon could not see further career advancement at Schlumberger, so he began to look for other opportunities. A recruiter sounded him out about moving to a bigger job with Western Atlas, and he grabbed the offer.

In his current position, Mixon is helping to develop an electronic sensing system that will be used to locate oil. In addition to working on the design of new circuitry, he is the point man delegated to work with manufacturing to bring the new gear into production quickly. And he's always on the lookout for new tasks to take on. Says Mixon, "It's better to ask for forgiveness than for permission." Mixon's ultimate goal is to build on his broad technical base by starting his own business.

Questions

1. *What skill(s) has been most important to Richard Mixon as his career has developed? Why?*
2. *Why are employees like Richard Mixon important to productivity in today's business environment?*
3. *What additional skills should Richard Mixon have if he indeed starts his own business?*
4. *What situations have been described in this case that relate to our lessons of product and process design? Explain.*

PART 3

Human Resources

CHAPTER 10

HUMAN RELATIONS, MOTIVATION, AND PERFORMANCE

When you have studied this chapter, you will be able to:

1. Define and explain the importance of human relations.
2. Describe the impact that scientific management and the Hawthorne studies had on motivation theories.
3. Define *motivation* and describe the role of needs in motivation.
4. Explain the two-factor concept of motivation.
5. Identify the role of reinforcement in motivation.
6. Describe Theory X, Theory Y, and Theory Z.
7. Discuss how performance goals affect motivation.
8. Describe management by objectives (MBO).

Sports coaches are supposed to inspire their players. When people talk about inspirational moments, they often tell stories about their favorite coaches. Perhaps the most famous story about an inspirational coach involved Knute Rockne and his Notre Dame football team. In 1928, his team was losing to a strong U.S. Army team. Rockne gave them a pep talk reminding them of George Gipp, a former teammate who had died, and urged his players to "win one for the Gipp." Inspired, his team rallied to beat the army cadets.

Motivational techniques to spur teams to victory didn't stop with Knute Rockne. Before a big game against Texas, Baylor coach Grant Teaff pulled a worm from his pocket and offered to swallow it if his team beat Texas. His emotionally charged players overcame Texas and later played in the Cotton Bowl that year. (Incidentally, Teaff never did swallow that worm.)

Vanderbilt coach Fred Pancoast once had a friend dress as General George Patton, ride out on the practice field, and give motivational talks to his players. Woody Hayes, former coach at Ohio State, used to smash watches and rip up baseball caps in "motivational" rages.

But are these motivational tricks worth it? Do pep talks and other gimmicks really inspire players to their best performances? Seppo Iso-ahola, a sports psychologist at Maryland, cautions that such gimmicks come with risks. They can insult the intelligence of athletes, who probably don't need to be reminded how important a game is. Also, pep talks may overarouse players, generating too much adrenaline and actually resulting in lower performance on the field. Iso-ahola believes the best motivational techniques may be positive reinforcement and mental imagery. But nothing guarantees victory like having better players than the other team.[1]

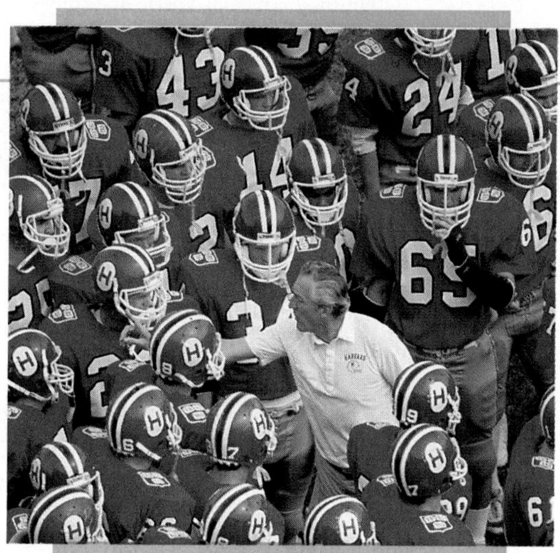

As a student, you already know something about motivation. For instance, you had to be motivated to continue your education beyond high school. Perhaps your parents or a teacher inspired you to work hard so you could get into college, because kids who stay in school get ahead in the business world. A personal drive like this can be a powerful source of motivation.

This chapter points out that effective managers realize the importance of motivating employees. It looks at some traditional theories of motivation and the relationship between motivation and performance.

HUMAN RELATIONS

Haworth, a family-owned company located in Holland, Michigan, is a global leader in the furniture manufacturing industry. Its mission statement says Haworth's employees are the company's most important resource. It says "the diversity of their races, genders, talents, and personalities enables Haworth to be more innovative, dynamic, and flexible. ...[the company] supports teams and individuals. Haworth encourages employee development and achievement through recognition, rewards, and opportunities for career growth."[2]

Human relations
The process by which the company manages and motivates people to achieve effective performance.

Human relations is the process by which the company manages and motivates people to achieve effective performance. Many business mission statements say something about human relations because managers know good people are essential to the company's success. Effective managers spend much time and effort dealing with human relations issues.

We began this chapter by discussing motivation on the athletic field. If you have played on a baseball, basketball, or soccer team, you know what coaches do to motivate players. But trying to motivate employees is not like trying to motivate athletes. While motivational pep talks may inspire outstanding one-game performances, they have little effect on long-term performance. Motivating employees to contribute good performances day in and day out over many years is a different human relations problem.

Obviously, people work at their jobs to get paychecks and possibly to get promoted. However, business theorists have known for some time that employees are also motivated by other things, such as recognition and accomplishment. Employees may be willing to work hard if they believe their work is important and appreciated by their managers.

THE EVOLUTION OF HUMAN RELATIONS CONCEPTS FOR BUSINESS

While the importance of such things as employee recognition and feelings of personal accomplishment seems obvious today, it was not always so. It took management theorists many years to understand how human relations can improve productivity. This section traces the development of management thinking about how to get better performance from people.

SCIENTIFIC MANAGEMENT: FREDERICK TAYLOR

Scientific management
The systematic study of the most efficient way to perform a job, training employees in that method, selecting employees with suitable skills, and redesigning tools used on the job.

Frederick W. Taylor is known as the founder of scientific management. Trained as a mechanical engineer, he was amazed at the inefficiencies he observed in workers. He saw that employees used widely differing techniques to do the same jobs and that they seemed to be "taking it easy" at work. He thought that worker output was only about one-third of what it could be. His book *The Principles of Scientific Management,* published in 1911, described various means to increase worker productivity.[3] Taylor's principles of **scientific management** involved the systematic study of the most efficient way to perform a job, training workers in that method, selecting employees with suitable skills, and redesigning tools used on the job. His principles included matching workers' skills to those their jobs required and redesigning the tools and methods used on the job. Some of his principles were similar to the time-and-motion work being done by Frank Gilbreth at about the same time.

In one classic study, Taylor observed workers loading pigs of iron weighing 92 pounds onto railroad cars. Without training, they loaded an average of 12.5 tons of iron a day. Taylor alternated various methods to see what impact different activities and movements, such as bending the knees while loading, would have on the workers' output. He also varied workers' rest periods, walking speeds, and carrying positions. These experiments gave him insights on how to best design the job and maximize productivity. By selecting only strong workers and having them adopt the most efficient means of carrying the pig iron, he increased productivity from 12.5 tons to 48 tons loaded per day.

Another experiment involved determining the right size of shovel to use for various jobs. Taylor had observed that every worker in the plant used the same size shovel regardless of the material being shoveled. He thought the size of the shovel should depend on the weight of the material being moved. His experiments revealed that the optimal weight to move with a shovel was 21 pounds. Thus, shovels were designed to handle different jobs. Heavy materials were moved with smaller shovels and lighter materials with bigger shovels, always maintaining a 21-pound load.

Taylor had great success using his scientific management principles for many different types of work. He would always find the one best way to do the job, select the right people for that job, and train them to do the job in this one best way. To motivate workers, he used incentive wage plans. With this approach, he achieved consistent improvements in productivity.

THE HAWTHORNE STUDIES: ELTON MAYO

Hawthorne studies
A series of studies from 1924 to the early 1930s that examined various sociological factors related to motivation.

The **Hawthorne studies** were a series of studies that began in 1924 and continued into the early 1930s which examined various sociological factors related to motivation. The studies were conducted at Western Electric Company's Hawthorne plant outside of Chicago.[4] Experimental groups of employees worked under varying intensities of light, while a control group worked under a constant light intensity. The industrial engineers conducting the experiments expected productivity to be related to the intensity of the light but found that productivity increased constantly over time, regardless of the lighting level. Productivity in the experimental group dropped only when the light intensity decreased to approximately that of moonlight.

The engineers asked professor Elton Mayo and his colleagues at Harvard University to join the study as consultants. Mayo and his associates experimented with many factors thought to influence productivity, including changes in the length of the workday and workweek, length and frequency of rest periods, and individual and group wage plans. The results of one study indicated that a group piecework incentive pay plan had less effect on workers' output than did group pressure and employees' beliefs that they were special. Mayo concluded that the social norms and standards of the group were key determinants of individuals' work behavior.

Some of Mayo's conclusions were as follows:

- The workers in the test room thought of themselves as a special, social group. The work atmosphere was informal and relaxed. Workers could talk freely and interacted sociably with the supervisor and the experimenters. Their feelings of being special motivated them, and they worked hard to stay in the group.
- The workers participated in planning the experiments and often gave the experimenters ideas for the study. They believed the supervisor valued their ideas and that their contributions to the company and to the study were important. Participating in management decisions regarding pay and working conditions also motivated them.
- The workers enjoyed the social environment of the test room and the additional pay they earned from being more productive. Job satisfaction increased dramatically during the study, as did their efforts.

For managers in today's highly competitive business world, motivating employees is essential. Managers now recognize that their companies' survival depends not only on financial and physical resources but also on their employees' skills and abilities. Despite today's sophisticated selection and hiring programs, managers often find that employees simply aren't applying their full energies to their jobs. This presents a big challenge to managers.

Hawthorne effect
The tendency for people to behave differently when they know they are being studied, especially in ways they think the researcher wants them to behave.

Researchers use the term **Hawthorne effect** to refer to the tendency for people to behave differently when they know they are being studied. This is partly what happened at the Hawthorne plant. Nevertheless, the findings in the Hawthorne studies led to new research and to different assumptions and concepts about employee motivation. Self-respect, a sense of belonging to a group, and being able to participate in company decisions about the work all seemed to have important effects on employee motivation.

From the early work of people like Taylor and Mayo, management theories regarding the motivation of employees began to emerge.

MOTIVATION IN CONTEMPORARY MANAGEMENT

Motivation
The arousal, direction, and persistence of a particular behavior.

Motivation is the arousal, direction, and persistence of a particular behavior. Most experts agree that motivation energizes, maintains, and guides behavior.[5] Managers are interested in the factors that prompt people to initiate a behavior, what affects their choice of behavior, and why they persist in that behavior for long periods of time. Although almost all human behaviors can be examined as a motivation process, we are specifically interested in how motivation affects work behaviors.

THE ROLE OF NEEDS IN MOTIVATION

Motivation of work behaviors has been studied for many years, and several concepts have been widely accepted by management writers. Exhibit 10.1 presents a simple model of motivation. This model suggests that people have basic needs for food, recognition, achievement, and so on. When these needs are not satisfied *(need deprivation),* an internal tension or drive is created. This drive motivates specific behaviors that seem likely to result in rewards that would satisfy the need. When the behavior is successful and the reward is received, the person learns that similar behavior in the future will probably get the same reward and satisfy the same need. Thus, employees might be motivated by being given rewards that satisfy their needs when they perform the job behaviors their managers desire.

Exhibit 10.1 **A SIMPLE MODEL OF MOTIVATION**

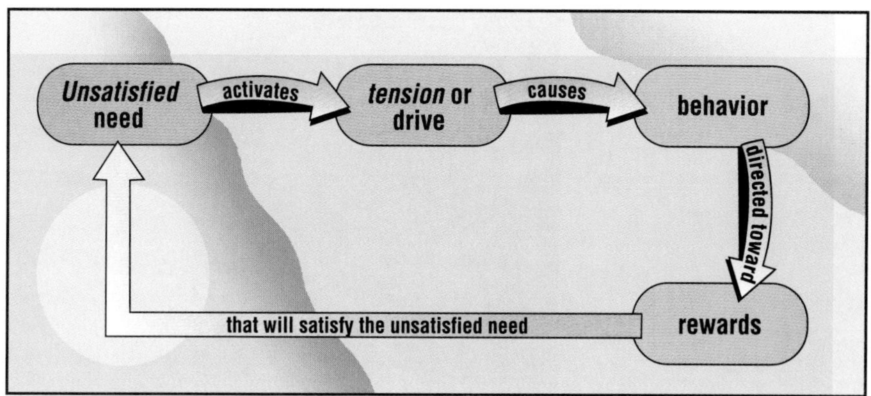

Of course, one problem with motivating employee performance based on satisfying their needs is that when the reward is appropriate to (satisfies) the need, the need is no longer unsatisfied. This means that the need-motivated behavior will not recur until the need is once again unsatisfied. Consider the need for food. A hungry person can be directed to perform many behaviors by being promised a good dinner as an incentive. But once the person is fed, he or she is no longer hungry, and until the person is hungry again (a wait of at least a few hours), it will be difficult to get the same level of motivated behavior by promising food. Thus, concepts of motivation that are based on needs must take this problem into account.

MASLOW'S NEEDS HIERARCHY

Psychologist Abraham H. Maslow proposed one of the most popular management theories of motivation: the needs hierarchy.[6]

Needs hierarchy
A hierarchical classification of human needs first proposed by Abraham Maslow that includes physiological, safety, social, self-esteem, and self-actualization needs.

The Five Needs in the Hierarchy. In his **needs hierarchy** theory, Maslow identified five human needs that exist in a hierarchical order, or pyramid. These needs include physiological, safety, social, esteem, and self-actualization needs (see Exhibit 10.2).

Physiological needs
The most basic of all human needs, including the need for food and water.

Physiological needs are the most basic of all human needs and include the need for food and water. At work, people need adequate heating and air conditioning, regular pay, and rest periods. Many incentive pay systems apply to the satisfaction of this need. When John J. Groch, Jr., an employee at Nalco Chemical Company, said, "I truly believe that money is a motivator," he was reflecting a largely physiological need.

Safety needs
The need for a secure environment.

Safety needs are the second most basic need and include the need for a secure environment in both a physical and emotional sense. Security is reflected in an environment that is nonviolent and has order and predictability. At work, this need can be satisfied by secure jobs, work rules that promote order, and jobs that are relatively free of hazards. Teaching jobs are often strong in satisfying safety needs. When college professors receive tenure, they are assured of job security. Union contracts with employers also provide considerable job security for union members. Thus, the need for safety is one of the primary motives for joining unions.

Social (belongingness) needs
The desire to be accepted by friends and colleagues, to be loved and to be part of a group.

Social needs or **belongingness needs** are found in the desire to be accepted by friends and colleagues, to be loved, and to be part of a group. At work, these needs can be satisfied by membership in a work group and by having friendly relationships with coworkers, customers, collaborators, and supervisors. Careers in social work, marketing, and human resource management offer high levels of satisfaction of this need. Many people choose careers in sales for the opportunity to meet and deal with people.

Exhibit 10.2 **MASLOW'S NEEDS HIERARCHY**

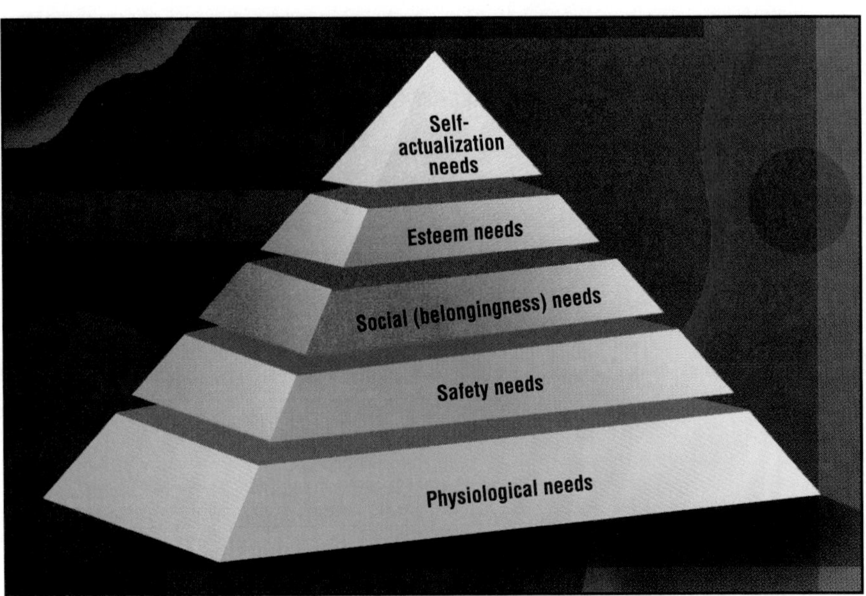

Esteem needs
The desire for a good perception of oneself and to receive recognition and respect from other people.

Esteem needs include the desire for a good perception of oneself, and to receive recognition and respect from other people. At work, these needs can be satisfied by praise from managers and coworkers, jobs with greater responsibility, and favorable performance evaluations. A person motivated by esteem needs will seek a career path that offers promotional opportunities, even if that path is a bit riskier than some others. Owning one's own business also provides satisfaction of esteem needs.

Self-actualization needs
The desire for fulfillment and for realizing all of one's potential.

Self-actualization needs include the desire for fulfillment and for realizing all of one's potential. Maslow wrote that even when a person is largely satisfied in the other need areas, dissatisfaction will develop if the individual isn't doing what he or she is fitted for. A musician must make music, a painter must paint, and a poet must write: "What a man can be, he must be."[7] Maslow said this tendency might be phrased as the desire to become more and more what one is, to become everything one is capable of becoming. Creativity and emotional growth are often associated with self-actualization. Jobs that provide opportunities to be creative, grow, and use all of one's talents and skills generally satisfy this need. Self-actualization is also satisfied when employees are given opportunities to make decisions and to have a positive impact on the company.

The Hierarchical Rules. The unique aspect of Maslow's needs hierarchy is not the five needs themselves but how they are related to one another. Their relationship is based on four rules. First, as Exhibit 10.1 shows, when a need is unsatisfied, it activates a drive that gives direction and purpose to one's behavior. Only unsatisfied needs serve this function. This leads to the second rule: Any need that is largely satisfied will no longer activate a drive.

The third rule in the hierarchy is that of prepotency. *Prepotency* means that the needs surface in a specific order (see Exhibit 10.2). If all five categories of needs are unsatisfied, the needs that will first give rise to a drive and thus to directed behavior are physiological needs, the most basic, or prepotent, need. Until that need is satisfied, the others will remain inactive, awaiting satisfaction of the most prepotent need. Then, when physiological needs are satisfied, the second most prepotent need, safety, will activate a drive and give direction to behavior; when the need for safety is satisfied, the third category, social needs, will become active, and so on.

The fourth rule is that people seek psychological growth; they seek to move up the hierarchy. This is a basic characteristic of humans. People are rarely content with what they have and constantly seek to improve themselves. Thus, some need is always active. As people satisfy a more basic need, a higher-order need arises, permitting the psychological growth they seek.

The Needs Hierarchy and the Real World. The needs hierarchy seems quite simple and easy to use. But in the real world of work, are people really motivated by anything besides money? Sometimes it seems that all employees really care about is the next raise or the next promotion.

In fact, however, businesses have been very successful in satisfying lower-order physiological and safety needs. American workers' salaries are among the highest in the world. Money is the traditional means by which managers have attempted to motivate employees to achieve high levels of performance. Given this truth, for the needs hierarchy to really apply to people, we must find that they continue to exert effort even when the lower-order needs are satisfied. They must, as Maslow proposed, move up the hierarchy and seek satisfaction of higher-order needs.

Stories about lottery winners in the past decade seem to bear this out. People who have won millions of dollars in various lotteries continue to work and seek new challenges. A teacher continued to teach because he liked to teach, indicating esteem and self-actualization needs. A carpenter continued to work because he would have been bored without a job, reflecting social and esteem needs.[8] This example suggests that Maslow's needs hierarchy is a fairly accurate depiction of how human needs act to motivate people.

MCCLELLAND'S ACQUIRED OR LEARNED NEEDS

Another psychologist, David McClelland, proposed that certain needs are not inborn as Maslow suggested; rather, people acquire or learn them. These needs are

1. **The need for achievement**—the desire to accomplish something difficult, reach a high level of success, master complex jobs, and surpass the achievements of others.
2. **The need for power**—the desire to influence others, control their behaviors and actions, be responsible for others, and have authority over them.
3. **The need for affiliation**—the desire to have close personal relationships, avoid conflict, and be friendly, warm, and close to others.

Need for achievement
The desire to accomplish something difficult, reach a high level of success, master complex jobs, and surpass the achievements of others.

Need for power
The desire to influence others, control their behaviors and actions, be responsible for others, and have authority over them.

Need for affiliation
The desire to have close personal relationships, avoid conflict, and be friendly, warm, and close to others.

These needs are closely associated with the jobs people have and the careers they follow. Individuals who have a high need for power see the company as a place where they can gain a position of status and authority. In fact, people with this need often seek careers in management and aspire to rise as high as possible in the company. They enjoy organizing the work of others and providing direction for them. They are not necessarily autocratic in their approach; they simply like to be responsible for directing the activities of others.

People who have a high need for affiliation see the company somewhat differently. They see it as a place where others are and therefore where they have an opportunity to form friendships and work in groups. They are motivated by tasks that promote social interaction and tend to choose careers such as personnel management and social work. If they have jobs in manufacturing or production, they prefer to work in self-managed teams rather than work alone.

People with a high need for achievement see the company as a place to work on challenging tasks and problems. It is a place where they can apply their skills and be recognized for their achievements. Careers in science, engineering, and product design appeal to them.

The need for achievement reflects a desire to accomplish something difficult, reach a high level of success, and surpass the achievements of others. The U.S. Navy recognizes outstanding achievements with a variety of decorations, medals, and ribbons. These rewards help satisfy sailors' need for self-esteem and recognition by others. Can you think of similar awards businesses give to satisfy the need for achievement?

Many become business owners, since owning their own businesses permits them to maximize their sense of achievement. It also allows them to unleash their creativity without the constraints that bosses would impose on them.

Some companies realize that employees with a high need for achievement can make important contributions if the organization can be structured to permit them to be creative. For example, 3M permits employees to use up to 15 percent of their work time to develop work-related projects in which they are personally interested. Two engineers, Arthur Fry and Spencer Silver, worked extra hours to develop Post-it™ Notes. Because they did this on their own time, they were able to take credit for the product, thus satisfying their need for achievement. 3M did not ignore their need for money, however; they receive a share of all profits on the sale of Post-it Notes.

To use McClelland's concepts of achievement, power, and affiliation needs, managers must give employees job assignments that appeal to employees' needs. Some employees prefer nonmanagerial jobs, some prefer scientific or engineering jobs, and some prefer to work with people. Many managers try to "put square pegs into round holes." But an employee who is highly motivated by working with people, such as a social worker, may be a terrible manager. What would seem to be a promotion to others might actually weaken the social worker's motivation and lead to a dissatisfied employee.

Two-factor concept
A theory of motivation based on hygienes and motivators.

Motivators
Factors related to employees' desire for growth in their work, which affect their level of satisfaction or motivation at work.

HERZBERG'S TWO-FACTOR CONCEPT

Practicing managers find the two-factor concept developed by Frederich Herzberg useful because it deals with designing the job itself to be a source of motivation.[9] The **two-factor concept** is a theory of motivation based on motivators and hygienes. From interviews with hundreds of workers, Herzberg found that there is a distinct set of conditions or factors that he called motivators. **Motivators** are factors related to employees' desire for growth in their work. These factors affect workers' levels of satisfaction or motivation at work and include achievement, recognition, work itself, responsibility, and advancement.

Exhibit 10.3 **THE TWO-FACTOR CONCEPT**

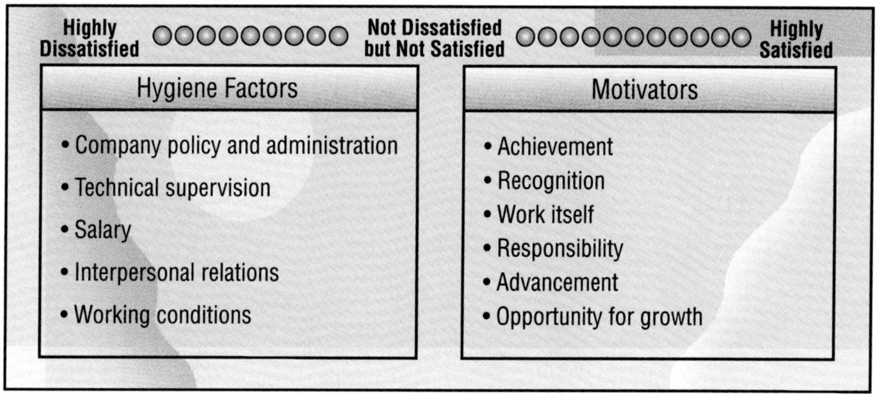

Highly Dissatisfied ○○○○○○○○○ Not Dissatisfied but Not Satisfied	○○○○○○○○○○○ Highly Satisfied
Hygiene Factors	**Motivators**
• Company policy and administration • Technical supervision • Salary • Interpersonal relations • Working conditions	• Achievement • Recognition • Work itself • Responsibility • Advancement • Opportunity for growth

Hygiene factors
Factors that describe employees' relationship to the environment in which they do their jobs and that affect their level of dissatisfaction at work.

Herzberg also found a second, different set of factors that he called hygiene factors. **Hygienes** are factors that describe employees' relationship to their job environment. Hygienes affect workers' levels of dissatisfaction at work and include company policy and administration, supervision, salary, interpersonal relations, and working conditions. The two-factor concept is illustrated in Exhibit 10.3.

While managers had previously thought that motivation and dissatisfaction are simply opposites of the same thing, Herzberg found they are quite different. Employees cannot be motivated simply by keeping them from being unhappy. Rather, to motivate employees, managers must provide entirely different things. More important, Herzberg found that to be motivated, employees must first *not be dissatisfied.* Thus, the two-factor theory proposes a two-step process to motivate employees:

1. First, make employees not dissatisfied by
   - Having sound, nonpunitive company policies that are administered fairly
   - Having good technical supervisors who permit employees to work without undue pressure and do not force employees to "do it my way!"
   - Paying salaries or wages that are adequate and fair
   - Establishing an environment that promotes good interpersonal relations between employees and supervisors
   - Creating good working conditions—comfortable offices, reasonable hours, and so on.
2. Then make employees motivated by
   - Permitting employees to achieve challenging goals with minimal interference
   - Recognizing employees' good performance and productivity and crediting them for their efforts
   - Giving employees more responsibility as they show the desire and ability to handle it
   - Providing a career path of meaningful advancements for productive employees
   - Designing jobs that are interesting and challenging
   - Providing training and educational opportunities that help employees grow, especially in skills that relate to their careers

The recognition that providing good working conditions and fair salaries will not necessarily motivate employees is important. Some managers think that being nice to employees and paying them good salaries will motivate them. But these actions simply keep them from being dissatisfied. Things given to us by others are not as motivating as things we give to

STREET SMART

Walking the Talk

Jack Welsch, CEO of General Electric for more than 12 years, offered the following advice to managers:

> I would argue that a satisfied work force is a productive work force. Back when jobs were plentiful and there was no foreign competition, people were satisfied just to hang around. Now people come to work with a different agenda.... Trust is enormously powerful in a corporation. People won't do their best unless they believe they'll be treated fairly—that there's no cronyism and everybody has a real shot. The only way I know to create that kind of trust is by laying out your values and then walking the talk. You've got to do what you say you'll do, consistently, over time.

ourselves. In addition, many companies find that giving monetary rewards often creates perceptions of inequity. "All recognition and perks are given to managers, but little or none are given to the nonmanagers who actually do most of the work," said an engineering manager with McClier Corporation in Atlanta.[10]

Motivation is accomplished only if employees first are not dissatisfied and second are provided with motivators. Thus, after providing fair salaries and good working conditions, managers must provide interesting and challenging jobs and opportunities for growth and responsibility. Frederick Schweizer, director of metallurgy at Special Metals Corporation in New Hartford, New York, says, "The best motivation is job satisfaction, which comes from responsibility, recognition, and reward."[11] In this way, employees achieve a sense of accomplishment and self-direction that motivates them to high levels of performance.

JOB ENRICHMENT: MANAGEMENT APPLICATION OF THE TWO-FACTOR CONCEPT

Job enrichment
The process of adding interest and challenge to jobs to make them more motivating to employees.

Herzberg believed one of the most important motivators is work itself. When jobs are interesting and challenging, employees will be more motivated. This idea formed the basis for a program called job enrichment. **Job enrichment** is the process of adding interest and challenge to jobs to make them more motivating to employees. Five essentials of job enrichment are

- Giving frequent feedback of performance results to the employee
- Creating the opportunity to experience psychological growth
- Providing opportunities to schedule components of one's own work
- Giving employees responsibility for some job costs
- Encouraging managers to be flexible and open to employee suggestions regarding their jobs
- Letting employees make some job decisions for which they have been trained.

Job enrichment is a very popular management process and has been successfully used by many organizations to achieve higher levels of employee motivation and productivity. Some surveys have found that employees rate interesting jobs far higher than good pay.

Japanese workers often take time out to engage in collective physical fitness activity. Japanese companies believe that these on-the-job exercises will help both the individual worker and the company. Companies with these programs believe they have enriched the workers' jobs.

A marketing assistant at a medium-size company began to feel she was going nowhere in her job. Her performance was still good, but she was losing interest in her work. She discussed the problem with her supervisor, who agreed to let her design a computer training program. She had a lot of interest in computers, and the company had a need for such a program. While continuing her marketing duties, the marketing assistant designed the training program and soon had trained over 40 employees in using the computers.

In one hospital, 500 employees were permitted to work with their supervisors to redesign their jobs. As a result, admission clerks are now patient representatives, admission managers also handle in-house contract negotiations with insurance companies, and nursing assistants receive professional training. Employee turnover has dropped from 34 percent to just 6 percent. These employees are now more productive and more satisfied—and so are the patients.[12]

THE ROLE OF REWARDS AND REINFORCEMENT IN MOTIVATION

Extrinsic rewards
The things other people give an employee (such as pay and promotions) in attempting to inspire better performance.

Intrinsic rewards
The good feelings people get when they have accomplished something important, such as completing a challenging job assignment.

Reinforcement theory
A motivation theory of the relationship between a given behavior and its consequences.

Extrinsic rewards and intrinsic rewards are the two basic categories of rewards. **Extrinsic rewards** are the things other people give an employee (such as pay and promotions) in attempting to inspire better performance. Short-term performance may be improved with extrinsic rewards, but long-term performance may depend more on the intrinsic rewards employees give to themselves. **Intrinsic rewards** are the good feelings people get when they have accomplished something important, such as completing a challenging job assignment. Managers may shape the nature of both extrinsic and intrinsic rewards.

Early 20th-century managers, such as Frederick Taylor, recognized that incentive pay plans might encourage employees to be more productive. But although managers have known about extrinsic rewards for a long time, pay for performance is a controversial issue for many people. Managers like the idea of rewarding employees according to their contributions, but it is hard to administer pay-for-performance systems. When properly administered, however, such systems can have a very positive effect on employee productivity and motivation.

Motivating employees by paying them according to their performance is based on principles of reinforcement theory. **Reinforcement theory** is a motivation theory of the relationship between a given behavior and its consequences. How rewards are administered to encourage desired behaviors is the focus of this theory. Immediate rewards and punishments

Exhibit 10.4 **AFFECTING WORK BEHAVIOR WITH REINFORCEMENT**

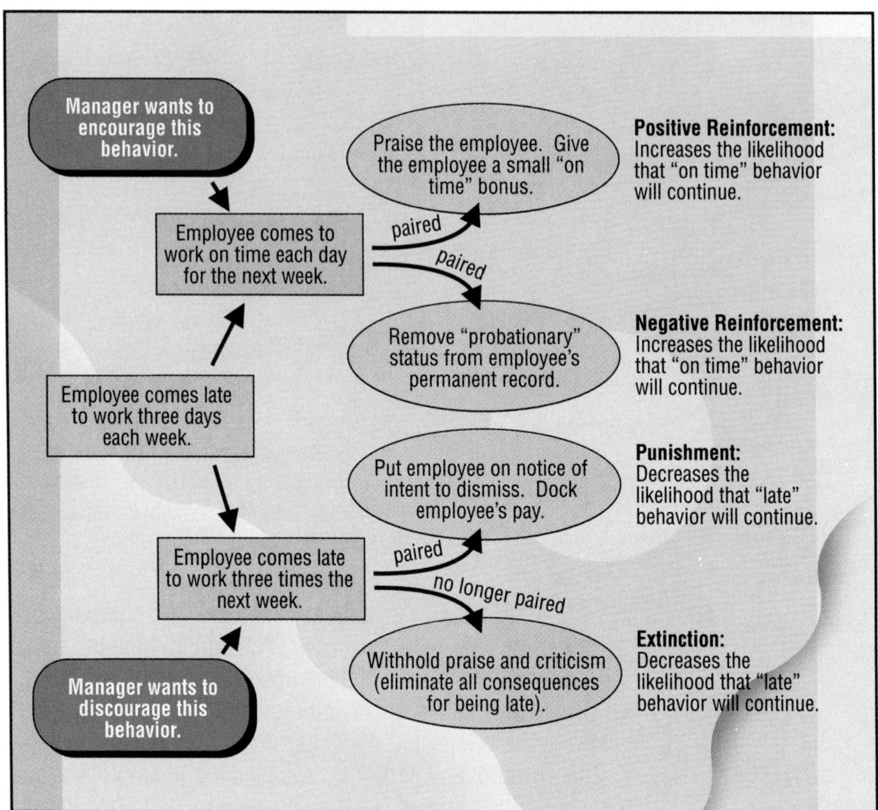

are used to change or modify employees' on-the-job behaviors that affect performance. The impact that rewards and punishments have on behavior is governed by the *law of effect,* which states that behavior that is rewarded tends to be repeated, while behavior that is punished tends to stop.

When a behavior is repeated because of a reward, it is said to be reinforced. Managers motivate employees using four basic effects: positive reinforcement, negative reinforcement, punishment, and extinction. Exhibit 10.4 illustrates these effects.

POSITIVE REINFORCEMENT

Positive reinforcement
The act of giving an employee a pleasant, valued consequence following a desired behavior.

Positive reinforcement is the act of giving an employee a pleasant, valued consequence following a desired behavior. Simply put, managers reward desired behavior, such as coming to work on time, with something pleasurable, such as a small bonus. Managers expect the reward will increase the likelihood that the employee will repeat the behavior. Many companies have used small bonuses and supervisor praise to increase "on-time" behavior of employees who previously were habitually late to work.

NEGATIVE REINFORCEMENT

Negative reinforcement
The act of removing some negative consequence following a desired behavior.

Suppose your friend is on academic probation, but then he or she gets a B average. Your friend's behavior is rewarded with the removal of the probation. **Negative reinforcement** is the act of removing some negative consequence after an employee performs a desired behavior. At work, timely attendance can be encouraged by removing unpleasant consequences such as probationary trainee status or unappealing night shift job assignments.

PUNISHMENT

Punishment
The act of giving a negative consequence following an undesired behavior.

Punishment is the act of giving a negative consequence following an undesired behavior. Pairing a negative consequence (like docking an employee's pay) with an undesired behavior such as tardiness will usually discourage that behavior. However, punishment does not always make it clear to the employee exactly what behavior is desired. For example, the chronically tardy employee may attempt to avoid punishment by finding ways to escape detection when she or he is late for work. Sometimes managers can successfully change this type of behavior by combining punishment with positive reinforcement. By punishing tardiness but systematically rewarding on-time behavior, the employee's undesirable behavior is discouraged at the same time the desired behavior is pointed out and encouraged.

EXTINCTION

Extinction
The withholding of all consequences, both positive and negative, following undesired behavior.

Extinction is the withholding of all consequences, both positive and negative, following undesired behavior. If a positive consequence does not follow a certain behavior, the behavior is less likely to be repeated. Thus, if a car dealer switches to a "no-haggling" pricing policy, sales personnel no longer receive rewards for "high-pressure" selling. They begin to realize that old behaviors no longer produce the desired outcomes.

USING REINFORCEMENT THEORY

While the basic idea of rewarding employees for desired behavior and punishing them for undesired behavior is simple, effective use of the theory is more complex. First, it is extremely important that the consequences (whether rewards or punishments) be given very soon after the behavior occurs. Otherwise the consequence and the behavior may not be "paired" in the employee's mind, and the old behavior will continue. Second, employees should be told why they are being rewarded or punished. This helps strengthen the pairing of the two events. Third, managers must determine how often to administer the consequences and how large the consequences should be.

FOCUS ON COMPANY

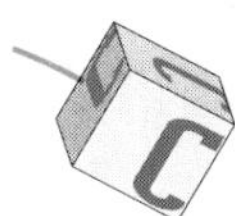

Participation and Rewards in Russia

For three-quarters of a century, Russian workers were part of the great experiment in socialism. If worker participation counted anywhere, it counted there. Has this changed since the breakup of the Soviet Union? To find out, several American researchers tested three motivational programs in the Kalinin Cotton Mill factory 90 miles northwest of Moscow. In the first, workers were given American goods as they increased the amount of top-grade fabric they produced individually. In the second, supervisors were trained to offer recognition and praise for productive behaviors, such as checking looms, changing rolls of fabric, and threading, and to criticize unproductive behaviors. In the third, workers' suggestions were solicited in open-ended discussions with supervisors.

The results? Participation actually led to *decreased* productivity. Extrinsic rewards, however, led to rapid improvements. Managers must recognize that different cultures in various stages of economic development may require somewhat different approaches to motivation.

THEORY X, THEORY Y, AND THEORY Z

How managers go about motivating employees depends greatly on their perceptions of the "typical" worker. Regardless of what they know about motivation theory, managers use only those concepts that correspond to their own view of the typical employee. Douglas McGregor, a management writer, proposed that managers tend to have two different perceptions of the typical worker that lead to entirely different motivation approaches. He called these two sets of perceptions *Theory X* and *Theory Y.*[13]

THEORY X

Theory X
The assumptions that employees are lazy and dislike work; must be forced, controlled, and threatened with punishment to be motivated to perform their jobs.

Some managers are relatively pessimistic about their subordinates' abilities and attitudes toward their jobs. These managers are called **Theory X** managers and hold the following assumptions:

- Employees dislike work and will avoid it if possible.
- Because they dislike work, employees must be forced, controlled, and threatened with punishment to be motivated to perform their jobs.
- Employees prefer to be directed, want to avoid responsibility, have relatively little ambition, and desire security.

Managers who hold these beliefs often seek to control all of their employees' behaviors and actions. They may use punishment to push employees to be more productive. They often threaten employees for poor performance and overlook their achievements. They withhold promotions because they believe employees lack ambition. They tend to be dictatorial in their leadership styles and do not consider employee inputs important. They tend to look down on management processes that allow employees to participate in setting objectives or determining how the organization is run.

THEORY Y

Theory Y
The assumptions that employees like work, seek out responsibilities, and can bring imagination and creativity to the job.

In contrast to Theory X managers, Theory Y managers are relatively optimistic regarding the abilities and attitudes of their subordinates. **Theory Y** managers believe that

- Employees like work; physical and mental work are as natural to them as play and rest.
- Employees do not want to be rigidly controlled or threatened with punishment.
- Employees will, under certain conditions, not only accept but also seek responsibility.
- Employees are capable of using a relatively high degree of imagination and creativity at work.
- Employees desire to satisfy social, esteem, and self-actualization needs as well as safety needs.

Rather than motivating employees by threat and punishment, Theory Y managers use rewards, incentives, and goals to create a motivational work environment. In such an environment, workers can help set their own objectives, use their creativity, and satisfy their higher-order needs. Theory Y managers emphasize self-control and participation.

While there probably are few pure Theory X or Theory Y managers, these two extremes illustrate important differences in motivational strategies used by managers. In fact, the trend in U.S. companies is toward the Theory Y approach. This approach corresponds to the major motivation approaches developed by Maslow, Herzberg, and other theorists. More recent concern about a possible loss of competitiveness to Japanese manufacturers has caused American companies to stress worker participation more heavily in their motivational strategies.

Exhibit 10.5 **THE THEORY Z MANAGEMENT APPROACH**

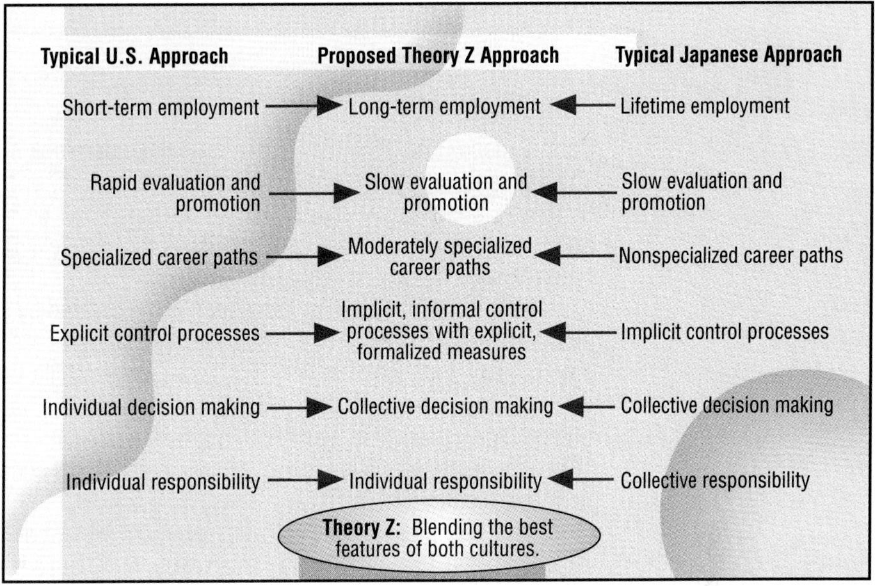

Typical U.S. Approach
Proposed Theory Z Approach
Typical Japanese Approach
Short-term employment
Long-term employment
Lifetime employment
Rapid evaluation and promotion
Slow evaluation and promotion
Slow evaluation and promotion
Specialized career paths
Moderately specialized career paths
Nonspecialized career paths
Explicit control processes
Implicit, informal control processes with explicit, formalized measures
Implicit control processes
Individual decision making
Collective decision making
Collective decision making
Individual responsibility
Individual responsibility
Collective responsibility
Theory Z: Blending the best features of both cultures.

THEORY Z

We explored the notion of total quality management (TQM) in previous chapters. We noted that Japanese companies have different relationships with employees than those in U.S. firms. W. Edwards Deming helped Japanese companies recognize the importance of employee participation in achieving high-quality products. Later William Ouchi, a professor of business at UCLA, studied Japanese manufacturers and concluded that their success was due not to the technology used in their production lines but to their special way of managing employees.

The Japanese approach to employee relations involved such arrangements as guaranteed lifetime employment, worker participation in decision making, nonspecialized career paths, and cooperative team building. The U.S. approach, in contrast, tended to focus on short-term employment arrangements, specialized career paths, and individual rather than team responsibility. Ouchi recognized that American culture differs greatly from Japanese culture and that the ways Japanese companies managed their employees might not work in the United States. However, he suggested a middle-of-the-road approach, illustrated in Exhibit 10.5. This approach, which blended the best features of both cultures, was labeled Theory Z.[14]

Theory Z
A management approach that emphasizes employee participation and modified Japanese and U.S. practices to improve motivation and productivity.

Theory Z suggests that worker participation is the key to increased performance. The **Theory Z** approach emphasizes long-term employment arrangements with employees rather than either short-term or lifetime ones. It provides job security and permits employees to focus on creativity and productivity. Employees receive varied training, broadening their skills and their value to the company. While promotions are somewhat slower to come by than typical in U.S. companies, this drawback is balanced by increased involvement and opportunity for growth.

The Theory Z firm is still somewhat rare in the United States, but it is on the increase. It is being tested in different labor markets, such as Mexico, by U.S. companies and will undoubtedly become more common in this country as well. Theory Z, which incorporates many of the concepts reviewed in this chapter, may indeed be the motivation approach of the future.

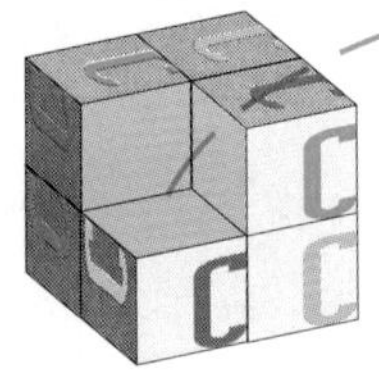

FOCUS ON COMPETITORS

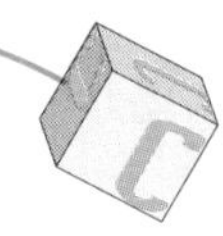

Mexican Workers

Dario Sanchez and his family live in a small cinderblock house in the city of Toluca, Mexico. The house is very basic, with no plumbing, furniture, or heat. But now the best thing about Sanchez's life is hope—hope that his lot in life will be far better than that of his parents. Sanchez works in a factory, and the pay is $78 a week. That's not much by U.S. standards, but in Mexico this pay is highly desirable.

The factory job is one of thousands being created by the movement of the auto industry south of the U.S. border. Each year, Mexican laborers are producing more cars and are now emerging as a low-cost, high-quality work force. While U.S. factories use costly robots and other mechanized approaches to control costs and improve quality, factories in Mexico are betting on highly motivated workers to produce quality at low cost. Ford, GM, and Chrysler have all opened major plants in Mexico, as have other global competitors such as Toyota, Mercedes, and Volkswagen.

In the automakers' view, Mexican workers are not only inexpensive but are motivated to deliver quality. The young work force adapts more quickly to new industrial methods than do experienced workers in the U.S. "Rust Belt." Workers in GM's Ramos Arizpe plant quickly mastered Japanese-style methods to become GM's number one "quality" plant. Mexican workers have taken to quality programs with near religious zeal. They have even recorded songs praising quality manufacturing. They take pride in work that they find intrinsically rewarding. In their culture, their jobs are held in high esteem.

At Ford plants in Mexico, workers are called "operators" or "technicians." They study statistics and ergonomics. They are grouped into teams and undergo intensive quality indoctrination. Graphs cover bulletin boards and remind the workers that they are producing higher-quality engines than their U.S. counterparts. It has been three years since GM auditors last found a defect in the plant at Toluca.

THE ROLE OF GOALS IN MOTIVATION

So far we have focused on motivating employees to achieve the "desired behavior." But what is the desired behavior? The answer lies in goal setting.

Most people have goals, such as what they want from their careers or from their private lives. Sometimes a goal is as simple as saving money for a new car. When you have saved up enough money, you purchase the car and thereby reach your goal. This act gives you a sense of accomplishment and pride. In this way, goals inspire people to take actions to achieve them. When employees reach goals that have been set for them on their jobs, they can have similar feelings of pride and accomplishment.

Goal-setting theory
A theory that explains how setting attainable goals and objectives can lead to high levels of motivation and accomplishment.

Goal-setting theory explains how setting attainable goals and objectives can lead to high levels of motivation and accomplishment. It examines the relationship between accomplishing goals and feelings of achievement and pride.

Performance goals
Targeted levels of performance that employees strive to achieve.

Performance goals act as targeted levels of performance that employees strive to achieve. When employees receive *feedback* that they have reached the goals, they feel good. Performance goals provide specific points toward which employees can focus their efforts. The setting of a performance goal is motivating because it makes it clearer to employees what they are to accomplish.

Exhibit 10.6 **EFFECT OF GOAL DIFFICULTY ON SENSE OF ACHIEVEMENT**

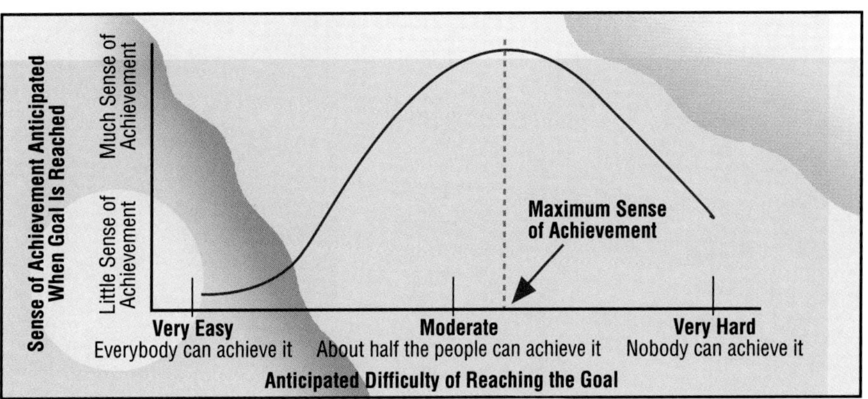

SETTING GOALS

There are four basic questions to answer when setting goals:

1. How difficult should performance goals be?
2. Who should establish the goals?
3. How specific should the goals be?
4. How much should employees be told about their progress toward achievement of the goals?

Goal Difficulty. The answer to the question "How difficult should performance goals be?" is found by examining the relationship between the difficulty of the goals and employees' perceived achievement. As Exhibit 10.6 shows, easy goals are those that nearly anyone can achieve. If everyone can reach them, people will not think their accomplishment is very special. Their achievement will have little meaning, and therefore the goals will not be very motivating to employees.

Goals that are very difficult to achieve are those that nobody, or almost nobody, will be able to reach. When employees look at these goals, they find it hard to imagine that they can reach them, no matter how hard they work. This discourages effort and decreases motivation. Furthermore, if they do manage to reach the goals, they will be considered quite lucky and will be unable to take individual credit for the achievement.

However, goals that are somewhere between moderate and difficult can be very motivating. Not everyone can reach these goals. When employees look at these goals, they can see that their own skills will make a large difference. If they do reach the goals, they will perceive it to be because they were skilled and worked hard—the two ingredients of a sense of high achievement.

Participative Goal Setting. Should a manager simply assign a performance goal for the employee, or should the employee have some say in what the goal should be? If moderate to difficult goals lead to higher motivation, the manager may conclude that it would be best to set goals at these levels without any employee participation. Some managers fear that if employees are allowed to set their own goals, they may set them low to avoid working too hard or out of fear of failing. Low goals will not motivate improved performance.

However, when employees participate in setting their performance goals, two things happen. First, they feel obligated to achieve the goals and are more committed to them than they would be to goals assigned to them by the manager. Commitment to the goals increases

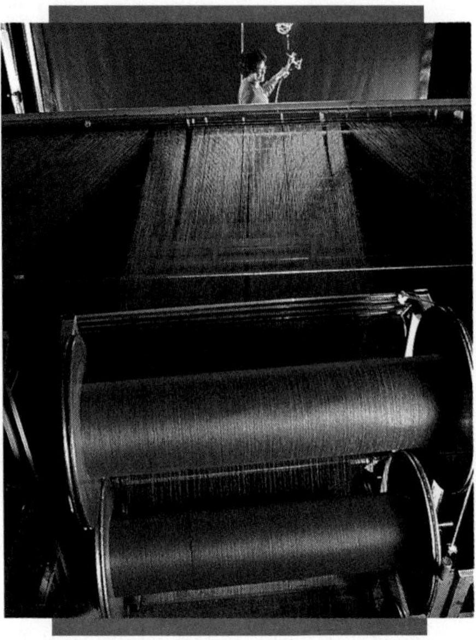

When carpeting giant Mohawk Industries acquired Horizon Industries and Fieldcrest's carpet division, the company extended its management philosophy to the new companies. David Kolb, Mohawk CEO, believes employees need to be involved in making decisions. "We would rather set broad objectives and get our people moving in that direction, and then reward them. When we acquired Horizon, we used a bonus program for hourly employees. . . . It rewarded people for reaching obtainable objectives. . . . It was a way to introduce them to our ideas about operations, incentives, and employee initiative."[15]

the motivation to achieve them. Second, employees actually set the goals at a more difficult level than they would with goals assigned to them. Goals that are more difficult (but not impossible) are more motivating.

Goal Clarity. Sometimes managers are not sure exactly what level of difficulty for goals is truly achievable. In some occupations goals can be easily described, such as "assemble 50 relay switches each day." In many others, this is not the case. For instance, how much should an engineer produce in terms of mechanical drawings or material specifications each day? Is it okay just to say, "Do your best" in cases like this?

When goals are hard to define, managers may prefer to say to employees, "Do your best," hoping they perceive this as a somewhat difficult challenge. But statements such as "Do your best" are not clear targets for employees to shoot for. They cannot tell whether their "best" is good enough as they go along. Therefore, managers must find ways to establish clear, specific goals to serve as performance targets that guide employee efforts along the way. In the case of the engineer, a goal such as "Finish this project in two weeks" is a much clearer target than "Do your best" because it refers to a definite requirement.

Feedback on Progress toward Performance Goals. Should employees be told how well they are progressing toward a goal, or should they find out only when the work ends, if ever? The motivational impact of feedback about progress toward performance goals is well documented. Feedback about progress toward goals helps employees assess how much effort is necessary to reach them. If employees are not exerting enough effort, it is better that they find out sooner than later. Late feedback does no good, but early feedback permits adjustments in effort. Also, feedback is necessary to feelings of achievement. If an employee finishes a pro-

Exhibit 10.7 **MANAGEMENT BY OBJECTIVES**

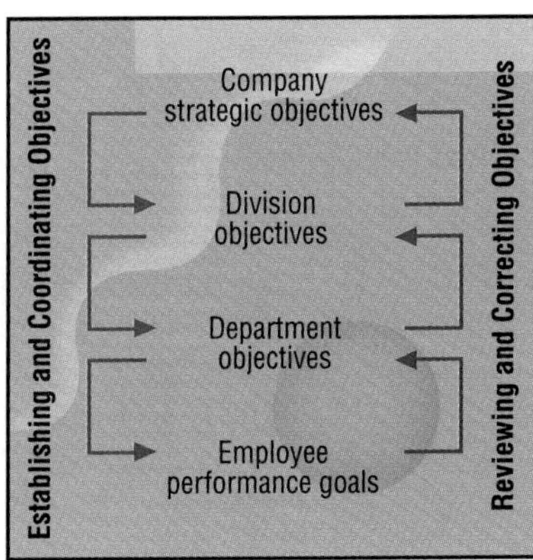

ject but has no idea whether or not the manager liked the work, he or she will feel no achievement, even if the manager liked it. Thus, feedback aids motivation by allowing employees to make adjustments as they work on the project and helping them to determine whether or not they indeed achieved the goal.

MANAGEMENT BY OBJECTIVES

There are many ways managers can use what they know about the motivational properties of performance goals. One of the most systematic applications of goal setting is called *management by objectives.* It is fairly easy to make individual goals motivating within the framework of goal setting, but tying all of the employees' individual goals together and relating them to the company's objectives is more challenging. **Management by objectives (MBO)** is a process for setting goals in which managers and their superiors define objectives for each division and department, and then managers and individual employees work together to set corresponding performance goals for the employees. Exhibit 10.7 illustrates this process.

Management by objectives (MBO)
A process for setting goals in which managers and their superiors define objectives for each division and department, and then managers and individual employees work together to set corresponding performance goals for the employees.

At each level in the goal-setting process, subordinates and superiors sit together and mutually set the goals and objectives. For example, company objectives might be discussed between top executives and division managers, and together they then set division objectives. Similarly, division managers might meet with their department managers and together set department objectives. Finally, department managers might meet with employees and together determine individual performance goals. These goals are then reviewed upward, with each manager checking with his or her superior, thus ensuring that complete coordination of goals has been achieved.

Under MBO, managers and subordinates regularly review progress toward goals. Adjustments in the employee's effort or in the goals are made as needed. This process incorporates all of the ingredients of goal setting (including goal difficulty, goal clarity, participation, and feedback), and employees are motivated to high levels of performance. At the end of the time frame for goal achievement, results are again reviewed. Employees receive rewards (or punishments) depending on their achievement levels, thus adding the properties of reinforcement to the MBO process.

MBO can be a very effective process for increasing employee performance. Surveys of employee attitudes toward MBO have generally found a high level of satisfaction with the process. However, MBO generates a great deal of paperwork, since goals and objectives must be reviewed at each level. Perhaps this problem will be overcome as managers increasingly apply computer techniques to the MBO process.

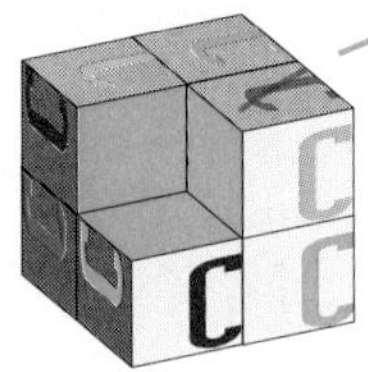

FOCUS ON CUSTOMERS

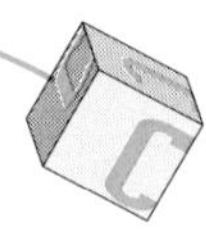

Roberts Express Values Its Customers

Jack Pickard, vice-president of sales and marketing at Roberts Express, a trucking company, believes a company must delight its customers and go beyond what they normally expect. One key to getting employees focused on customers and customer satisfaction is the inclusion of customer surveys in Roberts's MBO program. MBO provides clear direction to all employees and offers a strong financial incentive for performance that enhances customer satisfaction. Different employees have different goals depending on the nature of their jobs, but all employee goals are customer oriented. Roberts Express delights its customers by establishing goals such as making on-time deliveries, answering phones promptly, and providing friendly and competent customer service.

SUMMARY

1. ***Define and explain the importance of human relations.***
Human relations is the process by which the company manages and motivates people to achieve effective performance. Many business mission statements say something about human relations because good people are so important to the company's success. Effective managers spend much time and effort dealing with human relations issues.

2. ***Describe the impact that scientific management and the Hawthorne studies had on motivation theories.***
Scientific management, pioneered by Frederick W. Taylor, involved the systematic study of the most efficient way to perform a job and teaching workers those methods in the shortest time possible. Taylor's principles included matching workers' skills to those their jobs required and redesigning the tools and methods used on the job. With this approach, Taylor achieved consistent improvements in productivity.
The Hawthorne studies revealed the importance of the human or psychological factor in performance. Worker performances increased even in experiments designed to decrease performance, such as reducing the light intensity. The researchers decided that the increased motivation was due to feelings of being special due to membership in the work group, worker participation in decisions affecting the work, the social environment of the work group, and the additional pay workers earned from being more productive.

3. ***Define* motivation *and describe the role of needs in motivation.***
Motivation is the arousal, direction, and persistence of a particular behavior. One view of motivation is that people have basic needs and that when these needs are unsatisfied an internal tension or drive is created. This drive motivates specific behaviors that seem likely to result in rewards that would satisfy the need. Abraham Maslow identified a hierarchy of needs that includes physiological, safety, social, esteem, and self-actualization needs. David McClelland proposed that certain needs are acquired or learned and identified these as the needs for achievement, power, and affiliation.

4. ***Explain the two-factor concept of motivation.***
The two-factor concept of motivation was developed by Frederick Herzberg. Motivators are factors which are related to employees' desire for growth in their work, and which affect their level of satisfaction or motivation at work. Motivators include achievement, recognition, work itself, responsibility and advancement. Hygienes are factors which describe employees' relationship to

their job environment and which affect their level of dissatisfaction at work. Hygienes include company policy and administration, supervision, salary, interpersonal relations, and working conditions. The practical application of this theory in companies has been job enrichment—a focus on improving the content of the work itself.

5. ***Identify the role of reinforcement in motivation.***
Reinforcement theory focuses on rewards and how they are administered to encourage desired behaviors. Immediate rewards and punishments are used to change or modify employees' on-the-job behaviors that lead to performance. The impact that rewards and punishments have on behavior is governed by the law of effect which states that behavior which is rewarded tends to be repeated, but behavior which is punished tends to stop. When a behavior is repeated because of a reward the behavior is said to be reinforced.

6. ***Describe Theory X, Theory Y, and Theory Z.***
Theory X and Theory Y refer to assumptions managers hold regarding their subordinates. Theory X assumptions are that employees dislike work and will avoid it if possible; must be forced, controlled, and threatened with punishment to be motivated to perform their jobs; prefer to be directed, want to avoid responsibility, lack ambition, and desire security. Theory Y assumptions are basically the opposite: Employees like work, do not want to be controlled or threatened, will seek responsibility, are imaginative and creative at work, and seek to satisfy social, esteem, and self-actualization needs.
Theory Z blends the Japanese and U.S. approaches to employee relations. This approach emphasizes worker participation as the key to increased performance. Employment arrangements are long term. Employees are encouraged to focus on creativity and receive training to broaden their job skills. Promotion paths are slower, but worker participation and growth are increased.

7. ***Discuss how performance goals affect motivation.***
Performance goals serve as targets toward which employees can aim. When the goals are reached, employees experience feelings of pride and achievement. For goals to be motivating, they should be challenging but not impossible to achieve; employees should participate in setting the goals; the goals should be set in clear, measurable terms; and employees should receive feedback to let them assess their progress toward the goals.

8. ***Describe management by objectives (MBO).***
Management by objectives (MBO) is a process for setting goals in which managers and their superiors define objectives for each division and department, and then managers and individual employees work together to set corresponding performance goals for the employees. Managers and subordinates regularly review progress toward goals and make adjustments in the employee's effort or in the goals as needed. At the end of the time frame for goal achievement, results are again reviewed, and employees are rewarded (or reprimanded) for their achievement levels.

KEY TERMS AND CONCEPTS

Human relations (p. 214)
Scientific management (p. 214)
Hawthorne studies (p. 215)
Hawthorne effect (p. 216)
Motivation (p. 216)
Needs hierarchy (p. 217)
Physiological needs (p. 217)
Safety needs (p. 217)
Social (belongingness) needs (p. 217)
Esteem needs (p. 218)
Self-actualization needs (p. 218)
Need for achievement (p. 219)
Need for power (p. 219)
Need for affiliation (p. 219)
Two-factor concept (p. 220)
Motivators (p. 220)
Hygiene factors (p. 221)
Job enrichment (p. 222)
Extrinsic rewards (p. 223)
Intrinsic rewards (p. 223)
Reinforcement theory (p. 223)
Positive reinforcement (p. 224)

Negative reinforcement (p. 224)
Punishment (p. 225)
Extinction (p. 225)
Theory X (p. 226)
Theory Y (p. 226)
Theory Z (p. 227)
Goal-setting theory (p. 228)
Performance goals (p. 228)
Management by objectives (MBO) (p. 231)

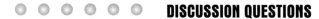

DISCUSSION QUESTIONS

Company

1. Why might the principles of scientific management, as applied by companies before the 1930s, fail in today's companies?
2. Why is it hard to administer pay-for-performance programs?
3. How difficult should performance goals be set to maximize employee motivation?

Customers

4. How might the ideas associated with need theories of motivation be applied to customer buying behavior?
5. How have some production line employees' jobs been enlarged to include responsibility for customer satisfaction? Give examples.

Competitors

6. In what ways might extreme competition among companies affect the usefulness of the two-factor concept for the companies' employees?
7. Do the strategic goals of a company relative to its position in a competitive market contribute to the sense of accomplishment and pride employees feel? Explain.

Collaborators

8. How important are outside activities, such as community service, in meeting employee needs?
9. What effects does government legislation have on the ability of companies to motivate their employees?

In Question: Take a Stand

Recent studies show that minority job applicants face discrimination in hiring at a rate about three times higher than that for nonminorities. Part of the hiring problem is blamed on inner-city issues, such as the trend to locate new plants in the suburbs. But Gary Orfield, professor of political science and education at the University of Chicago, believes racism is an important factor.

The effect on motivation is devastating. When qualified workers who live in the city cannot get to and from the suburban workplace, they lose self-esteem and are less inclined to try to find work. Lack of opportunity is one of the biggest obstacles to motivation. Supervisors must stop and ask how they can create an environment that will be fair and tap the potential of all individual employees.

This example suggests that many companies do not provide equal opportunities for all employees. How will this affect employee motivation? What can be done?

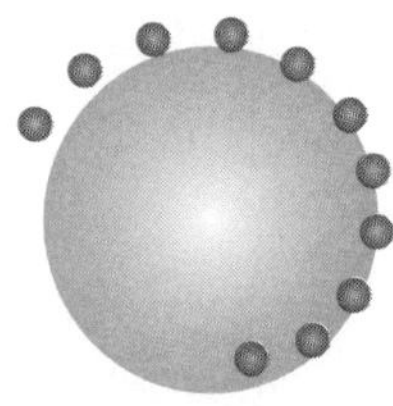

CASE 10.1
PAY FOR PERFORMANCE[16]

One of the most popular motivation programs used by managers is performance-based pay. A study of 630 companies found that 53 percent have some form of merit pay for nonexecutive employees.

John J. Groch, Jr., is one of the thousands of employees who are affected by pay-for-performance programs. He has worked at Nalco Chemical Company for more than twenty years and often has been recognized for high performance. This recognition has been in the form of an annual salary increase that is based on his productivity, and he likes it. "Pay for performance is something most people want," he says, "because if everyone gets the same compensation no matter how they do the job, there's no incentive. What it does is recognize those individuals who provide above-average performances. I truly believe that money is a motivator."

Nalco employees get only one pay raise each year, but they receive the merit pay on top of the regular salary increase program. At other companies, employees are given one-time, lump-sum incentive performance bonuses. Some top-level executives prefer employee pay for performance because the money paid for one-time bonuses does not become part of the annual salary expense and therefore does not count toward pensions, stock options, or profit sharing. Pay-for-performance bonuses are found at companies like Boeing, General Motors, and Nalco Chemical. Pay for performance is a growing trend because companies are trying to avoid fixed costs yet reward performance. The rationale is that performance-based pay dollars are aimed directly at the people who make the strongest contributions.

Questions

1. *Why is pay for performance at companies like Nalco Chemical Company so popular even though motivation is believed to be more affected by intrinsic rewards than by extrinsic rewards?*
2. *Does pay for performance have more applications to some types of jobs than to others? Explain.*
3. *Contrast the effects on employee loyalty, commitment, and job satisfaction to various pay programs such as pay for performance and straight salary.*

CHAPTER 11

HUMAN RESOURCE MANAGEMENT

When you have studied this chapter, you will be able to:

1. Define *human resource management* and identify four fundamental points of human resource management.
2. Identify the six steps of the human resource management planning process.
3. Describe the human needs forecast and the use of job analyses, job descriptions, and job specifications in the forecast.
4. Discuss the recruitment and selection processes.
5. Explain the role job and performance factors and labor market value play in the compensation of employees.
6. Discuss company training and development activities.
7. Describe the movements that occur among employees.
8. Discuss legal issues that affect human resource management.
9. Describe efforts by companies to improve quality of work life.
10. Explain the nature and importance of diversity programs.

In April 1992, McDonald's opened a flagship restaurant just off Tiananmen Square in Beijing, China. Local editorials described the company as a model employer. But soon the restaurant faced a public relations nightmare that took the shine off the golden arches.

Workers were enraged over poor conditions and low pay. One employee even distributed circulars demanding that workers unite in their dispute with management. The workers' complaints centered around McDonald's failure to keep salary increases in line with inflation and provide a decent benefits package. They also complained the work was too hard. News accounts stressed that these were the types of problems to be expected as socialist China adopts capitalist-style management techniques.

Tim Lai, managing director of the two-story restaurant, was surprised by the workers' complaints. McDonald's 600 workers in Beijing earned between 200 and 500 yuan each month ($35 to $88) compared with the average monthly Beijing wage of about 177 yuan ($31). They also received a housing allowance and coverage for medical, educational, and other social services that were normally provided by state employers in China's socialist system. Lai claimed the employee package was very competitive compared to those given by state employers. He also said workers were encouraged to communicate with management through a suggestion box and in monthly rap sessions with management.

McDonald's officials in Oak Brook, Illinois, painted the dispute as an isolated incident. They said such incidents are relatively rare at the chain, which has over 13,000 restaurants worldwide.[1]

As the business environment has become more global, situations such as that faced by McDonald's have become more common. Maintaining employee morale and productivity requires that managers effectively manage their human resources. The purpose of this chapter is to examine activities associated with human resource management.

OVERVIEW OF HUMAN RESOURCE MANAGEMENT

Human resource management
The process of recruiting, hiring, training, developing, and maintaining an effective work force within the company.

The management of human resources is a dynamic process that is facing rapid changes in our increasingly global business environment. **Human resource management** is the process of recruiting, hiring, training, developing, and maintaining an effective work force within the company.

To manage human resources effectively, managers need to understand four fundamental points. First, human resource management is the responsibility of *all* managers in the company. It is not a staff function carried out only by personnel specialists. Every manager in companies like McDonald's and in every business location must recruit, hire, train, develop, and maintain human resources.

Second, human resource management views employees as important resources or assets of the company. Despite all the emerging new technologies of production and information, and all the money being invested in buildings and equipment, human resources are what make a company competitive. This fact makes the expertise and skills needed to manage human resources critical to the organization's success.

Third, one of the major tasks of human resource management is to match employees and their skills and needs to the company's goals and objectives. This task is typically required each time an employee is hired for a particular job or receives specialized training. These activities are intended to perfect the match between the employee and the organization's goals.

Fourth, an increasing body of complex, comprehensive, and confusing laws governing relations between employers and employees is emerging. These laws affect all aspects of human resource management, and managers must be aware of them and comply with them. Failure to abide by the guidelines set forth in this legislation may result in enormous fines and penalties.

THE IMPORTANCE OF HUMAN RESOURCE MANAGEMENT

Increased competition, emphasis on productivity, legal constraints, advances in technology, and the changing nature of the work force are making human resource management increasingly important to companies. Unless human resource managers—and all managers in the company—perform their function effectively, employees may be mismatched to their jobs, reducing the company's competitiveness and productivity. A variety of examples illustrate the impact of human resource management on the company's operations:

- The Clinton health care reform plan, expected to be in place by 1995 or 1996, will drastically change how companies provide insurance benefits for employees. The costs of this program may be excessive for some employers.[2]
- Prospect Associates, a health research and communications company in Rockville, Maryland, lets employees bring their children to work if necessary, as long the children are well behaved and don't disturb the operation.[3]
- Provisions of the Americans with Disabilities Act of 1990 regulate a number of business activities ranging from questions permitted on

Parental leave at LinguiSystems gave Paul Johnson two weeks off with pay to be with his wife, Kenya, and their newborn daughter, Maureen. LinguiSystems provides both men and women with up to 12 weeks of parental leave. LinguiSystems is at the forefront of a human resource trend.[4]

application blanks, to width of grocery store aisles, to carpet pile height in public buildings.[5]

- Japanese employers, who once lauded their lifetime employment arrangements, are now struggling with the costs of this program. Faced with a loss of up to $300 million, Mazda is shifting white-collar workers to assembly line operations, and some companies are considering more drastic options.[6]

THE STAGES OF HUMAN RESOURCE MANAGEMENT

Exhibit 11.1 illustrates that human resource management consists of three stages. The first stage includes activities designed to attract productive employees to the company. The primary activities during this stage are planning, recruiting, and selecting employees. The second stage consists of activities to develop employees into a productive work force. Training and developing are the essential activities during this stage. The third stage includes activities that maintain the work force, such as compensating, promoting, transferring, demoting, and separating employees. This stage also includes innovation in methods that will maintain employee productivity.

GLOBAL DIMENSIONS OF HUMAN RESOURCE MANAGEMENT

Increased global competition has changed virtually every aspect of business, including human resource management activities. In the past, human resource management was a function devoted primarily to hiring and firing domestic employees and maintaining salary records. Then it evolved into a staff function, conducted by specialists called "personnel managers." Line managers were not involved in personnel activities except to give final approval in hiring and firing decisions. As unionization activities increased, personnel departments became involved in bargaining and negotiating union contracts.

However, the intense global competition of the last two decades led to manufacturing and marketing around the world. Companies began focusing more attention on human resource

Exhibit 11.1 **THREE STAGES OF HUMAN RESOURCE MANAGEMENT**

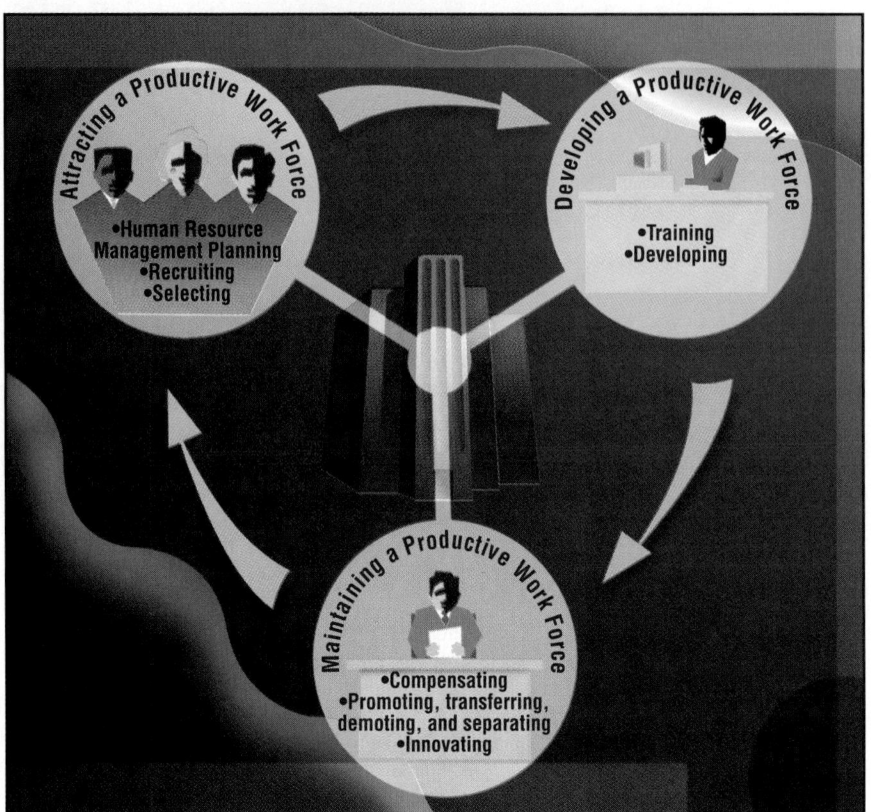

management as a global activity. Managers recognized the importance of human resources to the organization's ability to compete on a worldwide basis. Companies increased the involvement of line managers in human resource management activities. They also began to include human resource managers in the planning of corporate strategies.

DOWNSIZING

The term *downsizing*—reducing the work force—became commonplace during the turbulent 1980s. When huge companies like IBM, Texas Instruments, Sears, and United Air Lines found their profits dwindling, they released thousands of workers and eliminated many unprofitable business operations. Due to restructuring and reorganization, many employees found they had been declared a "surplus," and their positions had been eliminated. One research firm estimated that 615,186 jobs were lost in 1993 as a result of downsizing, nearly twice as many as in the recession year of 1990.[7] Downsizing is unpleasant and demoralizing to the remaining workers. But dramatic downsizing actions are less necessary if a company has an adequate human resource management plan.

HUMAN RESOURCE MANAGEMENT PLANNING

Six steps are involved in the human resource management planning process (see Exhibit 11.2):

1. The process begins with setting the organization's strategic objectives.

Exhibit 11.2 **THE HUMAN RESOURCE PLANNING PROCESS**

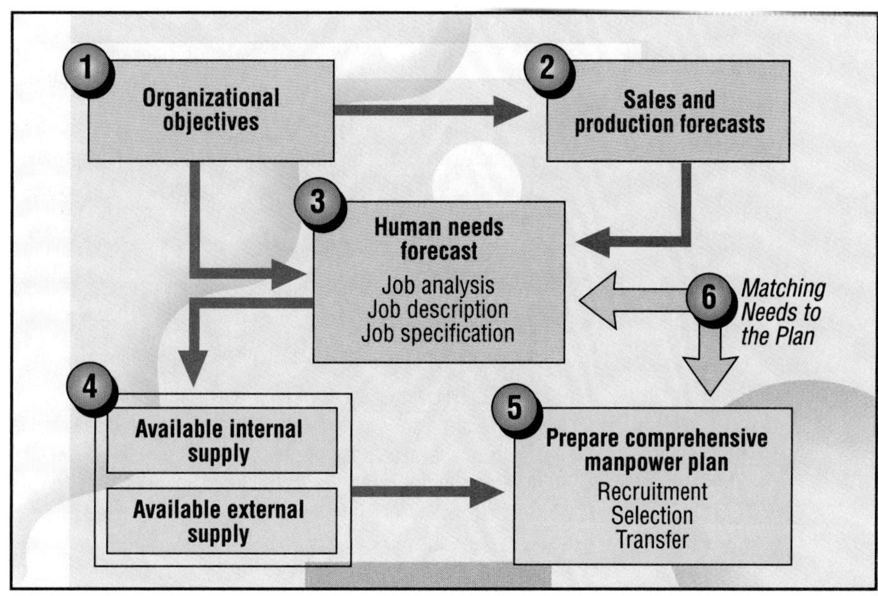

2. Sales and production forecasts are made from the company's objectives. These forecasts may also use sales projections based on past trends and economic forecasts.
3. Organizational objectives are combined with sales and production forecasts to generate a human needs forecast. This forecast is then refined through job analyses, job descriptions, and job specifications. This results in forecasts for specific numbers of employees who have sets of specified skills and abilities.
4. Managers analyze current supplies of employees having those skills and abilities (internal supply) and what is available in the labor market (external supply). Then they compare these supplies and skills to the human needs forecast to determine whether more or fewer employees will be needed.
5. The need for employees is compared to what is available, and a plan for recruiting, selecting, and transferring employees is developed.
6. The plan is compared to the human needs forecast to ensure that it will accomplish its purpose. The purpose is to have enough of the right types of employees in the right jobs at the right times to reach the company's goals.

THE HUMAN NEEDS FORECAST

Human needs forecast
A process that compares the current level of employment in various jobs to the numbers needed to fulfill the production and sales forecasts and to meet the company's strategic objectives.

The **human needs forecast** compares the current level of employment in various jobs to the numbers needed to fulfill the production and sales forecasts and to meet the company's strategic objectives. Before these numbers can be derived, managers must have a good understanding of the jobs to be performed and the employee skills and qualifications needed in those jobs. Generally, they get this information by using job analysis, job description, and job specification.

Job analysis
The systematic gathering of information about a job.

Job Analysis. **Job analysis** is the systematic gathering of information about a job. This information includes such items as job titles, supervisors, training, experience, and other qualifications needed to perform the job; responsibilities and activities involved in the job; and

Exhibit 11.3 **A JOB DESCRIPTION**

Wicker Hot Air Balloon Company
500 Main Street • Central City, USA

JOB DESCRIPTION
Accounting and Settlement Clerk

General Statement of Duties

Prepares, checks and distributes various accounting reports and statements to external and internal users. Posts to and prepares reports from general ledger accounts and performs other clerical duties as required.

Supervision Received

Works under close supervision of accounting supervisor or departmental manager.

Supervision Exercised

No supervisory duties assigned to this job.

Specific Job Duties

1. Prepares bank reconciliation statements and other financial summary statements for distribution to external clients and internal users.
2. Posts entries in various general ledger journals.
3. Prepares special reports from information generated from computer printouts and accounting statements.
4. Prepares on a monthly basis, complete financial reports and related trial balances for internal reporting purposes.
5. Performs certain routine office duties such as mailing, typing, report verification, and copy work.
6. Performs related activities as assigned by supervisor.

Minimum Qualifications

Education: High school degree required. Knowledge of accounting, math or information systems preferred.

Experience: Previous accounting experience desirable but not required.

Knowledge, skills and abilities: Position requires some knowledge of financial summary and bank reconciliation statements. Must work well with people. Ability to work quickly and accurately is of fundamental importance.

working conditions. The information also includes organizational data such as whether the job is dependent on other jobs and which jobs will follow the completion of this job.

Job analysis is performed by distributing employee questionnaires, interviewing employees holding the jobs, observing them as they perform their jobs, and soliciting supervisors' opinions. This information helps managers redesign the jobs, establish wage structures, and design training programs. Job analysis information is also used to create job descriptions and job specifications, two critical documents in the human resource planning process.

Job description
A document that describes the objectives for the job, the responsibilities and activities involved, how the job relates to other jobs, working conditions, and similar facts.

Job Description. A **job description** specifies the objectives for the job, the responsibilities and activities involved, how the job relates to other jobs, working conditions, and similar facts. It also has some career information, such as where the employee might expect to be promoted from the job. Exhibit 11.3 shows an example of a job description.

Job specification
A document that specifies the qualifications, skills, training, education, and other personal characteristics required of the person performing the job.

Job Specification. A **job specification** identifies the qualifications, skills, training, education, and other personal characteristics required of the person performing the job. The job specification lists such items as how many years of experience are needed to qualify for the job, required education levels, skills, special training, and, in some cases, psychological characteristics.

Exhibit 11.4 **JOB ADVERTISEMENTS**

R & D SECRETARY

Telectronics Pacing Systems, a world leader in cardiac device technology, has an immediate opening for an R & D secretary.

Responsibilities will include technical library maintenance, mail distribution, typing, file maintenance, coordination of travel arrangements and other special projects.

Requires: H.S. diploma, 55 wpm typing, computer experience (WP & DOS) and a minimum of two years previous office experience Must have excellent verbal and written communication skills.

We offer a competitive salary and benefits package including a 401K plan. Send resume and salary history to:

Telectronics Pacing Systems
Attn: Human Resources RDS
7400 S. Tucson Way
Englewood, CO 80112
EOE M/F/H/V

Medical Sales Representative
Denver Based

• Sherwood Medical, one of the most respected manufacturers in the disposable medical products industry, has an immediate opening for a qualified sales representative to sell our broad line of Kangaroo brand enteral feeding products, electronic thermometers and wound care products to hospitals and dealer networks in the Colorado/Utah area. • R.N. or Bachelor's Degree required with one to three years outside sales experience preferred. • In addition to a challenging career opportunity, we provide complete product and in-field training, company car, base salary, bonus opportunity, expenses, and an excellent benefits package. Qualified applicants are invited to send resume, including salary history to: Sherwood Medical Sherwood Regional Manager, P.O. Box 6549, Moraga, CA 94570 Equal Opportunity Employee, M/F/H. Agencies need not reply.

Condensed information from job descriptions and specifications is used to create job advertisements. Exhibit 11.4 gives some examples of job advertisements. These advertisements show both the job description and the job specification. In the Telectronics advertisement, for instance, the job description includes responsibilities such as technical library maintenance, mail distribution, typing, and file maintenance. The job specification includes a high school diploma, typing speed of 55 words per minute, computer experience, and a minimum of two years' previous office experience.

EVALUATING THE INTERNAL AND EXTERNAL SUPPLY OF EMPLOYEES

By conducting a job analysis, human resource managers can determine exactly what jobs are involved in reaching the company's objectives and how many employees will be needed. From the resulting job descriptions and job specifications, managers can then identify the qualifications of the employees needed for those jobs. The next step in the human resource planning process is to find out if the needed employees are already available within the company or whether the company must find new employees in the general labor market.

PREPARING THE HUMAN RESOURCE MANAGEMENT PLAN

The comprehensive human resource management plan includes estimates on the number of employees needed, where they will come from and how they will be recruited, selected, trained, and motivated to reach the desired levels of performance. Estimates of all associated costs are prepared and discussed with top executives. This discussion ensures that the plan is integrated with the strategic plan and that sufficient human resources will be available to achieve the company's objectives and goals.

RECRUITMENT AND SELECTION

After analyzing and describing jobs and determining the necessary qualifications, human resource managers must attract the required number of new, qualified employees to the company. Attracting new employees depends on two distinct human resource management activities: recruitment and selection.

RECRUITMENT

Recruitment
The process of informing qualified potential employees about job openings and encouraging them to apply for those positions.

Recruitment involves several activities designed to inform qualified potential employees about job openings and encourage them to apply for those positions. Although recruitment may sound like a fairly easy task, it is not. Legal restrictions and requirements, such as the Civil Rights Act of 1964, have dramatically altered this traditional process. Dun & Bradstreet is among the hundreds of companies seeking to increase diversity among its employees through an improved recruiting system. Its recruitment process focuses on minority recruitment and includes providing minority internships. Kraft General Foods puts its recruiters through its own diversity training program and has a program to encourage first-year Hispanic MBA students to study marketing.[8]

Employers can recruit from many sources, both within and outside the company. The first place many companies look is within the firm. In many cases, new job openings represent promotion opportunities for existing employees, who are already familiar with the company and its culture.

In other cases, employers either cannot find qualified employees from within or want to find "new blood" to inject new ideas and methods into the company. To minimize expense and time, these employers use collaborators to help them find qualified employees. Some collaborators used by companies include colleges, trade schools, state employment agencies, private employment agencies, labor unions, and professional organizations. Other outside sources include newspaper and professional journal advertisements and recommendations by current employees.

Employment agencies are very important collaborators for most companies. Typically an employment agency has a large pool of job applicants and has already tested them to determine their job skills. Thus, the recruitment pool it provides has already been refined to fit the company's needs.

At the higher management level, firms called "headhunters" provide a related service. Headhunters are even going global, finding qualified executives who can work anywhere in the world. Most of the candidates recruited by these agencies are experienced executives who are often fluent in two or more languages.

FOCUS ON COLLABORATORS

Finding the International Executive

One problem in finding international executives in the U.S. market is that few Americans have overseas work experience, speak foreign languages, or are familiar with the customs and business practices of other cultures. International jobs usually pay more than $75,000 annually, and the recruiting firm earns 35 to 40 percent of that amount from the hiring company.

So what do you need to find one of these international management jobs? Patrick W. Zilliacus is an engineer with a master's degree in business. He was chief executive at a multinational company based in Palo Alto, California, and speaks five languages. Dunhill Personnel System, Inc., found that most American managers are not "ready to compete globally" and don't think language fluency or understanding of cultures is important. However, the demand for language fluency is great. If you're a business school graduate fluent in Japanese and have spent a year in Japan, the field is wide open for you.

SELECTION

Selection
The process of screening applicants for the skills and abilities listed in the job specification to determine which ones are best suited for the job.

Once several people have applied for the job opening, human resource managers begin the selection process. The purpose of **selection** is to screen applicants for the skills and abilities listed in the job specification to determine which ones are best suited for the job. Effective evaluation of an applicant's ability to perform the job depends first on the type of information gathered on the applicant.

Information about the applicant may be gathered on the application blank itself, from the results of various job tests, and from recommendations by previous employers and personal acquaintances. Application forms request information such as name, address, previous work experience and salary, education, special training, and personal references. This information gives some insight into the candidate's work skills and interests. Job tests may include physical tests, such as for word processing skills, and psychological tests for attributes like assertiveness and sociability. Recommendations from previous employers will confirm past job skills and work attitudes, while personal recommendations may reveal various personality attributes.

FOCUS ON COLLABORATORS

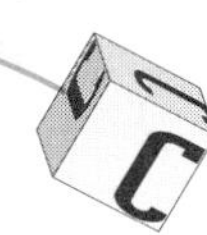

Avert Inc.

Like most small employers, Paul York's auto dealerships in Corpus Christi, Texas, don't have trained staff to check the backgrounds of prospective employees. So they use Avert Inc., a business that specializes in checking job applicants' resumes and backgrounds. Avert has uncovered problems like suspended driver's licenses and moving violations that would represent poor employment risks for York's dealerships.

Despite controversies arising from threats to applicant's privacy, firms like Avert Inc. are thriving. Employers of all sizes say they worry about a rising trend toward negligent-hiring suits, in which juries have faulted employers for failing to look thoroughly enough into the background of an employee who later committed a work-related crime.

Legal Considerations about Diversity. Various states and federal laws specify the proper use of information-gathering devices and the data they contain. Employers can discriminate among applicants only on the basis of job-related skills and attributes. It is generally illegal to discriminate on any other basis such as sex, age, race, religion, or ethnic background. Many states also have made it illegal to discriminate on the basis of sexual preference. Finally, it is often illegal to discriminate against candidates with disabilities if the job and work setting can be adjusted to accommodate the disability.

Managers must ensure that their selection procedures do not discriminate against applicants on any of these bases. But this can happen even when the managers are not personally biased if they have not carefully chosen their selection tests and procedures. Brooks Brothers, Inc., an apparel retailer in Massachusetts, settled a charge of hiring discrimination brought because it had said different things to African-American and white job applicants. White applicants were told an assistant manager position was open, but only an hour later an

STREET SMART

Reference Checks

Everyone understands the importance of checking identity, education, employment history, and references against information the job applicant provides. But some companies, pressured for time, drop their guard. Witness Hatteras Hammocks. In October 1991 the $10-million Greenville, N.C., company abruptly lost its controller. Executive vice-president Jay Branch interviewed several candidates for the position, but one man distinguished himself from the others. Recommended by someone Branch knew, the candidate came with a great resume—B.A. in accounting, M.B.A. from Indiana University, CPA, and several years as controller at a big local corporation. The following March, Branch hired him after a quick call to the previous employer. After a few months it became obvious that the new controller couldn't do the job, and by October Branch had fired him. His replacement quickly saw something wrong with the company's books. The man with the fancy resume had embezzled $60,000 from Hatteras Hammocks. A quick background check turned up no record of either of his degrees or his CPA credentials. The police arrested him and he confessed. Now his former employer, the large corporation, is also scrutinizing its books. Branch, who saw his own name forged on several checks, says, "The whole episode taught me the necessity of checking thoroughly, no matter how good a recommendation is."

African-American applicant was told the position was closed. William Roberti, president of Brooks Brothers, said the company was committed to equal employment opportunity and apologized for the incident.[9] This example stresses the need to exercise great care in the selection process to ensure equal treatment of all job applicants. Some of the laws that affect the selection process are discussed later in this chapter.

COMPENSATION

Compensation
All monetary payments and all nonmonetary goods and services given to employees in place of money.

One of the first steps in maintaining an effective work force is to establish proper compensation. **Compensation** consists of all monetary payments and all nonmonetary goods and services given to employees in place of money. Compensation of employees generally includes wages or salaries and fringe benefits such as health insurance, paid vacations and holidays, retirement plans, and profit bonuses. Effective compensation systems maintain equity among workers and promote loyalty and motivation. An effective system also helps the company during the recruitment and selection process. Ineffective compensation, in contrast, leads to high employee turnover, poor morale, and low levels of performance.

A COMPENSATION MODEL

As McDonald's discovered in Beijing, employees often complain about their salaries. Even when salaries appear to be competitive with those offered elsewhere, some employees perceive the pay system as inequitable, or unfair. Compensation structures that are equitable and also contribute to employee motivation are based on three factors: the job the employee holds, how well he or she performs it, and the general level of salaries paid by other employers.

Job evaluation
The process of establishing the general wage level for a job based on the skills, education, experience, and abilities required to perform the job.

Job Factors. Employee compensation first depends on the nature of the work performed. Not all jobs are worth the same amount of compensation from the company's viewpoint. The process of establishing the general wage level for a job based on the skills, education, experience, and abilities required to perform the job is called **job evaluation**.

Exhibit 11.5 **A MODEL OF COMPENSATION**

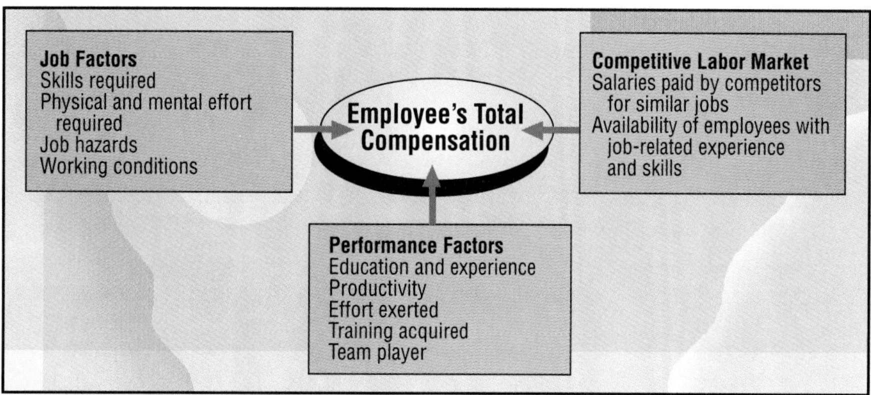

As Exhibit 11.5 shows, jobs may vary in the types and amounts of skills required and in working conditions and hazards associated with the job. They may also vary in the amount of physical or mental effort required of employees.

Working conditions (such as having to work outdoors in all kinds of weather) and job hazards are important compensation factors. Employees in extremely hazardous jobs, such as the firefighting crews who put out the oil well fires in Kuwait, often earn high salaries. Electrical engineers also earn high salaries, even though their jobs are not hazardous and are performed in nice office buildings, because their jobs demand great mental abilities, education, and special training.

Performance Factors. In addition to compensating employees according to the value of their jobs, companies must recognize the contributions made by individual employees. The evaluation of an employee's contributions in terms of current, real performance as well as potential for future contributions is called **performance appraisal**.

Performance appraisal
The evaluation of an employee's contributions in terms of current, real performance as well as potential for future contributions.

Not all electrical engineers are worth the same, for example. When one engineer works harder or creates a particularly valuable product, this contribution must be rewarded. Managers can measure and assess these types of direct performance factors and include them in employees' compensation.

One reason for differences in the value of individual employees is thought to be in employees' potential for assuming more responsible positions and developing new methods, products, or services. However, it is difficult to identify such potential, and many companies have used this factor as an excuse to discriminate against minorities. This practice is illegal and may result in substantial financial penalties, as Shoney's Inc., the nation's third largest family restaurant chain, discovered. Although Shoney's had 90 regional director positions, none were ever filled by African-Americans. These employees were assigned to kitchen duties, and few were hired for restaurants located in predominantly white areas. Obviously Shoney's was using race as a factor in identifying "potential" rather than skills related to job performance. In November 1992, Shoney's agreed to pay $105 million to victims of its discriminatory practices.[10]

Competitive Labor Market Value. The third factor in compensation is the general level of salaries for similar jobs in the competitive labor market. The most obvious example of how the labor market influences compensation is found in professional sports and entertainment. If a team wants to have superstars as gate and TV attractions, it must be willing to match the price paid by other teams.

Howard Schultz has transformed Seattle-based Starbucks Coffee Company from a local coffee manufacturer into a profitable $90 million national retailer. His radical growth strategy: Make every dollar you invest in your employees show up on the bottom line. He's convinced his employees work harder and smarter because they have a stake in the outcome and are committed to the organization's success.

Similar influences occur in most occupations. If there are relatively few plumbers, compensation for plumbers will increase because companies will compete for their services. If competitors pay between $15 and $25 per hour for a skilled plumber, a company that wants to hire a plumber must expect to pay somewhere in this range.

ALTERNATIVE COMPENSATION METHODS

The compensation model described in Exhibit 11.5 is common, but many companies use other methods to determine employee compensation. For example, pay-for-performance systems, described in Chapter 10, provide incentives for improving performance. Under a **piece-rate incentive system**, compensation is based on the amount of output an employee produces.

Piece-rate incentive system
A compensation system based on the amount of output an employee produces.

Another type of incentive system involves paying some base wage and then adding an incentive based on output. Thus, a salesperson might get a base salary of $1,500 a month plus 5 percent commission on the products he or she sells. Still another approach is a base salary plus an incentive based on what the work group (rather than the individual) produces. This is especially useful where the job requires considerable teamwork that individual incentives would disrupt. One common group-based incentive system, the Scanlon plan, is used by many manufacturers. A Scanlon plan consists of a plantwide wage incentive and an employee suggestion system. As employee productivity improves, increased profits are shared by the company and employees. Savings from employee suggestions are also passed to employees in some manner such as a plantwide bonus.

Finally, many companies pay a straight salary as described in the compensation model but add an incentive based on the profits earned by the company at the end of the accounting period. This is called **profit sharing** and is the most common incentive plan in the United States. It is estimated that more than 20 percent of U.S. companies use some form of profit-sharing plan.[11] Woodward Governor Company is one of many that find this approach worthwhile. At Woodward, daily figures for the company's sales, production, and profit are posted

Profit sharing
An incentive program in which some percentage of the company's profits are distributed to employees.

in the employee cafeteria. Thus, employees are kept current on progress toward production and profit goals. Woodward attributes its high levels of productivity and employee morale to this approach.

BENEFITS

Wages, salaries, and incentive payments are an important part of the total compensation package. Money provides a basic means by which companies motivate employees and encourage improvements in skills and productivity. However, maintaining an effective work force also depends on benefits that offer longer-term security. Benefits may not have the motivational impact of money, but they encourage loyalty, morale, and length of service to the company. Benefits are a central part of the pay structure, often adding more than one-third to a company's labor cost.

Companies may offer their employees a wide range of benefits. Common benefits include health and life insurance, retirement programs, paid vacations and holidays, sick time off, and child care. In addition, many companies offer on-premise medical and dental care, paid sabbaticals for long-term employees, company fitness and wellness programs, and on-premise barber services.

Company-sponsored fitness programs benefit not only employees but company productivity. Employee participation in such programs may reduce the employees' share of costs in other benefits, such as health insurance. Companies like Mesa Petroleum compensate employees for sick days they don't use and for reaching health goals set in the fitness program. Benefit programs like these improve the quality of the work force, which in turn improves the quality of the company's products and services.

FOCUS ON COMPANY

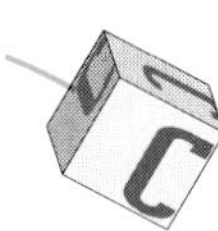

Employee Health Equals Company Health

For some time, companies have been paying for weight-loss programs, stress management seminars, and other wellness programs for employees. Some organizations, including the Bank of Delaware and U-Haul, shave the cost of insurance or deductibles for employees who exercise and quit smoking. Johnson & Johnson provides better benefits packages for employees who live healthy lifestyles. Adolph Coors Company and Control Data Corporation pay $10,000 more in death benefits if an employee killed in a car accident was wearing a seat belt. At Mesa Limited Partnership, employees who take no sick days, file no medical claims, control their weight, blood pressure, and cholesterol levels, and exercise at least 13 times a month earn up to $354 extra a year. One Manhattan real estate company pays $500 to employees who climb the 16 flights to their offices every day for a year. Turner Broadcasting System refuses to hire smokers.

The success of these programs is a tribute to the human resource managers who put them together. The programs are new, and their costs have not yet been determined. But the incentives paid are small, usually no more than a few hundred dollars a year. Companies believe the payoff is a healthier work force with lower absenteeism and fewer medical claims. And employees who are healthier are more productive.

Some benefits are paid completely by the employer, while others involve some type of cost-sharing arrangement by employer and employee. Some benefits are required by law, such as social security, which requires a contribution by both employer and employee. State unemployment compensation is widely required to provide temporary compensation for employees who are terminated from their jobs.

Flexible benefit plan
A benefit program in which employees are given specified dollar allowances which they allocate among benefits they prefer.

The newest approach to benefit programs is **flexible benefit plans**. These programs specify a dollar allowance for each employee based on the employee's salary and tenure. Generally employees must participate in a fixed base of benefits, such as the retirement program and a minimum health and life insurance program. However, employees may then decide how to distribute the remaining allowance among other available benefits. In this way, employees can customize benefits to meet their particular needs. For example, an employee with young children may decide to increase medical coverage or participate in the child care program. An older employee may prefer to increase contributions into the retirement program to increase his or her benefits upon retirement.

TRAINING AND DEVELOPMENT

Training and development activities are a systematic effort by companies to maintain and improve the quality of their work forces. In 1993, U.S. organizations budgeted $48 billion for the training of 47.2 million employees. Production workers received 378 million hours of training, followed by professionals at 317 million hours. In these two job categories nearly 21 million employees received training during 1993.[12]

The importance of training and development activities is underscored by weaknesses found in some of America's blue-collar workers. These workers lack the training or education to improve their skills and become discouraged as their jobs reach dead ends. This gives international competitors, with their better-trained work forces, a significant advantage.

China, which is emerging as a global competitor, has established many new training programs. For example, they recently established a joint venture with Airbus Industrie to establish a full flight simulator facility in Beijing by 1995 to train pilots to fly A300/310 and A330/340 aircraft. This $100 million training investment is viewed as essential to the country's full economic development.[13] China's attitude toward training is typical of companies and countries who wish to maintain the quality of their work force.

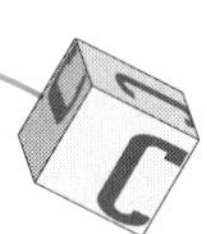

FOCUS ON COMPANY

Stihl Inc.

The Clinton administration earmarked $1.2 billion over four years to create school-to-work transition programs and funneled an additional $5.8 billion into worker training through the Department of Labor in 1993. Their recognition of the importance of training did not surprise many progressive companies that have been providing expensive training for many years. In the late 1970s, Stihl Inc., maker of chain saws, lawn trimmers, and snow blowers, found itself short of skilled craftspeople. The German company created an intensive four-year apprentice program in its American operations. Stihl took employees out of low-paying maintenance jobs and trained them in higher-paying machinist jobs. Stihl's U.S. operation has won seven of ten annual quality competitions among its international competitors. Stihl estimates the program costs $50,000 a year per apprentice, and other companies constantly try to hire these employees away from Stihl. But the payoff has been positive for Stihl, and it will continue to be a leader in providing employee training.

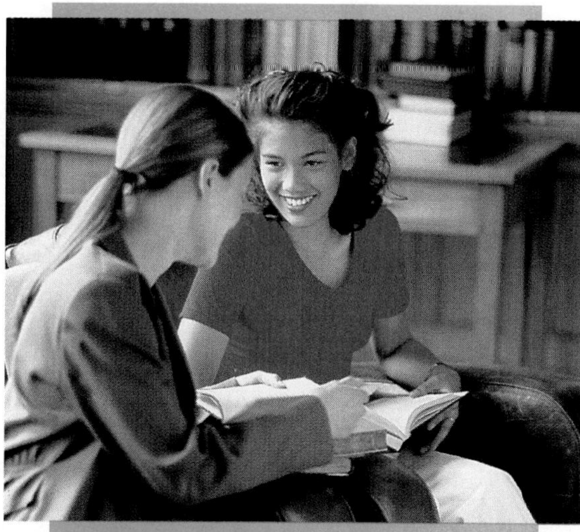

In Salt Lake City, women engineers have gotten enthusiastic responses from area junior high school girls. The 22 members of the Society of Women Engineers mentor young girls and spend a day with them on the job. The society hopes to encourage more young women to enter the engineering field. Women avoided this field because it offered few female role models or mentors for them.[14]

NONMANAGEMENT TRAINING APPROACHES

On-the-job training (OJT)
Training that occurs at the actual job site, at which experienced employees teach new employees how to perform their jobs.

The most common form of training for lower-level, nonmanagement employees is **on-the-job training (OJT)**. In OJT, experienced employees teach new employees how to perform their jobs. All of the job's activities are learned by trial and error and by seeking guidance from the experienced employees. However, learning the new job is basically a matter of "rolling up one's sleeves" and learning from mistakes.

If a systematic learning program is designed for OJT, it can be a very effective training approach. OJT has the advantages of being low cost, resulting in at least some productivity from new employees, and occurring in real-life job conditions.

Orientation training
Training that introduces employees to the company's structure and culture.

Classroom training
Training that occurs in an off-the-job setting; usually for learning mental skills, such as shop math.

Programmed instruction
Systematically designed materials, either text based or computer based, on which employees work at their own pace and are tested frequently to assess their learning.

Basic skills training
Classroom-type training that focuses on high school equivalency.

Other training approaches used with nonmanagement employees are

- **Orientation training,** in which new employees are introduced to the "company way" of doing things and learn about the company's structure and culture before learning the job duties and activities.
- **Classroom training,** in which both new and experienced employees learn job techniques by attending class in an off-the-job setting. The materials to be learned are presented using a variety of methods, including lectures, films, case studies, and simulations. This approach is especially useful for learning mental skills such as shop math.
- **Programmed instruction,** which may be either text based or computer based. In both cases, employees work through the material on their own, at their own pace. Materials are presented in a logical, systematic sequence, and learning is tested frequently with exercises or tests. The trainee must satisfactorily complete each exercise or test before going on to the more advanced material.
- **Basic skills training,** which is similar to classroom training except the focus is on high school equivalency.

Plumley Companies is one of many employers across the nation that sponsor employees who return to complete their high school education or equivalent. Here Plumley employees celebrate their graduation from high school equivalency classes.[15]

Management development
The process of training employees to become good managers, and continuing to develop their skills over time.

Case method
Training in which managers analyze problem situations and share their solutions with one another and the trainer.

Conference method
Training in which managers meet in groups of 15 to 30 and discuss various topics under the guidance of a professional trainer.

Performance coaching and counseling
Training in which the manager's direct superior discusses the manager's strengths and weaknesses and together they design a program for improving the manager's skills and performance.

Job rotation
A series of temporary assignments in various departments designed to increase managers' familiarity with the company's structure and operations.

MANAGEMENT DEVELOPMENT APPROACHES

Management development is the process of training employees to become good managers, and continuing to develop their skills over time. Management development differs from lower-level employee training in terms of both content and method used. While the job skills learned at lower levels tend to be specific, such as shop math, typing, or equipment operation, management skills are more diverse. In some cases, management development focuses on human relations, teamwork, and decision-making skills. Many experts believe these skills apply to any management position.

The primary training approaches for management development include

- **The case method,** in which managers analyze problem situations and share their solutions with one another and the trainer.
- **The conference method,** in which managers meet in groups of 15 to 30 and discuss various topics under the guidance of a professional trainer.
- **Performance coaching and counseling,** in which the manager's direct superior discusses the manager's strengths and weaknesses and together they design a program for improving the manager's skills and performance. This discussion is often a major part of the performance appraisal and serves as a developmental tool rather than as an evaluation for determining compensation.
- **Job rotation,** in which managers are given a series of temporary assignments in various departments. The assignments are designed to increase managers' familiarity with the company's structure and operations. This is a common approach for training young, inexperienced managers, but it is also used to develop junior executives who show potential for top management assignments.

STREET SMART

Mentors

Training of newly hired recent college graduates is often done on an informal basis by mentors who show younger employees "the ropes." Mentors send work back to be redone and redone until it meets their strict standards, but they also offer the new employee opportunities and challenges. A good mentor is determined to bring out the best in others and never loses sight of the need to reassure and encourage a young man or woman beginning a career.

The time will come when the younger employee will move up the ladder or move into a different job and will begin to break away from the mentor. He or she will begin to show independence, and the mentor will need to loosen the strings that bind the two of them. That may be unpleasant and difficult, much like when a child starts leaving home and parents, but mentoring is also extremely rewarding.

The importance of having well-trained managers is illustrated by companies' recent tendency to rehire former executives. During 1991 and 1992, over a dozen senior executives returned to major companies such as Westinghouse Electric, Ann Taylor, Rexene, and Lotus Development Corporation. This growing trend is due to the recession that stretched management talents and to weaknesses in management development programs.

When Mo Siegel returned to Celestial Seasonings after a six-year absence, he restored the creative zip that made Celestial a leader in the beverage industry. Siegel believed managers were not paying enough attention to developing new products and quickly made plans for a line of bottled herbal teas. Siegel obviously knew what strategies worked and how to implement them and how to pass that knowledge on to less experienced managers.[16]

PROMOTION, DEMOTION, TRANSFER, AND SEPARATION

To maintain an effective work force, companies must also consider employee movement between jobs and separation from the company. Promotions and demotions are useful management tools for rewarding and disciplining employees, and transfers may facilitate training activities.

However, as discussed earlier, unless such movements are planned for and managed, the company may hire too few or too many employees for the jobs it has. The flow of work may be disrupted. Unexpected job vacancies may be hastily filled with inexperienced, untrained employees, and productivity may suffer.

PROMOTIONS

Promotion
An assignment to a new job at a higher level and usually at a higher salary.

A **promotion** is an assignment to a new job at a higher level and usually at a higher salary. A promotion often means the employee will assume more responsibility and authority and have a greater number of subordinates to manage.

Promotions are an effective means of rewarding employees for superior performance in the previous position and are an important tool in management development programs.

However, many companies forget to plan for promotions and provide insufficient training for newly promoted employees. Skills that worked in the previous position may be inadequate for the new responsibilities. Therefore, promotions must be given on the basis of both previous performance and preparedness for the new position.

DEMOTIONS

Demotion
An assignment to a new job at a lower level and often at a lower salary.

A **demotion** is an assignment to a new job at a lower level and often at a lower salary. Good performers may be given demotions because they were assigned to a level beyond their abilities. This is related to a popular management theory called the Peter Principle, which states that people will be promoted until they reach their level of incompetency. When good performers are promoted to positions beyond their abilities, it is better to demote them than to leave them in the new positions. If left in their positions, they will become frustrated and stressed. Demoting them will relieve their performance anxiety and allow them additional time to learn the skills that go along with the higher positions.

Demotions may also serve disciplinary purposes. When an employee is continually disrupting the work of others, cannot get along with coworkers and managers, or has drug or alcohol problems, a demotion may be in order. Demoting is an alternative to more serious disciplinary actions, such as termination, and may force employees to deal with their problems. However, many companies are reluctant to use demotion as a disciplinary device, since it may make the employee's attitudes about the job or company even more negative. These negative attitudes can spread among coworkers and create serious problems that can lead to an outright dismissal.

TRANSFERS

Transfer
A horizontal or lateral movement from one job to another of equal or similar responsibilities and salary.

A **transfer** is a horizontal or lateral movement from one job to another of equal or similar responsibilities and salary. Transfers may serve a useful purpose in training programs. However, employees may desire lateral transfers for other reasons. In companies that are not growing, promotions that improve one's career may be infrequent. Employees' careers can stand still while they wait patiently for a promotion. But a lateral transfer permits them to learn new skills and increase their knowledge of the company. The importance of lateral transfers has increased as companies downsize. If you can't grow upward by being promoted, you must grow outward by learning new capabilities in new areas. Thus, a lateral move can be very beneficial.

FOCUS ON COLLABORATORS

Keeping Employees Motivated

In 1987, Helen E. R. Sayles made a lateral move within her company, Liberty Mutual Insurance Group in Boston, to become a writer in the corporate human resource division. She had been training coordinator in the information systems department. Her goal was to position herself in human resources—and it worked. Today she is vice president and manager of human resources. Now she suggests to other employees at Liberty Mutual that lateral transfers may be a critical part of their career plans because they will broaden their experience and learn more about the company.

Other companies, including large firms like IBM, Hartford Insurance Group, Atlantic Richfield, and Sheraton Hotels, are setting up new career ladders that downplay the importance of promotions at each step along the way. They are finding that more employees define opportunity not just in terms of promotion and salary but also as "the chance to develop more skills and have more autonomy."

SEPARATIONS

Separation
Occurs when an employee leaves the company due to layoff, involuntary termination, voluntary resignation, or retirement.

A **separation** occurs when an employee leaves the company. Separations can occur for many reasons, including layoffs, involuntary terminations (firing), voluntary resignations, and retirements. A *layoff* happens when the company faces financial difficulties and/or a decline in sales or production. Layoffs were common during the late 1980s and early 1990s, as the economic recession hurt the financial health of many firms. However, companies often expect such declines to be temporary. Accordingly, they do not wish to permanently separate employees from their jobs and prefer to lay them off temporarily. The company may arrange small payments to employees who are laid off to lessen their financial burden.

In contrast, an *involuntary termination,* or firing, is a permanent separation that is initiated by the company. Employees may be terminated for any number of reasons, including poor performance, breaking work rules, excessive absenteeism or tardiness, or similar problems. By terminating unsatisfactory employees, companies can ensure that the remaining work force consists of the best, most productive employees. Employers often cite the legal concept of **employment-at-will** when they fire employees. This concept holds that employers have the right to terminate employees for any reason whatsoever. In essence, this right is a property right of the business owner.

Employment-at-will
A concept holding that employers have the right to terminate employees for any reason they wish.

However, it may be hard for organizations to defend this right, as a recent case in Fort Collins, Colorado, suggests. When the city dismissed two veterans on the police force, it cited employment-at-will. However, the officers demonstrated that their performance ratings had been excellent for over 20 years, and the city was forced to rehire them and compensate them for damages.[17] *Evidently,* the city was allowed to terminate employees only for valid, performance-related reasons.

Voluntary terminations are permanent separations that occur when employees find reasons to leave the company. For example, employees may find more attractive or better paying jobs, or move to different cities. Most companies work hard to discourage voluntary terminations, since these employees are usually their best ones. When valuable employees resign, employers may offer increases in salary or promotions to help persuade these employees to stay with the company.

Retirement is still another reason for permanent separation from employment. Retirements are viewed as a reward for employees who have had long, productive careers. The Age Discrimination in Employment Act, as amended, raised the mandatory retirement age to 70 for most occupations. Thus, retirement is usually the decision of the employee rather than the company. Retirement is perhaps the most predictable form of employee turnover. Since managers know well in advance when most employees will retire, they should be able to plan ahead to train replacements. In fact, an effective manager will arrange for the retiring employee to assist in training the replacement. By doing this, the valuable experience and knowledge of the retiring employee will not be lost to the company.

LEGAL ISSUES IN HUMAN RESOURCE MANAGEMENT

Managers must keep current with the many laws that have been passed in the area of human resource management. State and federal legislators are constantly passing new laws, and companies that violate these laws can be subjected to heavy fines and penalties.

DISCRIMINATION

Perhaps the two most important laws are the Civil Rights Act of 1964 and the Equal Employment Opportunity Act (EEOA) of 1972, which is part of Title VII of the Civil Rights Act. The Civil Rights Act was recently amended by the Civil Rights Act of 1991. Both of these acts were intended to end discrimination in the workplace, specifically by prohibiting discrimination in hiring, firing, compensating, training, and terms, conditions, or privileges of employment based on race, religion, sex, and national or ethnic origin. Age-based discrimination was covered in a later amendment to the Civil Rights Act. Sexual harassment is also covered by this act. Since 1980, U.S. courts generally have used guidelines from the EEOC to define sexual harassment. Sexual harassment covers a wide range of behaviors, including suggestive remarks, unwanted touching and other sexual advances, requests for sexual favors, and other verbal and physical behavior of a sexual nature. The courts are increasingly holding employers accountable for such illegal behaviors on the part of their supervisors as well as third parties such as customers and suppliers.

The EEOA strengthened the Equal Employment Opportunity Commission (EEOC), the federal agency that enforces the Civil Rights Act. The EEOC is a powerful regulatory body in the arena of human resource management.

The 1991 amendment to the Civil Rights Act entitles victims of discrimination to trial by jury and punitive damages. As a result, the number of employees who file suit based on employer acts of discrimination is expected to increase throughout the 1990s. Martin Marietta Corporation is one of many companies finding this out. In June 1993, it was notified by the EEOC that its Denver-based astronautics unit discriminated against older workers when laying off employees. At least nine age discrimination lawsuits involving 21 former employees had been filed against the company.[18]

EMPLOYEE SAFETY

As described in Chapter 5, employees deserve to work in an environment that is as free of safety and health hazards as is humanly possible. Some jobs naturally entail risks, but those risks should be minimized. The right to work in safe, healthy environments was clearly established by the Occupational Safety and Health Act of 1970. This law is administered by the Occupational Safety and Health Administration (OSHA). This agency has established thousands of safety and health standards with which companies must comply. In most instances, companies must take steps to adhere to these standards.

As many companies have discovered, risks need not be life threatening. For example, many computer keyboarders suffer from a repetitive-stress (carpal tunnel syndrome) injury. Campbell Soup Company and Pepperidge Farm have been cited for violations in this area. Both companies have since moved to minimize the problem by redesigning jobs and providing appropriate tools.[19]

WAGES AND SALARIES

Wages and salaries have been the subject of considerable state and federal legislation since the depression of the 1930s. Wages and overtime pay are covered by the Fair Labor Standards Act of 1938, which established minimum wages and overtime pay for employees who worked more than 40 hours per week. By 1991 the minimum wage had increased to $4.25 per hour. Although most companies accept this law as necessary, some still debate whether it prevents employers from hiring entry-level workers who lack job skills. Thus, the poorest and least qualified people in our society may be unable to obtain jobs and training that would improve their living standards.

OTHER ISSUES

Exhibit 11.6 shows other laws important to the area of human resource management. There are laws that cover benefits programs, such as the Employee Retirement Income Security Act of 1974, which regulates company retirement programs. The Immigration Reform and Control Act of 1986 made it illegal to hire persons who do not hold valid work authorization. Employers must verify the eligibility of all their newly hired employees, including U.S. citizens. Several laws governing collective bargaining have been in place since 1935. These laws give employees the right to bargain collectively for wages, benefits, and working conditions. Obviously

Exhibit 11.6 **LAWS AFFECTING EMPLOYMENT PRACTICES**

Act	Provisions Affecting Employment Practices
Civil Rights Act of 1964	Prohibits discrimination in hiring, promoting, compensating, training, and dismissing employees on the basis of race, color, religion, sex, or national origin.
Age Discrimination in Employment Act of 1967 (amended in 1978 and 1986)	Prohibits discrimination in employment against anyone age 40 to 70 in hiring, promoting, compensating, training, and dismissing. Also prohibits mandatory retirement before age 70.
Executive Orders 11246 and 11375	Requires federal contractors to eliminate employment discrimination by creating affirmative action programs.
Vietnam-Era Veterans Readjustment Act of 1974	Prohibits discrimination against disabled Vietnam-era veterans and requires creation of affirmative action programs.
Vocational Rehabilitation Act of 1973	Prohibits discrimination based on physical or mental disability and requires that employees be informed about affirmative action plans. Similar laws have been passed in over 20 states, and court rulings have extended the coverage to include people with communicable diseases, including AIDS.
Americans with Disabilities Act of 1990	Extends the Vocational Rehabilitation Act. Prohibits discrimination in private sector employment, state and local governments, public accommodations, transportation, and telecommunications. Accessibility is a key component of the act.

managers must be alert to employment laws, because these laws have a great impact on a company's financial health.

INNOVATIONS IN QUALITY OF WORK LIFE

A recent study called *The National Study of the Changing Workforce* revealed that employees will trade compensation for a good quality of life.[20] The study concluded that companies that fail to address quality of work life issues will lose their best employees to companies that do care about them. Maintaining the effectiveness and motivation of the work force requires that managers continue to improve their human resource management activities.

Quality of work life (QWL)
Organizational programs that provide a high-quality workplace, treat employees with dignity, and contribute to employee motivation.

Quality of work life (QWL) refers to organizational programs that create a high-quality workplace, treat employees with dignity, and contribute to employee motivation. Job enrichment and Theory Z management, described in Chapter 10, are two motivational approaches that enhance quality of work life. QWL programs also include job sharing, flextime work arrangements, dependent care programs, parenting leaves of absence, and employee sabbaticals. Dependent care and parenting leaves of absence were described in Chapter 5 so this discussion will focus on job sharing, flextime, and employee sabbaticals.

JOB SHARING

Job sharing
A work arrangement in which two part-time workers share one full-time job.

Many people need to work but cannot work full time for a variety of reasons. However, many companies do not need part-time workers or have only full-time jobs. **Job sharing** is a work arrangement in which two part-time workers share one full-time job. Typically one works during the morning and the other works during the afternoon. This provides many parents who have child care responsibilities the opportunity to continue in their careers and maintain their work skills. Job sharing benefits companies as well, contributing to high employee morale and avoiding costly recruitment and training efforts when skilled employees can no longer work regular hours. It is also a recruitment source for full-time employees when job sharers are ready to return to full-time employment.

FLEXTIME

Flextime
A work arrangement that allows employees to set their own arrival and departure times.

A similar program helps employees who cannot conform to the typical nine-to-five workday. **Flextime** is a work arrangement that allows these employees to set their own arrival and departure times. Some employers have made flextime a companywide program, which has increased employee morale and productivity. However, when employees are assigned to work teams that require close coordination of work activities, the entire team must choose a common reporting time. Otherwise some workers may have to stand around waiting for the last employee to report to work.

FOCUS ON COMPANY

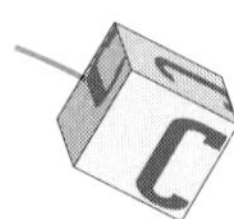

Flextime Is a Competitive Advantage

For some managers, flextime, work-at-home, job-sharing and other schedules are yielding rewards. James J. Bosco, a client services manager at an Automatic Data Processing Inc. office, believes flexibility gives the company a competitive advantage in attracting and retaining skilled workers. "I'm creating something here that the company down the street doesn't have," he says. Feelings are similar at Xerox Corporation. Thelma Spriggs, an operations manager for Xerox Corporation, put her 10-person department on flexible schedules. Productivity rose 10 percent while absenteeism plunged, and "it doesn't cost Xerox a dime to do this," she says.

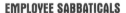

EMPLOYEE SABBATICALS

Sabbatical
An extended, paid release from the job for periods of time ranging from one to six months.

Still another QWL program that is increasing in use is the employee **sabbatical**, an extended, paid release from the job for periods of time ranging from one to six months. High-tech companies like Apple Computer find that valued employees may lose their skills unless they keep up with the rapid advances in their fields. Also, many of these jobs are highly stressful, and employees need relief from them periodically. Sabbaticals help meet this need.

The employee must apply for the sabbatical and have some idea of how the time is to be spent. Companies may be quite flexible regarding how employees spend the time. Some encourage employees to participate in community service; others require employees to take some type of schooling or training during the sabbatical. However, few companies consider the sabbatical a replacement for a paid vacation or holiday, and employees do not lose their entitlements to such benefits while they are on sabbatical leave.

DIVERSITY

Diversity
Intentionally creating a work force composed of people of all races, religions, genders, physical abilities, and beliefs.

Recently organizations have been embracing the concept of **diversity**—intentionally creating a work force composed of people of all races, religions, genders, physical abilities, and beliefs. Diversity, as described in Chapter 5, is similar to the affirmative action programs mandated by the federal government during the 1970s in response to the Civil Rights Act. Employers viewed affirmative action as something that was imposed on them and was not necessarily good for their business. Diversity, however, is a voluntary movement among employers and is viewed as a positive activity that is good for the organization.

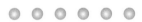

The willingness of employers to not only accept diverse members in their work force but to see this as desirable is a positive trend in our society. Recruitment of diverse members is seen in both the public and private sectors, in colleges and universities as well as businesses. Adolph Coors Company is one of many firms that are trying hard to recruit and accommodate a diverse work force. Coors employs between 600 and 800 people with disabilities and has trained managers in methods for accommodating the many different disabilities. Many believe that diversity programs will help blend all individuals in our society and lead to a more effective society as well as more effective companies.

Diversity programs will likely become more common human resource management programs in the future. Employees are a valuable asset to all companies, and great care must be taken to attract, develop, and maintain this resource.

SUMMARY

1. ***Define* human resource management *and identify four fundamental points that human resource managers need to understand.***
   Human resource management is the process of recruiting, hiring, training, developing, and maintaining an effective work force within the company. Managers need to understand four fundamental points to manage human resources effectively. First, human resource management is the responsibility of *all* managers in the company, not just personnel specialists. Second, human resource management views employees as important resources or assets of the company. Third, one of the major tasks of human resource management is to match employees and their skills and needs to the company's goals and objectives. Finally, an increasing body of complex laws governing employee-manager relations is affecting all aspects of human resource management.

2. ***Identify the six steps of the human resource management planning process.***
   The six steps in the human resource planning process are setting the company's strategic objectives; establishing sales and production forecasts; generating a human needs forecast; analyzing the current internal and external supplies of employees; comparing what exists to what is needed to establish a plan for recruiting, selecting, and transferring employees; and comparing the plan to the human needs forecast to ensure that it is appropriate. The purpose of the plan is to have enough of the right types of employees in the right jobs at the right times to reach the company's goals.

3. ***Describe the human needs forecast and the use of job analyses, job descriptions, and job specifications in the forecast.***
   The human needs forecast compares the current level of employment in various jobs to the numbers needed to fulfill the production and sales forecasts and to meet the company's strategic objectives. The job analysis gathers information about such items as the activities and responsibilities required to perform the job. The job description lists the objectives for the job, responsibilities and activities, working conditions, career information, and similar facts. The job specification identifies the qualifications, skills, training, education, and other personal characteristics required for the job. In this way, company recruiters have a good idea of what to look for in the job candidates.

4. ***Discuss the recruitment and selection processes.***
   The recruitment and selection processes are designed to obtain needed employees. Recruitment is the process of informing qualified potential employees about job openings and encouraging them to apply for those positions. Some employers recruit from among their current employees. Others use outside collaborators such as employment agencies. Selection consists of screening applicants for the skills and abilities listed in the job specification to determine which ones are best suited for the job.

5. ***Explain the role job and performance factors play in the compensation of employees.***
   Proper compensation of employees is essential to maintaining a motivated work force. Equitable compensation depends on three factors: the value of the job the employee holds, how well he or she performs it, and the general level of salaries paid by other employers. Different jobs have dif-

ferent value to the company and must be compensated accordingly. Job values are determined by job evaluation procedures. Companies must also recognize the contributions made by individual employees. The values of individual employees is determined through performance appraisal.

6. ***Discuss company training and development activities.***
Training and development activities are a systematic effort by companies to maintain and improve the quality of their work forces. Training and development activities exist at all levels in the company, although the objectives and methods differ between levels. The focus of lower-level employee training is on technical skills related to the employee's current job. The most common approach at this level is on-the-job training (OJT). At higher, management levels, the focus is on human relations, teamwork, and decision-making skills. The case method, the conference method, performance coaching and counseling, and job rotation are the primary training approaches used for management development.

7. ***Describe the movements that occur among employees of a company.***
Effective companies expect considerable movement of employees between jobs and away from the company. These movements must be anticipated and included in the overall human resource management plan. Promotions move employees to new jobs at a higher level and usually at a higher salary. Promotions are an effective means of rewarding superior performance. Demotions move employees to new jobs at a lower level and often a lower salary. Demotions are often preferable to leaving employees in jobs that are beyond their abilities. They are also used to discipline poor performers and can force employees to deal with their problems. Transfers are horizontal or lateral movements from one job to another of equal or similar responsibilities and salary. Lateral transfers may serve a useful purpose in training programs and help employees learn new skills and increase their knowledge of the company. Separations occur when employees leave the company, either voluntarily or involuntarily. Voluntary separations include voluntary resignations and retirement. Involuntary separations can be due to layoffs or involuntary termination.

8. ***Discuss legal issues that affect human resource management.***
The Civil Rights Act of 1964 and the Equal Employment Opportunity Act (EEOA) of 1972 were intended to end discrimination in the workplace. These acts prohibit discrimination in hiring, firing, compensation, training, and other terms of employment based on race, religion, sex, national origin, and age. This act also prohibits sexual harassment. Employee safety and health is covered by the Occupational Safety and Health Act of 1970. The Fair Labor Standards Act of 1938 established minimum wages. The Americans with Disabilities Act of 1990 prohibits discrimination against handicapped persons.

9. ***Describe efforts by companies to improve employees' quality of work life.***
To maintain the effectiveness and motivation of their work forces, many companies are experimenting with various quality of work life programs. Job sharing is a work arrangement in which two part-time workers share one full-time job. This allows employees to fulfill other responsibilities such as child care. Flextime permits employees to choose their arrival and departure times and thus match their personal schedules with their work schedules. Other QWL programs include dependent care programs, parental leaves of absence, and employee sabbaticals.

10. ***Explain the nature and importance of diversity programs.***
Organizations are now embracing the concept of diversity—intentionally creating a work force composed of people of all races, religions, genders, physical abilities, and beliefs. This is a voluntary movement and is viewed as a positive activity that is good for the organization. Many believe that diversity programs will help blend all individuals in our society and lead to a more effective society as well as more effective companies.

KEY TERMS AND CONCEPTS

Human resource management (p. 238)
Human needs forecast (p. 241)
Job analysis (p. 241)
Job description (p. 242)
Job specification (p. 242)
Recruitment (p. 244)
Selection (p. 245)
Compensation (p. 246)
Job evaluation (p. 246)
Performance appraisal (p. 247)
Piece-rate incentive system (p. 248)
Profit sharing (p. 248)
Flexible benefit plan (p. 250)
On-the-job training (OJT) (p. 251)
Orientation training (p. 251)
Classroom training (p. 251)
Programmed instruction (p. 251)
Basic skills training (p. 251)
Management development (p. 252)
Case method (p. 252)
Conference method (p. 252)
Performance coaching and counseling (p. 252)
Job rotation (p. 252)
Promotion (p. 253)
Demotion (p. 254)
Transfer (p. 254)
Separation (p. 255)
Employment-at-will (p. 255)
Quality of work life (QWL) (p. 257)
Job sharing (p. 257)
Flextime (p. 258)
Sabbatical (p. 258)
Diversity (p. 258)

DISCUSSION QUESTIONS

Company

1. Why is human resource planning essential to the achievement of a company's strategic objectives?
2. What is the relationship between job analysis and the design of a company's compensation program?
3. Do you believe the compensation top executives receive reflects their true value to the company? Why or why not?

Customers

4. How might changes in customer demands affect the human resource planning process?
5. In a company that markets services, what role does the selection of qualified employees play in the delivery of customer satisfaction?

Competitors

6. How does information regarding competitors affect a company's human resource planning process?
7. How does a company's training and development program help maintain the company's competitiveness?
8. Are competitors' employees a good source for recruitment?

Collaborators

9. In what ways do collaborators assist human resource managers?
10. How might a company president justify the costs associated with hiring outside employee benefit providers such as health and fitness specialists and child care services?
11. Call a local employment agency to learn about services they provide. Of what value are they to job seekers?

In Question: Take a Stand

Many employers use psychological tests to screen job applicants.[21] These tests screen for factors ranging from emotional disorders to drug or alcohol abuse to tendencies to violence or stealing. Some tests claim to measure the likelihood that a new employee will have accidents on the job or will quit. Some tests even question applicants about their religious beliefs and sexual habits. Is it ethical to use psychological testing for hiring? Are some of these tests an invasion of privacy? What can happen to a job applicant if the results of a test are unfavorable but incorrect?

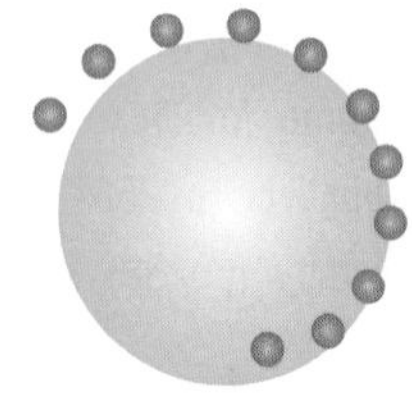

CASE 11.1
ALAGASCO[22]

After 13 years of paperwork and writing proposals in the equal employment opportunity and customer billing offices at Alagasco, a Birmingham, Alabama, utility, Thomas L. Wilder Jr. was looking for a change. "I wanted to see some more permanence to my work," he says, "something I could show my kids or grandkids. Something tangible, like a bridge." While a bridge trestle was out of the question, the trenches were wide open. One January, Wilder, 35, traded his suit and tie for company overalls and a hardhat. For six months he worked on Alagasco's construction crew, repairing gas lines and digging ditches. Says Wilder: "I think some of the people saw me as the guy from the ivory tower, so I made sure I got down in those ditches and got just as dirty as they did." After he returned to the air conditioning, Wilder said he feels "refreshed and a lot less bored." His field experience, which forced him to brave a freak winter snow storm and blistering summer heat, helped him realize he has it pretty good. He thinks, "If companies want to keep people like me and keep our minds on the work, they have to offer us something extra." So far, Alagasco has similarly reassigned 75 of its 1,300 employees, some to the United Way, others to summer jobs programs for disadvantaged youth. Explains President Michael Warren: "Given how slowly the energy industry is growing, we had to come up with a way to combat the `Is this all there is?' syndrome."

Questions

1. *What value does an employee sabbatical like that Thomas Wilder took have for a company?*
2. *What value do sabbaticals have for employees?*
3. *With the current trend toward downsizing, do you think employee sabbaticals will grow in popularity? Why or why not?*

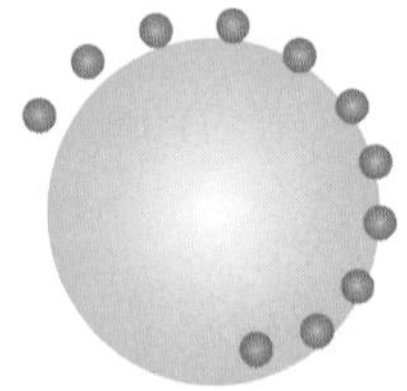

CASE 11.2
SPORTS ILLUSTRATED[23]

Lou Capozzola worked 10 years at *Sports Illustrated,* jetting from Super Bowls to the Olympics as a lighting specialist. He was on the road 180 days a year, working 15- to 20-hour days.

In February 1990 he was called into his boss's office and informed that his job was being eliminated, but that he could continue as an independent contractor. His base pay would be about halved to $20,000. His overtime pay would be cut by as much as two-thirds. And he could forget about his $20,000-a-year benefit package, including medical coverage.

Then he was asked to leave town on assignment. "They say 'We value you and your skills. We're just going to pull the rug out from under your feet because we want to save $20,000,'" he says.

In spite of the low pay and benefits, he agreed to stay on. He was the sole supporter of a wife and two children. "What could I do? They offered me some form of employment, I had to take it," he says.

Questions

1. *Do you believe that Lou Capozzola situation is unusual in today's business environment?*
2. *Does it make economic sense for Sports Illustrated to change Lou Capozzola's status from permanent employee to an independent contractor?*
3. *What does the term downsizing mean to you?*
4. *What are the ethical implications of downsizing?*

CHAPTER

12

EMPLOYEE RELATIONS

When you have studied this chapter, you will be able to:

1. Discuss the history of American labor unions.
2. Identify several important labor relations laws.
3. Describe the collective bargaining process.
4. Discuss the mediation and arbitration processes.
5. Discuss the issues of equal pay and equal employment opportunity.
6. Describe employee ownership of companies.

AT&T, one of the world's largest corporations, was built on a tradition of cooperation with unions. However, the nature of its business has changed during the past few years to largely nonunion ventures and acquisitions. For example, AT&T recently went into the consumer credit business with its Universal Credit Card operation. It also acquired NCR Corporation to boost its personal computer business.

These moves have caused serious problems for AT&T's relations with its two employee unions. Since 1984, the unionized work force at AT&T has shrunk from some 230,000 to only 130,000 employees, while its nonunionized work force has increased from 120,000 to 140,000. Union leaders now believe AT&T is trying to keep unions out of the growing parts of the company.

Both Paradyne Corporation, a maker of computer modems, and NCR have actively opposed unionization during the 1990s. NCR has cut unions to about 5 percent of its 27,000 workers in the United States. In two recent union certification elections, NCR hired an antiunion law firm and held one-on-one meetings with employees to stress that the union was an unnecessary third party.

All this activity by the new venture units has put AT&T chair Robert E. Allen in the hot seat. The unions are threatening strikes and customer boycotts unless the company becomes more receptive to the organizing efforts. But Allen has promised the new units autonomy in setting their own business strategies, including how they deal with the unions. Union leaders are fighting the trend at AT&T operations more aggressively. Recently some 30 union members were arrested for occupying NCR's Dayton, Ohio, headquarters. On the same day, the Communication Workers of America (CWA) held rallies in 11 cities and warned Allen that he couldn't have it both ways. The unions say Allen has to make up his mind whether his policy toward unions is what he says it is or what NCR says it is.

Later Morton Bahr, CWA president, walked out of a meeting with Allen when Allen chose to exclude NCR operations from discussions about relations between the company and the union. NCR's 12,000 nonunion employees far exceed the 3,300 unorganized workers at the other new businesses.

Allen's business plan is built on independent operations that set their own strategies. Now he may have to choose between his own business plan and increasing AT&T's labor problems.[1]

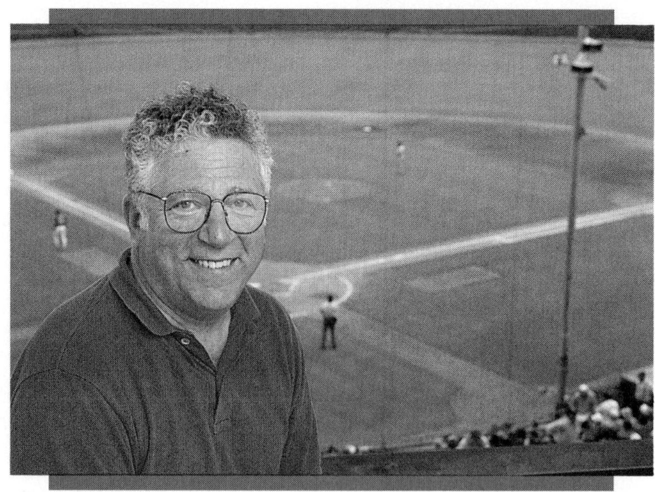

Dick Ravitch is the former head of New York City's Metropolitan Transportation Authority, a former mayoral candidate, and now a key player in negotiations with the Major League Baseball Players Association. In 1993, Ravitch convinced baseball team owners to reopen negotiations with the union after they fired Fay Vincent, who failed to successfully conclude negotiations with the players in 1992. Ravitch will test new ideas regarding revenue sharing, revenue participation, and salary caps in the coming years.[2]

The situation at AT&T is a common problem in many U.S. companies. Competitive pressures force managers to attempt to keep costs low and to maintain control over various production and service processes. Employees, however, are demanding increasing rights in the workplace and have many powers available to them as they bargain for salary and benefits. As our society struggles to meet global competition, unions often seem to be part of the problem rather than part of the solution.

This chapter examines labor unions and how they affect the management of business organizations. The history of unionization is an important framework for understanding the many issues faced by both employers and employees in our competitive business world.

LABOR UNIONS

Labor unions are a prominent force in American business and society. Unions affect the living and working standards of millions of U.S. workers. They also affect the political process as they support various candidates who promise to pass favorable union legislation.

Labor union
A group of workers who have joined together to more effectively achieve common goals such as improved working conditions, wages, and benefits.

A **labor union** is a group of workers who have joined together to more effectively achieve common goals such as improved working conditions, wages, and benefits. Many managers would argue that unions serve little purpose today and actually worsen the relationship between employees and managers. However, examination of working conditions before the passage of the National Labor Relations Act of 1935 (NLRA) shows that relationships between employers and employees have always been difficult.

The NLRA granted workers the right to form unions for the purpose of bargaining collectively (as opposed to individually) with their employers. Bargaining as a group rather than as isolated individuals gave workers much more power in negotiations with management. Prior to the NLRA, working conditions, wages, and benefits were determined solely by business managers. Many workers complained about unsafe working conditions, low wages, long hours, and the use of child labor. Workers were often paid subsistence (just livable) wages, and it was common for employees to work 12 hours a day 6 days a week. Vacations were rare, and insurance, retirement, and other fringe benefits were nonexistent.

As individuals, employees were unable to bargain with their employers for better wages and working conditions. If an employee asked for better conditions, the employer simply replaced him or her. In the few cases where employees attempted to bargain (or strike) for better wages as a group, prevailing laws favored the employer.

HISTORY OF U.S. LABOR UNIONS

Some improvement in employees' working conditions came about when Henry Ford decided to pay his employees a minimum of $5 per day. His decision brought bitter complaints from other industrial leaders, but Ford remained committed to that level of pay, and jobs in his factories were highly desired. Also, industrial theorists like Frederick Taylor and Frank Gilbreth influenced many employers to improve working conditions through scientific methods. However, at the onset of the Great Depression in the early 1930s, many American workers still suffered under autocratic and intolerant employers.

American Federation of Labor (AFL). Labor unions emerged periodically during the 1800s, but they had few powers and most failed to survive the ruthless tactics employers used to combat them. The first strong union, the Knights of Labor, was founded in 1869. At one point it had 700,000 members. However, division among members regarding the purposes and goals of the union and other issues caused it to break up into several smaller units. One of those units later became the **American Federation of Labor (AFL)**, a union that is still prominent today. Formed in 1886, the AFL became the major union representing affiliated craft unions such as carpenters and millwrights. Under the dynamic leadership of Samuel Gompers, the AFL focused on improving wages, hours, and working conditions for members of these unions.

American Federation of Labor (AFL)
A national union formed in 1886 to represent affiliated craft unions.

The AFL grew rapidly during its early years, but its growth slowed considerably after World War I. The world of business was rapidly becoming automated, and skilled craft jobs were being replaced by specialized, unskilled industrial jobs. In addition, the early years of the Great Depression led to widespread unemployment, and many employers simply fired workers who joined unions. It was easy to recruit replacements from among the ranks of the unemployed.

Congress of Industrial Organizations (CIO). While membership growth among crafts unions was slowing, several individual unions in the AFL began to organize workers in the mass production automobile and steel industries. Other unions began to recruit unskilled workers in the mining, newspaper, and communications industries. These unions were unhappy with their status in the craft-dominated AFL, which focused on nuts-and-bolts issues of concern mainly to skilled workers.

In 1935, a powerful group of industrial unions led by John L. Lewis, president of the United Mine Workers (UMW), separated from the AFL to form the **Congress of Industrial Organizations (CIO)**. The CIO soon rivaled the AFL in size as the trend toward assembly line production methods and automation continued. The growth of the CIO was aided by the passage of the National Labor Relations Act, which also occurred in 1935. For 20 years these two national unions competed for members, often challenging each other for representation of the workers of one employer. Finally, in 1955, through the efforts of George Meany, the two unions merged to become the AFL-CIO.

Congress of Industrial Organizations (CIO)
A national union formed in 1935 to represent affiliated industrial unions.

Today over 100 individual unions are affiliated with the AFL-CIO. Union membership in all unions today is about 17 million workers, many of them white-collar and professional employees. Women, at one time overlooked by unions, now make up over 30 percent of union membership. However, union membership as a percentage of the total U.S. labor force has declined steadily since 1953. We will see why later in the chapter.

Exhibit 12.1 **MAJOR FEDERAL LEGISLATION AFFECTING LABOR RELATIONS IN THE UNITED STATES**

Legislation	Major Provisions
Norris–La Guardia Act, 1932	Prohibited courts from issuing injunctions against nonviolent union activities. Outlawed employment contracts that forbade employees to join in union activities or unions themselves.
National Labor Relations Act (Wagner Act), 1935	Gave employees the right to form or join unions, collectively bargain with employers through elected union representatives, and engage in labor activities such as strikes and boycotts. Prohibited certain practices by employers to prevent employees from joining unions. Created the National Labor Relations Board to oversee the entire arena of labor activities.
Fair Labor Standards Act, 1938	Set a federal minimum wage and maximum hours for workers in industries involved in interstate commerce. Outlawed the use of child labor.
Taft-Hartley Act (Labor-Management Relations Act), 1947	Amended the NLRA, permitting states to pass laws prohibiting compulsory union membership. Determined methods for dealing with strikes that affect the general public health, safety, and welfare. Prohibited secondary boycotts, closed shops, and featherbedding.
Landrum-Griffin Act (Labor-Management Reporting and Disclosure Act), 1959	Amended the Taft-Hartley Act and the NLRA, guaranteeing individual rights of union members in relation to their own union leadership.

LABOR LEGISLATION

It is clear that labor unions faced significant problems in their early efforts to protect members' rights. Generally the political climate favored business owners, whose rights were founded in the "property rights" provisions of common law. However, the onset of the Great Depression signaled a change in the political climate. Public opinion was swayed by the great masses of unemployed workers and the realization that low wages were acting as a strong barrier to economic recovery. As a result of these changes, Congress passed the Norris–La Guardia Act in 1932, the first legislation favorable to unions in the 20th century.

As Exhibit 12.1 shows, Congress passed five national acts affecting labor-management relations, three of them during the Depression years. These acts tended to balance the powers of unions and companies and outlawed certain business practices, including the use of child labor.

Norris–La Guardia Act. The Norris–La Guardia Act, passed in 1932, was the first act passed during the Depression to protect unions. It greatly reduced management's power to prevent unionization and strikes. One of the primary weapons management had used against unions until this time was court injunctions prohibiting strikes, picketing, and sometimes even initial membership drives by unions. With these union activities forbidden, owners could act against unions without fear.

National Labor Relations Board (NLRB)
A Federal agency established by the National Labor Relations Act to supervise unionization activities and prevent antiunion practices by business owners.

National Labor Relations Act. The National Labor Relations Act (also called the Wagner Act), passed in 1935, legalized collective bargaining. The act required employers to bargain or negotiate in good faith with employees' elected representatives. Prior to this time, owners had invoked the Sherman Antitrust Act, claiming that unions represented a monopoly of labor. Courts had invoked the Sherman Act to prohibit collective bargaining.

The NLRA also established a federal agency, the **National Labor Relations Board (NLRB)**, to supervise unionization activities. It also prohibited many practices business owners had used to deter unions. Specifically, the act stated that owners could no longer fire workers for attempting to form or join a union and could not refuse to hire union sympathizers. It guaranteed workers the right to engage in union activities such as organizing, striking, picketing, and boycotting employers.

Fair Labor Standards Act. Although the Fair Labor Standards Act was not specifically designed as union legislation, it had an important impact on unions. Passed in 1938, the act set a federal minimum wage and maximum work hours for workers employed in interstate commerce. It also outlawed the use of child labor. The Fair Labor Standards Act has been amended several times, primarily to extend the coverage to more types of industries and to raise the minimum wage.

The basic work hours were established as 40 hours in one week and 8 hours in one day. The minimum wage was set at 25 cents per hour for most employees. Time-and-one-half was required for all hours in excess of 40, except for hospitals and agricultural workers, whose standards were somewhat different due to the nature of their work.

Based on the standards established in the act, employers typically set up three employee classifications: salaried exempt, salaried nonexempt, and hourly. Salaried-exempt employees are exempt from coverage. Usually the exempt classification includes only managers and certain professionals. This act successfully stopped employers from requiring employees to work seven 16-hour days, a practice that was contributing to high unemployment.[3]

Today many companies require fewer than 40 hours a week from their workers, and minimum-wage jobs tend to be held by part-time workers or others who are not primary wage earners. Most of these jobs are held by high school and college students working as food servers, as clerks, and in other retail positions.

Taft-Hartley Act. While the acts passed in the 1930s were deemed necessary to economic recovery, by 1945 the recovery seemed complete. At the end of World War II, unions became very aggressive in their demands. Strikes and boycotts were common, and the slowdown in business resulting from these activities threatened needed economic progress. Employment was at an all-time high, and companies badly needed assistance in coping with unreasonable union pressures. In response, Congress passed the Taft-Hartley Act (or Labor-Management Relations Act) in 1947 to prohibit unfair labor practices by unions.

Some of the practices unions were using to pressure companies included **secondary boycotts** against a company's suppliers, customers, or other neutral third parties; **featherbedding**, or creating unnecessary jobs for union members; and creating **closed shops** that kept companies from hiring nonunion workers. In some instances, strikes resulted not from disagreements with the company but from disputes between two or more unions that were fighting one another for the right to represent the company's employees. These strikes, called **jurisdictional strikes**, were prohibited by the Taft-Hartley Act. By prohibiting all of these practices, the Taft-Hartley Act helped to balance power between employers and unions.

Secondary boycott
A boycott against a company's suppliers, customers, or other neutral third party.

Featherbedding
Creating unnecessary jobs for union members.

Closed shop
A union contract requirement preventing companies from hiring nonunion workers.

Jurisdictional strike
A union strike resulting from a dispute between two or more unions that are fighting for the right to represent a company's employees.

Landrum-Griffin Act. Relations between employers and unions were not the primary reason for passing the Landrum-Griffin Act in 1959. Rather, the cause was a growing concern about corruption in unions and their leadership. Many unions were controlled by gangsters and hoodlums who were using unions to achieve personal goals. James Hoffa, president of the Teamsters Union, was perhaps the most notorious of the corrupt union leaders. Federal investigators found that at many elections held to choose Teamster leaders, members who opposed the current leaders were beaten by Hoffa's followers, and otherwise prevented from voting or attending union meetings. Union retirement and strike funds were being placed in the leaders' personal accounts, and under-the-table deals were being made with employers that filled the leaders' personal coffers while doing little for the union members.

In effect, the Landrum-Griffin Act was passed to protect union members from their own leaders. It ensured the right of union members to attend business meetings, vote on all

Exhibit 12.2 **EMPLOYEE RELATIONS AND COLLECTIVE BARGAINING ISSUES**

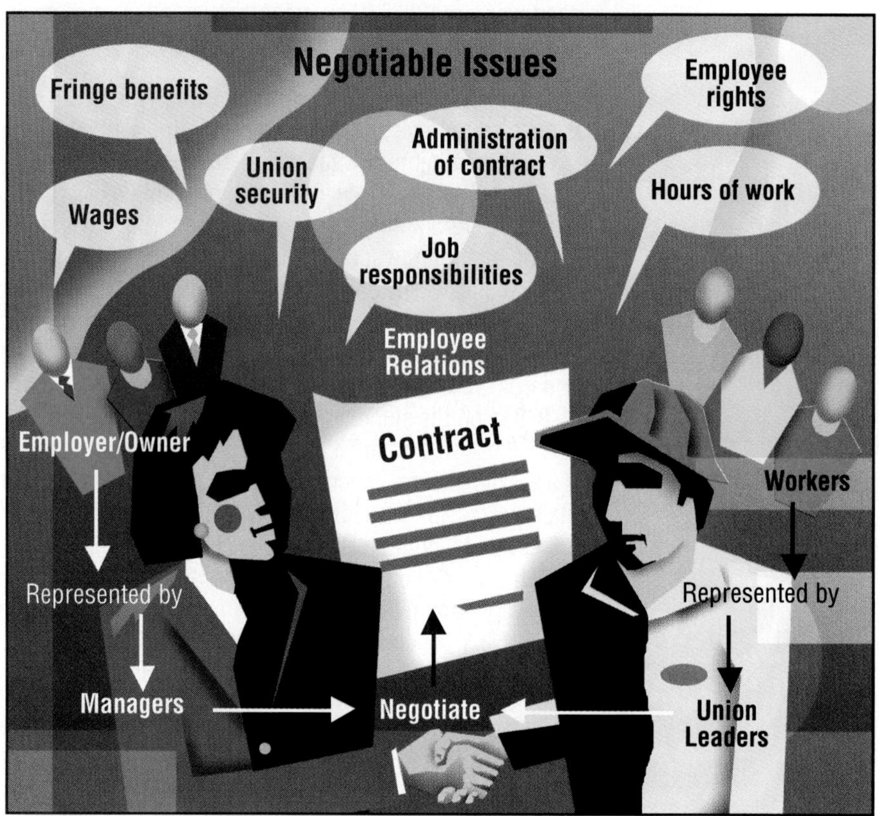

union matters, and vote for union leaders by secret ballot. The act also specified procedures for handling union funds.

THE COLLECTIVE BARGAINING PROCESS

Unions provide benefits to their members that may not be available when employees negotiate individually with their managers. The salaries of professional athletes highlight the advantage of having someone negotiate the terms of an employment contract. Often a star quarterback's agent is actively negotiating the terms of the next contract while the current football season is still going on.

But a forklift operator is not a star quarterback, and even the addition of an agent would probably result in few gains for that worker. Thus, for the typical worker, unions provide a "collective" voice, and it is this voice that has the power to negotiate better working conditions with employers. Unions protect their members from arbitrary employer actions and provide greater job security, better wages, and improved working conditions and benefits. They also minimize "playing favorites" by managers.

Collective bargaining
The process by which union representatives and management negotiate and administer written agreements of their understanding of the terms and conditions of employment.

Collective bargaining is the process by which union representatives and management negotiate and administer written agreements of their understanding of the terms and conditions of employment. If a union succeeds in organizing a company's employees, receives a majority of votes from the employees, and is certified by the National Labor Relations Board

(NLRB), it becomes the official representative of all the employees. As such, the union must be recognized by the company's managers as the legal bargaining agent for all employees (including those who are covered by the NLRB certification but choose not to join the union).

Collective bargaining activities center around establishing the terms of the contract (contract negotiation), strategies for achieving the bargaining goals, and administering the contract once it has been negotiated.

Contract Negotiations. As Exhibit 12.2 illustrates, the purpose of unions is to represent employees and bargain for them. The contract establishes the relationship between employer and employees. The contract is negotiated by management specialists, such as the head of human resource management or a trained negotiator, and their counterparts in the union, such as the chief union negotiator. Issues that can be negotiated include wages, fringe benefits, and conditions of work (such as work hours and job responsibilities). Employee rights (such as seniority) and union security are also negotiable items.

Wage-Related Issues. The most obvious issue of contract negotiations is wages and benefits. Although most people consider only the size of the resulting wage adjustments, many other wage items are negotiated. For example, unions seek agreement on how jobs will be evaluated, higher pay for workers who have to work undesirable hours, and bonuses and incentives.

During the recession of the early 1990s, companies were reluctant to grant wage increases. In fact, many companies sought various wage-related concessions from unions to stay in business. Several companies, including Continental Airlines, Eastern Air Lines, and LTV, filed bankruptcy in the late 1980s, prompting the need for cooperation from their union employees. Several unions agreed to pay cuts, pension plan freezes, and work rules more favorable to the companies. But as the economy improved, negotiations of wages and benefits were much tougher for many companies.

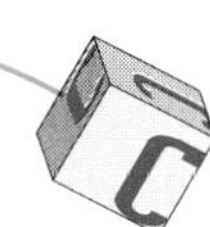

FOCUS ON COLLABORATORS

Unions at LTV

When LTV filed bankruptcy in 1986, its creditors opted for a reorganization and downsizing plan that would give them stock in LTV's steel unit. The steel unit ranked third in the steel industry, with revenues of $3.7 billion.

David Hoag, chair of LTV, hoped the company could exit Chapter 11 bankruptcy by the end of 1992, but that depended on the United Steelworkers. In 1986, the union agreed to a pay cut and a 10-year freeze in pension plan hikes. The union was asked to accept another concessionary contract in 1992. Unless additional concessions could be used to offset LTV's $3 billion pension obligation, stock that LTV would issue after the reorganization would be worth only $8 instead of $15 per share. This would hurt LTV's ability to raise badly needed money.

LTV claimed concessions were needed to cover pension expenses. "Creditors have all sacrificed, now it's labor's turn," said one financial adviser to LTV's unsecured creditors. But the union argued it had done enough.

After much negotiation, union members ratified a new, two-year contract by a vote of 6,503 to 1,505. The agreement, including minor concessions by the union, was expected to save LTV $60 million annually. Concessions included a freeze on wages at their current level throughout the term of the contract and the elimination of 218 jobs. But strangely enough, union employees received pension improvements.

American firms have become global corporations. Manufacturing now takes place around the globe, especially in countries where wages are low. The North Atlantic Trade Agreements have made it easier for American companies to produce products in Mexico. This has had a dramatic impact on labor union activity in the United States.

Conditions of Work and Employee Rights. There are a great many negotiable items related to working conditions and employee rights. While perhaps not as heated as wage issues, these items are very important to both employers and employees. Their importance was highlighted in 1992 when the Teamsters campaigned against Coca-Cola, claiming its bottlers were cutting health and retirement benefits, closing plants, and increasing workloads.[4] From the union's viewpoint, things didn't always go better with Coke.

AT&T is another example. A recent labor settlement between AT&T and two unions was nearly derailed because AT&T wanted to trim workers based on the "least-needed" technical skills. The company wanted to overturn two previous arbitrator rulings that favored seniority as the basis for layoffs. These rulings affected 13,000 employees. To maintain its global competitiveness, AT&T needed to consider job skills in cutbacks. The Communications Workers of America agreed to talk about future changes, such as cross-training workers in new skills, but resisted changes in the seniority work rules.[5]

Bargainable issues in working conditions and employee rights include

- Regular hours of work and total hours
- Holidays and vacations
- Overtime rules
- Rest periods
- Seniority rules
- Transfer procedures
- Layoff and recall rules
- Health and safety provisions

Some of these items are sometimes used as "bait" when the union really wants a wage increase, and vice versa. Arguing for a shorter workweek, for example, might weaken management's stance on the wage issue.

STREET SMART

The Five Characteristics of Successful Negotiations

Roger Dawson is an expert in negotiating. He offers street smart advice such as "never narrow negotiations down to just one issue." After years of experience, Dawson has identified five characteristics of a successful negotiation:

1. Both sides feel a sense of accomplishment.
2. Both sides feel the other side cared.
3. Both sides feel the other side was fair.
4. Each side would deal again with the other side.
5. Each side feels the other side will keep the bargain.

Union Security. A very important issue to union leaders and members is the union's security. *Union security* refers to contract provisions that strengthen the union. A strong union has more power when negotiating with management. A union is strengthened when its membership increases.

Union security clauses in the contract require employees who benefit from the union to either join it or at least pay dues to it. A closed shop (outlawed by the Taft-Hartley Act) would give great union security, since a worker would have to join the union before he or she could get a job with the company. In a **union shop**, however, employees who are not members at the time they are hired must join the union after some specified time, usually 90 days. This arrangement thus gives the union considerable security. Twenty-one states have passed **right-to-work laws** that give all employees the right to decide whether or not to join the union. When a union exists but the contract does not require joining it, the arrangement is called an **open shop**.

Union shop
A contract provision specifying that employees who are not union members at the time they are hired must join the union after some specified time, usually 90 days.

Right-to-work laws
Laws that give all employees the right to decide whether or not to join a union.

Open shop
A contract provision that makes union membership voluntary for all employees.

Although management typically prefers an open shop, certain advantages are gained from agreeing to a union shop provision in the contract. When some workers are union members but others are not, a certain amount of conflict will arise among workers. Also, any benefits gained by union negotiations will be given to the nonunion workers as well. Thus, management often agrees to require nonunion workers to pay a fee to the union equal to the union dues rate. This arrangement is called an **agency shop** and is the weakest form of union security that can be negotiated in the contract.

Agency shop
A contract provision that requires nonunion workers to pay a fee to the union equal to the union dues rate.

Strategies for Achieving Bargaining Goals. Negotiating a new contract is not an easy process. The employer needs to minimize costs to remain competitive, but employees desire improvements in their standard of living. Both the company and the union have goals to achieve in the negotiations, such as desired wage levels, benefits, working conditions and so forth.

Often bargaining is a pure conflict process in which the employer wins what the employees lose, and vice versa. This type of bargaining is called **distributive bargaining**. In distributive bargaining, each party uses whatever weapons it has available to win the most it can. Both the company and union negotiators have targets to shoot for, moderate concessions they will accept, and resistance points that will prompt them to use their weapons of last resort.

Distributive bargaining
A bargaining process in which the employer wins what the employees lose, and vice versa.

Exhibit 12.3 **BARGAINING STRATEGIES**

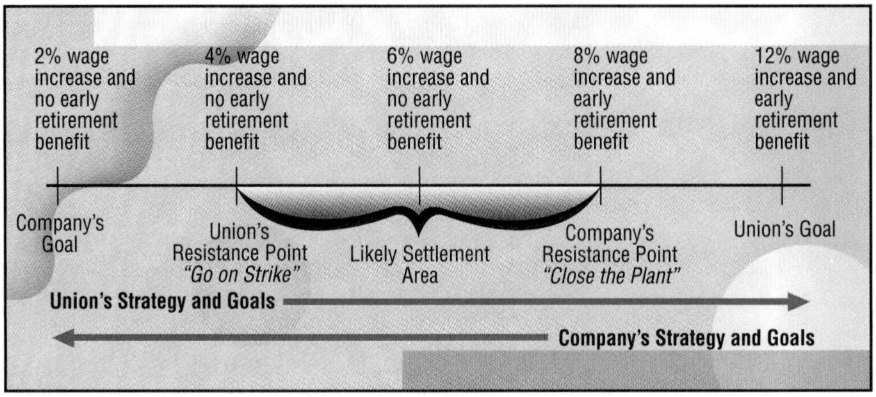

2% wage increase and no early retirement benefit
4% wage increase and no early retirement benefit
6% wage increase and no early retirement benefit
8% wage increase and early retirement benefit
12% wage increase and early retirement benefit

Company's Goal
Union's Resistance Point *"Go on Strike"*
Likely Settlement Area
Company's Resistance Point *"Close the Plant"*
Union's Goal

Union's Strategy and Goals →
← **Company's Strategy and Goals**

For example, in Exhibit 12.3 the two major bargaining issues are wages and a new early retirement program. The company's goal is to give a 2 percent wage increase and avoid paying early retirement benefits. The union's goal is to get a 12 percent wage increase and early retirement benefits for its members.

Typically, neither set of negotiators expects to reach its ideal goals and will settle for somewhat less as negotiations go on. However, the union will not accept less than a 4 percent wage increase with no early retirement benefits. This point is called the union's *resistance point.* Rather than accept less than this, the union will go on strike to try to force management to concede more. The company's negotiators are unwilling to agree to more than an 8 percent increase coupled with the early retirement benefit. This is the company's resistance point. Rather than agreeing to more than this, the company will close the plant (a lockout) to try to force the union to concede to the company. As we examine the strategies of the union and the company, it seems likely that the negotiators will come to an agreement somewhere between the two resistance points.

Neither the company nor the union wants to use its weapons of last resort, since either a strike or closing the plant means the workers will lose wages and the company will lose production and sales. However, sometimes the bargaining goals and resistance points are incompatible, and in these instances strikes, lockouts, or plant closings may occur. If a company with more than 100 employees decides to close the plant, it may have to give workers and local government officials an advance warning of 60 days. This is required by the Plant-Closing Notification Act of 1988, which is intended to minimize effects on local economies. Further, if a union decides to strike, the government may issue an injunction to prevent the strike for the same reason. Thus, the union may use lesser weapons such as boycotts, picketing, and work slowdowns, and the company may threaten to hire (or actually hire) replacement workers.

The effectiveness of these alternative weapons was illustrated in a recent strike by the United Auto Workers (UAW) against Caterpillar, Inc. The UAW, perhaps the country's strongest union, called a strike against Caterpillar in 1992. The strike went on for about six months, at which point the company threatened to hire permanent replacements for strikers who didn't return to work on Caterpillar's terms. Even though the union had an $800 million strike fund to help workers make it through the strike, the workers quickly agreed to return to work.[6]

Companies competing in a global economy need a better way to resolve labor disputes than strikes and shutdowns or the replacement of striking workers. If Caterpillar had accepted the union's demands, its ability to compete against its primary rival, Komatsu Ltd., would

Exhibit 12.4 **A TYPICAL GRIEVANCE PROCEDURE**

Stage	Parties Involved	Procedure
1	Employee and immediate supervisor	The employee discusses the grievance with the immediate supervisor, who has three days to prepare a response.
2	Employee, union officials, supervisor, and unit manager	Within seven days, the employee prepares the grievance in writing. After two union officials sign the grievance, it is submitted to the immediate supervisor and unit manager, who have seven days to prepare a response.
3	Union grievance committee and plant manager	Within 10 days the union grievance committee submits the grievance to the plant manager or his or her representative, who has 10 days to prepare a response.
4	Professional arbitrator	The grievance is taken to binding arbitration.

Mediation
The process of bringing in a third party who makes recommendations for resolving differences between two negotiating parties.

Arbitration
The process of bringing in a third party who makes a binding decision or judgment that both parties must agree to accept.

have been weakened. Mediation and arbitration of differences in negotiation are two traditional approaches to resolve labor disputes, but neither unions nor companies favor them. **Mediation** is the process of bringing in a third party who makes recommendations for resolving the differences. **Arbitration** means bringing in a third party who makes a binding decision or judgment that both parties must agree to accept. Arbitration removes control from the negotiators and is likely to make neither the union nor the company happy with the settlement.

Administering the Contract: Grievance Procedures. While union contract negotiations make the news, probably due to the ever present threat of a strike, the day-to-day administration of the contract requires most of the work. Even the best-written contract will not improve employee-management relations if employees and managers disagree over its interpretation. When a disagreements occurs, either the employee or a union steward may file a *grievance,* or complaint, against the employer.

A grievance may occur for many reasons. Perhaps the supervisor asked the employee to perform a task outside the written job description or sent the employee home early for suspected drinking on the job. The U.S. collective bargaining system has a well-developed private system for processing grievances. The grievance system protects workers from unfair treatment, yet takes the legitimate concerns of the company into account.

Grievance procedures are designed by the negotiators and incorporated into the contract. Although grievance procedures vary from contract to contract, some similarities exist. Exhibit 12.4 illustrates a typical grievance procedure.

Employers and unions generally prefer to resolve grievances at the lowest level possible, through discussion between the supervisor and the employee. Many companies train their supervisors in methods for avoiding and resolving grievances. A great many grievances are solved this way, thus avoiding further problems for the parties. If a solution cannot be reached at this level, company, union, and employee may continue to press the issue until, at the extreme, the dispute is taken to arbitration. Arbitrators hear evidence from both sides and then render a binding decision on the grievance.

An established grievance procedure has many advantages for a company. First, it enables the company to avoid costly disruptions to the production process that might occur if employees must resort to work slowdowns or strikes to have their complaints heard. Second, a grievance procedure provides feedback to upper management regarding trouble spots in its employee relations. If grievances are filed frequently on the same issue, a problem obviously exists, and managers should take action to correct it.

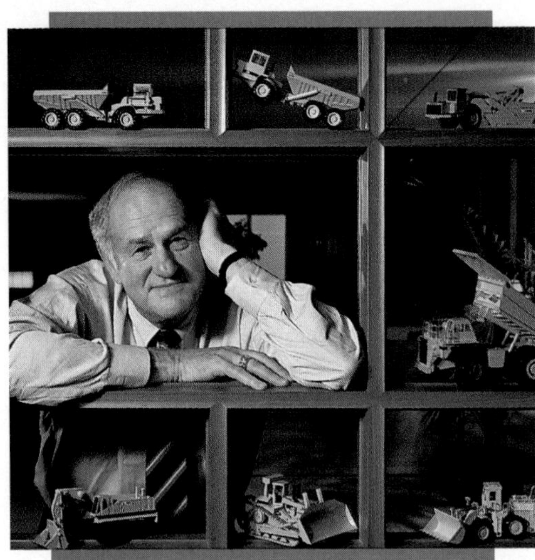

The European Union (EU) has a number of laws that apply to all member countries. One proposal in the EU's Social Action Proposal is to have worker representation on boards of directors. Furthermore, companies like Caterpillar, with operations in Britain, Belgium, and France, have found that some of the new agreements about common business policy are not popular with all its workers who prefer different ways to be compensated for overtime. In Britain, for example, workers could choose to take time off or to get overtime pay. However, under the new common rules, workers have to take time off.[7]

THE FUTURE OF UNIONS IN A GLOBAL ENVIRONMENT

Since the 1950s, union membership has lost popularity among American workers. As Exhibit 12.5 shows, union membership ran about 36 percent of the labor force in the mid-1940s but by 1992 had declined to only 16 percent of total employment and only 12 percent in the private sector. Some observers expect the total participation rate to fall below 5 percent in the near future.[8]

The decline in unionization appears to be connected to important changes in our economy. First, most of the new jobs created in the United States since the mid-1970s have been in the service sector, which today accounts for nearly two-thirds of the U.S. work force.[9] These workers generally have resisted unionization efforts. Second, as global competition has intensified, U.S. businesses have struggled to remain competitive. Corporate takeovers and mergers, the increased use of industrial robots, and the battle to maintain profits have caused thousands of union members to lose their jobs.

As employees in unionized factories have lost their jobs, those who find work at other locations are naturally reluctant to put their futures in the hands of union leadership. For example, workers at Nissan Motor Company in Smyrna, Tennessee, voted not to be represented by the United Auto Workers in the first certification vote at the company. The vote was more than two to one against the union after a long and bitter organizing campaign.[10] Perhaps working conditions, pay, and benefits were better at this plant than at unionized plants in Detroit, or maybe the workers simply were no longer interested in what the union had to offer.

Perhaps the most important factor working against unions is the increasingly tough stance against unions taken by U.S. companies. Economic pressures, especially from foreign competition, have increased employer resistance to unions. Union members receive, on average, 10 percent higher wages and, of course, limit managers' actions in assigning duties

Exhibit 12.5 **TRENDS IN UNION MEMBERSHIP IN THE UNITED STATES**

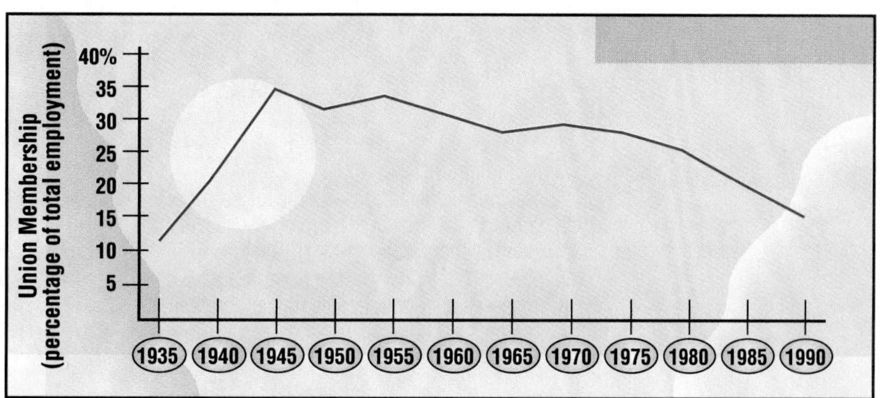

and maintaining discipline.[11] Also, some managers believe unions decrease the productivity of their workers, although this has not been verified. Still, higher wages, less flexible work rules, and lower productivity make companies ineffective in global competition.

Unions also affect other countries and their global businesses. Union participation rates are higher in many other countries, including Japan, as Exhibit 12.6 shows.[12] Thus, the complete answer to remaining globally competitive must be sought in other areas of labor-management relations.

OTHER ISSUES IN EMPLOYEE RELATIONS

Today all organizations face a number of employee relations issues, whether or not they are unionized. Some of these issues have arisen because of legislation. Others have arisen as the work force has become more educated, better skilled, and shifted from careers in manufacturing to careers in service. Chief among the issues affecting employee relations today are equal pay and equal employment opportunity, job security, and employee ownership.

EQUAL PAY AND EQUAL EMPLOYMENT OPPORTUNITY

Over the past three decades, several federal laws have been passed that are intended to stop the unequal treatment of men and women in the workplace. We discussed some of these laws

Exhibit 12.6 **UNION MEMBERSHIP IN EIGHT INDUSTRIALIZED COUNTRIES**

Country	Total Union Membership (thousands)	Union Membership as Percentage of Total Civilian Employment
United States	16,960	16%
Japan	12,227	26
United Kingdom	9,214	41
Germany	8,082	33
Italy	6,930	47
Sweden	3,415	84
Canada	2,536	33
France	1,970	11

STREET SMART

What Counts Is Being on the Field

Having female reporters in the locker room after a professional ballgame was very controversial when it began occurring in the 1970s. While some pro athletes have reservations about female trainers on their teams, many don't care as long as they are qualified. "When you can find someone, be it male or female, who can contribute to your success and your being on the field more than you're off the field, you're going to appreciate that," said St. Louis Cardinals shortstop Ozzie Smith.

in Chapter 11. The issues associated with the Equal Pay Act of 1963 are of special concern in employee relations. The Equal Pay Act prohibits using gender to establish pay rates for substantially equal work. In essence this means men and women should receive very similar pay levels when performing the same or similar jobs. Perhaps no issue other than sexual harassment can be so disruptive to employer relations with female employees.

Equal employment opportunity (EEO) legislation prohibits discrimination against women in terms of promotion. Yet surveys of employee relations practices in U.S. companies tend to show that little progress has been made in achieving full equality between women and men in the workplace. Although women's pay did increase during the 1980s, it averaged less than 75 percent of men's pay.

Many prominent companies have been charged with failure to comply with EEO requirements. For example, nearly 50 percent of employees at Wendy's International are women, yet most of Wendy's management positions are filled by men. A lawsuit charging Wendy's with failing to promote women was filed and subsequently settled when the company agreed to pay a total of $1.4 million to 700 women and fill 40 percent of upper-management and 50 percent of lower-management vacancies with women. It also agreed to hold seminars to educate all of its managers in issues of equal employment opportunity.

In another prominent lawsuit, AT&T agreed to pay over $15 million in back wages to women and some minority groups whose pay was determined to be too low due to illegal discrimination. In yet another case, a policewoman was awarded over $22,000 in back pay, and another received $24,000 in damages when the court found she had been sexually harassed and then retaliated against by management for filing a discrimination complaint.[13]

While some companies and public organizations are making good-faith efforts to correct pay and promotion inequities, many managers are overlooking the problem. Also, some aspects of the equal pay problem are not readily obvious. For example, some jobs are considered "men's jobs" and traditionally have paid more than so-called "women's jobs." Thus, pay for nurses ("women's work") is only 64 percent of pay for computer systems analysts ("men's work") employed by the state of Washington, even though state compensation specialists rated nurses' jobs as more valuable during a formal job evaluation.[14]

Not only can unequal pay and opportunity lead to court suits; it is also bad business practice. Managers must remember that women make up a large share of the buying public and may decide not to buy from a company that is known to be unfair to women employees. Also, poor relations with female employees may lead to high turnover rates in this segment of the company's work force. Finally, despite what some managers believe, job skills, abilities, and motivation of female employees are equivalent to those of male employees.

JOB SECURITY OF NONUNION EMPLOYEES

Job security of union members is always a major issue during labor negotiations. Rules governing layoffs, dismissals, and downsizing receive considerable attention from negotiators and often are the leading cause of a union strike. If the company is unionized, nonunion employees may benefit from job security rules negotiated in the labor contract.

But even companies that are nonunionized may experience improved employee relations when they provide some means of job security for employees. Many companies have gone to extreme lengths to build enviable records for employee job security. Hewlett-Packard, Eastman Kodak, and AT&T are noted for offering good job security. Hewlett-Packard has found it necessary to reduce its work force several times during the past 10 years, but it offers attractive early retirement and voluntary separation packages. These programs encourage employees who have other options to leave the company, permitting others to retain their jobs.

The issue of job security is especially important in a troubled economy, when many firms find it necessary to close inefficient operations. While such company actions impose hardships on employees and communities, the ability to bring operations to a successful end is as important as successfully starting up new operations.

FOCUS ON COMPANY

Downsizing at General Motors Corporation

Due to money problems, General Motors Corporation plans to close 21 plants and eliminate 74,000 jobs by mid-decade. At each plant, managers will have to close up while making sure everything runs smoothly until the last moment. Craig B. Parr, manager of the Pontiac-West assembly plant, must close that plant for good in 1994. But the plant is still running effectively. Just before the announcement that the plant would close, only 71 percent of the engines leaving the department were found to be of perfect quality. But six months later, 97 percent of the engines were perfect.

The plant is kept clean and neat. Unused areas are spotless, and there is fresh paint everywhere. Parr insisted that the annual Christmas party go on as usual after GM tried to cancel it. "If I show the work force that I haven't abandoned them, they're gonna hang in there with me," he says. His rules for plant closings are: Communicate, be visible, be honest, be positive, demand more, and keep the plant looking good. As this book went to press, the Pontiac-West assembly plant was scheduled to close at the end of 1994.

EMPLOYEE OWNERSHIP

Many issues among employees, managers, and the owners of a company arise simply because one group does the work but the other owns the results. Owners are not willing to part with too much of their profits, because they feel entitled to a return on their investment. Workers, however, believe their labor entitles them to a larger share of the pie. In addition, when economic conditions make it necessary to close a plant, owners often have other businesses and resources to maintain their standard of living. But workers have fewer resources and must rely on their jobs to support their families and living styles.

Employee stock ownership plan (ESOP)
A program that gives employees part ownership of the company.

Employee stock ownership plans (ESOP), which give employees part ownership of the company, are designed to give employees a share in improved profit performance. ESOPs have been used by small businesses to increase employee job security and motivation. They have helped prevent plant closings and have saved many jobs.

Avis, the world's second largest auto rental company, is owned by its employees. Since its employees acquired it, Avis has set many records for service and profitability. The employees share in gains and losses and in general work harder to ensure the company's success. All service employees participate in problem-solving teams in which they suggest methods for improving customer service and running the company more efficiently. Now they have designs on taking over number one from Hertz.[15]

Although a company that is largely owned by its employees would seem to have excellent employee relations, this is not always true. Sometimes employees are not very good at making management decisions. If the company does not hire professional managers, the owner-employees may have as many or more personnel problems than before. At employee-owned South Bend Lathe Inc., some employees picketed their own company when mistrust between employee groups occurred.[16]

Companies that maintain good employee relations do well because their employees are motivated and committed to the company. Companies that fail to solve the employee relations problems identified in this chapter will struggle to maintain their competitiveness and productivity in the future.

SUMMARY

1. ***Discuss the history of American labor unions.***
   A labor union is a group of workers who have joined together to more effectively achieve common goals such as improved working conditions, wages, and benefits. Labor unions existed during the 1800s, but most failed to survive. The first strong union was the Knights of Labor, founded in 1869. A subunit of this union later became the American Federation of Labor (AFL). The AFL was a craft-based union. The Congress of Industrial Organizations (CIO) was a group of industrial unions that separated from the AFL in 1935. In 1955, the AFL and the CIO merged to become the AFL-CIO. Union membership in all unions today is about 17 million workers.

2. ***Identify several important labor relations laws.***
   Traditionally the law favored the property rights of business owners. However, the Great Depression caused a change in the political climate. Congress passed the Norris–La Guardia Act in 1932. This act reduced management's ability to prevent unionization and strikes. The National Labor Relations Act, passed in 1935, required employers to bargain or negotiate in good faith with elected employee representatives. It also created the National Labor Relations Board (NRLB). The Fair Labor Standards Act, passed in 1938, set a federal minimum wage and maximum work hours for employees in interstate commerce and outlawed the use of child labor. The Taft-Hartley Act was passed in 1947 to limit strikes, boycotts, and other unreasonable union activities such as secondary boycotting, closed shops, and featherbedding. The Landrum-Griffin Act was passed in 1959 to protect union members from corrupt practices by union leaders.

3. ***Describe the collective bargaining process.***
   The collective bargaining process involves negotiations between management and the workers' elected representative. This process focuses on establishing the terms of the contract, strategies for achieving the bargaining goals, and administering the contract once it has been negotiated. Issues that can be negotiated include wages, fringe benefits, conditions of work, employee rights, and union security.

4. ***Discuss the mediation and arbitration processes.***
Mediation is the process of bringing in a third party who makes recommendations for resolving differences between the union and the company. Arbitration means bringing in a third party who makes a binding decision or judgment that both parties must agree to accept. The purpose of mediation and arbitration is to resolve differences without resorting to costly strikes or lockouts. However, neither unions nor companies favor these procedures.

5. ***Discuss the issues of equal pay and equal employment opportunity.***
Equal pay and equal opportunity laws have been passed to stop the unequal treatment of women in the workplace. The Equal Pay Act of 1963 prohibits using gender to establish pay rates for substantially equal work. Equal employment opportunity legislation prohibits discriminating against women in terms of promotion decisions. Nevertheless, little progress has been made in achieving full equality between women and men in the workplace. Women's pay continues to be lower than men's pay, on average, and many prominent companies have been charged with failure to comply with EEO requirements.

6. ***Describe employee ownership of companies.***
Many disagreements among a company's employees, managers, and owners occur because one group does the work but the other owns the results. Owners feel entitled to a return on their investment, while employees think their labor entitles them to a larger share of the pie. Employee stock ownership plans (ESOPs) give employees part ownership of the company. ESOPs have increased employee job security and motivation, have helped prevent plant closings, and have saved many jobs.

KEY TERMS AND CONCEPTS

Labor union (p. 266)
American Federation of Labor (AFL) (p. 267)
Congress of Industrial Organizations (CIO) (p. 267)
National Labor Relations Board (NLRB) (p. 268)
Secondary boycott (p. 269)
Featherbedding (p. 269)
Closed shop (p. 269)
Jurisdictional strike (p. 269)
Collective bargaining (p. 270)
Union shop (p. 273)
Right-to-work laws (p. 273)
Open shop (p. 273)
Agency shop (p. 273)
Distributive bargaining (p. 273)
Mediation (p. 275)
Arbitration (p. 275)
Employee stock ownership plan (ESOP) (p. 280)

DISCUSSION QUESTIONS

Company

1. In what ways can a company maintain good relations with its union employees without being unfair to its nonunion employees?
2. What benefits do companies receive from creating innovative programs such as flextime and job sharing?
3. Why do employees object to union shops?

Customers

4. How does collective bargaining affect a company's customers both positively and negatively?
5. What steps could management take to minimize the negative effects of a strike on its customers?

Competitors

6. What role do competitors play in the collective bargaining process?
7. How do labor relations laws affect the nature of business competition?

Collaborators

8. Why are mediators and arbitrators important to the collective bargaining process?
9. How has Congress helped maintain a balance between the powers of company owners and workers?

In Question: Take a Stand

I was laid off from my job after 16 years with a good work record, no time off, etc. The reason given was that the company was cutting down. I got four weeks' severance pay and four weeks' vacation. My boss came into my office at 11 A.M. and told me to pack up and leave. Does a company have a right to do this, or should I have been given 60 days' notice? If I quit my job, I'm supposed to give notice to the company. I think that after 16 years of dedicated service, an employee should at least be notified 24 hours in advance.[17]

This letter to the business section of the Chicago Tribune *suggests that employees often have little control over their own careers. Is it fair for an employee to be given such abrupt notice of a layoff? What can an employee do to protect himself or herself in situations like this? How can management deal with this situation, especially when the layoff was caused by financial problems that seemed to leave few alternatives?*

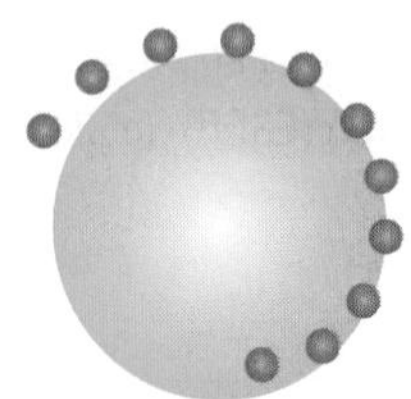

CASE 12.1
SILVER STAR MEATS INC.[18]

Silver Star Meats Inc. was sold by owner Richard Rzaca to company employees in a $1.5 million deal that offers long-term viability for the sausage and meat packaging firm. Mr. Rzaca said he feared alternatives other than an employee stock ownership plan would have resulted in liquidation. The 75 employees at McKees Rocks–based Silver Star have borrowed from Mellon Bank to complete the ESOP buyout. They will repay the loan through Silver Star income. Though the loan is to be repaid in seven years, Silver Star management hopes that rising profits will take care of the company's debt in four to five years. The company is being managed by a department-oriented team. Roger Krey is sales manager, Dominick Bovalina has been named plant superintendent and Randy Heit is the firm's controller. Though he admits that selling the company to his former employees was in his best interest, Mr. Rzaca said he had a desire to preserve Silver Star and the jobs of its employees. A chief concern of Mr. Rzaca and the firm's long-time employees was that an out-of-town meat producer would buy Silver Star just to plunder its sales list and inventory, leaving workers jobless once the company was abandoned. "I have employees that have worked for me for 30 years, and I didn't want to see them go out into the street to find a job," he said. "Who's going to hire someone who is 50 or 55 years old?"

Questions

1. *What are the advantages of an ESOP to Silver Star's employees?*
2. *What potential problems might the ESOP cause Silver Star?*
3. *Did Richard Rzaca get a good deal? Why or why not?*

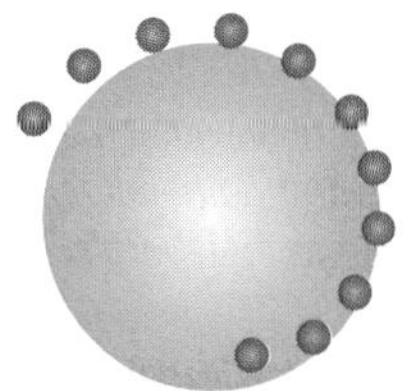

CASE 12.2
TEAMSTERS OBJECT TO NEW UPS WEIGHT LIMIT[19]

United Parcel Service operations were temporarily interrupted in February, 1994, when union members walked off their jobs to protest a company decision to raise the weight limit on UPS packages from 70 to 150 pounds. The teamsters said the higher weight limit endangers drivers and other workers who must lift the heavier loads.

A settlement was reached after a day of testy exchanges between the company and union officials. It spelled out that no Teamster is required to handle more than 70 pounds without help from another employee. It also said that UPS customers will have to label all packages that weigh more than 70 pounds. The company said it expects fewer than 1 percent of the 11 million packages it handles each day to exceed the old 70-pound limit.

Questions

1. *Is the new weight limit a legitimate strike issue? Why or why not?*
2. *How do union actions such as this affect UPS's ability to compete with other package delivery services such as Federal Express and the U.S. Post Office?*
3. *Should union members be permitted to walk off their jobs to protest changes by the company that affect their jobs, or is there a better alternative? Discuss.*

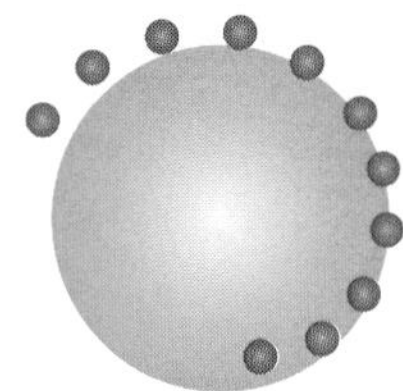

CASE 12.3
SPRINGFIELD REMANUFACTURING CORPORATION[20]

Jack Stack, a failed missionary who was kicked out of college, believes he has found a formula for business success: He shares all of his small company's financial information with employees.

For ten years, workers at Springfield ReManufacturing Corporation, an engine rebuilder in Springfield, Missouri, have gotten weekly peeks at everything from revenue and purchasing costs, to management and labor expenses. Partly because of this practice, the privately held concern pulled back from the brink and is posting record growth. Revenue climbed from $18 million in 1983 to more than $85 million in 1993.

"The more employees learned, the more they could do," says Jack Stack, SRC's 44-year-old president. "We matched up higher levels of thinking with higher levels of performance."

SRC employees, who also won 31 percent of the company, clearly have responded positively to this strategy, known as "open-book management." Many say they feel extremely loyal to the business, have a heightened sense of community, and will do whatever it takes to maintain competitiveness—including deferring wage increases. While SRC workers obviously value their big stock holding, they maintain that it's even more important to understand the company's numbers.

Limited information sharing has recently come into vogue among numerous small companies eager to enhance productivity. But few have embraced information sharing with as much gusto as SRC. Its open-book approach is generating intense interest among businesses big and small. SRC says about 1,500 companies, including many Fortune 500 concerns, have toured its facilities to learn more about the merits of disclosing everything to rank-and-file workers.

Ray Smiler, vice-president of the Center for Entrepreneurial Leadership says, "It's seen as an important way to involve employees in the growth of the enterprise. SRC is seen as a pioneer in the field. It is a stunning example of how well the idea works."

When SRC was a repair and services division of International Harvester, the division was poorly managed from the outset. Workers' distrust ran so deep that they often indicated their readiness for management's latest "snow job" by wearing raincoats and galoshes to company meetings. In 1979, as its own fortunes began to sag, International Harvester decided to close the division. But Stack, a managerial whiz kid at International Harvester persuaded them to let him try a turnaround.

He began by soliciting employees' opinions on how to improve the plant's operation. He also shared limited financial information with them and awarded bonuses to anyone who met financial targets. The results were immediate. For example, inventory accuracy, a measure of in-house availability of replacement parts, leapt to 99 percent from 48 percent between 1979 and 1980, and has remained at that level ever since. When International harvester was still facing serious financial losses, Mr. Stack and twelve other managers bought the unit, retaining 119 of its former employees. The company, renamed SRC, established an employee stock ownership plan later that year, stepped up the bonus program, and broadened its disclosure policy to cover all financial figures. Each week managers distribute the latest numbers and help employees evaluate them. Now employees speak glowingly of open-book management. "When I came here, I didn't realize that as a worker on the floor you could have a direct impact on the profit," says Candice Smalley, a nozzle rebuilder at SRC for ten years. "When we started seeing the financials and hearing about usage and overhead, it made us start trying to improve our quality."

Questions

1. *How does SRC's open-book management philosophy fit with traditional concepts of motivation, such as Herzberg's Two-Factor theory?*
2. *Describe Jack Stack's leadership style.*
3. *How does SRC's stock ownership approach affect its focus on customers and the quality of its service?*
4. *What are the disadvantages of letting employees know so much about the company's financial figures, and how does SRC overcome these disadvantages?*
5. *Based on what you see in this case, how would you describe SRC's human resource management philosophy?*

PART 4

Marketing Management

CHAPTER 13

MARKETING PRINCIPLES

When you have studied this chapter, you will be able to:

1
Define *marketing.*

2
Describe the marketing concept and trace its evolution.

3
Define the marketing mix and identify its components.

4
Describe the impact of the marketing environment.

5
Define *marketing strategy,* identify the basic marketing strategies, and describe the process for developing marketing strategies.

6
Define *market segmentation* and discuss the variables used to segment markets.

7
Discuss the consumer decision-making process.

8
Explain the marketing research process.

When LensCrafters started out in 1983, it began by investigating customer needs.[1] While quality topped customers' list of concerns, they made it clear that their current lifestyle needs were not being met. Most eyewear retailers were open only during regular business hours, and shopping for eyewear usually required a couple of trips. The growing number of dual-career families were finding it harder to squeeze eyeglass shopping into the hours they had available.

LensCrafters' strategy is to be heavily staffed evenings and weekends so there is little wait when customer demand is highest. Because its locations are in shopping malls, customers can take care of other business while they wait. Most glasses, LensCrafters promises, are ready "in about an hour."

Customers like the stores because they have everything—optometrists, labs, and a huge selection of frames—under one roof. This setup allows LensCrafters to create glasses quickly. Previously, the optometrist had to send prescriptions to an outside lab and wait days or even weeks for the finished glasses to arrive back at the store.

But at LensCrafters, the labs are right there behind a glass wall so customers can actually see what's going on. They can go into the lab and ask questions. The person who makes the glasses actually sees the customer, not as a number on a tray but as a real person. This kind of openness and visibility leads to high quality control. Under the old system, no one checked a pair of glasses except the person who made it. At LensCrafters, the optician who dispenses the glasses to the customer and the lab manager make second and third quality checks.

LensCrafters built itself around a marketing strategy that set it apart from its competitors. As this example illustrates, developing a marketing strategy is crucial to an organization's success. The basic principles underlying marketing strategy are the subject of this chapter.

WHAT IS MARKETING?

The LensCrafters example shows that marketing involves a company's relationship with its customers under competitive circumstances. A company's marketing task is to initiate the exchange of goods or services for a price.

The American Marketing Association's definition of marketing provides a more specific, yet broader, definition:

Marketing
The process of planning and executing the conception, pricing, promotion, and distribution of ideas, goods, and services to create exchanges that will satisfy individual and organizational objectives.

> **Marketing** is the process of planning and executing the conception, pricing, promotion, and distribution of ideas, goods, and services to create exchanges that will satisfy individual and organizational objectives.[2]

This definition stresses that marketing requires the business to conceive of a good, service, or idea and then develop it. In other words, marketers must have ideas for products that may be brought to market and purchased by buyers. Pricing, promotion, and distribution of the products help bring marketers (companies) together with buyers (consumers).

Effective marketing involves creating exchanges between the marketer and customers so that both parties are satisfied. Each party must gain something. Sales revenues satisfy the marketer's objectives. Products (goods, services, or ideas) satisfy customers' needs.

To say that marketing involves exchange means the fundamental purpose of marketing activities is to bring buyers and sellers together. At the beach, the thirsty sunbather seeks the Pepsi stand, whose owner, in turn, is interested in selling soft drinks to satisfy customers' thirst. Marketing activities such as locating the stand at the beach or advertising the price of a Pepsi on a sign help bring buyers and sellers together. The owner's goal is to make a sale that satisfies a customer.

This, of course, is a simple example. Most situations require more complex marketing activities. We will discuss more complex situations after we have looked at the fundamental aspects of marketing in more detail.

Marketing also stresses building *relationships.* Marketers want customers "for life." Once an exchange is made, marketing emphasizes managing the relationships that bring about additional exchanges. The marketer's job is to create, interpret, and maintain the relationship between the company and the customer.[3] In summary, marketing initiates and manages the relationship between the company and its customers.

MARKETING IN NOT-FOR-PROFIT ORGANIZATIONS

"Perform a death-defying act—eat less saturated fat." The American Heart Association offered this advice in an advertisement even though it does not seek to make a profit or charge a price for most of its services. Does the American Heart Association engage in marketing? Are your college, church, and local police department marketers? People who take a broad perspective of marketing unanimously say yes.

When analyzing a politician's campaign, a zoo's fund-raising drive, or an antismoking group's program, we can see marketing in action. Whether a donation is made to the American Heart Association, a zoo, a political campaign, or an antismoking effort, something is given and something is received. Even though the "something received" may be intangible, such as goodwill or a feeling of satisfaction, rather than a packaged good, a transaction (an exchange) has occurred either between an individual and a group or between two individuals. All of these instances illustrate marketing.

Exchange process
Occurs when two or more parties exchange or trade things of value.

What do these situations have in common with the buying and selling of a product? The common characteristic is exchange. The **exchange process**, in which two or more parties exchange or trade things of value, is a fundamental aspect of marketing. A business exchange of goods or services for a price expressed in monetary terms is the goal of a business.

However, the offering of a vote or a volunteer effort in exchange for a candidate's pledge to work hard for his or her constituents, the donation of blood to help the sick and injured, and time spent working for a United Way campaign, where the reward is a sense of satisfaction, are all exchange activities. As such, these activities may be viewed from a marketing perspective when they are planned to bring about an exchange.

THE EVOLUTION OF MARKETING

We have emphasized that effective marketers put the consumer at the center of the business world. As reasonable as this idea seems today, this was not always the case. Earlier in American business history, such as when rail transportation did not adequately connect all of America, companies held different basic philosophies about marketing. These philosophies can be categorized into three basic orientations for operating a company's marketing activities: the production orientation, the sales orientation, and the marketing concept.

PRODUCTION ORIENTATION

Production orientation
The philosophy that stresses the factory over the consumer.

In Chapter 1, we learned that at one time in American business history, the majority of businesses focused on production. Businesspeople of that era believed efficient mass production lowered production cost per unit. Producing a large number of items at lower production costs allowed marketers to sell more because they could charge consumers a lower price. A large sales volume meant large profits, even if profit margins were small. This **production orientation** philosophy stresses the factory over the consumer.

Henry Ford once said, "You can have any color you want as long as it's black." Making only one color reduced factory costs. Ford was oriented toward the construction of moving assembly lines, conveyors, and gravity slides. He and other businesspeople of his day were oriented toward production efficiencies.

SALES ORIENTATION

Sales orientation
The philosophy that a company should change consumers' minds to fit the product.

Organizations with a **sales orientation** believe in changing consumers' minds to fit the product. Managers that think this way stress aggressive sales and advertising campaigns to "push" their existing products. These businesses concentrate on "telling and selling." They sell what they make rather than learning what will best meet consumers' needs. Sales-oriented organizations emphasize short-run increases in sales of their existing products over long-run profits.

MARKETING CONCEPT

Marketing concept
The philosophy that a company must be consumer oriented in all matters and stress long-run profitability rather than short-term profits or sales volume.

The marketing concept is central to all effective marketing thinking, planning, and action. The **marketing concept** underscores two essential requirements:

1. The company must be consumer oriented in all matters.
2. The company must stress long-run profitability rather than short-term profits or sales volume.

This philosophy relates marketing to the organization's overall purpose: to survive and prosper by satisfying customers.

Consumer Orientation. A *consumer orientation* is the first aspect of the marketing concept. The consumer is seen as the center of the business universe. Sam Walton, founder of Wal-

Mart, said it this way: "There is only one boss. The customer. And he can fire everybody in the company from the chairman on down, simply by spending his money somewhere else."

Organizations that have adopted the marketing concept try to create products and services with the customer's needs in mind. In other words, to be consumer oriented the business must first determine what the customer wants and then design the product. The marketing concept says it is better to find out what the customer wants and offer that product than to make a product and then try to sell it to somebody. Consider the following examples.

For years, users of the U.S. Postal Service complained about slow package deliveries. Business customers and some individuals wanted packages delivered overnight, but the post office was not meeting this need. FedEx and some other companies filled the gap by offering private, overnight package courier services to customers who absolutely had to have next-day package delivery. Now the U.S. Postal Service offers express mail to compete with these package courier services.

At McDonald's restaurants, employees are taught the importance of the consumer orientation. While visiting one McDonald's outlet, a McDonald's marketing executive spied a sign ordering customers to "Move to the Next Position." He ordered that such signs be removed from all McDonald's outlets, stating, "It's up to us to move to the customer."

Progressive companies believe business success—indeed survival—depends on satisfying the consumer. When a company defines the broad nature of its business, it must take a consumer-oriented perspective.

Profit Orientation. The marketing concept also emphasizes marketing the product the consumer wants. This does not mean, however, that every trivial desire of every customer must be met. Consumers would prefer the price of a new Lexus to be under $10,000. But because the manufacturing and marketing costs associated with such a car far exceed that figure, Lexus's manufacturer and dealers would soon be out of business if they blindly fulfilled this unrealistic consumer desire.

Every business must operate in a profitable manner to continue to exist. Profits permit companies to grow and serve as an incentive to owners to further satisfy customer needs. Therefore, the marketing concept emphasizes *long-term* profits, in addition to *current* profitability.

Exhibit 13.1 summarizes the production, sales, and marketing orientations.

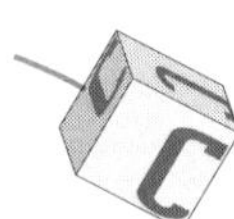

FOCUS ON COMPANY

You Can't Do That on Television

Nickelodeon is a marketing-oriented company. It is a network that understands kids. As the country's largest producer of original children's programming, it considers consumer orientation to be a top priority.

Nickelodeon offers saucy, flip, and hip programming because that's what its research shows kids want. Nickelodeon asked children what it thought were some straightforward questions, such as "What do you like about being a kid?" The kids responded with "some pretty amazing and alarming answers." Conventional wisdom maintains that preteens can't wait to grow up. However, the preteens Nickelodeon talked to kept insisting they *didn't* want to be teenagers. When Nickelodeon asked them why, "they started talking about all these horrible things about teenage life: drugs, AIDS, sex problems. They were worried about nuclear war, the environment, homeless people, their parents, and somewhere on that list they were worried about getting good grades."

Exhibit 13.1 **THREE PHILOSOPHIES OF MARKETING**

Orientation	Focus	Goal	Illustrative Comments
Production orientation	Make quality products	Produce as much as possible	If the factory makes a good product, people will buy it.
Sales orientation	Aggressive sales and persuasive advertising efforts to push existing products	Maximize sales volume	Sell this inventory no matter what it takes.
Marketing orientation	Consumer and profit orientation	Profits through customer satisfaction and long standing relationships	Learn consumers' wants before you produce goods or services.

So Nickelodeon decided its programming for school-age kids would provide escape and refuge rather than teach, preach, and inspire. Thus, on "Double Dare" kids get soaked with green slime, and on "You Can't Do That on Television" they take verbal potshots at stereotypical uncool parents. Nickelodeon's research helps the network provide an "enjoyable, fun, good, safe place on the TV dial for kids who are growing up in this kind of world—with a sort of us versus them attitude."

MARKETING ADDS VALUE

The marketing concept states that marketing's purpose in society is to satisfy consumers. As we saw in Chapter 2, a good's or service's ability to satisfy consumers' needs is called *economic utility.* Marketing helps production create *form utility* by communicating consumer needs for products of various configurations and formulations to production planners. By making products available at the right place—that is, where buyers want them—marketing creates *place utility.* By making products available when consumers need them, marketing creates *time utility. Possession utility* satisfies the consumer's need to own the product and have control over its use or consumption. It is created at the conclusion of a sale when the marketer transfers ownership to the consumer.

THE MARKETING MIX

Marketing mix
The result of management's efforts to creatively combine interrelated and interdependent marketing activities; consists of the four Ps of marketing: product, place, price, and promotion.

Our definition of marketing indicates that marketing entails many activities to encourage exchange. The term **marketing mix** describes the result of management's efforts to creatively combine interrelated and interdependent marketing activities. Facing a wide choice of product features, prices, distribution methods, and other marketing variables, the marketing manager must select and combine the "ingredients" of the organization's marketing mix.

The basic categories of marketing mix elements are *product, place, price,* and *promotion.* These ingredients are commonly referred to as the *four Ps of marketing.* Because virtually every marketing activity falls into one of these categories, the four Ps form a framework managers can use to develop a simple marketing plan.[4] Preparation of a marketing plan requires considering each mix element and involves decisions about the development of plans for each variable. Because marketing managers determine the nature of the marketing mix, the marketing mix is often referred to as the *controllable variables.*

PRODUCT

Product
What the company offers its perspective customers.

Product refers to what the company offers its prospective customers. A product may be a tangible good such as a cement truck, a service such as an airline trip, or an intangible idea such as saying no to drugs.

Because customers often expect more from a company than a simple, tangible good, the task of marketing management is to provide a complete offering—a "total product"—that includes not only the basic service or core product but all the "extras" that go with it. The core product of a city bus line may be transportation, but its total product offering should include courteous service, on-time performance, and assistance in finding appropriate bus routes.

The product variable includes the brand name, the package, the warranty, customer service, and the core product. Sometimes emotional aspects of the products are very important. We discuss these topics in Chapter 14.

PLACE

Place or **distribution**
The location where customers buy the product; how products get to the customer, how quickly, and in what condition.

The Mazda Miata is made in Japan. But American consumers do not go to Japan to buy this sports car because marketers make sure the car is available in the right place. The **place** element of the marketing mix involves the location where customers buy the product. Place is also called **distribution** because it involves how products get to the right place. The company must determine how goods get to the customer, how quickly, and in what condition. Decisions about transportation and storage are examples of distribution activities.

Not every company has the resources or ability to manage all the activities required in the distribution process. Thus, companies may concentrate on activities where they have a unique advantage. Retailers and various other collaborators, such as trucking companies, have evolved as specialists that make the distribution process more efficient. For example, Mazda Motor Corporation, which concentrates its efforts in the production and promotion of automobiles, finds it efficient to distribute through independent dealers, which are better equipped to sell cars and to provide service to buyers.

Chapter 15 discusses distribution in the global economy.

PRICE

Price
The amount of money, or sometimes goods or services, given in exchange for something.

Price is the amount of money, or sometimes goods or services, given in exchange for something. In other words, price is what is exchanged for the product. Price expresses the value of a product. Just as the customer buys a product with cash, so a manufacturer "buys" the customer's cash with the product. In not-for-profit situations, price may be expressed in terms of volunteered time or effort, votes, or donations.

Pricing involves establishing appropriate price levels. This can be difficult, because the price must be low enough to attract consumers but high enough to create sufficient profit. Companies also use discounts, rebates, and other tactics to adjust prices. For example, department stores almost always have after-Christmas sales.

Cost, competition, and desired profit determine prices. Prices are subject to rapid change. As cost or demand changes, so does price.

PROMOTION

Promotion
Applied communication such as advertising, personal selling, sales promotion, publicity, and public relations.

Promotion is applied communication such as advertising, personal selling, sales promotion, publicity, and public relations. Different companies use different combinations of these pro-

Exhibit 13.2 **BLENDING THE MARKETING MIX ELEMENTS**

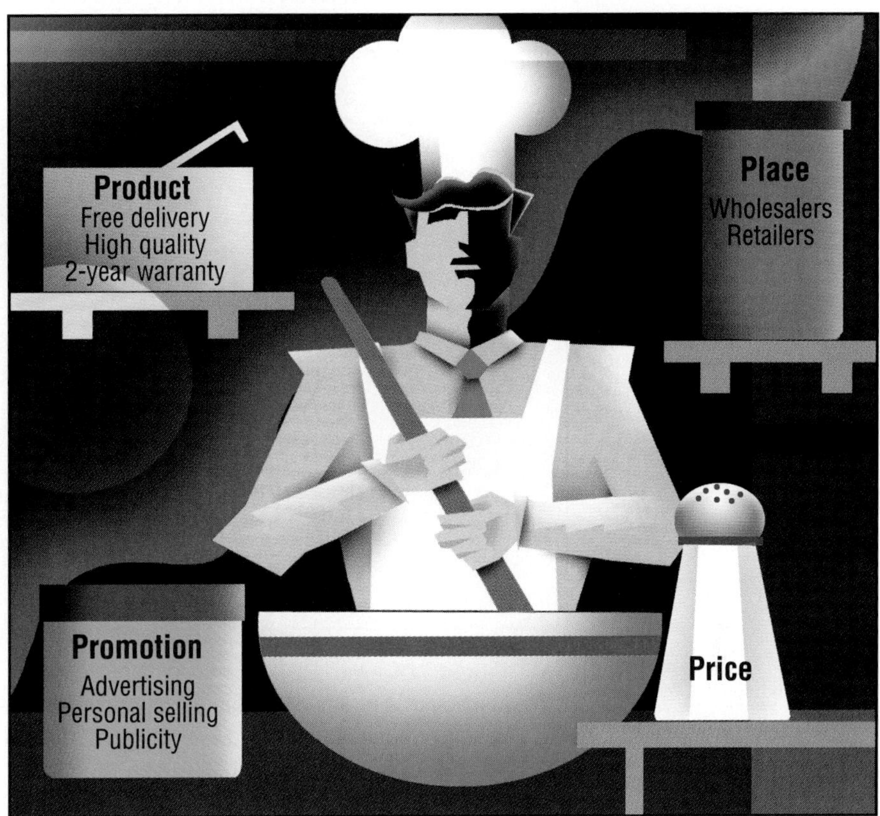

motion tools. Some companies emphasize advertising, while others hardly advertise at all. A television commercial advertising "Always Coca-Cola" reminds us of our experiences with a familiar cola. An IBM sales representative explains how a computer network will help our organization. An A&P supermarket offers a free sample of Eckrich sausage. Filmmaker Spike Lee created publicity when he urged African-Americans to skip school to see *Malcolm X.*

Promotion provides information about the company or its products. It may convey a message that encourages consumers to respond. Promotion usually tells why consumers should buy the product. It may communicate persuasive information about the other elements of the marketing mix, such as the new low price being offered during a sale or the names of stores where the product is sold.

THE ART OF BLENDING THE ELEMENTS

A manager's selection of a marketing mix may be likened to the chef who realizes there is no "one best way" to make a dish. Instead, different combinations of ingredients may be used, and the result will still be a satisfactory meal. In marketing, as in cooking, there is no standard formula for a successful combination of marketing elements. Marketing mixes will vary from company to company and from situation to situation (see Exhibit 13.2).

For example, the marketing mix strategies for Honda motorcycles vary greatly from those for Harley-Davidson bikes, even though both products are successful. Far greater differences in marketing mixes can be seen between different products, such as a Pearl Jam compact disk and a Steinway piano. The field of marketing uses such differing approaches because the planning and execution of a marketing mix are creative activities.

Exhibit 13.3 **ENVIRONMENTAL FORCES THAT SHAPE CONSUMER BEHAVIOR AND THE MARKETING MIX**

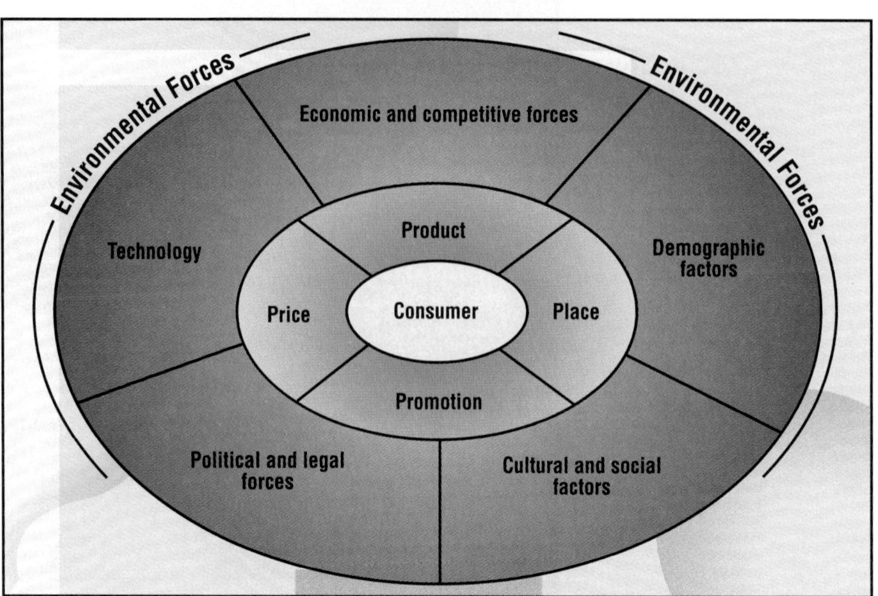

The distinctive nature of each marketing problem means there are no pat solutions in marketing. Even frequently encountered situations have unique aspects. This fact may trouble people who are accustomed to working math or accounting problems and arriving at one "right" answer. But marketing is different. Its relationship to the ever changing environment requires that it be dynamic, constantly adjusting its approaches to the marketplace.

THE MARKETING ENVIRONMENT

Marketers must deal with variables that occur outside the organization. External environmental forces influence all companies. Except in rare instances, managers cannot influence the nature of these external environmental forces; therefore, these forces are called *uncontrollable variables.*

Exhibit 13.3 illustrates the marketing environment and the uncontrollable influences that shape consumers' behavior and the company's marketing mix decisions. Reacting and adapting to economic and competitive forces, demographic trends, cultural and social values, technology, and political and legal forces are a major part of the marketing manager's job.

ECONOMIC AND COMPETITIVE FORCES

Economic and competitive forces have a strong influence on marketing activity. Organizations' reactions to high inflation rates are easy to spot in their pricing policies. During the past two decades, the U.S. Postal Service responded to inflation by raising the price of a first-class stamp from 20 to 22 to 25 to 29 cents. Increased postal charges, especially when they occur late in a calendar year, often contribute to declines in greeting card companies' sales. Other economic forces—for example, a shift in the business cycle to recession, shortages of materials, or high land prices—may lead to a decline in home building. Such a decline would then reduce the demand for bulldozers, concrete mixers, nails, and even work clothes.

Many companies face intense competition. A competitor's strategies or tactics may be the most important factor in the marketing organization's success or failure in achieving its objectives. A change in a competitor's marketing mix, such as a change in price, may call for an immediate response.

DEMOGRAPHIC TRENDS

Demographics
The study of the size and composition of the population.

Demographics is the study of the size and composition of the population. Knowledge about age, income, education, and other demographic characteristics is important for marketing managers. Meaningful demographic trends include the aging of the population, a general trend toward smaller families, the increasing number of single-parent households, and increasing immigration. These demographic trends have led to many changes in product design, pricing, distribution, and promotion. For example, at the turn of the century, only 1 person in 25 was over age 65. By the year 2000, one person in five will be over 65. To accommodate these older consumers, more firms are making easier-to-use products such as appliances with large letters and big knobs.

THE CULTURAL AND SOCIAL ENVIRONMENT

Culture
The social values, beliefs, and institutions in a society.

Every society has a culture. When discussing the business environment, the word *culture* does not refer to classical music, art, and literature. Instead, **culture** refers to the social values, beliefs, and institutions in a society. Culture includes everything we learn to know as members of society, but does not include the basic drives with which we were born. For example, we are all born with a need to eat, but what, when, and where we eat, and whether we season our food with ketchup or curry powder, are learned as part of our culture. The fact that many American women are "liberated," while few Saudi women are, is also related to culture. The value of products and the symbols associated with them also vary across cultures.

Social values
Represent the goals a society views as important and express a culture's shared ideas about preferred ways of acting.

A **social value** represents the goals a society views as important. Social values express a culture's shared ideas about preferred ways of acting. Marketing activity is shaped by the social values and social beliefs that guide a society's everyday life. It is the marketer's job to "read" the social environment and reflect the surrounding culture's values and beliefs in the marketing strategy.

For example, relaxing corporate dress codes and increasing trends toward casual living has caused sales of sheer pantyhose to decline. Managers must be able to accurately recognize and analyze subtle uncontrollable variables like these so that they can plan marketing mixes that are compatible with the environment.

TECHNOLOGY

Technology
The application of scientific knowledge to practical purposes.

Technology is the application of scientific knowledge to practical purposes. Technological advances can revolutionize or even destroy an industry. Think of the impact the development of superconductivity will have on the electronics industry or the effect of the discovery that getting a sunburn may cause cancer on sunscreen marketers. A dramatic example of this type of situation occurred when the *New England Journal of Medicine* published a study downplaying oat bran's cholesterol-reducing potential. The market share of oat bran cereals dropped to almost half within three months of the publication of the research.[5]

POLITICAL AND LEGAL FORCES

Political processes in other countries may have dramatic influences on international marketers. For example, the breakup of the Soviet Union opened new markets in Europe and Asia. Political forces have a critical impact when the U.S. government restricts the sale of weapons to countries like Cuba, Iraq, and Lebanon. In China, the student demonstrations in Tiananmen Square and the government's violent response in June 1989 illustrate the uncertainty of political forces and how swiftly political stability may change. After these events occurred, many Western corporations postponed or canceled plans for expansion into Chinese markets.

When conducting international business, it is essential to understand a country's culture and its normal way of conducting business. In Japan and many other Asian countries, the exchange of business cards is an important and complicated ritual. Unlike Americans, who typically take a casual glance at business cards before putting them away, Japanese executives carefully inspect the cards given to them. In South Korea, over half of the population has the family name Kim, Yi (Lee), or Pak (Park). They prefer to be addressed by their job title and family name, as in Plant Manager Yi.

Of course, many political and legal influences are quite stable. Laws in particular tend to have a long-term influence on marketing strategy.

THE INTERNATIONAL DIMENSION

Companies that operate outside of their home countries must contend with the international dimension of the external environment. Foreign cultures, global competition, political and legal factors in other countries, and the level of technology in other countries have a major impact on international business. For example, when Procter & Gamble first began producing and marketing Safeguard soap in China, it had to import most of its raw materials. Today the company can purchase most materials locally because of changes in China's economic policies.

Companies engaged in international marketing often work with collaborators. Kentucky Fried Chicken Corporation and Mitsubishi Corporation have collaborated to establish more than 1,000 restaurants in Japan. Legal requirements, different cultural values, and other environmental factors are often better understood by local collaborators who have experience doing business in the host country.

MARKETING FUNCTIONS

As we saw in Chapter 6, every business performs production, finance, management, and marketing functions. In most companies, performing the first three functions effectively strengthens marketing functions. For example, a music store cannot buy a large inventory of CDs without adequate financing. When it buys the CDs, it takes a risk that the items will become out of fashion with teenage CD buyers. *Risk taking* is a function of the business as a whole.

Certain business functions are primarily the responsibility of marketing managers. They are the conception and development function, the communication and exchange function, and the physical distribution function.

Product ideas must be born. Marketing is primarily responsible for the conception and development of products. Product ideas must be tested and refined with customers in mind.

This is the first function of marketing. It requires that marketers know the consumer, perhaps with the help of marketing research. It requires establishing standards of product quality and determining which suppliers are acceptable. The communication and exchange function involves selling, advertising, and other activities, such as pricing, that create exchanges and establish relationships between the marketer and its customers. Certain finance functions, such as granting credit, also facilitate exchange. Once the sale is made, marketing performs the physical distribution function, which involves transportation and storage so that products reach their final destination.

You should be able to recognize that the basic elements of the marketing mix and the functions of marketing have much in common. Although we have implied these are unique marketing functions, some of them, such as the granting of credit, are intertwined with the other functional areas of the business.

MARKETING STRATEGY

Marketing strategy
Consists of determining basic long-range goals and committing to a marketing plan that explains how the goals will be achieved.

Competitive advantage
Anything that makes a company's product superior or different from competitors in a way that is important to the market.

A **marketing strategy** consists of determining basic long-range goals and committing to a marketing plan that explains how the goals will be achieved. One of the most common strategic goals is to establish and maintain a **competitive advantage**: to be superior to or different from competitors in a way that is important to the market.

There are two basic marketing strategies. A manufacturer's low-cost/low-price strategy emphasizes producing a standardized product at a very low per-unit cost. The company gains a competitive advantage by producing at a lower cost than competitors, which allows it to underprice all competitors. Low prices increase demand, which increases the company's unit sales volume. This strategy is based on the belief that selling many units at a low price will bring greater profits than selling a small number of units at a higher profit margin. For example, the company that markets BIC pens, by capitalizing on cheaper resources in other countries, produces a *uniform standardized* product comparable in quality to its higher-priced competitors. It achieves a profit by selling a large volume at a rock-bottom price. Wal-Mart, Target, and other retailers using this strategy often advertise everyday low prices.

A differentiation strategy emphasizes offering a product that is unique in the industry, provides a distinct advantage, or is set apart from competitors' brands in some way other than price. Attractive product styling, distinctive product features, appealing advertising, faster delivery, or some other aspect of the marketing mix is planned to achieve a product consumers perceive as being different. The heart of a differentiation strategy is to create value for the consumer in a way that is different or better than what competitors offer. Goodyear Aquatrend's huge success was a result of the company's strategy of designing the best wet-weather tire that had ever been put on a car. To differentiate it from other tires, Goodyear developed a deep "aqua-channel" that evacuates water. This unique product feature is visibly different from those of other tires.

DEVELOPING MARKETING STRATEGIES

There are four major stages in the development of a marketing strategy that will satisfy customers' needs and meet the objectives and goals of the organization (see Exhibit 13.4):

1. Analyzing market segments and selecting target markets
2. Scanning the environment to identify and evaluate opportunities
3. Planning a market position
4. Developing a unified marketing mix

The various activities involved in developing a marketing strategy may be carried out by a number of people over varying time periods, and the actual sequence of decisions may differ among organizations. Nevertheless, each stage is crucial to effective strategy development.

Exhibit 13.4 **THE STAGES IN DEVELOPING A MARKETING STRATEGY**

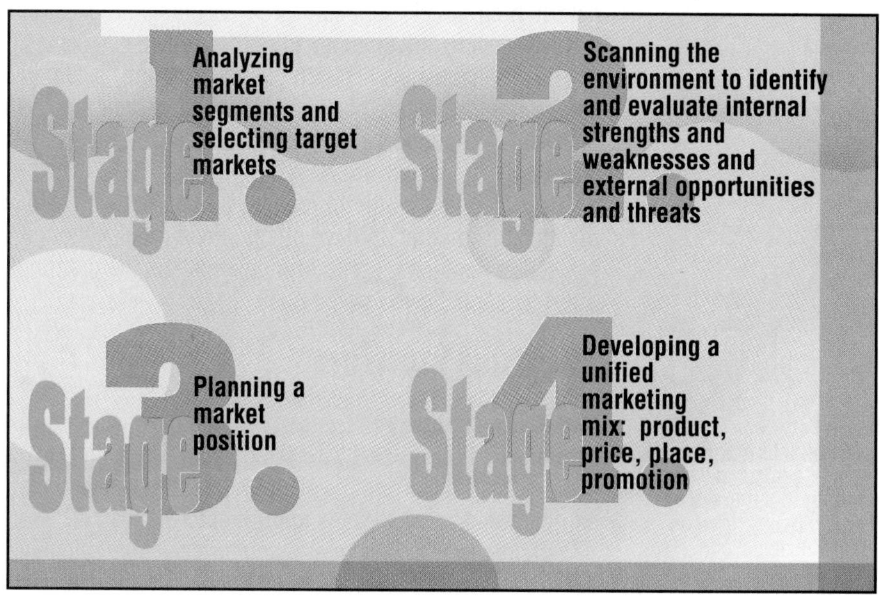

STAGE 1: ANALYZING MARKET SEGMENTS AND SELECTING TARGET MARKETS

Market
A group of individuals who are potential customers for the product being offered for sale.

A **market** is a group of individuals who are potential customers for the product being offered for sale. They are potential customers for the product because they are willing to spend their money or exchange other resources to obtain the product.

The term *market* can be confusing because it also refers to designated places (the Greater Houston Metropolitan Market), institutions (the stock market), and stores (the supermarket), as well as many other things. But each usage—even the name of a city in which business is carried out—suggests people or groups with purchasing power who are willing to exchange it for something else. It will become clear as you read this book that the nature of the market is a primary concern of marketing decision makers.

Consumer market
A market in which the buyers are individuals who will use the product to satisfy personal or household needs.

Organizational or **business market**
A market in which the buyers are organizations that will use the product in their operations or resell it later.

Many types of markets exist, but the most fundamental distinction among them is in terms of the buyer's use of the good or service being purchased. If the buyer is an individual who will use the product to satisfy personal or household needs, that person is a consumer. Thus, the product is a *consumer* product sold in the **consumer market**. When an organization purchases a product for use in its business (e.g., wood purchased by a furniture manufacturer) or to resell it later (a facsimile machine purchased by an office supply store), that product is an *organizational* or *business* product and is sold in the **organizational** or **business market**. A *business marketing transaction* takes place whenever a good or a service is sold for any use other than personal consumption.

To determine whether a product is a consumer product or an organizational product, the marketer asks these two questions:

1. *Who* wants to purchase it?
2. *Why* do they want to buy it?

Notice that it is not necessary to ask, "What do they want to buy?" For example, airline travel may be a consumer or an organizational product, depending on who bought it and why it was purchased; it does not matter what the actual service or good is.

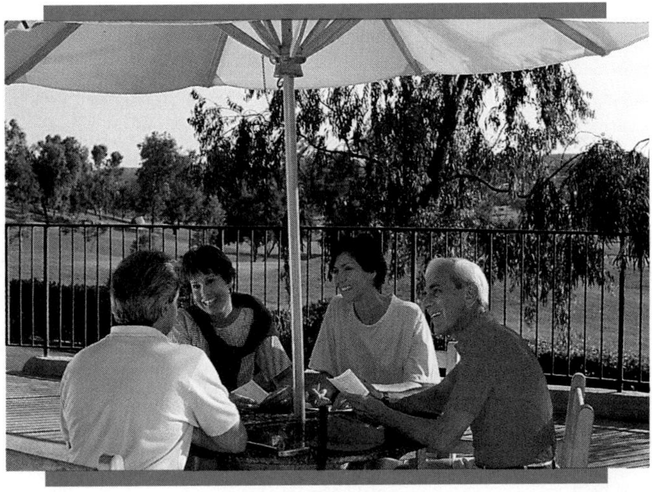

More than one-half of the population in Miami's Dade County were born outside the United States. Almost 60 percent of Dade County's population is bilingual. Hispanic-Americans comprise the majority of consumers in the county, and much business is conducted in Spanish. Marketers often target specialized products to markets such as Dade County.

Market segment
A portion of a larger market.

Market segmentation
Dividing a heterogeneous mass market into a number of smaller, more specific customer groups.

Target market
The specific group likely to buy the company's product.

Market Segmentation. **Market segments** are portions of larger markets. Thus, Asian-Americans comprise a segment of the total U.S. market. Asian-Americans between ages of 20 and 35 are a smaller, more narrowly defined segment. Female Asian-Americans, ages 20 to 35, who use gas rather than charcoal grills are a still smaller market segment. Market segments can be defined in terms of any number of variables, from race or sex to air travel behavior.

Market segmentation means dividing a larger, heterogeneous market into a number of smaller, more specific customer groups. Segments identified as having good potential for sales and services are likely to become the organization's **target markets**, that is, the specific groups likely to buy the company's product. Concentrating on one or a few target markets rather than trying to reach "everybody" allows the marketer to tailor a marketing mix to a group's specific needs. An old adage states, "You can't be all things to all people." A firm selects a target market because it believes it will have a competitive advantage in that particular segment. Some organizations target multiple market segments with different products or different marketing mixes.

Variables Used to Segment Consumer Markets. Marketers use many different variables as the basis for segmenting consumer markets. Exhibit 13.5 shows that geographic, demo-

Exhibit 13.5 **VARIABLES USED AS THE BASIS FOR MARKET SEGMENTATION**

Geographic Variables	Demographic Variables	Psychographic Variables	Buyer Behavior/ Product Usage Patterns
Continent	Age	Lifestyle	Heavy users versus infrequent users
Country	Gender	Personality	Loyalty to brand or store
Region	Income	Attitudes and opinions	Benefit expected (product needs)
Metropolitan area	Ethnicity (race)		Importance of price
Climate	Marital status		
	Household size		
	Education		
	Occupation		

graphic, psychographic, and buyer behavior/product usage are common ways to segment a market.

Geographic Variables. Most marketers use geography as a basis for segmenting markets. Virtually all marketers decide whether to engage in international business or market only in the United States. International marketers recognize that people in Mexico, Egypt, and Malaysia have different needs. In Argentina most Coca-Cola is consumed with food, but in many Asian countries it is consumed primarily as a refreshment and is rarely served with meals. Geographical differences are also important in the United States. Domestic marketers need to recognize that for many products, such as mass transportation, people in New York City have different needs than people in Wyoming.

FOCUS ON CUSTOMERS

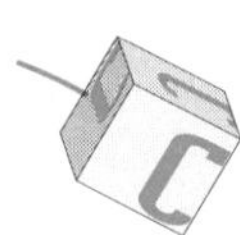

Diversity in the European Union

The 12 nations of the European Union (also called the European Community) are able to share a single market, and in the future there may be one currency.

But don't expect them to share identical tastes in toilet paper, pastries and pills. Marketers have discovered that there is no such thing as a typical European consumer; unlike the relatively homogeneous United States, the EU is divided by language, religion, climate and centuries of tradition. The message to American companies doing business in Europe is clear: Adapt to local attitudes and buying habits or watch your product fail.

Confronted with diverse national preferences, successful firms either develop new products, repackage existing ones or cleverly reposition them. Take toilet paper, for example. Scott Paper Company, the leading manufacturer of sanitary tissue in Europe, found that consumers in the United States, Britain and France are quite particular in the bathroom.

"The States is a nation of scrunchers, in contrast to the U.K., which is a nation of folders," says one executive. Thus Scott makes Andrex, its British brand, much tougher than domestic toilet paper. Because the French like individual strips, Scott obliges with its Le Trefle and Scottex brands.

Taste tests in London revealed that the English like their baked goods flaky and dry rather than moist and chewy, and they abhor strong flavors. Pillsbury changed recipes and, because U.K. consumers associate plastic tubes with cheap sausage, repacked its cookie-dough products in plastic tubs.

Almost every area of European commerce has potential cultural traps. Campbell Soup Company's familiar "M'm! M'm! Good!" ads featuring a smiling face and steaming bowl of soup won't work in the United Kingdom; apparently Britons prefer to make soup from scratch, reserving the condensed kind for use in recipes.

And Scantel Research, a British firm that advises companies on color preferences, found inexplicable differences in the way Europeans take their medicine. The French pop purple pills, while the English and Dutch prefer white ones. And pharmaceutical companies take note: Consumers in all three countries dislike bright red capsules, which are big sellers stateside.

Demographic variables Variables that describe people, including sex, age, and marital status.

Demographic Variables. Demographic variables, such as sex, age, and marital status, describe people. They are easily understood. Their relationship to different product needs has been well established. Families with five children generally buy different housing than single parents with one child.

Many products appeal to both men and women, and many do not. Gillette's Sensor for Women illustrates one company's response to a market segmentation opportunity. Men and

Owners of Harley-Davidson motorcycles come from all walks of life. But these individuals from different socioeconomic backgrounds are similar on psychographic variables. The mindset of the Harley owner revolves around freedom and independence, and a Harley bike projects independence and individuality. Harley ads reflect this lifestyle by showing Harleys on open roads and scenes of riders enjoying a laid-back lifestyle.

women have different shaving needs. Sensor for Women is designed with a wide handle, and the blade cartridges have more moisturizers than the regular Sensor razor used by men. Magazines like *Esquire* and *Working Woman* appeal to the different needs of these two market segments. If you scan a gender-specific magazine such as one of these, you will find many products, such as clothing, jewelry, soft drinks, and health care items, that appeal specifically to just one sex.

An important demographic trend is the increasing number of foreign-born people living in the United States. In 1990, 7.9 percent of the American population was foreign born, compared to 6.2 percent in 1980 and 4.7 percent in 1970. The many immigrants from a country like Mexico have unique consumer needs that marketers can satisfy.

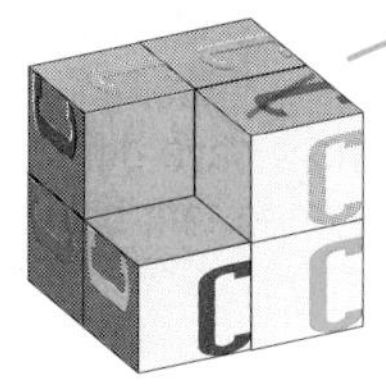

FOCUS ON CUSTOMERS

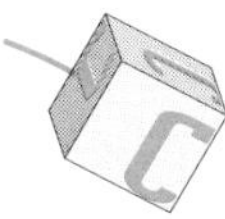

Texas Instruments

A is for "agua," *B* is for "bebe," *C* is for "casa"—simple ABCs to millions of U.S.-born children of Spanish-speaking parents. Now there are toys for reinforcement. Texas Instruments recently introduced new Spanish versions of its popular electronic toys. El Zoo Magico and El Lore Profesor are two of six toys targeted to kids who know the basics of Spanish but need help with vocabulary. Most children learn English at school. These new products give Hispanic-American children a way to study Spanish at home. A recent study shows that 93 percent of Hispanic-American parents want their kids to read and write competently in English, but an even larger group (98 percent) want their children to know Spanish perfectly.

Psychographic variables Lifestyle, personality, attitudes, and other psychological characteristics of consumers.

Psychographic Variables. **Psychographic variables** include lifestyle, personality, attitudes, and other psychological characteristics of consumers. A *lifestyle* reflects a pattern in the way a

The Olive Garden is the leading national Italian restaurant chain. To compete with the best "mom and pop" restaurants in every city, the chain serves five different regional sauces with its spaghetti and lasagna and varies its menu to cater to local tastes. Restaurants in Denver have more vegetarian entrees, while those in the Northwest or San Francisco Bay area offer more seafood dishes. The company's research shows that customers in metropolitan areas prefer more sophisticated, spicy dishes, while those in smaller cities prefer spaghetti and meatballs.

person lives his or her life. A lifestyle reveals an individual's life goals, and thus how a person spends his or her time and money. You probably know someone who has a "workaholic" lifestyle or someone with an "outdoor" lifestyle. An individual's activities, interests, and opinions are psychographic variables that measure a person's lifestyle. Using lifestyles is one way to segment markets based on psychographic variables. As you can imagine, psychographics is a complex topic that we cannot explore in great detail here.

Buyer Behavior/Product Usage Patterns. For airlines like United and American, product (service) usage and brand loyalty are the basis for their frequent-flyer programs. Some buyers use products very frequently, and others never buy or use the product. A Chicago Cubs season ticket holder is very different from the family from Iowa that vacations in the city and takes in a Cubs game to experience Wrigley Field. These consumers have different product needs. A buyer's purchase and product usage behavior can be an important basis for selecting target markets.

Geodemographic and Zip Code Segmentation. When segmenting markets, managers often combine geographic, demographic, psychographic, or buying pattern variables. For example, direct marketers, especially those who sell via catalogs sent through the mail, often use zip codes as a basis for market segmentation. The phrase "birds of a feather flock together" is appropriate here. People and households in the same zip code tend to be similar on demographic and socioeconomic characteristics.

Geodemographic segmentation
Combining demographic variables with a geographic variable to characterize clusters of similar individuals.

Geodemographic segmentation refers to combining demographic variables with a geographic variable, such as zip codes, to characterize clusters of similar individuals. This term is quite oversimplified, because most zip code marketers also use computer data about buying patterns and lifestyle.

Claritas Corporation's PRIZM system has analyzed each of the 36,000 zip codes in the United States and classified them into 40 market segments. Each segment has a colorful name

Exhibit 13.6 **MARKET SEGMENTS BY ZIP CODE TO REFLECT NEIGHBORHOOD CHARACTERISTICS**

Blue Blood Estates

1.1% of U.S. households
Median household income: $70,307
Age group: 35–44
Characteristics: wealthy, white, college-educated families, posh big-city townhouses
Buy: U.S. Treasury notes
Drive: Mercedes-Benzes
Read: *New York Times, Gourmet*
Eat: natural cold cereal, skim milk
TV: "David Letterman"
Sample zip codes: Beverly Hills, CA 90212; Potomac, MD 20854; Scarsdale, NY 10583; Lake Forest, IL 60045

Bohemian Mix

1.1% of U.S. households
Median household income: $21,916
Age group: 18–34
Characteristics: white-collar college graduates, singles, racially mixed
Buy: wine by the case, common stock
Drive: Alfa Romeos
Read: *Harper's*
Eat: whole wheat bread, frozen waffles
TV: "Nightline"
Sample zip codes: Greenwich Village, NY 10014; Dupont Circle, Washington, DC 20036; Lincoln Park, Chicago 60614; Shadyside, Pittsburgh 15232; Haight-Ashbury, San Francisco 94117

Middle America

3.2% of U.S. households
Median household income: $24,431
Age group: 45–64
Characteristics: high school educated, white families, middle-class suburbs
Buy: Christmas clubs, domestic air charters
Drive: Chevy Chevettes, Plymouth Sundances
Read: *Saturday Evening Post*
Eat: pizza mixes, T.V. dinners
TV: "Family Ties"
Sample zip codes: Marshall, MI 49068; Sandusky, OH 44870; Hagerstown, MD 21740; Oshkosh, WI 54901; Stroudburg, PA 18360; Elkhart, IN 46514

like Shotguns and Pickups (large, rural families with modest means) and Gray Power (active retirement communities). Exhibit 13.6 describes a few of these segments.

Segmenting Business Markets. Business markets may be segmented using geography and other variables similar to those discussed in the previous section. The obvious difference is that instead of using characteristics and behavior of individual consumers, the marketer uses characteristics and behavior of organizations. For example, business markets may be segmented on the basis of geography, organizational characteristics, purchase behavior and usage patterns, and organizational policies.

STAGE 2: SCANNING THE ENVIRONMENT TO IDENTIFY AND EVALUATE OPPORTUNITIES

We have seen that marketing activities are performed within a complex and ever changing environment. The impact of environmental factors presents opportunities and threats to every organization. But knowing that the environment has a major impact on marketing is not enough to ensure successful marketing strategies. The marketer must be able to accurately "read" the environment, identify any changes in it, and translate the analysis of trends into marketing opportunities.

Environmental scanning and analysis
The diagnostic activity of interpreting environmental trends in light of the organization's ability to deal with change.

Environmental scanning and analysis is the diagnostic activity of interpreting environmental trends in light of the organization's ability to deal with change. It serves as both a warning system that alerts managers to environmental threats (that is, the risk of potential problems) and an appraisal system to make managers aware of the benefits associated with certain opportunities.

Environmental scanning and analysis requires an inward look at the internal organization. The organization should evaluate its strengths and weaknesses in relation to the environment. The acronym **SWOT**—which stands for internal *strengths* and *weaknesses* and external *opportunities* and *threats*—should help you remember that the purpose of environmental scanning and analysis is to evaluate both the external and internal environments.

SWOT
Acronym for *strengths, weaknesses, opportunities,* and *threats.*

An environmental change may be interpreted as a threat or an opportunity depending on the product's competitive position. Declining per capita coffee consumption is clearly an unfavorable trend and thus is an environmental threat to the marketers of Hills Brothers coffee. The marketers of Pepsi-Cola, however, will see this trend as an opportunity to increase consumption of colas in the morning and thus sell more of their products.

Effective managers analyze threatening situations and foresee potential problems. Then they adapt their strategies in the hope of turning threats into opportunities. For example, Mr. Coffee developed an appliance for iced tea brewing because coffee consumption was declining. The company thus turned a threat into an opportunity.

An *environmental scan* of each competitor's strengths and weaknesses can be invaluable. A competitive analysis typically will identify competitors, review their marketing programs, assess their relative capabilities and resources, and evaluate how well they are serving their target markets. Although it is important to carefully examine what competitors have done in the past, it is equally important to anticipate what strategies and tactics they will use in the future. Also, marketing managers should consider the possibility of new competitors, such as overseas competitors, and what impact they will have on the company's marketing strategy. This can lead to the plan for a market position, discussed next.

STAGE 3: PLANNING A MARKET POSITION

Planning a market position is the third step in the development of a marketing strategy. After selecting a target market and identifying the influence of environmental factors, marketing managers plan the position they hope the brand will occupy in that market.

Positioning is highly related to the way consumers think about all the competitors in a market. A **market position** or **competitive position** represents the way consumers think about the brand relative to its competition. For example, consumers often position products according to quality or price. Motel 6, Holiday Inn, and Hyatt Regency all offer a room in which to spend the night. Chances are, however, that consumers position each of these places to spend the night in terms of budget, value, and quality.

Market position or **competitive position**
Represents the way consumers think about a brand relative to its competition.

Business Week positions itself with the slogan "Beyond news. Intelligence." It positions itself as giving a complete, well-thought-out perspective to business news compared to the "instant" news in *The Wall Street Journal.* The objective of positioning is to determine what distinct position in the prospect's mind is appropriate for the brand and then develop a marketing mix to accomplish that objective.

When marketing managers are confident that they understand the brand's position relative to the competition, they must decide whether to maintain that position or *reposition* the brand. Before the Butterfinger candy bar was repositioned, it was thought of as old and out of date, with no personality. The company was able to reposition Butterfinger as more hip by associating it with Bart Simpson, the mischievous fourth-grade cartoon character.

STREET SMART

Ways to Market Yourself

If you want to get ahead, being good at what you do is only half the battle. You've also got to know how to market yourself. Some suggestions:

- Make yourself the CEO of your career. Develop both short- and long-term goals. And come up with a way to measure these goals.
- Treat the boss like a client. Always cater to the boss's needs and go out of your way to make him or her look good.
- Become the person others can rely on. Volunteer to accept additional assignments that make others' jobs easier.
- Make yourself visible. Be seen in professional, civic and cultural circles outside of your job. Offer yourself as a panelist or speaker to local service clubs. And publish in both industry publications and the local papers, which often accept opinion pieces on vital topics.
- Watch your "packaging." Dress properly and make sure your non-verbal language projects a successful image.

Repositioning may require rethinking the customer benefits offered consumers via the marketing mix. Jello, which for years stressed its appeal as a dessert, was recently repositioned as a snack food. Its Jiggler recipe and Jiggler forms allow kids to eat Jello with their hands.

STAGE 4: DEVELOPING A UNIFIED MARKETING MIX

The target market strategy and the positioning strategy provide the framework for developing the marketing mix. Now marketing managers turn their attention to developing a unified marketing mix. However, we need to mention that market segmentation, target marketing, positioning, and the marketing mix are highly interdependent.

As we mentioned earlier, planning a marketing mix requires combining the four Ps: product, place (distribution), price, and promotion. Chapters 14, 15, and 16 discuss which marketing mix elements are appropriate under varying circumstances.

All of the elements of the marketing mix must come together as a synchronized, *integrated marketing plan.* The parts of the plan are so tightly interwoven that any change in one area will almost certainly affect all the others. For example, the story about LensCrafters at the beginning of the chapter shows how the entire marketing mix—one-hour service, location in shopping malls, after-five and weekend hours, and a huge selection—were all integrated into a unified marketing plan.

A formal *marketing plan* is a written statement of the marketing objectives and the specific courses of action to be taken when (or if) future events occur. It outlines the marketing mix, explains who is responsible for managing the specific activities in the plan, and provides a timetable indicating when those activities must be performed.

Marketing objective
A statement about the level of performance the company or a product is expected to achieve.

Establishing action-oriented objectives is a key element of the marketing plan. A **marketing objective** is a statement about the level of performance the company or a product is expected to achieve. Objectives are more focused than goals, because they define results in measurable terms. For example, "To increase our dollar volume share of the Japanese market from 7 percent to 11 percent by December 31" describes the nature and amount of change (a four-percentage point increase), the performance criterion (market share measured by percentage of dollar volume), and the target date for achieving the objective.

Marketing plans may be categorized by the duration of the plan: long term (five or more years), moderate in length (two to five years), and short term (one year or less). Most organizations prepare an *annual marketing plan* because marketing managers must determine not only where they want to be in the future (their marketing objectives) but also when and how to get there. A marketing plan establishes specific timetables for particular activities. However, certain aspects of the plan will ultimately be scrapped or modified due to changes in portions of the marketing environment.

CONSUMER BEHAVIOR

Marketing success requires satisfying the consumer. When a company defines the broad nature of its business, it must understand why consumers buy. Effective marketing begins with a knowledge of consumer needs. The company must avoid shortsighted, narrow-minded thinking that will lead it to define its purpose from a technical or production orientation. Marketers with a consumer orientation must understand consumer behavior.

Consumer behavior
Consists of the activities in which people engage when selecting, purchasing, and using products and services.

Consumer behavior consists of the activities in which people engage when selecting, purchasing, and using products and services. Such activities, which are intended to satisfy needs and desires, involve the decision-making process, emotional feelings, and physical actions.[6] A number of sound theories provide marketers with a means by which to understand why people buy. We will take a decision-making perspective of consumer behavior.

The consumer decision-making process has several steps. Consumers (1) recognize the problem, (2) search for and evaluate alternative solutions, (3) decide whether or not to buy, and (4) if a purchase is made, evaluate the product or service purchased. Many internal and environmental factors affect this process.

STREET SMART

Basic Rules for Car Shoppers

- Don't rush into signing contracts or paying deposits. The car will be there tomorrow. In fact, being willing to walk out the door may get you a better deal.
- Don't be lured by promises of easy financing. You may be approved quickly and have low monthly payments, but be sure to figure out your real total cost at the end of the loan.
- Don't rely on a salesperson's verbal promises about anything in your deal. Get everything in writing, and keep copies.
- With used cars, don't be swayed by shiny paint or a fancy sound system. They may be hiding an engine that is ready to self-destruct. Remember, "as is" means exactly that—any problems are your problems.

Suppose you read a newspaper article that announces that a new compact disk player displays sophisticated audio and video programs. The player allows you to call up an encyclopedia, a library of songs, and the complete works of Shakespeare using a hand-held controller. You think having one would be great. You have recognized a problem: You don't have an encyclopedia, a song library, or a Shakespeare collection. You may see an advertisement on TV that gives you some information. You go shopping with a friend to search for more information. You learn that both Commodore and Magnavox have versions of this product. You already own a Magnavox stereo, and you have a high opinion of the company. You learn the price of the new CD player is high. You decide you cannot afford to buy it right away, but you will ask your parents to pay part of the price as a birthday present.

From this simple description of the decision-making process, you can see how complex it can be and how many factors may influence a decision. Past experience (learning and habits), attitudes (feelings), stories in newspapers, information from advertising, advice from others, budget pressures, and many other psychological, sociological, and economic factors influence the decision-making process. In fact, this description of buying decision making assumes buyers use purely rational bases in making purchase decisions.

Many buying decisions, however, have emotional aspects. You may buy a hair-coloring product because it makes you feel more beautiful. You may buy a shaving cream because it has sex appeal. You may buy a pair of Air Jordans because all your friends want to have a pair.

In other buying situations, you may act in a routine manner. When you purchase a candy bar, you may act on impulse. You realize you are hungry (recognize problem), see a Snickers bar in a store, and buy it because that is the brand you always buy. You have a brand loyalty.

As you can see, consumer behavior is very complex. Marketers spend a great deal of time trying to find out exactly what makes consumers behave the way they do. They spend a lot of time doing marketing research, the subject of the next section.

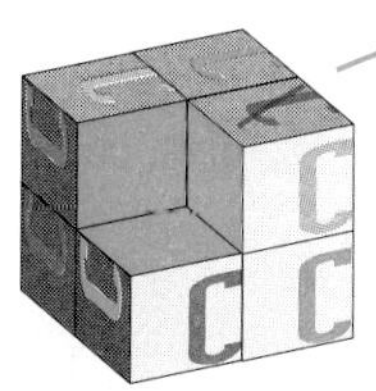

FOCUS ON CUSTOMERS

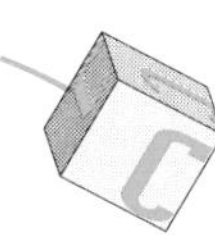

Armstrong World Industries

Armstrong World Industries, a company that markets sheet vinyl floor-covering products to do-it-yourselfers, learned that women were in charge of making the residential floor-covering purchase decision. Men, however, did the actual installation. Armstrong discovered consumers perceived a risk associated with the purchase: making that first cut. When the company asked people who examined but walked away from an in-store display the reason they did not buy the product, nearly 60 percent said they feared botching the job.

In response, Armstrong developed a marketing strategy to combat this fear. It introduced the Trim and Fit kit and promoted it with the message "Go on, cut. You'll be brilliant." When the small retail markup on the kit provided little incentive to retailers to push the product, Armstrong added a sure-fire risk reducer: a "fail safe" guarantee. If the do-it-yourselfer made a mistake, the company pledged to replace the floor covering at no cost. The biggest barrier to the purchase was largely removed. The strategy was a giant success.

MARKETING RESEARCH

During its first season in the National Hockey League, the San Jose Sharks recorded the worst won-lost record in the league. However, its Sharks crest logo, which depicts a black shark biting a hockey stick and darting out from a triangle, outsold all other NHL merchandise. First-year sales of licensed Shark merchandise of more than $100 million didn't occur by accident. The organization spent 13 months researching and planning a name and design that would create excitement rather than yawns. One of the team colors represents the Pacific Ocean. It was selected because when combined with black, it appealed to women and children as well as men.[7]

How do marketers learn what the customer wants? As the San Jose Shark example illustrates, marketing research is often the answer. Marketing research fulfills the marketing manager's need for information about the market. The emphasis of marketing research is to shift decision makers from risky decisions based on "gut feelings" to decisions based on carefully planned investigations.

Marketing research
The systematic and objective process of gathering information for aid in making marketing decisions.

Primary data
Data gathered and assembled specifically for the project at hand.

Secondary data
Data previously collected and assembled for some purpose other than the project at hand.

Marketing research is the systematic and objective process of gathering information for aid in making marketing decisions. This research information should be objective, not intuitive or haphazardly gathered.

Marketing research involves analysis of primary data or secondary data. **Primary data** are data gathered and assembled specifically for the project at hand. For example, a company that designs an original questionnaire and conducts a survey to learn about its customers' characteristics is collecting primary data. **Secondary data** are data previously collected and assembled for some purpose other than the project at hand. Secondary data come from both internal sources and sources external to the organization.

The difference between these two categories of data is based on whether the data are being used for the first or second time. Businesses, especially small businesses, usually find analysis of secondary data faster and cheaper than creating primary data. Thus, marketers usually begin research by collecting secondary data.

SECONDARY DATA

Internal records, such as accounting records of sales figures, can provide useful data for investigating market trends. Cost data, inventory data, sales data, and other regular data are routinely collected and entered into the computer. To the marketer these data, collected for the purpose of accounting, are secondary data.

Data already collected by the government or another source external to the company are external secondary data. Published external secondary data from government sources, trade associations, and companies that specialize in selling computerized databases are among the most common sources. For example, the *Statistical Abstract of the United States* provides many facts and figures about population trends, demographics, and changes in many economic variables.

Many businesses have learned that secondary data are most accessible when they are incorporated into management information systems. Chapter 17 discusses this topic in detail.

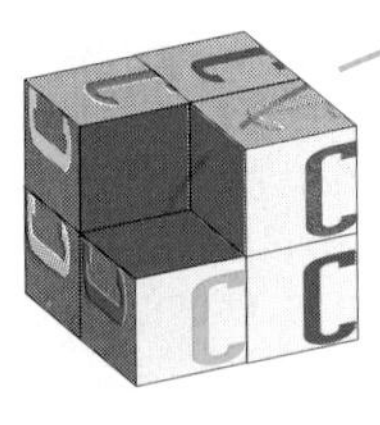

FOCUS ON COMPANY

Information Resources

Information Resources Inc. is an innovative organization that is leading the trend toward the use of new technologies in marketing research. It specializes in providing scanner data, information about brand and product sales. In supermarkets, optical scanners read and record universal product codes (UPCs) for each product sold. The UPC contains product identification information, such as package size, flavor, price, and so on. Information Resources organizes the scanner data into an appropriate format for competitive analysis. Marketers can analyze its reports to determine which package sizes sell best, what price is most effective, and how their brands are doing in relation to the competition. Modern computer and scanner technology make data from any given store available on a weekly or even daily basis.

PRIMARY DATA

When marketers find that secondary data are not available, they collect primary data. They may conduct surveys or observation studies. *Surveys* ask potential buyers questions. For example, Mary Anne Jackson was a working mother who was concerned about her daughter's nutrition during the workweek. She regularly prepared meals from scratch on Sundays so the baby-sitter had enough food to serve her daughter through the week. When she lost her job, she became inspired to market a line of nutritious convenience foods for the growing number of children of dual-career and single parents. Knowing the value of marketing research, she sent out 2,000 mail questionnaires to mothers. The responses revealed a huge unmet demand for foods that could be prepared quickly and easily. The mothers indicated they would prefer microwave meals that provided lots of nutrients but little salt or preservatives, wouldn't spoil if left at a baby-sitter's house all day, and tasted so good the kids would actually like eating it. My Own Meals, meals made of staples such as pasta, chicken, and lentils and packaged in shelf-stable packaging, was the result.[8]

Observation is another way to collect marketing research information. Marketing researchers at Nissan North America put video cameras and tape recorders in some Nissan cars to learn more about how people behave when driving. These observation studies suggested the need for changes in seat design ("Drivers want to feel in touch with the road, while passengers want to be insulated from it"), to include more individual storage space ("People always look uncomfortable when they want to put something away"), and to change the thickness and texture of the steering wheel ("You can tell if someone is touching it like a caress or with revulsion").[9]

Marketing research can be used to create or adjust product, price, distribution, and promotion strategies. The next chapter discusses product and pricing strategies.

SUMMARY

1. ***Define* marketing.**
   Marketing is the process of planning and executing the conception, pricing, promotion, and distribution of ideas, goods, and services to create exchanges that will satisfy individual and organizational objectives. The fundamental purpose of marketing is to bring buyers and sellers together and facilitate the exchange of goods and services. Once an exchange is made, marketing stresses relationships that bring about additional exchanges.

2. ***Describe the marketing concept and trace its evolution.***
   In different historical situations, companies have had different basic philosophies about marketing. These philosophies can be categorized into three basic orientations for operating a company's marketing activities: the production orientation, the sales orientation, and the marketing concept. The production orientation stresses the factory over the consumer and was a common philosophy earlier in American business history. Businesses in that era believed that producing a large number of items at lower production costs allowed them to sell more because they could charge consumers a lower price. The sales orientation emphasizes companies changing consumers' minds to fit the product. Companies that think this way stress aggressive sales and advertising campaigns to "push" their existing products. The marketing concept is central to all effective marketing, planning, and action. It emphasizes both a consumer orientation and a long-term profit orientation.

   Organizations that have adopted the marketing concept try to create products and services with the customer's needs in mind. Also, every business must operate in a profitable manner to continue to exist. Therefore, the marketing concept emphasizes long-term profits in addition to current profitability.

3. ***Define the marketing mix and identify its components.***
The marketing mix describes the result of management's efforts to creatively combine interrelated and interdependent marketing activities. The basic categories of marketing mix elements are product, place, price, and promotion. These ingredients are commonly referred to as the four Ps of marketing. Because virtually every marketing activity falls into one of these categories, the four Ps form a framework managers can use to develop a simple marketing plan. Product is what the company offers its prospective customers; it can be a tangible good or service or an intangible idea. Place is the location where customers buy the product. It is also called distribution because it involves how goods and services get to the customer, how quickly, and in what condition. Price is the amount of money, or sometimes goods and services, given in exchange for something. Promotion is applied communication such as advertising, personal selling, sales promotion, publicity, and public relations.

4. ***Describe the impact of the marketing environment.***
External environmental forces influence all companies. Except in rare instances, managers cannot influence the nature of these external environmental forces. Therefore, these forces are called uncontrollable variables and include economic and competitive forces, demographic trends, cultural and social values, technology, and political and legal forces. Economic forces like inflation and shortages of materials have a strong influence on marketing activity. In some highly competitive industries, a change in a competitor's marketing mix may call for an immediate response. Demographics, the study of the size and composition of the population, is also important for marketing managers. Another important force is the cultural and social environment with its values, beliefs, and institutions. Technological advances can revolutionize or even destroy an industry. Political processes in other countries may have dramatic influences on international marketers. However, many political and legal influences are quite stable. Laws in particular tend to have a long-term influence on marketing strategy. Finally, companies that operate outside of their home countries must contend with the international dimension of the external environment.

5. ***Define* marketing strategy, *identify the basic marketing strategies, and describe the process for developing marketing strategies.***
A marketing strategy consists of determining basic long-range goals and committing to a marketing plan that explains how the goals will be achieved. One of the most common strategic goals is to establish and maintain a competitive advantage: to be superior to or different from competitors in a way that is important to the market. There are two basic marketing strategies. A manufacturer's low-cost/low-price strategy emphasizes producing a standardized product at a very low per-unit cost. A differentiation strategy emphasizes offering a product that is unique in the industry, provides a distinct advantage, or is set apart from competitors' brands in some way other than price.

There are four major stages in the development of a marketing strategy: analyzing market segments and selecting target markets, scanning the environment to identify and evaluate opportunities, planning a market position, and developing a unified marketing mix. First, the company needs to divide a bigger market so that it can choose smaller market segments that can be better served. Environmental scanning and analysis is the diagnostic activity of interpreting environmental trends (threats and opportunities) in light of the organization's ability to deal with change (company strategies and weaknesses). After selecting a target market and identifying the influence of environmental factors, marketing managers plan the position they hope the brand will occupy in that market. A market position or competitive position represents the way consumers think about the brand relative to its competition. Finally, marketing managers attempt to develop a unified marketing mix. Market segmentation, target marketing, positioning, and the marketing mix are highly interdependent. Planning a marketing mix requires combining the four Ps: product, place (distribution), price, and promotion. All of the elements of the marketing mix strategy must come together as a synchronized, *integrated marketing plan.*

6. ***Define* market segmentation *and discuss the variables used to segment markets.***
Market segmentation means dividing a heterogeneous mass market into a number of smaller, more specific customer groups. Segments identified as having good sales potential are likely to become the company's target markets, that is, the specific groups likely to buy the company's product. Concentrating on one or a few target markets rather than trying to reach "everybody" allows the marketer to tailor a marketing mix to a group's specific needs. Some organizations target multiple market segments with different products or different marketing mixes.

Marketers use many different variables as the basis for segmenting consumer markets. Geographic, demographic, psychographic, and buyer behavior/product usage variables are common ways to segment a market. Most marketers use geography as a basis for segmenting markets. Demographic variables, such as sex, age, and marital status, describe people. Their relationship to different product needs has been well established. Psychographic variables include lifestyle, personality, attitudes and other psychological characteristics of consumers. When segmenting markets, managers often combine geographic, demographic, psychographic, or buying pattern variables. Geodemographic segmentation means combining demographic variables with a geographic variable, such as zip codes, to characterize clusters of similar individuals.

7. ***Discuss the consumer decision-making process.***
Consumer behavior consists of the activities in which people engage when selecting, purchasing, and using products and services. Such activities, which are intended to satisfy needs and desires, involve the decision-making process, emotional feelings, and physical actions. The steps in the consumer decision-making process are: (1) recognizing the problem, (2) searching for and evaluating alternative solutions, (3) deciding whether or not to buy, and (4) if a purchase is made, evaluating the product purchased. Many personal and environmental factors affect this process.

8. ***Explain the marketing research process.***
The emphasis of marketing research is to shift decision makers from risky decisions based on "gut feelings" to decisions based on carefully planned investigations. Marketing research is the systematic and objective process of gathering information for aid in making marketing decisions. This research information should be objective, not intuitive or haphazardly gathered. Marketing research involves analysis of primary data or secondary data. Primary data are data gathered and assembled specifically for the project at hand. Secondary data are previously collected and assembled for some purpose other than the project at hand. Secondary data come from both internal sources and sources external to the organization.

KEY TERMS AND CONCEPTS

Market position or competitive position (p. 304)	Consumer behavior (p. 306)	Primary data (p. 308)
Marketing objective (p. 305)	Marketing research (p. 308)	Secondary data (p. 308)

DISCUSSION QUESTIONS

Company

1. Identify a company that is production oriented, one that is sales oriented, and one that is marketing oriented.
2. How might a company create time, place, and possession utilities? Provide some examples.
3. Imagine that you are a marketing director for a local zoo. Of what would your marketing activities consist?
4. Compare and contrast the marketing mixes for Coca-Cola, Tide, and Hewlett-Packard LaserJet printers.

Customers

5. Ask several friends what companies they think are customer oriented and what companies are not.
6. Why do customers buy (a) Porsche sports cars, (b) Polo brand shirts, and (c) used textbooks?
7. How important is price in a consumer's decision to buy a package of gum? A car?

Competitors

8. What role do competitors play in determining whether or not a company adopts the marketing concept?
9. What role do competitors play in influencing the price component of the marketing mix?

Collaborators

10. Who collaborates with a company's marketing personnel?

In Question: Take a Stand

Both Theodore Levitt and Sterling Hayden have written about the consumption needs of humans. These two views appear below:

Theodore Levitt

The purpose of the product is not what the engineer explicitly says it is, but what the consumer implicitly demands that it shall be. Thus the consumer consumes not things, but expected benefits—not cosmetics, but the satisfactions of the allurements they promise; not quarter-inch drills, but quarter-inch holes....

The significance of these distinctions is anything but trivial. Nobody knows this better, for example, than the creators of automobile ads. It is not the generic virtues that they tout, but more likely the car's capacity to enhance its user's status and [sexuality]....

Whether we are aware of it or not, we in effect expect and demand that advertising create these symbols for us to show us what life might be, to bring the possibilities that we cannot see before our eyes and screen out the stark reality in which we must live.[10]

Sterling Hayden

What does a man need—really need? A few pounds of food each day, heat, and shelter, six feet to lie down in—and some form of working activity that will yield a sense of accomplishment. That's all—in a material sense. And we know it. But we are brainwashed by our economic system until we end up in a tomb beneath a pyramid of time payments, mortgages, preposterous gadgetry, playthings that divert our attention from the sheer idiocy of the charade.[11]

What would each author say about the other author's viewpoint? Does advertising create needs? Which of these two views is ethically correct?

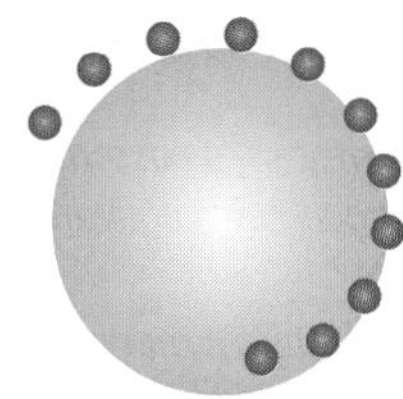

CASE 13.1 NORTHWESTERN UNIVERSITY[12]

The years 1973–1976 marked the absolute bottom of the post-boomer baby bust. The children born in those years have now reached 17–20 years old. With the student pool down, colleges and universities haven't been able to sit back and wait for students to come to them. Many schools are trying to take their cue from the business world and pitch themselves as "brands." The "product" they pitch is the intangible commodity of an education. Rebecca Dixon, associate provost of university enrollment at Northwestern University in Evanston, Illinois, explains how she is marketing the school.

> We stress both ethnic and socioeconomic diversity. Many of our students are the first in their families to attend college. Many are children of first- or second-generation immigrants.
>
> We're highly committed to giving financial aid, and have been for a long time. About 25 years ago, Northwestern decided it wanted broader ethnic and geographic diversity than our Midwestern feeder states could provide. To achieve that goal, we built up financial aid.
>
> All scholarships are based on need as opposed to merit alone. This is a statement for us. Our priority is to give students a chance.
>
> We introduce ourselves to the applicant pool in several ways: written brochures, local presentations, a campus video. All of this creates an image for the school. We present ourselves first as a medium-sized university. We can say that we're big enough to be varied, yet small enough for individual attention.
>
> We then point out that we're in a small city, immediately adjacent to a very attractive urban area. We don't downplay the cold weather or deny it if asked. We stress the beauty of the campus and the cultural richness of the region. We also say that since it's not *in* the large city, it's safe.
>
> We also note the diversity and high caliber of students and faculty. More than half of the students are from the Midwest. We think of our Midwest location as a strength. It sets us apart from our competition in the East or West, and we can talk about the open, Midwestern spirit, the hospitality and egalitarianism you find here.
>
> To some extent, the message varies by region. In the Midwest, we might say we are the only private school in the Big Ten, and the smallest among the Big Ten, with students from around the world. If we were speaking to students at a small private school in New England, we would more likely identify ourselves as a medium-sized school with choice and variety and small, even boutique programs.
>
> Unlike many institutions, we're actually several schools and therefore have sub-product differentiation. The largest is Arts and Sciences. Then we have the Schools of Engineering, Journalism, Music, Speech, and Education and Social Policy. Most people in our audience can identify with one of those areas.
>
> In the late 1960s, we radically changed our recruitment approach. We massively scaled down the high school visitation program and started buying names and addresses for direct marketing, mainly through the PSAT and SAT tests. Other schools do this, of course, but we started 25 years ago. This has allowed us to fine-tune a direct-mail strategy and be more efficient, freeing up money for other efforts.
>
> We send initial mailers to about 110,000 students, offering further information. Our response rate is 27%, which is pretty high. We contact those who reply, giving more information and inviting them to evening information sessions, held in about 80 cities, and to the campus.

We don't pepper people with publications. We send about an average amount. Surveys show that our publications are about as well-received as anyone else's.

Like all schools today, we've produced a video. This is shown at information sessions and offered, upon request, to applicants. The aim of the piece is to convey an accurate impression of Northwestern students. The video tells the story of six students, one from each school, from their arrival to graduation. The piece is not intended to be a synopsis of the catalog. Viewers aren't going to learn the names of the professors or the admissions rate, but they will know whether or not they identify with students here.

Our competitors are other large or medium-sized universities. We have the biggest overlap with the University of Michigan, Cornell, the University of Illinois, the University of Chicago and the University of Pennsylvania. Sometimes there's a "buzz" about a certain school, but we're not influenced by hype. We just try to do the best for the students we can. We have considered running an overt media campaign to generate excitement, but haven't pursued it so far. Athletics do not dominate here, as they might seem to at other schools. We've got big-time athletics *and* big-time academics—but the public may doubt the two are compatible. We won't give up the Big Ten berth because alums are loyal to that and it does attract students and media attention.

We can't sum up the school's character in three quick lines, but we have been getting our message across. While other schools have difficulty retaining faculty under budget restraints, that has not been our problem. Allowing for some fluctuation, applications have risen over the past decade. They're up 26% for next fall's freshman class.

Questions

1. *Can a university such as Northwestern implement a marketing concept? Who are its consumers?*
2. *What do Northwestern's customers buy? What is exchanged between Northwestern and its students?*
3. *Evaluate Northwestern's marketing mix. Compare it to the marketing mix that is used at your college.*

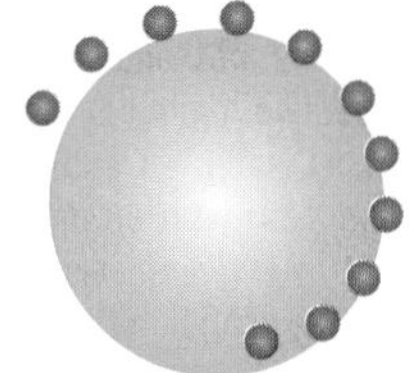

CASE 13.2
SPAM[13]

Almost five billion cans of the pink pork product known as Spam have been sold. Although some consumers described Spam as "mystery meat," Geo. A. Hormel & Co. likes to note that some 60 million people eat 3.8 cans per second. In 1994, Hormel spent $12 million in prime-time advertising to persuade America to reembrace the 58-year-old product with this advice—just cut it lengthwise and grill the slab like a hamburger. Spam is shown as Spam has never been seen before: decked with cajun spices; grilled on a barbecue by smiling youngsters on a California beach, and shrouded in neon on a giant, computerized bill board in New York's Times Square.

Questions

1. *What environmental forces influence the marketing of Spam?*
2. *What market segments purchase the most Spam? Describe how consumers' decide to purchase Spam.*
3. *In your opinion, what is the marketing mix for Spam?*

CHAPTER

14

PRODUCTS, BRANDS, AND PRICES

When you have studied this chapter, you will be able to:

1. Define *product* and describe the characteristics of products.
2. Describe the basic product categories.
3. Discuss the characteristics of services.
4. Explain the stages in new-product development.
5. Describe the product life cycle.
6. Explain the various types of brand strategy.
7. Discuss packaging strategy.
8. Describe customer service strategy.
9. Discuss the importance of price and pricing strategies.
10. Describe basic pricing objectives.
11. Identify the factors that affect pricing strategy.

Iwerks Entertainment, Inc., a movie production house founded by two Walt Disney veterans, started out seven years ago making films and motion-based simulators for amusement parks.[1] Today the company is designing a series of entertainment centers to be called Cinetropolis—a kind of high-tech amusement park in a box—that will offer stomach-churning thrill rides using motion simulators and big-screen film.

The new type of ride differs from the old roller coasters and Ferris wheels in the combination of physical thrills with the dramatic visual effects of a movie. You'll be able to take an imaginary ride on a submarine, immerse yourself in a rock concert, or don special headgear and play the latest in virtual reality war games. When you're tired of the rides, there will be Cinetropolis restaurants and retail shops to visit.

The first two of a planned sixty of these over $15-million complexes are under way in Japan and at the Foxwoods casino in Ledyard, Connecticut. At $4 for a 40-minute ride, a 14-seat ride simulator can generate as much revenue as a 180-seat theater in a third of the space.

Simulated thrill rides are a hot new product. Nearly all the top fifty U.S. theme parks have one or more big simulator rides in the works, usually keyed to movie hits and embellished with elaborate layouts and preride video scene setting. Theme parks like Universal Studios with its Back to the Future rides are major customers, but mega-shopping malls like Mall of America and hotel/gambling casinos like Circus Circus have also become interested in ride simulators with movie magic.

Knowing how to create products that satisfy customers' needs is essential to effective marketing. Product strategy is typically a focal point around which the entire marketing mix strategy is based. This chapter investigates how markets develop product and pricing strategies.

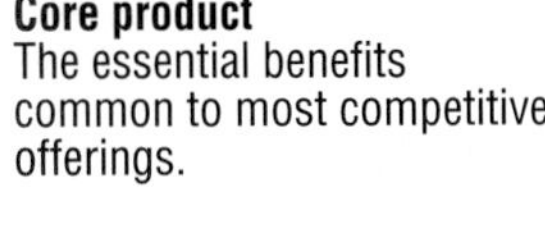

WHAT IS A PRODUCT?

The product a company offers to its market is not simply a can of cat food, a hotel room, or a charitable cause. There is more to "the product" than meets the eye. A product is a thing in a nuts-and-bolts sense, but it is also a reward offered to those willing to pay for it. For example, a beautiful, green lawn is the payoff for someone who buys fertilizer. Companies that view products in this way define a **product** as a bundle of customer benefits.

Product
A bundle of customer benefits.

Defining a product as a bundle of benefits stresses the satisfaction a product provides its consumers. Thus, it is a customer-oriented definition. It stresses what the buyer gets, not what the seller is selling. For example, a family visit at a Disney World Resort Hotel is more than a place to stay. It's sun and fun, relaxation and entertainment, and being a good parent.

Defining the product in terms of benefits allows a broad range of offerings, from tangible items to services to ideas, to be identified as products. Whether the company's offering is largely tangible (a ship), intangible (financial counseling), or even more intangible (the idea of racial harmony), it is a product. Thus, a product includes all the tangible and intangible benefits a buyer might gain once he or she has purchased it.

Every product has both primary characteristics and auxiliary dimensions. *Primary characteristics* are basic features and aspects of the core product. The **core product** provides the essential benefits common to most competitive offerings. Consumers expect a basic level of performance.[2] A half-inch drill is expected to operate to provide half-inch holes. *Auxiliary dimensions* include special features, styling, color, package, warranty, repair service contract, reputation, brand name, instructions for use, and so on. Any of these features may be important to a particular buyer. However, effective marketing strategies emphasize certain benefits over others.

Core product
The essential benefits common to most competitive offerings.

FOCUS ON COMPANY

Mazda

The Mazda Miata's exhaust system was designed to match consumers' perception of what a lightweight sports car should sound like. The company experimented with more than 150 variations of tunings for the Miata exhaust system before it was satisfied that this aspect of the product fit consumers' perception of the automobile's sound.

PRODUCT STRATEGY

Marketing managers must plan the product position and develop a unified mix of primary product features and auxiliary dimensions that provide the greatest benefits to consumers. This is the creative dimension of product strategy.

Product positioning concept
Defines the central idea underlying the product features and key benefits that appeal to the target market.

The **product positioning concept** defines the central idea underlying the product features and key benefits that appeal to the target market. The product positioning concept refers to the marketing strategist's selection and blending of a product's primary characteristics and auxiliary dimensions into a basic idea or unifying concept. The product positioning concept provides a reason for buying the product. The product positioning concept can be, and often is, described in the same terms used to characterize the competitive market position the product is expected to occupy in consumers' minds. For example, 7Up is positioned as The Uncola—clear and clean. The company wants soft-drink buyers to see 7Up as an alternative to Coca-Cola and Pepsi-Cola, the market leaders.

You can probably think of a company whose product positioning concept emphasizes that its product uses the most advanced technology, is of the highest quality, or was made in the USA. These are all popular product positioning concepts.

Successful product strategy requires analyzing all aspects of the product in light of competitive offerings. Calling buyers' attention to aspects of the product that set it apart from its competitors is called **product differentiation**. This may be accomplished by making some adjustment to the product to vary it from the norm or by promoting one or more of its tangible or intangible attributes. For instance, an automobile battery that has a selector dial to switch on a supplemental, booster backup battery when the primary battery fails to hold a charge will be more competitive than an ordinary battery. In other words, if the product differentiation is meaningful to consumers, it can create a *competitive advantage* for the company.

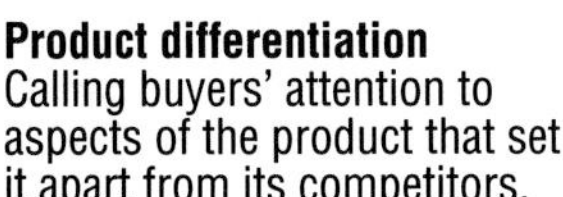

Product differentiation Calling buyers' attention to aspects of the product that set it apart from its competitors.

It is important to note that the differences need not be extra product features or scientifically demonstrable improvements. Color and shape differences, as well as technological differences, can all play a role in product differentiation. For example, Party Animals are "adult crackers" baked in animal shapes to visually set the brand apart from competitors such as Ritz. This is a less tangible, more symbolic difference. The bottom line is that if consumers see the variations as important, the variations by definition will serve to differentiate the product from its competitors.

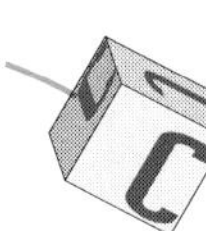

FOCUS ON COMPANY

General Electric

Most products are designed to be lighter so that they are easier to ship and handle. At General Electric's plastic division, product designers did just the opposite with GE's new valox plastic: They designed a plastic that is twice as heavy for a given volume than alternative materials. Why? Valox plastic is used to make faucets, packaging for cosmetics, piano keys, and housing for small appliances. It competes with materials such as ceramics, glass, porcelain, and metals in applications where customers equate weight with quality. General Electric adds weight to the plastic by mixing in 65 percent by weight of mineral filler. According to one product manager, this amounts to "blending rocks with cookie batter," but it produces a product that meets customer requirements.

CLASSIFYING CONSUMER PRODUCTS

Furniture, appliances, groceries, cosmetics, and many other types of products can be identified. The many and diverse products offered for sale make product classification a complicated task. Products may be classified on the basis of many criteria. For example, in Chapter 3 we distinguished between goods and services. In Chapter 13, we identified the difference between consumer products and organizational products sold in business markets. The following sections discuss widely accepted systems for classifying consumer products and organizational (business) products.

CLASSIFYING CONSUMER PRODUCTS BY CONSUMER BEHAVIOR

Consumer goods fall into three general categories: convenience, shopping, and specialty products. Although this classification describes the products involved, it is actually based on the *consumer's* reasons for buying, the *consumer's* need for information, and the *consumer's* shopping and purchase behaviors.[3]

CONVENIENCE PRODUCTS

Convenience product
A product that is relatively inexpensive, is purchased on a regular basis, and is bought without a great deal of thought.

Convenience products are relatively inexpensive, are purchased on a regular basis, and are bought without a great deal of thought. Convenience products reflect the consumer behavior of buying goods or services with a minimum of shopping effort. People buy these products at the most convenient locations (hence the term). Many dissimilar products, such as milk, shoe shines, soft drinks, and bread, are convenience products. How far out of your way would you go to buy a quart of a particular *brand* of milk? The answer to this question helps determine whether a given product is a convenience product.

Because extensive shopping effort rarely occurs, distribution is a central aspect of the marketing mix. The objective is to make the product available in almost every possible location. Thousands of retailers in every large city sell soft drinks and candy bars. These convenience goods are also common vending machine items. Convenience items that are purchased largely on *impulse,* such as candy bars, are sold in drugstores, discount stores, convenience outlets, and college bookstores. In fact, within individual stores, convenience items are usually placed at the most convenient spots, such as near the checkout counter. The fact that many of these products can be sold through vending machines reflects the lack of a need for in-store persuasive selling.

Of course, the other three elements of the marketing mix must also support the convenience product. The price must be appropriate, and the product must meet convenience criteria. Giant candy bars costing $5.50 do not meet convenience criteria as well as the standard Snickers bar does because the package size, as well as the price, places it into another product category. In the convenience goods classification, one brand is fairly easily substituted for another of its type, and personal selling efforts by retailers are almost nonexistent. Therefore, extensive advertising may be appropriate. The heavy advertising expenditures on Coca-Cola and Pepsi-Cola attest to this fact.

SHOPPING PRODUCTS

Shopping product
A product that generates a great deal of consumer effort.

Shopping products are goods and services that generate a great deal of consumer effort. Consumers feel the need to make product comparisons, seek out additional information, examine merchandise, or otherwise reassure themselves about quality, style, or value before purchasing a shopping product. In other words, prospective buyers of products such as clothing, shoes, furniture, and tableware want to shop around.

Decisions about shopping products are not made on the spur of the moment. Buyers want to mull things over before committing themselves. This is partly because shopping products are generally priced higher than convenience products. There is also greater consumer involvement with the purchase. Thus, the risks associated with shopping products, both monetary and social, are fairly high.

The distribution strategy for shopping products differs from that for convenience products. Since people are willing to shop around, the product should not be available everywhere; rather, it should be placed in selected spots. Managers often choose a selective distribution strategy, selling the product only in certain selected stores. Within a single store, shopping products will probably not be placed "up front." Furniture, for example, can be placed in distant areas of a department store because customers are willing to seek it out.

SPECIALTY PRODUCTS

In some cases, consumers believe they know exactly what they want. They have selected the brand in advance and will not accept substitutes. For example, they may insist on having Woody at A Cut Above The Others style their hair because they see his service as having a unique characteristic. At the moment of purchase, they no longer need to make shopping comparisons among alternatives. They have thought about their purchase. They regard the brand as having a particular attraction other than price. Products that are the object of this type of consumer concern are called **specialty products**. Many of these products are seldom-purchased items such as stereo equipment, pianos, wedding receptions, or expensive cars. Potential buyers may have gathered a great amount of information prior to making the purchase decision. They may even have bought and read books or magazines dealing with the product class. At the time of purchase, they may spend considerable time and effort to get to the appropriate store that carries the item, but they no longer need to make shopping comparisons. Their minds are made up.

Specialty product
A product perceived as having a particular attraction other than price.

Brand insistence can be strong. A shopper may have decided, after considerable thought, that only Wedgwood china and Waterford crystal will do for the dining room. As a result, these may be the only acceptable brands. This is important to retailers, because the customer will forgo purchases if the desired brand is out of stock.

The marketer of a specialty product may decide that exclusive distribution of the brand is the best distribution strategy. Dealers that stock Jaguar X-J6s are few and far between, in part because a potential buyer will travel considerable distances to purchase the car.

Some products do not fit neatly into this product classification scheme. Examples include the "purchase" of an ambulance service in an emergency or other *unsought* product purchases. However, classifying products into convenience, shopping, and specialty products does help in planning marketing strategy for most consumer products.

CLASSIFYING ORGANIZATIONAL PRODUCTS

Organizational products—products sold in the business market—can be categorized in much the same way as consumer products. The most commonly used classification system outlines the basic characteristics of each class of organizational product:

- *Raw materials:* basic ingredients that undergo processing in the factory
- *Component parts:* items used in the assembly of the finished product
- *Installations:* major capital purchases, such as a new factory building or an airport's computerized baggage system
- *Accessory equipment:* equipment that aids in the operation of the business, such as delivery trucks
- *Operating supplies:* paper, pencils, brooms, and other short-lived items that are routinely purchased and used up in the organization's operations
- *Services:* work provided by others, such as janitorial services, repair and maintenance services, and the services of lawyers and accountants

Derived demand
Demand for a product that depends on the demand for some other product.

All organizational products have one thing in common: derived demand. **Derived demand** means the demand for every organizational product depends on the demand for some other product. The auto mechanic's demand for metric tools is derived from the consumer's demand for imported cars. The demand for tempera paints, water colors, and chalk sold to the art departments of public schools is derived from the demand of students or their parents for a basic, well-rounded education. When the economy slows down and consumer demand for products drops, the volume of business travel declines. Hilton Hotels, "America's business address," may suffer accordingly. Ultimately the demand for all organizational products depends on consumer demand for finished goods and services.

SERVICES

Our discussion of consumer and business products includes both goods and services. Services are especially important because the service industry now accounts for more than half of personal consumption expenditures. While "service products" may be marketed somewhat differently from "goods products," the differences may not be as great as the marketing differences between a motorcycle and a box of Trix. Nevertheless, for many marketing decisions, the distinction between goods and services is important. We will discuss the characteristics of services and look at how marketing mix decisions for goods and services often differ.

Services have the following characteristics:

1. Intangibility
2. Perishability
3. Inseparability
4. Variability

INTANGIBILITY

Intangibility
The characteristic of something that makes it unable to be seen, felt, smelled, heard, or tasted.

Goods are tangible, whereas services are intangible. **Intangibility** means buyers normally cannot see, feel, smell, hear, or taste a service before making a purchase decision. Services, then, cannot be handled, examined, or tried out before they are purchased. This increases buyer uncertainty and necessitates marketing strategies and tactics to "make the intangible tangible." For example, a service marketer may develop and communicate projections of what the service can deliver. Architects do this with models and drawings of proposed buildings.

Although services are intangible, the production of a service may be linked to a tangible product. (The transportation service an airline provides is tied to its fleet of airplanes. Renting a videotaped movie is tied to the temporary use of the videocassette).

PERISHABILITY

Services "disappear" quickly. They are perishable and cannot be stored. If a computer salesperson loses a customer, the computer—a tangible good—remains to be sold to another. If a dentist's patient fails to keep an appointment, that half-hour of the dentist's time—the service to be sold—is gone forever.

INSEPARABILITY

Inseparability
A characteristic requiring that producer and consumer be present in the same place at the same time for the service transaction to occur.

A manufactured good may be produced by one firm and marketed by another; thus, the good can be separated from its producer. In contrast, as Pearl Jam's Eddie Vedder sings, his service is being consumed; thus, the service is inseparable from its supplier. **Inseparability** means producer and consumer may have to be present in the same place at the same time for the service transaction to occur.

A concertgoer who expects to see Eddie Vedder in a performance and is told a substitute singer will perform experiences feelings of disappointment. Fortunately, most services are not quite as unique as those of rock stars.

VARIABILITY

Most services are delivered by people. Because the quality of service provided is closely tied to the supplier's personal performance, there can be great variability among services provided.

Exhibit 14.1 **THE GOODS-SERVICES CONTINUUM**

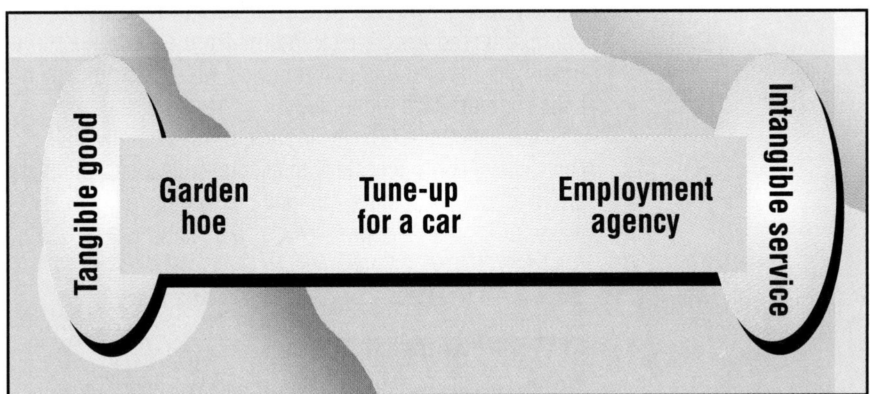

In other words, service quality is characterized by variability. Services are often heterogeneous because the quality of the service depends on who provides it and how quickly it is provided. You have probably experienced going to your favorite restaurant but receiving poor service from a new server.

Marketers of services strive to control service quality. One goal is to standardize services to reduce variability, but this is difficult. It is not possible to prescribe and deliver equal amounts of "smiling" by all employees at a bank. Nevertheless, companies that market services often use employee training and incentives, such as employee-of-the-month awards, as steps to control service quality.

THE GOODS-SERVICES CONTINUUM

If you think about a pasta dinner at a restaurant, you will realize that it is difficult to separate goods from services entirely. This reality has led some marketing experts to array products along a continuum from "mostly good" to "mostly service." A garden hoe is obviously a tangible good; an employment agency clearly provides a service. But a tune-up for your car provides both a good—spark plugs and other parts—and a service—measurement, tuning, and installation of the parts, as well as convenience of the location and other aspects of the total product offering. Thus, you will find a tune-up for a car in the middle of the goods-services continuum in Exhibit 14.1.

FOCUS ON CUSTOMERS

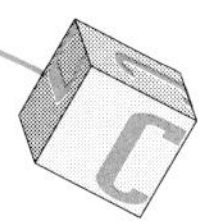

Marriott

You arrive at the hotel, pop your smart card in a doorway slot to introduce yourself, then go straight to your room which was assigned earlier by computer. To enter, say your name, and the door magically opens. You hang up your coat, punch in channel 162 on the TV, and hold a videoconference with colleagues. When the meeting ends, you flip to another channel to shop for a gift, then call home on the videophone to see how the family is faring while you are on the road.

Scenes like this will be commonplace soon because service companies like the hotel chain Marriott are listening to their customers and scurrying to satisfy their demands with just the right combination of high and low tech.

Because hotel guests frequently complain about time spent at check-in, Marriott launched a new program called First 10 that virtually eliminates the front desk. Pertinent information such as time of arrival and credit card number is collected when the reservation is made, thus reducing check-in time from an average three minutes (higher at big convention hotels) to one and one-half minutes. Marriott someday hopes to lower it to seconds with the help of smart card technology.

To make better use of the room, the chain will also provide videophones so that guests can visually communicate with clients, colleagues, and family. In-room videoconferencing may arrive at Marriott before the new century does.

NEW PRODUCTS

WHAT IS A NEW PRODUCT?

We all have ideas about what products are new. Consider the DentaCam, a tiny intraoral video camera in dentists' offices that goes directly into a patient's mouth. Developed by Fuji Optical Systems Inc., the DentaCam sends a high-resolution image to a standard color monitor screen, where dentist and patient view it simultaneously. Using foot pedals, the dentist can freeze the display and record it on a video floppy disk or print out an instant picture on a video printer. The system also keeps a database of patients' records and images.[4]

The DentaCam is undoubtedly a technological breakthrough. It is a new product by all standards. From a marketing point of view, however, a new product need not be a technological breakthrough or a major innovation. For example, a soft-drink company that has never marketed flavored iced tea cooler in a can before sees the canned iced tea cooler as a new product. The product is new because it is new to the company. Some new products are only variations of existing products. Thus, a "new and improved" version of an existing product or a "copycat" version of a competitor's product may be a new product. Simply defined, a *new product* is one that the company has never marketed before.

DEVELOPING NEW PRODUCTS

Developing new products is a vital marketing activity. At 3M, new products such as Scotch-Brite scour pads which use a technology combining abrasives with nonwoven fiber account for one-third of sales volume. Developing new products is the lifeblood of the company. Companies that do not introduce new products to keep up with changing consumer desires become vulnerable to more responsive and innovative competitors, and rarely survive in the long run.

Developing new products does not mean the company must be the "first mover," or the innovator that is first on the market. After all, developing completely new products is a risky venture that requires large financial investments. Competitors can serve as the source for new-products ideas. And quite often the company that is second on the market with an improved version will have a bigger success than the first mover. Caterpillar, a manufacturer of construction machinery, lets its competitors go through the trial-and-error process, then imitates them with the most trouble-free product on the market.

The failure rate for new products varies by industry. Estimates of new-product failures range from 10 to 90 percent. A precise figure is unavailable because not all failures are made public and definitions of failure vary. However, all evidence indicates that *most* new-product ventures fail to meet companies' expectations.

Even large corporations with experienced marketing staffs have product failures. For example, when General Mills introduced Benefit, a high-soluble-fiber psyllium cereal, it stressed the product's ability to reduce cholesterol. When sales did not meet expectations, the company learned that although consumers understood the role of oat bran, they were confused about the term *soluble fiber*. The death bell for the product rang when a barrage of publicity occurred questioning whether Benefit with psyllium was a drug or a cereal.[5]

Exhibit 14.2 **THE STAGES IN THE NEW-PRODUCT DEVELOPMENT PROCESS**

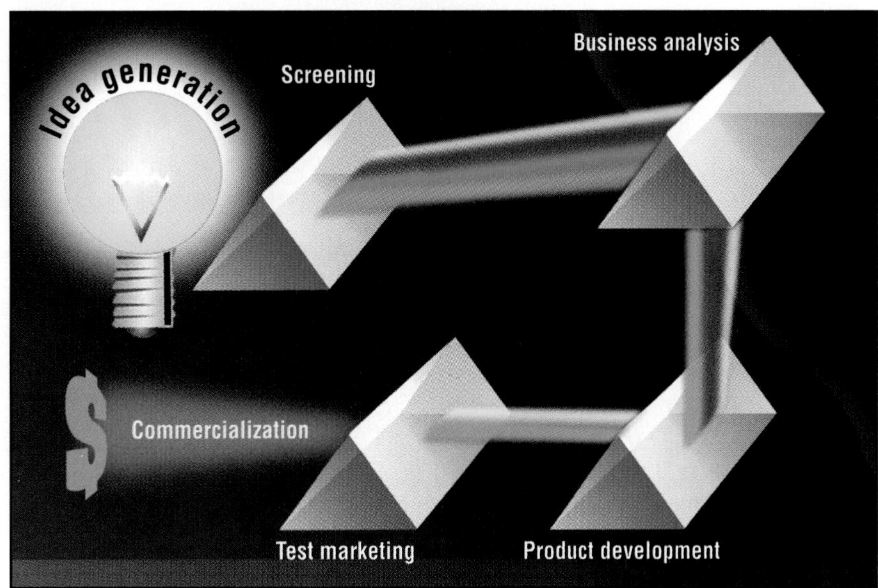

The new-product development process can result from a sudden flash of insight. In most cases, however, such as in the development of new computer software or other highly technical products, the process can take years. As Exhibit 14.2 illustrates, the new-product development process has six general stages: idea generation, idea screening, business analysis, product development, test marketing, and commercialization.

Idea generation stage
An ongoing search for product ideas that are consistent with target market needs and with the company's objectives.

Idea Generation. Because markets change constantly, marketers continually search for new-product ideas. The **idea generation stage** involves an ongoing search for product ideas that are consistent with target market needs and with the company's objectives. New ideas come from conducting environmental scans and from many other sources. Company employees, especially production workers, sales personnel, and research scientists, are often encouraged to submit new-product ideas. Customers and collaborators, who look at a company's products in a different light, may indicate their unfulfilled needs or suggest product improvements.

Idea screening stage
The stage in which managers evaluate which ideas are good and which are bad.

Idea Screening. In the **idea screening stage,** managers evaluate which ideas are good and which are bad. Good ideas fit with the company's resources, target markets, and business goals. Screening involves ranking and classifying ideas. Alternatives that are too risky are eliminated. Promising alternatives that are relevant to the company's mission undergo business analysis.

Business analysis
A critical examination of the new-product idea from all important company viewpoints.

Business Analysis. Business analysis is a critical examination of the new-product idea from all important company viewpoints. The company estimates market potential, cost of production, profitability, and other concerns about the product's overall business plan. Accountants, marketing researchers, and others may be involved in quantitative analysis of facts and figures to determine which ideas still show promise and which should be eliminated.

Product development stage
The stage in which the proposed new-product idea is transformed from a product concept to a working model or product prototype.

Product Development. In the **product development stage**, the proposed new-product idea is transformed from a product concept to a working model or product *prototype.* The product prototype is tested in the laboratory and with consumers. For example, before WordPerfect Corporation introduced its WordPerfect 6.0 software in 1993, it tested the software with thousands of customers, many of whom requested new features.

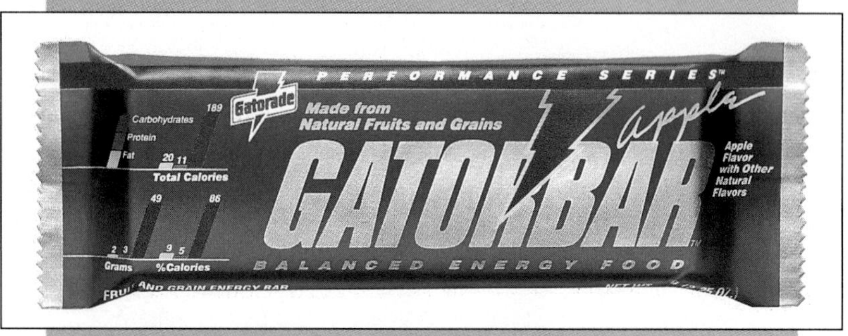

The Gatorade Company introduced Gatorbar into test markets in the summer of 1994. The fruit-flavored energy bar is Gatorade's first effort to extend its name beyond its sports drink. Gatorbar with only 110 calories is targeted toward active people seeking a low-fat, high-carbohydrate bar for snacking.

Gatorade is also introducing another new product—Sunbolt—which is a caffeinated drink positioned as a morning pickup for adults rather than as a beverage for athletes.

At the same time, managers develop the marketing strategy, especially decisions about target market, brand name, package, price, and promotional message. Marketing research investigates consumers' reactions to the product features to determine what they like and dislike about the product.

Test market
A city or small geographical area where a new product is sold in a typical retail setting.

Test Marketing. Once the product is fully developed, it may be test marketed. Many (but certainly not all) products are test marketed. **Test markets** are cities or small geographical areas where a new product is sold in typical retail settings. Test marketing requires a limited production of the product so that actual purchasing behavior and consumer reactions can be measured. The advantage of test marketing is that it provides a real-world test of the product under competitive conditions. However, as you can imagine, test marketing is extremely expensive.

McDonald's McPizza, a single serving of pizza, and McDonald's first attempt with McRib, a pressed meat and barbecue sandwich, failed in their initial test markets. Yet the company continues to experiment with innovative sandwiches and menu items. McDonald's, like many marketing-oriented organizations, realizes that successful launching of all new-product efforts is virtually impossible. However, the company also knows that successful organizations learn from their failures as well as their successes. Sometimes these products make a comeback when marketing strategies are adjusted and the timing is right. McDonald's is still working in test markets to develop a pizza item for its menu.

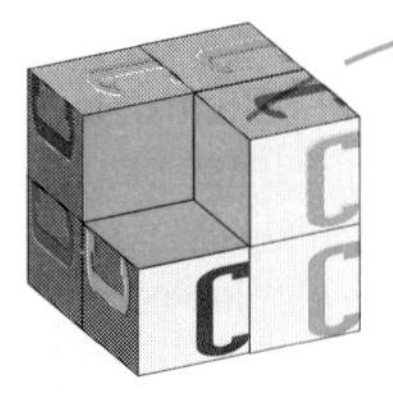

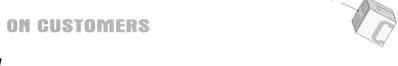

FOCUS ON CUSTOMERS

Pepsi A.M.

Americans' tastes have been shifting from hot, bitter beverages to cold, sweet ones. Soft drinks outsell most other beverages except during the morning, when coffee accounts for 47 percent of all beverages sold. Pepsico's marketing managers, armed with this information and the knowledge that coffee consumption has been declining for years, saw an opportunity to convert coffee drinkers to a "morning soft drink"—Pepsi A.M.

Research showed people wanted a morning beverage with the same cola taste but less fizz. So Pepsico reduced the level of carbonation and increased the level of caffeine to 4 milligrams per fluid ounce (compared to 3.2 for regular Pepsi). Pepsi A.M. had about one-fifth the caffeine in a cup of coffee.

Advertising in Waterloo, Iowa, where the product was test marketed proclaimed, "Pepsi A.M.—A refreshing break from the daily grind." Pepsi A.M. was marketed as a product that was cool and refreshing instead of hot and bitter. Pepsico asked grocers to stock the product in the coffee aisle. After six months of test marketing, sales were disappointing and Pepsico stopped testing. What went wrong? First, creating a new beverage is not easy. Pepsico was attempting to change the behavior of one of the most loyal consumer groups: morning coffee drinkers. Some consumers were concerned about the extra caffeine but the biggest problem was taste. Many described Pepsi A.M. as "flat" and the typical consumer reaction was "It doesn't taste very good."

Marketing managers, however, were glad they decided to test market, because the purpose of a test is to provide information to avoid a major failure in a nationwide introduction. Had the product succeeded, it would have gone into full-scale production and commercialization.

Commercialization
Process of going into full-scale production and the marketing process of launching the new product.

Commercialization. After product development and/or test marketing, the company makes the decision to "go for it" or to hold back. The process of going into full-scale production and the marketing process of launching the new product is known as **commercialization**. Planning for this stage requires that decisions be made for all the details of implementing the marketing plan.

When Domino's investigated marketing its pizza in Japan, the marketing research findings suggested that home delivery of pizza wouldn't work there. Japanese diets are heavy on raw fish, rice, and seaweed and consumers were known to dislike both tomatoes and cheese (which they thought looked and tasted like soap). Pizza was considered a snack food rather than a meal, which made it difficult to justify the high prices necessary to make the home delivery business profitable. Consumers who liked pizza the most were teenage girls, the market segment with the least disposable income. Further, the research showed that because Japanese families typically live in tiny apartments, those who were more likely to pay a premium price for a meal preferred to go out to a more spacious restaurant. Finally, Domino's guarantee of speedy delivery was perceived to be impossible in traffic-congested Tokyo.

Rather than being discouraged by what they learned, Domino's made three creative changes in its product strategy. The pizzas were made smaller: The U.S. sizes of 12 and 16 inches were reduced to 10 and 14 inches. Two optional toppings, corn and tuna (toppings that Americans might consider stomach curdling), were added to make the pizza more in harmony with the Japanese diet. To overcome Tokyo's narrow streets and congestion, Domino's used souped-up, streamlined motor scooters rather than cars to deliver the pizzas.

Although many factors determined Domino's success, its understanding of what was wrong and its willingness to adapt its product positioning concept played a major role.

THE PRODUCT LIFE CYCLE

Product life cycle
A graphic depiction of a product's sales history from its "birth," or marketing beginning, to its "death," or withdrawal from the market.

The **product life cycle** is a graphic depiction of a product's sales history from its "birth," or marketing beginning, to its "death," or withdrawal from the market. A product begins its life with the first sale, rises to some peak level of sales, and then declines until its sales volume and contributions to profits are insufficient to justify its continued presence in the market.

While this pattern is common, it varies from product to product. Products such as salt and mustard have been used for thousands of years. Arm and Hammer baking soda has been used for over 145 years. Cellular phones and facsimile (fax) machines are mere youngsters by comparison. Some products, such as Topp's Talking Baseball Cards, fail from the very start.

Whether a product has a very short, short, long, or very long life, the pattern of that life may be portrayed by a charting of sales volume.

Exhibit 14.3 portrays the product life cycle. According to the life cycle concept, each product's life typically flows through several distinct product life cycle stages as sales volume is plotted over time. These stages are *introduction, growth, maturity,* and *decline.* The length of time a product spends in each stage varies from case to case. Both sales volume and industry profit change during each stage of the product life cycle.

While useful for visualizing the stages of market acceptance, the product life cycle has its greatest practical use as a planning tool. Many successful marketers build their strategies around the concept, graph financial and market data against product life cycles, and develop long- and short-range plans that complement each stage.

THE INTRODUCTORY STAGE

During the period of product development and engineering, no sales are being made, yet assets are being spent. Thus, the company is making investments in the belief that later profitable sales will justify them.

During the introduction stage, the new product attempts to gain a foothold in the market. Sales are likely to be slow at first because the product is, by definition, new and untried. It takes time to gain acceptance. Sales volume and sales revenues are still low relative to the high expenses of developing the product and creating the marketing mix necessary to introduce it to the market. In most cases, profits are negative.

The introductory stage of the product life cycle focuses on gaining market acceptance. The marketing effort centers not only on finding first-time buyers and using promotion to make them aware of the product's existence but also on creating channels of distribution—attracting retailers and other middlemen to handle the product. In this stage, the bulk of research and development costs associated with the product needs to be recouped. Product alterations or changes in manufacturing may be required to "get the bugs out" of the new offering. The introduction stage, then, is typically a high-cost/low-profit period. Although it is an exciting time, it is also a time of uncertainty and anxiety, because the new product must survive this now-or-never situation.

Selecting strategies appropriate for the introductory stage of the product life cycle is critical. Organizations differ widely in their strategy choices. Some companies believe being a pioneer and a risk taker is the best approach—the greater the risk, the greater the reward. Thus, in many industries, such as tires and aircraft, the same companies are the leaders in new-product development over and over again. Other companies quickly follow the pioneer's lead and jump into the market during the introductory stage. Still others hold back and wait to see whether the new product will actually take off into a growth period. Each approach has obvious advantages and risks that management must weigh.

The length of the introductory stage varies dramatically. Personal computers and home video games gained market acceptance rapidly. Movies on laser disks, on the other hand, took years to achieve a reasonable degree of popularity.

The concentrated laundry detergent product category presents yet another example of slow market acceptance. The first serious effort to introduce a product that cleans a whole washload with only a quarter-cup of powder was made in 1976 with Colgate-Palmolive's Fresh Start, a powder in a plastic bottle. But this category did not achieve rapid sales growth until 1990, when two other brands, Ultra Tide and Fab Ultra, were successfully introduced. Their success was in part due to stressing the environmental advantage of small packages.

THE GROWTH STAGE

If the product earns market acceptance, it should at some point launch into a period of comparatively rapid growth. The classic product life cycle portrays this growth stage as sales

Exhibit 14.3 **THE PRODUCT LIFE CYCLE**

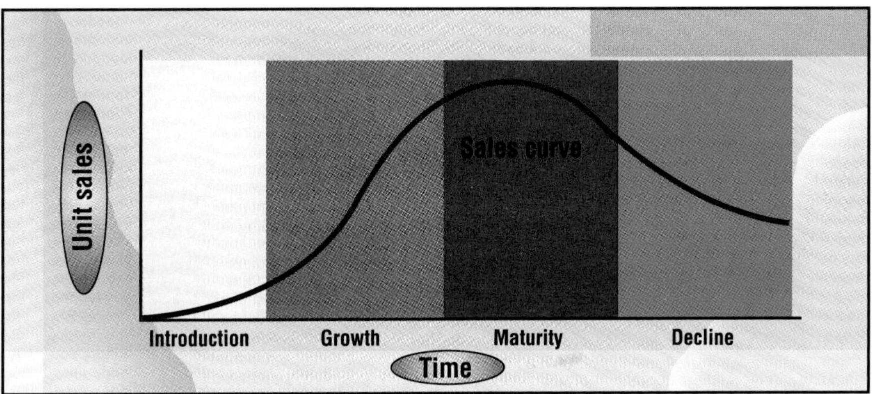

rising at an increasing rate. In other words, sales grow slowly at first but increase at a faster rate later on.

When the product enters its growth stage, profit margins are expected to be small. As sales continue to increase during the growth stage, profits can be expected to increase, partly because sales are increasing but also because the start-up expenses incurred at the start of the product life cycle will likely diminish. As a rule, profits peak late in the growth period.

When a product enters its growth stage, it has shown that it may have a future in the marketplace. As a result, the number of competitors and the level of marketing activity can be expected to increase. Pioneering firms are often forced to alter their products because competitors, having learned from the pioneers' mistakes and having the time to study the market, have improved on the original. Competition also increases because the industry has recognized an untapped potential market. Feeling that there is enough profit to go around, competing firms may be able to grab a sizable market share without taking any away from one another (as is the case during the maturity stage).

Products still in their growth stages include cellular phones, notebook computers, and computerized information and interactive shopping services. During their growth stages, the profits associated with these products will rise (although not for every company) and peak at the end of the period. Distribution costs will be brought under control as channels become more organized and better able to perform their tasks. Product quality will be stressed and improved. Persuasive efforts to create brand preference will become the emphasis of promotion. Promotion expenses will be adjusted as rising sales and profits indicate the product's potential.

THE MATURITY STAGE

As the product approaches the end of its growth period, sales begin to level off. A change in the growth rate, indicated by sales increasing at a decreasing rate, marks the end of the growth period and the beginning of the maturity stage. As Exhibit 14.3 shows, profits level off and then fall during the maturity stage. This is to be expected as competing firms try to operate within a static or slow-growth market. When sales peak, the product calls for marketing strategies and tactics appropriate for the maturity stage. During the mature stage, many products experience diminished popularity, product obsolescence, or market saturation (i.e., most target customers now own the product), the product begins to lose market acceptance.

Most products now on the market are in their maturity phase. During this stage, competition is likely to be intense. After all, one goal of effective marketing is to achieve brand

Services, like goods, follow a product life cycle. In most parts of Europe and South America professional soccer is in the mature stage of its product life cycle. In the United States, where the World Cup Games were held in the summer of 1994, professional soccer has yet to hit the growth stage of its product life cycle.

maturity status and maintain it for as long as the market supports the product. Further, because a product in the maturity stage has achieved wide market acceptance, the primary means for any one company to increase its market share is to take market share away from competitors. In the mature automobile business, for example, strategies for maintaining market share and defending against inroads from foreign competition are common.

Persuading existing customers to use more of the product may be a major objective for marketers of mature brands. For example, advertisements for many food products contain recipes that require the product as an ingredient. This strategy encourages increased usage.

THE DECLINE STAGE

The decline stage in the product life cycle is one of falling sales and profits. The number of firms in the industry is likely to drop as managers become aware that the product has entered the decline stage. A few firms, or even a single firm, may survive and even do well by catering to the remaining buyers. Makers of parts for Edsel and Hudson automobiles are neither large nor numerous, yet they can survive by catering to car collectors. Brylcreem, Ovaltine, Good & Plenty, and blacksmiths are less common than they once were, but they are still around.

In the decline phase, survivor firms compete within an ever smaller market, driving profit margins still lower. Ironically, the last surviving firm or firms may, as individual organizations, enjoy high profits at this point. This is because most competitors have withdrawn from the market, leaving what remains to one or two suppliers. What remains is a group of extremely loyal buyers—people who, for example, firmly believe that Camel unfiltered cigarettes are their brand. Profits for the remaining firms can be high. However, profits for the *industry* will be low, because only one or two producers are left. Eventually the decline stage ends with the disappearance of the product from the market.

EXTENDING THE PRODUCT LIFE CYCLE

Marketers use a number of strategies to extend the lives of products or brands. For example, *appealing to new target markets* may keep a product in the growth stage longer. *Finding new uses for the product,* such as creating new recipes for a food ingredient, and *increasing the frequency of use,* such as packaging the product in larger sizes, are also used to extend the product's life.

Product modification
Altering or adjusting the product mix.

Another strategy is **product modification**, the altering or adjusting of the product mix. Style or design changes or the discovery of a new technology may lead to "new and improved" products that extend the product's life. For example, after learning that kids favor bright crayon colors, Binney and Smith, maker of Crayola, replaced 8 of its 64 colors with more brilliant shades in the early 1990s. This was the first change of colors since 1958.[6]

BRAND STRATEGY

Brand name
The verbal part of a brand.

One of a product's most important auxiliary dimensions is the brand that identifies it. A **brand name** is the verbal part of the brand. Advil, Cover Girl, and MTV are brand names.

Brand mark
Anything that symbolically represents a product.

Trademark
A legally registered brand name or brand mark.

Many branded products rely heavily on some symbol for identification. Coca-Cola is closely associated with a certain style of script written in white on a red background. A rainbow-colored apple with a bite out of it symbolizes Apple computers. Businesspeople refer to these symbols as **brand marks**. When a brand name or brand mark is legally registered, it becomes a **trademark**.

Selecting a brand name is a major new-product decision. A brand name should be short, easy to read, and communicate something about the product. Brand names that are inappropriate to a market environment may "kill" an otherwise acceptable product. For example, in creating brand names, marketers must be aware of potential language problems. A vitamin product was introduced into the South American market under the name "Fundavit." The name was supposed to suggest that the product satisfied all the *funda*mental *vit*amin requirements. The English name had to be changed when objections were raised because the product's name was too close to a Spanish term used to refer to an attractive female's derrière.[7]

Manufacturer brand or **national brand**
A brand name owned and advertised by the firm that manufactures the product.

Many of the brand names with which we are most familiar are owned and advertised by the firms that manufacture those products. Black and Decker tools are made by the company of the same name. These brands are called **manufacturer brands** or **national brands**.

Distributor brand or **private brand**
A product whose name is owned by a retailer or other intermediary.

We also frequently encounter products whose names are owned by retailers. Sears's respected line of Craftsman tools is an example. Brands owned by Sears, A&P, Kroger, and other retailers are called **distributor brands** or **private brands**. Brands owned by wholesalers, such as IGA, are also called distributor brands.

A manufacturer that produces private brands for distributors hopes to increase its market share. Thus, private brands such as Sam's American Choice Cola often emerge in the mature stage of the product life cycle because an organization selling a mature product may be able to pick up new business among price-conscious consumers.

Generic brand
A general product name that any company can use.

Some companies market products that do not have names identifying the companies. Instead, a company marketing a product such as napkins or green beans may use a general name that any company can use. These products, which often have white packages with the generic product name in black, are called **generic brands**. The concept of generic brands is not new. Many years ago, shoppers bought most food products from bins and barrels. Those were truly generic goods. However, during economic periods when household budgets are strained, many no-frills products make gains in supermarket sales, particularly in such product categories as fabric softeners, canned vegetables, and facial tissues. Many of the same factors that encourage manufacturers to supply distributor brand goods lead them to produce generic goods.

World brand
An individual brand name common to all countries.

A product that is widely distributed throughout the world with a single individual brand name that is common to all countries is known as a **world brand**. Levi's, Marlboro, Sony, and Coca-Cola are marketed around the globe and are among the most widely known world brands.

License
A contractual agreement with some other firm that allows the second firm to use the company's trademark.

With a brand such as Coca-Cola, the product's greatest strength may be an intangible quality or the symbols associated with it. Companies such as Binney and Smith have learned that its brand name Crayola and logotype are valuable assets. In many cases, a brand name may be a company's strongest asset. Thus, the company may **license** the brand, that is, make contractual arrangements with another firm allowing the second firm to use the company's trademark. Mickey Mouse, Jurassic Park, Grateful Dead, and other trademarks from movies, television shows, and entertainment groups are examples of licensing.

PACKAGING STRATEGY

Packaging
Physical containers for individual product items, labels, inserts, instructions for product use, graphic design, and shipping cartons.

Packaging involves making decisions about labels, inserts, instructions for product use, graphic design, and shipping cartons, as well as decisions about the sizes and types of physical containers for individual product items within the package. In many situations, the packaging is more important than the product it contains. The Glue Stic and the hanging dispenser for Shower Mate are more than simple containers of a product. They offer considerable consumer benefits.

Packages perform many functions. They contain products and protect them until they are ready for use. Packages also facilitate the storage and use of products and aid in their use. Thus, packages should be designed to facilitate ease of handling by consumers and members of the channel of distribution. Products are often identified by their packages, and because distinctive packages on a shelf can attract consumers' attention, they can play a major part in promotional strategy. For example, Good Stuff Company markets oval pieces of cedar wood that help keep moths away from woolen clothing in closets and drawers. The wood chunks are called "Sweater Eggs" and are packaged in egg cartons. The packaging lends charm to the product and reinforces the brand name.

A package on a retailer's shelf may be surrounded by 10 or more packages competing for consumers' attention. In these days of self-service, every package design must attract attention and convey an easily identifiable image. The package must have shelf impact. It must tell consumers what the product is and why they should buy it.

Environmental considerations may strongly influence packaging decisions. Packaging waste is piling up, and there is a growing effort in many industries, such as the fast-food industry, to make all packaging biodegradable or easy to recycle.

In summary, packaging performs the following functions:

- Containment
- Protection in transit
- Storage
- Usage facilitation
- Promotion
- Ecological benefits

As you can see, designing a package is not unlike designing the product itself. The package designer must be as buyer oriented as the product designer.

CUSTOMER SERVICE STRATEGY

Customer service associated with a product is an intangible element of the product mix. Effective marketers, knowing that marketing does not end with the sale of the product, may create a competitive advantage by emphasizing the amount and quality of services. A new personal computer may provide little consumer satisfaction until the marketer loads the buyer's software onto the hard disk.

A service may be the primary product offering or a supportive offering that enhances a tangible product. Delivery, gift-wrapping, and repair services can all be important aspects of a product strategy for creating a competitive advantage. For example, every Thanksgiving the Butterball Turkey Talk-Line's telephone hotline staff of experts receive thousands of calls and provide cooking advice to help consumers prepare (and often rescue) their turkey dinners. Customer services like this create and maintain goodwill. They provide an opportunity to enhance consumer satisfaction.

THE PRODUCT LINE AND THE PRODUCT MIX

Product item
A specific version of a particular good or service.

Product line
A group of a firm's products that are fairly closely related.

Depth of product line
Describes the number of different product items offered in a product line.

In discussing consumer and organizational products, we have treated each product type separately, as though a given organization offered just one **product item**, or a specific version of a particular good or service. In reality, most organizations market more than one product. Even service marketers offer an array of products. Disney World, for example, consists of The Magic Kingdom, Epcot Center, and MGM Studios.

From a marketer's perspective, then, the firm's **product line** is a group of products that are fairly closely related. The term **depth of product line** describes the number of different product items offered in a product line. Louis Rich's food product line has grown to include several variations: turkey franks, turkey bologna, turkey pastrami, and several other lunchmeats made of turkey. Each item in Louis Rich's product line is within the same product class.

The products that make up a product line may be related to one another in several ways. Usually the items are in the same product class or perform a similar function. Procter & Gamble, for example, has a food products line, a bar soap products line, a cleaning products line, and a cosmetic/skin care products line. Clairol's hair coloring product line differs somewhat from its shampoo and conditioner line and certainly differs from its line of hair dryers, curlers, and other appliances. A product line may also be identified by price or quality. For example, Sears tool lines are often classified as good, better, and best.

PRICING

WHAT IS PRICE?

Value
Measures the power one product has to attract another product in exchange.

Price
The amount of money or other consideration given in exchange for a product or service.

As we have seen, marketing involves the exchange of a product for something of value. **Value** measures the power one product has to attract another product in exchange. An auto mechanic could exchange a tuneup for a month of coffee and doughnuts from a nearby diner. Such a trade is possible because the tuneup, the coffee, and the doughnuts all have value. When goods and services are exchanged for each other, the trade is called a *barter.*

While it would be possible to value every product in the world in terms of every other product, a barter system is too complicated. It is far easier to express value in terms of a single variable, money. **Price** is a statement of value because it is the amount of money or other consideration given in exchange for a product or service.

Price has many names that vary according to professional tradition or industry. For example, *rent, fee,* and *donation* are terms used in specific exchange situations to express price. Some sellers avoid the use of the word *price* to make a service offered for sale appear to be something other than a product offered at a given price. Thus, the student pays tuition, not a price, for education. The commuter pays a toll. The physician charges a fee for professional services. Universities, governments, and doctors all sell their services for a price, no matter what that price is called. In any case, marketing involves exchanges of things that have value. The term most commonly used to describe this value is *price.*

Price is special because it ultimately "pays" for all of the company's activities. Because *sales revenue* equals *price* times *unit sales volume,* the price of a product is one of the primary determinants of sales revenues. If a price can be increased while unit volume and costs remain the same, revenues and profits will increase.

PRICING OBJECTIVES

Although we are concerned here with pricing, you should remember that pricing objectives must be coordinated with the firm's other marketing objectives. These, in turn, must flow from the company's overall objectives. Thus, if a company seeks to gain a larger *market share*—that is, a larger percentage of the total industry sales—the pricing objectives and strategy must be consistent with that broad company goal.

A new company or a company that is struggling may see company *survival* as the fundamental pricing objective. This objective is usually set when the company's long-range future is much brighter than its short-range problems.

Most pricing objectives specify a *numerical target* or a measurable goal that the company hopes to reach. Managers typically set profit targets, sales volume targets, or market share targets.

Economists theorize about profit maximization as a pricing objective, but managers find this a difficult objective to achieve. It is hard to identify what maximum profits could be. Since objectives are best stated in measurable terms, most companies set profit targets rather than seek to maximize profit. Thus, a specific objective, such as a 15 percent profit margin, is more realistic.

Pricing objectives related to sales volume may be stated as short-term or long-term objectives. When managers concentrate on the long run, they recognize that changes in the external environment, such as changes in a competitor's strategy, may hinder the achievement of a sales volume target in the short run. Price often changes in the short run, but establishing a "base price" that will achieve the desired sales volume remains the objective.

A market share objective is a form of sales volume objective. The desired sales volume, however, is stated as a percentage of the market. A company whose objective is to always have the largest market share may use a strategy of always setting prices below competitors' prices. The advantage of market share objectives is that they always compare an individual company's performance with that of the rest of the industry.

Maintain the Status Quo/Stabilize Prices. The desire to avoid change and maintain the status quo is fairly common, but is particularly evident in the retailing of gasoline, produce, and dairy products. Though price wars in these areas are not unheard of, the normal practice is for all gas stations in town to charge roughly equal prices for fuel and for all grocery stores to charge approximately the same prices for lettuce and milk. A member of the business community seeking to avoid harmful price wars will set prices to maintain relative price differentials and help stabilize the general price level. If a pricing objective is to stabilize prices by either maintaining price differentials among companies or matching competitors' prices, this objective is called *price stabilization.*

Objectives Related to Market Position. Many companies realize that price alone cannot achieve a profit, sales, or market share target. Price is just one element in the marketing mix. Many marketers define pricing objectives by determining the role price plays in creating the proper market or competitive position.

A price serves as a marketing tool by adding symbolic value to a good or service and helping to position the brand in relation to competitors. A high price may suggest a status good, a low price may suggest a bargain, and a discount coupon or rebate may encourage purchases by people who would otherwise not buy the product. Entire marketing strategies may revolve around price. For example, Tiffany's, a chain of exclusive jewelry shops, maintains an image of the highest quality by stocking reliable products and providing special services—but also by charging comparatively high prices. Kmart and Target stress bargains and therefore must keep prices at the lowest levels.

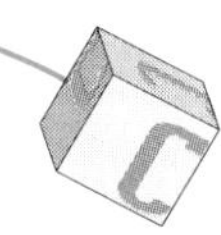

FOCUS ON COMPETITORS

American Floral Marketing Council

"A Rose Is A Rose Even When It's A Bargain." So reads the American Floral Marketing Council's poster in Roses Plus, one of many roses-only shops that have sprung up over the past few years.

The pricing of the country's national flower is undergoing a quiet revolution. A perennial best seller, roses generate $1.6 billion in sales annually. While a mere armful of the 889 million stems sold in the United States are purchased in roses-only shops like Roses Plus, the stores' sales are steadily growing. These stores offer blooms at impulse-purchase prices. A dozen roses may sell for as little as $6 to $16 instead of the usual $30 to $60. The bargain rates mean more people buy more roses. They also mean that roses, long prized for their quality and intrinsic value, are becoming a bargain.

Behind the roses-only shops are Latin American growers eager to increase their share of the U.S. market. The trend began when a few Guatemalan rose farmers became frustrated because U.S. wholesalers were not buying their entire crops. They decided to become their own retailers with wholesale-level prices. They arranged a three-month lease on a store in New York City. The store, Rosa Rosa, carried 12 varieties of roses in about 32 colors for $6 to $9 a dozen. It was so successful that the owners renewed the lease for 10 years and began seeking locations in Chicago, Washington, D.C., and Boston.

Because Latin American growers dramatically undersell U.S. rose farms, the impact on domestic growers has been devastating. Nearly one-third of the 250 U.S. rose farms are no longer productive. Rose imports from Latin America, on the other hand, are up dramatically. In 1971 imported roses accounted for only 2 percent of the blooms sold in the United States, but today 40 percent come from Latin America.

Some domestic rose marketers believe Colombian growers are using a "dumping" price strategy. They would like to see a base price agreement with the Colombian government, or maybe even a quota. Meanwhile, the American Floral Marketing Council recognizes that "People think roses are more valuable because they are expensive." Its promotional campaigns reflect an effort to show that quality isn't diminished just because blooms are plentiful and prices are down.

THE EFFECT OF DEMAND ON PRICE

Many factors affect the marketing manager's pricing decisions. One of the most important factors is demand by the organization's target market. The question the marketing manager must ask is "Who are our customers, and what do *they* want the price to be?" Of course, the forces of supply and demand, as discussed in Chapter 2, play an important part in buyers' expectations about market price. However, economists assume that perfect competition exists and that competing products are nearly identical. But this is rarely the case in our modern free enterprise system, and the traditional economic theory of demand becomes less important.

The ability to obtain a relatively high price for a brand indicates that the product and promotional strategies behind the item are competitively sound and well thought out. Lego's gets a price far above those of many of its competitors but still sells far more building blocks than any of them. This is fairly strong proof that price is only one element of the overall marketing strategy.

Lego's is better off than its competitors because effective nonprice competition allows the marketer to charge premium prices and to emphasize other marketing mix elements rather than relying solely on a lower price to gain customers.

However, intensive price competition exists in many industries where competing products are not distinct from one another. This is especially true for raw materials, such as crude petroleum. In these markets, price becomes the key marketing variable. If price is the sole basis of competition, the economic theory explained in Chapter 2 is a good description of how price is determined.

THE EFFECT OF COSTS ON PRICE

Marketers facing a pricing decision consider demand because the consumer is "king" in all marketing considerations. However, the seller's costs are equally important. Although some products may occasionally be sold at a loss, costs must be recouped sooner or later. Cost provides the "floor" on which to build a pricing strategy.

Before we continue our discussion of cost as the basis for pricing decisions, we need to define some accounting terms:

Variable costs fluctuate with some measure of volume.

Fixed costs expire with the passage of time, regardless of volume.

Total costs are the sum of fixed and variable costs.

For example, a building contractor that is constructing an office building would use the following formula to calculate price:

$$\textit{Selling Price} = \textit{Fixed Cost} + \textit{Variable Costs} + \textit{Profit.}$$

PRICE AND BREAKEVEN ANALYSIS

Breakeven point
The point at which total costs and revenues meet.

A manufacturing company must know how many units to produce and sell before it covers all its costs and breaks even. The **breakeven point** is the point at which total costs and revenues meet. Every time the company sells a unit above the breakeven point, it adds to its profits. Exhibit 14.4 shows how to derive the breakeven point.

The following formula is used to calculate the breakeven point:

$$\textit{Breakeven Point} = \frac{\textit{Fixed Costs}}{\textit{Selling Price} - \textit{Variable Costs}}$$

For example, suppose the selling price equals $10, variable costs equal $5, and fixed costs equal $50,000. Then the breakeven point is

$$\begin{aligned}\textit{Breakeven Point} &= \frac{\$50{,}000}{\$10 - \$5}\\ &= \frac{\$50{,}000}{\$5}\\ &= \textit{10,000 units.}\end{aligned}$$

Price clearly plays an important role in breakeven analysis. For example, raising the price of the product may allow revenues to catch up to cost more quickly, while lowering the price may have the opposite effect. Every product marketed by a company has a breakeven point. If that point is achieved and surpassed, the company makes a profit. Price thus determines when the breakeven point is met.

PRICING NEW PRODUCTS

Marketers have two basic pricing strategies to choose from during the introduction stage of the product life cycle: skimming pricing and penetration pricing.

Exhibit 14.4 **EXAMPLE OF BREAKEVEN ANALYSIS**

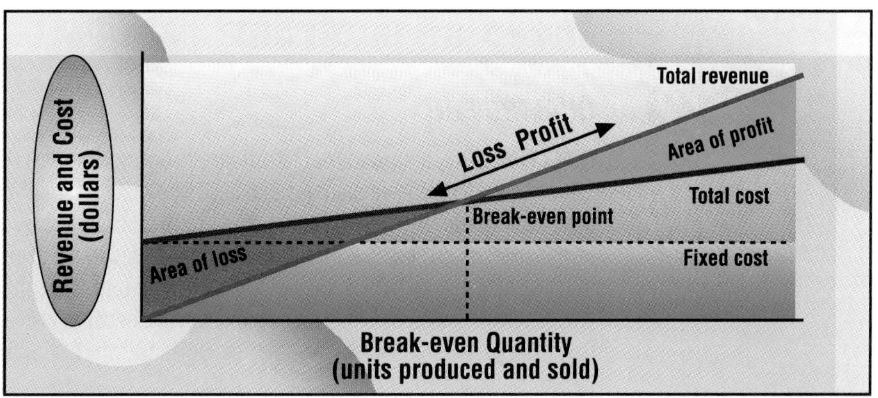

Skimming price
A relatively high introductory price that marketers plan to systematically lower as the product matures.

Skimming Price. A **skimming price** is a high introductory price intended to "skim the cream off the market." It is best used at the start of a product's life, when the product is novel and consumers are uncertain about its value. The initial high price will be lowered as the product matures. For example, compact disk players first sold at prices of around $800 but can now be purchased for as little as $100. When first introduced, the IBM personal computer sold for $5,455. Before it was replaced by the IBM System 2 computer, it was priced below $1,500.

Pricing high initially and then systematically reducing price over time allows companies to establish a flow of revenue that covers research and development expenses as well as the initial high costs of bringing the product to market. A skimming strategy assumes a relatively strong inelastic demand for the product, often because the product has status value or is a truly new, breakthrough item. Price is used to segment the market on the basis of discretionary income or degree of need for the product. As the product matures in the life cycle, competitive pressures reduce the price, and new market segments become the key targets.

Marketing strategists are most likely to adopt a skimming strategy when production capacity limits output or when some barrier to market entry exists. For instance, G. D. Searle and Company had a patent on NutraSweet, its aspartame artificial sweetener, until 1992. During the early stages of NutraSweet's product life cycle, Searle charged the highest possible prices to soft-drink companies like Coca-Cola and Pepsico—the customers with the greatest need for the product—until it was able to increase production capacity. It then progressively lowered prices as other food manufacturers began to desire NutraSweet for diet versions of their products. In 1991, recognizing that its "skimming-the-cream" days were almost over, Searle lowered its prices and began heavily advertising the NutraSweet brand name to solidify brand loyalty.

Penetration price
A low introductory price.

Penetration Pricing. A **penetration price** is a low introductory price. In the short run, it may even result in a loss. A penetration pricing strategy is used when a competitive situation is well established (or soon will be) and a low price in the introductory stage of the product life cycle will be necessary to break into the market. It is an alternative to skimming. Its objective is to enable the product to become established and survive in the long run. A penetration strategy achieves this objective by pricing so low that a profit is possible only if the company sells a relatively high volume and obtains a large market share. Thus, penetration pricing reduces the threat of competitor imitation because the small profit margin discourages low-cost imitators from entering the market. Further, by increasing the size of the total market and/or market share, the marketer establishes a strong brand loyalty and increases the brand's dominance in consumers' minds.

FOCUS ON COMPANY

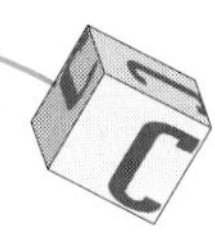

QUATTRO PRO

QUATTRO PRO, a spreadsheet software program regularly sold at $495, was offered at a special price of $99.95—a savings of $395. The clever aspect of this pricing strategy was that the offer was made via direct mail to owners of Lotus 123, Symphony, and Excel, members of a target market not likely to switch to a "me too" brand at the regular price. Even more clever was the fact that this offer was made shortly before the enhanced version, QUATTRO PRO 2.0, was to be introduced. Thus, converted buyers became more likely prospects for the new product. This inventive pricing strategy by Borland International, Inc., changed the nature of pricing in the software industry.

OTHER PRICING STRATEGIES

A penetration strategy may continue beyond the introductory stage of the product life cycle. Frequently the marketer will communicate the idea of *everyday low prices (EDLP)* when a penetration strategy has successfully allowed the product to move into the growth and maturity stages. A skimming strategy often leads to prestige pricing in those stages.

Prestige Pricing. The economic theory that the customer wants the lowest price is not always correct. Diamonds and Lexus automobiles are expensive partly because people expect them to be. A $100 bottle of perfume may cost less than $20 to produce; the other $80 goes to advertising, packaging, distribution, and profit. When consumers buy such perfume, they buy prestige, hope, the feeling of being someone special, and pride in having "the best." For many products, consumers use price to infer quality, especially when it is difficult to determine quality by inspection. Pricing a brand at high levels so that consumers believe that brand differs from other brands is known as **prestige pricing**.

Prestige pricing
Pricing a brand at high levels so that consumers believe that brand differs from other brands.

Why are prestige pricing strategies possible? Perfumes, furs, and gems are demanded in part because of their high prices. These products are status goods, and marketers often charge a prestige price for them to portray a quality image for the brand.

Of course, charging the highest price does not always work. The maker of Weight Watchers wanted a new line of frozen foods that would not take business away from its existing line. Candle Lite Dinners were priced higher than Le Menue, which was the highest-priced low-calorie frozen dinner. The prices were just too high, and the product flopped.

Odd and Even Prices. One seldom sees convenience and shopping products priced at $2, $5, or $10. Instead, they are normally sold at prices such as $1.99, $4.98, and $9.97. These are *odd prices.* Many marketers believe an odd number of $.99 suggests that the product's price is less than $1.00.

There is another, practical purpose. Odd pricing forces clerks to use the cash registers to make change, thus creating a record of the sale and discouraging employee dishonesty.

Exceptions to the logic of odd pricing immediately come to mind. *Even prices* may result in *more* sales, especially if the marketer deals in relatively inexpensive items. More bottles of soda will be sold from a machine that accepts 50 or 75 cents than from one that takes 49 or 73 cents.

Item Profit Pricing versus Total Profit Pricing. Many pricing strategists consider the product line rather than individual product items to be the appropriate unit of analysis. The objective is to maximize profits for the total product line rather than to obtain the greatest profits

Tourism in foreign countries is strongly influenced by the exchange rate. A favorable change in the exchange rate may dramatically reduce the costs of all services and goods consumed during a vacation or business trip.

Captive pricing
Pricing a basic product low but charging a compensating high markup on related supplies required to operate the product.

for any individual item in the line. A video game manufacturer may set low prices on its game player in the hope of making large profits on game software. Firms such as Schick and Gillette sell their razors at low prices to encourage long-term purchase of blades that fit the razors. In a **captive pricing** strategy, the basic product is priced low—often below cost—but the high markup on related supplies required to operate the basic product compensates for the low price. The loss on the basic product is recovered in profits from sale of the supplies. A newspaper costs more to produce and distribute than the price charged subscribers, but the increased circulation generated by the low price leads to more advertising revenue and greater overall profit. In all these cases, the marketer charges a reduced price on particular items to increase total profit.

Loss leader
A product that the seller prices at a loss to attract customers who might buy other goods.

Leader Pricing. A common pricing policy that sacrifices item profit for total profit is leader pricing. While most consumers are familiar with the **loss leader**—the product that the seller prices at a loss to attract customers who might buy other goods—they are less aware of the *cost leader* and the *low-profit leader.* In each instance, the product is priced to attract bargain-hunting customers who might make other purchases, but the leader item is sold at the seller's cost (cost leader) or at a very small profit (low-profit leader). For example, when a store like Target uses loss leader prices, managers may expect to triple store traffic. Goods so priced are usually frequently purchased items or familiar brands that customers will recognize as bargains.

Discounts. If you buy a swimsuit in September, will you expect to pay the same price that you would in July? Probably not, because seasonality affects the prices of many products, especially fashion items. Marketers discount prices as seasons change, for large quantity purchases, for cash payments, and for many other reasons. It is very common for marketers to offer cash discounts to customers who do not require 30 days to pay their bills.

PRICING IN GLOBAL MARKETS

In Chapter 3, we discussed exchange rates and how they influence international business. Of course, their biggest impact is on pricing. Pricing, as we have already seen, is influenced by many environmental factors. Supply and demand, competitive strategies, economic conditions, the target market's needs, and government regulations all play a major role in determining pricing strategies, especially those of international marketers.

Global marketers pay particular attention to prices in different markets around the world. For example, in the United States Levi's 501 jeans sell for about $35. In other markets, a pair of Levi's is a status symbol, so Levi Strauss uses prestige prices. In Tokyo, a pair of Levi's 501s costs over $70. In Paris, the price is about $90. Levi Strauss is a street-smart global competitor that has profit-oriented objectives for each international market it serves.

SUMMARY

1. ***Define* product *and describe the characteristics of products.***
A product is a bundle of customer benefits. Defining a product as a bundle of benefits stresses the satisfaction a product provides its consumers. Every product has both primary characteristics and auxiliary dimensions. Primary characteristics are basic features and aspects of the core product. The core product provides the essential benefits common to most competitive offerings. Consumers expect a basic level of performance. Auxiliary dimensions include special features, styling, color, package, warranty, repair service contract, reputation, brand name, instructions for use, and so on.

2. ***Describe the basic product categories.***
Products can be roughly classified into consumer and organizational products. Consumer goods fall into three general categories: convenience, shopping, and specialty products. This classification is based on the consumer's reasons for buying, the consumer's need for information, and the consumer's shopping and purchase behaviors. Convenience products are relatively inexpensive, are purchased on a regular basis, and are bought without a great deal of thought. They involve a minimum of consumer shopping effort. Shopping products generate a great deal of consumer effort. Consumers feel the need to make product comparisons, seek out additional information, examine merchandise, or otherwise reassure themselves before purchasing a shopping product. Specialty products are perceived as having a particular attraction other than price. Consumers will not accept substitutes.
Organizational products can be categorized in much the same way as consumer products. The most commonly used classification system outlines the basic characteristics of each class of organizational products. According to this system, these products can be classified as raw materials, component parts, installations, accessory equipment, operating supplies, and services. All organizational products have derived demand—demand based on the demand for some other product.

3. ***Discuss the characteristics of services.***
The basic characteristics of services are intangibility, perishability, inseparability, and variability. Whereas goods are tangible, services are intangible. Intangibility means buyers normally cannot see, feel, smell, hear, or taste a service before making a purchase decision. Services, then, cannot be handled, examined, or tried out before they are purchased. Services "disappear" quickly; they are perishable and cannot be stored. Inseparability means producer and consumer may have to be present in the same place at the same time for the service transaction to occur. Finally, most services are delivered by people. Because the quality of service provided is closely tied to the supplier's personal performance, there can be great variability among services provided.

4. ***Explain the stages in new-product development.***
The new-product development process has six general stages: idea generation, idea screening, business analysis, product development, test marketing, and commercialization. The idea generation stage involves an ongoing search for product ideas that are consistent with target market needs and with the company's objectives. In the idea screening stage, managers evaluate which ideas are good and which are bad. Ideas are ranked and classified, and alternatives that are too risky are eliminated. Business analysis is a critical examination of the new-product idea from all important company viewpoints.

The company estimates market potential, cost of production, profitability, and other concerns about the overall business plan for the product. In the product development stage, the proposed new-product idea is transformed from a product concept to a working model or product prototype. The product prototype is tested in the laboratory and with consumers. Many are test marketed. Test markets are cities or small geographical areas. Test marketing requires a limited production of the product so that actual purchasing behavior and consumer reactions can be measured in typical retail settings. After product development and/or test marketing, the company makes the decision to "go for it" or to hold back. Commercialization is the process of going into full-scale production and the marketing process of launching the new product.

5. ***Describe the product life cycle.***
The product life cycle is a graphic depiction of a product's sales history from its "birth," or marketing beginning, to its "death," or withdrawal from the market. Each product's life typically flows through several distinct product life cycle stages as sales volume is plotted over time. These stages are introduction, growth, maturity, and decline. During the introductory stage, the new product attempts to gain a foothold in the market. Sales are likely to be slow at first, and in most cases profits are negative. Selecting strategies appropriate for the introductory stage of the product life cycle is critical, and the length of this stage varies dramatically. If the product earns market acceptance, it should enter the growth stage. Sales rise at an increasing rate. Profits can be expected to be small but gradually to begin to increase. The number of competitors and the level of marketing activity can be expected to increase. As the product approaches the end of its growth period, sales begin to level off. A change in the growth rate, indicated by sales increasing at a decreasing rate, marks the end of the growth period and the beginning of the maturity stage. Profits level off and then fall in the maturity stage. Most products on the market are in their maturity phase. During this stage, competition is likely to be intense. The decline stage in the product life cycle is one of falling sales and profits. The number of firms in the industry is likely to drop as managers become aware that the product has entered the decline stage. A few firms, or even a single firm, may survive and even do well by catering to the remaining buyers.

6. ***Explain the various types of brand strategy.***
A brand identifies the product. A brand name is the verbal part of the brand. A brand mark is a symbol that identifies the product. Selecting a brand name is a major new-product decision. Brand names that are inappropriate to a market environment may "kill" an otherwise acceptable product. Many of the most familiar brand names are owned and advertised by the firms that manufacture the products. These brands are called manufacturer brands or national brands. Products whose names are owned by retailers or other intermediaries are known as distributor brands or private brands. Products that have names any company can use are generic brands. A product that is widely distributed throughout the world with a single individual brand name that is common to all countries is known as a world brand. A company with a very popular brand name may license the brand, or make contractual arrangements with another firm allowing the second firm to use the company's trademark.

7. ***Discuss packaging strategy.***
Packaging involves making decisions about labels, inserts, instructions for product use, graphic design, and shipping cartons, as well as decisions about the sizes and types of physical containers for individual product items within the outer package. In many situations, the packaging is more important than the product it contains. The functions of packaging include containment, protection in transit, storage, usage facilitation, promotion, and ecological benefits. A package designer must be as buyer oriented as the product designer.

8. ***Describe customer service strategy.***
Customer service associated with a product is an intangible element of the product mix. Effective marketers may create a competitive advantage by emphasizing the amount and quality of services. Delivery, gift-wrapping, and repair services can all be important aspects of a product strategy for creating a competitive advantage. Customer services create and maintain goodwill and provide an opportunity to enhance consumer satisfaction.

9. ***Discuss the concept of price.***
Price is a statement of value because it is the amount of money or other consideration given in exchange for a product or service. *Rent, fee,* and *donation* are terms used in specific exchange situations to express price. Price is special because it ultimately "pays" for all of the company's activities. Because sales revenue equals price times unit sales volume, the price of a product is one of the primary determinants of sales revenues. If a price can be increased while unit volume and costs remain the same, revenues and profits will increase.

10. ***Describe basic pricing objectives.***
Pricing objectives must be coordinated with the firm's other marketing objectives. These, in turn, must flow from the company's overall objectives. Pricing objectives may include market share, survival, profit targets, sales volumes, market share targets, profit maximization, maintenance of status quo, or price stability. Thus, if a company seeks to gain a larger market share, the pricing objectives and strategy must be consistent with that broad company goal. A new company or a company that is struggling may see company *survival* as the fundamental pricing objective. Most pricing objectives specify a numerical target or a measurable goal that the company hopes to reach. Managers typically set profit targets, sales volume targets, or market share targets. Since objectives are best stated in measurable terms, most companies set profit targets rather than seek to maximize profit. Pricing objectives related to sales volume may be stated as short-term or long-term objectives. A market share objective is a form of sales volume objective. The desire to avoid change and maintain the status quo is a fairly common objective. Price stabilization is the objective of stabilizing prices by either maintaining price differentials among companies or matching competitors' prices.

11. ***Identify the factors that affect pricing strategy.***
Many factors affect the marketing manager's pricing decisions. One of the most important factors is demand by the organization's target market, that is, "Who are our customers, and what do *they* want the price to be?" The forces of supply and demand play an important role in price determination. In markets where perfect competition does not exist, however, the traditional economic theory of demand becomes less important. Effective nonprice competition allows the marketer to charge premium prices and to emphasize other marketing mix elements rather than relying solely on a lower price. However, intensive price competition exists in many industries where competing products are not distinct. The seller's costs are equally important in pricing strategy. Although some products may occasionally be sold at a loss, costs must be recouped sooner or later. Cost provides the "floor" on which to build a pricing strategy.

KEY TERMS AND CONCEPTS

Product (p. 318)
Core product (p. 318)
Product positioning concept (p. 318)
Product differentiation (p. 319)
Convenience product (p. 320)
Shopping product (p. 320)
Specialty product (p. 321)
Derived demand (p. 321)
Intangibility (p. 322)
Inseparability (p. 322)
Idea generation stage (p. 325)
Idea screening stage (p. 325)
Business analysis (p. 325)
Product development stage (p. 325)
Test market (p. 326)
Commercialization (p. 327)
Product life cycle (p. 327)
Product modification (p. 331)
Brand name (p. 331)
Brand mark (p. 331)
Trademark (p. 331)
Manufacturer brand or national brand (p. 331)
Distributor brand or private brand (p. 331)
Generic brand (p. 331)
World brand (p. 331)
License (p. 332)
Packaging (p. 332)
Product item (p. 333)
Product line (p. 333)
Depth of product line (p. 333)
Value (p. 333)
Price (p. 333)
Breakeven point (p. 336)
Skimming price (p. 337)
Penetration price (p. 337)
Prestige pricing (p. 338)
Captive pricing (p. 339)
Loss leader (p. 339)

DISCUSSION QUESTIONS

Company

1. How does the marketing strategy of a company that markets a single product differ from that of a company that markets many products?
2. Should companies be actively involved in the development of new products? Why or why not?
3. How might a small business plan for a new-product development campaign?

Customers

4. What are the product positioning concepts for the following brands?
   a. Dodge Neon
   b. Southwest Airlines
   c. Walt Disney World
   d. Bazooka Bursts soft bubble gum
5. Which of the following would most customers perceive as convenience products? As shopping products? As specialty products?
   a. An airplane trip for a vacation
   b. A pair of scissors
   c. A postage stamp
   d. Silver dinnerware
   e. A man's tie
   f. A wedding dress
   g. Dental floss
6. Which of the following were carefully thought-out brand names?
   a. Holiday Inn
   b. La-Z-Boy
   c. Sam's American Choice
   d. Band-aid
   e. WD-40

Competitors

7. What role do competitors play in the new-product development process?
8. What should a company do if a competitor introduces a new product?
9. How are the product positioning concepts for Coca-Cola and Pepsi-Cola similar? How do they differ?

Collaborators

10. What collaborators might help a company in developing its product strategy?
11. How important are collaborators, such as marketing research companies, in the development of new products?

In Question: Take a Stand

Canandaigua Wine Company introduced a new product named Cisco. Cisco is a fizzy, fruit-flavored wine, packaged in 12-ounce clear bottles and sold in the coolers of convenience and liquor stores for about $1.50. Fortified with grape brandy, it is also as potent as five shots of vodka.

Shortly after Cisco's product launch, U.S. Surgeon General Antonia Novello called a press conference in Washington and criticized Canandaigua for deceptive positioning. Novello believed Cisco looked too much like a wine cooler, especially to underage drinkers. Joined by prominent health advocacy groups, she called for Canandaigua to immediately recall and repackage Cisco, which she called a "wine fooler," in bottles that resembled other fortified wines. "[Cisco] is a wolf in sheep's clothing," she said. "It is actually known on the streets as liquid crack." Experts from the Children's National Medical Center presented results of their study of acute alcohol poisonings recently treated at the center. Ten out of the 15 patients reported they had been drinking Cisco. Eight of them said they thought it was a wine cooler. Their average age was 15.

Canandaigua chief executive Marvin Sands disagreed. In his own press conference immediately after Novello's, he insisted he didn't believe the statistics about the threat to so-called Cisco Kids. In his view, the brand had been made a scapegoat for the problem of teen drinking.[8]

Should Cisco be allowed on the market?

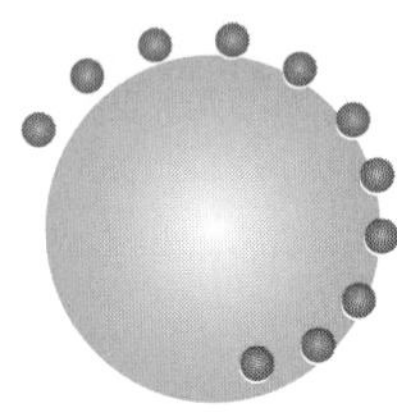

CASE 14.1 PARAMOUNT PICTURES[9]

Paramount Pictures and Edison Brothers Entertainment signed a licensing agreement to develop virtual reality entertainment centers using the theme of the TV series "Star Trek: The Next Generation." Edison Brothers will open its first Star Trek virtual reality center in a shopping mall. The company plans to test the concept before opening other centers across the nation.

The entertainment centers, which will feature Star Trek merchandise and restaurants, will take the concept of mall arcade virtual reality attractions into a new dimension. "For 25 years, Star Trek has been synonymous with the ultimate in technology," said Brandon Tartikoff, chair of Paramount Pictures. "Our agreement with Edison Brothers will, for the first time, permit Star Trek fans across the country to actually board the *USS Enterprise* and experience the excitement and adventure of the 24th century today."

Edison Brothers already features stand-alone virtual reality entertainment systems in its arcades. These systems allow a player to interact with characters and objects in a computer-generated world.

Questions

1. *The text classifies several types of products. What type of product best describes the new virtual reality center?*
2. *Is this a good idea? Is it a new product? Why or why not?*
3. *What brand name should Paramount use?*
4. *What pricing strategy would you recommend for the virtual reality centers?*

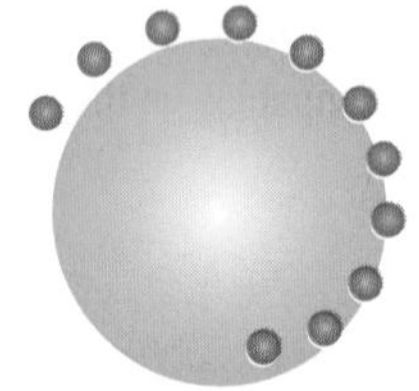

CASE 14.2 A NEW GUM[10]

Carl Kleber, a Fort Wayne, Indiana, dental scientist, has developed a formula for a gum that cleans and polishes teeth while you chew. He claims that tiny abrasives in the gum help remove up to 25 percent of the plaque on teeth. Kleber, who has been developing the gum since 1979 along with colleagues from Indiana University–Purdue University at Fort Wayne, recognizes that the taste has been the sticking point for years. The key question now is "How do you make this stuff appetizing to the average 10-year-old?"

When Kleber first started making the gum, the prototypes were like hunks of clay. Others were too abrasive and scratched tooth enamel. Indeed, the scientists had to devise a "mastication device" of human teeth and saliva to simulate chewing and protect innocent taste buds. An earlier version of the product was found to be slightly radioactive.

After years of slowly refining the gum's texture and flavor in clinical tests, it was time for human guinea pigs. "There's really no animal that chews gum besides humans," says Kleber.

"You can get a monkey to chew it for a couple of minutes, but then they just take it out and stick it in their hair." Fort Wayne elementary school pupils, whom the researcher dubs "professional gum chewers," became the first taste testers. While they seemed to like the gum, "what they really enjoyed was being able to chew gum in school." Small sample batches are now available in several flavors and a bubble gum.

Recently two California businesspeople acquired the rights to the product, and they say some companies are considering licensing it. A publicist for the still unnamed gum says, "There are 100 million people who simply don't go to the dentist. It's an untapped market."

Questions

1. *The text classifies several type of products. What type of product best describes the new gum?*
2. *Is this a good idea? Is it a new product? Why or why not?*
3. *What brand name should the California businesspeople use?*
4. *What pricing strategy would you recommend for the new gum?*
5. *Do you think this product will be a success? Why or why not?*

CHAPTER

15

DISTRIBUTION

When you have studied this chapter, you will be able to:

1
Discuss the collaborative nature of channels of distribution.

2
Describe the major types of channels of distribution.

3
Explain the distribution strategies used for market coverage.

4
Describe the different kinds of wholesalers.

5
Describe the various kinds of retailers.

6
Discuss several retail management strategies.

7
Understand that there are many approaches to international distribution.

When Steven K. Hindy, a foreign correspondent, began working in the Middle East, he had journalistic, not capitalistic, purposes in mind. That changed when Hindy sampled the home brew prepared by some of his compatriots in the U.S. Foreign Service. Because alcohol is forbidden by Islamic law, the diplomats had to acquire the necessary ingredients through diplomatic channels. Then they worked their brewing magic behind closed doors.

When he returned home in 1984, Hindy began experimenting. One of his early tasters was Thomas D. Potter, an assistant vice-president at Chemical Bank who had always dreamed of starting his own business. In 1986, Hindy convinced Potter that selling their own brand of beer was the opportunity Potter had been looking for.

In 1987, with $500,000 raised in a limited partnership offering, the two quit their jobs and started the Brooklyn Brewery. "Just the cost of getting the product into the marketplace turned out to be higher than [we] expected," Hindy admits. Merchants initially balked at the premium retail price of $22 per case. But once the retailers signed up, they became loyal customers. The Brooklyn Brewery's revenues grew from $400,000 in 1988 to more than $3 million. The company's line now includes Brooklyn Brown Ale, which, like the lager, is sold as far away as Japan.

It wasn't all clear sailing, however. Distribution had been a problem. Potter and Hindy, who mastermind their operation from a 30,000-square-foot warehouse in Brooklyn, handled their own local distribution from the beginning, but they relied on other companies to take care of distribution elsewhere.

"Our experience with outside distributors was very disappointing," says Potter. They were far more concerned about major brand sales than about promoting a new product. Potter and Hindy decided to expand their own distribution operation by providing a solution to other gourmet beer companies that had the same distribution problems.

Today the Brooklyn Brewery represents close to 50 microbreweries from around the world and distributes more than 100 distinctive beers. Potter and Hindy believe distributing a wide variety of gourmet beers is in all the breweries' best interests. "The whole category was being neglected, and that hurt everybody," says Potter.[1]

Exhibit 15.1 **A BASIC CHANNEL OF DISTRIBUTION**

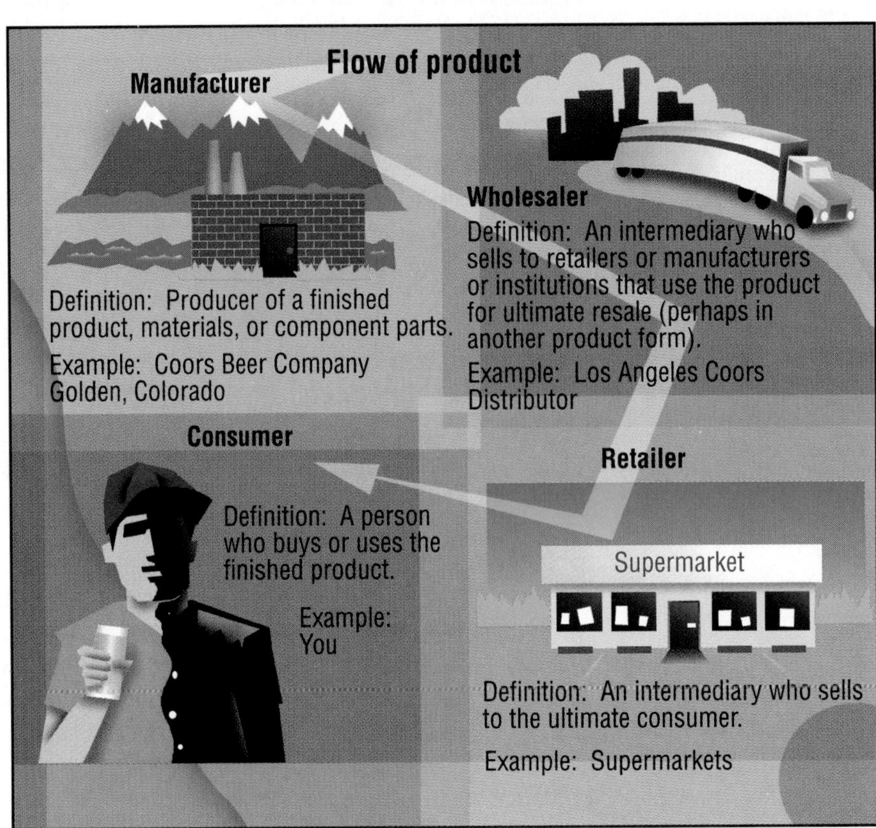

Flow of product
Manufacturer
Definition: Producer of a finished product, materials, or component parts.
Example: Coors Beer Company Golden, Colorado
Wholesaler
Definition: An intermediary who sells to retailers or manufacturers or institutions that use the product for ultimate resale (perhaps in another product form).
Example: Los Angeles Coors Distributor
Consumer
Definition: A person who buys or uses the finished product.
Example: You
Retailer
Supermarket
Definition: An intermediary who sells to the ultimate consumer.
Example: Supermarkets

The Brooklyn Brewery example highlights the importance of distribution to a business. The organizations that make up channels of distribution—retailers, wholesalers, and other specialized intermediaries—are vital to the marketing success of many goods and services. These organizations are the focus of this chapter.

THE NATURE OF DISTRIBUTION

Marketers manage distribution activities so that their products are sold in the right *places* at the right *times.* For example, Barbie dolls are made in Indonesia, but getting them to the United States for the Christmas toy season is a function of distribution. *Place* or *distribution* is one of the four major elements of the marketing mix.

The route that products follow from producer to final buyer is called a *channel of distribution.* A **channel of distribution** consists of the complete chain of marketing organizations that collaborate to bring a product from the producer to the ultimate consumer. Its purpose is to make transfer of ownership and/or possession of the product possible.

Channel of distribution The complete chain of marketing organizations that collaborate to bring a product from the producer to the ultimate consumer.

Exhibit 15.1 illustrates a basic channel of distribution consisting of the manufacturer, the wholesaler, the retailer, and the ultimate consumer. Each party in the channel collaborates with the others to make transactions that involve movement of the physical product and/or a transfer of title (ownership) of that product.

As the term *channel* suggests, products "flow" from the producer to other collaborating organizations. The path that some products follow can be extremely short. For example, when a local bakery sells its products directly to neighborhood customers, the path is short. Other

Intermediary
A middleman that buys and resells products and helps in other ways to get products into the hands of end users.

Wholesaler
An organization that buys products from producers and resells those products to retailers, other wholesalers, or industrial users.

Agent or **broker**
An intermediary that does not take title to the products it handles.

Retailer
An organization that sells products directly to consumers.

Physical distribution
The activities that move tangible products along in the channel of distribution.

channels include **intermediaries** or *middlemen* that buy and resell products and help in other ways to get products into the hands of end users. Intermediaries are important collaborators that often develop long-term relationships with producers.

Intermediaries fall into two major classifications: wholesalers and retailers. **Wholesalers** buy products from producers and resell those products to retailers, other wholesalers, and industrial users. In short, they do not sell to consumers like you. Other wholesalers work in a similar manner but do not actually buy the products handled. They do not "take title" to the products. These intermediaries are referred to as **agents** or **brokers**. Thus, we often hear marketers use the terms *merchant wholesalers* to refer to those wholesalers that take title to the goods they handle and *agent wholesalers* to refer to those that never own the products they sell. **Retailers** do sell to consumers—the people who will actually use the products. That is, retailers sell to customers who buy the product for their own use or for their household's consumption.

Excluded from the channel of distribution are numerous collaborators that perform specific facilitating activities for manufacturers, wholesalers, or retailers. For example, the airline or the freight train company that transports the product from Boston to Philadelphia is not a channel member, nor is the advertising agency that creates the advertising message and selects the appropriate media. These collaborators are hired because they are specialists that can perform a certain marketing activity more efficiently or more effectively. These collaborating enterprises, or *facilitators,* are excluded from the term *organizations* in our definition of a channel of distribution.

To move products along in the channel of distribution, members of the channel perform a number of activities that make up **physical distribution**. These include such activities as processing orders, managing inventory, transporting products, and storing and warehousing products. These logistical activities were discussed in Chapter 9.

It is important to realize that the nature of distribution can vary widely even among companies that sell directly competitive products. For example, Avon and Amway concentrate on using sales representatives to sell directly to consumers, while Gillette and Colgate-Palmolive, which sell similar products, deal with many wholesalers and retailers in their distribution systems.

DISTRIBUTION IN THE ECONOMY

Effective distribution brings consumers and organizations the products they need. If performed poorly, distribution activity can cause customer dissatisfaction, high prices, and even business failures. For example, citizens' frustration with inadequate distribution systems contributed to the collapse of the Soviet Union's economy. The starvation in Somalia was due to distribution problems caused by the tribal warlords.

THE INTERMEDIARY'S JOB

Whether the product is a box of crayons or a Caterpillar tractor, it must be moved from the producer to the buyer. In many cases, the product passes through an intermediary. It is surprising to some people that intermediaries actually *simplify* the distribution process and, in most cases, make it much more cost efficient. Exhibit 15.2 shows why this is true.

Note that without an intermediary in place, even a simple "economy" with only five buyers and five sellers would require over 100 interrelationships to allow each buyer to deal with each seller. The presence of an intermediary, however, greatly reduces the number of transactions and simplifies the system. This is because intermediaries perform a selling function for producers and a buying function for consumers or other buyers. You don't usually think of it in this way, but your local supermarket acts as a purchasing agent for you, gathering products from farmers, food processors, and wholesalers and storing them until you are ready to buy them.

Exhibit 15.2 **INTERMEDIARIES SIMPLIFY THE DISTRIBUTION PROCESS**

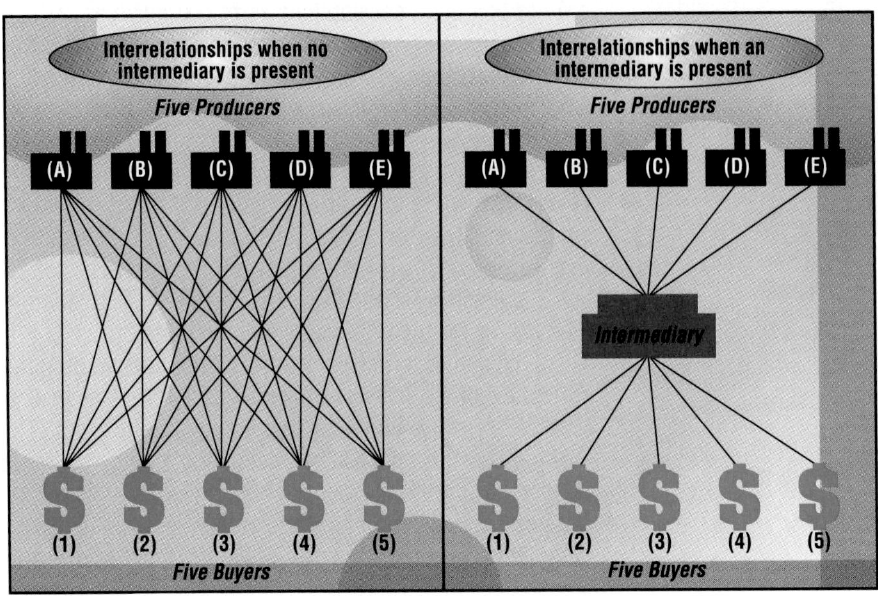

MAJOR CHANNELS OF DISTRIBUTION

Channels of distribution differ in structure from product to product and from industry to industry. Wm. Wrigley Jr. Company needs a different channel for its gum than does a builder of made-to-order office buildings. Wrigley must reach millions of consumers, whereas the builder may deal with only a few organizational buyers. Wrigley must use hundreds of wholesalers to reach many thousands of retailers that sell to millions of consumers, but the builder can deal with its business customers directly. Wrigley needs intermediaries to meet its goals, but the builder does not.

Notice that the key issue of customer satisfaction also comes into play here. The buyer of a building *wants* to deal directly with the builder. The gum purchaser does not care who sells the gum as long as it's fresh, reasonably priced, and available in a convenient location.

Exhibit 15.3 shows that some channels of distribution include many intermediaries and others contain none. Channels with many intermediaries are referred to as *long* channels, and those with few intermediaries are termed *short.* In almost every instance, channels are longer when the number of customers to be reached is high and shorter when the number of customers is small.

CONSUMER PRODUCTS CHANNELS

Channels 1 through 4 in Exhibit 15.3 are the most commonly used consumer products channels. Other, more complex channels exist, but extremely long channels are likely to be avoided because they tend to raise costs and decrease efficiency.

Channel 1, the direct-to-consumer channel, is used by some farmers, encyclopedia publishers, and small producers of baked goods, candies, and other products that are produced on the premises and sold directly to retail customers. This channel is, of necessity, the one used in most services marketing. A dentist deals directly with a patient, a restaurant with a diner, a bank with an investor, and so on.

Direct marketing
Marketing that uses mail-order catalogs or mass media to obtain orders by direct response via 800 telephone numbers or by mail.

Direct marketing is marketing that uses mail order catalogs or mass media to obtain orders by direct response via 800 telephone numbers, via computers, or by mail. Direct

Exhibit 15.3 **THE MAJOR CHANNELS OF DISTRIBUTION**

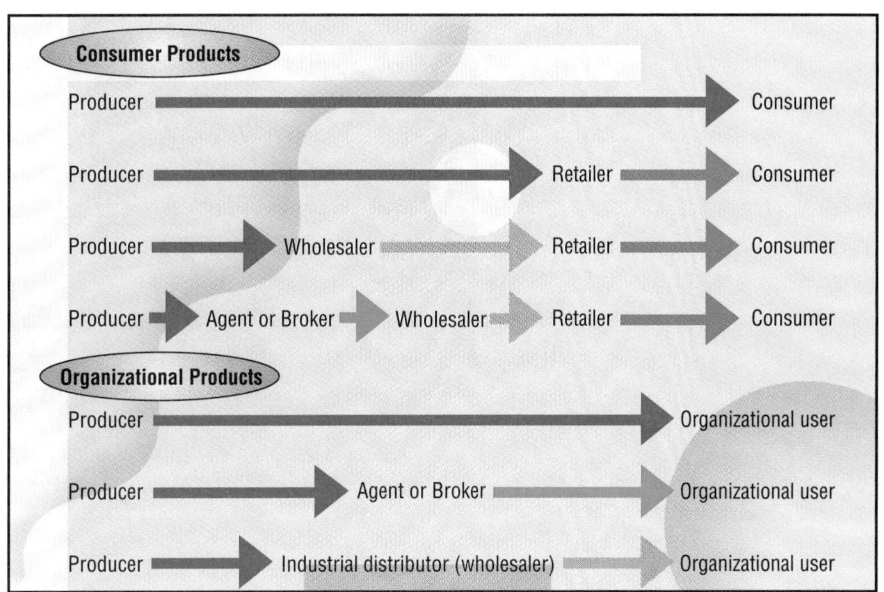

marketers, as the term suggests, use a direct-to-consumer channel. Although a telephone conversation may occur, there is no physical contact between the customer and the producer. Direct marketing has experienced tremendous growth in the last decade.

In channel 2, the producer deals directly with retailers. Clothing manufacturers often do this because they need to distribute certain types of apparel before it goes out of style. Retailers of these goods want to deal directly with manufacturers so that they can get the merchandise quickly and obtain the advice producers can offer them. Large retailers also use this channel frequently. Wal-Mart buys nearly all of its merchandise directly from manufacturers. Brooklyn Brewery's shipment from Fulton's Landing in Brooklyn to the Water Club in Manhattan is another example of this channel.

Channel 3 is the channel through which most consumer products flow. This is because so many people buy consumer products that manufacturers find it beneficial to use the transportation and storage services intermediaries can provide.

In channel 4, consumer products may be distributed through an agent or broker that facilitates sales to wholesalers but does not actually take title to the products. This channel is used when additional specialists can help with activities like negotiating price or determining the quality of products such as citrus fruits and other produce. It is commonly used when products are exported to other countries.

ORGANIZATIONAL PRODUCTS CHANNELS

Channels 5, 6, and 7 in Exhibit 15.3 illustrate three approaches to the distribution of organizational or business products.

Channel 5 shows the very common direct-to-organizational-user channel. For example, Rhino Foods in Burlington, Vermont, sells cookie dough directly to Ben & Jerry's Homemade, also of Burlington, Vermont, as an ingredient in one of Ben & Jerry's ice cream flavors. Many organizational users prefer to deal directly with producers, particularly when products are bought in large quantities, made to order, expensive, or highly technical in nature. Organizational users often need the producer's technical advice. Many believe they can get better quality or a better price by "dealing direct."

Services are often distributed through a direct channel. However, many service marketers, such as airlines, use agents to assist in the distribution process.

Channel 6 uses an agent intermediary that does not take title to the products. The agent performs the selling functions on behalf of the manufacturer. Use of an agent makes sense even when the products sold are highly specialized or made to order. Since the agent does not actually buy the goods, it cannot get "stuck" with them as a merchant wholesaler might. An intermediary would be foolish to take title to, say, a factory air-conditioning system in the hope of locating some potential customer whose building it happened to fit.

Industrial distributor
An intermediary that takes title to organizational products.

Channel 7 does use a wholesaler that takes title to the organizational products. This type of wholesaler is often called an **industrial distributor**. This intermediary is most likely to carry commonly used products such as small equipment, machine parts, oil, and other products in wide demand.

Before we move on to the problem of choosing among the various channel possibilities, we should note that each channel shown in Exhibit 15.3 involves channel intermediary *functions* even when no intermediary is actually present. When there is no "middleman," someone else—the manufacturer or the buyer—performs the absent intermediary's functions of transportation, storage, and so on. Thus, you can "eliminate the middleman," but you can't eliminate the middleman's functions. That is why eliminating intermediaries does not necessarily lead to lower prices or greater efficiency. Intermediaries, being specialists, may perform the necessary functions better than the producer or other organizations can.

SELECTING A CHANNEL

Which channel from among the many choices available should a company choose? The answer depends on many variables, but the most important factor is the customer. Channel management starts with the customer and works backward to the producer or other supplier. If the customer *wants* to deal directly with the manufacturer, the manufacturer must deal directly with the customer or find some good reason the customer would be better off dealing with an intermediary.

Other considerations are the organization's segmentation and positioning strategy. A perfume maker striving for a prestige image sells its product at a select number of shops, not at every possible drugstore. Also important is economics. If an organization has limited funds available, as a new venture might, it is more likely to use intermediaries than to maintain its own sales force. This is because intermediaries either *buy* the products they sell, providing a flow of cash to the producer, or charge a commission that need not be paid *until* they sell something. Hiring, training, and paying a sales force involve a far greater financial commitment.

Product characteristics and competitive considerations are also important. Goods that are easy to store and unlikely to go out of fashion are more suitable to channels involving intermediaries. Products such as fashion merchandise, products whose appeal depends on freshness, and complicated, high-tech goods suggest short channels of distribution. The marketer must also consider the channels competitors use. If competitors use trained internal sales forces to move their products, the marketer may be forced to do the same.

LEVELS OF DISTRIBUTION

Marketing managers often speak of *market coverage.* By this they mean the extent of distribution they seek for their products. Should the product be available nearly everywhere or only on a limited basis? Three levels of distribution determine how many collaborators the company will deal with.

INTENSIVE DISTRIBUTION

Intensive distribution
Making a product available in virtually every appropriate outlet.

As the term suggests, **intensive distribution** calls for making a product available in virtually every appropriate outlet. Candy bars, chewing gum, and soft drinks are examples of such products. They are sold in almost every kind of store as well as in vending machines. This is, of course, because they are convenience products that consumers replace frequently and will buy in the most convenient location. If one brand is not easily available, customers often buy another brand. Among organizational products, fan belts, paper clips, and office supplies are intensively distributed.

SELECTIVE DISTRIBUTION

Selective distribution
Placing the product in a relatively limited number of outlets.

Some marketers can count on their customers to spend a certain amount of effort seeking out preferred brands. When this is the case, **selective distribution**—placing the product in a relatively limited number of outlets—is appropriate. Shoes are a prime example among consumer products. Buyers who prefer Nike's Air Jordan shoes will exert some effort to locate that brand. Therefore, the maker can distribute the shoes selectively; they need not be available "everywhere." Some organizational products also are selectively distributed. Hewlett-Packard laser printers and professional-quality tools and building supplies are distributed in this fashion.

EXCLUSIVE DISTRIBUTION

Exclusive distribution
Placing the product in only a small number of outlets.

At the other end of the scale from intensive distribution is **exclusive distribution**—placing the product in only a small number of outlets. A medium-size city may have more than 1,000 sellers of Snickers bars, perhaps a dozen outlets for Nike Air Jordans, but only one or two Buick dealers and probably one BMW, Mercedes, or Volvo dealer. Even when there are two Buick dealers, the distribution is still exclusive in that the dealerships will almost certainly be located far apart from each other, reflecting the manufacturer's intent to assign "territories" to its dealers. The medium-size city will have *no* Rolls Royce dealers, since that company's concept of exclusive distribution is to create dealerships whose territories may include several states.

The categories of intensive, selective, and exclusive distribution are useful because they correspond quite well to consumer behaviors and buying patterns, to the various product categories discussed in Chapter 13, and to the desires of channel of distribution members. The investment in an auto dealership is so large that no one would operate one unless the manufacturer offered the dealer some exclusive rights to market the product. Adding a line of spark plugs at an auto supply store involves so little extra effort that the retailer would be unlikely to demand city- or statewide exclusive rights to the product. In general, the nature of the

Exhibit 15.4 **CHOICE OF DISTRIBUTION METHOD**

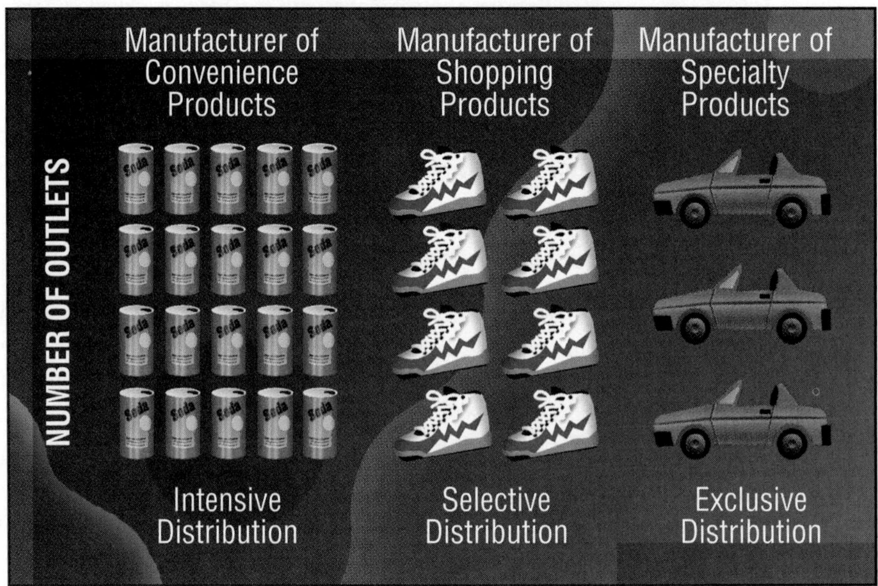

product, whether a convenience, shopping, or specialty product, influences the choice of distribution coverage (see Exhibit 15.4).

WHOLESALING

Although wholesaling activities go unnoticed by consumers, they are basic to the operation of many channels of distribution. As Exhibit 15.1 on page 348 shows, a wholesaler dealing in consumer products serves as an intermediary between manufacturer and retailer to facilitate the transfer of the products themselves or the exchange of title to those products. A wholesaler of organizational products sells to manufacturers or institutions that use the product for ultimate resale, perhaps in another product form.

Approximately 460,000 wholesaling businesses exist in the United States, with sales measured in trillions of dollars.[2] Such a vast sector of the economy includes many different types of operations. In this section, we will look at the operations of the major types of wholesalers.

Merchant wholesaler
An independently owned enterprise that takes title to the products it distributes.

Full-function or **full-service wholesaler**
An independent wholesaler that offers customers a full array of services, including delivery, warehousing, credit terms, merchandising advice, and other assistance.

INDEPENDENT MERCHANT WHOLESALERS

Merchant wholesalers are independently owned enterprises that take title to the goods they distribute. The majority of wholesalers are independent businesses. They represent about 80 percent of all wholesaling *enterprises* in the United States and account for about 50 percent of total U.S. wholesale *trade* (sales volume). Wholesalers are also extremely important in international marketing.

Independent wholesalers generally fall into two major groups. The first includes those that offer their customers a full array of services, including delivery, warehousing, credit terms, merchandising advice, and other assistance. These are called **full-function** or **full-service wholesalers.**

Limited-function wholesaler
An independent wholesaler that does not offer a full range of services but compensates by dropping its prices.

The second group is made up of businesses that do not offer a full range of services but compensate by dropping their prices. These are called **limited-function wholesalers**. A perfect example is the *cash-and-carry* wholesaler, which, as the term implies, requires that buyers come to the wholesaler's place of business, pick up the goods they want, and pay cash on the spot. The cash-and-carry wholesaler thus eliminates delivery and credit expenses, while the buyers save on merchandise cost.

The *drop shipper* is a wholesaler that merely handles the paperwork involved in the transaction and arranges to have products shipped from the producer directly to the retailer or other buyer. Drop shipping is common for bulky products such as coal and building materials.

MANUFACTURER-OWNED WHOLESALERS

Manufacturer-owned wholesaler
A manufacturer that does its own wholesaling.

Manufacturer-owned wholesalers—manufacturers that do their own wholesaling—make up the second most important group of wholesalers and account for roughly 40 percent of that trade. These "merchant" wholesaling organizations are most likely to be operated by producers of complex technical products or perishable goods or by those in industries where competition is intense. Independent wholesalers may simply not be large or aggressive enough to do the job.

Manufacturer-owned wholesalers operate two types of facilities. The *sales branch* holds inventory and fills orders from that inventory. The *sales office* serves as a headquarters for the sales force and does not hold inventories. Orders are filled from other points.

AGENTS AND BROKERS

As we saw earlier, agents and brokers are intermediaries that help bring buyer and seller together but do not take title to the products they sell. Some agents/brokers, such as art auctioneers, may take *possession* of merchandise. The key point is that they do not take *title*.

Manufacturer's agent
An independent business that calls on customers in a specific geographic territory and serves as its client's sales force in that area.

The **manufacturer's agent** is an independent business that calls on customers in a specific geographic territory and serves as its clients' sales force in that area. In effect, it is a "sales force for hire." Manufacturers' agents may represent several producers and receive a commission for their work. Manufacturers use these agents when they lack the expertise or resources to develop their own marketing programs, when they make too few products to justify maintaining a full marketing department, or where markets for their products are too "thin" to support a company-operated sales effort.

Manufacturers' agents are particularly important in the marketing of organizational products. We are all familiar with stockbrokers and real estate brokers. Scrap metal, coffee bean, lumber, and even radio station brokers also exist. Their great attraction is that even though they charge a fee or commission to bring buyer and seller together, the seller and the buyer need not use or pay them until they have actually completed the sale. Thus, buyers and sellers use brokers when they do not want to incur the expense of maintaining an on-going sales effort.

As you study business more closely, you will see that there are many kinds of wholesalers, each one of which has developed to meet particular market needs.

RETAILING

We now turn to retailing and a discussion of retail management strategies.

THE WHEEL OF RETAILING

Wheel of retailing
A theory explaining historical patterns of retail evolution.

Retailing has changed as the American consumer and American business have changed. The **wheel of retailing** is a theory explaining historical patterns of retail evolution. The history of retailing tells us that new retailer institutions enter the competitive environment as low-price

Exhibit 15.5 **THE WHEEL OF RETAILING**

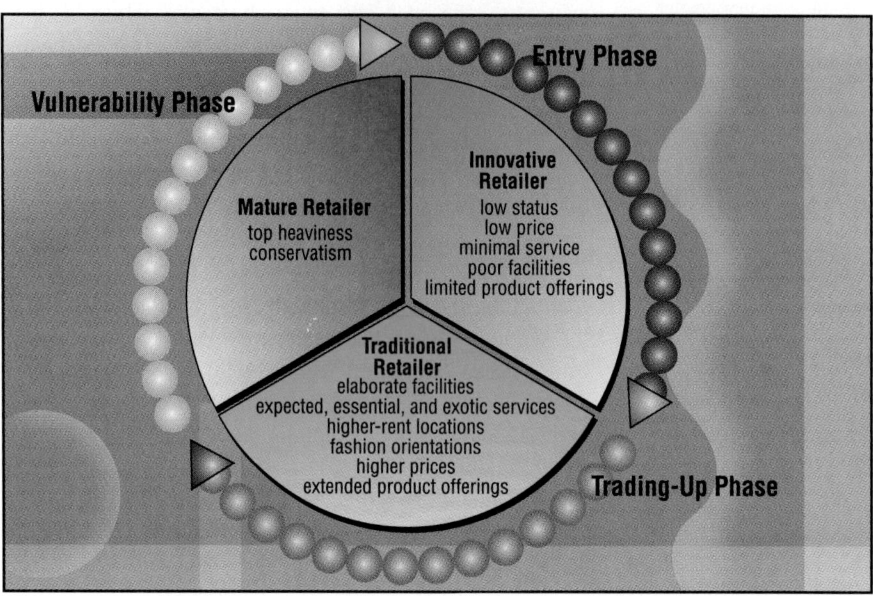

retailers. Exhibit 15.5 shows that during the entry phase, innovative retailers are low-status, low-price, and low-profit-margin operators that offer minimal services. Retail store interiors are designed for storage of goods rather than shopping comforts. As time passes, retailers move toward higher prices, higher profit margins, and higher status. Retailers add services, improve facilities, and increase costs. Charles Schwab, a discount stockbroker that does not offer all the financial services of traditional brokers, reflects the wheel of retailing.

FOCUS ON COMPANY

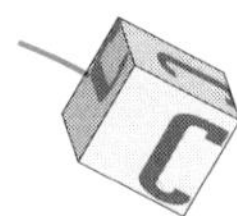

Old Capital Craft Company

Kay Kane knew immediately what went wrong when a customer brought a 96-cent teddy bear into her store. Kane's Old Capital Craft Company had been doing a brisk retail business selling the same "plain little naked" teddy bears for $1.79 each to craft hobbyists who dressed them up. At that moment, Kane knew what impact the new Wal-Mart was going to have on her business. The price at which she was buying the teddy bear from her wholesaler was higher than Wal-Mart's retail price.

Realizing that Wal-Mart could undersell her on many items, Kane sharpened her marketing skills and altered her retailing strategy. She decided she was not going to pack up her beads and bows and quit the way so many other retailers do when faced with Wal-Mart's retailing strength. She realized that the only way to survive was to provide outstanding customer service and specialize by providing a higher-quality assortment than the discounter's merchandise. She told her customers, "If you can get those teddy bears for 96 cents, then you get them from Wal-Mart. Then you come back here and buy your lace and your feathers to decorate them."

Kane listens carefully to her customers, tailors her offering to their needs, and stocks products in the quantities customers want. Customers can buy one feather or a thousand.

Exhibit 15.6 **CLASSIFYING IN-STORE RETAILERS BY PROMINENT STRATEGY**

Retailer Classification	Description
Specialty	Narrow variety, deep selection within a product category, traditional prices (no discount), personalized service, large bulk of all retailing operations (e.g., carpet store)
Department store	Generally chain operations, wide variety, full range of services
Supermarket	Wide variety of food and nonfood products, large, departmentalized operation featuring self-service aisles, centralized checkouts, discount strategy
Convenience store	Little variety, shallow selection featuring fast, courteous service, high prices
General discount merchandiser	Wide variety, shallow selection of high-turnover products, low prices, few customer services
Catalog showroom	Variation of general discount merchandiser using a catalog to promote items, low prices, wide variety, shallow selection
Warehouse club	Mass merchandiser that requires membership for shopping privileges. Variation of discount merchandiser using showroom as storage space
Off-price retailer	Uses discount merchandiser operation for a limited line of nationally known brand names, sometimes sells "seconds"

Customer service is a top priority. Customers get everything from a two-day turnaround on special orders to expert advice on craft projects. At Old Capital Craft Company, the prices may be higher but customers get benefits Wal-Mart doesn't offer.

TYPES OF RETAILERS

It is possible to classify retailers by type of ownership. Retailers may be independently owned or be chain stores owned by large corporations. This distinction is important. However, in this chapter we will focus on classifying the specific kinds of retailers based on their most prominent retail strategies.

A fundamental strategic decision involves choosing whether the retailer markets its goods and services with an *in-store retailing strategy* or a *nonstore retailing strategy.* This is such an important basis for classifying retailers that we will break our discussion of prominent retail strategies into these two major groups.

IN-STORE RETAILING

Many fundamental strategies differentiate in-store retailers. The variety of products they sell, their price levels relative to competitors, the degree of self-service, location, and other variables can be used to categorize retailers by long-range strategy. Each category has advantages and disadvantages, and each fits particular markets and situations.

Exhibit 15.6 classifies retailers based on price and services, width of merchandise assortment, and depth of product lines.

Price and Services. Many retailers, such as Kmart, stress a *discount strategy,* which usually means a large, self-service retail establishment that sells a variety of high-turnover products at low prices. Often retail pricing strategies are related to the customer service policy. A good part of a retailer's ability to hold prices down stems from the practice of offering few services. Other than the costs of the products they sell, most retailers find that personnel costs are their largest financial outlay. Thus, by eliminating most of the sales employees and services such as gift wrapping, discounters are able to reduce their prices. Other retailers, such as Tiffany

Direct marketers realize that two-income families have less time to shop in stores. Because of changes in the American workplace, nonstore retailing is becoming increasingly more important.

& Company, stress high or *prestige* prices. Well-informed sales personnel sell their merchandise in elegant surroundings.

Width of Merchandise Assortment. *Specialty stores* carry only one or a limited line of products, such as books. *Department stores* carry wider assortments. Some stores engage in *scrambled merchandising,* meaning that the product lines sold do not fit a traditional pattern. Sam's Wholesale Clubs sell almost everything ranging from fresh grapefruit to office furniture.

Depth of Product Line. The variety of items is another factor useful in classifying retailers. For example, Sportmart is very different from the typical family-owned sporting goods store. The Olive Garden restaurant has many more items on its menu than most Italian restaurants do. Because they have a limited line, most specialty stores have a deep merchandise selection. Mass merchandisers like Kmart generally have a limited selection within a product category.

NONSTORE RETAILING

Sears, Roebuck and Company began in the mail-order business and moved on to other types of marketing. Today the general mail-order catalog is no longer part of Sears's total business. Years ago, however, Sears' *Wishbook* created a new type of retailing that is extremely important to modern marketing. Many companies, such as Banana Republic and The Disney Store, combine both mail-order and in-store retailing. Others, like Sundance, are committed exclusively to mail-order retailing. This is just one of the many types of nonstore retailing (see Exhibit 15.7).

Exhibit 15.7 **CLASSIFYING NONSTORE RETAILERS BY PROMINENT STRATEGY**

Retailer Classification	Description
Mail-order/direct-response retailer	Low operating costs, emphasis on convenience, uses computerized lists
Vending machine	High-turnover products, low priced
Door-to-door retailer	High labor cost, image problems, declining in United States
Television home shopping	High capital costs for technology, products priced high

STREET SMART

Stop Shoplifting

Shoplifting causes a major expense to retailers. Alert store employees who know what to look for can often spot a shoplifter.

Here are various behavior traits and other clues that law-enforcement officials say can be tip-offs to shoplifting:

- *Nervous behavior.* Shoplifters are constantly on guard. They glance about nervously and look over their shoulders. Unlike most people, they are very aware of who may be watching them. Their attention is focused away from themselves rather than on merchandise immediately at hand.
- *Avoiding others.* Shoplifters tend to shun store personnel and other shoppers. Privacy means less scrutiny. They tend to move in low-traffic areas and prefer to "shop" when few other people are in the store.
- *Taking offense.* Since shoplifters fear scrutiny, they are sensitive to the attention of sales personnel. When you try to help them, they may become irritated or act rudely. They may even display annoyance if you stand in the same aisle. Legitimate shoppers, on the other hand, don't object to attentive service.
- *Aimlessness.* Shoplifters typically seem indecisive. Lacking a real shopping list, they often wander through the store, lingering here and there, stopping only to handle merchandise. They fold and drop things and may seem clumsy and overly interested in the items they handle. They are looking for the right time to conceal the merchandise.
- *Bulky baggage.* To help them steal from you, shoplifters often use items such as large purses, umbrellas, newspapers, and packages. The packages are known as "boosters boxes," which may even be gift-wrapped. Other tricks include the use of fake casts and slings, wheelchairs, and baby strollers.
- *Concealment techniques.* A common shoplifting tactic is to wear loose fitting or oversized apparel, which may seem out of place or out of season. Baggy clothing helps shoplifters conceal stolen clothing underneath their own. Female shoplifters have been known to leave a store with merchandise tucked under their skirts. Hairdos, bras, girdles, and devices that make a woman look pregnant are also used to hide loot.
- *Ploys.* Shoplifters sometimes work in teams. Together they fabricate distractions and diversions. They may fake an argument with store personnel or among themselves. One may monopolize an employee's time with pointless questions. Another may topple a display stand or stage a phony medical emergency.
- *Cash register flimflams.* Pay attention to price tags. Shoplifters sometimes switch them from low-cost to high-cost items. Also, you should require proof of purchase on returned items. Shoplifters may try to get a refund on an item lifted from your store.

Store employees should know what to do when they spot someone suspected of shoplifting. Here are guidelines:

- Simply offering the customer assistance may be enough to scare a would-be shoplifter away.
- If a customer who you are certain has lifted an item appears at a cash register to pay for other items, ask politely if he or she has forgotten to pay for the merchandise in question.
- Call the police immediately when you are sure that someone is shoplifting. Although attempting to detain a suspected shoplifter is lawful in most states it can be dangerous.

Authorities recommend that you check with your local and state law-enforcement agencies to determine what the laws in your area say about challenging or apprehending suspected shoplifters.

Though they can be most clever, shoplifters often give themselves away. If retailers are street smart they know what to look for.

Lillian Li Xu-Xuan bicycles through Guangzhoue, China's congested streets, ringing a handlebar bell to avoid collisions. Her wire basket doesn't hold squawking chickens or flapping fish like those of the other bikes she passes. Ms. Li's basket is full of Avon cosmetics, and she's hurrying to keep an appointment. Avon Products Inc. sample kit in hand, identification badge pinned on her shirt, lipstick carefully applied, Ms. Li knocks on the door and flashes a smile. "I'm from Avon Products and I'm here to demonstrate our line of cosmetics," she says in Cantonese. Ms. Li is one of 20,000 Chinese Avon ladies who make more than $8 million a year for Avon in China. Door-to-door selling is declining in the United States, but it is growing elsewhere in the world.[3]

Among the newer developments in nonstore retailing is the prospect of shopping at home by interacting with retailers via a personal computer. This is known as *computer interactive retailing.* For example, Prodigy, a prominent interactive personal service, allows owners of personal computers to book airline flights and hotel reservations, buy and sell stocks, and shop for thousands of items ranging from encyclopedias to china, crystal, and silver.

The coin-operated vending machine is an old retailing tool that has become increasingly sophisticated in recent years. Computer-based technological innovations, as evidenced by the new machines that personalize greeting cards, have permitted these machines to reach new markets and become more effective marketing tools.

RETAIL MANAGEMENT STRATEGIES

Like all marketers, retailers create marketing strategies. They analyze market segments, select target markets, and determine the competitive position they wish to occupy.

Also like all marketers, retailers must develop a marketing mix. The concept of the marketing mix is essentially the same in all applications of marketing. We have already discussed price and discount strategies as part of the retailer's marketing mix. Exhibit 15.8 shows some of the decision elements retail marketers consider in developing a retail marketing mix.

We cannot discuss all aspects of the retail marketing environment in this chapter. In the following sections, we will address four areas of special importance to retailers: merchandise assortment, location, atmosphere, and customer service.

Exhibit 15.8 **RETAILERS HAVE MARKETING MIXES TOO**

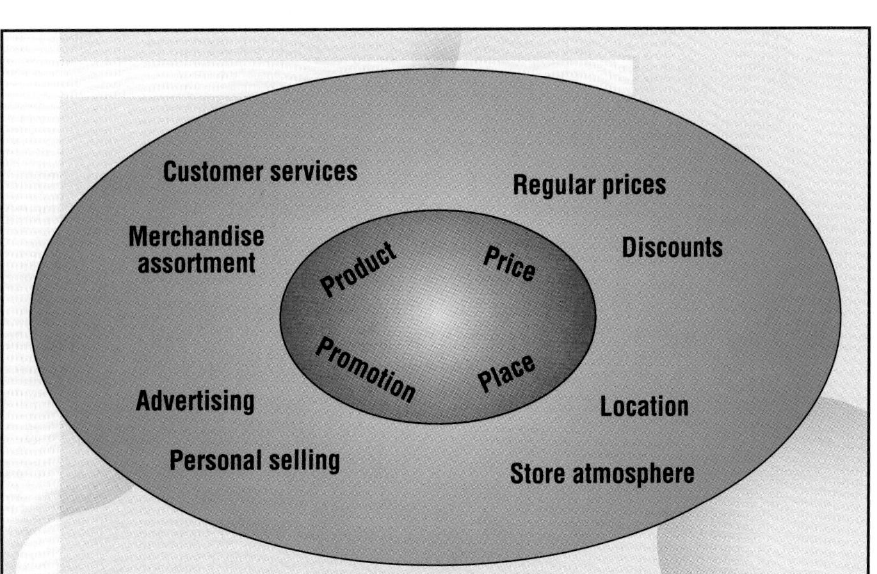

MERCHANDISE ASSORTMENT

From the individual customer's perspective, a major advantage of one retailer over a competitor is merchandise *assortment.* Other things are important, but no shopper will patronize a store without believing there is some chance that he or she will find the merchandise sought. How does a retail marketer decide what merchandise assortment to carry? The retailer must carefully consider the target market's needs and wants and match the merchandise selection to those needs and wants. This truth is fundamental to effective retail marketing. Yet retailers frequently make "buying mistakes" and absorb those costs through markdowns or other means. Buying errors cannot be totally avoided, but careful planning can minimize their occurrence.

LOCATION

An old adage says that the three most important factors in successful retailing are *location, location, and location.* But this is not always necessarily the case. An out-of-the-way location can be compensated for by other means, especially huge selections and low prices. Nonetheless, the adage makes a point. Retailers are justifiably concerned about locating in the right part of the right town. They must monitor changes that may affect the suitability of an existing location or make another site more attractive.

The right location depends on the type of business and the target customer, not on any formula or rule of thumb. As with merchandise assortment questions, the answer lies in careful marketing planning. Experience dictates certain guidelines, however. For example, Toys "R" Us requires that its outlets be placed in metropolitan areas with populations of at least 150,000 people, of which a specified percentage must be children. Ideally, each store is located in an unattached or *freestanding* building near a major mall. Today Toys "R" Us searches for good locations around the world.

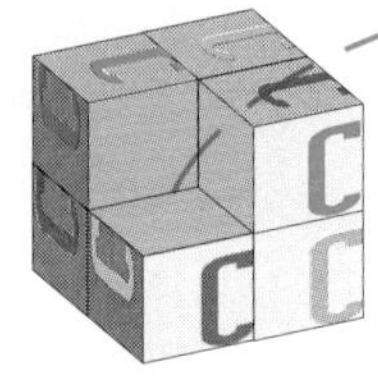

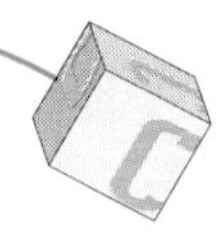

FOCUS ON COMPETITORS

JCPenney

As Terry S. Prindiville, a JCPenney executive, gazed at the women jammed into a bustling shop in Shanghai, he saw opportunity. All this tumult, he thought, to buy lingerie at higher prices and lower quality than his company could offer. Penney isn't selling goods in China yet, but Prindiville and his staff are masterminding an ambitious expansion to transform stodgy old JCPenney into a major international retailer.

Already Penney stores are under construction in Mexico. The company will soon add nearly 1 million square feet of retail space in Japan by offering its private-label apparel in 300 department stores. It has also been scouting sites in Chile.

Penney isn't alone in looking beyond the overbuilt U.S. market. The North American Free Trade Agreement is spurring many U.S. retailers, including giant Wal-Mart Stores, Inc., to enter Canada and Mexico. Led by specialty retailers such as Toys "R" Us, even traditionally cautious department store retailers like Nordstrom, Dillard, Saks Fifth Avenue, and Bloomingdale's are investigating expansion overseas. But few have gone after foreign markets in as many ways as Penney has.

Penney's recent foreign thrust began in 1990, when three managers took an eye-opening tour of seven European countries. They concluded that Penney was leagues ahead in marketing sophistication, in how to display products, in how to direct customer traffic, in how to group products—in short, in how "to develop an environment that invites the customer to shop."

Senior managers decided Penney would link up with local partners who were familiar with consumers' tastes and preferences. It would tailor its retailing strategy to each country, while banking on what it considered its strong suits: private labels and merchandise presentation. So Penney insisted that Liwa Trading, a licensee that opened its first Penney Collection store in Dubai in 1992 and plans to open 10 more stores in the Mideast by 1998, send people to Penney's headquarters in Dallas to learn Penney's merchandising, training, and accounting methods.

Several times a year, Penney inspects foreign stores to ensure that their displays stay within its guidelines. The licensees, Prindiville says, must "agree to replicate the way the merchandise is presented in the U.S." Penney's initial list of 30 promising countries was trimmed to 20 after executives analyzed factors such as political and economic stability, economic growth, and demographics.

Eventually the company settled on four fundamental strategies. In "understored" countries where real estate was affordable, laws allowed foreign ownership, and labor and construction regulations wouldn't hinder expansion, Penney would open and operate stores itself. In markets that were more saturated or had less favorable regulations, Penney would license local retailers to operate JCPenney Collection stores, which sell its branded apparel and other soft goods. In still tougher markets such as Singapore and Japan, where high property costs and regulations make it almost impossible to build large stores, Penney would license other retailers to operate in-store shops selling specific branded lines, such as the Hunt Club line. Finally, in markets with strong consumer demand but enormous barriers, Penney would sell through catalogs, typically distributing goods through a third party that would take orders, buy the goods from Penney in the United States, and ship them abroad.

Penney's efforts abroad are showing promising results. One of the most positive factors is the strong appeal of its private brands.

ATMOSPHERICS

Atmospherics
Physical characteristics of the store environment that contribute to the shopper's mental impression of what the store is.

Retail strategy includes managing every aspect of the store property and its physical characteristics to create an atmosphere that invites buying. **Atmospherics** are physical characteristics of the store environment, such as the store's exterior, interior appearance, store layout, and displays, that contribute to the shopper's mental impression of what the store is. Store atmosphere may influence the store's image, increase traffic, influence the amount of time shoppers spend in the store, and/or encourage shoppers to make impulse purchases.

Retailers may plan atmospheres that appeal to any of the shopper's five senses: sight, hearing, smell, touch, and taste. The Hard Rock Cafe is loud, crowded, and "happening." The Ralph Lauren store on Fifth Avenue in New York City has colors, lighting, decorations, and mahogany furniture designed to communicate that the environment is quiet, plush, and "upper class and quite British."

The exterior atmospherics may strongly influence a new customer's willingness to enter the store. The building's architecture, parking facilities, the storefront, and other aspects of the exterior appearance may either encourage or discourage patronage by communicating a certain message to potential shoppers. The architectural theme of a Taco Bell makes an impression on the consumer and communicates a message about the restaurant's product line.

Retailers plan the interior design and layout to influence the movement and mood of customers. A primary concern of many retailers is to keep "happy" consumers shopping in the store for as long as possible. Managers typically set objectives, such as avoiding a crowded appearance, and then design lighting, music, colors, fixtures, displays, and layouts to meet those objectives.

Store image
Reflects customers' mental impression of the store's personality.

Creating a store image is a primary aspect of retail atmosphere. The **store image** reflects consumers' mental impression of the store's personality. Do consumers see the store as friendly or reserved, traditional or contemporary, prestigious or economical? How do they feel about the store? Is it a place for them or a place where they would not like to be seen? Store personnel, merchandise, the store's immediate surroundings, its external and internal appearance, its prices, its customer services, and other aspects of the retailer's marketing mix all contribute to store image. In a sense, store image includes everything consumers *see* and *feel* about the store.

CUSTOMER SERVICE

The customer services a retailer provides may be as important—and sometimes more important—than the merchandise offered for sale. The courteous personal service and information provided by a salesperson may make the difference between success and failure in a retail setting. Services such as maintaining convenient store hours, providing parking facilities, and offering product information are essential to the operation of many retail establishments. Other services, such as delivery, alterations, repair, credit, return privileges, and gift wrapping, supplement the retailer's merchandise offerings. For some retailers, such as Domino's Pizza and Ho Lee Chow Chinese Food, the service offering—home delivery—is the primary reason for selecting one retailer over another.

Development of the retailer's marketing mix requires decisions about the *service level,* or the extent of "extra" services consumers will receive. Service level strategies are often interrelated with pricing strategies. An organization that desires to be competitive in price will typically match competitors' service levels. Retailers that emphasize nonprice competition may be full-service organizations that provide extra services to create a competitive advantage. Consumers' expected level of service is also a major determinant of service level. Many retailers regularly survey consumers to determine the amount and quality of services that are expected.

A Dunkin' Donuts franchise in Maiden, Massachusetts, installed a drive-up window at the shop. In less than five months, that window accounted for 30 percent of the store's business. Drive-in convenience is proving to be such a great sales stimulant that when it builds new Dunkin' Donuts franchises, the parent company plans to include drive-up and walk-up windows wherever the physical layout permits it.

In the early morning, most of the business at Dunkin' Donuts shops is at the drive-up windows. Customers on their way to work don't have time to park and go inside for their morning coffee and doughnuts. They prefer to wheel up to a window.

Like morning commuters, many other consumers are showing they prefer service while seated in their cars. And entrepreneurs of small and large businesses alike are finding that drive-up windows, by increasing convenience for customers, can increase their profits.[4]

Direct exporting
Dealing directly with overseas customers in their home countries without using independent wholesalers or retailers.

INTERNATIONAL DISTRIBUTION

Indirect exporting
Exporting using an intermediary, often located in another country, that performs the distribution function.

Export management companies
An intermediary that specializes in buying from sellers in one country and marketing the products in other countries, typically takes title to the goods, and reduces the risk for a company that lacks a great deal of exporting experience.

In today's era of global competition, obtaining distribution around the world may be a major business concern. There are many approaches to international distribution.

In the case of **direct exporting**, a business deals directly with overseas customers in their home countries without using independent wholesalers or retailers. The term *buyer for export* describes any customer that buys products for use in other markets. Buyers for export buy directly from a business in another country. Domestic-based manufacturers often serve such customers in essentially the same ways as other domestic customers. This direct channel of distribution is used by manufacturers of many industrial products. Direct exporting may be used when a firm wants greater control over foreign sales of its product.

Indirect exporting involves using an intermediary, often located in another country, to perform the distribution function. **Export management companies** are intermediaries that specialize in buying from sellers in one country and marketing the products in other countries. Export management companies, which typically take title to the goods, reduce the risk for a company that lacks a great deal of exporting experience. As with other wholesalers, the export management company performs many distribution functions for the seller. In most cases, however, selling and taking responsibility for foreign credit are their primary functions.

Finally, various types of *export agents* may represent manufacturers in overseas selling activities. They do not take title to goods, but they are efficient because they know the buyers in foreign markets.

A U.S. company with little international marketing experience may elect to periodically sell a portion of its inventory to some U.S.-based export management company that buys in the United States and distributes in other countries. In the past, many of these producers made no systematic effort to enter the international marketplace, which they viewed as a place to get rid of products. However, in today's globally competitive environment, effective marketers choose to export on a more continuous basis. They must plan regular distribution channels for international markets in the same way they plan for domestic distribution.

VERTICAL MARKETING SYSTEMS (VMSs)

Ideally, each channel member realizes that it is in the interest of all members for the channel to operate smoothly and cooperates with other channel members to accomplish this goal. The reality, of course, may not match the ideal. Channel members are often independent businesses, each with profit goals and ongoing concerns for its own welfare. When channel members pay too much attention to their own interests, *channel conflict*—and bad marketing—can result.

A common example is an athletic shoe retailer that wants to stock only the most popular styles of basketball shoes. The wholesaler attempts to force the retailer to stock all sizes. Channel conflict is the result. If the manufacturer seeks to "punish" the retailer by shipping only a few popular styles and many pairs of unpopular ones, the conflict worsens.

Something must be done to smooth over the conflict, but avoiding the problem would have been better. This would have been possible had one channel member been in a position to keep the others "in line." Realization of this fact has led to the development of *planned* distribution channels called **vertical marketing systems (VMSs)**. Three types of VMS are the administered, contractual, and corporate vertical marketing system.

Vertical marketing system (VMS)
A planned distribution channel designed to minimize conflict and increase efficiency among channel members.

ADMINISTERED VERTICAL MARKETING SYSTEMS

The **administered vertical marketing system** is a distribution system with a dominant member that is in a position to influence other channel members, thus keeping operations in order. Such a channel member, sometimes termed the *channel captain,* may draw power from its sheer size and importance, as does Wal-Mart, or from the extreme popularity of its products, as do Sony and Anheuser-Busch. In certain circumstances, especially where distribution rather than brand name is important, wholesalers may be channel captains. McKesson Corporation, a drug wholesaler, is one such example. McKesson serves about 50 percent of independent drugstores, 27 percent of chain drugstores, and 20 percent of hospitals in the United States.[5]

Administered vertical marketing system
A distribution system with a dominant member that is in a position to influence other channel members, thus keeping operations in order.

CONTRACTUAL VERTICAL MARKETING SYSTEMS

In a **contractual vertical marketing system**, channel members are linked by written contractual agreements. These agreements may be controlled by manufacturers such as Ford or Toyota, by service providers like Wendy's, or by wholesalers such as IGA Food Stores. Retailers too can control contractual vertical marketing systems. The True Value hardware stores chain is controlled by its retailer members.

Contractual vertical marketing system
A VMS in which channel members are linked by written contractual agreements.

CORPORATE VERTICAL MARKETING SYSTEMS

A **corporate vertical marketing system** is made up of organizations owned outright by one member of the VMS. For example, Sherwin-Williams Company completely controls the distribution of its paint by owning the entire distribution system.

Corporate vertical marketing system
A VMS made up of organizations owned outright by one member.

SUMMARY

1. ***Discuss the collaborative nature of channels of distribution.***
A channel of distribution is the complete chain of marketing organizations that collaborate to bring a product from the producer to the ultimate consumer. Its purpose is to transfer ownership and/or possession of the product. Most channels include intermediaries or middlemen who buy and resell products and help in other ways to get products into the hands of end users. Intermediaries fall into two major classifications. Wholesalers buy products from producers and resell those products to retailers, other wholesalers, and industrial users. Some wholesalers work in a similar manner but do not actually buy the products handled. These intermediaries are referred to as agents or brokers. Merchant wholesalers take title to the products they handle. Agent wholesalers never own the products they sell. Retailers sell to consumers—the people who will actually use the products. Excluded from the channel of distribution are numerous facilitators, collaborators that perform specific facilitating activities for manufacturers, wholesalers, or retailers. Physical distribution activities include processing orders, managing inventory, transporting products, and storing and warehousing products.

2. ***Describe the major types of channels of distribution.***
The major types of channels of distribution are consumer product channels and organizational product channels. The direct-to-consumer channel is used by some producers that sell directly to retail customers. It is also used in most services marketing. Other consumer product channels involve intermediaries such as wholesalers, retailers, and/or agents. Organizational product channels range from direct to organizational-user channels to channels that involve intermediaries like agents or industrial distributors.

3. ***Explain the distribution strategies used for market coverage.***
Market coverage means the extent of distribution that companies seek for their products. Three levels of distribution determine how many collaborators the company will deal with. Intensive distribution calls for a product to be available in virtually every appropriate outlet. Many convenience products are intensively distributed. Selective distribution involves placing the product in a relatively limited number of outlets and is used when the company can count on its customers to spend a certain amount of effort seeking out preferred brands. Exclusive distribution means placing the product in only a small number of outlets. The categories of intensive, selective, and exclusive distribution are useful because they correspond quite well to consumer behaviors and buying patterns, to the various product classifications, and to the desires of channel of distribution members.

4. ***Describe the different kinds of wholesalers.***
A wholesaler dealing in consumer products serves as an intermediary between manufacturer and retailer to facilitate the transfer of the products themselves or the exchange of title to those products. A wholesaler of organizational products sells to manufacturers or institutions that use the product for ultimate resale, perhaps in another product form. Merchant wholesalers are independently owned enterprises that take title to the goods they distribute. The majority of wholesalers are independent businesses. Independent wholesalers generally fall into two major groups. Full-function or full-service wholesalers offer their customers a full array of services, including delivery, warehousing, credit terms, merchandising advice, and other assistance. Limited function wholesalers do not offer a full range of services but compensate customers by dropping their prices. They include cash-and-carry wholesalers and drop shippers. Manufacturer-owned wholesalers—manufacturers that do their own wholesaling—are the second most important group of wholesalers. These "merchant" wholesaling organizations are most likely to be operated by producers of complex technical products or perishable goods or by those in industries where competition is intense. Manufacturer-owned wholesalers include sales branches and sales offices. Agents and brokers help bring buyer and seller together but do not take title to the products they sell. The manufacturers' agent is an independent business that calls on customers in a specific geographic territory and serves as its clients' sales force in that area. Manufacturers' agents may

represent several producers and receive a commission for their work. Manufacturers' agents are particularly important in the marketing of organizational products.

5. ***Describe the various kinds of retailers.***
   Specific kinds of retailers can be classified based on their most prominent retail strategies. The strategic decision determines whether the retailer markets its products and services with an in-store retailing strategy or a nonstore retailing strategy. Many fundamental strategies differentiate in-store retailers, including the variety of products they sell, their price levels relative to competitors, the degree of self-service, location, and other variables. Each category has advantages and disadvantages, and each fits particular markets and situations. Based on price and services, a store can follow a discount strategy, which usually means a large, self-service retail establishment that sells a variety of high-turnover products at low prices. Often retail pricing strategies are related to the customer service policy. Other retailers stress high or prestige prices. Well-informed sales personnel sell their merchandise in elegant surroundings. On the basis of width of merchandise assortment, retailers can be specialty stores that carry only one or a limited line of products. Department stores carry wider assortments. Some stores engage in scrambled merchandising, meaning that the product lines sold do not fit a traditional pattern. Other retailers differentiate themselves on the basis of depth of product line, or variety of items. Nonstore retailing may take the form of either mail-order retailing or door-to-door retailing. Among the newer developments in nonstore retailing is computer interactive retailing, shopping at home by interacting with retailers via a personal computer. Computer-based technological innovations are allowing vending machines to reach new markets.

6. ***Discuss several retail management strategies.***
   Like all marketers, retailers create marketing strategies. They also must develop a marketing mix. Four areas of special importance to retailers are merchandise assortment, location, atmosphere, and customer service. From the individual customer's perspective, a major advantage of one retailer over a competitor is merchandise assortment. The retailer must carefully consider the target market's needs and wants and match the merchandise selection to them. A good location is also crucial. The right location depends on the type of business and the target customer. As with merchandise assortment questions, the answer lies in careful marketing planning. Retail strategy includes managing every aspect of the store property and its physical characteristics to create an atmosphere that invites buying. Atmospherics are physical characteristics of the store environment, such as the store's exterior, interior appearance, store layout, and displays, that contribute to the shopper's mental impression of what the store is. Store atmosphere may influence the store's image, increase traffic, influence the amount of time shoppers spend in the store, and/or encourage shoppers to make impulse purchases. Finally, the customer services a retailer provides may be as important—and sometimes more important—than the merchandise offered for sale. The courteous personal service and information provided by a salesperson may make the difference between success and failure in a retail setting.

7. ***Understand that there are many approaches to international distribution.***
   When a marketer uses direct exporting, the business deals directly with overseas customers in the customers' home countries without using independent wholesalers or retailers. Indirect exporting involves using an intermediary, often located in a foreign country, to perform the distribution function. Export management companies are intermediaries that specialize in buying from sellers in one country and marketing the products in other countries. Export management companies, which typically take title to the goods, reduce the risk for a company without a great deal of exporting experience. There are various types of export agents that do not take title to goods, but represent the manufacturer in overseas selling activities.

KEY TERMS AND CONCEPTS

Channel of distribution (p. 348)
Intermediary (p. 349)
Wholesaler (p. 349)
Agent or broker (p. 349)
Retailer (p. 349)

Physical distribution (p. 349)
Direct marketing (p. 350)
Industrial distributor (p. 352)
Intensive distribution (p. 353)
Selective distribution (p. 353)
Exclusive distribution (p. 353)
Merchant wholesaler (p. 354)
Full-function or full-service wholesaler (p. 354)
Limited-function wholesaler (p. 355)
Manufacturer-owned wholesaler (p. 355)
Manufacturer's agent (p. 355)
Wheel of retailing (p. 355)
Atmospherics (p. 363)
Store image (p. 363)
Direct exporting (p. 364)
Indirect exporting (p. 364)
Export management company (p. 364)
Vertical marketing system (VMS) (p. 365)
Administered vertical marketing system (p. 365)
Contractual vertical marketing system (p. 365)
Corporate vertical marketing system (p. 365)

DISCUSSION QUESTIONS

Company

1. Assume your company manufactures the following products. What channel of distribution would you select for
   a. Potato chips?
   b. Computer chips?
   c. Commercial aircraft?
   d. Men's cologne?
2. What type of company might eliminate intermediaries?
3. Do service organizations have distribution strategies?

Customers

4. What benefits does distribution offer the consumer?
5. How do consumers' shopping behaviors influence the type of distribution channel?

Competitors

6. Think about a product like automobile engine oil. Do competing firms have similar channels of distribution? Explain.
7. How do retailers take competitor activity into account in their marketing strategies?

Collaborators

8. How important are collaboration and cooperation among different channel members to the efficient running of the channel?
9. What role do transportation companies play in distribution strategy?

In Question: Take a Stand

The original Spaghetti Warehouse, built in 1972 from an old warehouse on Dallas's depressed west side, was credited with helping to spark the area's comeback. The now trendy West End district attracts about 6 million visitors a year with its restaurants, bars, arcade, and upscale office space. In 1993, however, sales at the Dallas location, as at many of the company's downtown restaurants, were falling. The company blames urban woes, such as the Los Angeles riots, for tarnishing the downtown's image.

Some of the older Spaghetti Warehouse restaurants need armed guards in their parking lots. Spaghetti Warehouse executives say that in the wake of fears about urban crime, many people simply don't want to bring their families into the city. So, after two decades of doing business downtown, Spaghetti Warehouse is heading to the suburbs. The company, which made its mark braving urban America to transform old warehouses into family restaurants, decided to forgo the historic for suburban conformity. It is planning nine new restaurants in suburban strip centers, shopping malls, and other locations. The decision comes at a time when urban planners and city leaders still trumpet a renaissance of the nation's downtowns, urging the very kind of revitalization that Spaghetti Warehouse's presence has already triggered in a half-dozen areas.[6]

Does Spaghetti Warehouse have an obligation to communities with dying center-city areas? Should the company keep its restaurants downtown to help urban areas come back to life?

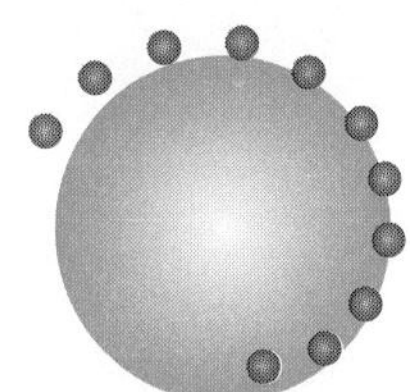

CASE 15.1
GOODYEAR TIRE AND RUBBER COMPANY[7]

For more than 60 years Goodyear tires could only be purchased on a new car or from its network of independent dealers.

In 1992 Goodyear Tire and Rubber Company decided the company needed wider distribution for its replacement market tires than its 1,000 company-owned stores and 2,500 independent dealers provided.[6] So the company began selling Goodyear tires through Sears, followed by Wal-Mart and several tire chains like Discount Tire. Many of Goodyear's smaller dealers were not happy. "I feel like they just stabbed me in the back," fumes Robert Wertz, owner of Goodyear dealer Wertz Tire & Auto Service in Flagstaff, Arizona. Wertz says last August he picked up the paper and saw an ad by Discount Tire that featured Goodyear Wrangler tires at $59.99, $17 less than Wertz paid for the same tires at wholesale. Another dealer, Fred Taylor of Glendale, Arizona, says a customer brought in an estimate from Discount Tire that quoted a price of $108 for a 16-inch Gatorback tire, $16 less than it cost Taylor. "They (the discount stores) are just using Goodyear as a bait and switch to sell their own private-label tires," Taylor says. In response to Goodyear, Wertz, Taylor, and other once loyal dealers are carrying competitors' tires and pushing the tires with the best markups. This is no small problem: The independent dealers still sell over 50% of Goodyear's replacement tires.

Top executives say Goodyear didn't have a choice. With competition getting tougher, the company needed the extra volume.

"We are doing more to support our dealers than any other manufacturer in the industry, and the dealers know that," says Goodyear's chief executive. "So we're not out there with some silly idea of taking business from dealers and giving it to Sears. But buying habits have changed. Fifty-one percent of the buyers are buying a tire within 48 hours of deciding they needed it." With tires more of an impulse item, marketing executives realized they needed broader distribution. People were no longer willing to seek out a specialty tire dealer when they wanted a replacement.

Questions

1. *Outline Goodyear's channel of distribution.*
2. *What type of distribution was Goodyear implementing before it began selling to Sears? What type of distribution strategy is Goodyear using now?*
3. *What marketing functions do Goodyear's retailers perform?*
4. *What are the pitfalls of Goodyear's distribution strategy? Will its strategy be successful?*

CHAPTER 16

PROMOTION

When you have studied this chapter, you will be able to:

1. Define *promotion,* explain its purposes, and identify several promotional objectives.
2. Describe the purposes and types of personal selling.
3. Identify the stages in the creative selling process.
4. Describe the major types of advertising.
5. Describe publicity and public relations.
6. Identify the various types of sales promotion.
7. Discuss several ethical issues involving promotions.

After almost being given up for dead, National Car Rental Systems is using a new advertising campaign to signal that it is healthy again. In the early 1990s, business was so bad for National that parent company General Motors considered liquidating it. But a change of management brought big improvements, and National is using promotion to tell consumers things have changed. The ads are part of a bid by National to zoom past Budget Rent-A-Car and take a solid hold on Number 3. The industry leaders are Hertz and Avis, Inc.

The advertising portrays National as offering "momentum" to business air travelers. The new ad campaign focuses on eliminating one of business travelers' leading concerns: delays at the car rental counter.

National's new television commercials show fast-moving business travel scenes set to Matthew Wilder's up-tempo song "Ain't Nothin' Gonna Break My Stride." The message is that National renters get through the airport quickly. At the end, a driver accelerates through a green traffic light to the punch line "Green means go"—a play on National's identifying color. A magazine ad in green ink says, "Only One Car Rental Company Makes All the Lights Green." Beneath this headline, a series of green traffic lights highlight selling points.

The new marketing strategy also focuses on personal selling. Management stopped grading reservations agents on seconds per call and started rewarding them for closing deals. National boosted employee morale by spending $95,000 on more comfortable chairs for agents. After paying for 25,000 hours of computer programming, National's management now has computerized car reservation and car management systems that "talk" to each other. And, according to National's executive vice-president for marketing and sales, "To deliver on our promises, our people have been empowered to deliver a no-hassle experience to the traveler." Both advertising and personal selling are part of an integrated promotional campaign designed to communicate the message customers want to hear: National renters will get through the airport quickly and with no hassles.[1]

You probably recognize television commercials and magazine advertisements, such as those for National Car Rental Systems, as examples of creative marketing and can appreciate the importance of personal selling to a marketing effort. This chapter explores the captivating world of promotion.

THE NATURE AND PURPOSES OF PROMOTION

The old saying "Build a better mousetrap and the world will beat a path to your door" contains a basic flaw: If the world doesn't know a better mousetrap exists, the consumers of the world will not know to which door to go. Having a great product and wonderful service is not enough. People must be aware of the company's brand and know its benefits. Thus, some form of promotion is necessary.

Promotion
Communication applied to business.

Promotion is communication applied to business. Marketers use promotion to exchange factual information and persuasive messages between buyers and sellers. Promotion's job is to communicate. Its task may be to *inform* consumers, *persuade* potential buyers to purchase, or *remind* past buyers not to forget to use the brand and to remember their satisfaction with past purchases.

PROMOTIONAL OBJECTIVES

Effective marketers plan their promotional efforts to achieve certain objectives. Companies may have several promotional objectives. This section discusses some of the most common objectives.

PROVIDING INFORMATION

Many companies wish merely to announce something, perhaps that a new movie will be released on July 4. Or maybe the company must inform car buyers about a product recall. (Of course, since this is a broad objective, most companies will make providing information the general purpose underlying their more specific objectives.)

DIRECT RESPONSE

A common promotional objective is to obtain a direct, measurable response such as an order, a donation, an inquiry, or a visit to the store.[2] Direct-response objectives are most often expressed as sales objectives. For example, a mail-order company, such as L. L. Bean, that sends out its catalog to make sales has a direct-response objective. Of course, most personal selling activity (discussed later this chapter) fits this category. However, the recent availability of highly targeted computerized databases has made direct-response promotions increasingly important. Sometimes direct-response activity via the mail, telephone, and other electronic media, such as fax machines, is called *direct marketing.*

PRODUCT DIFFERENTIATION

Creating *product differentiation* (discussed in Chapter 14) is often a promotional objective. Promoting some degree of product differentiation involves communicating some dimension of the product that competing brands or products do not possess. The communication highlights how use of the product solves a customer problem. Generally mature products are not truly unique, especially from a performance point of view. However, promoting Coors beer as brewed with Rocky Mountain spring water makes the brand appear to be different from the rest. Similarly Crayola Washable Crayons stresses a unique product difference as the foundation of its promotional campaign. The crayons' patented formula provides a unique benefit that competitors cannot match. It gives the buyer a reason for choosing this brand.

BRAND IMAGE

Brand image
The symbolic meaning associated with a particular brand.

Product distinctions often lie in the minds of consumers rather than in the products themselves. The symbolic meaning associated with a particular brand is known as the **brand image**. Though the image varies from consumer to consumer, the brand image remains a complex of symbols and meanings associated with the brand. People buy products not only for their functional purpose but also for their symbolic meanings. A brand image may be more important than the tangible ("real") product. Thus, a major promotional objective is to communicate a brand image or, in the case of a retailer, a store image.

FOCUS ON COMPANY

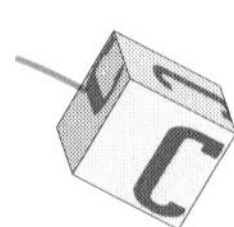

The Girl Scouts of America

Over the years, The Girl Scouts of America established a strong image for the organization. The image of a Girl Scout was one of dependability, trustworthiness, and honesty. But as the MTV era set in, the Girl Scouts began to see its membership decline, particularly among the 8-to-11 age group, or the so-called "tweens." Marketing research showed that preteens perceived Girl Scouts as childish, immature, and too squeaky-clean. So the organization's marketers decided the Girl Scouts had to move away from the uniformed, goody-goody image and show that the Girl Scouts are a fun, mature, cool place to be.

Past campaigns had tried to appeal to both girls and their parents. According to the Girl Scouts' advertising agency, Girl Scouts were "too soft, warm and fuzzy." That approach didn't work anymore, because in the 1990s girls are starting to want independence at an even younger age. The Girl Scouts were considered an organization that was "locked in time." To overcome the image problem, the Girl Scouts promotional campaign had to make the organization more relevant to the older age group while emphasizing the activities available to girls who join. The new image was to show Girl Scouts as part of the normal, straight life and culture of that age group. Girl Scouts are now portrayed as being hipper and more action oriented. For example, the cookie packages show Girl Scouts engaged in outdoor games such as volleyball.

Using MTV-style graphics, the TV advertising incorporates rap music, a TV teen sex symbol (Johnny Depp from "21 Jump Street"), and fantasy images such as windsurfing, skiing, and parachuting to suggest that the Scouts can offer girls a lot of fulfilling activities. One television ad closes with the line "The Girl Scouts. As great as you want to make it."

POSITIONING

Positioning campaign
Promoting a brand's position in relation to its competitors' to get consumers to view the brand from a particular perspective.

In Chapter 13, we defined a *competitive position* as the way consumers perceive a brand relative to its competition. Achieving a positioning objective is often the focal point of promotional campaigns. The **positioning** approach promotes a brand's position in relation to its competitors. The campaign objective is to get consumers to view the brand from a particular perspective.

Marketers assume that consumers have so much information about other brands, advertising, and similar products that the company must create a distinct position for the brand in the prospect's mind. The positioning approach slots a brand, in relation to its competition, within the target customer's mind. Bausch & Lomb's Clear Choice mouthwash is positioned as the brand without alcohol and other unnecessary ingredients to color it green, yellow, or red.

Michelin positions its tires as safe tires for the family car. Its advertising slogan (Michelin: Because So Much Is Riding On Your TIres.) and the photographs of infants and toddlers sitting inside its tires reinforces this position.

Marketers of organizational products also have positioning objectives. Today Xerox Corporation, long thought of as "the copier company," positions itself as "The Documents Company," involved in faxing, scanning, and printing in addition to copying. It wants to hold a position unoccupied by competitors.

Exhibit 16.1 identifies several positioning strategies. It also suggests that a brand image campaign or a product differentiation campaign can be thought of as *ways* to position the product. The important point about positioning is not what "selling point" is used as the basis for positioning but that promotion can be used to position a brand *relative to the competition.*

Positioning strategies often communicate what the product does. A positioning strategy may promote a single product attribute ("the car dealer with the lowest prices in town") or multiple attributes ("the high performance, luxury car"). It may identify whom the product is for (e.g., "for the working woman").

Benson & Hedges cigarettes were *repositioned* in promotions to reflect less affluent smokers because the market has become dominated by "blue-collar" smokers. Promotional campaigns stressing positioning are highly interrelated with the market segmentation strategy.

Exhibit 16.1 **COMMON POSITIONING STRATEGIES**

Positioning by	Example
Image of user	Guess Jeans (photographs of young, sexy people)
Image of price and/or quality	Hallmark (When you care enough to send the very best)
	Suave (When you know beautiful hair doesn't have to cost a fortune)
Product attributes or benefit	Indiglo by Timex (The watch's night light is the same kind they use in the cockpit of a Learjet)
Use or application	Arm & Hammer Baking Soda (Try adding Arm & Hammer [along with your laundry detergent] for a cleaner, fresher wash)
Product class	Raid Baits (There's no better way to kill bugs dead)
Competitor	Ford (Chevy Trucks are like unappealing rocks that don't go anywhere)
	Visa (The Olympics don't take American Express. It's everywhere you want to be.)

BUILDING RELATIONSHIPS

The relationship between marketer and buyer does not end when the sale is made. Long-term success often depends on the ability of advertising or the sales force to build a lasting relationship with the buyer. This is especially true in marketing to businesses. For many business-to-business marketers, the relationship intensifies after the sale is made. How well the marketer manages the relationship becomes the critical factor in the buying decision the next time around.[3] This can be the most important promotional objective.

INFLUENCING WORD-OF-MOUTH COMMUNICATION

We all recognize and appreciate creative advertising. You probably remember a humorous Nike commercial or a lively Diet Pepsi commercial that grabbed your attention. You may have even talked to your friends about some advertising you liked. The ability of creative advertising to stimulate people to talk to other people about products, services, and ideas is called *word-of-mouth communication.* It may be one of the most effective means of communicating a message to prospective customers. Thus, a promotional objective may be to influence word-of-mouth communication.[4]

THE ELEMENTS OF PROMOTION

Personal selling, advertising, publicity, and sales promotion are the four main elements of promotion. These promotional efforts are of two general types. They involve either direct communication, usually on a face-to-face basis, or indirect communication using television or some other mass medium. The marketer must determine which approach is best for each situation. The nature of the message strongly influences the choice of method. Few industrial buyers would feel comfortable buying plant equipment solely on the basis of a direct-mail or telephone communication. Few consumers need to talk to a salesperson to choose a certain brand of potato chip; most rely on advertising for most product information.

The following sections look at each element of promotion in turn.

PERSONAL SELLING

Personal selling
A person-to-person communication between the seller and the prospective buyer.

Personal selling is a person-to-person communication between the seller and the prospective buyer. Selling consists of human contact and direct communication rather than impersonal mass communication. Professional sales personnel are vital as business's "front-line troops in the battle for customers' orders."[5] They communicate the company's offer and show prospective buyers how the product can solve their problems.

When customers who already use a product or shop at a store are satisfied, they often tell friends or relatives about their purchases. Word-of-mouth communication can be extremely powerful, usually more persuasive than any commercial advertising.

The purpose of personal selling, whether face to face or over the phone, is to inform, persuade, or remind on a "one-on-one" basis. It involves discovering and communicating customer needs, matching the appropriate products with those needs, communicating product benefits, and developing customer relationships.[6]

In many instances, the one-on-one nature of this promotional technique makes it quite expensive. First, good salespeople make good money, often over $100,000 per year. Second, the salesperson must be properly trained. He or she may have to spend considerable time in developing and delivering a message suited to the individual customer. Finally, the salesperson may devote a lot of time to planning activities, traveling (in a company car), and/or waiting for the opportunity to deliver the message.

However, these costs are offset by the flexibility personal selling allows in delivering a promotional message. Questions can be asked, pauses can be taken at appropriate points to allow an idea to sink in, and responses can be tailor made to particular customer objections or questions about a purchase. Furthermore, the personal salesperson, unlike a TV or radio communication, can focus on the best prospects—those most likely to buy the product offered. Direct, and usually immediate, feedback from customers is among the major advantages of personal selling.

Field selling
Occurs when an "outside" salesperson travels to the prospective account's place of business.

Telemarketing
Using the telephone as the primary means of communicating with prospective customers.

Inside selling
Occurs when salespeople sell from the company's premises.

Field selling, telemarketing, and inside selling are the three basic methods for personal selling to organizations. **Field selling** occurs when an "outside" salesperson travels to the prospective account's place of business. **Telemarketing** refers to using the telephone as the *primary* means of communicating with prospective customers. **Inside selling** occurs when salespeople sell from the company's premises. This selling method is similar to retail selling by store clerks.[7]

ORDER TAKERS, ORDER GETTERS, AND SALES SUPPORT PERSONNEL

Many retail salespeople and telemarketing salespeople who handle catalog sales are considered *order takers.* Their main task is to properly record the order and make sure it is processed correctly.

Telemarketing is becoming a major activity of many inside order-taking sales representatives. Telemarketing uses computer technology for order taking. Of course, all salespeople telephone prospects and customers, and telephone selling is an important part of many order-getting sales jobs. However, we will use the terms *telemarker* and *telemarketing* to indicate that the company does all of its personal selling over the phone.

Many field salespeople are called *order getters* because they engage in creative selling. They evaluate prospects' needs and persuasively convince potential buyers that his or her company's product will be the solution to their problems.

Technical specialists and other *sales support personnel* provide information or customer service. Their job is to help in special selling situations. For example, a sales engineer may be required to explain how to install industrial equipment.

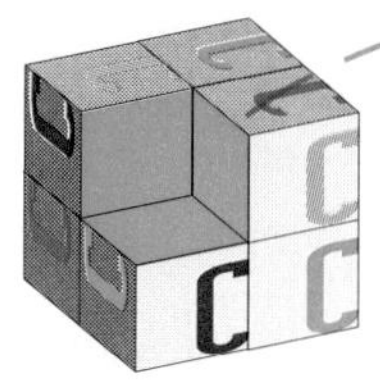

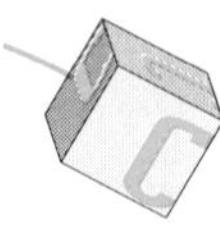

FOCUS ON CUSTOMERS

The Ideal House

One of the top real estate salespersons in New York state uses his other career—art teacher—to help him sell. Mike Fink, of U.S. One Laffey Real Estate Corp., in Williston Park, N.Y., spends until 2 P.M. each day teaching art to 6th, 7th, and 8th graders. Then he sells.

In his very first year selling, Fink sold $3-million worth of residential properties. By 1992, the number was $10.4 million. "I see no reason to level off," says Fink, predicting $18 million next year.

Not bad, for a second job.

Teaching until 2 P.M. works perfectly for him: "Most people can't go look at houses until after work, anyway. Plus, I'm free to sell on weekends and during vacations."

Art gives Fink his most powerful selling tool. "I do a lot of sketching. As people tell me what they're looking for in a house, I form a mental picture of the place. I ask them for details—what kind of neighborhood they want, what style of house, what schools they want to be near. By listening, I put together their ideal house—like those sketches police artists do—then I go out and find it. Sometimes the next day, sometimes not for a week. But I find it. I call it selling through *aesthetic intuition.*"

Fink personalizes the selling process, giving his clients a complete picture of himself before pitching them on a property: "Often people feel like a piece of meat or a number in a real estate office. So I tell them my story, and soon we're friends."

The most powerful tale Fink tells is that of his family. His son Dan suffered from a stroke as a child, but, guided and pushed by his father, he overcame its effects—spectacularly. Dan Fink became an athlete, and is now the first-ranked male gymnast in New York state, and 13th in the U.S. He got that way through total dedication to goals—paying his own way through gymnastics lessons by working as a party clown. "Dan had a total dedication to his goals. That's what every salesman needs, too."

THE CREATIVE SELLING PROCESS

In many sales jobs, established sales representatives spend most of their time making sales calls to regular customers. Exhibit 16.2 describes many of the activities a professional salesperson performs.

Keeping existing customers satisfied is an important—and in many businesses the most important—part of the sales job. However, growth comes from developing new customers or new accounts. Many sales jobs require the salesperson to engage in creative selling to get new business.

Exhibit 16.2 **ACTIVITIES OF ORDER-GETTING SALESPEOPLE**

Activity Name	Selected Activities
Selling function	Prospect for and qualify leads; prepare sales presentations; make sales calls; overcome objections
Working with orders	Order entry; expedite orders; handle shipping problems
Servicing the product	Test equipment; teach safety instructions; supervise installations, minor maintenance
Information management	Provide feedback to superiors; receive feedback from clients
Servicing the account	Inventory; set up point-of-purchase displays; stock shelves
Conferences/meetings	Attend sales conferences; set up exhibitions, trade shows
Training/recruiting	Recruit new sales representatives; train new sales representatives
Entertaining	Take clients to lunch, sporting events, golfing, tennis, etc.
Out-of-town traveling	Spend night on road; travel out of town
Working with distributors	Establish relations with distributors; extend credit; collect past-due accounts

Creative selling process
The process of locating and qualifying the prospect, approaching the prospect, creating awareness, arousing interest, making a specific proposal, handling objections and complaints, closing the sale, and following up to keep customers.

The **creative selling process** includes the following steps: (1) locating and qualifying the prospect, (2) approaching the prospect, (3) creating awareness, (4) arousing interest, (5) making a specific proposal, (6) handling objections and complaints, (7) closing the sale, and (8) following up to keep customers. As Exhibit 16.3 suggests, the ultimate goal of the creative selling process is customer satisfaction. Note that these steps are guidelines for helping salespeople to think about the tasks they face. They are not meant to be followed mindlessly.

Exhibit 16.3 **STEPS IN THE CREATIVE SELLING PROCESS**

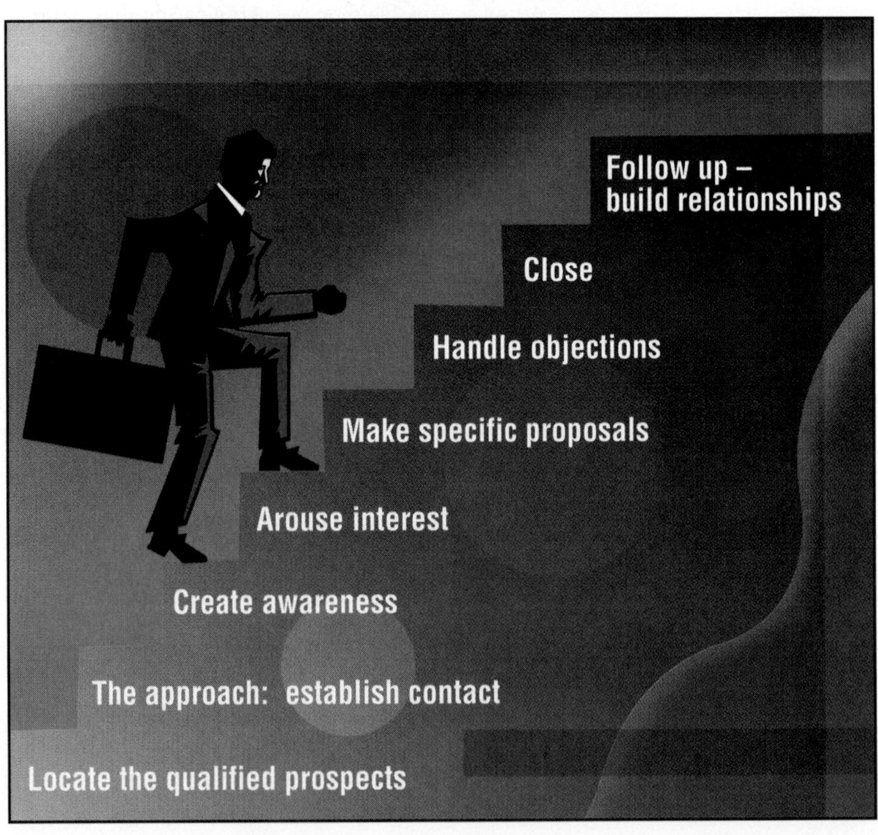

STREET SMART

Succeeding with Your Voice

The first 15 seconds of any telephone call are crucial. One key to success is knowing how to make your voice work for you. Some suggestions:

- Warm up your voice in the morning. Talk to yourself on the way to work. Read signs out loud.
- Record your voice and play it back. Be your own voice coach by using a simple cassette recorder. Just remember that most people dislike the sound of their voice.
- Use your natural pitch. Unconsciously "switching" your voice to create another image is not only artificial, but harmful to your voice over time.
- Sit up straight when your phone rings. It creates a more alert tone in your voice.
- Notice how your audience reacts to your voice. Do people often mistake who you are or ask you to repeat yourself? Do they hesitate when you expect them to speak? Chances are they may not be hearing you well.
- Listen actively. Let the person on the other end know you're listening. Use response signs, such as "Yes," "I understand" and "Certainly."
- Smile. People will "hear" your smile over the telephone. One symptom of not smiling is when people who know you ask if you're feeling all right. They hear stress and fatigue in your voice.

Prospecting
Activities to identify likely buyers from lists of previous customers, referrals, trade lists, advertising inquiries, and other sources.

Step 1. Locating and Qualifying Prospects. Locating likely prospects is called *prospecting.* **Prospecting** involves activities used to identify likely buyers from lists of previous customers, referrals, trade lists, advertising inquiries (such as postcards or coupons returned to the sales office by interested parties), and other sources.

Identification of possible prospects is only the beginning of effective creative selling. Prospects must be shown to be in need of the product and to be able to pay for it. Determining the company's need, its ability to pay, the possible order size, and the background of the specific person to be contacted is called *qualifying the prospect.*

Approach
An initial contact and establishing a good relationship with the prospect.

Step 2. Establishing Contact: The Approach. The **approach** involves making an initial contact and establishing a good relationship with the prospect. With established accounts or individuals already familiar with the salesperson and the company, the approach may be as simple as making a telephone call to request an appointment or knocking on the prospect's door with a friendly greeting.

Effective sales personnel recognize the importance of making a good impression during the first few seconds of the meeting. Experience is a great teacher in this matter, but planning the approach is important too. Good salespeople put themselves in the prospect's shoes. For example, not wearing a hard hat in a location that calls for protective gear may make the salesperson appear to be unfamiliar with the situation in which he or she is supposedly going to solve a client's problem. The importance of making a good impression should not be underestimated.

Step 3. Creating Awareness. Effective sales presentations begin with gaining the prospect's *attention.* Some salespeople do this by producing some physical object, such as the product itself (if it is both portable and eye catching), a model of the product, or something that relates to the product in an interesting or even humorous way. It is more common, however, to have an opening statement designed to attract attention, for example, "I'm here to show you how our computer networking system will save $5,000 a month in inventory cost."

Step 4. Arousing Interest. After gaining the prospect's attention, the salesperson needs to generate interest in the product offered. An opening comment that the salesperson can save the client a great deal of money may gain attention, but it must be followed by the development of *interest* in the product being sold as the means for saving the money. This step involves finding out the prospect's *problem* and then showing how the product is the solution to that problem. Describing the product's benefits in an interesting way, explaining how it works, or demonstrating the product's use can all be used to create interest.

Step 5. Making Specific Proposals. After arousing interest in the company's offer, the salesperson must create a *desire* to purchase the product by making a specific proposal. The salesperson attempts to persuasively communicate to the potential buyer the benefits of a specific course of action.

Step 6. Handling Objections or Complaints. After making a specific proposal, the salesperson attempts to move the prospect to *action.* This leads to closing the sale, but it may require handling objections before closing.

In most sales presentations, the salesperson does not make a one-way presentation of information while the customer passively listens. The customer, no matter how friendly or interested in the product, may be hesitant to commit money or other resources in a purchase agreement. Questions or strong objections are likely to arise. Because objections reveal the reasons for resisting or postponing purchase, the salesperson should listen and learn from them.

When an objection indicates that the prospect has failed to fully understand some point that was made, the salesperson can comment on the area of uncertainty. A question about a product characteristic may mean the prospect has not grasped how the product works or seen the benefits it can provide. A salesperson who encounters an objection of this type can go on to provide additional persuasive information, clarify the sales presentation, or offer the basic argument for the product in a different manner.

Closing
Bringing the sale to an end.

Step 7. Closing the Sale. Ultimately, the salesperson makes the sale. In selling, the term **closing** indicates that the sale is being brought to an end. The main advantage of personal selling versus other forms of promotion is that the salesperson is in a position to conclude negotiations by actually asking for an order. Closing or completing the sale, needless to say, is crucial in the selling process. The old adage "nothing happens until a sale is made" reflects the importance of selling to all aspects of a business.

Unfortunately, many salespeople are knowledgeable and convincing when making sales presentations but never get around to asking for the order. In any case, the point comes when the presentation must be drawn to its logical conclusion. At this point the salesperson asks for the order or uses a question to narrow the number of alternative choices.

Follow-up
Contacting the customer to make sure that everything was handled as promised and that the order was shipped promptly and received on schedule.

Relationship management
The sales function of managing the account relationship and ensuring that buyers receive the appropriate services.

Step 8. Building a Relationship: The Follow-Up. Modern marketers view the closing of the sale not as the end of the selling process but as the beginning of an organization's relationship with a customer. Satisfied customers will return to the company that treated them best if they need to repurchase the same product in the future. If they need a related item, these satisfied customers will know the first place to look. The professional salesperson knows that the best way to get repeat business is to keep customers. The best way to keep customers is to follow up after the sale. During the **follow-up**, the salesperson makes sure that everything was handled as promised and that the order was shipped promptly and received on schedule. Few things are worse than promising a delivery date and having the goods arrive weeks late. The salesperson should also ask the customer whether any problems occurred, such as missing parts or damage to the merchandise during shipping.

The term **relationship management** refers to the sales function of managing the account relationship and ensuring that buyers receive the appropriate services. The goal of relationship management is to help customer organizations expand their own resources and capacities through relationships. Buyers expect the products and services they buy to solve problems and contribute to the success of their organizations. The salesperson is the vehicle the marketer uses to achieve this goal.

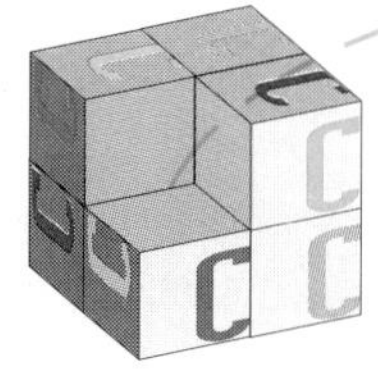

FOCUS ON COMPETITORS

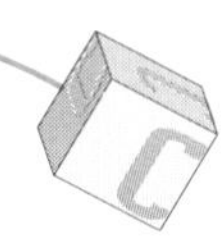

Beverly Hills Sports Council

Dennis Gilbert is doing a lot better in the major leagues than he ever did in the minors. As a sports agent, the one-time center fielder for teams like the Waterloo (Iowa) Hawks has hit several business home runs, negotiating some of the largest contracts in baseball history.

Gilbert's six-team bidding contest for free agent outfielder Bobby Bonilla resulted in a five-year contract with the New York Mets for $29 million. A month later, Gilbert signed Danny Tartabull to a five-year deal with the New York Yankees for $25.5 million. In 1992, he made a six-year deal for Barry Bonds worth $43.75 million. Gilbert was also able to get Mike Piazza (the 1993 National League Rookie of the Year award) a three-year guaranteed contract for $4.2 million—the highest salary ever for a second-year player. The deals will bring Gilbert's Beverly Hills Sports Council a 5 percent cut.

Gilbert spent five years riding the buses in the minor leagues. He hit .300 but never got close to the AAA clubs. In 1971 he retired and began selling insurance door-to-door in Los Angeles. He eventually started his own agency, which, he says, now does $100 million in policy sales a year. In 1982 he got back into baseball by taking over an embryonic sports agency from friend and former teammate Tony Conigliaro, who had suffered a brain-damaging heart attack.

In a field crowded with sharp lawyers, Gilbert's low-key, just-us-ballplayers approach serves him well in salary negotiations. He gets along with players because he can talk baseball with them. "I can relate to a player and I also know enough about baseball never to negotiate an incentive clause based on at-bats," he says. "You want a clause based on plate appearances to reward a player who walks or hits into a sacrifice, which are not at-bats, according to baseball statistics."

Today Gilbert has more than 50 major league clients—including Barry Bonds, José Canseco and Bret Saberhagen—all of whom get more than mere contract advice. Says Gilbert, "We'll do anything we can to advance a player's career. We've done everything from serve as marriage counselor to psychiatrist to business adviser."

Gilbert's successful career in selling insurance before he got back into baseball taught him the importance of personal selling. "You're selling something people can't smell, touch, see and hear, just like a player's contract. You're selling an intangible commodity the buyer hopes will pay off. No owner is going to want to buy a player for the price that we ask. He's got to be sold on the *idea.*"

ADVERTISING

Advertising is any communication carried by a mass medium and paid for by a sponsor whose product is identified in the message in some way. It consists of paid messages about an identified product, organization, or individual through nonpersonal media.

When we think of advertising, we normally think of television, radio, magazines, and newspapers, but any mass medium may be used for advertising. The ability to communicate to a large number of people at once is the major benefit of advertising. In this sense, advertising is a cost-efficient substitute for personal selling.

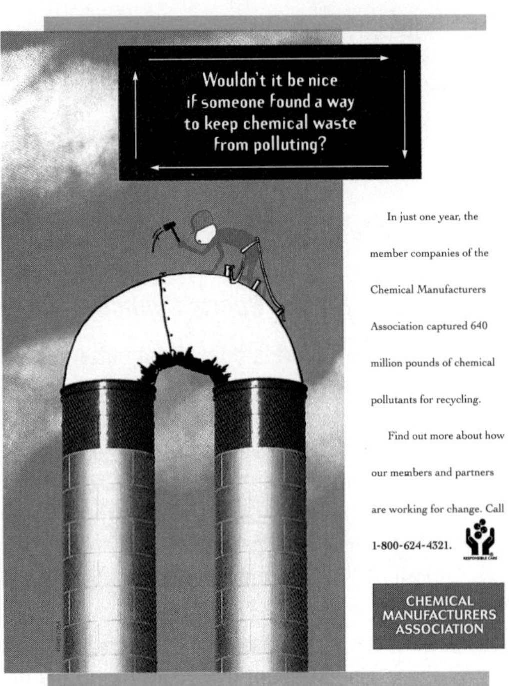

The Chemical Manufacturers Association runs institutional advertising. Its message, which portrays two "smokestacks" being linked together, communicates that the industry is actively working on recycling chemical pollutants.

Publicity also appears in mass media. However, publicity is free, whereas advertising is not. Advertisers must pay for their advertising messages.

Advertisers have a great deal of control over the content of the promotional messages. Also, a uniform and unvarying message can be repeated with great frequency. You may see a soft-drink commercial several times as you watch a basketball game on TV. You would never call a salesperson to repeat his or her message over and over again.

Advertising is not without disadvantages. Even though the cost per person may be low, using mass media such as national television often requires a major expenditure. This tends to restrict the use of advertising to larger, better-financed organizations. Also, advertising, unlike personal selling, does not allow the message to be tailored to the prospect, nor can it answer questions.

TYPES OF ADVERTISING

Advertising can be classified into three types according to its general purpose: selective, primary-demand, and institutional advertising.

Selective advertising
Advertising that attempts to create selective demand for a particular brand or store by promoting the brand's or store's attributes, benefits, uses, and images; also called *brand-specific advertising.*

Most advertising we see is selective advertising for a specific brand. **Selective advertising** (also called *brand-specific advertising*) attempts to create selective demand for a particular brand or store by promoting the brand's or store's attributes, benefits, uses, and images. Advertisements for Nike Air Jordans, Marriott Hotels, Kraft cheese, and many other brands are clearly intended to suggest purchasing a particular product, and indeed a particular brand. An advertisement for Ford trucks that declares "Ford trucks—the best never rests" and suggests that the viewer go down to the local Ford dealer to buy an F110 pickup truck is selective advertising because it features a specific product.

Some selective advertising is also called *comparative advertising* because the advertiser compares its brand against a competing brand. For example, Pizza Hut commercials

Exhibit 16.4 **ADVANTAGES AND DISADVANTAGES OF ADVERTISING MEDIA**

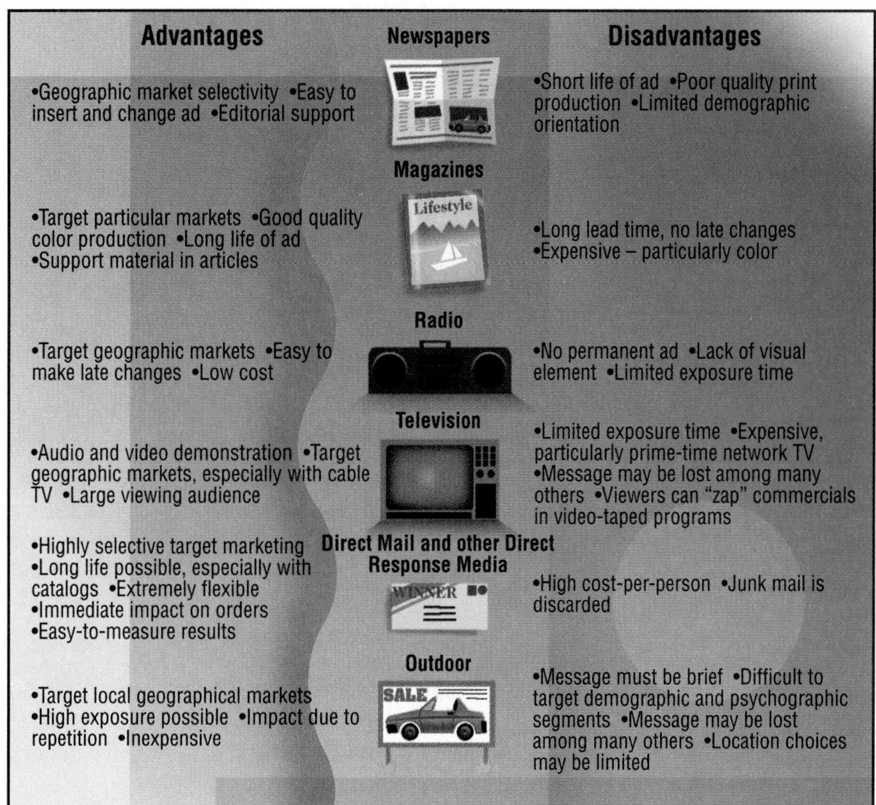

showed its home delivery system for its Bigfoot Pizza in a favorable light compared to Domino's. The idea of these ads is to build selective demand by saying your brand is better than that of the major competitor, which is often the market leader. Sometimes brand comparisons are made in demonstrations shown in the advertisement.

Primary-demand advertising Advertising that encourages generic demand for an entire product category.

Primary-demand advertising encourages generic demand for an entire product category. Ads sponsored by the government that urge you to wear a motorcycle helmet (any brand is okay) are primary-demand advertising.

Institutional advertising Advertising that promotes an industry or organization as a whole, stressing goodwill, corporate image, or contributions to society.

Institutional advertising promotes an industry or organization as a whole, stressing goodwill, corporate image, or contributions to society. The Chemical Manufacturers Association institutional advertising calls attention to the organization's involvement in recycling chemical pollutants. The intention is to promote goodwill by demonstrating that companies in the industry are socially responsible and productive.

ADVERTISING MEDIA

Communications media The means used to broadcast or print advertising messages.

Communications media are the means used to broadcast or print advertising messages. Network television, cable television, and radio are referred to as *broadcast media.* Magazines and newspapers are *print media.* Direct-mail catalogs, outdoor advertising (billboards), and other selective media are referred to as *specialty media.*

Each medium has its advantages and disadvantages (see Exhibit 16.4). Direct-response media, such as direct mail, can be very selective and can reach a clearly defined market such as families within a certain zip code or all holders of American Express cards. But it can also end up in the wastepaper basket. Television reaches a mass audience. Television allows the

Television is an advertising medium that allows for large audience-targeted geographic markets. Television programs such as "Sabado Gigánte" and "Latin MTV" are broadcast on Spanish-language television seen around the world. Don Francisco, the jolly host of "Sabado Gigánte," is well known not only in Latin America but to Hispanic audiences in the United States as well.

advertisers to show and tell because it can merge sight, sound, movement, cartoons, actors, and announcers who are not seen at all. Its strengths, however, may be outweighed by its relative expensiveness. Cable television with advertising rates lower than network television can be a good alternative for many products.

Media schedule or **media plan**
A time schedule identifying the exact media and the dates advertisements are scheduled to appear.

The **media schedule** or **media plan** is a time schedule identifying the exact media and the dates advertisements are scheduled to appear. Media planners not only select the general class of media (e.g., magazines, cable television) but also choose specific media vehicles (*Sports Illustrated,* "Sea Quest DSV").[8] Thus, specialization by type of television show or type of magazine is possible. For example, "Melrose Place" appeals to teens, and "Winnetka Road" appeals to older folks.

An objective of the media strategy is to select media that reach the desired audience. Certain media, such as broadcasts on The Nashville Network, have a greater appeal to different demographic and psychographic market segments than other media do.

Knowing which media will accomplish the promotional objective is important to the overall marketing strategy. Advertisers select their media by considering which media will hit the all-important target market. Knowing the target market—who the heaviest buyers are, what their demographic characteristics are—helps determine which media will deliver these prospects.

FOCUS ON COLLABORATORS

Fallon McElligott

Advertising agencies are independent companies that collaborate with clients to create advertising. They are advertising specialists. Fallon McElligott is an advertising agency known for its creativity. Lee Apparel Company, Timex, and Continental Bank are among its major accounts.

Exhibit 16.5 "ROLLING STONE" ADVERTISEMENT: PERCEPTION VERSUS REALITY

Perception.

Reality.

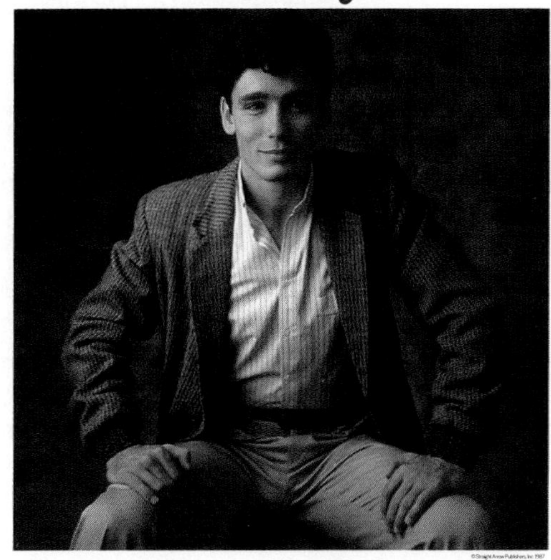

© Straight Arrow Publishers, Inc 1987

If your idea of a Rolling Stone reader looks like a holdout from the 60's, welcome to the 80's. Rolling Stone ranks number one in reaching concentrations of 18-34 readers with household incomes exceeding $25,000. When you buy Rolling Stone, you buy an audience that sets the trends and shapes the buying patterns for the most affluent consumers in America. That's the kind of reality you can take to the bank.

Source: Simmons 1986

The agency's advertising campaign for *Rolling Stone* magazine is considered an advertising classic. *Rolling Stone*'s customers, the people who buy advertising space in magazines, thought the magazine's audience was composed of a bunch of middle-aged hippies from the 1960s with little money or interest in purchasing much of anything, let alone upscale items. A perception/reality advertising theme (see Exhibit 16.5) compared old hippie images (the perception) with *Rolling Stone*'s readership's actual characteristic (reality).

Fallon McElligott's mission is "to be the premier, award-winning agency in America that produces extraordinarily effective work for a short list of blue chip clients." The agency believes it is important to have a true collaborative partnership with the client. It believes its job is to be involved in the client's business and to be a problem solver. Creative and research personnel work together to analyze available research to help them understand the client's marketing communication task. The agency focuses on creating great advertising that truly works for its clients.

Fallon McElligott's creative success has also worked in the marketplace. For example, its advertising for Lee jeans helped increase market share from 14.6 to 22.1 percent during the back-to-school selling season.

PUBLICITY AND PUBLIC RELATIONS

Publicity
Promotional activities that involve unpaid messages.

Both advertising and publicity appear in the mass media. Unlike advertising, however, **publicity** involves an *unpaid* message. Also unlike in advertising, the company cannot control the exact content of the message. When information about a product is considered newsworthy, the mass media tend to communicate that information "for free." Thus, the company being publicized neither directly pays for the message nor identifies itself as the message sponsor.

An important distinguishing characteristic of publicity is that it *always* involves a third party, such as a television reporter or a newspaper editor, who has the final say about the content of the message. Often consumers find publicity given by a third party more believable than advertising. The information is generally factual rather than persuasive. The reputation of the television news anchor may be associated with the company or its products.

Publicity can also be negative. In fact, because the message content is controlled by the media and is not in the hands of the company promoting the product, publicity can even be destructive. Nearly every recall of a popular product for repair or replacement makes the evening news and results in negative publicity. The makers of Saturn automobiles and Apple Powerbook computers spend millions of dollars to develop fine products. Bad publicity about defects, however minor, can easily offset their efforts.

Although publicity is "free" in the sense that mass media are not paid to communicate the message, this does not mean publicity should go unmanaged. For instance, you can be certain that every year the Macy Thanksgiving Day parade will generate a great deal of publicity. The parade is a carefully orchestrated annual publicity event that promotes the store and other sponsors who build floats or march in the parade. Marketers may spend considerable time and effort in getting news releases and interviews with company spokespersons placed in newspapers and on broadcasts so that a favorable organizational image will result.

Public relations
Activities that actively manage publicity (and sometimes other promotional elements).

When an organization carefully plans and distributes information to shape the nature of the publicity it receives, it engages in public relations. In other words, the purpose of **public relations** is to actively manage publicity (and sometimes other promotional elements). Public relations establishes and maintains a positive corporate image with customers, suppliers, stockholders, and the general public. It provides information to increase the public's knowledge about an organization's products.

FOCUS ON COMPANY

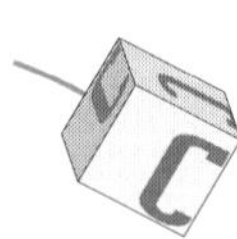

Franklin Sports Industries

When Mike Schmidt was under contract to endorse Franklin Sports Industries' baseballs and gloves, he advised marketing executives that batting gloves were an unexploited opportunity. Based on Mike Schmidt's suggestion, Franklin designed a spandex-and-leather glove that was contoured to improve the feel of a bat. Since the company lacked a large advertising budget, it decided to use public relations to generate publicity. The company gave every major league player a large supply of its gloves. Each glove had Franklin's name written in one-inch-high letters. Today, every time a TV camera takes a close-up shot of a professional batter's grip on the bat, the Franklin name gets "free" publicity. Kids see the players as heroes whom they wish to imitate. As a result of the company's efforts, Franklin's gloves are the market leader, and sales of its other baseball products have grown.

SALES PROMOTION

A sales promotion is a promotional activity other than personal selling, advertising, and publicity or public relations. **Sales promotions** are intended to encourage immediate purchases

Exhibit 16.6 **CONSUMER SALES PROMOTIONS**

Activity	Description	Features	Example
Product sampling	A free trial or trial sample of the brand is given to consumers.	An expensive method, but good for new brands in mature markets where brand loyalties exist.	A free sample of Fruitopia is given away.
Cents-off coupons	Temporary price reduction coupons; most often found in an advertisement, but may be located in the store or in the package.	Cutting price does not damage long-term quality or value image (many price-conscious consumers always clip coupons)	Save 50c on Cover Girl makeup
Rebates	Price reductions to induce immediate purchase; consumer gets money back from manufacturer rather than a price break at the retail level.	Lower cost than circulating coupons because rebate coupon is inside package. Coupons not always redeemed.	Mail-in rebate for $5 on Price Pfister faucet.
Contests and sweepstakes	Stimulate purchase because consumer has a chance to be a big winner.	Consumers like these exciting promotions. They may be tied to repeat purchases of a brand.	McDonald's Olympic Game Sweepstakes.
Premiums and self-liquidating premiums	Another product is offered free or at a reduced charge if the key brand is purchased. A self-liquidating premium is a giveaway.	Consumers see themselves as getting a deal on something for nothing.	T-shirt offer with purchase of charity ball ticket.
Multiple-purchases offers	Two-for-one deals or multiple purchases are tied to price or another promotion.	Induce heavier than normal purchase and maintain customer loyalty.	12-pack of Mountain Dew for the price of a 6-pack.

Sales promotion
A promotional activity that is intended to encourage immediate purchases or to induce distributors to work more intensely in a specific time period.

or to induce distributors to work more intensely in a specific time period. Sales promotions usually provide an incentive for certain behavior. Special "buy one, get one free" offers, coupon deals, free trial samples, and contests are examples of sales promotions. These are not routine but out-of-the-ordinary occurrences. Sales promotions differ from advertising because they are *temporary offers* of an uncommon reward to customers, retailers, or company salespeople. Sales promotions can be aimed at consumers or at the wholesale and retail trades (trade promotions).

CONSUMER SALES PROMOTIONS

The intent of *consumer sales promotion* programs is to intensify a company's advertising and personal-selling messages. Often the intensified effort occurs at the point of purchase. For instance, advertising may create an awareness of a new product like General Mills' Pop-Secret Pop Chips, but a cents-off coupon and the chance to participate in a sweepstakes give consumers an extra incentive to try the burger for the first time. Exhibit 16.6 lists the most common consumer sales promotions.

Often a consumer sales promotion's objective is to add an attention-getting quality to consumer advertising and to stimulate consumers to make an immediate purchase. Offering Lion King toys, with a purchase at Burger King gets the attention of members of a certain target market and stimulates them to visit the restaurant.

As Exhibit 16.6 shows, sales promotions can serve many purposes. Free samples or cents-off coupons encourage a first-time trial of a product. A premium offer or a sweepstakes may stimulate interest in a product and be used to encourage off-season sales. A contest may require that consumers visit the store or showroom to see if they have won. Whether they take the form of a rebate, a contest, or free calendars, the best sales promotions support and are coordinated with other promotional activities.

Consumer sales promotions may be especially important to small businesses. A small retailer may find that the expense of a promotion, such as giving away a free calendar or free ball point pen, may be affordable, while television advertising would be beyond its reach.

Overuse of sales promotions can cause problems, however. Some sales promotions, such as coupons, rebates, and premiums, lower the price of the product or enhance the product offering. But if these special incentives are used regularly, or if consumers can predict their timing, consumers may buy only during sales promotions. Marketers that continually use these types of sales promotion risk the loss of traditional sales to price-conscious consumers.

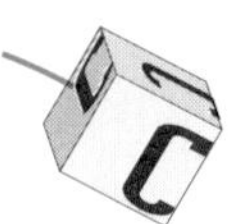

FOCUS ON COLLABORATORS

Abbott Laboratories

When Marcia Ryles gave birth to her first child, the hospital gave her a "survival kit" to take home. Along with a blanket and a toy bear came a large tin of powdered Similac, the leading brand of infant formula. When she discovered that her son, Alex, did not take to breast feeding, she tried the Similac. Alex liked the Similac, and Ryles did not try other brands. She said, "I just didn't want to risk upsetting him by switching formulas."

Abbott Laboratories, the marketer of Similac, and many of its competitors use trial sampling, that is, give free product samples as part of their marketing mixes to develop brand loyalty. However, the American Academy of Pediatrics believes giving free samples to mothers and marketing the products to doctors may hinder breast feeding. In a letter to its members, the academy urged doctors to pressure hospitals to stop accepting education and research grants from infant formula companies in exchange for not supplying other brands of infant formula.

TRADE SALES PROMOTIONS

The main purpose of a *trade sales promotion* is to provide an incentive to wholesalers and retailers to increase their promotional efforts. The company hopes to accomplish short-term objectives such as encouraging a retailer to put up special displays or inducing a wholesaler's sales force to sell to retailers more aggressively.

For example, a contest may be used to add some excitement to regular sales activity. In a sales contest, the wholesale salesperson with the highest sales volume for a particular period might win, say, a trip to Hawaii. The purpose of a contest is to motivate an intermediary's sales force to put out an extra effort.

Point-of-purchase materials
Items given to retailers to serve as reminders at the point of sale.

Trade allowance
A reduction in price, a rebate, merchandise, or something else given to a wholesaler or a retailer for performance of a specific activity or in consideration for a large order.

Trade show
An event at which a group of manufacturers (or other marketers) jointly exhibit their products in a convention hall.

Banners, pamphlets, coasters, and similar materials may be given to retailers. Such **point-of-purchase materials** remind consumers about brand names and advertising messages at the point of sale. Retailers like displays that provide both storage for products and reminders about messages used in consumer advertising.

A **trade allowance** is a reduction in price, a rebate, merchandise, or something else given to a wholesaler or a retailer for performance of a specific activity or in consideration for a large order. For example, a manufacturer may offer free merchandise to retailers that feature the product in point-of-purchase displays. Thus, a marketer of beer that wishes to increase beer sales for Halloween parties might provide a special promotional allowance to retailers that agree to place point-of-purchase displays in key locations within their stores.

At a **trade show**, a group of manufacturers (or other marketers) jointly exhibit their products in a convention hall. The major advantage of trade shows is that they bring a large number of buyers and sellers together at one time. The hardware, toy, fashion, consumer electronics, book publishing, and many other industries have annual trade shows.

THE PROMOTIONAL MIX

Promotional mix
The particular combination of all the elements of promotion—personal selling, advertising, publicity and public relations, and sales promotion—that will achieve the company's promotional objectives.

The particular combination of promotional elements a company uses is known as its **promotional mix**. The effective marketer integrates all the elements of promotion—personal selling, advertising, publicity and public relations, and sales promotion to achieve its promotional objectives. For example, advertising supports other promotional efforts. It may communicate information about a sales promotion or announce a public relations event. Advertising helps the salesperson get a "foot in the door" by preselling prospects. A salesperson's job can be made much easier if advertising informs the prospect about unique product benefits or encourages prospects to contact the salesperson. Without advertising, the salesperson's efforts may be hindered because the prospect will not know about the company or its products.

The promotional mix should be planned to meet the information requirements of all target customers. That is, it should not be exclusively designed to reach only the new buyer or only the regular buyer. Some elements of the mix may be aimed at the customers who know very little about the company or its products. At the other end of the scale, there may be a very well-informed customer who has some technical questions that only a qualified salesperson can answer. The elements of the promotional mix are selected to communicate to all prospective and existing customers.

Suppose you want to purchase a personal computer. You have probably advanced beyond total brand ignorance and are becoming increasingly aware of the different brands and their advertised benefits. Your interest in the product has led you to pay more attention to computer advertising and magazine articles about computers. Newspaper columnists may be writing about their own personal computers (publicity). Your friend the computer expert may regularly read the column and may have said something to you about recent improvements in personal computers. Sales promotions, such as the offer of a free software package or lessons on computer use, may ultimately bring you into the store, where personal selling communicates to you the benefits associated with a particular brand of computer. Then you make a decision to buy a particular brand such as Apple MacIntosh, IBM, or Gateway 2000. Each element of the promotional mix has its individual job to perform.

PUSH AND PULL STRATEGIES

Push strategy
A strategy that emphasizes promotional efforts aimed at members of the channel of distribution.

Pull strategy
A strategy that focuses promotional efforts at the ultimate consumer or industrial buyer located at the end of the channel of distribution.

A marketer may target a promotional strategy at members of the channel of distribution or at the ultimate consumers. Using the primary target of promotion as a basis for classification, the marketer may use either a *push* (pushing) strategy or a *pull* (pulling) strategy. A **push strategy** emphasizes promotional efforts aimed at members of the channel of distribution. Thus, the manufacturer of a product stresses personal selling to wholesalers and other dealers. The wholesalers then heavily promote the product to retailers. The retailers in turn direct their selling efforts at consumers. The term *push* comes from the fact that the manufacturer, with the help of other channel members, pushes the product through the channel of distribution. The push strategy may be thought of as a step-by-step approach to promotion.

A pull strategy reverses the direction of the effort. A **pull strategy** focuses promotional efforts at the ultimate consumer or industrial buyer located at the end of the channel of distribution. The marketer's purpose is to create consumer demand so that consumers will request the brand and encourage retailers and wholesalers to stock it. In other words, the demand at the buyer end of the channel of distribution *pulls* the product through the channel.

FOCUS ON COMPANY

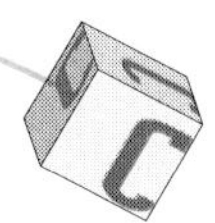

The Coca-Cola Company

When we first think about Coca-Cola, we envision the pull strategy it uses in the United States. However, if we think about how Coke expanded into each of its international markets, we realize the company had to build up a fairly complete local distribution system and use a push strategy to establish local demand. In Japan, consumers' long-established preference was for carbonated lemon beverages known as *saida.* Consumer demand did not "pull" Coke into this market; the company had to encourage the bottlers to "push" it. Today, because the company skillfully executed its expansion, Coke is a universally desired brand. But it got there because the company recognized the need for both push and pull strategies.

INTERNAL MARKETING

Internal marketing
Marketing efforts aimed at the marketer's own employees to help them recognize their role in the organization's effort to create customer satisfaction.

Marketers, especially service businesses, often use the term **internal marketing** when referring to marketing efforts aimed at their own employees who have contact with ultimate consumers or have a direct effect on those consumers' satisfaction with the product. The objective of a promotional effort may be to have employees recognize their role in the organization's effort to create customer satisfaction—perhaps to understand that the quality of service, which the employee provides, is essential to the firm's existence.

FOCUS ON COMPANY

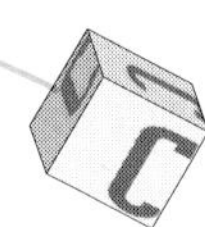

Disney World

At Disney World visitors are excited about the park's attractions, but many often comment that what they like even more are the park's sparkling cleanliness and the friendliness of Disney World employees.[9] This response is not a mere chance coincidence; it is the result of internal marketing by Disney. Company marketing executives know that the real "Disney Magic" lies in setting high standards of service excellence and exceeding the customer's expectations. A top priority at Disney World involves motivating employees to work as a team to provide top-quality service and teaching employees how to interact with customers to help them have fun. Employees are called "cast members" and are taught to be enthusiastic, helpful, and friendly. Internal marketing efforts communicate the idea that they are part of the "show" whether it's as a "security host" (police), "transportation host" (driver), or "custodial host" (street cleaner). Internal marketing efforts at Disney are based on the idea that if cast members love their jobs and feel a sense of pride in the "show," they will serve customers well.

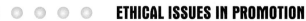

ETHICAL ISSUES IN PROMOTION

Social commentators frequently debate ethical issues about promotion, especially advertising. We will discuss three of these issues: deceptive and misleading practices, public standards, and promotions aimed at children.

DECEPTIVE AND MISLEADING PRACTICES

Our society grants consumers the right to be informed and prohibits deceptive practices and promotions that intentionally mislead consumers. For example, consumers have the right to know how likely they are to win a contest or sweepstakes. State and federal regulations now require that the odds of winning sales promotions be conveniently available to potential participants.

Misleading Advertising. Because of its direct effects on buyers, one area of particular concern is *misleading* or *deceptive advertising.* This emotional issue is based on the fact that almost all societies respect the truth and consider lying to be wrong. For example, advertising by Telefonica, Spain's telecommunications monopoly, promoting telephone calls to other European Union countries has been called deceptive. Telefonica advertisements claim that calls within the European Union cost 83 ptas a minute. In small letters at the bottom, however, they add a 38-ptas connection charge. Even then the rate is only for off-hours.[10]

In the United States, the Federal Trade Commission Act of 1914 makes it illegal to use dishonest advertisements. Thus, laws and court cases aimed at ending the worst abuses have long been part of the American business scene. Many recent incidents are traceable to consumerism and the right to be informed.

Bait and switch
Advertising a product at an amazingly low price to draw consumers to the store and then "switching" them to another, higher-priced item by claiming that the advertised item is no longer available.

Bait and Switch. Although our society and legal system disapprove of blatant deception, hard-and-fast rules are difficult to develop and enforce. Advertising that attempts to use the tactic known as *bait and switch* is a case in point. **Bait and switch** involves advertising a product at an amazingly low price. Consumers, drawn to the store by the advertising, are "switched" to another, higher-priced item by salespeople who claim that the advertised item is for some reason no longer available.

Although this tactic is clearly deceptive, proving intentional deception is difficult. Would anyone claim that the salesperson should not try to sell an item that was not mentioned in the store's advertisement? However, the sales tactic of trading up, whereby the salesperson tries to interest the customer in a higher-priced item than the one originally advertised, is a routine practice. The marketing concept stresses honest attempts at customer satisfaction. The debate about the ethics of switching revolves around the marketer's intentions and the actual availability of the product.

Puffery
The practice of making slight exaggerations.

Puffery. Although the law prohibits advertisements that are blatantly deceptive, a gray area known as *puffing* exists. Movie producers often publicize their films and publishers sometimes advertise their books by using *puffs* or *trade puffing.* **Puffery** is the practice of making slight exaggerations, which society in general considers harmless. "Most exciting movie ever!" and "Funniest book you'll ever read" are examples. Some critics think such statements should be banned because they are not provable.

Where does puffing stop and lying begin? Often the Federal Trade Commission or a judge is required to make the final decision.

PUBLIC STANDARDS

Matters of law and ethics are frequently decided on the basis of public standards or beliefs as to what is right and proper. Certain advertisements, such as the advertisement for Calvin Klein perfume showing nude men and women in provocative poses, cause a stir because they challenge public standards.

The public's sense of decency is a complicated thing to deal with. Television networks are often accused of offering too much sex and violence. Some groups condemn shows ranging from "Married with Children" to "Beavis and Butthead." Other groups condemn the self-proclaimed TV watchdogs, claiming no one should tell the American people what to watch, and "if you don't like it, you don't have to look at it."

Issues of public standards and concerns are not always clear-cut. In many cases, one market segment may have to be offended to satisfy the needs of another market segment. One need only think of the controversy concerning promotion of products such as CDs from "gangster rap" groups. Clearly many individuals find mass media advertising of a CD like *Strictly 4 My N.I.G.G.A.Z.* offensive, while other segments of the population find the advertising acceptable.

THE QUALITY OF CHILDREN'S LIVES

Marketing to children has always been an area of controversy. Critics argue that advertising aimed at children fosters materialism, highlights status inequalities, encourages the consumption of low-nutritional-value foods, and creates conflict within families. They claim children are susceptible and therefore should receive special protection. Others argue that children understand the purpose of commercials and must learn to be consumers. Marketing helps socialize them into the consumer role. Furthermore, parents—the ultimate arbitrators—have considerable influence on their children.

Because of their importance to growth and health, food products sold to children are objects of particular concern. General Mills advertised Mr. Wonderful's Surprise as "the only cereal with a creamy filling" in a test market. Consumer groups complained the product, like other sweetened cereals, was not nutritious; it contained 30 percent sugar and 14 percent fat. General Mills argued, however, that the product should be considered as part of the child's total diet and not as an item isolated "out of context."

SUMMARY

1. ***Define* promotion, *explain its purposes, and identify several promotional objectives.***
   Promotion is communication applied to business. Marketers use promotion to exchange factual information and persuasive messages between buyers and sellers. The purposes of promotion include informing consumers, persuading potential buyers to purchase, or reminding past buyers not to forget to use the brand and to remember their satisfaction with past purchases. Some common promotional objectives are to provide information, obtain a direct response, differentiate the product, create a brand image, position the brand, build relationships, and influence word-of-mouth communication.

2. ***Describe the purposes and types of personal selling.***
   Personal selling is a person-to-person communication between the seller and the prospective buyer. The purpose of personal selling is to inform, persuade, or remind on a one-on-one basis. It involves discovering and communicating customer needs, matching the appropriate products with those needs, communicating product benefits, and developing customer relationships. Field selling, telemarketing, and inside selling are the three basic methods for personal selling to organizations.

3. ***Identify the stages in the creative selling process.***
   Many sales jobs require the salesperson to engage in creative selling to get new business. The creative selling process includes the following steps: (1) locating and qualifying the prospect, (2) approaching the prospect, (3) creating awareness, (4) arousing interest, (5) making a specific proposal, (6) handling objections and complaints, (7) closing the sale, and (8) following up to keep customers. Locating likely prospects is called *prospecting.* Prospecting involves activities to identify likely buyers from lists of previous customers, referrals, trade lists, advertising inquiries, and other sources. The approach involves making an initial contact and establishing a good relationship with the prospect. Effective sales presentations begin with gaining the prospect's attention. After gaining the prospect's attention, the salesperson needs to generate interest in the product offered. The next step is to create a desire to purchase the product. The salesperson

attempts to persuasively communicate to the potential buyer the benefits of a specific course of action. After making a specific proposal, the salesperson attempts to move the prospect to action. This leads to closing the sale, but it may require handling objections before closing. During the closing stage the sale is made and orders are written up. During the follow-up, the salesperson makes sure that everything was handled as promised and that the order was shipped promptly and received on schedule. Relationship management refers to the sales function of managing the account relationship and ensuring that buyers receive the appropriate services.

4. ***Describe the major types of advertising.***
Advertising is any communication carried by a mass medium and paid for by a sponsor whose product is in some way identified in the message. It consists of paid messages about an identified product, organization, or individual through nonpersonal media. Most advertising we see is selective advertising for a specific brand. Selective advertising (also called brand-specific advertising) attempts to create selective demand for a particular brand or store by promoting the brand's or store's attributes, benefits, uses, and images. Primary-demand advertising encourages generic demand for an entire product category. Institutional advertising promotes an industry or organization as a whole, stressing goodwill, corporate image, or contributions to society.

5. ***Describe publicity and public relations.***
Publicity appears in the mass media. However, publicity is different from advertising because it involves an unpaid message. Unlike advertising the company cannot control the exact content of the message. When an organization systematically plans and distributes information to manage the nature of the publicity it receives it is engaged in public relations.

6. ***Identify the various types of sales promotion.***
Consumer sales promotion programs aim to intensify the company's advertising and personal-selling messages. Examples include product sampling, cents-off coupons, rebates, contests, sweepstakes, premiums, and multiple-purchase offers. The main purpose of a trade sales promotion is to provide an incentive to wholesalers and retailers to increase their promotional efforts. The company hopes to accomplish short-term objectives such as encouraging a retailer to put up special displays or inducing a wholesaler's sales force to sell to retailers more aggressively. Examples include contests, point-of-purchase materials, trade allowances, and trade shows.

7. ***Discuss several ethical issues involving promotions.***
Social commentators frequently debate ethical issues about promotion, especially advertising. Three major issues are deceptive and misleading practices, public standards, and promotions aimed at children. Our society grants consumers the right to be informed and prohibits deceptive practices and promotions that intentionally mislead consumers. In the United States, the Federal Trade Commission Act of 1914 makes it illegal to use dishonest or misleading advertisements. Matters of law and ethics are frequently decided on the basis of public standards or beliefs as to what is right and proper. Issues of public standards and concerns are not always clear-cut. Finally, marketing to children has always been an area of controversy. Some argue that children are susceptible and therefore should receive special protection. Others argue that children understand the purpose of commercials and that marketing helps socialize them into the consumer role.

KEY TERMS AND CONCEPTS

Promotion (p. 372)
Brand image (p. 373)
Positioning campaign (p. 373)
Personal selling (p. 375)
Field selling (p. 376)
Telemarketing (p. 376)
Inside selling (p. 376)
Creative selling process (p. 378)
Prospecting (p. 379)
Approach (p. 379)
Closing (p. 380)
Follow-up (p. 380)

Relationship management (p. 380)
Selective advertising (p. 382)
Primary-demand advertising (p. 383)
Institutional advertising (p. 383)
Communications media (p. 383)
Media schedule or media plan (p. 384)
Publicity (p. 385)
Public relations (p. 386)
Sales promotion (p. 387)
Point-of-purchase materials (p. 388)
Trade allowance (p. 388)
Trade show (p. 388)
Promotional mix (p. 389)
Push strategy (p. 389)
Pull strategy (p. 389)
Internal marketing (p. 390)
Bait and switch (p. 391)
Puffery (p. 391)

DISCUSSION QUESTIONS

Company

1. Select two well-known companies and identify their promotional objectives. How do their promotional strategies differ?
2. What promotional mix would you use for the following brands?
   a. Lexus automobiles
   b. Questran powder (a prescription drug for lowering cholesterol)
   c. Goodyear's Aquatread tires
   d. AC Delco spark plugs sold to General Motors
3. Discuss the type of personal selling performed at the following companies.
   a. Avis, Inc. (car rental)
   b. The Oakland Athletics
   c. Xerox copier division
   d. Entertainment and Sports Network (ESPN)
   e. Taco Bell
4. When should a company use institutional advertising? How does it differ from brand-specific advertising?
5. Pick a brand that is advertised on television, and evaluate the purpose behind its commercials.

Customers

6. How does advertising work?
7. What advertising media do you read, watch, or listen to most often? How do their advertising messages influence you?
8. How do "Star Trek: The Next Generation" and "Fresh Prince of Bel Aire" differ in terms of audience characteristics?
9. Think of a popular recording artist. How does he or she use public relations to manage publicity?
10. What is deceptive or misleading advertising? What examples can you provide of advertisements that have deceived consumers?

Competitors

11. Do competitors tend to use the same types of promotion? Explain.
12. What is primary-demand advertising?
13. How do competitors influence a company's positioning strategies?

Collaborators

14. What is the difference between a push strategy and a pull strategy?

15. How do collaborators help in a company's promotional efforts?
16. What role does the advertising agency play in developing advertising?
17. What promotional efforts are geared toward collaborators?
18. What role should government play in the regulation of advertising to children?

In Question: Take a Stand

Executives at Volvo and its advertising agency saw a video of a monster truck crushing cars. While other cars collapsed under the weight of the truck, the Volvo station wagon survived. What better way to demonstrate Volvo's durability and safety than to "recreate" the event for advertising?

In reality, the demonstration had been rigged. The Volvo station wagon had been altered, reinforced with metal and wooden struts that the camera would not detect. The other cars had had their B-pillars cut. For a close-up, the production crew rolled a single tire over the station wagon instead of having the truck drive over the car.

The car-crushing "competition" was staged by the advertising agency and production crew. After all, advertising is not reality. It is persuasive selling using the mass media and motion picture magic. Is this advertising practice ethical?[11]

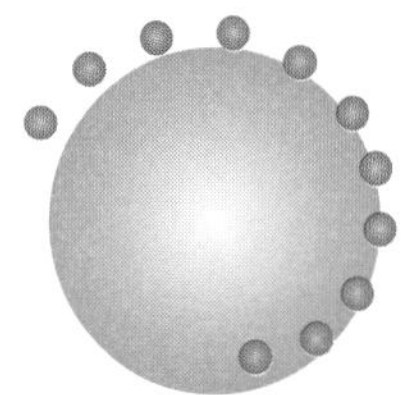

CASE 16.1
ACURA[12]

America Honda Motor Company's Acura division had watched a tightening competitive market before it decided to radically change its advertising. The upscale Japanese car marketer's advertising for the 1994 Acura Integra switched away from an emphasis on luxury and craftsmanship to "Hot Wheels" and a cool cartoon dog named Leonard. The "Hot Wheels" advertising campaign was aimed at young baby boomers (32-to-44-year-olds) who used to play with Hot Wheels, the toy cars marketed by Mattel. The advertising shows an Integra navigating an elaborate Hot Wheels track in the desert. As the car finishes a towering loop-the-loop the announcer says, "Not since Hot Wheels has a car been this much fun." The Acura logo then fills the screen before the camera returns to the car at rest. "Track sold separately," the announcer adds. (See photo below.)

The Leonard campaign was aimed at the so called Generation X consisting of 18-to-31 year olds. Acura believes this group represents 50 per cent of its prospective Integra buyers. These commercials are even wilder than the Hot

Wheels ads. The advertising uses custom animation and a cynical "spokes-dog" named Leonard. The dog never speaks directly, but the audience hears his thoughts spoken by comic Dennis Miller.

Honda went to great lengths to protect Leonard's "coolness." The company created a 10-point list of things dealers and their associations could not do with the character. For example, they did not want Leonard standing outside a car dealership waving to passing traffic.

Although the "Hot Wheels" commercials were broadcast on mainstream programs like "Home Improvement," the "Leonard" commercials were shown on cable programming, such as MTV and VH 1.

Eric Conn, Senior Manager of automotive advertising, said, "We're taking a leap of faith with this advertising." Even though he is in his 40s, Mr. Conn noted that the advertising is not designed to appeal to his generation. "If I understand it, it won't work," he says.

Questions

1. *In your opinion, what were Acura's advertising objectives for each advertising campaign?*
2. *In addition to advertising, what other promotional elements might Acura use in its promotional mix?*
3. *Do you think these advertising campaigns will be effective?*

PART 5

Tools for Business Decision Making

CHAPTER 17

INFORMATION FOR MANAGERS

When you have studied this chapter, you will be able to:

1. Identify the role of information in organizations.
2. List the characteristics of good information.
3. Define a *management information system (MIS)* and explain its role in the decision-making process.
4. Describe the most common computer hardware and software components in a computerized MIS.
5. Explain the steps in designing a management information system.
6. Discuss decision support systems and the types of decisions for which these systems are appropriate.
7. Describe various technologies now emerging in the communications field.

United Parcel Service (UPS) is one of the world's largest private package delivery companies. At any moment on any day, UPS can track the status of its shipments around the world. UPS drivers use a delivery information acquisition device (DIAD), a hand-held electronic clipboard on which they record appropriate data about each pickup and delivery. Then the data are entered into the company's main computer for recordkeeping and analysis. Using a satellite telecommunications system, UPS can track any shipment for its customers.

It wasn't always this way, however. In the early 1980s, the company's manual packaging-handling procedure was so sophisticated that UPS had the lowest cost in the industry. But by 1983 it became apparent that to keep pace with competitors like FedEx, UPS would have to improve its information technology system. Executives believed that computer-based systems could identify, route, and track packages better than any human being could. So UPS invested $50 million in a global data network, $100 million in a data center in Mahwah, New Jersey, and $350 million in electronic clipboards. It also committed $150 million to create a cellular data net and a machine-readable label.

The company learned a lot during the decade-long changeover process. Most important, it learned that the key to successfully implementing a high-technology information system is to step back and examine exactly what it is that the company does and how every process can be changed to do a better job.

Before, when a UPS package was lost, finding out who signed for it meant rummaging through countless paper receipts. The process sometimes took as long as a week. Today's improved information technology allows a driver to use a hand-held computer to electronically capture and record the signature of the recipient. Once the delivery information is transferred to New Jersey, all a customer needs to do is call to find out what happened to the package.

For UPS, the biggest problems in implementing the changes were in the human element. Many managers feared the technology would be inflexible, expensive, and prone to failure. So UPS sent selected, high-performing managers to school to learn the technology. The result was a group of managers who were supportive rather than critical of the changes.

The costs of automation and international expansion weakened UPS profits during the late 1980s, but after a few years earnings made a remarkable recovery.[1]

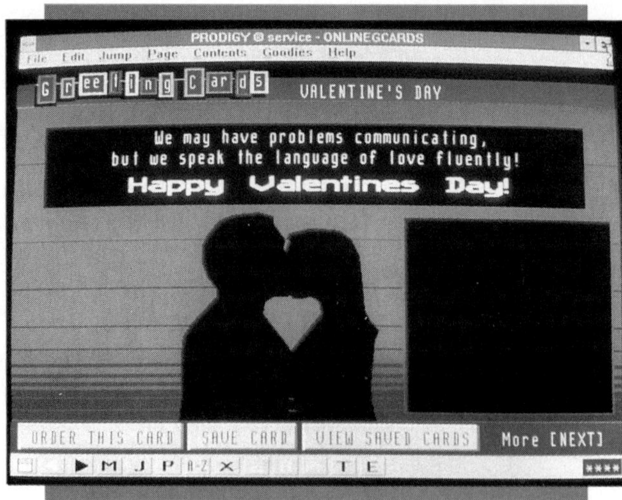

Information networks are penetrating almost every aspect of life in the United States. The world of electronic information exchange has attracted millions of Americans with PCs and modems. On Valentine's Day in 1994, thousands of people sent Cupidgrams to their Valentines on CompuServe and swapped sweet nothings on a Prodigy bulletin board.[2]

As the UPS example illustrates, computers reduce the time needed to collect and distribute information to managers and employees who need that information. This chapter looks at how information has changed the nature of business.

BUSINESS IN THE INFORMATION AGE

Most managers understand that information is a vital tool for effective management. Accurate, timely information is critical for coordinating and controlling complex business systems and for making major decisions. Large organizations like UPS are spending millions of dollars to create procedures for obtaining, distributing, and using information.

In Chapter 1, we mentioned that our modern business era is often called the *information age* or the *global era.* The impact of electronic information technology has been greater than any other force shaping business around the world. Contemporary information technologies have dramatically altered the nature of international trade. Global competition has intensified over the last decade because electronic information technology gives businesspeople access to so much timely information. It is now possible to *instantaneously* communicate to virtually any location around the world. Modern computer, satellite, cellular, and fax (facsimile) technology has shattered communication borders across the globe.

Today's businesspeople have personal computers on their desks. They routinely use fax machines, electronic mail, electronic libraries, and satellite technology for videoconferencing. Computer and electronic technology have moved business into an arena where competition is based as much on information and time (speed) as on price and quality.

The information age has radically changed the complexion of our work force. Factories and offices have become automated. Industrial robots have revolutionized the manufacturing process. These changes in manufacturing have made factory workers more productive and reduced the number of workers needed. Today fewer Americans work in factories. Most are engaged in the delivery of services rather than the production of manufactured goods. Many are engaged in the provision of information services.

Exhibit 17.1 **PRIMARY AND SECONDARY DATA FOR AN MIS**

Type	Description	Examples
Primary Data	Data that are gathered directly from the original source.	Total sales: as taken from cash register receipts. Sales calls by telemarketer: as recorded by telephone billing. Customer attitudes toward product: collected by survey questionnaires sent to customers. Cash on hand: recorded in check book and verified by bank statement.
Secondary Data	Data that are reported elsewhere, and then recorded in the information system.	Building permits issued by the city: reported by county clerk. Gross Domestic Product: reported by federal government. Total sales in the industry: reported in various industry publications. Catalogue mailing list: bought from a mailing list service

Changes in electronic technology have dramatically changed the nature of jobs in large organizations. For example, new technology has increased companies' ability to work with collaborators. Many American companies, such as The Limited, now link their computers with the computers of collaborating suppliers around the globe.

Improvements in information technology are also partly responsible for the downsizing of organizations. As companies shrink their work forces, personal computers, fax machines, and other information tools must increasingly be used to improve productivity. Already there are signs that information technology is making a difference. Since 1989, white-collar productivity has been improving, due in part to improvements in the methods for handling information.

Many small companies are reluctant to make the investment necessary to improve their information technologies. But more than ever, American businesses of all sizes need information technology that works. They need information systems that can help them get closer to customers and collaborators.

THE ROLE OF INFORMATION IN ORGANIZATIONS

All managers, regardless of the size of their business, face two major information issues. The first is getting access to disorganized data. The second is turning the disorganized data into useful information.

DATA AND INFORMATION

The terms *data* and *information* are often used interchangeably. In the context of information systems, however, they mean very different things. *Data* are raw facts that have not yet been processed or organized for useful purposes. For example, each sale at a department store is recorded at the cash register. If the store keeps a record of each sale, the recordings are data. Unless these long lists of transactions are organized, the data are not very useful, except perhaps to arrive at some total sales figure. As we saw in Chapter 13, various types of data can be collected. Original data gathered directly from transactions are called *primary data.* Existing data from others' reports of transactions or past investigations are called *secondary data.* Exhibit 17.1 lists examples of each type of data.

When the data are sorted, organized, and processed, they become *information* that may serve many purposes for the store. For example, a store typically enters each sale into a computerized inventory control system directly from the cash register. As each customer transaction is recorded, the item identification number triggers an entry that determines the remaining stock of that item. At some point, a new sales transaction will trigger a stock reorder, which will prevent the store from running out of the product. In addition, the computerized system will total sales volume, calculate state and local taxes, and record bank deposits. All of these business transactions are important to the store. An effective means of collecting and organizing such information is critical for all organizations.

CHARACTERISTICS OF GOOD INFORMATION

Effective management of any company requires having and using good information. But what makes information "good"? Many attributes make information useful, but four factors are especially important for good information: timeliness, accuracy, completeness, and relevance.[3]

Timeliness
The degree to which information is available in time to make decisions.

Timeliness. Information that is received in time to make decisions is said to have **timeliness**. One important attribute of computerized information systems is that events can be recorded and the information made available soon after they occur. The time span between the collection of data and the availability of processed information is critical to many business decisions. At Toys "R" Us, for example, the information system is programmed to alert managers about slow-moving toys several weeks before Christmas (the peak selling season for toys). This timely information allows managers to put slow-moving items on sale before Christmas to avoid getting stuck with a large inventory after the holidays.

Knowing that a timely supply of information is necessary to remain competitive, businesses are relying more and more on computerized information systems. Computers can shorten new-product development time and permit managers to respond quickly to changing business conditions.

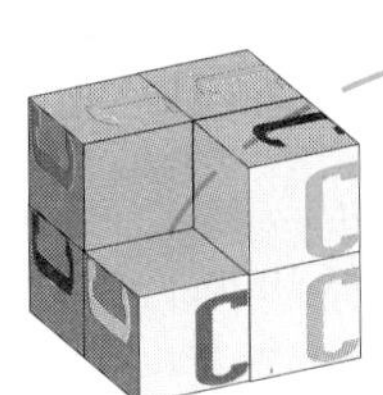

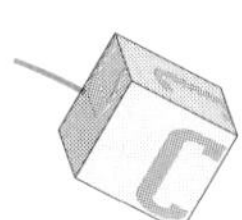

FOCUS ON COMPETITORS

Wal-Mart Stores, Inc.

Ten years ago, Wal-Mart Stores trailed Kmart in sales and profit. Because of its greater purchasing power, Kmart could negotiate lower wholesale prices. But Wal-Mart used its highly effective information system to compete with Kmart's purchasing power. By collecting and analyzing sales data from stores daily, Wal-Mart could immediately determine which merchandise was moving too slowly and thus avoid overstocking. Now many products enter one Wal-Mart loading dock and leave from another without ever sitting on a storage shelf. Although Kmart's information system has vastly improved in recent years, the competitive advantage of Wal-Mart's information system caused Kmart to lose a great deal of business.

Accuracy
The degree to which information reflects reality.

Accuracy. Information that reflects reality is said to have **accuracy**. Accurate information contains data that are adequate, complete, and correct. Information often loses its accuracy at two points in the information system: at the point of data entry and in the equations used in computer programs to process the data into information. If a supermarket clerk enters an incorrect inventory item, adjustments to inventory balances will be inaccurate. If the equations used to process the sale entry are inappropriate, the resulting inventory balance will be incorrect even if the clerk made the correct entry. Thus, most modern supermarkets use scanners at the cash register to record sales from the bar code labels on products. This practice, coupled with testing the computer equations for accuracy, results in highly accurate inventory counts on an hourly basis.

STREET SMART

Knowing Where to Find the Information

Too many students spend their college years memorizing class notes and book passages. They fail to see that what's really important is learning how to uncover information, then using that information to solve problems.

One day, a reporter was interviewing Albert Einstein in his office. Toward the end of the interview, the reporter asked Einstein for his home phone number. Einstein reached over for the phone book, looked up his number, and gave it to the reporter. The reporter was astounded. "You don't know your own phone number?" he asked. Einstein smiled and replied that he didn't want to clutter his mind with such trivia. The important thing, he said, is knowing where he could find the information when he needed it.

Completeness
The degree to which information contains the appropriate amount of data.

Completeness. Information **completeness** refers to having the appropriate amount of data. Too little data will fail to tell the complete story about the transaction or problem. Too much data may cause confusion and information "overload." Both extremes will result in ineffective information systems and ineffective decision making.

In designing the information system, it is important that the system designer work with managers and employees to determine how much information is required to be useful. One advantage of a computerized information system is that it permits the gathering of much more data, which can be collapsed into a manageable amount of information. This is how American Airlines maintains its ticket reservation system to schedule the appropriate-size aircraft. However, even the most advanced system can break down under the load of great volumes of data, as angry victims of an overbooked flight will tell you.

Relevance
The degree to which information relates to the problems, decisions, and tasks for which it is collected.

Relevance. To be useful, information must relate to the problems, decisions, and tasks for which it is collected. This characteristic is called information **relevance**. Production managers need information on production schedules, inventory balances, and the number of unacceptable parts produced. Airline clerks need information on seating capacity, passenger reservations, and weather conditions. Insurance adjusters need information on claim rates and typical costs of various medical services. Information like this is relevant because it helps managers and employees perform their tasks.

MANAGEMENT INFORMATION SYSTEMS

Management information system (MIS)
An organized system for collecting and organizing information and distributing it to organizational decision makers

Now that we know the characteristics of useful information, we can focus on how managers gain access to that information and how they use it in making decisions. A **management information system (MIS)** is an organized system for collecting and organizing information and distributing it to organizational decision makers. As Exhibit 17.2 shows, an MIS is designed to improve both the handling of information and the decision-making process.

THE MIS AND DECISION MAKING

The MIS is designed as a support mechanism around various organizational decision makers. It gathers, sorts, and organizes good information and delivers it to the appropriate decision

Exhibit 17.2 **THE MIS AND THE DECISION-MAKING PROCESS**

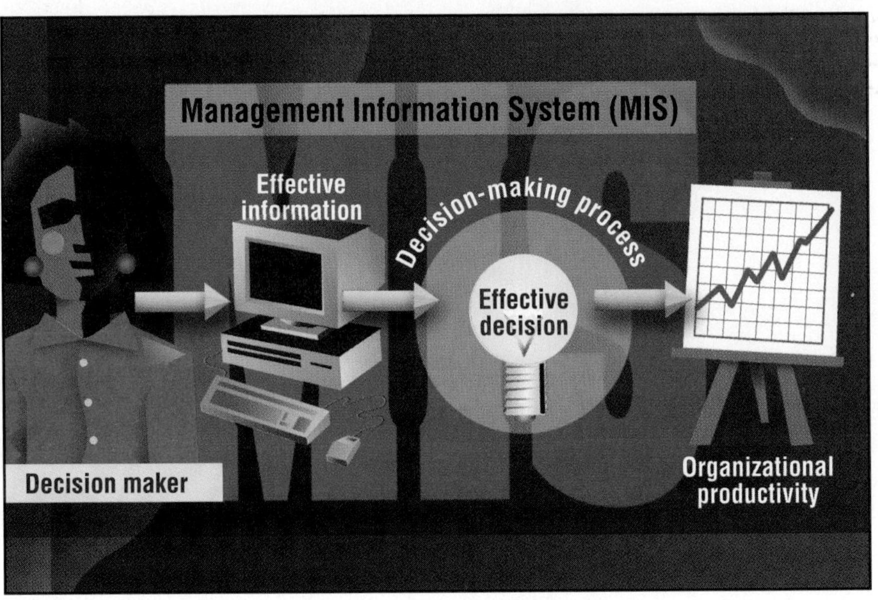

makers. Then these managers use an effective decision-making process to arrive at decisions that will enhance the organization's effectiveness. In some cases, the calculations involved in making the decision may be included in the MIS itself. In other cases, the calculations will be a part of the decision-making process.

For example, calculations for inventory levels and reordering may be included directly in the MIS. Thus, as data are gathered and entered in the MIS, calculations will be performed automatically. In this way, the manager can manage inventories without having to rely on possibly less accurate human judgments. Alternatively, decisions regarding a new plant location may involve considerable human judgment. The MIS will gather and organize relevant data about various locations, perhaps including location costs, available labor supply, potential customer traffic, and local laws or ordinances. The MIS then generates a report on the information, which various executives and managers can use as they consider each location. But the final decision will rest on their judgment rather than on the calculations performed by the MIS.

The MIS is an indispensable tool for effective decision making. Some decisions for which an MIS is needed would include the following:

- Which products should we emphasize in the European market?
- What effect would a 5 percent increase in price have on sales?
- How many new salespeople should we expect to hire next year?
- What level of production should we maintain during the coming month?
- Is the inventory of product A at the right level?

DATABASES

An information system is only as good as the data that support it. The data that are stored, saved, and maintained until needed for some decision purpose are called a *database.* A

Database
A centralized, organized, and integrated collection of data from a great many sources that is designed to meet the information needs of decision makers.

database is a centralized, organized, and integrated collection of data from a great many sources that is designed to meet the information needs of decision makers.

Databases often reside in computer storage devices such as hard disks. Other types of data are found in file cabinets or telephone books. A mailing list of customer names and addresses is one type of database, as is a collection of biographical data gathered from job applicants. Data such as these can be stored until needed for decisions or other purposes. When a new catalog is ready for mailing to customers, the mailing list can be retrieved and applied to the task. When a company needs a new employee, its database on applicants may yield a qualified employee much more quickly than a newspaper advertisement can.

Databases on financial aspects of the business, competitor prices, and economic trends have obvious uses for the company. If databases are not maintained on a wide variety of company issues, the management information system will be less useful. Out-of-date databases may lead to costly delays, especially if decisions are urgent.

The importance of databases to a company's health were underscored when Hurricane Andrew roared through Florida and Louisiana in August 1992. Many companies along the Gulf of Mexico feared that the storm would wipe out their databases. AIM Management Group, Inc., based in Houston, was concerned about losing its mutual fund database. It sent 20 portfolio managers to Englewood, Colorado, where they used the backup computers and database of Data Assurance Corporation to continue trading stocks. Data Assurance is one of a few companies specializing in helping clients deal with the loss of their databases from hurricanes and other catastrophies. Data Assurance offers its 250 clients backup computers and holds backup computer tapes that contain months or even years of data.[4]

THE ROLE OF COMPUTERS IN THE MANAGEMENT INFORMATION SYSTEM

Computerized management information systems have become commonplace. The many advantages of computerizing an MIS include speed, savings on storage space, accuracy, and ease of use. In addition, creators of MIS software have developed some very innovative programs. Thus, the use of computers in an MIS can lead to new and creative solutions to management problems.

The major disadvantage of a computerized MIS is its cost. But the much greater accuracy and efficiency a computerized system provides often offsets the cost.

FOCUS ON COLLABORATORS

Philippe Kahn

Philippe Kahn is greatly admired by industry leaders for his technical innovation and marketing wizardry. Kahn has built his eight-year-old company, Borland International Inc., into a fierce competitor. In 1991, Borland became the third largest maker of personal computer software when Kahn acquired Ashton-Tate Corporation in a $439 million stock swap. Only Microsoft Corporation and Lotus Development Corporation are bigger.

Borland was built on the success of computer languages and consumer-oriented specialty programs like Sidekick, an electronic calendar, address book, and calculator combination. But new database and spreadsheet programs like Quattro and Paradox have demonstrated Borland's ability to succeed with corporate accounts. Borland offered Paradox at deep discounts to users of dBASE and discounted Quattro to users of Lotus 1-2-3. Borland is now one of the great success stories in the world of information systems.

Exhibit 17.3 **A COMPUTERIZED MIS**

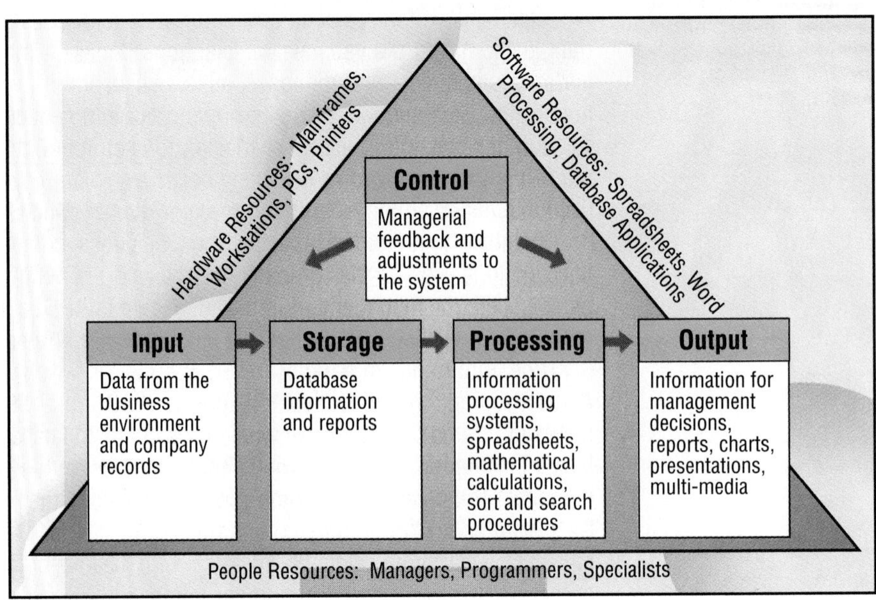

Hard disk
A thin, rigid metallic platter coated with a magnetizable substance that allows data to be recorded as magnetized and non-magnetized spots, and which is permanently encased within a hard disk drive.

Floppy disk
An inexpensive portable magnetic disk created from mylar plastic coated with a magnetizable substance on which data can be recorded as magnetized and non-magnetized spots, which can be inserted and withdrawn from floppy disk drives.

Magnetic tape
A storage medium created from thin plastic coated with a magnetizable substance on which data are stored as magnetized and non-magnetized spots on the tape.

Optical storage disks
Plastic coated disks on which data are recorded and read by using a laser beam rather than through magnetic means.

AN MIS MODEL

Exhibit 17.3 presents a model of one computerized information system. The major phases of this system are inputs, storage, processing, output, and control.

Inputs. Inputs to an MIS include the company's goals and objectives, facts and other data needed to evaluate problems, and other specific information that managers need. Many different types of data are needed as inputs to company problems and decisions. For example, when Columbia Sportswear Company needs to decide what styles and sizes of winter ski jackets to offer, it must have data on customer preferences, winter weather forecasts, and economic trends. It may also have other types of inputs such as scanned artwork that can be used for designing advertisements.

Often data are gathered not for a particular problem or task but for some unspecified future use. In these cases, MIS specialists simply anticipate that certain data may prove useful. For instance, Columbia Sportswear Company may gather population trends with the expectation that changes in the population may affect future decisions on the location of new warehouses.

Storage. In the storage phase of the MIS model, data and information are stored in databases. Databases are kept on hard disks, floppy disks, magnetic tape, or optical storage devices such as CD-ROM disks. A **hard disk** is a thin, rigid metallic platter coated with a magnetizable substance that allows data to be recorded as magnetized and non-magnetized spots, and which is permanently encased within a hard disk drive. A **floppy disk** is an inexpensive portable magnetic disk created from mylar plastic coated with a magnetizable substance on which data can be recorded as magnetized and non-magnetized spots, which can be inserted and withdrawn from floppy disk drives. **Magnetic tape** is a storage medium created from thin plastic coated with a magnetizable substance on which data are stored as magnetized and non-magnetized spots on the tape. **Optical storage disks**, such as CD-ROMs, are plastic coated disks on which data are recorded and read by using a laser beam rather than through magnetic means.

Raw data that have not yet been processed may be stored to await processing when they are needed for decisions or problem solving. Data that have been processed into information also may be stored to avoid the need to reprocess the information in the future. Also, processed information that is stored may be used later in more complex calculations. Thus, stored information comes from both initial input and processed data.

Processing. Once gathered, data must be organized, stored, and transformed into information that managers can use to solve problems or make decisions. Processing involves the use of a wide variety of programming applications, such as spreadsheets, statistical packages, and mathematical equations. The type of processing may range from simply sorting the data alphabetically to complex statistical analysis.

Octel Communications Corporation is a small company that sells voice information services that electronically link voice, data, and image processing over the telephone network. Customers can use a touch-tone telephone to call up the processed information. Traveling salespeople can use PowerCall to call their companies' computers and check the inventory (processed data) for an item that has been sold to a customer. Also using similar processing equipment, a university student can listen to course descriptions recorded in a professor's own words, find out whether a course still has space available, register for it, and get documents like transcripts and financial aid forms by fax.[5]

Output. Output consists of reports, charts, presentation materials, and, more recently, multimedia materials. For instance, to persuade a store owner to allot shelf space to Sylvania light bulbs, a salesperson will present a multimedia demographic map of the store's clientele within a ten-mile radius. The database also will have information about their bulb-buying habits. Color-coded hot-cold maps of their territories tell salespersons which neighborhoods are most likely to use their light bulbs.[6]

Control. The control phase of the MIS model ensures that the MIS is producing the type of information needed and that the information is timely, relevant, and accurate. Control generally goes on throughout the MIS, but we show it following the output phase, since this is the point at which the entire process can be evaluated. Feedback from the people using the output is critical, since only they are in a position to evaluate the output. If the MIS is determined to be operating improperly, it must be modified. Modifications may include changing the nature of the data collected, changing the processing method, or revising the output. Only by establishing control over the MIS can managers ensure that the information generated meets their own and other users' needs.

COMPUTER HARDWARE

Computer *hardware* consists of the actual machinery that makes up the computer system. Hardware includes input devices such as keyboards, scanners, mouses, and sound and video input devices. Output devices such as monitors, printers, and plotters are integral parts of computer hardware. Storage devices include large hard drives that may have several gigabytes of memory and floppy drives that store about 360 kilobytes of data.

THE MICROPROCESSOR

Microprocessor
An integrated circuit, or chip, on the computer's main circuit board that processes the instructions supplied to it by the software.

Perhaps the least understood part of the computer is the microprocessor. The **microprocessor** is an integrated circuit, or chip, on the computer's main circuit board. This tiny chip processes the instructions supplied to it by the software. When the microprocessor receives an instruction, it interprets it and "tells" the other parts of the computer system—the disk drives, the video display, and so on—what they should do.

The instructions the microprocessor receives are in the microprocessor's own vocabulary, known as its *instruction set.* Each microprocessor on the market understands its own set of instructions. Software programs are normally designed to run on specific microprocessors, which explains why some software will run only on certain computers. For example, software designed for the IBM will not run on the Macintosh, and software designed for the NeXT computer will not run on either the IBM or the Mac, without special software. Some progress in making software compatible among brands of computers is expected in the near future, but true compatibility depends more on the microprocessor than on the software design.

MEMORY

Read-only memory (ROM)
Computer memory that contains permanent information that cannot be erased or changed.

Random access memory (RAM)
Computer memory that stores the information the microprocessor needs to run an application.

Computers use two types of memory, both of which are contained in more chips connected to the computer's main circuit board. **Read-only memory (ROM)** contains permanent information that cannot be erased or changed. This information remains intact when the computer is turned off, because it is needed again when the computer is turned back on. Computer routines, such as how to start the system, how to move data to and from disks and peripheral devices, and how to manage the memory space in RAM, are contained in the ROM. These routines are accessed by the microprocessor and used to operate the computer software.

Random access memory (RAM) stores the information the microprocessor needs to run an application, such as word processing software. RAM is contained in separate memory chips, also connected to the main circuit board. Information in RAM is stored electronically and is retrieved much more quickly than information retrieved from a mechanical device such as a floppy or hard disk drive. However, because it is stored electronically, information can be lost when the computer is turned off. For this reason, computer users are urged to "save" their work regularly and often.

When an application is started, the microprocessor finds the application at its permanent location on the disk and transfers a temporary "copy" into RAM. Large applications such as desktop publishing require large amounts of RAM. Thus, any software that manipulates large databases will probably require four or more megabytes of RAM.

DISK DRIVES

The primary way to load software information and instructions into RAM is with floppy disks and disk drives. *Disk drives* record information on thin, circular disks that are coated with a magnetic surface. The disk drives contain read-write heads similar to the recording heads in a cassette recorder. When the disk is inserted, these heads will read any software instructions on the disk, as well as any information stored by the user. Hard drives contain permanent disks that may store as much as several gigabytes of information, equivalent to several hundred volumes of encyclopedias. Floppy disks may contain as much as two megabytes of data, enough for several term projects.

OUTPUT DEVICES

Output devices consist of hardware that display information, such as monitors and printers. Monitors typically use cathode-ray tubes similar to those found in common television sets. A moving electron beam inside the picture tube scans across the screen, turning on and off to create tiny dots called pixels (short for picture elements). The monitor is the primary output device, displaying the information as the user enters it. Any changes to the information are instantly displayed on the screen, permitting the user to check his or her work.

There is an almost endless variety of printers, including dot-matrix printers, ink jet printers, laser printers, and different types of color printers. Printers display information on paper, but only when the user instructs the program to "print." Users typically print only when their work is in its final version, to eliminate unnecessary waste of paper. Printed copies of the output, often called hard copies, let users distribute their information to other persons to be read and analyzed.

COMPUTER SOFTWARE

Computers use two basic types of software: the system software and application software. *System software* is a collection of programs the computer needs (in addition to the instructions contained in ROM) before you can use it. Among the files contained in typical system software are

- Computer language–specific information needed for communication with various application software
- Information on keyboard layouts
- Fonts (styles of type)
- The finder information needed to manage the contents of the disks and disk drives
- Resources that drive the printers, networks, and displays

Application software refers to the specific applications—word processing, spreadsheets, graphics programs, and so on—that are used to manipulate or process data in particular ways. The most popular application software packages include

- WordPerfect, Microsoft Word, MacWrite (word processing)
- Lotus 1-2-3, Excel (spreadsheets)
- MacDraw, Harvard Graphics, Adobe Illustrator (graphics)
- PageMaker, QuarkXPress (desktop publishing)
- Aldus Persuasion, PowerPoint (presentation software)
- MacroMind Director, HyperCard (multimedia)
- SPSS—Statistical Package for the Social Sciences, SAS—Statistical Analysis System (statistics)

Many of these application software packages are available in versions for different computers. For example, PowerPoint, PageMaker, Lotus 1-2-3, Excel, and WordPerfect are available for both IBM-compatible and Macintosh computers. Thousands of application software programs exist for most computer systems. Different users have their favorite programs, and there is little general agreement regarding which is best. Generally, a company should use the software that best meets its needs and the information needs of the users.

TYPES OF COMPUTERS

We have seen that many different brands of computers exist. You are probably familiar with the small, desktop computers called *microcomputers* or *personal computers* that include the Macintosh, the IBM-PC, and a large number of IBM compatibles that run MS-DOS software programs.

The revolution in computers in business actually began with much larger computers called *mainframe computers.* Mainframe computers are very large, in terms of both physical size and memory and processing speeds. Three decades ago, mainframes consisted of thousands of vacuum tubes used to store data. These tubes tended to burn out frequently, and the computer was subject to short circuits caused by moths that were attracted to the warm, bright interior of the computer. Technicians then had to replace the vacuum tubes and remove the moths, which led to the expression "debugging the computer."

AT&T suffered after the U.S. government severed it into seven regional operating companies, and left AT&T only with long-distance and Western Electric operations. But those long-distance networks put AT&T in a unique position to create the largest information network in the world. Its core telecommunications network, a vast intricate web of wire, computers, optical fiber, and software, contributes more than $40 billion to AT&T's profits.[7]

Today mainframe computers are far more reliable. They are much larger in terms of storage and processing speed but are physically much smaller. They may cost several million dollars. Very large business and government organizations use mainframes to keep track of their complex operations. The term *supercomputers* emerged during the 1980s to describe the many advanced computer systems that were being built for scientific projects around the country. These very fast, very large computers often were shared by users at different companies. However, rapid advances in computer technology soon made these computers obsolete. Today the trend is toward the use of workstations or minicomputers.

The *minicomputer* is about the size of a small desk. It is somewhat slower in processing speed than the mainframe and has much less storage capacity. However, it is also much less expensive and can be used for complex business and scientific applications. Some businesses have joined two or more minicomputers to create faster, larger computer systems that approximate mainframe capabilities at far less cost.

The most obvious advances in business use of computers has occurred in the microcomputer. This is the smallest type of computer. It is much slower and has much less storage capacity than mainframes and minicomputers do. Nonetheless, vast numbers of American businesses and other organizations, as well as individuals, have adopted personal computers.

The typical microcomputer is an IBM-PC, an IBM compatible, or a Macintosh. Generally these desktop computers contain a speedy microprocessor, internal hard disks that can store 40 or more megabytes of data, 2 megabytes of RAM, and a floppy disk drive. Monitors are available in a wide range of prices, in both black-and-white and color. Many of these computer systems can be upgraded in terms of speed and memory. Some systems contain 256 megabytes of RAM, hard drives that can store over 5 gigabytes of data, and monitors as large as 21 inches.

NETWORKED COMPUTERS

Although minicomputers are designed to stand alone, they can be networked to other microcomputers, minicomputers, and mainframes. *Networked computers* can share information, printers, and application programs. For example, a salesperson can gather data and enter them in the computer as a sale is made. In a networked system, the regional sales manager can access the sales data from a second computer and then pass them along to the production department or other people who need that information. Similarly, a salesperson can take a portable computer with a modem along on a long sales trip. Simply by plugging the hotel phone line into the modem, the salesperson can call company offices, access inventory information, and determine which products can be shipped immediately to customers.

Networked computers can help a company in other ways as well. For example, managers can communicate over computer networks and share ideas. Companies such as Boeing Corporation use networked computers to conduct group brainstorming sessions. In this way, the participants avoid arguments and reach decisions faster than they would in an ordinary brainstorming session. Other companies find that collaborative projects can be completed more quickly, and out of the reach of the sometimes disruptive influence of the boss.

FOCUS ON COMPANY

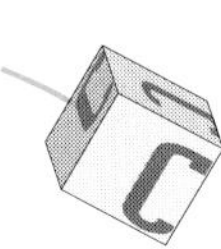

Software for Brainstorming

After years of complaints that office computing doesn't pay for itself, new software for meetings—called groupware—can reduce the time needed to complete complex projects. In some cases, the time savings may approach 90 percent. Many companies have used GroupSystems software, developed by Jay Nunamaker at the University of Arizona, to tap creative energy in brainstorming sessions. The participants still sit around a table, but instead of arguing, they enter their thoughts into networked personal computers to keep track of what everyone has to say. Participants can sift through far more material and reach decisions much more quickly than they could in ordinary brainstorming sessions.

Productivity gains around the conference table are common benefits of this software, but companies can achieve much more by linking departments or coworkers in different locations. Collaborative projects can be completed without costly time delays and travel budgets as employees communicate and coordinate their decisions with help from the software.

Price Waterhouse, a large accounting firm, uses a different groupware program—Notes by Lotus Development Corporation—to coordinate activities among employees at diverse worldwide locations. Notes provides interlinked electronic bulletin boards that allow people in different locations who have insights or expertise on a particular problem to find one another. A typical Notes conversation can include employees from five or six cities around the world. A question from London may be responded to by someone in Toronto and a third comment contributed by an employee in Los Angeles. Before Notes, only four members of Price Waterhouse's 15-person senior executive committee used PCs. Now they all do.

Exhibit 17.4 illustrates a very simple computer network. In this network, four computers are connected over a communication network and share one printer. In addition, depending on how they want the system to work, network users may share designated data files or application programs with one another over the network. However, if any user wants to keep certain information private, he or she can designate that information as a file not to be shared. Thus, all users get to control their own information.

Exhibit 17.4 **A SIMPLE COMPUTER NETWORK**

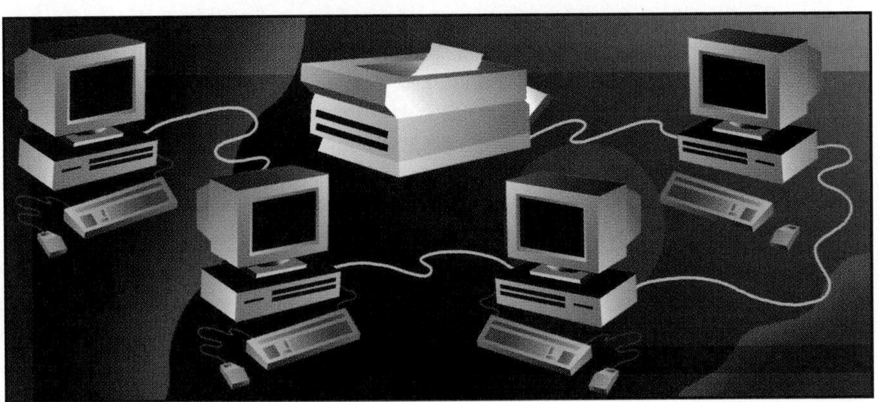

More complex networks may include linkages among departments, linkages among different types of computers (for example, both IBM-PCs and Macintoshes can be put on the same network), and a wide variety of peripheral equipment such as scanners and printers. Computer networks can also control lighting and heating equipment, production lines, and other manufacturing processes.

Finally, computers can be networked to television systems, and the output of computer processing can be displayed directly over the system. Mind Extension University (MEU), which offers college degree programs over public television, is one example of this capability. MEU courses often include displays of computer processing taken directly from the computer screen during the television broadcast.

DESIGNING A MANAGEMENT INFORMATION SYSTEM

The purpose of any management information system is to provide information to managers and employees who need the information to perform their jobs. It is important that the MIS provide useful and relevant information in a form that managers and employees can use. Effective design of an MIS typically involves four steps.[8] As with most management activities, the design of an MIS begins with planning, after which the system is designed, implemented, and evaluated (see Exhibit 17.5).

PLANNING

MIS planning focuses on the types of information managers need. Information specialists will need to decide how the data and information will be processed and presented to the users. Thus, MIS planning involves both managers (users) and technicians, since only managers can identify their information needs and only technicians can design the processing system. During this stage, users and technicians try to determine the exact types of data and information needed, who will need them, and how they will be distributed to users. In addition, estimates of the cost of the MIS and a determination of how the existing MIS (manual or computerized) will be converted to the new system must be made.

DESIGN

One of the most important design considerations will be whether or not to computerize the new MIS. During the past few years, even the smallest companies have opted for computerized MISs. A computerized MIS can be relatively inexpensive if microcomputers are used, and

Exhibit 17.5 **DESIGNING A MANAGEMENT INFORMATION SYSTEM**

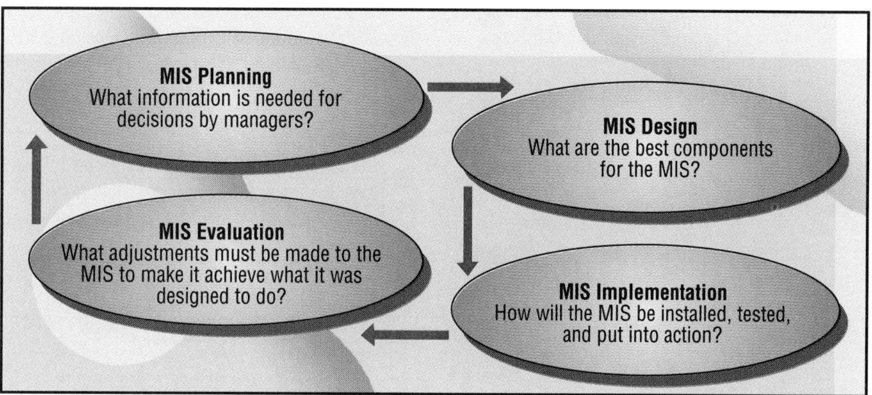

the costs of these systems are quickly recovered due to their efficiency and accuracy. Once decisions are made regarding the design of the MIS, a prototype can be built to pretest various parts of the system.

In a computerized management information system, accounting, payroll, and other financial recordkeeping and processing activities are often the first functions to be computerized. Effective processing of this type of information will depend heavily on the hardware and software the MIS uses.

Another design consideration is whether the MIS will be centralized or more widely distributed among users. In a *centralized* MIS, a group of specialists and key managers control the hardware and software. Although the security of a centralized system is high, the system is slow to respond to the needs of individual users. In a *distributed* MIS, smaller computers are distributed at different locations where data are received or used. These systems are very responsive to individual department needs, but sometimes lead to inefficient coordination among the various locations. A well-designed MIS will balance the advantages and disadvantages of centralized and distributed systems, arriving at an MIS that meets the needs of all users.

A poorly designed MIS can have devastating impacts on a company. Blue Cross, one of the world's most prominent health insurers, lost millions of customers and spent large sums of money on an MIS that was improperly designed. Analysts suspect that technologists made too many design decisions without input from managers and other users. Ultimately, Blue Cross had to hire an outside consulting firm to handle its MIS.[9]

IMPLEMENTATION

In the implementation step, MIS plans and designs are converted into operational MIS systems. This involves purchasing all hardware and software, hiring the personnel who will operate various parts of the system, and installing, testing, and modifying the equipment. If there is an existing MIS, implementation will include removing the old equipment and installing the new.

Implementation also includes training all personnel who will be involved with the MIS. These include managers and other employees who need to have information for their daily activities and decision making. If they were accustomed to an "old" way of doing things, they may resist the new MIS. Thus, money invested in training them will be well spent, since it will make the new system easier for them and reduce their resistance to it. The more the users of the MIS are involved in implementing the system, the more effective it is likely to be.

Exhibit 17.6 **TYPES OF DECISIONS IN A DECISION SUPPORT SYSTEM**

Functional Area	Types of Decisions
Marketing	What would be the effect of increasing prices by 5, 8, or 10 percent? Where should a new product be test marketed? What market segments are likely to become more important to our industry in the next 10 years?
Finance	What impact will deferring dividends to shareholders have on the price of our stock? What impact will a new stock offering have on our credit rating? How will a proposed union contract affect future liabilities and our ability to meet them?
Production	Should we purchase new, expensive production equipment or give more business to outside vendors? What will be the impact of a strategic policy to reduce delivery time to customers by five days? What are the key factors in determining labor costs for each product we manufacture?
Strategic management	What level of business should we plan for in the next five years? What impact would be felt on our business as a result of potential antitrust action? Should we expand our manufacturing operations into a politically unstable nation?

EVALUATION

After the MIS is installed, it must be evaluated periodically to ensure that it is accomplishing its purposes. MIS evaluations typically examine four areas:

- Effectiveness: How has the MIS helped the organization and its managers?
- Efficiency: How well does the MIS use the company's resources?
- Reliability: To what extent does the MIS provide information when needed?
- Security: How safe from abuse and theft are the stored data and the equipment in the system?

Evaluation of the MIS also should involve managers and other users. A survey of these people, along with a review of computer and MIS activities, will provide valuable information on the effectiveness of the MIS. If the evaluation reveals that new information needs have occurred or that new technology would be more efficient, the process of MIS planning, designing, implementing, and evaluating must begin anew.

DECISION SUPPORT SYSTEMS

Decision support system (DSS)
An interactive, computer-based information system designed to support specific decisions made by managers.

When designing an MIS, engineers and programmers may focus too heavily on how to package and manipulate information. Management decision making may be overlooked in the process of designing an effective information processing system. A more advanced type of MIS focuses on the types of decisions managers make and how they make those decisions. A **decision support system (DSS)** is an interactive, computer-based information system designed to support specific decisions made by managers. The types of decisions that form the core of a DSS are those made by top managers, such as strategic planning and forecasting. Decision support systems are designed more to assist in complex, unstructured management decisions, while MISs are designed more for relatively structured activities such as inventory control. Information that a DSS database might contain includes pricing histories

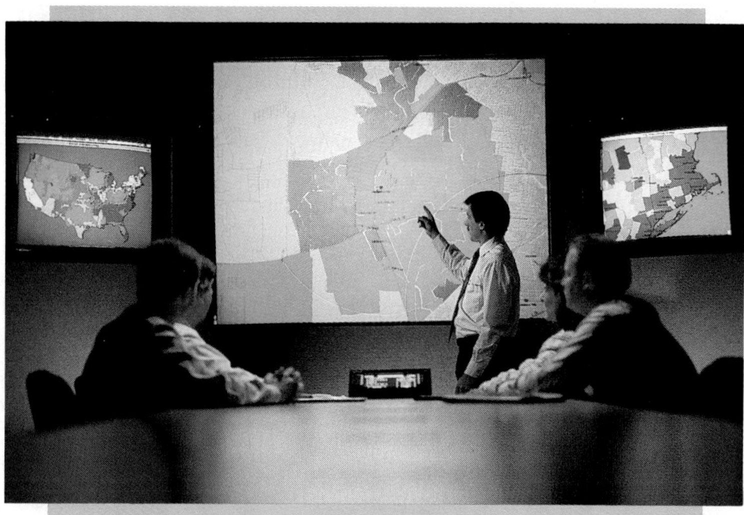

When Frank St. Onge, manager of marketing analysis for Osram/Sylvania, really wants to impress customers, he brings them into the high-tech "War Room" at headquarters, dims the lights, and turns on the equipment. The room is designed for teleconferencing and state-of-the-art multimedia presentations, but what most lights up visitors are the maps—big, computerized maps, rich with useful data, displayed on a six-foot color videoscreen. Says St. Onge, "We show them where are our competitors, where are the customers, and what areas of the country have the greatest sales potential, down to the block level. ... we could give them the same data on ... spreadsheets, but illustrating the information with a map is a much more powerful tool." [10]

of the company's and competitors' products, seasonal variations in demand, and general economic data such as gross domestic product (GDP) and inflation rates. Exhibit 17.6 lists some types of decisions that a decision support system might address.

Thus, managers who use a DSS can manipulate the data and interact with the system. Rather than just receiving printouts on information in a preset format, managers can change the way the information is presented, apply different formulas to the data, and combine the computerized facts with other information based on the managers' judgment. In this manner, the system focuses on decisions rather than on the information contained in the system.

Geographic information system (GIS)
A decision support system that displays data on digitized maps.

A **geographic information system (GIS)** is a decision support system that displays data on digitized maps. For example, the GIS at Cigna, the giant insurance company, helps sales representatives sell managed-care plans to brokers who buy health insurance policies for corporations. A broker might ask, for instance, what percentage of the client's employees will find at least two Cigna-affiliated doctors within eight miles of their homes. Instead of responding with many pages of tabular data, a sales representative can now provide a broker with maps showing the distribution of physicians and employees. People recognize details on maps that they would not understand if the data were organized in another way.[11]

Expert system (ES)
A computer program that is based on the expertise, rules of thumb, and knowledge of specialists in a field.

Another development in decision support systems is the expert system. An **expert system (ES)** is a computer program that is based on the expertise, rules of thumb, and knowledge of specialists in a field. Thus, the analyses and decisions made by humans (managers) can be imitated by using the knowledge and rules of thumb of the experts.

EMERGING COMMUNICATIONS TECHNOLOGIES

The entire field of communications technology is changing rapidly. Today's ideas will, in all likelihood, be tomorrow's reality. Emerging technologies in information processing, computers, and information exchange will affect many areas of business.

COMPUTERS AND HARDWARE

The changing nature of the information revolution and its effect on organizations is evidenced by changes at the world's largest computer company, IBM. In late 1992, IBM announced changes in its organizational structure. The company's focus shifted from mainframe computers to the manufacture of mini- and microcomputers. The IBM AS/400 minicomputer competes directly with the small IBM ES/9000 mainframe. Because of the increased processing speeds in mini- and microcomputers and the ability to network large numbers of these computers, networked systems of small computers may outperform mainframe computers, and at a lower cost.[12] The trend is definitely toward more powerful microcomputers.

Furthermore, IBM, Apple, and Motorola collaborated to develop a new type of computer chip, the Power PC. The Power PC chip promises to make IBM and Macintosh computers highly compatible.

TELEPHONES AND THE EXCHANGE OF INFORMATION

With modems, voice messaging systems, and cellular phone technology, the field of information exchange and communication over telephone systems is changing rapidly. You are probably already familiar with the use of modems for exchanging information over telephone networks. Today notebook computers, often using cellular technology, can be equipped with modems for use by business travelers. Other interfaces among telephone systems, computers, and users of information are being implemented.

AT&T recently announced a successful test of a telephone system that also displays a televised picture of the person on the other end of the phone. The technology is new, and the video picture is displayed at only 11 frames per second (in contrast to a normal rate of 60 frames per second). Because the signal is slow, synchronizing words and lip movements is a problem. But it is clear that technologies like this will continue to improve. This means managers and their subordinates may be able to "meet face to face" over a telephone.

Videoconferencing
A business meeting at which telephones or satellites and TV screens link participants located in different cities or remote locations.

Videoconferencing refers to a business meeting at which telephones or satellites and TV screens link participants located in different cities or remote locations. Videoconferencing eliminates the cost of having individuals travel to company headquarters or a central meeting place such as an airport hotel.

Voice mail
A sophisticated, computerized telephone answering system that digitizes incoming spoken messages, stores them in the recipient's voice mailbox, and converts them to spoken form when retrieved.

Voice mail systems have changed the way businesspeople get their messages. **Voice mail** is a sophisticated, computerized telephone answering system that digitizes incoming spoken messages, stores them in the recepient's voice mailbox, and converts them to spoken form when retrieved. Voice mail allows a manager to be away from his or her desk and still receive messages. Voice mail, coupled with the increased use of microcomputers by managers, has substantially reduced the cost of secretarial help.

FAX MACHINES

Facsimile (fax) machine
A machine which copies a sheet of paper at one location and then transfers it via telephone to a fax machine at another location.

Facsimile (fax) machines seemed revolutionary only a few years ago. Today **fax machines**, which copy a sheet of paper at one location and then transfer it via telephone to a fax machine at another location, have changed many aspects of business. For example, mail-order computer company Gateway 2000's technical support hotline offers to fax documentation to users having problems with the company's products. There is no need to wait for "snail mail" from the post office. Fax modems, which allow sending and receiving computer files, can now be inexpensively installed on most business computers.

Communications technology has greatly changed the way companies work with their collaborators. Today videoconferencing lets company employees and collaborators work on the same document simultaneously and talk to and see one another. This allows collaborators such as engineering consultants, product designers, and computer system analysts to work closely with manufacturing and operations personnel in client companies—even those thousands of miles away—without visiting the clients' headquarters.[13]

TELEVISION AND INFORMATION EXCHANGE

When the former Soviet Union created the world's first satellite, few people would have predicted the dramatic impact these artificial stellar bodies would have on our everyday lives. Today most of the television we watch, many of the telephone conversations we conduct, and much of the weather information we receive involve satellites. Using satellite transmissions, companies can access remote locations from their headquarters and exchange larger volumes of information than ever before.

Cable Television. The marketing of products using cable television and personal information services such as Prodigy has changed the nature of some consumer markets. The Home Shopping Network, for example, airs programs that show a wide variety of products, much like a television version of a mail-order catalog. Consumers can call in to ask questions or order products. This system allows communication of product information and product demonstration more easily and inexpensively than many other methods.

Interactive media
Technology that promotes messages to groups of similar prospects, and then allows for responses customized to buyers' wishes.

Interactive Media. An emerging growth market using new technologies to exchange information involves the use of interactive media. **Interactive media** promote messages to groups of similar prospects and then allow for responses customized to the buyers' wishes. For instance, interactive media might show an "advertisement" for a series of vacation packages and then allow a shopper to request more detailed information to be sent to his or her computer screen. In selected test cities in the United States, interactive media are already linked to cable television systems, and there is no need for a computer. The shopper, movie viewer, or information seeker needs only a television set with a remote.

TELE-EDUCATION

Educational television has expanded far beyond "Sesame Street." Today a person can earn a university degree by attending classes offered on television by several universities in local areas and nationally over networks like Mind Extension University. These systems broadcast campus classrooms and allow adult learners who cannot attend regular classes to continue their education via television.

Also, experimental programs like the American Memory Project (AMP) undertaken by the Library of Congress promise to change the type of information students have available in their classrooms. The Library of Congress has vast volumes of historical movie clips, photographs, and speeches that most Americans cannot access. The AMP is designed to record most of this information to videotape and subsequently to laser disk. Then computer programs will access that information over cable television networks. In this manner, a student can sit in a classroom and use the school's computer to call up a particular movie clip or speech from laser disks at the television station. Thus, great volumes of educational information may become available to any citizen with a computer and a tie-in to the cable system.

FOCUS ON COLLABORATORS

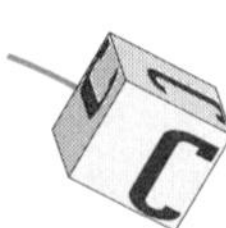

Jones Intercable Inc. and BCE, Inc., Deal

As the cable and telephone industries began to converge, Glenn Jones, chair and CEO of Jones Intercable Inc., formed an alliance with BCE, Inc.(parent of Bell Canada), Canada's largest publicly held company. BCE purchased a 30 percent stake in Jones to form the cross-border alliance. Jones hopes to make Colorado the distance education capital of the world. Mind Extension University, a major product for Jones, offers distance education and college degree programs 24 hours a day to some 2.6 million students. Jones is also planning a health network and a language network and is an active player in interactive and educational software publishing.

THE INTERNET

Internet
A huge, global web of 25,000 computer networks.

The **Internet** is a huge, global web of 25,000 computer networks. In 1993 the Internet doubled in size, and an estimated 20 million people had access to it. Many companies, including General Electric, IBM, J. P. Morgan, Merrill Lynch, Motorola, and Xerox, are making use of this information superhighway.

Companies use the Internet to increase communication, improve collaboration with strategic partners, and access the world's largest public library for an endless range of information. Most of the corporate traffic that crosses the Internet is E-mail. Electronic messages cross the globe instantly, making rapid decisions possible.

The Internet is also used for direct marketing of products and services. Since the 20 million users identify themselves as members of various interest groups, marketers have a much better idea of who will buy what types of products and services.

In addition to organizations, millions of individuals have plugged into the Internet through their computers and modems. E-mail zooms between private citizens, and many subscribe to formal information services such as Prodigy and America Online. The Internet is certain to become an important part of the growing future of information services.[14]

BREAKING LANGUAGE BARRIERS

As business has become increasingly global, serious problems have arisen from language differences. When managers in one nation cannot communicate with managers in a second country, coordination between the business units suffers. Information needed to make decisions in different locations needs to be translated, without loss of meaning and without costly time delays.

The Japanese language, for example, has more than 7,000 characters, which has made even the use of personal computers in Japan very difficult. However, computer programmers have created *voice recognition systems* for many languages, including Japanese. Using these systems, Japanese workers can speak to the computer, which then makes the correct typed entries. While voice recognition systems are still in their early stages, such systems could eventually record words spoken in one language and type a version translated into another language. Thus, a manager in Japan could simply give a verbal message in Japanese to his or her computer in Tokyo and send the message by modem or satellite to an office in San Francisco where it would be instantly translated into English for an American manager.

FOCUS ON COLLABORATORS

Fuji Xerox and Kurzweil Applied Intelligence

Kazuhiko Sumiya spoke softly but clearly into a telephone handset. *Teikiatugaari,* he said, looking at the Sun Microsystems workstation perched on a nearby desk. In seconds, the Japanese phrase appeared on the screen in phonetic English, followed by several rows of Japanese *kanji* characters. *Taikio,* Sumiya added. Again Japanese characters appeared on the screen. The message: "There is a low-pressure system that makes the atmosphere unstable." The voice recognition system had correctly identified the spoken Japanese words on the first try, but also offered several choices in case it had misunderstood some words.

Ray Kurzweil, a busy inventor of high-tech products, is behind the new system. Kurzweil began researching speech recognition technology more than a decade ago. In 1982, he started Kurzweil Applied Intelligence to build the first computerized voice recognition system. This system requires that the speaker pause briefly after each word. But in Japanese, where distinctions among phrases are subtle, continuous speech is a requirement. That means faster, more powerful microprocessors will be needed before such a system is economically feasible.

As you learned in this chapter, you need not be a computer programmer to understand and use computerized information systems. Information has become critical for business decisions and organizational effectiveness. It is likely that management information systems will be computerized in the future and that great strides will be made in the types of information these systems manage.

SUMMARY

1. ***Identify the role of information in organizations.***
   All managers face two major information issues: getting access to disorganized data and turning the disorganized data into useful information. Data are raw facts that have not yet been processed or organized for useful purposes. When data are sorted, organized, and processed, they become information that may serve many purposes for a company.

2. ***List the characteristics of good information.***
   Four major characteristics of good information are timeliness, accuracy, completeness, and relevance. Information that is received in time to make decisions is said to have timeliness. Information that reflects reality is considered to have accuracy. Information completeness refers to having the appropriate amount of data. To have relevance, information must relate to the problems, decisions, and tasks for which it is collected.

3. ***Define a* management information system (MIS) *and explain its role in the decision-making process.***
A management information system (MIS) is an organized system for collecting and organizing information and distributing it to organizational decision makers. It is designed to gather, sort, and organize good information and deliver it to the appropriate decision makers. Some decisions for which an MIS would be useful include the type of product to offer, the likely effect of a price increase on sales, how many new salespeople to hire, what level of production to maintain, and whether the inventory of a given product is at the right level.

4. ***Describe the most common hardware and software components in a computerized MIS.***
A computerized MIS has the advantages of speed, savings on storage space, accuracy, and ease of use. Computer hardware consists of the actual machinery that makes up the computer system, including input, output, and storage devices. The microprocessor is an integrated circuit, or chip, on the computer's main circuit board. It processes information supplied to it by the software and "tells" other parts of the computer system what they should do. Computers use two types of memory. Read-only memory (ROM) contains permanent information that cannot be erased or changed. Random access memory (RAM) stores the information the microprocessor needs to run an application. Disk drives record information and will read software instructions and information stored by the user. Hard drives contain permanent disks that may store as much as several gigabytes of information. Floppy disks may contain as much as two megabytes of data. Two common output devices are monitors and printers. Monitors display information as it is entered by the user, while printers provide hard copies of the information in its final form.
Computers use two basic types of software: system software and application software. System software is a collection of programs the computer needs before you can use it. Application software is the specific applications that are used to manipulate or process data in particular ways. Software applications include word processing, spreadsheets, statistical analysis, graphics, desktop publishing, presentation software, and multimedia applications.

5. ***Explain the steps in designing a management information system.***
Effective design of an MIS involves four steps: planning, designing, implementing, and evaluating the system. MIS planning focuses on determining the exact types of data and information needed, who will need them, and how they will be distributed to the users. One of the most important design considerations will be whether or not to computerize the new MIS. Another is whether the MIS will be centralized or more widely distributed among users. Implementing the system involves purchasing all hardware and software, hiring and training all personnel who will be involved with the system, and installing, testing, and modifying the equipment. Finally the MIS must be evaluated periodically to ensure that it is accomplishing its purposes. MIS evaluations typically examine the system's effectiveness, efficiency, reliability, and security of information.

6. ***Discuss decision support systems and the types of decisions for which these systems are appropriate.***
A decision support system (DSS) is an interactive, computer-based information system designed to support specific decisions made by managers. The types of decisions that form the core of a DSS are those made by top managers, such as strategic planning and forecasting. Information that a DSS might contain includes pricing histories, seasonal variations in demand, and general economic data. Managers who use a DSS can manipulate the data and interact with the system, apply different formulas to the data, and combine the computerized facts with other judgmental information.

7. ***Describe various technologies now emerging in the communications field.***
The entire field of communications technology is changing rapidly. The need for faster processing speeds and the ability to network computers is creating a trend toward more powerful microcomputers. With modems, voice messaging systems, and cellular phone technology, the field of information exchange and communication over telephone systems is changing rapidly. Videoconferencing is eliminating many of the costs of holding meetings, and voice messaging systems have changed the way businesspeople get their messages. Facsimile (fax) modems can

now be inexpensively installed on most business computers. Using satellite transmissions, organizations can access remote locations from their headquarters and exchange larger volumes of information than ever before. The marketing of products using cable television and personal information services has changed the nature of some consumer markets. Interactive media promote messages to groups of similar prospects and then allow for responses customized to the buyers' wishes. Tele-education allows a person to earn a university degree by attending classes offered on television by several local universities. The Internet, a huge, global web of 25,000 computer networks, is being used by both organizations and individuals to increase communication and improve information exchange. Finally, voice recognition systems may eventually permit instantaneous translations of messages from one language to another.

KEY TERMS AND CONCEPTS

Timeliness (p. 402)
Accuracy (p. 402)
Completeness (p. 403)
Relevance (p. 403)
Management information system (MIS) (p. 403)
Database (p. 405)
Hard disk (p. 406)
Floppy disk (p. 406)
Magnetic tape (p. 406)
Optical storage disks (p. 406)
Microprocessor (p. 407)
Read-only memory (ROM) (p. 408)
Random access memory (RAM) (p. 408)
Decision support system (DSS) (p. 414)
Geographic information system (GIS) (p. 415)
Expert system (ES) (p. 415)
Videoconferencing (p. 416)
Voicemail (p. 416)
Facsimile (fax) machine (p. 416)
Interactive media (p. 417)
Internet (p. 418)

DISCUSSION QUESTIONS

Company

1. Why might employees view a company's high-tech information system as a threat?
2. What factors should a company consider in determining whether or not to computerize its management information system?
3. What information might the following organizations use in their decision support systems?
   a. A 7-Eleven store
   b. A local horse-racing track
   c. The production department of Firestone Tire & Rubber Company

Customers

4. What kind of information does a company need to provide high-quality products and services to its customers?
5. What effects might emerging technologies have on a company's relationship with its customers?
6. What information about customers might the following organizations have?
   a. McDonald's Corporation
   b. A local McDonald's restaurant
   c. A Safeway supermarket
   d. The Lexus division of Toyota Motor Corporation

Competitors

7. How will inaccurate, untimely, incomplete, and irrelevant information in a company's management information system benefit the company's competitors?
8. What types of information might a company collect and process regarding its competition, and how might it use this information?

Collaborators

9. In your opinion, are software designers important collaborators in achieving a company's objectives? Why or why not?
10. Should a company provide access to parts of its management information system to its suppliers and other collaborators? Why or why not?

In Question: Take a Stand

As the amount of information companies collect increases, many Americans find their privacy being invaded. Telemarketers obtain names from credit card companies, magazine subscription lists, and other sources, and suddenly you are flooded with unwanted junk mail. Often incorrect credit information is entered into a credit bureau's computer system and negatively affects the credit ratings of hundreds of consumers.

What responsibility do companies have to protect their customer information from unwanted distribution to other organizations? What are the individual's rights in these instances? What can be done?

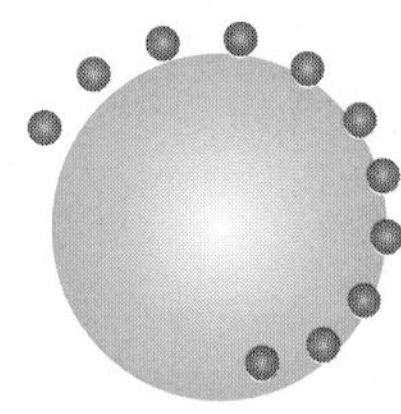

CASE 17.1
BLUE CROSS & BLUE SHIELD[15]

Blue Cross & Blue Shield of Massachusetts had experienced a swelling load of paperwork that was getting information to managers too late to make important decisions. So Blue Cross & Blue Shield spent six years and $120 million to develop an information system

System 21, a new computer system that would be cheaper and more responsive to customers, was heralded as the future of Blue Cross. But early in 1992, behind schedule and far over budget, the project was junked.

After approving the budgets, top management had let professional programmers assume total command of the project. Top management failed to establish a firm set of priorities that would state which features were essential, which ones should be done first, and so on. No executive was assigned to keep tabs or head the project. When the programmers showed the executives their finished project, missing reports and incorrect analyses led to needed changes that led to many of the cost overruns.

Blue Cross still trails other insurers in managing the swelling load of paperwork. It has nine different claims-processing systems on hardware dating from the early 1970s. Now Electronic Data Systems Corporation (EDS) has been hired to take over the information systems and other computer operations for Blue Cross. Interestingly, management had refused an earlier recommendation to turn over data processing to EDS, claiming that EDS charged too much and lacked key technology.

Questions

1. *What type of data does a company like Blue Cross & Blue Shield collect?*
2. *What type of information does the company need?*
3. *Blue Cross & Blue Shield put a lot of money into the new information system. In your opinion, what did the company do wrong when it attempted to create the new system?*
4. *What key characteristics of a decision support system would be most important to a company like Blue Cross & Blue Shield?*

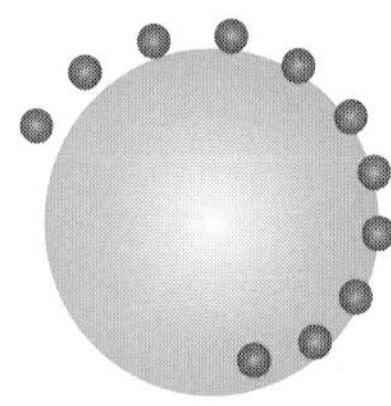

CASE 17.2
TECHNOLOGY IN THE DEPARTMENT OF DEFENSE[16]

The U.S. Army now has some of the most sophisticated information systems in the world. Commanders now see the battle unfold on computer screens, and can make critical adjustments in the deployment of their troops at a pace never before possible. The Army is trying to control the tide of battle, reduce friendly-fire deaths, and accomplish more with a smaller budget through affordable, off-the-shelf technology.

Tanks, helicopters and, eventually, soldiers will be fitted with radios that send their locations based on the global positioning system already on the commercial market. That information will be supplemented by reports from satellites, planes, and ground patrols monitoring the enemy. The data then will be combined in computers so the force can be given the information they need on displays right in their tanks, armored transports, or aircraft.

"The military has a lot to learn from Motorola," says Andrew Krepinevich, director of the watch-dog group Defense Budget Project. Jim Quinlivan, a vice president with the Rand Corporation working with the Army, says the new equipment will require a new mindset and new tactics. The new tactics include the fact that "You'll know where he's (the enemy) coming from before he's visible, and can ambush or take other counter-measures."

The army faces complex decisions on how to allocate this flood of information. Each soldier, from general down to tank gunner, must get all necessary information. The goal of the improved battlefield information system is a better "force exchange ratio." That is, the number of our dead soldiers to the number of the enemy's dead soldiers. Before the implementation of the system, the U.S. military enjoyed a ratio of 2-to-1. With the battlefield information system in place, the goal is between 15- and 20-to-1. This goal is very reachable, given the lopsided victory in Desert Storm.

Questions

1. *In what ways have information systems improved the effectiveness of the U.S. Army?*
2. *What uses of information in business organizations seem similar to those of the military, and how can business leaders take advantage of advances made in battlefield technologies?*
3. *What are the ethical issues raised by this case, and how can they be resolved?*

CHAPTER 18

ACCOUNTING

When you have studied this chapter, you will be able to:

1. Explain the purposes of accounting information.
2. Define the accounting equation and describe its components.
3. Describe the accounting process.
4. Discuss the types and purposes of financial statements.
5. Explain the various types of accounting.
6. Describe the financial ratios used to analyze and interpret accounting information.

At the Universal Studios theme park in Orlando, Florida, you can ride an oversized bicycle with E.T. the Extraterrestrial. The bicycle twists and turns as it escapes government scientists and police officers attempting to capture E.T. Ultimately you find yourself in a strange land surrounded by huge, exotic plants. These plants, the scientists, and the police officers are entertainment robots.

Many entertainment robots at this and other theme parks are built by Sally Industries Inc. as part of a specialized business called animatronics, which turns imagination into real characters. Each robot results from a precise mix of latex, wires, tubes, and artistry that must be carefully managed. This is accomplished by combining art, technology, management, and accounting.

Entertainment robots are very expensive. Prices range from $15,000 for the simplest robot, made with off-the-shelf parts, to $250,000 for a scripted show starring a group of elaborately costumed robots. To be profitable, Sally must manage its revenues and expenses carefully. Sally's management estimates the cost of the robot components by using information for the direct material, direct labor, and overhead costs related to the robot's construction. This information is obtained from the accounting system.

All employees must log on to a project each time they work on it and log off at the end of the day. This information becomes part of the labor cost database. In this manner, all labor costs are correctly assigned to each robot and automatically transferred to the job cost and payroll modules of the accounting system. Finally, the production, management, labor, cost estimation, and general accounting systems are coordinated with accounting information used at each stage of manufacturing. By tracking all of this information, managers can determine labor costs, material usage, and the profitability of each robot.[1]

This determination is important because Sally can continue in business only as long as it is profitable. This doesn't apply only to Sally, however, as profitability is essential to the success of any company.

THE IMPORTANCE OF ACCOUNTING

To determine their profitability, companies must be able to track their production, labor, and material costs. Sophisticated methods of gathering and processing accounting information are sometimes necessary. Effective business decisions depend on having reliable information regarding the company's costs and revenues.

Accounting
An information system designed to analyze, summarize, record, and report financial information related to a business.

Accounting provides a means for gathering this information. **Accounting** is an information system designed to analyze, summarize, record, and report financial information related to a business. Accounting also provides a language for communicating the information to interested parties such as investors, bankers, creditors, government agencies, and employees. Investors in a company need information about the company's financial condition and future prospects. Bankers and creditors use financial information about a company to assess the risk related to providing loans or extending credit. Government agencies rely on financial data for the purposes of regulation and taxation. Employees have a vested interest in the company and benefit from having information about its financial condition. For these reasons, accounting plays a vital role in American business.

Information from an accounting system consists of financial data related to business transactions. The data are expressed in money terms. Analyzing, summarizing, recording, and reporting the information in financial statements make the data meaningful.

ACCOUNTING FOR A BUSINESS

To illustrate the accounting process, let's look at a specific example. Catherine Tai had always wanted to operate her own business. One day, she decided to open a jewelry store. She had saved $75,000, which she used to start her business. To get additional money for the business, she borrowed $100,000 from her local bank on April 1, 1994. She agreed to pay interest annually at a rate of 12 percent and to repay the $100,000 at the end of two years.

Tai used the $175,000 to obtain the items necessary to start her jewelry business. She purchased an inventory of watches, rings, necklaces, and pins at a cost of $100,000 in cash. In addition, she purchased showcases for $2,000 in cash. She leased a shop at a rent of $500 a month. She also spent $300 in cash on promotion and advertising.

Initially, Catherine Tai had a number of business objectives. One was to show a profit at the end of the first month of business. Toward that end, she solicited customers and by the end of the month had sold jewelry merchandise for $80,000 in cash. The goods sold had a cost of $50,000.

Tai also wanted to be able to determine how efficiently she was operating her company. In addition, she wanted to be able to make good business decisions. By keeping records of her company's financial transactions, Tai established an accounting system and implemented accounting procedures. This system enabled her to determine the profitability of her business. It also provided her with the information she needed to make sound business decisions and permitted her to assess how well she was achieving her business objectives.

BUSINESS TRANSACTIONS AND THE ACCOUNTING EQUATION

From an accounting viewpoint, a *business transaction* refers to an event that has occurred and has had a financial impact on the business. All of the transactions that occurred during the period should be analyzed in terms of the financial impact they had on the company and their effect on the accounting equation. The *accounting equation* is the basic principle on which

Assets
The economic resources a company owns that are expected to provide a benefit in the future.

Liabilities
What the company owes to others, such as creditors.

Owner's equity
Resources invested in a business by the owner and the undistributed earnings.

Accounting equation
Assets = Liabilities + Owner's Equity.

accounting is based. It describes the relationship between the company's assets and its liabilities and owner's equity. **Assets** are the economic resources the company owns that are expected to provide a benefit in the future. **Liabilities** are what the company owes to others, such as creditors. **Owner's equity** is the resources invested in the business by the owner and the undistributed earnings. Mathematically, the **accounting equation** is expressed as

Assets = Liabilities + Owner's Equity

After the transactions have been analyzed, they must be classified and recorded. To illustrate, we will use the transactions described for Catherine Tai's Jewelry Store, a sole proprietorship. Business transactions for the store included (1) the initial investment of $75,000, (2) the bank loan of $100,000, (3) the purchase of inventory for $100,000, (4) the purchase of showcases for $2,000, (5) the payment of $500 for rent, (6) the expenditure of $300 for promotion and advertising, and (7) the sale of merchandise for $80,000 in cash.

Transaction 1. The first business transaction was Catherine Tai's initial investment of $75,000. This amount represents her ownership interest. It is the equity that she has in her business. It also represents the amount of capital she can spend on business-related activities. The equity of the owner is commonly referred to by using the owner's name, followed by the word *Capital,* such as *Tai's Capital.* Hence, the status of Tai's jewelry business at this point is

	Cash	**=**	**Tai's Capital**
(1)	$75,000	=	$75,000

Notice that the two financial items, cash and capital, are equal. This makes sense, since $75,000 in cash was received from the initial investment.

The cash is a result of a past transaction. It is also an economic resource that will provide a future benefit. Thus, it is classified as an *asset.* As we already saw, Tai's Capital represents the resources Tai has invested in her business and is thus classified as *owner's equity.* So the relationship between the business's assets and owner's equity can be expressed more completely as

	Assets	**=**	**Owner's Equity**
	Cash	=	Tai's Capital
(1)	$75,000	=	$75,000

Transaction 2. The second transaction occurred when Tai obtained the loan from the bank. This increased cash in the amount of $100,000 and created an equivalent liability. The *liability* represents an obligation to transfer assets ($100,000) to the bank at the end of two years. The effect of this transaction would be recorded as

	Assets		**=**	**Liabilities**	**+**	**Owner's Equity**
	Cash		=	Loan Payable	+	Tai's Capital
Balance	$75,000		=			$75,000
(2)	100,000		=	$100,000		
Balance	$175,000		=	$100,000	+	$75,000
		$175,000	=	$175,000		

Notice that the amount owed to the bank, plus the sum of money Tai invested, is exactly equal to the cash balance. This satisfies the accounting equation.

Transaction 3. Tai's third business transaction was the purchase of jewelry for sale to customers. It is clear that the $100,000 jewelry inventory will provide a benefit to the business when sold and is therefore listed as an asset. Now the financial status of the business can be expressed as

	Assets		=	**Liabilities**	+	**Owner's Equity**
	Cash	+ Inventory	=	Loan Payable	+	Tai's Capital
Balance	$175,000		=	$100,000	+	$75,000
(3)	−100,000	+ $100,000				
Balance	$75,000	+ $100,000	=	$100,000	+	$75,000
	$175,000		=	$175,000		

Since Tai paid cash of $100,000 for the inventory, the business's cash decreased by that amount. At this point, assets equal $175,000, as do liabilities *plus* equity. Thus, the accounting equation still holds.

Transaction 4. Buying the showcases was Tai's fourth transaction. The purchase required a cash outlay of $2,000. The effect on the accounting equation is as follows:

	Assets			=	**Liabilities**	+	**Owner's Equity**
	Cash	+ Inventory	+ Equipment	=	Loan Payable	+	Tai's Capital
Balance	$75,000	+ $100,000		=	$100,000	+	$75,000
(4)	−2,000		+ $2,000				
Balance	$73,000	+ $100,000	+ $2,000	=	$100,000	+	$75,000
		$175,00		=	$175,000		

This transaction has no effect on the store's total assets, liabilities, or equity. However, it does change the mixture of assets, decreasing cash while increasing equipment by $2,000.

Expenses
Payments necessary for the normal operations of the business.

Transactions 5 and 6. The $500 paid for rent and the $300 paid for advertising and promotion are payments that are necessary for the normal operations of the business and are therefore classified as **expenses**. These payments cause both cash and owner's equity to decrease, with the following results:

	Assets			=	**Liabilities**	+	**Owner's Equity**
	Cash	+ Inventory	+ Equipment	=	Loan Payable	+	Tai's Capital
Balance	$73,000	+ $100,000	+ $2,000	=	$100,000	+	$75,000
(5)	−500						−500
(6)	−300						−300
Balance	$72,200	+ $100,000	+ $2,000	=	$100,000	+	$74,200
		$174,200		=	$174,200		

Generally speaking, the use of assets or services in conducting business activities is called an expense. Normal operating expenses might include wages paid to employees and payment for utilities, rent, and insurance. For Catherine Tai's Jewelry Store, the business expenses incurred and paid during the month included rent and advertising. The effect of these transactions was to reduce cash and owner's equity by $800. Again, this is consistent with the accounting equation.

Revenue
An increase in resources resulting from business activities.

Transaction 7. Throughout the month, merchandise inventory is sold and results in business-related cash receipts totaling $80,000. The $80,000 represents an increase in resources resulting from business activities and would therefore be classified as **revenue**. The earning of revenue increases both assets and owner's equity.

Cost of goods sold
The cost of inventory that has been sold.

As the merchandise is sold, the inventory decreases. The decrease is in the amount that the goods cost. This is called **cost of goods sold** and, for Catherine Tai's Jewelry Store, amounts to $50,000. This is another expense of doing business. The financial effects of the seventh transaction are recorded as follows:

	Assets					=	Liabilities	+	Owner's Equity
	Cash	+	Inventory	+	Equipment	=	Loan Payable	+	Tai's Capital
Balance	$72,200	+	$100,000	+	$2,000	=	$100,000	+	$74,200
(7a)	80,000								80,000
(7b)		−	50,000					−	50,000
Balance	$152,200	+	$50,000	+	$2,000	=	$100,000	+	$104,200
			$204,200			=		$204,200	

After the effects of the sales of merchandise have been recorded, assets remain equal to liabilities plus owner's equity of $204,200. By using the accounting equation relationship, those events that had a financial impact on the jewelry store during the month have been analyzed, classified, and recorded. Revenue-producing assets in the form of cash, inventory, and equipment have been identified and quantified. Also identified are the claims against these assets, by both the creditors (the bank) and the owner.

THE ACCOUNTING PROCESS

Notice that through the use of the accounting equation and the basic relationship among assets, liabilities, and equity, all transactions for the month of April were recorded. This was possible, though, because only a few transactions occurred. The procedure used here becomes awkward and inefficient as the number and types of transactions increase. Thus, the accountant needs a far more effective means of recordkeeping and reporting than Catherine Tai has used so far. That means maintaining separate records for each item that appears in the company's financial statements by using accounts that are recorded in journals and ledgers.

ACCOUNTS

Account
A detailed record of the changes that have occurred in a particular asset, liability, or owner's equity item during the accounting period.

A detailed record of the changes that have occurred in a particular asset, liability, or owner's equity item during the accounting period is called an **account**. For Catherine Tai's Jewelry Store, we can create an account by referring to the transactions that occurred during April that affected cash. Initially, Catherine Tai's Jewelry Store had no cash. After her investment, the store had $75,000 in cash. We can summarize all the events that had an effect on cash as follows:

Cash

Increase or Decrease in Cash			Transaction or Event
Beginning balance		0	April 1, 1994
	+	75,000	Investment
	+	100,000	Loan
	−	100,000	Inventory purchase
	−	2,000	Equipment purchase
	−	500	Rent payment
	−	300	Advertising expense
	+	80,000	Merchandise sales
Ending balance		$152,200	April 30, 1994

By focusing on the changes that occurred in cash during the month, we can see that cash either increased or decreased. Therefore, to provide a detailed record of the changes in cash or any asset, liability, or owner's equity item, it is necessary only to establish a means of recording increases and decreases.

In its simplest form, an account has a right side and a left side. It also has a title, which is the name of the asset, liability, or equity item to which it relates, for instance *Cash.* The account for cash at Catherine Tai's Jewelry Store is as follows:

	Cash		
Beginning balance	0		
(1)	75,000	100,000	(3)
(2)	100,000	2,000	(4)
(7)	80,000	500	(5)
		300	(6)
Ending balance	$152,200		

DEBITS AND CREDITS

Debit
An entry recorded on the left side of an account.

Credit
An entry recorded on the right side of an account.

Since cash is an asset, increases in cash (transactions 1, 2, and 7) are recorded on the left side of the account; that is, the account is debited. In accounting, **debit** means an entry on the left side of the account. Decreases (items 3, 4, 5, and 6) are recorded on the right side, and the cash account in this case is credited. Hence, a **credit** is an entry recorded on the right side of the account.

All *increases in assets* are recorded on the left side of the asset account, while all decreases are recorded on the right side. Conversely, an *increase in a liability or owner's equity item* is recorded by making an entry on the right side of the account (crediting). A decrease is recorded by making an entry on the left side (debiting). Hence, any entry made on the left is a debit, and any entry made on the right is a credit. Here is a summary of the effects of debits and credits on various accounts:

Account	Increased	Decreased
Assets	Debit	Credit
Liabilities	Credit	Debit
Equity	Credit	Debit
Revenues	Credit	Debit
Expenses	Debit	Credit

Chart of accounts
A list of all the accounts and their account numbers.

All financial items have their own accounts. For Catherine Tai's Jewelry Store, inventory, equipment, loan payable, and Tai's capital would all be separate accounts. Any additional financial items arising from other business transactions also would have assigned accounts. These accounts are listed, along with their account numbers, in the company's **chart of accounts**. The chart of accounts acts like a table of contents for the accountant.

DOUBLE-ENTRY SYSTEM

Double-entry system
A bookkeeping system based on the fact that in any business transaction, at least two accounts are always affected.

The account, then, is the means of recordkeeping and is especially important in a double-entry system of bookkeeping. The term **double-entry system** comes from the fact that in any business transaction, at least two accounts are always affected. For example, Tai's purchase of inventory affected both the inventory and cash accounts.

The double-entry system assumes that all business transactions create both a benefit and a sacrifice. Therefore, under a double-entry system, each transaction is recorded with at least one debit and one credit so that the total dollar amount of the debit(s) equals the total dollar amount of the credit(s).

JOURNALS

Journal
The chronological accounting record of a company's transactions.

The **journal** is the chronological accounting record of the company's transactions. All transactions are recorded first in the journal. It is the accountant's "diary." In the journal, a sepa-

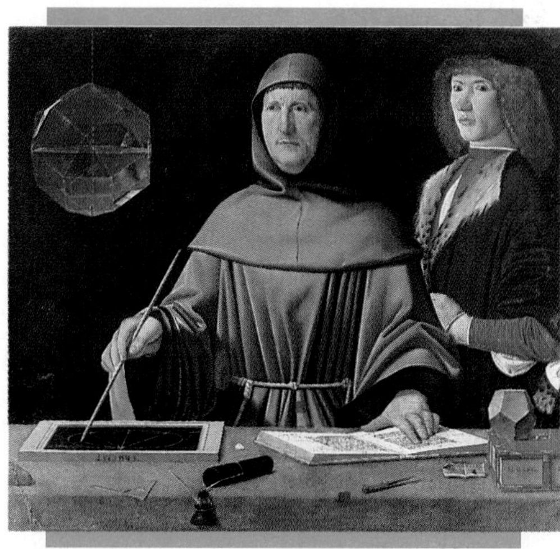

Five centuries ago, Luca Pacioli, a Franciscan monk, published a mathematics text that contained an explanation on double-entry bookkeeping for merchants. The book was illustrated by Leonardo da Vinci. Recently two Seattle University professors created plans for a big celebration in Sansepolcro, Italy, Pacioli's birthplace. The celebration, for 1994, marks the 500th anniversary of the publication of his work on double-entry bookkeeping. The two professors persuaded four of the six biggest accounting firms to contribute $125,000 to make a 27-minute video for the event. The professors believe that a person of Pacioli's stature helps accountants to be "less apologetic" about their work.[2]

rate entry is written for each transaction, in the order in which it occurred. Exhibit 18.1 shows examples of journal entries. Information in a journal entry typically includes the date, the names and numbers (Post. Ref.) of the accounts affected, and the amounts of the transactions.

LEDGER ACCOUNTS

Ledger
A group of related accounts that make up a complete unit.

To reflect the events that have been entered in the journal, the transaction amounts are transferred to ledger accounts. A **ledger** is a group of related accounts that make up a complete

Exhibit 18.1 **A GENERAL JOURNAL**

General Journal					Page 1
Date		**Description**	**Post. Ref.**	**Debit**	**Credit**
1994					
April	1	Cash	112	75,000	
		Catherine Tai's Capital	313		75,000
		To record owner's investment in jewelry store.			
	1	Cash	112	100,000	
		Loan Payable	215		100,000
		To record money borrowed from bank.			

Exhibit 18.2 **A GENERAL LEDGER ACCOUNT**

General Ledger

Cash — **Account No. 112**

Date		Item	Post. Ref.	Debit	Credit	Balance Debit	Balance Credit
1994	1	Owner Investment	J1	75,000		75,000	
April	1	Loan Payable	J1	100,000		175,000	
	7	Rent Exp.	J1		500	174,500	
	8	Adv. Exp.	J1		300	174,200	
	8	Inventory	J1		100,000	74,200	
	8	Showcase	J1		2,000	72,200	
	27	Revenue	J1	80,000 *		152,200	

*To simplify the illustration, the $80,000 received from customers is shown as one deposit. But in practice, it is more likely that this amount is received in several smaller sums throughout the month and would be individually posted in those amounts.

unit, such as all of the accounts of a specific company. Exhibit 18.2 illustrates a ledger account for cash.

Posting
The process of transferring amounts from the journal to the ledger accounts.

Trial balance
An initial listing of all ledger accounts to determine the equality of the debits and credits.

The process of transferring amounts from the journal to the ledger accounts is called **posting**. Posting is done periodically, at the end of each day or even less frequently. Exhibit 18.3 illustrates this process.

Exhibit 18.3 illustrates a manual posting process, but computers are commonly used to post the entries after they have been recorded. They can also be used to prepare a trial balance. A **trial balance** is an initial listing of all ledger accounts used to determine the equality of the debits and credits. The trial balance is entered on a worksheet, which is used to prepare financial statements.

FINANCIAL STATEMENTS

Financial statements are prepared in order to provide information to interested parties about the profitability and financial condition of the company. The process by which financial statements are prepared is referred to as the *accounting cycle.* The accounting cycle begins with setting up the ledger accounts and ends with preparing the financial statements (see Exhibit 18.4). The accounting cycle is divided into work done during the period (e.g., recording in the journal and posting to the ledger) and work performed at the end of the period (preparing the financial statements).

Accountants routinely prepare four basic financial statements: the balance sheet, the income statement, the statement of cash flows, and the statement of owner's equity. These statements form the basis for a wide variety of decisions that company owners and managers must make. Exhibit 18.5 illustrates the relationship among the preparers, users, and auditors of financial statements.

Balance sheet
A statement that reports the company's resources (assets) and claims against those resources (liabilities and owner's equity); sometimes called the *statement of financial position.*

BALANCE SHEET (STATEMENT OF FINANCIAL POSITION)

The **balance sheet**, sometimes called the *statement of financial position,* is a statement that reports the company's resources (assets) and claims against those resources (liabilities and

Exhibit 18.3 **THE POSTING PROCESS**

General Journal — Page 1

Date		Description	Post. Ref.	Debit	Credit
1994 April	1	Cash	112	75,000	
		Catherine Tai's Capital	313		75,000
		To record owner's investment in jewelry store.			
	1	Cash	112	100,000	
		Loan Payable	215		100,000
		To record money borrowed from bank.			

General Ledger

Cash — **Account No. 112**

Date		Item	Post. Ref.	Debit	Credit	Balance Debit	Balance Credit
1994 April	1	Owner Investment	J1	75,000		75,000	
	1	Loan Payable	J1	100,000		175,000	
	7	Rent Exp.	J1		500	174,500	
	8	Adv. Exp.	J1		300	174,200	
	8	Inventory	J1		100,000	74,200	
	8	Showcase	J1		2,000	72,200	
	27	Revenue	J1	80,000 *		152,200	

General Ledger

Catherine Tai's Capital — **Account No. 313**

Date		Item	Post. Ref.	Debit	Credit	Balance Debit	Balance Credit
1994 April	1	Owner Investment	J1		75,000		75,000

Exhibit 18.4 **THE ACCOUNTING CYCLE**

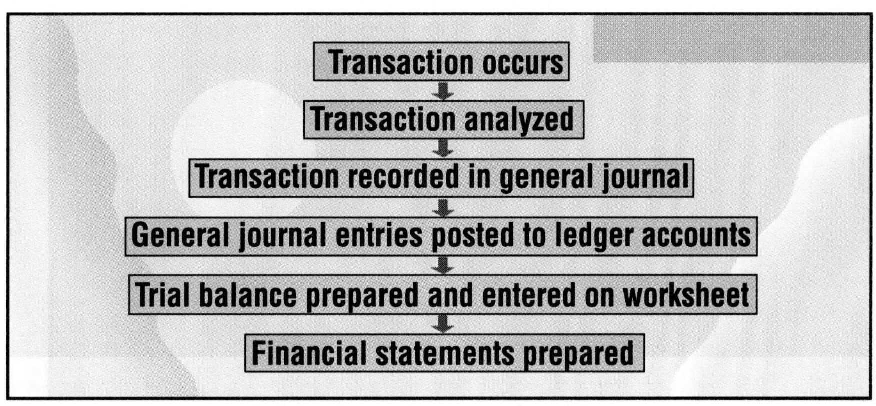

Exhibit 18.5 **INDIVIDUALS INVOLVED IN THE PREPARATION OF FINANCIAL STATEMENTS**

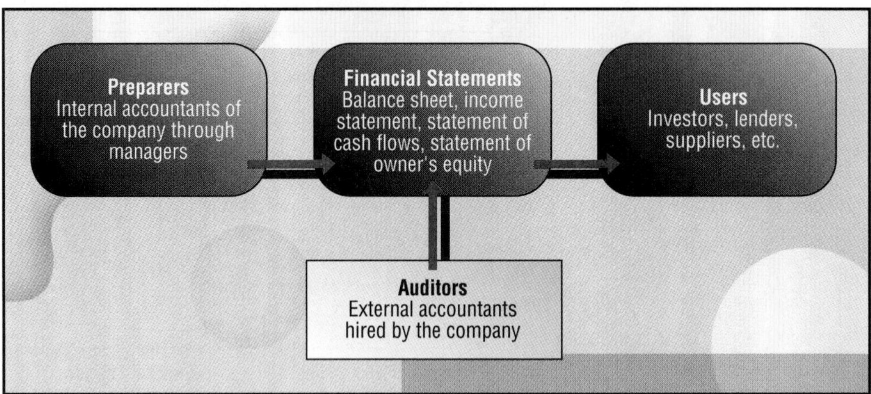

owner's equity). This information gives a monetary picture of the company's financial condition at a particular point in time. It is called the *balance sheet* because both sides of the statement must be equal (in balance). The accounting equation, Assets = Liabilities + Owner's Equity, is the basic principle underlying the balance sheet.

Balance sheets are typically shown in detail. Assets and liabilities are classified as *current* and *noncurrent.* Exhibit 18.6 shows a balance sheet for Catherine Tai's Jewelry Store.

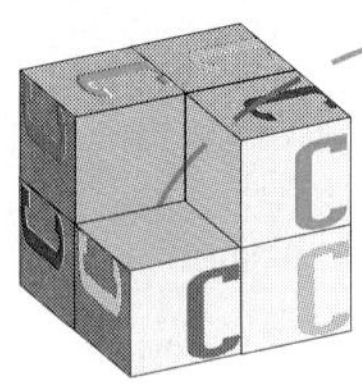

FOCUS ON COMPETITORS

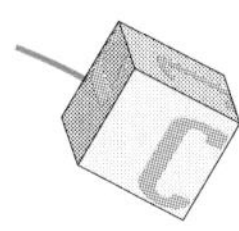

Chambers Development Company

Increasing volumes of solid waste have created an unhealthy competition among the titans of trash removal, generally increasing stock prices and earnings. To keep their investors happy, some companies have resorted to clever bookkeeping. Chambers Development Company was forced by its auditors to publicly disclose changes made to the company's 1991 earnings. The

Exhibit 18.6 **BALANCE SHEET**

Catherine Tai's Jewelry Store
Balance Sheet
April 30, 1994

Assets			**Liabilities and Equity**	
Current Assets			Current Liabilities	
Cash		$152,200	Interest Payable	1,000
Inventory		50,000	Noncurrent Liabilities	
Noncurrent Assets			Loan Payable	100,000
Equipment	2,000		Owner's Equity	
Accumulated Depreciation—Equipment	(17)	1,983	Tai, Capital	$103,183
Total Assets		$204,183	Total Liabilities and Owner's Equity	$204,183

recalculation showed that Chambers had not earned 83 cents a share, as originally reported; rather, its earnings were an embarrassing 3 cents per share.

Many of the major waste management companies are fudging their figures. One area that is especially vulnerable is the "landfill," which is a major asset for these firms. Nobody knows for sure how long it takes to fill them up, which gives their accountants lots of room to maneuver.

Operating cycle
The average time it takes for the company to spend cash for inventory, sell the inventory in exchange for accounts receivable, and collect the receivables in cash.

Current Assets. Assets are classified as *current* if they are cash, convertible into cash, or will be consumed within one year or within the operating cycle, whichever is longer. An **operating cycle** is the average time it takes for the company to spend cash for inventory, sell the inventory in exchange for accounts receivable, and collect the receivables in cash.[3]

Since Catherine Tai's Jewelry Store is a relatively new business and has had few transactions, the items listed in the balance sheet in Exhibit 18.6 are minimal. The company reports only two assets that are classified as current: cash and inventory. A larger company's current assets also commonly include temporary investments and accounts receivable. Current assets are normally listed in the order of how easily they are converted into cash, with cash first. The most common current assets are cash, temporary investments, receivables, inventory, and prepaid expenses.

Temporary investments consist of debt or equity securities, such as stocks or bonds of other companies. These securities are purchased by management as a means of investing idle cash. Because they can be readily marketed, they are resold when the need for cash arises.

Receivables such as accounts receivable and notes receivable represent claims to cash. In the case of accounts receivable, the claim is the result of a credit sale to a customer. Receivables are reported in the amounts the company expects to collect. If doubt exists as to whether the receivables will be collected, a provision for *uncollectible accounts* may be made and reported along with the receivables.

Inventory, as in the case of Catherine Tai's Jewelry Store, is merchandise held for resale. For manufacturing companies, inventories typically include raw materials, work in process, and finished goods.

Prepaid expenses are amounts paid in advance for rent, supplies, insurance, and the like. These items are current assets not in the sense that they will be converted into cash but in the sense that if they had not been paid for in advance, they would require the use of current assets during the following year or operating cycle.

Noncurrent Assets. *Noncurrent assets* provide a benefit over extended periods of time. They include property, plant, equipment, long-term investments, and intangible assets.

Property, plant, and equipment are assets such as land and buildings that are tangible and long-lived. Also referred to as *plant assets* or *fixed assets,* these assets are reported in the amounts paid to acquire them, less depreciation which will be discussed with the income statement.

Long-term investments include various types of investments that management intends to hold for periods longer than one year. For example, plant assets that are not currently used in operations would be reported as a long-term investment.

Intangible assets such as patents or trademarks lack physical substance. However, they have value because they convey certain rights to the business.

Liabilities. Liabilities are also classified as current and noncurrent. *Current liabilities* such as accounts payable, taxes payable, and interest payable are obligations that will be paid within the year. Moreover, the payments will require the use of resources classified as current assets.

Noncurrent liabilities include obligations that will not be paid within the year, such as Catherine Tai's loan payable. Examples include notes payable, bonds payable, and mortgage payable.

Registered trademarks are often valuable intangible assets. Ferrara Pan Candy Company has made Lemonheads candy for over 35 years. Now a popular rock band, the Lemonheads, has taken its name directly from the candy. Ferrara is trying to decide whether to seek a promotional relationship with the band or to ask them to stop using the name Lemonhead, which is a registered trademark.[4]

Owner's Equity. The third section of the balance sheet is owner's equity. Since Catherine Tai's Jewelry Store is a sole proprietorship, its owner's equity is entirely represented by Tai's capital account. This account reflects all of Tai's investments, as well as earnings of the business and any withdrawals Tai makes from the business. Thus, the capital account solely reflects the owner's ownership interest. The capital account is used in exactly the same manner by partnerships to record the partners' ownership interest.

For a corporation, owner's equity is depicted somewhat differently. First, the term used to designate owner's equity is *stockholder's equity,* because the owners of the corporation are the stockholders. Investments of the stockholders are recorded in the *Common Stock* and *Preferred Stock* accounts. Common stock records the amount received from the sale of common stock (the amount invested by the common stockholder). Preferred stock records the amount invested by the preferred stockholders. In either case, the accounts pertain only to the investment and do not include earnings generated by the business. Earnings are accounted for separately in an account entitled Retained Earnings. This account provides information about a firm's undistributed earnings.

We should note that individuals can benefit from keeping good records of their personal "equity," or net worth. This is not a concern only for companies; individuals should know what their value is as well.

INCOME STATEMENT

Income statement
A report of the revenues and expenses for a particular period that provides a measure of the results of operations and profitability.

The **income statement** reports the revenues and expenses for a particular time period. It provides a measure of the results of operations and the profitability of the business during that period. Exhibit 18.7 provides an income statement for the month of April for Catherine Tai's Jewelry Store.

Net income measures the success Catherine Tai enjoyed as a result of the first month of business. By using the income statement, Tai can determine whether or not she met her goal of earning profits in the first month of operation. The income figure is computed by match-

STREET SMART

Calculating Your Net Worth

The first step in taking control of your personal finances is to calculate your net worth. To figure your net worth, add up the value of all your assets. Start with what you have in checking, savings, and money market funds. Add the current value of other assets you own, such as your car, bike, skis, books, or a home. Don't overlook items such as the cash value of an insurance policy, jewelry, or collectibles. Once you have determined the value of your assets, you must subtract any outstanding obligations such as the amount you owe to a credit card company, your student loan, or what you owe to the bank. The difference between the two is your net worth.

You should recalculate your personal net worth at least once a year. Some debt counselors tell clients to figure out their net worth immediately before they start Christmas shopping, presumably to keep them from overspending. "Don't spend what you don't have" is street-smart advice.

ing the revenues generated during the period ($80,000 in cash sales) to the expenses incurred in generating those revenues.

The expenses included the $500 for rent and the $300 spent for promotion and advertising. Although interest is not actually paid in April and depreciation does not require a cash payment, they are nonetheless recognized as expenses incurred during the month. The interest expense was recognized because one month had passed, and a liability to pay $1,000 interest had been incurred ($100,000 x 12% x 1/12 year).

Depreciation
The process of spreading the costs of fixed assets over the assets' expected useful lives.

Accountants spread the costs of fixed assets, such as Tai's showcases, over the assets' expected useful lives. This process is called **depreciation**. Assuming the showcases will last for 10 years and have no value at the end of that time, depreciation expense for April would

Exhibit 18.7 **INCOME STATEMENT**

Catherine Tai's Jewelry Store
Income Statement
For the Month Ended April 30, 1994

Revenues		$80,000
Cost of goods sold		50,000
Gross profit		30,000
Operating Expenses		
Rent expense	$ 500	
Advertising expense	300	
Interest expense	1,000	
Depreciation expense	17	
Total operating expense		(1,817)
Net income		$28,183

All companies have assets such as buildings, vehicles, and equipment that may be depreciated over their expected useful lives. This adjustment is needed to make the reporting of income more realistic.

be $17. The accrual of interest and the recording of depreciation recognize expenses when they are incurred, regardless of whether or not cash was paid.

It is important that all transactions that affect a company's income be accurately reported. Otherwise investors may be misled as to the company's performance.

FOCUS ON COMPANY

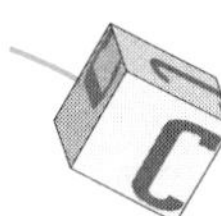

Leslie Fay Company

In 1993, Leslie Fay Company's stock lost more than a third of its value. Why? The company had to announce that correction of "alleged accounting irregularities" could wipe out its 1992 net income and force the company to restate its 1991 earnings. That announcement caused its stock to fall from $7.375 per share to only $4.625 in one day.

The false entries were largely related to inventory adjustments and the cost of goods sold. According to the company's corporate controller, he and another employee inflated inventory and decreased the cost of goods, thereby increasing the reported profits. One financial analyst said that not knowing the company's true earning power was a calamity. When accounting information is misstated, it is very difficult to know what the stock is really worth and what the stock price should really be.

STATEMENT OF CASH FLOWS

Statement of cash flows
A statement that reports the cash receipts and payments related to the company's operating, investing, and financing activities during the accounting period.

The **statement of cash flows** reports the cash receipts and payments related to the company's operating, investing, and financing activities during the accounting period. The detailed explanation of cash inflow and outflow provided in the statement enables users to assess the company's ability to generate future cash for operations.

At the beginning of business on April 1, 1994, the cash balance for Catherine Tai's Jewelry Store was zero. Cash at the end of April was $152,200, representing an increase of $152,200. Catherine Tai's statement of cash flows appears in Exhibit 18.8.

Exhibit 18.8 **STATEMENT OF CASH FLOWS**

Catherine Tai's Jewelry Store
Statement of Cash Flows
For the Month Ended April 30, 1994

Cash Flow from Operating Activities		
Cash collected from customers	$80,000	
Cash paid for merchandise	(100,000)	
Cash paid for operating expenses	800	
Cash used in operating activities		$(19,200)
Cash Flows from Investments		
Purchase of equipment	(2,000)	
Cash used for investment		(2,000)
Cash Flows from Financing Activities		
Proceeds from bank loan	100,000	
Proceeds from investment	75,000	
Cash provided from financing		175,000
Net increase in cash		152,200
Cash, April 1, 1994		000
Cash, April 30, 1994		$152,200

The statement of cash flows is closely tied to the income statement and the balance sheet, but presents information on a cash rather than an accrual basis. It is considered to be equal in importance to the income statement and the balance sheet.

FOCUS ON COMPANY

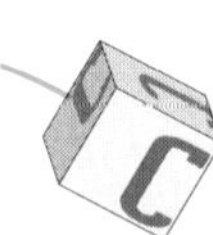

Major League Baseball

Spring training is, or used to be, a laid-back, casual experience. In pregame practice, fans sit close by the field and even talk to the players. Spring training means sun and fun. Accountants, however, think differently about spring training.

Do Major League teams make or lose money on spring training? That's a matter of debate. The teams themselves say they make no money from the preseason games. "There are no profits in spring training," said John Schuerholz, general manager of the Atlanta Braves. Referring to the new kinds of deals being struck by teams, he added: "You have to have these new deals just to minimize your losses. The function of spring training is to try to bring in as much money as you can so that you limit what you lose."

That claim cannot be verified because the 28 Major League teams historically do not make their income statements public and each uses slightly different accounting methods. But many independent analysts disagree with Mr. Schuerholz. "I think the teams are probably making a lot of money because there is quite a bit of money to be made," said Andrew Zimbalist, a professor at Smith College and the author of *Baseball and Billions: A Probing Look Inside the Big Business of Our National Pasttime.* "You are selling out most games at ever higher ticket prices, you're getting a healthy chunk of concessions, advertising and parking, and your player salary expenses are virtually nonexistent" because players generally do not receive extra pay for preseason games.

Indeed, a team's revenues during spring training can exceed $2.5 million, depending on the size of the park and the contract each team has with its host city. By contrast, the average operating cost of spring training per team in 1991 was a mere $750,000, according to a study commissioned by the Florida Commerce Department.

STATEMENT OF OWNER'S EQUITY

Statement of owner's equity A statement that summarizes the events that caused owner's equity to change during a specified period of time.

The **statement of owner's equity** summarizes the events that caused owner's equity to change during a specified period of time. The transactions that would affect owner's equity include capital contributions or withdrawals and income or loss.

Two types of transactions affected the equity of Catherine Tai's Jewelry Store during the month of April. Catherine Tai, the owner, made an original investment of $75,000. Also, the store earned income of $28,183. Both activities would be disclosed in the statement of owner's equity prepared for the month ending April 30, 1994. Exhibit 18.9 shows this statement.

TYPES OF ACCOUNTING

Because financial information is used for a variety of purposes, many specialized types of accounting exist. The most important forms are financial, managerial, and public accounting.

FINANCIAL ACCOUNTING

Financial accounting Preparation, reporting, analysis, and interpretation of accounting information in reports for external users.

Financial accounting involves the preparation, reporting, analysis, and interpretation of accounting information in reports for external users. External users of accounting information include collaborators such as current and prospective investors, creditors and suppliers, and customers. Other users are financial analysts, stock exchanges, regulatory agencies, and the general public.

The reporting typically takes the form of the general-purpose financial statements discussed in the previous section. These statements disclose information "comprehensible to those who have a reasonable understanding of business and economic activities."[5] Potential investors, lenders, and suppliers use these financial statements to determine whether an investment in the company is reasonably safe, whether the company can pay dividends, and whether the value of the stock is likely to increase. Regulatory agencies such as the Securities and Exchange Commission (SEC) often use accounting information contained in the company's annual report to evaluate planned issues of stock.

In collecting and analyzing accounting information, financial accountants conform to generally accepted accounting procedures (GAAP). The most important rules and procedures were created by the Financial Accounting Standards Board (FASB). The FASB has seven members and is responsible for establishing sound guidelines for accounting practices. These rules

Exhibit 18.9 **STATEMENT OF OWNER'S EQUITY**

Catherine Tai's Jewelry Store
Statement of Owner's Equity
For the Month Ended April 30, 1994

Catherine Tai, Capital, April 1, 1994		$ 000
Investment during month	$75,000	
Net income for the month	28,183	
Increase in owner's equity		103,183
Catherine Tai, Capital, April 30, 1994		$103,183

assure external users that the financial reports are fairly presented. Without such rules, the general public would be skeptical of accounting reports.

MANAGERIAL ACCOUNTING

Managerial accounting
Information-gathering and reporting activities and related accounting procedures designed to assist people inside the company in making various decisions.

Managerial accounting consists of information-gathering and reporting activities and related accounting procedures. It is designed to assist people inside the company in making various decisions. Managerial accounting supports decision making by providing financial information that various managers need. For example, a production manager needs information on product costs. Costs of materials, labor, and factory overhead, and the like, must be controlled, since they ultimately affect the pricing of the product. Production planning and scheduling, product line management and development, cash management, capital expenditures, and selling and distribution expenses are all areas where production managers need accounting information.

Bank managers must keep accurate internal accounting records to prepare for inspections by federal and state officials. Bank managers typically use a cash-balancing and monitoring system, budgets and cash management reports, and capital expenditure decision analyses. Retail store managers need accounting information with which to evaluate advertising campaigns, product displays, and customer traffic.

PUBLIC ACCOUNTING

Certified public accountant (CPA)
An accountant from outside the company who has been certified by passing a comprehensive public accounting exam and demonstrating work experience with a public accounting firm.

Financial statements that a company issues are prepared by accountants employed by the company and are the responsibility of management. However, interested parties often request the company to present financial reports that have been audited or certified by independent, external accountants. Banks, for example, may request audited financial statements in making loan decisions. These independent accountants are called **certified public accountants (CPAs)**. To become certified, a public accountant must pass a comprehensive public accounting exam and demonstrate work experience with a public accounting firm.

In auditing the financial statements, the CPA examines the company's records. The process typically includes verifying such items as inventory, payroll, and the value of physical assets like buildings. Ultimately, the CPA prepares a report attesting to the fairness of the company's financial information and presentation.

The competence and reputations of the public accounting firm and its CPAs are critical. An auditor is considered competent if he or she is knowledgeable about both generally accepted accounting principles and generally accepted auditing standards. This is why the designation of certified public accountant is so important for external auditors.

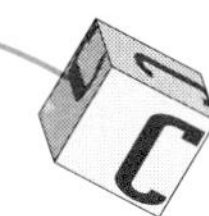

FOCUS ON COLLABORATORS

A New Focus for External Auditors

By the year 2000, massive new disclosure requirements for corporations may dramatically change the nature of public accounting. Auditors could just as likely be chemical engineers as CPAs, and audits may be so automated that financial statements are issued untouched by human hands. Accountants will be compiling, reporting, and certifying a whole new collection of nonmonetary information. They will be expected to give opinions about a vast range of areas from science to economics. Audit teams could require non-CPA experts in the sciences, law, and public affairs. This trend is consistent with a survey of 1,600 executives who said they need "better nonfinancial information on customer satisfaction, safety and environmental performance, energy efficiency, product defect rates, brand awareness, employee turnover, market share data, and technology trends."

Public accounting firms range from one-person practices to large, international organizations that employ thousands of professional accountants. The largest of these multinational accounting firms are commonly referred to as "The Big Six." The Big Six firms and some of their audit clients include the following:[6]

Firm	Selected Audit Clients
Arthur Anderson	Texaco, Sara Lee Corporation, Circus Circus Inc., Delta Air Lines, FedEx
Coopers & Lybrand	Ford Motor Company, Johnson & Johnson, AT&T, 3M, Kraft General Foods, Inc., Dunn & Bradstreet Corporation, Avon Products, Inc.
Deloitte and Touche	Sears, Roebuck and Company, General Motors, Boeing Company, American Express, The Gap, Chrysler Corporation, Procter & Gamble
Ernst & Young	McDonald's Corporation, Wal-Mart Stores, Inc., Coca-Cola Company, American Express, Apple Computer, Texas Instruments
KPMG (Klynveld Peat Marwick Goerdeler)	General Electric, Pepsico, JCPenney, USAir, General Mills, Ryder System, Inc., Trans World Airlines, Gillette Company, Pillsbury Company
Price Waterhouse	IBM, Kmart, The Walt Disney Company, Kellogg Company, Eastman Kodak, Hewlett-Packard, Goodyear Tire & Rubber, Campbell Soup Company

In addition to auditing services, public accounting firms provide tax services that include preparation of federal tax returns and tax planning. Tax planning involves considering the tax consequences of various business activities. These are only a few of the diverse types of services public accountants provide.

COMPUTERS AND ACCOUNTING INFORMATION SYSTEMS

As companies have grown to become large, international operations, the sheer volume of financial information has become overwhelming. Even in small companies, keeping accounting records on computers may be more effective than maintaining the records manually. Dozens of accounting software programs are commercially available to smaller companies at local computer stores. In addition, many public accountants have developed accounting programs that will calculate and print every financial statement and report imaginable.

Computerized accounting information systems are designed to meet companies' financial and managerial information needs. The design includes flowcharts and identifies the responsibilities of particular employees. In some cases, the design includes computerized software for tracking such items as labor and payroll, accounts payable and receivable, and inventory. Multifunctional software programs that support a computerized accounting information system have made it possible to fully integrate managerial accounting within the financial accounting system.[7]

USING ACCOUNTING INFORMATION

As we have seen, financial statements provide information about a company's financial condition and performance. But the facts and figures they report cannot by themselves give a complete picture. To make the information meaningful, managers use a number of financial ratios that allow users to compare items such as inventory and earnings per share from one year to the next and thus detect favorable or unfavorable trends in the company's performance. This kind of analysis enables managers, investors, lenders, and other users to make better decisions.

Analysts typically are interested in financial ratios that focus on short-term solvency, long-term solvency, and profitability.

Deltek is one of many companies now offering sophisticated accounting software. One of its products, the Government Contractor Software Series, is a fully integrated accounting system designed to meet the reporting requirements mandated by the federal government. Deltek advertises its line along with a photo of Mount Rushmore, seeking an analogy between the "hard-nosed" government and the "rock-hard noses" of the four presidents.

SHORT-TERM SOLVENCY RATIOS

Current ratio
Current assets divided by current liabilities.

Solvency ratios help assess the company's ability to pay its debts. Favorable short-term solvency ratios indicate that the company is likely to remain solvent for the near future. One of the more useful ratios for analyzing short-term solvency is called the *current ratio.* The **current ratio** compares the company's current assets to its current liabilities:

$$\text{Current Ratio} = \frac{\text{Current Assets}}{\text{Current Liabilities}}.$$

From Catherine Tai's Jewelry Store's balance sheet (Exhibit 18.6), we can see that the store's current ratio would be

$$\frac{\text{Current Assets (Cash of \$152,200 + Inventory of \$50,000)}}{\text{Current Liabilities (Interest Payable of \$1,000)}} = \frac{\$202,200}{\$1,000} = 202.2.$$

This means that Catherine Tai's has $202.20 for each dollar of short-term obligation.

Quick ratio
Cash, plus temporary investments, plus short-term receivables divided by current liabilities; also called the *acid-test ratio.*

A second ratio for analyzing short-term solvency is called the *quick ratio* (or sometimes the *acid-test ratio*). This ratio considers only those assets that can be converted into cash for repaying short-term debts (for instance, accounts receivable are easier to convert into cash than inventory is). "Quick" assets include cash, temporary investments, and current receivables. Thus, the **quick ratio** is expressed as follows:

$$\text{Quick Ratio} = \frac{\text{Cash + Temporary Investments + Short-Term Receivables}}{\text{Current Liabilities}}.$$

For Catherine Tai's Jewelry Store, the only quick asset is cash of $152,200. The current liability is still interest payable of $1,000; therefore the quick ratio is $152,200 ÷ $1,000 or 152.2. This means that if the creditor asked for repayment tomorrow, Tai would have $152.20 immediately available for each dollar owed.

To be even more meaningful, the current and quick ratios can be evaluated together. They can also be compared to the ratios of previous years and to competitors' ratios.

LONG-TERM SOLVENCY RATIOS

Both creditors and owners have claims against the company's assets. The relationship between debt and equity provides an indication of the company's long-term solvency. It is measured by dividing the total debt (current plus noncurrent liabilities) by owner's equity.

$$\text{Debt to Equity Ratio} = \frac{\text{Current Liabilities + Noncurrent Liabilities}}{\text{Owner's Equity}}.$$

Debt to equity ratio
Total debt (current plus noncurrent liabilities) divided by owner's equity.

This ratio is called the **debt to equity ratio** and measures the extent to which the company is financed by debt rather than owner's equity. If the claims of the creditors exceed those of the owners, interest payments will likely be substantial. If earnings decline and the business cannot make interest payments, creditors might take control of the business. For Catherine Tai's Jewelry Store, the debt to equity ratio is

$$\frac{\text{Current Liabilities (\$1,000) + Noncurrent Liabilities (\$100,000)}}{\text{Owners Equity (\$103,183)}} = \frac{\$101{,}000}{\$103{,}183} = 0.98.$$

The debt to equity ratio for the store indicates that the company relies almost equally on debt and equity to finance its operations. This fact might affect Tai's future attempts to borrow money.

PROFITABILITY RATIOS

Other types of ratios measure a company's ability to generate profits. Profitability ratios include earnings per share, return on sales, and return on equity. The term *return* is used to measure profitability.

Return on sales
Net income divided by sales.

In computing **return on sales**, net income is divided by sales.

$$\frac{\text{Net income}}{\text{Net sales}}.$$

For Catherine Tai's Jewelry Store, the return on sales is

$$\frac{\text{Net income (\$28,183)}}{\text{Net sales (\$80,000)}} = .35.$$

High returns on sales indicate that more of the sales dollar is going into profit. Low returns would be a red flag signaling that expenses are out of line with the product price. If this were the case managers might wish to examine ways to decrease expenses.

Return on equity
Net income divided by owner's equity.

Return on equity is used to evaluate the return in relation to the amount invested by the owners. This ratio is calculated by dividing net income by owner's equity.

$$\frac{\text{Net Income}}{\text{Owner's Equity}}.$$

For Catherine Tai's Jewelry Store, the return relates to Tai's capital investment and is

$$\frac{\text{Net Income (\$28,183)}}{\text{Owners Equity (\$103,183)}} = .27.$$

This return is favorable, especially when compared to the 3 percent Tai might currently earn at a bank. But it may be less favorable when compared to returns from previous years or to returns earned by competitors.

Earnings per share
Net income available for common stock shares (net income minus preferred dividends) divided by the number of shares of common stock outstanding.

The most often used profitability measure is earnings per share. **Earnings per share** reports the amount each share of common stock would receive if available earnings were distributed. Therefore, earnings per share pertains only to corporations. It is calculated by dividing net income available to common stock (net income minus preferred dividends) by the number of shares of common stock outstanding.

$$\textit{Earnings per Share} = \frac{\textit{Net Income} - \textit{Preferred Stock}}{\textit{Share of Common Stock Outstanding}}.$$

If there is no preferred stock, the calculation is simply net income divided by the number of shares of stock outstanding. Since Catherine Tai's Jewelry Store is a sole proprietorship, there is no common stock, and earnings per share cannot be computed.

Corporations regularly report their earnings per share in newspapers such as *The Wall Street Journal* and in their annual reports. For example, in 1993 Sears, Roebuck and Company reported a fourth-quarter loss of $1.8 billion. This amounted to a loss of $4.84 per share and greatly affected Sears's stock price.[8] CBS Inc posted fourth-quarter net income of $33.3 million, or $2.14 per share, which was up from $9.4 million or $0.61 per share the previous year.[9] Also, companies often use earnings per share to gauge their progress toward achieving their objectives. Avon Products, Inc., reported that it should meet its objectives of 10 to 13 percent growth in profit from operations in 1993. Avon's profits increased from $239 million to $264 million in 1993, a jump from $3.32 to $3.67.[10]

Accounting ratios such as *inventory turnover* and *accounts receivable turnover* provide a way to assess the company's ability to generate revenues and earnings through the productive use of its assets. **Inventory turnover** is determined by dividing the cost of goods sold by the average inventory for the period. This ratio measures the number of times a company sells its average level of inventory during the period. It may signal obsolete inventory or pricing problems.

Inventory turnover
Cost of goods sold divided by the average inventory for the period.

Accounts receivable turnover
Net credit sales divided by average net accounts receivable.

Accounts receivable turnover measures a company's ability to collect cash from credit customers. It is determined by dividing net credit sales by average net accounts receivable. The resulting amount indicates how many times during the year the average level of receivables is converted into cash. Generally the higher the ratio, the more success the business has in collecting cash.

Financial executives report that ratios play an important role in analyzing financial results and managing a business. Some companies incorporate financial ratios into their organizational objectives. The ratios that are relied on most heavily are the ones that measure the company's ability to generate profit, such as return on equity and earnings per share.[11]

SUMMARY

1. ***Explain the purposes of accounting information.***
   Accounting provides a means for gathering financial information about a business. Accounting also provides a language for communicating this information to interested parties such as investors, bankers, creditors, government agencies, and employees. Investors in a company need information about the company's financial condition and future prospects. Bankers and creditors use financial information about a company to assess the risk related to providing loans or extending credit. Government agencies rely on financial data for the purposes of regulation and taxation. Employees have a vested interest in the company and benefit from having information about its financial condition.

2. ***Define the accounting equation and describe its components.***
The accounting equation is the basic principle on which accounting is based. It describes the relationship between the company's assets and its liabilities and owner's equity. Assets are the economic resources the company owns that are expected to provide a benefit in the future. Liabilities are what the company owes to others, such as creditors. Owner's equity is the resources invested in the business by the owner and claims by the owner against the company's assets. Mathematically, the accounting equation is expressed as Assets = Liabilities + Owner's Equity.

3. ***Define the accounting process.***
Most modern companies maintain separate records for each item that appears in their financial statements. An account is a separate record used to record specific financial elements. In its simplest form, an account has a right (credit) side and a left (debit) side. The account is especially important in a double-entry system of bookkeeping. The double-entry system assumes that all business transactions create both a benefit (debit) and a sacrifice (credit). All transactions are recorded first in the journal. A separate entry is written for each transaction, in the order in which it occurred. Periodically the accounts are posted, or transferred from the journal to the ledger accounts. A ledger is a group of related accounts that make up a complete unit, such as all of the accounts of a specific company. Following posting, the entries are used to prepare a trial balance to determine the equality of the debits and credits in the ledger accounts. The trial balance is entered on a worksheet, which is then used to prepare financial statements.

4. ***Discuss the types and purposes of financial statements.***
Accountants routinely prepare four basic financial statements: the balance sheet, the income statement, the statement of cash flows, and the statement of owner's equity. These statements form the basis for a wide variety of decisions that company owners and managers must make. The balance sheet, or statement of financial position, reports the company's resources (assets) and claims against those resources (liabilities and owner's equity). This information gives a monetary picture of the company's financial condition at a particular point in time. The income statement reports the revenues and expenses for a particular time period. It provides a measure of the results of operations and the profitability of the business during that period. The statement of cash flows reports the cash receipts and payments related to the company's operating, investing, and financing activities during the accounting period. This information enables users to assess the company's ability to generate future cash for operations. The statement of owner's equity summarizes the events that caused owner's equity to change during a specified period of time.

5. ***Explain the various types of accounting.***
The most important forms of accounting are financial, managerial, and public accounting. Financial accounting involves the preparation, reporting, analysis, and interpretation of accounting information in reports for external users such as creditors, suppliers, customers, stockholders, lenders, and the general public. In collecting and analyzing accounting information, financial accountants conform to generally accepted accounting procedures (GAAP). The Financial Accounting Standards Board (FASB) is responsible for establishing sound guidelines for accounting practices. Managerial accounting consists of information-gathering and reporting activities and related accounting procedures. Managerial accounting supports managerial decision making by providing financial information that various managers need. Public accounting firms employ certified public accountants (CPAs). A CPA audits a company's financial statements to determine that the information contained is fairly presented. In addition to auditing services, public accounting firms provide tax services.

6. ***Describe the financial ratios used to analyze and interpret accounting information.***
Managers use a number of financial ratios to make accounting information on financial statements more meaningful. Analysts typically are interested in financial ratios that focus on short-term solvency, long-term solvency, and profitability. Short-term solvency ratios help assess the company's ability to pay its debt in the near future. One short-term solvency ratio is the current ratio, or current assets divided by current liabilities. Another is the quick ratio (or acid-

test ratio): cash, plus temporary investments, plus short-term receivables divided by current liabilities. A long-term solvency ratio is the debt to equity ratio, which measures the extent to which the company is financed by debt rather than owner's equity. The formula is total debt (current plus noncurrent liabilities) divided by owner's equity. Profitability ratios measure a company's ability to generate profits. Return on sales is calculated by dividing net income by sales. Return on equity is obtained by dividing net income by owner's equity. The most often used profitability measure for corporations is earnings per share. It is calculated by dividing net income available for common stock shares (net income minus preferred dividends) divided by the number of shares of common stock outstanding. Other profitability ratios assess the company's ability to generate revenues and earnings through the productive use of its assets. Inventory turnover—cost of goods sold divided by the average inventory for the period—may signal obsolete inventory or pricing problems. Accounts receivable turnover—net credit sales divided by average net accounts receivable—measures a company's ability to collect cash from credit customers.

KEY TERMS AND CONCEPTS

Accounting (p. 426)
Assets (p. 427)
Liabilities (p. 427)
Owner's equity (p. 427)
Accounting equation (p. 427)
Expenses (p. 428)
Revenue (p. 428)
Cost of goods sold (p. 428)
Account (p. 429)
Debit (p. 430)
Credit (p. 430)
Chart of accounts (p. 430)
Double-entry system (p. 430)
Journal (p. 430)
Ledger (p. 431)
Posting (p. 432)
Trial balance (p. 432)
Balance sheet (p. 432)
Operating cycle (p. 435)
Income statement (p. 436)
Depreciation (p. 437)
Statement of cash flows (p. 438)
Statement of owner's equity (p. 440)
Financial accounting (p. 440)
Managerial accounting (p. 441)
Certified public accountant (CPA) (p. 441)
Current ratio (p. 443)
Quick ratio (p. 443)
Debt to equity ratio (p. 444)
Return on sales (p. 444)
Return on equity (p. 444)
Earnings per share (p. 445)
Inventory turnover (p. 445)
Accounts receivable turnover (p. 445)

DISCUSSION QUESTIONS

Company

1. Explain the steps a company follows in recording business transactions.
2. Why do companies use external auditors to verify the accuracy of financial statements?
3. How is financial statement information used to evaluate a company's objectives?
4. Discuss the various types of accounting information most companies routinely use.

Customers

5. Under what circumstances might a customer benefit from having access to a company's financial statements?

Competitors

6. How might a competitor use information provided in a company's annual report? How can a company protect itself against such uses?
7. How might financial ratio analyses be used to make comparisons among competing companies in the same industry?

Collaborators

8. How does classifying assets and liabilities as current and noncurrent provide collaborators with useful information?
9. How might collaborators incorporate financial ratios into their decision-making process?

In Question: Take a Stand

When a Phar-Mor Inc. employee asked an auditor from the CPA firm Coopers & Lybrand, "Do you know about the second set of books?" a $500 million fraud was disclosed that caught the auditor completely off guard. Coopers & Lybrand had audited Phar-Mor since 1984 and claims it had no inkling of the massive fraud that went on, perhaps the largest in U.S. corporate history. The U.S. government accused top executives in Phar-Mor's finance department of inflating the company's inventory and accounts receivable to attract $1.1 billion from external investors.[12]

What is the responsibility of public accountants such as Coopers & Lybrand in cases of corporate fraud? Should the executives or the auditors of the bankrupt company pay for losses suffered by investors and creditors?

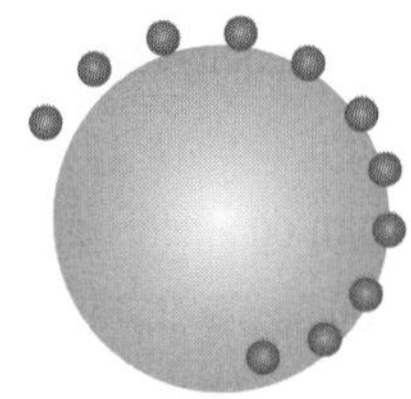

CASE 18.1
ALL IN THE FAMILY?[13]

Goody's Family Clothing, Inc., announced that its internal auditor found accounting irregularities related to the chief executive officer's personal expenses. Following the announcement, Goody's chief financial officer, Donald VandenBerg, resigned. The problem stemmed from stock investments in the company made by CEO Robert Goodfriend, the company founder's son. Goodfriend purchased stock investments from the company for $6.6 million. The check Goodfriend wrote was not cashed but was recorded as "cash on hand." VandenBerg held the check until Goodfriend got a bank loan for that amount. But Goodfriend used company money to pay off the bank loan and then wrote another check for $6.6 million. Again the company held the check and recorded it as "cash on hand."

Questions

1. *In your opinion, is the chief financial officer or the chief executive officer at fault in this case? Why?*
2. *Should company officers and accountants be held legally liable for losses to investors when actions such as these are uncovered?*
3. *What procedures could a company implement to prevent further abuses on the part of its officers?*

PART 6

Finance

CHAPTER 19

MONEY AND FINANCIAL INSTITUTIONS

When you have studied this chapter, you will be able to:

1. Define *money* and list five criteria for effective money.
2. Identify the components of the money supply.
3. Describe the structure of the Federal Reserve System.
4. Explain the most important tools the Federal Reserve System uses to control the supply of money.
5. Discuss the major functions of the Federal Reserve System.
6. Explain the differences between depository and nondepository institutions.
7. Discuss the regulation of the financial institutions.
8. Discuss federal deposit insurance programs in use today.
9. Describe trends that are changing banking in the United States and throughout the world.

Ilira Steinman went out shopping one day wearing a hat she had stitched together from some fabric scraps. The owner of a clothing boutique noticed the hat and asked Steinman to make four more for her.

Suddenly, Steinman was in the millinery business. Her business expanded, but her sales income barely covered costs because she didn't have enough money to buy fabric in volume.

Then Steinman heard about Working Capital, a nonprofit organization based in Cambridge, Massachusetts. Working Capital lent her $500, which she used to buy fabric wholesale. Thanks to that loan, she now has a credit line with a fabric wholesaler, produces over 100 hats a week, and employs three part-time workers.

Working Capital is one of at least 200 "microlenders" that have emerged across the country over the last three years to lend bits of money—usually between $500 and $1,500—to very small, struggling entrepreneurs.

Jeffrey Ashe started Working Capital in 1990 after working with a non-profit group called Accion International. Accion specialized in community development in Latin America. After helping Accion make microloans in Latin America for 11 years, Ashe wanted to bring the concept to poor neighbors in the U.S. "Tiny businesses here [in the U.S.] have the same problems informal businesses have anywhere else in the world," says Ashe.

Jeffrey Ashe borrows his capital from commercial banks and relends it to his small borrowers at a spread of about five percentage points over his cost of capital. He finances his overhead with private donations. Most microlenders depend on grant money, usually from private foundations, for the money they lend as well as for their overhead.

The rate of defaults on microloans is surprisingly small. One reason: Microlenders often use peer pressure to ensure repayment. Working Capital has its borrowers form "business loan groups" whose members act as informal advisers to one another. Working Capital will not lend to any member of a group unless every member is current on his loan. The group is also responsible for paying Working Capital back on delinquent loans. Working Capital has a 2% default rate.

"We're not robbing from the rich and giving to the poor," says Working Capital's Jeff Ashe. "We're creating capitalists."[1]

A billion dollars is a lot of money! Invested in a safe, tax-exempt municipal bond yielding a mere 5.6 percent interest, $1 billion would shower you with $153,425 in interest each and every day. No wonder Bill Gates, chair of Microsoft Corporation, can afford this huge mansion on Lake Washington in Seattle—Gates is worth more than $6.7 billion.[2]

This example shows the importance of money—even a small amount—to a business. Because money is so essential to a business, one of the most important collaborators for a company is its bank. This chapter is about money and how businesses obtain it.

WHAT IS MONEY?

A Harvard Business School professor wrote, "A business is about only two things—money and customers. It takes money to get started, customers to keep going, and more money to hold on to existing customers."[3] Money is so important that almost every society uses some form of it. American Indians used strings of beads and various shells as wampum, their form of money. American colonists used tobacco and whiskey as items to exchange for other goods. During World War II, prisoners of war used cigarettes as a substitute for money. These are only a few examples of the types of money societies have used.

But not all forms of money are equally effective. Money is effective when it meets five criteria:

1. Its value is easy to assess.
2. It is widely accepted by the society (or societies) that uses it.
3. Its units are divisible, making it easy to make change.
4. It is easily transported (as in a wallet or pocket).
5. It does not deteriorate quickly, either in value or physically.

Money
Anything that is generally accepted in a society as a means of payment or exchange.

Currency
Coins and paper money.

Economists define **money** as anything that is generally accepted in a society as a means of payment or exchange. Coins and paper money, commonly called **currency**, fit this definition and provide a ready example of one type of money. Since checks are also an acceptable form of payment, they too are thought of as money.

FUNCTIONS OF MONEY

Regardless of the form money takes, money performs three functions: It serves as a unit of account, a medium of exchange, and a store of value.

UNIT OF ACCOUNT

Unit of account
A common means by which the value of goods and services is measured.

Just as weight is measured in pounds, ounces, and/or grams and distance in miles, feet, and/or meters, the value of goods and services is measured in money terms. Therefore, money is the **unit of account** by which value is measured.

To see the importance of this aspect of money, let's look at a hypothetical barter economy consisting of three goods: chocolate bars, soda water, and coconuts. To exchange the goods, three prices are necessary: the price of soda water in terms of coconuts, the price of coconuts in terms of chocolate bars, and the price of chocolate bars in terms of soda water. In this three-good economy, establishing an exchange price is relatively easy. But when an economy consists of many goods, as most modern economies do, the problem of measuring value becomes more complex. For example, in a 1,000-good barter economy, 499,500 (N[N – 1]/2) prices would be needed. Using money as a unit of account is an efficient way to measure value. Money, or currency, is the common denominator by which all goods and services can be compared in terms of value.

MEDIUM OF EXCHANGE

Medium of exchange
A common means of facilitating exchanges of goods and services.

Since money facilitates the exchange of goods and services, it serves as a **medium of exchange**. Money is useful because it eliminates much of the time required to make an exchange. In a barter economy, a person who makes furniture and wants to buy a new computer would have to find someone who sells computers and also needs some new furniture. This transaction would require a good deal of time. When money is used in an exchange, however, the furniture maker is given money by anyone who needs new furniture and in turn can use the money to buy the new computer. No longer is it necessary to find a seller of computers who needs new furniture. The use of money thereby promotes economic efficiency by reducing the time required to exchange goods and services.

STORE OF VALUE

Store of value
The ability of money to maintain its buying power over time.

Liquidity
The relative ease with which an asset can be converted into the medium of exchange.

In addition to being a unit of account and a medium of exchange, money must provide a **store of value**; that is, money must maintain its buying power over time. Other assets, such as diamonds, houses, artwork, and stocks and bonds, are also stores of value. But the chief advantage money has is its liquidity. **Liquidity** is the relative ease with which an asset can be converted into the medium of exchange. Money is the most liquid store of value because it *is* the medium of exchange. Its liquidity explains why money is held even during inflationary periods, when it is not the best store of value. *Inflation* erodes the ability of money to maintain its store of value, because as prices rise, the buying power of money decreases.

FOCUS ON COMPANY

The Effect of Inflation

At the Luna boutique in Serbia, a Snickers bar costs 6 million dinars, at least until the manager reads the overnight fax from his boss. "Raise prices 99 percent," the fax states. For the second time in three days, Tihomir Nikolic sets about raising prices. New price tags are prepared and placed directly on the goods, which have so many price stickers that it is hard to tell what the prices really are. Since the international community imposed economic sanctions on Serbia, inflation in that country has approached 10 percent daily (an annual rate in the quadrillions). The government mint churns out dinars 24 hours a day, trying to keep up with the inflation that is fueled, in turn, by its nonstop printing.

THE MONEY SUPPLY

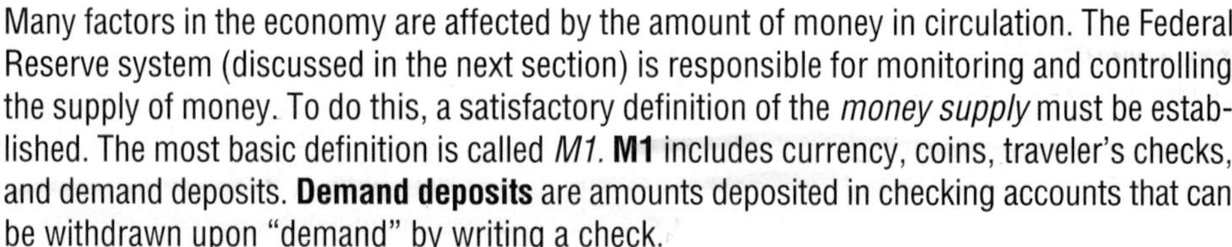

M1
The most basic definition of the money supply; includes currency, coins, traveler's checks, and demand deposits.

Demand deposit
An amount deposited in a checking account that can be withdrawn upon "demand" by writing a check.

Many factors in the economy are affected by the amount of money in circulation. The Federal Reserve system (discussed in the next section) is responsible for monitoring and controlling the supply of money. To do this, a satisfactory definition of the *money supply* must be established. The most basic definition is called *M1.* **M1** includes currency, coins, traveler's checks, and demand deposits. **Demand deposits** are amounts deposited in checking accounts that can be withdrawn upon "demand" by writing a check.

The Federal Reserve System sometimes uses other measures of the money supply that include less liquid assets than M1 does. These measures are called *M2* and *M3* and include savings deposits and money market accounts.

THE FEDERAL RESERVE SYSTEM

HISTORY

During the 19th century, Americans were very skeptical about the centralization of power. Due to this skepticism, coupled with a general distrust of monied interests, there was little support for the formation of a coordinated central bank. Two unsuccessful attempts to establish a central bank were made. First, in 1791 the government sought to establish a government-sponsored bank. The First Bank of the United States, as it was known, was chartered for 20 years and was intended to regulate the issuance of bank notes by state banks and to serve the U.S. Treasury by maintaining deposits and executing its payments. The charter of the First Bank was not renewed in 1811 because of political pressure. The second attempt came five years later, when Congress tried to reestablish a central bank. It chartered the Second Bank of the United States, which performed functions similar to those of the First Bank. The Second Bank suffered the same fate when its charter was allowed to expire in 1836.

Throughout the 19th century, *bank panics*—in which depositors, fearing that their banks would fail, attempted to withdraw their deposits—led to widespread bank failures. Following the panic in 1907, the American public became convinced that a central bank was needed to prevent future panics. The Federal Reserve Act was passed in 1913, and the Federal Reserve System was born.

STRUCTURE

Federal Reserve System
A network of 12 regional Federal Reserve banks, a board of governors, and approximately 5,000 member commercial banks.

Unlike the central banks of most countries, which are single institutions, the **Federal Reserve System** (or *the Fed,* for short) consists of 12 regional districts, each with a Federal Reserve bank; a board of governors; and approximately 5,000 member commercial banks. In addition, several councils advise the board on banking, consumer, and economic matters.

Federal Reserve Banks. As Exhibit 19.1 shows, each of the 12 Federal Reserve districts has one main *Federal Reserve bank,* the largest being the Federal Reserve Bank of New York. This regional bank holds more than 30 percent of the total Federal Reserve assets. It is the most influential bank because it has direct contact with the major financial markets that operate in New York.

Congress established the Federal Reserve banks as the operating arms of the Federal Reserve System. Exhibit 19.2 illustrates the structure of the Federal Reserve System. The Reserve banks hold the cash reserves of depository institutions and make loans to them. They

Exhibit 19.1 **THE FEDERAL RESERVE SYSTEM**

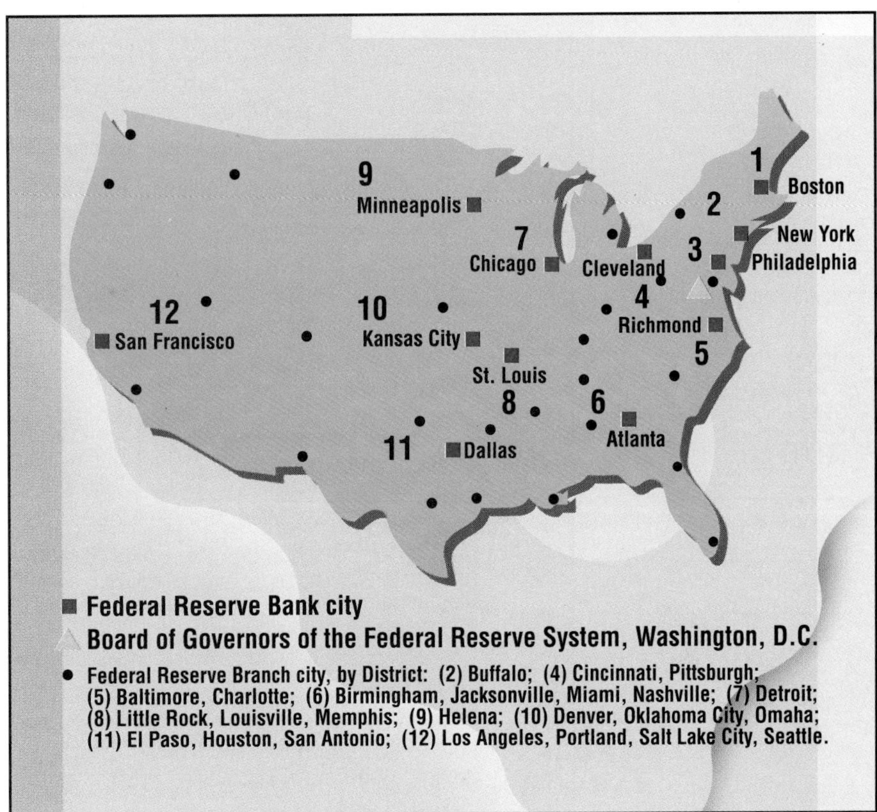

move currency and coins into and out of circulation and collect and process millions of checks each day. They provide checking accounts for the U.S. Treasury, issue and redeem government securities, and act as the fiscal agent for the U.S. government. They also participate in setting monetary policy.[4]

Board of Governors. While the district banks have some effect on the establishment of monetary policy, the most influential factor is the *Board of Governors of the Federal Reserve.* The seven-member Board of Governors is appointed by the president of the United States and confirmed by the U.S. Senate. Each appointee serves one 14-year term that is not renewable. The appointees' terms expire in rotating fashion, one every second year. To ensure that the interests of a particular district are not overrepresented, the governors are required to come from different districts. The chairperson, who serves a four-year term, is selected from the seven-member board. The tasks of the board are many and varied, but they all relate to monetary policy. One primary responsibility is participation in the Federal Open Market Committee (FOMC).

Federal Open Market Committee (FOMC)
The most important monetary policymaking body of the Federal Reserve System; creates policies to promote economic growth, full employment, stable prices, and international trade and makes key decisions regarding open market operations.

The Federal Open Market Committee. The **Federal Open Market Committee (FOMC)** is the most important monetary policymaking body of the Federal Reserve System. It is responsible for creating policies to promote economic growth, full employment, stable prices, and international trade. It makes key decisions regarding the conduct of *open market operations*—purchases and sales of U.S. government securities—that affect the cost and availability of money and credit in the U.S. economy. The FOMC meets about every six weeks to make these decisions.

Exhibit 19.2 **STRUCTURE OF THE FEDERAL RESERVE SYSTEM**

Board of Governors
Seven members appointed by the President

- Sets reserve requirements and approves the discount rate as part of monetary policy
- Supervises and regulates member banks, bank holding companies and foreign-owned banks operating in the United States
- Establishes and administers protective regulations governing consumer credit
- Exercises general supervision over the Reserve Banks

Federal Open Market Committee
Board of Governors and five Reserve Bank Presidents

- Directs open market operations (the buying and selling of U.S. Government securities), the primary tool of monetary policy

Advisory Councils

- Consumer Advisory Council
- Federal Advisory Council
- Thrift Institutions Advisory Council

Federal Reserve Banks
Twelve district Banks serve as the operating arms of the central bank. Five presidents of the Reserve Banks sit on the Federal Open Market Committee

- Propose discount rate
- Hold reserve balances for depository institutions and lend them at the discount window
- Furnish currency and coin
- Collect, clear, and transfer funds for depository institutions
- Act as fiscal agent for Treasury Department

FOCUS ON COLLABORATORS

The Chairperson of the Federal Reserve

Although each member of the Federal Reserve's Board of Governors has an equal vote, the chairperson of the Fed has special powers as spokesperson for the nation's monetary policy. Thus, the financial community takes great interest in the chair's monetary philosophy. The two most recent chairs—Alan Greenspan, reappointed to a second term in 1992, and his predecessor, Paul Volcker—have been extremely influential.

Volcker was appointed chair by President Jimmy Carter in l979. Having previously served as president of the Federal Reserve Bank of New York and in the Department of the Treasury, Volcker was considered an authoritative and knowledgeable figure in monetary affairs. Most notable among his many accomplishments was his fight to curb inflation. Volcker put the economy through two back-to-back recessions in the early 1980s and let interest rates spiral. By the end of 1982, the inflation rate was less than 5 percent.

The success of Volcker's anti-inflation policy continued throughout the rest of his term as chair. Unemployment fell steadily from a rate of more than 10 percent, and the inflation rate remained below 5 percent. However, new appointments to the Board of Governors by President Reagan created a large gap between Volcker and the administration.

In mid-1987, Alan Greenspan replaced Volcker as chair of the Federal Reserve Board. Formerly chair of the Council of Economic Advisers under President Ford, Greenspan was widely regarded as the best possible replacement. Greenspan committed himself to Volcker's policies. In an address to the Senate in 1992, Greenspan stated that the central bank's most important task was to promote price stability.

MONETARY POLICY

The Federal Reserve uses several means to influence the supply of money and the availability of credit. The tools of monetary policy include the reserve requirement, the discount rate, and open market operations.

THE RESERVE REQUIREMENT

Reserve requirement
The percentage of a bank's total deposits that must be held in reserve at the Federal Reserve bank.

All depository institutions (commercial banks, savings and loans, mutual savings banks, and credit unions) are required to maintain reserves against their deposit liabilities. The Federal Reserve periodically sets a **reserve requirement**—the percentage of a bank's total deposits that must be held in reserve at the Federal Reserve Bank. For example, if the reserve requirement is 10 percent (the requirement in effect in May 1994), $10 in reserves must be held for every $100 in demand deposits. Thus, when a customer deposits $100 in his or her checking account, the bank must send $10 to the Federal Reserve bank in its district and can loan only $90 to a borrower. By varying the reserve requirement, the Federal Reserve controls the ability of the depository institutions to loan funds.

THE DISCOUNT RATE

Discount rate
The rate of interest the Federal Reserve charges to banks that borrow to meet their reserve requirements.

Sometimes banks experience temporary shortages in their required reserves and find it necessary to borrow from the Federal Reserve. The **discount rate** is the rate of interest the Federal Reserve charges to banks that borrow to meet their reserve requirements. Any change in the cost of borrowing from the Federal Reserve will affect a bank's willingness to borrow from the Federal Reserve. A decrease in the discount rate will stimulate borrowing, while an increase will tend to discourage borrowing.

OPEN MARKET OPERATIONS

Open market operations
The buying and selling of U.S. Treasury securities by the Federal Reserve.

The third tool of monetary policy is **open market operations**—the buying and selling of U.S. Treasury securities by the Federal Reserve. Open market operations are the major tool used to influence the total amount of money and credit available in the economy. By purchasing and selling government securities, the Federal Reserve attempts to encourage expansion of money and credit while achieving price stability and growth in economic activity.

FEDERAL RESERVE BALANCE SHEET

Since assets and liabilities are the result of financial activity, the Federal Reserve Balance Sheet in Exhibit 19.3 will be used as a vehicle to discuss what the Fed does.

ASSETS OF THE FEDERAL RESERVE

Assets held by the Federal Reserve include gold certificates, loans to member banks, U.S. government securities, cash items in process of collection, and miscellaneous assets.

Gold Certificates. Although the Treasury is no longer required to hold gold to support the supply of money, it can still own gold. When the Treasury wishes to obtain funds, it can sell the gold to the general public or sell *gold certificates*—warehouse receipts for gold issued by the Treasury—to the Federal Reserve.

Exhibit 19.3 **A SIMPLIFIED FEDERAL RESERVE BALANCE SHEET**

Assets	
Certificates (gold and other)	$19,071,286,000
Loans to member banks	93,975,000
U.S. government securities	349,865,718,000
Cash items in process of collection	7,173,331,000
Other assets	33,766,201,000
Total assets	$409,970,511,000
Liabilities	
Federal Reserve notes	$343,925,294,000
Deposits	
Member bank reserves	34,951,228,000
U.S. Treasury	14,809,011,000
Foreign	386,345,000
Other	396,563,000
Other liabilities	8,699,548,000
Capital	$6,802,522,000
Total liabilities and capital	$409,970,511,000

U.S. Government Securities. U.S. government securities are purchased and sold by the Federal Reserve. These transactions alter the money supply and the ability of banks to create credit.

Federal funds
Short-term loans by the Federal Reserve that enable banks to meet reserve requirements.

Loans to Member Banks. Loans made by the Federal Reserve to member banks, sometimes referred to as **federal funds**, are short-term loans enabling the banks to meet reserve requirements. The interest charged to the banks is called the *federal funds rate.* This interest rate is one way of knowing whether the Federal Reserve is increasing or decreasing the supply of money. When the rate is lower, the supply of money grows.

Cash Items in Process of Collection. Also included in the asset section in Exhibit 19.3 is an item called Cash items in process of collection. In this case, *cash* refers not to cash per se but to the clearing of checks, which is an important service of the Federal Reserve. In 1993, the Federal Reserve handled more than 19 billion checks, which cost $555 million to process.

Float
The time it takes checks to clear through the Federal Reserve System.

The time it takes checks to clear through the Federal Reserve System is commonly called the **float**. It may take several days from the time a company writes a check until the time its bank finally reduces the company's account by that amount. During this time, the company continues to earn interest on the amount. Also, some companies may write checks for more than they actually have on deposit with their banks and use the float period to find other money to cover the amounts of the checks. The Federal Reserve continues to find ways to reduce the float. The advent of electronic and computer technology is the most effective weapon in this struggle.

Other Assets. This classification of assets includes foreign currencies held by the Federal Reserve. The need for a supply of foreign currency arises when Americans travel abroad and when U.S. firms invest in foreign businesses. In these instances, American dollars must be exchanged for local currency. The exchange is conducted by Federal Reserve banks, which have deposits of foreign currencies.

LIABILITIES OF THE FEDERAL RESERVE

Activities of the Federal Reserve cause it to incur various liabilities. These liabilities include Federal Reserve notes, deposits, and other, miscellaneous liabilities.

Since 1992, the Federal Reserve has been distributing technologically improved paper money. In recent years, technological advances such as color photocopiers have made counterfeiters' jobs quite easy. The new notes, however, have two new features to discourage counterfeiters: a security thread and microprinting. These features will make illegal copies much easier to detect.[5]

Federal Reserve notes
Paper currency of the United States issued by the Federal Reserve.

Federal Reserve Notes. The primary liability of the Federal Reserve is the paper currency that is in circulation. **Federal Reserve notes** are the paper currency (those green dollar bills in your wallet) issued by the Federal Reserve. Several billions of dollars of this currency are printed each year, primarily to replace old and worn paper money that is taken out of circulation.

Deposits. Another liability is deposits. Deposits include those made by the U.S. Treasury, member banks, and other countries. Of all the different deposits, the most important are those made by member banks. Deposits of member banks refer to the reserves deposited by commercial banks, savings and loans, mutual savings banks, and credit unions. As stated earlier, by altering the required reserves and the amount of Federal Reserve notes outstanding, the Federal Reserve Bank is able to regulate the supply of money and credit.

Other Liabilities. Other liabilities refer to miscellaneous obligations that exist at fiscal year end. Sundry liabilities such as accounts payable are included in this classification.

DEPOSITORY INSTITUTIONS

Depository institution
A financial institution that directly offers federally insured checking and savings accounts.

The authority of the Federal Reserve to influence the supply of money was increased by the Depository Institution Deregulation and Monetary Control Act of 1980. Under this act, all commercial banks, mutual savings banks, savings and loan associations, and credit unions became subject to regulation by the Federal Reserve. These organizations are generally referred to as **depository institutions**, because they are the only ones that directly offer federally insured checking and savings accounts.

Commercial bank
A bank that receives deposits from individuals and companies and uses these funds to make loans and conduct other business.

COMMERCIAL BANKS

Commercial banks are used by more than three-fourths of all U.S. households.[6] A **commercial bank** receives deposits from individuals and companies and uses these funds to make loans and conduct other business. Approximately 11,000 commercial banks make loans by

Exhibit 19.4 **FUNCTIONS OF A COMMERCIAL BANK**

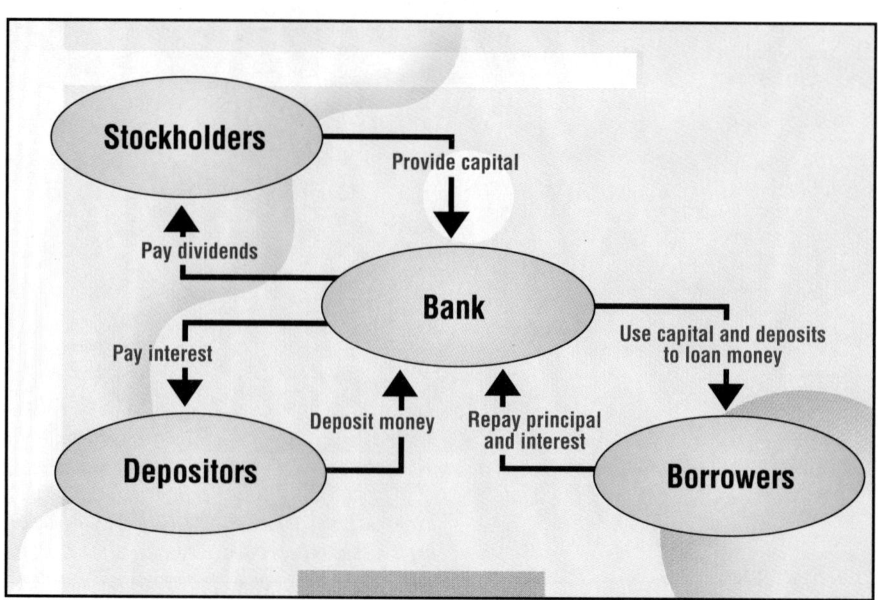

using funds deposited in checking and savings accounts.[7] Exhibit 19.4 illustrates the functions of commercial banks.

The *National Banking Act of 1863* created national currency and provided for the national chartering of banks. It also established the Office of the Comptroller of the Currency to supervise nationally chartered banks. Today banks are chartered by both the federal and state governments and operate in a dual banking system.

Commercial banks are service oriented and depend on customer deposits for operating funds. Therefore, banks must satisfy customers by providing a variety of services. This means getting to know customers and serving all of their banking needs. This includes providing for loans, checking and savings accounts, money market transactions, trust arrangements, discount brokerage services, and safety deposit boxes.

Negotiable order of withdrawal (NOW) account
A checking account that pays annual interest as long as the depositor maintains some minimum balance.

Super NOW account
A form of NOW account that pays higher interest and gives free and unlimited check-writing privileges, but requires a much larger minimum balance.

Certificate of deposit (CD)
A time deposit that earns higher interest than does the traditional passbook savings account.

Checking and Savings Accounts. Traditionally commercial banks limited checking account services to such activities as processing checks, preparing and sending monthly bank statements, paying interest, and cashing checks. Also, savings accounts, called *time deposits,* were confined mostly to the standard passbook types. However, a revolution has occurred in commercial banks that has greatly expanded the services they provide.

Most checking accounts now pay interest to depositors. This type of account, called a **negotiable order of withdrawal (NOW) account**, typically pays annual interest as long as the depositor maintains some minimum balance. In addition, the bank may restrict the number of checks the depositor can write. A variation of the NOW account called the **super NOW account** pays higher interest and gives free and unlimited check-writing privileges, but requires a much larger minimum balance.

Savings accounts also have changed substantially in the past two decades as banks have struggled to increase deposits. A **certificate of deposit (CD)** is a time deposit that earns higher interest than does the traditional passbook savings account and thus encourages savings. A CD is established for a specified period of time, during which the depositor cannot withdraw the money without paying a hefty early-withdrawal penalty. During the high inflation of the late 1970s and early 1980s, interest rates on CDs often exceeded 15 percent. Today you are lucky to get 5 percent unless the period is for at least five years.

Exhibit 19.5 **WHO GETS WHAT IN A CREDIT CARD TRANSACTION**

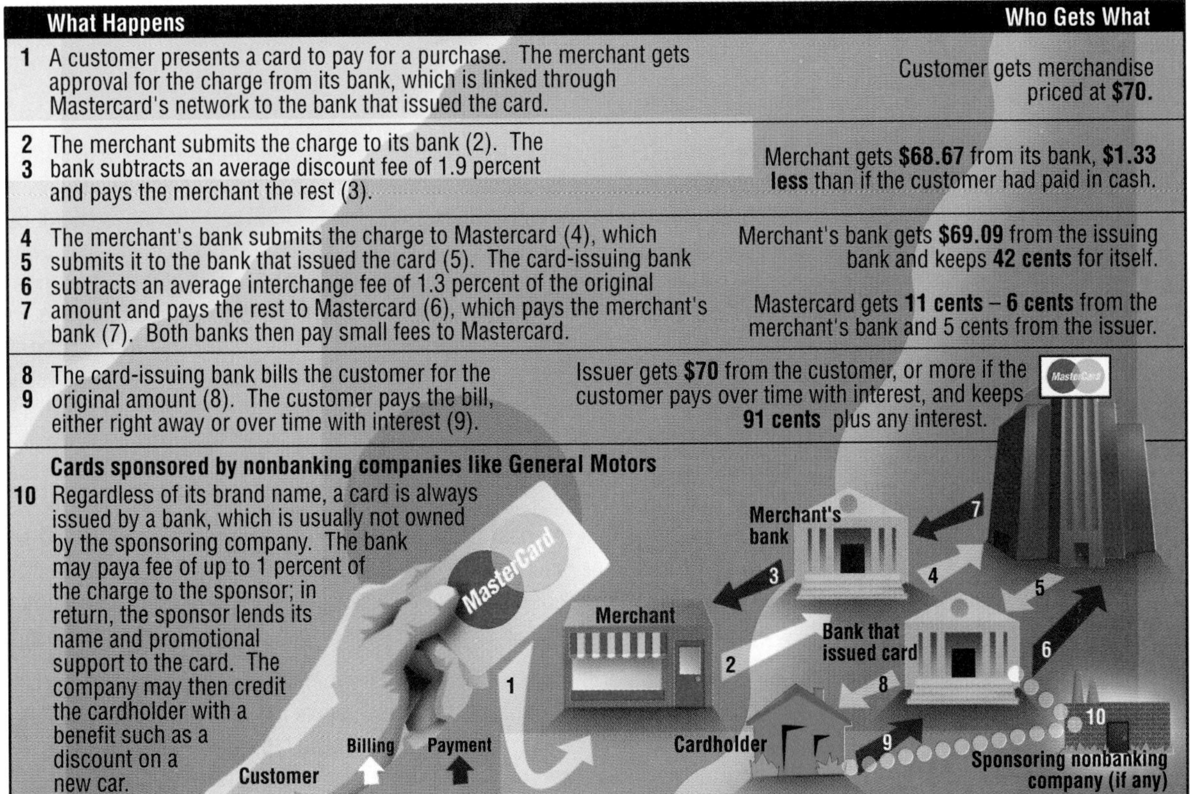

What Happens
Who Gets What
1 A customer presents a card to pay for a purchase. The merchant gets approval for the charge from its bank, which is linked through Mastercard's network to the bank that issued the card.
Customer gets merchandise priced at $70.
2 The merchant submits the charge to its bank (2). The
3 bank subtracts an average discount fee of 1.9 percent and pays the merchant the rest (3).
Merchant gets $68.67 from its bank, $1.33 less than if the customer had paid in cash.
4 The merchant's bank submits the charge to Mastercard (4), which
5 submits it to the bank that issued the card (5). The card-issuing bank
6 subtracts an average interchange fee of 1.3 percent of the original
7 amount and pays the rest to Mastercard (6), which pays the merchant's bank (7). Both banks then pay small fees to Mastercard.
Merchant's bank gets $69.09 from the issuing bank and keeps 42 cents for itself.
Mastercard gets 11 cents – 6 cents from the merchant's bank and 5 cents from the issuer.
8 The card-issuing bank bills the customer for the
9 original amount (8). The customer pays the bill, either right away or over time with interest (9).
Issuer gets $70 from the customer, or more if the customer pays over time with interest, and keeps 91 cents plus any interest.
Cards sponsored by nonbanking companies like General Motors
10 Regardless of its brand name, a card is always issued by a bank, which is usually not owned by the sponsoring company. The bank may paya fee of up to 1 percent of the charge to the sponsor; in return, the sponsor lends its name and promotional support to the card. The company may then credit the cardholder with a benefit such as a discount on a new car.
MasterCard
Merchant
Merchant's bank
Bank that issued card
Cardholder
Customer
Billing
Payment
Sponsoring nonbanking company (if any)

Bank Credit Cards. Credit cards are another area where commercial banks have expanded their services. Used by 56 percent of American households, bank credit cards are the most widely used credit product.[8] Many companies, including JCPenney, Sears, and Macy, developed customer charge accounts before World War II. With these accounts, customers could buy merchandise without having to pay cash. After the war, Diner's Club initiated a national credit card program for use in restaurants throughout the United States. American Express and Carte Blanche developed similar programs. In the late 1960s, two bank card programs were created: MasterCard and Bank Americard, which is now VISA. Today bank credit cards number about 200 million.

Credit cards generate sizable profits to banks, since they stem from both interest charged to credit card holders and payments made by the stores that sell the goods and services (see Exhibit 19.5). As competition has increased among credit card companies and banks, interest rates and annual fees have dropped dramatically. By the end of 1993, many issuers were waiving first-year fees and the average interest rate had declined to 16.3 percent.[9]

Banks have also experimented with debit cards, which deduct the amount of a purchase directly from the cardholder's checking account. The customer avoids interest charges, but the amount is usually deducted from the checking account within 24 hours. These cards have not yet become popular.[10] Also, banks are moving toward working with collaborators to offer co-brand credit cards. For example, Citibank has collaborated with American Airlines to offer the VISA/AAdvantage card, which adds air travel miles to the credit card holder's frequent-flyer account.[11]

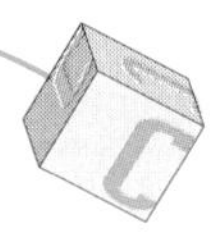

FOCUS ON COMPETITORS

NationsBank Start Card

As the competition among credit card issuers heats up, NationsBank thinks it has come up with a winner. Recently it formed an alliance with Start Inc., a Virginia marketing company that patented the frequent-saver idea. Under the program, holders of the new NationsBank Start co-brand card will receive rebates ranging from 0.5 to 7 percent on purchases. This amount will be set aside in an annuity for retirement. Start charges a $25 membership fee and has agreements with 20 companies, including MCI, Hertz, Spiegel, and Club Meditterranee Food Service. Negotiations are under way to add more than 30 other companies to the program. NationsBank will contribute from 0.5 to 1 percent for purchases made with its cards, regardless of whether or not the merchant is a participating company.

Automated teller machine (ATM)
An electronic machine that permits customers to make deposits and withdrawals and transfer funds among their accounts.

Automated Teller Machines (ATMs). Automated teller machines (ATMs) became standard in commercial banks within the past decade. These electronic machines offer 24-hour banking at convenient locations such as the local supermarket or the student union on campus. Bank customers can make deposits and withdrawals and transfer funds among their accounts by using a personalized access card.

Loans. Making loans is one of the key functions of commercial banks. Loans to companies represent 20 percent of commercial banks' total assets, while loans to individual consumers account for 11.5 percent of their assets.[12] Loans to businesses typically are classified as either short-term or long-term. *Short-term loans* must be repaid within one year and are used for the company's immediate needs, such as to build seasonal inventory. *Long-term loans* may be granted for periods of up to 20 years but most often run from 3 to 5 years. They are used to acquire equipment, buildings, and other long-term assets.

STREET SMART

How Much Debt Can You Stand?

It is clear that Polonius's advice in *Hamlet,* "Neither a borrower nor a lender be," is generally not followed in this country. Many people borrow substantial amounts of money, for a home, a car, education, clothing, and furniture. Financial institutions are only too anxious to lend you this money. But be careful: Unnecessary debt can ruin your finances. Professionals advise you to minimize use of high-interest credit cards, steer clear of six-year and seven-year car loans some lenders offer, and take advantage of low-interest, 15-year home mortgages if possible. Above all, watch your cash flow when agreeing to any loan.

Panic reigned for depositors at the Old Court Savings and Loan of Randallstown, Maryland, as they waited in line to claim savings held in the failed savings and loan..

SAVINGS AND LOAN ASSOCIATIONS

Savings and loan association (S&L), or **thrift**
A depository institution that accepts deposits and makes home mortgage loans.

Savings and loan associations (S&Ls), also called **thrifts**, are the next largest group of depository institutions used by 40 percent of all households.[13] S&Ls are depository institutions that accept deposits and make home mortgage loans. They can be state or federally chartered.

S&Ls grew rapidly during the 1950s and 1960s, but when interest rates began to increase in the late 1960s to early 1980s, their growth slowed. This slowdown was attributed to the ceiling on interest that S&Ls could pay on depositors' savings accounts. Depositors were switching to *money market mutual funds,* which paid a higher rate of interest and also offered check-writing privileges. The tremendous popularity of these funds was partly explained by the fact that investors received the market rate of interest and reasonable safety of principal. Assets of money market mutual funds exploded from $3.8 billion in 1977 to an astounding $271 billion in 1992.[14]

Since savings deposits are a primary source of funding for S&Ls, their ability to grant mortgage loans diminished. This in turn had a strong impact on the construction industry, as demand for homes depends on the availability of mortgage loans. The *Depository Institutions and Monetary Control Act of 1980* mandated that interest rate ceilings be phased out over a six-year period. But this act did not completely stop the transfer of deposits from S&Ls to money market funds. The *Garn–St Germain Act of 1982* permitted S&Ls to offer competitive interest rates and subsequently led to new money market accounts at most commercial banks and S&Ls.

The S&L Scandal of the 1980s. The savings and loan scandal of the 1980s was unparalleled in terms of the extent of fraud and its ultimate cost. The price tag for the failure of S&Ls during this time is estimated at somewhere between $500 billion and $1 trillion.[15] Although it is hard to identify all the causes of these bank failures, the trouble probably began in the 1970s and early 1980s, when inflation and interest rates soared. To make S&Ls more competitive, deregulatory laws were passed in 1980 and 1982 that permitted S&Ls to make new, far riskier investments. Thus, S&Ls began to invest in land acquisition, construction loans to commercial real estate developers, junk bonds, and Ferrari dealerships.[16]

In addition, unscrupulous investors scrambled to use S&L funds for personal enrichment. Perhaps the most notorious of these investors was Charles Keating, who purchased California-based Lincoln Savings and Loan in 1983. At the time the bank had $1.1 billion in assets, 30 percent of which were in residential loans. In five years, Keating expanded the bank to over $6 billion in assets, but less than 2 percent was in residential loans. Among the excesses Keating directed was an investment in a luxury Phoenix resort built at a record cost of $500,000 per room. The bank's investment in junk bonds jumped from zero to $779 million. Keating paid exorbitant salaries to members of his family, including $1 million a year to his son, whom he appointed chair of the thrift.

Keating was skilled in enlisting help from important U.S. politicians. Five U.S. senators were cited for ethical violations for helping Keating obtain favorable treatment from the Federal government. Keating even fooled financial experts such as Alan Greenspan, current chair of the Federal Reserve. Greenspan once wrote letters to key members of Congress citing Keating and his management team as "seasoned and expert," with a "record of outstanding success in making sound and profitable direct investments."[17] Keating was sentenced to 12-1/2 years in prison for bank fraud and racketeering. He was also ordered to pay $122.4 million in restitution to the U.S. government, but few expect this to ever be paid.[18]

MUTUAL SAVINGS BANKS

Mutual savings bank
A bank that is owned by its depositors and managed by a board of trustees.

Mutual savings banks are owned by their depositors and managed by a board of trustees. They are similar to S&Ls in that they obtain funds from depositors and then loan the funds, primarily for mortgages.

Most "mutuals" were started in the northeastern United States to promote savings deposits among working people. This explains some of the unique names of these banks, such as Bowery Savings Bank and Merchant Seaman's Bank. They also provided consumer loans, which most other banks did not offer at that time.

Before 1980 mutual savings banks, like S&Ls, were restricted to making mortgage loans and suffered similar problems when interest rates rose. The Depository Institutions Deregulation and Monetary Control Act of 1980 thus also affected mutual savings banks. Today mutual savings banks can make all types of loans to consumers and provide checking account services. Mutual savings banks have not spread to other parts of the country, probably because S&Ls and credit unions serve the same purpose.

CREDIT UNIONS

Credit union
A cooperative depository institution organized to meet savings and loan needs of a particular group of people.

Credit unions are organized to meet savings and loan needs of particular groups of people, such as government employees, teachers, and union members. Originating in Europe in the 1880s, credit unions are small cooperatives that can be chartered either by the federal government or by states. Funds from members' deposits are used to make consumer loans to other members. A credit union is distinguished from a mutual savings bank by the common bond that exists among its members, namely their place of employment.

Since credit unions do not have shareholders, the profits they generate can be passed on to members in the form of lower fees or increased services. Their charters, which limit them to making loans to members, have generally prevented them from making large real estate loans or loans to less developed countries. Thus, credit unions have not experienced the problems that have plagued S&Ls and commercial banks.[19]

The regulations of the early 1980s that affected depository institutions have resulted in a wider variety of authorized services by credit unions. These services are similar to those offered by other depository institutions and include checking accounts, automated teller machines, and mortgage and home equity loans. Some credit unions even offer safety deposit boxes, mutual fund investments, and financial planning services.[20]

NONDEPOSITORY INSTITUTIONS

Nondepository institution
A financial institution that cannot offer federally insured savings and checking accounts.

Unlike depository institutions, **nondepository institutions** cannot offer federally insured savings and checking accounts. However, nondepository institutions play as important a role in transferring funds from lenders (savers) to borrowers as banks do. They are also subject to state regulations, but the restrictions are less severe than those imposed on depository institutions.

Nondepository institutions include insurance companies, pension funds, and finance companies.

INSURANCE COMPANIES

Insurance companies receive premiums paid on policies and invest those funds in assets such as stocks, bonds, mortgages, and other loans. Income generated from these investments is used to pay policy claims. Thus, insurance companies convert one type of financial asset into another. We will discuss the insurance industry in greater detail in Chapter 22.

PENSION FUNDS

Pension funds
A third-party trustee to which employers and/or employees contribute money that accumulates assets to provide income to employees at retirement.

A **pension fund** is a third-party trustee to which employees and/or employers contribute money periodically. The purpose of the pension fund is to accumulate assets so that employees will have a source of income at retirement.

The deposited funds are invested in income-producing assets. Thus, the funds grow over time as additional amounts are contributed and the funds already in the plan earn income. Pension plan assets generally consist of government securities, mortgage loans, and stocks and bonds. Some pension funds are very large and serve as a major source of investment funds for businesses. For example, Teachers Insurance & Annuity Association, a nationwide pension fund for teachers, has over $50 billion, nearly one-fourth of which is loaned directly to corporations.[21]

COMMERCIAL AND CONSUMER FINANCE COMPANIES

Commercial and consumer *finance companies* acquire funds by issuing commercial paper (unsecured short-term notes in denominations of $100,000 or greater) and selling shareholder stocks and bonds. They use this money to make loans to borrowers who do not meet the credit requirements of banks. Typically finance companies charge higher rates of interest than banks do, since the loans are riskier. These loans are usually small in amount and are designed to fit consumer and small-business needs. Thus, finance companies borrow large amounts but lend in small amounts. This process is quite different from that used by commercial banks, which typically receive small deposit amounts but often make large loans.

Although states regulate the maximum amount that finance companies can loan and the terms of loan contracts, there are no restrictions on branching, the types of assets that can be held, or how funds can be raised. Thus, finance companies are virtually unregulated, which enables them to better accommodate customer needs.

There are three types of finance companies: sales, consumer, and business finance companies.

Sales Finance Companies. A sales finance company makes loans to customers to purchase items from a particular retailer or manufacturer. Sears, Roebuck Acceptance Corporation finances purchases of goods and services acquired at Sears stores. General Motors Acceptance Corporation finances GM products. These companies are able to compete directly with banks for consumer loans, since they earn profit from the sales, as well as interest on the loans.

Consumer Finance Companies. A consumer finance company makes loans to consumers who are typically higher credit risks and cannot get loans elsewhere. For example, Household Finance Corporation and Person-to-Person Finance Company make loans to consumers to buy items such as furniture and home appliances. Because of the higher loan risk, consumer finance companies tend to charge high rates of interest.

Business Finance Companies. A business finance company provides special types of credit to businesses. Two ways companies may borrow from a business finance company are to sell their accounts receivable to the finance company and to lease equipment from that company.

The sale of accounts receivable is called *factoring.* The cash the selling company receives is less than the face amount of the receivables and is called a *discount.* The finance company collects the accounts receivable, earning profits due to the discount.

Business finance companies also specialize in the leasing of equipment. First they acquire the equipment and then lease it to other businesses for specified periods of time.

REGULATION OF FINANCIAL INSTITUTIONS

As we saw earlier, the Federal Reserve System was created to ensure stability of the banking system. From the establishment of the Federal Reserve in 1913 until 1929, the banking system enjoyed great stability, and the Federal Reserve was credited with making tremendous improvements. However, the stock market crash of 1929 and the onset of the Great Depression raised serious questions about the effectiveness of the Federal Reserve. Between 1929 and 1933, approximately 9,000 banks—almost one-half of the banks in operation in the United States—failed. This crisis led to legislation to reform the banking industry. The most important legislation was the National Banking Act of 1933, which we described earlier.

REGULATORY RELATIONSHIPS

Depository institutions are subject to multiple regulatory agencies. *Comptroller of the Currency,* a federal agency that charters and examines national banks, has supervisory authority over the 4,000 federally chartered banks. The Federal Reserve System and the states have joint authority over those commercial banks that are both state chartered and members of the Federal Reserve. The Federal Reserve also has sole regulatory authority over bank holding companies and secondary authority over the national banks. The *Federal Deposit Insurance Corporation (FDIC)* is the agency of the federal government that supervises commercial banks and insures depositors' accounts. The FDIC and state banking authorities jointly supervise banks that are state chartered and have FDIC insurance but are not members of the Federal Reserve System. Finally, state banking authorities regulate those state banks that do not have FDIC insurance. Exhibit 19.6 illustrates some of the regulatory relationships for commercial banks.

Regulation begins when a bank is chartered, either by the Comptroller of the Currency or by state banking authorities. The chartering process begins when the bank submits an application showing how it will be operated. Once chartered, the bank is required to submit periodic financial statements. In addition, bank records are examined regularly to assess the bank's financial condition. The Comptroller of the Currency examines large banks more frequently when, as has been the case recently, the banking system is in difficulty.

The FDIC allows a maximum of 36 months between bank examinations. The Federal Reserve audits bank records every 18 months. The Comptroller of the Currency examines national banks, the Federal Reserve examines state banks that are members of the Federal Reserve System, and the FDIC examines banks that are not members of the Federal Reserve System. To avoid duplication of effort, the three federal regulators typically work together and accept one another's examinations.

Exhibit 19.6 **REGULATORY RELATIONSHIPS FOR COMMERCIAL BANKS**

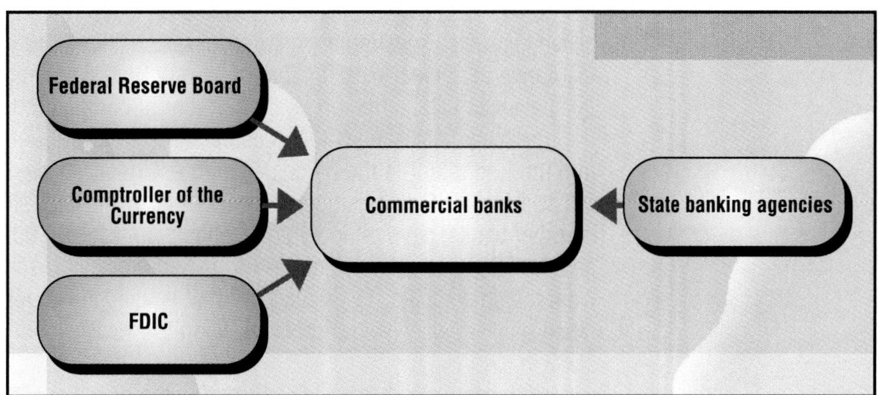

BANK EXAMINATIONS

A bank examination occurs with an unannounced visit by a bank examiner. The examiner determines whether or not the bank is complying with rules and regulations regarding the bank's holdings of assets. The examiner has considerable authority and can force the bank to sell assets he or she believes are too risky and to write off loans determined to be uncollectible. If the examiner concludes that the bank has insufficient capital or some other problem exists, the bank is declared a problem bank and will be examined more frequently.

FOCUS ON COLLABORATORS

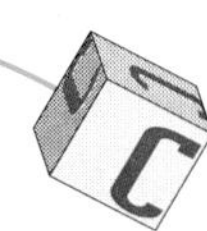

Federal Reserve Board Regulators

Federal bank examiners, or regulators, have the tough job of inspecting commercial bank operations to ensure compliance with all federal regulations. Following the bank crisis of the 1980s, these regulators have pursued their jobs with a vengeance. Some banks believe the regulators have become too tough and hold up economic recovery. But regulators like George Masa, director of the Federal Deposit Insurance Corporation's San Francisco region, feel differently. Among their pet peeves are "character loans" based on a banker's trust in a borrower, incomplete loan applications, and overvalued collateral. Making our banks safer places to keep our money is no easy job.

BANK FAILURES AND DEPOSIT INSURANCE SYSTEMS

Commercial Bank Failures. During the Great Depression, bank failure meant that depositors had to wait to get their money until the bank's assets had been converted into cash. Often the depositors had to settle for a fraction of what they had deposited. The number of commercial bank failures averaged over 2,000 per year during the Depression.

In contrast, the number of banks that failed from 1934 to 1981 averaged only 10 per year. The reason for the sharp reduction in bank failures was the creation of the Federal Deposit Insurance Corporation (FDIC). Since FDIC insurance protects depositors with deposits under $100,000, they are less likely to withdraw their funds (which may cause a bank to fail).

The number of bank failures has dropped dramatically, but they have not been completely eliminated. In 1984, 206 banks failed, and since 1985 bank failures have been occurring at a rate of over 100 a year. In 1992, 120 failures occurred among banks holding more than $46 billion in assets. Covering depositor's losses cost the FDIC some $4.6 billion. In 1991, the FDIC insurance fund was $7.03 billion in the red. But by the end of 1993 the fund showed a positive balance of $13.1 billion as the number of bank failures dropped to only 41 in 1993.[22]

If a bank fails, the FDIC can use either the payoff method or the purchase and assumption method to settle the bank's accounts. Under the *payoff* method, the bank is allowed to fail and the FDIC, by using funds acquired from deposit insurance premiums paid by all member banks, pays off individual deposits up to $100,000. Then the bank's assets are sold, and the FDIC and other creditors of the bank receive their respective shares of the proceeds from the sold assets. The payoff method is used infrequently for guaranteeing deposits of a failed bank. It was used, however, when the Penn Square Bank of Oklahoma failed in July 1982.[23]

Under the *purchase and assumption* method, the FDIC reorganizes the bank. This typically involves finding another bank that is willing to merge with the failed bank and assume all of its liabilities. The FDIC may assist the merger partner by providing subsidized loans. This method is more commonly used than the payment method and ensures full protection for deposit accounts.

S&L Failures. Savings and checking deposits at S&Ls were insured by the *Federal Savings and Loan Insurance Corporation (FSLIC)* up to $100,000 per depositor. By 1986, growing losses in the S&L industry were bankrupting the FSLIC. In 1987, Congress attempted to remedy the situation by passing the Competitive Equality Banking Act. This act provided a $10.8 billion addition to the insurance fund, but this amount proved inadequate as losses in the industry mounted.

In August 1989, the *Financial Institution Reform Recovery and Enforcement Act (FIRREA)* was signed into law. This act shifted the regulatory role to a bureau of the U.S. Treasury, the Office of Thrift Supervision. It also shifted supervisory responsibilities of the FSLIC to the FDIC. The FDIC then became the sole administrator of federal deposit insurance programs. The FDIC created two separate deposit insurance funds. The Bank Insurance Fund (BIF) applies to deposits at commercial banks. The Savings Association Insurance Fund (SAIF) covers deposits at S&Ls. In addition, the Resolution Trust Corporation was formed to manage insolvent S&Ls and to sell more than $300 billion in real estate owned by failed institutions.

BANKING TRENDS IN THE UNITED STATES

American financial institutions are caught up in a rapidly changing business environment. These changes are due to the globalization of competition, rapid developments in information technology, and lessons learned in the 1970s and 1980s. Two of the most important developments are the emergence of electronic funds transfers and megabanks.

ELECTRONIC FUNDS TRANSFERS (EFTS)

Electronic funds transfer (EFT)
A computerized system for performing many financial transactions such as making purchases, depositing paychecks, and paying bills.

By 1992, about three-fourths of all U.S. households had access to some form of **electronic funds transfer (EFT)**, a computerized system for performing many financial transactions such as making purchases, depositing paychecks, and paying bills. Automated teller machines (ATMs) are the most widely used EFT service; more than half of all American households have ATM access cards. The monthly number of ATM transactions was over 605 million by 1993.[24] In fact, ATMs are now emerging as global networks. Already tourists from Chicago can walk up to an ATM in Tokyo and withdraw cash, in yen, from their home banks. In about 10 seconds, they can transfer funds between their savings and checking accounts or make deposits.

Direct deposit, in which employees have their paychecks deposited directly into their accounts, is another widely used EFT service.

Point-of-sale (POS) system An electronic machine located in a store that immediately transfers funds from the buyer's checking account to the retailer's when a debit card is used.

The newest innovation in the EFT field is **point-of-sale (POS) systems**, electronic machines located in stores that immediately transfer funds from a customer's checking account to the retailer's account when a debit card is used. With such a system, a retailer can put your debit card into a slot in its cash register. When the amount of the sale is calculated, an electronic signal is sent to your bank, immediately transferring funds from your account to the retailer's.

Finally, many consumers are using their home computers and modems to pay bills and perform other financial transactions over interactive computer networks like Prodigy.[25] There seems to be no end in sight for creative ways to use technology to speed up financial transactions.

MEGABANKS

One consequence of the banking crisis of the 1980s and of increasing competition among giant international banks has been the consolidation of the U.S. banking structure. Furthermore, competition with other providers of financial services such as brokers, pension funds, and investment banks has forced strong responses from banks. Mergers of large banks have resulted in megabanks called superregional or supercommunity banks, depending on their size and business strategy. A *superregional bank* typically has assets totaling more than $20 billion and operates in several states. A *supercommunity bank* usually has assets of around $5 billion and has a strong community service orientation.

Mergers have swept across state lines. President Clinton recently approved a banking policy that permits nationwide branching, which will encourage even more growth.[26] Just how large banks should be to achieve efficiency in operations yet remain sensitive to customer needs is debatable. For example, KeyCorp, a supercommunity bank with assets of $32 billion, has grown 10 times in size since 1982. This bank's strategy has been to move into smaller communities and emphasize good service rather than low prices. KeyCorp earned $245.6 million with this strategy in 1992.[27] In contrast, NationsBank, the largest superregional, had assets of $125 billion and net income of $900 million in 1992.[28]

Megabanks are pushing beyond traditional lines of banking business as they struggle to maintain profitability. Traditional services, such as credit cards and loans, have met competition from nondepository institutions. In an effort to become more competitive, these large banks are pushing stock, mutual funds, financial planning, real estate, and other products and services.[29] Mergers of large banks and expansion of services into nontraditional areas will likely continue into the future.

FOCUS ON COLLABORATORS

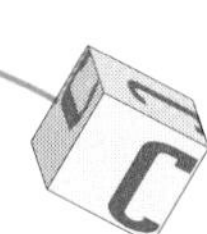

Founders National Bank

Many of the nation's smallest banks are minority owned. Carlton Jenkins is managing director of one of these banks, Founders National Bank. Founders serves African-American communities in and around South Central Los Angeles. With assets of $72 million, Founders seeks several million dollars in equity from major banks and corporations to increase its ability to make loans to local minority-owned small businesses. BankAmerica Corporation is one large bank that has shown a willingness to help. The motivation is simple: a mix of social consciousness and self-interest. It's good public relations, and many of the small banks are very sound investment risks.

Exhibit 19.7 **THE 10 LARGEST BANKS IN THE WORLD**

Bank	Assets (Billions of Dollars)
1. Dai-Ichi Kangyo Bank (Japan)	480
2. Sakura Bank (Japan)	458
3. Sumitomo Bank (Japan)	458
4. Sanwa Bank (Japan)	452
5. Fuji Bank (Japan)	448
6. Mitsubishi Bank (Japan)	428
7. Industrial Bank of Japan (Japan)	325
8. Credit Agricole (France)	307
9. Credit Lyonnais (France)	306
10. Deutsche Bank (Germany)	295

INTERNATIONAL BANKING AND FINANCIAL TRANSACTIONS

In 1960, only eight U.S. banks had operations outside the United States. Today over 100 U.S. banks have branches in other nations, with total assets of more than $500 billion. In addition, Japanese banks now have over 20 percent of the U.S. banking market. The United States is no longer number one in banking. In the early 1980s, Citicorp and BankAmerica were the two largest banks in the world in terms of asset size. By 1992, 7 of the 10 largest banks in the world were Japanese owned (see Exhibit 19.7). Citicorp, the largest U.S. bank, was listed only 26th.

In the United Kingdom and Canada, five or fewer banks dominate the banking industry. In Japan, only about 150 commercial banks exist. In contrast, approximately 12,000 commercial banks operate in the United States. U.S. commercial banks not only are more numerous but also tend to be smaller than those in other countries. The contrast could become even sharper as the economic integration of Europe progresses. Since January 1, 1993, any bank licensed by the European Union (formerly the European Community) has been able to provide banking services in any European Union country. This is leading to a Europe-wide banking system.

Perhaps one of the most interesting developments in international banking at the present time is the struggle in Russia for control over its central bank. As Russia attempts to shed 74 years of centralized, communist rule, reform of the central bank is proving difficult. Russian bankers complain they don't have checks or a clearing house and that they have no interest rate policies. The struggle for capitalistic freedom may depend on how quickly the central bank is able to develop the trappings of an effective banking system.[30]

EURODOLLARS AND INTERNATIONAL CURRENCIES

Eurodollar
Funds created when deposits in accounts in the United States are transferred to a European bank but kept in the form of dollars.

The Eurodollar market is an important source of growth for international banking. **Eurodollars** are created when deposits in accounts in the United States are transferred to a European bank but kept in the form of dollars. Thus, when a business sells goods in the United States for dollars and then deposits the dollars in its European bank, Eurodollars are created. The total amount of Eurodollars outstanding exceeds $2 trillion, making the Eurodollar market an important international source of funds.

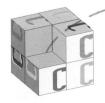

FOCUS ON COMPETITORS

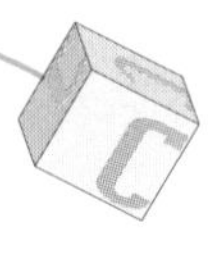

Capitalism, Communism, and Dollars

During the height of the Cold War in the early 1950s, the Soviet Union had accumulated substantial dollar balances held by banks in the United States. Fearing that the United States might freeze those assets in this country, the Soviets moved the deposits to Europe, where they would be free from expropriation. However, they also wanted to keep the deposits in the form of dollars, since the dollar was the strongest currency in the world. By moving the dollars to European banks under the condition that they be kept in the form of dollars, the Soviets actually created the Eurodollar market.

It is important to understand that the value of *all* international currencies, in addition to Eurodollars, varies from day to day. For example, the exchange rate for dollars and yens (Japanese currency) may be 100 yen for 1 dollar today but only 95 yen for 1 dollar tomorrow. This makes the acquisition of goods and services in a foreign country a far riskier venture than when a company buys them in its own country. Successful financial managers closely follow the fluctuations of currencies and time their purchases to enhance their companies' financial position.

The internationalization of banking has made financial markets around the world more integrated. This trend may lead to internationalization of bank regulation and stabilization of international politics.

SUMMARY

1. ***Define* money *and list five criteria for effective money.***
   Money is anything that is generally accepted in a society as a means of payment or exchange. Early societies used such items as beads, shells, and tobacco. But not all items are equally effective as money. Money is effective when it meets five criteria: (1) Its value is easy to assess, (2) it is widely accepted by the society (or societies) that uses it, (3) its units are divisible, (4) it is easily transported, and (5) it does not deteriorate quickly, either in value or physically.

2. ***Identify the components of the money supply.***
   The most basic definition of the money supply is called M1. M1 includes currency, coins, traveler's checks, and demand deposits (amounts deposited in checking accounts). Other measures of the money supply, called M2 and M3, include savings deposits and money market accounts.

3. ***Describe the structure of the Federal Reserve System.***
   The Federal Reserve System consists of 12 regional districts, each with a Federal Reserve bank; a board of governors; and approximately 5,000 member commercial banks. In addition, several councils advise the board on banking, consumer, and economic matters. Congress established the Federal Reserve banks as the operating arm of the Federal Reserve System. The Board of Governors consists of seven members appointed by the president of the United States. The board's many and varied tasks all relate to monetary policy. The Federal Open Market Committee (FOMC) is the most important monetary policymaking body of the Federal Reserve System.

4. ***Explain the most important tools the Federal Reserve System uses to control the supply of money.***
   The primary tools of monetary policy are the reserve requirement, the discount rate, and open market operations. The reserve requirement is the percentage of a bank's total deposits that must be held in reserve at the Federal Reserve Bank. By varying the reserve requirement, the Federal Reserve controls the ability of depository institutions to loan funds. The discount rate is the rate of interest the Federal Reserve charges to banks that borrow to meet their reserve requirements. Any change in the cost of borrowing from the Federal Reserve will affect a bank's willingness to borrow from the Federal Reserve. Open market operations—the buying and selling of U.S. Treasury securities by the Federal Reserve—are the major tool used to influence the total amount of money and credit available in the economy. By purchasing and selling government securities, the Federal Reserve attempts to encourage expansion of money and credit while achieving price stability and growth in economic activity.

5. ***Discuss the major functions of the Federal Reserve System.***
The Federal Reserve System performs several functions, including selling gold or gold certificates, buying and selling U.S. government securities, making loans to member banks, clearing checks written by depositors of member banks, issuing paper currency (Federal Reserve notes), and maintaining deposits to the Federal Reserve Bank. Although the U.S. Treasury is no longer required to hold gold, it can own or sell gold to the general public or sell gold certificates to the Federal Reserve to raise money. Transactions in U.S. government securities alter the money supply and the ability of banks to create credit. By making loans to member banks—sometimes referred to as federal funds—the Federal Reserve may earn additional interest. These activities all represent assets on the Federal Reserve's balance sheet. However, Federal Reserve notes and deposits are liabilities, since they are obligations of the Federal Reserve to other parties.

6. ***Explain the differences between depository and nondepository institutions.***
The primary difference between depository and nondepository institutions concerns whether they can offer federally insured checking and savings accounts. Depository institutions—commercial banks, mutual savings banks, savings and loan associations, and credit unions—may offer these accounts. Nondepository institutions such as insurance companies, pension funds, and finance companies deal in other types of financial services that affect the money supply but cannot offer federally insured checking and savings accounts.

7. ***Discuss the regulation of financial institutions.***
Depository institutions are subject to multiple regulatory agencies. The Comptroller of the Currency has supervisory authority over federally chartered banks. The Federal Reserve System and the states have joint authority over commercial banks that are both state chartered and members of the Federal Reserve. The Federal Reserve has sole regulatory authority over bank holding companies and secondary authority over the national banks. The FDIC and state banking authorities jointly supervise banks that are state chartered and have FDIC insurance but are not members of the Federal Reserve System. State banking authorities regulate those state banks that do not have FDIC insurance. Regulation begins when a bank is chartered. Once chartered, the bank is required to submit periodic financial statements. In addition, bank records are examined regularly to assess the bank's financial condition and to ensure that the bank is complying with banking rules and regulations. The FDIC examines banks at least every 36 months. The Federal Reserve audits bank records every 18 months.

8. ***Discuss federal deposit insurance programs in use today.***
The Federal Deposit Insurance Corporation (FDIC) supervises commercial banks and insures depositors' accounts in amounts up to $100,000. Prior to 1989 the Federal Savings and Loan Insurance Corporation (FSLIC) supervised S&Ls and insured the accounts of S&L depositors. With the passage of the Financial Institution Reform Recovery and Enforcement Act (FIRREA), the FDIC assumed the supervisory responsibilities of the FSLIC and became the sole administrator of federal deposit insurance programs. The FDIC created two separate deposit insurance funds. The Bank Insurance Fund (BIF) applies to deposits at commercial banks. The Savings Association Insurance Fund (SAIF) covers deposits at S&Ls.

9. ***Describe trends that are changing banking in the United States and throughout the world.***
American financial institutions are caught up in a rapidly changing business environment. Two of the most important developments in U.S. banking are the emergence of electronic funds transfers and megabanks. Automated teller machines (ATMs) are the most widely used EFT service. The newest innovation in the EFT field is point-of-sale (POS) systems. In addition, many consumers are using their home computers and modems to perform various financial transactions over interactive computer networks. Competition with other providers of financial services has resulted in mergers among large banks. These mergers have created megabanks, which include superregional and supercommunity banks. To maintain their profitability, megabanks are expanding their services into nontraditional banking areas.

   Today over 100 U.S. banks have branches in other nations, but 7 of the 10 largest banks in the world are Japanese owned. As the economic integration of Europe progresses and formerly communist nations centralize their banking structures, many new developments in international banking are likely to emerge. The integration of financial markets around the world may lead to internationalization of bank regulation.

KEY TERMS AND CONCEPTS

Money (p. 452)
Currency (p. 452)
Unit of account (p. 453)
Medium of exchange (p. 453)
Store of value (p. 453)
Liquidity (p. 453)
M1 (p. 454)
Demand deposit (p. 454)
Federal Reserve System (p. 454)
Federal Open Market Committee (FOMC) (p. 455)
Reserve requirement (p. 457)
Discount rate (p. 457)
Open market operations (p. 457)
Federal funds (p. 458)
Float (p. 458)
Federal Reserve notes (p. 459)
Depository institution (p. 459)
Commercial bank (p. 459)
Negotiable order of withdrawal (NOW) account (p. 460)
Super NOW account (p. 460)
Certificate of deposit (CD) (p. 460)
Automated teller machine (ATM) (p. 462)
Savings and loan association (S&L), or thrift (p. 463)
Mutual savings bank (p. 464)
Credit union (p. 464)
Nondepository institution (p. 465)
Pension fund (p. 465)
Electronic funds transfer (EFT) (p. 468)
Point-of-sale (POS) system (p. 469)
Eurodollar (p. 470)

DISCUSSION QUESTIONS

Company

1. How does the reserve requirement of the Federal Reserve System affect companies?
2. How can a company speed up the collection of money from noncash sales?
3. How does the use of money promote efficiency in a company's business transactions?

Customers

4. How do monetary policies of the Federal Reserve System affect a company's customers?
5. How are bank credit cards important to customers?

Competitors

6. What impact did the passage of the Depository Institution Deregulation and Monetary Control Act of 1980 have on competition within the banking industry?
7. What services have banks implemented to increase their competitive advantage?
8. What effects might branch banking have on commercial banking competition?

Collaborators

9. What functions does the Federal Reserve perform that relate to its role as a collaborator of American business?
10. How do banks function as collaborators?
11. What collaborative role do regulatory agencies play in the banking industry?

In Question: Take a Stand

You make a mistake in your checkbook, writing a check for $30 to your supermarket without having adequate funds in your account. Your bank *returns the check to the supermarket, indicating there are insufficient funds. The bank charges you $10 for your mistake, and the supermarket charges you $15. The following month, you are balancing your checkbook and notice that the bank recorded a $100 deposit as $10. You go to your bank. The bank identifies its error and puts the extra $90 back into your account. You tell the teller you want an extra $25 from the bank because its mistake cost you time and effort as well as $15 charged by the supermarket. The teller says it is not the bank's policy to pay for its mistakes although it will refund the $10 it charged to your account. Yet the bank made you pay for your mistake. Is the bank's policy fair?*

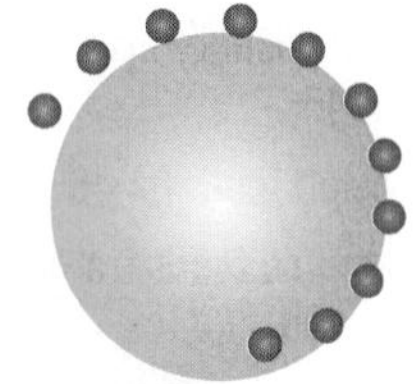

CASE 19.1
THE FOOTHILL GROUP[31]

The Foothill Group is a fast-growing specialty finance company headquartered in Los Angeles. It lends to midsize companies that can't get unsecured commercial bank credit and it buys distressed loans from banks at a deep discount. Foothill earns good money for these services—over $15 million in the first 9 months of 1993—and a stock price that nearly doubled in 12 months during that year.

Foothill's secret to success: dig deeper, know more than your competitors. Commercial banks usually lend against a company's cash flow projections which may not always be accurate. But Foothill lends on accounts receivable, inventory, and other hard assets. The company's strength lies in its ability to appraise these assets. This is a costly, labor-intensive process that requires expertise in sizing up a collateral base that changes daily. Foothill knows how to evaluate troubled companies.

Allnet Communications Services near Detroit could not borrow from commercial banks or raise equity because it was losing $20 million a year and had a negative net worth of $102 million. But Foothill was impressed by Allnet's 300,000 commercial customers who were producing a steady stream of accounts receivable. It gave Allnet a $30 million line of credit, and closely monitored its cash receipts. Allnet earned $40 million 1993 and was able to replace Foothill's costly loan with regular bank credit.

Questions

1. *How is The Foothill Group able to compete with commercial banks?*
2. *What lesson is to be learned from The Foothill Group's success?*
3. *Under what circumstances might a customer require the services of The Foothill Group?*

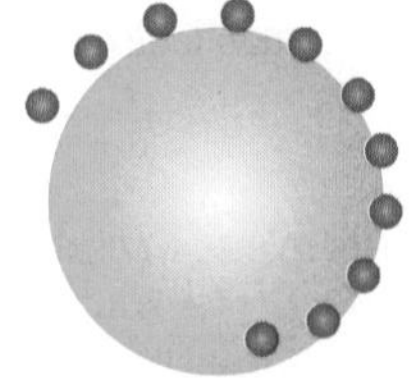

CASE 19.2
SUPERMARKET BANKS[32]

Cruising the aisles of a Kroger supermarket in Memphis, Tennessee, Maria Kittrell is shopping for customers. But instead of offering salami samples, she's selling certificates of deposit.

Ms. Kittrell is an employee of National Commerce Bank, which has a branch in the Kroger store. Passing through the frozen-food section without a pause, she explains that it's tough to sell CDs where it's cold. But somewhere between the cookies and the crackers she spots a prospective customer and launches into a rapid-fire sales pitch, detailing everything from interest rates for credit cards to the tax advantages of home-equity loans.

Michelle Gwin, a government tax examiner, is impressed by the credit card's 7.9% rate of interest. "I'm going to fill out an application right now," she says.

There are currently about 2,100 supermarket bank branches in the United States, up from about 900 in 1990, and their number is growing fast. The reason: As banks are confronted by intensifying competition from mutual funds and other nonbank suppliers of financial services, bankers are concluding that free-standing branches are too expensive to build and operate. Worse still, many of the most desirable customers don't even use branches; they prefer automatic-teller machines.

Today's most successful supermarket bankers are aggressively marketing their profitable products. In addition to sending employees into the aisles, National Commerce plants ads throughout stores. In the produce section, so-called talking signs show vegetables juxtaposed with images of financial products. One depicts a head of lettuce and a credit card under the headline "No Fat, No Fee."

The signs work. Ava Petreman bought a $25,000 certificate of deposit after she noticed a sign offering six-month CDs with a 4.5% interest rate, higher than she had seen elsewhere.

John Presley, an executive of National Commerce Bank says 400-square-foot supermarket branches, which cost less than $200,000 to build, break even with just $4 million in deposits. Free-standing branches, which generally have 4,000 square feet and cost at least $800,000 to build, need at least $15 million in deposits to cover costs.

Supermarket officials also seem pleased with their resident bankers. Store managers say the bankers are so integrated into stores that customers routinely ask tellers to help them find everything from chicken breasts to dog food. One shopper plopped a large ham on the bank counter and asked a branch manager if she could carve it into thin slices.

Not only does the bank pay rent for its space, but supermarket store officials believe that bank branches enhance the loyalty of their customers and give them another reason to visit the store.

Questions

1. *What regulatory changes have led to the creation of supermarket bank branches?*
2. *How has competition with other financial institutions contributed to this development?*
3. *Describe the collaborative relationship between supermarket banks and the supermarkets where they are located.*

CHAPTER 20

THE SECURITIES MARKETS

When you have studied this chapter, you will be able to:

1. Define *investing* and explain the importance of financial markets in the investing process.
2. Describe the types of equity securities.
3. Discuss the types of debt securities.
4. Explain the nature and types of mutual funds.
5. Describe the various organized securities exchanges.
6. Discuss the process of purchasing and selling securities.
7. Explain the difference between a bull market and a bear market.
8. Describe legislation passed to regulate securities trading.
9. Explain how information published in the financial press can help investors.

After 10 years of investing in safer, more predictable bank and money market accounts, investors are once again switching to stocks and bonds to obtain higher rates of return. Many now do business with Charles Schwab & Company, the largest discount brokerage firm in the United States. Schwab has 163 offices in 41 states and serves nearly 2 million clients.

Charles Schwab has been capitalizing on opportunities since he was a boy. After years of struggling with dyslexia, an impairment that makes it difficult to process information, he founded a company that does exactly that—process information. Schwab is proud of his ability to "empower" his customers with information from many sources so that they can make informed investment decisions. In 1979, he purchased state-of-the-art computer equipment for $2 million. By 1982, his technology was well ahead of that of most Wall Street firms.

TeleBroker, one of Schwab's newer innovations, enables customers to buy and sell securities, get quotes, and check their account balances via any Touch-Tone phone 24 hours a day. Directed by a computer, callers never speak to a human being. Schwab shaves off 10 percent of its commissions if customers use this procedure, which greatly cuts costs for the company. In 1991, its first year of nationwide operations, TeleBroker answered more than 14 million calls as investors let their fingers do the walking through 600,000 of the 4.6 million transactions the company completed that year.

Another innovative move is the establishment of multilingual centers to handle inquiries from various non-English-speaking groups. Schwab's Asia Pacific service center is staffed with representatives that speak Mandarin, Cantonese, Japanese, and Vietnamese. A center for Spanish-speaking clients recently opened in Miami.

Many people entering their high saving and investing years (ages 45 to 64) are investing in mutual funds. At the beginning of 1994, Schwab had sold $23.7 billion of mutual funds. Schwab's total mutual fund assets of $90 billion still pale beside large mutual funds like Fidelity Investments. But Schwab is growing rapidly, and Charles Schwab himself is still driven by the need to succeed.[1]

Exhibit 20.1 **THE PROCESS OF INVESTING**

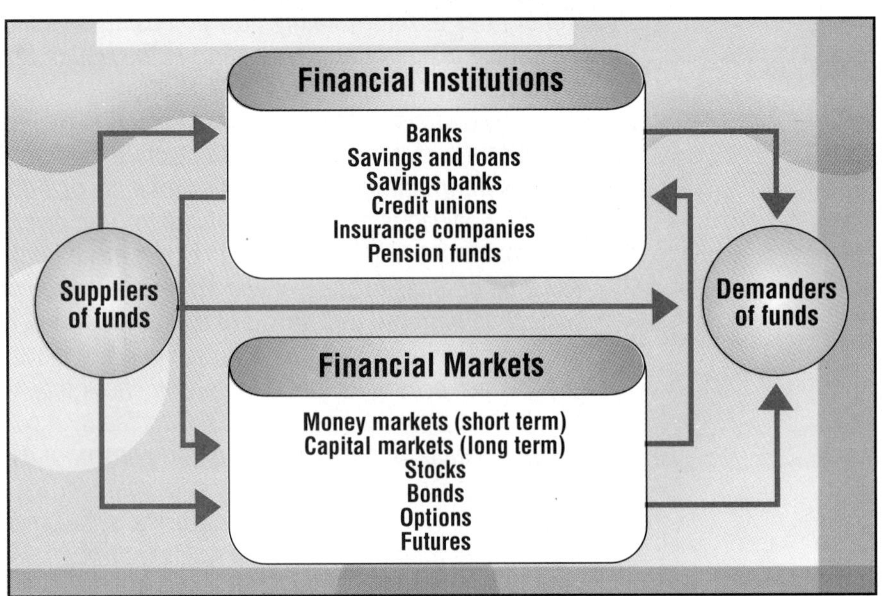

Each year, millions of Americans become collaborators of U.S. companies as they invest their savings in corporate stocks and bonds. Those companies use the investments to improve their operations, finance growth, build new plants, and develop new products and services. Brokerage firms like Charles Schwab thus perform a valuable service as they match individual investors with companies that need capital. This chapter looks at how such companies use the securities market to finance their growth.

INVESTING AND THE SECURITIES MARKETS

Investing
The process by which suppliers of funds (those with surplus money) are brought together with demanders of funds (those needing money).

Investing is the process by which suppliers of funds (those with surplus money) are brought together with demanders of funds (those needing money). Financial institutions (discussed in Chapter 19) and financial markets bring suppliers and demanders together. Financial markets include capital markets such as stock, bond, and option markets, as well as money markets. Exhibit 20.1 illustrates the investing process.

Money markets permit short-term transactions, usually in amounts of $100,000 or more. The transactions conducted in capital markets tend to be long term. Capital markets consist of various kinds of securities exchanges through which investors can purchase stocks, bonds, options, and futures. Capital markets are classified as primary markets or secondary markets.

PRIMARY MARKETS

Primary markets
Capital markets that sell new securities to the public.

Primary markets sell new securities to the public. *Securities* are investments that relate to debt, ownership of a business, or the legal right to acquire or sell an ownership interest in the business. The need to issue new securities might arise when the company's resources are inadequate to finance the company's efforts at growth and borrowing money from a financial institution is not desirable. In this instance, the company may issue securities to the general public.

On November 9, 1993, investors rushed to buy stock of Boston Chicken, Inc. By the following day, the price had jumped from $20 to $48.60 a share, a net gain of 143 percent in one day. When Franchisee Marion Lewis opened the doors to his Atlanta restaurant, customers immediately started asking about the stock. By mid-December, the price had fallen to $37 a share. Gambling on IPOs can indeed be risky.[2]

The company seeking potential investors can sell securities itself by advertising or selling the securities door to door. Both of these methods, however, would be very time consuming and divert the company's managers from day-to-day operations. To avoid problems associated with selling their own securities, companies engage investment bankers that underwrite (sell) the newly issued securities.

Initial public offerings (IPOs)
A special category of common stock issued by new firms going public for the first time.

Initial public offerings (IPOs) are a special category of common stock issued by new firms going public for the first time. A record 859 IPOs came to market during 1993. Not all of them succeeded. Wilt Chamberlain's Restaurants Inc., for example, collapsed in two days. Many IPOs, however, are issued by established companies that simply need to obtain funds for capital projects and growth.[3] For instance, Northwest Airlines, Inc., offered 20 million shares at $13 to $14 per share to reduce its sizable debt load.[4]

UNDERWRITING

Underwriting
A process whereby an investment banker purchases new issues of securities from the issuing company and then sells them to the investing public.

Underwriting is a process whereby an investment banker purchases new issues of securities from the issuing company and then sells them to the investing public. Once the company and the underwriter have reached an agreement, the company receives a specified amount of money and the underwriter assumes the risk of sale.

The underwriter and the issuing company prepare a preliminary *prospectus* that provides information about the company's financial condition and other details about the company. When the securities are approved for issuance, a final prospectus is prepared and distributed. The information it contains is similar to that in the preliminary prospectus, but also includes the security price, the underwriting fees, and the amount to be received by the issuing company. To spread the risk involved in selling the securities, the underwriter brings in other investment bankers as partners to form a syndicate. Then the syndicate assembles a large number of brokerage firms, called a *selling group*. Each brokerage firm is responsible for selling a certain portion of the securities issue. Then the selling group contacts individual investors and sells the securities to them. Exhibit 20.2 illustrates this process.

Exhibit 20.2 **THE PROCESS OF SELLING SECURITIES**

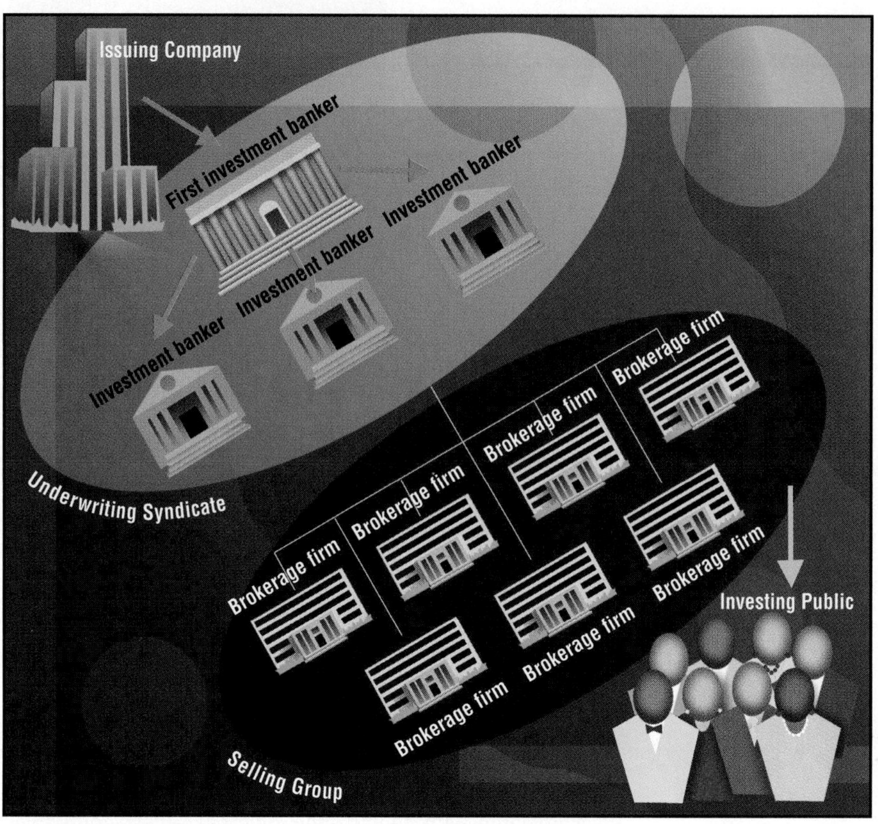

Investment bankers are kept busy, as the profits they earn show. Goldman, Sachs & Company's 1993 pretax profit was $2.7 billion, Merrill Lynch & Company earned $2.42 billion, and Salomon Brothers Inc. earned $1.46 billion.[5]

SALE OF SECURITIES

Eventually the securities are sold, and the purchaser may opt to leave them with the brokerage firm. This frees the purchaser from worries about the securities' safety and makes it easier to resell them. However, since the securities held by the brokerage firm are registered in the firm's name rather than in the purchaser's, the company that issued the securities will send its annual reports and other announcements to the brokerage firm. Therefore, the purchaser may prefer to take receipt of the securities.

The purchaser can pay for the securities in part or in full. If only partial payment is made, the securities are acquired on margin. *On margin* refers to the purchase of securities on credit provided by the broker. The **margin** is the portion of the selling price that must be paid with the purchaser's own funds. The arrangement itself is called *margin trading.*

Margin
The portion of the selling price for an issue of securities that must be paid with the purchaser's own funds.

Margin requirements are set by the Federal Reserve System. By raising or lowering margin requirements, the Federal Reserve can stimulate or depress activity in the securities markets and, consequently, in the economy. After nearly disappearing in the early 1990s, the practice of buying stock on margin is regaining popularity. The New York Stock Exchange reported a record $60.3 billion in margin loans in December 1993.[6]

Resales of securities from the initial purchaser to another investor occur in one of the secondary markets.

STREET SMART

Stock Certificates Get a Makeover

Companies have always used their stock certificates to project their images and goals. Now certificates are changing because companies want a more modern image. Reliance Electric Company's original certificate, designed in the 1950s, depicted an industrial landscape with smoking factories. To show the company's environmental awareness, the new certificates have eliminated the smokestacks. Kmart Corporation replaced the mother and daughter in its old certificates with male and female executives standing in front of Kmart's corporate headquarters. James M. Herron, senior vice president and general counsel for Ryder System, Inc., expressed the attitude of many corporate leaders: "We felt we wanted to project a more up-to-date image. People in the business of image-making tell you this is important."

SECONDARY MARKETS

Secondary markets
Capital markets in which previously issued securities are bought and sold.

Capital markets in which previously issued securities are bought and sold are called **secondary markets**. Thus, transactions in the secondary markets simply involve transfers of securities from one investor to another. The prices quoted in the financial press relate to buyers and sellers who are coming together to conduct exchanges in the secondary markets. Financial instruments traded in secondary markets include equity and debt securities. Equity securities include common and preferred stock, while debt securities consist primarily of bonds.

EQUITY SECURITIES

Equity securities
Securities that represent ownership interest.

Equity securities represent ownership interest. The ownership interest is a function of the number of shares obtained by the purchaser in relation to the total shares issued by the company. By selling ownership interest in the form of stock, companies can obtain large amounts of capital. Chrysler Corporation raised slightly more than $2 billion when it sold an additional 52 million shares of common stock at $38.75 per share. Chrysler plans to use at least half of the new capital to reduce its $3.9 billion unfunded pension liability.[7]

A group of shares of similar stocks is called a *class of stock.* All the shares within the class have the same rights and restrictions. The class of stock that controls the board of directors, shares in the success of the company, and bears the risk of failure is called **common stock**.

Common stock
The class of stock that controls the board of directors, shares in the success of the company, and bears the risk of failure.

Common Stock. Common stock carries certain rights that are outlined in the stock contract associated with it. Normally there are four rights. First, and probably most important, is the right of stockholders to share in company profits in the form of dividends. Second, the right to vote allows stockholders to participate in the election of the board of directors. Third, the right to share in the company's assets if the company is liquidated ensures that stockholders will receive a proportionate distribution of assets once all other claims are settled. Fourth, if new issues of the stock are sold, stockholders have the right to purchase enough shares to maintain their ownership interest. This right is referred to as the *preemptive right.*

The stock certificate provides evidence of corporate ownership. The face of the certificate gives the name of the owner, the issuing company, and the number of shares. In some states, a par value will be stated for certain stock. The par value, or face value, differs from the amount for which the stock could be sold in the secondary market. That amount is referred to as the stock's *market value.*

Common stocks appeal to investors because most stocks pay dividends regularly and therefore provide a steady source of income. In addition, a wide range of common stocks are available, from relatively stable stocks to stocks that promise attractive capital gains. These factors are reflected in the market's classification of stock as blue-chip, income, growth, or speculative.

Blue-chip stocks
Stocks of companies that have long been recognized as leaders in their industries.

Blue-Chip Stocks. **Blue-chip stocks** are stocks of companies that have long been recognized as leaders in their industries. The name probably stems from the blue chips used in poker that have the highest value. These companies are known for their long record of stable earnings and dividends. For this reason blue-chip stocks, such as H. J. Heinz and AT&T, are particularly attractive to investors seeking quality investments that offer respectable dividends.

Income stocks
Stocks whose attractiveness stems solely from their dividend yields.

Income Stocks. The attractiveness of **income stocks** stems solely from their dividend yields. These stocks have a long history of paying larger than average dividends. Income stocks are suitable for individuals seeking relatively predictable and high levels of income from their investments. Since earnings that are not retained for growth and expansion are usually distributed to stockholders, companies with higher payouts may lack growth potential. In fact, many income stocks have moderate or even low earnings growth rates. This doesn't mean that companies associated with income stocks are unprofitable. On the contrary, most are quite profitable and have good prospects for the future. Income stock companies include General Motors, Bank of New York, and most public utilities.

Growth stocks
Stocks of companies that are experiencing growth in both operations and earnings.

Growth Stocks. Stocks of companies that are experiencing growth in both operations and earnings are called **growth stocks**. Solid growth stocks can have an increase in earnings of 15 to 18 percent, while the average earnings increase of common stocks in general may be 5 or 6 percent. Whereas the growth of income stock companies levels out, that for growth stocks does not. Rubbermaid Incorporated, Marriott Corporation, and Shaw Industries are examples of growth stocks. Shaw Industries, a carpet manufacturer, recently improved earnings by expanding overseas.[8]

Normally growth stocks pay little or no dividends, since most of the earnings are reinvested in the company. For these stocks, the major source of return to the stockholder is from a continual increase in the price of the stock. Thus, growth stocks appeal to investors looking for capital gains rather than dividends and to those who are willing to accept greater risk.

Speculative stocks
Stocks of companies whose earnings are unstable and uncertain.

Speculative Stocks. Generally, **speculative stocks** are stocks of companies whose earnings are unstable and uncertain. Speculative stocks are subject to tremendous price fluctuations. In addition, they pay few or no dividends. The stock of many high-tech and biotech companies can be classified as speculative because they are just starting up or are on the verge of innovative discoveries, and are therefore unproven. Speculative stocks are very risky. When John Scully, former CEO of Apple Computer, moved to Spectrum Information Technologies, Inc., Spectrum's credibility and stock price both rose. But when he resigned because he discovered improper accounting practices and that the Securities and Exchange Commission was investigating Spectrum, the company's stock fell 60 percent.[9]

Dividends. In choosing among several investment possibilities, such as General Electric, Westinghouse, and Teledyne, an investor might compare the dividend yields of their common stocks. A common method of determining the dividend yield of a common stock is to calculate it on a percentage basis relative to the stock's price. The formula for the calculation of dividend yield is

$$\textit{Dividend Yield} = \frac{\textit{Dividends Received per Share Annually}}{\textit{Current Market Price per Share}}.$$

Instead of distributing cash dividends, an increasing number of companies automatically reinvest the dividends in additional shares of their common stock. Approximately 1,000 companies including IBM, Homestake Mining, and Sears, Roebuck and Company offer dividend reinvestment plans. These plans are attractive because they provide the stockholder with a convenient and inexpensive way to accumulate capital. A stockholder can join the plan by contacting the company. Once enrolled, the stockholder receives an increasing number of shares at each dividend payment date. Note, however, that even though the dividends are not actually received, they are taxable as though they were.

Preferred stock
Stock whose holders have a prior claim over common stockholders on the company's earnings and assets.

Preferred Stock. The primary feature of **preferred stock** is that its owners have a prior claim over common stockholders on the company's earnings and assets. They have preference with respect to dividends. That is, once dividends have been declared, the preferred stockholders receive their share before the common stockholders do.

Typically, preferred stock is issued with a par value, and the dividends paid are expressed as a percentage of the par value. Thus, a holder of 10 percent preferred stock with a $100 par value would receive annual dividends of $10 per share. Although preferred stock tends to be nonvoting, preferred stockholders have preference over common stockholders in the distribution of company assets at liquidation.

To make the preferred stock more marketable, the issuing company may offer various features. Currently most preferred stock (approximately 90 percent) is issued with a *cumulative* feature. This feature assures preferred stockholders that undeclared dividends in any given year will be paid in any following year in which dividends are declared.

Preferred stock may also have the privilege of *convertibility*. In this case, stockholders have the option to exchange their preferred stock for shares of common stock at some specified ratio. Preferred stockholders might wish to do this when the price of the company's common stock is growing in the secondary market. The convertibility feature makes preferred stock particularly attractive to some investors.

DEBT SECURITIES

Debt securities
Securities that represent IOUs; investors who purchase these securities are creditors.

Bond
A long-term debt instrument having a specified rate of interest and a specified maturity date.

The second way a company obtains funding in the secondary markets is by issuing securities. **Debt securities** represent IOUs; investors who purchase these securities are creditors.

Debt securities consist primarily of bonds. A **bond** is a long-term debt instrument having a specified rate of interest and maturity date. The company pays interest over a specified period, at the end of which (the maturity date) it repays the principal. Whereas stockholders are owners of the corporation and hold securities that have unlimited lives, bondholders hold debt that eventually matures and are therefore creditors of the company.

The bond market is huge. At the end of 1990, the value of debt was $11.1 trillion. In contrast, the value of equities was $4.2 trillion. Like stocks, bonds are initially sold in the primary market and then traded in the secondary market.

Government Bonds. The U.S. government is the largest issuer of bonds. The U.S. Treasury issues bonds to finance the federal government deficit. Various agencies of the federal government issue bonds as well. These securities vary in denomination and maturity date. They are purchased by the Federal Reserve, banking institutions, households, and other investors. You can buy Treasury notes or bonds directly from Uncle Sam by calling your nearest Federal Reserve bank or branch. Savings bonds are available with no fee through most banks and financial institutions.

Revenue bond
A bond paid from revenues associated with a specific income-generating project.

Like the federal government, state and local governments issue a variety of bonds. These bonds are usually sold as general obligation bonds, meaning they are backed by the full faith, credit, and general taxing authority of the issuer. State and local governments also issue revenue bonds. **Revenue bonds** are paid from revenues associated with specific income-

The city and county of Denver issued $100 million in municipal bonds to help finance construction of the new Denver International Airport. These bonds paid between 5.00 and 6.35 percent interest.

generating projects. The money raised from the sale of either type of bond is used to fund capital projects such as the construction of airports, sports stadiums, and bridges.

A unique feature of municipal bonds is that the interest they pay is tax exempt. This advantage permits state and local governments to issue bonds at a lower interest rate. Despite the lower rate of interest, municipal bondholders benefit because the after-tax return is competitive with those of corporate bonds. Still, municipal bonds are not a favorite investment for investors who should benefit the most: those in the 36 and 39.6 percent federal tax brackets. Fully three-quarters of those investors keep all of their cash in taxable bank accounts, money market funds, or taxable bonds.[10]

Corporate Bonds. Corporations are the major issuer of nongovernment bonds. Many types of corporate bonds exist, each with distinct characteristics.

Some corporate bonds are secured. These include mortgage bonds and equipment trust certificates. **Mortgage bonds** are secured by claims on real property, such as a warehouse or a manufacturing facility. These fixed assets secure the debt. If the issuer defaults, the bondholders obtain title to the assets. **Equipment trust certificates** are issued primarily by railroads and airlines. The proceeds from the sale of the certificates are used to purchase freight cars, engines, and airplanes. These assets then become collateral that can be easily sold to other railroads or airlines if the issuer defaults.

Mortgage bond
A bond secured by a claim on real property.

Equipment trust certificate
A bond that is secured by the equipment purchased with the money raised from the bond issue.

In contrast to these secured bonds are unsecured bonds known as *debentures.* **Debentures** are promissory notes that are supported only by the general credit of the issuing company. Debentures are riskier than secured bonds, because if the company defaults, secured debt is repaid first. However, debentures usually pay bondholders a higher rate of interest.

Debenture
An unsecured bond supported only by the general credit of the issuing company.

Even riskier are *subordinated debenture bonds,* which have the lowest priority relative to other debts of the company, even unsecured debt. Since subordinated debentures carry a high degree of risk, they pay an even higher rate of interest and are often accompanied by some feature such as convertibility.

Convertible bonds, like convertible preferred stock, can be converted into a specified number of shares of common stock at the option of the holder. These bonds pay interest and have a maturity date like all other bond debt. The conversion feature, however, makes them similar to equity securities. This "hybrid" nature of convertible bonds often results in a

Convertible bond
A bond that may be converted into a specified number of shares of common stock at the option of the bondholder.

market price for the bonds that depends on both the bond interest and the value of the common stock.

Zero coupon bond
A bond that pays no interest, is initially sold at a discount, and redeemed at par value.

In 1989, JCPenney sold the first publicly marketed bonds that pay no interest. These bonds are called **zero coupon bonds** or *deep discount bonds.* They are sold at a discount (less than their face amount), which is the buyer's only source of payoff and it comes at maturity. More recently, The Walt Disney Company offered a different kind of unique bond, the 100-year bond. The company expected to sell $150 million of 100-year bonds at a yield of 7.5 percent. Apparently the slightly higher interest attracted investors who were tired of returns below 6 percent.[11]

FOCUS ON COMPANY

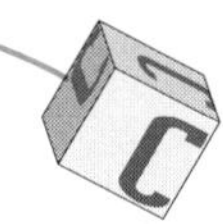

Pennzoil Company

An unusual move by Pennzoil Company has made the best of a not-so-good situation. Pennzoil holds 17.2 million shares of Chevron Corporation, which it bought as an investment from 1989 to 1991. The investment didn't work out as expected, since the stock didn't appreciate in value. So Pennzoil sold $402.5 million of an unusual variety of debentures (bonds) that allows holders to exchange them for some of the common stock the company owns in Chevron.

The debentures, priced at par value to yield 6.5 percent, are convertible into Chevron shares at $84.125 each, which is about 20 percent above Chevron's price in January 1993. The debenture holders receive interest income while betting that Chevron's stock price will rise above $84.125.

Bond Ratings. Regardless of the type of bond, all bonds that are new issues are sold in the primary market through an underwriter. Prior to issuance, bond-rating agencies such as Moody's Investors Service and Standard & Poor's are notified of the pending sale. The agencies, in turn, rate the bonds. They determine the quality of the bonds and assign them a letter grade, such as AAA. Exhibit 20.3 lists and explains Moody's and Standard and Poor's bond ratings.

Exhibit 20.3 **BOND RATINGS**

Bond Rating		
Moody's	**Standard & Poor's**	**Description**
Aaa	AAA	*High-grade investment.* The highest rating assigned. Indicates strong ability to pay principal and interest.
Aa	AA	*High-grade investment.* Coverage not quite as strong, but still high quality.
A	A	*Medium-grade investment.* Possibility of unfavorable conditions may be present, even though positive investment elements exist.
Baa	BBB	*Medium-grade investment.* Adequate ability to pay principal and interest, but lacking certain protective elements.
Ba	BB	*Speculative.* Moderate protection of principal and interest in the face of unfavorable economic conditions.
B	B	*Speculative.* Generally lacking in characteristics associated with investment quality.
Caa	CCC	*Default.* Poor-quality issues that may be either in default or in danger of default.
Ca	CC	*Default.* Highly speculative and often in default.
C		*Default.* Extremely poor investment quality.
	C	*Default.* Relates to income bonds on which no interest is paid unless income is sufficient to pay all other expenses and interest.
	D	*Default.* Bonds that are actually in default, with principal or interest in arrears.

Since Matt Seto launched his Matt Seto Fund, it has soared 38 percent. The 16-year-old high school sophomore's mutual fund has about $30,000 in assets. . . . His top stock pick, electronics retailer Best Buy Company, climbed 52 percent for a profit of $3,100 on his 150 shares.[12]

In addition to the letter grades, Moody's uses numerical ratings of 1 to 3 to indicate high, middle, and low ratings within a class of bonds. Standard and Poor's uses plus and minus signs to indicate degree of strength within a category. For example, Aa(1) or AA^+ indicates a high rating in the AA category. Aa(3) or AA^- indicates that the issue is on the low end of the AA category.

The purpose of the rating is to indicate the likelihood of default by the issuer and the investment quality of the bonds. The company's earning power, the stability of the company's income, and the company's ability to make interest payments on existing debt are some of the factors reflected in the bond rating. Note that the bond issue, not the company, is being rated. Thus, the same company can have different ratings assigned to all of its bond issues.

In addition to rating new issues, bond-rating agencies regularly review outstanding issues. A review can change the rating. For example, Standard & Poor's lowered its rating on $8 billion of GTE Corporation's debt because of the debt burden of its investments in Venezuelan Contel Corporation.[13] Both Moody's and Standard & Poor's upgraded Chrysler Corporation's debt rating when Chrysler issued 40 million new shares of common stock and introduced a line of profitable new products.[14] Although most issues have the same rating until they mature, changes in market conditions or the company's financial structure, as was the case for GTE and Chrysler, may invalidate the first rating.

Most investors consider ratings important and depend on them as indicators of the company's creditworthiness. Ratings can also have a strong effect on a bond's market price and interest rate. The higher the rating, the lower the interest rate. At the low end of the rating scale are the poorest-quality bonds, referred to as *junk bonds.* These bonds have a high degree of risk and thus pay much higher interest than other bonds. Although junk bond purchases contributed to the failure of many savings and loans, they remain popular with investors. The junk bond market had its best year in 1993, when $68 billion of these bonds were issued.[15]

Bond Retirement. Unlike common stock, all bonds must be retired, or repaid, on the maturity date. Term bonds and serial bonds are distinguished on the basis of their maturity. A *term bond* has a single, usually lengthy date to maturity, while a *serial bond* matures in installments.

Serial bonds are frequently sold by school districts or other taxing authorities that borrow funds to be repaid in installments financed by a special tax levy.

MUTUAL FUNDS

Mutual fund
Investment company that combines the funds of several investors with similar investment goals and invests them in a wide variety of securities.

Many investors who lack the time, knowledge, or desire to manage their own investments turn to mutual funds for professional management. A **mutual fund** is an investment company that combines the funds of several investors with similar investment goals and invests them in a wide variety of securities. Investors receive shares in the mutual fund and benefit from a wider diversification of investments than they would otherwise obtain.

The first mutual fund was begun in 1924. By 1940, 68 funds held $448 million in assets that were managed for 300,000 shareholder accounts. By the end of 1993, the assets of all mutual funds exceeded $2 trillion.[16]

Every mutual fund has an established investment objective. The objectives of mutual funds are as varied as the objectives of individual investors. *Growth funds* focus on appreciation of capital. They tend to invest in common stock that has growth potential, but offer little in the way of dividends. Growth funds are viewed as long-term investments. *Equity-income funds* invest primarily in securities that have a high dividend yield, but also consider price appreciation in the long run. They tend to invest in high-quality stocks of blue-chip companies and utilities. The purpose of *balance funds,* as the name implies, is to maintain a balance between income and capital appreciation. They invest in bonds to generate income and acquire stocks for their growth potential.

Specialty funds are available for those who wish to invest in specific industries. The most popular are those that invest in aerospace and defense, financial services, gold, leisure and entertainment, natural resources, electronics, computers, telecommunications, and health care. Other popular specialty funds are international funds that invest almost exclusively in foreign securities.

Money market mutual fund
A mutual fund that pools funds from a large number of investors, uses them to purchase high-yield, short-term securities, and provides check-writing privileges.

In 1972, **money market mutual funds** were created to pool funds from large numbers of investors. The accumulated funds are used to purchase high-yield, short-term securities such as U.S. Treasury bills, corporate commercial paper, and certificates of deposit. Money market mutual funds provide check-writing privileges that enable investors to easily access their money. These advantages help money market mutual funds to compete effectively for investment dollars.

The growth of money market mutual funds and the movement of money into them from low-interest savings accounts led to the deregulation of interest rates and the emergence of interest-bearing checking accounts. It is little wonder that *The Wall Street Journal* has hailed the money market mutual fund as one of the 10 most important financial innovations.

ORGANIZED SECURITIES EXCHANGES

It takes trillions of dollars to meet the financial needs of American companies. Meeting these needs requires the efforts of both large institutions and individual investors.

Financial institutions such as banks, pension funds, insurance companies, and mutual funds have large amounts of money that need to be invested to earn a return. Professional money managers, called *institutional investors,* are often hired to manage these large sums. Since they represent organizations that have billions of dollars to invest, their presence in securities markets has a major impact. For example, The Walt Disney Company issued $400 million in notes available only to large institutional investors. The return on these notes is based on the success of Disney movies connected to the notes. If the movies are big hits, investors stand to realize profits far above prevailing interest rates.[17]

As we saw earlier, both institutional and individual investors purchase original-issue securities in the primary market, and subsequent transactions occur in the secondary

Exhibit 20.4 **LISTING REQUIREMENTS OF THE NEW YORK AND AMERICAN STOCK EXCHANGES**

Listing Requirements (Minimum)	New York Stock Exchange	American Stock Exchange
Number of shares held by the general public	1,100,000	400,000
Number of stockholders owning 100 or more shares	2,000	1,200, of which 500 must own between 100 and 500 shares
Pretax income for latest fiscal year	$2,500,000	$750,000
Pretax income for preceding two years	$2,000,000	
Aggregate value of shares publicly held	$18,000,000	$300,000
Tangible assets (e.g., plant, equipment, land, inventory)	$18,000,000	$4,000,000

market. The secondary market includes various securities exchanges and the over-the-counter (OTC) market.

Organized securities exchanges are either regional or national. Both types are similar in structure and facilitate the trading of stocks and bonds of companies listed on the exchanges. To become listed, a company must file an application and meet the exchange's listing requirements. Exhibit 20.4 gives the listing requirements for the two largest exchanges, the New York Stock Exchange and the American Stock Exchange.

Getting its securities listed gives a company prestige, because it indicates that the company has grown in size and importance. Once its securities are accepted for trading, a company must continue to meet the exchange's listing requirements. The major securities exchanges include the New York Stock Exchange, the American Stock Exchange, regional stock exchanges, foreign stock exchanges, and the over-the-counter market.

THE NEW YORK STOCK EXCHANGE (NYSE)

Fifty million Americans own stock, and two-thirds own shares of the 1,700 companies listed on the *New York Stock Exchange (NYSE).* The NYSE is the largest securities exchange in the United States, accounting for over 2,200 stocks and 3,300 bonds. Companies such as IBM, 3M, General Mills, Coca-Cola, and Anheuser-Busch are listed on the NYSE.

Only designated individuals who are members of the NYSE are permitted to trade on the floor of the exchange. Membership is selective, as there are a total of 1,366 seats (in practice, though, members of the NYSE conduct trades standing up). Membership is also expensive. Seats on the NYSE sell for as much as $1.25 million.

THE AMERICAN STOCK EXCHANGE (AMEX)

The *American Stock Exchange (AMEX)* has 660 seats and lists 950 stocks and 325 bonds. Its procedures are similar to those of the NYSE, but as Exhibit 20.4 shows, its listing requirements are less strict. The Amex also operates in New York and, in terms of listed companies, is the second largest exchange in the United States. However, its dollar value trading is less than that of both the Midwest and Pacific regional exchanges, 2 of the 13 regional exchanges that operate in the United States.

REGIONAL STOCK EXCHANGES

Between 100 and 500 companies are listed on each of the *regional stock exchanges* below.

- Boston Stock Exchange
- Cincinnati Stock Exchange
- Colorado Stock Exchange
- Detroit Stock Exchange
- Honolulu Stock Exchange
- Intermountain Stock Exchange
- Midwest Stock Exchange
- Pacific Stock Exchange

Philadelphia Stock Exchange
Pittsburgh Stock Exchange
Richmond Stock Exchange
Spokane Stock Exchange
Wheeling Stock Exchange

Most regional exchanges are patterned after the NYSE. However, their listing and membership requirements are much more lenient. Typically, each exchange lists companies of particular interest to the geographic region. Some companies are listed on both a regional and national exchange. This double listing often increases trading of the security.

FOREIGN STOCK EXCHANGES

In addition to U.S. exchanges, a number of *foreign stock exchanges* exist. The largest foreign exchange is the Nikkei in Tokyo. Until recently U.S. stock markets were the largest in the world, but foreign stock markets have grown increasingly important. Today the United States is not always the largest trader of stocks and bonds. Japan's trading often exceeds that of the United States. Other prominent foreign exchanges include the Paris Stock Exchange, the London Stock Exchange, the Toronto and Montreal Stock Exchanges, and the Hong Kong Stock Exchange.

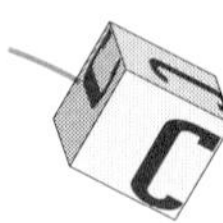

FOCUS ON COLLABORATORS

Stock Trading in China

The Hong Kong stock market continues to grow thanks to the flood of investors in Southern China. Also soaring are the stocks that trade in China itself. Fifty investment funds have been established worldwide to buy shares in Chinese companies or in organizations with significant interests in China.

To expand China's stock markets, each province will select one or two share-holding companies to be listed on the two official stock exchanges in Shenzhen and Shanghai. The success of China's efforts is evident in the 873 million new shares issued during 1993.

Like the U.S. regional exchanges, the foreign exchanges operate much like the NYSE. They offer a market for the trading of securities of companies located in the various countries.

Advances in technology have spurred the internationalization of financial markets. Dealers around the world can trade 24 hours a day, thanks to globewide instantaneous electronic transmission of share prices and other information. Progress in low-cost international communication has dramatically enhanced overseas trading.

THE OVER-THE-COUNTER MARKET (OTC)

In addition to the organized securities exchanges, stocks and bonds can be traded in the *over-the-counter market (OTC).* Companies whose securities are traded in the OTC are usually younger and more innovative. A large number of high-tech companies, such as Apple Computer and Microsoft, trade over the counter. Traders in this market are linked by a sophisticated telecommunications network that accounts for one-third of all shares traded.

Bid price
The highest price a dealer is willing to pay for a security.

Asked price
The lowest price a dealer will accept for a security.

Unlike the organized exchanges, the OTC has no central location where brokers conduct transactions for buyers and sellers. Trading occurs by telephone or electronically as dealers acquire securities for their own accounts. They buy securities at a **bid price**, which is the highest price the dealer is willing to pay. They sell at an **asked price**, which reflects market conditions and is the lowest price the dealer will accept. The difference between the two prices, called the *spread,* is the dealer's profit.

More than 50 Chinese funds manage some $3 billion for institutions and individual investors in the West. You can invest in most of these funds, either directly or through a U.S. broker. This new entertainment center in Guangzhou was completed with investments from U.S. pension funds.[18]

OTC dealers are linked with buyers and sellers through the National Association of Securities Dealers Automated Quotation (NASDAQ) system. This system provides up-to-the-minute quotations on over 5,000 highly active OTC securities and enables buyers and sellers to locate each other quickly. Approximately 2,900 NASDAQ stocks meet listing requirements for inclusion in the national market system. OTC listing requirements are less restrictive than those of the New York Stock Exchange. Fewer shareholders, fewer assets, and lower net incomes are required for OTC listing, permitting many small companies to be included in the system. However, many large companies, including MCI Communications and Intel Corporation, are also members. NASDAQ estimates that more than 600 companies in the national market system would be eligible for listing on the NYSE.

PURCHASE AND SALE OF SECURITIES

Once an investor has decided to invest and identified investment goals, he or she should select an investment broker.

Following the selection of the broker, the investor should consider alternative investment strategies and select the one that best meets his or her investment objectives. If income is important, for example, an investment that provides a steady cash flow from dividends or interest might be preferable to one that focuses on growth stocks that pay no dividends.

FOCUS ON COLLABORATORS

Learning from the Pros

Many individual investors find it difficult to choose investment strategies. But they might use the Wall Street professionals as unknowing collaborators in making good investment decisions. Whether an investor has only a few dollars to spend or several billion, many of the investment principles are the same. Individual investors can learn important lessons from the big players. For example, pension fund managers construct their portfolios from the top, beginning with an overall investment strategy and asset mix. Here are 10 basic strategies and techniques of institutional investing that can help individual investors:

1. Plan first, then pick investments.
2. Match investments with objectives.
3. Construct a core portfolio.
4. Emphasize stocks for retirement.
5. Develop a stock-picking style.
6. Focus on prospects, not past results.
7. Formulate a strategy for when to sell.
8. Diversify into foreign markets.
9. Review holdings regularly.
10. Monitor results against proper benchmarks.

Rules like these yield a consistent investment approach and reduce the costs of investing.

When an investment strategy has been determined, the investment broker executes the order to purchase securities. The orders are transmitted to the floor of the exchange or to the OTC dealer.

TYPES OF ORDERS

Basically three types of orders can be placed: a market order, a limit order, and a stop-loss order.

Market order
An order to purchase or sell a security at the best price available at the time the order is placed.

Limit order
An order to buy (or sell) a security at a specified or lower (or higher) price.

Stop-loss order
An order to sell a security when the market price reaches or falls below a specified level.

Market Order. A **market order** is an order to purchase or sell a security at the best price available at the time the order is placed. Since market orders are usually transacted as soon as they reach the exchange floor or the OTC dealer, they are often the fastest way to fill an order.

Limit Order. A **limit order** is an order to buy (or sell) at a specified or lower (or higher) price. The limit order is transmitted to an individual on the exchange floor who specializes in the security. The order is executed as soon as the specified price is reached and all other orders that take precedence have been filled.

Stop-Loss Order. A **stop-loss order** is an order to sell a security when the market price reaches or falls below a specified level. The order is activated once the stop price is reached. After being activated, it becomes a market order to sell the security at the best price possible.

SIZE, PAYMENT, AND COSTS OF TRANSACTIONS

In considering an investment, an investor needs to ask three important questions:

1. How much will I have to buy?
2. How will I pay for it?
3. How much will the transaction cost?

Size of the Transaction. Securities can be purchased in round or odd lots. A *round lot* is a unit of 100 shares or multiples of 100. An *odd lot* is fewer than 100 shares. So, for example, a purchase of 150 shares would be a combination of round and odd lots. Theoretically, there is no lower limit to the number of shares one can buy. However, buying only one or a few shares would be both expensive and unrealistic.

Payment for the Transaction. Payment for the securities purchased is made through accounts set up with the broker. The most common type of account is the cash account. This account permits the investor to make only cash transactions. If the balance in the cash account is insufficient to cover the cost of a purchase, the investor has five business days to make payment in full. An investor can also use borrowed funds to purchase securities.

Costs of the Transaction. Costs of the transaction are paid by the investor to the broker. With the passage of the Securities Act Amendment of 1975, brokers are permitted to charge whatever commission they believe is appropriate. Most brokerage firms have developed a fixed commission schedule that applies to small transactions and negotiate commissions on large, institutional transactions. The Securities and Exchange Commission, however, is concerned that commissions are based only on the investment dollars a broker brings in. This encourages brokers to push for more sales without regard to the match between the investment and the investor's needs.[19]

Many full-service brokerage firms now charge extra for doing research on investments. As a result, many investors do the research themselves and then use discount brokers, such as Charles Schwab & Company, to make the actual transactions. Discount brokers charge 30 to 80 percent less than full-service brokers.

Both full-service and discount brokers have been busy in recent years. With bank interest rates at their lowest in 30 years, investors have pulled some $70 million out of savings accounts and certificates of deposit and put those funds into the stock market, where prices generally have been increasing. The higher returns have been a good substitute for interest earnings.[20]

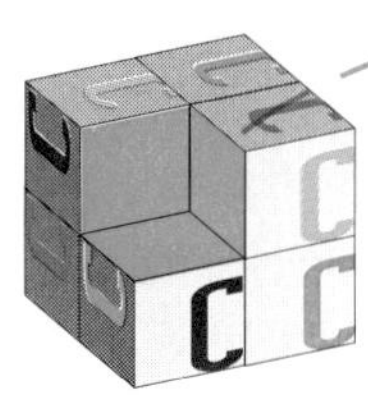

FOCUS ON CUSTOMERS

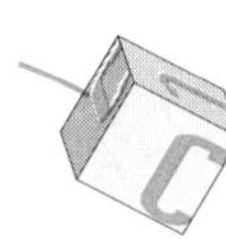

Appealing to Female Investors

Many Wall Street brokerage firms and financial planners believe women investors represent a brand-new market. A survey by Shearson Lehman Brothers concluded that women desire to have more confidence in making investment decisions. Another study reported that women also want more investment knowledge and experience.

Traditionally, when brokers and financial planners targeted women customers, they focused on widows and wealthy divorcées. In the past, these women tended to be the only ones with large amounts of money to invest. But now working women have accumulated billions of dollars in employer-sponsored savings plans, such as profit-sharing and 401(k) plans. When they change jobs, they often receive a lump-sum payment from these plans, and brokers are eager to tap into this investment potential. One trade magazine for brokers, the *Registered Representative,* offered tips on targeting women: "Prospect work places, sponsor seminars targeted at women business owners...hold investment classes for women only, distribute information for the newly single."

STOCK MARKET FLUCTUATIONS

Bull market
A stock market indicator of favorable economic conditions, investor optimism, and generally rising stock prices.

Bull markets are commonly associated with favorable economic conditions, investor optimism, and generally rising stock prices. Five bull markets have occurred since the end of World War II. The longest-running bull market lasted 97 months, from June 1949 to July 1957. The most recent one started in August 1982 and peaked in August 1987.

Bear market
A stock market indicator of unfavorable economic conditions, investor pessimism, and stock price declines.

In contrast, **bear markets** indicate unfavorable economic conditions, investor pessimism, and stock price declines. The most recent bear market started in October 1987 with the largest and most devastating stock market crash in U.S. history.

The stock market actually had begun to decline in late August 1987, and the Dow Jones Industrial Average (referred to as the *Dow* or the *DJIA*) had experienced a 15 percent decline by mid-October. Then came October 19, 1987, "Black Monday," when the Dow declined by nearly 23 percent in one day. On that day, the stock market lost approximately a half-trillion dollars in value. A record-breaking 600 million shares were traded on that historic day.

A personal insight into the crash was provided by the late Sam Walton, at the time one of America's richest people. When reporters noted that Walton had lost a half-billion dollars that Monday, he replied, "It's only paper."[21]

Many investors have come to fear October, the month of the stock market crashes of both 1929 and 1987. But in fact, the worst month for the Dow Jones Industrial Average is September. September has had an average loss of 0.90 percent. Excluding the two crashes, October has shown an average gain of 0.38 since 1915.[22]

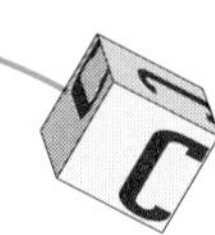

FOCUS ON COLLABORATORS

The Lesson of Black Monday

On Black Monday, the Dow Jones Industrial Average took a terrifying 508-point plunge. But unlike 1929, investors did not panic. It didn't take investors long to learn the central lesson of this crash: Don't sell in a panic. Within months, the Dow rebounded, and in the next five years the index rose 83 percent from its October 19 low.

The October 1987 crash was triggered by an overvalued stock market and troubling economic events, including the breakdown of cooperation between the United States and Germany on interest rate policy and a proposal in Congress that would have curbed leveraged buyouts. Although investors now see that the 1987 crash was an isolated event, it does emphasize the importance of economic collaboration.

SECURITIES REGULATION

The stock market crash of 1929 had a tremendous impact on this country. One result was the passage of several acts to regulate securities trading.

THE SECURITIES ACT OF 1933

Following the 1929 stock market crash, extensive fraud in securities trading was revealed. Demands for regulation resulted in the passage of the Securities Act of 1933. The act requires full disclosure of all relevant information related to new securities issues. A registration statement providing detailed information about new issues must be filed. Only after all of the necessary information has been filed and approved can a new issue be sold.

THE SECURITIES EXCHANGE ACT OF 1934

The Securities Act of 1933 applied only to new issues. The Securities Exchange Act of 1934 was passed to regulate trading in the secondary markets. This act created the Securities and Exchange Commission (SEC). The SEC was given the power to regulate the securities exchanges and their listed companies. The exchanges are required to register with the SEC, which in turn monitors and regulates exchange activities. The Securities Exchange Act of 1934 also set forth specific guidelines pertaining to insider trading, that is, activities by people who have exclusive knowledge about the company. The act defined insiders as the company's officers, directors, major stockholders, employees, and relatives of these individuals. Recently the term has been expanded to include anyone who has information that is not public knowledge. These people include financial analysts, loan officers, accountants, lawyers, investment bankers, and any others who do business with the company.

A highly celebrated case of insider trading is that of Ivan Boesky, a Wall Street arbitrageur. Boesky had an arrangement in which he paid cash to Dennis Levine, an investment banker. Because Levine's bank was financing the deal, he would have known when a takeover was about to occur. Levine would sell this information to Boesky, who would purchase the stock of the takeover target and sell it after the stock price rose. Some believe Boesky's insider-trading activities netted him hundreds of millions of dollars. He had to enjoy his ill-gotten gains from a distance, however, as he was sentenced to three years in jail. He was also fined $100 million and banned from the securities business.

OTHER LEGISLATION

The Securities Act of 1933 and the Securities Exchange Act of 1934 are the key pieces of legislation that protect participants in the securities markets. Another act is the Maloney Act of 1938, which provides for the establishment of trade associations for self-regulatory purposes. To date, only one trade association, the National Association of Securities Dealers (NASD), has been formed.

The Investment Company Act of 1940 authorized the SEC to regulate the practices of investment companies such as mutual funds. This act protects investors by requiring adequate and accurate investment company financial statement disclosure. It also prohibits excessive commissions and fees.

Investor protection is also provided by the Securities Investor Protection Act of 1970, which established the Securities Investor Protection Corporation (SIPC). This agency operates

STREET SMART

Avoid Affinity Fraud

It's easy to lose your money to con artists. *Affinity fraud*—investment fraud that targets members of a particular ethnic, political, religious, or professional group—seems to dupe professionals more than any other groups of investors. Federal regulators suggest the following tips for avoiding affinity fraud:

- Beware of testimonials from other group members. Scam artists often pay high initial returns to early investors to sucker in money from later investors.
- Do your homework by getting a prospectus or other form of written information.
- Get professional advice by asking a neutral outside expert to evaluate the investment.
- Check up on the seller. The North American Securities Administrators Association (202-737-0900) and the National Fraud Information Center (1-800-876-7060) can direct you.

Exhibit 20.5 **STOCK QUOTATIONS FROM "THE WALL STREET JOURNAL"**

52 Weeks Hi	52 Weeks Lo	Stock	Sym	Div	Yld %	PE	Vol 100s	Hi	Lo	Close	Net Chg
7⅞	5	BioWhit	BWI		...	28	19	6⅝	6½	6⅝	+ ⅛
32⅝	20¾	BirmghamStl	BIR	.40	1.6	38	6389	25¾	24⅝	24¾	+ ¼
22⅞	17	BlackDeck	BDK	.40	2.3	17	1142	17⅜	17⅛	17⅜	+ ⅛
27⅛	17⅞	BlackHills	BKH	1.32	7.1	11	101	18¾	18½	18⅝	− ⅛
10¾	8½	BlackRockAdv	BAT	.73	8.3	...	70	9	8¾	8¾	− ¼
15⅞	13⅛	BlkrkCal2008	BFC	.86	6.3	...	134	13⅞	13¾	13¾	...
15¾	13⅞	BlkrkFla2008	BRF	.86	6.0	...	65	14¼	14⅛	14¼	+ ⅛
9⅛	6⅝	BlackRockIncTr	BKT	.75	10.7	...	969	7⅛	7	7	− ⅛
10⅞	9⅛	BlkrkMuni	BMT	.62	6.4	...	242	9¾	9⅝	9¾	...
15½	13¼	BlkrkMuni2008	BRM	.89	6.1	...	209	14½	14⅜	14½	+ ⅛
14¾	11⅝	BlackrockInvQty	BKN	.90	7.6	...	98	12	11⅞	11⅞	...
10	7⅜	BlackRockInv	BQT	.70	9.0	...	1226	8	7¾	7¾	− ⅛
10⅞	9⅜	BlackRockMuni	BMN	.62	6.3	...	321	10	9¾	9⅞	+ ⅛
15⅞	13⅜	BlkrkNY2008	BLN	.86	6.2	...	110	14⅛	13⅞	13⅞	...
12⅞	9¼	BlackRockNoAm	BNA	1.05	10.4	...	633	10¼	10	10⅛	+ ⅛
10¼	7⅝	BlackRockStrat	BGT	.70	8.7	...	711	8⅛	8	8	− ⅛
10½	8⅝	BlackRockTgt	BTT	.70	7.7	...	878	9⅛	9	9⅛	...
10¼	8	BlackRock1998	BBT	.62	7.0	...	481	8⅞	8¾	8⅞	+ ⅛
10	8⅛	BlackRock1999	BNN	.63	7.5	...	112	8⅜	8¼	8⅜	...
9¾	7¾	BlackRock2001	BLK	.68	8.6	...	2305	8⅛	7⅞	7⅞	− ⅛
23½	15¾	BlanchHldg	EWB	.24e	1.2	20	18	21	20¾	20¾	− ¼
48¾	34½	BlockHR	HRB	1.25f	3.2	21	4134	39¾	39	39½	...
34¼	21⅞	BlockbstrE	BV	.10	.4	23	9384	27¼	26½	27¼	+ ⅝
8⅝	6⅝	BluChipValFd	BLU	.46e	6.6	...	29	7	6⅞	7	+ ⅛
n 23⅞	18¼	BlythInd	BTH		...	...	5	23⅞	23⅞	23⅞	+ ⅛
50⅛	35⅜	Boeing	BA	1.00	2.1	13	13258	47½	46½	46¾	− ⅝
27¾	19	BoiseCasc	BCC	.60	2.5	dd	1928	24¼	23¾	24¼	+ ⅜
27	19	BoiseCasc pfE		1.79	7.5	...	64	23¾	23⅜	23¾	+ ¼
27¾	24¼	BoiseCasc depF		2.35	9.4	...	31	24⅞	24⅝	24⅞	...

52 Weeks Hi	52 Weeks Lo	Stock	Sym	Div	Yld %	PE	Vol 100s	Hi	Lo	Close	Net Chg
51⅞	40	CPCInt	CPC	1.36	2.7	23	1689	50½	49⅞	50	− ¾
18⅜	13¾	CPI Cp	CPY	.56	3.2	23	43	17⅝	17½	17½	− ⅛
9⅝	5¼	CRI Liq	CFR	3.20e	56.9	...	132	5⅝	5⅜	5⅝	+ ¼
13¼	8¼	CRSS	CRX	.12	1.1	30	10	11⅜	11¼	11¼	− ¼
9⅝	7⅜	CS FstBsInco	FBF	.72	9.3	...	90	7¾	7⅝	7¾	...
10⅞	8½	CS FstBsStrg	FBI	.81	9.3	...	30	8⅞	8¾	8¾	...
92⅜	68¾	CSX	CSX	1.76	2.4	18	969	75½	74⅝	74⅝	− ½
39¾	25	CUC Int	CU		...	36	5389	29½	28⅞	29½	+ ½
11½	9	CV REIT	CVI	1.08	11.5	9	62	9⅜	9¼	9⅜	...
11¾	7	CWM Mtg	CWM	.64	8.1	30	1034	7⅞	7⅝	7⅞	+ ⅛
s 25⅛	17⅛	CablWirels	CWP	.47e	2.3	...	945	20½	20¼	20¼	...
132½	82⅝	CabltrnSys	CS		...	23	3270	107⅞	106	106¾	+1¾
58½	46¼	Cabot Cp	CBT	1.04	2.1	21	104	50⅞	50⅜	50⅝	− ¼
27	17⅝	CabotO&G	COG	.16	.8	cc	888	22⅛	21⅛	21⅛	− ¾
17½	9¾	CadenceDsgn	CDN		...	dd	3169	17¼	16⅞	16⅞	− ¼
59	35¾	CaesarWld	CAW		...	11	649	39⅞	39¼	39⅜	− ⅛
33⅜	24⅛	Caldor	CLD		...	12	81	30⅛	29⅞	30	+ ¼
15⅜	9⅞	CalgnCarb	CCC	.16	1.3	22	218	12⅝	12½	12½	− ⅛
16¾	9⅛	CalFedBk A	CAL		...	dd	817	12¼	12	12⅛	...
23	16⅛	CalFedBk pfA		1.94	9.2	...	21	21	21	21	...
20⅜	15¾	CalEngy	CE		...	16	116	16⅞	16⅝	16¾	..
2⅝	1¾	CalifREIT	CT	.15e	8.0	dd	3	1⅞	1⅞	1⅞	− ⅛
41¼	33¾	CalifWtr	CWT	1.98	5.6	13	5	35⅝	35⅜	35⅝	+ ¼
s 43⅜	20¾	CallwyGlf	ELY	.20	.5	31	2122	40⅝	39⅞	39⅞	− ⅝
25⅝	16⅜	CalMat	CZM	.40	1.9	37	435	21⅛	21	21⅛	+ ⅛
n 21½	15	CamcoInt	CAM	.10e	.5	...	207	21	20⅞	20⅞	− ¼
n 27⅝	22	CamdenProp	CPT	1.76	7.0	...	372	25	24¾	25	+ ⅛
1¼	13/32	CampblRes g	CCH		...	...	408	7/16	13/32	7/16	...
43¼	34¼	CampblSoup	CPB	1.12	3.1	15	1563	36	35⅝	35¾	− ⅛

similarly to the Federal Deposit Insurance Corporation; its purpose is to oversee the liquidation of bankrupt brokerage firms. It also insures investor accounts to a maximum of $500,000.

In addition to federal legislation, various state laws protect investors. These laws regulate the sale of securities within some states. Since they are designed to prevent investors from purchasing nothing but "blue sky," they are called *blue sky laws.*

INVESTMENT FRAUD

Despite the passage of legislation to protect investors, investment-related fraud still results in a billion-dollar-a-year activity that keeps getting bigger. Certain U.S. cities seem to be hotbeds for such activities, but fraud can occur anywhere. The investor's best defense is not to talk to strangers who promise "guaranteed" high rates of return, either in person or over the phone. Instead, the wise investor will thoroughly check out the credentials of the investment adviser, periodically visit the brokerage firm, and request to see his or her account statement.[23]

GETTING FINANCIAL INFORMATION

Whether interested in buying, selling, or simply tracking the price of a stock or bond, an investor should be familiar with the ways securities prices are quoted. Staying current on the movement of a security's price is essential to making good investment decisions.

STOCK QUOTATIONS

Stock quotations appear daily in the financial press and in various on-line services such as Prodigy and America Online. They are an easy way to get financial information. Exhibit 20.5 is a sample of quotations for the New York Stock Exchange published in *The Wall Street Journal.*[24] Quotations such as these are published each weekday and report on the trading the previous day. Several other financial newspapers use a similar format.

Several large corporations appear in the quotations in Exhibit 20.5, including Boeing (Boeing), Black & Decker (BlackDeck), H & R Block (BlockHR), Blockbuster Video (BlockbstrE) and Campbell Soup Company (CampblSoup). We will use Campbell Soup to see how quotations are read.

52-Week High-Low Range. The first two columns are labeled *Hi* and *Lo.* Prices reported here are the high and low stock price for the preceding 52-week period. This period includes the current week, but not the latest trading day. The high and low for Campbell Soup Company were 43 ¼ and 34 ¼, respectively. Stock prices are quoted in one-eighth of a dollar, so Campbell Soup's prices are $43.25 and $34.25 per share.

Company Name and Type of Stock. The company name appears in the third column, labeled Stock. If no special letters follow the company name, it is a common stock. If the abbreviation *pf* follows the name, it is a preferred stock. Other symbols that can appear in this column and in the area to the left of the 52-week high/low range are discussed daily in the footnotes box on page C-3 of *The Wall Street Journal.*

Ticker Symbols. The abbreviation that follows the company name is used as a symbol for that stock on market ticker tapes, electronic information systems, and computer databases. The symbol for Campbell Soup is CPB.

Dividend Payment. Column 5 is labeled *Div* and provides information about the annual per share cash dividend declared by the company. The dividend for Campbell Soup was 1.12, meaning the company's stockholders received $1.12 for each share owned.

Percentage Yield. The column labeled *Yld %* reports the dividend return that an investor can expect for each share of stock. It is determined by dividing each share's dividend by the share's current market price and is expressed as a percentage. The percentage yield for Campbell Soup was 3.1 on the day this quotation was published.

Price-Earnings Ratio. The column labeled *PE* gives the price-earnings ratio. The *price-earnings ratio* is the ratio of the price of the stock to the stock's earnings per share. This calculation is used to evaluate a stock's relative performance and worth. Higher ratios mean investors are more optimistic about the company's future financial prospects. Lower ratios indicate a more pessimistic attitude. The price-earnings ratio for Campbell Soup on this day was 15.

Trading Volume. The column labeled *Vol 100s* provides information about the total number of shares traded for the day. The number reported, in hundreds, for Campbell Soup is 1563, meaning 156,300 shares of Campbell Soup were traded. When the letter *z* appears to the left of the volume number, the actual number traded is being reported. For example, if a *z* appeared before the number 13, the number of shares traded would be only 13, not 1,300.

Trading Price Range. The second set of columns labeled *Hi* and *Lo* provide information about the highest and lowest prices for the day. For Campbell Soup on this day, the high price was $36.00 and the low price was $35.625.

Closing Price. The column labeled *Close* gives the trading price at the time the market closed the previous day. Campbell Soup's closing price was $35.75.

Price Change from Previous Day. The final column, *Net Chg,* reports the difference between the closing price the day before and that two days before. For Campbell Soup, the closing price the day before was 12¢ higher than it was the previous day.

BOND QUOTATIONS

Quotations for corporate bonds are given in a manner similar to that for stock quotations. The name of the issuing company is listed, followed by the stated annual rate of interest and year of maturity for the bond. The current yield, which is determined by dividing the annual inter-

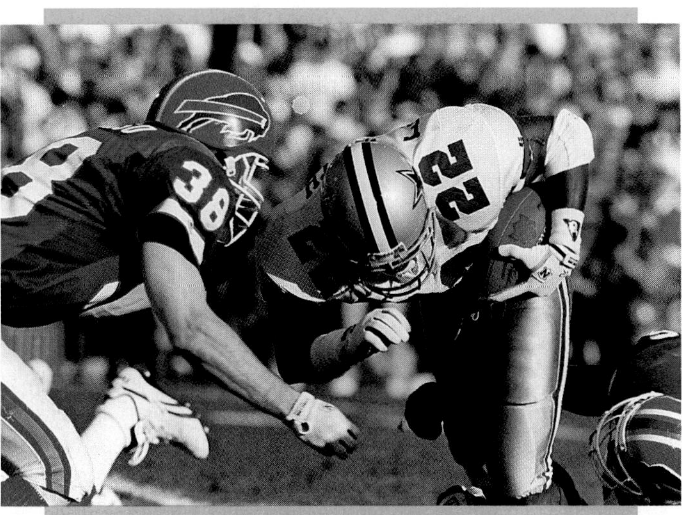

Many investors wish to predict the direction of the Dow Jones averages. Some look to the Super Bowl for help. In the 28 Super Bowls from 1967 to 1994, 26 out of 28 times the market rose by year's end when a team from the original NFL won the championship or fell when a team from the American Football League (now the NFL's America Football Conference) won. Most likely this is mere coincidence, but with a 95 percent prediction rate, many investors still root for the old NFL teams on Super Bowl Sunday.

est by the current market price, is also provided. Information about the number of bonds traded, the closing market price, and the net change in the price of the bond over the previous day complete the bond quotation.

STOCK INDEXES

Stock prices vary daily, and a number of indexes are used to monitor the fluctuations. The most widely quoted index is the Dow Jones Industrial Average (DJIA), which consists of 30 of the largest and best-known companies (listed below).[25]

Allied-Signal
Alcoa
American Express
AT&T
Bethlehem Steel
Boeing
Caterpillar
Chevron
Coca-Cola
DuPont
Eastman Kodak
Exxon
General Electric
General Motors
Goodyear
IBM
International Paper
J. P. Morgan
McDonald's
Merck
3M
Philip Morris
Procter & Gamble
Sears, Roebuck
Texaco
Union Carbide
United Technologies
Walt Disney
Westinghouse
Woolworth

Companies included in the DJIA are major forces in their industries, and their stocks are widely held by individual and institutional investors. Changes in the composition of companies used in the average are rare. In addition, Dow Jones & Company computes the averages for 15 utilities and 20 transportation stocks, along with a composite index for all 65 companies used in the three averages.

A number of major companies such as Johnson & Johnson are not included in the Dow Jones Industrial Average. This has been cited as a shortcoming of the index. Other indexes, such as Standard and Poor's 500 and the New York Stock Exchange Index, include larger numbers of stocks. Although the averages of the various indexes occasionally differ, they are an excellent source of information for people who wish to invest in the U.S. stock market.[26]

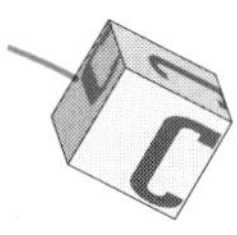

FOCUS ON COMPANY

Dow Jones Goes Global

Dow Jones & Company, which publishes *The Wall Street Journal,* recently introduced a new benchmark of stock performance for global investors: the Dow Jones World Stock Index (DJWSI). This index provides a comprehensive measure of stock performance worldwide for investors who are interested in global markets. The DJWSI is a global expansion of the four-year-old Dow Jones Equity Market Index for the United States. The world index consists of stocks of 2,200 companies from countries around the globe organized into nearly 120 industrial groups.

The DJWSI is said to offer superior measures of stock market performance, since it gives investors two comparative views: geographic and industrial. Investors can assess the political, economic, and financial forces affecting the global market and determine how an individual issue has performed against its peers on a global, regional, or national basis. For example, they can look at the computer industry in the United States, Europe, the Far East, or around the world.

SUMMARY

1. ***Define* investing *and explain the importance of financial markets in the investing process.***
   Investing is the process by which suppliers of funds (those with surplus money) are brought together with demanders of funds (those needing money). Financial institutions and financial markets bring suppliers and demanders together. Financial markets include capital markets such as stock and bond markets, as well as money markets. Money markets permit short-term transactions, while transactions in capital markets tend to be long term. Capital markets are classified as primary markets or secondary markets. Primary markets sell new securities to the public. Purchases and sales of securities are performed by investment bankers, which buy new issues of securities from the issuing companies and sell them through a selling group to individual investors. Secondary markets deal in previously issued securities and are used to transfer securities from one investor to another. Financial instruments traded in secondary markets include equity and debt securities.

2. ***Describe the types of equity securities.***
   Equity securities represent ownership interest. By selling ownership interest in the form of stock, companies can obtain large amounts of capital. Equity securities consist of common stock and preferred stock. Common stock controls the board of directors, shares in the success of the company, and bears the risk of failure. Also, common stock carries four rights for stockholders: (1) the right to share in company profits in the form of dividends, (2) the right to vote, (3) the right to share in the company's assets upon liquidation, and (4) the right to purchase enough shares of new issues of stock to maintain their ownership interest (the preemptive right). Common stocks are generally classified as blue-chip, income, growth, or speculative stocks. These classifications reflect a stock's stability and potential for attractive capital gains. Preferred stockholders have a prior claim over common stockholders on the company's earnings and assets. Once dividends have been declared, the preferred stockholders receive their share before the common stockholders do. Typically, preferred stock is issued with a par value,

and the dividends paid are expressed as a percentage of the par value. Preferred stock can have cumulative and convertibility features.

3. ***Discuss the types of debt securities.***
   Debt securities represent IOUs, and consist primarily of bonds. A bond is a long-term debt instrument having a specified rate of interest and a specified maturity date. The company pays interest over a specified period, at the end of which (the maturity date) it repays the principal. The U.S. government is the largest issuer of bonds. State and local governments also issue bonds to finance various capital projects. Corporations are the major issuer of nongovernment bonds. Corporate bonds include mortgage bonds, equipment trust certificates, debentures, and convertible bonds. Prior to issuance, a bond-rating agency determines the quality of the bonds and assigns them a letter grade. The rating indicates the likelihood of default by the issuer and the investment quality of the bonds. All bonds must be retired, or repaid, on the maturity date.

4. ***Explain the nature and types of mutual funds.***
   Many investors who lack the time, knowledge, or desire to manage their own investments turn to mutual funds for professional management. A mutual fund is an investment company that combines the funds of several investors with similar investment goals and invests them in a wide variety of securities. Mutual funds include growth, equity-income, balance, and specialty funds. The money market mutual fund is an important development in mutual funds. This type of fund uses funds pooled from a large number of investors to purchase high-yield, short-term securities and offers check-writing privileges.

5. ***Describe the various organized securities exchanges.***
   National and regional securities exchanges facilitate the trading of stocks and bonds of companies listed on the exchanges. The largest securities exchange in the United States is the New York Stock Exchange (NYSE). The NYSE has the strictest listing requirements of all the exchanges. The American Stock Exchange (AMEX) is the second largest securities exchange in terms of listed companies. Its listing requirements are less strict than those of the NYSE. Regional stock exchanges list companies of particular interest to the geographical regions in which they are located. A number of foreign stock exchanges also exist. The largest is the Nikkei in Tokyo. In addition to the organized securities exchanges, stocks and bonds can be traded in the over-the-counter market (OTC).

6. ***Discuss the process of purchasing and selling securities.***
   Once an investor has decided to invest and identified investment goals, he or she should select an investment broker and decide on an investment strategy that will best meet the investment objectives. The investment broker then executes the order to purchase securities. Three types of orders can be placed: a market order, a limit order, or a stop-loss order. When making an investment, an investor needs to consider (1) how many shares of the security to buy (a round lot versus an odd lot), (2) how to pay for the transaction (cash versus credit), and (3) how much the transaction will cost (broker fees and commissions).

7. ***Explain the difference between a bull market and a bear market.***
   Bull markets are commonly associated with favorable economic conditions, investor optimism, and generally rising stock prices. Bear markets indicate unfavorable economic conditions, investor pessimism, and stock price declines.

8. ***Describe legislation passed to regulate securities trading.***
   Following the stock market crash of 1929, demands for regulation of the securities industry resulted in the passage of the Securities Act of 1933. This act requires full disclosure of all relevant information related to new securities issues. The Securities Exchange Act of 1934 was passed to regulate trading in the secondary markets. This act created the Securities and Exchange Commission (SEC), which regulates the securities exchanges and their listed companies. It also set forth specific guidelines pertaining to insider trading. The Maloney Act of 1938

provides for the establishment of trade associations for self-regulatory purposes. The Investment Company Act of 1940 authorized the SEC to regulate the practices of investment companies. The Securities Investor Protection Act of 1970 established the Securities Investor Protection Corporation (SIPC), which oversees the liquidation of bankrupt brokerage firms. Finally, several state laws regulate the sale of securities within the states.

9. Explain how information published in the financial press can help investors.
Whether interested in buying, selling, or simply tracking the price of a stock or bond, an investor should be familiar with ways securities prices are quoted. Staying current on the movement of a security's price is essential to making good investment decisions. Stock quotations appear daily in the financial press and are an easy way to get financial information. *The Wall Street Journal* and other financial newspapers publish stock quotations each weekday. Quotations for corporate bonds are given in a manner similar to that for stock quotations. Stock prices vary daily, and a number of indexes are used to monitor the fluctuations. The most widely quoted index is the Dow Jones Industrial Average (DJIA). Other indexes include Standard and Poor's 500 and the New York Stock Exchange Index.

KEY TERMS AND CONCEPTS

Investing (p. 478)
Primary markets (p. 478)
Initial public offerings (IPOs) (p. 479)
Underwriting (p. 479)
Margin (p. 480)
Secondary markets (p. 481)
Equity securities (p. 481)
Common stock (p. 481)
Blue-chip stocks (p. 482)
Income stocks (p. 482)
Growth stocks (p. 482)
Speculative stocks (p. 482)
Preferred stock (p. 483)
Debt securities (p. 483)
Bond (p. 483)
Revenue bond (p. 483)
Mortgage bond (p. 484)
Equipment trust certificate (p. 484)
Debenture (p. 484)
Convertible bond (p. 484)
Zero coupon bond (p. 485)
Mutual fund (p. 487)
Money market mutual fund (p. 487)
Bid price (p. 489)
Asked price (p. 489)
Market order (p. 491)
Limit order (p. 491)
Stop-loss order (p. 491)
Bull market (p. 492)
Bear market (p. 493)

DISCUSSION QUESTIONS

Company

1. Discuss the effect that securities regulation has had on American companies.
2. What sources of capital do American companies have available to them?
3. What types of company information do stock quotations provide?

Customers

4. What advantages does a discount broker offer its customers?
5. How can customers (i.e., investors) protect themselves against investment fraud?
6. What effects does the Federal Reserve have on brokerage firms' customers?
7. How might ethical issues related to insider trading affect a company's customers?

Competitors

8. What effects has the discount broker had on competition among brokerage firms?
9. What effect does competition have on stock prices?

Collaborators

10. How do investors serve as collaborators to American companies?
11. How do investors benefit from securities regulation?
12. How has insider trading affected the relationship between companies and their investment collaborators?

In Question: Take a Stand

As the assistant to the president of a major corporation, Kyle is in a position to learn important information about the company's performance before it becomes available to investors outside the company. Recently, he was approached by a wealthy friend who offered to give Kyle 5 percent of her profits based on stock trades made on information Kyle provided. What is the ethical concern here? Should Kyle strike a deal?

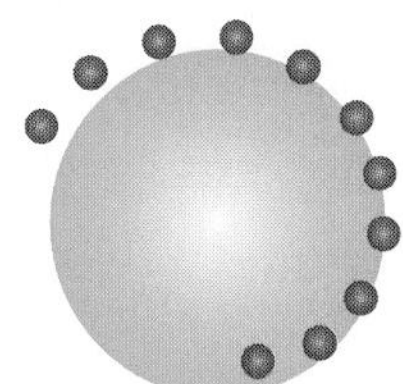

CASE 20.1
BOOK VALUE PROBLEMS IN THE STOCK MARKET[27]

Stocks of well-known companies like Kmart and Digital Equipment are currently selling below book value. That's a sure sign the stocks are out of favor, and a hint that some of them may be bargains. Book value is a company's per-share net worth—the sum of its assets minus its liabilities divided by the shares of common stock. In classic investment theory, stocks selling below book are potential buys. Stocks can stay at a discount to book value for months or years, but often return to favor with the stock market in a short time.

Stocks selling at or below book were scarce in 1994. The average stock in May 1994 sold for close to three times its book value. Only 29 stocks in the *Standard & Poor's 500 Stock Index* were selling below book value. One stock selling at less than its book value was Digital Equipment, which sold for more than $200 per share in the late 1980s. It is now just over $21 a share. Although Digital's Alpha computer chip is about the fastest chip in the market, its hardware business has been a consistent loser, and it is hard to tell when things will turn around.

Questions

1. *What measures other than the company's book value can be used in making an investment decision?*
2. *Why would stocks selling for less than their book value be potential buys?*
3. *What factors might explain why a company's book value is more than its stock price?*

CHAPTER

21

FINANCIAL MANAGEMENT

When you have studied this chapter, you will be able to:

1. Define *finance* and explain the role financial managers play in a company's long-term success.
2. Describe the financial planning process.
3. Discuss the importance of establishing financial control.
4. Explain how float can benefit a company.
5. Describe the importance of managing accounts receivable.
6. Discuss the importance of managing inventory.
7. Explain three major uses of funds in a company.
8. Describe the major sources of funds for a company.
9. Discuss the use of leasing as an alternative method for acquiring capital assets.

Jean H. Barr is an enterprising business owner who has her own philosophy about financing a company. Her business began with her interest in sewing and travel. Some 25 years ago, she was planning a trip to Europe and promised a friend to bring back some buttons for some ski sweaters the friend was making. While in Vienna, she found a style of button she really liked and bought the store's complete inventory of the item for cash.

Recognizing a business opportunity, Barr bought buttons every time she went to Europe, brought them back home, and sold them for a profit. For five years, her ski sweater friend and a local department store were her only customers.

Today Barr's wholesale button company, JHB International, Inc., is a multimillion-dollar business that occupies 28,000 square feet of industrial space, plus two semitrailers. The company's growth—28.9 percent during 1992—has been carefully monitored and controlled. Ms. Barr says, "I've grown only as I could afford to grow. I borrowed money once, paid it back in 30 days, and never borrowed money again." Some call this type of financing bootstrap financing, *defined by one professor as "making do with as little financial commitment up front as humanly possible. ...Bootstrapping is really paying as you go."*

JHB grew slowly, with hands-on money management. Barr describes herself as financially "frugal." Initially she offered no discounts even to large customers, charging all customers the same price. Today she does offer discounts, based strictly on volume. Money that's not put back into the company is invested. Now Jean Barr's company is so solid that she can promise quick turnaround and high quality on a huge volume of buttons.

Barr still travels extensively, searching for new sources for buttons and building up a list of export customers. Her advice to aspiring entrepreneurs is that success is possible "as long as you grow as you can afford to grow.... There's no sense being in business unless it's profitable and you can keep it under control."[1]

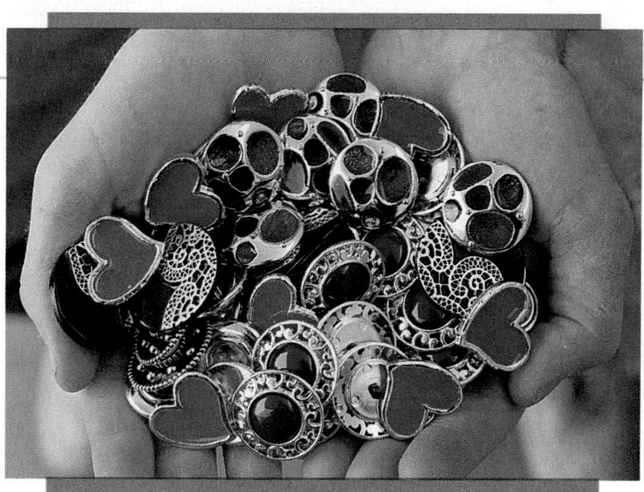

JHB is a successful company, due in large part to Jean Barr's ability to obtain funds and manage its financial assets. This chapter examines the reasons companies need funds, how they obtain and use funds, and how they manage their financial assets.

THE ROLE OF FINANCE

Finance
The business function of obtaining and using funds to maximize company profit or shareholders' wealth.

Finance is the business function of obtaining and using funds to maximize company profit or shareholders' wealth. Simply put, finance focuses on coordinating money matters within the company. For a start-up company, finance means finding enough money to meet the company's cash needs and "make the payroll" every month. In well-established corporations, finance involves managing the company's numerous financial assets and liabilities to maximize the wealth of the company's owners. Whether a company is a start-up or a 100-year-old organization, how its assets and liabilities are managed is critical to the company's long-term success.

Financial manager
A manager who constructs financial plans and budgets, obtains funds needed to run the business, determines how financial resources will be used, and makes investment decisions.

Financial managers construct financial plans and budgets, obtain funds needed to run the business, determine how financial resources will be used, and make investment decisions. Financial activities include making loans, selling stocks and bonds, establishing credit policies for customers, arranging payment terms with suppliers, and managing taxes.

The field of finance is closely related to the fields of accounting and economics. To do their jobs effectively, financial managers need to understand the relationship among these three fields.

Accounting is sometimes called the language of finance because it provides the financial information managers need to make their decisions.[2] Financial managers must know how to interpret the information from income statements, cash flow statements, balance sheets, and other accounting statements. Accounting information allows financial managers to assess whether they are maximizing profit-generating opportunities and using the company's financial resources effectively.

Economic principles provide a foundation for financial decisions. The price of money (i.e., interest rates) is based on supply and demand relationships. Another very important economic concept is that of risk. Financial managers must balance the risks involved in various investments against the potential for profits or losses. Economics also helps explain the economic environment in which companies operate. Financial managers must understand economic factors such as gross domestic product, inflation, interest rates, and taxes in making their decisions.

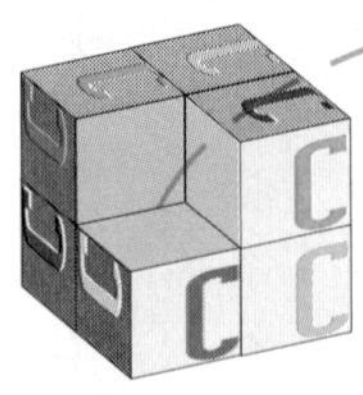

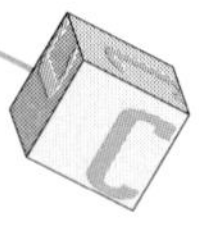

FOCUS ON COMPETITORS

GE Capital

During the last decade, many large companies tried to increase their profits by offering various financial services in addition to their basic business. Perhaps the most successful company involved in this trend is General Electric. In 1992, nearly one-third of GE's profits came from GE Capital, the company's financial services branch.

The ability to offer loans to both consumers and large businesses distinguishes GE Capital and enhances its competitive power in the electronics industry. Its financial strength is built on shrewd financial management and a AAA credit rating on Wall Street. GE Capital makes money from leasing activities and earns interest income from lending and insurance operations. It is also among the world's best at collecting receivables and planning cash flow. Four times a year, GE Capital business managers meet with top executives. The team maps out financial strategies and evaluates and adjusts operating plans for the current year.

Competitors have virtually ceded the industry to GE Capital. Banks fear regulations, insurers are plagued by weak real estate holdings, and companies like Sears are being pressured by angry shareholders to return to their core businesses—which they have done. GE Capital is using its competitors' weaknesses against them, gobbling up their assets and expanding its own.

FINANCIAL PLANS

As with all business activities, financial success depends first on effective planning of activities. To avoid unexpected money problems, financial managers must examine how money comes into and leaves the company and then develop appropriate financial plans.

Managers' failure to understand the need for the right amount of money at the right time can be one of the most critical problems a company faces. For example, a product that is selling well offers great potential, but it also creates a need for money to allow the company to meet consumer demand for the product. If sales of the product double from $500,000 to $1,000,000, the company may require an additional $250,000 in equipment and supplies. But if the profit margin is only 15 percent, profits will provide only $150,000 of the money needed for expansion (0.15 × $1,000,000). The additional $100,000 must come from somewhere.

Financial plan
A plan that forecasts the company's short-term and long-term needs for funds, develops budgets to meet those needs, and establishes financial control.

A **financial plan** forecasts the company's short-term and long-term needs for funds, develops budgets to meet those needs, and establishes financial control. Financial planning typically includes three major activities: forecasting financial needs, developing budgets to meet those needs, and establishing financial control.

FORECASTING FINANCIAL NEEDS

The financial forecast is based on a comprehensive review and analysis of the company's objectives and operations. Several forecasts should result from this review, including a forecast of sales, a forecast of marketing expenditures, and a production forecast that includes an analysis of inventory, labor costs, overhead, and general administrative costs.

Sales forecasts focus on revenues that should flow to the organization as it sells its goods and services. A long-term forecast usually covers a period of 5 to 10 years. A short-term forecast applies to a period of less than one year. The production budget and almost all other aspects of financial planning are the result of projections based on the sales forecast for the time period being considered.

Exhibit 21.1 shows how the long-term and short-term sales forecasts, the resulting budgets, and the calculation of the various financial statements are interrelated in the financial planning process.

One of the best methods for determining a company's financial needs is to develop projected financial statements called *pro forma statements.* The discussion that follows shows the process leading up to the development and use of pro forma income statements, cash budgets, and balance sheets.

BUDGETING FOR FINANCIAL NEEDS

Budget
A detailed plan that outlines the acquisition and use of financial and other resources over a specific time period.

A **budget** outlines the planned acquisition and use of financial and other resources over a specific time period. An operating budget outlines planned activities of company operations and the resources needed to accomplish them.[3] A small company may need only a single operating budget indicating what will be spent on salaries, wages, advertising, and other expenses related to operations. A large company may have separate operating budgets for the production department, the marketing department, and general administration. Such a company uses expense budgets outlining essential operational activities performed in various departments and the expenditures needed to complete them. For example, the production

Exhibit 21.1 **FINANCIAL FORECASTING**

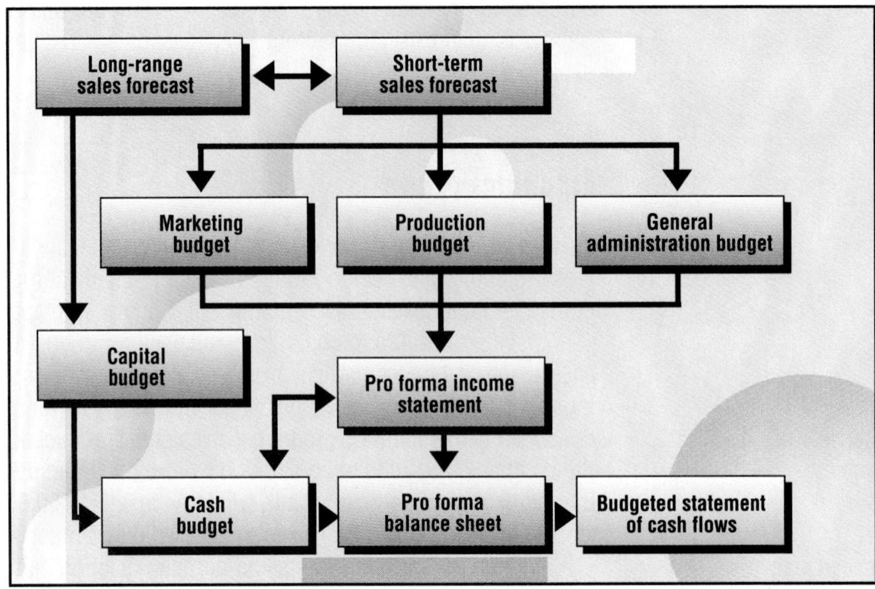

department may have a direct labor budget and a direct materials budget. An expense budget might help a production manager develop production and inventory schedules or a marketing manager to plan for advertising, sales personnel, and other necessary expenses that support the sales forecast.[4]

Capital Budgets. A capital budget is a detailed plan for spending money on major (capital) assets such as new plants, equipment, and land. These budgets are particularly important for companies that are expanding their operations, since acquiring capital assets often requires large amounts of money. Capital asset purchases often need to be financed by borrowing money through long-term loans, issuing bonds, or selling ownership equity.

Capital assets can speed up production and improve quality. Many companies routinely budget for capital spending. Cooper Industries, a $6.2-billion-a-year manufacturer in Houston, has doubled its capital spending since 1990. New equipment has made Cooper's manufacturing processes faster and improved the quality of its products.[5]

As these budgets come together, the financial manager can estimate and develop a cash budget, a pro forma income statement, and a pro forma balance sheet. By examining these budgets, the financial manager will know where money will come from, when it will be used, and when the company will have too much or too little cash.

Cash budget
A detailed plan showing how cash resources will be acquired and used over a specified time period.

Cash Budgets. A **cash budget** is a detailed plan showing how cash resources will be acquired and used over a specified time period. Generally, a cash budget is prepared for each quarter, and each quarter is combined into the totals for the year (see Exhibit 21.2). This budget is critical, since cash is required to support the various activities of the business. It consolidates much of the information contained in the other budgets and forecasts.

The cash budget consists of four major elements:

1. Receipts of cash
2. Disbursements of cash

Exhibit 21.2 **A CASH BUDGET**

The Johnson Company
Cash Budget
For the Year Ended December 31, 19XX

	Quarter				
	1	**2**	**3**	**4**	**Year**
Cash balance, beginning	$ 43,600	$ 41,000	$ 41,000	$ 40,500	$ 43,600
Add receipts					
Collections from customers	240,000	495,000	765,000	540,000	2,040,000
Total cash available before current financing	283,600	536,000	806,000	580,500	2,083,600
Less disbursements					
Direct materials	59,600	76,000	120,500	89,350	345,450
Direct labor	83,000	193,600	210,000	124,000	610,600
Manufacturing overhead	69,000	98,000	104,000	76,000	347,000
Selling and administrative	94,000	133,700	187,000	124,150	538,850
Income taxes	17,000	20,000	18,000	18,000	73,000
Equipment purchases	25,000	18,700	3,500	—	47,200
Dividends	15,000	15,000	15,000	15,000	60,000
Total disbursements	362,600	555,000	658,000	446,500	2,022,100
Excess (deficiency) of cash	(79,000)	(19,000)	148,000	134,000	61,500
Financing					
Borrowings (at beginning)	120,000	60,000	—	—	180,000
Repayments	—	—	(100,000)	(80,000)	(180,000)
Interest (at 10% per year)	—	—	(7,500)	(6,500)	(14,000)
Total financing	120,000	60,000	(107,500)	(86,500)	(14,000)
Cash balance, ending	$ 41,000	$ 41,000	$ 40,500	$ 47,500	$ 47,500

3. A statement of cash excess or deficiency
4. A statement of financing

As Exhibit 21.2 illustrates, the receipts section contains the opening cash balance. Any cash receipts expected during the quarter are added to the opening balance. The disbursements section reports all cash payments planned for the quarter. These include payments for direct (raw) materials, labor, overhead, income taxes, and so on. The cash excess or deficiency is the difference between the totals for cash receipts and cash disbursements. If a deficiency exists, financial managers must decide how to obtain the needed funds. If an excess results, financial managers must decide how to invest the idle cash.

The financing section of the cash budget provides a borrowing plan. It identifies the amount to be borrowed and projects the interest that will be paid on the borrowed money. Since the company has planned for both borrowing and interest payments well in advance of its need, a bank or other collaborator will likely approve the loan request.

Anticipating cash requirements for routine operating expenses can help companies finance growth. For example, Hi-Tech Manufacturing Company in Longmont, Colorado, which assembles printed-circuit boards, expected 1993 sales to triple. So it hired more than 100 people supplied by Western Temporary Services. Western permitted High-Tech to pay for its services 30 days after the temporary workers started. That gave Hi-Tech an extra monthly pool of $50,000 to finance growth.[6]

Failure to invest in capital assets led to the decline of the U.S. steel industry. While the rest of the world was modernizing its steel foundries, U.S. steelmakers were relying on inefficient manufacturing processes. Could other U.S. industries go the way of this steelworks near Pittsburgh? Absolutely—unless they budget for capital spending.[7]

Pro Forma Financial Statements. Managers prepare three pro forma financial statements from information gathered in the financial plan. The first, the pro forma income statement, projects anticipated sales, expenses, and income. It is important to distinguish between income and cash flow. Cash flow is affected by customer payments, cash payments for expenses, borrowing, and similar transactions. Although income includes cash related to revenues and expenses, it is also affected by noncash items such as depreciation. Income is the better indicator of a company's ability to generate returns for its owners, whereas cash flow reflects the company's ability to finance income-producing operations.

The second statement, the pro forma balance sheet (sometimes called the master budget), projects future assets, liabilities, and owner's equity. The pro forma budget ensures that all other budgets and items in the financial plan fit together. It also helps managers determine whether the financial plan is yielding results that are in the best interests of the company and its owners.

Finally, the budgeted statement of cash flows reflects changes in the pro forma balance sheet accounts resulting from cash transactions. This statement permits financial managers to forecast and evaluate their receipts and payments of cash.

ESTABLISHING FINANCIAL CONTROL

Financial control
The process of periodically comparing the actual revenues, costs, expenses, and cash flow with the budgets.

After a company has identified short-term and long-term financial needs and created appropriate budgets, the next step in financial planning is to establish financial control. **Financial control** is the process of periodically comparing the actual revenues, costs, expenses, and cash flow with the budgets. Inadequate financial control over expenses and insufficient cash flow are two of the three most common reasons for business failure. The third is undercapitalization. Consider, for example, the experience of Rochelle Zabarkes, who opened the popular Adriana's Bazaar in New York. Although daily revenues averaged $1,100, the company was undercapitalized. Zabarkes defaulted on a $145,000 bank loan and was so desperate for cash that she once misappropriated a New York state check for $5,000. The check had been made out to Zabarkes to pay a business consultant but she used the check to pay other creditors.[8]

Financial control permits managers to detect deviations from the financial plan and decide on corrective actions. For example, suppose an operating budget calls for factory expense of $150,000 during one quarter. If managers discovered that actual expenses were $175,000, they would need to determine the cause of the deviation. If sales were unexpectedly high, the higher than expected factory expense might seem justified. However, this expense may have a negative effect on cash flow. Only by evaluating all deviations from the financial plan can financial control be maintained.

Financial control is more effective with the use of computers. Software programmers have designed many financial planning computer programs. These include simple spreadsheet programs such as Excel and Lotus 1-2-3, as well as more sophisticated financial software designed for specific financial analyses.

But computers can do more than just process data. They also reduce the number of employees needed. Payroll costs are one of the biggest drains on cash, so when Merrill Lynch faced escalating costs and declining profits, it turned to computers. By using computer technology that reduced paperwork and duplication of tasks, Merrill Lynch was able to eliminate nearly 8,000 jobs, restoring cash flow and profits.[9]

CASH MANAGEMENT: USES AND SOURCES OF FUNDS

Companies use various resources to produce goods and services. Managers must determine what the best uses for the company's resources are and where to obtain the funds for those uses. Financial managers sometimes refer to this aspect of cash management as *uses and sources of funds.* The focus of attention when evaluating the uses and sources of funds is the company's cash.

CASH MANAGEMENT

Managing cash is becoming increasingly complex in today's global and technologically sophisticated business world. Companies are finding it critical to squeeze all possible profits out of their resources. While cash is indeed a desirable resource, it earns no profits unless it is invested in other profit-earning assets. Idle cash ties up operating funds just as excess inventory and production facilities do. Thus, it is the job of financial managers to keep cash at a minimum but have it available when needed. For this reason, financial managers spend considerable time controlling the company's cash flow and finding ways to invest excess cash balances profitably.

Managing Cash Flows. Jack Welch, CEO of General Electric Company, advises, "The three most important things you need to measure in a business are customer satisfaction, employee satisfaction, and cash flow...cash flow is the pulse—the key vital sign of a company."[10] **Cash flow** refers to the inflows and outflows of cash that occur as a company conducts its daily operations.

Cash flow
The inflows and outflows of cash that occur as a company conducts its daily operations.

While a business should not hold large sums of excess, idle cash, maintaining an adequate level of cash is important. Perhaps the most important reason is to have money on hand to cover expenses when cash flows are less than normal. For companies in seasonal industries, such as landscapers, building contractors, and toy manufacturers, cash inflows in any given period are uncertain. This uncertainty increases the importance of effective cash management.

Cash balances are strongly affected by the cash flowing through the company. Cash flow relies on the payment pattern of customers, the speed with which suppliers and creditors process payments, and the efficiency of the banking system. Thus, managing cash flow requires a large amount of timing and a small amount of luck.

In the simple cash flow cycle shown in Exhibit 21.3, the sale of the company's products and services generates either cash or an account receivable that will be collected at a later time.

Exhibit 21.3 **THE CASH FLOW CYCLE**

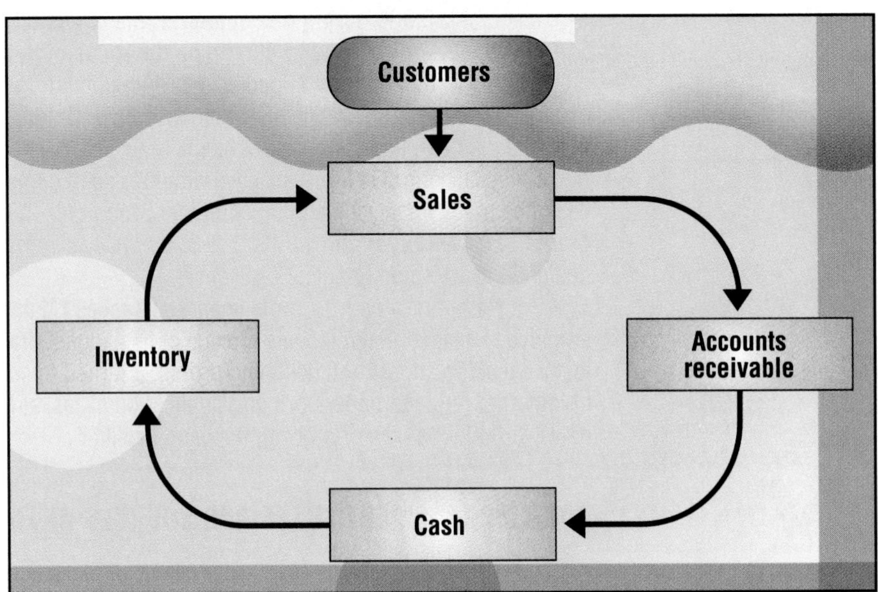

At collection the receivable becomes cash, which is used to pay for supplies and materials and to support the company's operations. Cash management requires that managers know when checks written for payments will arrive at the company's bank, when collections of receivables are expected, and when inventory must be paid for.

Managing Float. As we discussed in Chapter 19, the cash balance recorded in a company's checking account ledger may differ quite sharply from the company's "real" cash balance at the bank. The difference between the real balance at the bank and the balance shown in the company's records is called the *float.* Float arises from time delays in mailing, processing, and clearing checks through the banking system. Float gives the financial manager an opportunity to manage the timing of check clearing through activities such as collection of accounts receivable.

Some companies actually operate with a *negative* cash balance on their bank records, knowing that the float will carry them through to the next cash receipts. This saves them sizable interest payments on funds they would otherwise have to borrow. But collections of accounts receivable and cash sales must be dependable, or the company may end up overdrawn at the bank.

Managing Accounts Receivable. Many small businesses use accounts receivable to generate sales. A recent Dun & Bradstreet survey of small businesses showed that 77 percent extend credit. An important aspect of cash flow management is collecting money owed to the company. This is especially true for accounts receivable. Payments often are delayed because invoices are hard to read and understand or are not addressed to the person who processes payments and arrive 30 to 45 days after the goods or services are delivered.[11]

Managers can take a number of actions to ensure prompt conversion of receivables into cash. Perhaps the most common strategy is to offer discounts to customers who pay their accounts promptly. Carpet manufacturers, for example, commonly offer a cash discount for

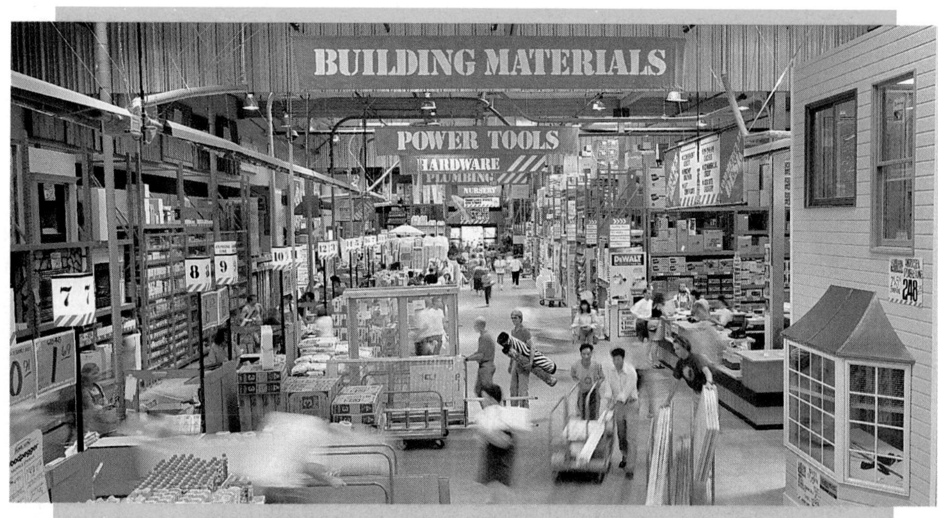

Home Depot stores like this one in Campbell, California, stock over 35,000 items that shoppers need for their homes. The inventory is set up so that shoppers can easily find their way around. Home Depot is successful because it uses its financial resources to buy income-producing inventory.[12]

prompt payment of invoices. Typical discounts are expressed in terms such as 2/10, n/30. In this case, the buyer may deduct 2 percent from the invoice price if payment is made within 10 days of the invoice date. After 10 days, the net price (full) must be paid. Thus, if a roll of carpeting costs $3,000, a 2 percent discount amounts to $60, and the buyer needs to send only $2,940 rather than the full $3,000. This is equivalent to an effective annual interest rate of 36.7 percent—an exceptionally high rate. Furthermore, if a retailer buys 20 rolls of carpeting each month, taking advantage of discounts may add $1,200 to monthly profits. This is a major incentive for the retailer to pay promptly and improves the manufacturer's cash flow.

Managing Disbursements and Inventory. From the carpet retailer's viewpoint, some advantage can be gained by delaying payment as long as possible. This is sometimes difficult to manage, however, since excessive delays may cause the retailer to lose discounts from the supplier. Also, when suppliers experience consistent payment problems with their customers, they may refuse to extend any more credit to them. Still, managers attempt to delay disbursements as long as possible without jeopardizing their companies' credit ratings or losing discounts.

One way to delay disbursements is to keep more than one bank account and use the account located the farthest geographical distance away to pay the supplier. This way the supplier receives the money on time, but the float is extended.

The most common way to manage disbursements is to manage the inventory of raw materials. For many firms, the largest use of cash is for inventory. Companies hold inventory to ensure that customer demands are met and that the items required for production are available when needed. Inventory management means balancing the costs of carrying inventory against the costs of stockouts. Using techniques like just-in-time and materials requirement planning (discussed in Chapter 9), can dramatically reduce the funds required for inventory. Procter & Gamble saves nearly $1 billion annually by using just-in-time arrangements with its suppliers.[13]

FOCUS ON COMPANY

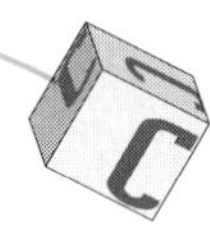

Rizzo Associates

Bill Rizzo, cofounder and CEO of Rizzo Associates, an environmental engineering company based in Natick, Massachusetts, knows the importance of monitoring a company's accounts payable and receivable. These two financial items can have dramatic effects on the company's cash flow and ultimate success. When Rizzo's company was much smaller—about 50 employees—he hired specialists in accounts payable and receivable. In addition, he meets weekly with the company's controller, the accounts payable clerk, and the collections manager. Since they can't devote equal attention to all receivables and payables, they assign priorities. Finally, they analyze all payable invoices when they arrive and all receivable invoices before they mail them to customers. This way, they can establish dates on which they will follow up if the accounts have not been cleared. Rizzo has a steady cash flow and now employs about 100 people.

USES OF FUNDS

Uses of funds fall into three areas:

1. Reducing liabilities (repaying short-term and long-term loans)
2. Reducing net worth (which arises from paying shareholder dividends, retiring company stock, and operating losses)
3. Increasing assets (inventory, accounts receivable, plant and equipment)

Reducing Liabilities. Corporate debt has increased more than tenfold since World War II. The growth in corporate debt is attributed to increasing costs of new technologies, the rapid growth of many companies, the impact of inflation, bad investing decisions, and inadequate operating income to fund growing operations.[14] Interest payments on a company's debt can reduce income to owners, so it is important to budget and use funds to service a company's debt.

Jack Nicklaus, the millionaire golfing legend, is a good example of the importance of reducing liabilities. Like most athletes, Nicklaus has investments in a variety of businesses, including gas and oil fields, travel agencies, and golf courses. At one point, his company had total liabilities of $150 million on businesses that were earning only $6 million a year. He sold some assets to generate cash and used $12 million of his own money to substantially reduce his liabilities. As a result, both his income and his cash flow improved, as did his golf game.[15]

Reducing Net Worth. Although it may seem strange to use funds to reduce a company's net worth, there are many good reasons for doing this. First, this is how owners receive cash from the company. While dividend payments reduce the company's net worth, they represent increases to an owner's personal net worth.

Corporate stock repurchase The use of company assets—usually cash—to buy back shares of stock from existing shareholders.

Second, a company with excess cash may choose to make a **corporate stock repurchase**, that is, use assets—usually cash—to buy back shares of its stock from shareholders. Repurchasing stock may increase the demand for the shares and thus benefit company owners. Stock repurchases also tend to increase earnings per share and the share market price.

Third, the use of funds may reduce net worth when a company loses money as a result of operations. As you learned in Chapter 18, profits and losses are recorded against owner's

Exhibit 21.4 **SOURCES OF FUNDING**

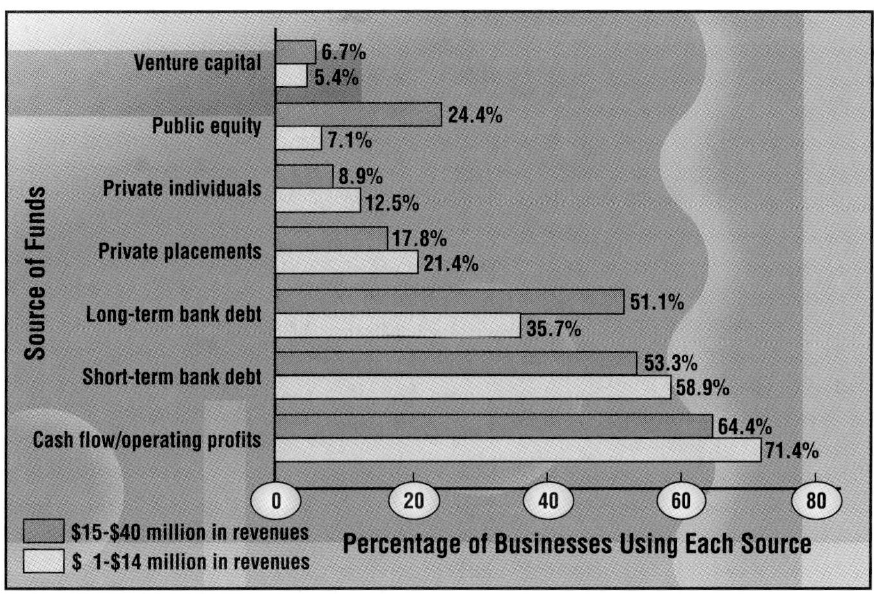

equity or net worth. Losses reduce the value of the company. Owners who then sell their shares of ownership must accept less for them.

Increasing Assets. One of the most aggressive uses of funds is to increase income-producing assets. Such assets include plant and equipment, inventory, and accounts receivable. For retailers and other service-oriented companies, inventory is their competitive advantage. Home Depot is the top-ranked service company in the United States based on 10-year growth in earnings per share. Its net income was over $360 million by 1993. It achieved this remarkable growth by investing in an extensive and high-quality inventory of products for home care and repair. The stores are packed to the rafters with plywood, paint, power tools, and 35,000 other items for the home.[16]

SOURCES OF FUNDS

Companies obtain funding from three major sources: equity funding, debt funding, and leasing.

Equity funding
Funds raised from owners; also called *equity capital.*

Equity Funding. Equity funding, also called *equity capital,* refers to funds raised from owners through means such as

1. Initial sale of stock to investors
2. Additional investments by shareholders
3. Investments made by venture capitalists (who receive a share of ownership in return)
4. Profits from operations that are plowed back into the company instead of being distributed to shareholders

As Exhibit 21.4 shows, companies differ in their approaches to funding growth. Growth requires cash, and managers must decide how they will get the cash to finance growth. Some corporations emphasize growth through the use of retained earnings, funds generated internally and kept in the business rather than distributed to owners. These earnings are used to finance future growth. The owners or shareholders benefit from the increasing value of the companies' stocks rather than from earnings paid to them in the form of dividends. It is common for growth oriented companies to retain as much as 80 to 90 percent of their profits.[17]

Other companies, however, need additional money to finance growth. High-tech companies such as Apple Computer, Pioneer Electronics, and Texas Instruments often face rapid growth in demand for their products, far above what they can finance through retained earnings. They must either find other sources of money or pass up the growth opportunities. These companies may borrow money or issue additional stock. For example, when Werner Enterprises, an interstate trucking company, expanded its service into three new markets, it had to upgrade its fleet of 3,300 tractors and 8,000 trailers. It also had to equip its trucks with portable computers that connect to headquarters by satellite. The company used the proceeds from a new stock offering to pay off debt that had financed the new truck purchases.[18] Spectrum Holobyte, Inc., which has sold more than 12 million copies of video games for personal computers, has also used equity funding to finance growth. In 1994, Spectrum offered 2 million shares in the company to raise $19 million to fund new software developments and pay off debt.[19]

Venture Capitalists. The need for cash is never greater than when a company is just starting out. At this time, the company has few assets other than the ideas, hopes, and dreams of its founders. The new-business owner often lacks enough personal assets to finance the company through its first year or two of operations. During this time, the company's cash flow will be under heavy pressure. Until the public gets to know the firm's products and services, rev-

STREET SMART

How to Be a Venture Capitalist

Being a successful venture capitalist is a tough job. About two of three new businesses fail, so the one that succeeds must be a real winner, to pay for the losses incurred on the other two. Successful venture capital investors suggest a checklist of things to look for before plunging into a new venture.

- Are you convinced that there is a market for the product or service? Read the business plan carefully to be sure you believe there really is a demand for the product or service.
- Has management laid out a detailed plan for expanding the business? If the business plan is general, without specifics on how to get from A to B, the chances are that a real plan doesn't exist.
- Does the management team have enough experience in the field and a record of past successes? New businesses succeed only if the product is right and the execution is excellent.
- Is management truthful? Some venture capital firms even hire private detectives to do background checks of the principals.
- Are your rights adequately protected? Make sure the investment agreement safeguards your interests and provides you with the right options whether the business succeeds or fails. A major mistake is not providing a way to get your money out when the business succeeds, and being frustrated with small returns.

enues will be low. Expenses, however, will be great, especially if buildings and production equipment need to be acquired. To begin a new company, the owner(s) may seek additional money from friends and family. But even this may not be enough.

For these reasons, many new companies seek money from venture capital firms. *Venture capital companies* look for promising investments that offer large returns on their money. In 1980, the average venture capital company had assets of $15 million to $40 million. Today more than a dozen large capital funds have over $100 million to invest in promising companies. Managers of these funds seek investments in the range of $250,000 to $1,500,000.

In the typical arrangement, the venture capital company receives shares of either common or preferred stock in the new company in return for its long-term investment. Most venture capital companies ask for 30 to 40 percent ownership, since demanding a larger share may destroy the original owner's incentive to make the company succeed. To obtain this type of financing, the owner must have a sound business plan and a solid proposal for how the money will be used. The average venture capital firm receives more than 1,000 proposals a year and will fund fewer than 5.[20]

Venture capitalists are responding to our changing culture. For years the venture capital industry ignored companies owned by women. But recently several venture capital funds have emerged to provide female entrepreneurs with capital. Among them are Women's Equity Fund in Boulder, Colorado, New Era Capital Partners in Los Angeles, and Inroads Capital Partners in Chicago.[21]

Other sources of venture capital are available to needy entrepreneurs, including some quasi-government agencies. The most prominent source is the Small Business Investment Companies (SBICs), created in 1958. Although an SBIC is not a government agency, it is licensed by the Small Business Administration (SBA), which is a federal agency. An SBIC is operated as a private lending institution, often as a subsidiary of a commercial bank or holding company. An SBIC provides capital to small businesses, especially during a company's early years, when normal sources of funds are limited. In exchange, the company sells common stock or long-term convertible debt that the SBIC can, at its option, convert into shares of common stock.

Investment Bankers. Many companies avoid venture capital firms because they do not want to give up so much ownership control to one investor. In addition, more mature companies can obtain equity funding with more favorable terms. Many of these companies turn to investment bankers.

Investment bankers provide a link between the company in need of cash and the actual investor. An **investment banker** designs and packages a security offering by the company and then sells the offering to the general public. These offerings typically take the form of stock, either common or preferred, although a number of alternatives exist. As an intermediary, the investment banker performs a number of functions, including underwriting the securities issue as discussed in Chapter 20.

Investment banker
A firm that specializes in designing and packaging a security offering by a company and then sells the offering to the general public.

There are many advantages and disadvantages to raising cash by issuing stock (see Exhibit 21.5). Perhaps the chief advantage to the company is that it eliminates the legal obligation to repay the money (as is the case with all loans).

Debt Funding. Debt funding, sometimes called *debt capital,* consists of money borrowed from lenders such as banks.

Debt funding
Money borrowed from lenders such as banks; sometimes called *debt capital.*

Short-Term Financing. Companies frequently need cash on a short-term basis to manage problems caused by cyclical or seasonal fluctuations in inventory, accounts payable, and cash. Short-term financing—money that is to be repaid in less than two years—is appropriate for these situations. The most common sources of short-term financing are trade credit, bank loans, factoring, and commercial paper.

Exhibit 21.5 **ADVANTAGES AND DISADVANTAGES OF SELLING STOCK TO RAISE FUNDS**

Advantages	Disadvantages
Since shareholders are owners, the company is not obligated to repay the cash that was raised. This means the money can be used on a long-term basis for such purposes as buying land, buildings, and expensive equipment.	Shareholders can vote on company matters, unlike lenders. Thus, owners give up some control of the company when they issue stock.
The company has no legal obligation to pay dividends. Thus, all earnings can be retained by the company and reinvested in the business.	If dividends on the stock issues are declared, taxes will be paid on earnings *before* the dividends are computed. Interest, on the other hand, is a business expense, and taxes are paid *after* interest has been deducted.
Owner's equity does not adversely affect the company's ability to borrow money from banks. In fact, because there is more owner's equity, banks may be more willing to loan money in the future.	The need to satisfy shareholders sometimes distracts managers from the need to make hard decisions. Sometimes, for instance, managers may feel obligated to pay dividends, even though they need the money for cash flow purposes.
Selling stock is relatively quick and easy, especially if investment bankers are used.	

Trade credit
The practice of buying goods or services on credit.

Trade Credit. **Trade credit** is the practice of buying goods or services on credit and is offered by most sellers of goods and services. Trade credit represents an account payable for the company and is usually extended for 30 to 60 days. It is often accompanied by discount terms to induce the company to make timely payments. As mentioned earlier, such discounts are an important source of earnings for the company and should be taken if possible. Thus, while managers might be tempted to stretch out the payment period (as an indirect way to obtain additional short-term financing), they should think twice before doing so to avoid losing discounts. In addition, if the company builds a reputation among its suppliers of not paying its accounts payable promptly, suppliers will be less willing to grant favorable terms and prices. Suppliers may even refuse to do business with companies that abuse their trade credit privileges.

Prime interest rate
The base rate that banks charge their most creditworthy customers.

Bank Loans. Banks may provide funds for short-term and seasonal needs as well as for long-term growth. Two-thirds of business loans by commercial banks and lending institutions are short term in nature.[22] Often companies establish long-term relationships with their banks that include many services such as checking account services, long-term loans, and a variety of short-term financial arrangements. For reliable business customers, the interest rate charged on short-term bank loans is near the prime interest rate. The **prime interest rate** is the base rate that the bank charges its most creditworthy customers. The average business customer can expect to pay 1 or 2 percent above this rate.

Unsecured loan
A loan for which the borrower pledges no collateral but simply signs a promissory note.

The most common type of short-term business loan is an **unsecured loan**, for which the borrower pledges no collateral but simply signs a promissory note. Most promissory notes are due in one to six months, usually in one lump sum rather than in monthly installments. In addition to unsecured loans, a company may be able to arrange a line of credit. A line of credit is an agreement between the bank and the borrower that specifies some amount of funds that the bank will lend over a stated period of time. Thus, the company need not complete a loan application each time it borrows money as long as it has not used more than is available in the line of credit. The New Line Cinema Corporation, which has distributed a string of profitable movies such as *Nightmare on Elm Street* and *Teenage Mutant Ninja Turtles,* has a $75 million line of credit from several banks, including Chemical Bank. This permits New Line to gamble on big-budget blockbusters like Robert Altman's recent movie, *The Player.*[23]

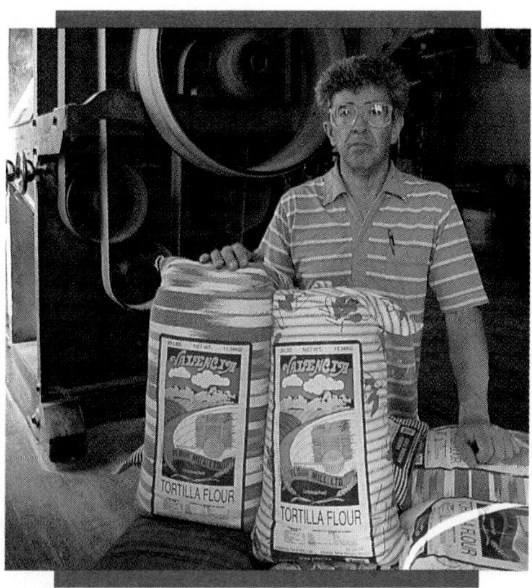

José Cordova is an engineer with a degree in milling technology and 22 years' experience in helping 3M improve its products and quality systems. When he decided to return to his native village in Jarales, New Mexico, and reopen the mill his grandfather founded in 1914, he knew how to do it. Backed by personal savings, a small bank loan, and a financial plan, his small company, Valencia Flour Mill Ltd., now produces specialty flours for tortillas and sopaipillas.[24]

Secured loan
A loan that is backed by collateral pledged by the borrower to support the loan in the event of default.

Inventory loan
A loan that uses specific inventory items as collateral.

Banks also make a variety of short-term secured loans. A **secured loan** is backed by collateral pledged by the borrower to support the loan in the event of default. In general, short-term loans are collateralized by short-term or current assets rather than by long-term assets such as buildings. The most common short-term secured business loans are **inventory loans**—loans that use specific inventory items as collateral. Sometimes called *floor planning,* inventory loans are commonly used by automobile, appliance, and furniture retailers. To serve as collateral, the inventory items must be individually identifiable, such as by serial numbers. They must also be of significant value, usually several hundred dollars. Each item in the inventory is then pledged separately to secure the loan. The total amount of the loan is adjusted each time a new item is added or an old item is sold. If the value of the items is quite large, as in the case of automobiles, the bank may hold the title to each item. This ensures that when the item is sold, the loan will be reduced by that amount.

Factoring. Accounts receivable can also be used as collateral for secured loans. However, they are more difficult for the lender to track than other forms of collateral. There is no easy way to tell whether the company is paying back the loan at the same rate as money is collected from its customers. Thus, while a company can use its accounts receivable to help meet its short-term need for cash, companies more commonly factor their receivables.

Factoring involves selling the accounts receivable to some financial institution, often one that specializes in this activity. As you learned in Chapter 19, a *factor* buys the accounts receivable at a discount, paying cash to the company. The factor then collects its money from the accounts receivable customers according to the arrangements the company had with them. A major advantage of using factors to finance receivables is that the factor usually provides all credit and collection services.[25] At one time, Sears arranged to factor $550 million of its accounts receivable at 99 percent of face value, which allowed it to collect from all customers with minimal effort.[26]

FOCUS ON COLLABORATORS

Gotham Apparel

When Michael and Patricia Kipperman opened Gotham Apparel in New York in 1990, they lacked the financial resources they needed to fill the large number of orders they received. Their business assets were not sufficient as collateral for a bank loan, so they turned to another source of capital: factoring. Now the Kippermans sell their accounts receivable to Merchant Factors Corporation. If cash advances are required against receivables before the accounts are due for payment, the factor disburses up to 80 percent of the value of the receivables. The Kippermans must pay interest on this amount until their customers pay the invoices. When the invoices are paid, the Kippermans receive the balance of the receivables, minus interest charges and Merchant's commission.

Factoring has helped Gotham Apparel achieve remarkable growth in a short time. Annual sales zoomed from $8 million in its first year to over $20 million in its third year.

STREET SMART

The Five Questions Every Money Source Asks

Because the competition for financing is so fierce, don't even *think* about approaching lenders or investors unless you've done your homework. Each money source, of course, has his or her own list of favorite areas to probe. But here are some of the basic questions all will want you to answer:

- How much money do you need? Instead of being coy, financial people say, it's important to be specific about the amount of money you're seeking. Saying how much you need helps set a framework for the discussion and helps show how well you understand your business. Indeed, some people say if you can't provide a figure, you're not ready to ask for money.
- What do you plan to use it for? Lenders and investors will always want to know how you plan to use their money. Do you need it for working capital? For marketing? Or is it to buy out your partner? Different sources have different biases and different tolerances for risk. Your answer will help reveal your priorities and your approach to the business.
- How will this money improve the business? Nobody wants to pour money into a bottomless pit. Lenders and investors want to see how their loan or equity lowers your costs, expands your capability, and moves you closer to being self-sustaining. If you're not able to provide credible cash-flow projections showing this, it will be hard to drum up serious interest.
- How are you going to pay it back? Obviously, this is of paramount concern to banks these days. The first thing bankers want to understand is how you can pay off the loan from cash flow. (They'll ask you to pledge collateral—usually business or personal assets—but only as a secondary source.) While equity investors aren't asking for the same level of predictability, they'll still want to hear your thoughts on how—and when—they might become liquid.
- If Plan A doesn't work, what's your backup plan? If the business runs into trouble, banks and other lenders will attempt to recover their money by liquidating the collateral. But equity investors won't have that alternative. For them, the big concern is, What if you need more money? The more you can show you have other options for generating revenues and financing, the better off you'll be.

Commercial paper
A short-term unsecured promissory note issued to the general public in minimum units of $25,000.

Commercial Paper. For large, well-known firms, commercial paper is an important source of short-term financing. **Commercial paper** is a short-term, unsecured promissory note issued to the general public in minimum units of $25,000. Commercial paper usually matures in nine months or less. Since it is unsecured, small companies and businesses with poor credit ratings are unable to sell commercial paper.

Interest rates on commercial paper tend to be a little lower than rates charged on unsecured bank loans. But for many people, that rate is higher than what they can earn in the money market or savings accounts. Thus, there is a ready supply of individuals willing to buy commercial paper.

The commercial paper market is affected by unfavorable experiences. When the Penn Central Railroad went bankrupt in 1970, it defaulted on $85 million in commercial paper. This experience made investors unwilling to buy commercial paper for some time. Companies that had abandoned their banks in favor of lower-cost commercial paper as a source of short-term financing had to go back to the banks. However, many banks would no longer lend them money at the favorable prime interest rates charged to "loyal" customers. The lesson here is that it pays to preserve good relationships with your banker.

Long-Term Financing. Companies that need funds to acquire long-term assets, such as a new building, or expensive production equipment, often seek long-term sources of funds. Long-term financing refers to money that is to be repaid to lenders over a period longer than two years.

Long-term financing is an alternative to selling stock to venture capitalists and investment bankers. The most common long-term financing arrangement is a simple long-term loan.

New companies rarely get long-term loans from banks, since banks view them as high risk. However, once a company is established and has dependable cash flows, bank loans are fairly easy to get. *Long-term loans* are usually repaid in 3 to 10 years but can go for as long as 12 or 15 years.

Long-term business loans are offered by commercial banks, insurance companies, and business finance companies. In addition, some sellers of large equipment may offer long-term repayment terms. This arrangement is similar to the loans made by divisions of automobile manufacturers such as Ford. If you buy a new Ford, you can obtain a loan for that purchase from Ford Motor Credit Company. This is one way the manufacturer can increase sales and earn a return on its equipment loans as well.

However, the cost of long-term loans is often high. In addition, interest and principal payments will affect cash flow in the future, so the borrower must be sure that additional revenues will offset the additional cash outflow. These drawbacks make other sources of long-term debt attractive.

FOCUS ON COMPANY

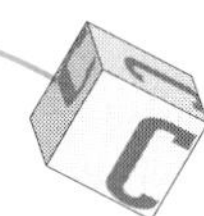

Euro Disney

When The Walt Disney Company planned to build Euro Disney, it did not plan to lose $1 million a day. But that is what is happening at its resort and theme park on the outskirts of Paris. Sky-high overhead and interest payments on loans are threatening the project less than two years after its grand opening.

Although European visitors love the park, which enjoys just under 1 million visitors a month, it may be the largest financial disaster ever experienced by the popular American company. Heavy reliance on debt just as interest rates started to rise and poor financial planning have proven to be its undoing. Former Disney executives, bankers, and others say Disney's biggest mistakes were overambitious plans to develop the site and Euro Disney's financial plan.

Exhibit 21.6 **TYPES OF BONDS**

Type of Bond	Description
Secured Bonds	
Collateral trust	Bonds secured by the general credit of the company as well as specific property for which it was used. For example, if the bond proceeds were used to buy a fleet of trucks, the trucks would serve as collateral.
Mortgage bonds	Bonds secured by real property, such as buildings or equipment.
Unsecured Bonds	
Convertible bonds	Bonds that can be exchanged for another security, usually common stock.
Debenture bonds	Bonds secured only by the general credit of the firm, plus any unpledged assets.
Bonds with Special Repayment Features	
Coupon bonds	Bonds with coupons attached that the bondholder must submit to an agent for repayment. No longer used.
Zero coupon bonds	Bonds that pay no interest prior to maturity. The investor's earnings come from the difference between the purchase price and the par value.

The financial plan depended on a highly optimistic financial scenario with no room for glitches. It placed the risk on outside investors, keeping much of the profit potential for the company. A finance company was set up to own the park and lease it back to an operating company, Euro Disney SCA. Disney kept only a 17 percent stake in this company but kept 49 percent of the equity in the operating company. Euro Disney would manage the resort for hefty fees and royalties. But none of this has worked as Disney hoped—and certainly not as its lenders hoped.

Corporate bonds are the most common alternative to long-term loans for large U.S. corporations. Exhibit 21.6 shows various types of bonds and their features. As discussed in Chapter 20, a bond is a contract of indebtedness issued by a corporation. The bond agreement specifies basic terms such as the par value, the interest rate, and the maturity date. **Par value** refers to the principal or face value, which commonly is $1,000. All details about the bond issue are contained in a legal document called the bond **indenture**. The two major items in the indenture pertain to the security provisions of the bond and the methods of repayment.

Par value
The principal or face value of a bond.

Indenture
A legal document that contains all details about a bond issue.

Secured bonds contain pledges of specified assets to the investor in the event of default by the borrower. Mortgage bonds, discussed in Chapter 20, are the most common secured bonds and typically pledge real property such as equipment. Mortgage bonds are intended to offer some security to the investor. But that is not always the case, as many bondholders of Continental Airlines learned in 1990. Fine print provisions in $350 million in mortgage bonds allowed Continental to sell many of the most valuable planes that secured the bonds to raise cash. This decreased the value of the bonds which Continental then bought back for much less than $350 million.[27]

Secured bond
A bond that pledges specific assets to the investor in the event of default by the borrower.

Leasing. When a company lacks the resources to purchase capital assets, it may arrange a long-term lease. A **lease** is a contractual agreement between a *lessor* (the owner of the equipment) and a *lessee* (the user of the equipment) that calls for the lessee to pay the lessor an agreed-upon payment for using the equipment. Leasing has become a popular means of acquiring equipment such as airplanes, computers, and satellites. Airlines and railroads lease huge amounts of equipment. Many retail chains lease the bulk of their retail buildings and warehouses.[28]

Lease
A contractual agreement that calls for the lessee to pay the lessor an agreed-upon payment for using equipment owned by the lessor.

When Goudreau Corporation, a Massachusetts construction company, needed to acquire equipment, owner Henry Goudreau negotiated 36-month capital leases on nearly $200,000

Atmel Corporation, a medium-sized microchip manufacturer in San Jose, California, competes effectively against Intel Corporation, the industry leader. George Perlegos, Atmel's founder and CEO, defied the conventional wisdom that chipmakers must own their own factories. Instead, Atmel leased chipmaking factories from bigger companies with excess capacity. Atmel didn't own a plant until 1989, when it bought one from Honeywell Inc. Atmel then expanded its wafer fabrication facilities extensively, adding a 180,000-square-foot building.

Atmel has a strong cash flow, with a $25 million cash pile and $51 million in long-term marketable securities. Its biggest expense—about 13 percent of revenue for R&D—is essential to its business, while fancy buildings are not.[29]

worth of trucks, machinery, office furniture, and a computer system. Goudreau explained, "Leasing helps us satisfy our bonding company without getting too tied up at the bank."[30]

As we saw in this chapter, financial management is a key to survival in our increasingly competitive economy. Managing cash flow and arranging short-term and long-term financing are important managerial responsibilities.

SUMMARY

1. ***Define* finance *and explain the role financial managers play in a company's long-term success.***
   Finance is the business function of obtaining and using funds to maximize company profit or shareholders' wealth. Whether a company is a start-up or a 100-year-old organization, how its assets and liabilities are managed is critical to its success. Financial managers construct financial plans and budgets, obtain funds needed to run the business, determine how financial resources will be used, and make investment decisions. Their financial activities include making loans, selling stocks and bonds, establishing credit policies for customers, arranging payment terms with suppliers, and managing taxes.

2. ***Describe the financial planning process.***
   Financial planning typically includes three major activities: forecasting financial needs, developing budgets to meet those needs, and establishing financial control. The financial forecast is based on a comprehensive review and analysis of the company's objectives and operations. Several forecasts should result from this review, including forecasts of sales, marketing expen-

ditures, and production costs. Sales forecasts yield projections on which most other aspects of financial planning are based. In the budgeting stage, financial managers plan for the acquisition and use of financial and other resources over a specific time period. The cash budget consolidates information contained in other budgets and forecasts and shows how cash resources will be acquired and used over a specified time period. Managers also prepare pro forma financial statements from this information.

3. ***Discuss the importance of establishing financial control.***
After a company has identified short-term and long-term financial needs and created appropriate budgets, the next step in financial planning is to establish financial control. Financial control is the process of periodically comparing the actual revenues, costs, expenses, and cash flow with the budgets. Financial control permits managers to detect deviations from the financial plan and decide on corrective actions.

4. ***Explain how float can benefit companies.***
Float is the difference between a company's real balance at the bank and the balance shown in the company's records. Float arises from time delays in mailing, processing, and clearing checks through the banking system. Float gives the financial manager an opportunity to manage the timing of check clearing through activities such as collection of accounts receivable. Float can save companies sizable interest payments on funds they would otherwise have to borrow.

5. ***Describe the importance of managing accounts receivable.***
An important aspect of cash flow management is collecting money owed to the company. This is especially true for accounts receivable. Managers can take a number of actions to ensure prompt conversion of receivables into cash. Perhaps the most common strategy is to offer discounts to customers who pay their accounts promptly. Discounts can help boost profits for customers and improve the company's cash flow.

6. ***Discuss the importance of managing inventory.***
For many firms, the largest use of cash is for inventory. Companies hold inventory to ensure that customer demands are met and that the items required for production are available when needed. Inventory management means balancing the costs of carrying inventory against the costs of stockouts. Using techniques like just-in-time and materials requirement planning can dramatically reduce the funds required for inventory.

7. ***Explain three major uses of funds in a company.***
Companies use funds to reduce liabilities, reduce net worth, and increase assets. By repaying liabilities, companies can eliminate interest payments and increase profits. When net worth is reduced by paying dividends or retiring company stock, the owners of a company benefit either from receiving cash or having the value of the company's stock increase. But when net worth is reduced as a result of operating losses, the owners also suffer financial losses. Funds also are used to acquire income-producing assets. This may be the most important use of assets, which should increase profits and ultimately the net worth of the company.

8. ***Describe the major sources of funds for a company.***
Companies obtain funding from two major sources: debt and equity. Debt funding consists of money borrowed from lenders such as banks. Equity funding includes funds raised from owners through means such as the initial sale of stock, additional investments by owners, investments by venture capitalists, and retained earnings. Venture capital companies look for promising investments that offer large returns on their money. Investment bankers specialize in designing, packaging, and selling securities of other companies to the general public. Debt funding can take the form of either short-term or long-term financing. Short-term financing—money to be repaid in less than two years—is appropriate in cases of cyclical or seasonal fluctuations in business. The most common sources of short-term financing are trade credit, bank loans, factoring, and commercial paper. Trade credit is the practice of buying goods or services on credit. Bank loans can be secured or unsecured. Factoring involves selling accounts receivable to some financial

institution. Commercial paper is a short-term, unsecured promissory note issued to the general public. Long-term financing—money to be repaid over a period longer than two years—is used by companies that need funds to acquire long-term assets such as buildings. Common sources of long-term financing include venture capitalists, investment bankers, and debt financing. The most common forms of debt financing are long-term loans and corporate bonds.

9. ***Discuss the use of leasing as an alternative method for acquiring capital assets.***
Leasing is an important alternative to the use of equity or debt financing. A lease is a contractual agreement between a lessor (the owner of the equipment) and a lessee (the user of the equipment) that calls for the lessee to pay the lessor an agreed-upon payment for using the equipment. The lessee can thus acquire the equipment but avoid using large amounts of cash or debt.

KEY TERMS AND CONCEPTS

Finance (p. 504)
Financial manager (p. 504)
Financial plan (p. 505)
Budget (p. 505)
Cash budget (p. 506)
Financial control (p. 508)
Cash flow (p. 509)
Corporate stock repurchase (p. 512)
Equity funding (p. 513)
Investment banker (p. 515)
Debt funding (p. 515)
Trade credit (p. 516)
Prime interest rate (p. 516)
Unsecured loan (p. 516)
Secured loan (p. 517)
Inventory loan (p. 517)
Commercial paper (p. 519)
Par value (p. 520)
Indenture (p. 520)
Secured bond (p. 520)
Lease (p. 520)

DISCUSSION QUESTIONS

Company

1. What are the relative merits of various sources of short-term financing?
2. Why is the cash budget an important component of a company's cash management?
3. What factors influence a company's financial plan?

Customers

4. What benefits might customers obtain from a company's effective management of accounts receivable and inventory?
5. How does trade credit affect a retailer?

Competitors

6. How does taking advantage of cash discounts give a company an advantage over its competitors?
7. How does managing float give a company a competitive advantage?

Collaborators

8. What roles do financial collaborators play in meeting a company's financial needs?
9. How do venture capitalists serve as collaborators for a new business?

In Question: Take a Stand

You are CEO of a struggling motorcycle manufacturer. Although the company has a loyal following of customers, it also has $70 million in debt and a severe cash flow problem. During the last two years, it lost $57 *million. You think the cash flow and operating loss problems must be immediately resolved or the company will have to declare bankruptcy within two years. Some of the cash flow problems could be reduced by using a just-in-time (JIT) approach, which would shift inventory responsibilities to suppliers. But many of the suppliers are also struggling financially, and increasing their own inventories could create a cash management problem for them.*

What is the responsibility of your company to others that might be affected by your financial management solutions? Should you offer to help these suppliers as you shift to a JIT approach? Why or why not?

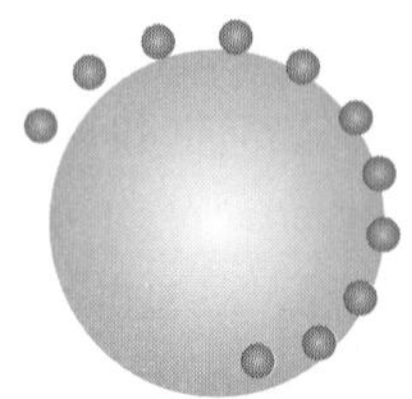

CASE 21.1
CENTRAL GARDEN & PET[31]

Central Garden & Pet is a growing distributor headquartered in Lafayette, California. It stocks over 18,000 gardening, pet, and pool supplies in its 30 warehouses and then delivers these products to retail customers such as Kmart, Target, and Home Depot. Central helps the retailers stock shelves and manage their inventories. It also instructs the retailers in the use of products ranging from pesticides to garden hoses.

In 1991, Central diversified by buying a pet supply distributor. Since then, it has acquired six small gardening and pet distributors with $70 million in annual sales. Securities analysts expect the company's 1994 net income to rise 65 percent, to $6.6 million and experience a 21 percent increase in revenues, to $411 million.

Questions

1. *What are some potential threats to financial success for Central Garden & Pet?*
2. *What would be the best means for funding Central's strategy of growing through acquisition?*
3. *If you were Central's financial manager, what would you recommend regarding the 30 warehouses and 18,000 items of inventory? Why?*

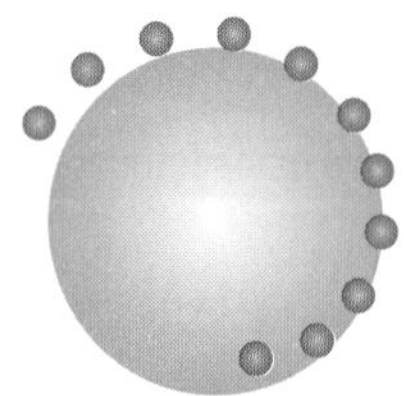

CASE 21.2
FINANCING THE GROWTH OF INTUIT[32]

Entrepreneurial graveyards are littered with the corpses of fast-rising companies that couldn't keep up as business grew more complex. Scott Cook of Intuit saw that moment coming in 1990 when sales of his Quicken personal financial software exploded.

Today Intuit is the largest maker of personal financial software. David Farina, a stock analyst at William Blair & Co. in Chicago, estimates that operating earnings will increase 30 percent in 1994, to $20 million on sales of $240 million. In a recent survey by *Soft Letter,* an industry publication, Intuit's peers voted it the best-managed software company—better than even Microsoft.

Cook, a former P&G brand manager and consultant at Bain & Co., started Intuit in 1983 with Tom Proulx, a college student studying programming. All of the thirty personal finance programs then on the market took longer to use than paying bills by hand. Their bright idea was to apply consumer marketing techniques—many of which Cook learned at P&G—to software. They got feedback from potential customers with surveys and product tests. When Quicken went on sale in 1984, it cut the average bill-paying time of three hours in half. Still, it took Cook and Proulx almost two years to break into the marketplace with their unknown company. Sales took off only after they gambled their last $100,000 on direct-response ads in publications like *PC Magazine* and *Byte.* By 1990, revenues were up to $33 million and growing fast.

That's when Cook realized that they had to shift from an entrepreneurial mind-set to one suitable to running a complex company. After interviewing dozens of venture capitalists, he recruited the aid of four who bought 20 percent of Intuit. Each contributed up to 20 hours a week of his time. Their advice didn't stop with financial matters. They also advised Cook and Proulx on strategic planning, operations, and other business issues. For instance, they suggested that Proulx should quit as head of R&D and concentrate on acquisitions and future business. The new R&D chief, experienced in product development, was able to greatly expand the number of products launched. Proulx went on to play a key role in Intuit's successful merger in 1993 with $70-million-a-year Chipsoft, maker of Turbo Tax.

Bringing in venture capitalists isn't for everyone. You need to have strong management skills in the first place and a company with a winning product.

Questions

1. *What alternatives (collaborators) to venture capitalists might Cook and Proulx have had available?*
2. *What were the advantages to Intuit of going the route of the venture capitalists?*
3. *What kinds of management skills are needed, besides financial management, in creating a successful growth company like Intuit?*

CHAPTER

22

MANAGING RISK AND INSURANCE

When you have studied this chapter, you will be able to:

1

Describe the two basic types of risk.

2

Define *risk management* and describe its critical elements.

3

Define *insurance* and explain what an insurance policy includes.

4

Describe the unique characteristics of insurance.

5

Discuss the characteristics of insurable risk.

6

Describe the various types of insurance.

7

Explain some of the major issues in the insurance industry today.

Natural disasters may seem unpredictable, but in fact they occur with some regularity. Fire swept the hills around Oakland, California, in 1993; earthquakes devastated the San Francisco area in 1989 and Los Angeles in 1994. Hawaii suffered from Hurricane Iniki in 1993, and the Midwest endured record flooding in 1993. Tornadoes regularly leave unpredictable paths of destruction in Texas, Oklahoma, Ohio, and other states.

When Hurricane Andrew roared through Miami it cost insurers some $16.5 billion. State Farm, the largest insurer in the United States, posted a $1.2 billion loss in 1992. Uninsured home and business owners also lost several billion dollars. Hurricane Andrew was the costliest insurance disaster in U.S. history, including the 1994 Los Angeles earthquake, which caused $7 billion in insured damages. Within a month of the hurricane, some 700,000 homeowners had filed insurance claims.

The thousands of claims created a new business opportunity for independent public insurance adjusters. Some adjusters were charging fees as high as 30 percent of the claim settlements until the Florida insurance authorities ruled that they could charge a maximum of 10 percent. Insurance commissioner Tom Gallagher claimed that some adjusters were encouraging homeowners to commit insurance fraud by reporting nonexistent losses.

The losses from Hurricane Andrew and other disasters have caused insurance companies nationwide to reconsider their insurance strategies. Fearing that a single South Florida storm could cost the industry over $75 billion, insurers in Florida have canceled policies of some 500,000 individuals and raised premiums for countless others. Insurance companies in other states have stopped writing new policies in afflicted areas.

This trend has forced newly created state-run associations to pick up the high risks. One association in Florida, headed by a Floridian whose policy was canceled, provides policies for residents who lack coverage. But the premiums typically run 25 to 35 percent higher than comparable coverage from private insurers. In Massachusetts, premiums in the state pool can run 60 percent higher than private rates. Insurers claim the risks of loss far exceed what current regulations allow them to charge for premiums. Until this gap closes, insurance companies are unlikely to resume writing policies in these high-risk areas.[1]

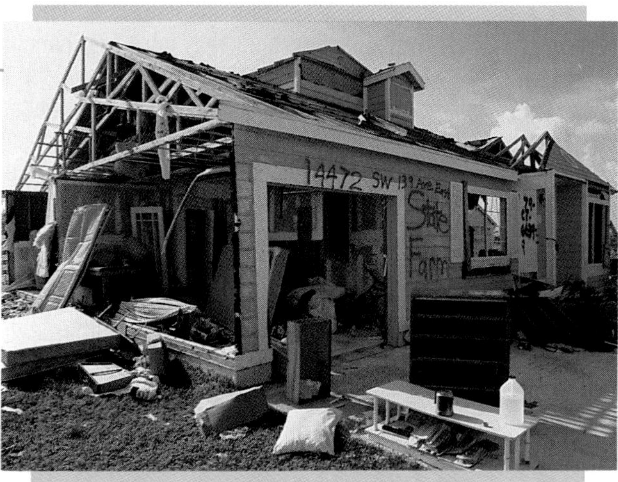

Feng shui—*meaning* wind *and* water—*is a 4,000-year-old technique for improving your chances in life by arranging furniture, travel dates, and company to take maximum advantage of the interplay of luck and natural forces. Many Hong Kong business tycoons will not proceed with a building or an investment without calling in the* feng shui *guru. This is a unique approach to risk management.*[2]

Disasters such as Hurricane Andrew can lead to financial ruin for individuals, businesses, and insurers. Businesses face a unique set of risks, including lost or damaged inventory, lawsuits, on-the-job injuries, and employee theft. This chapter is about how companies manage these and other risks.

RISK MANAGEMENT

The very nature of business requires that owners and managers take risks. Choosing to invest money in the development of a new product or a new marketing strategy involves taking a risk. Hiring a new employee involves taking a risk, since at the time of hiring it is unknown whether or not the employee will be productive. But these types of business decisions involve risk that the owner or manager can minimize and control. While their business decisions may not produce the results they hope for, managers can control the outcomes of these decisions by applying their business skills and talents. This type of risk is called **speculative risk**, since it involves deliberate actions managers take to generate profits. Any losses suffered from these actions are thus part of planned business activity.

Speculative risk
Risk that involves deliberate actions managers take to generate profits.

Another type of risk businesses face is not as easy to manage. **Pure risk** refers to the possibility of loss that is unplanned or accidental. From these risks the company can expect only loss or no loss.[3] There is no profit to be gained when things go well. Pure risk is the type of risk associated with hurricanes, fires, theft, and similar events. As many businesspeople learned from Hurricane Andrew, no additional profits were earned during any years when no hurricanes occurred but substantial loss was suffered in the one year in which a hurricane struck.

Pure risk
The possibility of loss that is unplanned or accidental, and the company can expect only loss or no loss.

Risk management involves managerial actions aimed at minimizing the adverse effects of accidental loss on the company. While it is tempting to think that managing accidental losses is simply a matter of buying insurance, that is a very shortsighted—and a very expensive—solution. Some types of losses cannot be compensated for with money alone. For example, the loss of a customer mailing list when the computer breaks down cannot be compensated for with money. The business needs the list, and nothing else will do. Thus, a major

Risk management
Managerial actions aimed at minimizing the adverse effects of accidental loss on the company.

Exhibit 22.1 **THE RISK MANAGEMENT PROCESS**

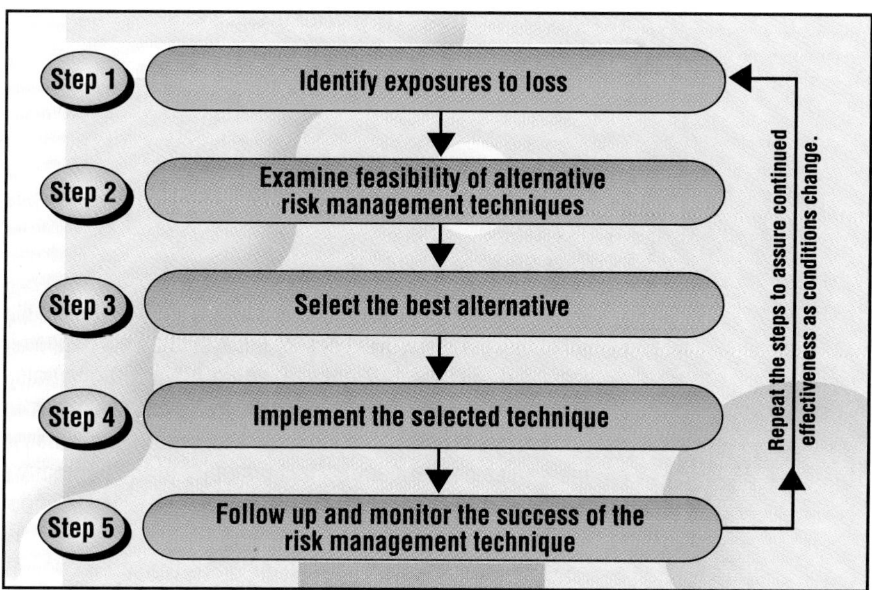

aspect of risk management is finding ways to avoid or minimize all types of accidental losses. Risk management is therefore a decision-making process, as Exhibit 22.1 illustrates.

Two critical aspects of risk management are identifying the exposures to risk the business faces and discovering alternative ways to manage those risks.

IDENTIFYING EXPOSURES TO RISK

A *loss exposure* is the possibility of financial loss arising when a particular peril strikes a thing of value. In examining the company's risk exposure, a manager will assess the type of asset exposed to loss, the perils that might cause the loss, and the financial consequences of the loss. Most businesses face four categories of significant losses: property loss, net income loss, liability loss, and personnel loss.

Property Loss. Property loss is unexpected financial loss resulting from interruption of business or physical damage to property. The owner of a small floral shop, for example, faces a variety of loss exposures. A power outage could cause the refrigeration to break down, damaging the florist's flower inventory. A short circuit in the electrical wiring could start a fire, wiping out the building. Perils such as these threaten the business's property.

Net Income Loss. The breakdown of refrigeration would cause an additional loss for the florist, since he or she would have no flowers to sell. Thus, any sales that might have been made will be lost, while the business expenses will remain. For most companies, this is a type of double jeopardy. When income-producing property is lost, both the property and the income such property produces are lost.

Liability Loss. Another exposure occurs when a snowstorm deposits snow and ice on the sidewalk in front of the store. If a passerby slipped on the sidewalk, the florist might be held liable for any injuries suffered. Similar liability exposures arise when hazards exist where employees work or where customers are present.

Personnel Loss. Personnel losses arise from the death, disability, retirement, or resignation of critical employees, managers, or partners. When the success of a company depends heavily on the unique skills of an individual, that individual becomes critical to the company. Inventors, engineers, and partners are often critical in this respect. If the florist has a partner who is an expert on plant diseases, the death of this partner may threaten the success of the business.

FOCUS ON COMPANY

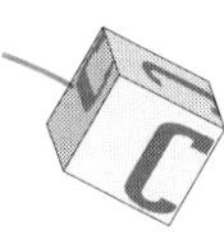

CEO Illness

When a chief executive officer develops a life-threatening illness, the business may suffer emotional turmoil and a good deal of uncertainty. This happened at Tenneco when Michael Walsh, chair and CEO, was diagnosed with a brain tumor. It also happened at Time Warner when Steven Ross, chair and co-CEO, died of prostate cancer.

For shareholders, suppliers, and customers, illnesses and deaths of high-level managers raise concern about the continuity of the company's plans and strategies. Employees and executive colleagues must grapple with worries about their boss and how the situation will affect their own lives and careers.

The best approach for managing this type of risk seems to be complete honesty. Tenneco, in fact, has a regulatory obligation to disclose such illnesses, as do all publicly held companies. As soon as his illness was confirmed, Walsh informed the presidents of Tenneco's operating companies and prepared a three-page press release. These actions permitted Tenneco to minimize and control concerns by investors and employees regarding this situation.

ALTERNATIVE RISK MANAGEMENT TECHNIQUES

Risk management involves preventing losses from occurring, minimizing losses that do occur, and paying for those losses. Common risk management approaches include exposure avoidance, loss prevention, loss reduction, segregation of loss exposures, contractual transfer, and risk financing.

Exposure Avoidance. *Exposure avoidance* means removing the possibility of loss. This is done by abandoning an activity or passing up an opportunity that exposes the company to risk. For example, cigarette manufacturers today face increasing liability lawsuits from relatives and survivors of lung cancer victims. They could avoid such lawsuits in the future by abandoning the manufacture of tobacco products. However, avoiding risk also means abandoning the profits that activity can generate. Thus, it is unlikely that all cigarette manufacturers will abandon this activity. Rather, they may find alternate ways to manage the liability risk.

Loss Prevention. *Loss prevention* involves taking steps to reduce the frequency or likelihood of a particular loss. The local florist can shovel the sidewalk during a snowstorm to reduce the likelihood that someone will slip on the sidewalk. If a power outage would threaten refrigerated inventory, the florist can buy an emergency generator.

Loss Reduction. The goal of *loss reduction* is to decrease the severity of a particular loss. In many states, shoveling a snow-covered sidewalk in front of a store may reduce the owner's liability for damages when someone does slip. If the sidewalk has not been shoveled, the owner can be held liable for a much larger amount.

Loss reduction is a common strategy of oil companies that ship crude oil by ocean tankers. When an oil tanker such as the Exxon *Valdez* ruptures, the company is exposed to great loss. The loss of valuable product may be small compared to the liabilities incurred from environmental damage assessments. Therefore, oil tankers are designed to withstand many types of accidents. Multiple bulkheads and honeycomb construction ensure that less oil will be lost when accidents do occur.

A common loss reduction technique used by both companies and individuals is the use of alarm systems, including fire alarms and theft deterrent systems. Alarm sales now total $6 billion a year. Honeywell's home theft deterrent system, TotalHome, sells for as little as $2,000 and as much as $100,000. Motion sensors detect intruders at windows, at doors, inside rooms, and in yards. Most companies have at least some type of alarm system, at least strong locks on the doors and a sprinkler system for fires.[4]

Loss reduction techniques would have been useful during the Persian Gulf war when retreating Iraqi soldiers set fire to hundreds of Kuwaiti oil wells. Emergency cutoff valves and other catastrophe-preventing measures might have saved considerable economic and environmental losses. Of course, the Iraqi soldiers might have circumvented many devices, but losses would have been reduced.

Segregation of Loss Exposure. *Segregation of loss exposure* means arranging activities and resources so that no single peril can cause a simultaneous loss of all resources. Professional sports teams often do this by sending some of their athletes on one plane and the rest on another. Thus, a plane crash will not completely destroy the team. A less dramatic example is found among companies in Florida that maintained duplicate financial records in other states. Although they suffered property damage from Hurricane Andrew, they did not lose their records.

STREET SMART

Safety First: A Management Checklist

A poor safety record is almost always a symptom of other more basic problems in a business, says Hank Sarkis, president of The Reliability Group, a consulting firm in Miami. While there may be no quick fix for the apparent underlying organizational problems, Sarkis says, most businesses can achieve results quickly by applying the following general recommendations:

1. All accidents can be prevented. Do not settle for less than perfect safety results.
2. The best consultants are a company's own workers. Allow them flexibility to decide how the work gets done.
3. Do not pressure people to work safely without first knowing the specific causes of accidents in your operation.
4. Encourage first-line supervisors to do everything they can to make the workplace more fun and cheerful.
5. Keep things simple. Don't burden workers with a lot of written procedures.
6. Develop a system for reporting events that almost resulted in accidents in the workplace, but design the system so that it doesn't threaten or blame the employees.
7. Do not place too much emphasis on incentives such as awards or prizes to make an operation safe.
8. Never hire employees; hire partners. All workers should have part of their compensation tied to the long-term financial health of the organization.
9. Provide a method for workers to give supervisors both positive and negative feedback on all operational matters.
10. Don't be satisfied with short-term accomplishments. Always strive for continuous improvement.

Segregation is an excellent risk management approach for minimizing inventory loss. If all of a company's inventory is in one building, a fire will destroy the entire inventory. If inventory is kept in two or more locations, however, a fire at any one location will not destroy it all.

Contractual Transfer. *Contractual transfer* of an asset or activity refers to transferring financial responsibility for a loss to another party. This is a common practice in the construction business, where subcontractors bear the financial responsibility for worker injuries. Another example is the shipping industry, where the carrier bears the responsibility if the manufacturer's goods are damaged during shipment.

Risk Financing. *Risk-financing* techniques focus on methods for generating funds to pay for losses that other risk management techniques do not completely prevent. Two major risk-financing techniques are retention and transfer. **Retention** is a risk management technique in which the firm retains part or all of the losses resulting from a given loss exposure. It includes activities directed at generating cash from within the company to pay for losses. **Transfer** is the process of transferring financial responsibility for a loss by either contract or indemnification by a third party.

Retention
A risk management technique in which the firm retains part or all of the losses resulting from a given loss exposure.

Transfer
The process of transferring financial responsibility for a loss by either contract or indemnification by a third party.

Many types of organizations use retention as at least part of their risk management strategy. Companies can use several approaches to fund accidental losses internally. Perhaps the most common retention approach is to treat such losses as current expenses. The advantage of this approach is that it is simple. But unless the losses are small and infrequent, it is a risky approach that may threaten the company's cash flow and disrupt business operations. There is no assurance that cash will be available if a significant loss occurs.

The second method is to create an **unfunded loss reserve**, which recognizes in advance that the company may suffer a loss. It is much like a depreciation account. However, the cash is rarely set aside to cover the anticipated loss. Rather, it is diverted into other needs, such as meeting salary or dividend costs.

Unfunded loss reserve
An account that recognizes in advance that the company may suffer a loss but holds no money to cover an anticipated loss.

The third common method is to create a funded loss reserve. A **funded loss reserve** contains money set aside to cover the costs of accidental losses. Many public organizations, such as universities, use this approach to manage potential property losses. Since a university may have more than 100 buildings, property insurance can be very costly. Some universities use a funded loss reserve to which they make annual deposits to self-insure their properties. Unless they lose all of their buildings at once, the funded reserve is likely to cover accidental losses. However, if natural disasters like Hurricane Andrew occur with any frequency, this approach may not be feasible.

Funded loss reserve
An account that contains money set aside to cover the costs of accidental losses.

In one variation of the funded reserve approach, several organizations pool their accidental risks and create a common reserve account. State governments often do this for the many agencies that have buildings and properties. This is a very practical approach for many states, since the properties are spread throughout the state and a common catastrophic loss is less likely.

FOCUS ON COMPANY

Silver Creek Industries

Many companies use some form of self-insurance to pay health care losses to their employees. Silver Creek Industries has shown that this approach is not just for large, cash-rich companies. Silver Creek, a small electronics manufacturer in Wisconsin, switched to a partial self-insurance plan for its 20 employees. Kevin Edgar, co-owner and treasurer, said, "We had to take some type of cost-control action. Our insurance broker told us we faced a 50 percent premium increase for the plan we had been offering, which required the insurer to reimburse 80 percent of all claims above a $100 deductible."

Edgar devised a simple but effective self-insurance plan. After getting renewal quotes from the insurance company at $250, $500, and $1,000 deductibles, he calculated what it would cost the company to cover the difference between $100 deductible and the three new levels. Keeping its employees at the $100 deductible, Edgar decided to pay the difference up to $1,000, after which amount the insurance company would pay.

Now Silver Creek pays about $2,000 in self-insurance costs, plus an $18,000 annual premium for the $1,000 deductible policy. This represents a substantial savings from the original premium quote of $27,000 for the $100 deductible policy.

INSURANCE

Insurance
An agreement in which an insurance company protects the insured against losses associated with specified risks in return for a fee, or premium payment.

Although several alternatives for avoiding or reducing risk are available, some risks are best managed by shifting them to insurance companies. **Insurance** is an agreement in which an insurance company protects the insured against losses associated with specified risks in return for a fee called the *premium payment.* Insurance policies are written, legal contracts that specify all of the terms of the agreement, including the types of risks covered, the types of actions by the insured that will void the policy, the maximum amount the insured can collect for losses, and how the premiums are to be paid. In the event of a loss, the insurer will pay for the loss up to the amount specified in the insurance policy.

CHARACTERISTICS OF INSURANCE

All insurance policies share several characteristics that distinguish insurance from other risk management techniques. These characteristics include (1) pooling of losses, (2) the law of large numbers, (3) payment of fortuitous losses, (4) risk transfer, and (5) indemnification.

Pooling of Losses. Insurance is similar to a funded loss reserve. An internal funded loss reserve is created by setting aside a smaller amount on a regular basis. Over time, the fund builds to an amount large enough to cover larger losses. External funded loss reserves are created by making regular premium payments to an insurance company. The premiums are "set aside" by the insurance company, which adds the premiums to those submitted by other insureds. This creates a large, pooled fund reserve to cover losses suffered by any insured individual.

Pooling
The spreading of losses incurred by a few parties over the many parties who have purchased insurance.

The pooling of losses is one of the central characteristics of insurance. **Pooling** is the spreading of losses incurred by a few parties over the many parties who have purchased insurance. Thus, the party suffering the loss is compensated in full from the fund created from premium payments made by all policyholders. Exhibit 22.2 illustrates the pooling process.

The state of Florida recently resorted to pooling to obtain insurance coverage for thousands of homeowners who could not get insurance following Hurricane Andrew. The state created an insurance pool, which by law had to charge 25 percent more for coverage than the commercial market charged. But at least the homeowners were covered.[5]

Law of large numbers
The concept that the larger the number of exposures, the more predictable the occurrences of perils on which the insurance premiums are based.

The Law of Large Numbers. The **law of large numbers** states that the larger the number of exposures (policyholders), the more predictable the occurrences of perils on which the insurance premiums are based. Although individual events, such as a fire at Johnson & Johnson's warehouse, are not predictable, the occurrence of 3.5 fires among all insureds during a specified period is predictable. Such predictions are called *probabilities* and are calculated using statistical principles. But making such calculations depends on having a large number of insureds, or policyholders. By calculating the expected number and amount of

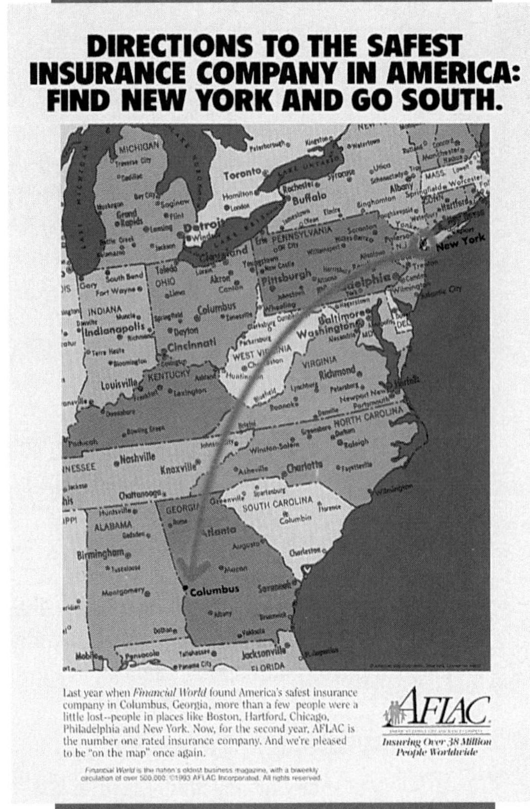

Financial World *rated AFLAC America's safest insurance company. Safety and reliability are extremely important when selecting insurance for a business.*

losses, the insurance company can determine the amount of premium payment it must collect from the insureds.

Fortuitous loss
A loss that is unforeseen and occurs as a result of chance.

Payment of Fortuitous Losses. Another characteristic of insurance is the payment of fortuitous losses. A **fortuitous loss** is a loss that is unforeseen and occurs as a result of chance. This may seem inconsistent with the calculation of expected losses among *all* policyholders (the law of large numbers), but it is not. Rather, it means only that any *individual* loss is unforeseen and results from chance events. This very fact of *accidental loss* is what makes the law of large numbers work. Thus, if a policyholder intentionally starts a fire in his or her warehouse, the insurer will not cover the loss.

Risk transfer
The transfer of a loss associated with pure risk to an insurer.

Risk Transfer. Risk transfer is similar to contractual transfer of risk. But rather than transferring the risk by such means as physical transfer of the property, **risk transfer** means that the loss associated with pure risk is transferred to the insurer, who is in a better financial position (due to premium collections) to pay the loss than the insured is. Pure risks that can be transferred to an insurer include risks of premature death, loss of property, liability, and poor health.

Indemnification
The process of restoring an insured to his or her financial status prior to a loss.

Indemnification. A final characteristic of insurance is **indemnification** for losses. This means the insured is restored to his or her approximate financial status prior to the loss. Thus, if a company's warehouse burns to the ground, the insurer will indemnify the company, or restore it to its previous position. The company will recover sufficient funds from the insurer to rebuild the warehouse.

Exhibit 22.2 **THE PRINCIPLE OF POOLING**

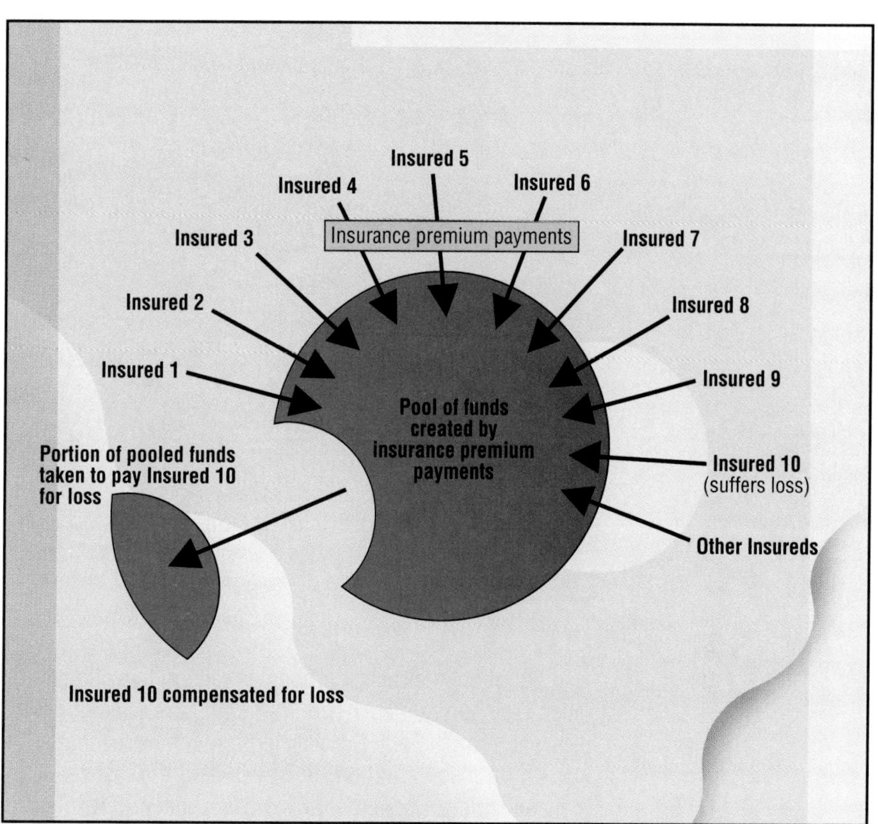

CHARACTERISTICS OF INSURABLE RISKS

Not all losses are insurable. While damages suffered in a warehouse fire might be insurable, some types of fires are excluded from fire policies. As mentioned earlier, fires intentionally set by business owners (arson) are not insurable. Insurers typically insure only pure risks. If the risk is affected by factors other than chance, such as an arson fire, it is impossible to calculate the probabilities on which insurance depends. However, not all pure risks can be insured. Whether a risk is insurable depends on six characteristics of the risk:

- There must be a large number of homogeneous exposure units.
- The loss must be accidental and unintentional.
- The loss must be determinable and measurable.
- The loss should not be catastrophic.
- The chance of loss must be calculable.
- The premium must be economically feasible.[6]

Large Number of Homogeneous Exposure Units. The first characteristic of insurable risks is that they must be part of a large number of homogeneous exposure units. This means there must be many similar units, such as homes or people, that are subject to the same peril or group of perils. Residential homes meet this criterion. They are many, and they face the same group of perils such as fire, wind storms, and hail. This characteristic of risk is related to the law of large numbers. Since there are many units and they all face the same group of perils, it is possible to calculate or predict losses.

The insurance industry paid over $500 million for damages caused to the World Trade Center by a terrorist bomb. While such disasters may be isolated events, they are insurable because of the large number of office buildings throughout the United States.[7]

Although insurance companies rely on this characteristic to determine the insurability of risks, they sometimes insure items that are "one of a kind." One of the most famous examples was actress Betty Grable's legs, which were insured for $1 million during the 1940s. This was an unusual situation, however, and the insurer, Lloyd's of London, may have viewed the policy as an advertising expense, since it resulted in much publicity for Lloyd's. But Lloyd's is unlikely to issue policies like this in the future. Lloyd's lost $7.6 billion between 1988 and 1990 (Lloyd's doesn't close its books for three years) and faces huge claims from Hurricane Andrew.[8]

Accidental and Unintentional Loss. The law of large numbers does not work when losses result from intentional actions rather than by chance. Losses need to result from chance events outside the insured's control. If an individual deliberately causes a loss, it should not be paid. Thus, if a business owner sets fire to his or her warehouse to collect on fire insurance, the insurer will not pay the claim—and the owner will have committed a criminal act. Some life insurance policies also have clauses reducing the insured's claim if she or he commits suicide.

Determinable and Measurable Loss. A third characteristic of insurable risks is that the loss must be determinable and measurable. This means the cause, time, place, and amount of the loss must be calculable. The purpose of this characteristic is to determine whether the loss is covered under the policy and, if so, how much should be paid. For most perils, this information is known and the insurer can quickly determine and pay the loss. Other losses are much harder to determine, such as in the case of physical disability or illness. Whether the insured can or cannot return to work is hard to determine, and thus the amount to be paid for the disability or illness is unclear.

Noncatastrophic Loss. The fourth characteristic is that the loss should not be catastrophic. For the insurer to be able to cover losses, it is essential that not all of the units suffer losses at the same time. Catastrophic losses in late 1993, including the Los Angeles earthquake and winter storms, caused the insurance industry to lose $7 billion in the first quarter of 1994.[9] This is why insurance companies sometimes cancel policies in an area following a major storm

STREET SMART

How to Switch Insurance Carriers

Rick Kislia, CEO of Crescent Laundry, an 85-employee commercial laundry in Davenport, Iowa, has been forced by astronomical premium rate hikes to switch health insurance carriers twice during a five-year period. He offers two pieces of advice on how to switch carriers without alienating the local insurance agents.

First, survey the marketplace annually. Coverages and rates can change quickly, especially if a new insurance company enters your local market and forces the competition to lower prices. Shopping aggressively during such a period can result in substantial savings and shift the cause of the switch to the new insurer rather than to the company.

Second, obtain independent insurance advice. It pays to investigate all your options through independent sources. Insurance agents have their own interests at stake and will not tell you whether lower rates or better coverage is available elsewhere.

like Hurricane Andrew. Many insurers had written too many policies for the area, and the storm destroyed too much property insured by these companies. Thus, they are now reducing the number of policies they have in Florida to prevent future catastrophic losses. This, of course, leaves many individuals and businesses uncovered and seeking either new policies or new risk management strategies.

Calculable Chance of Loss. The fifth important characteristic of insurable risks is that the chance of loss must be calculable. Both the average frequency and the average size of losses due to common perils must be known. Some perils occur with regular and predictable frequency, and the predicted size of losses is easy to calculate. Other perils, such as floods and war, occur very irregularly, and the size and frequency of losses are hard to predict. As stated earlier, if the size and frequency of loss cannot be estimated, an insurer has no idea of what premium to charge. This makes such perils uninsurable or subject to unusually large premiums.

Economically Feasible Premium. The final characteristic of insurable perils is that the premium must be affordable by parties that need the insurance. The premium must be much lower than the amount insured, and thus the chance of loss must be small. This way, both insured and insurer benefit from the insurance agreement.

ADVERSE SELECTION

Adverse selection
Process in which the exercise of choice by insureds leads to higher than average loss levels since those with a greater probability of experiencing a loss are most likely to seek that kind of insurance coverage.

To maintain affordable insurance premiums, insurance companies attempt to match premiums to the degree of risk involved. This means people who pose a higher risk of loss will likely pay a correspondingly higher premium. This practice is an attempt to control for adverse selection. **Adverse selection** is a process in which the exercise of choice by insureds leads to higher than average loss levels since those with a greater probability of experiencing a loss are most likely to seek that kind of insurance coverage. For example, people who find out they have cancer will then seek to increase the amount of life insurance they carry. But people whose doctors declare them to be in perfect health will not seek additional insurance. Thus, an insurance company that insures people who pose higher risk may experience higher than predicted losses. Unless insurers protect themselves against adverse selection, they stand to lose more money than they have collected in premiums.

Insurers protect themselves against adverse selection by excluding coverage for "pre-existing" conditions in the policy provisions. A second approach is to charge higher premiums only for the higher risks, as is often done for automobile insurance. People who pose higher risk, such as young drivers or drivers convicted of alcohol-related offenses, may obtain insurance, but their premiums are higher.

TYPES OF INSURANCE

Many types of insurance are available to protect against a wide variety of perils and risks. The most important types of insurance for business include liability insurance, property insurance, fidelity bonds, surety bonds, criminal insurance, and employee benefit insurance.

LIABILITY INSURANCE

Liability insurance
Insurance protection against claims caused by injuries to others or damage to their property.

One of the most important types of insurance for business owners is liability insurance. **Liability insurance** protects against claims caused by injuries to others or damage to their property. Unlike other types of insurance, liability insurance pays nothing to the insured when loss occurs. Rather it pays third parties for injuries caused by actions of the insured. Like all insurance policies, however, it is designed to protect the insured from loss. It does this because the third party may be able to collect damages for the injury caused by the insured, and the insurance indemnifies the insured against those damages.

Liability insurance includes four types: premises, operations, contingent liability, and product liability insurance.

Premises Insurance. *Premises insurance,* sometimes called *owners', landlords', and tenants' insurance,* covers the insured when other people trip on the sidewalk, fall into a hole in the lawn, walk into the glass patio door, or fall down the stairs. Business owners face many of these perils, since customers are regular visitors to their premises. For example, a grocery store can be sued by a parent whose child fell out of a grocery cart. Premises insurance would cover this peril.

Most businesses are required to maintain safe premises. For example, sidewalks must be cleared during a snowstorm, and customers must be alerted to dangerous conditions such as a recently waxed floor. Failure to maintain safe conditions will either raise the premium rates or cause the insurer to cancel the policy. Premiums are also affected by the number of customers and the type of business.

Operations Insurance. Many everyday business operations create liability exposure for the company. If the business uses forklifts, trucks, or automobiles in its operations, special liabilities exist. Both customers and employees may be exposed to hazard from these operations. Employees will likely be covered by public insurance programs, such as workers' compensation. However, customers and the general public must be covered by special liability insurance. A common example of this type of liability policy is seen in typical automobile insurance policies. These policies cover third parties who are injured by the insured's car and protect the owner from financial loss as a result of those injuries.

This type of liability insurance is often called *operations insurance* or *manufacturers'* and *contractors' insurance.* The premium is calculated after the size of the company's payroll, gross sales, and the natural risk involved in the company's operations have been determined. Contractors' premium rates would naturally be higher than would premiums for comparable-size grocery stores.

Contingent Liability Insurance. Not all injuries to third parties are caused by the company itself. Individuals or businesses that work for the company, such as employees or independent contractors, may cause injury to a third party. Since many businesses contract with collaborators, such as carpenters, plumbers, janitorial services, deliverypeople, and construction firms, this type of insurance coverage should not be overlooked.

Product Liability Insurance. As many manufacturers can tell you, their liabilities do not stop when the product leaves the door. Liability for injuries caused by faulty products may continue throughout the products' useful lives. Manufacturers do not readily admit to product liability, as the highly publicized case of the General Motors pickup truck indicates. The federal government claimed that GM's side-mounted gasoline tanks made its trucks 3.5 times more dangerous than Ford's. Risk of fire was claimed to be 2.4 times greater. The U.S. Department of Transportation asked GM to voluntarily recall millions of the trucks in April 1993. GM, however, debated the accuracy of the government's statistics, and cited NBC's rigged videotape of an exploding Chevrolet pickup as failing to prove the truck was unsafe. The government warned that it was willing to pursue the case for years, if necessary. The last time it pursued a case against GM, it lost, but the case was in the federal courts for eight years.[10]

The makers of silicone breast implants had even more at risk as they fought the claims of injured consumers. While they did not admit fault, the major makers of these products, including Bristol-Myers Squibb Company, Baxter International Inc., 3M, General Electric Company, and McGhan Medical Corporation, agreed to fund a $4 billion liability settlement plan. This plan will compensate women with ruptured implants and for other specific purposes, including removal of implants and diagnosis of illness.[11]

PROPERTY INSURANCE

Property losses may arise from a variety of perils, such as fire, explosion, lightning, wind, vandalism, and theft. Property losses can be classified into two groups: direct and indirect losses. Direct losses are those incurred on the property itself. For instance, if a warehouse is damaged by a hailstorm, the costs of repair are direct losses. Similarly, if a water pipe breaks and ruins the interior of an office building, this loss is a direct loss. Direct property losses involve the costs of returning the property to its original condition following a peril covered by the policy.

Indirect property losses involve incidental losses associated with a direct loss. For example, it may take several days for repairpeople to finish repairs on a damaged warehouse. The warehouse cannot be used during this time, and the company may suffer losses in sales revenue. Losses of revenue are sometimes called **business interruption losses**. When an office building is damaged, as in the World Trade Center explosion in 1993, businesses may have to relocate their operations for a period of time. Costs of moving, setting up, and preparing the new premises are indirect losses.

Business interruption losses Indirect losses (of revenue) caused by direct losses to company assets.

There are nearly 3,800 insurers who provide property and liability insurance. These include some of the largest and best-known companies, such as State Farm, Allstate, Travelers, and Aetna Life and Casualty. The major lines of property insurance are classified by the types of perils they cover, such as fire, transportation, nature (wind, storm, lightning), employee crime, crimes committed by others (vandalism, theft, arson), and failure to meet contracted performance requirements.

FOCUS ON CUSTOMERS

Rental Car Customers

It used to be said that personal automobile insurance follows you no matter what car you drive. But that is changing in the face of insurance company losses. Now several of the nation's largest auto insurers are saying their policies don't automatically cover their customers when they drive rental cars. State Farm is pulling its automatic collision and liability coverage for policyholders who rent cars for business purposes. Instead it now sells this coverage as optional coverage for $40 a year.

Insurance experts predict other insurers will follow State Farm's lead. American Express pulled its automatic car rental insurance from its corporate cards, and Nationwide Insurance eliminated coverage entirely for autos rented for business purposes. In the complex world of car rental insurance, this move by insurers is sure to add further confusion for consumers. It may cause travelers to buy extra insurance whether or not they need it.

Fire Insurance and Allied Lines. *Fire insurance* covers losses to real and personal property due to fire, lightning, and removal from the premises. Insurers can add other perils such as wind, hail, tornadoes, and vandalism. They can also add indirect losses to these policies to cover extra expenses incurred as a result of a loss from business interruptions.

Marine Insurance. *Marine insurance,* sometimes called *transportation insurance,* covers goods in transit against pure risks associated with transportation. Marine insurance may cover goods shipped over the ocean (hence its name), but may also cover goods shipped by land.

Casualty Insurance. Casualty insurance is an important and very large line of insurance. It covers whatever fire, marine, and life insurance do not. Some of the more unusual policies include nuclear insurance, crop-hail insurance, glass insurance, and boiler and machinery insurance.

Multiple-Line Insurance. *Multiple-line insurance* combines both property and casualty coverages into one policy. This is a common type of insurance for businesses today, since buying separate policies for the many and varied risks they face is often impractical.

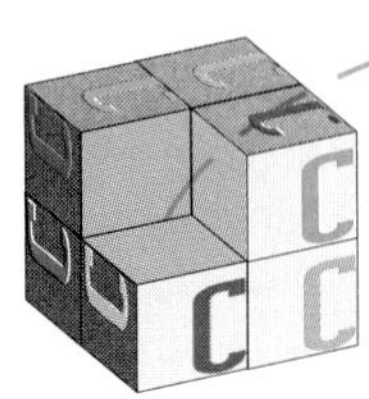

FOCUS ON COMPETITORS

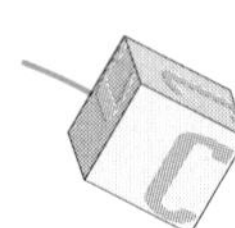

Pressure on the Insurance Giants

Zurich Insurance Group is the world's largest insurance company, with gross annual premiums of almost $14.3 billion. It has many lines of business in almost every insurance market across North America and Europe. Now, however, the giant is attempting to restructure its operations around certain key markets. Rolf Hueppi, president and CEO, says, "This is the evolution of the industry: The less specific you are, the more difficult it will be to survive."

Hueppi's strategy is driven by competition. When competition continues to force lower and lower prices, a company must add value for its customers in the form of improved, customized products and services. U.S. giant Cigna has outlined a similar strategy for its property and casualty companies. In 1990, it announced that it would focus on six core markets. One outside insurance consultant supports this move, saying, "Who wins in insurance? It's the most focused companies, like the mutuals. They always do better than the generalist. You've got to put all your eggs in one basket."

FIDELITY BONDS, SURETY BONDS, AND CRIMINAL INSURANCE

Two important types of insurance available to companies are called *fidelity bonds* and *surety bonds.* While many people think only of natural perils in connection with insurance, other unplanned losses can be insured. One such type of loss is due to theft and other criminal behaviors of employees.

Employees who are placed in positions of trust—especially positions that require handling money, such as cashiers, accountants, bartenders, and loan collectors—can embezzle or steal large sums of money from the company. Curry Printing & Copy Centers in Panama City, Florida, discovered that the company's accountant had failed to submit $150,000 in payroll taxes to the Internal Revenue Service. Instead, the accountant had taken the money for her own personal use.[12] **Fidelity bonds** protect employers against losses caused by dishonest and fraudulent acts of employees.

Fidelity bond
A bond that protects an employer against dishonest or fraudulent acts of employees.

A second type of unplanned loss occurs when a company is unable to meet the performance terms of a contract. For example, a customer who asks a contractor to build a new warehouse may lose money if the warehouse is not completed by some specified date. In this case, the customer may ask the contractor to purchase a **surety bond**, a bond that provides monetary compensation if the bonded party fails to meet the performance terms of a contract. If the contractor fails to meet the completion deadline, the surety bond will compensate the customer for the face amount of the policy. Without the surety bond, the contractor might be obligated to compensate the customer directly.

Surety bond
A bond that provides monetary compensation if the bonded party fails to meet the performance terms of a contract.

A related type of insurance protects the company against the criminal acts of others. This is especially important in the case of burglary, robbery, and theft. Each of these perils requires a separate policy, because the risks differ and require different premiums. **Burglary insurance** covers losses when the company's property is taken by forced entry. If a "cat burglar" breaks into the premises at night and steals expensive display items, burglary insurance will cover the loss. **Robbery insurance** covers losses when the company's property is taken by force or threat of force, such as frequently happens during a holdup of a bank or convenience store. **Theft insurance**, which is general coverage, applies to all losses due to any act of stealing, including burglary and robbery. Note that employee theft may be covered by either fidelity bonds or theft insurance.

Burglary insurance
Insurance for losses when property is taken by forced entry.

Robbery insurance
Insurance for losses when property is taken by force or threat of force.

Theft insurance
Insurance for losses when property is taken by any act of stealing, including burglary and robbery.

Video cameras are used to record shoplifting and other criminal acts in shopping centers and banks. In addition to installing alarms and video cameras, business owners can purchase criminal insurance to cover associated losses.

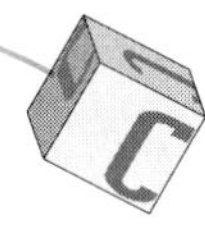

FOCUS ON COMPANY

Insurance Fraud by a Doctor

Insurance fraud costs the American public millions of dollars each year. Are medical doctors above all that? Indeed not! One recent legal case pointed out that doctors are as susceptible to temptation as anybody else. A federal jury convicted a California doctor of racketeering and ordered him to forfeit $50 million and his home in one of the largest medical insurance fraud cases in U.S. history. William Kupferschmidt was a ringleader in a scheme that cheated insurance companies and government programs out of $1 billion.

Kupferschmidt set up three medical clinics in Torrance, Tustin, and San Diego. Every patient was subjected to a battery of high-tech diagnostic tests, regardless of the patient's need for them. In many instances, the tests were performed before the patient was examined by the doctor. Kupferschmidt supervised medical doctors, technicians, and nonmedical personnel who performed physical exams and then placed phony diagnoses on the patients' health insurance claim forms.

EMPLOYEE BENEFIT INSURANCE

Employee benefit insurance
Insurance that protects employees against losses due to illness, injury, or death.

A very important group of insurance policies covers losses due to sickness, injuries, or deaths of employees. Partners may purchase life insurance policies that cover them for the unexpected death of one partner. In this section, however, we focus on insurance that provides benefits to employees and their survivors. This type of insurance, called **employee benefit insurance**, is for the benefit of employees and is intended to protect them rather than the company in the event of fortuitous loss. Employee benefit insurance includes health insurance, life insurance, and annuities.

Health insurance
Insurance that covers losses suffered by employees due to illness or injury.

Health Insurance. The rising costs of health care have caused great concern for many Americans and their elected officials, including the Clinton administration. Although medical research has led to cures and treatments for many serious illnesses, the costs of treatments may be excessive. In addition to the direct cost of treatment, employees may lose wages and other benefits while they are sick. **Health insurance** is designed to cover losses suffered by employees due to illness or injury. These policies typically have a deductible amount which the employee pays when the loss occurs.

Coinsurance
A provision in insurance policies that requires the insured to pay a certain percentage of eligible medical expenses.

It is common for employers to provide group health insurance coverage for employees, in which employees pay part of the premium and the employer pays the other part. Health policies typically cover hospital, surgical, and other common expenses. Major medical expenses, such as those for cancer treatment, are often covered by specific clauses in the policy. Many policies require **coinsurance** for some medical expenses, meaning the insured employee must pay a certain percentage of eligible medical expenses, such as 20 percent. In addition, certain costly, experimental medical treatments, such as bone marrow transplants, may be excluded.

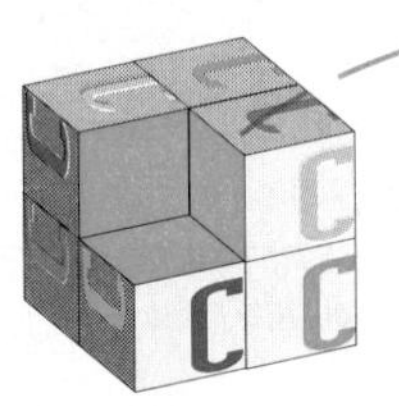
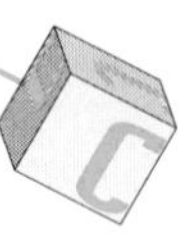

FOCUS ON CUSTOMERS

Health Care Fraud

The $800 billion health care industry is a prime target for fraud. More doctors, pharmacists, clinics, laboratories, hospitals, and other providers of health care engage in fraud than ever before. They defraud the health care system by charging for services they never delivered and by falsifying diagnoses to get the maximum payments possible. Sometimes they deliberately provide more services than were necessary to inflate medical bills. Sometimes they receive kickbacks for prescribing a certain type of medical equipment. Pharmacies bill for brand-name drugs but sell patients generic brands. Medical labs get kickbacks for delivering false test results.

Experts estimate that health care fraud has two critical impacts on society: poor treatment for some patients and an estimated $50 billion in unnecessary charges. "It's not the insurance companies or the government who carry the cost, it's all of us who pay for fraud in the end," says William Mahon, executive director of the National Health Care Anti-Fraud Association. "When you have 35 million people with health insurance, we have an obligation to try to eradicate [fraud]."

Health maintenance organization (HMO)
An organized system of health care that provides comprehensive health services to its members for some fixed fee.

A popular alternative to traditional health care insurance is the **health maintenance organization (HMO)**, an organized system of health care that provides comprehensive health services to its members for some fixed fee. Its focus is on preventing more serious health problems. Thus, certain items such as doctors' office visits are paid, whereas typical group health policies do not cover office visits. Most HMOs require that the insured choose a doctor from a list of qualified practitioners provided by the HMO. HMOs are often less expensive than group premiums, but offer fewer choices in terms of doctors and hospitals.

A major problem for health insurance providers involves catastrophic illnesses. Treatments for breast cancer, for example, often cost more than $100,000, as do bone marrow transplants. Since treatments for diseases like cancer are often classified as experimental, insurance companies routinely deny coverage.

However, recent court decisions may force insurers to rethink their responsibilities and options. A California HMO, Health Net, lost a high-profile court case involving a 37-year-old woman who was denied coverage for a bone marrow transplant. She paid for the treatment on her own and later died, but a jury awarded her estate $89 million in damages.[13]

In addition to providing basic health insurance, some employers help employees obtain coverage for dental expenses. Dental insurance pays for various dental procedures, including the costs of braces, annual checkups, and oral surgery.

Life insurance
Insurance that provides for payment of a stipulated sum to a designated beneficiary upon death of the insured.

Group term life insurance
Life insurance provided to a number of persons on a single master contract.

Life Insurance. **Life insurance** provides for payment of a stipulated sum to a designated beneficiary upon death of the insured. Life insurance is one of the most important investments wage earners can make for their dependents. As long as the primary wage earner is alive, the well-being of his or her family is reasonably safe. If the primary wage earner dies, however, the family survivors may be hard pressed to find financial support. Life insurance, especially for the primary wage earner, is one of the basic means by which survivors can be assured of a reasonably comfortable lifestyle. Group life insurance accounts for some 40 percent of the total life insurance in force in the United States.[14]

The most common form of group life insurance is **group term life insurance**. This insurance provides low-cost protection for employees, and the employer often shares the cost as part of the employees' benefits package. The face value of an employee's policy is usually some multiple of the employee's annual salary, such as 1.5 to 2 times the salary. This would provide substantial protection for the employee's survivors, but many insurers believe it may not be enough. Insurers often recommend that a person carry up to five times his or her annual salary in life insurance protection. Many group policies permit employees to convert all or some of the coverage to an individual term life insurance policy upon retirement. Many group life insurance plans permit employees to enroll their dependents for a certain minimal amount of life insurance, typically $1,000 for dependent children and up to $10,000 for a spouse.

In addition to group term life plans, some employers provide *group accidental death and dismemberment insurance.* These policies pay additional benefits if an employee dies in any type of accident or suffers certain types of injuries in an accident. These are very low-cost policies, since they cover only a narrow range of the possible causes of death.

Annuity
A periodic payment to a person that continues either for a fixed period or for the duration of the person's life.

Annuities. Annuities provide individuals with retirement income. An **annuity** is a periodic payment to a person that continues either for a fixed period or for the duration of the person's life. While a life insurance policy pays when an individual dies, an annuity pays while a person lives.

The insurable risk associated with annuities is that of excessive longevity, that is, the possibility that a person will outlive his or her financial resources. As with premature death, this risk can be pooled by an insurable group, and the necessary premium can be calculated. The result is a type of retirement program wherein employees are assured of a certain level of income following their retirement. In fact, many employers use annuities as the basis of their retirement programs. Premiums for the annuity are usually shared by employer and employee. This arrangement often results in a higher retirement income than would be available if the employer paid the total premium.

SOCIAL INSURANCE PROGRAMS

Social insurance
Insurance programs provided by government agencies and regulations, generally financed entirely by mandatory contributions from employers and/or employees rather than by general (tax) revenues

Social insurance programs are provided by government agencies and regulations. Generally, these programs are financed entirely by mandatory contributions from employers and/or employees rather than by general (tax) revenues. The contributions are set aside for the social insurance programs and kept separate from other government funds. The major social insurance programs in the United States are

- Old-age, survivor's, disability, and health insurance (social security)
- Unemployment insurance
- Workers' compensation
- Compulsory temporary disability insurance
- Railroad Retirement Act (an alternative to social security available to employees of railroads)
- Railroad Unemployment Insurance Act

We covered many of these government programs in earlier chapters and will not repeat that discussion here. However, social security is so important to Americans that it deserves some mention. This program, which began in 1935, covers more than 90 percent of American workers. Many employees are covered by both a private retirement program and social security. For many citizens, however, the only source of income following retirement will be the benefits paid by social security.

Social security is funded by a contribution tax paid by both the employer and the employee. Self-employed people pay a special tax that is higher than an employee's share but lower than the employer-employee total would be for a person of that income level. Benefits provided by social security include lump-sum payments upon death, survivor's income payments, disability income payments, hospital and medical payments through the Medicare program, and retirement income payments. While many skeptics have criticized the social security program, it remains strong. It pays substantial sums to retired and disabled persons and has yet to borrow funds from general revenues to meet its obligations.

ISSUES IN THE INSURANCE INDUSTRY TODAY

Like the victims of Hurricane Andrew, people who need insurance are discovering that it is harder to find and that when they do find a willing insurer, the premiums are often excessive. The escalating cost of automobile insurance has forced many college students to either give up their cars or work extra hours to pay for the premiums. In many states, skyrocketing malpractice insurance premiums have caused many doctors, especially obstetricians, to give up their practices. Perhaps the major issue the insurance industry faces today is making insurance available to those who need it at a price they can afford. As we saw earlier, one of the criteria of insurable risk is that the premium be economically feasible.

What has caused this problem? Several factors seem to be responsible, including unsound investments of premiums by insurance companies, abuses by insurance agents, and increasingly large settlements in lawsuits against insureds and their insurance companies. Many experts argue that the largest single factor is excessive awards by juries in lawsuits. Manufacturers, as one affected group, have found that product liability insurance is practically unavailable today. This is a severe problem and, in fields such as pharmaceuticals and medicine, may have very negative effects on society in general. Already several medical products, such as certain vaccines, are no longer manufactured despite statistics that show society is far better off with them than without them. However, manufacturers have lost millions of dollars when juries found them liable for allergic reactions to the vaccines. Many are unwilling to expose themselves to further risks of lawsuits by continuing to manufacture these useful products.

Abuses by insurance agents also add substantial cost to insurance premiums. For example, one agent sold a $100,000 annuity to a client who had just won a $331,000 court settlement arising from a malpractice suit. He then sold the customer's wife a $100,000 life insurance policy, but increased it to $1,000,000 by carefully adding a zero. The customers didn't find out about the fraud for two years, since the agent had the insurance premiums withdrawn from the annuity payments and forged the wife's signature on the withdrawal authorization slips. When the husband died, a court awarded the widow $21 million from the insurance company.[15] Such abuses add greatly to the premiums all insureds must pay.

Until laws are passed to prevent excessive damage claims, premiums will continue to be economically unfeasible for many businesses. In the meantime, companies must rely on other risk management techniques.

SUMMARY

1. ***Describe the two basic types of risk.***
   The two basic types of risk are speculative risk and pure risk and depend on whether or not the risk can be controlled. Speculative risk involves deliberate actions managers take to generate profits. Any losses suffered from these actions are thus part of planned business activity. Pure risk refers to the possibility of loss that is unplanned or accidental. From these risks, the company can expect only loss or no loss. Pure risk is associated with hurricanes, fires, theft, and similar events.

2. ***Define* risk management *and describe its critical elements.***
   Risk management is managerial actions aimed at minimizing the adverse effects of accidental loss on the company. Two critical aspects of risk management are identifying the exposures to risk the business faces and discovering alternative ways to manage those risks. In examining the company's risk exposure, a manager will assess the type of asset exposed to loss, the perils that might cause the loss, and the financial consequences of the loss. Most businesses face four categories of significant losses: property loss, net income loss, liability loss, and personnel loss. Risk management also involves preventing losses from occurring, minimizing losses that do occur, and paying for those losses. Common risk management approaches include exposure avoidance, loss prevention, loss reduction, segregation of loss exposures, contractual transfer, and risk financing. Exposure avoidance means removing the possibility of loss. Loss prevention involves taking steps to reduce the frequency or likelihood of a particular loss. The goal of loss reduction is to decrease the severity of a particular loss. Segregation of loss exposure means arranging activities and resources so that no single peril can cause a simultaneous loss of all resources. Contractual transfer of an asset or activity refers to transferring financial responsibility for a loss to another party. Risk-financing techniques focus on methods for generating funds to pay for losses that other risk management techniques do not completely prevent. Two major risk-financing techniques are retention and transfer. Retention involves management activities

directed at generating cash from within the company to pay for losses. Transfer refers to generating cash from outside the company to pay for losses.

3. ***Define* insurance *and explain what an insurance policy includes.***
   Insurance is an agreement in which an insurance company protects the insured against losses associated with specified risks in return for a fee, or premium payment. Insurance policies are written, legal contracts that specify all of the terms of the agreement, including the types of risks covered, the types of actions by the insured that will void the policy, the maximum amount the insured can collect for losses, and how the premiums are to be paid. In the event of a loss, the insurer will pay for the loss up to the amount specified in the insurance policy.

4. ***Describe the unique characteristics of insurance.***
   All insurance policies share several characteristics that distinguish insurance from other risk management techniques. These characteristics include pooling of losses, the law of large numbers, payment of fortuitous losses, risk transfer, and indemnification. Pooling is the spreading of losses incurred by a few parties over the many parties who have purchased insurance. The law of large numbers states that the larger the number of exposures (policyholders), the more predictable the occurrences of perils on which the insurance premiums are based. A fortuitous loss is a loss that is unforeseen and occurs as a result of chance. Risk transfer means that the loss associated with a pure risk is transferred to the insurer. Indemnification means the insured is restored to his or her approximate financial status prior to the loss.

5. ***Discuss the characteristics of insurable risk.***
   Whether a risk is insurable depends on six characteristics of the risk. First, there must be a large number of homogeneous exposure units. This means there must be many similar units, such as homes or people, that are subject to the same peril or group of perils. Second, the loss must be accidental and unintentional so that the law of large numbers is satisfied. Third, the loss must be determinable and measurable. This means the cause, time, place, and amount of the loss must be calculable. Fourth, the loss should not be catastrophic. For the insurer to be able to cover losses, it is essential that not all of the units suffer losses at the same time. Fifth, the chance of loss must be calculable. Both the average frequency and the average size of losses due to common perils must be known. Finally, the premium must be economically feasible, that is, affordable by parties that need the insurance.

6. ***Describe the various types of insurance.***
   Many types of insurance are available to protect against a wide variety of perils and risks. The most important types of insurance for business include liability insurance, property insurance, fidelity bonds, surety bonds, criminal insurance, and employee benefit insurance. Liability insurance protects against claims caused by injuries to others or damage to their property. Liability insurance includes premises, operations, contingent liability, and product liability insurance. Property losses are classified as either direct or indirect losses. Direct losses involve the costs of returning the property to its original condition following a peril covered by the policy. Indirect losses involve incidental losses associated with a direct loss. The major lines of property insurance are classified by the types of perils they cover. They include fire, marine, casualty, and multiple-line insurance. Two important types of insurance available to companies are fidelity bonds and surety bonds. Fidelity bonds protect employers against losses caused by dishonest and fraudulent acts of employees. Surety bonds provide monetary compensation if the bonded party fails to meet the performance terms of a contract. A related type of insurance protects the company against the criminal acts of others and includes burglary, robbery, and theft insurance. Employee benefit insurance is intended to protect employees and their survivors rather than the company in the event of fortuitous loss. It includes health insurance, life insurance, and annuities. Health insurance is designed to cover losses suffered by employees due to illness or injury. Life insurance is one of the basic means by which primary wage earners can assure their survivors of a reasonably comfortable lifestyle in the event of the wage earners' death. Annuities provide individuals with retirement income. An annuity is a periodic payment to a person that

continues either for a fixed period or for the duration of the person's life. Finally, social insurance programs are provided by government agencies and regulations. Generally, these programs are financed entirely by mandatory contributions from employers and/or employees rather than by general (tax) revenues. These contributions are set aside for programs such as social security, unemployment insurance, and workers' compensation.

7. ***Explain some of the major issues in the insurance industry today.***
   One major issue faced by the insurance industry is making insurance available to those who need it at a price they can afford. Rising costs have led to sharp increases in premiums, forcing some people to give up their policies. Related issues are unsound investments of premiums by insurance companies, increasingly large settlements in lawsuits against insureds and their insurers, and abuses by insurance agents. These problems have led some companies to abandon manufacture of useful products like vaccines and some doctors to leave their practices. Until these issues are resolved, premiums may continue to be economically unfeasible for many businesses.

KEY TERMS AND CONCEPTS

Speculative risk (p. 528)
Pure risk (p. 528)
Risk management (p. 528)
Retention (p. 532)
Transfer (p. 532)
Unfunded loss reserve (p. 532)
Funded loss reserve (p. 532)
Insurance (p. 533)
Pooling (p. 533)
Law of large numbers (p. 533)
Fortuitous loss (p. 534)
Risk transfer (p. 534)
Indemnification (p. 534)
Adverse selection (p. 537)
Liability insurance (p. 538)
Business interruption losses (p. 539)
Fidelity bond (p. 541)
Surety bond (p. 541)
Burglary insurance (p. 541)
Robbery insurance (p. 541)
Theft insurance (p. 541)
Employee benefit insurance (p. 542)
Health insurance (p. 542)
Coinsurance (p. 542)
Health maintenance organization (HMO) (p. 543)
Life insurance (p. 543)
Group term life insurance (p. 543)
Annuity (p. 544)
Social insurance (p. 544)

DISCUSSION QUESTIONS

Company

1. What are the characteristics of insurable risks?
2. How does the nature of a company's business operations influence the type(s) of insurance from which the company would obtain maximum benefit?
3. Why is it important for an insurance company to integrate coinsurance and deductibles into insurance agreements?

Customers

4. What benefits do customers obtain from a company's implementation of a sound risk management program?
5. How do the increasing amounts awarded in liability suits affect insurance companies and their customers?
6. What types of coverage are available to the customers of insurance companies?

Competitors

7. What are some competitive techniques insurance companies can use to attract customers?
8. What effect does social insurance have on competition in the insurance industry?

Collaborators

9. Why are companies tending to rely on collaborators less and on themselves more in managing their risks?
10. What does a company gain by providing employee benefits?

In Question: Take a Stand

Before the Americans with Disabilities Act was passed, some employers avoided paying the costs associated with employees' deteriorating health and rising medical bills by canceling their health insurance policies and substituting contracts that excluded particular ailments. When H&H Music, a retail chain in Houston, learned that an employee had AIDS, it switched to an insurance plan that put a $5,000 lifetime cap on benefits for an AIDS patient. But the plan retained the $1 million maximum for those who suffered from other diseases. The courts have upheld H&H.

Denying a worker benefits for AIDS or other catastrophic illnesses seems cruel. Yet it seems equally unfair to shift the responsibility to a small employer or union. Such calamities can cost insurance companies and, ultimately, the insured workers $500,000 or more. More critical, perhaps, the insurance company might cancel the employer's policy or raise the premiums out of reach.[16]

What ethical issues are involved in situations like that faced by H&H Music? What alternatives to cancellation of coverage might there be for coverage of employees with catastrophic illnesses? If you were the owner of a small business, how would you deal with this problem?

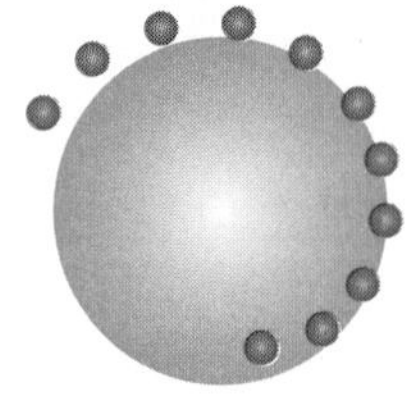

CASE 22.1
MID-ATLANTIC PACKAGING INC.[17]

The high cost of workplace accidents and injuries threatened the future of Mid-Atlantic Packaging Inc. in the spring of 1991. During the previous year, the Montgomeryville, Pa., company's 80 employees had racked up 17 injuries and more than $400,000 in workers' compensation claims. But the potential toll for the company—a manufacturer of corrugated cardboard boxes—added up to far more than the sum of its workers' comp insurance claims. The company's financial health was suddenly in jeopardy because of the steep premium increases expected to follow its poor accident record.

"We told the employees clearly that if we did not improve, this could put the company out of business," recalls Andrew Pierson, the general manager. "We could not have $400,000 in workers' comp claims and stay in business."

Questions

1. *Is the situation at Mid-Atlantic Packaging unusual? Explain.*
2. *How important has workers' compensation insurance been to you when seeking a job? How important has it been to your parents?*
3. *What steps should Mid-Atlantic Packaging take to reverse its disastrous workers' compensation record?*

PART 7

Business Opportunities and Constraints

CHAPTER 23

BUSINESS LAW AND GOVERNMENT REGULATION

When you have studied this chapter, you will be able to:

1. Explain the basis of the legal system.
2. Discuss the general organization of the American court system.
3. Identify the conditions for a legally valid contract.
4. Explain the nature of sales law.
5. Discuss the characteristics of property law.
6. Discuss the agency relationship and the conditions that govern it.
7. Describe intellectual property and the law that applies to it.
8. Explain the types of bankruptcy permitted by bankruptcy law.
9. Discuss tax law and the revenue it provides to the government.
10. Describe the laws that regulate business and the benefits of deregulation in some industries.
11. Discuss the nature of ethics in business.

Operating a franchise, such as an Arby's, a Kwik Kopy, or a Brakemaster, is one way to pursue the American dream of owning your own business. Franchises account for some 13 percent of retail sales. A franchise can be almost anything these days, from a steel bungee-jumping tower (Air Boingo) to a gun shop (Strictly Shooting).

However, concern is growing about abuses by franchisors, the people who sell the franchises to the local operators. Franchise contracts, often 50 or more pages long, heavily favor franchisor rights. Competitive pressures sometimes lead franchisors to oversell franchises and misrepresent their business potential. For example, several franchisees recently charged that Car Checkers of America Inc. provided references from franchisees who had never actually owned a franchise. They also claimed the company misrepresented advertising costs and broke numerous promises to new franchisees. Denny's was accused by the Justice Department of discriminating against African-American franchisees, customers, and suppliers.

As a result of such conflicts between franchisors and franchisees, Congress has written legislation that could regulate the entire franchising industry. The final draft of new franchise disclosure guidelines was completed in March 1994. The guidelines would require franchisors to rewrite key brochures given to prospective franchisees disclosing, for instance, information about franchisee failures and turnover.

Some states are drafting laws and regulations aimed at creating some balance of power between franchisors and franchisees. Texas legislators have proposed a bill that would protect franchisees from competition with company-owned restaurants, prevent terminations of franchises without good cause, and prohibit reprisals against franchisees who organize themselves. This regulation is aimed at Taco Bell, a unit of Pepsico, Inc., which some legislators believe is particularly abusive of franchisee rights. Iowa passed a tough franchise law in 1992. Franchisors claim the law takes away their right to run their systems as they see fit. They also think the law gives too much power to the courts, which are beginning to favor franchisees in contract disputes.[1]

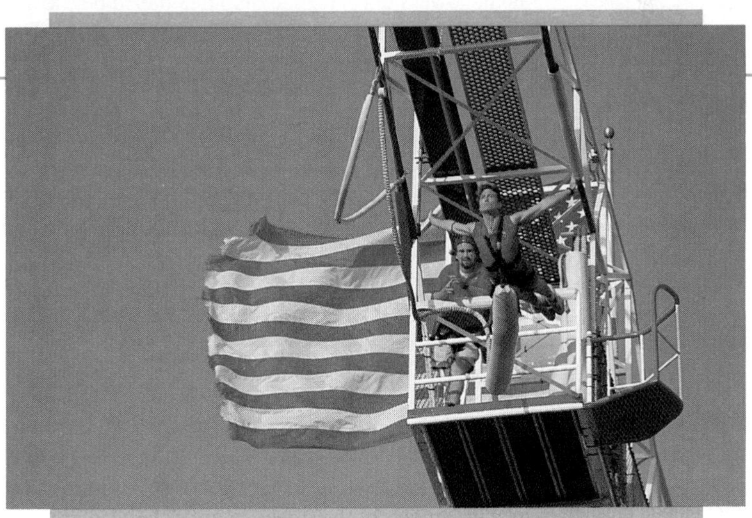

As the opening vignette illustrates, business transactions often give rise to disputes between the parties. Without laws and regulations, disputes such as these may never be resolved. This chapter discusses many of the laws and regulations that affect business activities.

THE U.S. LEGAL SYSTEM

Law
Enforceable rules that govern relationships among individuals and between individuals and their society.

Law consists of enforceable rules that govern relationships among individuals and between individuals and their society.[2] Most legal scholars agree that ideals, logic, history, and customs have influenced the development of law. Due to our colonial heritage, much of our legal system is based on English law.

COMMON LAW

When the Normans conquered England in 1066, William the Conqueror began to unify the country using a consistent base of law. Before the conquest, disputes had been settled according to local customs. This system was inefficient, however, because the means of settling disputes differed from one area to another. Thus, the King's Court was established to create a uniform set of rules across the country. The body of rules that evolved from this court was called **common law**—law that was common to the entire country.

Common law
Law that is common to the entire country.

When settlers came to America from England, they brought with them English laws and rules of behavior. Many of these laws and rules were subsequently incorporated into the laws of the United States, since they were used as the basis for settling disputes. Legislators at both the federal and state levels can change common law as societal changes dictate the need. For example, common law once set the legal age of majority at 21, but most states have changed the age of majority to 18. It is interesting to note that in Louisiana, Roman or civil law, rather than common law, prevails. This is due to the early French influence in Louisiana.

CASE LAW

As English judges decided disputes, they recorded important and unique decisions in *Year Books.* Later cases having similar circumstances were decided by using the earlier cases as **precedent**. This practice has carried forward to our modern legal system and forms the doctrine of *stare decisis.* Today, all decisions reached by judges are filed in court reports by court reporters. Interpretations by judges become binding on lower courts in the same jurisdiction, as the lower courts decide disputes based on the same points of law. Thus, judges create law as their decisions become law for the lower courts. Such law is known as **case law**.

Precedent
A court decision that establishes a point of law for deciding subsequent cases having similar circumstances.

Case law
Rules of law based on earlier court decisions.

CONSTITUTIONAL LAW

The U.S. Constitution is the supreme law of the United States. Any law that violates the Constitution, no matter what its source, will be declared unconstitutional and will not be enforced. The Constitution, for instance, grants the federal government the power to regulate interstate commerce, which is a major influence on business activities.

Each state also has its own constitution that establishes the powers of the state government. States retain the power to regulate intrastate commerce, which affects activities such as establishing a corporation and obtaining a license to sell liquor.

ADMINISTRATIVE LAW

Statutory laws
Laws enacted by Congress and state legislatures.

Administrative law
Rules and regulations created by an administrative agency to implement constitutional and statutory laws.

Laws enacted by Congress and the state legislatures are called **statutory laws**. **Administrative law** is devoted to rules and regulations created by an administrative agency to implement constitutional and statutory laws. An administrative agency is created when the executive or legislative branch of the government delegates some of its authority to a unit called an *agency* or a *commission.* For example, the Securities and Exchange Commission (SEC) was created to carry out the Securities Exchange Act of 1934. The SEC, like other administrative agencies,

Furniture manufacturers sell and distribute to retailers across the country. Contracts for these sales are covered by the Uniform Commercial Code. Furniture is both a tangible and a movable good.

has a good deal of clout with business. For example, pressures from the SEC have forced stock exchanges and brokerage firms to better police themselves and eliminate many misleading and fraudulent practices.[3] Hundreds of other administrative agencies exist, including the Federal Trade Commission (FTC) and the National Labor Relations Board (NLRB).

Both state and federal administrative agencies have the power to make rules for implementing laws, and the rules have the strength of law. When a person or a business has a dispute with an agency, administrative law applies.

THE UNIFORM COMMERCIAL CODE

Uniform Commercial Code (UCC)
A body of statutory law that governs the design, production, marketing, and interstate distribution of tangible, movable products.

The body of law that addresses commercial dealings is commonly called *commercial* or *business law.* The most important body of commercial laws is contained in the **Uniform Commercial Code (UCC)**. The UCC governs the design, production, marketing, and interstate distribution of tangible, movable products.

The UCC evolved because various states had their own unique laws pertaining to the conduct of business. This system made conducting business very difficult, especially when a transaction occurred between businesses in different states. Therefore, the National Conference of Commissioners on Uniform State Laws met in the late 1800s to create uniform statutes governing business transactions. Once these uniform codes were created, state legislatures were encouraged to adopt them.

Adoption of the UCC is at the discretion of state legislators, who may reject all or part of a code or rewrite it as they deem necessary. The UCC is designed to facilitate business transactions by assuring companies that their contracts, if entered into in a valid manner, will be uniformly enforced by state courts.

THE COURT SYSTEMS AND RESOLUTION OF DISPUTES

Jurisdiction
The power of a court to hear and resolve a dispute.

The United States has 52 separate court systems, each of which settles legal disputes. Each state and the District of Columbia has a court system, and there is a separate federal court system. Which court hears a case is a matter of jurisdiction. **Jurisdiction** is the power of a court to hear and resolve a dispute. Generally, a state court's jurisdiction is limited to the territorial boundaries of the state, not including constitutional issues, which the federal courts must decide. Some state courts have decided cases that had important national implications.

FOCUS ON COLLABORATORS

Pepsico, Inc., and The Soviet Union

Twenty years ago, Pepsico patriarch Donald Kendall struck an innovative deal with the Soviet Union: the trade of Pepsi-Cola for vodka. Now Pepsico can sell Pepsi in the former Soviet Union if it imports a proportionate amount of Stolichnaya vodka to the United States.

This deal sounds simple enough. However, various state regulations bar companies that serve alcohol from owning liquor distributors in the United States. Pepsico owns Pizza Hut, which serves alcohol, and previously owned Monsieur Henri, which is now the sole supplier of Stolichnaya vodka. Facing these state regulations, Pepsico set up separate ownership and operation of Monsieur Henri. But company insiders and corporate documents suggest that Pepsico has a major influence in the operation of Monsieur Henri, even to the extent that its employees are part of Pepsico's stock option and health benefits plan.

Now several states are examining the relationship, and Pepsico may have to defend its operations in state courts across the country. Texas is one of those states. The general counsel for Texas's Alcoholic Beverage Commission says, "We would view it with suspicion.... The fact that they are providing business services is *prima facie* a violation, and something we'd have to investigate very carefully." In 1994 the Bureau of Alcohol, Tobacco and Firearms fined Monsieur Henri Wines Ltd. $150,000 for failing to disclose that Pepsico actually controlled the liquor-importing business.

STATE COURTS

Most state court systems consist of four levels. Exhibit 23.1 depicts the typical state court system.

State inferior court
The lowest level of state trial court, often having limited jurisdiction.

State Inferior Courts. State inferior courts are the lowest level of state trial courts and often have limited jurisdiction. These courts hear disputes involving specialized subject matter. State inferior courts include *probate courts* (will and estate settlements), *divorce courts* (domestic disputes and child custody), *criminal courts* (criminal violations), and *small claims courts* (small monetary claims). These courts may not hear or decide disputes outside their special jurisdictions. For instance, a probate court cannot hear a case involving a traffic violation.

State court of general jurisdiction
A state trial court that has broad jurisdiction.

State Courts of General Jurisdiction. State courts of general jurisdiction have broad jurisdiction in terms of subject matter. They are called by various names such as *county court, district court, superior court,* or *circuit court.* General jurisdiction trial courts hear and decide disputes involving nearly all subject matter.

All legal disputes are heard in trial courts, either general jurisdiction or inferior courts. Cases that were decided in inferior courts may be appealed to the general jurisdiction courts. However, many cases are heard first in general jurisdiction courts. Whether a case begins in an inferior or a general jurisdiction court often depends on the general court's caseload.

State appellate court
A state court that decides questions of law.

State Appellate Courts. Appellate courts are usually not trial courts. State trial courts settle *questions of fact,* for example, whether the person who signed a contract had authority to do so. **State appellate courts** decide *questions of law,* such as whether the trial court committed an error. Every state has at least one appellate court. The jurisdiction of appellate courts

Exhibit 23.1 **A TYPICAL STATE COURT SYSTEM**

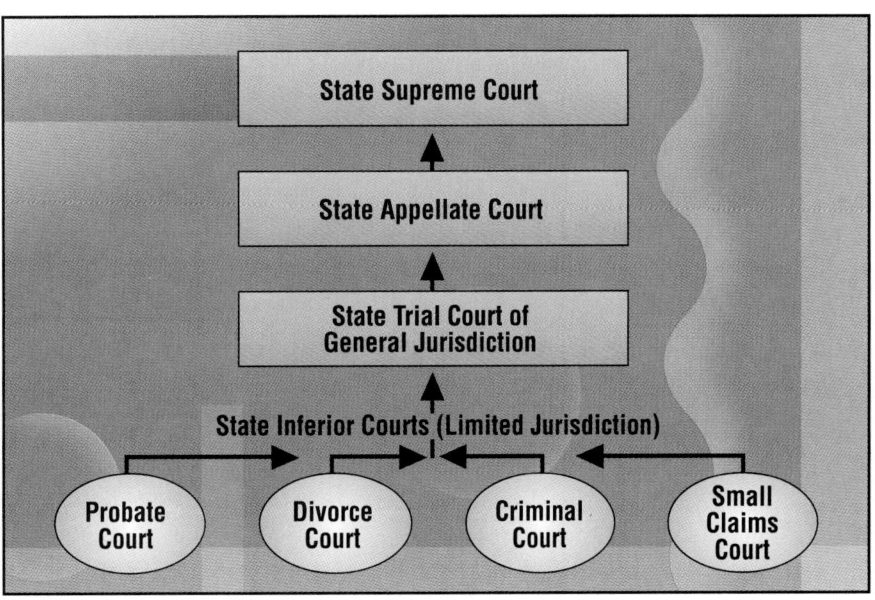

is basically limited to hearing appeals. Most appellate courts have multijudge panels that examine cases being appealed.

State supreme court
The highest state court to which cases involving questions of law can be appealed.

State Supreme Courts. State supreme courts are the highest level of state courts. Like an appellate court, a state supreme court decides questions of law and is the final state court to which a case can be appealed. In most instances, state supreme courts consist of a panel of five to nine judges who listen to lawyers' arguments regarding points of law involved in the cases they appeal. If a case involves no federal issue, the decision of the state supreme court terminates the case. If it involves some federal law or issue, the case may be appealed to the U.S. Supreme Court.

FEDERAL COURTS

The federal court system is authorized by the U.S. Constitution. Article III, section I of the Constitution says, "The Judicial Power of the United States shall be vested in one Supreme Court and in such inferior courts as the Congress may from time to time ordain and establish." Thus, the highest court in the land is the U.S. Supreme Court, which is supported by a system of lower-level courts (see Exhibit 23.2).

Federal district court
The trial-level court in the federal court system.

Federal District Courts. Federal district courts, sometimes called *federal trial courts,* are the trial-level courts in the federal court system. Thus, a federal district court is the federal equivalent of a state court of general jurisdiction. Each state has at least one federal district court, and more populous states have several. U.S. district courts have original jurisdiction in federal matters. Thus, most federal cases originate in these courts.

Other Federal Courts and Administrative Tribunals. At the same level as federal district courts are several courts of limited jurisdiction. For example, the *U.S. Tax Court* handles cases involving questions of federal taxation. Individuals seeking administrative remedies must first proceed through the Internal Revenue Service (IRS) before appealing to the U.S. Tax Court. The *U.S. Claims Court* deals with claims made by individuals against the U.S. government.

Exhibit 23.2 **THE FEDERAL COURT SYSTEM**

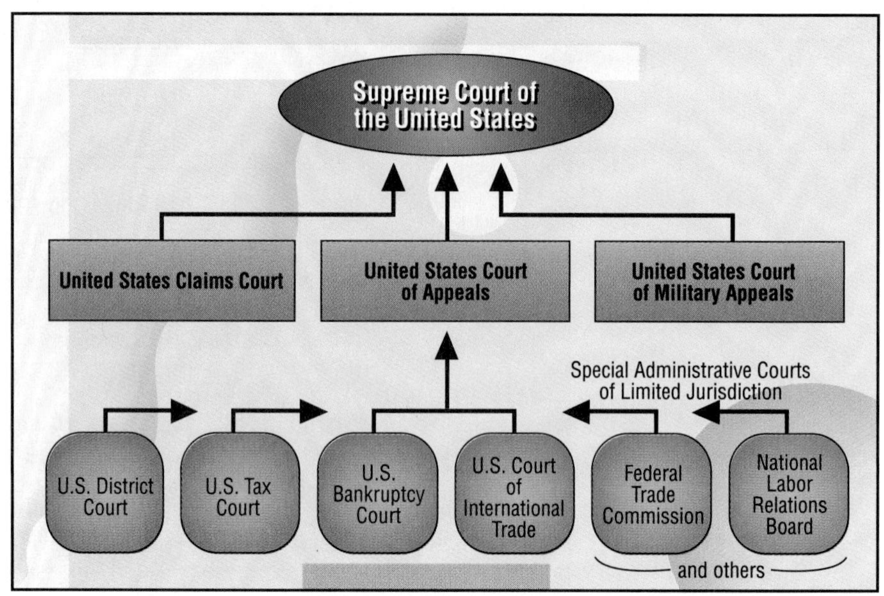

In addition, several administrative agencies have hearings boards to decide special jurisdiction issues. For example, the National Labor Relations Board settles issues arising from union and employee activities.

U.S. court of appeals
One of 13 courts that hear appeals of cases from the district courts located in their respective circuits.

U.S. Courts of Appeals. Congress established 12 judicial courts, sometimes called circuit courts or U.S. courts of appeals. The **U.S. courts of appeals** hear appeals of cases from the district courts located in their respective circuits. They also hear appeals from federal administrative agencies such as the National Labor Relations Board. In 1982, Congress created a thirteenth circuit court, called the *Court of Appeals for the Federal Circuit.* This court has national jurisdiction over certain matters, including public contracts, patents, and international trade.

Federal district and appeals courts have endorsed the view that civil rights statutes don't protect fired employees if their conduct would have gotten them fired had their employers known about it. In a case heard by the federal appeals court in Cincinnati, the court ruled that the plaintiff was not allowed to claim she was fired because of her age, since she took home copies of company financial records to prepare her lawsuit. Since the company would have fired her for this action, the age discrimination claim was voided.[4]

U.S. Supreme Court
The highest court in the federal court system.

U.S. Supreme Court. The highest court in the federal system is the **U.S. Supreme Court**. Most cases heard in the Supreme Court are appeals from the federal courts of appeals, and some are from cases decided in state courts. Occasionally the Supreme Court hears original trials.

A case involving Honda Motor Company illustrates the types of business-related lawsuits the U.S. Supreme Court hears. An Oregon jury had awarded $5 million in punitive damages to a plaintiff who was badly injured when his Honda three-wheel, all-terrain vehicle overturned. The Oregon state supreme court affirmed the trial results. Honda appealed to the U.S. Supreme Court, which agreed to hear the case. The appeal was based on a prior U.S. Supreme Court decision stating that at least some judicial review of punitive awards is needed, and such a review did not occur in Oregon.[5]

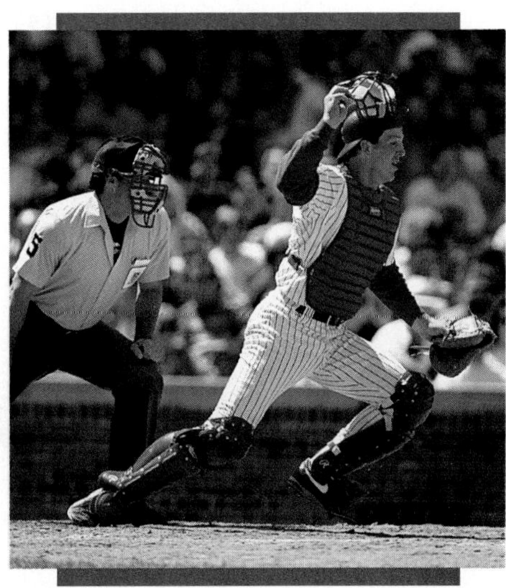

Sports is a business. Baseball players who realize their entertainment value to teams often command high salaries. But young players without free-agency status are often disappointed with the offers they get from teams' general management. When no agreement results, the dispute often goes to arbitration. The year after Rick Wilkens had a .303 batting average with 30 home runs and established himself as the Chicago Cubs' number one catcher, his salary went to arbitration.

ALTERNATIVE DISPUTE RESOLUTION

Seeking remedies in court is expensive for all parties in a dispute. It is also time consuming, since the courts are very crowded. Therefore, managers and companies involved in disputes often seek solutions outside the courtroom. Mediation and arbitration, discussed in Chapter 12, are the primary means of alternative dispute resolution. In *mediation,* a third, impartial person (the mediator) assists the parties in reaching an acceptable solution but does not make a decision for the parties regarding the solution. In *arbitration,* a more formal process, the third party (the arbitrator) makes a legally binding decision by which the disputing parties must abide. These methods are common in disputes between companies and unions regarding interpretation of labor contracts.

LAWS AFFECTING BUSINESS ACTIVITIES

Since owners of businesses are at the same time citizens of the country, all law is business law. In earlier chapters, we discussed laws that pertain to employee relations, securities exchanges, consumer protection, environmental issues, taxation, and other areas. In this section we look at other major laws affecting business, including contract law, sales law, property law, agency law, intellectual property and computer law, bankruptcy law, and tax law.

CONTRACT LAW

Contract law
A body of law intended to ensure compliance with contracts or to provide some remedy for those harmed when contracts are broken.

A *contract* is a promise enforceable by law. **Contract law** is intended to ensure compliance with contracts or to provide some remedy for those harmed when contracts are broken. Contract law is based on common law and applies to all contracts except when modified or replaced by statutory or administrative law. Contracts relating to services, real estate, employment, and insurance are typically covered by general contract law. Contracts for the sale of goods are covered by statutory law, specifically the Uniform Commercial Code.

Exhibit 23.3 **ELEMENTS OF A CONTRACT**

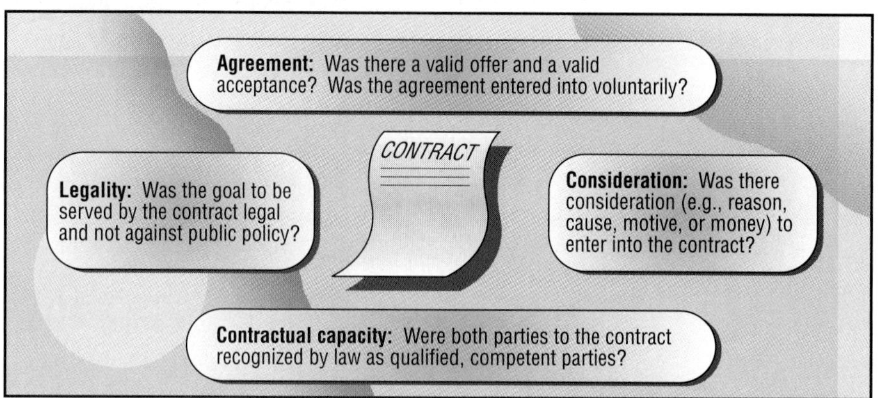

Without contract law, managers and other employees would have to rely solely on the good faith of others. Such reliance may be adequate in certain cases, but other situations require the strength of law.

Basic Conditions for a Valid Contract. Not all promises are legal contracts. However, a contract need not be written in legal jargon to meet the basic conditions for being legally valid. The four basic conditions, known as the *elements* of a contract, are agreement, consideration, contractual capacity, and legality (see Exhibit 23.3).

1. *Agreement.* An agreement includes a valid offer and a valid acceptance. One party must voluntarily offer and another must voluntarily accept some promise to perform.
2. *Consideration.* Consideration is the inducement for the parties to enter into a contract. Consideration is something of value, such as money, that a person earns for entering into the agreement. For example, a company orders several computers and pays $5,000 as a down payment. The $5,000 is legal consideration from the company.
3. *Contractual capacity.* Each party entering into a contract must have the legal capacity to do so. A person who is a minor or is mentally ill is unlikely to have contractual capacity. For instance, if the party who promised the computers is under 18 years of age, the contract may be invalid.
4. *Legality.* The contract must be intended to accomplish some legal purpose. A loan contract that specifies an interest rate higher than that allowed by law may not be enforceable.

In addition to meeting the four conditions for a valid contract, the contract must be in a form appropriate for the contracted purpose. While not all contracts must be written, some transactions require a written contract. For example, a contract for the sale of goods valued at more than $500, or a contract for real property, must be in writing. Also, contracts that cannot be fulfilled in less than a year must be written.

Breach of contract
The failure to perform a contractual duty.

Breach of Contract. A **breach of contract** is the failure to perform a contractual duty. Any breach of contract entitles the nonbreaching party to sue for damages. This does not mean, however, that the nonbreaching party is excused from fulfilling his or her contractual duty. In some cases, especially if the breach of contract is easily remedied (such as the case of a late delivery), the other party may simply be entitled to some monetary compensation.

Exhibit 23.4 **CLASSIFICATIONS OF PROPERTY**

Classification	Characteristics
Real property	Immovable property—the land and all things permanently attached to it. Includes the buildings, trees, plants, and lakes. May also include air space and subsurface rights.
Personal property	Anything that is not real property, including both living and inanimate property. For instance, livestock and cars are personal property.
Tangible personal property	Things of physical existence, such as cars, furniture, computers, and file cabinets.
Intangible personal property	Things lacking physical existence, such as stocks, bonds, patents, trademarks, and copyrights.

In general, the person who breaches a contract may be liable for monetary damages or forced to uphold the promised performance. But such compensation may be denied unless it can be proven that a contract existed in the first place. Thus, it is good practice to have all contracts in writing and to make sure they contain the four elements of a valid contract.

SALES LAW

Today's sales law evolved from customs and traditions of merchants and traders in previous centuries and is contained in the Uniform Commercial Code (UCC). The UCC, as we saw earlier, is the most comprehensive body of law governing commercial transactions. The UCC views the entire commercial transaction for the sale of goods as a single legal occurrence with numerous facets.[6] Thus, facts applying to sales transactions are best discussed with an attorney.

Like all contracts, sales contracts must contain the elements of agreement, consideration, capacity, and legality. Also, the UCC deals only with contracts for the sale of *goods,* not real property such as real estate, or services, or intangible property, such as stocks and bonds. To be characterized as a good, an item must be both tangible and movable.

A *tangible* item has physical existence. It can be seen, heard, smelled, tasted, or touched. Items that lack physical existence, such as stocks, bonds, promissory notes, patents, and copyrights, are intangible and are thus not covered by sales law in the UCC. A *movable* item can be carried from place to place. Hence, real estate, which cannot be moved, is covered by property law rather than by sales law in the UCC. However, sales of crops or timber, which can be separated from the land, are sales of goods and are covered by sales law.

PROPERTY LAW

A major characteristic of our society is the right of individuals to own *property.* People may own land, houses, furniture, and cars. They may also own factories, machinery, trucks, patents, and copyrights.

As Exhibit 23.4 shows, property can be either *real property* or *personal property,* and personal property can be either *tangible* or *intangible.* Ownership of real and tangible personal property is fairly easy to establish, whereas ownership of intangible property is difficult to establish.

This difficulty was illustrated in a recent lawsuit involving Apple Computer, Inc., and Microsoft Corporation. Apple sued Microsoft for allegedly violating its ownership rights to the icon-based look and feel of its "user-friendly" computers. Microsoft Windows software indeed appears to duplicate the Apple icons. However, Microsoft claimed that Windows' program instructions differed from Apple's, and therefore did not violate Apple's intangible property rights. The court generally found in favor of Microsoft, but the final outcome of the case may not be decided for some time.[7]

Property law
A body of law that deals with the various ways ownership rights in property can be held and with rights regarding mislaid, lost, or abandoned property.

Property law deals with the various ways ownership rights in these forms of property can be held and with rights regarding mislaid, lost, or abandoned property.

Property Ownership. Property ownership conveys a number of rights, including the right to possess the property and the right to dispose of it through sale, gift, rental, lease, and so on. The law permits various forms of ownership. The most common forms of ownership are fee simple, tenancy in common, and joint tenancy.

Fee Simple. When one person holds all of the property rights, he or she is said to be the owner in *fee simple.* Fee simple owners are entitled to use, possess, and dispose of the property as they choose.

Tenancy in Common. People can also own property jointly. *Tenancy in common* occurs when each of two or more parties owns a fractional interest in the property, where the fractions may not be equal. In the event one person dies, his or her interest in the property passes to that person's heirs. The heirs then become tenants in common with the other owners. Tenancy in common can be a headache for owners unless they can agree on how to "share" their property.

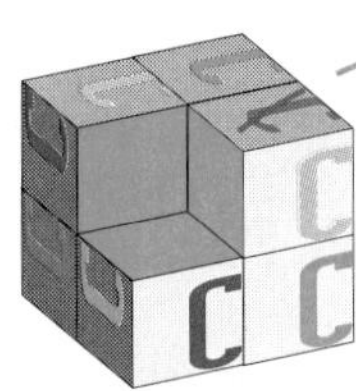

FOCUS ON CUSTOMERS

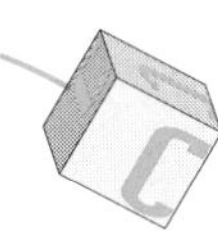

Timesharing

Front Street in Lahaina, Hawaii, has 17 tourist information booths that are really hawking timeshare properties. These companies buy or build resort condominiums and then sell blocks of time in them. Big, reputable companies such as The Walt Disney Company, Marriott Corporation, and Hilton Hotels Corporation are among those competing for buyers. Although some of the early "bugs" have been worked out, the industry is still plagued by complaints of fraud and deception. Visitors to the booths accept free rides on parasails or dinner invitations on restaurant-ships, then get subjected to high-pressure sales pitches that go on for hours.

Those who buy slices of ownership find high maintenance fees, inconvenient time slots for enjoying their "time" at the resort, and few ways to rid themselves of ownership when they grow discontented. Under pressure, the Maui mayor's office has begun to investigate, and the state has sent in undercover sleuths to check out some of the complaints. Some locals even warn tourists to "Beware [the information booths], they are really selling timeshare properties. Ignore them."

Joint Tenancy. *Joint tenancy* ownership also involves two or more parties who own undivided interests in the whole property. In the event of the death of one party, the deceased party's ownership interest passes to the surviving joint tenant(s). Most homes owned by married couples are owned in joint tenancy. When one spouse dies, the ownership interest passes to the surviving spouse.

Rights Regarding Mislaid, Lost, or Abandoned Property. An old adage says, "Possession is nine-tenths of the law." In fact, one method of acquiring ownership of property is to simply possess it. However, just finding something and holding onto it does not necessarily entitle the finder to own it. When property is voluntarily placed somewhere and then forgotten—that is, *mislaid* property—the finder becomes the caretaker of the property. It still belongs to the true owner, since he or she is likely to return for it.

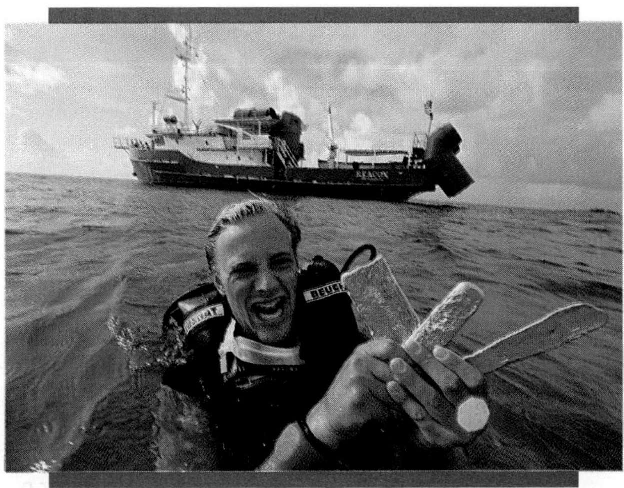

Recently the U.S. Supreme Court dealt a blow to treasure hunters by rejecting the "finders, keepers" principle. The case involved $1 billion worth of treasure from a ship sunk in 1857. Insurance companies sued the treasure finder, claiming they had insured the treasure in 1857. The court ruled that the original owners of sunken treasure retain their rights to it but that the finder was entitled to a substantial salvage award.[8]

Property that is left behind involuntarily is *lost* property. A finder of lost property holds ownership rights against all others *except the true owner.* If the true owner demands the return of the lost property, it must be returned.

Finally, property that the owner has discarded is *abandoned* property. This would include cases where property was lost and the owner gave up attempts to find it. Any finder of abandoned property becomes the owner of the property, even above the original owner. Often the courts decide whether or not property has been abandoned.

AGENCY LAW

Agency law
A body of laws that applies to transactions involving agents and principals.

Agency law applies to transactions involving agents and principals. An *agency* is a legal relationship in which two parties, a principal and an agent, agree that one will act on behalf of the other and under that person's control. A *principal* is the person who wishes to have some task or purpose performed, and the *agent* is the person acting on behalf of the principal to accomplish that task or purpose. Within the scope of the agency agreement, the agent may negotiate contracts and transactions, and the principal will be legally bound by those arrangements.

All businesses rely on agents to conduct business. Owners of businesses hire managers, who hire employees. Together managers and employees conduct business on behalf of the owners. Therefore, owners are principals and managers and employees are agents. Companies also use advertising, real estate, and insurance agencies to perform certain transactions on their behalf. Agency law applies to all these individuals and the transactions they perform for the companies. Exhibit 23.5 illustrates the basic agency relationship.

Agency law is somewhat complex. The essential ingredients of agency relationships and transactions are

1. The actual versus apparent authority of the agent
2. Whether the principal is known (disclosed) to a third party doing business with the principal

Exhibit 23.5 **BASIC AGENCY RELATIONSHIPS**

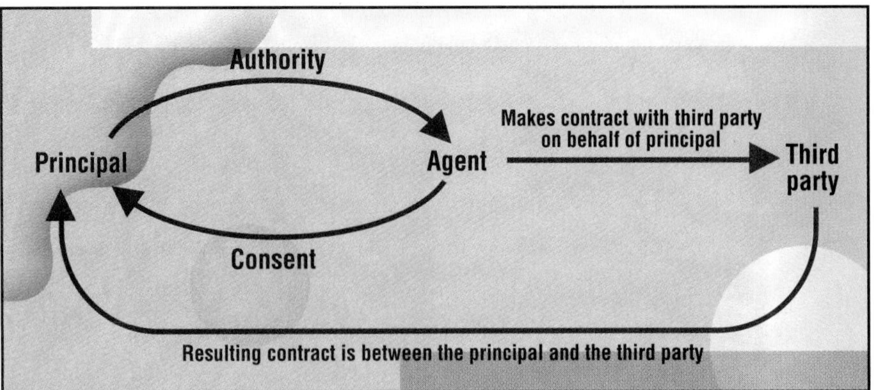

3. Whether the principal has the right of control or exercises control over the agent
4. Whether the agency relationship is formalized with a power of attorney

Actual and Apparent Authority of the Agent. An agent gains *actual* authority when the principal assigns authority to that agent and the agent consents to that authority. The authority can be general or limited to certain transactions. However, any person can have *apparent* authority when the principal merely tells a third party that the person is the principal's agent. When an agent acts within the scope of either actual or apparent authority and makes a contract with a third party, the principal is liable on the contract.

Disclosure of the Principal to a Third Party. If the third party knows, or reasonably should know, who the principal is, the principal is called a *disclosed principal.* If the third party knows there is a principal but not who the principal is, the principal is a *partially disclosed principal.* If the third party does not know, or cannot reasonably know, that a principal exists (that is, thinks the agent is acting on his or her own behalf), the principal is an *undisclosed principal.*

Agents are not liable for contracts between third parties and disclosed principals, since the contract is between those two parties only. However, if the principal is only partially disclosed, both principal and agent are liable. In the case of an undisclosed principal, the parties to the contract are the agent and the third party.

Control over the Agent by the Principal. To the extent that a person has the right of control, or exercises control, over another person, he or she is liable for the other person's conduct. But that liability is limited to the actual conduct over which the principal has control. For example, supervisors typically do not have control over employees' behavior after normal working hours. Thus, if an employee stopped at a bar on the way home and got drunk, the employer would not be liable for any automobile accident involving the employee when he or she left the bar. Alternatively, the employer might be responsible if the employee got drunk at work and had an accident while delivering goods to a buyer.

Power of attorney
A document authorizing another person to act as one's agent.

Power of Attorney. A **power of attorney** is a document authorizing another person to act as one's agent. A power of attorney grants an agent either full or restricted authority to act on behalf of the principal. Most often the power of attorney is notarized. Powers of attorney are often used in the sale of real estate and sometimes in the sale of automobiles. If the owner of property expects to be absent at the time the title will be signed and transferred, a specific power of attorney may give the agent the right to transfer ownership.

INTELLECTUAL PROPERTY AND COMPUTER LAW

Business assets are commonly thought to consist largely of tangible assets such as land, buildings, inventory, and cash. However, some of the most valuable business assets include intangible assets called *intellectual property.* Intellectual property consists of the products of people's minds—their inventions, trademarks, copyrights, and patents. In our technology-oriented society, computer software has become an important intellectual property.

Intellectual property and computer law
A body of law designed to protect patents, copyrights, and trademarks.

Intellectual property and computer law is designed to protect the rights of those who create intellectual properties. It consists of separate laws covering patents, copyrights, and trademarks.

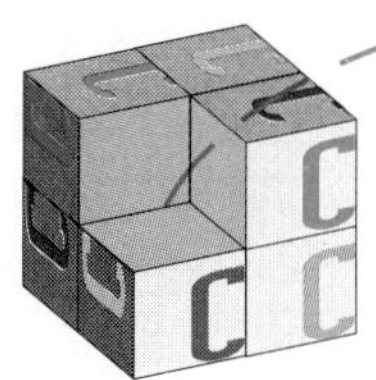

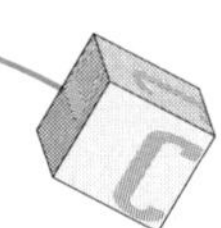

FOCUS ON COMPETITORS

Trademark Laws in Southeast Asia

Pressure by the United States and other countries led to the passage of new trademark laws throughout Southeast Asia. However, the laws have not been very effective. Clothing makers Levi Strauss, Pierre Cardin, and Alfred Dunhill of London Inc. saw some of their most profitable trademarks stolen by an Indonesian company. Indonesia's previous trademark law gave a trademark to the first company to file for it, even if the trademark was already used by another company. Using this law, PT Makmur Perkasa Abadi registered the trademarks of more famous companies. In the United States such disputes would be resolved quickly, because foreign companies generally win trademark protection if they have already registered the marks in their home countries.

Patent
A government grant giving inventors the exclusive right to make, use, and sell their inventions for a period of 17 years.

Copyright
The exclusive right of an originator of a literary or artistic production to sell and profit from his or her work for the life of the originator, plus 50 years.

Fair use
A doctrine that permits limited reproduction of copyrighted works without the payment of royalties.

The federal government grants inventors **patents**, which give them the exclusive right to make, use, and sell their inventions for a period of 17 years. **Copyrights** are given to the originators of certain literary or artistic productions. These works include novels, poems, textbooks, movies, videos, songs, and similar creations. Works created after January 1, 1978, receive statutory copyright protection for the life of the originator, plus 50 years. Although the author has the exclusive right to sell and profit from his or her work, a **fair use** doctrine permits limited reproduction without the payment of royalties.

The Computer Software Copyright Act of 1980 included computer programs in the list of creative works protected by federal copyright law. Computer programs are defined as a set of statements or instructions used in the computer to bring about a certain result. Because of the unique nature of computer programs, the courts have had difficulty applying the act. As we saw earlier, one major issue the courts are dealing with is the "look and feel" of computer programs and software.

Additional laws cover computer crimes, such as using a computer to break into bank records. Business students must be aware of the seriousness of these crimes as they learn to program and operate computers for business applications.

FOCUS ON COMPETITORS

High-Tech Privacy

A recent ruling by a federal judge in Austin, Texas, sheds new light on privacy laws in our technological age. The court explicitly ruled that the Privacy Protection Act applies to electronically stored information and that computer bulletin boards and electronic mail are safeguarded by federal wiretap laws against government eavesdropping. In the case heard before the court, a U.S. Secret Service raid had been conducted against an Austin-based publisher of games and books. The Secret Service was looking for electronic documents it thought had been stolen from Bell-South. The ruling says the government cannot monitor electronic mail any more than it can monitor U.S. mail. The raid, spurred by a crackdown on computer hacking, is being closely examined by agencies responsible for enforcing copyrights and other software protection laws.

BANKRUPTCY LAW

Bankruptcy
A legal condition of insolvency in which the court administers the company's or individual's estate for the benefit of the creditors.

Although most individuals and companies repay all of their legal debts, some cannot meet their financial obligations. The financial management of a company is complex and risky. When no reasonable alternative for meeting financial obligations exists, the person or business may file for bankruptcy. **Bankruptcy** is a legal condition of insolvency in which the court administers the company's or individual's estate for the benefit of the creditors.

Some of the nation's most respected companies have filed for bankruptcy to reorganize debts with their creditors. R. H. Macy & Company, the giant New York retailer, filed for bankruptcy with the support of its major creditors, General Electric Capital and Fidelity Investments. An improved debt structure enabled Macy to repay its creditors and continue doing business until it merged with Federated Department Stores.[9]

Bankruptcy law permits three basic types of bankruptcy: Chapter 7, Chapter 11, and Chapter 13 bankruptcy. *Chapter 7 bankruptcy* requires that the business be dissolved and its assets sold or distributed to its creditors. The proceeds from the sale of assets are distributed among creditors to help settle the debts. *Chapter 11 bankruptcy* temporarily frees a business from its financial obligations while it reorganizes and works out amended repayment plans with creditors. Chapter 11 has been used by Continental Airlines, Texaco, and other companies in recent years. *Chapter 13 bankruptcy* is similar to Chapter 11, but applies only to individuals. It permits individuals to establish three-to-five-year plans for repayment of their obligations while retaining most of their assets.

FOCUS ON COMPANY

USG Corporation

USG Corporation, a leading producer of gypsum wallboard used in home construction, filed for bankruptcy protection in 1993, an action that lasted only 37 days. The move was prompted by a $1.4 billion debt, accumulated after the company fought off an unfriendly takeover attempt by two Texas raiders, Jack Brown and Cyril Wagner, Jr. Cash rich at the time, USG paid off its shareholders with cash, debentures, and new stock. Then the price of wallboard fell, leaving the company in a shaky position. Interest and principal payments were eating up all the cash flow. As a result of the bankruptcy, interest payments were reduced by half and debt maturities were extended.

TAX LAW

Perhaps the most far-reaching body of law—one that directly affects all businesses and individuals in the nation—is *tax law.* Nearly 30 percent of the gross national product is taken by taxes, including federal, state, and local taxes.

Both individuals and businesses are subject to federal taxes. In fact, some 37 percent of 1992 federal budget receipts came from individual income taxes, 7 percent from corporate taxes, 30 percent from social security taxes, and 3 percent from excise taxes.[10] State and local governments also collect taxes, including income, sales, excise, and property taxes.

Although any tax tends to affect business, some have more direct effects. These taxes are income, property, transaction, and employment taxes.

Income Taxes. Although various federal taxes have been imposed over the years, it was not until the Revenue Act of 1913 was passed that Congress authorized a consistent federal income tax. Today's prevailing federal income tax law is contained in the Internal Revenue Code of 1986 as amended in 1987 and 1988.

Sole proprietorships and partnerships are affected primarily by individual income taxes, since the incomes of these businesses flow to the owners, where they are taxed. Tax rates for individuals now fall between 15 and 39 percent. These rates are likely to change under the Clinton administration.

Corporations' net incomes are taxed at the prevailing corporate rate—currently 34 percent (after subtracting operating expenses). However, certain types of investments and incomes receive special treatments. For example, income earned abroad is treated differently, and there is an alternative minimum tax on corporations of 20 percent.

Property Taxes. Property taxes are sometimes referred to as *ad valorem taxes,* since they are based on the value of the property. They apply to both individuals and businesses. Property taxes fall into two categories: those imposed on real property and those imposed on personal property. The definition of *real property* for tax purposes includes land and any permanent structures and fixtures attached to it.

Personal property taxes can be imposed on items devoted to personal use, such as household furnishings and jewelry, but this is rather uncommon. However, businesses are often taxed on inventories, trucks, machinery, and equipment.

Transaction Taxes. Transaction taxes, which are typically imposed at the point of transaction, include sales and excise taxes. These taxes are collected from buyers of goods by sellers, and must be submitted to the taxing authority on a regular basis.

Employment Taxes. Employers must collect state and federal income taxes from their employees. They do this by withholding specified amounts and submitting them to the Internal Revenue Service or to the state's revenue department. Failure to collect or submit these taxes will subject a business to substantial penalties.

In addition, a business must collect FICA (Federal Insurance Contributions Act) taxes, commonly referred to as the social security tax. FICA taxes are shared by employee and employer. FICA rates for an employee depend on the employee's income, but are maximized at a total of $5,328.90. The employer must match whatever the employee pays.

Finally, employers must pay FUTA (Federal Unemployment Tax Act) taxes. FUTA provides funds that states can use to administer unemployment benefits. FUTA is applied at a rate of 6.2 percent on the first $7,000 of covered wages paid during a year to each employee. However, if the employer does not terminate very many employees, it may qualify for much lower rates.

REGULATION AND DEREGULATION OF BUSINESS

Laws such as those discussed in this chapter regulate business practices in many ways. Laws establish the basis for business relationships and provide a means for the remedy of illegal acts. Government also affects companies by directly regulating competition and other business practices to achieve societal objectives. Regulation of business is intended to control undesirable business behavior as well as to protect and provide opportunities for businesses.

Exhibit 23.6

TYPES AND PURPOSES OF REGULATIONS

Type of Regulation	Characteristics	Regulatory Acts and Agencies
Functional regulation	• Helps the government carry out its duties and expresses government interest in a general aspect of business • Applies in an equal manner to most businesses • Is compatible with major values of business	Internal Revenue Service Social Security Administration National Labor Relations Board Federal Trade Commission Sherman Antitrust Act Securities and Exchange Commission
Industry regulation	• Benefits most companies in an industry • May or may not affect companies in other industries • Is compatible with some, but not all, business values	Interstate Commerce Commission Civil Aeronautics Board Federal Reserve Board Department of Agriculture
Social regulation	• Implements noneconomic objectives of society • Applies in an equal manner to most businesses • Is not implemented on the basis of compatibility with business values	Environmental Protection Agency Occupational Safety and Health Administration Equal Employment Opportunity Commission Consumer Product Safety Commission

Regulatory acts by the government are classified into three types: functional, industry, and social regulation.[11] Exhibit 23.6 lists these types and the objectives they serve.

FUNCTIONAL REGULATION

Functional regulation of business is intended to help government carry out its functions and to help business in general. These regulations are generally compatible with business values and tend to control undesirable competition and establish basic guidelines for business. Tax laws and social security regulations help government carry out some of its social functions.

Other regulations are more specifically designed to promote healthy competition. The first regulation of competition occurred when the Sherman Antitrust Act was passed in 1890. This act prohibits all contracts and conspiracies in restraint of trade, such as price fixing, and makes monopolies illegal. The Clayton Act of 1914 also forbids contracts between companies that restrict competition, mutual membership on boards of directors, and certain types of stock acquisitions, which tend to act as restraints of trade.

Two recent cases remind us that the federal government still enforces these acts. In the first, Allen-Myland Inc. sued IBM, claiming IBM's pricing policy regarding parts needed to upgrade mainframe computers amounts to an illegal scheme to prevent competition. At stake is more than $30 billion in business from 1991 to 1996.[12] In the second, the Justice Department filed a criminal indictment against General Electric Company and De Beers Centenary AG for alleged price fixing in 1994. The companies were charged with fixing prices in the $600-million-a-year world market for industrial diamonds.[13]

FOCUS ON COMPETITORS

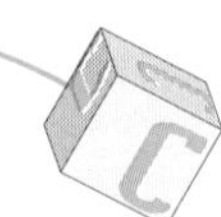

AT&T Loses Exclusive Right to 1-800

Since AT&T was broken into separate companies in 1984, competitors have atttacked the telephone giant in virtually all segments of the long-distance phone business except the profitable toll-free 1-800 service. But as of May 1, 1993, the Federal Communications Commission opened up the $7.5 billion market to full competition.

Competitors believe they can reduce AT&T's market share to less than 60 percent in the near term. MCI began offering 100 free days of long-distance service, spread over two years, as an incentive to AT&T customers to make the switch. Sprint and AT&T quickly matched the offer. MCI also charged that AT&T was using pressure tactics to keep customers. Observers expect that AT&T will hold on to most of the 1-800 business but that prices will drop and profits will decrease. Of course, that is the very point of open competition in a free market economy.

INDUSTRY REGULATION

Many government regulations apply to specific industries. Some of these regulations include the Pure Food and Drug Act of 1906, the Fair Debt Collections Practices Act of 1978, and regulations by such agencies as the Interstate Commerce Commission, the Civil Aeronautics Board, the Federal Reserve Board, and the Department of Agriculture. These laws and agencies impose restrictions on specific industries such as the trucking industry, the aviation industry, banks, and farming. For example, the Food Safety and Inspection Service, a regulatory agency, enforces legislation regarding meat inspection. When customers of Sizzler International Inc.'s restaurants in Oregon contracted food poisoning, inspectors closed the restaurants.[14]

In addition to restricting certain industry practices, some regulations grant protection to favored businesses by imposing barriers to entry, price controls, and subsidies. Such regulations require all businesses to adhere to standard practices.

SOCIAL REGULATION

Social regulation often results when society's goals and objectives conflict with those of business. For example, pollution and environmental protection regulations cost businesses a great deal of money, but are highly desirable from a social viewpoint. Regulatory agencies such as the Environmental Protection Agency and the Consumer Product Safety Commission are charged with protecting the rights of workers and consumers and making their environment

The aviation industry is regulated by the Civil Aeronautics Board. Regulation of aviation permits air traffic controllers to schedule and control the flights of competing airlines to avoid accidents caused by heavy air traffic. All commercial and private airplanes are required to conform to instructions from air traffic controllers.

safer. This, of course, requires businesses to spend considerable sums to develop safer work methods and products. Businesses must also spend more money on product recalls and face the threat of being sued by consumers injured by defective products.

DEREGULATION

While most observers would admit that our society has benefitted from reasonable regulation activities, the rapid growth of agencies has created many headaches. For example, the specific regulations associated with occupational safety and health at one time were contained in a stack of books that stood over six feet high. Any manager or owner would be hard pressed to read, much less understand, all these regulations. In addition, regulations tend to create unnecessary paperwork. Many agencies impose large fines on businesses for simple paperwork violations. Thus, a businessperson who broke no laws might have to pay heavy penalties just for forgetting to fill in one piece of information on a required form.

While these problems with regulation are obvious, the effect of regulation on business competition is less apparent. In the past two decades, several industries have been deregulated, with positive results. Before the telephone industry was deregulated, AT&T dominated most of the market. Deregulation resulted in new companies and new technology. Today telephone service is better, prices tend to be lower, and customers who are dissatisfied with their service have choices. Similar effects occurred after deregulation of the airline industry in 1978. Since that time, 26 new interstate carriers have entered the industry and 19 have left. Increased competition has led to lower fares, but it has also caused the demise of some long-respected airlines.

Dealing effectively with issues of regulation and deregulation requires recognition of circumstances faced by the business or industry. Government needs a variety of approaches, including laws and regulations, monitoring and information services, and incentive structures to ensure healthy competition and sound business practices.

ETHICS IN BUSINESS

In recent years, companies and their managers have been severely criticized for engaging in seemingly unethical business practices. Insider trading, defective products, workplace dis-

STREET SMART

Balancing Profits and Ethics

Calling the 1990s the decade of ethics and the environment, Max Clarkson, professor of management at the University of Toronto, declared that business ethics is no longer a contradiction. His 30 years of business experience before becoming dean of the Faculty of Management at the university has provided unique insight into business problems. He stated that the business of business is not just business but "business in society." Corporations cannot survive and prosper apart from the communities in which they do business. But Clarkson made it clear that "if you don't make a profit, you can't fulfill any social responsibilities at all." Thus, the real challenge for companies is to balance profits with ethical behaviors.

Exhibit 23.7 **ETHICAL, LEGAL, AND PROFIT TRADEOFFS**

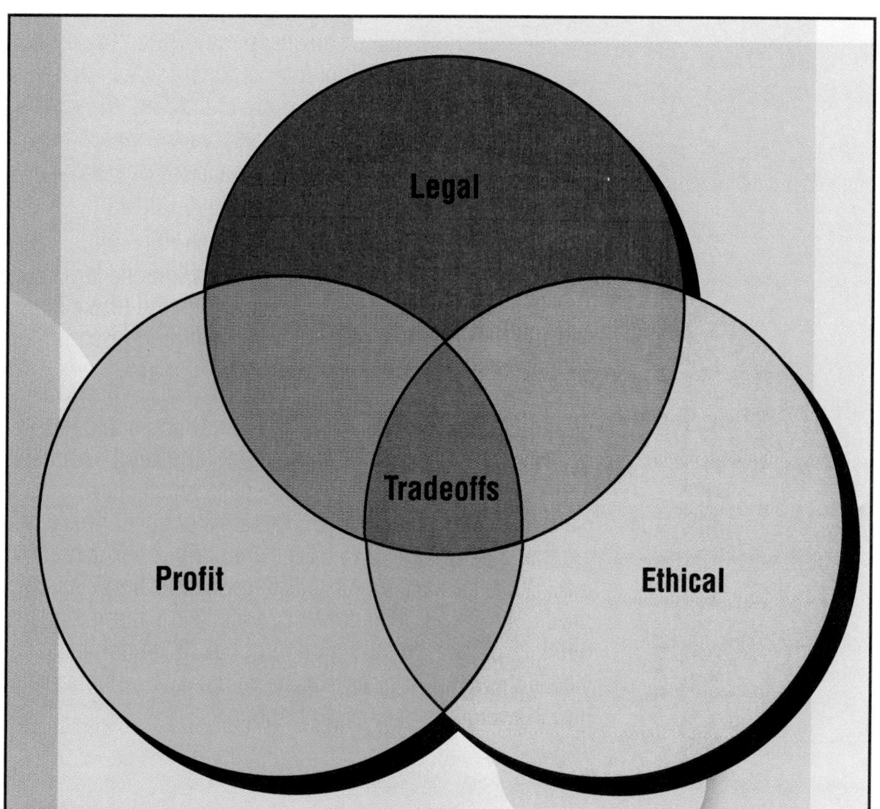

crimination, price gouging, and other issues have filled the business pages of local newspapers. This has led to a focus on how to increase the presence of ethics in business decisions and activities.

As you learned in Chapter 5, *ethics* is a branch of philosophy that deals with morality and the ways moral principles apply to life. It is the study of what constitutes right or wrong behavior. Questions such as what is fair and what is right are central to understanding ethical behavior. Business ethics focuses on what are right or wrong behaviors in the world of business.

Nearly all the laws we have discussed are related to business ethics, because law is an expression of ethical principles. Law answers the questions of what is fair and what is right. However, some argue that ethical behaviors should go beyond the law. That is, one should not have to consult a lawyer or go to court to find out what is right or fair. Perhaps ethics can be found in religion or in codes of conduct that are based at the company level rather than in the courts.

Increasingly, however, managers are recognizing that business decisions require tradeoffs. As Exhibit 23.7 illustrates, no matter what business decision is to be made, the manager must trade off legal, ethical, and profit consequences. It is a matter not only of doing the right thing but doing the legal thing and the profitable thing as well. This point of view does not make the life of a manager any easier. If a manager acts *only* ethically, will he or she also meet profit objectives and meet the letter of the law?

LAW AND INTERNATIONAL BUSINESS

As we have seen throughout this book, transactions among companies in different countries are becoming the rule of business rather than the exception. But each country has its own laws, and one major risk of international trade is that a company will unintentionally violate laws or regulations of one or more countries. While we cannot cover all of the complexities of international law, a few areas deserve mention.

First, contracts for the international sale of goods between firms located in different countries are governed by the United Nations Convention on Contracts for the International Sale of Goods (CISG). This international sales law is similar to the Uniform Commercial Code, and applies to contracts between entities located in countries that have ratified the CISG.

Second, currency differences among nations (as discussed in Chapter 19) can complicate international transactions. It is important to specify the currency in which payment is to be made and the method of payment.

Third, some U.S. laws affect how American firms may do business with international organizations. Two laws are especially important in this regard: the Foreign Corrupt Practices Act of 1977 (FCPA) and the Sherman Act (antitrust) as amended in 1982. The FCPA was passed to prevent companies from giving payments in cash or other form to foreign government officials to obtain business contracts. Although bribery may be normal business practice in another country, any U.S. citizen who bribed a foreign official would be guilty of violating U.S. law. The Sherman Act, originally passed to break up large monopolies in the United States during the 1800s, also prevents price fixing, dumping, and other attempts to control the production, price, or distribution of goods. Both domestic and foreign firms can be sued if they violate this act. It is clear that the complexities of international laws are becoming increasingly important to business organizations.

SUMMARY

1. ***Explain the basis of the U.S. legal system.***
   Law consists of enforceable rules that govern relationships among individuals and between individuals and their society. Much of our legal system is based on English law. Common law evolved from the King's Court and is common to the entire country. Legislators at both the federal and state levels can change common law as societal changes dictate the need. The U.S. legal system also consists of case law, rules of law based on earlier court decisions. The U.S. Constitution is the supreme law of the United States and grants the federal government certain powers. Each state also has its own constitution that establishes the powers of the state government. Administrative law is devoted to rules and regulations created by administrative agencies to implement constitution and statutory laws. Commercial or business law addresses commercial dealings. The most important body of commercial laws is contained in the Uniform Commercial Code (UCC). The UCC governs the design, production, marketing, and interstate distribution of tangible, movable products.

2. ***Discuss the general organization of the American court system at both the state and federal levels.***
   The United States has 52 separate court systems, each of which settles legal disputes. Each state and the District of Columbia have a court system, and there is a separate federal court system. Most state court systems consist of four levels. At the lowest level are state inferior courts, which hear disputes involving specialized subject matter. These courts include probate courts, divorce courts, criminal courts, and small claims courts. The next level is state courts of general jurisdiction, which hear and decide disputes involving nearly all subject matter. Next come state appellate courts, which are not trial courts but instead settle questions of law. The jurisdiction of appellate courts is basically limited to hearing appeals. Finally, state supreme courts are the highest level of state courts. These courts also decide questions of law and are the final state courts to which cases can be appealed. The federal court system is authorized by

the U.S. Constitution. Federal district courts are the federal equivalent of state courts of general jurisdiction. Most federal cases originate in these courts. At the same level are several courts of limited jurisdiction, including the U.S. Tax Court and the U.S. Claims Court. In addition, several administrative agencies have hearings boards that decide special jurisdiction issues. Cases heard in federal district courts can be appealed to one of 13 U.S. courts of appeals. The highest court in the federal system is the U.S. Supreme Court. Most cases heard in the Supreme Court are appeals from the federal courts of appeals, and some are from cases decided in state courts.

3. ***Identify the conditions for a legally valid contract.***
A contract is a promise enforceable by law. A legally valid contract contains the four basic elements of agreement, consideration, contractual capacity, and legality. An agreement includes a valid offer and a valid acceptance. Consideration is something of value and is the inducement for the parties to enter into a contract. Contractual capacity means each party entering into a contract must have the legal capacity to do so. Legality means a contract must be intended to accomplish some legal purpose. A contract must also be in a form appropriate for the contracted purpose. While not all contracts must be written, some transactions require a written contract.

4. ***Explain the nature of sales law.***
Today's sales law is contained in the Uniform Commercial Code (UCC). Sales law generally applies only to the sale of goods, which are defined as items that are both tangible and movable. It does not pertain to real or intangible property, which is covered by property law.

5. ***Discuss the characteristics of property law.***
Property can be classified as either real property or personal property, and personal property can be either tangible or intangible. Property law deals with the various ways ownership rights in these forms of property can be held. The law permits various forms of property ownership. When one person holds all of the property rights, he or she is said to be the owner in fee simple. People can also hold property jointly. Tenancy in common occurs when each of two or more parties owns a fractional interest in the property that passes to that person's heirs upon his or her death. Joint tenancy also involves two or more parties who own interest in the property, but if one party dies, his or her ownership interest passes to the surviving joint tenant(s). Property law also provides for rights in cases of mislaid, lost, and abandoned property.

6. ***Discuss the agency relationship and the conditions that govern it.***
An agency is a legal relationship in which two parties, a principal and an agent, agree that one will act on behalf of the other and under that person's control. Within the scope of the agency agreement, the agent may negotiate contracts and transactions, and the principal will be legally bound by those arrangements. The essential ingredients of agency relationships and transactions are (1) the actual versus apparent authority of the agent, (2) whether the principal is disclosed to a third party doing business with the principal, (3) whether the principal has the right of control or exercises control over the agent, and (4) whether the agency relationship is formalized with a power of attorney. A power of attorney is a notarized document that grants an agent either full or restricted authority to act on behalf of the principal.

7. ***Describe the types of intellectual property and the law that applies to it.***
Intellectual property consists of the products of people's minds—their inventions, trademarks, copyrights, and patents. Another important intellectual property in our modern society is computer software. Intellectual property and computer law is designed to protect the rights of those who create intellectual properties. It consists of separate laws covering patents, copyrights, and trademarks.

8. ***Explain the types of bankruptcy permitted by bankruptcy law.***
Bankruptcy is a legal condition of insolvency in which the court administers the company's or individual's estate for the benefit of the creditors. Bankruptcy law permits three basic types of bankruptcy: Chapter 7, Chapter 11, and Chapter 13 bankruptcy. Chapter 7 bankruptcy requires that the business be dissolved and its assets sold or distributed to its creditors. Chapter 11

bankruptcy temporarily frees a business from its financial obligations while it reorganizes and works out amended payment plans with creditors. Chapter 13 bankruptcy permits individuals to establish three-to-five-year plans for repayment of their obligations while retaining most of their assets.

9. ***Discuss tax law and the various sources of revenue it provides to the government.*** Perhaps the most far-reaching body of law is tax law. Both individuals and businesses are subject to federal taxes. Taxes that directly affect business are income, property, transaction, and employment taxes. Sole proprietorships and partnerships are affected primarily by individual income taxes. Corporations' net incomes are taxed at the prevailing corporate rate. Property taxes are imposed on real and personal property owned by both individuals and businesses. They are based on the value of the property. Transaction taxes include sales and excise taxes and are collected from buyers by sellers. Employment taxes include amounts withheld for federal and state income taxes, FICA (social security) taxes, and FUTA (unemployment) taxes.

10. ***Describe the laws that regulate business and the benefits of deregulation in some industries.*** Government affects companies by directly regulating competition and other business practices to achieve societal objectives. Regulatory acts by the government are classified into three types: functional, industry, and social regulation. Functional regulation is intended to help government carry out its functions and to help business in general. These regulations are generally compatible with business values and tend to control undesirable competition and establish basic guidelines for business. Industry regulation applies to specific industries. In addition to restricting certain practices, some of these regulations grant protection to favored businesses by imposing barriers to entry, price controls, and subsidies. Social regulation often results when society's goals and objectives conflict with those of business. Several regulatory agencies charged with protecting the rights of workers and consumers have required businesses to develop safer work methods and products. In the past two decades, several industries have been deregulated, with positive results. For example, increased competition among telephone companies has resulted in better service, lower prices, and more choices for customers.

11. ***Discuss the nature of ethics in business.*** Ethics is a branch of philosophy that deals with morality and the ways moral principles apply to life. Business ethics focuses on what are right or wrong behaviors in the world of business. Nearly all laws that affect business are related to business ethics, because law is an expression of ethical principles. Ethical issues in business apply to all activities and transactions in which managers engage. These include the treatment of customers, collaborators, and competitors and perhaps even managers' treatment of their own companies.

KEY TERMS AND CONCEPTS

Law (p. 552)
Common law (p. 552)
Precedent (p. 552)
Case law (p. 552)
Statutory laws (p. 552)
Administrative law (p. 552)
Uniform Commercial Code (UCC) (p. 553)
Jurisdiction (p. 553)
State inferior court (p. 554)
State court of general jurisdiction (p. 554)
State appellate court (p. 554)
State supreme court (p. 555)
Federal district court (p. 555)
U.S. court of appeals (p. 556)
U.S. Supreme Court (p. 556)
Contract law (p. 557)
Breach of contract (p. 558)
Property law (p. 560)
Agency law (p. 561)
Power of attorney (p. 562)
Intellectual property and computer law (p. 563)
Patent (p. 563)
Copyright (p. 563)
Fair use (p. 563)
Bankruptcy (p. 564)

DISCUSSION QUESTIONS

Company

1. How do companies benefit from the Uniform Commercial Code?
2. Identify an agency relationship that might exist between a company and a collaborator. What are some points of law that might apply?
3. Why must companies consider tax consequences when making business decisions?

Customers

4. Who are the customers of the various state courts? Discuss.
5. In what ways does government protect the customers of businesses?
6. What are some ethical issues that might arise in making business decisions that would affect customers?

Competitors

7. What role does computer law play in maintaining competition among companies in the computer industry?
8. What ethical issues might a company have to consider in dealing with competitors?

Collaborators

9. How do state appellate and supreme courts serve as collaborators of the legal system?
10. In what different capacities do companies use agents?
11. What protection does bankruptcy law provide to collaborators of businesses?

In Question: Take a Stand

In March 1993, Continental Airlines was preparing to emerge from Chapter 11 bankruptcy. When it begins to operate without bankruptcy protection, Continental will face fierce competition, a smaller cash balance, and unhappy employees who have weathered two rounds of pay cuts.

Continental's reorganization plan called for paying most creditors a fraction of what they are owed, collapsing the company's 54 units into 4, and authorizing a $450 million transaction giving 55 percent of the airline's equity to Air Canada and Air Partners. Chapter 11 gave Continental time to improve its balance sheet. When it went into bankruptcy, the company had $3.96 billion in debt. When it emerged, it had about $1.8 billion in debt and about $635 million in cash.[15]

Is it fair for companies like Continental to stay in business when many of their creditors lose millions of dollars when the companies file bankruptcy? What benefits, if any, does society derive when companies file bankruptcy? If you were manager of a company that was filing for bankruptcy, how would you explain the situation to your suppliers? What actions would you take to be able to continue doing business with them?

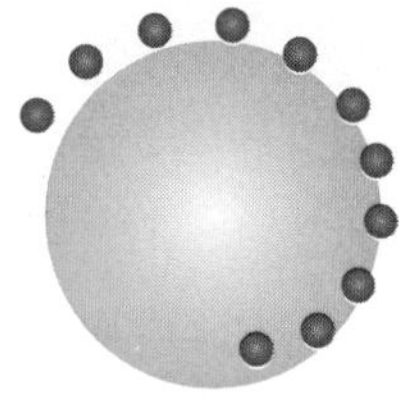

CASE 23.1
PEARLE VISION INC.[16]

Pearle Vision Inc. is well known for making low-priced eyeglasses. Customers like the ease and speed with which they can order and receive glasses at Pearle Vision Centers around the country. However, few Americans realize that Pearle centers are franchises. Pearle is franchised by London-based Grand Met, whose franchising operations include Burger King and Häagen-Dazs. Pearle has over 400 franchised units in the United States.

Many of these units are in financial distress because of Pearle's price-slashing programs. To meet competition from U.S. Shoe Corporation's Precision LensCrafters Inc., Pearle forced franchises to cut their prices but did not reduce the royalties it charges them for using the Pearle Vision name and processes. Franchisees complained to the Federal Trade Commission that Pearle had violated federal rules governing disclosures to prospective franchisees. In fiscal year 1993, Pearle operations lost $91.5 million.

Questions

1. *What obligations does a franchiser such as Pearle Vision Inc. have to ensure that its franchisees make a fair profit?*
2. *What, if any, information should a franchisor not have to disclose to prospective franchisees? Why?*
3. *Should Pearle Vision Inc. cut the royalties it charges franchisees and share in the price-slashing programs it has demanded of them? Why or why not?*

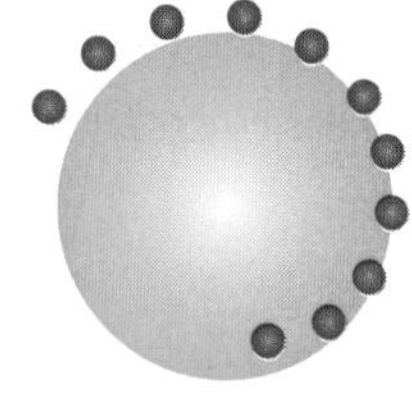

CASE 23.2
AT&T AGAINST THE BABY BELLS[17]

For twelve years the obstinate offspring of the old AT&T have strained at the decree that broke up the Ma Bell monopoly, spun them off, and barred them from AT&T's rich long-distance and equipment markets. Now they are bidding to win deregulation and eliminate the consent decree that has hobbled them for a decade. But the story is more interesting than that.

In 1991, outside the oversight of regulators, AT&T and the seven regional Bell companies held a year of secret talks aimed at crafting terms for urging the federal court to dissolve the decree. The plan was code-named Acorn, from the old saying, "Tall oaks from little acorns grow." But the talks collapsed over how soon the Bells should be allowed into the long-distance business, according to people familiar with the discussions.

Frustrated, the Bells set out on a 2 and 1/2 year effort to plot their own strategy for getting the consent decree voided. As one result of this effort four Baby Bells filed an unprecedented legal motion demanding an end to the decree, the core of U.S. telecommunications policy since the 1984 breakup. The Bells say the decree, based on evidence and market data now two decades old, is antiquated and counterproductive.

That pits the Bells against AT&T and the rest of the industry. It draws hard battle lines just when federal authorities must begin making decisions that will determine the structure of, and ground rules for, the $300 billion telecommunications business for years to come. Even as the Bells begin their court action, Congress is weighing sweeping changes in telecommunications law, and the Bells are lobbying for relief. To succeed, they must win on both fronts. At the heart of this fight is whether the United States should tear down the barriers segregating AT&T and the Baby Bells and unleash the seven multibillion-dollar monopolies—and whether the Bells should sacrifice monopoly control for more freedom.

Once freed, could the Bells resist leveraging their control over the phone lines that reach into 100 million homes and businesses and should they have to? The Bells' style is "to act the way they have traditionally—take advantage of their position and engage in anti-competitive behavior," says Bradley Stillman of the Consumer Federation of America.

Consumers have much to gain or lose in the clash of telecommunications titans. The size of their local monthly phone bills, how low long-distance prices go, what kind of newfangled features they can get, how soon they may enter the much-hyped information highway—all could be affected by the Bells' assault on court and on the Capitol.

Questions

1. *In your opinion, how has government regulation of the telecommunications industry affected competition and customers?*
2. *Should secret meetings between competitors, such as the one held between the Baby Bells and AT&T be permitted? Why or why not?*
3. *What points of law, discussed in this chapter, seem relevant to the case for the Baby Bells?*

YOUR FUTURE IN BUSINESS

After graduating from St. Mary's College in South Bend, Ind., Karen Siegel moved to Chicago and became an internal auditor for a large consumer products company. At the same time, she began volunteering about three hours a week for the Illinois Special Olympics, an organization her family had always supported.

Although Siegel says she has an aptitude for numbers, she wasn't having much fun using the analytical skills her job required. "Something was wrong in my professional life," she says. To compensate, Siegel began spending evenings, weekends and days off at her volunteer job, devoting as much energy to it as she did to her paid career.

Four years later, despite a promotion to senior corporate accountant, Siegel opted for some radical career surgery. She resigned her accounting job for a position that required completely different skills: director of training and management for the Texas Special Olympics in Austin.

Siegel says her Special Olympics position was more satisfying because it "used my stronger abilities," such as public speaking, writing, organizing and training volunteers and staffers, she says. "I'm happier and more naturally suited to" that type of work, says Siegel. "I could spend twelve hours a day doing it and still have more energy than if I spent eight hours doing accounting."[1]

Now that you have read this textbook, we hope you regard business as a fascinating subject. Many interesting, even exciting careers are available in business. However, as Karen Siegel's experience shows, to be truly satisfied with your job, you must find the career that will be most fulfilling to you.

GET AN EARLY START

Most career experts agree that the key to finding the ideal job is to get an early start on your search. This means thinking about your future and planning what you need to get there. Connie Moser, coordinator of student job placement at Tulsa Junior College, says, "It is important to develop job-search skills. You need to know the market and know your goals."[2] Remember the old adage: "If you do not know where you are going, any road will take you there." The key to determining which career is best for you is to identify your abilities (both strengths and weaknesses) and interests and then match them with an occupation. After you decide where you are going, you can select the best road to take you there.

Career opportunities exist in many specializations, including accounting, finance, computer systems, marketing, management, insurance, production, and human resource management. This epilog reviews some of the many career options and explains how you might set about choosing a career in business.

CAREER INFORMATION

An important question for many students is "How do I get information on careers and decide which is best for me?" You should begin by asking the people closest to you—your family, friends, classmates, professors, and part-time employers. Personal contacts can give you many insights as to the kinds of careers available and how you might get started in them. In addition, most college campuses have a student career center, with professional job counselors who can assist you in finding a career that fits your aptitudes and goals. We strongly suggest that you contact the student career counselors early in your college studies to help you select a college major that will meet your career needs.

In addition, most states offer career services to their residents. Career information delivery systems are often available in public libraries, schools, and vocational rehabilitation centers. State employment agencies also carry career information.

You can also obtain career information from various professional associations, such as the American Management Association, the American Marketing Association, and state associations of certified public accountants. The *Encyclopedia of Associations* lists and describes most trade associations and professional societies. Information from one of these many sources will supplement the brief descriptions of career opportunities presented in this epilog.

CAREER OPPORTUNITIES IN BUSINESS

During the past few years, students have become concerned by news accounts describing major layoffs and downsizing of U.S. corporations. To be sure, news that a large, well-known company is reducing its work force by 40,000 should cause concern. But government statistics show that employment levels are actually higher than they have been in previous years. In fact, although career opportunities in some fields are decreasing, in other fields opportunities are greater than ever. Some of the forces contributing to this turbulence in business include population growth, increasing education of our citizens, the globalization of business, and rapidly changing technologies for products and production processes. This turbulence means you must plan your career with great care.

Exhibit E.1 **PERCENTAGE CHANGE IN EMPLOYMENT, 1990–2005**

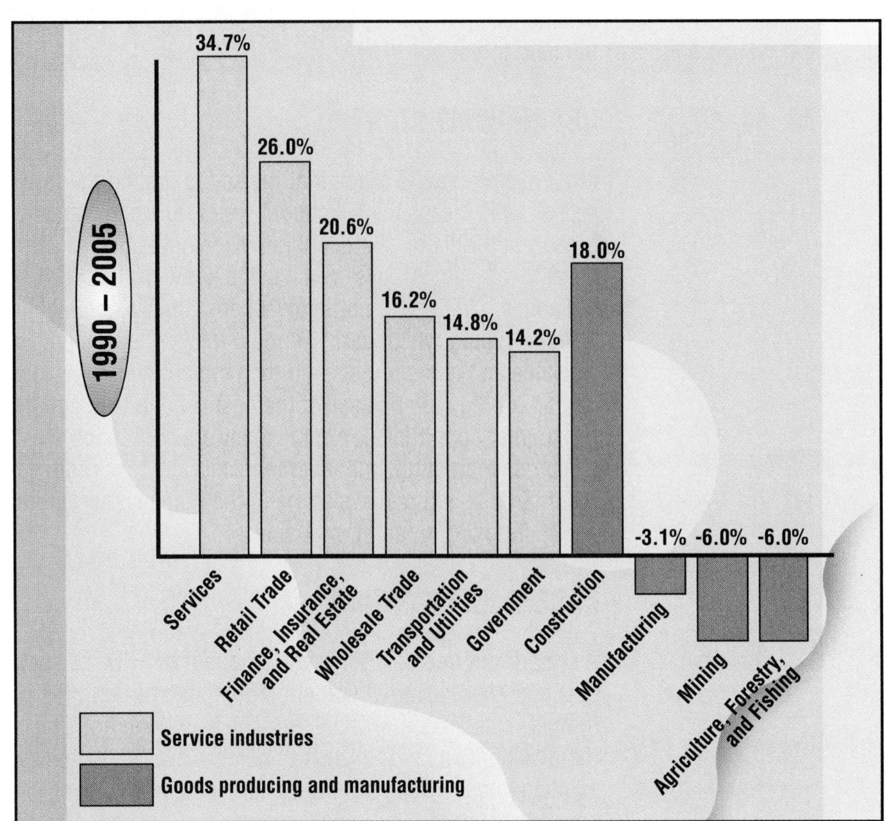

The U.S. Department of Labor predicts that total employment in the United States will increase from 125 million in 1990 to 151 million in 2005, a 21 percent rate of growth.[3] However, not all sectors of our economy will grow at the same rate. You should consider important employment trends when choosing a career field. One of the most important trends is the strong growth in careers that require high levels of education or training relative to blue-collar and other nonprofessional jobs.

As Exhibit E.1 shows, job growth will be much faster in the service sector than in manufacturing. Health care will be one of the fastest-growing industries, reaching 12.8 million jobs by 2005. Retail trade and the finance, real estate, and insurance industries will grow rapidly as well.

Although we cannot describe career opportunities in all of the hundreds of fields in business, we can discuss the major categories of career opportunities. The following sections describe these categories in the general order in which we discussed them in the text.

GENERAL MANAGEMENT

It is difficult to estimate the entire range of management jobs in the United States. All organizations, both public and private, need managers. Examples of general managers include chief executive officer, executive vice-president for marketing, department store manager, office manager, college president, school principal, hotel manager, and police chief. The responsibilities of managers vary according to the size of the company and the management level.

Exhibit E.2 **OCCUPATIONAL FIELDS WITH FASTEST AND SLOWEST EXPECTED GROWTH, 1990–2005**

Fastest-Growing Occupations	Slowest-Growing Occupations
Home health aides	Telephone operators
Paralegals	Electrical equipment assemblers
Systems analysts	Private child care helpers
Physical therapists	Precision assembly workers
Operations research analysts	Textile machine operators
Psychologists	Utilities meter readers
Travel agents	Machine tool operators
Corrections officers	Farm workers
Flight attendants	Garment sewers
Management analysts	Bank tellers

Success in management careers requires long hours, including some weekends and evenings. Lots of travel may be required among international, national, regional, and local offices. Job transfers among offices is common as managers build their careers.

Education and Experience. The educational backgrounds of managers and top executives vary, but most of these individuals have bachelor's degrees in liberal arts or business administration. Liberal arts degrees are more common for the public sector, while business degrees dominate the private sector. The most obvious skills required of successful managers are interpersonal skills. Also, managers with analytical minds, who are able to quickly and accurately assess large amounts of information and data, are more likely to move upward in the management hierarchy.

Career Opportunities. Career opportunities for general managers and top executives are expected to increase at about the average rate for all occupations. However, opportunities in some industries will be much greater, depending on industry growth rates. Although some managers and executives are among the highest-paid people in the country, salary levels vary greatly. Average salaries for CEOs of 200 major companies are over $2.5 million, including bonuses and stock options. Top human resource managers earn nearly $100,000 a year, while computer networking managers earn about $60,000.

Related Opportunities. As Exhibit E.2 shows, managers in the health care industry may expect unusually high growth during the next few years. Top executives in this field should not expect the lavish compensation offered by the Fortune 500 firms, but they will earn very respectable salaries. Half of all hospital CEOs earned more than $120,000 a year in 1993 while managers of selected services earned a good deal less. For example, the average salaries for managers of medical records was about $42,000, while the median salary for managers in group practices was nearly $60,000. Job openings in this management field are expected to grow rapidly.

PRODUCTION MANAGEMENT

Production managers coordinate activities related to producing goods and direct the work of first-line supervisors. Great variety exists among manufacturing plants and in the specific activities of production managers at those plants. However, most production managers are responsible for scheduling production, staffing their operations, acquiring equipment, controlling quality and inventory, and coordinating production with the needs of other departments.

Production managers usually report to the plant manager or vice-president of manufacturing. In large plants with several operations, as in aircraft assembly, individual production managers are in charge of each major operation, such as machining, assembly, and finishing. Most production managers divide their time between the shop floor and their offices. They often work more than 40 hours a week, especially when production deadlines are tight.

Education and Experience. Many production managers have a college degree in business or industrial engineering. Some also have a master's degree in business (MBA). Employers prefer candidates with these degrees, but some hire students with associate degrees as well. People entering this field directly from college may spend their first few months in training. This training familiarizes them with the production line, company policies, and job requirements. They may also rotate between related departments, such as purchasing and accounting. Once they become managers, they must keep current with new production technologies and management practices. Thus, continuing education and training are required. Some employers require their production managers to be members of professional associations such as the American Production and Inventory Control Society.

Career Opportunities. At the start of this decade, about 210,000 production management jobs were available in the United States. About half of these positions were in five industries: industrial machinery and equipment, transportation equipment, fabricated metal products, food products, and chemicals. The U.S. Department of Labor expects this field to grow at the average rate for all occupations through 2005. Automation of facilities may decrease the need for production workers, but will have little effect on the need for qualified production managers. However, automation will cause firms to seek better-educated production managers. Median annual salaries range from $50,000 to $85,000, depending on firm size. Production managers often receive additional bonuses based on productivity.

Related Opportunities. Production trainees have other career opportunities as well. Company operations that require similar training and education include materials, operations, purchasing, and traffic management. Many individuals with production training achieve success as sales engineers, manufacturers' sales representatives, and industrial engineers.

HUMAN RESOURCE MANAGEMENT

The field of human resource management, sometimes called personnel management, offers many management opportunities. Human resource managers may specialize in recruiting and selecting employees, training, labor relations, compensation, and fringe benefits analysis. In small organizations, one human resource manager may be responsible for all of these activities. Larger organizations often have a director of human resources who oversees several specialized departments, each headed by an experienced personnel manager. Human resource managers work in offices, and a 40-hour workweek is standard. Some overtime work is required periodically, especially during contract negotiations with unions. Some travel is required, such as when recruiting on college campuses.

Education and Experience. The responsibilities of human resource managers are many and varied. Thus, the education and experience of these managers are also diverse. A college degree is typically required for entry-level positions. Some companies prefer degrees in human resource management, personnel management, or industrial and labor relations. Others prefer liberal arts or humanities degrees. Regardless of the major, some coursework in social sciences, business, and behavioral science will be useful. Many specialized positions, such as collective bargaining, require previous experience. Positions such as these are often filled by people with line management experience.

Career Opportunities. Openings for human resource managers are expected to grow at a somewhat faster rate than the average for other jobs. But competition for these positions will be keen due to an abundant supply of college graduates who have acceptable qualifications. The median annual salary of human resource specialists is about $30,000. However, human resource managers typically earn more than $36,000, and in larger firms salaries may be considerably higher. Industrial and labor relations directors earn more than $60,000 a year, training directors about $50,000, and affirmative action specialists around $32,000. Many jobs exist in the federal government, where people with bachelor's degrees or three years' experience generally start at $17,000 a year.

Related Opportunities. All personnel, training, and labor relations positions are related. Occupations that share the skills and general duties of human resource managers include employment counselors, rehabilitation specialists, college career planning counselors, placement counselors, psychologists, sociologists, public relations specialists, and teachers.

MARKETING AND SALES MANAGEMENT

Many interesting careers are available in marketing and sales management. Some of the more obvious career opportunities include product and brand management, advertising, sales and sales management, public relations, and retail management.

Jobs in personal selling, which require learning about the company's products and customers, are often the starting point for people hoping to become corporate marketing managers. Almost all sales jobs require the development of human relations skills. A variety of sales jobs, ranging from retail sales to professional selling positions, typically require considerable travel. Don't confuse professional selling with the stereotype of the low-paid used-car salesman. The best sales representatives who work on commission can make hundreds of thousands of dollars.

Product and brand managers supervise marketing activities connected with a single brand or a small family of products. For example, Procter & Gamble has separate brand managers for Tide, Cheer, and Ivory Snow.

Advertising attracts many business majors because of the glamour associated with it. Some companies have one in-house person who is responsible for their advertising. It is more common, however, for companies to hire advertising agencies to produce their advertising campaigns. In addition to advertising managers, positions exist for account executives, copywriters, and art directors. Account managers are responsible for handling relationships with clients and coordinating ad campaigns. Copywriters create the text for print ads and scripts for radio and TV ads. Art directors are responsible for the visual appearance of ads, including arrangement on the page, type style, photographs, and illustrations.

Public relations positions are also likely starting points for people trained in marketing because of their skills in advertising and personal presentation. Retail careers also take advantage of marketing skills, since retailing involves sales training and sales work in the beginning. Retail careers, like other professional positions, may require long hours at initially low wages. But salaries of top retail managers can be quite high. Sales positions typically require a lot of travel.

Education and Experience. Many educational backgrounds are suitable for entry-level positions in marketing, advertising, and public relations management jobs. Broad liberal arts backgrounds with courses in sociology, psychology, and literature are acceptable. For marketing, sales, and promotion management positions, many employers prefer bachelor's or master's degrees in business with an emphasis on marketing. Companies typically fill management positions in these careers by promoting experienced staff. Experience, ability, and leadership are emphasized for promotion, but advancement is even faster for employees who participate in management training programs. Successful marketing, advertising, and public relations managers are confident, creative, highly motivated, able to cope with stress, and flexible yet decisive. Good communication skills are essential.

Career Opportunities. Positions in the general field of marketing are expected to increase much faster than the average for other occupations through 2005. Increasingly intense competition for domestic and foreign products and services will require greater marketing skills and efforts. Growth will be faster in most service industries and in automobile dealerships. Salary levels vary greatly, depending on the level of management responsibility, education, and firm size. The median annual salary of marketing, advertising, and public relations managers is typically more than $40,000, but the top 10 percent earn $78,000 or more. Regional sales managers earn about $65,000, advertising managers about $45,000, and product and brand managers around $55,000.

Related Opportunities. Since marketing skills are important in many jobs, people trained in marketing have several interesting and fulfilling career opportunities. Some of these positions are lobbyists, public relations specialists, graphic artists, technical writers, and editors.

COMPUTERS AND INFORMATION SYSTEMS MANAGEMENT

Computers have become central to most U.S. businesses. Thus, in the past few years many careers related to business uses of computers have opened up. Perhaps the fastest-growing occupation, other than computer programmer, is that of computer systems analyst. Computer systems analysts define business, scientific, or engineering problems and design solutions using computers. This may include planning and developing new computer systems or devising ways to apply existing systems to identified problems. Systems analysts work about 40 hours a week, with occasional overtime when necessary to meet deadlines.

Education and Experience. Education and experience required for this work depend greatly on the field in which you work. Prior work experience is very important. For example, an auditor in an accounting department may become a systems analysts specializing in computer applications for accounting. A college degree is required, and some employers prefer graduate degrees. Analysts with backgrounds in business management or related fields are usually desired for work in business environments. Preferred degrees are in computer science, information science, computer information systems, or data processing. Systems analysts must be able to think logically, have good communication skills, and like working with ideas and people. Willingness to take continuing education courses in rapidly changing computer technology is critical.

Career Opportunities. The field of systems analysis is growing very rapidly. Annual earnings of computer systems analysts average about $40,000. Entry-level positions pay in the low $20,000s, but experienced systems analysts can earn more than $60,000 per year.

Related Opportunities. Other careers that require the use of research, logic, and creativity to solve business problems are computer programming, financial analysis, urban planning, operations research analysis, and management analysis.

ACCOUNTING

Accountants and auditors prepare, analyze, and verify financial reports used by managers in all business, industrial, and government organizations. Major fields of accounting include public accounting, management accounting, government accounting, tax accounting, and internal auditing. Public accountants have their own businesses or work for accounting firms. They audit accounting records of organizations needed by a variety of users including investors and various government agencies. Public accountants also prepare tax reports for their clients. Management accountants work for medium-size and large companies; they prepare financial records used by organization managers. Internal auditors also work for private companies. They verify the accuracy of their organizations' records, checking for mismanagement, waste, or fraud. Government accountants and auditors maintain and examine the records of government agencies and audit private businesses and individuals whose activities are subject to government regulations or taxation. Accountants and auditors work in offices, but may be required to travel while conducting audits. Most accountants work a standard 40-hour week, but public accountants often work long hours during tax season.

Education and Experience. Accounting positions nearly always require a bachelor's degree in accounting or a related field. Some employers prefer a master's degree in accounting or business. Previous experience is useful in finding a starting position. Summer internships and part-time work in related fields help get a career off the ground. Professional certification is required by many employers and is critical for building a career in public accounting. People planning a career in accounting must have good math skills, know how to analyze, compare, and interpret facts and figures, and be able to make good decisions based on this knowledge. Communication skills and interpersonal skills are important when dealing with clients and managers.

Career Opportunities. Career opportunities for accountants and auditors are expected to grow faster than the average for other occupations during the next decade. Complex tax laws and increasing demands of investors will keep the demand for qualified accountants high. Accountants with computer skills will have excellent career opportunities. Starting positions for college graduates with degrees in accounting typically average $27,000 a year. Those with master's degrees often start in the low $30,000s. Experienced management accountants' salaries average over $80,000, and internal auditors earn more than $55,000.

Related Opportunities. Training in accounting is important in many other occupations. Some related positions for people with degrees or training in accounting include appraisers, budget officers, loan officers, financial analysts, bank officers, actuaries, underwriters, tax collectors and revenue agents, special agents of the Federal Bureau of Investigation (FBI), brokers, and purchasing agents.

FINANCIAL MANAGEMENT

Nearly all businesses have one or more financial managers, including treasurer, controller, credit manager, cash manager, and chief financial officer (CFO). Financial managers oversee the company's cash flow and financial resources and assess the company's present and future financial status. Chief financial officers in large organizations help CEOs develop financial strategies and procedures, delegate authority, and oversee the implementation of financial strategies. Controllers direct the preparation of all financial reports and oversee the accounting, audit, or budget departments. Cash and credit managers monitor and control the flow of cash receipts and disbursements. Risk and insurance managers oversee programs to minimize risks and losses associated with business operations. Financial institutions such as banks, savings and loan associations, and credit unions have many positions for financial specialists. These opportunities include bank branch managers, consumer credit officers, and loan officers. Financial managers work a standard 40-hour week, although overtime is occasionally required.

Education and Experience. Successful careers in finance require a bachelor's degree in accounting or finance. An MBA degree is a plus. Experience, ability, and leadership are major requirements for promotion, and specialized training will speed up advancement. Continuing education at local universities and colleges is common. Financial managers should enjoy working independently, dealing with people, and analyzing detailed financial information. Good communication skills, both written and oral, and computer skills are important.

Career Opportunities. In 1990 there were about 700,000 financial management positions in the United States. About one-third of these were in financial institutions, and another third were in service industries. The field is expected to continue to grow rapidly, as events such as the savings and loan crisis have prompted the need for skilled financial managers. Competition for positions in this field is expected to be severe as universities and colleges have improved their programs. The median annual salary of all financial managers is

$37,000. But, in large organizations, a top financial executive's compensation often exceeds $100,000 per year. Financial managers often become CEOs of their companies.

Related Opportunities. There are many related occupations in which persons with financial management skills can excel. These include activities in lending, credit operations, securities investment, insurance, and pension funds. Financial training also is important for accountants, auditors, budget officers, credit analysts, loan officers, insurance agents, pension consultants, real estate advisors, securities consultants, and underwriters.

THINK SMALL

Not all students will go to work for Microsoft, General Electric, or other Fortune 500 companies. Small companies also offer many challenging and rewarding careers. In fact, some of the best career opportunities exist in small companies. Small, entrepreneurial companies often have the edge in innovation, marketing, and financial wizardry. Often they offer better advancement opportunities and fringe benefit programs than their larger counterparts do. For example, the founder of Quad/Graphics Inc., a rapidly growing printing company headquartered in Pewaukee, Wisconsin, boasts a long list of training courses, an on-site sports center, and a stock ownership program. It also sets up every press crew as an independent profit center responsible for its own operations. Prime Technology Inc., a machine tool distributor in Grand Rapids, Michigan, has fewer than 30 people on its payroll. But it offers spirited, team-based management, generous bonus programs, and open-book policies.

Thousands of small companies like Quad/Graphics and Prime Technology offer high-quality career opportunities. However, they are less likely than large companies to recruit on college campuses, so be prepared to seek them out.[4]

FOCUS ON CAREER

Forget the Fortune 500

Joanna George joined retailer Toys 'R Us because she wanted to work in an informal, innovative atmosphere where she could develop close friendships with co-workers. Unfortunately, she didn't last long.

A lack of feedback from her bosses and the inaccessibility of company decision-makers prompted George to jump ship. She left the national toy-store chain to join Palmetto Promotions, a 13-person firm in Columbia, South Carolina.

"I find the informal atmosphere of the smaller organization more comfortable," says George, who earned a marketing degree at Clemson University. "I've also had the opportunity to [get to] know my co-workers personally, which was important to me since I was making a career change from management to sales." Her advice to new college grads: "Begin your work experience in a small business rather than at a more impersonal larger company."

THINK ENTREPRENEURIAL

This book began with the story about The Body Shop, the company founded by Anita Roddick. Roddick was not an experienced businessperson when she decided to start her own business. Roddick's career in business began as an entrepreneur. For many students, owning their own business is the proper career path. Chapter 6 discussed the benefits and pitfalls of this career path.

THINK INTERNATIONAL

This book has stressed that business operates in a world economy. Business will be even more global in the 21st century. Today's students should consider pursuing careers in international business as accountants, managers, and marketing specialists. The increasing internationalization of business is spawning numerous career opportunities in these fields. Even small, entrepreneurial companies are finding they need employees who are willing to travel and do business internationally. People pursuing these careers need to know more than just their specialties. They must also know geography, have good foreign language skills, understand international customs, and be familiar with business procedures in other countries.

PREPARING FOR A CAREER IN BUSINESS

Many observers of the U.S. labor force predict that nearly 20 million college graduates will enter the workplace during the next decade. As you saw in the previous section, there are many good opportunities for fulfilling careers, but competition for jobs is very intense.

Although business profits are up, output is growing, and the economy is recovering, there has been no great surge in job growth. Downsizing by some of America's best-known companies, including IBM, Sears, and General Motors, is becoming all too common. Rather than hiring new employees in some fields, many larger companies are either working their old ones harder or replacing them with technology. Recent college graduates in some fields are facing the toughest job market in 20 years. Thus, finding an entry-level career position will require much planning, creativity, and persistence.

FOCUS ON CAREER

Job Search Tips

When good jobs are hard to get, standard advice for getting a job is not enough. Taking risks, being creative, and being smart are the extra ingredients—layered over solid technical skills and experience—that often result in a job. Jack Erdlen, an outplacement and career counselor, recommends putting energy into networking, sending out résumés, doing follow-ups, and going out on interviews. But he has seen some extraordinary efforts pay off as well. One candidate pestered the hiring manager for the company he wanted to work for until the manager, impressed with his determination, hired him. Another sent a résumé to a prospective employer with a toy electric magic wand. An enclosed note suggested that she could "work magic" with sales and should be hired. Yet another enclosed a state lottery ticket with her résumé and a note that said, "The odds of winning the lottery are 3 1/2 million to 1. Also enclosed is my résumé, but there is absolutely no gamble if you want to hire me. I'm a proven performer."

Still, it is a candidate's skill that interests employers. The tricks are merely attention getters, and not all employers like them. Patricia Davis, who handles recruitment and employee relations for Waste Management, Inc., says the best strategy is "Tell me what you can do and why I should hire you rather than someone else—in one paragraph."

FINDING YOUR FIRST JOB

While successful applicants for entry-level jobs take many different approaches, their efforts can be grouped into four basic guidelines:

- Know what kinds of jobs you will enjoy most.
- Build experience.
- Build a résumé.
- Build interview skills.

KNOW YOURSELF

Before you start your career search, you need to know the kinds of activities you enjoy and the things you do well. For various reasons, many new graduates pursue careers that aren't right for them. Some eventually land more satisfying jobs, while others never realize the joy of doing what they really love. Being smart and motivated may not be enough if you aren't suited to your career.

Charles McVinney, vice-president of Whole Brain Corporation, a Cambridge, Massachusetts, consulting firm, suggests that the brain plays a big role in determining the match between you and your career. Research shows that the human brain is split into two halves, each of which is responsible for certain abilities. The left side is the active, verbal, logical, rational, and analytical part. It tends to process words and numbers in an orderly way and is capable of quickly processing information. The right side of the brain is the intuitive, creative, largely nonverbal part. It deals with images, metaphors, analogies, and new ideas. Thus, left-brain thinkers are better at solving problems, working with numbers, and dealing with concrete decisions. Right-brain thinkers are more comfortable with complex problems and like to apply unique, creative solutions.

Thus, good career matches depend on finding job choices that require activities compatible with your brain dominance. If you are a left-brain thinker, good career choices are likely to be in fields that require the use of logic and rationale and the application of quantitative skills. These careers are found in production, planning, financial analysis, marketing management, accounting, computer information systems, market research, and insurance. If you are a right-brain thinker, good career choices are probably those that require the use of creativity in solving complex problems. Such careers are likely to be in marketing and advertising, entrepreneurship, sales, human resource management, social work, public relations, and customer service.[5] Knowing whether you are more left or right brained can help you make a better choice of careers.

BUILD EXPERIENCE

Nothing is more discouraging to a recent graduate than the words "experience required." How can you get the experience if no one will give you that first job? But there are many things you can do to build the experience portion of your résumé. Human resource managers point out that experience need not be obtained only on a job. For example, leadership skills can be acquired through work in student organizations and volunteer activities.

Summer jobs can provide more than just money to pay tuition. Although few internships are available, some students volunteer to do something "extra" for employers during the summer. That extra, unpaid work might be something like rearranging the inventory or designing a computerized information system for a small business. Simply cooking hamburgers will add little to a résumé, unless you are seeking a career in hotel or restaurant management. In that case, even that little extra activity may pay dividends. Among students who received job offers during on-campus recruiting, nearly three-quarters have held internships or had related summer job experience. Among those receiving no offers, fewer than one-third have had such experience.[6] The key to building experience is to think in terms of skills and activities that fit with the career you are seeking.

STREET SMART

Detective Skills for Job Seekers

One problem in locating employers with good career potential is that many are not what they seem to be in terms of career opportunities. Thus, detective skills are as important as work skills in finding that first job. *Inc.* offers these tips for checking out potential employers:

- *Hit the phones.* Small private companies often don't show up in business journals and trade publications, so it is hard to learn about them. For them, the best sources of information are local trade associations or chambers of commerce, local business reporters, and people associated with the company, such as suppliers and customers.
- *Run a credit check.* Want to know if your prospective employer is financially sound? Request the annual report or ask TRW's Business-to-Business Credit Report System for a profile. It costs $28.
- *Compare benefits and compensation.* Trade association publications print benefits-and-compensation surveys, broken down by region and job level.
- *Inspect the corporate culture.* When you visit for an interview, look around. One consultant advises clients to ride the elevator, eat in the cafeteria, and listen. Hang around the parking lot in the mornings and after work to see how people dress and at what times they come and go. If you're called back for further interviews, ask to speak with a few employees, and ask how they learn about company news. Or ask how decisions are made, and what kinds of behaviors are rewarded in the company.

If the company really is a good place to work, with good career opportunities, the owners, managers, and employees will be glad you asked.

BUILD A RÉSUMÉ

Although both education and experience are important in finding a job, unless you can build an attractive résumé, prospective employers may not even learn about your talents. A résumé is a summary of your career objective, educational background, work experience, major interests, and other personal information relevant to an employer. Information can be presented in a résumé in several different ways, and it is best to seek help from a professional résumé writer. Generally, you can get help in writing a résumé by contacting your student placement center, a state employment agency, or an instructor of business communications. Seeking professional help in building résumés is a smart thing to do. An example of a résumé appears in Exhibit E.3.

BUILD INTERVIEW SKILLS

If all goes as planned, experience and an appropriate résumé will result in an interview with a prospective employer. It is important that you plan for the interview and be prepared to make a positive impression on the interviewer. Preparation includes finding out as much about the company as you can. In the case of large, international companies, you can find much information in your library or student placement center. You can also find current news items in magazines such as *Business Week* and *Fortune.* Much less information is available about small companies, but you should still try to research them as much as you can. Local business publications, the Chamber of Commerce, and the credit bureaus are good sources of information for small businesses.

In addition to researching the company, it is important to have some idea of the types of questions to ask an interviewer. Questions about salary, fringe benefits, and location may be

Exhibit E.3 **SAMPLE RÉSUMÉ**

Melissa A. Middleton
1400 Lakeview Road
College Town, U.S.A. 90524
(301) 555-1632

OBJECTIVE

A challenging career that would provide personal growth and an opportunity to participate in the growth of the company through the utilization of my leadership and communication skills.

EDUCATION

- Major: Industrial/Organizational Psychology
- GPA In Major: 3.6 CSU Overall: 3.5
- Colorado State University, Fort Collins, Colorado
- Graduated with B.S.: May 1995

QUALIFICATIONS

Leadership: Panhellenic President, Vice President, & Vice President of Judicial Affairs Board. Learned to use empowerment and delegation in an organization understood the importance of effective communication, developed the ability to look to the future, and discovered the importance of self-motivation.
Training: Founded CARE (Cultural & Racial Education Program), developed and assisted with alcohol awareness & educational programs, planned and worked with several student leadership conferences and retreats, and worked in University Administration on numerous committees.
Planning: Designed, promoted, and executed leadership conference in Fall 1991 for sorority women. Instructed a psychology lab with the assistance of another undergraduate student.

EXPERIENCE

Sales Associate/Dept. Head. Gart Brothers, Fort Collins, CO 1995. Assisted customers, arranged store displays, handled inventory control, and represented Gart Brothers positively. Outstanding sales associate, 1995.
Student Orientation Leader/ Management Team. Preview Colorado State, Fort Collins, CO. 1993–1995. Promoted and represented Colorado State University in positive ways. Maintained various financial accounts.
Hostess/Bookkeeper. University Club, Fort Collins, CO. 1992–1994. Presented the club positively while serving faculty and staff members. Helped keep financial accounts and inventory.

ACTIVITIES AND INTERESTS

- Member of Delta Delta Delta 1991–1995
- Panhellenic 1992–1995
- Homecoming Parade Coordinator 1990
- Golden Ram 1992
- Student Hall Government Representative 1991–1992
- Coordinator of CARE (Cultural and Racial Education)

HONORS & AWARDS

- Golden Key National Honor Society 1994
- President's Honor Roll Spring 1994
- Faculty/Staff Scholarship 1994–1995
- Gamma Sigma Alpha Honor Society 1993
- Outstanding Greek Woman Spring 1995
- Colorado State University Pacesetter 1994
- Greek Honor Roll all semesters 1991–1995
- Dean's Honor Roll—7 of 8 semesters
- Palmer Leadership Award 1995

REFERENCES

Available upon request.

important to you, but may turn off the interviewer if they dominate the interview. Questions about opportunities the company offers for growth and learning are far more impressive. They will let the interviewer know about your objectives and assessments of your own strengths and weaknesses. Employers are also interested in a candidate's honesty, integrity, and ambition, qualities that your questions will reflect.

You must also be prepared for questions that interviewers like to ask. Some of the most often asked questions include

STREET SMART

Prepare, Prepare, and Prepare!

The Workforce Development Center helps out-of-work people find new careers. It believes one of the most important things people can do is learn how to sell themselves better. The center teaches candidates how to dress properly for an interview and how best to prepare themselves mentally. It advises, "One of the biggest mistakes you can make is not being prepared, not knowing enough about the company to ask intelligent questions. They want to know that you've done some research on them, where you see yourself in five years, what you feel you can offer to the company, why you want to work there." There are three keys to a successful interview: prepare, prepare, and prepare.

- What are your long-term career objectives?
- What are your greatest strengths (weaknesses)?
- How much money do you want to earn in five years?
- If you could have any job in the world, what would it be? Why?

Often the most difficult part of an interview is keeping it moving in a direction that maintains the company's interest in you. This is a subtle skill that you can acquire only by practice. It is a good idea to go through several "mock interviews" before going on an actual job interview. Such mock interviews can be arranged by your career counselor and may be videotaped so that you can review your interview behaviors.

Choosing a career and finding your first career position are very important. Your decisions regarding your career will last a lifetime, and they deserve considerable thought. Use all the resources at your disposal as you embark on this critical part of your life.

APPENDIX A

SAMPLE BUSINESS PLAN: LITTLE LEARNERS PARENT–TEACHER STORE

The following pages present a business plan for a fictional small business, the Little Learners Parent-Teacher Store. While this plan is shorter and less detailed than an actual business plan, it illustrates the basic style of such a plan.

A computerized version of this business plan is available. Your instructor will provide a copy if it is needed for this class.

Business Plan
Little Learners Parent-Teacher Store
Fiscal Year 1995
Robin Lee, President

Submitted to:

Pat Johnson
Commercial Loan Officer
Commerce National Bank
March 1, 1995

CONTENTS

Table 1 **COMPARATIVE INCOME STATEMENTS: FISCAL YEARS 1992–1995**

	FY 1992	FY 1993	FY 1994	FY 1995*
Sales revenue	$86,000	$177,000	$232,000	$321,000
Expenses:				
Cost of goods sold	44,000	94,000	119,000	165,000
Administrative costs	5,000	2,000	2,000	3,000
Salaries	50,000	66,000	68,000	84,000
Rent and utilities	20,000	21,000	22,000	40,000
Advertising and PR	1,500	1,500	2,000	7,000
Other expenses	1,000	1,500	1,500	2,000
Income before taxes	($35,000)	($9,000)	$17,500	$20,000

*Projected, with expansion.

EXECUTIVE SUMMARY

Little Learners Parent-Teacher Store is an 1,100-square-foot retail store specializing in educational games and teaching aids. Its primary customers are elementary school teachers who want additional resources for the classroom and parents seeking educational resources to supplement their children's learning in school.

In 1995 the owners would like to expand in response to the opportunity presented by a retail vacancy next to the existing store. Expanding into the existing space will increase square footage which is expected to boost monthly sales. The sales increase would more than offset the additional operating costs.

INTRODUCTION

Little Learners Parent-Teacher Store is an 1,100-square-foot retail store specializing in educational games and teaching aids. Its best-selling products include workbooks, science experiments, and classroom decorations such as posters and bulletin board art. The store has been in operation since 1992 in the downtown business district of Palo Alto, California. Its primary customers are elementary school teachers who want additional resources for the classroom and parents seeking educational resources to supplement their children's learning in school. The owners of Little Learners are two former teachers in the Palo Alto school system. All salespeople in the store have teaching experience, enabling them to better help shoppers evaluate the products for sale.

In each of the first three years of its operation, the store has exceeded its revenue projections. For fiscal year 1994, ending May 31, 1995, the business is expected to post its first profit: $17,500 before taxes. Table 1 summarizes income statements for the past three years. To achieve its sales, the store has relied primarily on recommendations among teachers and weekly advertisements in the local newspaper, the *Palo Alto Times.* Because the store has little direct competition, it has been able to maintain an average 48 percent gross margin, avoiding price reductions except to clear out seasonal items.

CUSTOMER ANALYSIS

Palo Alto, California, is a middle- to upper-class community of mostly professionals. With Stanford University and many research-oriented employers nearby, the people of this community place high value on learning and education. Thus, a major environmental opportunity is that this area is a strong supporter of educational resources for parents and teachers, including the Little Learners store.

In fact, we believe that we have only begun to tap the demand for the types of products we sell. Our sales have so far been limited by a small budget for advertising and public relations, as well as space constraints that prevent us from stocking as broad a selection as would interest most parents. A telephone survey of 50 households within a five-mile radius found that only 24 percent were aware of the store, but 43 percent expressed interest in the categories of merchandise offered.

Population trends support the view that demand for a parent-teacher store will continue to grow. Over the last decade, the population of Palo Alto has grown by only 1 percent, but the strongest growth (11.5 percent) was among households with children under 15. Furthermore, most of the population consists of professional people, a group that generally has a sizable amount of disposable income and values high-quality toys and educational opportunities for its children.

COMPETITIVE ANALYSIS

Research into the stores located within a 20-mile radius uncovered only one store that directly competes with Little Learners. This store, called Educational Resources, has been operating for ten years in Santa Clara, California. The location is somewhat less desirable, but the costs of operating there are lower. As the store is privately owned, no data are available on its sales volume. However, on a recent Saturday, a steady flow of customers was seen entering the store.

We do not expect major competition from new stores over the near term. Because Educational Resources has operated for ten years without expanding or even, to all appearances, updating its interior, we believe that aggressive expansion is not in its owners' plans. Furthermore, because our own expansion into adjacent space is likely to attract less notice than opening new locations would, we expect that our expansion will attract few, if any, new competitors.

Thus, the major sources of competition for Little Learners are other types of retailers of educational products for children. Examples are toy stores, which sell some toys considered educational, bookstores, catalog retailers, and companies such as Discovery Toys that sell quality products in the home. Despite these environmental threats, we believe that our major strengths—the year-round availability of the store and the expertise of the owners and sales staff—set Little Learners apart as an easy-to-use source of guidance in selecting toys, games, and other materials that enhance learning by children.

COMPANY PLANNING

This section describes our growth objective and how we plan to achieve it. The retail space adjacent to Little Learners became vacant in February 1995, when the jewelry store occupying the space relocated. This vacancy presents an attractive opportunity, given the strong sales Little Learners has experienced with minimal advertising. The remainder of this business plan details how the owners intend to take advantage of this expansion opportunity.

Company Objectives. Our objective is to achieve a 55 percent increase in sales by the end of fiscal year 1995. The increase is to be achieved by expanding the total square footage of the store to include the vacant space next door, for a total of 2,000 square feet (an increase of approximately 80 percent). The increase in sales is to be measured on a monthly basis in comparison to the previous year. In spite of the costs associated with increased size, we intend to keep our profit margin above 6 percent in fiscal year 1995. We seek to return to our current pretax profit margin of 7.5 percent by the end of fiscal year 1996.

Target Markets. The target markets for the store have been teachers working within a 20-mile radius of the store and "active parents" living within a 10-mile radius. By "active parents," we mean parents who devote a relatively great amount of time and money to their children's growth and development—for example, signing them up for swimming lessons, sending them to the "best" preschools, selecting toys that purportedly have educational value, joining parents' groups, visiting classrooms.

Active parents are the target market for the store's planned expansion. Not only are they interested in the kinds of products sold by Little Learners, they are willing to spend heavily on such products. They tend to be less budget conscious than the teachers who shop at the store.

Company Strategy. To attract the target market of "active parents," Little Learners will use most of the additional space to expand its offerings of educational toys and games. Compared to such materials as workbooks and posters, these are the items most often requested by the parents who shop at the store. The focus will be on top-quality, high-margin items that are hard to find at most toy stores. For example, there will be an extensive line of materials for science experiments, as well as top-quality arts and crafts supplies suitable for children. Top-quality, high-margin items support the store's image as a place to find materials superior to those available at a toy store. This focus appeals to parents who are willing to spend more if it means giving their children an edge.

The strategy to build revenues depends on increasing sales among parents who already visit the store and attracting more of the parents who live within a 10-mile radius. The primary means of increasing sales among current customers is the expanded product line. To attract new customers, we will rely on several types of communications. First, we will increase the frequency of display advertisements the store runs in the *Palo Alto Times* from twice a month to once a week. To build awareness, each ad will feature a different product or product line available at the store, along with the slogan "The Store Dedicated to Joyful Learning."

In addition, Little Learners will sponsor quarterly lectures on topics of interest to parents. The store will arrange for child development experts to speak at the public library. Posters and press releases announcing these events will mention the store's sponsorship.

To supplement these regular communications activities, the store will seek to take advantage of other opportunities to receive publicity. These will include events at the store, such as a writing contest among elementary-school students.

Itemized costs for this strategy appear in the appendix to the business plan.

COLLABORATORS

Little Learners plans to use Commercial National Bank as a collaborator to supply funds. M. A. X. McGee, a C.P.A. located in Palo Alto, will help with the accounting work. A key to Little Learners' strategy is to offer top-quality, high-margin items that are hard to find in most toy stores. Thus, a close relationship with suppliers, such as Fisher-Price and MicroSoft Inc., will be important to fulfill the company's goals.

IMPLEMENTATION AND CONTROL

The owners of Little Learners Parent-Teacher Store will be responsible for implementing this business plan. As shown in Figure 1, the timetable for implementing the plan involves occupying the new space by June 1, 1995, and opening for business there by August 15. We expect to achieve the 55 percent increase in sales by the end of the fiscal year (May 31, 1996). Success in carrying out this plan will be measured in terms of completing activities according to the schedule shown in Figure 1 and meeting the objectives of the plan.

If costs should be higher than projected, our contingency plan is to proceed as long as we can keep costs within 15 percent of the projected amount. This will delay our

Figure 1 **SCHEDULE FOR BUSINESS PLAN: FISCAL YEAR 1995**

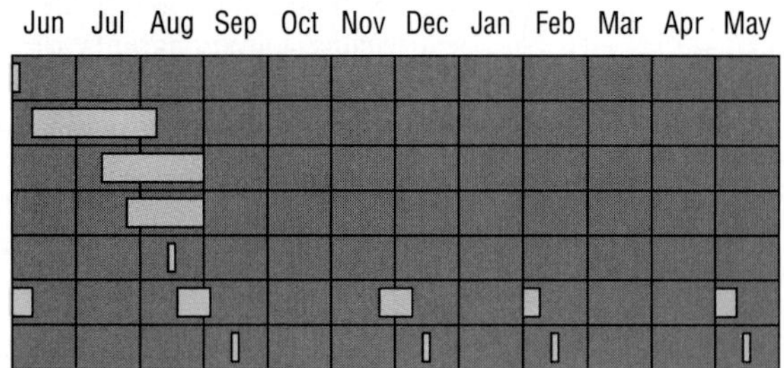

ability to profit from the expansion until fiscal year 1996. If the adjacent retail space should no longer be available, our contingency plan is to forgo expanding the size of the store at the present time and to reevaluate the mix of products offered in the current store. We may be able to increase sales and profits by replacing some current offerings with more of the kinds of products we are planning to sell in the additional space. However, in adjusting the product mix, we will avoid changing in ways that detract from fulfilling our mission of serving teachers as well as parents in their efforts to promote learning.

APPENDIX: FINANCIAL ANALYSIS

This appendix presents a sales forecast and budget in support of the marketing plan.

Sales Forecast. Little Learners Parent-Teacher Store sells to parents and teachers. By offering teachers a free subscription to a company-produced, two-page monthly newsletter, the store can identify which sales go to which category of buyers. Figure 2 shows the pattern of sales to each category during the three years of the store's operations.

The marketing plan targets its expansion efforts at parents. Thus, sales to teachers are expected to follow the historical trend of increasing at an average of 5 percent per year. The additional communications efforts should increase sales beyond historical patterns. A telephone survey of area households found that only about one-quarter were familiar with the store but that almost half were interested in the types of products sold. Therefore, we anticipate that more intensive communications will lead to approximately a 45 percent increase in sales to parents.

Figure 2 **SALES HISTORY BY CATEGORY**

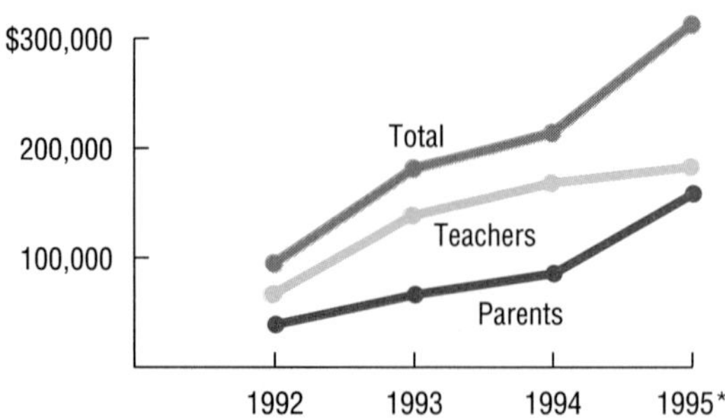

*Projected.

Table 2 **COMPANY BUDGET: FISCAL YEAR 1995**

Assitional Company Expenses	
Sales staff	$34,000
Advertising, newspaper	6,300
Seminar speakers (4 @ $100)	400
Other, including posters, in-house PR	300
Total company expenses	$41,000
Costs for Additional Space	
Preparation of space	$20,000
Additional rent and utilities @ $1,500 per month	18,000
Total for additional space	$38,000

Budget. The budget for this business plan appears in Table 2. The additional salesperson would cost about $16,000 per year, bringing the total cost for sales staff to $34,000. The additional communications expenses would be $5,000, bringing the total budget for promotion to $7,000. The total costs to expand into the new location are $20,000 to prepare the space, plus an additional $1,500 per month in rent and utilities.

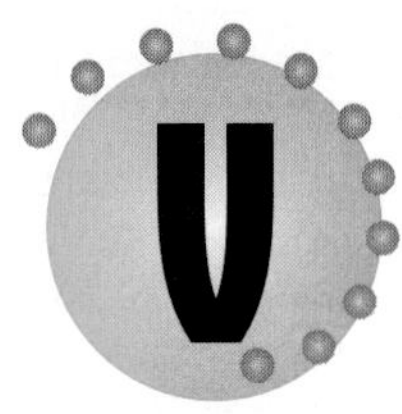

INTEGRATIVE VIDEO CASE
SPECIALIZED BICYCLE COMPONENTS

Most interdepartmental meetings at Specialized Bicycle Components are scheduled for 12 noon. Yet everyday at that time, the conference rooms are empty. Everyday at noon the employees at Specialized Bicycles hop on their bikes and take off for the hills surrounding the company's Morgan Hill, California, headquarters located ten miles south of San Jose. The employees, nearly all of whom are serious cycling fanatics, use the time to test Specialized's new products—including bikes, helmets, wheels, tires, shoes, components, and even water bottles—in order to make sure they pass the enthusiasts' test before they are offered to consumers.

By harnessing this fervor into product development, Specialized has climbed to the top of the international bicycling business. Specialized's 1981 introduction of the Stumpjumper, the first mass-produced mountain bike, heralded the international boom in mountain bikes. Slightly more than ten years later, sturdy off-road bikes account for roughly two-thirds of the market's unit sales.

"Cycling is our passion," says Mike Sinyard, president and founder of Specialized. "We make bikes that we want to ride ourselves. Our lunchtime rides are more than recreation. They are the source of our most exciting product innovations."

A quick glance through Specialized's catalogue affirms this. The ProLong saddle was the result of employees' wish for a seat with a longer nose and tapered back edge. The Sub 6 helmet answered the call for a lighter, stronger, more aerodynamic, and more attractive racing helmet.

Specialized has remained on the cutting edge by remaining close to the authentic cycling experience. In addition to hiring enthusiasts, the company sponsors Team Specialized, the premier off-road racing team. Specialized uses the team as factory test pilots for all of its newest technologies. The company maintains that if a product can stand up to the rigorous testing of world-class racers, it is ready for consumers.

The key to innovative product development is a synthesis of spirit, vision, and energy, according to David Haygood, vice president of research and design. To that end, Specialized created the S-works design unit in 1991. The spirit of this elite group is embodied in its "Innovate Or Die" motto.

"S-Works bikes are the coolest, most outrageous off-road racing bikes we could imagine," says Haygood. "We were never satisfied with existing bicycle technology. Through S-Works we can really stretch out and test the limits of what is possible and design our own dream bikes."

For 1993, the S-Works designers have broken the mold with two new futuristic concept bikes. The two bikes combine industrial engineering and bicycle technology with design innovations that range from inspired to outrageous. "These bikes are an important part of S-Works, " said Robert Egger, the S-Works designer who created the prototypes. "In order to truly innovate we must challenge ourselves to think in entirely new directions for bicycle design. We want to push the limits of existing technology and make people dream a little."

One of the bikes is a rideable, race-ready, full-suspension mountain bike called Synergy. It is made with a one-piece, six-layer carbon fiber frame and is ergonomically designed for comfort during riding and inevitable portages and transport. The second concept bike is a throwback to the old "big wheel" Penny Farthing bikes from the turn of the century. The Retro is four feet tall, and uses the most cutting-edge design techniques in the industry. The Retro has a racing design for Penny Farthing races, although no such event exists.

For 1993, S-Works also introduced the FSR, the most advanced full suspension bicycle in the world. Like automobile suspension, bicycle suspension systems act as shock absorbers and also keep the wheels in contact with the ground. The FSR allows the rider to adjust the suspension action based on personal preference and terrain. This engineering innovation reduces rider fatigue, provides superior traction, and improves rider control.

Specialized is an international leader in high-end bicycle equipment, but it was not always this way. Mike Sinyard founded the company in 1974 when he began importing hard-to-find Italian components to the United States. Without any capital available to sink into inventory, Sinyard persuaded his customers, primarily bicycle shop owners, to pay in advance for each order.

This unusual supplier/customer trust remains the foundation for Specialized's relationship with its international network of dealers. More than 6,000 retailers in 25 countries now sell Specialized products. It makes a full range of bicycles including high-end and entry-level road bikes, mountain bikes, hybrids, city bikes, and children's bikes. Despite its rapid growth, Specialized's humble origins enable the company to identify with the needs—and sometimes the limitations—of smaller independent bicycle dealers.

Specialized's role as a market leader comes from much more than shrewd financial acumen. For many years, Specialized has grown its customers' business by creating and sponsoring regional mountain bike races throughout the world. Mike Sinyard believes that by popularizing the sport of mountain biking he can cause the market to grow as well.

Its technical support crews travel throughout the country setting up mountain bike race courses and providing free repair services to racers in need. Its support of Team Specialized, featuring six-time national champion Ned Overend, has created a set of heroes and superstars in the emerging sport. Specialized also sponsors frequent free clinics teaching the essentials of mountain biking technique, equipment maintenance, and safety.

Specialized also holds itself to the highest standards on environmental and safety issues. Land access disputes among hikers, bird watchers, equestrians, and cyclists still limit the growth of mountain biking. Where other manufacturers seem to ignore the problem, perhaps hoping it will go away, Specialized has come forward to address it aggressively.

Mike Sinyard has hired a land access coordinator at the company whose sole function is to mitigate disputes between outdoor enthusiasts. Specialized donates thousands of dollars annually to local, grassroots organizations to further land access concerns. This year, Specialized created a non-branded public service advertising campaign educating cyclists about the issue of land access and their responsibility to "share the trail."

Safety is always a consideration in product design. When designing its new children's mountain bikes, Specialized focused on safety and started from scratch. "Many manufacturers take adult bikes and simply shrink them to make kids' bikes," said Chris Murphy, product manager for bicycles at Specialized. "By including children as test pilots in our research and design process we created bikes that kids prefer, that fit better, and have children-friendly features. All of these design specifications make these bikes ultimately safer for kids to ride."

The primary safety focus for adults has come in the area of helmet safety. The company estimates that more than 80 percent of cycling related fatalities involve people who did not wear helmets. In response, Specialized has given away more than $2 million worth of helmets since 1991. "Helmets must be standard equipment for all cyclists," says Sinyard. "I consider them the equivalent of airbags in motor vehicles. Never ride a bike without a helmet. It is that simple."

Combining Sinyard's statesman-like leadership with a continuing stream of innovative products has proven a winning recipe for success at Specialized. The company has enjoyed more than thirty percent annual growth in sales during the last five years. An independent Canadian subsidiary opened in 1991 and several more have since opened in Europe.

What's next for Specialized? On the business side, the company hopes to consolidate its recent expansions in the Pacific Rim and South America, according to Erik Eidsmo, executive vice president of sales and marketing. He believes that significant, untapped opportunity still exists in these regions for mountain bikes. On the product side it is hard to predict the future, but chances are good that it may be discovered one day soon at lunchtime in the hills surrounding Morgan Hill.

Questions—Business Foundations

1. *In your own words explain the basic nature of this company.*
2. *Who are Specialized's customers?*
3. *Who are Specialized's competitors?*
4. *Who are Specialized's collaborators?*
5. *Is Specialized a small business? Is Mike Sinyard an entrepreneur?*
6. *If you were asked to write a business mission statement for Specialized, what would it contain?*
7. *Specialized holds itself to the highest standard on environmental and safety issues. How important is social responsibility to its business?*

Questions—Management

1. *How would you describe Specialized Bicycle's use of teams in its product design*

and testing processes? In what ways do Specialized's teams resemble quality teams, and in what ways do they differ?

2. *How does carrying a wide variety of products, such as the Stumpjumper bike, the Synergy bike, the Retro bike, and the ProLong saddle, affect the typical production process? What other issues, such as inventory management, are affected by carrying multiple products, and how does Specialized deal with these issues?*
3. *How does Specialized integrate design of products with design of the manufacturing processes?*
4. *How would you describe Mike Sinyard's leadership style? What impact does this style have on the motivation and attitudes of Specialized's employees?*
5. *Discuss Specialized Bicycle's business mission and objectives. What strengths and weaknesses do you see in the mission and objectives?*
6. *As Specialized expands into the Pacific Rim and South American markets, how should it design the organization?*
7. *What employee relations programs does Specialized have for its employees, and what programs might you suggest as the company grows?*

Questions—Marketing

1. *What target markets does Specialized appeal to most?*
2. *Identify Specialized's marketing mix.*
3. *In what stage of the product life cycle are Specialized brand bicycles?*
4. *How important is new product development to Specialized's operation?*
5. *What collaborators are important to the marketing effort?*

Questions—Accounting and Finance

1. *What options were available to Specialized in financing the company during its formative years? What are the pros and cons of using advance customer payments as the primary source of capital investment?*
2. *How would advance payments from customers show up on the company's financial statements?*
3. *Specialized incurs substantial costs from its use of technical support crews, setting up mountain bike race courses and providing free repair services to racers. Are these short-term or long-term investments, and how should they be treated in the company's financial statements?*
4. *Specialized employs a land access coordinator to mitigate disputes between outdoor enthusiasts. What are the advantages and disadvantages to using this person to settle disputes rather than a qualified attorney?*
5. *Specialized expends considerable effort to ensure the safety of their products, including giving away more than $2 million worth of helmets. What impact does this have on their ethical and legal obligations? How would accountants treat the $2 million?*
6. *Specialized has enjoyed more than thirty percent annual growth in sales during the past five years and has opened operations in Canada, Europe, the Pacific Rim, and South America. How does this growth affect the company's need for funds, and what sources should it look to for these funds?*

GLOSSARY

Account A detailed record of the changes that have occurred in a particular asset, liability, or owner's equity item during the accounting period.

Accounting equation Assets = Liabilities + Owner's Equity.

Accounting An information system designed to analyze, summarize, record, and report financial information related to a business.

Accounts receivable turnover Net credit sales divided by average net accounts receivable.

Accuracy The degree to which information reflects reality.

Acquisition The result of one firm simply buying the assets and obligations of another company.

Administered vertical marketing system A distribution system with a dominant member that is in a position to influence other channel members, thus keeping operations in order.

Administrative law Rules and regulations created by an administrative agency to implement constitutional and statutory laws.

Adverse selection Process in which the exercise of choice by insureds leads to higher than average loss levels since those with a greater probability of experiencing a loss are most likely to seek that kind of insurance coverage.

Affirmative action programs Programs that attempt to remedy historical problems of discrimination by increasing the number of minority employees in organizations.

Age of Titans Also called the Second Industrial Revolution, the second half of the 19th century and the first decades of the 20th century, when big-business tycoons owned large industrial corporations in urban areas.

Agency law A body of laws that applies to transactions involving agents and principals.

Agency shop A contract provision that requires nonunion workers to pay a fee to the union equal to the union dues rate.

Agent or broker An intermediary that does not take title to the products in handles.

American Federation of Labor (AFL) A national union formed in 1886 to represent affiliated craft unions.

Annuity A periodic payment to a person that continues either for a fixed period or for the duration of the person's life.

Approach An initial contact and establishing a good relationship with the prospect.

Arbitration The process of bringing in a third party who makes a binding decision or judgment that both parties must agree to accept.

Asked price The lowest price a dealer will accept for a security.

Assets The economic resources a company owns that are expected to provide a benefit in the future.

Atmospherics Physical characteristics of the store environment that contribute to the shopper's mental impression of what the store is.

Authority The right to make decisions due to the organization's delegation of that right.

Automated teller machine (ATM) An electronic machine that permits customers to make deposits and withdrawals and transfer funds among their accounts.

Bait and switch Advertising a product at an amazingly low price to draw consumers to the store and then "switching" them to another, higher-priced item by claiming that the advertised item is no longer available.

Balance of payments A record of the flow of money between a nation and the rest of the world.

Balance sheet A statement that reports the company's resources (assets) and claims against those resources (liabilities and owner's equity); sometimes called the *statement of financial position.*

Bankruptcy A legal condition of insolvency in which the court administers the company's or individual's estate for the benefit of the creditors.

Barter The exchange of one good for another.

Basic skills training Classroom-type training that focuses on high school equivalency.

Bear market A stock market indicator of unfavorable economic conditions, investor pessimism, and stock price declines.

Benchmarking Comparing a company's products and manufacturing processes to those of competitors to help gauge how much the company needs to improve.

Bid price The highest price a dealer is willing to pay for a security.

Blue-chip stocks Stocks of companies that have long been recognized as leaders in their industries.

Board of directors Group of individuals selected by the corporation's stockholders to hire the chief executive officer (CEO), make decisions about the corporation's stocks and dividends, and oversee major policy decisions.

Bond A long-term debt instrument having a specified rate of interest and a specified maturity date.

Brand image The symbolic meaning associated with a particular brand.

Brand mark Anything that symbolically represents a product.

Brand name The verbal part of a brand.

Breach of contract The failure to perform a contractual duty.

Breakeven point The point at which total costs and revenues meet.

Budget deficit Exists when the federal government's spending exceeds its tax revenues for a given year.

Budget A detailed plan that outlines the acquisition and use of financial and other resources over a specific time period.

Bull market A stock market indicator of favorable economic conditions, investor optimism, and generally rising stock prices.

Burglary insurance Insurance for losses when property is taken by forced entry.

Business analysis A critical examination of the new-product idea from all important company viewpoints.

Business cycle Reflects recurring fluctuations in general economic activity.

Business ethics Concerns the principles that guide an organization's conduct and the values the company expects to express in certain situations.

Business interruption losses Indirect losses (of revenue) caused by direct losses to company assets.

Business mission A statement defining what the company business is and how the company will operate the business.

Business plan Lays out a direction for the company; describes the business operations and outlines the goals of the business.

Business value chain A system of activities and relationships, both inside and outside the firm, that a company needs to run its business.

Business All activities involved in the production and distribution of goods and services for profit to satisfy consumer needs and wants.

Capital Material resources intended for use in the production of other goods and services

Captive pricing Pricing a basic product low but charging a compensating high markup on related supplies required to operate the product.

Case law Rules of law based on earlier court decisions.

Case method Training in which managers analyze problem situations and share their solutions with one another and the trainer.

Cash budget A detailed plan showing how cash resources will be acquired and used over a specified time period.

Cash flow The inflows and outflows of cash that occur as a company conducts its daily operations.

Centralization Keeping most authority at the top levels of management and maintaining control through several layers of intermediate management.

Certificate of deposit (CD) A time deposit that earns higher interest than does the traditional passbook savings account.

Certified public accountant (CPA) An accountant from outside the company who has been certified by passing a comprehensive public accounting exam and demonstrating work experience with a public accounting firm.

Chain of command An unbroken hierarchy of authority that links managers and subordinates.

Channel of distribution The complete chain of marketing organizations that collaborate to bring a product from the producer to the ultimate consumer.

Chart of accounts A list of all the accounts and their account numbers.

Classroom training Training that occurs in an off-the-job setting; usually for learning mental skills, such as shop math.

Closed shop A union contract requirement preventing companies from hiring nonunion workers.

Closing Bringing the sale to an end.

Code of conduct Establishes a company's or professional organization's guidelines indicating its ethical principles and specifying what behavior the organization considers proper.

Coinsurance A provision in insurance policies that requires the insured to pay a certain percentage of eligible medical expenses.

Collaborator A person or an organization that works with the company but is not part of it.

Collective bargaining The process by which union representatives and management negotiate and administer written agreements of their understanding of the terms and conditions of employment.

Commercial bank A bank that receives deposits from individuals and companies and uses these funds to make loans and conduct other business.

Commercial paper A short-term unsecured promissory note issued to the general public in minimum units of $25,000.

Commercialization Process of going into full-scale production and the marketing process of launching the new product.

Committee organization A structure in which authority is given to a group of individuals rather than to one person.

Common law Law that is common to the entire country.

Common stock The class of stock that controls the board of directors, shares in the success of the company, and bears the risk of failure.

Communications media The means used to broadcast or print advertising messages.

Company An arrangement for running the business. The term *company* refers to the business itself: the organization of people, the buildings and equipment, and other resources needed to operate the business.

Compensation All monetary payments and all nonmonetary goods and services given to employees in place of money.

Competitive advantage Anything that makes a company's product superior or different from competitors in a way that is important to the market.

Competitive advantage Having an edge or being superior to or different from competitors in some beneficial way.

Competitors Rival companies engaged in the same business.

Completeness The degree to which information contains the appropriate amount of data.

Computer-aided design (CAD) The use of computers that are specially programmed to aid in the design of parts, products, and buildings.

Computer-aided manufacturing (CAM) A production technology in which computers guide and control the manufacturing process.

Conceptual skills Skills that require the ability to understand the whole organization, analyze and evaluate information, and make appropriate plans and decisions.

Conference method Training in which managers meet in groups of 15 to 30 and discuss various topics under the guidance of a professional trainer.

Conglomerate merger The combining of firms that do business in completely unrelated industries.

Congress of Industrial Organizations (CIO) A national union formed in 1935 to represent affiliated industrial unions.

Consumer behavior Consists of the activities in which people engage when selecting, purchasing, and using products and services.

Consumer market A market in which the buyers are individuals who will use the product to satisfy personal or household needs.

Consumer orientation A business philosophy that believes customer needs and wants are the focus of a business enterprise.

Consumer price index (CPI) A measure that reflects the average prices for many goods and services purchased by the typical household.

Consumer spending An early indicator of an economy's well-being that measures how much people are buying.

Contract law A body of law intended to ensure compliance with contracts or to provide some remedy for those harmed when contracts are broken.

Contractual vertical marketing system A VMS in which channel members are linked by written contractual agreements.

Controlling The process of monitoring and evaluating the organization's performance and determining how to correct problems that detract from that performance.

Convenience product A product that is relatively inexpensive, is purchased on a regular basis, and is bought without a great deal of thought.

Convertible bond A bond that may be converted into a specified number of shares of common stock at the option of the bondholder.

Cooperative A business that is owned and managed by its customers or members, who pay annual dues or membership fees and share in any profits made.

Copyright The exclusive right of an originator of a literary or artistic production to sell and profit from his or her work for the life of the originator, plus 50 years.

Core product The essential benefits common to most competitive offerings.

Corporate stock repurchase The use of company assets—usually cash—to buy back shares of stock from existing shareholders.

Corporate vertical marketing system A VMS made up of organizations owned outright by one member.

Corporation An entity owned by stockholders and granted by government charter certain powers, privileges, and liabilities separate from those of the individual stockholders.

Cost of goods sold The cost of inventory that has been sold.

Cost The value of all inputs used to produce the product or service, including raw materials, labor, plant and equipment overhead and similar factors.

Creative selling process The process of locating and qualifying the prospect, approaching the prospect, creating awareness, arousing interest, making a specific proposal, handling objections and complaints, closing the sale, and following up to keep customers.

Credit union A cooperative depository institution organized to meet savings and loan needs of a particular group of people.

Credit An entry recorded on the right side of an account.

Culture The social values, beliefs, and institutions in a society.

Currency Coins and paper money.

Current ratio Current assets divided by current liabilities.

Customers Those who buy the company's products or services.

Database A centralized, organized, and integrated collection of data from a great many sources that is designed to meet the information needs of decision makers.

Debenture An unsecured bond supported only by the general credit of the issuing company.

Debit An entry recorded on the left side of an account.

Debt funding Money borrowed from lenders such as banks; sometimes called *debt capital.*

Debt securities Securities that represent IOUs; investors who purchase these securities are creditors.

Debt to equity ratio Total debt (current plus noncurrent liabilities) divided by owner's equity.

Decentralization Delegation of considerable authority to lower, operational levels and minimizing the number of intermediate levels of management.

Decision making Choosing one action from among several possible alternatives.

Decision support system (DSS) An interactive, computer-based information system designed to support specific decisions made by managers.

Demand curve A graphic representation of the relationship between the various prices sellers charge for a good or service and the amount of that product or service buyers will desire at each price

Demand deposit An amount deposited in a checking account that can be withdrawn upon "demand" by writing a check.

Demand The quantity of a good or service consumers are willing and able to buy at a given price

Demographic variables Variables that describe people, including sex, age, and marital status.

Demographics The study of the size and composition of the population.

Demotion An assignment to a new job at a lower level and often at a lower salary.

Departmentalization The logical grouping of jobs into distinct units located within the organizational structure.

Depository institution A financial institution that directly offers federally insured checking and savings accounts.

Depreciation The process of spreading the costs of fixed assets over the assets' expected useful lives.

Depression The low phase of the business cycle, in which unemployment is highest and consumer spending and business output are low.

Depth of product line Describes the number of different product items offered in a product line.

Derived demand Demand for a product that depends on the demand for some other product.

Direct exporting Dealing directly with overseas customers in their home countries without using independent wholesalers or retailers.

Direct marketing Marketing that uses mail-order catalogs or mass media to obtain orders by direct response via 800 telephone numbers or by mail.

Directing The process of guiding and motivating employees to accomplish the organization's objectives.

Discount rate The rate of interest the Federal Reserve charges to banks that borrow to meet their reserve requirements.

Distributive bargaining A bargaining process in which the employer wins what the employees lose, and vice versa.

Distributor brand or **private brand** A product whose name is owned by a retailer or other intermediary.

Diversity training programs Programs that attempt to get workers to understand and value individual cultural differences within the organization's work force.

Diversity Intentionally creating a work force composed of people of all races, religions, genders, physical abilities, and beliefs.

Division of labor Subdividing a company's work into different components.

Double-entry system A bookkeeping system based on the fact that in any business transaction, at least two accounts are always affected.

Durable good A good that lasts over an extended period of time.

Earnings per share Net income available for common stock shares (net income minus preferred dividends) divided by the number of shares of common stock outstanding.

Economic order quantity (EOQ) The amount of material that should be ordered at one time to minimize the cost of storing it in inventory.

Economic utility A product's ability to satisfy potential customers' wants

Economics Concerned with the production, distribution, and consumption of goods and services.

Economics The study of the way society uses its limited resources, which have alternative uses, to produce goods and services for present and future consumption

Effectiveness The degree to which the company's goals are being attained.

Efficiency The ratio of benefits to costs as resources are used and depleted to produce goods and services.

Electronic funds transfer (EFT) A computerized system for performing many financial transactions such as making purchases, depositing paychecks, and paying bills.

Employee benefit insurance Insurance that protects employees against losses due to illness, injury, or death.

Employee stock ownership plan (ESOP) A program that gives employees part ownership of the company.

Employment-at-will A concept holding that employers have the right to terminate employees for any reason they wish.

Enterprise A company or business organization consisting of one or more establishments under the same ownership or control.

Entrepreneur Someone who takes a financial risk in the hope of making a profit

Environmental scanning and analysis The diagnostic activity of interpreting environmental trends in light of the organization's ability to deal with change.

Equilibrium The market situation where the quantity supplied equals the quantity demanded

Equipment trust certificate A bond that is secured by the equipment purchased with the money raised from the bond issue.

Equity funding Funds raised from owners; also called *equity capital.*

Equity securities Securities that represent ownership interest.

Establishment Any single physical location where a company conducts its business.

Esteem needs The desire for a good perception of oneself and to receive recognition and respect from other people.

Ethical dilemma A predicament in which the businessperson must resolve whether an action, although benefiting the organization, the individual, or both, may be considered unethical.

Ethics Involves values about right and wrong conduct.

Eurodollar Funds created when deposits in accounts in the United States are transferred to a European bank but kept in the form of dollars.

European Union (EU) Also called the **European Community (EC)**, an economic and potential political union of western Europe.

Exchange process Occurs when two or more parties exchange or trade things of value.

Exchange rate Indicates the value of one country's currency relative to another country's currency.

Exclusive distribution Placing the product in only a small number of outlets.

Expenses Payments necessary for the normal operations of the business.

Expert system (ES) A computer program that is based on the expertise, rules of thumb, and knowledge of specialists in a field.

Export management companies An intermediary that specializes in buying from sellers in one country and marketing the products in other countries, typically takes title to the goods, and reduces the risk for a company that lacks a great deal of exporting experience.

Exports Products that are produced in the home country and sold in other countries.

Extinction The withholding of all consequences, both positive and negative, following undesired behavior.

Extrinsic rewards The things other people give an employee (such as pay and promotions) in attempting to inspire better performance.

Facsimile (fax) machine A machine which copies a sheet of paper at one location and then transfers it via telephone to a fax machine at another location.

Factors of production The resources used in the production process include material resources (land and capital) and human resources (labor and entrepreneurship)

Factory system A simple concept for mass production in the industrial age in which unskilled workers use machines to manufacture interchangeable parts and other workers assemble the parts into a standardized product.

Fair use A doctrine that permits limited reproduction of copyrighted works without the payment of royalties.

Featherbedding Creating unnecessary jobs for union members.

Federal antitrust legislation Laws prohibiting acts such as restraint of trade, monopoly, price fixing, price discrimination, and other behavior that tends to lessen competition.

Federal district court The trial-level court in the federal court system.

Federal funds Short-term loans by the Federal Reserve that enable banks to meet reserve requirements.

Federal Open Market Committee (FOMC) The most important monetary policymaking body of the Federal Reserve System; creates policies to promote economic growth, full employment, stable prices, and international trade and makes key decisions regarding open market operations.

Federal Reserve notes Paper currency of the United States issued by the Federal Reserve.

Federal Reserve System A network of 12 regional Federal Reserve banks, a board of governors, and approximately 5,000 member commercial banks.

Federal Trade Commission (FTC) A major federal agency with broad powers of investigation and jurisdiction over unfair methods of competition.

Fidelity bond A bond that protects an employer against dishonest or fraudulent acts of employees.

Field selling Occurs when an "outside" salesperson travels to the prospective account's place of business.

Finance The business function of obtaining and using funds to maximize company profit or shareholders' wealth.

Financial accounting Preparation, reporting, analysis, and interpretation of accounting information in reports for external users.

Financial control The process of periodically comparing the actual revenues, costs, expenses, and cash flow with the budgets.

Financial manager A manager who constructs financial plans and budgets, obtains funds needed to run the business, determines how financial resources will be used, and makes investment decisions.

Financial plan A plan that forecasts the company's short-term and long-term needs for funds, develops budgets to meet those needs, and establishes financial control.

Fiscal policy A policy that involves the government's power to tax and spend.

Flexible benefit plan A benefit program in which employees are given specified dollar allowances which they allocate among benefits they prefer.

Flexible manufacturing system (FMS) A small or medium-size automated production line that can be adapted or modified quickly to produce different products.

Flextime A work arrangement that allows employees to set their own arrival and departure times.

Float The time it takes checks to clear through the Federal Reserve System.

Floppy disk An inexpensive portable magnetic disk created from mylar plastic coated with a magnetizable substance on which data can be recorded as magnetized and non-magnetized spots, which can be inserted and withdrawn from floppy disk drives.

Follow-up Contacting the customer to make sure that everything was handled as promised and that the order was shipped promptly and received on schedule.

Form utility Economic utility created by conversion of raw materials into finished goods with a more useful form

Fortuitous loss A loss that is unforeseen and occurs as a result of chance.

Franchise An individually owned business that is operated as a part of a network of businesses; a contractual agreement between a franchisor and a number of franchisees.

Full-function or full-service wholesaler An independent wholesaler that offers customers a full array of services, including delivery, warehousing, credit terms, merchandising advice, and other assistance.

Funded loss reserve An account that contains money set aside to cover the costs of accidental losses.

Gantt chart A chart that lists necessary activities, their order of accomplishment, who is to perform each activity, and the time needed to complete it.

General Agreement on Tariffs and Trade (GATT) A series of agreements reached by member nations that are located in different parts of the world but want to encourage global trade by reducing international trade restrictions and tariffs.

General partner A partner who participates in managing the business and has unlimited liability for its debts.

Generic brand A general product name that any company can use.

Geodemographic segmentation Combining demographic variables with a geographic variable to characterize clusters of similar individuals.

Geographic information system (GIS) A decision support system that displays data on digitized maps.

Goal-setting theory A theory that explains how setting attainable goals and objectives can lead to high levels of motivation and accomplishment.

Golden parachute Compensation given to an executive whose company is purchased by another company in a hostile takeover.

Gramm-Rudman-Hollings Act A law passed in 1985 to achieve automatic spending cuts to help reduce the deficit.

Greenmail The practice of threatening to take over a company and buying a significant portion of the company's stock in the hope of making a quick profit.

Gross domestic product (GDP) Measures the value of all the goods and services produced by the workers and capital in a country.

Gross national product (GNP) Measures the value of all the goods and services produced by a country's residents or corporations regardless of location.

Group term life insurance Life insurance provided to a number of persons on a single master contract.

Growth stocks Stocks of companies that are experiencing growth in both operations and earnings.

Hard disk A thin, rigid metallic platter coated with a magnetizable substance that allows data to be recorded as magnetized and non-magnetized spots, and which is permanently encased within a hard disk drive.

Hawthorne effect The tendency for people to behave differently when they know they are being studied, especially in ways they think the researcher wants them to behave.

Hawthorne studies A series of studies from 1924 to the early 1930s that examined various sociological factors related to motivation.

Health insurance Insurance that covers losses suffered by employees due to illness or injury.

Health maintenance organization (HMO) An organized system of health care that provides comprehensive health services to its members for some fixed fee.

Hierarchy of objectives An arrangement of objectives beginning with the company's broad, long-term strategic objectives and ending with increasingly specific, shorter-range employee objectives.

Horizontal merger The joining of firms in the same industry.

Hostile takeover Occurs when a firm acquires another company whose managers do not want the company to be sold.

Human needs forecast A process that compares the current level of employment in various jobs to the numbers needed to fulfill the production and sales forecasts and to meet the company's strategic objectives.

Human relations skills Skills that require the ability to get along with others and to lead and motivate them to accomplish what the organization needs.

Human relations The process by which the company manages and motivates people to achieve effective performance.

Human resource management The process of recruiting, hiring, training, developing, and maintaining an effective work force within the company.

Hygiene factors Factors that describe employees' relationship to the environment in which they do their jobs and that affect their level of dissatisfaction at work.

Idea generation stage An ongoing search for product ideas that are consistent with target market needs and with the company's objectives.

Idea screening stage The stage in which managers evaluate which ideas are good and which are bad.

Import quotas Limits on the number or types of imported goods.

Imports Products that are produced in other countries and sold in the home country.

Income statement A report of the revenues and expenses for a particular period that provides a measure of the results of operations and profitability.

Income stocks Stocks whose attractiveness stems solely from their dividend yields.

Indemnification The process of restoring an insured to his or her financial status prior to a loss.

Indenture A legal document that contains all details about a bond issue.

Indirect exporting Exporting using an intermediary, often located in another country, that performs the distribution function.

Industrial distributor An intermediary that takes title to organizational products.

Industry market A market consisting of all buyers and all sellers who engage in the exchange of a good or service

Industry All competitive producers of a good or service.

Inflation A rise in price levels over an extended period of time.

Information age The current era of global business where electronic information is communicated worldwide. A business enterprise must try to gain competitive advantage, yet put a greater emphasis on its social responsibilities.

Infrastructure The basic, underlying framework of an economic system that is necessary for a healthy economy.

Initial public offerings (IPOs) A special category of common stock issued by new firms going public for the first time.

Inseparability A characteristic requiring that producer and consumer be present in the same place at the same time for the service transaction to occur.

Inside selling Occurs when salespeople sell from the company's premises.

Insider trading Occurs when a person buys or sells stocks of a company because he or she has inside information about the company's plans.

Institutional advertising Advertising that promotes an industry or organization as a whole, stressing goodwill, corporate image, or contributions to society.

Insurance An agreement in which an insurance company protects the insured against losses associated with specified risks in return for a fee, or premium payment.

Intangibility The characteristic of something that makes it unable to be seen, felt, smelled, heard, or tasted.

Intellectual property and computer law A body of law designed to protect patents, copyrights, and trademarks.

Intensive distribution Making a product available in virtually every appropriate outlet.

Interactive media Technology that promotes messages to groups of similar prospects, and then allows for responses customized to buyers' wishes.

Intermediary A middleman that buys and resells products and helps in other ways to get products into the hands of end users.

Internal marketing Marketing efforts aimed at the marketer's own employees to help them recognize their role in the organization's effort to create customer satisfaction.

Internet A huge, global web of 25, 000 computer networks.

Intrapreneur A person who works for a large corporation and experiments with new ideas, takes the initiative to do different things, and takes risks just as an entrepreneur does.

Intrinsic rewards The good feelings people get when they have accomplished something important, such as completing a challenging job assignment.

Inventory loan A loan that uses specific inventory items as collateral.

Inventory turnover Cost of goods sold divided by the average inventory for the period.

Inventory The goods (raw materials, work in process, and finished products) that the company keeps on hand to produce the product or service.

Investing The process by which suppliers of funds (those with surplus money) are brought together with demanders of funds (those needing money).

Investment banker A firm that specializes in designing and packaging a security offering by a company and then sells the offering to the general public.

Job analysis The systematic gathering of information about a job.

Job depth The degree of responsibility, autonomy, and freedom an individual has in planning, organizing, and controlling his or her own work.

Job description A document that describes the objectives for the job, the responsibilities and activities involved, how the job relates to other jobs, working conditions, and similar facts.

Job design A conscious effort to group activities and tasks into logical units of work.

Job enrichment The process of adding interest and challenge to jobs to make them more motivating to employees.

Job evaluation The process of establishing the general wage level for a job based on the skills, education, experience, and abilities required to perform the job.

Job rotation A series of temporary assignments in various departments designed to increase managers' familiarity with the company's structure and operations.

Job scope The variety of tasks that are included within a job.

Job sharing A work arrangement in which two part-time workers share one full-time job.

Job specification A document that specifies the qualifications, skills, training, education, and other personal characteristics required of the person performing the job.

Joint venture An alliance in which two or more people or companies join together to undertake a specific, limited, or short-term project.

Journal The chronological accounting record of a company's transactions.

Jurisdiction The power of a court to hear and resolve a dispute.

Jurisdictional strike A union strike resulting from a dispute between two or more unions that are fighting for the right to represent a company's employees.

Just-in-time (JIT) An inventory management technique designed to create a zero inventory level by having materials arrive just in time for immediate use in the production process.

Labor union A group of workers who have joined together to more effectively achieve common goals such as improved working conditions, wages, and benefits.

Law of large numbers The concept that the larger the number of exposures, the more predictable the occurrences of perils on which the insurance premiums are based.

Law Enforceable rules that govern relationships among individuals and between individuals and their society.

Leader A person who guides others, often by example, to ensure that their work is done correctly and on time.

Lease A contractual agreement that calls for the lessee to pay the lessor an agreed-upon payment for using equipment owned by the lessor.

Ledger A group of related accounts that make up a complete unit.

Liabilities What the company owes to others, such as creditors.

Liability insurance Insurance protection against claims caused by injuries to others or damage to their property.

License A contractual agreement with some other firm that allows the second firm to use the company's trademark.

Life insurance Insurance that provides for payment of a stipulated sum to a designated beneficiary upon death of the insured.

Limit order An order to buy (or sell) a security at a specified or lower (or higher) price.

Limited partner A partner who does not participate in managing the company and is liable for its indebtedness only to the extent of his or her investment in the firm.

Limited partnership A partnership in which some partners invest money or other assets but have no managerial responsibilities or liability for losses.

Limited-function wholesaler An independent wholesaler that does not offer a full range of services but compensates by dropping its prices.

Line departments Departments that perform activities directly associated with company objectives, such as production, marketing, finance, and customer service departments.

Line-and-staff organization A structure that combines the direct flow of vertical (line) authority with staff who specialize in a limited set of activities that support the line activities.

Liquidity The relative ease with which an asset can be converted into the medium of exchange.

Logistics The entire process of moving raw materials and component parts, in-process inventory, and finished goods into, through, and out of the firm.

Loss leader A product that the seller prices at a loss to attract customers who might buy other goods.

M1 The most basic definition of the money supply; includes currency, coins, traveler's checks, and demand deposits.

Macroeconomics The study of how scarce resources are allocated within the economy as a whole or within an entire industry

Magnetic tape A storage medium created from thin plastic coated with a magnetizable substance on which data are stored as magnetized and nonmagnetized spots on the tape.

Management by objectives (MBO) A process for setting goals in which managers and their superiors define objectives for each division and department, and then managers and individual employees work together to set corresponding performance goals for the employees.

Management development The process of training employees to become good managers, and continuing to develop their skills over time.

Management information system (MIS) An organized system for collecting and organizing information and distributing it to organizational decision makers.

Management pyramid A hierarchy of authority relationships among managers at different levels in the organization..

Management The effective and efficient integration and coordination of resources to achieve desired objectives.

Manager A person responsible for integrating and combining human, capital, and technological resources in the best way possible to ensure that the organization's objectives are achieved.

Managerial accounting Information-gathering and reporting activities and related accounting procedures designed to assist people inside the company in making various decisions.

Manufacturer brand or **national brand** A brand name owned and advertised by the firm that manufactures the product.

Manufacturer's agent An independent business that calls on customers in a specific geographic territory and serves as its client's sales force in that area.

Manufacturer-owned wholesaler A manufacturer that does its own wholesaling.

Manufacturing resource planning (MRP II) An inventory management method that coordinates inventory management with other company systems, such as capacity planning, accounting, and financial planning.

Margin The portion of the selling price for an issue of securities that must be paid with the purchaser's own funds.

Market economy An economy in which competition exists and supply and demand determine the prices of goods and services

Market order An order to purchase or sell a security at the best price available at the time the order is placed.

Market position or competitive position Represents the way consumers think about a brand relative to its competition.

Market segmentation Dividing a heterogeneous mass market into a number of smaller, more specific customer groups.

Market segments A portion of a larger market.

Market A group of customers.

Market A group of individuals who are potential customers for the product being offered for sale.

Marketing concept The philosophy that a company must be consumer oriented in all matters and stress long-run profitability rather than short-term profits or sales volume.

Marketing mix The result of management's efforts to creatively combine interrelated and interdependent marketing activities; consists of the four Ps of marketing: product, place, price, and promotion.

Marketing objective A statement about the level of performance the company or a product is expected to achieve.

Marketing research The systematic and objective process of gathering information for aid in making marketing decisions.

Marketing strategy Consists of determining basic long-range goals and committing to a marketing plan that explains how the goals will be achieved.

Marketing Planning and distributing products to satisfy customer needs at a profit.

Marketing The process of planning and executing the conception, pricing, promotion, and distribution of ideas, goods, and services to create exchanges that will satisfy individual and organizational objectives.

Master limited partnerships Similar to a limited partnership, except that shares of ownership can be traded on stock exchanges.

Materials requirement planning (MRP) An inventory management technique used when the demand for some materials depends on the demand for others.

Matrix organization A structure that is built around a specific project or problem and usually has a line-based manager and a project manager in one work group.

Media schedule or media plan A time schedule identifying the exact media and the dates advertisements are scheduled to appear.

Mediation The process of bringing in a third party who makes recommendations for resolving differences between two negotiating parties.

Medium of exchange A common means of facilitating exchanges of goods and services.

Merchant wholesaler An independently owned enterprise that takes title to the products it distributes.

Merger The result of two firms formally joining their assets, liabilities, and ownership.

Microeconomics The study of the economic behavior of individual firms

Microprocessor An integrated circuit, or chip, on the computer's main circuit board that processes the instructions supplied to it by the software.

Middle management Managers responsible for implementing the strategies and plans developed by top management.

Mixed economy An economy in which there is a mixture of free enterprise and government regulation of economic resources

Monetary policy Policy that promotes or restricts economic activity by controlling the size of the country's money supply.

Money market mutual fund A mutual fund that pools funds from a large number of investors, uses them to purchase high-yield, short-term securities, and provides check-writing privileges.

Money Anything that is generally accepted in a society as a means of payment or exchange.

Monopolistic competition An industry in which a large number of sellers sell similar products differentiated only by minor changes in product design, style, or technology.

Monopoly An industry that has only one producer firm and in which no substitute products are available.

Moral behavior Reflects how well an individual's or organization's business activities demonstrate ethical values.

Mortgage bond A bond secured by a claim on real property.

Motivation Energizing employees to exert high levels of effort and achieve superior performance.

Motivation The arousal, direction, and persistence of a particular behavior.

Motivators Factors related to employees' desire for growth in their work, which affect their level of satisfaction or motivation at work.

Mutual fund Investment company that combines the funds of several investors with similar investment goals and invests them in a wide variety of securities.

Mutual savings bank A bank that is owned by its depositors and managed by a board of trustees.

National debt Money borrowed by the federal government to finance budget deficits over several years.

National Labor Relations Board (NLRB) A Federal agency established by the National Labor Relations Act to supervise unionization activities and prevent antiunion practices by business owners.

Need for achievement The desire to accomplish something difficult, reach a high level of success, master complex jobs, and surpass the achievements of others.

Need for affiliation The desire to have close personal relationships, avoid conflict, and be friendly, warm, and close to others.

Need for power The desire to influence others, control their behaviors and actions, be responsible for others, and have authority over them.

Needs hierarchy A hierarchical classification of human needs first proposed by Abraham Maslow that includes physiological, safety, social, self-esteem, and self-actualization needs.

Negative reinforcement The act of removing some negative consequence following a desired behavior.

Negotiable order of withdrawal (NOW) account A checking account that pays annual interest as long as the depositor maintains some minimum balance.

Nondepository institution A financial institution that cannot offer federally insured savings and checking accounts.

Nondurable good A good that is quickly used, worn out, or outdated and is consumed in a single usage or a few uses.

Norms Suggest what ought to be done under given circumstances.

North American Free Trade Agreement (NAFTA) This agreement, approved in 1993, allows for increased trade among Mexico, Canada, and the United States.

Objectives Targets, or desired levels of achievement.

Oligopoly An industry controlled by a few large firms.

On-the-job training (OJT) Training that occurs at the actual job site, at which experienced employees teach new employees how to perform their jobs.

Open market operations The buying and selling of U.S. Treasury securities by the Federal Reserve.

Open shop A contract provision that makes union membership voluntary for all employees.

Operating cycle The average time it takes for the company to spend cash for inventory, sell the inventory in exchange for accounts receivable, and collect the receivables in cash.

Operational plans Plans that are set are for very short periods of time and outline activities and goals at department, work group, or individual employee levels.

Optical storage disks Plastic coated disks on which data are recorded and read by using a laser beam rather than through magnetic means.

Organization chart Diagram illustrating the chain of command, division of work activities, and departmentalization within the organization.

Organization Culture A pattern of shared expectations and norms that affects relationships among employees and their individual and group behaviors.

Organizational or business market A market in which the buyers are organizations that will use the product in their operations or resell it later.

Organizational structure A formal grouping of employees and their tasks into logical working arrangements that will maximize the achievement of the organization's objectives.

Organizing Establishing the basic framework of formal relationships among tasks, activities, and people in the company.

Orientation training Training that introduces employees to the company's structure and culture.

Owner's equity Resources invested in a business by the owner and the undistributed earnings.

Packaging Physical containers for individual product items, labels, inserts, instructions for product use, graphic design, and shipping cartons.

Par value The principal or face value of a bond.

Partnership agreement A written document stating the terms of the partnership for the protection of each partner.

Partnership An arrangement in which two or more people co-own the business.

Patent A government grant giving inventors the exclusive right to make, use, and sell their inventions for a period of 17 years.

Penetration price A low introductory price.

Pension funds A third-party trustee to which employers and/or employees contribute money that accumulates assets to provide income to employees at retirement.

Pension A fixed amount of money paid to a retired employee on a regular basis.

Performance appraisal The evaluation of an employee's contributions in terms of current, real performance as well as potential for future contributions.

Performance coaching and counseling Training in which the manager's direct superior discusses the manager's strengths and weaknesses and together they design a program for improving the manager's skills and performance.

Performance goals Targeted levels of performance that employees strive to achieve.

Personal selling A person-to-person communication between the seller and the prospective buyer.

PERT (Program Evaluation and Review Technique) Chart A chart that analyzes the tasks involved in completing a project, estimates the time needed to complete each task, identifies the minimum time needed to complete the total project, and identifies the path along which delays will hold up the project.

Philanthropy Company donations to charities and other social causes.

Physical distribution The broad range of activities concerned with efficient movement of finished products from the end of the production line to the customer.

Physiological needs The most basic of all human needs, including the need for food and water.

Piece-rate incentive system A compensation system based on the amount of output an employee produces.

Place or distribution The location where customers buy the product; how products get to the customer, how quickly, and in what condition.

Place utility Economic utility created by making products available at the right place, or where buyers want them to be

Planning The process of assessing future business conditions and anticipating actions the business should take to reach its objectives..

Point-of-purchase materials Items given to retailers to serve as reminders at the point of sale.

Point-of-sale (POS) system An electronic machine located in a store that immediately transfers funds from the buyer's checking account to the retailer's when a debit card is used.

Pooling The spreading of losses incurred by a few parties over the many parties who have purchased insurance.

Positioning campaign Promoting a brand's position in relation to its competitors to get consumers to view the brand from a particular perspective.

Positive reinforcement The act of giving an employee a pleasant, valued consequence following a desired behavior.

Possession utility Economic utility created by ownership, which satisfies the consumer's need to have control over a product's use or consumption

Posting The process of transferring amounts from the journal to the ledger accounts.

Power of attorney A document authorizing another person to act as one's agent.

Power The ability to influence another person's behavior.

Precedent A court decision that establishes a point of law for deciding subsequent cases having similar circumstances.

Preferred stock Stock whose holders have a prior claim over common stockholders on the company's earnings and assets.

Prestige pricing Pricing a brand at high levels so that consumers believe that brand differs from other brands.

Price The amount of money or other consideration given in exchange for a product or service.

Price The amount of money, or sometimes goods or services, given in exchange for something.

Primary data Data gathered and assembled specifically for the project at hand.

Primary markets Capital markets that sell new securities to the public.

Primary-demand advertising Advertising that encourages generic demand for an entire product category.

Prime interest rate The base rate that banks charge their most creditworthy customers.

Process layout A facilities design in which all production equipment that performs similar tasks is grouped together.

Producibility The extent to which a product or service can be easily produced using existing facilities and processes.

Product development stage The stage in which the proposed new-product idea is transformed from a product concept to a working model or product prototype.

Product differentiation Calling buyers' attention to aspects of the product that set it apart from its competitors.

Product item A specific version of a particular good or service.

Product layout A facilities design in which equipment and activities are arranged for a single product or service in the sequence of steps that will be used to produce it.

Product life cycle A graphic depiction of a product's sales history from its "birth," or marketing beginning, to its "death," or withdrawal from the market.

Product line A group of a firm's products that are fairly closely related.

Product modification Altering or adjusting the product mix.

Product positioning concept Defines the central idea underlying the product features and key benefits that appeal to the target market.

Product A bundle of customer benefits.

Product What the company offers its perspective customers.

Production orientation A business philosophy during the era of the factory systems that stressed production and engineering to mass produce products.

Production orientation The philosophy that stresses the factory over the consumer.

Production The use of people, capital, and other resources (inputs) to convert raw materials into finished goods and services (outputs).

Productivity A measure indicating how constructive or efficient a person, operation, or enterprise is; a ratio of output to input.

Productivity The total output of goods and services in a given period of time divided by the inputs needed to produce that output.

Profit center A highly independent unit or division that is given broad decision-making authority as long as it makes acceptable profits.

Profit sharing An incentive program in which some percentage of the company's profits are distributed to employees.

Profit A company's reward for taking risks and doing a good job of management

Programmed instruction Systematically designed materials, either text based or computer based, on which employees work at their own pace and are tested frequently to assess their learning.

Promotion An assignment to a new job at a higher level and usually at a higher salary.

Promotion Applied communication such as advertising, personal selling, sales promotion, publicity, and public relations.

Promotion Communication applied to business.

Promotional mix The particular combination of all the elements of promotion—personal selling, advertising, publicity and public relations, and sales promotion—that will achieve the company's promotional objectives.

Property law A body of law that deals with the various ways ownership rights in property can be held and with rights regarding mislaid, lost, or abandoned property.

Prospecting Activities to identify likely buyers from lists of previous customers, referrals, trade lists, advertising inquiries, and other sources.

Prosperity The phase of the business cycle in which the economy operates at or near full employment and both consumer spending and business output (GDP) are high.

Psychographic variables Lifestyle, personality, attitudes, and other psychological characteristics of consumers.

Public relations Activities that actively manage publicity (and sometimes other promotional elements).

Publicity Promotional activities that involve unpaid messages.

Puffery The practice of making slight exaggerations.

Pull strategy A strategy that focuses promotional efforts at the ultimate consumer or industrial buyer located at the end of the channel of distribution.

Punishment The act of giving a negative consequence following an undesired behavior.

Pure capitalism An economic system characterized by private property, free enterprise and freedom of choice, profit incentives, and a free market economy with competition.

Pure communism An economic system characterized by public ownership of property, central planning, an absence of economic incentives for workers, and an absence of entrepreneurship

Pure competition An industry in which no barriers to competition exist

Pure risk The possibility of loss that is unplanned or accidental, and the company can expect only loss or no loss.

Push strategy A strategy that emphasizes promotional efforts aimed at members of the channel of distribution.

Quality of life A value that reflects a lessening concern with being economically well off and an increasing concern with people's general well-being.

Quality of work life (QWL) Organizational programs that provide a high-quality workplace, treat employees with dignity, and contribute to employee motivation.

Quality The serviceability and value of the product or service.

Quick ratio Cash, plus temporary investments, plus short-term receivables divided by current liabilities; also called the *acid-test ratio.*

Random access memory (RAM) Computer memory that stores the information the microprocessor needs to run an application.

Read-only memory (ROM) Computer memory that contains permanent information that cannot be erased or changed.

Recession The downward phase of the business cycle, in which consumer spending, business output, and employment are decreasing.

Recovery The upward phase of the business cycle, in which employment, consumer spending, and business output are rising.

Recruitment The process of informing qualified potential employees about job openings and encouraging them to apply for those positions.

Reinforcement theory A motivation theory of the relationship between a given behavior and its consequences.

Relationship management The sales function of managing the account relationship and ensuring that buyers receive the appropriate services.

Relevance The degree to which information relates to the problems, decisions, and tasks for which it is collected.

Reliability The degree to which the product or service will perform its intended function for a reasonable length of time.

Reorder point (ROP) The inventory level at which an order for new material should be placed.

Reserve requirement The percentage of a bank's total deposits that must be held in reserve at the Federal Reserve bank.

Resources The people, financial capital, technology, and time used in achieving the organization's objectives.

Retailer An organization that sells products directly to consumers.

Retention A risk management technique in which the firm retains part or all of the losses resulting from a given loss exposure.

Return on equity Net income divided by owner's equity.

Return on sales Net income divided by sales.

Revenue bond A bond paid from revenues associated with a specific income-generating project.

Revenue An increase in resources resulting from business activities.

Reverse discrimination Discrimination that makes it more difficult for nonminority groups to be hired or promoted.

Right to be informed Right to be protected against fraudulent, deceitful, or grossly misleading information, advertising, labeling, or other practices, and to be given the facts one needs to make an informed choice.

Right to safety Right of customers to use products that do not unnecessarily put them in danger.

Right-to-work laws Laws that give all employees the right to decide whether or not to join a union.

Risk management Managerial actions aimed at minimizing the adverse effects of accidental loss on the company.

Risk transfer The transfer of a loss associated with pure risk to an insurer.

Robbery insurance Insurance for losses when property is taken by force or threat of force.

Robot A machine that can be programmed to perform a variety of tasks without direct employee involvement.

S corporation (subchapter S) A form of business that is distinct from other corporations only in the way it is taxed; taxed similarly to sole proprietorships and partnerships.

Sabbatical An extended, paid release from the job for periods of time ranging from one to six months.

Safety needs The need for a secure environment.

Sales orientation The philosophy that a company should change consumers' minds to fit the product.

Sales promotion A promotional activity that is intended to encourage immediate purchases or to induce distributors to work more intensely in a specific time period.

Savings and loan association (S&L), or **thrift** A depository institution that accepts deposits and makes home mortgage loans.

Scarcity The concept that there are only finite resources to meet infinite human needs and wants

Scientific management The systematic study of the most efficient way to perform a job, training employees in that method, selecting employees with suitable skills, and redesigning tools used on the job.

Secondary boycott A boycott against a company's suppliers, customers, or other neutral third party.

Secondary data Data previously collected and assembled for some purpose other than the project at hand.

Secondary markets Capital markets in which previously issued securities are bought and sold.

Secured bond A bond that pledges specific assets to the investor in the event of default by the borrower.

Secured loan A loan that is backed by collateral pledged by the borrower to support the loan in the event of default.

Selection The process of screening applicants for the skills and abilities listed in the job specification to determine which ones are best suited for the job.

Selective advertising Advertising that attempts to create selective demand for a particular brand or store by promoting the brand's or store's attributes, benefits, uses, and images; also called *brand-specific advertising.*

Selective distribution Placing the product in a relatively limited number of outlets.

Self-actualization needs The desire for fulfillment and for realizing all of one's potential.

Separation Occurs when an employee leaves the company due to layoff, involuntary termination, voluntary resignation, or retirement.

Service Any task (work) performed by another person or business.

Shopping product A product that generates a great deal of consumer effort.

Skimming price A relatively high introductory price that marketers plan to systematically lower as the product matures.

Small Business Administration (SBA) A federal agency charged with protecting and assisting small businesses.

Small Business Development Centers (SBDCs) Agencies that sustain and encourage the small-business community through low-cost training and free one-on-one counseling programs.

Small business A business that is independently owned and operated, is not dominant in its field, and has fewer than 500 employees.

Social (belongingness) needs The desire to be accepted by friends and colleagues, to be loved and to be part of a group.

Social audit A form of self-regulation in which the company attempts to monitor managers' and employees' ethical behavior.

Social insurance Insurance programs provided by government agencies and regulations, generally financed entirely by mandatory contributions from employers and/or employees rather than by general (tax) revenues.

Social responsibility Refers to the ethical consequences of a person's or organization's acts as they might affect the interests of others.

Social value A value that reflects the goals a society views as important and expresses a culture's shared ideas about preferred ways of acting.

Social values Represent the goals a society views as important and express a culture's shared ideas about preferred ways of acting.

Socialism An economic system in which private property is allowed but the government owns primary industries

Sole proprietorship A business that is owned by only one person.

Span of control The number of subordinates who report directly to a manager.

Specialization Assigning different activities to different individuals to attain greater efficiency.

Specialty product A product perceived as having a particular attraction other than price.

Speculative risk Risk that involves deliberate actions managers take to generate profits.

Speculative stocks Stocks of companies whose earnings are unstable and uncertain.

Staff departments Departments that perform specialized activities that support line departments in activities such as human resources management, engineering, and accounting.

State appellate court A state court that decides questions of law.

State court of general jurisdiction A state trial court that has broad jurisdiction.

State inferior court The lowest level of state trial court, often having limited jurisdiction.

State supreme court The highest state court to which cases involving questions of law can be appealed.

Statement of cash flows A statement that reports the cash receipts and payments related to the company's operating, investing, and financing activities during the accounting period.

Statement of owner's equity A statement that summarizes the events that caused owner's equity to change during a specified period of time.

Statutory laws Laws enacted by Congress and state legislatures.

Stop-loss order An order to sell a security when the market price reaches or falls below a specified level.

Store image Reflects customers' mental impression of the store's personality.

Store of value The ability of money to maintain its buying power over time.

Strategic planning The process of setting organizational objectives, determining overall strategy for the business, and deciding on the appropriate allocation of resources for the business to reach its objectives.

Super NOW account A form of NOW account that pays higher interest and gives free and unlimited check-writing privileges, but requires a much larger minimum balance.

Supervisory management Managers responsible for directing and coordinating the work of nonmanagement employees.

Supplier A person or a company that provides goods or services needed to make a final product.

Supply curve A graphical representation of the amount of goods or services marketers will supply at various prices

Supply The quantity of a good or service marketers are willing and able to sell at a given price in a given time period

Surety bond A bond that provides monetary compensation if the bonded party fails to meet the performance terms of a contract.

SWOT Acronym for *strengths, weaknesses, opportunities,* and *threats.*

Tactical planning Focuses on specific actions to take to implement the organization's long-range strategies.

Target market The specific group likely to buy the company's product.

Tariff A tax imposed by a nation on an imported good.

Technical job skills Skills that require the ability to understand and use the specific tools, knowledge, and techniques of a discipline or function.

Technology The application of scientific knowledge to practical purposes.

Telemarketing Using the telephone as the primary means of communicating with prospective customers.

Tender offer An offer to the shareholders of a company to purchase all of their stock at a price above current market value.

Test market A city or small geographical area where a new product is sold in a typical retail setting.

Theft insurance Insurance for losses when property is taken by any act of stealing, including burglary and robbery.

Theory X The assumptions that employees are lazy and dislike work; must be forced, controlled, and threatened with punishment to be motivated to perform their jobs.

Theory Y The assumptions that employees like work, seek out responsibilities, and can bring imagination and creativity to the job.

Theory Z A management approach that emphasizes employee participation and modified Japanese and U.S. practices to improve motivation and productivity.

Time utility Economic utility created by storing products so they are available when consumers need them

Timeliness The degree to which information is available in time to make decisions.

Top management Managers who are responsible for setting the overall direction of the business and determining the organization's business strategy.

Total quality management (TQM) A business philosophy that a company must operate with an emphasis on customer-driven quality throughout the organization.

Total quality management (TQM) A company-wide effort that includes all employees, suppliers, and customers and seeks to continuously improve the quality of products and services to meet customer expectations.

Trade allowance A reduction in price, a rebate, merchandise, or something else given to a wholesaler or a retailer for performance of a specific activity or in consideration for a large order.

Trade credit The practice of buying goods or services on credit.

Trade show An event at which a group of manufacturers (or other marketers) jointly exhibit their products in a convention hall.

Trademark A legally registered brand name or brand mark.

Transfer A horizontal or lateral movement from one job to another of equal or similar responsibilities and salary.

Transfer The process of transferring financial responsibility for a loss by either contract or indemnification by a third party.

Trial balance An initial listing of all ledger accounts to determine the equality of the debits and credits.

Two-factor concept A theory of motivation based on hygienes and motivators.

U.S. court of appeals One of 13 courts that hear appeals of cases from the district courts located in their respective circuits.

U.S. Supreme Court The highest court in the federal court system.

Underwriting A process whereby an investment banker purchases new issues of securities from the issuing company and then sells them to the investing public.

Unemployment rate A measure of the percentage of individuals in the work force who are willing and able to work but cannot find full-time jobs.

Unfunded loss reserve An account that recognizes in advance that the company may suffer a loss but holds no money to cover an anticipated loss.

Uniform Commercial Code (UCC) A body of statutory law that governs the design, production, marketing, and interstate distribution of tangible, movable products.

Union shop A contract provision specifying that employees who are not union members at the time they are hired must join the union after some specified time, usually 90 days.

Unit of account A common means by which the value of goods and services is measured.

Unity of command A principle of organizing stating that each employee should be responsible to only one manager.

Unsecured loan A loan for which the borrower pledges no collateral but simply signs a promissory note.

Value Measures the power one product has to attract another product in exchange.

Vertical marketing system (VMS) A planned distribution channel designed to minimize conflict and increase efficiency among channel members.

Vertical merger The combining of firms engaged in related businesses.

Videoconferencing A business meeting at which telephones or satellites and TV screens link participants located in different cities or remote locations.

Voice mail A sophisticated, computerized telephone answering system that digitizes incoming spoken messages, stores them in the recipient's voice mailbox, and converts them to spoken form when retrieved.

Wheel of retailing A theory explaining historical patterns of retail evolution.

Whistle blower An employee who informs management, a union, the press, or a government agency that some behavior within the organization is not as it should be.

Wholesaler An organization that buys products from producers and resells those products to retailers, other wholesalers, and industrial users.

World brand An individual brand name common to all countries.

Zero coupon bond A bond that pays no interest, is initially sold at a discount, and redeemed at par value.

REFERENCES

Chapter 1

1. Martha T. Moore, "Selling the Social Ethic in Soap, Shampoo," *USA Today,* March 20, 1990, p. b4; Bo Burlingham, "This Woman Has Changed Business Forever," *Inc,* June 1990, pp. 35–45; Philip Elmer-DeWitt, "Anita the Agitator," *Time,* January 25, 1993, pp. 52–54; Carl Mortished, "Body Shop Reviews Retailing Strategy," *The (London) Times,* May 13, 1993, pp. 27, 29; Maggie Urry, "Dull Performance in UK behind 15% Decline at Body Shop," *Financial Times,* May 13, 1993, p. 26.
2. Richard S. Tedlow, *New and Improved: The History of Mass Marketing in America* (New York: Basic Books, 1990), p. 5.
3. The Four Cs of Business is copyright by William G. Zikmund, 1991. Use of this conceptual scheme elsewhere is not permitted without written permission from William G. Zikmund. For an alternative conceptualization, see Kenichi Ohnae, *The Mind of The Strategist* (New York: Penguin Books, 1982), p. 91.
4. Rosabeth Moss Kanter, "How to Compete," *Harvard Business Review* (July-August 1990), p. 7.
5. Tedlow, *New and Improved,* p. 5.
6. Richard Hofstadter, William Miller, and Daniel Aaron, *Since 1965,* vol. 2 of *The American Republic* (Englewood Cliffs, N.J.: Prentice-Hall, 1959), p. 194.
7. Mary Beth Norton et al., *To 1877,* vol. 1 of *A People and a Nation: A History of the United States* (Boston: Houghton Mifflin, 1982), pp. 220–247.
8. Tedlow, *New and Improved,* p. 120.
9. Adapted with permission from H. Lee Murphy, "Driving for the Green: Area Golf Club Maker Clearing Start-up Hazards," *Crains Chicago Business,* November 8, 1993.
10. Excerpts reprinted from "Companies to Watch: Treadco," *Fortune,* January 10, 1994, p. 109.

Chapter 2

1. Excerpt adapted from Andrew Tanzer, "This Time It's for Real," *Forbes,* August 2, 1993, pp. 58–61. Reprinted by permission of FORBES magazine. © Forbes Inc., 1993.
2. Milton H. Spencer, *Contemporary Economics* (New York: Worth Publishing, 1990), p. 2.
3. Ibid., p. 27.
4. Ibid.
5. Steven Prokesch, "Discontent in Equalitarian Sweden Threatens Socialists in Vote Today," *The New York Times,* September 15, 1991, p. Y-10.
6. Richard S. Tedlow, *New and Improved: The Story of Mass Marketing in America* (New York: Basic Books, 1990), p. 165.
7. Kenneth M. Prager, "Soviet Health Care's Critical Condition," *The Wall Street Journal,* January 29, 1987, p. 28.
8. Mark Memmott and Susan Antilla, "In U.S.S.R., Free Markets Frighten Many," *USA Today,* August 21, 1991, p. b-1.
9. Excerpted from Andrew Tanzer, "This Time It's for Real," *Forbes,* August 2, 1993, p. 59. Reprinted by permission of FORBES magazine. © Forbes Inc., 1993.

Chapter 3

1. Excerpts from Richard Lacay, "Give Me Your Rich, Your Lucky ...," *TIME,* October 14, 1991, p. 26. Copyright 1991 Time Inc. Reprinted by permission.
2. Peter D. Bennett, *Dictionary of Marketing Terms* (Chicago: American Marketing Association, 1988).
3. Kenneth P. Uhl and Gregory D. Upah, "The Marketing of Services: Why and How Is It Different?", in Jagdish N. Sheth, ed., *Research in Marketing,* vol. 6 (Greenwich, Conn.: JAI Press, 1990), p. 236.
4. U.S. Bureau of Labor Statistics, *Outlook 2000* (Washington, D.C.: U.S. Government Printing Office, 1990), pp. 27, 59; U.S. Bureau of Labor Statistics, *Bulletin #2340 April 1990* (Washington, D.C.: U.S. Government Printing Office, 1990), pp. 90–95, 557–558; portions adapted with permission from *Time,* February 2, 1987, p. 52.
5. This section is based on Paul Wonnacott and Ronald Wonnacott, *Economics* (New York: John Wiley & Sons, 1990), p. 7; and Harold T. Shapiro, George C. Dawson, and Gerson Antell, *Applied Economics* (Colorado Springs, Col.: Junior Achievement, 1990), p. 21.
6. Many economists include economic security, equity of income, reduction of pollution, and economic freedom in the list of economic goals. We address these issues from the perspective of the company elsewhere in this book.
7. Robert D. Hershey, Jr., "Why Economists Fear the Deficit," *The New York Times,* May 26, 1992, pp. D1, D3.
8. *Random House Dictionary of the English Language* (New York: Random House, 1968), p. 684.
9. See Michael R. Czinkota, Ilkka A. Ronkainen, and Michael H. Moffett, *International Business* (Fort Worth, Tex.: Dryden Press, 1994), pp. 12–16, for a more detailed discussion of this topic.
10. Denise Kaletk, "French Pocket a Landmark," *USA Today,* September 25, 1991, p. 1-A.
11. Reprinted with permission from Bob Herbert, "Ticket Trust Busters," *New York Times,* OP-ED, June 5, 1994, p. E-17.

Chapter 4

1. Adapted from Rita Koselka, "Society Girl Makes Good," *Forbes,* December 9, 1991, pp. 90–92.
2. *Statistical Abstract of the United States, 1993* (Washington, D.C.: U.S. Department of Commerce, 1993), pp. 540–541.
3. Ibid., p. 541.
4. John J. Curran, "China's Investment Boom," *Fortune,* March 7, 1994, pp. 116–124.
5. Jeffrey L. Hiday, "Hasbro Welcomes Mattel Rivalry," *The Providence Journal-Bulletin,* August 21, 1993, Dowquest.
6. *Statistical Abstract of the United States: 1993,* p. 543.
7. David Kirkpatrick, "Could AT&T Rule the World?" *Fortune,* May 17, 1993, pp. 55–66.
8. Alan Murray and Monica Langley, "Relatively New Form of Business Structure Is Causing Controversy," *The Wall Street Journal,* June 30, 1987, p. 1.
9. James R. Healey, "New Models Fuel Mazda's Market Push," *USA Today,* October 21, 1992, p. 7B.
10. Catherine Romano, "All A-board! The Composition of the Board Room Is Changing—Albeit Slowly," *Management Review,* October 1, 1993. Copyright American Management Association, 1993.

Chapter 5

1. Excerpt from Richard Lacayo, "Death on the Shop Floor," *TIME,* September 16, 1991, p. 28. Copyright 1991 Time Inc. Reprinted by permission.
2. James A. Belasco, *Teaching the Elephant to Dance* (New York: Crown Publishers, 1990), p. 111.
3. Janice Castro, "Making It Better," *Time,* November 13, 1989, pp. 78–81; David A. Gavin, "Competing on the Eight Dimensions of Quality," *Harvard Business Review* (November/December 1987), pp. 101–108.
4. "Burger King Opens Customer Hot Line," *Marketing News,* May 28, 1990, p. 7.
5. Peter D. Bennett, *Marketing Terms* (Chicago: American Marketing Association, 1988), p. 189.
6. Ray Billington, *Living Philosophy: An Introduction to Moral Thought* (London: Routledge, 1988), p. 17.
7. John R. Schermerhorn, Jr., James G. Hunt, and Richard N. Osborn, *Managing Organizational Behavior* (New York: John Wiley and Sons, 1991), p. 27.
8. Ian Robertson, *Sociology* (New York: Worth Publishing, 1987), pp. 64–65.
9. For a general discussion of ethical issues see Schermerhorn, *Managing Organizational Behavior,* p. 27.

10. U.S. Bureau of the Census, Associated Press, "Women's Pay Short for Equal Work," *Tulsa World,* November 14, 1991, p. B-5; Joan E. Rigdon, "30 Years After Equal Pay Act Women's Wages Far From Parity," *The Wall Street Journal,* June 9, 1993.
11. "Jobless Rate Sinks to 6%," *AP Newswire,* Prodigy Information Service, June 3, 1994.
12. U.S. Department of Labor, Bureau of Labor Statistics, *Monthly Labor Review* (November 1989).
13. Adapted from Talila Baron, "Sun Micro Sees Diverse Future," *The Business Journal-San Jose,* August 23, 1993. Copyright City Business/USA, Inc. 1993.
14. Ibid.
15. Melissa Lee, "Enterprise: Diversity Training Brings Unity to Small Companies," *The Wall Street Journal,* September 2, 1993.
16. "Sexual Harassment Is Real Problem; Treat It That Way," *USA Today,* October 9, 1991, p. 10a.
17. The research was conducted in a 1987 study by the U.S. Merit Systems Protection Board. See Karen DeWitt, "As Harassment Drama Plays, Many U.S. Employees Live It," *The New York Times,* October 13, 1991, p. y-9.
18. "Eisner The Top-Paid Executive," Prodigy Interactive Personal Service, April 15, 1994. Suzan Wong, "Pay Checks of the Super 50," *Forbes,* May 10, 1993, p. 105; Del Jones, "$1 Billion in Profits Taken on Options," *USA Today,* March 23, 1993, pp. B-1–B-2; Michelle Osborn, "Author's Recipe for CEO Pay," *USA Today,* October 9, 1991, p. B-4.
19. ITT Code of Corporate Conduct.
20. R. Eric Reidenback and Donald P. Robin, *Ethics and Profits* (Englewood Cliffs, N.J.: Prentice-Hall, 1989), p. 11.
21. Schermerhorn, *Managing Organiza-tional Behavior,* p. 27.
22. Adapted from Myron Magnet, "Small Business's Big New Worries," *FORTUNE,* July 26, 1993, p. 65. © 1993 Time Inc. All rights reserved.

Chapter 6

1. Adapted from Sally Bell, "Surviving and Thriving," p. 18. Excerpted by permission, *Nation's Business,* March 1990. Copyright 1990, U.S. Chamber of Commerce.
2. Much of the information in this section appeared in materials provided by the Small Business Administration.
3. This definition is from the *Small Business Administration Answer Desk Directory* (Washington, D.C.: U.S. Small Business Administration, November 1986).
4. Press release on Small Business Week, May 7–13, 1989, Small Business Administration, Washington, D.C.
5. Adapted from Myron Magnet, "Small Business's Big New Worries," *FORTUNE,* July 26, 1993.
6. *Starting Your Own Business: Answers to Some of Your Questions* (Washington, D.C.: U.S. Small Business Administration, 1990).
7. "Mother's Helper," *Entrepreneurial Woman,* December 1991, p. 8.
8. See Michael H. Morris and Joan M. Jarvi, "Making Marketing Curriculum Entrepreneurial," *Marketing Educator* (Fall 1990), pp. 1, 8.
9. Robert D. Hisrich and Michael P. Peters, *Entrepreneurship: Starting, Developing, and Managing a New Enterprise* (Homewood, Ill.: Irwin, 1992), p. 51.
10. Ibid., p. 62.
11. Much of this section reflects material published in SBA booklets.
12. Adapted from *Starting Your Own Business: The Isuzo Guide to Small Business Success,* by the editors of *Income Opportunities Magazine.*
13. Kent Gibbons, "Black-Owned Firms Feel Pinch of Law, Economy," *USA Today,* May 6, 1991, p. 3E.
14. Ibid.
15. James Kim, "'Mom-preneurs' Tend to Kids, Corporate Accounts at Home," *USA Today,* October 17, 1991, p. 48.
16. "Women Start Firms Faster Than You Can Say 'Glass Ceiling'," *USA Today,* May 6, 1991, p. 3E.
17. This section is adapted from *Starting Your Own Business: The Isuzo Guide to Small Business Success,* by the editors of *Income Opportunities Magazine.*
18. Ibid.
19. Adapted from Sharon Nelton, "The Man Who Transformed T-Shirts from Underwear into Fashion," p. 14. Adapted by permission, *Nation's Business,* January 1991. Copyright 1991, U.S. Chamber of Commerce.
20. Lisa Gubernick, "You Don't Have To Be a Rocket Scientist, *Forbes,* January 3, 1994, pp. 82–83. Reprinted by permission of FORBES magazine. © Forbes Inc., 1994.

Chapter 7

1. Jennifer Boice, "Southwest Air's Leader Takes 'Radical' Approach," *Tucson Citizen,* October 22, 1993; Roderick Gary, "Southwest Airlines' CEO Shares Tips with Student Entrepreneurs," *Arizona Daily Star,* October 25, 1993; and "Prince of Midair," *Time,* January 25, 1993.
2. Neal Templin, "GM's Saturn Subsidiary Is Fighting for Its Future," *The Wall Street Journal,* June 16, 1993, p. B4.
3. "The Fortune 500: The Largest U.S. Industrial Companies," *Fortune,* April 18, 1994, pp. 220–221.
4. "New Pony: How a 'Skunk Works' Kept Mustang Alive on a Tight Budget," *The Wall Street Journal,* September 21, 1993.
5. Howard Banks, "The Best Defense...," *Forbes,* January 3, 1994, p. 106.
6. Bill Saporito, "And the Winner Is Still Wal-Mart," *Fortune,* May 2, 1994, pp. 62–70.
7. Tricia Welsh, "Best and Worst Corporate Reputations," *Fortune,* February 7, 1994.
8. Brian Dumaine, "Payoff from the New Management," *Fortune,* December 13, 1993, pp. 103–110.
9. G. Dumaine, "Unleash Workers and Cut Costs," *Fortune,* May 18, 1992, p. 88.
10. G. P. Zachary, "Theocracy of Hackers Rules Autodesk, Inc., A Strangely Run Firm," *The Wall Street Journal,* May 28, 1992, p. A1.
11. Brian Dumaine, "The New Non-Manager Managers," *Fortune,* February 22, 1993, pp. 80–84.
12. "A Japanese 'Flop' that Became a Launching Pad," *Business Week,* June 8, 1992.
13. Thomas Peters and Robert Waterman, Jr., *In Search of Excellence* (New York: Warner Books, 1982).
14. James W. Dean, Jr. and James R. Evans, *Total Quality Management, Organization, and Strategy* (Minneapolis/St. Paul, Minn.: 1994), pp. 8–23.
15. Ibid.
16. G. Dumaine, "Unleash Workers and Cut Costs," *Fortune,* May 18, 1992, p. 88.

Chapter 8

1. Joseph Weber, "A Big Company That Works," *Business Week,* May 4, 1992, pp. 124–132.
2. Peter Drucker, *The Practice of Management* (New York: Harper & Brothers, 1954), pp. 65–83.
3. Saturn Corporation, Publication no. S02 00027 0890, 1990.
4. Sam Walton with John Huey, *Made in America: My Story* (New York: Doubleday, 1992); and Bill Saporito, "And the Winner Is Still Wal-Mart," *Fortune,* May 2, 1994, pp. 62–68.
5. Laura Zinn, "Can These Guys Revive Macy's?", *Business Week,* May 11, 1992, p. 38.
6. Brenton R. Schlender, "How Toshiba Makes Alliances Work," *Fortune,* October 4, 1993, pp. 116–120.
7. A. Wilkins and W. Ouchi, "Efficient Cultures: Exploring the Relationship Between Culture and Organizational Performance," *Administrative Science Quarterly* 28 (September 1983), pp. 468–481.
8. Sam Walton, *Made in America,* p. 157.
9. Dow Jones Information Service, "HILTON ANNOUNCES NEW CORPORATE ORGANIZATION," PR NEWSWIRE, STORY 62, page 1 of 4, January 28, 1994, Beverly Hills, CA. Reprinted by permission of the DOW JONES NEWS SERVICE. © 1994 Dow Jones & Company, Inc. All Rights Reserved.

Chapter 9

1. Alan Farnham, "America's Most Admired Company," *Fortune,* February 7, 1994, pp. 50–54.

2. "Even American Know-how Is Headed Abroad," *Business Week,* March 3, 1986, pp. 60–63.
3. Louis E. Boone and David L. Kurtz, *Contemporary Business,* 6th ed. (Hinsdale, Ill.: The Dryden Press, 1990), pp. 222–224.
4. William Echikson, "The Trick to Selling in Europe," *Fortune,* September 20, 1993, p. 82.
5. *Therblig* is a term coined by reversing the letters of the last name of Frank Gilbreth, a pioneer in the time-and-motion field.
6. "Top-Flite Puts New Spin on Golf-Ball Wars," *USA Today,* November 20, 1992, p. B-1.
7. Otis Port, "The Best-Engineered Part Is No Part at All," *Business Week,* May 8, 1989, p. 150.
8. Richard L. Daft, *Management,* 2nd ed. (Hinsdale, Ill.: The Dryden Press, 1991), p. 574.
9. Daft, *Management,* p. 574.
10. "Brace for Japan's Hot New Strategy," *Fortune,* September 21, 1993, p. 63.
11. Fleming Meeks, "Be Ferocious," *Forbes,* August 2, 1993.
12. "Business 2000: The New World Order," *Inc.,* special advertising section, December 1993, p. 51.
13. James C. Johnson and Donald F. Wood, *Contemporary Physical Distribution and Logistics* (New York: Macmillan, 1990), p. 18.
14. "Quality Standards That Can Open Doors," *Nation's Business,* November 1992, pp. 32–33.
15. "Business 2000: The New World Order," *INC.,* special advertising section, December 1993, p. 51.
16. "Quality Programs Show Shoddy Results," *The Wall Street Journal,* May 14, 1992, pp. B1, B9.
17. Otis Port and John Carey, "Questing for the Best: In Itself, the Search for Quality is Creating a Revolution," *Business Edge for Tomorrow's Leaders,* May, 1992, pp. 18–22.
18. "Turning a Stew of Old Tires into Energy," *The New York Times,* December 27, 1992, p. F-8.
19. Joseph M. Sieger, "A Need to Crunch the Right Numbers," *The New York Times,* October 27, 1991, p. F13.
20. Sue Shellengbarger, "Indicators of Quality in Day Care Worsen," *The Wall Street Journal,* May 6, 1992, p. B1.
21. "Quality Winning Its Own Place in Executive Suite," *Chicago Tribune,* November 3, 1991, p. 8-1.
22. Myron Magnet, "The Truth about the American Worker," *Fortune,* May 4, 1992, pp. 48–65.
23. "Chevron Tries to Show It Can Protect Jungle While Pumping Oil," *The Wall Street Journal,* June 9, 1992, pp. A1, A12.
24. Excerpts from Louis S. Richman, "The New Worker Elite," *FORTUNE,* August 22, 1994, p. 58. © 1994 Time Inc. All rights reserved.

Chapter 10

1. Greg Boeck, "Coaches Pull Out All Stops in Pep Talks," *USA Today,* September 23, 1992, p. 10c.
2. Sharon Nelton, "Putting Your Purpose in Writing," *Nation's Business,* February 1994, p. 62.
3. Frederick W. Taylor, *Principles of Scientific Management* (New York: Harper and Brothers, 1911).
4. Alex Carey, "The Hawthorne Studies: A Radical Criticism," *American Sociological Review* (June 1967), pp. 403–416. See also J. F. Rothlisberger and W. J. Dickson, *Management and the Worker* (Cambridge, Mass.: Harvard University Press, 1939).
5. John J. Hudy, "The Motivation Trap," *HR Magazine,* December 1992, pp. 63–67.
6. Abraham F. Maslow, "A Theory of Human Motivation," *Psychological Review* 50 (1943), pp. 370–396.
7. Frank G. Goble, *The Third Force: The Psychology of Abraham Maslow,* (New York: Grossman Publisher, 1970). Also see Edward Hoffman, "Abraham Maslow: Father of Enlightened Management," *Training,* September, 1988, pp. 79–82.
8. Bonnie Angelo, "Life at the End of the Rainbow," *Time,* November 4, 1991, pp. 80–81.
9. Frederick Herzberg, "One More Time: How Do You Motivate Employees?", *Harvard Business Review* (January/February 1968), pp. 53–62.
10. Shari Caudron, "Motivation? Money's Only No. 2," *Industry Week,* November 15, 1993, p. 33.
11. Ibid.
12. Carol Kleiman, "If You Don't Like Job, You Can Redesign It," *Chicago Tribune,* November 24, 1991, p. 8-1.
13. Douglas McGregor, *The Human Side of Enterprise* (New York: McGraw-Hill, 1970).
14. William G. Ouchi, *Theory Z: How American Business Can Meet the Japanese Challenge* (Menlo Park, Cal.: Addison-Wesley, 1981).
15. "Team Building Melds Cultures," *Business Atlanta,* September 1, 1993.
16. Carol Kleiman, "Performance-based Pay Merits Debate," *Chicago Tribune,* December 17, 1989, p. 8-1.

Chapter 11

1. "A Beijing Battle for McDonald's," *Chicago Tribune,* January 14, 1993, Sec. 3, p. 3.
2. Christopher Connell, "Major Features Listed in Clinton's Health Reform Plan," *Tulsa World,* September 23, 1993, p. 6.
3. Sharon Nelton, "A Flexible Style of Management," *Nation's Business,* December 1993, pp. 24–31.
4. Ibid.
5. Mimi Hall, "More Access Due under Landmark Law," *USA Today,* July 22, 1993, pp. A1–A2.
6. Andrew Pollack, "Japan Finds Ways to Save Tradition of Lifetime Jobs," *The New York Times,* November 28, 1993, pp. Y-1, Y-9.
7. Frank Swoboda, "U.S. Companies Speed Pace of Downsizing," *Washington Post,* February 9, 1994.
8. Leon E. Wynter, "Employers Go to School on Minority Recruiting," *The Wall Street Journal,* December 15, 1992, p. B1.
9. Ron Suskind, "Brooks Bros. Settles Job-Bias Suit; Inquiry Used Controversial 'Tests'," *The Wall Street Journal,* April 21, 1993, p. B6.
10. Brett Pulley, "Culture of Racial Bias at Shoney's Underlies Chairman's Departure," *The Wall Street Journal,* December 21, 1992, p. A1+.
11. Michael Schroeder, "Watching the Bottom Line Instead of the Clock," *Business Week,* November 17, 1988, pp. 134, 136.
12. Bob Filipczak, "Training Budgets Boom," *Training,* October 1993, pp. 37–51.
13. Michael Mecham, "Airbus to set up Chinese Simulators," *Aviation Week and Space Technology,* November 1, 1993, p. 43.
14. "Women Mentors Hope to Make Lasting Impact," *The Wall Street Journal,* April 28, 1993, p. B1.
15. Martha E. Mangelsdorf, "Ground-Zero Training," *Inc.,* February 1993, p. 83.
16. Joann S. Lublin, "Seeking Wisdom of Seasoned Veterans, More Firms Rehire Former Executives," *The Wall Street Journal,* April 29, 1992, pp. B1, B6.
17. Personal experience of one of the authors, who served as an expert witness for the police officers in this case.
18. Jeffrey Leib, "Martin Denies Age-Bias Finding," *Denver Post,* June 4, 1993, p. C1.
19. Kevin G. Salwen, "OSHA Fine Against Pepperidge Farm of $1.4 Million Is Largely Reversed," *The Wall Street Journal,* March 22, 1993, p. B2.
20. Barbara P. Noble, "Dissecting the 90's Workplace," *The New York Times,* September 19, 1993, p. F21.
21. Michael Cronin, "This Is a Test," *Inc.,* August 1, 1993.
22. Excerpt from Jaclyn Fierman, "Beating the Midlife Career Crisis," *FORTUNE,* September 6, 1993, p. 54. © 1993 Time Inc. All rights reserved.
23. Excerpt from Clare Ansberry, "Workers Are Forced to Take More Jobs with Fewer Benefits," *The Wall Street Journal,* March 11, 1993, p. A-1. Reprinted by permission of The Wall Street Journal. © 1993 Dow Jones & Company. All Rights Reserved Worldwide.

Chapter 12

1. "What's the Right Choice for AT&T?", *Business Week,* April 13, 1992, pp. 35, 38.

2. Claire Smith, "Hardball Isn't New to Top Negotiator," *The New York Times,* December 20, 1992, p. Y-27.

3. R. Dennis Middlemist, Michael A. Hitt, and Charles R. Greer, *Personnel Management: Jobs, People, and Logic* (Englewood Cliffs, N.J.: Prentice-Hall, 1983), p. 280.

4. "Teamsters: Things Go Better with Coke," *Business Week,* July 13, 1992, p. 38.

5. "Seniority vs. Skills: The Debate Arises Again Amid New Downsizings," *The Wall Street Journal,* July 7, 1992, p. A1.

6. Ronald Grover, "After CAT: What Does the Right to Strike Mean Now?", *Business Week,* May 4, 1992, pp. 36, 37.

7. Michael R. Czinkota, Ilkka A. Ronkainen, and Michael H. Moffett, *International Business* (Ft. Worth, Tex.: The Dryden Press, 1994), p. 603.

8. National Labor Relations Board, *A Guide to Basic Law and Procedures under the National Labor Relations Act* (Washington, D.C.: U.S. Government Printing Office, 1991).

9. Raymond A. Noe, John R. Hollenbeck, Barry Gerhart, and Patrick M. Wright, *Human Resource Management: Gaining a Competitive Advantage* (Burr Ridge, Ill.: Austen Press, 1994), pp. 478–479.

10. Bureau of National Affairs, "Union 'No' at Nissan," *Bulletin to Management,* August 10, 1989, pp. 249–250.

11. S. B. Jarrell and T. D. Stanley, "A Meta-Analysis of the Union-Nonunion Wage Gap," *Industrial and Labor Relations Review,* 44 1990, pp. 54–67.

12. C. Chang and C. Sorrentino, "Union Membership in 12 Countries," *Monthly Labor Review,* 113, no. 12, 1991, pp. 53–56.

13. Richard L. Daft, *Management,* 3rd ed. (Hinsdale, Ill.: The Dryden Press, 1994), p. 346.

14. Joan E. Rigdon, "Three Decades After the Equal Pay Act, Women's Wages Remain Far from Parity," *The Wall Street Journal,* June 9, 1993, pp. B1, B10.

15. Christopher Farrell and John Hoerr, "ESOPs: Are They Good for You?", *Business Week,* May 15, 1989, pp. 116–123.

16. "They Own the Place," *Time,* February, 1989, pp. 50–51.

17. Lindsey Novak and Lauren Spier, "No Guaranteed Notice for Layoff," *Chicago Tribune,* June 14, 1992, Section 8, p. 1.

18. Excerpt from David Welch, "Silver Star Meats Sold to 75 Employees in ESOP Deal," *Pittsburgh Business Times & Journal,* September 27, 1993.

19. Steven Wilmsen, "Teamsters End UPS Walkout," *The Denver Post,* February 8, 1994, p. C1, C10.

20. Adaptions and excerpts from Timothy L. O'Brien, "Company Wins Workers' Loyalty by Opening Its Books," *The Wall Street Journal,* December 20, 1993, pp. B1, B2. Reprinted by permission of The Wall Street Journal, © 1993 Dow Jones & Company, Inc. All Rights Reserved Worldwide.

Chapter 13

1. Judith D. Schwartz, "LensCrafters Takes the High Road," *AdWeek's Marketing Week,* April 1990, pp. 26–27.

2. This is the American Marketing Association's definition of marketing as reprinted in *Marketing News,* March 1, 1985, p. 1.

3. Regis McKenna, "Marketing Is Everything," *Harvard Business Review,* January/February 1991, pp. 65–79.

4. E. Jerome McCarthy, *Basic Marketing* (Homewood, Ill.: Richard D. Irwin, 1960).

5. Julie Liesse, "Oat Bran Popularity Hitting the Skids," *Advertising Age,* May 21, 1990, p. 3.

6. William L. Wilke, *Consumer Behavior* (New York: John Wiley & Sons, 1989).

7. "Marketing 100," *Advertising Age,* July 6, 1992, p. S-18.

8. "Marketer's Report Card 1989," *Adweek,* November 27, 1989, p. 26.

9. Claudia H. Deutsch, "In Search of New Products," *The New York Times,* February 24, 1991, p. F-25.

10. Theodore Levitt, "The Morality (?) of Advertising," *Harvard Business Review,* July/August 1970, pp. 84–92. Reprinted with permission of the President and Fellows of Harvard University.

11. Sterling Hayden, *The Wanderer* (New York: Alfred Knopf, 1963).

12. Judith D. Schwartz, "The School as Brand: Marketing Northwestern," *Brandweek,* November 8, 1993, pp. 28–29. © Adweek L. P. Used with permission from *Brandweek.*

13. Source: Based on Kevin Goldman, "BBDO Creates Spots Spicing Up Ways to Serve 58-Year-Old Spam," *The Wall Street Journal,* May 3, 1994.

Chapter 14

1. James Norman and Nikhil Hutheesing, "Hang on to Your Hats—and Wallets," *Forbes,* November 22, 1993. Adapted by permission of FORBES magazine. © Forbes, Inc., 1993.

2. Theodore Levitt, *The Marketing Imagination* (New York: Free Press, 1986), p. 79.

3. This classification is based on a "typical" consumer's reasons for buying. It makes good sense across the board, but in the case of a specific shopper, especially if that shopper is very poor or very rich, the classification scheme is less useful.

4. Lawrence M. Fisher, "Molar Movies and Other Dentists' Aids," *The New York Times,* April 29, 1990, p. 8f.

5. Julie Liesse, "General Mills May Try Again with Psyllium," *Advertising Age,* January 8, 1990, p. 4.

6. Cara Appelbaum, "Crayola Launches Hip, Bright Ads for Kids," *AdWeek Marketing Week,* September 5, 1990, p. 8.

7. David A. Ricks, *Big Business Blunders* (Homewood, Ill.: Dow Jones–Irwin, 1983), p. 52.

8. Adapted with permission from Laura Bird, "Novello Brands Cisco a 'Wine Fooler,'" *AdWeek's Marketing Week,* January 14, 1991, p. 6.

9. Adapted from Robyn Taylor, "Beam Me Out of This Mall, Scotty," *Brandweek,* October 12, 1992, p. 9. © Adweek L. P. Used with permission from *Brandweek.*

10. Adapted from Carl Quintanilla, "If You Walk, Chew This Gum, You'll Stumble with a Smile," *The Wall Street Journal,* June 8, 1993, p. B1. Reprinted by permission of The Wall Street Journal, © 1993 Dow Jones & Company, Inc. All Rights Reserved Worldwide.

Chapter 15

1. Maxine Lipner, "A Beer Brews in Brooklyn," p. 18. Adapted by permission, *Nation's Business,* November 1992, Copyright 1992, U.S. Chamber of Commerce.

2. *Statistical Abstract of the United States,* 112th ed. (Washington, D.C.: U.S. Department of Commerce, 1992), p. 526.

3. Excerpted from Drew Wilson, "Avon Ladies Calling in China Provinces," p. 19. Reprinted with permission by *Crain's New York Business,* September 13, 1993.

4. Julie Candler, "Window Shopping at the Drive-In," p. 43. Adapted/excerpted by permission, *Nation's Business,* February 1993. Copyright 1993, U.S. Chamber of Commerce.

5. Gene G. Marcial, "McKesson's Hard Sell Success," *Business Week,* June 30, 1986, p. 58.

6. "Spaghetti Warehouse: Not Abandoning Downtown Stores," *The Wall Street Journal,* July 6, 1993; Tara Parker Pope, "Spaghetti Warehouse Treks to Suburbs from Downtown," *The Wall Street Journal,* July 6, 1993.

7. Seth Lubove, "The Last Bastion," *Forbes,* February 14, 1994, p. 58. Adapted by permission of FORBES magazine. © Forbes Inc. 1994.

Chapter 16

1. Adapted from Robert L. Simison, "National Car Rental Stresses Speed, Challenges Budget," *The Wall Street Journal,* March 24, 1994, p. B3. Reprinted by permission of The Wall Street Journal, © 1994 Dow Jones & Company, Inc. All Rights Reserved Worldwide.

2. Herbert Katzenstein and William Sacks, *Direct Marketing,* 2d ed. (New York: Macmillan, 1992), p. 5.

3. Theodore Levitt, *The Marketing Imagination* (New York: Macmillan, 1986), p. 111.

4. It is interesting ot note that with Internet, word-of-mouth commmunications no longer have geographical borders.
5. D. J. Dalrymple and L. J. Parsons, *Marketing Management* (New York: John Wiley and Sons, 1980), p. 538.
6. Gerald L. Manning and Barry L. Reece, *Selling Today: A Personal Approach* (Boston: Allyn and Bacon, 1990), p. 6.
7. Thomas N. Ingram and Raymond W. LaForge, *Sales Management: Analysis and Decision Making* (Hinsdale, Ill.: The Dryden Press, 1989), p. 37.
8. The term *medium* (plural *media*) is, unfortunately, used to describe both the general classes and the specific vehicle.
9. Paul Burka, "What They Teach You at Disney U.," *Fortune,* November 7, 1988, p. 176; Charles Leerhsen, "How Disney Does It," *Newsweek,* April 3, 1989, pp. 48–54; and Christopher Knowlton, "How Disney Keeps the Magic Going," *Fortune,* December 4, 1989, pp. 111–132.
10. "Telephone Ads Attacked," *Euromarketing,* November 17, 1992, p.3.
11. David Kiley, "Candid Camera; Volvo and the Art of Deception," *Adweek,* November 12, 1990, p. 5; Raymond Serafin and Gary Levin, "Ad Industry Suffers Crushing Blow," *Advertising Age,* November 12, 1990, pp. 1, 54; Jennifer Lawrence, "How Volvo's Ad Collided with the Truth," *Advertising Age,* November 12, 1990, p. 76; Gary Strauss, "Smashing Event," *USA Today,* November 12, 1990, p. b-1; Stuart Elliot, "Volvo Says It's Crushed over Misleading Ads," *USA Today,* November 6, 1990, p. b-1.
12. Adapted with permission from Cleveland Horton, "Acura Integra Ads Swerve to Avoid Conventional," *Advertising Age,* July 12, 1993, pp. 3, 37.

Chapter 17

1. Peter Coy, "The New Realism in Office Systems," *Business Week,* June 15, 1992, pp. 128–133.
2. Nicole Winfield, "Heartthrobs Go On-line," *The Denver Post,* February 14, 1994, p. 1C.
3. J. A. O'Brien, *Computers and Information Processing,* 2nd ed. (Homewood, Ill.: Richard D. Irwin, 1987), pp. 499–500.
4. Janet Day, "Storm Chases Clients to Data Assurance," *The Denver Post,* August 27, 1992, p. C-1.
5. Gene Bylinsky, "How to Shoulder Aside the Titans," *Fortune,* May 18, 1992, pp. 87–88.
6. Rick Tetzeli,"Mapping for Dollars," *Fortune,* October 18, 1993, p. 92.
7. David Kirkpatrick, "Could AT&T Rule the World?" *Fortune,* May 17, 1993, pp. 55–66.
8. Vincent R. Ceriello, "Human Resources Management: Toy or Tool?", *Journal of Systems Management,* May 1980, p. 38.
9. Geoffrey Smith, "The Computer System That Nearly Hospitalized an Insurer," *Business Week,* June 15, 1992, p. 133.
10. Excerpted from Rick Tetzeli, "Mapping for Dollars," *FORTUNE,* October 18, 1993, pp. 91–92. © 1993 Time Inc. All rights reserved.
11. Ibid.
12. John W. Verity, "It's PCs vs. Mainframes—Even at IBM," *Business Week,* September 21, 1992, pp. 66–67.
13. Tim Clark, "Intel Enters Videoconferencing," *Advertising Age,* January 31, 1994, p. 14.
14. Rick Tetzeli, "The Internet and Your Business," *Fortune,* March 7, 1994, pp. 86–96.
15. Smith, "The Computer System."
16. Steve Komarow, "Army Adding Byte to the Battle," *USA Today,* April 4, 1994, p. 5A.

Chapter 18

1. Thomas L. Barton and Frederick M. Cole, "Accounting for Magic," *Management Accounting,* January 1991, pp. 27–31.
2. Lee Berton, "Father of Accounting Is a Bit of a Stranger to His Own Progeny," *The Wall Street Journal,* January 29, 1993, pp. A1, A5.
3. Jan Williams, Keith Stanga, and William Holder, *Intermediate Accounting* (New York: Harcourt Brace Jovanovich, 1987), p. 130.
4. Eben Shapiro, "Candy Man Wonders, Is Rock Idol Tarnishing the Lemonhead Name?", *The Wall Street Journal,* March 1, 1994, p. B1.
5. "Objectives of Financial Reporting by Business Enterprises," *FASB Statement of Financial Accounting Concepts,* no. 1, 1978, paragraph 34.
6. *Who Audits America* (Menlo Park, Cal.: The Data Financial Press, 1992).
7. Thomas P. Houck, "Have PCs Really Made Auditors More Efficient?", *Accounting Today,* July 19, 1993, p. 33.
8. Gregory Patterson, "Sears Registers Quarterly Loss of $1.8 Billion," *The Wall Street Journal,* February 10, 1993, p. A3.
9. James Hyatt, "CBS Net Soared in 4th Quarter; 1993 Gains Seen," *The Wall Street Journal,* February 11, 1993, p. B4.
10. "Avon Expects to Meet Its Targets on Growth in '94 Profit, Revenue," *The Wall Street Journal,* February 10, 1993, p. A4.
11. Charles Gibson, "How Industry Perceives Financial Ratios," *Management Accounting,* April 1982, pp. 13–19.
12. Jay Greene, "Phar-Mor and Coopers Provide Textbook Example," *The Denver Post,* March 21, 1993, pp. 1G, 5G.
13. "Goody's Family Clothing Finds Accounting Problem," *The Wall Street Journal,* November 17, 1993, p. A5.
14. Glenn A. Cheney, "Can Accounting Keep Up?" *New Account,* September 1993, pp. 22–24.

Chapter 19

1. Michael Schuman, "The Microlenders," *Forbes,* October 25, 1993, pp. 164,166. Adapted by permission of FORBES magazine. © Forbes, Inc., 1993.
2. Susan Caminiti, "What $1 Billion Can Buy," *Fortune,* June 28, 1993, p. 42.
3. Theodore Levitt, *Thinking about Management* (New York: The Free Press, 1991), p. 109.
4. *A Series on the Structure of the Federal Reserve System, No. 3: Federal Reserve Banks,* Board of Governors of the Federal Reserve System, 1993.
5. *79th Annual Report, 1992* (Washington, D.C.: Board of Governors of the Federal Reserve System, 1993), p. 242.
6. *Federal Reserve Bulletin,* March 1992, p. 172.
7. Anat Bird, *Super Community Banking: A SuperStrategy for Success* (Chicago: Probus Publishing, 1994), p. 312.
8. *Federal Reserve Bulletin,* March 1992, p. 174.
9. Stephen Frank, "Card Users May Be the Winning Targets of a Raging Battle in Credit Industry," *The Wall Street Journal,* August 31, 1993.
10. Steven Lipin, "Banks' Push to Sell Debit Cards Is Mostly Uphill," *The Wall Street Journal,* October 19, 1993, p. B1.
11. Bruce Knecht, "American Express Embraces Co-Brands," *The Wall Street Journal,* February 17, 1994, p. B1.
12. Herbert B. Mayo, *Finance: An Introduction* (Hinsdale, Ill.: The Dryden Press, 1989), p. 30.
13. *Federal Reserve Bulletin,* March 1992, p. 173.
14. CDS/Wiesenberger Investment Companies Service yearbook, 1993, p. 18.
15. Robert Emmet Long, *Banking Scandals: The S&Ls and BCCI* (New York: H. W. Wilson Company, 1993), p. 7.
16. Ibid., p. 25.
17. Kathleen Day, *S&L Hell* (New York: W. W. Norton, 1993), p. 210.
18. Amy Stevens, "Keating Is Given Sentence of 12 1/2 Years for Bank Fraud in Thrift-Scandal Case," *The Wall Street Journal,* July 9, 1993, p. B7.
19. Lynn Asinof, "Looking for Better Rates and Lower Fees? Credit Unions Are Favorites These Days," *The Wall Street Journal,* September 2, 1992, p. C1.
20. Ibid.
21. Catherine Yang, Howard Gleckman, and Mike McNamee, "The Future of Banking," *Business Week,* April 22, 1991, pp. 72–76.
22. Kenneth H. Bacon, "FDIC Discloses Big Turnaround in Insurance Fund," *The Wall Street Journal,* February 23, 1994, p. B9.

23. Frederic S. Mishkin, *The Economics of Money, Banking, and Financial Markets,* 3rd ed. (New York: HarperCollins, 1992), p. 332.
24. *79th Annual Report, 1992,* p. 201.
25. Floyd E. Egner III, *The Electronic Future of Banking* (Naperville, Ill.: Financial Sourcebooks, 1991), pp. 183–204.
26. Kenneth H. Bacon, "Clinton Backs Bank Policy That Includes Nationwide Branches, Help Overseas," *The Wall Street Journal,* October 22, 1993, p. A3.
27. Terence Paré, "Unconventional Wisdom Pays Off," *Fortune,* March 8, 1993, p. 78.
28. Martha Brannigan, "NationsBank Grows Rapidly via Innovation and a Slew of Mergers," *The Wall Street Journal,* December 28, 1992, pp. A1, A4.
29. Martha Brannigan, "Two Big Rival Banks in Southeast Take on New-Age Competitors," *The Wall Street Journal,* July 8, 1993, pp. A1, A6.
30. Claudia Rosett, "Rooted in Soviet Past, Russia's Central Bank Lacks Grasp of Basics," *The Wall Street Journal,* September 23, 1993, pp. A1, A4.
31. Nancy J. Perry, "Why These Bulls Love Bad News," *Fortune,* January 24, 1994, pp. 86–88.
32. Excerpts from Bruce Knecht, "Banks Bag Profits With Supermarket Branches," *The Wall Street Journal,* May 20, 1994, pp. B1, B6. Reprinted by permission of The Wall Street Journal, © 1994 Dow Jones & Company, Inc. All Rights Reserved Worldwide.

Chapter 20

1. Terence P. Paré, "How Schwab Wins Investors," *Fortune,* June 1, 1992, pp. 52–63; Robert McGough, "Schwab's Swellin' Girth Holds Sway in the Fund Field," *The Wall Street Journal,* November 9, 1993, pp. C1, C18.
2. Walencia Konrad, "Fowl Play," *Smart Money,* February, 1994, pp. 92–99.
3. Ibid.
4. Warren Getler and Carl Quitanilla, "Northwest Air Is Slashing Its IPO Price," *The Wall Street Journal,* March 17, 1994, pp. C1, C5.
5. Alexandra Peers, "Goldman Sachs Is Leading the Pack with Its '93 Results," *The Wall Street Journal,* March 8, 1994, p. A11.
6. Anita Raghavan, "Record Margin Borrowing Stirs Some Doubt on Stocks," *The Wall Street Journal,* January 31, 1994, p. C1.
7. "Chrysler Stock Sale Raises Slightly over $2 Billion," *The Wall Street Journal,* February 10, 1994, p. A4.
8. Steven E. Levingston, "Growth Investing May Be Poised to Make a Comeback," *The Wall Street Journal,* July 26, 1993, p. C1.
9. "Sculley Quits Spectrum, Sues," *The Denver Post,* February 8, 1994, p. C1.
10. Al Ehrbar, "You Mean You Still Don't Own Munis?", *Smart Money,* February 1994, p. 45.
11. Thomas T. Vogel, Jr., "Disney Amazes Investors with Sale of 100-Year Bonds," *The Wall Street Journal,* July 21, 1993, p. C1.
12. Steven E. Levingston, "Teen Fund Manager Shows Big Boys: Investing Is Kid Stuff," *The Wall Street Journal,* March 8, 1994, p. A1.
13. "GTE Debt, Preferred Totaling $8 Billion Get Lower Ratings," *The Wall Street Journal,* July 3, 1992, p. C16.
14. Douglas Lavin, "Chrysler to Sell Shares Valued at $1.46 Billion," *The Wall Street Journal,* January 12, 1993, p. A3.
15. Laura Jereski, "Junk-Bond Market Had Another Record Year in 1993," *The Wall Street Journal,* January 3, 1994, p. 26.
16. Robert McGough, "Stock Funds Had Record Inflows in December," *The Wall Street Journal,* January 28, 1994, p. C1.
17. Thomas T. Vogel, Jr., "Walt Disney to Sell Notes Tied to Films' Results, with Initial Yield Linked to U.S. 7-Year Issue," *The Wall Street Journal,* February 17, 1994, p. C22.
18. John C. Curran, "China's Investment Boom," *Fortune,* March 7, 1994.
19. Christi Harlan, "SEC Turns Up Heat on Brokers' Commissions," *The Wall Street Journal,* December 2, 1993, p. C1.
20. Paré, "How Schwab Wins Investors."
21. Sam Walton with John Huey, *Made in America: My Story* (New York: Doubleday, 1992), p. 3.
22. Steven E. Levingston, "Stock Investors' Fear of Octobers Is Probably Overdone, Data Show," *The Wall Street Journal,* September 27, 1993, p. C1.
23. "Scams, Dupes, Crafts, and Goldbricks," *Private Clubs,* November–December 1988, pp. 10–13.
24. "Understanding Financial Data—Part 1: Stock Prices and the Stock Markets; How to Read Quotations and Market Indexes," *The Wall Street Journal,* 1992/93 Educational Edition, pp. 7–8.
25. Dow Jones & Company, Inc., "The Dow Jones Averages: A Non-Professional's Guide," 1993.
26. Douglas R. Seaser, "Divergence of Industrial Average and S & P 500 Foreshadows 'Correction' in Stocks, Some Argue," *The Wall Street Journal,* July 13, 1992, p. C1.
27. John R. Dorfman, "Stocks Selling Below Book Value Can Be Bargains in Light of Today's Valuations," *The Wall Street Journal,* May 18, 1994, pp. C1, C2.

Chapter 21

1. Adapted from Kris McGovern, "JHB Buttons Up Deals," *The Denver Post,* February 1, 1993, section 1C, 5C.
2. Stanley Block and Geoffrey Hirt, *Foundations of Financial Management,* 6th ed. (Homewood, Ill.: Richard D. Irwin, 1992), p. 6.
3. Ricky W. Griffin, *Management,* 4th ed. (Boston: Houghton Mifflin, 1993), p. 632.
4. Stephen P. Robbins, *Management,* 4th ed. (Englewood Cliffs, N.J.: Prentice-Hall, 1994), p. 250.
5. Edmund Faltermayer, "Invest or Die," *Fortune,* February 22, 1993, pp. 42–52.
6. Michael Selz, "Firms Find Ways to Grow without Expanding Staffs," *The Wall Street Journal,* March 18, 1993, p. B1.
7. Edmund Faltermayer, "Invest or Die."
8. Brent Bowers, "This Store Is a Hit, but Somehow Cash Flow Is Missing," *The Wall Street Journal,* April 13, 1993, p. B2.
9. Antony J. Michels, "Get Lean When the Times Are Fat," *Fortune,* May 17, 1993, pp. 97, 100.
10. "Jack Welch's Lessons for Success," *Fortune,* January 25, 1993, pp. 86–93.
11. William Bak, "Make 'Em Pay," *Entrepreneur,* November 1992, pp. 64–67.
12. Patricia Sellers, "Companies That Serve You Best," *Fortune,* May 31, 1993, p. 76.
13. Barnaby J. Feder, "Moving the Pampers Faster Cuts Everyone's Costs," *The New York Times,* July 14, 1991, p. F5.
14. Block and Hirt, *Foundations of Financial Management,* p. 466.
15. Jaime Diaz, "In Bear Market, Nicklaus Is Bullish on His Business," *The New York Times,* February 2, 1992, pp. Y23, Y27.
16. Sellers, "Companies That Serve You Best," pp. 74–88.
17. Lawrence J. Gitman and Michael D. Joehnk, *Fundamentals of Investing* (New York: Harper & Row, 1990), p. 250.
18. John Labate, "Companies to Watch: Werner Enterprises," *Fortune,* November 29, 1993, p. 105.
19. Gautam Naik, "Spectrum Faces Big Cash Needs to Stay Ahead," *The Wall Street Journal,* March 18, 1994, p. A5A.
20. Norman M. Scarborough and Thomas Zimmerer, *Effective Small Business Management,* 3rd ed. (Columbus, Ohio: Merrill, 1991), p. 241.
21. Udayan Gupta, "Venture Capitalists Target Women-Owned Businesses," *The Wall Street Journal,* January 6, 1994, p. B2.
22. Block and Hirt, *Foundations of Financial Management,* p. 203.
23. Kevin Goldman, "Hollywood Movie Maker Thrives with Different Script," *The Wall Street Journal,* May 22, 1992, p. B4.

24. William P. Diven, "Flour Power," *Entrepreneur,* November 1992.
25. Bruce J. Blechman, "The High Cost of Credit," *Entrepreneur,* January 1993, pp. 22–25.
26. Donald E. Kieso and Jerry J. Weygandt, *Intermediate Accounting,* 6th ed. (New York: John Wiley & Sons, 1989), p. 305.
27. Linda Sandler, "Continental Air Bonds' Terms Spur Turbulence," *The Wall Street Journal,* December 17, 1990, pp. C1–C2.
28. Block and Hirt, *Foundations of Financial Management,* pp. 484–487.
29. Timothy O'Brien, "Atmet Harnesses Cash, Skill to Battle Big Chip Makers," *The Wall Street Journal,* March 5, 1993, p. B2.
30. Jan R. Williams, Keith G. Stanga, and William W. Holder, *Intermediate Accounting,* 4th ed. (Fort Worth: The Dryden Press, 1992), p. 1086.
31. "Central Garden & Pet," *Fortune,* February 7, 1994, p. 137.
32. Adapted and excerpted from Brian Dumaine, "A New Remedy for Growing Pains," *FORTUNE,* April 4, 1994, p. 144. © 1994 Time, Inc. All rights reserved.

Chapter 22

1. "Quake Costliest in California History?", *The Denver Post,* January 19, 1994, p. 8A; Morris Newman, "Collecting on Insurance in Oakland's Fire," *The New York Times,* January 24, 1993, p. Y26; Earl Gottschalk, Jr., "In Hurricane Andrew's Wake, Settling Insurance Claims May Be Next Disaster," *The Wall Street Journal,* September 25, 1992, pp. C1, C12; Chris Roush, "The Weather Has Home Insurers Running Scared," *Business Week,* April 5, 1993, p. 30.
2. "The Splash of the Cockerel," *The Economist,* January 23, 1993, p. 75.
3. George Head and Stephen Horn II, *Essentials of Risk Management: Volume I,* 2nd ed. (Malvern, Pa.: Insurance Institute of America, 1991), p. 8.
4. Andrew E. Serwer, "Crime Stoppers Make a Killing," *Fortune,* April 4, 1994, pp. 109–111.
5. Greg Steinmetz, "Allstate Insurance to Let Policies Lapse in Florida to Lower Hurricane Exposure," *The Wall Street Journal,* April 23, 1993, p. A3.
6. George Rejda, *Principles of Risk Management and Insurance* (New York: HarperCollins, 1992), p. 24.
7. Greg Steinmetz, "Trade-Center Blast to Cost Insurers about $510 Million," *The Wall Street Journal,* March 30, 1993, p. C20.
8. Richard A. Melcher, "Lloyd's Uneasy Rider," *Business Week,* April 26, 1993, p. 84; "Lloyd's of London Proposes Allowing Corporate Investors to Join Syndicates," *The Wall Street Journal,* April 30, 1993, p. A3.
9. Leslie Scism, "Insurers' Losses on Catastrophes Reach $7 Billion," *The Wall Street Journal,* March 29, 1994, pp. A2, A9.
10. Martin Tolchin, "GM Asked to Recall Pickups," *The Denver Post,* April 10, 1993, p. 2A.
11. Thomas M. Burton, "Funding Set for Settlement over Implants," *The Wall Street Journal,* February 14, 1994, pp. A3, A4.
12. Frances Huffman, "Embezzlement," *Entrepreneur,* November 1992, pp. 194–197.
13. George Anders, "More Insurers Pay for Care That's in Trials," *The Wall Street Journal,* February 15, 1994, pp. B1, B5.
14. Rejda, *Principles of Risk Management and Insurance,* p. 492.
15. Greg Steinmetz, "Life Insurers Now Find They Are Held Liable for Abuses by Agents," *The Wall Street Journal,* January 21, 1994, pp. A1, A6.
16. "Does the Boss Know You're Sick?" *Fortune,* August 9, 1993, p. 91.
17. Excerpts from Roger Thompson, "Taking Charge of Worker's Comp," pp. 18, 21. Reprinted by permission, *Nation's Business,* October 1993, U.S. Chamber of Commerce.

Chapter 23

1. Jeffrey Tannenbaum, "New Head of Franchiser Group Stresses Self-Regulation," *The Wall Street Journal,* March 11, 1993, p. B2; Michele Galen and Laurel Touby, "Franchise Fracas," *Business Week,* March 22, 1993, pp. 68–73; Eleena De Lisser and Benjamin A. Holden, "Denny's Begins Repairing Its Image—and Its Attitude," *The Wall Street Journal,* March 11, 1994, pp. B1, B3.
2. Kenneth Clarkson, Roger Miller, Gaylord Jentz, and Frank Cross, *West's Business Law* (St. Paul, Minn.: West, 1992), p. 2.
3. Amy Stevens, "Wall Street Turns to a New Breed of In-House Lawyer," *The Wall Street Journal,* January 14, 1994, p. B1.
4. Milo Geyelin, "Courts Are Raising the Bar for Employee Suits," *The Wall Street Journal,* December 31, 1993, pp. B9–B10.
5. Paul M. Barrett, "Justices Agree to Hear Honda Appeal for Cap on Punitive-Damage Awards," *The Wall Street Journal,* January 17, 1994, p. B3.
6. Clarkson et al., *West's Business Law,* p. 357.
7. Kathy Rebello, Michele Galen, and Evan Schwartz, "It Looks and Feels as if Apple Lost," *Business Week,* April 27, 1992, p. 35.
8. David Savage, "Treasure Finders Sunk by Court," *The Denver Post,* March 23, 1993, pp. 1A, 13A.
9. Patrick M. Reilly and Laura Jereski, "Vance Is Named as a Mediator in Macy Case," *The Wall Street Journal,* February 23, 1994, pp. A3, A5.
10. William Hoffman, Jr., James Smith, and Eugene Willis, *West's Federal Taxation: Individual Income Taxes* (St. Paul, Minn.: West, 1992), p. 1-4.
11. Donna Wood, *Business and Society* (Boston: HarperCollins, 1990), p. 340.
12. Wade Lambert, "Old Antitrust Decree Figures in IBM Case," *The Wall Street Journal,* February 24, 1994, p. B8.
13. William M. Carley and Amal Kumar Naj, "Price-Fixing Charges Put GE and De Beers under Tough Scrutiny," *The Wall Street Journal,* February 22, 1994, pp. A1, A5.
14. Catherine Yang and Amy Barrett, "In a Stew over Tainted Meat," *Business Week,* April 12, 1993, p. 36.
15. Bridget O'Brian, "Continental Airlines Gets Ready to Fly Without a Net," *The Wall Street Journal,* March 19, 1993, p. B4.
16. Jeffrey A. Tannenbaum, "Franchisees Take Complaints Against Pearle to FTC," *The Wall Street Journal,* February 16, 1994, p. B2.
17. Excerpts from Leslie Cauley, John Keller, and Dennis Kneale, "Battle Lines Harden As Baby Bells Fight to Kill Restrictions," *The Wall Street Journal,* July 22, 1994, pp. A1, A4. Reprinted by permission of The Wall Street Journal, © 1994 Dow Jones & Company, Inc. All Rights Reserved Worldwide.

Epilog

1. Eugene Raudsepp, "Finding the Perfect Career," *The College Edition of the National Business Employment Weekly,* Fall 1992, p. 7. Excerpt reprinted by permission from the National Business Employment Weekly, © 1992, Dow Jones & Co. Inc.
2. Ray Tuttle, "One Step Ahead: The Key to Job Hunting Is Getting an Early Start," *Tulsa World Magazine,* May 23, 1993, p. 4.
3. *Occupational Outlook Handbook* (Washington, D.C.: U.S. Department of Labor, 1993), p. 8.
4. John Case, "The Best Small Companies to Work for in America," *Inc.,* November 1992, pp. 89–99.
5. Raudsepp, "Finding the Perfect Career," pp. 7–11.
6. "Interns Have Edge on Jobs," *Fortune,* May 17, 1993, p. 14.

CREDITS

Chapter 1

Street Smart Box (p. 7) Source: Holland Cooke, "Be Nice; Customers Aren't Crackpots," *Marketing News*, August 14, 1989, p. 7. Reprinted with permission of the American Marketing Association.

Photo Credits

p. 3 Christopher Pillitz 1991 Network/Matrix. p. 5 Zoological Society of San Diego. p. 8 Doug Goodman, Advertising Age, Crain Communications, Inc. p. 13 Courtesy of Up Software, Inc. p. 14 © 1993, Michael Simpson, FPG International Corp.

Chapter 2

Street Smart (p. 27) Source: Richard S. Tedlow, *New and Improved: The History of Mass Marketing in America* (New York: Basic Books, 1990), p. 261. Focus on Collaborators (p.35) Source: "Boone Set For Showdown with Japanese Business Culture," *Tulsa World*, June 27, 1990, p. 2B.

Photo Credits

p. 21 Hu Yong, Gamma Liaison. p. 24 Michael L. Abramson. p. 25 Hugh Sitton/Tony Stone Images. p. 29 Bruce Ayres/Tony Stone Images. p. 30 Haroldo de Faria Castro, FPG International Corp.

Chapter 3

Exhibit 3.1 Source: Adapted from *The New York Times*, July 4, 1993, p. V6. Exhibit 3.3 Source: 1993 budget of the U.S. government; and Beth Belton, "Clinton Likely to Tout His Move on Economy," *USA Today*, January 25, 1994, p. B1. Exhibit 3.4 Source: Peter Passell, "Regional Trading Makes Global Deals Go Round," *The New York Times*, December 19, 1993, p. E4. Exhibit 3.5 Source: U.S. Department of Commerce. Focus on Customers (p. 47) Sources: "Confidence Hits Another Low," *Tulsa World*, February 26, 1992, p. B-1; "Business Milestones 1993," *Fortune*, January 10, 1994, p. 15. Focus on Competitors (p. 51) Source: Andrew Pollack, "Japan, Relenting, Plans to Allow Import of U.S.-Made Sushi," *The New York Times International*, October 4, 1992, pp. 7–4. Street Smart (p. 52) Source: Northwest Airlines Advertisement. Focus on Collaborators (p. 54) Sources: Bryan Iwamoto, "1992: A Wake Up Call," *Express Magazine*, September 1989, pp. 2–4; Shawn Tully, "Now the New Europe," *Fortune*, December 2, 1991, pp. 136–144. Focus on Customers (p. 56) Source: Adapted from Joseph J. Romm, "The Gospel According to Sun-Tzu," *Forbes*, December 9, 1991, pp. 157-158. Reprinted with permission of Joseph J. Romm.

Photo Credits

p. 41 © 1993, Jeffrey Sylvester, FPG International Corp. p. 44 Daniel Bosler/Tony Stone Images. p. 49 © 1989, Larry Grant, FPG International Corp. p. 50 Darwin R. Wiggett/First Light. p. 53 Courtesy of Kellogg Company.

Chapter 4

Exhibit 4.1 Source: Data supplied by Statistics of Income Division, Internal Revenue Service, Washington, D.C., personal communication, 3/24/94 Exhibit 4.2 Source: *Statistical Abstract of the United States, 1993* (Washington, D.C.: U.S. Department of Commerce, 1993), p. 539. Exhibit 4.3 Source: Sidney Wolf, *The Accountant's Guide to Corporation, Partnership, and Agency Law* (New York: Quorum Books, 1989), pp. 126–126. Exhibit 4.5 Source: 1993 data compiled for three quarters and extrapolated to 4 quarters, from *Mergers and Acquisitions*, January/February, 1994. Statistical Abstract of the United States: 1993, 113th ed., U.S. Department of Commerce, Bureau of Census, Washington, D.C., 1993. Focus on Competitors (p. 70) Source: Jeffrey Leib, "Boyer Boys Lose Battle; Company Renamed," *The Denver Post*, September 27, 1992, pp. 1l, 5l. Focus on Competitors (p. 73) Source: Shelley Neumeier, "Betting on China's Boom," *Fortune*, June 1, 1992, pp. 24+. Focus on Collaborators (p. 79) Source: Stephen Yoder and G. Paschal Zachary, "Digital Media Business Takes Form as a Battle of Complex Alliances," *The Wall Street Journal*, July 14, 1993, pp. A1, A6.

Photo Credits

p. 63 © 1994 Black/Toby Photography. All rights reserved. p. 75 Used by permission of Fisher-Price, Inc. p. 79 Ford Motor Company. p. 80 The Advertising Council, Inc.

Chapter 5

Exhibit 5.3 Source: U.S. Bureau of the Census and Associated Press, "Women's Pay Short for Equal Work," *Tulsa World*, November 14, 1991, p. B-5. Exhibit 5.4 Source: Employment and Earnings, June 1993, U.S. Department of Labor, Bureau of Labor Statistics, current population survey. Exhibit 5.5 Source: Susan Chin, "The Biggest Bosses," *Forbes*, May 11, 1992, p. 176. Focus on Collaborators (p. 96) Source: Excerpt adapted from "Headliners: After the Curtain Falls," *The New York Times*, October 13, 1991, p. E-7. Copyright © 1991 by The New York Times Company. Reprinted by permission. Street Smart (p. 97) Source: Robert E. Allen, "An Explicit Policy Toward Harassment," *The New York Times*, October 20, 1991, p. 15. Copyright © 1991 by The New York Times Company. Reprinted by permission. Courtesy of AT&T Archives. Focus on Customers (p. 101) Source: Adapted from Meryl Davids, "Rainforest Goods," *Adweek*, November 1990, page H.P./H.M. 6. © 1990 Adweek, L.P. Used with permission from *Adweek*. Focus on Company (p. 103) Source: Excerpts from Sandy Sheehy, "Raising the Levels of Hope and Expectations," *Forbes*, October 21, 1991, p. 332. Adapted by permission of FORBES magazine. © Forbes Inc., 1991. Take a Stand Source: Adapted from Diana Henriques, "To American Women: Sayonara," *The New York Times*, August 27, 1989, p. E-10. Copyright © 1989 by The New York Times Company. Reprinted by permission.

Photo Credits

p. 87 THE CHARLOTTE OBSERVER/BOB LEVERONE. p. 90 Courtesy of Russell Corporation. p. 94 ©, 1994, Comstock, Inc. p. 95 © 1992, Arthur Tilley, FPG International Corp. p. 100 Courtesy of Wrangler, Inc.—a VF company... A leader in quality apparel.

Chapter 6

Exhibit 6.1 Source: Excerpts from *A Guide to the Small Business Administration's Definition of Small Business* (Washington, D.C.: U.S. Small Business Administration). Street Smart (p. 119) Source: Stanley R. Rich and David E. Gumpert, "Packaging Is Important," *Harvard Business Review* (May/June 1985), p. 162. Focus on Customers (p. 120) Source: Adapted from Alyssa A. Lappen, "You Just Work Your Heart Out," *Forbes*, March 5, 1990, pp. 74–77. Focus on Company (p. 123) Source: Fleming Meeks and R. Lee Sullivan, "If at First You Don't Succeed...," *Forbes*, November 9, 1992, p. 172. Adapted by permission of FORBES magazine. © Forbes Inc., 1992. Focus on Company (p. 125) Source: David Paschal, "Risky Business, Big Rewards," p. 6. Excerpted by permission, Nation's Business, March 1990. Copyright 1990, U.S. Chamber of Commerce. Street Smart (p. 128) Source: Bradford McKee and Sharon Nelton, "Building Bridges to Minority Firms, *Nation's Business*, December 1992, p. 33.

Photo Credits

p. 111 Mark Perlstein. p. 113 © Michael L. Abramson. p. 114 TED WOOD/TIME MAGAZINE. p. 124 Courtesy of Ernst & Young. p. 127 Don Smetzer/Tony Stone Images. p. 129 ©, 1992, Comstock, Inc.

Chapter 7

Exhibit 7.5 Source: Adapted from T. Peters and R. Waterman, Jr., *In Search of Excellence* (New York: Warner Books, 1982). Focus on Collaborators (p. 142) Source: Raymond Serafin, "The Saturn Story," *Advertising Age*, November 16, 1992, pp. 1, 13, 16. Focus on Company (p. 145) Source: G. P. Zachart, "Theocracy of Hackers Rules Autodesk Inc., A Strangely Run Firm," *The Wall Street Journal*, May 28, 1992, p. A1+.

Photo Credits

p. 139 © 1994 Louis Psihoyos Matrix. p. 141 Swatch, a division of SMH (US) Inc. p. 143 PHOTO BY DICK KELLEY 1993. p. 151 © Brian Smith/Outline. p. 156 Bob Jones, Jr.

Chapter 8

Focus on Company (p. 169) Source: Sam Walton with John Huey, *Sam Walton: Made in America,* (New York: Doubleday, 1992), p. 55. Focus on Competitors (p. 174) Source: Andrew Erdman, "Staying Ahead of 800 Competitors," *Fortune,* June 1, 1992, p. 111. Street Smart (p. 175) Source: Adapted from Kenichi Ohmae, "The Equidistant Manager," *Express Magazine,* Fall 1990, pp. 17–18. Street Smart (p. 176) Source: Gilbert Fuchsberg, "Decentralized Management Can Have Its Drawbacks," *The Wall Street Journal,* December 9, 1992, pp. B1, B8. Focus on Collaborators (p. 176) Source: Adapted from: Carla Rapoport, "A Tough Swede Invades the U.S.," *Fortune,* June 29, 1992, pp. 76–79.

Photo Credits

p. 163 Photo courtesy of Ted Kawalerski and Johnson & Johnson. p. 164 3M Company. p. 167 Courtesy of Saturn Corporation. p. 180 Reprinted with permission of Compaq Computer Corporation All Rights Reserved.

Chapter 9

Exhibit 9.1 Source: Adapted from Michael A. Hitt, R. Dennis Middlemist, and Robert L. Mathis, *Management: Concepts and Effective Practice* (St. Paul, Minn.: West, 1989), p. 527. Focus on Company (p. 191) Source: Michael Clements and James R. Healy, "Big 3 Earnings Accelerate ... As Detroit Learns Efficiency // Detroit's New Approach Pays Off," *USA Today,* February 10, 1994, p. B-1. Copyright 1994, USA TODAY. Reprinted with permission. Street Smart (p. 196) Source: John Holusha, "Pushing the Envelope at Boeing,: *The New York Times,* November 10, 1991, pp. 3–1, 3–6. Focus on Customers (p. 192) Source: John Harris, "Dinnerhouse Technology," *Forbes,* July 8, 1991, pp. 98–99. Focus on Company (p. 202) Source: Michael Barrier, "When 'Just In Time' Just Isn't Enough," *Nation's Business,* November 1992, pp. 30–31. Focus on Competitors (p. 203) Source: Barnaby J. Feder, "Formica: When a Household Name Becomes an Also-ran," *The New York Times,* August 12, 1990, p. F-12.

Photo Credits

p. 187 © 1992 Rubbermaid Incorporated Used with permission. Rubbermaid and Draintainer are trademarks of Rubbermaid Incorporated. p. 191 © Shawn Henry/SABA. p. 195 Reproduced with permission from General Motors Corporation. p. 197 Copyright, Peter Sibbald 1992. p. 206 © 1994 CHRIS SHINN.

Chapter 10

Street Smart (p. 222) Source: Jack Welch's Lessons for Success," *Fortune,* January 25, 1993, p. 92. Focus on Company (p. 225) Source: Lisa Mainiero, "Participation? nyet: Rewards and Praise? da!" *Academy of Management Executive,* (August, 1993). pp. 86–88. Focus on Competitors (p. 228) Source: "Detroit South," *Business Week,* March 16, 1992, pp. 98–103. Focus on Customers (p. 232) Source: Jack Pickard, "Motivate Employees to Delight Customers," *Training and Development Journal* (July 1993), p. 48. Take A Stand Source: Carol Kleiman, "Minorities Isolated from Job Hot Spots," *Chicago Tribune,* July 28, 1991, p. 8-1; Shelia M. Poole, "With Diversity Comes the Need to Understand," *Chicago Tribune,* July 28, 1991, p. 8-1.

Photo Credits

p. 213 COMSTOCK, INC./Stuart Cohen. p. 216 COMSTOCK, INC. p. 220 Robert Burke/Gamma Liaison. p. 223 Martin Rogers/Tony Stone Images. p. 230 © 1988, Mason Morfit, FPG International Corp.

Chapter 11

Exhibit 11.1 Adapted from Richard L. Daft, *Management,* 2nd ed. (Hinsdale, Ill.: The Dryden Press, 1991), p. 337. Exhibit 11.4 Source: *The Denver Post,* July 5, 1992, pp. 17J–18J. Focus on Collaborators (p. 244) Source: Carol Kleiman, "For Executive Search Firms, Global Marketplace Is Now," *Chicago Tribune,* August 4, 1991, p. 8-1; "Language Fluency Can Translate into Career Success," *Chicago Tribune,* August 4, 1991, p. 8-1. Focus on Collaborators (p. 245) Source: Eugene Carolson, "Business of Background Checking Comes to the Fore," *The Wall Street Journal,* August 31, 1993, p. B2. Street Smart (p. 246) Source: Michael Cronin, "This is a Test," p. 64. Reprinted with permission, *Inc.* magazine, August, 1993. Copyright 1993 by Goldhirsh Group, Inc., 38 Commercial Wharf, Boston, MA 02110. Focus on Company (p. 249) Source: Claudia H. Deutsch, "Rewarding Employees for Wellness," *The New York Times,* September 15, 1991, p. F-21. Focus on Company (p. 250) Source: Kevin G. Salwen, "German-Owned Maker of Power Tools Finds Job Training Pays Off," *The Wall Street Journal,* April 13, 1993, pp. A1, A7. Street Smart (p. 253) Source: Harvey Gittler, "Give Yourself a Present: Becoming a Mentor to an Employee," *Industry Week,* December 6, 1993. Copyright Penton Publishing Inc. 1993 Focus on Collaborators (p. 254) Source: Carol Kleiman, "These Days You Can Score with a Lateral," *Chicago Tribune,* May 5, 1991, p. 8-1. Focus on Company (p. 257) Source: Sue Shellenbarger, "Managers Navigate Unchartered Waters Trying to Resolve Work-Family Conflicts," *The Wall Street Journal,* December 7, 1992, pp. B1, B10.

Photo Credits

p. 237 © 1992, Dennis Cox, FPG International Corp. p. 239 Fred Zwicky. p. 248 © ROBERT HOLMGREN 1994 ALL RIGHTS RESERVED. p. 251 Telegraph Colour Library, FPG International Corp. p. 252 © Mark Tucker.

Chapter 12

Focus on Collaborators (p. 271) Source: "Steelworkers Ratify Contract with LTV," *Employee Benefit Plan Review,* December 1992, p. 75; "A Brawl with Labor Could Block LTV's Rebirth," *Business Week,* March 16, 1992, p. 40. Street Smart (p. 273) Source: Reprinted from Roger Dawson, *The Secret of Power Negotiating* (Chicago: Nightingale-Conant Corporation), 1987, Card 9. Street Smart (p. 278) Source: Denise Tom, "Competence the Key, Not Gender, Say Many Players in Pro Ranks," *USA Today,* November 11, 1992, p. 14C. Focus on Company (p. 279) Source: "Doing It Right, Till the Last Whistle," *Business Week,* April 6, 1992, pp. 58–59.

Photo Credits

p. 265 © Ann States/SABA. p. 266 Tom Burton/Silver Image. p. 272 Charlie Archambault, U.S. News & World Report. p. 276 BRENDA BLACK & LEWIS TOBY.

Chapter 13

Exhibit 13.6 Source: Michael J. Weiss, *The Clustering of America* (New York: Harper and Row, 1988) Focus on Company (p. 290) Source: Based on Joseph M. Winski, "Addicted to Research, Nick Shows Strong Kids' Lure," *Advertising Age,* February 16, 1992, p. S-2. Focus on Customers (p. 300) Source: Phil Davies, "You Say Tomato, I Say Tomahto," *Express Magazine,* Spring 1992, p. 19. Reprinted by permission of *Express Magazine,* a publication of Federal Express, copyright 1992. Focus on Customers (p. 301) Source: Adapted from "New Electronic Toys Speak to the Needs of Hispanic Tots," *USA Weekend,* October 16–18, 1992, p. 26. Copyright 1992, USA WEEKEND. Reprinted with permission. Street Smart (p. 305) Source: Adapted from *Radio Only,* 1930 E. Marlton Pike, Cherry Hill, NJ 08003. As in *Communication Briefings,* Volume IX, No. XI, p. 2. Street Smart (p. 306) Source: Reprinted from Mitch Maurer, "Knowing the Lingo Can Help," *Tulsa World,* October 18, 1992, p. 6-5. Focus on Customers (p. 307) Source: Edward DiMingo, "The Fine Art of Positioning," *Journal of Business Strategy,* March/April 1988, pp. 34–38.

Photo Credits

p. 287 © 1991, TRAVELPIX, FPG International Corp. p. 296 Larry Dale Gordon/The Image Bank. p. 299 MCMXC Del Sol Productions/The Image Bank. p. 301 CATHERINE KARNOW. p. 302 The Olive Garden.

Chapter 14

Focus on Company (p. 319) Source: John Holusha, "Giving Good Weight to Plastic," *The New York Times,* September 9, 1990, p. F-9. Focus on Company (p.323) Excerpted from Faye Ricé, "The New Rules of Superlative Service," *Fortune,* Autumn/Winter 1993, p. 50. © 1993 Time Inc. All rights reserved. Focus on Customer (p. 326) Source: Christy Fisher, "Wake Up and Smell the Tacos, Pepsi," *Advertising Age,* September 14, 1989, p. 4; Michael J. McCarthy, "Tests Show That Pepsi's Rival to Coffee So Far Isn't Most People's Cup of Tea," *The Wall Street Journal,* March 30, 1990, p. B-1. Focus on Competitors (p. 335) Source: Debra Nussbaum, "Will the National Flower Become an Import Too?", *AdWeek's Marketing Week,* July 9, 1990, p. 24. Take a Stand Adapted from Laura Bird, "Novello Brands Cisco a 'Wine Fooler'," *Adweek's Marketing Week,* January 14, 1991, p. 6. © 1991 Adweek L.P. Used with permission from *Brandweek.*

Photo Credits

p. 317 COPYRIGHT 1994 BY SETH RESNICK. p. 326 COURTESY OF THE GATORADE COMPANY. p. 330 AP/WIDE WORLD PHOTOS. p. 339 Michael Salas/The Image Bank.

Chapter 15

Exhibit 15.5 Source: Reprinted with the permission of Macmillan College Publishing Company from RETAILING 5/E by Dale M. Lewison. Copyright © 1994 by Macmillan College Publishing Company, Inc. Focus on Company (p. 356) Source: Jacalyn Carfagno, "When Wal-Mart Comes to Town," *USA Today,* August 23, 1990, p. 4b. Street Smart (p. 359) Source: Joe Dacy II, "To Catch a Shoplifter," p. 72. Excerpted by permission, Nation's Business, November 1992. Copyright 1992, U.S. Chamber of Commerce. Focus on Competitors (p. 362) Source: Adapted from Bob Ortega, "Penney Pushes Abroad in Unusually Big Way as It Pursues Growth," *The Wall Street Journal,* February 1, 1994, pp. A1, A6. Reprinted by permission of The Wall Street Journal, © 1994 Dow Jones & Company, Inc. All Rights Reserved Worldwide.

Photo Credits

p. 347 ALAN DOROW. p. 358 David Young-Wolff/Tony Stone Images. p. 360 Avon Products, Inc. p. 364 Dunkin' Donuts, Inc.

Chapter 16

Exhibit 16.1 Source: Based on David A. Aaker and John G. Meyers, *Advertising Management third edition,* (Englewood Cliffs, N.J.: Prentice-Hall, 1987), p. 375; and George E. Belch and Michael A. Belch, *Introduction to Advertising and Sales Promotion,* (Homewood, Ill.: Irwin, 1990), pp. 213–222. Exhibit 16.2 Source: Adapted from William C. Moncrief, "Selling Activity and Sales Position Taxonomies for Industrial Salesforce," *Journal of Marketing Research* 23 (August 1986): 261–270, published by the American Marketing Association. Used with permission. Exhibit 16.5 Source: By Straight Arrow Publishers, Inc. 1987. All Rights Reserved. Reprinted by Permission. Focus on Company (p. 373) Source: Adapted from Jane Weaver, "Girl Scout Campaign: Shedding Old Image for MTV Cool," *Adweek,* September 11, 1989, p. 68. Focus on Customers (p. 377) Source: Excerpts from "The Sales Arsenal," pp. 29–30. First appeared in SUCCESS May 1993. Written by Duncan Anderson. Reprinted with permission of SUCCESS Magazine. Copyright © 1993 by Hal Holdings Corporation. Street Smart (p. 379) Source: Excerpt adapted from *The Book of Checklists and Other Tools for Small-Business Decision Making,* by the John H. Melchinger Company, 15 Cypress St., Suite 207, Newton Centre, MA 02159. As in Communication Briefings—Volume ix, No. V, p. 5. Focus on Competitors (p. 381) Source: John H. Taylor, "Not-So-Free Agent," *Forbes,* April 13, 1992, pp. 128–129. Adapted by permission of FORBES Magazine. © Forbes Inc., 1992; Skip Hollandsworth, "Batting A Million," *USA Weekend,* July 9–11, 1993, pp. 4–6; "Piazza Signs," *USA Today,* February 11, 1994, p. B-4. Focus on Collaborators (p. 384) Source: David M. Steward, "Twin Piques," *Advertising Age,* June 3, 1991, pp. 20c–25c; Joyce Rutter Kaye, "Group Therapy," *Advertising Age,* July 2, 1990, pp. s16–s17. Focus on Collaborators (p. 388) Source: Adapted from "The Furor over Formula Is Coming to a Boil," *Business Week,* April 190, p. 52. Focus on Company (p. 390) Source: Keichi Ohmae, "The Equidistant Manager," *Express Magazine,* Fall 1990, pp. 10–12. Focus on Company (p. 390) Paul Burka, "What They Teach You at Disney U.," *Fortune,* November 7, 1988, p. 176; Charles Leerhsen, "How Disney Does It," *Newsweek,* April 3, 1989, pp. 48–54; and Christopher Knowlton, "How Disney Keeps the Magic Going," *Fortune,* December 4, 1989, pp. 111–132.

Photo Credits

p. 371 NATIONAL CAR RENTAL SYSTEMS, INC. W.B. DONER & CO. (AGENCY). p. 374 Used with permission of Michelin Tire Corporation. All rights reserved. p. 376 Gary Gladstone/The Image Bank. p. 382 Chemical Manufacturers Association. p. 384 Don Francisco of "Sabado Gigante." p. 395 © 1993 Acura Division of American Honda Motor Co., Inc.

Chapter 17

Focus on Competitors (p. 402) Peter Coy, "The New Realism in Office Systems," *Business Week,* June 15, 1992, p. 130. Street Smart (p. 403) Robert Troutwine, "Prepare Now and Succeed Later," Managing Your Career, (*The Wall Street Journal,* Fall, 1990), p. 10. Focus on Collaborators (p. 405) Lawrence M. Fisher, "From Bad Boy to Big Business," *The New York Times,* July 14, 1991, p. F-12. Focus on Company (p. 411) David Kirkpatrick, "Here Comes the Payoff from PCs." *Fortune,* March 23, 1992, pp. 93–100. Focus on Collaborators (p. 418) Dinah Zeiger, "Jones' Converging Universe," *The Denver Post,* February 13, 1994, p. 1l, 6l. Focus on Collaborators (p. 419) Glenn Rifkin, "Toward the Voice-Literate Computer," *The New York Times,* February 24, 1991, pp. 45–49.

Photo Credits

p. 399 ©John Abbott. p. 400 AP/WIDE WORLD PHOTOS. p. 410 © TED HARDIN. p. 415 John Madere. p. 417 Intel Corporation.

Chapter 18

Focus on Competitors (p. 434) Source: Gabriella Stern, "Audit Report Shows How Far Chambers Would Go for Profits," *The Wall Street Journal,* October 21, 1992, pp. A1, A8; Julia Flynn, "Burying Trash in Big Holes—on the Balance Sheet," *Business Week,* May 11, 1992, pp. 88–89. Street Smart (p. 437) Source: Marshall Loeb, *1990 Money Guide* (Boston: Little, Brown, 1989), p. 18. Focus on Company (p. 438) Source: Teri Agins, "Leslie Fay Says Irregularities in Books Could Wipe Out '92 Profit; Stock Skids," *The Wall Street Journal,* February 2, 1993, p. A4. Focus on Company (p. 439) Source: Excerpt from Larry Rohter, "The Games, The Practice; The Money, Real," *The New York Times,* March 13, 1994, p. F-6. Copyright © 1994 by The New York Times Company. Reprinted by permission. Focus on Collaborators (p. 441) Source: Rick Telberg, "GAAP Be Damned: Accounting Moves Beyond Money," *Accounting Today,* December 13, 1993, pp. 12–17. Photo 18.5 Source: VISaVIS, August 1992, p. 88.

Photo Credits

p. 425 Copyright Universal Studios Inc., all rights reserved. p. 431 Scala/Art Resource, NY. p. 436 (left) Ferrara Pan Candy Co. p. 436 (right) Siaud/Stills/Retna Ltd. p. 438 Walter Bibikow/The Image Bank. p. 443 Photograph provided courtesy of DELTEK, McLean, VA.

Chapter 19

Exhibit 19.5 Source: Patirck J. Lyons, "What Happens When a Customer Says 'Charge It'," *The New York Times,* March 7, 1993, p. F8. Copyright © 1993 by The New York Times Company. Reprinted by permission. Focus on Company (p. 453) Source: Roger Thurow, "Special, Today Only: Six Million Dinars For a Snickers Bar," *The Wall Street Journal,* August 4, 1993, pp. A1, A4. Focus on Collaborators (p. 456) Source: Statement by Alan Greenspan before the Committee on Banking, Housing, and Urban Affairs, U.S. Senate, January 29, 1992, *Federal Reserve Bulletin,* March 1992, p. 201. Focus on Competitors (p. 462) Source: Martha Brannigan, "NationsBank's 'Start' Credit Card Adds New Wrinkle to Retirement Planning," *The Wall Street Journal,* January 7, 1993, p. A4. Street Smart (p. 462) Source: Georgette Jasen, "Taking on Debt: First Keep the Basics in Mind," *The Wall Street Journal,* December 10, 1993, pp. C1, C14. Focus on Collaborators (p. 467) Source: Fred R. Bleakley, "'Regulators from Hell' Frighten Some Banks but Also Win Praise," *The Wall Street Journal,* April 27, 1993, pp. A1, A4; Dean Foust and Kelley Holland, "Taking a Sharper Look at Bank Examiners," *Business Week,* April 19, 1993, pp. 99–100. Focus on Collaborators (p. 469) Source: John R. Emshwiller, "Minority-Owned Banks Seek Boosts from Big Rivals," *The Wall Street Journal,* December 16, 1992, p. B2. Focus on Competitors (p. 000) Source: Frederick S. Mishkin, *The Economics of Money, Banking, and Financial Markets,* 3rd ed. (New York: HarperCollins, 1992), p. 243.

Photo Credits

p. 451 1993 Seth Resnick. p. 452 © Rich Frishman. p. 459 1992, Nesbit Grammar, FPG International Corp. p. 463 AP/WIDE WORLD PHOTOS.

Chapter 20

Exhibit 20.3 Source: Moody's *Bond Record* and Standard & Poor's *Bond Guide.* Street Smart (p. 481) Source: Steven E. Levingston, "Stock Certificates Get a Makeover for the '90s," *The Wall Street Journal,* January 19, 1993, p. C1. Focus on Company (p. 485) Source: Caleb Solomon, "Pennzoil Sells a $402.5 Million Issue

Exchangeable into Chevron Common," *The Wall Street Journal,* January 8, 1993, p. A16. Focus on Collaborators (p. 489) Source: "China to Allow More Firms to Publicly Issue Securities," *The Wall Street Journal,* January 4, 1993, p. C15; John J. Curran, "China's Investment Boom," *Fortune,* March 7, 1994, pp. 116–124. Focus on Collaborators (p. 490) Source: Karen S. Damato, "Ten Lessons to Learn from Wall Street's Pros," *The Wall Street Journal,* January 8, 1993, p. C1. Focus on Customers (p. 492) Source: Ellen E. Schultz, "Wall Street Courts Women with Pitch They Have Different Financial Needs," *The Wall Street Journal,* June 11, 1992. Focus on Collaborators (p. 493) Source: Douglas R. Sease, "Black Monday Taught Investors to Lose Fear," *The Wall Street Journal,* October 16, 1992, pp. C1, C18. Focus on Company (p. 498) Source: "Journal Launches Index Tracking World Stocks," *The Wall Street Journal,* January 5, 1993, p. C1.

Photo Credits

p. 477 © George Lange/ONYX. p. 479 © Jeffrey Lowe/ONYX. p. 484 Richard Shock/Gamma Liaison. p. 486 Courtesy of Matt Seto. p. 490 Forrest Anderson - Gamma-Liaison. p. 497 JOE TRAVER/GAMMA-LIAISON.

Chapter 21

Exhibit 21.4 "Where Do You Plan to Get Money?," *Inc.,* November, 1992, p. 43. Focus on Competitors (p. 504) Source: Tim Smart, "GE's Money Machine," *Business Week,* March 8, 1993, pp. 62–67. Focus on Company (p. 512) Source: "Setting Receivables and Payables Priorities," *Inc.,* February 1993, p. 39. Street Smart (p. 514) Source: Al Ehrbar, "First Come, First Served," *Smart Money,* February, 1994, pp. 132–138. Street Smart (p. 518) Source: Excerpted from Bruce G. Posner, "How to Finance Anything—The Five Questions Every Money Source Asks," p. 66. Copyright 1993 by Goldhirsch Group, Inc., 38 Commercial Wharf, Boston, MA 02110. Reprinted with permission, *Inc.* magazine, February 1993. Focus on Collaborators (p. 518) Source: Joan C. Szabo, "Alternative Ways to Find Capital," *Nation's Business,* April 1992, pp. 33–35. Focus on Company (p. 519) Source: Peter Gumbel and Richard Turner, "Fans Like Euro Disney, but Its Parent's Goofs Weigh the Park Down," *The Wall Street Journal,* March 10, 1994, pp. A1, A12.

Photo Credits

p. 503 Denver Post/Martin. p. 508 1993, Photo by Patrick Tehan. p. 511 Andy Freeberg ©. p. 517 William P. Diven. p. 521 Atmel Corporation.

Chapter 22

Focus on Company (p. 530) Source: Amanda Bennett, "CEO's Illness May Endanger Company's Health as Well," *The Wall Street Journal,* January 21, 1993, pp. B-1, B-5. Street Smart (p. 531) Source: Roger Thompson, "Taking Charge of Worker's Comp," p. 21. Reprinted by permission, Nation's Business, October 1993. Copyright 1993, U.S. Chamber of Commerce. Focus on Company (p. 532) Source: "Savings Through Self-Insurance," *Inc.,* November 1992, p. 48. Street Smart (p. 537) Source: "When to Switch Carriers," *Inc.,* January 1993, p. 39. Focus on Customers (p. 539) Source: James Hirsch, "Insurers Retreat on Rental Cars Used for Work," *The Wall Street Journal,* December 30, 1992, p. B-1. Focus on Competitors (p. 540) Source: Charles Fleming, "Zurich Insurance Group Is Looking for a New Focus," *The Wall Street Journal,* June 26, 1992, p. B-4. Focus on Company (p. 542) Source: Thomas R. King, "Doctor Convicted in Case Involving Insurance Fraud," *The Wall Street Journal,* July 26, 1993, p. B5A. Focus on Customers (p. 542) Source: Judith Graham, "Health-Care Prime Target of Insurance Fraud," *The Denver Post,* January 16, 1992, p. C-7.

Photo Credits

p. 527 John Berry/Gamma Liaison. p. 528 1993 Mary Beth Camp/Matrix. p. 534 Ad furnished courtesy of AFLAC Incorporated. p. 536 AP/WIDE WORLD PHOTOS. p. 541 © 94 Tom Sobolik/Black Star.

Chapter 23

Exhibit 23.7 Source: Adapted from Kenneth Clarkson, Roger Miller, Gaylord Jentz, and Frank Cross, *West's Business Law* (St. Paul, Minn.: West, Company, 1992), p.34. Focus on Collaborators (p. 554) Source: Michael McCarthy, "Pepsico Still Sways Firm That State Law Required It to Sell," *The Wall Street Journal,* July 24, 1992, pp. A1, A9; Michael McCarthy, "Pepsico Linkage to M. Henri Wines Draws U.S. Fine," *The Wall Street Journal,* May 17, 1994, p. B8. Focus on Competitors (p. 563) Source: Junda Woo and Richard Borsuk, "New Trademark Laws in Asia Are Less Effective Than Firms Hoped," *The Wall Street Journal,* February 16, 1994, p. B8. Focus on Competitors (p. 563) Source: Bob Ortega, "Ruling Gives Laws on Privacy a Hi-Tech Edge," *The Wall Street Journal,* March 18, 1993, pp. B1, B6. Focus on Company (p. 564) Source: Bill Saporito, "The Benefits of Bankruptcy," *Fortune,* July 12, 1993, p. 98. Focus on Competitors (p. 566) Source: Mark Lewyn, "800 Numbers: No Longer AT&T's Private Line," *Business Week,* March 29, 1993, pp. 85–86. Focus on Customers (p. 568) Source: Jim Carlton, "Timeshare Condo Sales Are Climbing Rapidly Amid Many Gripes," *The Wall Street Journal,* March 18, 1993, pp. A1, A6. Street Smart (p. 568) Source: Mimi Deitsch, "A Canadian Perspective: What's the Code of Business for the '90s?", *Financial Executive,* September-October 1990, pp. 68–71.

Photo Credits

p. 551 PHOTO BY GUS GUSTOVICH. p. 553 © 1987, Steven Gottlieb, FPG International Corp. p. 557 Stephen Green. p. 561 Mark Greenberg/Liaison International. p. 567 Eric Sander/Gamma Liaison.

Epilog

Exhibit E.1 Source: *Occupational Outlook Handbook* (Washington, D.C.: U.S. Department of Labor, 1993). Exhibit E.2 Source: "Job Trends Across the Millennia," *Forbes,* January 6, 1992. Focus on Career (p. 584) Source: Constance J. Pritchard, "Forget the Fortune 500," *The College Edition of the National Business Employment Weekly,* Fall 1992, p. 12. Excerpt reprinted by permission from the National Business Employment Weekly, © 1992, Dow-Jones & Co. Inc. Focus on Career (p. 585) Source: Carol Kleiman, "A Little Inventiveness Helps Get You Noticed," *The Chicago Tribune,* September 6, 1992, p. 8-1. Street Smart (p. 587) Source: Michael Cronin, "Due Diligence," *Inc.,* November 1992, p. 93. Street Smart (p. 589) Source: Toni Griffith-Byers, "Many Avenues of Help for Those on Job Hunt," *The Vidette-Messenger,* August 23, 1992, p. D-1.

Photo Credit

p. 576 Courtesy of Karen Siegel Cunningham.

NAME INDEX

SUBJECT INDEX

Bold face type indicates pages on which key terms and concepts are defined.

COMPANY INDEX